The Complete Book of Classical Music

edited by David Ewen

ROBERT HALE · LONDON

First published in Great Britain 1966
First paperback edition 1989

Robert Hale Limited
Clerkenwell House
Clerkenwell Green
London EC1R 0HT

British Library Cataloguing in Publication Data

The complete book of classical music.
1. Music, to 1965
I. Ewen, David, 1907–85
780.'19

ISBN 0–7090–3865–8

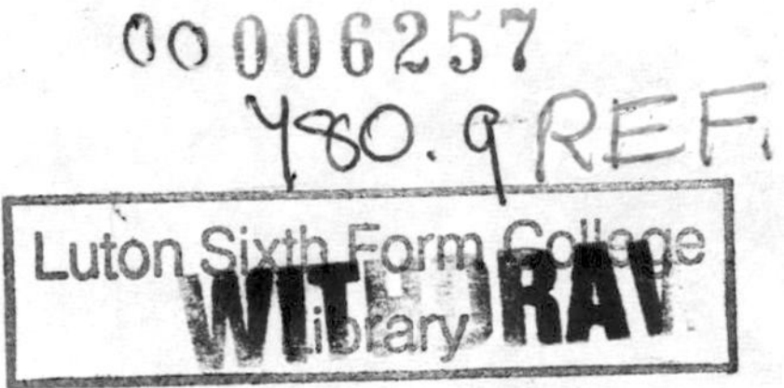

Printed and bound in Great Britain
by Mackays of Chatham, Kent

To Fabien and Mary Sevitzky –
an expression of my admiration,
an earnest of my affection

CONTENTS

The Complete Book of Classical Music

GUILLAUME DE MACHAUT

1300–1377

Guillaume de Machaut is perhaps the first composer to lift music to an artistic status. One of the truly significant creative figures of the fourteenth century, Machaut was a leading exponent of "Ars Nova," the "new art" that flourished in the 1300's. The so-called "old art"—Gregorian melodies and plain chants—had been developed by the "Notre Dame" Gothic School of composers headed by Leonin and Perotin in the twelfth century. "Ars Nova" in general—and Machaut in particular—built a new musical structure on these old foundations.

The greatest single change effected by "Ars Nova" was in rhythm, which now acquired variety for the first time. Machaut was one of the first composers to use extensively a new technique in rhythm: the "isorhythmic" (or equal rhythm) device in which a rhythmic pattern of notes and rests was repeated at fixed points throughout a composition, sometimes in the tenor voice, sometimes in all the voice parts.

But beyond this significant innovation in rhythm, "Ars Nova" and Machaut were responsible for other significant changes: for a new and more flexible manner of polyphonic writing, often by means of successive instead of simultaneous entry of the voices; for a more original polyphonic texture through the avoidance of parallel fifths and octaves; for a firmer harmonic structure; for a more extensive use of instruments; and for the development of new forms —the motet and the Mass in liturgical music, the ballade, in secular.

Machaut produced both secular and liturgical music—ballades, rondeaux, and virelais; motets and Masses. To his writing he brought an expressiveness unknown in the "old art," for as Machaut himself once said, "He who writes and composes without feeling spoils both his words and music." With Machaut, music became not only a "new" art but also a "modern" one.

He was born in the diocese of Rheims in France in or about 1300. Early in life he took holy orders. From about 1323 to 1340, he was employed by the King of Bohemia, first as almoner, then as notary, and finally as secretary. After that, he was a member of the musical household of Charles V, King of Navarre. From 1337 until his death in 1377, he was canon at Rheims. Machaut was a distinguished poet as well as a significant composer.

1364. THE NOTRE DAME MASS, for four voices.

This, Machaut's masterwork, is the earliest known polyphonic setting of a Mass by a single composer. The only other known work in this form is the

Mass of Tournai, written in or about 1300, the product of several composers, all unknown to us.

Machaut wrote the *Notre Dame Mass* for the coronation of Charles V of France at Rheims. The entire composition is based on the plainsong, "David," which is repeated three times by the tenor over a consistent rhythm, and then is stated a fourth and last time over a completely different rhythmic arrangement. The isorhythmic technique is utilized throughout the Mass with considerable subtlety. It serves as a kind of catalyzing agent to bind together the ten brief sections from the opening "Kyrie" to the concluding "Ite Missa Est." Another integrating factor is the repetition of a seven-note melodic idea which recurs frequently, often in a modified or altered form.

In describing this composition, F. L. Harrison wrote: "For the shorter movements he followed the procedure of the motet in the isorhythmic design and in the disposition of his four-part texture, though here the lower parts (tenor and countertenor) need not be given to instruments and are quite suitable for vocal performance. The longer movements ("Gloria" and "Credo") are essentially vocal in style, and the words are treated in largely syllabic fashion, apart from the long section sung at the end of each movement to the single word "Amen" (isorhythmic in the "Credo"). Machaut rounded off his Mass with an isorhythmic setting of "Deo gratias," the choir's response to the celebrant's "Ite Missa Est," from which the service of the Mass (Latin, Missa) took its name."

Machaut's Mass looks backward in time through its use of Gregorian chants and plainsongs. But it also looks into the future. It was one of the earliest works in musical history in which the music suggests some of the emotional or spiritual content of the text. In the "Et Incarnatus Est" section, for example, the music broadens majestically to suggest the awe, mystery, and mysticism of the Virgin birth.

JOHN DUNSTABLE 1370–1453

John Dunstable was England's first significant composer, England's leading exponent of "Ars Nova." He wrote almost exclusively for the church—motets, Masses, and other settings of liturgical texts. His only contribution to secular music came with three delightful ballads in a chanson style: "Durer ne puis," "Puisque m'amour," and "O rosa bella."

To his polyphonic writing, Dunstable brought an eloquence and beauty unknown in his time. Even more than Machaut he sought out the musical equivalent of his text in his attempt to interpret words through music. One of his innovations was the adaptation of the rhythm of his declamation to that of the spoken word. "Not only is the musical form in its main outlines determined by the text," explains Donald Jay Grout, "but the outline of many phrases is molded to the rhythms of the words." Another of his technical contributions was the development of the six-three chord. In his fresh concept of melody and harmony, in his striking originality in the use of ornamentation, in his heightened expressiveness, he represents after Machaut a significant step forward—away from the archaic, toward the modern.

John Dunstable was born in or about 1370, probably in Dunstable, in Bedfordshire, England. From 1419 to 1440, he served as canon at the Hereford Cathedral, and as prebendary of Putson Manor. Later in life he was a member of the musical court of John, Duke of Bedford, with whom he probably visited France. Dunstable died in London on December 24, 1453, and was buried in St. Stephen's, in Walbrook, in the city of London.

———. QUAM PULCRA ES, antiphon.
VENI SANCTE SPIRITUS, motet.

An antiphon is a composition in the simple syllabic style of a Gregorian chant, its text derived from the Scriptures. It is sung either before or after a psalm. *Quam Pulcra Es,* one of Dunstable's finest compositions, is in two sections. All voices move in the same rhythm, often even pronouncing the same syllables together. At times this movement is in parallel thirds and sixths, to which English composers were partial. The sonorities of this antiphon are more full-bodied than those generally encountered in the polyphonic music of this period.

In the motet, *Veni Sancte Spiritus,* Dunstable employs the isorhythmic technique in all four voices. It is twice repeated in each of the three sections. The main melody, heard in the lowest voice, is based on the hymn, "Veni Creator Spiritus." When first sung, this melody is extended to such lengths that it is hardly recognizable; but it serves as a convenient base on which to build the moving upper voices. In the second section, the notes of the hymn lose one-third their value; and in the third section, two-thirds of their value is lost. It is in the third section that the hymn tune at last becomes recognizable.

GUILLAUME DUFAY 1400–1474

The first important school of polyphonic music in the fifteenth century was the Burgundian, whose dean was Guillaume Dufay.

The Burgundian school was concentrated in Belgium, Holland, and northern France; its culture was a blend of the French and the Latin.

Dufay was first influenced by the French Gothic composers of the thirteenth century, then by Dunstable. After that he proceeded on his own to advance the art of vocal polyphony. He helped reduce the complexities of Gothic counterpoint to a simpler, more easily assimilable style. He established for the first time the technique of four-part harmony. With Dufay, canonic writing ceased to be a technical exercise and became the means for the production of beauty of sound and musical texture.

One of Dufay's salient contributions was the introduction of secular tunes into the Mass as a replacement for Gregorian chants. Dufay was the first composer to make extensive use of the folk song, "L'Homme armé"—a favorite with virtually every major composer of polyphonic music up to Palestrina and Carissimi. With Dufay, the secular song became a unifying factor for the Mass, a single melody being repeated throughout all the sections.

Into the dark corners of the polyphonic music for the church, Dufay brought the sunshine of brilliant instrumental colors and the shining hues of voices in the high register. His church music embraces motets, Masses, and Magnificats. In secular music, he produced over sixty chansons.

Guillaume Dufay was born in Hainault, Burgundy, in or about 1400. Between 1426 and 1428, he served as the Maître de Chapelle in Cambrai, and for many years after that, he was a singer in the papal choir. He entered the church in 1437, becoming canon at Cambrai, and later in Bruges. From 1438 to 1444, he resided in Savoy. In 1445, he returned to Cambrai to become canon at its Cathedral, holding this post till the end of his life. Dufay died in Cambrai on November 27, 1474.

1464. AVE REGINA COELORUM, motet.

This deeply moving composition plumbs emotional depths not often encountered in fifteenth century polyphonic music. It was completed by the composer a decade before his death with the hope that it might be sung at his deathbed. ("Have mercy on the failing Dufay" is one of its lines.) This motet was not performed for Dufay in his last hours, as he had requested, but it was sung at his funeral services.

——— MISSA CAPUT.

This is the most significant of Dufay's seven Masses. The meaning of its title has long been subject to conjecture. A Mass usually used as its title the opening words of the plainsong or secular song that served as its *cantus firmus*. Manfred Bukofzer, however, points out that Dufay drew the name of *Missa Caput* from the closing line of the concluding antiphon, "Venit ad petrum," whose last word is "Caput." The use of this antiphon points up Dufay's indebtedness to Dunstable. The Mass is cyclic in form, unified by a recurring melodic idea and by a tenor common to all four sections.

——— CHANSONS: "Ce jour de l'an"; "Se la face ay pale"; "Je Languis en piteux martire."

Dufay's first chansons had been influenced by Dunstable's ballades. But in time Dufay evolved a style richer and more poetic than that of his predecessor. With Dufay's chansons we encounter the first flowering of a song form in which mood and emotion are affected by the text. Tender and gracious moods abound. Instrumental interludes provide delightful changes of color and feeling. The technique of imitation is often a unifying device. "Quiet, profound, transcendent feelings are their domain," wrote Paul Henry Lang, "and self-restrained and tasteful expression is their ideal."

The gamut of emotion is wide. "Ce jour de l'an" is lively and gay; "Se la face ay pale" is reflective. And "Je Languis en piteux martire" is deeply emotional—the entreaty of a man to the woman he loves to pity his immeasurable misery.

JOSQUIN DES PRÉS 1450–1521

The Burgundian school of polyphony was succeeded by the Flemish (or Netherland) school of polyphonic composers, which dominated European music from the middle of the fifteenth century to the end of the sixteenth. Josquin des Prés was the dominating figure of this new school. He evolved a musical art that was individual, and for his time incomparable. To the contrapuntal and technical processes of the Burgundian composers, he brought the beauty, symmetry, clarity, transparency, and at times radiance of Italian music. Josquin des Prés was one of the first composers anywhere to give importance to melody and harmony, and to endow both with such warm, rich colors. With Josquin, counterpoint became a pliable instrument for the expression of emotion. He was truly a child of the Renaissance; his music reflects the Renaissance in its serenity, grandeur, sentiment, and humanity. As the venerable historian Ambros remarked: "There speaks in his music a warm sensitiveness, a capacity for urgent emotion, a mystic awe of worship."

Josquin des Prés was born in Hainault, Burgundy, in or about 1450. He is believed to have been a pupil of Jean de Ockeghem (1430–1495). For five years Josquin was employed in the musical court of Duke Galeazzo Maria Sforza in Milan; after that he served at the court of Lorenzo the Magnificent in Florence. From 1486 to 1494, he sang in the Papel choir, and from 1494 to

1499, he was the choirmaster of the Cambrai Cathedral. His first publications —Masses and motets—appeared in 1502. In or about 1516, he was appointed canon of the Collegiate Church at Condé. Josquin des Prés died in Condé-sur-Escaut on August 27, 1521.

1502. L'HOMME ARMÉ, Mass.

Josquin completed seventeen Masses. *L'Homme armé,* found in his first publication, is one of the most famous. "L'Homme armé" is a French chanson of unknown origin. Charles Burney is convinced that this is an air that the hero Roland sang at the head of his army while advancing to attack the enemy. In any event, "L'Homme armé" enjoyed enormous popularity. There is hardly a major composer in the fifteenth and sixteenth centuries who did not use it within the context of the Mass. Josquin's use of the song is of particular interest, since he transposes it to each of the successive steps of the hexachord—beginning with "C" for the "Kyrie", "D" for the "Gloria," and so on.

Burney has singled out some of the points of interest in this Mass. "In the 'Sanctus,' the soprano leads off the subject in D . . . moving in breves and semibreves accompanied by the tenor in a free and airy melody; and after six bars the countertenor sings the theme in F major and in augmentation. . . . The 'Osanna' has many curious contrivances in contrary motion and double counterpoint, in three parts, while a fourth is still singing 'L'Homme armé.' In the next two movements, 'Benedictus' and 'In Nomine,' by a curious species of contrivance, duos are formed by two parts singing the same intervals in different measures; that is, while one performs the melody in semibreves, the other sings it in minims, and *e contra.*"

——— AVE MARIA, motet.

In a discussion of Josquin's motets, Robert Stevenson wrote that the composer "followed two main courses. Either he drew some ancient fragment of Church melody through the motet, like a strand of white yarn through a piece of multicolored knitwork, or he took the text and divided it where punctuation occurred, constructing the music for each phrase of the text as if it were a separate square in a patchwork quilt." Stevenson then goes on to explain: "He was fond of sequences, that is, repetitions of melody higher or lower than the original statement, and in the same voice. At times he resorted to strong rhythmic accents, or conflicting accents in different voices, in order to enforce the emotional meaning. Whatever techniques he chose to employ, his music showed infinite variety of texture, of light and shade."

The *Ave Maria,* for four voices, is characteristic of Josquin's style and approach within the motet form. The thematic material is derived from the Gregorian chant, the melody being continually embellished, and treated with the utmost freedom. Contrapuntal devices are subordinated to the emotional content, which reaches a moving climax with the closing line, "O mater dei memento mei."

Donald Jay Grout points out that each phrase of the text has its own musical motive "which is first presented in imitation by each voice in turn; the musical sentence thus initiated comes eventually to a cadence, and a similar sentence on the next phrase of the text, and with its own musical motives, begins." Grout adds that the cadences are hidden by an overlapping process in which, while some voices are still finishing one sentence, others are beginning the next. Thus "the music continues without obvious division into sections."

ORLANDO DE LASSO 1532–1594

Orlando de Lasso (or Roland de Lassus) was the last, and possibly the greatest, representative of the Flemish (or Netherland) school of polyphonic music. He was also one of the most prolific and versatile. The number of his compositions passes the fifteen-hundred mark. He handled several different styles of several different countries with equal mastery and richness of invention. His secular music includes French chansons, Italian madrigals and villanellas, and German choral songs. Among his numerous works for the church are some one thousand motets, over fifty-three Masses, together with Magnificats and psalms. In his religious music, he combines Italian warmth and passion, brilliance of color and decorative figurations with the more severe contrapuntal art and science of Josquin des Prés. Orlando de Lasso could be gay, witty, and lighthearted when he wrote drinking songs or set bawdy verses to music. Some of his madrigals are intense and passionate. In his most significant church music, he reaches down into profound emotional depths or ascends to exalted spiritual heights. With Palestrina, he was a leading musical spokesman for the Renaissance. But where Palestrina tended toward deepest religious convictions and mysticism, Orlande de Lasso was often human, vivacious, and vital.

He was born in Mons, Hainault, in 1532. As a boy he was a chorister at the St. Nicolas Church in his native city. He had such an extraordinary voice that he received the nickname of "the Belgian Orpheus," and on three occasions was kidnapped to sing in various choral groups. In 1544, he joined the entourage of Ferdinando Gonzaga, Viceroy of Sicily, with whom he traveled to Sicily and Italy. From 1553 to 1554, he was chorusmaster at the St. John the Lateran Church in Rome. He settled in Antwerp in 1555, the year in which his first two publications (both made up of madrigals) appeared; a volume of motets followed a year later. In 1556, he settled permanently in Munich at the court of Albert V, Duke of Bavaria. There he served first as a member of the chapel, and from 1563 until his death, as Kapellmeister. In 1558, he married Regina Wechinger, an aristocrat. One of his most celebrated works, the *Sacrae cantiones,* for five voices, was published in 1562. A year later he completed what most musicologists regard as his magnum opus, the *Seven Penitential Psalms of David.* Though he continually received tempting offers to leave Munich and work in other courts, he remained with Duke Albert V until the end of his life. Lasso died in Munich on January 14, 1594.

1563. THE SEVEN PENITENTIAL PSALMS OF DAVID.

Most of the *Seven Penitential Psalms of David* are for five voices, but some are also for two, three, four, or six voices. A polyphonic practice identified as "musica reservata" is employed throughout this masterwork. This is a style, prominent in the sixteenth century, emphasizing realistic pictorial settings of texts. Claude Palisca, a present-day musicologist who has done a considerable amount of research in this subject, explains that "musica reservata" is the equivalent of "mannerism in painting, whose most celebrated exponent was El Greco." He adds: "Like its artistic and architectural counterparts, 'musica reservata' tends toward overstatement. It is full of restless activity, rapid changes of mood and texture, sharp color contrasts, unresolved tensions and asymmetrics, clambering ornamentation."

These *Psalms* are remarkable for the way in which the text is set to music and also for the rich emotional veins that are tapped. The verses inspired in Lasso, now music of profoundly tragic content, now music of rare exaltation. Van den Borren writes: "Without any failure of inspiration he makes to pass before us all the states of soul which the Psalmist describes, ranging from the profoundest grief to the brightest hope. . . . All this he has depicted in musical language, ideally concise, in which the madrigalesque element intervenes largely, but with the utmost discretion and with a most exquisite sense of proportion."

The *Psalms* were written at the request of Duke Albert V, who thought so highly of them that he had the composition transcribed on parchment, and illustrated by the court painter; the Duke then bound them into two beautiful folio volumes in rich red morocco leather, decorated with silver clasps.

1568–1604. MOTETS: "Adoremus te, Christe" and "Tristis est anima mea," for five voices; "In hora ultima," for six voices.

The motet, more than any other form, lifted Orlando de Lasso to the heights. He wrote almost a thousand such works—for two, three, four, five, six, seven, eight, nine, ten, and twelve voices. Some are, explains Caldwell Titcomb, "Franco-Flemish, some are severely Roman, some are brilliant polychoral in the Venetian manner." In works like "Adoremus te, Christe" and "In hora ultima (1604), and "Tristis est anima mea" (1568) he was truly "incomparable." "Compared with Palestrina," continues Titcomb, "Lasso employs a richer palette, is more human and deeply expressive, as well as more harmonically oriented. In general, his style falls between that of Palestrina and de Monte on the one hand, and that of Victoria and Marenzio on the other. He wonderfully summarizes the whole Renaissance, while at the same time looking forward to the Baroque."

JAN SWEELINCK 1562–1621

As the creator of motets, psalms, and chansons, grounded in the techniques and methods of the Flemish composers, Sweelinck proved the last significant exponent of that school. But his significance in music history lies not in his choral music but in his compositions for harpsichord and organ. Here he opened a new world by becoming one of the earliest creators of Baroque instrumental music. In these efforts, he was influenced partly by the early English virginalists, from whom he learned the art and science of variations; partly by the Venetian school with its partiality for embellishments, ornamentations, antiphonal effects. But in spite of such derivations, his organ works are the individualized products of a singularly original creative force. Their impact on German organ music can hardly be overestimated. Sweelinck's instrumental works (often intended to be played interchangeably by organ or clavier) fall into three convenient groups: sacred and secular variations, toccatas, and fantasias.

He was born in Amsterdam in 1562. His principal training at the organ came from his father, organist of the Old Church in Amsterdam. In 1577, Sweelinck received his first appointment as organist. Three years after that, he inherited his father's organ bench at Old Church, which he held for the remainder of his life. In the ensuing years, he became famous throughout Europe as composer, organist, and teacher. He died in Amsterdam on October 16, 1621.

——— COMPOSITIONS FOR ORGAN:

VARIATIONS: "O Mensch, bewein dein Suende Gross"; "Mein Junges Leben hat ein End."

FANTASIAS: "Fantasia Chromatica"; "Fantasias in Echo Style."

Sweelinck's secular and sacred music for the organ consists mainly of variations on psalm tunes and chorales. Though affected by the style of the

English virginal composers, Sweelinck makes their technique subservient to liturgical needs. Sweelinck can be said to have originated the practice during German Protestant services of prefacing congregational hymn singing with organ variations on the hymn melody. In his variations on these church tunes, the melody, says Manfred F. Bukofzer, is "subjected to mechanical elaboration in abstract rhythmic patterns. The patterns constantly challenged the imagination of the composer. . . . Each variation contained a great variety of upbeat patterns, complementary rhythms, and motives in double counterpoint."

As important in Sweelinck's literature for the organ as his variations are his fantasias. Here he laid the foundation stones of the fugue form—a form in which he demonstrated such mastery that some musicologists regard him in this department second only to Johann Sebastian Bach. Sweelinck's fantasias are usually based on a single subject in long notes, subjected to various changes of rhythm. Variation becomes a salient method in these fantasias, but variation is confined not to the main subject but to countersubjects. In the *Chromatic Fantasy,* the initial basic subject, as the title suggests, is chromatic; it remains basically unchanged throughout the piece. But fascinating contrast is achieved through the variety of the rhythms, lively countersubjects, and fascinating scale passages and ornamentations. The work ends with a brilliant display of virtuosity. In the *Fantasias in Echo Style,* the middle part makes effective use of an echo effect reminiscent of the antiphonal writing of the Venetian polyphonists.

GIOVANNI GABRIELI 1557–1612

The Flemish polyphonists were succeeded by the Venetian school of composers, one of whose founders was Adrian Willaert (1490–1562). Willaert helped evolve the antiphonal style characterizing so much of Venetian choral music of this period. The St. Mark's Cathedral in Venice, where Willaert was employed as Maestro di Cappella, boasted two organs and two choirs. Utilizing the means he had at hand to attain a new artistic end, Willaert created contrapuntal music for two choirs. Sometimes they were used alternately, one making a soft statement, the other making a loud reply. Sometimes they were combined with extraordinary sonorous effect. In addition to this new antiphonal technique, the Venetian school created a solid harmonic style through the use of chords; it developed the Italian madrigal as a medium for secular polyphonic writing; it increased the resources of instrumental music.

Among the preeminent masters of this Venetian school were Andrea Gabrieli (1520–1586) and his remarkable nephew, Giovanni Gabrieli. Giovanni took on where his uncle had left off. He extended contrapuntal techniques and forms, increased harmonic colorations, introduced new subtleties of nuances and a boldness of modulation unknown at that time. It was particularly in his instrumental music that he became a musical pioneer of first significance. More than any of the Venetians who had preceded him, Giovanni Gabrieli devised an instrumental style as opposed to a vocal one. He handled instruments with such mastery and such variety of means that the history book is sometimes inclined to describe him as "the father of orchestration." He inaugurated a variety of dynamics and a blending of timbres then new to music. In addition, he was also one of the first composers to create religious and secular music exclusively for the organ.

His contemporaries recognized his worth. The sixteenth-century theorist and composer, Michael Praetorius, described him as "the most eminent and most famous of us all." Later generations also valued him highly. Hugo Riemann maintained that Giovanni Gabrieli exerted an even greater influence on the music of the first half of the seventeenth century than did the Florentine masters (the Camerata), who invented recitative and the opera. And Hermann Kretzschmar wrote that Gabrieli was "the chief representative" of the "golden age of a really solemn, elevated, and noble style of orchestral music . . . rooted in the spirit of the times in which, during the sixteenth and seventeenth centuries, churches, states, cities, and corporations held grand festivals. The music is marked with the stamp of Venetian art: the splendor and sumptuousness, the loftiness and grandeur which stir and exalt us in the masterpieces of Montegna, of Paolo Veronese, and Titian."

Giovanni Gabrieli was born in Venice in or about 1557. After studying with his uncle, Andrea, he went to Munich where, from 1575 to 1579, he was both an assistant to and a pupil of Orlando de Lasso. By 1584 he was back in Venice, where he substituted for Claudio Merulo as first organist of St. Mark's Cathedral. In 1585, he became second organist there, and upon the death of his uncle in 1586, first organist. His fame as organ virtuoso was second only to his reputation as composer and teacher. In 1587, he made his first appearance in print, when five of his madrigals and five of his motets appeared in a volume to which his uncle also contributed several pieces. This was followed in 1593 by a book of *Intonazioni* for organ, and in 1579, by the first volume of his monumental *Sacrae symphoniae,* for voices and instruments. Giovanni Gabrieli died in Venice on August 21, 1612.

1597–1615. SACRAE SYMPHONIAE, two sets for voices and instruments.

Gabrieli published two sets of *Sacrae symphoniae* for voices, the first in 1597, and the second (posthumously) in 1615. These are mostly motets for any number of voices: up to sixteen in the first volume, and up to nineteen in the second. These volumes also included canzoni, sonatas, and Masses for instruments, and utilized instrumental accompaniments (organ or a small orchestra) for the voices.

In his vocal writing, Gabrieli made use of modulations so daring, and so technically demanding, that one unidentified critic of his day remarked it was difficult to remember that this music was intended for voices. The antiphonal writing is particularly noteworthy in most of these motets, often yielding stunning colors and effects.

No less advanced was Gabrieli in his instrumental technique. He endowed his instrumental backgrounds with dynamics, nuances, blendings, and contrasts rarely, if ever, encountered in the music of the sixteenth century.

Characteristic of the compositions in these two volumes is the motet "In Ecclesiis" from the second book for two four-part choruses, organ, and brass, described as "processional and ceremonial music."

——— CANZONI, for organ or instruments.
SONATA PIAN' E FORTE, for instruments.

The "canzon," whose development came largely through the efforts of Andrea and Giovanni Gabrieli, is one of the earliest known forms of instrumental music. Originally, it was a piece for the organ. But after a while, it developed into a form for several instruments modeled after the French chanson. Hugo Riemann considered the "canzon" identical with the earliest sonatas; in fact, Gabrieli used the term "sonata" and "canzon" interchangeably. Other authorities see in the "canzon" the seeds of the later concerto grosso.

Giovanni Gabrieli produced a set of *Canzoni e Sonate* toward the end of his life, and it was published posthumously in 1615. It was written for from three to twenty-two instrumental voices. Individual melodic parts are often grouped into several choirs. The *Canzon Quatri Toni a 15*, for example, was written for fifteen voices grouped in three instrumental choirs of five parts each. Here, we are informed by Leopold Stokowski, "Gabrieli gave brilliant characteristics to each of the three instrumental choirs—some brilliant and high, another less high and brilliant, and a third soft and mystical in quality."

The *Canzon in the Ninth Tone* is one of the finest in this medium. It was written for two four-part choirs that sometimes play antiphonally and sometimes are combined. "No specific instruments are called for," explains Gustave Reese. "Where this happens, it seems reasonably clear that brass instruments were sometimes used in the performance of ensemble pieces."

The *Sonata Pian' e Forte* is one of the first instances in music history to contain indications for "piano" and "forte" performance. "Here," says Gustave Reese, "the term sonata simply means a piece to be sounded by instruments rather than to be sung." This work is for two four-part instrumental choirs. "In each of these the three lowest parts are indicated as being for trombones.

In the first choir the top part is for cornetto (not the equivalent of our modern cornet, but a gentle woodwind instrument). In the second choir the top part is for violino, by which is meant an instrument more like the modern viola than the violin. By using the two choirs antiphonally, Gabrieli obtains impressive color contrasts, and still another color effect is obtained by combining them."

GIOVANNI PIERLUIGI DA PALESTRINA 1525–1594

The Roman school of polyphony—like the Venetian—was an offshoot of the Flemish. But where the Venetians were progressive and forward-looking, always seeking to uncover new methods, the Roman polyphonic masters adhered faithfully to the past.

The leading figure of this Roman school—indeed, the leading musician of the Renaissance and possibly the greatest composer before Bach and Handel—was Palestrina. He created no new styles or techniques. His art represented transformation rather than revolution. It was deeply rooted in medieval music—specifically the Gregorian chant. Palestrina is the summit of medieval music, the ultimate point of technical and artistic development beyond which sixteenth-century a cappella music could not go.

He stands at the crossroads where the Renaissance meets the Counter-Reformation. Though Palestrina wrote some eighty secular madrigals (which, later in life, he regretted having produced), his music is of the Catholic Church, freed of secular associations and connotations. Sir Donald Tovey once remarked that, like Spinoza, Palestrina was a God-intoxicated man. As such, and as a child of the Counter-Reformation, he wrote with discipline, concentration, other-worldliness, with rigid adherence to authority and principle. But he was at the same time a son of the Renaissance. And so, to techniques and idioms inherited from the Flemish polyphonists, he added an Italian warmth and glow, an Italian partiality for color, proportion, and balance. In the last phase of his artistic evolution, he was finally able to part company with the Flemish masters and arrive at a style all his own. That style had no rivals in the sixteenth century for mysticism, exaltation, spirituality, equilibrium of form and content, adaptability to the singing voice, and purity of texture.

His real name was Giovanni Pierluigi, but he is known as Giovanni Pierluigi da Palestrina because he was born in the town of Palestrina, near

Rome, in or about 1525. In 1544, he was made organist and chorusmaster of the St. Agapit Cathedral in his native town. While holding this post he married Lucrezia Gori, in 1547, who bore him two sons. In 1551, he was made the director of the Julian Choir in Rome, and three years later his first publication appeared, a volume of Masses. During the next quarter of a century, Palestrina held several major posts. Between 1555 and 1560, he was the musical director of St. John Lateran Church in Rome; and from 1561 until 1567, he held a similar post at Santa Maria Maggiore. His first volume of motets was issued in 1563; and his most famous Mass, the *Missa Papae Marcelli,* came out in 1567. After leaving Santa Maria Maggiore, Palestrina was employed by Cardinal Ippolito d'Este. Then, in 1571, Palestrina reassumed his former post as musical director of the Julian Choir, which he now occupied until the end of his life. He died in Rome on February 2, 1594.

1567–1570. MASSES:
Missa Papae Marcelli; Missa Assumpta Est Maria; Missa Brevis.

Palestrina wrote ninety-three Masses. Two of the most famous were written in 1567, the *Missa Papae Marcelli* and the *Missa Assumpta Est Maria.* Both are for six voices. The first is for soprano, alto, two tenors, and two basses; the second, for two sopranos, alto, two tenors, and bass.

A legend about the *Missa Papae Marcelli* has circulated for so many years that it came to be accepted as fact. In 1562, the Council of Trent ordered a major reform in church music. The aim was to strip it of its complexity while ridding it of all secular influences. To achieve this goal, a commission of Cardinals was created to examine the existing repertory of church music and suggest necessary changes. The fiction was subsequently created that Palestrina wrote the *Missa Papae Marcelli* to convince the Cardinals that church music could be written with beauty and majesty without reducing it to simplicity; that Palestrina's Mass made such a deep impression on the jury that the Cardinals agreed no reform was necessary.

There is evidence to support the belief that Palestrina wrote the *Missa Papae Marcelli* to help prevent a change in church music; and it is possible that some of Palestrina's music was responsible for avoiding unnecessary reforms. Certainly it stands to reason that, when the Cardinals examined the existing church repertory, they must have studied some of Palestrina's Masses. Palestrina himself told the Jesuit fathers in Rome on one occasion that the projected reform in church music had been abandoned after some of his works had been heard.

One of the reasons why the *Missa Papae Marcelli* has erroneously been singled out as the work that most influenced the Cardinals, was the composer's own statement in the preface of the second volume of his Masses. Here he explained that in the *Missa Papae Marcelli* he tried "to adorn the Mass with music of a new order in accordance with the views of the most serious and religious-minded personages in high places."

We know now that the *Missa Papae Marcelli* had no part at all in preserving the status quo in church music. Nevertheless, it remains one of Palestrina's most significant creations—a giant edifice that towered over the polyphonic creations of the sixteenth century. As Zoë Kendrick Pyne wrote: "If today the Mass can still work its wondrous spell on the jaded senses of the modern music, what must have been its effect in the sixteenth century, in all the freshness of its revelation? Those heavenly harmonies surely seemed little short of miraculous as they echoed through that marvelous nave in Santa Maria Maggiore."

Pyne's analysis of this Mass may be regarded as definitive. "The introductory portion . . . is written in the Hypolydian mode with occasional incursion to the Mixolydian. Beginning on the fifth, it rises to the highest note of the mode, sweeping down to its final C, and beyond. But nothing in this fragment of analysis could convey to the reader the exquisite balance and repose of the opening phrase. It is like a benediction, quieting the spirit with a heavenly sense of peace; or it suggests a vision of the white wings of a dove folding as they come to earth. The short phrases forming the points of imitation seem not so much contrapuntal devices as passages of sheer inevitability. . . . Perhaps the most striking feature is simplicity. In the score, the erudition must astonish, but in performance the voices blend so naturally they impress the hearer with a sense of fortuitous confluence.

"The entire Mass is written within the compass of two octaves and a fifth, but never for a moment is the ear wearied by so small a range. The absence of mechanical rhythm, or a strong or weak beat arbitrarily applied, permits an unbroken flow of sound and the sense of a calm, sweet, ordered progress, only interupted as the voices rest on their allotted points of repose. In the 'Credo,' the choice of phrase is extraordinarily expressive, but it is in the 'Sanctus' that Palestrina reaches that fullness of sound, that suave harmony transfiguring the words as a nimbus adorns the pure, pale face of a saint. . . . Such an experience tranquillizes and relieves the spirit, and the four-part 'Benedictus' suggests the sending of an earthly embassy on high with a message of thankfulness and praise. Once again, it must be insisted that the apparent simplicity marks the perfection of achievement, the plasticity of materialism won after endless toil. Considered from this point of view, the old Netherlanders, with their compound time-measurements, their canons and all the rest of their diabolical ingenuities, all had a hand in the *Missa Papae Marcelli,* though the master mind was necessary to divine the ultimate end."

Whenever Palestrina utilized a text about the Virgin Mary he produced music of unearthly radiance and purity. The *Missa Assumpta Est Maria* is a work of such surpassing beauty and spirituality that many Palestrina authorities place it at the top of the composer's Masses. Henry Coates described this work as "an outstanding example of Palestrina's skill in what has been appropriately termed vocal orchestration. . . . Here much of the light, brilliant effect of the music is due to the choice of voices . . . and the continual use of the upper registers, the frequent crossing and interlacing of the parts helping to create a tonal fabric of luminous yet brilliant quality. There is a supremely effective touch in this Mass, where, after the outburst of rejoicing which the opening 'Kyrie' suggests, the six voices are reduced to four, and in a hushed homophonic passage, one is reminded that after all it is a prayer for mercy that is being sung."

The *Missa Brevis* for four voices, which appears in Palestrina's third book of Masses (1570), is one of the simplest and most spare of his compositions, yet without a loss of elevating feeling. This work is based on a theme from *Audi filia,* a Mass by Claude Goudimel (1510–1572). Says Lehman Engel: "The harmonic style could not be more pure, consisting entirely and without exception of the plain triadal progressions. The tonality, according to modern systems, is built around F, its dominant, subdominant, and their relative minor keys. The melodic flow is generaly restricted in a single section to a few notes in range—undoubtedly a direct result of the influence of the Gregorian chant. And in one sense the Mass may be said to be without rhythm, since there is a greater feeling of phrase (and this usually without repeated time pattern) than of beat. . . . In the Mass, the meaning and significance of the text governed entirely the tempo and frequent tempo changes in the music. For example, in the 'Gloria' the words 'Et Incarnatus Est' are slower than those which precede them; in the 'Sanctus' the attack of 'Hosanna' is faster. The miracle is that Palestrina's music in every case propels the tempo change, for in Palestrina, the man, the word, and their every degree of meaning had a complete and irresistible integration."

1950. STABAT MATER, for a double choir of eight voices.

The Stabat Mater was a religious poem of medieval origin describing the sorrow of the Blessed Virgin at the Cross. It is attributed to Jacopone da Todi, a thirteenth-century Franciscan monk. Originally it was not liturgical, nor did it have a musical setting. But the early polyphonic masters, including Josquin des Prés, started to set the words to music. In Palestrina's *Stabat Mater,* "the opening phrase—a progression of three major common chords on a bass descending in major seconds—is one of the most beautiful effects in polyphonic music," says Rosa Newmarch, "and forms the leading motive of the work." Richard Wagner prepared a modern edition of Palestrina's *Stabat Mater* in Leipzig in 1877.

TOMÁS LUIS DE VICTORIA 1548–1611

Though of Spanish birth, Victoria belonged to the Roman school of polyphony. He believed that music should be directed only to "the praise and glory of God." Consequently, all of his almost two hundred compositions are for the church, and place him at the side of Palestrina as a leading composer of the Counter-Reformation. Though he was strongly influenced by Palestrina and the Roman school, and though he was an extension of that school, Victoria remains identifiably Spanish in the fervor and ecstasy of his language, in the fierce intensity of his emotion, and most of all in his asceticism. Henri Prunières has noted: "He makes use of the madrigalesque style and of all the musical symbolism then current in Italy in order to express mystical emotions of such poignancy and tragic grandeur as none before him had attained. Every idea suggested by the text is in some manner illustrated by the music with an extraordinary inventiveness, force, and color. More dramatic, more passionate, more graphic than Palestrina, Victoria has been described as the El Greco of music, where Palestrina was its Raphael."

Tomás Luis de Victoria (or Vittoria) was born in Avila, Spain, in or about 1548. He received his preliminary musical training in his native city, where he served as boy chorister in the Cathedral. In 1565, he came to Rome to prepare for the priesthood. His friendship with Palestrina—and a probable period of study with that master—lured him from the church to music. In 1569, he became Maestro di Cappella at S. Maria di Montserrato in Rome, and in 1571, he succeeded Palestrina as Maestro di Cappella at its Seminary. Victoria's first publication was a volume of motets in 1572. One year later he became Maestro di Cappella at the Collegium Germanicum. After finally being ordained a priest in 1575, Victoria served for four years as choirmaster of S. Apollinare, and for seven as chaplain of San Girolamo della Carità. He returned to his native land in or about 1595, becoming organist and choirmaster of the Descalzas Reales convent in Madrid, and chaplain to the Empress-Mother Maria, sister of Philip II. Victoria's last, and probably greatest, work was a Requiem Mass in memory of Maria, who died in 1603. Victoria died in Madrid on August 27, 1611.

1572. O VOS OMNES, motet for four voices.

Victoria's first publication—a set of three motets—already finds him in full maturity, with a clearly identified creative personality. *O Vos Omnes,* from this collection, is one of his finest motets, and by the same token one of the shining adornments in motet literature. "Instead of the gentle, even rhythms of Palestrina," explains Donald Jay Grout, "the lines are broken as if into sobbing ejaculations; arresting vivid phrases with repeated notes ('Attendite') give way to cries of lamentation underlined by poignant dissonances ('Sicut dolor meus')."

1603. REQUIEM MASS (OFFICIUM DEFUNCTORUM), for six voices.

Victoria's last composition, which he described as his "swan song," came eight years before his death. It was written in memory of the Empress-Mother Maria upon her death in 1603 and in all probability was sung at her funeral. The composer dedicated this music to Maria's daughter, the Infanta Margarita, who was a nun in the Descalzas Reales convent where Victoria officiated as choirmaster and organist. The Mass is officially described as an "Office for the dead on the occasion of the death and obsequies of her Sacred Majesty the Empress."

This Requiem has been described as "the crown" of Victoria's compositions, and as "the greatest triumph of his genius." "Nothing in a cappella literature," states Paul Henry Lang, "can equal its glowing dark color and its passionate lamentation."

The work consists of an "Introit," with a "Kyrie," "Gradual," "Offertorium," "Sanctus," "Benedictus," "Agnus," and "Communio." J. R. Milne goes on to explain that each section is "preceded by the unison plainsong intonation, but also with the plainsong melody continued more or less freely in the second soprano." On a larger scale than any of his earlier Masses—and with a dramatized harmonic structure—this work is a masterpiece in which, as Milne adds, "there is no display of "art for art's sake." Its greatest strength, perhaps, lies in its "subordination of art to the sincere expression of religious devotion."

LUCA MARENZIO 1553–1599

The Italian madrigal came to full flower during the Renaissance with Marenzio. Previously, it had passed through several stages of technical development. The most important change that had taken place before Marenzio's time came with Willaert and Orlando de Lasso, among others, all of whom made a conscious attempt to give their texts a faithful and at times a realistic musical representation.

It is with Marenzio that the Italian madrigal enters the final phase of its evolution. Through Marenzio it acquires a definitely homophonic character, as a more extensive use is made of solo voices; it passes from the older modality to a modern tonality; it patterns the musical phrase after the accents of language, rather than pursuing a set meter; it increases dramatic interest, and intensifies poetic feeling; and it endows musical writing with pictorial images and details.

Luca Marenzio was born in Coccaglio, near Brescia, Italy, in 1553. He received some music instruction while serving as a chorister at the Brescia Cathedral; then some additional training in Rome, where from 1572 to 1578, he was Maestro di Cappella to Cardinal Madruzzo. For seven years, beginning with 1579, he was in the musical service of Cardinal Luigi d'Este. Marenzio's first volume of madrigals (for five voices) appeared in 1580. It proved so successful that during the next twenty-two years it went through six editions. Marenzio published eight more volumes of five-voice madrigals, together with several volumes of six-voice madrigals, and a single volume of *Madrigali Spirituali*. He also produced motets and villanelle. From 1591 to 1595, Marenzio was employed in Rome by Cardinal Aldobrandini; from 1596 to 1598, he was a member of the musical court of Sigismund III in Cracow. Upon returning to Rome, he worked for various establishments until his death in that city on August 22, 1599.

1580–1599. MADRIGALS, for five voices:
I piango ed ella il volto; Strider faceva; Solo e pensoro.

Marenzio was particularly partial to the love and pastoral poems of Petrarch, to whose verses he brought some of his finest musical inspiration. As Alfred Einstein has noted, Marenzio set many of the poems that reveal some of the facets of Petrarch's personality—"the sweet melancholy, the fluctuation between joy and grief, the sensuously supersensual." But, adds Einstein, Marenzio sought out in Petrarch "the pastoral, the playful, the contrast, the pathos, indeed, the extreme pathos. In general, he knows how to reconcile the most violent antithesis."

I piango ed ella il volto is one of Marenzio's shortest madrigals. But Alfred Einstein takes pains to point out that this brevity is the result of "the wealth of means placed at his disposal by the long history of the madrigal—these include chromaticism and freedom of declamation—and because he is a supreme master in the use of these means for the purpose of suggestion." With a quick stroke, and within a constricted area, Marenzio was here able to "recreate the whole situation: the dream, the finespun transparent web of illusion that precedes the awakening of the sleeper."

Marenzio's concern with his text led to vivid, at times realistic, pictorialism. In *Strider faceva* he imitates the droning of a bagpipe and the singing of birds for a poem that begins: "At dawn the shepherd made his bagpipes screech." In *Solo e pensoro* he fixes the feeling of loneliness and pain encountered in the opening line of the poem ("Alone, thought-sick, I pace where none has been") in a slow chromatic scale in the upper voice, against poignant descending figures in the other voices.

CARLO GESUALDO 1560–1613

Gesualdo (like Marenzio) was a genius of the madrigal. The fact that he was a dilettante and a nobleman, that his famous picaresque adventures served storytellers including Brantôme and Anatole France, may tend to obscure the more salient fact that he was a significant musical figure during the Renaissance. The bulk of his more than a hundred madrigals are gems, still capable of affording pleasure to a discriminating public. In addition, he was a prophetic voice in music. Nobody in his time was bolder than he in the use of discords and daring modulations; freer in the deployment of structure; more original in the progress of the melodic line; more advanced in the utilization of chromatic harmonies that anticipate Wagner. To his contemporaries he was an *enfant terrible*.

Gesualdo's main interest was not melody for its own sake but dramatic and emotional expression. For the sake of emotion and drama, he was compelled to write often in an unvocal style, to exploit unusual and at times bizarre sounds, to break rules and part company with tradition.

He was born in Naples in or about 1560 to an old, distinguished family. His first significant instruction in music came from Pomponio Nenna, a distinguished madrigalist, who taught him singing, composition, and lute playing. Gesualdo married Donna Maria d'Avalos in 1586. Four years later he achieved notoriety by arranging the murder of his wife and her lover. To escape punishment, he went into hiding. The death of his father brought him back to Naples, where he assumed the title of Prince of Venosa. In 1594, he settled in Ferrara and later married Leonora d'Este, daughter of the Duke. There he issued his first two volumes (both made up of five-voice madrigals), which became extremely popular. Four more volumes of madrigals appeared between 1595 and 1611, while a seventh was published posthumously in 1626. Gesualdo returned to Naples in or about 1597 and died there on September 8, 1613.

1611. MADRIGALS, for five voices:
Moro lasso al mio duolo; Resta di darmi noia.

Both of these madrigals, among the most celebrated by their composer, reveal him to be the rebel who side-steps rule and tradition in search of emotional or dramatic effect. "Moro lasso" is characterized by harmonic freedom and what Robert Craft describes as an "extravagant but tortured" and "dramatic but theatrical" art. Craft points to "Morro lasso" as an example of Gesualdo's "musical mannerism." He explains: "The tendency now called Mannerist was first distinguished by Vasari in reference to a group of his contemporaries among Florentine artists. They had begun to paint, Vasari noted, *di maniera* rather than *di natura*. But another expression of Vasari's can be applied more concretely to music. This is *lo sforzato,* the strained effect. In fact, Gesualdo might well be dubbed the master of *lo sforzato*. . . . The perfect example of musical mannerism . . . is Gesualdo's most famous madrigal, 'Moro lasso.' To understand Mannerism, in fact, one has only to compare this flamboyant music to the mathematical simplicity and the expressive control of a motet by Ockeghem. But Gesualdo's musical means are the tried and traditional tools of the contrapuntists, too. Gesualdo has only developed and used them in Gesualdo's way."

Equally bold in exploitation of new means and methods to arrive at greater expressiveness is the madrigal, "Resta di darmi noia." This one, like "Moro lasso" comes from the composer's sixth volume of madrigals. "Tortured harmony and restless declamation," says Alfred Einstein, "have been transformed from mannerism into full-blown expression, and this expression is more affecting if one considers the piece as an autobiographical confession."

ORAZIO VECCHI 1550–1605

Orazio Vecchi successfully combined a number of unaccompanied madrigals into a unified sequence intended for stage performance. It is through this medium that he reached the summit of his art, though much of his church music (Masses, motets, hymns) boasts a consummate craftsmanship in contrapuntal techniques. In his madrigal sequences—of which *L'Amfiparnaso* is his masterwork—he combined the gay (*piacevole*) and the grave (*grave*). Moving and affecting though his more sober and serious pages are, it is the infectious gaiety and buffoonery of his lighter moments that make him unique among the Italian madrigalists of his day.

Orazio Vecchi was born in Modena, Italy, in 1550. Music study took place mainly in Bologna with Salvatore Essenga, who published a Vecchi madrigal in 1566. Vecchi's first published volume, made up of canzonette, appeared in 1580. Meanwhile, he had taken holy orders, and in 1586, was made canon of the Correggio Cathedral. There, five years later, he was elevated to the post of archdeacon. Upon returning to his native city in 1596, he became Maestro di Cappella at its Cathedral. From this post he was removed in 1604 for having defied a minor order from the bishop. After that Vecchi went into a rapid physical decline. He died in Modena on February 19, 1605.

1594. L'AMFIPARNASO, "comedia harmonica" in three acts and fourteen scenes, with text by the composer.

L'Amfiparnaso consists of fourteen five-part unaccompanied madrigals, with which the art and science of the madrigal soars to Alpine heights. Since it had a plot and was intended for the stage, *L'Amfiparnaso* represents a significant link between the polyphonic era that preceded it and the age of opera that followed. But it must be remembered that its music did not employ the monodic or recitative style of the later opera, but was entirely polyphonic.

In the prologue, Vecchi informs his audience that the spectacle about to unfold is "to be seen through the mind, which it enters by ears and not be by eyes." In other words, he wanted his audience to concentrate on listening to the music rather than becoming absorbed by the visual spectacle. Nevertheless, Vecchi insisted on describing his work, not as a madrigal sequence, but as a "comedia harmonica," or "comedy in music," and he demanded a stage production.

There are two plots. The first, the "lirico tragica," describes the courtship of Lucio and Isabella, rudely interrupted when Isabella receives the false information that her beloved is dead. She plans suicide, but at the zero hour is saved when her servant comes with the happy tidings that Lucio is still alive. This part of the work concludes with the wedding of the lovers.

The second plot, "grottesco comica," deploys characters from the Commedia dell' arte. Here the main thread ties together Old Pantalone and the courtesan, Hortensia, while the love affair of Lelio and Nisa intertwines as a subplot.

When *L'Amfiparnaso* was given at the Berkshire Music Center in Lenox, Massachusetts, during the 1950's in what was probably the first time the work had been staged in the United States, Olin Downes described it as follows: "It is polyphonic—madrigal feeling its way towards monodic aria and recitative, in a word-play of delicious nonsense, poetry, sensuality, and wit, and adroit characterization of the figures on the stage. . . . The work is a madrigal variation, or sublimation, of the comedy of masks, that semi-provisional form of dramatic entertainment that for two centuries and more delighted the Italian public and represented the most popular form of musico-dramatic representation that they knew."

"Vecchi," explains Prof. Edward J. Dent, "set the comedy of masks to music, not because he wished to be dramatic, but because music without words was practically unthinkable. The comedy of masks was familiar to his singers in such a way that his setting was virtually wordless. The characters represented would not be made real to their minds through what they said on one particular occasion; they were not individuals, but eternal types, personifications of phases of character that every hearer could recognize more or less in some aspect of his personality."

L'Amfiparnaso was performed for the first time in Modena in 1594, and published three years later. On the occasion of the four-hundredth anniversary of the composer's birth, the work was revived in a stage presentation in Modena, in 1950.

WILLIAM BYRD 1543–1623

Tudor England boasted many composers of impressive gifts and achievements; perhaps the most remarkable of them all was William Byrd. "He not only excelled in every branch of musical composition in his own day," says E. H. Fellowes, "but ventured into new paths hitherto untrodden; and in every branch he met with success at least as conspicuous as that attained by any of his contemporaries. . . . The largeness of his output, even apart from its exceptional merit, gives it a degree of importance which cannot pass unnoticed." The motets Byrd contributed to *Cantiones sacrae* in 1575 (his first publication), together with those written for the same volume by Thomas Tallis, represent the first time that Latin motets were written and published by Englishmen. After that, Byrd issued two more volumes of *Cantiones sacrae* (1589, 1591) and two sets of *Gradualia* (1605, 1607). Besides his Latin church music, Byrd also created music for the English prayer book where, with "nothing available for immediate use" (as Fellowes has pointed out) and "with no tradition as to form or method of setting the canticles," Byrd produced services and anthems that have remained indestructible monuments.

Remarkable as his church music was, Byrd is most familiar to present day music lovers through his madrigals, songs, and music for the keyboard. Here, too, he was a pioneer, often creating his own forms, styles, traditions. Whatever medium he worked in, whatever form he utilized, Byrd touched his music with the imprints of a master. No wonder, then, that to his contemporaries and successors he was the "miracle man of music," the "parent of British music." No wonder, too, that a musicologist of the stature of E. H. Fellowes can place him "unhesitatingly in the first flight of the world's composers."

William Byrd was born in 1543, probably in Lincolnshire. He is believed to have attended the St. Paul's School. Later he received musical instruction from Thomas Tallis. From 1563 to 1572, he was organist at the Lincoln Cathedral. During this time, in 1568, he married Juliana Birley. From 1572 on, he was the organist of the Chapel Royal in London, initially sharing the post with Tallis, and then (after Tallis's death) occupying it alone. Byrd's first publication was *Cantiones sacrae,* in 1575, a volume of thirty-four motets, sixteen by Byrd and the other eighteen by Tallis. This was the first publication of a house of which Byrd and Tallis were joint proprietors under a license granted them by the Queen. Byrd ran the firm himself after Tallis's death; in the ensuing decades, he issued several more volumes of his own compositions. Byrd died in Stondon Massey, Essex, on July 4, 1623.

1588–1589. MADRIGALS:

"Though Amaryliss Dance in Green"; "Come to Me Grief, Forever"; "Come, Woeful Orpheus"; "I Thought That Love Had Been a Boy"; "In Winter Cold"; "Who Made Thee, Hob, Foresake the Plough?"

Byrd's madrigals were among the earliest such pieces appearing in England. Stylistically and structurally they differed sharply from the English madrigals of Morley, Wilbye, and Gibbons that came afterwards. The Byrd madrigal was almost an art song. Many of his madrigals were designed, as Fellowes explains, "to be performed alternatively, either by combined voices or by solo voice accompanied by strings." The main voice (referred to by the composer as "the first singing part") presented a continuous melodic line, in place of a repetition of phrases to which later madrigalists were partial. The other voices, or viols, served as an accompaniment.

"Though Amaryliss Dance in Green" was Byrd's first madrigal and first piece of secular music; it is still one of his most popular compositions. Here rhythm rather than melody is emphasized. The equivalents of 3/4 and 6/8 time are used, either in succession or simultaneously, with intriguing effect.

Essentially an austere personality, Byrd preferred treating madrigal subjects that were contemplative, at times even somber. In this vein we find "Come to Me Grief, Forever" and "Come Woeful Orpheus." But Byrd also had a lighter side, as Fellowes has remarked. "'I Thought That Love Had Been a Boy' is in the best vein of light lyrical setting; 'In Winter Cold' is treated with subtle touches of satire; and in 'Who Made Thee, Hob, Foresake the Plough?', Byrd has caught exactly the spirit of the blunt rustic humor of the words."

——— COMPOSITIONS FOR THE VIRGINAL:

The Earl of Salisbury; Wolsey's Wilde; Sellinger's Round; The Earl of Oxford's March; The Bells.

Byrd wrote about one hundred and forty pieces for the virginal. Eight of these pieces (including the famous *The Earl of Salisbury*) appeared in *Parthenia,* issued in 1612–1613, the first collection of music for the virginal ever issued in England, and one of the earliest publications in England to be printed from engraved plates.

Byrd had no precedent to guide him in writing keyboard music. The only such pieces produced up to that time had consisted merely of adaptations of vocal polyphonic music or popular dances. Nevertheless, Byrd managed to create a library of keyboard music with which English instrumental music emerges for the first time. Singlehandedly, he devised technical effects for the keyboard and crystallized for English instrumental music such forms as the fantasia and the variation. Byrd produced preludes, voluntaries, courantes, pavanes, galliards, airs, rounds, as well as fantasias and variations. One of his most celebrated pieces, *The Earl of Salisbury,* consists of two dances, a pavane and a galliard. Another popular composition, *Wolsey's Wild,* is in variation form. The melody here is broken up into separate sections, each section in turn receiving variation. *Sellinger's Round* and *The Earl of Oxford's March* are, as their titles indicate, respectively a round and a march. Byrd's gift at pictorial writing can be found in *The Bells.*

The twentieth-century English composer, Gordon Jacob, arranged three of these Byrd pieces for orchestra and combined them into a suite: *The Bells, The Earl of Oxford's March*, and *Wolsey's Wilde.*

THOMAS MORLEY 1557–1603

The thirty-year period during which the madrigal prospered in England was one of the richest eras in that country's musical history. The year of 1588 may be regarded as the year of decision for the English madrigal. It was then that William Byrd wrote the first such piece by an Englishman. It was also during the same year that the Italian madrigal achieved in England a new wave of popularity through the publication of Nicolas Yonge's *Musica Transalpina,* a collection of Italian madrigals with texts translated into English.

On the wave of this newly aroused interest in madrigals, Thomas Morley was swept to greatness. In 1593, he published a volume of three-voice canzonets, in which a madrigal style was suggested. One year later, he emerged as one of the foremost English madrigal composers of his age with the issue of his first book of madrigals, for four voices. In 1601, he edited a monumental edition of English madrigals by twenty-three different composers: *The Triumphs of Oriana,* published in 1603. Here each madrigal ended with the words, "Long live the fair Oriana," as a tribute to Queen Elizabeth, who was called Oriana in pastoral poetry. In this collection are found two gems by Morley, together with madrigals by Wilbye and Gibbons. The madrigal was now a fixture in the musical life of England. By the time its heyday had passed, in or about 1627, more than forty books of such pieces had been published—a remarkable library that led Ernest Walker to regard it as "on the whole the greatest music treasure England possesses."

Morley also produced significant balletts for voices, and an "ayre" for a Shakespeare play ("It Was a Lover and His Lass"). This "ayre" is one of the few surviving songs from the late sixteenth century.

Thomas Morley was born in 1557, the precise place in England not known. After serving as a boy chorister at St. Paul's in London, he studied music and mathematics with William Byrd. In 1588, he received a baccalaureate in music from Oxford. In or about 1589, he became organist of St. Paul's Cathedral, and in 1592, he was made Gentleman of the Chapel Royal. Poor health compelled him to resign from the Chapel Royal in 1602. He died in London, probably in 1603.

1594–1601. MADRIGALS, for four voices:

"April Is in My Mistress' Face"; "Now in the Gentle Season"; "Since My Tears and Lamenting"; "Hard By a Crystal Fountain."

The first three of these madrigals come from Morley's first book issued in 1594; the fourth appeared in the *Triumphs of Oriana* in 1603. All four are masterpieces that bring into focus the stylistic traits that set the English madrigal sharply apart from its Italian counterpart. These gems are all characterized by a lightness of touch; vivid pictorialism; vitality and grace of rhythm; pithy and forcefully expressive melodies; sharpness of detail; a sunny warmth of feeling; effectiveness of declamation. Here Morley set a standard of madrigal writing toward which all his contemporaries reached, but which few surpassed.

A. E. F. Dickinson, in comparing Morley's madrigals with those written before his time, finds them "more objective, . . . less dramatic or emotional, while achieving a lightness of touch Byrd had not known. A picturesque verbal phrase was an opportunity not to be missed. Failing this, skilful imitation and flowing counterpoint must fill the gap. . . . 'Insouciance' is Walker's word and it is a true one. There is little sense of spiritual adventure. . . . Morley was a true Elizabethan, rejoicing, while it lasted, in the exercise of creative vitality, technical introspection, and stately gloom."

1595. BALLETTS, for five voices:

"Now Is the Month of Maying"; "Fire, Fire My Heart"; "My Bonny Lass, She Smileth"; "Sing We and Chant It."

The ballett was a vocal form introduced to England by Morley, and of which he was the most significant creator. The ballett was a madrigal-like piece of music. However, where the madrigal was through composed, the ballett was strophic, the same music being repeated through several stanzas. Once again, where the madrigal was sophisticated and subtle, the ballett was light-hearted and buoyant in feeling. Most balletts were homophonic, with the melody (in dance meter) set off in the top voice, and divided into sections that were frequently repeated.

"Now Is the Month of Maying" is Morley's most popular ballett. It is in triple meter, with the melody built from four-bar phrases, except for the ending, which is in a three-bar phrase. What Karl Nef said about this ballet applies equally to "Fire, Fire My Heart," "My Bonny Lass, She Smileth," and "Sing We and Chant It." The melodies are all characterized "by the same vernal freshness and charm," springing "genuinely from native soil" and fashioned "with true artistry."

JOHN WILBYE 1574–1638

John Wilbye shared with Morley the leadership of the English school of madrigal composers. His sixty-five madrigals, for three to six voices, are some of the finest flowers in this wondrous garden. His technical mastery is equal to Morley's, and so is his consistently high level of inspiration. There are some musicologists who even regard him as Morley's superior in the flexibility of adapting the mood and feeling of text to music, and in the variety of the subjects treated.

Wilbye was born in Diss, Norfolk, England, in 1574. In 1595, he became a household musician for Sir Thomas and Lady Elizabeth Kytson at Hengrave Hall, near Bury St. Edmunds. Three years later, he published the first of his two volumes of madrigals, the second appearing in 1609. He left the employ of the Kytson family in 1628 to become attached to the household of Lady Rivers in Colchester. He died there in September, 1638.

1598–1609. MADRIGALS, for four and five voices:

"Flora Gave Me Fairest Flowers"; "Sweet Honey-Sucking Bees"; "Adieu, Sweet Amaryllis"; "All Pleasure Is of This Condition"; "Happy, Oh, Happy He."

Like Morley, Wilbye could be light, gay, and amorous with irresistible charm. But he could also sound deeper and more somber notes with little diminution of imagination or power. In fact, some of Wilbye's finest madrigals are in an elegiac mood.

The five madrigals here under discussion are among the composer's finest, as well as most characteristic. Here is how Ernest Walker described them: "The works by which he is best known—'Flora Gave Me Fairest Flowers' and 'Sweet Honey-Sucking Bees' (both for five voices)—represent him in his delicately graceful and lighter mood; they are marked by exquisite polish and charm. . . . We see him in rather more reflective mood, tender and expressive, with a vein of quiet sadness in . . . the four-part, 'Adieu, Sweet Amaryllis.' . . . But he is seen at his greatest when the words give him emotional chances . . . [in] the four-part 'Happy, Oh, Happy He' and the five-part 'All Pleasure is of This Condition.' The latter of these two is throughout gray in mood, with its feeling, so to speak, dulled and resigned; but just at the end, to the words 'with gnawing grief and never-ending smart,' the voices, after some most striking anticipatory harmonic progressions, build themselves up in a sort of last cry of despair—superbly managed both technically and emotionally —and then sink slowly back. But perhaps even more wonderful is the close of 'Happy, Oh, Happy He'—the words of which form what is practically a religious poem—. . . on which Wilbye's somber and restrained music fades slowly into darkness with one poignant utterance of extraordinary pathetic dignity."

ORLANDO GIBBONS 1583–1625

Gibbons ploughed three fields of music productively. In English church music he was perhaps without an equal—an outstanding exponent of the new church style then being evolved in England and to which he brought (as Henri Prunières noted) "a primitive type of mysticism, noble, dignified, and severe."

But it is by the two other fields he fertilized and enriched that Gibbons is most often remembered today. One is the madrigal, of which he was a master in the class of Morley and Wilbye. The other was instrumental music—more than forty pieces for the virginal (fantasias, fancies, In Nomines, courantes, pavanes, galliards, and so forth) and some remarkable fantasias for viols.

Orlando Gibbons was born in Oxford, England, in 1583. In 1598, he was matriculated from King's College, Cambridge, where he had served as boy chorister. In 1605, he was made organist of the Chapel Royal, holding this post for the remainder of his life. He also served as a chamber musician to the king and as the organist of Westminster Abbey. Gibbons died in Canterbury, England, on June 5, 1625.

1605–1613. FANTASIAS, for three viols.

Gibbons' various fantasias for viols (nine of which were published during his lifetime) are the cream of the instrumental crop produced in Tudor England. Gibbons was impelled to write fantasias through his dissatisfaction with the way in which vocal madrigals were being adapted for instruments. He aimed to write music *intended* for instruments, with an instrumental rather than vocal technique, an instrumental gamut of expression, instrumental nuances. Thus he realized one of the earliest forms of English instrumental composition. His fantasias were in a free fugal style (anticipating later fugal writing). His fantasias were usually made up of several sections, in each of which themes of varying length were developed contrapuntally, subjected to frequent changes of tempo and mood. These fantasias, says J. A. Fuller Maitland, "are so masterly in design, so highly inventive, and so splendidly carried out" that they find few equals in the instrumental literature of this period."

1612–1613. THE EARL OF SALISBURY, pavane for virginal.

Gibbons contributed six pieces for the virginal to *Parthenia:* a prelude, two galliards, a four-art fantasia (*The Queen's Command*), and what is probably his most famous composition for the keyboard, *The Earl of Salisbury.* The last is an extraordinary example of an instrumental pavane—the pavane being an old Italian dance with a slow and stately rhythm. The Italian pavane had by then gone out of fashion, but *The Earl of Salisbury* was one of several important works during the Tudor period that restored this dance form to instrumental music.

1614. MADRIGALS, for five voices:

"The Silver Swan"; "What Is Our Life?" "How Art Thou Thrall'd"; "Dainty, Fine Bird."

Gibbons published only a single volume of madrigals, all of them for five voices. The texts deal with sadness, renunciation, unrequited love, death, when they do not try to point up some moral. Musically, these madrigals are as massive in structure as they are somber in mood. Technically, they demonstrate a progressive point of view toward harmony and melody.

"The Silver Swan," perhaps Gibbons's best-known madrigal, is described by Ernest Walker as "exquisite, . . . none could be more polished in expression." To Walker, Gibbons's finest madrigals are those that combine strength with subtlety, as, for example, "the lengthy, solemnly impressive 'What Is Our Life?' and 'How Art Thou Thrall'd,' . . . the last pages of which are magnificent." Commenting upon "Dainty Fine Bird," Walker points to the "beautiful close . . . so as to show how Gibbons treats words that come as close as any used by him ever do to the typical madrigalian sentiments."

JOHN BULL 1562–1628

English keyboard music took a giant forward step with the one hundred and fifty or more pieces that Bull wrote for the virginal or the organ. As a brilliant virtuoso on both these instruments—and as a creator of virtuoso music for each—Bull is sometimes described as the Franz Liszt of his time. In writing for the keyboard, Bull continued where Byrd had left off. Wanda Landowska said: "Each one of them brings popular music to the same destination. The prowess of augmentation and diminution is as familiar to the one as to the other. And both are intoxicated with perpetual movement, with a harsh and robust rhythm. Notice those clusters of semiquavers which, with Byrd and Bull, roll, overflow, and spread out the exuberance of life over the measure bars."

He was born in Somersetshire, England, in or about 1562. Music study took place first with William Blitheman at the Chapel Royal, then at Oxford and Cambridge, from which Bull received his musical baccalaureate and doctorate. Meanwhile, in 1582, he was appointed organist of the Hereford Cathedral. Three years later he became a Gentleman of the Chapel Royal, where, in 1591, he was appointed organist. Between 1596 and 1607, Bull occupied the then newly created chair of music at Gresham College. From 1603 to 1613, he was music master to the royal children. In 1613, he left England for good, under mysterious circumstances. He settled in Antwerp where he became organist of the Notre Dame cathedral. He died in Antwerp on March 12 or 13, 1628.

——— COMPOSITIONS FOR VIRGINAL:
Walsingham Variations; The King's Hunt; Queen Elizabeth's Pavane; Spanish Pavane.

With his brilliant runs, scale passages, arpeggios, cross rhythms, cross-hand harmonies, broken octaves, and intervallic leaps, Bull introduced a new virtuosity to English keyboard music. It is quite true that in some of his pieces virtuosity seems an end in itself. The famous *Walsingham Variations* is a case in point. It offers such a remarkable display of pyrotechnics that Margaret H. Glyn is led to say that it contains "nearly all present piano technique, if allowance be made for the limited treble compass and the absence of octave passages." Other Bull pieces for virginal are rich in pictorial imagery or are singularly expressive, melodically and harmonically. *The King's Hunt* is such a composition. The main theme represents the call of the hunting horn. A series of variations follows in which the interest is focused, not only on the way the melody changes shape and form, but also on the way in which the chase is programmatically depicted in runs, arpeggios, and cross rhythms. Bull's expressive lyricism distinguishes his two pavanes, the *Queen Elizabeth's Pavane* (whose heart is a stately melody) and the *Spanish Pavane* (a series of variations on a delightful dance tune).

JOHN DOWLAND 1563–1626

The lute songs (or "ayres") of John Dowland mark the beginnings of the art song. Dowland published his first book of songs in 1597, the earliest English musician to issue such a collection. By doing so, he may be said to have helped deliver the blow that destroyed the vogue for the madrigal. Here, and in his later volumes of songs, he achieved such a high artistic standard, and was so successful in realizing a song style, that Ernest Newman did not hesitate to place him with a half-dozen or so of the greatest song composers the world has known.

Dowland was born, probably in Ireland, in or about 1563. He came to London when he was fifteen, and soon found employment in the household of Sir Henry Cobham, with whom he stayed until 1583. For a period of time after 1583, Dowland worked for Sir Edward Stafford, with whom he visited France. In 1588, Dowland received a bachelor degree in music from Christ Church, Oxford, and had his first piece of music published (an instrumental galliard). After 1593, he traveled about a good deal in Europe, and for a while studied with Marenzio in Italy. Back in England in 1595, he issued a volume of lute pieces in 1596, and his first book of songs in 1597. The latter proved so successful that within sixteen years it went through five editions. In 1598, Dowland was engaged as lutenist at the court of Christian IV of Denmark. He stayed several years in Elsinore, issuing two more volumes of songs, in 1600 and 1603. A set of instrumental compositions—the *Lachrymae, or Seven Tears*—appeared in 1605, and a last collection of songs—*The Pilgrim's Solace*—in 1612. Dowland died on January 21, 1626, probably in London.

1600–1603. SONGS (OR AYRES), with lute:
"Flow, My Tears"; "Sorrow, Sorrow, Stay"; "I Saw My Lady Weep"; "Say, Love"; "Weep You No More, Sad Fountains."

Dowland published three volumes of songs (or "ayres"), and a fourth, which he called *The Pilgrim's Solace*. The composer's most celebrated song, "Flow, My Tears," comes from his second volume, issued in 1600. (He used this melody again as the first composition in an instrumental work entitled *Lachrymae, or Seven Tears*.) "Sorrow, Sorrow Stay" and "I Saw My Lady Weep" also come from this second volume, while "Say, Love" and "Weep You No More, Sad Fountains" are found in the third volume, issued in 1603.

The lute song, or ayre, is actually a simplified madrigal. The basic melody is placed in the solo voice, while supplementary voices and the lute serve as a background. Where the madrigal is pictorial, the ayre is lyrical, with an even greater and more conscious attempt to have the melody give a faithful rendering of the text. Castiglione, Dowland's contemporary, regarded the lute song as superior to the polyphonic madrigal. He maintained: "To sing to the lute is much better, because all sweetness consisteth in one voice alone, and singing to the lute with dittie is more pleasant than rest, for it addeth to the words such a grace and strength that it is a great wonder." By suggesting a homophonic character, by realizing the expressive qualities of the solo human voice, Dowland became the first of that royal line of great composers of song that included Schubert, Schumann, and Brahms.

Most of Dowland's songs are melancholy. An exception is "Say, Love," which is as light and frolicsome as a Morley ballett. "Sorrow, Sorrow, Stay" is remarkable, not only for its lyricism, but also for the richness and expressive character of the lute accompaniment.

JACOPO PERI 1561–1633

The Baroque era in music, extending from about 1600 to 1750, followed the Renaissance. The term "baroque" is borrowed from art and architecture. It denotes over-all grandeur, massive designs, ornamental details, decorative effects. Baroque music placed emphasis on dramatic values within new spacious forms: the oratorio in church music, for example, and the opera, in secular. Instrumental music became as important as vocal. Baroque, consequently, saw the development of instrumental virtuosity, and the birth and early development of the orchestra. With the Baroque period, a "new music" ("Nuove musiche") appeared. In this "new music," the polyphonic style, combining several different melodies of equal importance, gave way to homophony, in which a single melody was prominently set against a harmonic instrumental background.

"New music"—and with it opera—was the achievement of a group of Florentine dilettantes known as the "Camerata," of which Jacopo Peri was a member. It met regularly at the palace of Count Giovanni Bardi, beginning with 1680. Fired by the spirit of the Renaissance, and by humanism, the Camerata sought to revive Greek drama with music. Polyphony, it was at once realized, was poorly suited for dramatic purpose. Drama, after all, emphasized the solo voice rather than a group of voices; besides, polyphony tended to obscure the articulation of the text. Giovanni Battista Doni explained this problem a century later as follows: "Means must be found in the attempt to bring music closer to the classical times, and to bring out the chief melody prominently so that the poetry could be understandable." Going back to the Greeks for guidance and a solution, the Camerata came upon a treatise by Aristoxenus maintaining that song must be patterned after speech; it also found a Plato quotation saying that music had to be "first of all language and rhythm, and secondly tone, and not vice versa." With these signposts providing a direction, the Camerata veered toward an altogether new kind of music: the "stile rappresentativo," or "stile recitativo," which Vincenzo Galilei first described in his *Dialogues of Ancient and Modern Music* (1581), sometimes described as the declaration of war against polyphony. This new music was in a monodic or declamatory style. It consisted of a recitative-like melody, patterned after the inflections of speech, accompanied by an instrument. With the appearance of stile rappresentativo, homophony emerges at last. This was a style that could be used as the musical spine of classical drama. The marriage of declamation, or recitative, with classical drama gave us opera.

Though Peri was not the first to use the stile rappresentativo (see page 35, EMILIO DE' CAVALIERI), he was the first to set a stage text entirely to music. In doing this, he helped evolve "dramma per musica" ("drama through music"), as opera was originally called.

Jacopo Peri was born in Rome, Italy, on August 20, 1561. He received his musical training from Cristofano Malvezzi. Later he became attached as singer and composer to the musical establishment of the De Medicis in Florence. All this while, he was a member of the Camerata, which met regularly to discuss art and culture. Stimulated by these conversations—and by the invention of stile rappresentativo—Peri wrote *Dafne* in 1597, the first time a stage work was set entirely to music. In 1600, he completed a second opera, *Euridice*. After that, he wrote two more operas that were never produced and collaborated with other composers on two others, besides writing music for various court spectacles and entertainments, and some church music for the choir of San Nicola in Pisa. Peri died in Florence on August 12, 1633.

1597–1600. OPERAS:
Dafne; Euridice.

In *Dafne,* the libretto by Ottavio Rinuccini is built around a simple mythological episode. Dafne, beloved of Apollo, is being pursued by a god. To protect her, Dafne's mother transforms her into a laurel tree, which from then on becomes sacred to Apollo.

The score has been lost. But we do know that Peri's music was made up mainly of recitatives, accompanied by a lyre, lute, or harpsichord. Occasionally, variety of interest was introduced through the interpolation of brief choral episodes and dances.

Dafne was seen for the first time in 1597, at the Palazzo Corsi in Florence, during the Carnival. The cast included Peri himself, playing the part of Apollo. The drama proved such a huge success that during the next two or three years it was repeated several times, with various changes and interpolations.

The acclaim given to *Dafne* encouraged Peri to write a second opera, *Euridice,* in 1600, to honor the wedding of Henry IV of France to Marie de Medici. This music, fortunately, has been preserved. The opera was produced for the first time at the Palazzo Pitti in Florence during the marriage ceremonies—on October 6, 1600. Once again, Peri was a member of the cast, this time as Orfeo.

The text by Rinuccini represents the first time that the legend of Orpheus and Eurydice was given a musico-dramatic treatment. From this time on, this story would be the one favored most often by opera librettists, and with good reason. It is ideal material for operatic treatment. The central character being a singer and poet provides ample opportunities for song. In addition to this, the drama is partial to musical treatment: in the gamut of its emotions; in the dramatic interest implicit in the rescue of Eurydice from Hades by her husband's love and devotion; in the description of Elysium and Hades; and in the contrasts between the tragic opening and the happy ending. It is, therefore, significantly appropriate to find that the first opera to survive is one that was built around this legend.

Peri's *Euridice* has neither an overture nor instrumental interludes. Four instruments were utilized backstage as accompaniment (harpsichord, bass lute, lute, and lyre). Their main function was to support the voice with solid and, at times, expressive harmonies. The action is carried entirely by the solo voices through recitatives. Though these recitatives tend to follow speech patterns, they nevertheless manage to have a great deal of musical interest, at least for the early seventeenth century. Indeed, a few of the recitatives almost suggest a song-like character. In addition to these solo passages, this opera includes a few dances and some polyphonic and monophonic choruses.

In 1963, the first recording ever made of Peri's *Euridice* was released by Amadeo Records in a performance prepared and conducted by Angelo Ephrikian. In reviewing this release, Alan Rich had this to say about the opera in the *New York Times:* "One can admire the simple plasticity of Peri's melodies and his graceful subservience to the demands of the prosody of Ottavio Rinuccini's libretto. But the music remains an experiment, not a realization. Where the genius of Monteverdi transcends the early innovators in his ability to choose the best of the new and the old, and to combine them with a keen awareness of musical and dramatic needs. Peri, as an ardent proselytizer, constantly overstates the need for the new simplicity and ends with a piece that is dramatically so flaccid as to have no musical life at all." Rich sums up by saying that *Euridice,* as far as present-day audiences are concerned, has far greater interest "as a historical document than as a genuinely exciting musical experience."

EMILIO DE' CAVALIERI 1550–1602

While Jacopo Peri was the first composer to set a stage work entirely in the new monodic or recitative style (see sketch above), he was not the first composer to use this style successfully. This achievement fell to another member of the Florentine Camerata, Emilio de' Cavalieri. In 1590—about half a dozen years before Peri wrote *Dafne*—Cavalieri completed the music for several "favole pastorali" ("pastoral fables"), with texts by Laura Guidiccioni. These fables represented the first attempts to use the stile rappresentativo, or recitative. Cavalieri's success in this experiment might well have been the stimulus Peri needed for the writing of the first "dramma per musica."

Cavalieri's masterwork in the monodic style was *La Rappresentazione di anima e di corpo,* an extended morality play with music. In its own way it proved as influential as Peri's operas in establishing and solidifying the concepts of "Nuove musiche."

Emilio de' Cavalieri, son of a nobleman, was born in or about 1550, place unknown. After completing his musical studies, he became the organist of the Oratorio del Santissimo Crocofisso in Rome. From 1588 to 1596, he served as the Inspector General of Arts and Artists at the Tuscan court. This was the period in which he became actively involved in the discussions of the Camerata at the Palazzo Bardi (see sketch on PERI). In 1589, Cavalieri wrote the music for an intermezzo performed during the wedding ceremonies of Ferdinand I, Grand Duke of Tuscany, and Christine of Lorraine. A year later came his first experiments with a monodic style, with the pastoral fables *Il Satiro* and *La Disperazione di Fileno.* His chef d'oeuvre, *La Rappresentazione di anima e di corpo,* came a decade later. Cavalieri died in Rome on March 11, 1602.

1600. LA RAPPRESENTAZIONE DI ANIMA E DI CORPO, a morality play with music.

La Rappresentazione received its first performance in the Oratorio della Vallicella at St. Philip Neri's Church in Rome in February 1600. Later choral works for the church were designated "oratorios" because their predecessors in a similar format had been performed in this Oratory. It is for this reason that *La Rappresentazione* has long been described as the first oratorio ever written—which is not the case at all. *La Rappresentazione* is not an oratorio in any sense of that term. It is a morality play. Agostino Manni's text—an allegory personifying Time, Life, Body, Soul, Pleasure, Intellect, and so forth—was intended to teach churchgoers the basic elements of a good religious life. In the preface to the published score, the specific instructions on methods of stage production point strongly to the fact that *La Rappresentazione* is more of an opera than anything else.

This work is made up of a succession of recitatives delivered by the various characters. Several choral passages (notably the choruses of the Blessed and the Damned Spirits) and a few instrumental interludes, between the acts, provide contrast. The composition is divided into three acts, a fact of no small historical significance, since this is the first musico-dramatic work to assume such a pattern.

What is perhaps the first stage presentation of this morality play, since its premiere in 1600, took place in Cambridge, England, on June 9, 1949. For this presentation, Prof. Edward J. Dent provided a new English translation for the text.

CLAUDIO MONTEVERDI 1567–1643

It took just ten years for the "dramma per musica" (see PERI) to develop into a compelling art form; to transform the stile rappresentativo, or recitative, into rich, fluid, and varied melody. Only a genius could have taken the primitive means devised by the Camerata, and Jacopo Peri, and used them with a wealth of imagination, dramatic force, and creative richness. That genius was Claudio Monteverdi. He was the first composer to write operas with a full awareness of the artistic potential of this musico-dramatic genre; he was the first musical dramatist. He created the first operas that a present-day audience can listen to with appreciation and pleasure. We can, therefore, readily understand why his contemporaries should have referred to him as "music's prophet."

He began as a polyphonist. His first published volume was a set of three-part motets issued when he was only fifteen. This was followed by a book of three-part canzonettas, and the first three of his eight volumes of madrigals. Vital and original and singularly eloquent though he proved to be in his greatest madrigals, it is in the opera that he became a prophet and a seer. Compared to the archaic vocabulary and methods of a Peri, Monteverdi's operas represent an entirely new art. This is not revolution: there was nothing before Monteverdi that he could have revolutionized. This is invention, the discovery of a brave, new world. Monteverdi was the innovator of an altogether new concept of dramatic music—with new methods, techniques, style, and idioms. He used rhythm, discords, instrumental colors, key changes, to project dramatic action or interpret characters or project moods and emotions, and in a way completely unknown before or during his time. He was the first one to understand and appreciate the role of the orchestra in an opera, to use an instrumental style and resources as an ally for his dramatic mission. He was the first to realize that wind instruments and percussion, for example, were effective in projecting military moods; that flutes were apt for pastoral scenes; that violas and lutes were best suited for sentimental or amatory episodes. To use instruments for the purpose of mood painting and characterization was simply without precedent. He also had to devise instrumental techniques to create the kind of agitation or passion or emotional intensity ("stile concitato") his dramas needed—pizzicato and tremolo, for example. He knew how to make his characters, not the abstractions they had been with Peri, but human beings. What he created was so different from anything that had been done before him that his greatest operas seem to have been "issued from the void," as Domenico de Paolo once said, "almost as Minerva sprang from the brain of Jupiter."

Claudio Monteverdi was born in Cremona, Italy, in 1567. He was a boy chorister at the Cremona Cathedral, where he studied music with Marc' Antonio Ingegneri, and published his volume of three-voice motets. Between 1587 and 1592, he issued a volume of three-part canzonettas and his first three volumes of madrigals. In or about 1590, Monteverdi became a viol player and madrigal singer at the court of Vincenzo Gonzaga, the Duke of Mantua; and in 1602, he assumed there the post of Maestro di Cappella. Meanwhile, in 1595, he married Claudia Cattaneo, a singer at court. Her premature death in 1607 left him with two infant sons.

Between 1603 and 1605, Monteverdi issued two more volumes of madrigals; and in 1607, a volume of three-voice *Scherzi musicali* and his first opera his magnum opus, *La Favola d'Orfeo.* One year later, he completed a second opera, *Arianna,* of which only a single fragment has survived, the remarkable "Lament," the most deeply moving operatic song written before Gluck. From 1613 until the end of his life, Monteverdi served as Maestro di Cappella at the St. Mark's Cathedral in Venice. There he produced three more volumes of madrigals, and several operas, beginning with *Il Combattimento di Tancredi e Clorinda,* produced in 1624. An outbreak of the plague in Venice in 1631, from which he emerged untouched, seems to have impelled Monteverdi to take holy orders in 1632. In 1639, his first opera in almost a decade, *Adone,* was produced at the Teatro San Moïse. His last opera, a masterwork—*L'Incoronazione di Poppea*—was given in 1642. Just before his death, Monteverdi revisited his native city of Cremona. Soon after resuming his musical duties in Venice, he died there on November 29, 1643, and was buried in the chapel of St. Ambrosius in the church of Santa Maria dei Frari.

1607. LA FAVOLA D'ORFEO (THE FABLE OF ORPHEUS), dramma per musica in five acts, text by Alessandro Striggio. First performance: Mantua, February 22, 1607.

It is significant that in his title Monteverdi did not include the name of Eurydice, something that most of the subsequent composers did in treating the Orpheus legend. In the Monteverdi opera, Eurydice is a subsidiary character to whom only a few numbers are assigned. The principal action, and most of the emotion surrounding it, involve Orpheus; and it is for Orpheus that Monteverdi produced his most eloquent music.

The opera opens with the celebration of the marriage of Eurydice and Orpheus. No sooner has Orpheus extolled the beauty of his bride to his shepherd friends whan he learns that Eurydice has just died, the victim of a snake bite. Orpheus insists upon following her into the kingdom of the dead. His eloquent plea wins over Charon's support, who permits him to cross the river Styx into the inner recesses of Hades. There Proserpine prevails on Pluto, ruler in Hades, to allow Eurydice to return with Orpheus into the upper world. Pluto consents, but only on the condition that Orpheus not look at his bride until he is back on earth. A violent clap of thunder, however, makes Orpheus involuntarily look back at her. Eurydice returns to Hades. Back again on earth, Orpheus gives voice to his terrible despair, vowing to renounce love forever. But the god Apollo pities him, descends to earth and lifts Orpheus to the stars, where he can be reunited with his beloved Eurydice.

Monteverdi utilized every resource at his command—and some he had to devise—to carry over into his music all the drama, tenderness, and pathos of this story. Peri had also written an opera about Orpheus and Eurydice in *Euridice,* but Monteverdi "turned the aristocratic spectacle of Florence into modern musical drama overflowing with life and bearing, in its mighty waves of sounds, the passions which make up the human soul," as Henri Prunières has written. Peri's monodic style becomes in Monteverdi's hands, not just a recitative following speech inflections, but a melody filled with such beauty and feeling that it anticipates the aria writing of later Italian opera composers. "Ecco purch'a voi ritorno" with which Orpheus rhapsodizes over Eurydice's beauty in the opening of the second act; "Tu se' morta," in which he cries in anguish over Eurydice's demise; and "Possente spirito," with its remarkable embellishments, with which Orpheus appeals to and wins over Charon—all this is so far removed from the stylized and stilted recitatives of Peri that they represent a completely new world of sound. In addition to solo vocal numbers, the opera is studded with duets, trios, and polyphonic choruses, providing a continual change of pace and mood.

The vocal numbers, solo and ensemble, are set against an expressive harmony—sometimes a simple scheme based on common chords, sometimes exciting and dramatized discord and chromatic harmonies. "To hear one scene in this manner, the common chords endowing the music with a truly Hellenic beauty," wrote Domenico de Paoli, "is to realize what a marvelous dramatic harmonist Monteverdi was. To listen to those rarely employed discords which trouble this purity like anguished cries, at the tense moments of the drama, is to find ourselves face to face with the deep things of the world, and with that economy of means which is nothing short of mysterious. . . . Written in an age when everything musical had yet to be discovered in the realm of harmony, *Orfeo* nurses its powers, reserving the high lights for the supreme moments of the drama; and the effect produced is astonishing, even for us who are surfeited with the audacious experiments of modern times."

The human voice was not the sole ally Monteverdi had in projecting the drama. The orchestra also played an all-important role—the first time in music history it was required to do so. Where Peri had used only a lyre, lutes, and a harpsichord to accompany the voices, Monteverdi required forty instruments, including flutes, cornets, trumpets, trombones, a family of strings, and a harpsichord. For this orchestra Monteverdi wrote twenty-six numbers including an overture (a brief fanfare that is repeated several times in the opera), introductory pieces (or sinfonias), and brief interludes between the stanzas of a vocal number (ritornelli). The ensemble thus utilized may very well be regarded as the first symphony orchestra.

The truly instrumental style evolved by Monteverdi for his ensemble, makes the composer music history's first orchestrator.

Monteverdi wrote *Orfeo* at the behest of the two sons of Vincenzo Gonzaga, Duke of Mantua, for the wedding ceremonies of Francesco Gonzaga and the Infanta of Savoy. That first performance—at the Accademia degli Invaghiti in Mantua in 1607—was so successful, that Francesco Gonzaga insisted that a public performance be given for the people.

The American stage première of Monteverdi's *Orfeo* took place in Northampton, Massachusetts, at Smith College, on May 12, 1929. At that time a new-edited version, by Gian Francesco Malipiero, was used. Before then, the opera had been heard several times in the United States in concert versions. A notable stage revival took place in New York City during the fall season of 1960, at the New York City Opera, with Leopold Stokowski conducting.

1590–1638. MADRIGALS, for five voices:

Ecco mormorar l'onde; Non si levava ancor; A un giro sol.

Lamento di Arianna, four madrigals: 1. Lasciatemi morire. 2. O Teseo. 3. Dove e la fede. 4. Ahi che non pur rispondi.

Lagrime d'amante al sepolcro dell'amata, madrigal sequence (sestina): 1. Incenerite spoglie. 2. Ditelo o fiumi. 3. Darà la notte. 4. Ma te raccoglie. 5. O chiome d'oro. 6. Dunque amate reliquie.

Lamento della Ninfa "Amor", for three voices.

The eight books of madrigals that Monteverdi published in his lifetime—the first when he was fifteen; the last, five years before his death—carry the madrigal to its final sphere of technical and artistic evolution. With Monteverdi, more than with any of his predecessors, the madrigal becomes a passionate, intensely felt medium of human expression. Here, too, as in his operas, Monteverdi is the supreme dramatist, utilizing every device he can think of or invent in order to heighten the capacity of music to interpret its text. Here, too, he is a reformer and an iconoclast, startling many of his contemporaries with his bold innovations. He was, as Alfred Einstein said of him, "the greatest representative of a period of revolution in which the very foundations of tradition were shaken."

Discords abound in the first four book of madrigals. In the second, published in 1590, these and other techniques are used to project pictorial images. The poem "Ecco mormorar l'onde" by Tasso describes how the dawn and morning breezes bring balm to an anguished heart. The madrigal opens in a somber mood in the lower voices, but the atmosphere lightens considerably as the music describes the break of dawn and the flutter of gay breezes. "A series of appropriate motives, [is used] to convey the murmuring waves, the rustling leaves, and the mountains catching the glow of the morning," writes Denis Arnold, "motives which are then worked out contrapuntally in a most magical way." Vivid tone setting characterizes another madrigal in this set, *Non si levava ancor* (poem again by Tasso), "a rising figure in one part negatived by a descending scale in another," as Denis Arnold points out.

In the third book (1592), days Arnold, Monteverdi "chooses more passionate poetry and interprets it more vividly. Sometimes he writes deliberately angular melodic lines, using awkward intervals to create tension. Dissonance becomes a primary means of expression, and the agony of love seems to require one discord to resolve into yet another." *A un giro sol* from the fourth book (1603) finds Monteverdi becoming increasingly subtle and penetrating in fixing the nuances of text (by Guarini) into appropriate tones. "'When you turn your eyes, the air itself smiles,' says the poet," explains Denis Arnold, "and Monteverdi provides first a 'turn' (musical ornament) for the word giro, then a melisma (long chain of notes to one syllable) for the Italian word ride ('smiles'). This literally makes the singer smile. The approval of sea and winds is given in a gentle consonant motion, as near to realism as such can be. Suddenly the concrete images disappear; the lover laments, 'Only I am sad, being killed by your cruelty'; and the music immediately becomes agonized with a chromatic change. . . . Dissonance and awkward intervals rend the heart."

A new harmonic language begins to appear in the fifth book (1605) through the use of dominant seventh and ninth chords without preparation. At the same time a radical structural change is apparent through the deployment of a continuo or thorough bass (madrigale concertato).

In the sixth book (1614), we encounter the *Lamento d' Arianna,* four five-voice madrigals adapted from one of his most celebrated and significant operatic monodies, the Lament from *Arianna* (1608). In the opera, Arianna bemoans her fate at being abandoned by Theseus. In her narrative, skips in the melody, dissonant harmonies, chromatic intervals, all help to project high tragedy. To give the poem an even greater depth of feeling, Monteverdi rewrote the monody into a quartet of madrigals to avail himself of the greater richness of expression afforded by the additional voices.

This sixth book contains still another immortal lament—a sequence of six madrigals (or sestina) collectively entitled *Lagrime d'amante al sepolcro dell' amata* (*Tears of a Lover at the Tomb of the Beloved*), poems by Scipione Agnelli. This is one of the greatest threnodies in madrigal literature. To Alfred Einstein, it represents "a strange mixture of old and new." Einstein adds: "He sees the mourning lover—the name Glauco is a literary pretense—as he stands at the open grave, like Tancred at Clorinda's tomb; with this picture in mind, he makes the tenor the dominant voice and gives the 'chorus' the lugubrious responses that follow the lines, leaving the way open, however, for lyricism, the madrigalesque, and the *contrapposto,* especially in the Terza parte."

Still another remarkable lament, this time of a nymph, comes out of the eighth volume (1638)—*Lamento della Ninfa "Amor"*. In this volume are concentrated madrigals about love and war, the gamut of style and mood more expansive than those found in earlier books. *Lamento della Ninfa "Amor"* is one of the most emotional and dramatic in this set. A trio of male voices describes a nymph wandering through a meadow while lamenting her fate. The madrigal is built up from a sequence of four descending notes in the bass, recurring throughout the piece.

1642. L'INCORONAZIONE DI POPPEA (THE CORONATION OF POPPEA), opera in three acts, with text by Giovanni Busenello. First performance: Venice, fall of 1642.

This was Monteverdi's last opera. Written when he was seventy-four, it is the fruit of his full maturity as a composer for the stage, "an autumnal masterpiece," as Kathleen Hoover described it in *Opera News,* "paralleled only by the last two operas of Verdi." This is one of the earliest examples of opera with text based on history rather than mythology. *L'Incoronazione* is a surging human drama of surpassing grandeur. The librettist, as Kathleen Hoover adds, "had the insight to draw subject matter from human history, and from one of its lustiest chapters." She concludes: "Monteverdi could apply his ripened technique to a text in every way dramatically valid. The wealth of styles and structures he had mastered went into his re-creation of pagan Rome. His music has, in addition, a new sensuousness as powerful as that of Titian in his last canvases, though its flow is restrained by an unerring sense of symmetry. The fusion of form and expression for which he had always striven is here achieved with a mastery that set an example to composers of every era."

The plot involves Poppea, beloved of Ottone. When Nero, the Roman emperor, falls in love with her, he banishes Ottone from his realm, divorces his own wife, Ottavia, and places Poppea at his side on the throne.

When *L'Incoronazione* was revived in Glyndebourne, England, in 1962, Howard Taubman wrote in the *New York Times:* "*Poppea* is uncannily modern. It is composed in a style of sustained song. Declamation melts almost imperceptibly into arioso, and arioso into full-blooded, soaring aria. . . . *Poppea* abounds in musical riches. It is astonishing to discover how truly Monteverdi characterized his people in musical terms. Listen to Ottavia . . . describe her humiliation, rage and suffering in an anguished lament in the first act, and notice the nobility of her sorrowing farewell to Rome in the second act. Observe the brilliance of Poppea's music, which leaves no doubt of the courtesan's self-centered ambition. . . . So it goes throughout the piece. Nero, weak-willed and besotted, is admirably realized in tone. So are Seneca, the wise and doomed philosopher; Ottone, the hapless lover of Poppea; Drusilla, the girl who loves Ottone; and Arnalta, Poppea's shrewd and faithful old nurse. Monteverdi has even provided an enchanting little intermezzo for comic relief, between a young man and a pretty serving maid."

So enriched is the monody of Monteverdi that we are now just a short step away from the da capo aria and bel canto, soon to be fully realized by the early Neapolitan masters. The two arias of Ottavia singled out by Taubman —"Addio, Roma, Addio, Patria" and "Disprezzata regina"—and Ottone's deeply affecting first-act air, "E pur io torno," are recitatives no longer, but elevated pages of affecting lyricism, which find no equal in the operatic music of Monteverdi's time. This aristocratic lyricism is matched by the composer's ever-sure feeling for good theater—in the relentless surge of the action toward a powerful climactic denouement; in the psychological penetration into character; in the subtle and effective projection of atmosphere and mood. "The caprice of time is powerless against it," says Henri Prunières of this opera, "and it remains one of the most precious ornaments of the musical drama, along with *Don Giovanni, Tristan und Isolde,* and *Pelléas et Mélisande.*"

L'Incoronazione di Poppea was written five years after the first public house anywhere opened its doors in Venice. The world première of this opera took place in such a public theater, at the Teatro SS Giovanni e Paolo in Venice, in the fall of 1642. It proved so successful that during the next few years the opera was repeatedly given in Venice. *L'Incoronazione* was probably the first opera ever mounted in Naples; this took place in 1651. The American première had to wait until the twentieth century, when it was mounted at Northampton, Massachusetts—at Smith College—on April 27, 1926. The first New York production took place at the Juilliard School of Music on February 23, 1933.

GIACOMO CARISSIMI 1605–1674

The oratorio, like the opera, was a child of the Baroque era. In the closing decades of the sixteenth century, St. Philip Neri used to stage scenes from the Scriptures in the Oratory of his church in Florence, the Santa Maria in Vallicella. These productions came to be known as "oratorios." One such spectacle was Emilio de' Cavalieri's *La Rappresentazione di anima e di corpo,* which, however, was a morality play with music, with none of the characteristics we now ascribe to the oratorio (see EMILIO DE' CAVALIERI). More in line with what the later oratorio became—though still highly primitive—was a work like *Il Martirio dei SS. Abbundio ed Abbundanzio* by Domenico Mazzocchi (1592–1665), first produced in Rome in 1631.

Giacomo Carissimi was the first master of the oratorio. He developed some of the conventions that were henceforth to govern that genre. With Carissimi, the oratorio began to take recognizable shape as a dramatized setting of a Biblical (or some other form of sacred) text, for solo voices, chorus, and orchestra. But where earlier such dramas had been staged, those by Carissimi were among the first to dispense with scenery and costumes. He introduced the Narrator (called Historicus, or Testo) to keep the story line moving through recitatives. The story is never really completely unfolded, but is rather suggested, not only through recitatives, but also through duets, choral passages, and orchestral interludes. Carissimi's masterwork was *Jepthe,* but he produced numerous other oratorios, whose subjects had also been drawn from the Old Testament—Job, Jonah, Solomon, and so forth.

While the significance of Carissimi's oratorios can hardly be denied, it is important to remember that he produced works in other media as well, including 12 Masses, 210 motets, and 145 cantatas. The cantata was for Carissimi a form second in importance only to the oratorio. These works, most of which came between 1640 and 1672, "range from the simple strophic composition," says Gloria Rose, "to the large dramatic work for two or three characters. . . . Carissimi sought a variety of musical forms and styles, whether or not they were suggested by the poem. . . . If any one trait may be said to dominate the cantatas of Carissimi it is variety. Form, texture, melody, rhythm, harmony, indeed all the elements of musical composition are marked by diversity. . . . Carissimi's works, from basic structure to minute detail, are masterpieces of vocal chamber music; they represent the height of artistic achievement in the cantata of the middle *seicento.*"

Giacomo Carissimi was born in Marino, near Rome, in 1605. He served first as a singer, then as an organist, at the Cathedral of Tivoli from 1624 to 1627. After a brief period of service as Maestro di Cappella in Assisi, he assumed the post of Maestro di Cappella at S. Appollinare in Rome, which he held from 1628 until the end of his life. He died in Rome on January 12, 1674.

c.1660. JEPTHE, oratorio for solo voices, chorus, and orchestra.

Jepthe is the first modern oratorio. Here the narrator, or Historicus, is not a single character; his part is distributed among various male and female soloists. The chorus, representing the crowd (turba) is utilized with telling impact as a commentator on the dramatic episodes. "Apart from the main (six-part) turba choruses," explains Anthony C. Lewis, "the sorrowful chant of the Ammonites (three-part) and the succeeding paean of the Israelites (two-part) are particularly effective elements in the tonal scheme." The writing is at times remarkably realistic in descriptive passages, while for moments of tragedy, dissonance is used most effectively. Most of the solo passages are recitatives—frequently expressive and emotional in describing the various incidents in the Biblical tale. Two of the noblest of these recitatives are Jephtha's poignant lament, "Heu, mihi!" and the song of Jephtha's daughter, "Cantate mecum Dominio."

In his text, Carissimi makes slight revisions in the actual Bible story, in addition to including a few interpolations of his own. Jephtha, a leader in Israel, vows to God that, if he proves successful in destroying the Ammonites, he will sacrifice the first person he meets from his household upon his return home. The oratorio then describes how the Ammonites are defeated, in pictorial passages vivid with programmatic details. The narrator next describes how Jephtha comes home in triumph to be welcomed with songs of rejoicing by his beloved daughter and her companions. Since she is the first to meet him, it is she whom he must sacrifice to God. When, heartbroken, Jephtha reveals his vow to his daughter, she implores him to permit her to go off with her companions into the mountains to await her death there. The oratorio ends with a mighty six-part lamentation for Jephtha's daughter.

HEINRICH SCHUETZ 1585–1672

Heinrich Schuetz was Germany's most significant composer before the age of Bach and Handel. He represents the transition between not only two epochs but also two cultures. As a student in Venice, he was introduced to, and assimilated, the polyphonic art of the Venetian masters. The impact of Venice is felt in Schuetz's first publication—a volume of five-part madrigals, issued in Venice in 1611. Later on he was brought into contact with Monteverdi's operas. This experience led Schuetz to write *Dafne,* the first German opera in music history, produced in Dresden in 1627. (The score has been lost.)

Thus Schuetz is a connecting link between Italian and German cultures. To German music he brought all the contrapuntal skill, the richness of color, and depth of feeling of the Italian polyphonists. He also carried over into German music the recitative writing of the first Italian opera composers. But Schuetz was no man's imitator. He was a powerful creator in his own right. His structure may be based on Italian foundations—but it is his. To the then primitive music of Germany, he brought a new grandeur, a new capacity to translate texts to musical sound, a new dramatic force and humanity. His works represent the noble beginnings of German music.

Schuetz is also a link between the past and the future. Stylistically and technically, he often reminds us of the Italian polyphonists who preceded him; at times he even carries memories of the Mysteries of the Middle Ages. But at the same time, he anticipated Johann Sebastian Bach in the majesty and nobility of his thought and style. If Schuetz had not lived, it is hardly likely that the giant structures of Baroque choral music would have developed with Bach and Handel they way they did.

Heinrich Schuetz was born in Koestritz, Saxony, on October 8, 1585. As a boy he received not only music instruction but also a thorough training in languages and the sciences. Later he studied law at the University of Marburg. In 1609, he came to Venice, where he was a pupil of Giovanni Gabrieli, and where his first publication (a volume of five-voice madrigals) appeared in 1611. In or around 1613, he returned to Germany and was appointed organist at the court of the Landgrave in Cassel. In 1615, Schuetz went to work for the Elector Johann Georg of Saxony in Dresden, becoming his Kapellmeister in 1617. Schuetz married Magdalene Wildeck in 1619; she died six years later.

During the 1620's, Schuetz reached full maturity as a composer, beginning with the publication in 1619 of *Psalmen Davids,* a collection of psalms and motets in which the Italian monodic style was offically introduced into German music. This was followed by such major works as the Easter oratorio, *Historia der Auferstehung Jesu Christi* in 1623; *Cantiones sacrae,* a volume of motets, in 1625; and the opera *Dafne,* introduced in Torgau on April 23, 1627. In 1633, Schuetz left Dresden to serve for two years as Kapellmeister for King Christian IV in Copenhagen. He returned to his Kapellmeister post in Copenhagen in 1637, and once again in 1642. In 1655, Schuetz was back in Dresden for good, reassuming his one-time assignment as Kapellmeister, which he now held until his death. Toward the end of his life Schuetz went deaf. He spent his time reading the Scriptures, most frequently the Psalms. His last composition was a setting of Psalm CXIX. Schuetz died in Dresden on November 6, 1672.

1619–1650. MOTETS:
Zion spricht; Saul, Saul was verfolgst du mich?

Zion spricht—one of the most inspired of Schuetz's many motets—is found in the collection *Psalmen Davids* (1619), with which both Schuetz and German music enter upon a new era. Two four-part choruses and two six-part ensembles of voices and instruments are here deployed in a giant composition. So skilful is Schuetz's polyphony that each stave is virtually an independent melody. At the same time, Schuetz utilizes an accompaniment with a virtuosity and a richness of timber and color, unheard of in Germany at that time.

Saul, Saul was verfolgst du mich? is the eighteenth number in *Symphoniae sacrae* (1650). With a remarkable feeling for effect and emotion, and with programmatic realism, Schuetz here tells the story of Saul en route to Damascus. Anthony C. Lewis notes how eloquent is the effect produced by the cry "Saul, Saul," which rises "from the lowest depths of the vocal register until the whole of the six-part solo group, and then the entire choral mass as well, join in a tremendous insistent call." The call is interrupted by the warning cry of other voices, and then is resumed "with even greater urgency" and "repeated with steady emphasis until the final cadence on two voices only—seeming infinitely remote yet compellingly near—repeats for the last time the reproach, 'Why persecutest thou me?'" This motet calls for three choruses, with an accompaniment of wind instruments.

1645. DIE SIEBEN WORTE JESU CHRISTI AM KREUZ (THE SEVEN LAST WORDS OF CHRIST AT THE CROSS), oratorio for solo voices, chorus, and orchestra.

This is one of the works by which the oratorio in Germany finally came into its own. It is an account of the last scene of the Passion, narrated by Biblical characters, each represented by a solo voice. The role of the Evangelist is assumed by three solo voices of different registers, and a quartet. The Evangelist's narratives are accompanied by a thorough bass (basso continuo) in the organ. String accompaniments serve as the background for the words of Christ. This use of a basso continuo for the narrator and instrumental accompaniment for Christ is a practice followed by Johann Sebastian Bach.

Die sieben Worte opens with a chorus based on the chorale melody, "Da Jesu an dem Kreuz stund" (Introitus). This is followed by an instrumental sinfonia (also in the style of a chorale), which, in turn, leads into the narrative. The story is then told in declamations often suffused with piety, devotion, or spiritual exaltation; the reaction of the crowd (turba) is dramatized in choral passages. The first chorale-like sinfonia returns right after the Seventh Word, and just before the deeply moving final chorus.

1665. THE PASSION ACCORDING TO ST. MATTHEW, for solo voices and *a cappella* chorus.

Two decades after he had written the *Seven Last Words,* Schuetz made settings of the Crucifixion story according to the accounts of each of the four Evangelists—St. Matthew, St. Mark, St. Luke, and St. John. He called this quartet of compositions the *Historia des Leidens und Sterbens unsers Herrens Jesu Christi.* The most celebrated work in this set is *The Passion According to St. Matthew,* certainly the finest setting of the Crucifixion according to St. Matthew made before the one by Johann Sebastian Bach. Schuetz's *St. Matthew Passion* reminds us of Bach in several ways, but most of all in the dramatic surge and sweep of the choruses, and in the deeply religious character of some of the recitatives.

The Schuetz *St. Matthew Passion* is scored for solo voices and chorus but without any instrumental accompaniment. These are the characters: the Evangelist, who serves as a narrator (tenor); Christ (bass); Judas (baritone); Peter (tenor); the two false witnesses (soprano and contralto); Pilate (tenor); and Pilate's wife (contralto). The chorus describes the people's reactions to the stirring events transpiring, frequently in pages dramatically filled with movement and color. Though the declamations have great austerity and simplicity, they never lack emotional appeal, and at times overflow with compassion or are touched with exaltation.

The *Passion* opens and ends with a choral section in which the sentiments of the crowd watching the Crucifixion are described. The introductory chorus (Introitus) prepares the listener for the coming drama. The final chorus (one of the score's high peaks of inspiration) is a song of thanksgiving by the faithful for having been redeemed through the Lord's suffering. In between these opening and closing choral passages come numerous descriptive episodes underscoring the tensions and high drama of the text. A descending movement of the melody tells of Christ prostrating himself before His Father. Effective modulations speak of Peter's three denials of Christ. A theatrical change of register points up the Evangelist's grief when he repeats Jesus's last words, "Eili, Eili."

In *The St. Matthew Passion,* Schuetz reduced his style to barest essentials. Many of his declamations are almost like plainchants; many of his choruses are stripped of the one-time rich palette of colors he had formerly utilized in earlier works. Only the most economical, the most direct means, are exploited for each sought-after effect. It was almost as if "the composer at the end of his career wished to present his music in its purest form," says Anthony C. Lewis, "and he achieves thereby an intensity that is deeply impressive. . . . Behind the apparent simplicity . . . lies a concentration of power born of ripe experience."

There is also in this music a radiance that Cecil Gray once described as an "abstract and disembodied quality and thought"; notes of "wistful and tender resignation," which make us think of Beethoven's last quartets. It has been suggested that the other-worldly feeling that pervades the Schuetz *Passion*—like that encountered in Beethoven's last quartets—could only come from a man who was deaf.

GIROLAMO FRESCOBALDI 1583–1643

The development of instrumental music was a major development of the Baroque period. In organ music, the Baroque era found a master in Girolamo Frescobaldi. Before him, Sweelinck and Gabrieli had written organ music in the contrapuntal style of their choral compositions. It took a while for the organ to free itself from what has been described as "vocal tyranny"; for composers to begin writing music that belonged to the organ and not to the voice. Frescobaldi was one of the first significant composers to do this. Recognized as the foremost organ virtuoso of his generation, Frescobaldi brought a new style and new techniques to the organ keyboard. To him we owe the solidification and enlargement of such basic structures in organ music as the toccata, canzone, ricercare, and fantasia. Frescobaldi's style was still mainly polyphonic—especially in the fugue form, in which he proved to be such a consummate craftsman that today he is sometimes described as "the Italian Bach." Nevertheless, Frescobaldi did frequently suggest, and at times develop, a homophonic concept. In 1624, he published *Capriccio sopra un soggetto* (*capriccio on a single subject*), in which a single thematic idea is presented in lieu of multiple themes, and is then elaborated and varied to its fullest potential.

In his toccatas and fantasias, Frescobaldi introduced a style that was romantic and passionate, marked by exciting changes of tempo and rhythm, by bold modulations, brilliant passage work and ornaments, effective chromaticisms and discords. These toccatas and fantasias are not just exercises in virtuosity and improvisation. They are personal utterances, at times poetic, at times dramatic, and at times the essence of serenity.

Girolamo Frescobaldi was born in Ferrara, Italy, in 1583. In Ferrara, he studied the organ with Luzzaschi, soon achieving recognition not only as an organ virtuoso but also as a singer. After being the organist at the Santa Maria church in Rome, he settled in Flanders in 1607. In 1608, his first two publications appeared. One was a volume of five-part madrigals, and the other a collection of four-part organ fantasias. During this same year, he received an appointment as organist of St. Peter's in Rome, where his fame as a virtuoso rapidly spread throughout Europe. Between 1615 and 1616, he published two significant volumes for the organ and cembalo, including the important *Second Book of Pieces for Organ and Cembalo,* released in Rome in 1616. In 1628, he took a five-year leave of absence from St. Peter's to serve in Florence as organist for the Grand Duke of Tuscany, Ferdinand II. Once back at St. Peter's, he stayed there for the rest of his life. His last publication in 1635, was one of his greatest, the *Fiori musicali* for organ. Frescobaldi died in Rome on March 1, 1643.

1635. FIORI MUSICALI (MUSICAL FLOWERS), a collection of pieces for the organ.

Frescobaldi's last publication was a collection for the organ made up of toccatas, ricercari, canzoni, capriccios, and other numbers intended for performance at Mass. Here, says Martin Bukofzer, Frescobaldi transformed "the traditional counterpoint by a highly sensitive chromaticism, a brilliant keyboard technique, and an effective tempo rubato." So highly did Johann Sebastian Bach regard this volume that he copied it all out by hand.

Perhaps the most celebrated single piece in the entire volume is the *Toccata per l'elevazione,* or *Toccata for the Elevation* (No. 31). This is music of magnificent breadth of style and nobility of thought. Also famous is the *Toccata avanti la messa della Domenico* (No. 1), and the *Toccata avanti il Ricercare* (No. 43), each of "a transfigured, heavenly purity." *Canzona dopo l'Epistola* (No. 27) is remarkable for its contrasting sections and for the way in which a musical thought is subjected to imaginative transformations.

DIETRICH BUXTEHUDE 1637–1707

In the writing of organ music and church cantatas, none exerted a greater influence upon Johann Sebastian Bach than Buxtehude. Bach's biographies tell us how, in 1703, he walked a distance of some two hundred miles to Luebeck just to hear Buxtehude play the organ. So impressed was he by these performances, and by the quality of Buxtehude's compositions, that he overstayed his leave of absence. From then on, Bach never wavered in his high regard for Buxtehude. In his own compositions he often drew guidance from his predecessor. As C. Hubert Parry said: "In Johann Sebastian Bach's organ works the traces of the influence of Buxtehude are more plentiful than those of any other composer. It is not too much to say that unless Dietrich Buxtehude had gone before, the world would have had to do without some of the most lovable and interesting traits in the divinest and most exquisitely human of composers."

Buxtehude's organ music embraces chaconnes, fantasias, fugues, passacaglias, toccatas—and possibly most important of all, chorale preludes. He developed these varied structures to a point where hey begin to differ only slightly and in superficials from those utilized by Bach. To his writing, Buxtehude brought a power of invention, a gift at variation and embellishment, a romantic ardor, a mastery of keyboard technique, a strength of harmony and attention to detail, that compelled Philipp Spitta to regard Buxtehude as "one of the greatest composers of organ music, except the one and only Johann Sebastian Bach." And Charles Sanford Terry referred to Buxtehude as "one whose genius was touched by the poetic fires that lit Bach's own."

Buxtehude was one of the earliest masters to write music for a concert audience as well as for the church. In doing so, explains Romain Rolland, "he felt the need of making his music a kind which would appeal to everyone . . . . Buxtehude sought nothing but clear, pleasing, and striking designs, and even aimed at descriptive music. He willingly sacrificed himself by intensifying his expression, and what he lost in abundance he gained in power . . . . The neatness of his beautiful melodic designs and the repetition of phrases which sink down into the heart are all essentially Handelian traits. No less is the magnificent triumph of the ensembles, and his manner of painting in bold masses of light and shade."

Dietrich Buxtehude was born in Helsingör (Elsinore), then under Danish rule, in 1637. He received his principal instruction on the organ from his father, the organist of the Olai Church in Helsingör. After that, Buxtehude held organ posts in Helsingborg and Helsingör. When he was thirty, he was appointed organist of the Marienkirche in Luebeck, a position he held for forty years. There he became celebrated, not only for his organ performances, which attracted pilgrims from all parts of Europe, but also for his *Abendmusiken,* the earliest public concerts ever given. For these concerts Buxtehude wrote a considerable amount of secular music. Dietrich Buxtehude died in Luebeck on May 9, 1707.

—— CHORALE PRELUDES, for organ:

Ich ruf' zu dir; In dulci jubilo; Ein feste Burg; Ich dank dir, lieber Gott.

The chorale prelude was an organ piece played during religious services, just before the congregational singing of a chorale. The organist here revealed his skill at improvisation, sometimes by embellishing a chorale melody with interweaving melodic parts, and sometimes by erecting a new tonal edifice on the foundation stones of the first few notes of the chorale tune. The chorale prelude was passed down to Buxtehude by such early composers for the organ as Sweelinck and his pupil Samuel Scheidt (1587–1654). But it was Buxtehude who first endowed the form with artistic dimension and content through his extraordinary gift at variation. In his hands, a simple chorale melody like *Ich ruf' zu dir,* or *In dulci jubilo,* or *Ich dank dir, lieber Gott* would unfold and expand into the most formidable designs and contours. Cecil Gray noted that Buxtehude raised the chorale prelude to "an unexampled pitch of elaboration and enriched it with every conceivable device of contrapuntal and decorative resource at his disposal. In his hands, indeed, the theme is frequently so varied and adorned with arabesques as to become totally unrecognizable, and even when presented textually it is often hidden from sight altogether under the exuberant welter of ornamentation with which it is surrounded."

Buxtehude's organ setting of "Ein feste Burg" is one of the earliest significant uses of this hymn in instrumental music. "Ein feste Burg" is Martin Luther's setting of the 46th Psalm, which became the battle song of the Reformation. Johann Sebastian Bach also used this melody for an organ chorale prelude.

—— CHURCH CANTATAS, for solo voices, chorus, and orchestra.
O froehliche Stunden; Singet dem Herrn; Alles was ihr tut.

The church cantata was still another area in which Buxtehude's talent flourished, and in which his influence upon Johann Sebastian Bach was far-reaching. The church cantata had been crystallized by Franz Tunder (1614–1667), who made the chorale the spine of this form of religious composition. Like its secular counterpart, the church cantata was written for one or more solo voices, chorus, and instrumental accompaniment. Arias, duets, recitatives, and choral passages were combined into a several-movement structure. To the church cantata, Buxtehude brought not only a mastery at polyphony but also the same kind of spiritual values that we encounter so frequently in Bach.

O froehliche Stunden and *Singet dem Herrn* are of comparatively smaller dimension. For all that, they occupy a major position among Buxtehude's church cantatas. Both are for a single voice—soprano. *O froehliche Stunden* is an Easter cantata, utilizing for its accompaniment two violins and a continuo. As its title implies ("O Happy Hours"), the music overflows with jubilant feelings, which come to a stirring climax in an exultant Alleluia, to which the violins provide exquisite filigree work. *Singet dem Herrn* is accompanied by a single violin and continuo. A setting of four lines from Psalm 98, it opens with a religious sinfonia and continues on with an aria, recitative, sinfonia, and aria.

Alles was ihr tut is more spacious in structure, and more dramatic in musical content, than either one of the two cantatas mentioned above. It is scored for soprano, alto, bass, chorus, orchestra, and continuo. The text of the first chorus (which gives the entire work its name) is from the service for the fifth Sunday after Epiphany; the other texts are hymns. The nine sections begin with a sinfonia. After that, we hear a rousing opening chorus in homophonic style, "Alles was ihr tut." A repetition of the opening sinfonia brings an expressive alto aria, "Dir, Dir Hoechster Dir allein." Two solos follow.

One is for bass and the other for soprano. After that, the chorus enters, its melody based on the final strophe of the hymn of the preceding soprano aria. A short ritornello in three sections prefaces the final chorus. Here the textual material from the opening chorus is repeated verbatim, and its musical material is embellished upon.

—— CHACONNE IN E MINOR, for organ.

The E minor Chaconne, the third item in Vol. I of Spitta's edition, has become most familiar to the concert audiences of our time through the highly effective orchestral transcription prepared by Carlos Chávez. In listening to the Buxtehude Chaconne, it is not difficult to see where Bach got both his inspiration and example in writing his incomparable work in the same form for solo violin.

"The theme," explains John Briggs in his program notes for the Philadelphia Orchestra, "is a simple four-bar descending phrase . . . introduced in the pedal and repeated nine times with constantly varied embellishments in the upper voices." After the bass line is omitted, the theme is again heard in the tenor voice (organist's left hand) with various embellishments. "The theme is combined and recombined, undergoing many ingenious transformations, and finally emerges in still a different form, as a powerful restatement in the bass."

ARCANGELO CORELLI 1653–1713

The increasing importance of instrumental music during the late Baroque period is emphasized most strongly by the fact that Corelli, one of the most eminent composers of this era, wrote nothing at all for the voice. To Corelli, music owes the early development of two of the most significant forms of instrumental music—the sonata and the concerto.

"Sonata" was a term devised to describe a composition meant to be "sounded" or "played"—as opposed to the cantata, which was to be "sung." One of the earliest appearances of the term "sonata" is found with the Venetian master, Giovanni Gabrieli, who published in 1615 a volume of instrumental *Canzoni et sonate*. The sonata was actually an offshoot of the canzone (or, as it was more officially baptized, canzone da sonare). This was a composition either for the keyboard or for a combination of instruments in a polyphonic style. Actually, two forms sprang out of the canzone. One was the sonata da chiesa (church sonata), in a stately and dignified style; this was the predecessor of the classical sonata. The other was the sonata da camera (chamber sonata), lighter in mood, consisting of a series of dances; this was the forerunner of the classical suite.

Corelli produced four volumes of sonatas for two instruments and figured bass (opus 1 through opus 4), and a volume of sonatas for a single violin and figured bass (opus 5). It was in the last publication that he made monumental advances in writing sonata music for the violin. As one of the foremost violin virtuosos of his day, Corelli proved to be a significant force in perfecting and crystallizing for the first time a modern style and technique of violin performance. For this reason, he is sometimes singled out as music's first violin virtuoso. He devised a technique of using the bow that his contemporaries and successors adopted. He amplified and enriched the language of the violin through the skilful use of double stops, arpeggios and chords, trills and appoggiaturae. In his sonatas, he was not an innovator introducing new methods. His technique, as a matter of fact, was a comparatively limited one, never progressing beyond the third position. He was actually a reformer, one who took what he found and used it to its fullest advantage. At the same time he rejected that which was cumbersome and ungrateful to his instrument. Thus he helped establish violin technique on sound principles for the first time, perfecting a style of writing for the violin that served that instrument exclusively. He also helped to bring into existence a new potential for homophonic style through some of his beautiful slow movements.

In his opus 6 he was the first successful composer of the concerto. The concerto was a sonata da chiesa for a group, or several groups, of instruments. The word "concerto" originated with Ludovico Viadana (1564–1645) for polyphonic motets with organ accompaniment, which he designated as "concerti ecclesiastici." As additional instruments were added to the organ for the purpose of accompaniment, these compositions came to be known as concerti da chiesa: for example, Giovanni Gabrieli's *Concerti ecclesiastici* (1587), in which instrumental group were used antiphonally. The genre of the concerto, however, was not realized until Giuseppe Torelli (1658–1709) published a set of concertos for solo instruments and accompaniment in 1686. And it was not until Corelli issued his epoch-making opus 6—actually the parent of the later concerto for solo instrument and accompaniment—that the style and structure of the concerto were finally and firmly established.

Arcangelo Corelli was born in Fusignano, Italy, on February 17, 1653. He studied the violin with Giovanni Benvenuti and Leonardo Bragnoli. By the time he was seventeen, he had achieved such renown as a violin performer that he was elected a member of the Accademia Filarmonica in Bologna. In 1671, Corelli settled in Rome, where, except for brief trips, he stayed for the rest of his life. After playing the violin in the orchestra of the St. Louis of France Church, and directing the orchestra at Teatro Capranica, he acquired the patronage of some of Rome's most powerful noblemen and princes of the church. Among the latter was Cardinal Pietro Ottoboni, who appointed Corelli Maestro di Cappella at his palace. Corelli now achieved renown, not only as a violinist and composer, but also as a teacher of the violin; he helped found the first significant school of violin performance. Arcangelo Corelli died in Rome on January 8, 1713, and was buried in the Pantheon near Raphael's tomb.

1700. SONATAS FOR VIOLIN AND FIGURED BASS, op. 5:

Sonata No. 1 in D major. I. Grave; Allegro; Adagio. II. Allegro. III. Adagio. IV. Adagio; Allegro.

Sonata No. 8 in E minor. I. Prelude. II. Allemande. III. Sarabande. IV. Gigue.

Sonata No. 12 in D minor, "La Folia."

In this volume, we encounter examples of both the sonata da camera and the sonata da chiesa. The eighth work, in E minor, belongs to the former category. It opens with a prelude dominated by a deeply moving melody in 3/4 time. After that we get three dances. The Allemande is vigorous; the Sarabande is stately; the Gigue is sprightly.

It is within the Sonata da chiesa form that Corelli poured some of his finest inspiration. These works are usually in four movements. Quick and slow sections alternate with one of the quick sections in fugal style. There is a good deal here to suggest the direction the classical sonata would eventually take. Each movement is divided into two sections. The first offers a melody that modulates to a different key at the cadence, while the second presents a new melody in that key before returning to the original tonality. Thus Corelli anticipates the binary, or two-theme, form so basic to the later sonata form. The Corelli sonatas are further characterized by a strong rhythmic sense and by a contrast, not only of keys, but also of polyphonic and homophonic procedures.

The first sonata, in D major, is one of Corelli's finest works in the da chiesa structure. Two slow introductory measures lead into a brisk Allegro, which in turn is followed by a seven-bar Adagio. These three parts are repeated, but the Adagio section with which the movement ends is considerably amplified. The second movement is polyphonic in style, and a fantasia in structure. After the presentation of two subjects, they are developed in thirty or so measures. The third movement is entirely homophonic. The finale begins with an Adagio before exploiting polyphonic devices in a vigorous Allegro.

The most celebrated composition in opus 5 is not, strictly speaking, either a sonata da camera or a sonata da chiesa, but a theme and variations. It is the Sonata in D minor, No. 12, entitled *La Folia.* A "folia" (or "Folies d' espagne") is a familiar tune dating from the early sixteenth century, probably of Portuguese origin. This stately melody is presented without preliminaries by the violin. Twenty-three short variations follow. Like so many other composers (including Frescobaldi, Lully, Vivaldi, Cherubini, and Johann Sebastian Bach), Corelli found the "folia" useful for variation purpose.

Melodies from opus 5 were lifted by transcribers for three different symphonic works sometimes performed today. Two of these compositions are the work of John Barbirolli: the Concerto in F major, for oboe and string orchestra, and the Concerto Grosso, each in five movements. The oboe concerto borrows material from Sonatas No. 7 in D minor and No. 10 in F major. (I. Preludio. II. Vivace. III. Sarabande. IV. Gavotte. V. Gigue). The Concerto Grosso goes for its thematic material to Sonatas No. 1 in D major, No. 3 in C major, No. 4 in F major, and No. 7 in D minor (I. Grave. II. Allegro. III. Adagio. IV. Sarabande. V. Allegro).

Fernández Arbós prepared a popular three-movement *Suite for Strings* (I. Sarabande. II. Giga. III. Badinerie). The sarabande comes from the third movement of Sonata No. 7 in D minor; the second movement Giga, from the second movement of Sonata No. 9 in A major; the concluding Badinerie, from the fifth movement of Sonata No. 11 in E major.

1628–1710. CONCERTI GROSSI, for orchestra, op. 6:

Concerto Grosso No. 3 in C minor. I. Largo; Allegro. II. Adagio; Grave. II. Vivace. IV. Allegro.

Concerto Grosso No. 8 in G minor, "Fatto per la notte di Natale" (Christmas Concerto). I. Vivace; Grave. II. Adagio; Allegro. III. Adagio. IV. Vivace. V. Allegro. VI. Pastorale.

Concerto Grosso No. 9 in G major. I. Allemande. II. Corrente. III. Gavotte. IV. Adagio. V. Minuet.

This volume, published posthumously in 1714, established the conventions of the concerto grosso, the predecessor of the solo concerto. With Corelli, the concerto grosso became a composition in several movements (usually from four to six), for two or more instruments and orchestra. The solo instruments were known as the "concertino"; the rest of the orchestra as "ripieno" or "concerto grosso." The concertino was used in combination with, or set against, the ripieno, contrasting color to the principal themes being provided by means of light and shade.

Corelli scored his twelve concerti grossi for two violins and cello as the concertino, with string orchestra and continuo as the ripieno. The first eight concerti grossi were intended for performance in church; the other four were secular music. Alfred Einstein pointed out that "proportion, repose and equality" were "the very elements of life" in these compositions. He adds: "The harmonic symmetry, . . . the construction of and relationship between two dissimilar tonal masses of sound are brought to perfection." Abraham Veinus states further: "In style and in musical structure, the Corelli concertos are models of quiet dignity and sober repose. His harmonies are sonorous and full, applied like warm flesh tones over a perceptible framework of well-joined bone and muscle. His melodic units are usually simple and brief. Clarity and proportion are his guiding principles, and concertino and concerto grosso (or ripieno) are meticulously equalized as factors in the formal structure."

Concerto No. 3 in C minor opens with a stately slow section, before embarking on a robust Allegro. A brief, expressive Adagio then serves as a preface to a more extended Grave section. Following a fermata, the vigorous Vivace enters, to be followed by an equally robust Allegro.

Concerto No. 8 in G minor is the most frequently played of Corelli's concerti grossi. It is popularly known as the *Christmas Concerto* since its title bears the legend that it was "composed for the night of the Nativity." About the only association this music seems to have with the Christmas season is found in the finale, a deeply religious and spiritual pastorale. The lovely melody in thirds, in a Sicilian rhythm, depicts the scene in Bethlehem at Christ's cradle. This movement was the forerunner of several other devout pieces of music, also called Pastorales—notably those in Handel's *Messiah* and Johann Sebastian Bach's *Christmas Oratorio.*

The *Christmas Concerto* opens with a seven-bar introductory Vivace in 3/4 time. A stately Grave follows, its melody—presented by the solo instruments—interrupted after every other phrase by an orchestral interjection. An eight-measure Adagio, and an equally brief Allegro follow; the latter concludes with a cadenza for first and second solo violins. Next we hear a twelve-measure Adagio, a two-section Vivace, and an Allegro that has the character of a graceful courtly dance. The Pastorale brings the concerto to a reverent conclusion.

Concerto No. 9 in G major consists of a series of delightful dances after a slow, dignified introduction. First come an Allemande, Corrente, and Gavotte, the latter two in binary structure. A brief Adagio section provides contrast before the concerto ends with still another dance, a graceful Minuet.

JEAN-BAPTISTE LULLY 1632–1687

Since opera had originated, and had first developed, in Italy before penetrating the rest of Europe, it is appropriate to find an Italian and not a Frenchman as the founder of French opera. He was Jean-Baptiste Lully.

The French had not been interested in the early Italian operas of the Camerata and its immediate successors. The first contact France had with opera was through *Orfeo,* by Luigi Rossi (1597–1653); later, several operas by Pier Francesco Cavalli (1602–1676) were produced in Paris. The importance that these and other Italian operas placed on music over the drama did not meet with a responsive chord in France. Partial as they were to the classical tragedies of Corneille and Racine, the French failed to respond to the formula-ridden texts and to the stilted and plebian poetry dominating Italian opera librettos. Besides, the French were convinced that their language was poorly disposed to recitatives, then the spine of opera.

Lully's operas squarely met and overcame the French resistance. In Philippe Quinault, he found a poet and dramatist who could provide him with tragedies filled with those soaring flights of poetry and stirring dramatic episodes so dear to the hearts of French theatergoers. Lully catered to the French enthusiasm for ballet by making it integral to his operas, and by writing ballet music that was elegant and refined in the French manner. After having made a most painstaking study of the diction of La Champmeslé, the celebrated actress of the *Comédie française,* Lully succeeded in adapting the recitative to the accents and inflections of the French language. He avoided music with excessive emotion and passion in favor of that which was polished, controlled and well mannered in the best traditions of French culture. He filled his operas with the kind of spectacles the French doted on—feasts for eye and ear, even though they made no basic contribution to the plot—and with pastoral scenes, for which the French had a preference. In doing all this, he not only built up in France an audience for opera but also established a tradition of operatic writing to which French composers would adhere for many years.

Lully was, first and foremost, a master of the recitative. In his hands it became a supple instrument for dramatic expression and strongly felt emotion. His recitatives helped to carry the action on, to identify characters, to pinpoint moods. Meticulously, Lully fitted his music to his poetic text, in place of distorting and contorting the poetic line to fit the musical one as the Italians were apt to do. Only occasionally did he permit the expressiveness of his recitative writing to erupt into full-grown arias. When he did, Lully achieved a most moving, a most eloquent lyricism—as in "Bois épais" from *Amadis de Gaule* (1684), "Par le secours" from *Roland* (1685), "Plus j'observe" from *Armide et Renaud* (1686), and "J'ai perdu la beauté" from *Persée* (1682).

Lully gave the orchestra an importance it had not previously known, even with Monteverdi. Lully's orchestra was made up mainly of strings; but it also included flutes, oboes, trumpets, drums. The orchestra was used frequently in each of his operas: for the overture; for ritornelli; for ballets; for spectacles and pastoral episodes; to double the choral parts; to accompany recitatives and arias. Instrumentation was now utilized more effectively than heretofore in implementing the text to project mood and atmosphere. Lully's orchestra also often provided realistic programmatic representations of battles, storms, and scenes in Hades. He recruited flutes for nocturnal scenes, oboes for pastoral episodes, trumpets and drums for martial effects, strings for lyrical or sentimental moods.

One of Lully's contributions was the establishment of a new kind of overture, which French composers were to use extensively. It came to be known as the "French Overture" as opposed the "Italian." An outgrowth of the sonata da chiesa, the "French Overture" was made up of two sections. The first, slow and majestic, was in duple meter. The second, lively and often in a fugal style, was either in duple or triple meter.

Jean-Baptiste Lully was born in Florence, Italy, on November 28, 1632. After having received some instruction on the guitar and in the rudiments of music, he came to Paris, in or about 1646. There he was employed at the household of Mlle. de Montpensier, cousin of Louis XIV. It was not long before Lully joined the orchestra at the court of Louis XIV. In this capacity he wrote many instrumental compositions, and, between 1658 and 1671, some thirty ballets for presentation at Versailles. He rose to high station and was the recipient of royal favors. In 1661, he was made "composer to the king"; in 1662, he was made "Maître de musique" to the royal family. He also acquired a patent of nobility and, in 1672, a license to give public performances of opera at the Académie Royale de musique. Meanwhile, in 1662, he had acquired wealth through marriage with Mlle Lambent.

As the head of an opera company, Lully's creativity was inevitably directed into stage channels. On November 15, 1672, the Académie Royale presented *Les Fêtes de l'amour et de Bacchus,* a skilful stringing together of pastoral scenes from various ballets and comédie-ballets. On April 27, 1673, came *Cadmus et Hermione,* Lully's first "tragédie en musique" (or opera), text by Quinault. After that, Lully wrote the music for eleven more tragedies by Quinault, and three to texts by Corneille and Campistron. It is in these works that French opera—and Lully's fame as a composer—was planted on a solid footing. Lully's most famous operas were *Thesée* (1675), *Atys* (1676), *Psyché* (1678), *Persée* (1682), *Phaéton* (1683), *Amadis de Gaule* (1684), *Roland* (1685), *Armide et Renaud* (1686). In 1681, Lully was made "Secrétaire du roi," an appointment that carried with it an exalted social station. Lully died in Paris on March 22, 1687, a victim of gangrene.

1686. ARMIDE ET RENAUD, "tragédie en musique" in five acts, with text by Quinault, based on Tasso's *Gerusaleme liberata*. First performance: Paris, February 15, 1686.

Armide et Renaud, Lully's penultimate opera, was produced posthumously, less than a year after the composer's death. It was acclaimed at its première, and remained popular in Paris for many years after that. Lecerf de la Viéville described it as "a supremely beautiful piece of work, with a beauty that increased in every act. . . . I do not know how the human mind could imagine anything finer than the fifth act."

Most of Lully's operas were cast in the same mold. After the "French overture" came a patriotic prologue in pastoral style, either glorifying king and country, or singing the praises of some recent victory. The five-act tragedy that followed invariably involved the supernatural powers of either a god or a sorceress and a pair of lovers. The story usually provided a good excuse for magical scene changes, excursions into the underworld, tempests. Most of the plot unfolded in the recitatives. But three or four arias invariably allowed a richer lyrical treatment for the voice. Ballets, spectacles, pastoral scenes introduced welcome contrasts for the eye.

Armide et Renaud followed such a pattern. The overture is in two parts, the first presenting a stately subject, the second brisk and lively. The curtain then rises on the prologue, in which two female voices, representing Glory and Wisdom, sing the praises of Louis, "the august hero," accompanied by chorus. Three dances follow: an entrée, a minuet, and a gavotte en rondeau. The drama, set during the first Crusade, involves Armida, a beautiful Syrian sorceress. She inhabits an enchanted palace to which she lures knights, who become so enchanted by her beauty that they forget their mission. In the first act, to the accompaniment of a stately march, Hidraot, Prince of Damascus, comes to visit Armida at her palace. After a number of dances are performed for the entertainment of the Prince and the sorceress, a messenger arrives with the news that the knight Renaud had been responsible for rescuing Armida's prisoners. Enraged, Armida joins Hidraot in a plot to destroy the knight.

The second act finds Renaud sleeping at the banks of a river. He is being lulled gently by music from the strings. Nymphs perform a ballet around him. After Renaud awakens, he sings one of the most beautiful airs in the opera, "Plus j'observe." Armida then appears, captures Renaud, and raises her voice in an exultant hymn of triumph.

In the third act, Armida realizes to her horror that she has fallen in love with her prisoner. She calls to Hatred to rescue her from this dilemma. Hatred, accompanied by Cruelty and Vengeance and other members of her entourage, sing and dance for Armida.

The fourth act involves the efforts of two of Renaud's friends to rescue the knight from the clutches of the sorceress. They come with a magic shield of diamonds and a golden scepter and confront numerous obstacles and difficulties.

The fifth act opens with a passacaglia, which the attendants of Armida dance before Renaud. (This musical episode is built from four descending notes in the bass, around which fascinating variations are spun.) Renaud is finally rescued by his friends. With a cry of terror, "Renaud! Ciel!," Armida realizes she has lost Renaud for good.

Many of Lully's operas boast instrumental episodes known as "symphonies de sommeil," which have considerable pictorial interest. *Armide et Renaud* is no exception. Henri Prunières points it out: "There is a passage [in the second act] . . . in which a description of a slowly flowing river is combined with an impression of Renaud's sweet torpor. At the words, 'Un son harmonieux se mêle au bruit des eaux,' a sound rising from the bass bursts at the surface like a bubble of air. Here is impressionism in every detail."

HENRY PURCELL 1659–1695

Though he is acknowledged to be the most "English" of all English composers—and though he is certainly one of the greatest—Purcell was not altogether free of foreign influences. He himself confessed that in his sonatas he "faithfully endeavored a just imitation of the most famed Italian masters." By way of Italy, too, come many of Purcell's instrumental fantasias and vocal recitatives. In his anthems, Purcell betrays the impact upon him of the French motet.

But the strongest of all the foreign forces to shape his style and musical thinking was Jean-Baptiste Lully. From Lully, Purcell learned how to project powerful dramatic scenes, how to write dance music for the stage with skill and good taste. It is even probable that Lully's success in adapting French diction and poetry to recitatives was the stimulus and example Purcell needed to accomplish a similar end in England for English poetry. Certainly, as J. A. Westrup has noted, "no other composer, before or since, has succeeded so well in translating into music the accents of the English language."

The influence of Italy and France—and of Lully, specifically—notwithstanding, Purcell is unmistakably himself, and unmistakably English. "His melodies," wrote Paul Henry Lang, "are most personal and of an expressiveness found only in a Monteverdi. His unbridled imagination, his free and original forms, transformed every inspiration, however French or Italian in appearance, into his own creation."

There was no area of music cultivated in Purcell's day that he did not enrich. He is most famous for *Dido and Aeneas,* the only opera by an Englishman written before World War II that has held the stage throughout the world. Purcell produced a vast amount of other music for the theater, with which emerges a new age for English dramatic music. In addition, Purcell completed a vast repertory of church music—hymns, psalms, odes, anthems, Services, sacred songs with chorus, cantatas. This includes the anthem "My Heart Is Inditing," written for the coronation of James II, and regarded as one of the summits in seventeenth century English church music.

With musical England passing from the age of the madrigal to the era of homophony, Purcell gave the new movement a powerful forward push with his sonatas, chaconnes, suites, and sundry other instrumental compositions. In his fantasias for viols, as in so much of his church literature, Purcell draws style and materials from the past, though the harmonies are often strikingly modern. In his sonatas, as in so many of his compositions for the stage, he once again looks into the future. He is, in his instrumental works, as Peter Warlock remarked, "a Janus-like figure in the history of music. . . . The quality of his music reveals Purcell as a man of genius far above his age; the forms in which it was cast were for the most part dictated by his age, and it is the unsatisfactory character of these forms that is largely responsible for the neglect of his music."

Like Bach, Purcell was forgotten for many years after his death. It took almost a century for England to discover the extent of his genius, and for the rest of the music world to follow suit. The Purcell revival started in 1876 with the founding of the Purcell Society, formed to publish Purcell's complete works. This project took over half a century and resulted in more than forty volumes. Performances of Purcell's music in celebration of the bicentenary of his death, in 1895, further popularized him. Today, as J.A. Westrup remarks, "when the revival of Baroque music is so widespread, Purcell is recognized as one of the greatest and most individual composers of the seventeenth century." Throwing a *coup d'oeil* on the variety of Purcell's compositions, Alec Robertson adds: "The journey from the abstract music of the fantasias, by way of the church music, to the crowded canvas of the masques and the single opera, with a dive down into the Rabelaisianism of the catches, is an enormously long one for a man who died at the age of thirty-seven to have traversed."

Henry Purcell was born in London in or about 1659. He was the son of Thomas Purcell, a renowned musician and a Gentleman of the Chapel Royal. Henry Purcell was a chorister at the Chapel Royal, where he received music instruction from Cooke, Humfrey, and John Blow. When Purcell's voice broke in 1673, he was appointed "keeper of the king's instruments." Four years later he was made "composer to the king's band." Meanwhile, in 1676, he contributed a song to Playford's *Choice of Ayres,* his first publication.

In 1679, Purcell succeeded Blow as organist of Westminster Abbey, and in 1682, he became an organist of the Chapel Royal. During this period, between 1680 and 1683, he completed his fantasias for viols and twelve trio sonatas. In 1689, he wrote and had produced *Dido and Aeneas,* his magnum opus, and his only music for the stage that can be regarded as an opera. In the few years that followed, Purcell wrote incidental music for numerous plays by Dryden, Congreve, John Fletcher, Shakespeare, and others. Henry Purcell died of tuberculosis in London on November 21, 1695. He was buried beneath the organ in Westminster Abbey.

1680. FANTASIAS, for viols, in three, four, and five parts.

In these fantasias Purcell reached into the past, to the form and style English composers had been cultivating since the sixteenth century. Fantasias (or "fancies") were instrumental exercises in polyphony in which a number of short themes were deployed. Such compositions had been successfully produced before Purcell's time by Byrd and Morley. Purcell took this form and, as Alec Robertson said, "virtually breathes new life . . . into its expiring corpse, avoiding its excesses of learning, its dry pedantry, and far surpassing its greatest achievements of beauty." The reason why Robertson here refers to the fantasia as a "dry corpse" is because, by 1680, the form was out of fashion among English composers. It was well known in England that the king detested fantasias, and for that reason this type of music lost its popularity. Purcell himself never again wrote fantasias after his twenty-first year.

In his fantasias, Purcell alternated slow and quick movements. The work is generally set into motion by a fugal passage in which either one or two themes are presented simultaneously. In a preface to his transcription of Purcell's fantasias in 1927, Peter Warlock described these works as follows: "Many who hear . . . these fantasias of Purcell for the first time will doubtless find them 'modern' in the sense of being in advance of their age; and assuredly we must go forward to Bach before we can find any music which displays such consummate mastery of all the devices of counterpoint allied to so wide a range of profoundly expressive harmony. . . . It is in these early fantasias, modeled on the old English tradition that was already considered *vieux jeu* in his own time, that he shows his greatest originality and finest musicianship . . . . In the fantasias . . . there is a perfect relation between form and content, and there can be no doubt that within a short time these works will be generally recognized as one of England's most significant contributions to the world's great music."

The Fantasia No. 4 in C minor, in four parts, has tragic overtones. "Nothing more lovely has been written for music," wrote A. K. Holland. "The haunting close has a pathos which Wagner, with the whole apparatus of the orchestra, scarcely excelled, and a striking affinity with a passage at the close of the Prelude to Act 3 of *Die Meistersinger*."

Fantasia No. 5 in D minor, also in four parts, has a kind of ceremonial dignity. But the most celebrated of all these Fantasias is the one in F major in five parts, published independently. Known as the *Fantasia on One Note,* this remarkable piece of music sustains the note of "C" in one of the viols throughout the composition, while the other viols weave around it the most fanciful melodic figures. To Robertson, "the one note . . . sounds the death knell of a form of instrumental composition whose requiem was indeed long overdue. . . . The theme, like the angels on Jacob's dream ladder, ascends and descends simultaneously—music, being of the spirit, can do this as well as angels!—and in two other sections of the piece the same theme is developed in a downward direction. . . . Along this road instrumental music could travel no further."

1683. SONATA IN F MAJOR ("GOLDEN"), for two violins and bass. I. Largo. II. Adagio. III. Allegro. IV. Allegro.

CHACONNE IN G MINOR, for two violins and bass.

Both these compositions, which rank high among Purcell's instrumental works, are found in a volume of ten sonatas published posthumously in 1697. Nobody knows why the Sonata in F major is dubbed the "Golden." It is in four movements, in the sonata da chiesa form, and in the style of Corelli. A dignified Largo proceeds to a supremely beautiful Adagio movement, which has been described as a "beautiful little elegy." The third movement Allegro is in three parts in which extensive use is made of imitation. The finale, also an Allegro, emphasizes an energetic dance tune.

The celebrated G minor chaconne appears as the sixth Sonata. The ground bass is a five-bar theme, which is repeated no less than forty-four times. Around it are woven melodies of varying lengths, moods, and emotions.

1689. DIDO AND AENEAS, opera in three acts, with text by Nahum Tate, based on the fourth book of Virgil's *The Aeneid*. First performance: Chelsea, England, 1689.

Purcell wrote a considerable amount of incidental music for plays. These scores are often so abundant with varied numbers and so rich in musical content that the temptation to call some of them operas is irresistible. But Purcell actually produced only a single work that can accurately by termed an opera, since it is his only stage work in which the entire text is set to music. That work is *Dido and Aeneas,* the most significant opera by an Englishman; the only English opera of the past that is continually revived; one of the few operas before the time of Gluck that carries few suggestions of the archaic or the obsolete; an opera that remains from first bar to last vibrantly contemporary in musical interest and emotional appeal.

A good deal in *Dido and Aeneas* is derived from Lully. The overture is in the French style. The music, continually the servant instead of the master of the text, is used with compelling force both for characterizations and for mood painting. The ballets are integral to the work as a whole. The recitatives are deployed with uncommon mastery and expressiveness. The setting of the inflections and diction of the English language is throughout remarkable. In addition, the note-against-note style of some of the duets, and the grandeur of some of the choral pages, bear the further imprints of Lully.

Lully's operas are almost never given any longer; and the few times that one is revived, it usually appears like a museum piece of greater historical than aesthetic interest. But *Dido and Aeneas* remains today "one of the most original expressions of genius in all opera," as Gustav Holst once wrote, "the only opera of the seventeenth century . . . that is performed as a whole nowadays for the sheer pleasure it gives as an opera." Having written what critics have long described as a "perfect opera," and the only one of its kind in English, Purcell never attempted a second.

Purcell was commissioned to write *Dido and Aeneas* for a girls' boarding school in Chelsea. Nahum Tate's libretto was based on the tragic love story of Dido and Aeneas, as recounted by Virgil in *The Aeneid*. Aeneas, the Trojan hero, fleeing from ravaged Troy, is sent by the gods to Latium to found a new empire. A violent storm sweeps his ships to the coast of Carthage, where the hero is welcomed by the queen, Dido. She falls in love with him. But two witches and a sorceress join to rob her of her love and thus destroy her. One of them disguises herself as Mercury and comes to Aeneas to remind him he must leave Carthage without delay and fulfill his destiny. Aeneas promises to go, much to the joy of the evildoers. Learning of Aeneas's departure, Dido gives voice to her terrible grief in what is one of the noblest pages in early opera, "Dido's Lament." She then falls dead of a broken heart in the arms of her maid, Belinda. Her courtiers chant an elegy to her passing in "With Drooping Wings."

Purcell's effective use of the recitative proved his uncommon dramatic powers. This type of recitative, as Prof. Edward J. Dent explains, has little relationship with the recitative of the Italian opera. On the contrary, Purcell's recitative, as Donald Jay Grout described it, is "free arioso, admitting expressive florid passages, and always maintaining a clear, rhythmic, formal, and harmonic organization, yet without sacrificing correctness of declamation or expressive power." When the emotion in the text called for it, Purcell's lyricism expanded from expressive recitative into airs of the most compelling eloquence, as, for example, in "Dido's Lament." Flanked on the one side by a poignant recitative, "Thy Hand, Belinda," and on the other by the elegiac chorus, "With Drooping Wings," "Dido's Lament" remains one of the most touching episodes encountered in the opera before Gluck.

Purcell's dramatic powers are also in evidence in his instrumental episodes. With extraordinary vividness, the orchestra conjures up a storm in "The Grove"; paints the dark mystery of the witches in "The Cave"; re-creates the stir and bustle of a harbor just before sailing time in "The Ships."

But beyond its recitatives, arias, and orchestral pages, *Dido and Aeneas* boasts a wealth of choral numbers and dances, many of a striking English identity. The finest choruses include "To the Hills and the Vales" with its madrigal-like identity; the witches' chorus, "Ho, ho, ho"; and the sailors' chant with which the third act opens. The memorable ballet interludes include the first-scene "Triumphing Dance," the "Echo Dance of the Furies" with which the first act closes, and the "Witches' Dance" ending the second act.

Of its many strong points, perhaps the strongest of all is the opera's dramatic power. Here, maintains Hubert J. Foss, lies "the special greatness of

Purcell's achievement. He has the power to vivify each of the characters, puppet-like though they appear to be in the libretto; he enlivens each scene, so that it seems as if paper flowers and property trees had blossomed into real fragrance and were oozing the real sap of spring. His gaiety is as lively as his sorrow is poignant; his crowds are as sharply characterized as his principles. This music carries out its dramatic purpose by sheer swiftness of style."

1691. KING ARTHUR (or THE BRITISH WORTHY), a play in five acts by John Dryden, with incidental music by Purcell. First performance: London, April 1692.

Though *King Arthur* is not completely set to music the way *Dido and Aeneas* is, it contains so many outstanding musical episodes and of such variety, that it is sometimes referred to as an opera. But strictly speaking, it is a play with incidental music. Though the entire score has not come down to us intact, and though some confusion exists as to what belongs where (or if it belongs at all), enough of the surviving Purcell material from *King Arthur* is pure gold, to place it among the composer's most treasurable achievements for the stage. "The bulk of it," says J. A. Westrup, "is full of the most lively inspiration. . . . The best movements in this opera, whether simple songs or elaborate contrapuntal structures, have that quality inseparable from fine craftsmanship—they appear inevitable."

The plot of the play is both complicated and confused, "a quaint mixture," says Westrup, "of historical legend and pure fantasy." Here is the way Westrup outlines the story in brief. "Arthur, king of the Britons, and Oswald, Saxon king of Kent, are rivals for the hand of Emmeline, the blind daughter of the Duke of Cornwall. Already ten bloody battles have been fought, and the Saxons have been driven back. . . . The British leaders [take] encouragement from the omen of St. George's Day. Oswald has the cooperation of a magician, Osmond, who is further assisted by two familiar spirits, Grimbald and Philidel, one of the earth, the other of the air. Philidel, however, is persuaded by Merlin to transfer his services to the British side. When Grimbald tries to mislead Arthur and his troops, Philidel counteracts his malice by setting them on the right path. Meanwhile, Emmeline and her attendant. Matilda, are captured by Oswald. . . . More unpleasant experiences follow when Osmond presses his unwelcome attentions on her, and, to impress her with love's power—her sight having by this time been restored—produces an impromptu display, in which a frozen countryside and people are warmed to life again by Cupid. Right begins to triumph when Arthur, after successfully resisting the charms of two sirens, captures Grimbald, who had been masquerading as Emmeline, and so breaks the enchantments that are against him. In the last act the opposing armies come together. . . . Arthur meets Oswald in hand-to-hand combat and, disarming him, offers him his freedom. Emmeline is reunited to her royal lover, while Merlin announces that Arthur is the first of 'three

Christian worthies' and exercises his magic arts. The winds are banished and Britain's island rises from the sea. The whole company unites to sing the praises of St. George, and a general dance concludes the celebrations."

Westrup singles out the best pages in the score. In the second act are found the rival choruses of Grimbald's and Philedel's spirits, and Grimbald's soaring song, "Let Not a Moon-born Elf Mislead Ye." In the third act there is the extraordinary music describing the frozen wastes out of which the Cold Genius arises. "What distinguished Purcell's music for this scene is . . . the extraordinary suggestiveness of the harmonic progressions, from the strange sliding semitones of the instrumental introduction to the discordant melancholy of the Cold Genius's concluding words." The fourth act boasts the unforgettable song of the two sirens, "Two Daughters of This Aged Stream Are We," followed by the impressive passacaglia, "How Happy the Lover." The high moments of the fifth act include the baritone air, "Ye Blustering Brethren," dramatized by bravura passages in the accompanying strings; the pastoral trio in Italian style, "For Folded Flocks"; and the tune in English folk-song style, "Your Hay It Is Mow'd."

ALESSANDRO SCARLATTI 1660–1725

The center of operatic activity eventually shifted from Venice to Naples—from Monteverdi and his followers to Alessandro Scarlatti and his school. The techniques and methods developed in Naples were adopted by Italians for many years after that—until Gluck chartered a new course for opera. Even a non-Italian like Handel was influenced by, and imitated, the Neapolitans.

Scarlatti was the first major composer to establish the rules by which, first, his fellow Neapolitans and, then, the rest of Europe wrote their operas. Scarlatti created over a hundred operas. All are forgotten. Even those works regarded by his contempraries as masterworks are never given today—*Mitridate Eupatore* (1707), *Tigrane* (1715), and *Griselda* (1721), for example.

The new techniques found in these and other Scarlatti operas changed the format and style of Italian opera. Scarlatti was one of the first to establish the aria as an entity apart from the recitative. He helped evolve the da capo form (A-B-A), to which Italian composers after him remained faithful for many decades and which assumed a place of dominant importance within the operatic scheme. The aria grew so popular that an inflexible rule was tacitly conformed to, whereby every scene had to end with one. Hand in hand with this new importance of the aria came a new status for the singer. Composers began writing florid melodies—full of runs and embellishments—to exploit and glorify the human voice, and particularly, the voice of the castrato, now come to fashion.

To provide contrast, the opera composer saw to it that no singer be allowed to deliver two arias in succession, nor would he permit two arias of the same emotional character to follow one another. Recitative was still being used to carry the plot along, but it now also served the purpose of setting the stage for the aria. With Scarlatti, the old-time stile rappresentativo made way for two types of recitatives. One was called "secco"—a harpsichord accompanying the voice with formal chords. The other came to be known as "stromentato"—a richer and more varied background provided by the orchestra.

We encounter in Scarlatti operatic ensembles—vocal quartets, for example. Scarlatti also developed the so-called Italian Overture—as distinct from the French Overture of Lully. An outgrowth of the old sonata da chiesa, the Italian Overture was in three movements, with a slow one flanked by two fast ones.

While Scarlatti was thus invoking a new age and a new tradition for opera, he was not neglecting other forms of composition. He wrote over six hundred chamber cantatas. These, says Martin Bukofzer, are full "of the most audacious harmonic progressions." Here Scarlatti imbued "his arias with the complex harmonies of the tonal idiom, achieving startling, yet most convincing, melodic progressions."

Scarlatti's twelve Sinfonie di concerto grosso—a cross between the Italian Overture and the concerto grosso—gave orchestral writing in Italy a new direction and purpose. He produced a library of church music—Masses, motets, madrigals, oratorios, and a remarkable Stabat Mater—and he was the first composer to write a string quartet. "He has gathered up all that was best of the tangled materials produced by that age of transition and experiment, the seventeenth century," says Prof. Edward J. Dent, "to form out of them a musical language, vigorous and flexible as Italian itself, which has been the foundation of all music of the classical period."

Alessandro Scarlatti was born in Palermo, Sicily, on May 2, 1660. In 1672, he came to Rome, where he studied with Carissimi, made his first significant attempts at composition, and in 1678, married Antonia Anzalone. His debut as an opera composer came with *Gli equivoci nel sembiante,* introduced in Rome in February 1679. Its success brought him an appointment as Maestro di Cappella from Queen Christina of Sweden. In 1682, he made his home in Naples, where he became Maestro di Cappella at the royal chapel. During the next two decades, he completed many operas as well as sundry compositions for various entertainments at the palace.

Political disturbances in Naples in 1702 brought him to Florence for a visit. He then settled once again in Rome. Gaining the patronage of the powerful Cardinal Pietro Ottoboni, he was made Maestro di Cappella of the Ottoboni palace, and of the Santa Maria Maggiore Church. During this period, Scarlatti devoted himself to the writing of church compositions and chamber cantatas. His most ambitious and significant opera up to then, *Mitridate Eupatore,* was successfully produced in Venice in 1707.

In 1709, Scarlatti resumed his old Maestro di Cappella post in Naples. Except for brief trips, he now stayed in Naples for the rest of his life, devoting himself not only to composition but also to teaching. *Tigrane,* one of his most highly acclaimed operas, was seen in Naples in 1715; and *Il Trionfo dell' onore,* one of his best, came to the same city three years later. Now one of Italy's most celebrated musicians, Scarlatti was the recipient of many tributes and honors, including knighthood and the Order of the Golden Spur. Alessandro Scarlatti died in Naples on October 24, 1725.

1718. IL TRIONFO DELL 'ONORE (THE TRIUMPH OF HONOR), opera in three acts, with text by Francesco Antonio Tullio. First performance: Naples, November 26, 1718.

This is the only opera by Scarlatti to become familiar to twentieth-century audiences. It has enjoyed several revivals in England and Italy since 1938, most frequently in an edition prepared by the Italian musicologist, Virgilio Moratri; and it has been recorded in its entirety, an Italian release distributed in the United States by Cetra-Soria.

Il Trionfo has particular importance in opera history by virtue of being one of the earliest comic operas ever written. It preceded Pergolesi's *La Serva padrona*—with which opera buffa was finally crystallized—by fifteen years. Yet it would be a mistake to describe *Ii Trionfo* as an opera buffa. None of the conventions of this genre are as yet realized here. Strictly speaking, *Ii Trionfo* is an opera seria with comic episodes.

The plot gravitates around the escapades of a young rake, Riccardo. He has made love to and abandoned two women—Leonora and Doralice. Now he has come to Lucca to seek out his uncle so that he can replenish his sadly depleted purse. Erminio—Leonora's brother, and a former sweetheart of Doralice—follows Riccardo to Lucca. The first time he tries to engage Riccardo in a duel, he is stopped by Doralice, who begs him to spare the life of the man she still loves. But Doralice is not at hand when Erminio encounters and challenges Riccardo a second time. In the ensuing battle of swords, Riccardo is wounded. For the first time Riccardo has begun to repent his dissolute ways. He begs for forgiveness and promises to atone for his sins by marrying Leonora. Thus—as the concluding chorus explains—does honor triumph.

We find realized in *Il Trionfo* most of the innovations for which Scarlatti and his Neaplitan colleagues became famous: the effective three-part Italian Overture; beautiful da capo arias, of which the most significant are "Con quegl'occhi" in the first act, "È ben far" in the second, and "Ne vuoi pìu" in the third; fully realized ensemble numbers, such as the skilful quartet that closes the second act; effective recitatives of the secco and stromentato variety.

c. 1750. SONATA A QUATTRO IN D MINOR. I. Allegro. II. Grave. III. Allegro; Menuetto.

Scarlatti wrote two quartets in which, for the first time in chamber music, the figured bass of a harpsichord is dispensed with as the four stringed instruments are permitted to play independently of such a harmonic background. As the first composer to produce a quartet for two violins, viola, and cello, Alessandro Scarlatti is singled out as the creator of the string quartet. He wrote two such works, both appearing in a London publication entitled *Six Concertos for Two Violins and Violoncello Obbligato with Two Violins More, a Tenor, and Thoroughbass*. The composer took special pains to point out that none of the works in this volume required the use of a harpsichord.

The *Sonata a Quattro* in D minor is a three-movement composition. The first is in fugal style, betraying the composer's dependence on old polyphonic techniques. In the second movement, he progresses toward homophony with a stately melody set against a harmonic background. The concluding movement is a suave minuet, such as Lully might have written for his operas.

—— STABAT MATER, for soprano, contralto, and orchestra.

Scarlatti's *Stabat Mater* is one of the most eloquent in a form distinguished before him by Josquin des Prés and Palestrina. We do not know when Scarlatti wrote this music. The complex, often cerebral, contrapuntal devices of Josquin des Prés and Palestrina here make way for a simple and direct expression of sorrow. Brooding melancholy is immediately encountered in the chromatic melody for soprano and contralto, with its dramatized accompaniment, in the opening "Stabat Mater." The figurations on the word "dolentem" in the second section ("Cuius anima") and the pervading austerity of the entire third part ("O quam tristis") deepen the gloom. But in several of the succeeding sections, vigor or gentle serenity or an other-worldly radiance dispel the tragic atmosphere, at least temporarily. Tragedy returns in the poignant tenth section ("Quando corpus"). The eleventh, and concluding, part is an "Amen" for two voices. The florid writing here helps to carry the composition to an exultant, rather than tragic, denouement.

JOHANN KUHNAU 1660–1722

As Johann Sebastian Bach's predecessor at the Thomasschule in Leipzig, Kuhnau was responsible for the writing of church music of such high quality that many of his contemporaries regarded him as one of the foremost composers of his age. But today Kuhnau is remembered neither for his motets nor his cantatas. He survives by virtue of his compositions for the clavichord. There are two good reasons why this is so. For one thing, Kuhnau was the first German composer to use the term "sonata" in piano (or clavichord) music. For another, in some of his later sonatas he proved a significant pioneer in the writing of program music.

His first sonata is found in the *Neue Clavieruebung* published in 1692. The work is in three movements—Allegro, Adagio, Allegro. Thus did the Italian sonata da chiesa invade German music. In 1696, Kuhnau published another volume of clavichord music, the *Frische Clavier Fruechte*. Here we find seven sonatas, all in the sonata da chiesa form. Some are in four movements, others in five. Two themes of a contrasting character are sometimes found in a single movement, while some of the slow movements clearly define a homophonic style. In a few of his last movements, fugal writing carries a reminder of the old polyphonic methods. In 1700, Kuhnau published a set of six sonatas collectively entitled *Biblische Historien,* or *Biblical Stories*. In these works, Kuhnau tried to tell, often with naive literalness, tales from the Bible within the instrumental forms then in general use, from dance movements to the chorale prelude. It is in this collection that we encounter Kuhnau's best-known—and today most widely played—clavichord composition, *Der Streit zwischen David und Goliath* (*The Combat between David and Goliath*).

While there is only a remote relationship between Kuhnau's sonatas and the later classical works in that form, Kuhnau did manage to point a finger to the musical future by his "lucid sense of form," as Wanda Landowska once described it, and his use of "an outline that is graceful and elegant." Mme. Landowska added: "He had a fine fluidity of musical expression and a wonderful resourcefulness in enriching melodic materials."

Johann Kuhnau was born in Geising, Saxony, on April 6, 1660. His academic and musical studies took place in Dresden and Zittau. In the latter city, he wrote a motet for two choirs, which brought him an appointment as cantor. From 1682 to 1684, he studied law at the University of Leipzig; and in 1684, he was appointed organist of the St. Thomas Church. In 1686, he became a lawyer; and in that same year, he founded the Collegium Musicum for the presentation of public concerts. For about thirteen years, Kuhnau pursued the study of both law and music. In 1700, he was made music director of the University of Leipzig and of two Leipzig churches. For twenty years, beginning with 1701, he served as cantor of the Thomasschule. Upon getting this last appointment, he gave up law for good to concentrate on music. He died in Leipzig on June 5, 1722, his post at the Thomasschule being taken over by Johann Sebastian Bach.

1700. DER STREIT ZWISCHEN DAVID UND GOLIATH (THE COMBAT BETWEEN DAVID AND GOLIATH), sonata for the clavichord.

This programmatic description of the Biblical story of David and Goliath is one of six sonatas in *Biblical Stories* (*Biblische Historien*). Other sonatas tell how David cured Saul's madness with his harp music; how Jacob got married; how Hezekiah fell ill. A fourth is called *Gideon,* and a fifth, *The Tomb of Jacob.*

The Combat between David and Goliath is the most famous of this group—indeed, Kuhnau's most popular work. It is in six movements, each with a title to provide a clue to its programmatic content. The movements are as follows: "The Bravado of Goliath," "The Terror of the Israelites and Their Prayer to God," "David's Courage before the Terrible Enemy," "The Dispute and the Slinging of the Stone by David," "The Plight of the Philistines," and "Paeans of Victory by the Israelites."

Chords, scale passages, changing dynamics—the simplest possible resources—are utilized to translate into tones such extra-musical concepts as Goliath's boasts, David's defiance, the flight of the stone from David's sling, the escape of the Philistines. But as McKinney and Anderson explain in their book, *Music in History,* there are at least two sections in which Kuhnau "goes much deeper and attains something of true expressive and suggestive power." The first is when Kuhnau describes both the dejection of the Israelites and their implicit faith and trust in God. "Here the chromatic dropping background of repeated-note accompaniment is genuinely poetic; above it rises a chorale tune, the plea to God." The other comes with the death of Goliath. "Here a weighty descending figure suggests the gradual crumpling up of the body, and another may well stand for the departing breath as the giant's life ebbs away." The sonata ends in a dance movement telling of the Israelite rejoicing over David's victory.

FRANÇOIS COUPERIN LE GRAND 1668–1733

Couperin's pieces for the harpsichord are a landmark in French instrumental music. Couperin extended the virtuosity of the keyboard; established a modern method of fingering; developed the techniques and art of ornamentation. Wanda Landowska wrote: "The resources of the instrument are wonderfully extended and immeasurably enriched by this early French master, who must be considered one of the earliest masters of the keyboard."

Couperin evolved a French instrumental style that had grace, precision, a sense of balance, clarity, purity of expression. Indeed, to Couperin goes the distinction of having crystallized the elegant galant-style of homophonic instrumental writing, a style that flourished in Europe up to the mid-eighteenth century. In addition to all this, Couperin made the suite more flexible and more varied than it had been up to this time. And most significantly, perhaps, he was the first major French composer to write short programmatic pieces with descriptive titles in the style and manner of Robert Schumann, who came two centuries after Couperin. Through these programmatic items, new vistas were opened for tone painting and a new articulateness was achieved by instrumental music.

But harpsichord music was by no means the only area in which Couperin achieved greatness. He wrote some of the most remarkable church music of his age. He was one of the first in France to write sonatas. His *Concerts royaux* represent an early attempt, and a highly successful one, to produce French chamber music. The Couperin Mass, as Donald Jay Grout has remarked, "is one of the glories of the Baroque era in France, as was Buxtehude's in Germany."

François Couperin is known as "the great one," or "le grand," to distinguish him from all the other Couperins, who for several generations had been successful musicians in France. He was born in Paris on November 10, 1668, and studied the organ first with his father (the organist of St. Gervais Church) and later with Jacques-Denis Thomelin. When he was seventeen, he took over his father's organ post at St. Gervais, holding it until 1723. He married Marie-Anne Ansault in 1689. A year later, his first child, and his first publication (a volume of Masses for the organ) were born. In 1693, he competed successfully for Thomelin's post as organist to the king. Couperin now also taught music to the royal princes and princesses, and in 1701, was made harpsichord virtuoso to the king. While serving at court, he composed the *Concerts royaux*—among the earliest examples of French chamber music—for performance at the Sunday concerts at Versailles. After giving up his court post as harpsichordist in 1730, Couperin went into complete retirement. He died in Paris on September 12, 1733.

1695. LA SULTANE, sonata for two violins, two cellos, and bass.

Couperin wrote his first four sonatas for two violins and bass in 1692. With these compositions, the Italian form of the sonata da chiesa invaded French music. With *La Sultane,* in 1695, Couperin had succeeded in bringing a Gallic personality and charm to his sonata writing. "*La Sultane,*" explains Wilfrid Mellers, "is conceived on a grand scale and is remarkable not only for its extensive development but also for the fact that it includes two more or less independent cello parts. It thus has four string parts in all; the second cello sometimes, but by no means habitually, doubles the bass of the continuo."

The work opens with an extended stately Grave movement. A spacious Allegro in contrapuntal style follows. After that comes an eloquent "Air tendre," a dialogue between the two cellos and two violins. A second Grave section, this time brief, leads into two fast movements, one of which is a gigue.

Darius Milhaud, the eminent twentieth-century French composer, orchestrated the first two movements of *La Sultane* in 1940. Renamed *Introduction and Allegro,* it was played for the first time by the St. Louis Symphony Orchestra under Vladimir Golschmann on January 17, 1941.

1714–1715. LEÇONS DES TÉNÈBRES, for one or two voices, with organ and viol continuo. I. Incipit lamentatio Jeremiae Prophetae. II. Et egressus est filia. III. Manum suam misit hostis.

In or about 1714, Couperin began writing the *Leçons des ténèbres* for some unidentified religious establishment. He planned nine such pieces, but managed to complete only three. This triumvirate of church compositions finds Couperin at the height of his creative powers. The text is made up of the Latin words of the prophet Jeremiah, with ritualistic Hebrew phrases continually interjected. These Hebrew interpolations allow Couperin to indulge in remarkable vocalise elaborations. Otherwise, his style is a French adaptation of the Italian aria, marked by an intensity and passion not often encountered in Couperin's works. "The opening of the first 'Leçon,' explains Wilfrid Mellers, "indicates admirably . . . [a] breadth of line and also shows how the ornamentation is both an expressive part of the line's contour and a concomitant of the harmony. If the third 'Leçon' impresses one as being the greatest, it is largely because, being conceived for two soloists instead of one, it offers opportunities for a combination of the vocalise technique with polyphony. Its clear counterpoint, mated with lucid tonal architecture, shows that in his last and greatest church work Couperin is still, like Bach, poised between two worlds, and making the best of them both."

1722. APOTHÉOSE DE LULLI, sonata in G minor, for two violins and bass.

This—probably Couperin's masterwork within the form of the sonata—boasts an elaborate descriptive program. Wilfred Mellers tells us that "Couperin first gives, as it were, a summing up of the tradition on which he had been nurtured; and then demonstrates how he has, through his career, managed to incorporate the Italian sonata in it." Mellers adds: "The Overture—Lully in the Elysian Fields—moves with grave simplicity in a regular crochet pulse, achieving a noble pathos through groupings of a falling scale passage . . . . The airs of the *ombres liriques,* the *Vol de Mercure,* the *Descente d'Apollon* (contrapuntal but dance-like), and the *Rumeur souteraine* of Lully's contemporaries and rivals, are all chamber-music versions of operatic devices. The *Tendres plaintes* of Lully's contemporaries . . . is a beautiful instance of Couperin's rarefied sensuousness. . . . The *enlèvement de Lully* to Parnassus introduces for the first time the contrapuntal method of the Italian canzona and makes fascinating play with a syncopated rhythm. When Lully reaches Parnassus he is met by Corelli and the Italian muses, who greet him with a Largo strictly in the da chiesa manner, majestically proportioned, with acrid augmented fifths. The *Remerciement de Lulli à Apollon* is a symmetrical operatic aria which illustrates the absorption of the Lullian aria into the tonally more developed Italian arias of Handel. . . . Next Apollo persuades Lully and Corelli that the unions of *Les Goûts françois et italiens* would create musical perfection; so the two muses sing together an *Essai, en forme d'ouverture, élégamment et sans lenteur*. This opens with a brilliant fanfare in dotted rhythm, which is followed by a 3/4 tune in flowering quavers making considerable use of arpeggio figures. Then come two little *airs légers* for the violins without continuo; in one of them Lully plays the tune and Corelli the accompaniment, in the other the roles are reversed. And the whole work is rounded off with a full-scale sonata da chiesa in which Lully and Corelli play together, the Italian technique being finally, as it were, translated into French."

1722. CONCERT ROYAUX NO. 2 IN D MAJOR, for harpsichord and unspecified instruments.

Couperin wrote four suites for harpsichord and various unspecified instruments for the Sunday court concerts attended by Louis XIV and his entourage at Versailles. These works were intended to "soften and sweeten the king's melancholy," and consequently they are all light and melodious. Each of the four works is a dance suite. Unity is achieved through a consistent tonality among the respective parts. The four *Concerts,* published in a single volume in 1722, are in the keys of G, D, A, and E. Thus it will be seen that each succeeding work proceeds by a fifth to the key of the dominant.

The second *Concert royaux* opens with a Prelude that has the stately pace of a minuet. After that come an Allemande in fugal style, and an expressive "Air tendre" in minor mode. All three movements thus far have been in a comparatively slow tempo. The fourth, "Air contre fugue," provides a change of pace through its vigorous motion. The suite ends with a beautiful slow movement in rondo form entitled "Echos."

In 1725, Couperin published a second volume of *Concerts royaux* under the title of *Les Goûts réunis;* there are ten works in this volume.

1713–1730. PIÈCES DE CLAVECIN, four volumes.

FIRST VOLUME: 1. L'Auguste. 2. Courantes I and II; 3. La Majestueuse. 4. Gavotte. 5. La Milordine. 6. Menuet. 7. Les Silvains. 8. Les Abeilles. 9. La Nanète. 10. Les Sentiments. 11. La Pastorelle. 12. Les Nonètes. 13. La Bourbonnaise. 14. La Manon. 15. L'Enchanteresse. 16. La Fleurie. 17. Les Plaisirs de Saint-Germain-en-Laye. 18. Sicilienne. 19. La Laborieuse. 20. Courantes I and II. 21. La Prude. 22. L'Antoine. 23. Gavotte. 24. Menuet. 25. Canaries et double. 26. Passepied. 27. Rigaudons. 28. La Charoloise. 29. La Diane. 30. Fanfare pour la suite de la Diane. 31. La Terpiscore. 32. La Florentine.

33. La Garnier. 34. La Babet. 35. Les Idées heureuses. 36. La Mimi. 37. La Diligente. 38. La Flateuse. 39. La Voluptueuse. 40. Les Papillons. 41. La Ténébreuse 42. Courantes I and II. 43. La Lugubre. 44. Gavotte. 45. Menuet. 46. Les Pélerines. 47. Les Laurentines. 48. L'Espagnolète. 49. Les Regrets. 50. Les Matelotes provençales. 51. La Favorite. 52. La Lutine. 53. La Marche des gris-vêtus. 54. Les Baccanales. 55. La Pateline. 56. Le Réveil-matin. 57. La Logivière. 58. Courantes I and II. 59. La Dangereuse. 60. Gigue. 61. La Tendre Fanchon. 62. La Badine. 63. La Bandoline. 64. La Flore. 65. L'Angélique. 66. La Villers. 67. Les Vendageuses. 68. Les Agrémens.

SECOND VOLUME: 1. Les Moissonneurs. 2. Les Langueurs tendres. 3. Le Gazouillement. 4. La Bersan. 5. Les Baricades mistérieuses. 6. Les Bergeries. 7. La Commère. 8. Le Moucheron. 9. La Ménetou. 10. Les Petits âges. 11. La Basque. 12. La Chazé. 13. Les Amusements. 14. La Raphaèle. 15. L'Ausoniène. 16. Courantes I and II. 17. L'Unique. 18. Gavotte. 19. Rondeau. 20. Gigue. 21. Passacaille. 22. La Morinète. 23. Allemande a deux clavecins. 24. La Rafraîchissante. 25. Les Charmes. 26. La Princesse de Sens. 27. L'Olimpique. 28. L'Insinuante. 29. La Séduisante. 30. Le Bavelot-flotant. 31. Le Petit deuil. 32. Menuet. 33. La Triomphante. 34. La Mézangère. 35. La Gabrièle. 36. La Nointèle. 37. La Fringante. 38. L'Amazône. 39. Les Bagatelles. 40. La Castelane. 41. L'Etincelante. 42. Les Grâces naturèles. 43. La Zénobie. 44. Les Fastes de la grande et ancienne Mxnxstrxdxxx. 45. Les Jumèles. 46. L'Intime. 47. La Galante. 48. La Coribante. 49. La Vauvré. 50. La Fileuse. 51. La Boulonoise. 52. L'Atalante.

THIRD VOLUME: 1. Les Lis naissans. 2. Les Rozeaux. 3. L'Engageante. 4. Les Folies françoises. 5. L'Âme-en-peine. 6. Le Rossignol-en-amour. 7. La Linote éfarouchée. 8. Les Fauvètes plaintives. 9. Le Rossignol-vainqueur. 10. La Juillet. 11. Le Carillon de Cithère. 12. Le Petit-rien. 13. La Régente. 14. Le Dodo. 15. L'Évaporée. 16. Musète de Choisi. 17. Musète de Taverni. 18. La Douce et piquante. 19. Les Vergers fleuris. 20. La Princess de Chabeuil. 21. Les Grâces incomparables. 22. L'Himen-Amour. 23. Les Vestales. 24. L'Aimable Thérèse. 25. Le Drôle de corps. 26. La Distraite. 27. La Létiville. 28. La Superbe. 29. Les Petits moulins à vent. 30. Les Timbres. 31. Courante. 32. Les Petits Crémières de Bagnolet. 33. La Verneuil. 34. La Verneuillète. 35. Soeur Monique. 36. Le Turbulant. 37. L'Atendrissante. 38. Le Tic-toc-choc. 39. Le Gaillard boiteux. 40. Les Calotins et les calotines. 41. Les Calotines. 42. L'Ingénue. 43. L'Artiste. 44. Les Culbutes Jxcxbxnxs. 45. La Muse-Plantine. 46. L'Enjouée.

FOURTH VOLUME: 1. La Princesse Marie. 2. La Boufone. 3. Les Chérubins. 4. La Crouilli. 5. La Fine Madelon. 6. La Douce Janneton. 7. La Sézile. 8. Les Tambourins. 9. La Reine des cours. 10. La Bondissante. 11. La Couperin. 12. La Harpée. 13. La Petite Pince-sans-rire. 14. Le Trophée. 15. Airs pours la suite du Trophée. 16. Le Point du jour. 17. L'Anguille. 18. Le Croc-en-jambe. 19. Menuets croisés. 20. Les Tours de passe-passe. 21. L'Audacieuse. 22. Les Tricoteuses. 23. L'Arlequine. 24. Les Gondoles de Delos. 25. Les

Satires chèvre-pieds. 26. Les Vieux seigneurs. 27. Les Jeunes seigneurs. 28. Les Dars homicides. 29. Les Guirlandes. 30. Les Brinborions. 31. La Divine babiche. 32. La Belle Javotte autre fois l'Infante. 33. L'Amphibie. 34. La Visionaire. 35. La Mistérieuse. 36. La Montflambert. 37. La Muse victorieuse. 38. Les Ombres errantes. 39. La Convalescente. 40. Gavotte. 41. La Sophie. 42. L'Épineuse. 43. La Pantomime. 44. L'Exquise. 45. Les Pavots. 46. Saillie. 47. Les Chinois.

With Couperin's four volumes of pieces for the clavecin, or harpsichord, the history of French keyboard music embarks upon its first fruitful era. The more than two hundred items gathered into the four volumes are divided by the composer into twenty-seven suites—or "Ordres," as Couperin preferred to designate the suite. There are five "ordres" in the first book; eight "ordres" in the second; and seven "ordres" each in the next two volumes. An "ordre" is a grouping of little pieces in dance patterns in related keys and with picturesque titles. These dance movements are not in the stylized structures of the keyboard suite so long in use, but frequently sophisticated little pieces in the manner of the ballet episodes written by Lully for his operas. The numbers in each of the "ordres" are so self-sufficient that each one can be played independently of the others. The relationship between one and another is also so flexible that the order of the pieces within any given group can be rearranged. The individual numbers are in the forms of allemandes, chaconnes, rondeaux, musettes, sarabandes, passacaglias, or theme and variations.

There is hardly a phase of French society in the seventeenth and early eighteenth centuries that is not touched upon in these little compositions. Court life, the sights and sounds of Parisian streets, customs and dress, daily routines, the dances and tunes of the times—these are only a few of the many facets of the life and times of Couperin as described here in music. Other pieces venture into an altogether different direction by describing insects, jugglers, gossip, the weather, a fortuneteller, harvesters, a prude, a seductress, hurdy-gurdy players, bells, windmills, and so forth. Sometimes it is just a passing mood that is touched upon.

In the first volume (1713), the finest single piece is "La Favorite," a chaconne in C minor re-creating the pomp and circumstance of court life in Versailles. Other impressive numbers in this set include "La Tendre fanchon," "La Bandoline," "La Ténébreuse," and "La Lugubre."

In the second book (1716–1717), some of the more famous individual numbers include "Les Moissonneurs," a peasant gavotte with a strong rhythmic pulse in a lute figuration; "Les Baricades mistérieuses," with its effective series of resonant suspensions; and "Les Langueurs tendres," one of the most impressive mood pieces in the volume. But the crown of the collection is the "Passacaille," which Wanda Landowska once described as "the queen of harpsichord pieces." This is not only one of Couperin's most important compositions in any medium or form, but also one of the noblest ever conceived for the harpsichord. "The tragic effect of this movement," explains Wilfrid Mellers, "is attributable to the tension between the audacious fluidity of the harmonies and the rigid repetition, not merely of the bass, but of the whole opening period. . . . Each couplet adds to the intensity. . . until a shattering climax is reached in the seventh couplet with its great spread of discords and anguished suspensions percussively exploiting the whole range of the instrument."

In this second volume, the fourth item in the eleventh "Ordre" is something of a curiosity—due to its strange title. It is called "Les Fastes de la grande et ancienne Mxnxstrxdxxx." The last garbled word was intended by the composer to suggest "Ménéstrandise," a musician's guild or trade union in Couperin's time. The guild was using pressure to get the court musicians to join up. Since the guild was composed primarily of tavern musicians, the court people balked; and so did Couperin. As an expression of protest, Couperin wrote a composition that is in the nature of a little play in five acts for the harpsichord. In the first, whose mood fluctuates from sobriety to broad humor, the officers and jury members of the guild stride into the hearing room. The complaints of barrel-organ players and musical beggars are heard. Jugglers, tumblers, and clowns, leading monkeys and bears, now come upon the scene, followed by musicians who have been crippled in the service of music. In the concluding part, the rout of the whole troupe is depicted. In this work, Couperin makes effective, and at times witty, use of popular music, street songs, and the tunes of street fiddlers and hurdy-gurdy players.

In the third volume (1722), will be found the remarkable twelve-part *Les Follies françoises*. Structurally, this work is a chaconne—a series of variations on a ground bass. The composition as a whole is an amusing and pictorial experiment in correlating human attributes with colors: modesty with red; hope with green; loyalty with blue; ardor with scarlet; jealousy with gray; frenzy or despair with black. The music tries to reproduce not only the emotion being portrayed but also the color with which that emotion is associated. "The work," says Mellers, "is a microcosm of Couperin's art, its tragic passion, its witty urbanity, its sensuous charm. . . . Though in duration in time it is not long, through the variety of its mood and the architectural precision of its structure, it seems to be a work of imposing dimensions."

This third volume also includes such descriptive pieces as "Le Carillon de Cithère," with its effective suggestions of tolling bells; "Les Petits moulins à vent"; "Le tic-toc-choc"; and an impressionistic cameo, "Les Vergers fleuris," which evokes the feelings engendered by the heat and haze of summer.

The fourth volume appeared in 1730, three years before the composer's death. Of particular interest here is "L'Arlequine," Couperin's interpretation of Harlequin in which his tragic as well as comic nature is pointed up. A sarabande, "Les Vieux seigneurs," is completed by a second piece, "Les Jeunes seigneurs," in which various types of court society are satirized. Stately chords with trills describe the old lords, while the younger ones are portrayed through tripping figures with echo effects. A mood of mystery is created in "La Mistérieuse" through subtle key changes, while heat and languor are magically interpreted in tones in "Les Pavots."

DOMENICO SCARLATTI 1685–1757

In writing new music for the harpsichord, and in opening thereby new vistas for harpsichord performance, only Domenico Scarlatti can rival the significance of Couperin-le-Grand. Though Domenico Scarlatti wrote twelve operas that were highly popular in his day; and though his collected works provide a rich yield of church music, including four oratorios and many chamber cantatas, it is by his remarkable harpsichord pieces that he has secured a historic place in music. Everything he did in the larger forms has become obscured by the wit, charm, and vitality of his harpsichord sonatas, which stand with dignity and a sense of belonging with the greatest music written for that instrument. So different is Scarlatti's instrumental writing from anything that preceded it, that C. Hubert Parry is strongly tempted to believe that "the work of his prototypes had been lost." Parry concludes: "His instinct for the requirements of his instrument was so marvelous and his development of technique so wide and rich, that he seems to spring full-armed into the view of history."

Domenico Scarlatti was the son of the distinguished Neapolitan opera composer, Alessandro Scarlatti (which see). Domenico was born in Naples on October 26, 1685. He received a thorough musical training from his father. In 1701, Domenico Scarlatti became organist and composer at the royal chapel in Naples. Two years later, his first opera, *Ottavia risituita al trono,* was produced. Two more operas were written and produced before 1704 was over. In 1708, Scarlatti came to Venice, where for a while he studied with Gasparini and then achieved renown as a harpsichord virtuoso. For a while after that, Scarlatti lived in Rome. There he engaged Handel in a competitive performance on both the harpsichord and the organ, with Scarlatti emerging as the victor on the harpsichord, and Handel on the organ. In 1709, Scarlatti was engaged as house musician of Queen Maria Casimira of Poland, who was then residing in Rome. Scarlatti wrote seven operas for her. When the Queen left Rome, Scarlatti became Maestro di Cappella at the Vatican, an office that led him to write many church compositions.

While serving in Lisbon as Maestro di Cappella at the royal chapel, a post he assumed in or about 1720, Scarlatti made a brief return visit to Rome, where, in 1728, he married Maria Caterina Gentile. In 1729, Scarlatti and his wife settled in Madrid, where he stayed for the rest of his life. There he served as Maestro di Camera at the royal palace and as teacher of the harpsichord to Maria Barbara, the Queen. It was for the Queen that Scarlatti wrote his first harpsichord sonatas, the first volume of which was issued in 1738. In 1738, also, Scarlatti was knighted. After the death of his wife in 1739, Scarlatti married a second time—Anastasia Maxarti. Between them, his two wives had given him nine children. Scarlatti died in Madrid on July 23, 1757.

—— SONATAS (ESSERCIZI), for harpsichord.

E major, "Cortège," L. 23; B minor, "Andante Mosso," L. 33; C major, "Allegro," L. 104; A major, "Barcarolle," L. 132; B minor, "Bourree", L. 263; G minor, "Burlesca," L. 338; C minor, L. 352; E major, "Capriccio," L. 375; D minor, "Pastorale," L. 413; D minor, "Toccatina," L. 422; D major, L. 461; D major, "Tempo di ballo," L. 463; G minor, "Cat's Fugue," L. 499.

Scarlatti completed over five hundred short compositions for the harpsichord which today are called "sonatas" but which he himself identified as "Exercises" or "Essercizi." Scarlatti's identification is more suitable than ours. These pieces are not sonatas in the later concept of that form (no more than those of Johann Kuhnau were sonatas). They are miniatures, "short pieces taking from two to six minutes to perform," as Robert Stevenson described them in *Music Before the Classic Era*. "They are usually divided in the middle, with both halves repeated. They begin with some pungent melodic or rhythmic figure, then proceed to something fresh, though not necessarily in a new key or in another mood. The effect produced is one of cheerfulness and bonhomie. In the second half, the composer often switches on to a new track without, however, changing the general mood or tempo. The ends of the first and of the second half are customarily alike; the first half will end in the key of the dominant, and the second will return to the tonic."

Most of these compositions are exercises in various techniques of harpsichord performance, with which an altogether new virtuosity is developed for keyboard music. One piece emphasizes the trill; another, arpeggios; a third, scale passages; a fourth, shakes. These works abound with leaps across the keyboard in intervals larger than the octave, with contrary motion, broken chords, tremolos, repeated notes, passages for crossed hands. But while the composer's principal aim seemed to have been to clarify a specific problem—and while he himself described his music as "only a frolic in art intended to increase confidence in the clavier"—he achieved far more than he had intended. Like Chopin in his études, Scarlatti brought such a remarkable creative inventiveness and imagination to his exercises that they rise above the utilitarian to become vibrant works of art, extraordinary for the variety of expression and emotional nuances.

In many of his sonatas, Scarlatti gives us a glimpse into the society of his time—even as Couperin did in the *Pièces de clavecin.* "His fancy," Wanda Landowska once wrote, "draws him, for the most part, to people. He does not depict the sumptuousness of palaces, and he scorns the grandezza of princes. It is above all the street that attracts him, with its guitars, castanets, its clapping of hands, and all its motley, swarming life. Shaken by the excitement of the dance, by the fever of desire, this rollicking and unbridled music derives its life from perpetual motion itself. The major and minor intervals change unpredictably; the flames flare up and disappear with a rapidity that leaves us breathless. In the pastorales, melancholy as they are, or in the smooth gliding barcarolles, even when the composer is most contemplative and serene, his music still retains its intensity and vitality."

Sometimes we can detect the influence on Scarlatti of his native city, Naples—the C major Sonata (L. 205), for example, which is a Neapolitan dance. But the Spanish influence on him is far more profound. Scarlatti often employed rhythms of the Spanish dance—the jota primarily. In using repeated notes, Scarlatti occasionally tried to simulate the clicking of castanets. The imitation of guitar strumming gives some of his accompaniments their unique character and is responsible for some of the discords. "When we hear his music," says Wanda Landowska, "we know we are in the climate of sunlight and warmth. . . . It is Spain—the spirit of the Latin countries and of the god of the Mediterranean; we are in the presence of that same deity who has been truly called 'the god who dances.'"

The Sonata in E major (L. 23), known as the "Cortège," describes, in Mme. Landowska's words, "an approaching procession, with its hammering of horses' hoofs, ringing of silver bits, and jingling of spurs, which first come to us from a distance, and then reach us in a magnificent cortège. Fifths ring out and pursue one another in imitation; trills carry on a dialogue and vibrate in echo. The parade passes before us, moves on, and finally disappears."

The names of "Capriccio" and "Pastorale" were given to the Sonatas in E major (L. 375) and D minor (L. 413) by Karl Tausig in his famous transcriptions for the piano.

One of the most frequently heard of all the Scarlatti sonatas in the one in D major (L. 461). To Mme. Landowska, this work "reads like a page from a music drama. What other term can we use to describe the sudden changes of mood which demand corresponding changes in tempi, or the opposing motifs, the batteries, rolls, and cascades unexpectedly interrupted here and there by a love theme like an arietta accompanied by guitars?"

The Sonata in G minor (L. 499) is sometimes known as the "Cat's Fugue," because the leaps in the melody sound as if a cat had run across the keyboard.

It should be explained that the letter "L" and the adjoining number, used to identify Scarlatti's sonatas refer to the place of each sonata in the definitive Longo edition.

Two twentieth-century Italian composers used themes from the Scarlatti sonatas for significant works. One was Vincenzo Tommasini, composer of the ballet score to *The Good-Humored Ladies* (see below). The other was Alfredo Casella, whose *Scarlattiana* is a divertimento for piano and orchestra. It was performed for the first time anywhere in New York City on January 23, 1927.

—— THE GOOD-HUMORED LADIES (LE DONNE DI BUON UMORE), a one-act ballet, based on Carlo Goldoni's comedy of the same name, with choreography by Léonide Massine. Vincenzo Tommasini's music was derived from seven Scarlatti sonatas. First performance: Rome, April 12, 1917, by the Ballet Russe de Monte Carlo.

The scenario of this ballet concerns amatory diversions and escapades during the Carnival celebration in a small town near Venice. Here is how the program described the plot when the ballet was first introduced: "The Good-Humored Ladies can think of nothing but roguery. They send to the love-sick Rinaldo a note in which a lady wearing a rose-colored ribbon offers him a rendezvous. Five ladies, all wearing rose-colored ribbons, present themselves, and finally Rinaldo remains alone with old Silvestra. The soubrette Mariuccia, in love with Leonardo, arranges for a supper with the rake, Battista, during the course of which they play many jokes on the old Marquis Luca, who finally courts the two young people, both disguised as ladies. In the end, the Good-Humored Ladies give to old Silvestra as partner the inn-keeper Nicoclo, whom they have dressed up as a lord. Through all this roguery passes the melancholy and charming figure of Constanza, fiancée of Rinaldo, with whom the other women are carrying on flirtations. Throughout, one sees episodical figures which seem to have been drawn from Longhi or Hogarth."

Before getting down to work on his score, Tommasini went through all of the five hundred or more Scarlatti sonatas. He put aside a dozen, and finally selected seven: B minor (L. 33), G major (L. 209), D major (L. 361), F major (L. 385), G major (L. 388), D major (L. 463), and G minor (L. 499).

Later on, Tommasini lifted five numbers from his ballet score and gathered them into a now-popular orchestral suite (I. Presto. II. Allegro. III. Andante. IV. Non presto, in tempo di ballo. V. Presto).

ANTONIO VIVALDI 1669–1741

Vivaldi's output was vast. He wrote some forty operas, a hundred or so major choral works, four hundred concertos, about twenty-five secular cantatas, seventy-three sonatas, and various other items.

It is through his concertos that we know him best and revere him highly—his concertos for a solo instrument (or solo instruments) and orchestra, and his concerti grossi. To the solidly established concerto structure of Arcangelo Corelli and Giuseppe Torelli (1658–1709)—to their idiomatic writing for the violin in the solo concertos, and to their sound structures and vigorous styles in the concerto-grosso form—Vivaldi contributed a personal note. His was a varied lyricism, particularly eloquent in the slow movements; a robust rhythm that gives his fast movements an irresistible drive; and, whether in slow movements or fast, a nobility of concept. Vivaldi carried the concerto grosso to its ultimate development before Bach and Handel, making it a mold into which he could pour a wealth of poetic thought and sensitized emotion. In some of his concerti grossi he demonstrates an altogether new approach to program music. And while Torelli had preceded him in writing solo concertos, Vivaldi was the one who managed to personalize the solo instrument.

Henri Prunières described the Vivaldi concerto as follows: "The three-movement scheme (Allegro, Largo, Allegro) is the one usually adopted. All the quick movements are in two sections: in the first, the themes are stated; in the second, the principal motive is developed; and the opening theme is repeated at the end. Vivaldi appears to have been the first to break away from the system of repeats and ritornelli in the Allegros and to conceive them as a continuous stream. His flowing counterpoint is a marvel of rhythmic energy and harmonic power. In the Largos and Adagios the melodies blossom forth regardless of symmetry, obeying only the instinct which had prompted their creation. Some of the slow movements in the concerti and in the violin and cello sonatas are as sublime as anything in music. . . . The passionate Allegros with which the concerti end are cast in a free rondo form with regular return of the ritornello in various keys. Vivaldi's work reveals a new conception of the orchestra, which is later adopted by the early symphonists, and by Haydn and Mozart. Horns and oboes now no longer double the violins, but mark the rhythm and punctuate the discourse of the strings by appropriately placed accents."

Vivaldi's influence was decisive. We know how profoundly Johann Sebastian Bach was affected by his music; how he used to copy out Vivaldi's concertos by hand; how he transcribed some of them for different instruments; how he kept Vivaldi in mind when he set to write his own concertos.

Though the concerto was the area cultivated most fruitfully by Vivaldi, his best choral music and some of his other works are well worth exploring. His creative power—regardless of the medium he selected—was both varied and rich. When one of his forgotten masterworks is revived, we invariably confront new vistas in his art. Here is how Alfredo Casella described these vistas: "The prodigious wealth of musical invention; the dramatic force (which recalls so imperatively the brilliance and fire of the great Venetian painters); the mastery of choral polyphony; the marvelous dynamism of the instrumental parts; the incessant movement of which, independent of the voices and chorus, plainly forecasts the Wagnerian style; and finally, the high quality of the emotion which animates his works—all these put Vivaldi in a wholly new light."

Antonio Vivaldi was born in Venice, Italy, in or about 1669. Though he received intensive music instruction from his father and from Giovanni Legrenzi, he was directed to the church. In 1693, he took the tonsure, and sometime before 1703, received holy orders. All the while he continued musical activity by perfecting himself as a violinist and by writing a considerable amount of music. In 1703, he became a teacher of the violin; after 1709, he served as Maestro di Concerti at the Ospedale della Pietà in Venice. For his concerts, he produced many of his concertos. In 1740, Vivaldi left Venice for Vienna, hoping to get a desirable assignment at court. But his expectations were not realized. During the last years of his life, Vivaldi suffered extreme poverty and neglect. He died in Vienna in July 1741 and was consigned to a pauper's grave.

1712. CONCERTO IN A MINOR, for violin and orchestra, op. 3, no. 6. I. Allegro. II. Largo. III. Presto.

—— CONCERTO GROSSO IN D MINOR, op. 3, no. 11. I. Maestoso. II. Largo. III. Allegro.

The dozen concertos assembled in opus 3 are collectively entitled *L'Estro armonico,* or "Harmonic Inspiration." This volume includes four solo concertos and eight concerti grossi. Of the latter, Nos. 2, 4, and 7 are in the four-movement structure of the sonata da chiesa; the others are in the three-movement form of the sonata da camera.

Of the solo concertos, that in A minor for solo violin and orchestra—the sixth of the set—is perhaps the most popular. The first movement is somewhat less vigorous than that generally encountered in Vivaldi concertos, dominated by a yearning subject introduced at the outset by the orchestra before being taken over and transformed by the solo violin. The writing is in the best traditions of the concerto grosso, with alternations of light and shade, and with the solo instrument now being set against, now being combined with, the accompanying orchestra. The slow movement is an exalted song for the solo instrument, and the finale is robust in fiber and athletic in pace.

The Concerto Grosso in D minor—the eleventh in the set—is today one of the most frequently played of Vivaldi's concertos, though usually in modern adaptations. The version favored most by our present-day concert halls is that of Alexander Siloti, because, while utilizing a modern orchestra, it sticks most closely to the composer's original intentions. The work has three movements. The first movement has spacious design. It opens with a powerful figure in the strings that is worked out dramatically. A sedate three-measure passage leads into a fugal section. The second movement is the most eloquent in the entire work. It is dominated by a melody of incandescent beauty, of a reverent mood and a contemplative character rarely encountered in concerto-grosso writing before Johann Sebastian Bach. The entire movement has the quality of an opera aria, the singing melody set against an even rhythm. The finale is in the vigorous style of the first movement. A strong phrase against powerful chords is given striking contrasts of dynamics and harmonic colors as it is worked out.

1716. JUDITHA TRIUMPHANS (JUDITH TRIUMPHANT), oratorio for solo voices, chorus, and orchestra.

Vivaldi wrote two oratorios, in which he anticipated some of the powerful choral writing and the spiritual lyricism that Handel carried over into his greatest works in this medium. Despite the fact that Vivaldi's *Judith* suffers from an execrable text—the work of Giacomo Cassetti—the composer succeeded in rising above the limitations of his words to create a work of powerful drama and, at times, towering majesty.

The Biblical subject of Judith had been favored by composers for operatic and oratorio treatment from the seventeenth century on. Between 1700 and 1716, there were at least eight musical adaptations of the Judith story. The year that Vivaldi completed his oratorio, three other operas and oratorios on the same subject were introduced. Since Vivaldi's time, the tale of Judith has been exploited by numerous composers, including Arthur Honegger and William Schuman in the twentieth century.

Judith is a native of Bethulia. When her native city is besieged by the Assyrians—headed by its king, Holofernes—she enters the camp of the enemy, ostensibly to betray her people. But there she enraptures Holofernes with her ravishing beauty. When he succumbs to a drunken sleep, she slays him.

Vivaldi's text concentrates on what transpires in the camp of the Assyrians as Judith wins the love of Holofernes and then destroys him. But Cassetti intended his libretto to be something more than just the retelling of a Biblical episode. He used it to symbolize Venice's problems at that time. Judith is meant to represent Venice; Holofernes and the Assyrians stood for the Turks; Bethulians pointed to the Christian congregation in Venice.

In his music, as we learn from a program annotator who has not been identified, Vivaldi "follows the Baroque tradition of alternating without variety, recitative and aria." He skilfully balanced Holofernes and Judith (bass and alto) with their respective servants (tenor and soprano). But here, the annotator continues, "the resemblance to contemporary oratorio practice stopped. His intent was symphonic: he could have given each character a separate musical entity, but he chose instead to let each one, at another time, carry the same theme and thus develop the *Judith* as a whole. There are programmatic indications, like the sawing of the strings at Judith's words, 'I sever Holofernes' head'; but these are minimal. The instrumental combinations are sometimes unusual: violas d'amore and muted strings, oboes and bassoons with nothing in the middle, and even two solo mandolins. The center of gravity in the orchestral parts is always in the strings, which seem to fulfil the function of the orchestral foundation to which the winds add only color. Instrumentally, there are many indications of a polyphonic style; the aria lines follow contemporary practice without undue stress on bravura; but all three choruses are, like Gluck's, completely monodic."

—— LE QUATTRO STAGIONI (THE FOUR SEASONS), four concerti grossi for violin and string orchestra, op. 8, nos. 1–4. I. La Primavera (Spring). II. L'Estate (Summer). III. L'Autunno (Autumn). IV. L'Inverno (Winter).

A fifth set of concertos, successor to opus 3, was issued under the title of *Il Cimento dell' armonia e dell' Inventione* (*The Trial of Harmony and Invention*). This volume, opus 8, is essentially made up of violin concertos, which adhere basically to the structure and identity of the concerto grosso. Many of these works are realistic tone pictures. The first four concertos describe literally the four seasons of the year. The fifth concerto is entitled *Il Tempesta* (*The Storm*); the sixth, *Il Piacere* (*The Delight*); the tenth, *La Caccia* (*The Hunt*). All other concertos are absolute music with no identifying titles or other frames of reference.

The most important concertos in this grouping are the first four, collectively known as *The Four Seasons*. Each bears the name, and is descriptive of, one of the four seasons of the year, beginning with Spring. At the head of each concerto appears a sonnet intended to provide the clue as to the purpose and meaning of the music that follows. No identification is given to the author of these poems; it is strongly suspected Vivaldi himself wrote them. What is especially interesting, and unusual, about this union of sonnets and music is a device invented by the composer. Parts of the sonnets are given identifying letters. These letters are then used in the music over some passage to point to the place where a specific line (or lines) of the poems receives musical description. So realistic is Vivaldi's music in its program writing that each of the four concerti grossi, or violin concertos, almost resembles a tone poem.

The first concerto, about Spring (E major), opens ebulliently, with a joyous frame of mind ("Spring is come"). The excitement dies down by the fourteenth measure to permit three violins to warble like birds ("The festive birds salute it with their merry songs"). Various descriptive passages follow: playing fountains, and a storm, are particularly favored. In the latter, unison strings suggest the steady downpour of the rain; runs in the violins depict streaks of lightning; loud passages rumble like thunder. But when the storm is over, calm returns, with three solo violins resuming their bird-like carols. In the slow movement, only thirty-nine bars in length, we see a picture of a "flowery meadow" on which "sleeps the goatherd with his faithful dog at his side." The lovely melody is scored for solo violin over muted strings.

The finale provides a vivid tonal translation of the following program: "To the festal sounds of pastoral pipings, nymphs and shepherds dance on their beloved heath to celebrate the coming of the radiant spring." The entire movement has the character of a rustic dance; the solo violin engages in the brusque accents of dance rhythms. The movement, and the concerto, ends serenely, since by now the shepherd and the nymphs have grown weary of the festivities.

The same kind of vivid tonal descriptions, with identifying code letters relating to passages in an appended poem, characterize the other three concertos. In *Summer* (G minor), we hear the voice of the cuckoo, the coo of the turtledove, and the voice of the goldfinch in the solo violin. This is found in the first movement where, later, the same solo violin re-creates the weeping of a shepherd, terrified at the approaching storm. In the slow movement, the shepherd is disturbed by flies and gnats, who buzz about realistically in the orchestration. Loud tremolos in the orchestra suggest thunder and lightning. The storm erupts in the third movement, with sweeping scale passages in the violins, and with rumbles of thunder in basses and cellos.

In the *Autumn* concerto (F major), a gay scene is painted of farmers celebrating harvest time with their merry songs and dances. Fatigue eventually sets in; the merrymakers yield to their weariness and fall into a sound slumber. This concerto ends with music detailing a hunting scene.

The *Winter* concerto (F minor) is one of the most vividly pictorial of this group. In the first eleven measures, winter induces "shivering, tingling, with the chilling snow." We hear teeth chattering in the wind, and people stamping their feet to induce warmth. In the slow movement, an idyllic winter evening is set forth, as people enjoy the warmth of a fireside. But in the finale, winter once again becomes oppressive, as the music tells of ice, snow, and winds. The work ends with an evocation of "Boreas with all the winds at war," and with the message that, for all its ferocity and cruelty, winter can also bring a measure of joy.

One of the most frequently played modern adaptations of *The Four Seasons* was made by Bernardino Molinari, published in 1927.

—— CONCERTO IN G MINOR, for violin and orchestra, op. 12, no. 1. I. Allegro. II. Adagio. III. Allegro.

Among Vivaldi's eighty or so violin concertos, that in G minor (together with the one in A minor discussed earlier) are among those played most often today. It opens strongly in the orchestra before the solo violin arrives with a moving subject, accompanied by the orchestra. A powerful mood is maintained throughout the movement, the opening strong idea getting varied treatment for each of its phrases. The slow movement is prefaced by an eloquent introduction by the orchestra. The solo violin then engages a soaring melody that sounds like an opera aria. The finale is highlighted by a spirited dance tune with which the movement opens. A momentum is forthwith created that carries this movement to its dynamic conclusion without relaxation.

—— GLORIA MASS, for two sopranos, chorus, and orchestra.

Vivaldi's church music is a world all its own—and it is *terra incognita.* On the infrequent occasions that some adventurous musical organization, or recording company, embarks on this unfamiliar music, it usually finds itself involved with a work of deep religious conviction, surpassing majesty of thought, and a complete mastery of polyphonic technique. Such a work is the *Gloria Mass.* As Bach later did in his Mass in B minor, Vivaldi takes each phrase of the Gloria (the second of the five parts of the Catholic Mass) and devotes an entire section to it. In *Music before the Classic Era,* Robert Stevenson suggests how strongly Vivaldi's *Gloria Mass* resembles Bach's B minor Mass. "It will be found that Bach followed Vivaldi, not only in the division of the text, but also in the assignment of certain sections to solo voices and others to chorus. Vivaldi split up the Gloria into eleven different numbers, Bach into eight."

The Mass opens with a "Gloria" section made brilliant by trumpet calls; the chorus enters with a powerful utterance. The graceful, reflective music of "Et in Terra Pax" and a lovely duet, "Laudamus te," follow. A dramatic fugal episode, "Propter magnam," precedes one of the most deeply moving sections of the entire composition, a Pastorale, "Domine Deus," which Marc Pincherle says "can stand comparison with the most beautiful arias in the Bach Passions." An "Agnus Dei" then offers another effective melody, this time mainly for solo cello and basses. The chorus now interjects a robust interpolation with "Cum Sancto Spiritu." After the "Gloria," which arrives at an impressive climax with a fugal section, the Mass concludes with a powerful "Amen."

GEORG PHILIPP TELEMANN 1681–1767

"If we wish to understand the extraordinary blaze of music that illumined Germany from the time of Haydn, Mozart, and Beethoven" wrote Romain Rolland, "we must have some acquaintance with those who prepared this magnificent beacon; we must watch the lighting of the fire." One of those whom Rolland regarded as significant in the pro paration of that beacon, and in the lighting of that fire, was Georg Philipp Telemann.

In his own time, Telemann was one of the most highly esteemed musicians of Germany. Bach and Handel venerated him. Mattheson, in a celebrated couplet, placed him above Lully and Corelli. To Johann Adolph Schiebe, he was "one of the greatest composers of the century." But to the twentieth century, Telemann is hardly more than a name.

He was one of the most prolific composers of all time. His vast output includes some forty operas, seven hundred church cantatas, forty-four Passions, six hundred French Overtures, and innumerable other orchestral, chamber, and harpsichord compositions. It is quite true that he wrote too much and too hastily. "He admitted," said Lawrence Gilman, "too many shady guests to the banquet of his inspiration. There are more lapses from distinction and sincerity, there are more formulas, more platitudes in his scores, than a great master would have allowed. Yet Telemann stood securely in the outer court. And sometimes . . . he had his hand almost upon the door." Romain Rolland is of the belief that if Telemann had "been more careful of his genius . . . his name would perhaps have left a deeper mark on history than that of Gluck."

Even so, Telemann left the impress of his genius on the music of his generation. He carried the Baroque era in music to its culmination; and at the same time, he proved a transition to the rococo age that followed. His technique was second to none, as Handel asserted when he said that Telemann could write an eight-part motet as easily as others wrote letters. He had a gracious style in the best traditions of rococo; the gamut of his expression was wide; his lyrical invention was superior. Though he was not one to experiment or innovate, he was responsible for bringing chamber music to the threshold of modernity by dispensing with the basso continuo to which his predecessors and contemporaries clung; and, as he himself put it, he contrived to make "the bass . . . a natural melody, forming, with the other parts, an appropriate melody."

Georg Philipp Telemann, the son of a Lutheran pastor, was born in Magdeburg, Germany, on March 14, 1681. He was extraordinarily precocious. As a child, he could play several instruments competently, including the violin and the flute; by the time he was twelve, he had written an opera. For all that, he planned a career in law, and for this purpose entered the University of Leipzig in 1700. But the success of some of his church music convinced him where his destiny really lay. Abandoning legal studies, he became the organist of the Neue Kirche in Leipzig in 1704. After that, he had various posts in different parts of Germany: Kapellmeister and Konzertmeister of court music for Prince Erdemann von Promnitz in Sorau; court Kapellmeister in Eisenach; Kapellmeister to the Prince of Bayreuth.

In 1721, he was appointed musical director of the city of Hamburg, where he was put in charge of five churches and made cantor of the Johanneum. He held this post for the remainder of his life. Besides his official church duties, he supervised the musical instruction in the city schools; conducted the Hamburg Opera; founded the Collegium Musicum, which gave public concerts; and published the first music journal to appear in Germany. When the post of cantor was vacated by Kuhnau at the Thomasschule, Telemann was offered it. He turned it down, preferring to spend the rest of his days in Hamburg, and the post went to Johann Sebastian Bach. Bach's high regard for Telemann had long since been proved by the fact that he had asked Telemann to be the godfather of his son, Carl Philipp Emanuel Bach. Telemann died in Hamburg on June 25, 1767.

—— DON QUICHOTTE, suite for orchestra.
SUITE IN A MINOR, for flute, strings, and harpsichord.

Telemann had a flair for pictorialism and a wit, both of which are demonstrated to good advantage in *Don Quichotte,* a delightful suite for orchestra, inspired by the Cervantes classic. The Don's absurd encounter with the windmills and the heavy-footed gait of his horse (in contrast to the stumbling movement of his squire's donkey) are some of the episodes providing the composer with an opportunity to spice his writing with irony. The suite opens with a classic overture, its slow section intended to depict the nobler side of Don's personality, the quick part pointing up his quixotic nature. The second section relates the circumstances surrounding "Don Quixote's Awakening." In rapid succession there now come several romantic or adventurous episodes of Don's picaresque career.

The melodious Suite in A minor, for flute and strings (with harpsichord), is in seven parts. The opening movement is an overture in the French style, beginning with a slow and stately part, continuing with a brisk episode, and ending with a slow movement. Six light, airy dances or dance-like tunes follow, beginning with a movement entitled "Les Plaisirs," or "The Pleasures," continuing with a buoyantly lyrical "Italian Air," and progressing through a minuet, polonaise, and Passepieds to the gay finale movement called "Réjouissance."

—— DIE TAGESZEITEN (TIMES OF DAY), cantata for solo voices, chorus, and orchestra.

This cantata describes the four different periods of the day, the reason why it is in four sections respectively subtitled "Morning," "Noon," "Evening," and "Night." Each section features two arias for one of the soloists, separated by a recitative, and concluded by a chorus. The soprano is heard in the first part, the alto in the second, the tenor in the third, the baritone in the fourth. Nathan Broder explains that the text "combines descriptions of nature with religious devotion." In commenting on Telemann's music, he adds: "The work gets better as it goes along. 'Morning' is rather routine, but 'Noon' has one charming aria, and 'Evening' and 'Night' remain consistently on a higher plane of inventiveness and expressivity."

—— FANTASIAS, for harpsichord.

Telemann wrote some three dozen fantasias for harpsichord to which he brought the structures of the French and Italian overtures. The first and third dozen are in the form of the Italian Overture; for this reason, they utilize Italian terms for tempo, and instrumentation. The second dozen uses the French language for the various designations because it employs the French Overture structure. Telemann planned to have each pair of consecutive fantasias played as a unit, the first fantasia to be repeated when the second had been performed. Each individual fantasia is characterized by fluidity and grace of the melodic line, and by the clarity of the overture structure.

JOHANN SEBASTIAN BACH 1685–1750

Practically all of those who were his superiors at the St. Thomas Church in Leipzig, and most of those who attended the services there regularly, had little idea that their cantor, Johann Sebastian Bach, was one of music's elect. The church rector, Johann August Ernesti, treated him with contempt, never losing an opportunity to humiliate him. Other church officials seemed ever on the alert to defraud him of his due. The congregation was hardly more appreciative of him. It considered him little more than a hard-working musician, who deserved no more than the humble salary and the appalling living and working conditions that came with the post of cantor. On several occasions, the congregation completely failed to comprehend the greatness of Bach's musical conceptions. When Bach first played his *Passion According to St. Matthew* at his church in 1729, the worshipers were "thrown into the greatest wonderment," reported one of Bach's pupils, "saying to each other, 'What does it all mean?' while one old lady exclaimed, 'God help us! 'Tis surely an opera-comedy!'"

So little was Bach's music appreciated in Leipzig that immediately after his death a bundle of his cantatas sold for forty dollars, and some of the manuscripts of his solo sonatas were used by the local merchants to wrap their ware. Two years after Bach's death, the plates of *The Art of the Fugue* were disposed of for their value as metal.

The fact that Bach was buried in an unidentified grave is both significant and symbolic: Bach's contemporaries—his own sons, even—were ready to consign him to permanent anonymity. For seventy-five years after Bach's death, the name of "Bach" conjured to mind one of the sons, rarely Johann Sebastian. Only a fraction of Johann Sebastian Bach's vast output had by then reached publication, and even that fraction was little known to the general music public. A handful of discerning musicians—Mozart, Beethoven, Mendelssohn, and Schumann were a few—valued him highly; but even they could hardly have been aware of the extent of the master's fabulous achievements, since most of what Bach had written was still lying around in manuscript.

In dramatic contrast to this appalling lack of understanding, and this amazing neglect, suffered by Bach for so long a time, is the evaluation our present generation places on his work. Bach wrote so much that, according to one estimate, it would take a copyist seventy years just to transcribe his scores on paper! Even more amazing than the quantity is the quality of this production. "His message to humanity," says W. G. Whittaker, "is the purest, the noblest, the most fruitful that musician has ever delivered." Charles Sanford Terry said: "Bach is dateless, his art perennial, immortalized by the intense individualism that informed it. Directed by a faith childlike in its simplicity, he used it to interpret the infinite, saw the heavens opened, and was prophetically oracular." Cecil Gray remarked: "Bach belongs to no age and cannot be placed in any category or pigeon-hole whatsoever . . . . None of the elaborate systems of weights and measures we employ in dealing with lesser men are applicable to him: he is too big. Every generation sees a different aspect of him; all schools, however opposed in tendency, unite in claiming him as their master."

It is not difficult to explain why there should exist such a wide gulf between two generations in their evaluation of Bach. To Bach's immediate successors, he was the voice of a dying, or dead, musical epoch. Bach had been an exponent of the Baroque, and he had adhered for the most part to polyphonic traditions. With the new age of classicism at hand, and with the development of homophony, Bach's music seemed at first glance to be terribly old-fashioned. His son, Carl Philipp Emanuel Bach, referred to him as "that old peruque." What Bach's successors failed to realize was that the master had carried the Baroque style and tradition to such advanced stages that he had left his predecessors and contemporaries far behind. Where others had built basilicas, Bach had constructed cathedrals—edifices incomparable for magnificence, majesty, grandeur. Together with a formidable, even incomparable skill at polyphony, Bach possessed a humanity, a nobility, a spirituality, and a religious exaltation rarely confronted in the music of his age. After Bach, a new epoch *had* to come, for Bach himself had exhausted all the possibilities of the older one.

Ernest Newman put it this way: "Bach bestrode the whole world of music of his day; the music of the half century that followed him, indeed, rich as it was in new achievements, has often the air of having gone back to the nursery after having become with him a grown man. There is nothing in the epoch of 1750–1800 to compare with the far-flung luxuriance of Bach's melody . . . or the intensity of his harmony, or the way he could force the most complex polyphony into the service of the profoundest emotional expression, or the freedom and variety of musical speech to which he could attain even while he fettered himself with seemingly the most crabbed forms . . . . Within the . . . older forms that lay ready to his hands . . . he could indulge himself to his heart's content in the sounding of the very depths of the human soul; no other contemporary instrumental form, for instance, would have afforded him such opportunities, both for the intensity and spaciousness of poetic expression, as that of the organ chorale prelude; it is safe to say that in these works of his alone, there is hardly an emotion that is not expressed, and with a poignancy that remains undiminished even after three generations of post-Tristan developments."

There is one other fact that Bach's immediate successors could not comprehend, because so little of Bach's music was available to them. Bach was not merely the culmination of an old era; he was the dawn of a new one. In clarifying the sonata structure, in further developing instrumental techniques, in evolving a homophonic style in many of his wonderful slow movements, and in experimenting with new idioms, Bach already was speaking in terms of the new language that his son, Carl Philipp Emanuel Bach—and Haydn and Mozart after him—were to develop so fruitfully. It was because Bach had this vision of a new world and a new age that Schumann was led to say: "Music owes as much to Bach as religion to its founder."

Johann Sebastian Bach came from a family that for several generations had been producing professional musicians. He was born in Eisenach, Germany, on March 21, 1685. His parents died when he was ten. Young Bach went to live with his brother, Johann Christoph, who gave him a thorough musical training. In 1700, Johann Sebastian became a chorister at St. Michael's Church in Lueneburg, and in 1704, he was engaged as organist of the church at Arnstadt. It 1707, following his appointment as organist of St. Blasius Church in Muehlhausen, Bach married his cousin, Maria Barbara.

His first productive period of composition came in Weimar, where, in 1708, he had been made court organist and chamber musician. This is the epoch in Bach's life when he became a pre-eminent organ virtuoso and when he wrote many of his masterworks for that instrument. Between 1717 and 1723, he worked as Kapellmeister and director of chamber music at Coethen, at the court of Prince Leopold of Anhalt. During these years, he cultivated instrumental music, producing a rich library of sonatas and concertos. Meanwhile, in 1720, his wife Maria Barbara died. In 1721, Bach married a second time. She was Anna Magdalena Wuelken, who bore him thirteen children.

In 1723, Bach assumed the post he was to hold for his remaining years, that of Cantor at the St. Thomas Church (or Thomasschule) in Leipzig. His duties included the writing of music for Leipzig's leading churches and directing it; playing the organ; teaching a class of boys in Latin and music. Though his regimen was severe and exacting, though he was continually at odds with his employers, and though he was compelled in live in dark and unsanitary quarters, his creative output was prodigious. It was for these church services at Leipzig that Bach wrote many of his most important cantatas, together with the *Passion According to St. Matthew* and the B minor Mass. Not even partial paralysis or blindness could arrest his creativity. In his last year, Bach completed *The Art of the Fugue* and the choral prelude, *Vor deinen Thron*. Just before his death, sight returned briefly, enabling him to revise and copy out the parts of *The Art of the Fugue*. He died in Leipzig on July 28, 1750, and was buried in an unidentified grave in the churchyard of St. John's Church. His coffin was finally recovered in 1894 and reburied within the church.

c. 1700. FUGUE IN G MINOR, "LITTLE," for organ.

Though one of Bach's earliest works for the organ, the "little" G minor Fugue already demonstrates his immense technique at fugal writing. This work has been dubbed "little," not because it is small in design, but to distinguish it from the monumental fugue in the *Fantasia and Fugue in G minor* (see 1708–1717). Indeed, the subject of this supposedly smaller fugue is more spacious than one usually employed by Bach in his later compositions—a free flowing melody, which becomes the basis of fugal writing charged throughout with dramatic interest and marked by the most extraordinary rhythmic effects. Leopold Stokowski and Lucien Cailliet are among those who transcribed this fugue for orchestra; it has also been adapted for solo piano and for two pianos.

1704. CAPRICCIO WRITTEN ON THE DEPARTURE OF A FAVORITE BROTHER (CAPRICCIO SOPRA LA LONTANAZZA DEL SUO FRATELLO DILETTISSIMO), for clavier.

In 1704, Johann Sebastian Bach's brother, Johann Jakob, left for Poland. His departure impelled Johann Sebastian to write a short descriptive composition for the clavier in which he depicted programmatically the departure and the reaction of friends. This work is a curiosity in that it is the only one where Bach is literally programmatic in his musical writing. It has six brief sections, played without interruption; to each is appended a descriptive heading. In the first part, Johann Jakob's friends plead with him not to embark on the journey. This is followed by their recital of possible misfortunes and disasters that might befall him in foreign lands. The argument between Johann Jakob and his friends reaches an amusing and lively climax with a fugue. The third section is a "Lament," the grief of Johann Jakob's friends at realizing that he is determined to go. The sound of the postillion is made the basis of the fourth section. In the fifth, this postillion horn motif is treated fugally. The coach than embarks on its journey.

1707–1735. CHURCH CANTATAS:

ACH GOTT, VOM HIMMEL SIEH DAREIN, for solo voices, chorus, and orchestra (No. 2).

ALSO HAT GOTT DIE WELT GELIEBT, for soprano, bass, chorus, and orchestra (No. 68).

AUS DER TIEFE, for solo voices, chorus, and orchestra (No. 131).

CHRIST LAG IN TODESBANDEN, for solo voices, chorus, and orchestra (No. 4).

EIN' FESTE BURG IST UNSER GOTT, for solo voices, chorus, and orchestra (No. 80).

HERZ UND MUND UND TAT UND LEBEN, for solo voices, chorus, and orchestra (No. 147).

ICH STEH' MIT EINEM FUSS IM GRABE, for solo voices, chorus, and orchestra (No. 156).

ICH WILL DEN KREUZSTAB GERNE TRAGEN, for bass, chorus, and orchestra (No. 56).

NUN KOMM, DER HEIDEN HEILAND, for solo voices, chorus, and orchestra (No. 61).

SCHLAGE DOCH, GEWUENSCHTE STUNDE, for alto and orchestra (No. 53).

WACHET AUF, for solo voices, chorus, and orchestra (No. 140).

WAS GOTT TUT, for solo voices, chorus, and orchestra (No. 98).

The almost two hundred church cantatas by Johann Sebastian Bach are without equal in liturgical music. If Bach had written nothing else, his place in music would still have been enduring. So varied is Bach's invention here, so frequently is it poised on an elevated plane, so bountiful are his technical resources, so penetrating is his insight and so subtle his expression, that to Albert Schweitzer everything else Bach wrote is just a supplement to his cantatas.

Bach wrote these works as functional music for the Sunday and Saints Day services at the St. Thomas Church in Leipzig. The church cycle of five years required 295 cantatas, if no single work is to be repeated. Bach apparently completed this vast cycle, but only a little less than two hundred of his cantatas are in existence, almost a hundred apparently having been lost, and three existing in an incomplete state. Bach wrote his first cantata in 1704, his last in 1744. During his twenty-one years in Leipzig, he produced on an average of one cantata a month. The text was prepared expressly for the performance for which it was intended, at times suggested by the Scriptural lesson of the day, at times made up of hymn verses, at times borrowing some Biblical text. While there was no story line, each cantata had some unifying thought to provide integration. Bach's cantatas range in length from twelve to forty minutes in performance time. The cantata usually opens and closes with a chorus, the concluding one being a chorale. Between these two choral extremities lie recitatives and arias, at times duets and trios and instrumental interludes, at times chorales accompanied by instruments.

"We are amazed," writes W. G. Whittaker in surveying the Bach cantatas, "to find how few pages there are in which his spirit does not soar. Here we find his conception of Jesus presented from every aspect, his treatment of the subject of death, occurring not once but a hundred times, his reverence for dogma, his detestation of the infidel and the unbeliever; we see the heart of a great man and a profound believer revealed in a way unlike anything else in the history of religious art." Whittaker then concludes: "There is music of all moods except that of utter despair; there are choruses of the utmost sublimity, of praise, of mourning, of peace, of strife, of defiance; there are arias tender and bold, of denunciation and ecstatic bliss, which face death benignly, which express all the experiences in the life of a Christian; there are even dances in profusion, for Bach's happiness in religion was so great that he turned naturally to the gavotte, the bourree, the siciliano, the gigue, to express his joy. An extraordinary thing about these dance movements is that, in the solemn aisles of a cathedral, they sound perfectly fitting, they never jar our sensibilities, they are always in perfect keeping with the rest of the work. To understand Bach fully, we must know his cantatas well.

Ach Gott, vom Himmel sieh darein (1740) was intended for the second Sunday after Trinity. It is unusual among Bach's cantatas in that it has no instrumental introduction, the voices entering immediately accompanied by instruments. The chorale tune, "Ach Gott, vom Himmel sieh darein," upon which the entire work is built, enters in the tenor voice, before being taken over by the bass, soprano, and alto in augmentation. This is followed by a tenor recitative, an aria for alto with violin obbligato, a recitative for bass, and a second aria for tenor. The cantata concludes with a vigorous recall of the chorale tune in four-part harmony.

Also hat Gott die Welt geliebt (1735) was written to be performed on Whit Monday. Here the second section—"Mein glaeubiges Herz," an aria for soprano—is an enlargement of a melody Bach had used in his secular cantata, *Phoebus and Pan;* it is one of Bach's most celebrated compositions for the voice. The free flowing and deeply moving air is here joined, as André Pirro explains, "by a sort of instrumental peroration, based on the motif of the violoncello piccolo. The violin and the oboe, which have not figured in the accompaniment, now take up and imitate this motif. It is a prolongation in which the lyricism of the poem is allowed to develop freely, delivered from the burden of the words." This beautiful air has been transcribed for various solo instruments, including cello, solo piano, organ, and string quartet.

Aus der Tiefe is one of Bach's earliest cantatas, dating from 1707, when the composer was employed in Muelhausen. To the text of Psalm 130, Bach produced five movements. Three utilize the chorus, one is for bass solo with oboe obbligato, and one is for tenor solo. Above each of the two solo numbers, Bach introduced the melody of a sixteenth-century hymn, "Herr Jesu Christ, du hoechtest Gut."

Christ lag in Todesbanden (1724) is a cantata for Easter Sunday with words by Martin Luther. This is Bach's only cantata where the hymn melody, and its verses, are used exclusively throughout the entire work. The opening fourteen-measure Sinfonia, in the style of Buxtehude, is followed by seven verses, each receiving its own musical treatment "as if chiselled in music," says Albert Schweitzer, each almost a variation of the chorale tune. Though the opening Sinfonia is touched by the sorrow of death, the cantata as a whole represents the triumph of faith. For his chorale, Bach borrowed a twelfth-century hymn, "Christ ist erstanden." In the opening chorus, it is heard in the soprano over a contrapuntal background. In the second verse (a duet for soprano and alto), a dramatic effect is realized through a running bass figure used to represent the words "force" and "power" in the text. There is an outpouring of joy in the third verse, for tenor solo. In the fourth verse, for chorus, where the cantus firmus is assigned to the alto, the music makes us see, says Schweitzer, "a knot of bodies in conflict, as in a picture of Michaelangelo." To Spitta, the fifth verse, for bass solo, is "an expression of mystical emotion." This is followed by a duet for soprano and tenor, and the concluding chorale.

Ein' feste Burg ist unser Gott (1716–1730) is, to be sure, based on Martin Luther's famous setting of the 46th Psalm. Bach used the same melody for one of his organ preludes. With Luther's hymn as his point of departure, Bach went on to create what Schweitzer described as "a dramatic art work of the most perfect kind imaginable" for performance during the Reformation Festival. There are eight sections, beginning with a mighty choral embellishment of the hymn, and concluding with the chorale, "Das Wort sie sollen lassen stahn." The third verse of Luther's chorale is used in the fifth part of the cantata—"Und wenn die Welt voll Teufel waer," for chorus—in order "to paint the picture of the fiends of Hell struggling against the bands of true believers, with the imagery of a true mystic." Individual vocal passages of special significance include the aria for solo bass and soprano choir, "Mit unser Macht ist nicht getan," and the wondrous duet for alto and tenor, "Wie selig sind doch die, die Gott im Munde tragen."

Herz und Mund und Tat und Leben (1716) is best known through one of its parts, the celebrated "Jesu bleibt meine Freunde," or as it is familiar in the United States, "Jesu Joy of Man's Desiring." This is the tenth number—a broad, devotional chorale melody against a flowing accompaniment in triplets. Terry has called this music "a highway to heaven." Among the many existing transcriptions are those for orchestra (Lucien Cailliet), piano (Myra Hess), two pianos (Horne), organ (E. Power Biggs), solo voice and piano (Hess). The cantata as a whole, text by Salomon Franck, was written in Weimar for performance on the fourth Sunday in Advent; Bach is believed to have revised it many years later in Leipzig.

The most celebrated section of *Ich steh' mit einem Fuss im Grabe* (1730) is its wonderful opening Sinfonia for oboe and strings. Here the strings suggest graphically the steps leading to the grave with a descending Adagio figure receiving several variants in the bass. A syncopated form of the same motive is used in a subsequent aria, "Ich steh' mit einem Fuss im Grabe" with "all possible rhythmical nuances in the upper strings," explains Schweitzer, "to express quite clearly the picture suggested in the words. . . . In order to mitigate the rhythmical unrest, Bach accompanies the song with the chorale, "Machs mit mir, Gott, nach deiner Guet." This cantata, text by Picander, was intended for the third Sunday after Epiphany.

Ich will den Kreuzstab gerne tragen, (1731) text once again by Picander, was heard on the nineteenth Sunday after Trinity. It is made up of two recitatives and two arias, all for the bass, concluding with the chorale, "Komm o Tod." An unusual procedure is followed here by having each of the two arias precede rather than follow the recitative, as is customary elsewhere. The bass, explains André Pirro, "is the sole interpreter of Bach's mystical desires. The first air has a melodic texture and a rhythmical variety which are very remarkable ("Ich will den Kreuzstab gerne tragen") . . . . The third part ("Endlich, endlich") is animated by a new tempo. Instead of points, repeated notes, stressed phrases which so far have given the composition a tormented character, in this conclusion now appear motifs in triplets, which hover in relief above an accompaniment cradled by the equal cadence in the bass."

Nun Komm, der Heiden Heiland (1714)—for the first Sunday after Advent—is based on Christ's words, "See thou, see thou I stand before the door and knock thereon" from Revelation, iii, 20. Here we find a remarkable example of the way in which Bach often makes instruments point up and illuminate the text. Eva Mary and Sidney Grew explain: "The accompaniment is a series of pizzicato chords in crotchet rhythm. The concrete subject is not, however, what at first fancy it might seem to be, namely the *knocking,* for that is a subject that could not be applied mystically. It is rather the conception of a swinging pendulum of time that marks with awful solemnity the movement of creation to the Second Coming." The Grews then pay special attention to the recitative, "Siehe, siehe!," and the ensuing aria, "Komm Jesu." "The music in this piece of accompanied recitative moves from E minor to G major. The voice ends on an interrupted cadence. The instruments complete the cadence with four chords . . . symbolically . . . expressive of some such thought as 'the elder brother found, the younger melts with fondness in His arms.' The aria preceding this recitative—a piece for tenor, unison strings, and bass—is an ideal example of the da capo aria in primitive form, and of Bach's practice of working one musical subject throughout a movement and in all the parts. The subject itself, which is sixteen bars long, is an example of extended melody." Of the concluding chorale, the Grews say: "[It] is equally an ideal example of the use of a chorale to finish a work. It is a portion of 'Wie schoen leuchtet der Morgenstern,' which is one of the most beautiful and appealing of German hymns and hymn tunes. It rises into being here as much as the Passion chorale does in the *Matthew Passion.*"

Spitta is of the belief that *Schlage doch, gewuenschte Stunde* (1723–1724) was intended for private rather than public worship. An unorthodox device employed in this cantata is the tolling of obbligato bells. This cantata consists of a single number for contralto, accompanied by strings and bells. The music is consistently gentle and resigned, and is in the three-part song structure.

Wachet auf, or *Sleepers Awake* (1731), for the twenty-seventh Sunday after Trinity, is based on the Gospels. The text deals with the parable of the wise and foolish virgins, and the coming of the Bridegroom for whom they make ready the lamps. Musically, the work is based on a hymn, also named *Wachet auf,* by Philipp Nicolai, published in 1599. In the first two verses of Nicolai's hymn, the story line of the parable is carried, while the last verses sing the praises of God and the heavenly hosts. To Arnold Schering, this festive wedding cantata symbolizes the marriage of the faithful soul to Christ. The cantata opens with an elaborate chorus in which the crowd describes the awakening of the sleeping virgins and awaits the arrival of bride and groom. A tenor recitative announces His approach. After a moving duet for soprano and baritone, there appears the cantata's most famous portion—the chorus singing of the joy of Zion and the arrival of Christ the Bridegroom in "Zion hoert die Waechter singen." Bach himself adapted this music into a celebrated chorale prelude for organ, *Wachet auf.* A baritone recitative with comforting words about the Bridegroom in the bridal chamber, and the exultant duet for soprano and baritone, lead to the magnificent concluding chorale, "Gloria sei dir gesungen," in praise of the Lord and the heavenly hosts.

1708–1717. COMPOSITIONS FOR ORGAN:

Fantasia and Fugue in G minor, "The Great"; Passacaglia in C minor; Prelude and Fugue in C minor; Toccata in C major; Toccata and Fugue in D minor.

Eight Little Preludes and Fugues: 1. C major. 2. D minor. 3. E minor. 4. F major. 5. G major. 6. G minor. 7. A minor. 8. B-flat major.

Orgelbuechlein (*The Little Organ Book*), forty-six chorale preludes for organ. 1. Nun komm der Heiden Heiland. 2. Gott, durch deine Guete. 3. Herr Christ, der ein'ge Gottes-Sohn. 4. Lob sei dem allmaechtigen Gott. 5. Puer natus in Bethlehem. 6. Gelobet seist du, Jesu Christ. 7. Der Tag, der ist so freudenreich. 8. Vom Himmel hoch da komm' ich her. 9. Vom Himmel kam der Engel Schaar. 10. In dulci jubilo. 11. Lobt Gott, ihr Christen, allzugleich. 12. Jesu, meine Freude. 13. Christum wir sollen loben schon. 14. Wir Christenleut'. 15. Helft mir Gottes Guete preisen. 16. Das alte Jahr vergangen ist. 17. In dir ist Freude 18. Mit Fried' und Freud' ich fahr' dahin. 19. Herr Gott, nun schleuss den Himmel auf. 20. O Lamm, Gottes, unschuldig. 21. Christe, du Lamm Gottes. 22. Christus, der uns selig macht. 23. Da Jesus an dem Kreuze stund. 24. O Mensch, bewein' dein' Suende gross. 25. Wir danken dir, Herr Jesu Christ. 26. Hilf Gott, das mir's gelinge. 27. Christ lag in Todesbanden. 28. Jesus Christus, unser Heiland. 29. Christ ist erstanden. 30. Erstanden ist der heil'ge Christ. 31. Erschienen ist der herrlich' Tag. 32. Heut' triumphiret Gottes Sohn. 33. Komm, Gott, Schoepfer, heiliger Geist.

34. Herr Jesu Christ, dich zu uns wend.' 35. Liebster Jesu, wir sind hier. 36. Liebster Jesu, wir sind hier. 37. Dies sind die heil'gen zehn Gebot. 38. Vater unser im Himmelreich. 39. Durch Adams Fall ist ganz verderbt. 40. Er ist das Heil uns kommen her. 41. Ich ruf' zu dir, Herr Jesu Christ. 42. In dich hab' ich gehoffet, Herr. 43. Wenn wir in hoechsten Noeten sein. 44. Wer nur den lieben Gott laesst walten. 45. Alle Menschen muessen sterben. 46. Ach wie nichtig, ach wie fluechtig.

While holding the office of court organist and chamber musician to Duke Wilhelm Ernst in Weimar, Bach devoted a good deal of his time to playing the organ in the chapel. For these performances, he completed a repertory of organ music that to this day stands without any parallel. Here all the earlier tendencies in organ music were swept to their ultimate destiny, both as to style and structure. Here a new world of effect, nuance, and techniques was explored. "Nurtured in the traditions of German polyphony, but gifted to endow it with a new life," says Charles Sanford Terry, "he combined a felicity of melodic exuberance with harmonic inventiveness and resource never excelled or equalled."

The organ was Bach's favorite instrument. "With its ample resources," wrote Harvey Grace, "[the organ] gave him a sense of freedom, security, and power that he could obtain from no other source. Forkel relates that he would improvise organ music by the hour—long series of movements on some favorite hymn tune. He won his greatest personal triumphs and expressed his deepest feelings in the organ loft; and we shall probably be right in supposing that, given his choice, the organ is the medium through which he would wish his memory to be kept green."

Most of the organ works by Bach with which we are most familiar today (whether in its original version or in transcription) come from his Weimar period.

The Fantasia and Fugue in G minor combines one of Bach's greatest inventions within the fantasia form with one of his giant fugues. The fantasia is rhapsodic, made up of dazzling cadenza-like passages punctuated with dramatic chords. "It is," says Alec Robertson, "a remarkable example of ordered freedom. . . . Its passage writing is expressive and rich in harmonic implications . . . controlled by a structural balance that the older composers never knew, and vitalized by harmonic devices that are arresting even today." The fugue is known as "The Great" to distinguish it from another G minor Fugue, "The Little" (see 1700). Like the "little" fugue, the "great" one in G minor has an expansive rather than an epigrammatic subject—a fully stated lyric thought all by itself. Two countersubjects follow, and the three themes are then used in triple counterpoint. Excellent orchestral transcriptions of the Fantasia and Fugue in G minor were made by Leopold Stokowski and by Dimitri Mitropoulos; Franz Liszt transcribed it for the piano.

The Passacaglia in C minor is one of the Alpine summits in all organ music —probably the finest Passacaglia ever conceived. The eight-measure theme has solemnity. Ten eight-measure variations follow in the pedal, and five after that exclusively for the manuals. All the while, a mighty tension is created that seeks and finds release in the next five variations. But the tension returns in the concluding five variations, in which the passacaglia subject reverts to the pedals. At the peak of this drama comes the fugue as a logical culmination, its subject derived from the first half of the passacaglia theme. "This Passacaglia," says Leopold Stokowski, whose orchestral transcription is well known, "is one of those works whose content is so full and significant that its medium of expression is of relative unimportance. . . . It is one of the most divinely inspired contrapuntal works ever conceived. Bach's Passacaglia is in music what a great Gothic cathedral is in architecture—the same vast conception—the same soaring mysticism given eternal form." Eugene Ormandy, Fabien Sevitzky and Ottorino Respighi are others who adapted the passacaglia for orchestra; Pochon arranged it for string quartet.

The Prelude and Fugue in C minor is one of many preludes and fugues for organ completed by Bach in Weimar. The Prelude has a majestic twenty-four bar introduction. The fugue—preceded by a declamatory section—is described by Harvey Grace as "a walk up from tonic to dominant and back again."

The Toccata in C major is in three sections. First, we get the toccata, a display piece with brilliant passages on the manual and a remarkable pedal solo. After that comes an Adagio, which Lawrence Gilman once described as "a grave and beautiful instrumental song of unusual character, for it is sustained by a homophonic accompaniment of a type almost unparalleled in Bach's music." Gilman further called this music an utterance of "rapt meditation so typical of him [Bach] in his more emotional moods." A series of suspensions lead into a lively fugue. Leo Weiner's and Leopold Stokowski's transcriptions for orchestra are celebrated; so is Busoni's arrangement for solo piano. This toccata has also been transcribed for two pianos, for viola and piano, for cello and piano, and for string quartet.

The Toccata and Fugue in D minor ranks with the most famous of all Bach organ compositions. It is a study in contrasts. The toccata at times is a brilliant display piece; at times it is a stormy and dramatic exposition. Pirro described it picturesquely as follows: "The dazzling lightning, the clap of thunder, rumbling formidably in the repercussions of a long, broken chord, above the crash of a profound pedal; the wind, then the hail; we are in a classical storm." The fugue, on the other hand, has an almost classical serenity. Stokowski, Ormandy, Lucien Cailliet, Sir Henry J. Wood, Melichar, and Fabien Sevitzky have all made orchestral adaptations of this Toccata and Fugue, while Busoni arranged it for solo piano.

The *Eight Little Preludes and Fugues* was intended as instruction material for Bach's sons. They are neither "little" nor exclusively functional, but are among Bach's masterworks. The Preludes, explains E. Power Biggs, "have an easy melodic flow, and they combine in varying degree the best of Italian and German influence. We may well believe that Bach's instructive interest was stylistic as well as technical. . . . Fugal subjects are brief and to the point." Harvey Grace singles out for special attention the Prelude No. 3 as "a thoughtful little piece with the real Bach spirit, especially in its gravely expressive close." In the sixth Prelude and Fugue, there is a thematic kinship between the two parts.

The *Orgelbuechlein,* or *Little Organ Book,* is a treasury of forty-six chorale preludes for organ. The chorale prelude was an outgrowth of the chorale. Its purpose was to introduce the chorale melody to the congregation, at times even to replace communal hymn singing. "Here," says W. G. Whittaker, "Bach gave full rein to his exuberant fancy." Here we encounter the "most wonderful fantasies expressing the inner meaning of his favorite hymns. Sometimes we are given a general expression of a mood of verse or hymn, the melody becomes the material for a glorious arabesque, harmonies of wonderful richness and free counterpoints are added below until the simple plain tune is transfigured. At other times, he will take each separate line and amplify the meaning of the corresponding portion of the text by means of derived or independent ideas which serve to introduce and accompany the line of the tune, and to serve it to a conclusion. At others again, he will construct a kind of scena, using the hymn verse as a foundation; sometimes he will build a fantasia on melodic fragments."

Known as "the church year in music," *The Little Organ Book* provides choral preludes for the various seasons of the church calendar from Advent through Whitsuntide. A concluding group concerns itself with the Christian life ("The Catechism," "Penitence and Amendment," "Christian Conduct and Experience," "In Time of Trouble," "Death and the Grave," and "The Life Eternal"). Albert Schweitzer points out that the chorale preludes are grouped in such a way that those for Christmas constitute a miniature Christmas oratorio; those for the Passion time, a mininature Passion; and those for Easter, a miniature Easter overture. *The Little Organ Book,* continues Schweitzer, is "a lexicon of Bach's musical speech" and one of the greatest achievements in all music.

Here is the way E. Power Biggs analyzes both the structure and the content of these chorale preludes: "The form . . . is simple in the extreme. Around the melody, employed as a Cantus Firmus, and usually in the soprano, Bach weaves little pictorial tapestries illustrating the mood and emotion and frequently the circumstantial detail of the words of each chorale. Here lies the essential significance of *The Little Organ Book,* and the great advance of Bach's art over that of his predecessors, Pachelbel, Buxtehude, and others. Not content, as they were, to elaborate the chorale on purely formalistic lines, Bach created a tone speech of his own, painting through the medium of this characteristic counterpoint the poetic content of the text. The changing seasons of the church year are depicted in these miniatures, portraying moods of tenderness, of hearty jubilation, of deepest sorrow, of grave and solemn joy, and abounding in symbolical and even frankly pictorial suggestion. The voice of Bach communing with his Maker, bewailing the fate of the Saviour on the cross, rejoicing at the triumph of Easter, is as eloquent and as deeply moving for this age as for his own."

1716–1732. SECULAR CANTATAS:

"Schafe koennen sicher weiden" from *Was mir behagt,* No. 208, for solo voices, chorus, and orchestra.

Weichet nur, betruebte Schatten (*Wedding Cantata*), No. 202, for soprano and orchestra.

Schweiget stille, plaudert nicht (*Coffee Cantata*), No. 211, for soprano, tenor, baritone, chorus, and orchestra.

Der Streit zwischen Phoebus und Pan (*The Dispute Between Phoebus and Pan*), No. 201, for solo voices, chorus, and orchestra.

Mer Hahn en neue Oberkeet (*Peasant Cantata*), No. 212, for soprano, bass-baritone, chorus, and orchestra.

Bach produced about forty secular cantatas, of which only twenty-four have survived. They offer a marked contrast to those he wrote for the church. We do not hear in them the exalted speech of the devout Cantor of the St. Thomas Church, but the burgher given to wit, satire, at times even broad burlesque. Bach's secular cantatas are, for the most part, *pièces d'occasion* written for specific ceremonies or parties, to welcome visiting royalty, or to celebrate the installation of a new ruler. They abound with lighthearted attitudes and often make extended use of popular-type tunes and dance melodies.

The exception to the rule stated above is the familiar "Schafe koennen sicher weiden," or "Sheep Shall Safely Graze," from the cantata *Was mir behagt.* This is pastoral music in which a serene melody (aria of Pales) is set against two flutes. This idyllic composition has become familiar through numerous transcriptions, notably for orchestra by Sir John Barbirolli, also by Sir William Walton; for two pianos (Mary Howe); for piano solo (Percy Grainger); and for organ (E. Power Biggs).

The work of which this idyll is just a segment is Bach's first secular cantata —text drawn from mythology. Bach's score is made up of a dozen recitatives, eight arias, and two choruses. This cantata was written in 1716, at the request of Bach's employer in Weimar, Duke Ernst Wilhelm. The Duke had been invited to a hunting party celebrating the birthday of Duke Christian von Sachsen-Weissenfels. He commissioned Bach to write a musical composition appropriate for such an occasion. Bach's cantata was heard during a banquet held at the gamekeeper's lodge.

The Wedding Cantata (1720) is much more popular in style and musical content than *Was mir behagt,* its text describing the passing of the winter and the arrival of spring. Schweitzer says: "To this expressive poem, Bach has written some particularly beautiful music. The vaporous semiquavers ascending in the strings in the opening aria ("Weichet nur, betruebte Schatten") depict the mists vanishing before the breeze of spring, while the oboes sing a dreamy yearning melody of the type of which Bach alone seems to have the secret." The six ensuing sections—four arias and two recitatives, all for soprano—end with a joyous gavotte expressing wishes for the couple's continued happiness ("Sehet in Zufriedenheit").

From the light and jovial mood of *The Wedding Cantata* we pass on to the broad comedy of *The Coffee Cantata,* in which echoes of a later buffo style can be detected. Charles Sanford Terry believes that Bach completed this work in 1732 as a kind of "domestic comedy" for performance at home. Others are of a different mind, maintaining it had been planned for performance at some festivity as a comic interlude. In any event, the text by Picander makes sport of woman's passion for coffee. To this text, Schweitzer says, Bach wrote music that seems "to come from Offenbach rather than from the old cantor." It is not too farfetched to look upon *The Coffee Cantata* as a one-act operetta.

There are ten sections, beginning with the tenor's admonition to his audience to listen to what has befallen to Herr Schlendrian ("Schweigt, stille, plaudert nicht"). And this is what has happened. Schlendrian's daughter, Lieschen, has become addicted to coffee, as Schlendrian himself explains in his aria, "Hat mann nicht mit seinen Kindern." Lieschen extols the delights of coffee drinking in an ebullient air, "Ei, wie schmeckt der Coffee suesse." The pros and cons of coffee drinking are then explored in several recitatives and arias. In the ninth section, the tenor explains that Lieschen has no intention of marrying anybody who is not addicted to coffee ("Nun geht und sucht der alte Schlendrian"). The work ends with a gay commentary by the chorus on the undeniable fact that, since the older folk have a weakness for coffee, they cannot properly deny the drink to girls ("Die Katze laesst das Mausen nicht").

In the year of 1732, Bach also completed *Phoebus and Pan,* where the accent once again was on humor and satire. Picander here uses the old Greek legend of the song contest between Phoebus and Apollo. To Bach, this offers an opportunity to air his views about the ponderous music then being written for operas; through the character of Midas (who prefers Pan to Phoebus), Bach caricatures Johann Adolph Schiebe, who was so critical of his efforts. (The similarity of aim, and at times execution, between *Phoebus and Pan* and Wagner's *Die Meistersinger* is remarkable.) Bach's music passes from the pictorial (as in his vivid descriptions of a storm and of the passing of a dust cloud) to the plebian (as in Pan's peasant tune, "Zu tanze, zu Sprunge"). He progresses from pure and unadulterated lyricism (Tmolus's hymn to music, "Phoebus deine Melodie") to parody. In the concluding chorus, a hymn is sounded to the kind of music that brings joy to men and gods alike ("Labt das Herz").

The Peasant Cantata, comprising twenty-four sections, was written in 1742 to celebrate the assumption of the office of Gutsherr (Lord of the manor) by Karl Heinrich von Dieskau. Since this office requires the collection of taxes, music and text make some snide and witty comments on tax collectors (the basso aria, "Ach Herr Schoesser," for example, a fervent plea to the tax collector to have a heart). A tonal description of the squire Karl Heinrich is found in the soprano aria, "Unser trefflicher lieber Kammerherr," and a picture of the little town of Zschocher is provided by the soprano aria (with flute and strings), "Klein Zschocher muesse." The cantata ends with a chorus entreating the people to go off to the nearby inn to celebrate with wine and song, "Wir geh'n nun wo der Tudelsack."

1717–1723. CONCERTOS FOR ONE AND TWO VIOLINS AND ORCHESTRA:

Concerto No. 1 in A minor, for violin and orchestra. I. Allegro II. Andante. III. Allegro assai.

Concerto No. 2 in E major, for violin and orchestra. I. Allegro. II. Adagio. III. Allegro assai.

Concerto in D minor, for two violins and orchestra. I. Vivace. II. Largo ma non tanto. III. Allegro.

Two of Bach's concertos for solo violin and orchestra are the earliest in music history to survive in the present-day repertory. Bach wrote his violin concertos while serving in Coethen. They are derived from Italian concerto methods, with the two outer movements fast, and the middle one slow and lyrical. The solo instrument is accompanied by strings with a clavier continuo.

Generally speaking, the outer movements employ a single theme, repeated consistently, though with changes of key. The concerto-grosso technique of contrasting the solo and the tutti, and with its rapid changes of dynamics, are here employed liberally. The A minor Concerto opens with a two-section theme in orchestra extending twenty-four measures. The first part is then used consistently throughout the movement to accompany the solo instrument. In the finale, the main theme is immediately presented by the orchestra fugally.

The main subject of the first movement of the E major Concerto is constructed from three sharply accented quarter notes. Toward the middle of this movement, these three notes become an accompanying figure in the orchestra, as the solo violin embarks on a magical lyrical passage in the relative minor key of C-sharp. In the finale, the vigorous opening subject is repeated several times, with equally robust subsidiary material contributed by the solo instrument.

It is perhaps in the slow movements that Bach is most inspired. Here, as C. Hubert Parry has said, "he reveals the actual intention to use music as the vehicle of psychological concepts. . . . The Adagio movement of the Violin Concerto in E is particularly illuminating in this sense and has even a dramatic character, owing to the very definite manner in which the dialogue is carried on." In comparing the slow movements of these two violin concertos, Albert Schweitzer notes: "The beauty of the A minor Concerto is severe, that of E major full of unconquerable joy of life that sings its song of triumph in the first and last movements."

Bach's Concerto for Two Violins and Orchestra, in D minor, is not only one of the most exalted works in Baroque literature for the violin, but also the most celebrated two-violin concerto ever written. In the vigorous flanking movements, the energetic main themes are given fugally. In the first movement, after a second subject has been introduced, it is set contrapuntally against the opening theme; in the finale, the second subject in the first violin provides an eloquent emotional contrast to the hearty spirits of the rest of the movement. Once again, the jewel of the concerto lies in the slow movement—a melody of surpassing radiance, presented canonically by the two violins.

1717–1750. SUITES, for orchestra:

No. 1, C major. I. Ouverture. II. Courante. III. Gavottes I and II. IV. Forlane. V. Menuetti I and II. VI. Bourrees I and II. VII. Passepieds I and II.

No. 2, B minor. I. Ouverture. II. Rondeau. III. Sarabande. IV. Bourrees I and II—Polonaise and Double. V. Menuet. VI. Badinerie.

No. 3. D major. I. Ouverture. II. Air. III. Gavotte. IV. Bourree. V. Gigue.

No. 4, D major. I. Ouverture. II. Bourrees I and II. III. Gavotte. IV. Menuetto. V. Réjouissance.

In Bach's time, the terms "suite" and "overture" were often used interchangeably. This was because the first movement of a suite was a French Overture and was the most significant part of the entire work. Bach himself referred to his four orchestral suites as "overtures."

The first two suites were completed while Bach was serving as music director at the court of Prince Leopold of Anhalt between 1717 and 1723. The last two came at a later period, some time after Bach had assumed his office as cantor in Leipzig.

The first suite is scored for two oboes, bassoons, and strings. The French Overture opens with a Grave section in which two oboes play in unison with the first violins, bassoons, and cellos. This is followed by a fugal Vivace. When the Grave returns, the opening material is modified and revised, both in the way the themes are given and in the instrumentation. The dance movements that follow are in expected Baroque style.

The second suite—scored for flute and strings—once again opens with a French Overture, in which a stately slow section precedes and follows a four-voice fugal episode. The more memorable dance movements to follow include the stately sarabande, a delightful polonaise in which the flute plays an octave above the first violins, and a playful badinerie.

In the third suite (for two oboes, three trumpets, drums, and strings) the most popular movement is the second, an "Air." This spiritual melody is enriched by the subtle interweaving of the accompanying voices. The melody is familiar to violinists everywhere through a transcription by August

Wilhelmj, which he entitled *Air on the G String*. This version is often dubbed a "derangement" rather than an "arrangement." Donald Francis Tovey said: "Imagination boggles at the idea of Bach's reception of Wilhelmj's piety in leaving the inner voices undisturbed and in crassly ungrammatical relation to the melody in its new position."

The suite once again opens with a French Overture. After the "Air," we get a succession of light, graceful, lively dances.

The rarely played fourth suite is scored for three oboes, bassoon, three trumpets, drums, and strings. Its French Overture was again used by the composer for his cantata, *Unser Mund sei voll Lachens*. Several Baroque dance tunes are concluded with a "Réjouissance" for full orchestra. The "Réjouissance" (French for "enjoyment") is a lively piece of music occasionally encountered as an accessory piece in a Baroque suite.

1718–1723. 6 SONATAS, for violin and clavier: I. B minor. II. A major. III. E major. IV. C minor. V. F minor. VI. G major.

3 SONATAS, for unaccompanied violin: I. G minor. II. A minor. III. C major.

3 PARTITAS, for unaccompanied violin: I. B minor. II. D minor. III. E major.

3 SONATAS, for cello and clavier: I. G major. II. D major. III. G minor.

6 SUITES, for unaccompanied cello: I. G major. II. D minor. III. C major. IV E-flat major. V. C minor. VI. D major.

Bach's most celebrated single work for the violin—indeed, one of the noblest achievements in all violin literature—is the Chaconne. The Chaconne, —though often given at concerts all by itself—is actually a movement for a larger work, the Partita No. 2 in D minor, for unaccompanied violin (I. Allemande. II. Courante. III. Sarabande. IV. Gigue. V. Chaconne). This remarkable piece of music consists of a melody of cathedral-like grandeur, presented in full chords. Thirty-one variations follow. "The master's spirit," wrote Philipp Spitta, "inspired the instrument to express the inconceivable. At the end . . . the music swells like organ-tone, and at times one hears a whole chorus of violins." Numerous transcriptions have popularized this work for media other than the solo violin. Stokowski was one of several to orchestrate it; Busoni adapted it for the piano, and Brahms for piano left hand. Andrés Segovia transcribed it for guitar. Mendelssohn prepared a piano accompaniment for the violin part. But whatever terms it is translated into, the Chaconne remains music of surpassing majesty.

Bach utilized the terms "partita," "sonata," and "suite" for his large compositions for violin or for cello, whether with or without clavier accompaniment. "Partita" and "suite" are terms used interchangeably to connote a work made up of dance movements. Consequently, in Bach's Partitas for solo violin and in his Suites for solo cello, such old dance forms as the Allemande, Courante, Sarabande, Minuet, and Gigue are used. In the sonatas, the customary tempo markings are found. Most of Bach's sonatas are in four movements, the first and third in slow tempo and the second and fourth, fast.

The unaccompanied sonatas and partitas for violin, or for violoncello, are "another instance," writes Hans T. David and Arthur Mendl in *The Bach Reader,* "of Bach's taking hints from the past and basing structures of the utmost complexity upon them. Once the figured bass had been introduced, chamber music without it was a rarity. By the end of the seventeenth century, on the other hand, the technique of polyphonic playing on a stringed instrument had been fully developed. . . . But [no one] of these men had written unaccompanied music for a stringed instrument on any such scale as even one of Bach's works, let alone such a series of them as his two sets of six each."

The Chaconne from the D minor Partita gives testimony to Bach's capacity to bring to his polyphonic writing whether for violin or for cello, a wealth of emotion as well as thought. Frequently, effects suggesting the organ, or even an orchestra, are simulated. In addition, the technique of violin or cello performance is greatly enhanced—so much so in the case of the cello that it is often maintained that here the cello achieves full emancipation as a solo instrument.

An example of Bach's remarkable polyphonic writing can be found in the third movement of the Sonata No. 2 in A major, for violin and clavier (I. Andante. II. Allegro assai. III. Andante un poco. IV. Presto). To C. Hubert Parry, this music "appears to be a pathetic colloquy between the violin and the treble clavier part, to which the bass keeps up the slow constant motion of staccato semiquavers; the colloquy at the same time is in strict canon throughout, and, as a specimen of expressive treatment of that time-honored form, is almost unrivalled." Other sonatas and partitas boast remarkable polyphonic pages, particularly in fast or slow fugal movements—notably the first movement of the unaccompanied violin Sonata in C major (I. Adagio; Fugue—Molto moderato. II. Largo. III. Allegro assai).

It is in his slow movements that Bach most often scaled the heights in these compositions for the violin or for the cello. Here, as C. Hubert Parry noted, we find "a point of rich and complex emotional expression which music reached for the first time in Bach's imagination." Sublimity is the keynote of movements like the third in the C minor Sonata for violin and clavier (I. Siciliana. II. Allegro. III. Adagio. IV. Allegro). Sublimity also prevails in the slow movements of the first two cello sonatas with clavier: the first, in G major (I. Adagio. II. Allegro ma non tanto. III. Andante. IV. Allegro moderato); the second in D major (I. Adagio. II. Allegro. III. Andante. IV. Allegro).

The Chaconne is one of two excerpts from these Partitas, Sonatas, and Suites to have been transcribed most frequently into other media. The other excerpt is the opening Prelude of the Partita No. 3 in E major for solo violin. It was adapted for orchestra by various musicians, including Lucien Cailliet,

Stokowski, Sir Henry J. Wood, and Pick-Mangiagalli. Bach also orchestrated it when he interpolated it into his twenty-ninth Cantata. Robert Schumann and Fritz Kreisler each arranged it for violin and piano; Rachmaninoff, for piano solo; and Andrés Segovia, for guitar.

1720–1724. INVENTIONS, in two and three parts, for clavier.
CHROMATIC FANTASY AND FUGUE IN D MINOR, for clavier.

The fifteen two-part and fifteen three-part Inventions for the clavier are part of the *Clavierbuechlein vor Anna Magdalena Bach* (1720), which the composer concocted as instruction pieces for his wife. Bach himself explained that these minor items were planned as "a guide for clean performance, with special emphasis on the cultivation of a cantabile style of playing and the acquisition of a strong foretaste of composition. The *Inventions* have become basic to piano study in general and to an introduction to, and preparation for, Bach's more complex clavier literature in particular. "Invention" was a term that Bach probably inherited from Francesco Antonio Bonporti (1672–1749), who wrote several pieces in that form which Bach had copied out by hand. But as Martin F. Bukofzer remarks, Bach made the form entirely his own. "Written in fugal style without being fugues, the Inventions represent the triumph of obbligato part-writing. . . . They are arranged like the *Well-Tempered Clavier* in the ascending order of keys but with the omission of those involving more than four accidentals." To Wanda Landowska, the "miracle of Bach's inspiration finds itself in its purest, most beautiful, most succinct form in the two-part Inventions. It is here that Bach's 'singing style' can be found not only in epitome but in flowering. Here, the melodic line of Bach is perpetually alive, merry, full of life."

There is nothing functional about the *Chromatic Fantasy and Fugue* (1720–1724); this is concert music of the highest order. The title comes from the chromatic modulations in the opening fantasy and in the chromatic structure of the fugal subject. What endows this work with particular interest is the way in which the recitative style is carried over to instrumental music. The piece opens with a dramatic recitative, preceding the rhapsodic fantasia with its brilliant runs and arpeggios. The three-part fugue begins softly and sedately, but is built up toward a powerful climax.

1722–1744. DAS WOHLTEMPERIERTE CLAVIER (THE WELL-TEMPERED CLAVIER), forty-eight preludes and fugues, for clavier.

Bach wrote two books of preludes and fugues for the clavier. The first twenty-four pieces came in 1722; the succeeding twenty-four, in 1744. Like a good many of Bach's clavier works, these were intended primarily as instruction material for his wife and children. But, like a good many of Bach's instruction pieces, they also were lifted by his genius to exalted art.

But there is a particular historical significance to *The Well-Tempered Clavier* not encountered in his other clavier music. Each of the preludes and fugues is in a different key; each of the two books covers all the twelve major and minor scales. Bach's purpose was to prove that the "well-tempered," or "well-tuned," clavier was uniquely effective and practical for the writing of music—something that the early eighteenth century had not as yet accepted. In doing this, he was carrying out a concept first established by Andreas Werckmeister, a pioneer in dividing the octave into twelve equal semitones. This process, identified as "equal temperament," made it possible to have each tone approximately in tune, through the discrepancy in pitch being more or less equally distributed through the twelve tones of the octave. The value of this new system of tuning lay in the fact that transposition from one key to the next could be effected more simply. Bach was convinced of the significance of this method; to prove that significance, he created the *Well-Tempered Clavier*.

"The old method of tempering (or tuning) the keyboard," explains W. R. Anderson, "was based on a system which (to put it as briefly and as untechnically as possible) left some keys well in tune and some out of tune. Bach advocated little adjustments so that music in *every* key be equally pleasant, even if the tune were not mathematically exact. Such tuning is, of course, commonplace today, but it was by no means so in Bach's time or even for a good while afterwards."

In Bach's hands, functional music proving a technical system becomes art of surpassing imagination, daring in its harmonies, rich and varied in emotional content, inexhaustible in its polyphonic devices. The *Well-Tempered Clavier* is unquestionably one of the supreme masterworks in piano literature. As W. G. Whittaker says: "It bears undoubtedly the seeds of many flowers and fruits of the future, besides forming a glorious garden for present happiness. No composer ever spoke such widely different thoughts. . . . One can find music there to meet all needs, to synchronize all states of emotion."

This is Wanda Landowska's estimate of *The Well-Tempered Clavier:* "The poetry, the atmosphere, the intensity of expression, the beauty of the preludes and fugues, grip, overwhelm, and stimulate us. . . . The scholarly music unfolds as freely as if the rules of counterpoint did not exist. . . . Let us never forget that the preludes and fugues are not abstract speculations. They come from the brain and heart of a great creator, who is a poet. Bach understands everything. He is equally happy in describing a pastoral scene, the majesty of a Gothic cathedral, or the overwhelming joy of a dance."

1721. 6 BRANDENBURG CONCERTOS, for orchestra:
I. F major. I. Allegro. II. Adagio. III. Allegro. IV. Menuetto.
II. F major. I. Allegro. II. Andante. III. Allegro assai.
III. G major. I. Allegro moderato. II. Allegro.
IV. G major. I. Allegro. II. Andante. III. Presto.
V. D major. I. Allegro. II. Affettuoso. III. Allegro.
VI. B-flat major. I. Allegro. II. Adagio ma non tanto. III. Allegro.

Being a collector of concerto music, Christian Ludwig, the Margrave of Brandenburg, made it a practice to commission composers he admired to write such works for him. In or about 1719, he met Johann Sebastian Bach, and was so deeply impressed with him that he commissioned him to create several concertos. Bach completed the assignment early in 1721. "Humbly" he submitted the final product to his benefactor with the plea that he not judge "their imperfections too harshly," and that he try to find in them "the profound respect and the very humble allegiance that they seek to convey." It is extremely doubtful that the Margrave regarded these works highly. He failed to list them in the catalog of his collection; and when they were disposed of after the Margrave's death in 1734, each Brandenburg Concerto was valued at about ten cents apiece.

Bach here makes free use of the Italian concerto-grosso form inherited from Vivaldi. In contrasting the concertino with the ripieno, Bach hit upon the happy idea of utilizing a different set of solo instruments for each of his concertos. The exception to this rule is the third, where the orchestra is divided into three parts to replace the solo instruments. Bach also departs occasionally from the traditional three-movement structure of the concerto grosso. Bach's first concerto has four movements (an extended minuet appearing after the three usual parts); the third concerto has only two movements.

The first concerto is the most opulently orchestrated work in the set, calling for solo violin, three oboes, bassoon, two horns, and strings. Twelve measures precede the presentation of the concertino in a conversation between oboes and horns. The slow movement (once described as a "most impassionated song of woe") offers a recitative-like melody for oboes and solo violin. The vigorous Allegro movement was later transcribed by Bach for chorus for one of his cantatas. There, explains Michael Sternberg, "the solo violin has become a glory of four-part choral polyphony, the horn parts are ignited into the brilliance of high trumpets, and the result is altogether stunning." For his finale, Bach used a minuet in several sections. The minuet theme for full orchestra is heard first, followed by a polacca for strings, a return of the minuet, a trio for horns and oboes, and a final statement of the minuet.

The second concerto has unusual instrumental colors obtained through the deployment of a quartet of four high-pitched instruments. One is a trumpet, used to provide brilliant and fanciful figurations around the main theme. The trumpet, however, does not appear in the slow movement, which is music of incandescent beauty and religious ardor, scored for flute, oboe, and violins to an accompaniment by cellos and harpsichord.

There are only two movements in the third concerto, scored for three violins, three violas, three cellos, double bass, and harpsichord. The usual slow section is replaced by two chords. There is good reason to believe that Bach had intended these chords as the point of departure for an improvisation by the harpsichord. Some present-day conductors like to interpolate into this work a slow movement from one of Bach's other works. This concerto has an unusual structure in that three string choirs are used, each divided into three segments (three violins, three violas, three cellos). The three instruments within their respective choirs are sometimes heard in unison, sometimes as individual voices.

A lightness of touch sets the fourth concerto apart from the others in the Brandenburg set. This delicacy is particularly evident in the concertino writing. The slow movement is the aristocrat of the entire work, with a melody of surpassing nobility and elegance. Bach later transcribed this Brandenburg Concerto as a piano concerto, in F major. (The fourth concerto is scored for violin, two flutes, strings, and harpsichord.)

The fifth concerto enlists the services of a solo harpsichord, flute, violin, and strings. Here the harpsichord assumes such importance that the work almost has the appearance of a harpsichord concerto. Perhaps nothing more notable for this keyboard instrument can be found within a Baroque orchestral composition than the extended first movement cadenza. This is a rhapsodic episode. With the rest of the orchestra silent, the solo instrument embarks upon an exalted monologue.

The scoring of the sixth concerto is most unusual. Violins are completely deleted from the string section, which includes the mellow tones of a viola da gamba. Through such instrumentation, the work acquires a consistently subdued—at times even somber—personality. In addition, Bach pays particular attention to the violas. In the first movement, they are used canonically in the opening tutti; in the slow movement, the main melody is assigned to them; and in the finale, two violas imitate each other playfully while introducing a lighter tone into otherwise solemn proceedings.

1722–1725. 6 ENGLISH SUITES, for clavier: I. A major II. A minor. III. G minor. IV. F major. V. E minor. VI. D minor.

6 FRENCH SUITES, for clavier: I. D minor. II. C minor. III. B minor. IV. E-flat major. V. G major. VI. E major.

A completely convincing explanation of why Bach named six of these clavier suites "English," and six more "French," has not as yet been offered by musicologists. It is Forkel's belief that the so-called "French Suites" were written in the style of Louis Marchand (1669–1732) and Couperin-le-Grand; that the English Suites were so designated because of their greater sobriety and reserve. In any event, these dozen suites are among Bach's most significant productions for the solo clavier.

Each of the English Suites opens with a prelude, while the French Suites are introduced with an allemande. Generally speaking, the movements of the French Suites are shorter than those in the English, and contain lighter and more graceful material. In both the French and English Suites, says Schweitzer, "Bach . . . follows tradition in placing the dances that were not originally part of the suite between the sarabande and the gigue, so that the latter forms the conclusion. He generally places the extraneous movements at the beginning. . . . Naturally some of these dances were somewhat altered in clavier style. . . . Bach . . . always vitalizes the form, and gives each of the principal dance forms a definite musical personality. For him the allemande represents vigorous but easy motion; the courante represents a measured haste, in which dignity and elegance go side by side; the sarabande represents a grave and majestic walk; in the gigue, the freest of all the forms, the motion is quite fancy free. He thus raises the suite form to the plane of the highest art, while at the same time he preserves its primitive character as a collection of dance pieces."

1723. THE PASSION ACCORDING TO ST. JOHN, for solo voices, chorus, and orchestra.

It is believed that Bach wrote five Passions. Only two have survived in their entirety (the other one being the monumental *Passion According to St. Matthew*). The *St. John* was Bach's first setting of the Passion of Christ. Bach completed it soon after he had assumed the office of cantor at the St. Thomas Church; he introduced it there in 1723, probably on Good Friday.

Barthold Heinrich Brockes derived the text mainly from the eighteenth and nineteenth chapters of St. John, which detail dramatically the arrest, trial, and crucifixion of Christ in a series of secco recitativos for the Evangelist (tenor). The words attributed to Christ, Pontius Pilate, and Peter—spoken by the Evangelist—are also set to recitatives.

In all these recitatives, maintains Schweitzer, "Bach has preserved in the most admirable way the special tint of the narrative as it is in St. John. His setting of the words of Jesus reproduced the super-terrestrial, almost abstract, elevation that characterizes the Christ of the fourth Gospel, from the beginning." Charles Sanford Terry adds: "Bach's recitative speaks a language spontaneous and natural, unfolding the narrative with the inflexions of a good reader, restrained but conscious of its dramatic force and poignancy."

After an episode has been described, a solo written to a specially prepared text remarks on the emotional impulse aroused by this incident. Here Bach often rises to lofty heights of lyricism, giving voice to the most moving tenderness and compassion. Two cases in point are the arias for contralto and for basso respectively, the "Es ist vollbracht" and the "Betrachte, meine Seel".

The chorus speaks for the crowd—for the soldiers, priests, the populace—reflecting the mob reaction to the mighty drama. Here the poignancy and elevation of the solo arias give way to powerful dramatic utterance: the outcries to crucify Jesus ("Kreuzige!"); the derision of the people in "Sei gegruesset, lieber Judenkoenig"; the fanaticism of the mob in "Waere dieser nicht ein Uebeltaeter," which Schweitzer described as "unsurpassably dreadful in its effect."

Music of a completely contrasting nature can be found in the chorales—music radiant and profoundly devout. Here the congregation would join in the singing. "By a marvelous pliancy in the treatment of the parts," explains

Spitta, "and an inexhaustible wealth of harmonic resource, he was able to distribute over the whole a fresh and varied vitality with a subtle and significant illustration of details." It is on such a note of eloquence that the Passion ends, with the chorale, "Ach, Herr, lass dein Lieb' Engelein." Here, says Hugh Ross, Bach "is, as he alone knew how to be, the sublime comforter, the maker of music so transcendent in its divine benignity that there are no words with which to speak of it that would not seem impertinent."

1723. MAGNIFICAT IN D MAJOR, for solo voices, chorus, and orchestra.

Bach made two settings of the Magnificat for performance after the sermon on high festivals. Both were based on a text from Luke I: 46–55. The first, written in 1723, was intended for the Christmas evening service. This version (in the key of E-flat major) boasts four Christmas hymns, which are not part of the text but inserted between the verses. The hymns were sung not by the regular choir but by several choristers in an opposite gallery, accompanied by a smaller organ. On the other feast days, these hymns were removed from the context. But the Magnificat as performed today is Bach's second version. This is in the key of D major and does not include the Christmas hymns.

The Magnificat is Bach's ode to joy. "Of all his Latin works," wrote André Pirro, "this is without doubt the one most directly and scrupulously inspired by the text. The first chorus, written for five parts, is one long jubilation, which bursts out, is developed and repeated to express the joy of the first verse, 'Magnificat anima mea Dominum.' In the following verses, Bach also translates with almost naïve care in the primitive manner the musical images suggested by the words. The motifs rise; the rhythms become animated to express the exultation of the soul chosen by God. A descending theme symbolizes the humility of the Lord's handmaiden. The whole choir suddenly intervenes in a soprano aria to symbolize the voices of 'All the generations.' The contrast in significance of the word 'deposuit' and 'exultavit' is achieved by the contrast in the direction of the themes which accompany them. But in the midst of these familiar archaic devices we find deep allusions such as only Bach could have conceived. In the verse 'Suscepit Israel puerum suum,' the ancient melody to which the German Magnificat was sung hovers over the trio of the two sopranos and alto. The old liturgical theme of the 'Tonus peregrinus' thus mingles with the hymn of the actions of grace which the voices develop. It recalls the compassion which God at all times and under all laws reserves for his chosen people. In a single bouquet, the musician assembles the blessings promised to those who have served the Lord in the sincerity of their soul, whatever the discipline of their religion."

1723. JESU, MEINE FREUDE, motet for five-part a cappella chorus.

Bach completed five unaccompanied motets. *Jesu, meine Freude* is one of the greatest. Unaccompanied choruses were rarely written in Bach's time, belonging as they did to an earlier polyphonic age when instrumental music had not as yet been developed. It is Donald Francis Tovey's view that in Bach's unaccompanied choruses "there are hardly two consecutive pages in all . . . without some passage which proves that Bach has imagined the basses to be supported by some instrument an octave below them." Tovey then goes on to explain that Bach had "no such view of choral music as had Palestrina and his army of sixteenth-century fellow masters, to whom the unaccompanied chorus was the one real instrument of music, and all artificial instruments the merest crutches. To Bach, the unaccompanied can exist, if it exists at all, only as a tour de force alike for composers and performers."

Jesu meine Freude has eleven sections. The first and last are chorales in which different texts are set to the same music. "A glance at the list of movements . . . shows that they are arranged in a remarkable symmetry," Tovey explains. "Six verses of a chorale alternate with five passages from the eighth chapter of the Epistle to the Romans; the sixth chorale is set to the same music as the first; of the prose scriptural choruses, the last resumes the music of the first, while the two scriptural numbers that are for three-part semi-chorus or solo voices (Bach gives no indication) are at equal distances the one from the beginning, the other from the end."

Tovey singles out the ninth movement (the first verse of the chorale) as one of Bach's "great choral variations . . . a stupendously complete and clear form which only Bach has achieved. . . . The essence of this form is that, while one voice or part sings the chorale phrase by phrase, with pauses so long between each as to stretch the whole out to the length of a long movement, the other parts execute a complete design which may or may not have some connection with the melody of the chorale, but which in any case would remain a perfectly solid whole if the chorale were taken away."

1729. THE PASSION ACCORDING TO ST. MATTHEW, for solo voices, chorus, and orchestra.

The *St. Matthew Passion* is the second of two famous Bach settings of Christ's last suffering and death. It followed the *Passion According to St. John* by six years, and was performed for the first time, under the composer's direction, at the St. Thomas Church in Leipzig on April 15, 1729.

The text was prepared by Christian Friedrich Hinrici from the twenty-sixth and twenty-seventh chapters of St. Matthew. In essence, the *St. Matthew Passion* is a more devout and spiritual work than its predecessor and companion, which, on the other hand, is more dramatic. In the *St. Matthew Passion,* for example, the words of Christ are accompanied by strings (an accompaniment that has been happily compared to a halo around the Savior's head); in the *St. John Passion* the accompaniment consists merely of chords in the harpsichord. In the *St. Matthew Passion,* Bach scales the peaks of sublimity in such incandescent arias as the one for alto, "Buss' und Reu," another for soprano, "Blute nur," the contralto aria with violin obbligato, "Erbame dich, mein Gott," and the haunting soprano aria, "Aus Liebe will mein Heiland sterben." Only rarely do the choral episodes soar to such heights. They did so in the opening funereal chant, "Kommt ihr Toechter" and in the closing threnody, "Wir setzen uns mit Traenen nieder."

A new concept of tonal speech enters in the *St. Matthew Passion,* as Leonard Bernstein remarked in *The Joy of Music*. We discover, he says, a "mystic fusion of words and notes" resulting "in a whole new Bachian language. It is in this language that Bach writes his drama, not only in the recitative sections where the story is being told, but everywhere in the Passion." Bernstein then points to the tonal images utilized by Bach to shape the Cross, the gesture of Christ's hand, the ascent to the mount of Olives. "For instance," continues Bernstein, "there . . . comes a chorale which is heard no fewer than five times throughout the course of the work. . . . Each time this chorale appears, it is presented in a new way: with different words in different keys, and with different harmonizations. And through these differences of tone speech, Bach is able to communicate a variety of meaning that is phenomenal."

The *St. Matthew Passion,* then, is a marriage of the theater and the church; a work which, in Arthur Loesser's words, is "an act of worship which . . . has the animation of a play. . . Bach definitely reinstated the primacy of the devotional atmosphere into his Passion music. The Bible text was kept in its original purity: in fact, in his manuscript of the *St. Matthew Passion* he underlined the words of Scripture with red ink. The chorales, representing a liturgical element, were reintroduced and were provided with Bach's matchless harmonies." Loesser than singles out those parts of the *Passion* in which the spiritual and the elevated make room for the dramatic. "The speeches of the various personages, such as the Evangelist, Christ, Peter, Judas, Pilate, and so forth, are directly represented by the various singers, although the same singer at different times has to take several different parts. The emotional values of the story are vividly brought out in the music. The mob's terrifying cry of 'Barabbas,' the cruel intervals of the passage, 'Let Him Be Crucified,' the manner in which the false witnesses parrot each other in exact imitation—in all these and many other passages the composer aims to portray the inner, psychological truth of the words."

It was the *St. Matthew Passion* that first set into motion the revival of Bach, which finally lifted the master out of the obscurity into which he had lapsed following his death, and in which he stayed for almost a century. This happened in Berlin on March 11, 1829, when Felix Mendelssohn revived the *St. Matthew Passion,* which had not been heard since Bach's own time. In 1829, few indeed could have expected such awesome grandeur from a forgotten work by a forgotten master as confronted them with this music. The impact of *St. Matthew Passion* was, consequently, overwhelming. "Everyone," Mendelssohn wrote to his sister Fanny, "was filled with the most solemn devotion. One heard only an occasional involuntary ejaculation that sprang from deep emotions." The *Passion* had to be given a second time, and once again it stirred its hearers profoundly. The first step in the restoration of Bach and his music had been taken.

c. 1730. CONCERTOS, for solo clavier and orchestra:
No. 1, D minor. I. Allegro. II. Adagio. III. Allegro.
No. 4, A major. I. Allegro. II. Larghetto. III. Allegro ma non tanto.
No. 5, F minor. I. Allegro. II. Largo. III. Presto.

Bach was the first significant composer to write a clavier concerto. He produced seven of them, in or about 1730, intending them for performance by his sons or pupils. Some are transcriptions of his violin concertos. Spitta is of the opinion that, in writing his violin concertos, Bach always kept the keyboard style in mind. Thus, when he embarked on writing concertos for the clavier, it was logical for him to transform some of his violin concertos for the piano.

According to Hans T. David, Bach "actually created a new form" in his clavier concertos. "The keyboard instrument had been used for centuries as a solo instrument. . . . But in Bach's time, the keyboard instrument was still confined to a secondary role whenever it was used together with the other instruments."

The first time Bach used the clavier for the concerto form was in the famous D minor, one of three clavier concertos by Bach heard most frequently today. The first theme is a powerful six-measure subject in unison, which dominates the entire movement and provides it with its motor energy. In the second movement, a richly decorated melody in the clavier soars above a recurring bass in the orchestra. The finale is set into motion by a vigorous twelve-bar subject.

The fourth concerto opens with a ritornel motive that recurs throughout the first movement, but from time to time alternating with an important episode in the clavier. In the Larghetto, we hear the string orchestra in a bold melody in the minor, around which the clavier weaves fanciful figures. A powerful, exciting theme provides the finale with its stout vigor and brisk pace.

In the fifth concerto, both piano and orchestra embark on a fourteen-measure passage to open the first movement. The clavier then engages new expressive material. A recurrence of the opening subject precedes a new effective melodic idea. In the second movement, a vocal-like aria unfolds luxuriously in the clavier against attractive accompanying figures in the orchestra. The finale, in triple time, is vigorous and dramatic, beginning with a vigorous motive that attacks the movement and sweeps it relentlessly on to an exciting climax.

1730–1733. CONCERTO NO. 1 IN D MINOR, for three claviers and orchestra. I. Allegro moderato. II. Alla siciliana. III. Allegro.

CONCERTO NO. 2 IN C MAJOR, for three claviers and orchestra. I. Allegro. II. Adagio. III. Allegro.

CONCERTO IN A MINOR, for four claviers and orchestra. I. Allegro. II. Largo. III. Allegro.

CONCERTO IN D MINOR, for violin, oboe, and orchestra. I. Allegro. II. Adagio. III. Allegro.

It is Spitta's contention that Bach wrote his two concertos for three claviers so that he might have material to play with his sons, Wilhelm Friedemann and Carl Philipp Emanuel. The exact date of composition is not known—though it is generally assigned to Bach's Leipzig period; but it is usually believed that the D minor concerto came first, and the C major afterwards. To Albert Schweitzer, the second concerto is "planned on larger lines that the first, and the orchestra plays a more important part in it." Schweitzer then adds: "The tonal and rhythmical effects that Bach has achieved with the three claviers are indescribable. At every hearing of these works we stand amazed before the mystery of so incredible a power of invention and combination."

Max de Schauensee, the program annotator for the Philadelphia Orchestra, describes the D minor Concerto as follows: "The first movement is without tempo indication in the manuscript but in the ritornello form. From its general nature it must be considered as the normal opening Allegro. The Siciliana that follows in the relative major key, is a richly harmonized slow movement—a memorably lovely adaptation of the old dance form with its leisurely, swaying six-beats-to-a-measure lilt. One notices that in these two movements the first piano is quite predominant, the others more or less providing an accompaniment. However, the fugal finale that ends the work supplies each soloist with a florid piece of bravura—an unaccompanied cadenza. Here the solo instruments emerge as equal partners in a brilliant culminating display."

The C major Concerto opens with the three pianos in unison before they embark their separate ways on new material. The slow movement is introduced by the strings in a polyphonic passage. The three claviers then offer the main subject. Toward the end of the movement, we hear the solo instruments in a cadenza charged with unusual chromatic harmonies. In the finale, the thematic material is treated fugally, as each of the three solo instruments is provided an opportunity to assert his own individuality in virtuoso passages.

The Concerto in A minor, for four claviers, is a transcription of a concerto by Vivaldi—the B minor, for four violins and orchestra, op. 3, no. 10. The music is essentially Vivaldi's, except for one measure in the finale, the change of key throughout the entire work, and the filling out of the harmonic structure in the solo instruments. The main material of the first movement consists of a forcefully rhythmic subject heard without preliminaries, to which the four solo claviers give reply. The second movement is in three-part song form, the middle assigned to the four solo instruments without accompaniment. The dynamic finale enters without a break.

The Concerto in D minor, for violin, oboe, and orchestra is a modern adaptation of Bach's C minor Concerto for two claviers. In the first movement, the two solo instruments are heard in the main subject immediately after a brief orchestral introduction. The middle movement is an eloquent melody for the two solo instruments, presented in imitation over a pizzicato accompaniment. There is no break between the second and third movements. Following a robust orchestral introduction, the two instruments offer the vital main theme, which is then extensively developed.

1731–1735. 6 PARTITAS, for clavier: I. B-flat major. II. C minor. III. A minor. IV. D major V. G major. VI. E minor.

CONCERTO NACH ITALIENISCHEN GUSTO IN F MINOR (ITALIAN CONCERTO, or CONCERTO IN THE ITALIAN STYLE), for solo clavier. I. Allegro. II. Andante. III. Presto.

The six clavier Partitas (1731) comprise the first part of the *Clavieruebung*—this being the collective title for an anthology of Bach's keyboard music published between 1726 and 1742. (In the second part are found the *Italian Concerto* and the *Overture in the French Manner;* in the third part, four duets, the prelude and St. Anne fugue for organ, and chorale preludes; in the fourth part, the *Goldberg Variations*.)

Like other Bach Partitas, those for clavier are essentially suites—made up of dance movements. Bach himself described these works as "galanteries composed for the mental recreation of art lovers."

The Partita No. 3 in A minor departs from the norm by its inclusion of two humorous episodes, a scherzo and a Burlesca (I. Fantasia. II. Allemande. III. Corrente. IV. Sarabande. V. Burlesca. VI. Scherzo. Vll. Gigue). The Partita No. 4 in D major has a remarkable Sarabande, one of those noble utterances that set the Leipzig cantor apart from the other masters of his generation (I. Overture. II. Allemande. III. Corrente. IV. Aria. V. Sarabande. VI. Menuet. VII. Gigue). The Partita No. 5 in G major has an almost consistent serenity and sobriety throughout most of the movements (I. Praeambulum II. Allemande. III. Corrente. IV. Sarabande. V. Tempo di minuetto. VI. Passepied. VII. Gigue).

The *Italian Concerto* (1735), from the second part of the *Clavieruebung,* is for unaccompanied solo clavier, even though concertos were traditionally for solo instrument *and* orchestra. Bach here attempted a solo concerto in the form and style previously established by such Italian masters as Corelli—the reason why he entitled the work a "Concerto in the Italian Style." The vigor and muscular strength of the Italian concerto are found in the outer fast movements—the Presto being particularly distinguished for its rhythmic invention. But surely the most eloquent part of the concerto comes in the slow movement. This is a soaring aria for the clavier in which the new age of homophony is not only anticipated but even realized.

1733–1738. MASS IN B MINOR, for solo voices, chorus, and orchestra.

When Bach made a bid for the post of composer at the Saxon Royal Chapel in 1733, he submitted two movements of the B minor Mass as "a trifling example of my skill"—the "Kyrie" and the "Gloria." Five years later, Bach completed the other parts of the Mass. The entire work was never heard in Bach's time. That première took place almost a century after Bach's death—in Berlin. There the first half was heard on February 20, 1834, and the second half, a year later, on February 12.

Bach derived less than one-third of the music from this Mass from earlier works, most notably church cantatas. But as Charles Sanford Terry has said: "Even in their adaptation, the borrowed movements reveal their creative genius, while a collation of them with their originals exposes the sensitiveness of his judgment and self-criticism." The old material and the new were joined into one of the mightiest, most grandiose edifices music has known. This, says, Terry, is "the design of a superb architect, perfect in proportion and balance." Rosa Newmarch considers the Mass the "culmination of Bach's spiritual development. The deep inwardness, the brooding spirituality, which breathe in the church cantatas and Passions, were the outcome of that Protestant piety which lay at the root of his nature. But to this masterpiece of his fullest maturity . . . a new element is added: a Catholicism in the highest and broadest sense of the word."

The question has long been posed as to why Bach, a Protestant, sought to write a Mass belonging to Catholic ritual. Rosa Newmarch poses a satisfactory answer by pointing to "the unusual profundity and breadth of his religious views. He was probably one of the very rare devout spirits of his age who could discern the essential God in both churches. At any rate, when we are uplifted by the mystic grandeur and beauty of the B minor Mass, we cling to the conviction that when Bach thus drew to the forms and spirit of the older faith, he was actuated by some nobler ideal and purpose than to prove himself serviceable to a Court which had accepted Catholicism as the price of the Polish crown."

The five sections of the Mass in B minor—the "Kyrie," "Gloria in excelsis," "Credo," "Sanctus," and "Agnus Dei"—are further subdivided into twenty-four smaller, self-sufficient parts. The Mass opens with a resplendent four-bar introductory Adagio for full chorus and orchestra. Here, says Spitta, "the elect of God [are] crying to the Redeemer from the very first introduction of sin into the world." The orchestra takes over the "Kyrie" theme, after which the chorus returns in a five-voice fugal treatment stretching for forty-three bars. The grandeur of this music suggests to Schweitzer "nations innumerable ever joining with one accord to this prayer of mercy." The prayer continues with a supplication to Christ—the duet "Christe eleison," and a dramatized return of the opening "Kyrie," this time for four-part chorus.

In the five-part "Gloria," the music steps from minor to major to sound a mighty hymn to God. This act of glorification continues on into the florid "Laudeamus te" for mezzo-soprano, which is embellished with descending figures in the solo violin and culminates in the four-part chorus, "Gratias agimus tibi."

The glorification of God the Father now yields to a similar paean to Christ the Son, beginning with "Domine Deus," a duet for soprano and tenor. A profound sadness and an all-encompassing tenderness overflow in the choral music of "Qui tollis." An aria for contralto, "Qui sedes," and a stronger one for bass, "Quoniam," lead to a mighty chorus of praise to Christ in "Cum sancto Spiritu." Here the full orchestra and chorus combine in a powerful utterance, which flows into a mighty fugue.

The "Gloria" section now ended, the third part of the Mass, the "Credo," arrives to affirm proudly the unity of God. The strength of the true faith is thundered by the chorus in the opening "Credo" and continues on into "Patrem omnipotentem." After that, we hear a beautiful duet for soprano and contralto, "Et in unum Deum," followed by "Et incarnatus est," a chorus whose poignancy is enhanced by its unaffected simplicity and directness. The "Crucifixus" for chorus, now heard, is one of the most awe-inspiring pages in the score, "one of the supreme moments in music," as C. Hubert Parry once described it. "Its wonder lies in its combining, like a psychological condition, many different phrases. While the rare harmonies and the melody descending to the lowest available notes in the voice express the depths of overwhelming sorrow, the subtle alternation of the progression of the bass from the long reiterated formula which has persisted throughout the movement, suggests to the mind mysteriously the sense of something great that is coming . . . the premonition of the triumphant 'Resurrexit'."

In "Et in Spiritum Sanctum," an atmosphere of peace and tranquillity is invoked by the baritone, with obbligato by oboe d'amore. The "Credo" section then concludes with the five-part chorus, "Confiteor."

With the opening of the "Sanctus," the fourth section, we are being lifted to still higher spheres of inspiration. To Rosa Newmarch, its opening chorus surpasses "all that has gone before. We learn now, if we have never learned before, the true meaning of the word 'sublime.' . . . The massive orchestration is rendered brilliant by the participation of drums and three trumpets. As the music continues we hold our breath, marveling what can appropriately follow upon the consummate grandeur of this chorus. But Bach goes on from strength to strength and we soon find ourselves borne along on the current of another superb figure at the words, 'Pleni sunt coeli,' in which all the concentrated radiance of the picture seems to be reflected as in a river flashing under the midday sun."

From the thunder and lightning of the "Sanctus," we proceed to the radiant sunshine of the "Benedictus," an aria for tenor, to which solo violin provides an eloquent background. This exalted mood is maintained in the concluding section of the Mass, the "Agnus Dei," an air of incomparable tenderness for the contralto, accompanied by tutti violins. The Mass then ends with a wondrous prayer for peace and a song of thanksgiving for chorus in "Dona nobis pacem."

1734. WEIHNACHTS ORATORIUM (CHRISTMAS ORATORIO), for soloists, chorus, and orchestra. I. Am ersten Weihnachtsfeiertage. II.

Am zweiten Weihnachtsfeiertage. III. Am dritten Weihnachtsfeiertage. IV. Am Neujahrstage. V. Am Sonntage nach Neujahr. VI. Am Feste der Erscheinung Christi.

Bach's so-called *Christmas Oratorio* is not an oratorio, strictly speaking, since it is not a single, integrated, unified work based on a Biblical test. The *Christmas Oratorio* is actually a collation of six church cantatas, each to be performed at one of the six church events between Christmas and Epiphany. The first cantata was heard under Bach's direction at the St. Thomas Church during the morning service of Christmas day in 1734. The remaining five cantatas were given on the second and third days following Christmas, on New Year's Day, on the Sunday after New Year, and on the Feast of Epiphany. In Bach's time, the six cantatas were never presented at a single performance.

C. Hubert Parry explains that Bach's purpose in this work was to keep "the worshipers' minds occupied with the successive events commemorated throughout the Christmas season, and make them ponder well the suggestive thoughts and reflections which are appended."

Michael Hauptmann explains that the work as a whole consists of "lyrical meditations in the form of arias, ariosos, and choral passages, held together by the recitations of the Evangelist (tenor), relating to the story of the birth of Christ as set forth in the Gospels of Matthew and Luke." Hauptmann goes on to say: "The completeness of each cantata is established not only by mere formal designation but also by factors of internal harmonic and key relationships within each section and recurrent figuration in the bass." Hauptmann finally feels that the Christmas Oratorio is one of "the most satisfying musical experiences among Bach's larger works" because of the "brilliance of Bach's orchestra, with high D trumpets, timpani, choirs of flutes and oboes" together with "the sheer melodic joy of the arias, the animated drive of the choruses and chorales, and the brilliant virtuosity demanded of singers and obbligato instruments."

There is only one instrumental preface in the oratorio. This comes at the opening of the second section (all other divisions beginning with a chorus). It is called "Pastorale"—in Germany referred to as "Hirtenmusik" or "Shepherd's Music"—and is probably the work's most celebrated single excerpt. It is in G major, in the rhythm of a siciliano, and scored for flutes, oboes, strings, and organ continuo. In music of incomparable tranquillity, this piece describes the announcement to the shepherds of the birth of Christ and the praises sounded to the Almighty by the angelic host. The main melody is repeated in the chorale ending the oratorio, each line of the final hymn being followed by a brief recollection of the shepherds' melody.

1736. KOMMT, EILET, UND LAUFET (EASTER ORATORIO), for solo voices, chorus, and orchestra

In 1725, Bach wrote a cantata, *Entfliehet, verschwindet, entweicht, ihr Sorgen* (which was lost to the world until 1942). In 1736, Bach used the same music for a new German text suitable for Easter. The story of the Resurrection was here told in rhymed madrigal verses—the action advanced by the recitatives; the emotional content stressed by the arias. The Easter episode tells about the two Marys come early in the morning to the sepulchre only to find the tomb empty.

This is the only one of Bach's so-called oratorios that deserves that designation. Others are merely a stringing together of cantatas, as was the case with the *Christmas Oratorio* (see above). But the *Easter Oratorio* follows the oratorio form as established by the Italians.

The work opens, not with one, but with two instrumental sections. The first is a brilliant Sinfonia in D major, which, with trumpets and timpani, sets the mood of joy and celebration dominating the entire composition. This is followed by a more introspective Adagio in the relative minor key. A melody for oboe over a dotted rhythm in the strings describes the suffering of Jesus before the Resurrection. The narrative proper begins with the duet of Peter and John expressing their joy in learning of Christ's resurrection ("Kommt, eilet, und laufet"). Ten lyrical sections follow. Most memorable for their expressive melodic content are Peter's exquisite lullaby, "Sanfte soll mein Todeskummer nur ein Schlummer" and Mary Magdalene's exquisite air, "Saget, saget, mir geschwinde." The oratorio ends with a resounding hymn of glory to the Lord in "Preis und Dank."

1742. ARIA MIT 30 VERABENDERUNGEN (GOLDBERG VARIATIONS), for clavier.

It may come as a shock to some music lovers to discover that the Goldberg Variations—one of the most monumental creations for the piano in variation form—was written to serve as a mild musical tranquillizer or soporific. But this is fact, not fiction. Count Kayserling, Russian ambassador at the court of Dresden, suffered from insomnia. To help him relax before bedtime, his chamber musician, Johann Gottlieb Goldberg, played him soothing music. It was for just such a performance that Count Kayserling commissioned Bach to prepare for him a piece of music that would be "soft and yet a little gay." Apparently, Bach filled the bill successfully; the Count presented him with a golden goblet filled with a hundred louis d'or.

The air that precedes the variations—and upon which they are based—is a sedate and reflective sixteen-measure sarabande-type melody divided into two eight-bar periods. Thirty variations follow, not all of them directly based on the opening air; many are derived from the sequences of harmonies supporting the main melody. While most of the variations have a gentle pastoral quality, others (like the fourth and fifth) are animated and at times even joyful, and some are even playful (the fourth). Still others are majestic (twelfth), or introspective (thirteenth), or delicate (seventeenth), or full of splendor (sixteenth and twenty-eighth). To Wanda Landowska, the twenty-fifth variation is "the supreme pearl of the necklace, the black pearl; the reflections are somber, and the unrest romantic." The twenty-ninth and thirtieth variations carry the work to a climactic point, after which the opening aria returns to conclude the music as it had begun, in a serene mood.

1747. DAS MUSIKALISCHE OPFER (MUSICAL OFFERING), contrapuntal compositions for instruments.

In 1747, Bach visited the court of Frederick II in Berlin, where his son, Carl Philipp Emanuel, was then employed. The appearance of the master caused quite a stir at court. The king welcomed him with considerable ceremony. On one occasion during the visit, Bach asked the king for a fugal subject which, when given, was forthwith elaborated extemporaneously by Bach into a fully realized three-part fugue. Then feeling that this theme was unsuitable for such a treatment, Bach proceeded to extemporize a six-part fugue on one of his own subjects. Later on, Bach wrote down the three-part fugue on the king's theme and his own six-part fugue. From this point, he went on to use the king's theme as material for a sonata for flute, violin, and thorough bass, and for ten instrumental canons. He later issued this entire work as the *Musical Offering,* dedicating it to Frederick II. It proved Bach's last chamber-music work, and the only one he himself had published. Though Bach left the choice of instruments up to the performers themselves, there is reason to believe that he intended his canons to be played by an instrumental ensemble and the sonata by a trio comprising a transverse flute, violin, and continuo.

The *Musical Offering* consists of a dozen one-movement compositions and a four-movement sonata. All are in the key of C minor; all are in the polyphonic style. The work opens with a three-part fugue and continues with five canons. The heart of the work is a trio sonata (I. Allegro. II. Largo. III. Andante. IV. Allegro). After that, five more canons are heard. The entire work ends with a six-part fugue, which in the description of Hans T. David, has "a solemn intensity and abundant beauty that make it excel even among Bach's own instrumental works. Thus it forms the overwhelming finale of a work which demonstrates the flawless craftsmanship as well as the essential profundity of Bach's art."

c. 1750. COMPOSITIONS FOR ORGAN:

Prelude and Fugue in E-flat major, "St. Anne"; Prelude and Fugue in C major; Prelude and Fugue in E minor, "Wedge."

Though the majority of Bach's most celebrated works for the organ came while he was employed in Weimar, several masterworks were created in Leipzig. Of these, the Prelude and Fugue in E-flat major, found in the third part of the *Clavieruebung,* is among the most notable. Here is how C. Hubert Parry described it: "[It] is indeed massive and dignified, but unusually harmonic and melodious in style. . . . It was certainly written under Italian influences and contains many traces of the Italian concerto type in passages which suggest alternations of tutti and soli."

The fugue is known as "St. Anne" because its subject resembles the opening phrase of the St. Anne tune popular in churches in Bach's time. To Albert Schweitzer, the three distinct sections of the fugue, all on the same subject, are a "symbol of the Trinity." Schweitzer explains: "The same theme recurs in three connected fugues, but each time with another personality. The first fugue is calm and majestic, with an absolutely uniform movement throughout; in the second, the theme seems to be disguised and is only occasionally recognizable in its true shape, as if to suggest the divine assumption of an earthly form; in the third, it is transformed into rushing sixteenth-notes, as if the Pentecostal wind were coming roaring from the Heaven."

Arnold Schoenberg is among those who made orchestral transcriptions of the E-flat major Prelude and Fugue; Frederick Stock is another. Busoni transcribed it for the piano.

The Prelude in the Prelude and Fugue in C major has for the most part a pastoral character; but dramatized episodes occur in the mounting sonorities and in the use of detached chords. A one-bar theme serves as the subject of the five-voice fugue.

The Prelude and Fugue in E minor, known as the "Wedge," is significant for its architectonic grandeur. The prelude is in the form of a rondo, its main theme making five appearances with various melodic and harmonic changes. The fugue, called the "Wedge," is more distinguished for its countersubject than for the subject. The latter, says Alec Robertson, "usurps the main interest of the fugal portion of the movement. The reason for the expression 'fugal portion' lies in the fact that Bach deserts his fugue after the expository section of fifty-nine bars and indulges in a hundred and twenty bars of a middle section based on a little theme . . . and a series of ascending scale passages."

c. 1750. CONCERTOS FOR TWO CLAVIERS AND ORCHESTRA:

No. 1, C minor. I. Allegro. II. Adagio. III. Allegro.

No. 2, C major. I. Allegro. II. Adagio ovvero Largo. III. Fuga.

In writing a concerto for two claviers and orchestra, Bach once again traveled in a new direction: A two-clavier concerto with orchestra was unknown before Bach. Bach wrote two such works, probably during his Leipzig period. (A third is an arrangement of his celebrated D minor Concerto for two violins.)

Hans T. David describes the first movement of the C minor Concerto as "elegiac . . . but . . . full of vigor and intensity." The use of an echo effect in the ritornello is "one of the many original traits found in the score." In the second movement, an Adagio in E-flat major "accompanies the fine lines of the solo instruments with strings playing pizzicato throughout." The finale "has almost the character of a rustic dance."

The first movement of the C major Concerto, says David, "established almost entirely by means of thematic differentiations the contrast between a ritornello and solo episodes." The beautiful slow movement, a siciliano, is for the two solo instruments without accompaniment. The finale is one of the rare instances in which Bach uses the fugal form within a concerto.

"The first exposition," David explains, "is entrusted to the solo instrument" with the first tutti parts entering "only after the sixth entrance of the four-measure theme, opening an exposition of three more entrances."

1749–1750. DIE KUNST DER FUGE (THE ART OF THE FUGUE), for unspecified instruments.

In the dusk of his life, the greatest master the fugue has known set out to demonstrate the full extent of his technical and creative resources. He completed one of the most ambitious, one of the most grandiose fugal projects every attempted. Taking a single subject in D minor, Bach subjected it to every possible treatment and method provided by the fugal technique. The result was a set of sixteen fugues, two canons, two fugues for two claviers, and a final uncompleted fugue. Only the composer's death kept him from bringing the giant venture to its final resolution. As his son, Carl Philipp Emanuel, noted, in the last fugue, "where the name Bach had been brought in as a countersubject, the composer died." This fugue stops at the 239th bar. It has since become a custom, in performances of *The Art of the Fugue,* to conclude this work with a presentation of a chorale prelude Bach had dictated just before his death.

Except for the two fugues for two claviers, Bach gave no clue as to what instrument he had in mind, nor did he provide an indication of dynamics or tempo. It is more than probable that Bach had no intention of having the work performed publicly, wanting it to serve as a manual of instruction on ways and means of constructing canons and fugues. It is also not altogether certain that Bach himself gave the work the name by which it is now identified.

The first edition appeared a year after Bach's death. Since at that time the world of music considered the fugue and the polyphonic technique as obsolete, it paid no attention whatsoever to the publication. A second edition came out in 1752. Only thirty copies were sold within a four-year period; in the end, the copper plates were disposed of for their value as metal.

It was many years before the world came to realize that *The Art of the Fugue* is not just a theoretical treatise, nor just a tour de force, but music of "unaccountable power," as John N. Burk once described it, "wherein each complexity resolves and unfolds naturally, easily, inevitably—and even spontaneously. The imagination has free play in episodic invention as if unaware of constricting bounds." Today the work is performed most often on harpsichord or piano. But numerous transcriptions offer it to us in other media as well. It has been adapted for orchestra by Wolfgang Graeser, Hans T. David, Hermann Diener, and Paul Graener, among others; for string quartet, by Roy Harris in collaboration with M. D. Herter Norton; for organ solo, by E. Power Biggs; for two pianos, by Erwin Schwebsh.

In his program notes for the Boston Symphony Orchestra, John N. Burk explains: "The music was theoretical in concept and presentation. It is significant that Bach did not call each number a fugue but a contrapunctus (counterpoint). The parts (usually four) are written in open score, each voice on a separate staff, fo that the contrapuntal texture stands out clearly to the eye. The pattern is the thing."

Hans T. David has provided a valuable bird's-eye view of this vast project: "(1) two fugues on the subject and two on its inversion; (2) three fugues: (a) the subject in notes of the same value; (b) the subject in diminution; (c) the subject in diminution and augmentation; (3) two fugues, two double fugues; (4) two triple fugues; (5) four "mirror" fugues; (6) unfinished triple fugue which if terminated should have been a quadruple fugue. (It is in this subject that the theme on the name 'Bach' appears as countersubject.) Aside from these groups there are four canons." Mr. David concludes: "The principal subject appears in myriad forms and transformations, by means of enlargements, contractions, passing notes, skips, inversions, extensions, rhythmic alterations and shifts, and other applications of the variations principle."

—— THE WISE AND FOOLISH VIRGINS, ballet suite for orchestra, arranged by Sir William Walton from the music of Johann Sebastian Bach.

The Wise and Foolish Virgins is a ballet produced in 1940 at Sadler's Wells in London under the direction of Constant Lambert. The scenario was based on the parable of the Wise and Foolish Virgins as recounted in the twenty-fifth chapter of St. Matthew. Sir William Walton derived his ballet score from various Bach compositions. The production was described by a reviewer for the London *Musical Times* as "a masque-like presentation . . . delicately poised between the spiritual and the actual." The ballet suite, adapted from the score, consists of five sections. The first is the initial chorus from the church cantata, No. 99, *Was Gott tut.* This is followed by the chorale from *The Passion According to St. Matthew,* "Lord, Hear My Longing." The third movement is a tenor aria from the church cantata, No. 85, *Ich bin ein guter Hirt* ("Seht, was die Liebe tut!"). The opening chorus of the church cantata, No. 26, *Ach wie fluechtig,* and "Schafe koennen sicher weiden" from secular cantata No. 208, *Was mir behagt,* conclude the suite.

GEORGE FRIDERIC HANDEL 1685–1759

Though Handel's best concerti grossi and orchestral suites is music of uncommon distinction, and though he filled his solo concerti and sonatas with the most infectious ideas, he is essentially a dramatic and not an instrumental composer. He gained his fame through operas—his immortality, through oratorios. But whether he wrote oratorios or operas, he was a man of the theater, whose greatest creations, as Winton Dean wrote, are notable for their "breadth of human sympathy, love of pageantry, manipulation of contrasts on however large or small a scale, the first-time response to stimuli, whether presented by a situation, a verbal image or a musical idea, the ability to project himself into any mood at short notice without losing formal balance, the eye for the sudden patch of color that transforms the commonplace into the sublime, and the constant subordination of logical design to immediate effect—of what looks right to what sounds right."

When the phrase "Handelian style" is summoned, it usually connotes the nobility and grandeur of his oratorio choruses. But Handel strummed on more strings than one. He could be vividly pictorial and descriptive, contemplative and introspective, religious and spiritual, and often surpassingly tender. That last trait—tenderness—is something that Philip Hale singles out for special attention. "This giant of music could express a tenderness known only to him and Mozart, for Schubert with all his melodic wealth and sensitiveness could fall at times into sentimentalism, and Schumann's intimate confessions were sometimes whispered. Handel in his tenderness was always manly." Then Hale adds: "No one approached him in his sublimely solemn moments. Few composers, if there is anyone, have been able to produce such pathetic or sublime effects by simple means, by a few chords even. He was one of the greatest melodists. His fugal pages seldom seem labored; they are distinguished by amazing vitality and spontaneity. In his slow movements, his instrumental airs, there is a peculiar dignity, a peculiar serenity, and a direct appeal that we find in no other composer."

Of Handel's many operas only parts remain—arias of surpassing beauty, radiance, majesty, tenderness, humanity, or sublimity. These are representative: "Care selve" from *Atalanta* (1736); "Alma mia" from *Floridante* (1721); "V'adoro, pupille" from *Giulio Cesare* (1724); "La Speranza è giunto in porto" from *Ottone* (1732); "Vanne sorella ingratia" and "Sommi dei" from *Radamisto* (1720); "Lascia ch'io pianga" from *Rinaldo* (1711); "Dove sei" from *Rodelinda* (1725); "O Sleep, Why Dost Thou Leave Me?" and "Wher'er You Walk" from *Semele* (1734); "Ombra mai fu" (the famous *Largo* in instrumental transcriptions) from *Serse* (1738); "Non lo dirò col labbro" from *Tolomeo* (1728). It is for the sake of such wondrous lyrical pages as these that some of Handel's operas are today occasionally revived. Unfortunately, in writing for the stage, Handel adhered so rigidly to the conventions of opera seria as established by Alessandro Scarlatti and his Neapolitan school, that few of his operas as a whole carry conviction or dramatic interest for present-day audiences. For, as C. E. Abdy Williams noted, Handel was essentially "a man of his own times. He made no effort to advance the art; he simply took the forms he found ready-made and adorned them with all the beauty and solidity he was capable of producing, which far surpassed the operatic efforts of his contemporaries. He did not anticipate future developments; his effort was to attract his own public by the best possible art he could give them." Basically, Handel's operas, as far as the twentieth century is concerned, are a "storehouse of hundreds of splendid arias, inexhaustible treasure of noble songs, all stamped with the hallmark of the same genius, and yet endlessly varied."

Handel's instrumental music belongs to the Baroque era. Some of it is touched with his genius. But most of it, like his operas, conform to rather than rise above the existing formulas and methods of his age. In structure and style, many of Handel's instrumental works fail to give warning of the new classical age soon to dawn in music.

But in his oratorios, Handel was the genius *in excelsis,* and it is primarily through his oratorios that he won and held his exalted place in music history. Here he combined the dramatic and vocal resources he had perfected in his operas, with religious and spiritual values and the noblest and purest musical inspiration of which he was capable. In writing for the chorus, he married nobility of style to the fullest resources of polyphonic technique. His oratorios represent sacred dramas of monumental design, spoken with a language exalted and compassionate, tender and powerful, contemplative and vividly pictorial. He expanded the dramatic, aesthetic, and structural possibilities of the oratorio form to such proportions that all such works that had preceded him lose stature in comparison, while those that followed him generally appear to be imitations.

Many and varied are the attractions of his greatest oratorios, but as Anthony Lewis notes, perhaps the one quality that sets then apart from other oratorios is their "titanic strength, strength that is more majestic for its capacity to be gentle without weakness, expressive without loss of sinew. Breadth and fundamental power are of its very essence, and it has the enduring quality of the truly monumental."

George Frideric Handel (as he himself Anglicized his name) was born in Halle, Saxony, on February 23, 1685. His basic music study took place in his native city with Friedrich Zachau. Handel was only twelve when he officiated as assistant organist at the Halle Cathedral and completed several ambitious works, including motets and sonatas. For a brief period, he attended the University with the intention of becoming a lawyer. But he soon discarded this plan and went on to Hamburg to begin a career as musician. There he was employed as violinist in the orchestra of the Hamburg Opera and wrote his first two operas—*Almira* and *Nero*—produced in Hamburg in 1705. He left Hamburg in 1706 to embark on a tour of Italy, where he wrote a few more operas and his first two oratorios. Performances of these works, and his remarkable virtuosity on both the organ and the harpsichord, made him famous throughout Italy. In 1710, Handel was appointed Kapellmeister at the court of the Elector of Hanover. One year after that, he paid his first visit to London, where he scored a major success with *Rinaldo,* an opera produced at the Haymarket Theater on February 24, 1711. In 1712, he took a second leave of absence from his Hanover post to revisit England. The triumphs of *Il Pastor fido* in 1712 and *Teseo* in 1713 finally convinced him to stay in England for good. In 1713, he received an annuity from the English court which a year after that was doubled; in 1716, he was in the royal entourage that visited Hamburg; and at about this time, he was engaged as music master to the royal family.

From 1717 to 1720, Handel was employed as Kapellmeister to the Duke of Chandos in Cannons, near London. In 1720, he was appointed director of the Royal Academy of Music in London, recently founded to present Italian operas. Beginning with *Radamisto,* on April 27, 1720, Handel wrote a succession of operas for that theater, which made him the most highly esteemed composer in England. But he also made enemies who resented him because he was dictatorial, boorish, and disagreeable. To dim some of the luster of Handel's popularity, these enemies invited Giovanni Bononcini (1670–1755), one of Italy's most successful composers, to visit England and help produce some of his operas. A lively rivalry ensued in London between Handel and Bononcini, from which Handel emerged victorious. But other forces were gathering to bring about Handel's decline. English audiences, weary of the ritual and set patterns of Italian opera, were now beginning to direct their enthusiasm to the ballad opera, in which John Gay and Pepusch had scored a triumph with *The Beggar's Opera* in 1728. The deficits mounted at the Royal Academy of Music until that theater was forced to close down. On several occasions Handel tried to woo his opera public back but with so little success that, not only was he dragged to the brink of financial ruin, but also his health and spirit became shattered.

Having written his first "English" oratorio in 1732 (*Esther*), and having followed this work with several more oratorios, including *Saul* and *Israel in Egypt,* Handel now decided to concentrate his enormous energies and creative powers on the oratorio after 1741. A number of masterworks followed, which Arnold Schering regards as the greatest single epoch in oratorio history: the *Messiah, Judas Maccabaeus, Solomon, Theodora,* and *Jephtha.* With these works, Handel's creative genius soared to new heights, while he reassumed his former exalted station in English music.

Handel was working on his last oratorio, *Jephtha,* in 1751, when he discovered that his sight was beginning to fail. Blindness followed. But that did not keep him from giving concerts on the organ or directing performances of his oratorios. Handel made his last public appearance on April 6, 1759, when he directed the *Messiah.* Eight days after that, he died in London, and was buried in Westminster Abbey.

1711. RINALDO, opera in three acts, with text by Giacomo Rossi, based on a sketch by Aaron Hill derived from Torquato Tasso. First performance: London, February 24, 1711.

Handel's first opera, *Almira,* was produced in Hamburg on January 8,

1705. Six years—and four operas—later, he paid his first visit to London when he forthwith established his fame on a solid basis with his most successful opera up to that time—*Rinaldo*. Handel completed his score in two weeks' time (using some material he had written earlier). *Rinaldo* took London by storm. It was given fifteen times between February and June, always to capacity houses. "The *Rinaldo* tunes swept with swift insidiousness," says Newman Flower, "To all drawing rooms. To drinking dens. Years afterwards Pepusch used some of them for his *Beggar's Opera*. They paraphrased them. They danced to them." And there was good reason for such contagious popularity. "The notes of *Rinaldo*," continues Flower, "carried in them all of Handel's surging youth, all his mentality, fresh and unspoiled. The work came at a time when his whole soul was in tune with his task. . . . *Rinaldo* was a masterpiece, and it reshaped the whole fabric of London music at the time."

Nevertheless, *Rinaldo,* like other Handel operas, followed meekly in the footsteps of his Italian predecessors and contemporaries. It struck no new paths. Handel was partial to librettos in which the main characters were heroes from history or mythology; in which the story was often set into motion by women disguised as men and vice versa, and by sorcerers or sorceresses working their evil magic. The voice, particulatly the solo voice, was the spine of the musical fabric—with particular attention paid to the virtuosity of the castrato. Recitatives, both the secco and the accompagnato varieties, narrated the main facts of the story. Da capo arias commented on what was taking place. Little use was made of choral or ensemble episodes. The orchestra was confined mainly to the overture, to ballet sequences, and to ritornelli which helped to emphasize the emotional content of the arias.

It was a rigid formula. Into it, however, Handel poured a flood of melodic beauty. Almirena's air "Lascia ch'io pianga" is a page of incomparable majesty; the airs of Armida ("Ah crudel") and Rinaldo ("Cara sposa") are hardly less wondrous. The battle music from this score was utilized by Sir Thomas Beecham for his ballet music to *The Origin of Design* (see below).

The hero of the opera is a young knight in love with Almirena. It is the time of the Crusades. But Rinaldo is being pursued by the sorceress, Armida. She imprisons Almirena in an enchanted garden. Rinaldo comes to the rescue of his beloved. Then, having taken the sorceress as prisoner, he is able to effect her conversion to Christianity.

1717. WATER MUSIC, suite for orchestra, arranged by Sir Hamilton Harty. I. Overture. II. Air. III. Bourree. IV. Hornpipe. V. Andante. VI. Finale: allegro deciso.

In 1717, there took place a royal pageant on the Thames River in London. The royal family, and members of the nobility, floated on barges up and down the river. The trip was accompanied all the way by special music written for that occasion, and directed, by Handel. This music—consisting of all kinds of dances, airs, and fanfares—so delighted the king that he requested the orchestra to repeat all the numbers three times.

Legend would have us believe that this music was responsible for bringing about a reconciliation between Handel and the king. This story would have us believe that when the king had been the Elector of Hanover, and Handel had been his Kapellmeister, the employer became enraged at Handel's prolonged absence in London. Thus, when the Elector mounted the throne of England as George I, he was supposed to have refused to have any further traffic with his one-time Kapellmeister—that is, until Handel was restored to his favor through the writing of the *Water Music*. Facts, however, give the lie to the legend. George I ascended the English throne in 1714. By the time the *Water Music* was written (1717), Handel had for some time been gainfully employed by the king as music master to the royal family. Besides, in 1716. Handel had been a member of the king's entourage during a royal visit to Hanover. Finally, it was the king who had asked Handel to write the music for the aquatic pageant.

When the *Water Music* was published in 1741, it consisted of some twenty-five pieces. Only some of these had been done for the 1717 pageant, the others being written both before and after that year. In any event, as most often heard today either in performance or recordings, the *Water Music* is given in an arrangement and modern orchestration by Sir Hamilton Harty—a suite made up of six movements. An Overture in the French style, with brilliant fanfares, precedes a melodious air in the style of an English folk song. Two lively dances follow, a bourree and a hornpipe. A second beautiful lyrical page leads into a robust finale, in which effective use is made of trumpets, befitting the pomp and ceremony of the royal pageant.

c. 1720. 6 CONCERTI GROSSI, for orchestra, op. 3: I. B-flat major. II. B-flat major. III. G major. IV. F major. V. D minor. VI. D major.

Different authorities place the writing of the opus 3 concerti grossi at different periods of Handel's life. In his *History of Music,* Sir John Hawkins maintained they were written in 1733 for the marriage ceremonies of Princess Anne and the Prince of Orange. Chrysander was of another mind, insisting that some of these concertos had been written while Handel was still employed as Kapellmeister in Hanover. But Samuel Arnold, who published this set in 1797, placed them in or about the year of 1720 while Handel was in Cannons, and this is the period accepted today by most Handel authorities.

Handel had been stimulated into writing his opus 3, his first concerti grossi, through his admiration for similar works by Corelli, which he had encountered in Rome in or about 1706. But there is little imitation here. Continually we encounter instrumental and solo combinations unusual for the concerto grosso, the solo combinations sometimes changing from one movement to the next. A new symphonic breadth was brought to the concertino passages. On the other hand, the modern solo concerto is anticipated in some of the solo passages and cadenzas (as in the Allegro movement of the sixth concerto). A departure from Corelli's Baroque traditions can be found in the extraordinary invention and freedom of structure of some of Handel's free fantasia sections (the Maestoso from the fifth concerto being a case in point).

Time and again in opus 3 we come across music that Handel used in other compositions. The fugues of the third and fifth concertos are carry-overs from earlier clavier compositions. Parts of the fourth and fifth concertos are also found as overtures to *Amadigi* (1715) and *Ottone* (1723).

The oboe plays a prominent role in all six concertos. In the first concerto, there are two oboes, sometimes playing in thirds, sometimes doubling the first violins. This work also calls for two cembalo parts, one for the solo instruments, the other for the ripieno. This is the only work in the set in three movements (I. Allegro maestoso. II. Andante con moto. III. Allegro).

The second concerto in B-flat major, is one of the most interesting of the group (I. Vivace. II. Largo. III. Allegro. IV. Menuetto. V. Gavotte). The strong-fibered first movement, in the style of a sarabande, features a theme with octave leaps. A stately three-measure introduction precedes the lyrical second movement, where a solo oboe appears with a haunting melody set against broken chords. The third movement is a double fugue, while the last two movements are graceful eighteenth-century dances.

The five-movement structure reappears in the third and fifth concertos; there are four movements in the fourth concerto, and only two in the sixth.

1720. THE HARMONIOUS BLACKSMITH, for harpsichord.

The title "Harmonious Blacksmith" is not an invention by the composer himself, nor is there anything in this music suggesting a blacksmith—harmonious or otherwise. A myth has been fabricated saying Handel, stimulated by the rhythm of the struck anvil, invented the basic tune while seeking refuge from a storm in a blacksmith's shop. This is sheer fiction. In or about 1822, a publisher in Bath, England, issued this music under the title of *Harmonious Blacksmith,* having concocted this name through the circumstance that a Bath blacksmith often hummed the Handel tune and thus was often identified as the "harmonious blacksmith." Actually, this composition—one of Handel's most popular for the keyboard—comes out of a larger work, though it is often played independently of the other movements. The larger work is the Suite No. 5 in E major (*Suites des pièces pour clavecin*), Handel's first published instrumental composition. The *Harmonious Blacksmith* is in the form of theme and variations. The theme is a pleasing eight-bar melody in two parts.

1720. ACIS AND GALATEA, masque (or serenata) for vocal quartet, chorus, and orchestra.

Acis and Galatea has been variously identified as a masque, serenata, cantata, and at times even as an oratorio. Since it is dramatic music based on a mythological subject; since it has no action to speak of; and since it employs dance as well as song, it conforms most closely to the English masque (even though in Handel's own day the work was advertised as a "serenata"). Handel wrote it during his period of employment in Cannons for the Duke of Chandos, where it was introduced in 1721. (An earlier Handel pastoral on the same subject, *Aci, Galatea e Polifemo,* produced in Naples in 1708, has an altogether different score.) For the next quarter of a century, *Acis and Galatea* received some notable revivals, including a few presentations in 1723 at the Royal Academy of Music, for which Handel interpolated some new numbers. On this occasion an announcement explained that there would be "no action on the stage, but the scene will represent in a picturesque manner a rural prospect with rocks, groves, fountains, and grottos, amongst which will be disposed a chorus of nymphs and shepherds, the habits, and every other decoration, suited to the subject."

Most of the text is the work of John Gay, but parts are by Dryden and Pope. Its source is the seventh fable in the thirteenth book of the *Metamorphoses,* which tells about Acis, a shepherd, who is crushed by the monster Polypheme and is transformed by his beloved Galatea, a shepherdess, into a fountain. It is an idyllic theme for which Handel created a score, which, starting with its overture, is mostly pastoral in mood; which, as Herbert Weinstock once wrote, "throbs with sunlight, sweet passion and terror."

There are thirty musical numbers in all, most of them in the da capo aria form. Six choruses—often closely knit with the solo voices—include the lustrous opening, "Oh, the pleasures of the plains"; the sparkling chant, "Happy We," which closes the first section; the electrifying opening chorus of the second part, "Wretched Lovers"; and the tender admonition of the shepherds and their swains, "Galatea, Dry Thy Tears," with which the masque ends.

These are some of the notable airs: by Acis, "Love in Her Eyes Sits Playing," "Love Sounds the Alarm," and "Where Shall I Seek?"; "As When the Dove Laments Her Love" by Galatea; and Polypheme's air, "O Ruddier Than the Cherry", probably the most popular number in the entire score.

1724. GIULIO CESARE IN EGITTO (JULIUS CAESAR IN EGYPT), opera in three acts, with text by Niccolò Francesco Haym. First performance: London, February 20, 1724.

Giulio Cesare was Handel's fifth opera after *Radamisto* had so triumphantly ushered in his regime as director of the Royal Academy of Music in 1720. Enjoying uncommon success, *Giulio Cesare* was given fourteen performances in its first two months, and enjoyed quite a number of revivals in Handel's lifetime. It has also received attention in the twentieth century both in concert versions and on the stage. In July 1952, it received a memorable performance in the picturesque setting of the Teatro Grande in the ruins of Pompeii, with a cast headed by Renata Tebaldi and Cesare Siepi. In 1956–1957, it was magnificently mounted at La Scala in Milan, Giulietta Simionato and Nicola Rossi-Lemeni assuming the principal roles. In 1959, it was one of four Handel operas produced in Halle commemorating the bicentenary of the composer's death. The American Opera Society produced the work in New York on November 18, 1958.

Giulio Cesare survives by virtue of the lofty inspirations of its greatest pages. These include Caesar's magnificent airs, "Alma den gran Pompeo" and "Dall' ondoso periglio"; and those of Cleopatra, "Voi, che mie fide ancelle" and "V'adoro, pupille." Herbert Weinstock points out, in addition, that the instrumentation of this opera is "intensely expressive," particularly in Handel's use of four horns to enrich the orchestral sound. The "Battle Music" from this opera was incorporated by Sir Thomas Beecham in his ballet score, *The Gods Go A-begging* (see below).

The opera opens with the arrival of Julius Caesar in Egypt as a conquering hero. As a token of this victory, Caesar is presented with the head of the defeated Pompey, the latter having been murdered by Ptolemy, Cleopatra's brother. Caesar is shocked at this gift, denounces the bearer, and later expresses his grief at Pompey's tomb. Cleopatra, rival of Caesar for the Egyptian throne, summons all her irresistible feminine wiles to win his love. She arranges a magnificent feast, during which she sings to him seductively. Caesar, mistaking Cleopatra for Lydia—Cleopatra's handmaiden to whom he had become powerfully attracted—proposes marriage. But Cleopatra reveals her true identity when the news in brought her that an avenging mob is seeking the conqueror's head. Caesar is forced to flee, as Cleopatra prays for his safety. But Caesar manages to return to Egypt in triumph. Now hopelessly victimized by Cleopatra's beauty, Caesar crowns her queen. Caesar and Cleopatra exchange ardent vows of love as the people sing their praises.

1725. RODELINDA, opera in three acts, with text by Niccolò Francesco Haym, based on a libretto by Antonio Salvi. First performance: London, February 13, 1725.

Rodelinda is one of Handel's finest operas; like *Giulio Cesare,* it has enjoyed a number of important revivals in the twentieth century. *Rodelinda* helped bring about a Handel revival, or renaissance, in Germany between the two world wars, after successful presentations at Goettingen (in a German translation) in 1930. On May 1931, it was given in English at Smith College, at Northampton, Massachusetts. In 1939, it was presented at Old Vic in London. An excellent performance was given by the Handel Opera Society at Sadler's Wells in London in 1959 with Joan Sutherland in the title role.

In writing *Rodelinda,* Handel hoped it would bolster his then sagging fortunes at the Royal Academy of Music, which was about to close shop after six years of successful activity. To bring his audiences into his theater with *Rodelinda,* Handel scoured all Europe for the best available singers;

among those he acquired were Francesca Cuzzoni, Giuseppi Boschi, and the highly favored castrato, Senesino. But when *Rodelinda* was first performed, neither the singers nor the music caused half the stir that did the brown silk gown trimmed with silver worn by Mme. Cuzzoni. That gown forthwith launched a new vogue in women's wear in London for brown and silver colors.

The heroine, Rodelinda, is a Lombardian queen deserted by her husband, King Betriarch. The king had been exiled by the tyrant Griswold, who had usurped the throne. When the king makes a secret return to his realm, he overhears Griswold making advances to Rodelinda, threatening her that, if she did not yield, he would kill her son, Flavius. With the help of his sister, Hadwig, King Betriarch manages to cause the downfall of the tyrant and to return in triumph to his wife and his throne.

One of the exalted moments in this opera comes in the first act with the king's aria, "Dove sei? Amato bene." Upon his secret return home, the king has come upon his own tombstone in the castle cemetery; he then sings this beautiful air to his wife, whom he has not yet seen. Equally appealing are the king's dramatic accompanied recitative, "Pompe vane di morte"; Grimaldo's moving air, "Fatto inferno," in which R. A. Streatfeild finds anticipations of Beethoven's *Fidelio*; and Rodelinda's song of springtime, "Mio caro bene."

1735. ALCINA, opera in three acts, with text probably by Antonio Marchi, based on Ariosto's *Orlando Furioso*. First performance: London, April 16, 1735.

Alcina was written at a time when the composer was wracked with pain through rheumatism, and his spirits depressed by recent failures of his operas. Nevertheless, this music reveals nothing of Handel's sufferings. Light in style, infectious in mood, it is to Newman Flower the "most exquisite" of Handel's stage works in a less serious or ambitious style. Its ballet music reveals the composer "in his richest mood." Ruggiero's air, "Verdi prati," is one of Handel's finest melodic pages, even though the castrato Carestini did not look upon it with favor and sang it under protest. Alcina's air, "Ombre palide" (in which she invokes the supernatural spirits) and the ballets of Pleasant and Bad Dreams that follow, are also on a lofty plane. In addition, Herbert Weinstock notes that the first scene in Alcina's palace "intermingles choral passages and dances in a powerful suggestive pattern that Gluck was to adopt." An orchestral suite made up of ballet episodes from this opera is sometimes heard at symphony concerts and has been recorded.

Alcina is a sorceress who has lured Ruggiero from his betrothed, Bradamante. Disguised as the boy, Ricciardo, Bradamante sets forth to find her lover, and locates him on a magic island. A clap of thunder brings Alcina's palace to full view. Inside, Alcina entertains her guests with festive ceremony and elaborate ballets. When Bradamante comes upon Ruggiero, she finds he has forgotten her completely. But the spell that has thus far seized Ruggiero is broken through the power of a magic ring. Despite Alcina's incantations, in which she summons the help of the spirits of the underworld, Ruggiero recognizes Bradamante and returns to her, fleeing with her from Alcina's island.

1736–1739. ALEXANDER'S FEAST, ode for soloists, chorus, and orchestra.

ODE FOR ST. CECILIA'S DAY, for soloists, chorus, and orchestra.

From the time of Purcell and John Blow (1648–1708), the practice had been established in London to honor St. Cecilia's Day on November 22 with musical performances. St. Cecilia, of course, was the patron saint of music. Poems were written to St. Cecilia by Dryden, Congreve, and Pope among others, some set to music by various composers including Purcell, Blow, and Handel. The Dryden poem in praise of St. Cecilia—*Alexander's Feast,* or *The Power of Music* (1697)—was set by Handel twice, first in *Alexander's Feast* in 1736, and again in *Ode for St. Cecilia's Day* in 1739. The Dryden poem had also been used by other composers, among them Jeremiah Clarke (c. 1637–1707) and Giovanni Battista Draghi (seventeenth century).

With *Alexander's Feast* Handel enjoyed one of his greatest successes during his middle years. "The grandeur of his music," says Newman Flower, "the majestic choruses, reflective of all the pomp and richness of the story, the beautiful words of Dryden . . . all these circumstances bore upward to success." The first performance, at Covent Garden on February 19, 1736, was a gala event. The London *Post* reported: "There never was upon the like occasion so numerous and splendid an audience at any theater in London, there being at least thirteen hundred persons present." The audience was most enthusiastic, the applause being "such as had seldom been heard in London."

Two of the more familiar airs from this score are "War Is Toil and Trouble" for tenor and "Revenge, Timotheus Cries" for bass.

Even more impressive musically than *Alexander's Feast* is the *Ode for St. Cecilia's Day,* completed in 1739, and introduced in London that year on St. Cecilia's Day. Though Handel lifted some of his musical ideas from two harpsichord suites by the Austrian composer, Gottlieb Muffat (1690–1770)—including the magnificent fugue with which the ode ends—Handelian alchemy could turn base metal into gold. Muffat was a competent craftsman and a master of the Baroque style; but he was incapable of lifting his own material to such noble elevation as Handel was able to do in this *Ode.*

The *Ode* has twelve sections, opening with an overture, and concluding with a giant fugue. The first vocal number is the tenor recitative, "From Harmony, From Heavenly Harmony," with its vivid portrayal of natural phenomena. A powerful chorus then leads to the lovely soprano aria, "What Passion Cannot Music Raise," in which Jubel's lyre is represented by a solo cello. A tenor aria with chorus, "The Trumpet's Loud Clangors," makes an intentional quotation from Purcell's *King Arthur*. A march for orchestra precedes four arias that are shared by soprano and tenor alternately. "The Soft Compelling Flute" for soprano uses flute and lute as suggested in he text; in the tenor aria, "Sharp Violins Proclaim," effective use is made of detached violin playing. The soprano recitative, "But Bright Cecilia," brings on an air for soprano and chorus, "As from the Power of Sacred Lays," which in turn precedes the concluding fugue.

1738. SAUL, oratorio for solo voices, chorus, and orchestra.

By 1738, Handel had come to the grim realization that his career as an opera composer was coming to an end. The recently introduced *Serse* (April 15, 1738)—the opera that contains the wonderful air, "Ombra mai fu," which has become even more famous in its instrumental transcriptions under the title of *Largo*—had been a fiasco. Before that season ended, the King's Theater was forced to close down. The truth of the matter was that the London music public was weary of Italian operas, and of Handel's operas. It was now rallying to the more popular form of stage entertainment known as the ballad opera. Handel realized sadly that no longer could he turn defeat into victory, as he had done in the past, unless he redirected his prodigious gifts and energies into different channels. He was not unaware of the fact that he had exhausted all his creative potentials in opera, that he had nothing more to contribute through that medium. It was at this juncture that he went back to the oratorio, only to find renewed strength and a revitalized inspiration, and at the same time to get a new lease on fame.

The oratorio was, of course, no new medium for Handel in 1738. As far back as 1708, in Italy, he had written two oratorios: *La Resurrezione* and *Il Trionfo del tempo e del disinganno*. Not until a quarter of a century later did he write another oratorio.

A masque he had written while working for the Duke of Chandos—*Haman and Mordecai*—had been revived in London in 1732 at a private performance given by children in costumes and with scenery. The Bishop of London raised vehement objections, maintaining it was sacrilegious to dramatize the Bible; further performances were forbidden. Eager to get *Haman and Mordecai* heard again, Handel side-stepped the Bishop's interdiction by asking Samuel Humphreys to expand the masque libretto into a large-scale text that could be performed at concerts devoid of stage paraphernalia. The new work was named *Esther*. It was Handel's first "English" oratorio. Performed for the first time on May 2, 1732, *Esther* proved such a triumph that four days later the royal family attended a second presentation.

Handel's second English oratorio was *Deborah* in 1733. His full giant strides came five years after that, with two masterworks, *Saul* and *Israel in Egypt*.

Saul was begun on July 23, 1738, and completed two months later. The text was the work of Charles Jennens, the first time that the collaborators of the *Messiah* joined forces. For his libretto, Jennens remained faithful to the Bible story of David and Saul, beginning with David's victory over Goliath, and the jealousy of Saul at seeing the Israelites acclaim David as a hero, and ending with the death of Saul and Jonathan.

Beyond its affecting arias and stirring choruses, *Saul* is memorable for two familiar orchestral excerpts. The first is an extraordinary four-part overture, one of the most spacious by Handel. It begins with an Allegro; proceeds on to a Largo in which the organ is heard in impressive solo passages; continues with an Allegro; and concludes with a Minuet. The second popular orchestral episode is the "Dead March." This is an eloquent threnody following the announcement of the death of Saul and Jonathan. "The trumpets and trombones, with their sonorous pomp, and the wailing oboes and clarinets make an instrumental pageant which is the very apotheosis of grief." So wrote Felix Borowski. He continues: "The effect of the march is all the more remarkable when it is considered, in contradistinction to all other dirges, it is written in the major key."

The following are some of the remarkable vocal pages in the score: Jonathan's assurance to David he will never do him harm ("But Sooner Jordan's Stream I Swear"); Michael's stirring song, "No, Let the Guilty Tremble"; and David's poignant lament over the death of Jonathan, "In Sweetest Harmonies."

These are some of the more dramatic choruses: the opening hymn of the Israelite soldiers, "How Excellent Thy Name, O Lord"; the song of the Israelites in praise of David, "Welcome, Welcome, Mighty King"; and the powerful chorus that ends the oratorio.

1738. ISRAEL IN EGYPT, oratorio for solo voices, chorus, and orchestra.

Hardly was the ink dry on the *Saul* manuscript, when Handel embarked upon an even more monumental work—the oratorio, *Israel in Egypt*. He started only four days after he had put the final strokes on *Saul*, and completed it within twenty-seven days. In spite of such haste, *Israel in Egypt* remains one of the towering peaks in oratorio music, "the most gigantic effort ever made," as Romain Rolland once said.

Handel compiled his own text with excerpts from the Bible and the prayer-book version of the Psalms. Originally he named his work *Exodus,* and planned it as a cantata. This later became the second part of *Israel in Egypt*. But Handel soon realized that this material called for a larger design and greater scope than a cantata. He then decided to append to it another huge section, describing the dramatic events in Egypt preceding the exodus. In this first part, he related how the Israelites were enslaved in Egypt; how Moses emerged as their leader and deliverer; how plagues were inflicted by God on the Egyptians; how the Israelites passed out of Egypt and through the Red Sea. The second part, now called "Song of Moses," became for the most part a succession of hymns to the Lord and His might, and of songs of victory by the

Israelites. This section ends with an exultant song of triumph by Miriam ("Sing Ye, to the Lord"), supplemented by an eight-part chorus ending with the giant choral movement, "The Lord Shall Reign Forever and Ever."

Many of Handel's oratorios, though based on Biblical subjects, are essentially secular rather than religious, drawing copiously from Handel's experiences as a composer of operas. *Israel in Egypt* is no exception. Handel can be vividly pictorial and theatrical. The six sections in the first part of the oratorio describe the plagues with remarkable realism. All the resources of rhythm, harmony, and counterpoint are recruited to depict the rain of hail and stones, the fury of a storm, the buzzing of flies, the hopping of frogs, the descent of a thick darkness over the land, and the smiting of the first born.

Israel in Egypt is second in popularity only to the *Messiah* among Handel's oratorios. The two works are poles apart in style and mood and purpose. Where the *Messiah* is consistently devout, spiritual, and exalted, *Israel in Egypt* is dramatic to the point of being operatic. Where the *Messiah* divides its musical interest equally between the solo voices and the choruses, *Israel in Egypt* finds its most powerful utterances and its most elevated thought in the choral pages. The *Messiah* has an overture, while *Israel in Egypt* has none. The latter begins at once with the statement of the Narrator, "Now there arose a new king in Egypt who knew not Joseph." That Narrator is still another way in which *Israel in Egypt* differs from the *Messiah*. There is none in the latter, while in the former, he is used to tell the story through recitatives and to serve as a catalyzing agent.

The majesty and greatness of this oratorio lie mainly in the choruses: in expressive pages, such as "He Led Them Through the Deep," or "I Will Sing Unto the Lord," or "The People Shall Hear and Be Afraid"; in tranquil, at times pastoral, passages, such as "But for His People, He Led Them Forth Like Sheep." But there are also parts for individual voices that command interest; and the most significant of these is the ever popular martial duet for two basses, "The Lord Is a Man of War."

1739. 12 CONCERTI GROSSI, for orchestra, op. 6: I. G major. II. F major. III. E minor. IV. A minor. V. D major. VI. G minor. VII. B-flat major. VIII. C minor. IX. F major. X. D minor. XI. A major. XII. B minor.

On October 29, 1739, there appeared the following item in the London *Daily Post:* "This day are published proposals for printing by subscription with His Majesty's royal license and protection, Twelve Grand Concertos in seven parts, for four violins, a tenor, a violoncello, with a thorough bass for harpsichord. Composed by Mr. Handel. Price to subscribers two guineas. Ready to be delivered by April next. Subscriptions are taken by the author at his house in Brook Street, Hanover Square." The concertos appeared the following April, and soon thereafter were played at the Theater Royal in Lincoln's Inn Fields.

Together with Bach's Brandenburg Concertos (written twenty years earlier), these concerti grossi, op. 6, represent the outer posts of concerto-grosso writing. Here the concerto grosso achieves the ultimate in structural development and aesthetic significance. Handel wrote these masterworks with a flying pen. The entire set was completed in a single month (between September 29 and October 30 of 1739). Sometimes a concerto was written in one day, sometimes even at a single sitting. But one would be at a loss to detect haste in any of these works, so rich is each in musical ideas, so varied in emotional expression, so sure-handed in technique and structure.

The concerto-grosso method of alternating and combining the concertino and ripieno is employed here in the manner of Corelli and Vivaldi. But, as Winton Dean remarks, "the range of mood and design not only between different works but within the same work is wide. Plain melodic statements and technical feats of high virtuosity, rustic dances, and intimations of profound tragedy, grow together in a satisfying whole. Many of the basic ideas are commonplaces of the age. Subjected to Handel's characteristic rhythmic energy, which splits and recombines them in periods of irregular shape, they emerge in a fresh and personal light. Handel had the peculiar gift of transcending his models without hiding them. Corelli and Vivaldi here, like Scarlatti and Purcell elsewhere, are raised to the highest degree."

Where Bach generally used a three-movement structure for the *Brandenburg Concertos,* Handel resorted to from four to six movements. Some critics blame Handel for "oscillating between the suite and the sonata, with a glance towards the symphonic overture." But Romain Rolland is of a far different mind, finding this variety of structure an asset rather than a detriment. "For," Rolland says, "he does not seek to impose a uniform cast on his thoughts, but leaves it open to himself to fashion the form as he requires, and the framework varies accordingly, following his inclinations from day to day. The spontaneity of his thought . . . constitutes the great charm of these works. They are, in the works of Kretzschmar, grand impression pictures, translated into a form, at the same time precise and supple, in which the least change of emotion can make itself easily felt."

Concerto No. 6 in G minor is one of the most celebrated of the set. It is in five movements (I. Largo affettuoso. II. A tempo giusto. III. Musette: larghetto. IV. Allegro. V. Allegro). The first movement has some of the majesty of the nobler pages from the oratorios. The second, is a freely conceived fugue on a chromatic chord. The third movement, however, is the jewel of the work. It is a melancholy musette, which Rolland described as "one of the most delightful dreams of pastoral happiness. A whole day of poetic and capricious events gradually unrolls itself over the beautiful echoing refrain, then the movement slackens, nearly going to sleep, then presses forward again, acquiring a strong joyous rhythm, a pulsating dance of robust youth, full of bounding life." This is followed by two energetic Allegros, each exciting for its rhythmic drive.

Concerto No. 10 in D minor has four movements (I. Overture: allegro.

II Air: lento. III. Allegro. IV. Allegro moderato). The Overture is in the French style, the Allegro part being a three-voice fugue. The lyrical air that follows is presented first by the concertino in alternate passages, then by the concertino in conjunction with the ripieno. The Allegro that comes next is the longest movement in the work, with a robustness and an infectious spirit that spill over into the concluding Allegro moderato.

Concerto No. 12 in B minor has five movements (I. Largo. II. Allegro. III. Aria larghetto e piano. IV. Largo. V. Allegro). The first movement is in a sober mood, with the concertino and the ripieno alternating continually. The solo instruments are given considerable attention in the second movement, often in themes with bold leaps in the melody. An enchanting two-part aria is embroidered with several imaginative variations in the third part. Another slow section follows. Then a six-bar Largo for harpsichord leads into the finale, a four-part fugue.

1740. L'ALLEGRO, IL PENSEROSO ED IL MODERATO, for tenor, soprano, bass, chorus, and orchestra.

In 1740, Charles Jennens offered Handel a text, the first two parts of which were adapted from Milton, while the third part, *Il Moderato,* was a hodgepodge of his own invention. Having recently suffered a major defeat in the opera house, Handel hoped to recoup both his fortunes and his reputation with a work slighter in texture and lighter in tone than his operas. He decided to set Jennens's text, uneven though it was.

L'Allegro, extolling pleasure, is represented by a tenor; Il Penseroso, which dwells on the rewards of melancholy, by a soprano. The work begins, without the preliminaries of an overture, with a vigorous recitative in which L'Allegro banishes melancholy and in which Il Penseroso replies with a denunciation of "vain, deluding joys." Both L'Allegro and Il Penseroso then embark on lilting airs. The former presents "Come, Come, Thou Goddess Fair," while the latter offers "Divinest Melancholy." Now comes one of the most delightful pages in the score, and perhaps one of the merriest to come from Handel. This is a sunny passage aglow with laughter in which L'Allegro summons a nymph to bring on "jest and youthful jollity," after which he launches into a minuet-type song, "Come and Trip It as You Go."

These are some of the highlights in the pages that follow: Il Penseroso's brilliant song accompanied by the voice of the nightingale, "Sweet Bird that Shun'st the Noise of Folly," and the air that follows immediately, "Oft on a Plat of Rising Ground," to which a far-sounding curfew provides a background; and L'Allegro's descriptive "Populous Cities Please Me Then," evoking images of knights and their ladies.

1742. MESSIAH, oratorio for solo voices, chorus, and orchestra.

The *Messiah* is Handel's supreme achievement, and an epic in oratorio literature without a rival. Its writing came at a time when the composer's fortunes and spirits were at their lowest ebb. His last opera—*Deidamia,* in 1741—had been a fiasco. Handel needed no further proof that he was through as a composer for the stage. However, the oratorio—the medium that had begun to absorb his interest and energies since 1732—still failed to win him back his audiences. Both *Saul* and *Israel in Egypt* in 1738 made little impression. It seemed that, even as an oratorio composer, Handel was rejected. Never before in his life had Handel's career plunged to such depths.

Then, in 1741, Handel was invited to Dublin by the city's Lord Lieutenant, the Duke of Devonshire, and the directors of several charities. They wanted him to direct one of his compositions for charity. For this visit, Handel decided to write a new oratorio, utilizing a script prepared for him by Charles Jennens from the Scriptures.

Handel went to work with a dedication and a passion unique even for him. Aroused by religious ardor that had always smoldered deep within him, and inspired by an exaltation that was completely new, he wrote his music as if he were under some spell. The huge score took him only twenty-five days to complete. All the while he worked he refused to leave his house, and frequently did without food or sleep. "He was," as Stefan Zweig described him in *Tides of Fortune,* "as if intoxicated. When he marched up and down the room, beating time with his hand and singing at the top of his voice, his eyes looked distraught; if someone addressed him he started, and his answers were vague and disconnected. . . . Time and space during these feverish days were obliterated as far as Handel was concerned; day and night he kept hard at his task, living wholly in the realm where rhythm and tone reigned supreme." He felt at one with the Maker. When he completed the 'Hallelujah Chorus,' he told his servant: "I did think I did see all Heaven before me, and the great God Himself." And when his giant task was over, and all his music was on paper, he remarked simply: "I think God has visited me."

The première of the *Messiah* was anticipated with a good deal of excitement. Handel had never really lost any of his popularity in Dublin, nor had his formidable stature been dwarfed by his recent failures in London. A new work by Handel, therefore, was an artistic event to which all Dublin rallied. In addition, Dublin knew that the city's finest musical resources had been placed under Handel's direction: an excellent orchestra; two choirs from leading Cathedrals; and such outstanding vocal soloists as Mesdames Avolio and Cibber.

Long before the day of the concert, all seats at the Music Hall on Fishamble Street were gone. A preliminary performance (the last general rehearsal, open to the public) was held on April 8, 1742. Then on April 13, the official première took place. "Words are wanting," reported the *Faulkner Journal,* "to express the exquisite delight it afforded the admiring, crowded audience." Thus the *Messiah* began its fabulous career with a success of the first magnitude.

Unfortunately, it cannot be said that this triumph was repeated when the *Messiah* was heard in London for the first time, on March 23, 1743. Handel in 1743 was considered passé, and the public had lost interest in him. Others objected to a prose text, and still others maintained that to perform a work like this in a concert hall was a desecration. But one part of the *Messiah* did create an overpowering impact—the "Hallelujah Chorus." King George II, who was present, was so moved that involuntarily he rose in his seat and stood throughout the "Hallelujah" section. When the audience saw its king standing, it also rose to its feet. In this way, a tradition was started that has prevailed up to the present day—for the audience to stand during the singing of the "Hallelujah Chorus."

The great popularity of the *Messiah* in London began in 1749 when Handel led a benefit performance. This time the audience reaction was most enthusiastic. During the next nine years, Handel conducted the *Messiah* in London annually for the benefit of the Foundling Hospital; by the end of that decade, the *Messiah* had established itself solidly and permanently as a prime favorite with English music audiences. Since that time, *Messiah* has been played continually, not only in London, but throughout the world. It is undoubtedly the most frequently performed oratorio ever written, as well as the most highly esteemed.

"*Messiah,*" wrote C. E. Abdy Williams, "towers above all the other oratorios of Handel's in the estimation of the English people. The highest ideals of the Christian religion are here set forth and enhanced by music which in its strength, its sincerity, and its entire fitness to the subject appeals to learned and unlearned with equal force. The massive choruses, the powerful solos and recitatives, in which the highest skill of composer and performer are called forth, drive home to every hearer the truths of religion more powerfully than the finest oratory can do."

The *Messiah* is in three parts. In the first, the coming of the Messiah is prophesied. After a French-type overture, which begins with slow and stately measures and progresses toward a vigorous fugue, there come the tenor recitative, "Comfort Ye," a joyous air for soprano, "Every Valley Shall be Exalted," and the first radiant chorus, "And the Glory of the Lord." This is followed by an incandescent melody for contralto, "O Thou That Tellest Good Tidings to Zion" and two powerful, at times sublime, choruses, "And the Glory of the Lord" and "For Unto Us a Child is Born." Now we hear the poignant "Pastoral Symphony" for muted strings in which the Nativity is described. From this level, the music soars to heights of eloquence with the soprano air, "Rejoice Greatly, O Daughter of Zion," the devout aria for soprano, "He Shall Feed His Flock," and the sensitive chorus, "His Yoke Is Easy."

The second part tells about the suffering and death of Christ. This section opens with the exultant chorus, "Behold the Lamb of God," followed by the poignant one, "Surely He Hath Borne Our Grief." Two memorable arias come next, one for alto ("He Was Despised") and the other for soprano ("How Beautiful Are Thy Feet"). At this point, the summit of the whole oratorio rises like the Matterhorn above the surrounding geography—the "Hallelujah Chorus." "The glorious choral effects," wrote César Saerchinger, "the stirring polyphony, now simultaneous, now imitative, reflect a potency and spiritual elevation that perhaps will never be surpassed."

The third part not only maintains this exalted level of inspiration, but almost, in certain pages, touches new heights. This part opens with the wonderful soprano aria, "I Know That My Redeemer Liveth" and ends with the incandescent three-part chorus, "Worthy Is the Lamb."

C. E. Abdy Williams explains how Handel's treatment of the Passion story differs from that of Bach. "In Bach's Passions, the Evangelist narrates the events, which are emphasized by the chorus, who represent Jews, apostles, and so forth, and the Savior Himself speaks. The music for the soloists and congregation represents the emotion that is aroused by the events narrated. In *Messiah,* the congregation takes no part, the soloists are impersonal, and they and the chorus carry on the narrative by means of passages of Scripture bearing the story. The Passion is a religious service; *Messiah* is a sermon."

1743. DETTINGEN TE DEUM, for solo voices, mixed chorus, and orchestra.

This ceremonial work, completed in thirteen days, helped celebrate the victory of the English over the French at Dettingen during the War of Austrian Succession. The Te Deum was first performed for the royal family at the St. Paul's Cathedral as a hymn of thanksgiving, on November 27, 1743. Always bearing in mind the ceremonial purpose of his composition, Handel made effective use of high-sounding trumpets. "One striking feature here," says Werner Menke, "is the frequent climbing of instrumental parts so that now the second trumpet rises above the first, now the third above the second." Another unusual aspect of Handel's orchestration is the way in which bassoons are used as part of the continuo rather than as independent voices.

For his text, Handel went to the Hymn of St. Ambrose of Milan in the Book of Common Prayer. The Te Deum is divided into eighteen sections, opening with the rhapsodic chorus, "We Praise Thee, O God." An affecting alto solo with chorus follows, "All the Earth Does Worship Thee." After that come two stirring choruses, "To Thee All Angels Cry Aloud" in three parts, and the paean, "To Thee Cherubim and Seraphim Continually Do Cry." "The Glorious Company of the Apostles that Praise Thee," which follows, is for vocal quartet and chorus. In the ensuing two parts, the baritone is prominent, the first time heard with chorus in "Thou Art the King of Glory," and the second time as a solo in "When Thou Tookest Upon Thee to Deliver Man." Two more choruses, a trio for alto, tenor, and baritone, and a brilliant trumpet fanfare are now given. In the next eight sections, we get four consecutive choruses. The work ends exaltedly with the air for alto with chorus, "Oh Lord in Thee Have I Trusted."

Much has been written about Handel's continual tendency to borrow ideas from other composers. There is much in the *Te Deum* that apparently was lifted from a *Te Deum* by an obscure composer-priest named Francesco Antonio Urio (possibly as many as ten numbers!). But Herbert Weinstock remarks: "If it was in truth by Urio, Handel was a plagiarist to about the same extent as Shakespeare, and with about the same results as to the fate of his sources, and the magnificent use he made of them."

1744. SEMELE, a secular choral work, with text by William Congreve, adapted possibly by Newburgh Hamilton. First performance: Covent Garden, London, February 10, 1744.

Semele is neither an oratorio nor an opera, but a mixture of the two. Herbert Weinstock describes it as an "actionless opera." It has been heard both in concert version (à la oratorio) and in staged presentations (like operas). Some authorities prefer to describe it as a "pastoral."

Like so many other Handel operas or pastorals, *Semele* is best known to us through parts rather than as a whole. These include two of the most moving airs Handel ever wrote: Semele's song, "Oh, Sleep Why Dost Thou Leave Me?." and that of Jupiter, "Where'er You Walk." This score also boasts a remarkable chorus in "Now Love That Everlasting Joy" and Juno's haunting air, "Above Measure."

The heroine, Semele, daughter of King Cadmus of Thebes, is about to celebrate her marriage to Prince Athmas, even though she is in love with Jupiter. She goes through a period of agonizing doubt. A peal of thunder suddenly destroys the Temple of Juno, and an eagle is despatched by Jupiter to lift Semele to heaven. This enrages Juno, who is bent on destroying Semele. Juno now induces Semele to ask Jupiter to reveal himself to her in his divine rather than assumed human form. When Jupiter visits Semele, she extracts from him a promise to fulfil any of her wishes. Semele now expresses the wish to see Jupiter in his bodily shape. Suddenly Jupiter becomes transformed into a burst of lightning and fire in which Semele is destroyed. Back in Thebes, the people mourn her death. The high priestess prophecies that her ashes shall raise the phoenix, which will prove mightier than love and thus will banish all sorrow.

1746. JUDAS MACCABAEUS, oratorio for solo voices, chorus, and orchestra.

Judas Maccabaeus completed what the *Messiah* had begun—to reestablish Handel's fame, to restore him to the good graces of royalty and nobility, to make him a favorite of the musical public. Still another group was won over to Handel's side through *Judas*—the Jewish community of London. Based on the exploits of a Biblical hero, *Judas Maccabaeus* provided for England an all too rare favorable representation of a Jew

Frederic, the Prince of Wales, commissioned Handel to write *Judas Maccabaeus* in celebration of the victorious return of the Duke of Cumberland, following his military triumph at Culloden, Scotland. Handel's text was prepared by Reverend Thomas Morell, based on the first book of the Maccabees and the twelfth book of Josephus's *Antiquities of the Jews*. First given at Covent Garden, on April 1, 1747, *Judas Maccabaeus* was such a huge success that it had to be repeated seven times that season. Several years later, Handel made important interpolations into his score: the chorus of the Israelite maidens and youths hailing Judas, "See the Conquering Hero Comes," which Handel lifted from his oratorio *Joshua* (1748); and the chorus, "Sion Now Her Head Shall Raise," one of the greatest pieces of choral music, he was destined to write.

"See the Conquering Hero Comes" is the most famous single excerpt from the oratorio, and has become a favorite piece of music to help celebrate victories. Felix Borowski said of it: "It is very simple in construction, like many others of Handel's most effective numbers, and first sung as a three-part chorus, then as a duet and chorus of virgins, again by the full power of all voices, and gradually dies away in the form of an instrumental march."

Judas Maccabaeus is, of course, the central character of this oratorio. He is the Jewish military hero who, in the struggle of Israelites against Antiochus IV, won a decisive victory over the Syrians while winning religious freedom for his people. It is to commemorate his consecration of the Temple of Jerusalem in December of 165 B. C. that the Jews today celebrate the holiday of Chanukah.

The oratorio opens with the deeply moving chorus of the Israelites, "Mourn Ye Afflicted Children" and ends with an exultant "Hallelujah." In between come such grandiose choral pages as "Oh Father, Whose Almighty Power," "Fallen Is the Foe," and "Sing unto God." Among the more memorable solo vocal and ensemble numbers are the following: "How Vain Is Man" for tenor; the duet for soprano and alto, "Come Ever Smiling Liberty"; the moving prayer of the priest with which the third part of the oratorio opens, "Father of Heaven"; and Judas's unforgettable battle song, "Sound an Alarm."

1748. SOLOMON, oratorio for solo voices, chorus, and orchestra.

After *Judas Maccabaeus,* Hebraic characters from the Bible continued to interest Handel. In *Susanna* (1748), he described the Jewish captivity in Babylon. *Solomon,* which came hard on the heels of *Susanna,* was built around the personality of that celebrated Hebrew king. Both *Susanna* and *Solomon* were well received when first performed. *Solomon* was heard for the first time on March 17, 1749, after which it received three more performances. Significant revivals took place in London in 1836 and 1870. In our own time, magnificent presentations of this oratorio were given both by Sir Thomas Beecham and Sir Henry J. Wood, though with radical changes and modernizations.

The text of *Solomon* is by Thomas Morell. It has three parts, each intended to provide a different facet of Solomon: "The Piety of Solomon," "The Wisdom of Solomon," and "The Splendor of Solomon." Like so many other Handel oratorios, *Solomon* is more secular than religious. "Indeed," says Sir Thomas Beecham, "in hardly another of his great oratorios does the purely religious side play so modest a part."

Rosa Newmarch has carefully singled out those parts of the oratorio pointing to the variety of Handel's style and the wide gamut of his expression. His uncommon dramatic power is demonstrated in the scene between the two mothers. His "sure and penetrating art of portraiture" is illustrated by Solomon himself and the Queen of Sheba. Handel's "wonderful mastery of choral writing" is proved by such pages as "With Pious Heart," "From the Censer Curling Rise," "Shake the Dome," and "Praise the Lord." The chorus, "May No Rash Intruder," is to Newmarch "idyllic in sentiment, and echoing the nightingale's song, and the remarkable tone picture, 'Thus Rolling Surges,' is equally perfect in a less monumental manner. The lovely solo, 'Bless'd the Day,' which has a pastoral intermezzo between the first and final vocal parts, is so fresh and lively that, as Leichtentritt says, it might have been signed by Purcell."

An orchestral excerpt also demands our interest and attention. This is the remarkable sinfonia highlighting a duet of oboes that accompanies the entrance of the Queen of Sheba. It is known as "The Arrival of the Queen of Sheba."

1749. THE ROYAL FIREWORKS MUSIC, suite for orchestra, arranged by Sir Hamilton Harty. I. Overture. II. Largo alla siciliana. III. Allegro. IV. Bourree. V. Minuets I and II.

When a peace treaty was signed at Aix-la-Chapelle, in 1748, to end the conflict between France and England, a huge celebration was arranged at Green Park, London, for April 27, 1749. Accident, however, marred the proceedings. A fire, started by some misguided fireworks, almost created a panic when the people went scurrying for safety. The structure built for that event was completely destroyed.

The festivities opened with an overture which, in Handel's original orchestration, required the services of twenty-four oboes, twelve bassoons, nine trumpets, nine horns, one contrabassoon, three pairs of timpani, and a now obsolete instrument in the cornet family then known as a "serpent." After the overture came a royal salute from one hundred and one brass cannon. Then were heard various pieces by Handel (all of them originally scored for winds, though subsequently Handel also arranged them for full orchestra). These items symbolized different aspects of the celebration.

It was only after Handel's score had been completely performed that the pandemonium was let loose, Handel's *Royal Fireworks Music* was heard again (this time under more favorable auspices) on May 27, 1749. At that time a much smaller band played it in the chapel of the Foundling Hospital during a benefit concert attended by the Prince of Wales, and an audience numbering over a thousand.

When the *Royal Fireworks* is performed today, it is usually in the arrangement and orchestration prepared by Sir Hamilton Harty. In this suite, a brief overture precedes a siciliano movement entitled "Le Paix," celebrating the peace. A third movement, called "La Réjouissance," is a festive number in the spirit of rejoicing that marked the happy occasion. Three charming little dance movements follow, a bourree, and two courtly minuets.

c. *1750.* CONCERTOS FOR ORGAN AND ORCHESTRA:

No. 10, D minor. I. Adagio. II. Allegro, III. Adagio. IV. Allegro.

No. 13, F major, "The Cuckoo and the Nightingale." I. Larghetto. II. Allegro. III. Adagio. IV. Larghetto. V. Allegro.

Concerto in D major, adapted by Sir Hamilton Harty. I. Adagio. II. Allegro moderato. III. Allegro con brio.

Among Handel's various concertos for solo instruments and orchestra are three fine sets for organ and orchestra. The first volume (opus 4) was written in or about 1735, and published in 1738. The composer suggested that these compositions might be played by either the organ or harpsichord. In the second set (no opus number)—completed in 1739 and published in 1749—Handel suggested the harp as an alternate to the organ as solo instrument. But the third set, written between 1740 and 1751 (and published as opus 7 in 1761) is specifically designated by the composer as exclusively for organ and orchestra.

The tenth concerto in the last set (opus 7) is one of the most popular in this group. The first movement is stately music, robust in rhythm, and in its thematic material elevated in thought. Another vigorous movement comes after that. An emotional Adagio then allows the organ to take the limelight with an eloquent improvisation. The finale abounds with vital statements in which the virtuosity of the performer is frequently exploited.

Independent of the three sets described above, there exists another popular organ concerto known as "The Cuckoo and the Nightingale." Its name comes from the fact that in the second movement the calls of these birds are simulated. In this concerto, Handel utilizes material from earlier compositions. In the first and last movements, we get reminders of subjects from his Trio

Sonatas Nos. 5 and 6, and from one of the movements of his Concerto Grosso, op. 6, no. 9.

The frequently heard Organ Concerto in D major is an adaptation by Sir Hamilton Harty made in 1933 from a work he found in the Handel Gesellschaft edition, vol. 47.

—— THE GODS GO A-BEGGING, ballet suite for orchestra, arranged from Handel's music by Sir Thomas Beecham.

THE GREAT ELOPEMENT, ballet suite for orchestra, arranged from Handel's music by Sir Thomas Beecham.

THE ORIGIN OF DESIGN, ballet suite for orchestra, arranged from Handel's music by Sir Thomas Beecham.

Several important orchestral suites have been arranged by twentieth-century musicians from Handel's compositions and have become an integral part of the symphonic repertory. Three of these were prepared by Sir Thomas Beecham for ballets.

The *Gods Go A-Begging* is a one-act ballet with choreography by George Balanchine and book by Sobeka (pseudonym for Boris Kochno). The first performance took place in London on July 16, 1928. The scenario is an evocation of a Watteau-like "fête-champêtre," relating a love episode between a servant maid and a shepherd in a forest glade. After they have aroused the displeasure of the maid's employers, the humble lovers reveal themselves as divinities. The orchestral suite adapted from this score comprises an Introduction, Minuet, Hornpipe, Musette, Ensemble, Dream, Tamburino, Gavotte, and Bourree. This material was derived mainly from Handel's operas *Terpischore* and *Alcina;* the Hornpipe comes out of the Concerto Grosso, op. 6, no. 7.

Sir Thomas Beecham himself prepared the plot and scenario of *The Great Elopement,* which he introduced over the facilities of the American Broadcasting Company on April 7, 1945. His description of the story is as follows: "The scene of the ballet is the city of Bath, in England, at that time—the second half of the eighteenth century—one of the most fashionable pleasure resorts in Europe. The celebrated Beau Nash was the Master of Ceremonies, and the Director of Music was Thomas Linley, one of the most popular composers of the day. His daughter, Elizabeth, a beautiful girl and an accomplished singer, is sought in marriage by a local squire. There appears upon the scene a brilliant young stranger, Richard Brinsley Sheridan, as yet unknown to fame, but the future author of *The Rivals* and *The School for Scandal.* The two young people fall in love to the chagrin of Linley. With the assistance of Beau Nash, the lovers elope to London." Beecham's ballet suite—consisting of eleven numbers—is derived from airs, choruses, and instrumental passages from Handel operas and secular choral works, *Il Pastor Fido, Rodrigo,* and *Il Parnasso in Festa.*

The Origin of Design is a ballet produced in London in 1932 by the Camargo Society. The concert suite comprises a Bourree, Rondeau, Gigue, Musette, Battle, and Finale, taken from various Handel operas, including *Ariodante, Terpischore, Rinaldo,* and *Giulio Cesare.*

JEAN-PHILIPPE RAMEAU 1683–1764

With Jean-Philippe Rameau, the golden age of French classical opera is at hand. Lully was the founder of French opera, and in essence Rameau's operas were an extention of Lully, and not a departure. This fact makes all the more ridiculous the bitter war waged against Rameau by the Lully faction, which came to regard Rameau as an arch enemy, the negation of what Lully stood for and accomplished. This opposition started with Rameau's first opera, *Hippolyte et Aricie* in 1733. It continued unabated through the productions of such Rameau masterworks as *Castor et Pollux* and *Dardanus*. Originally, the opposition of the Lullists sprang from a fear that Rameau might displace their own favorite composer in public esteem. But in time, the Lullists fought Rameau with specious issues: that Rameau's preoccupation with harmony and orchestration was a denial of Lully's principles; that Rameau's lyricism and embellished vocalism were a reversion from French to Italian methods. In a lengthy introduction to his ballet-opera, *Les Indes galantes,* Rameau protested that he had only the highest admiration for Lully, that in his own operas he aspired to fulfil what Lully had begun. But even if we did not have Rameau's printed word for it, we do have his operas, each one of which is a step forward from the point where Lully had come to a stop, and along the same road.

It is quite true that in comparison with Lully before him, and Gluck after him, Rameau had some serious shortcomings as a musical dramatist. He was too easily satisfied with the mediocre texts provided him by his librettists; too ready to put to music verses that made a pretense at poetry but more often than not were just plain doggerel. Rameau always maintained that a good composer could set *anything* to music. He was incapable of endowing his characters with human qualities; for the most part, they remain stereotypes of classical figures. He was too often preoccupied with details, too often incapable of maintaining a dramatic flow, too often ready to use his plot as an excuse for elaborate scenes, ballets, and ceremonials not integral to the dramatic action.

Nevertheless, he did possess pronounced dramatic instincts in other areas, and a musical invention of an order far superior to Lully's. More than his eminent predecessor—indeed, more than any composer of opera who had preceded him—Rameau enriched harmony and orchestration, carrying over to the orchestra a dramatic impulse and a symphonic breadth it had heretofore not known. Rameau was particularly adept in representing through orchestral sound such natural phenomena as storms and earthquakes, and such scenes as country landscapes, sunrises, and flowing brooks. His arias had a soaring and poetic flight, often incomparable for nobility and grandeur. His recitatives were rich in dramatic interest and his monologues—a cross between the aria and the recitative—were the media for some of his most grandiose utterances. Of one of these monologues—that of Pollux in *Castor et Pollux*—Debussy said: "This magnificent air has so personal an accent, such novelty of construction that space and time are forgotten and Rameau seems our contemporary." To ballet music, Rameau brought an incomparable grace, together with a variety of rhythm and color. And to the chorus, he carried not only a majestic speech but also a clearly defined personality that often made it a significant protagonist in the play.

"Grandeur and pride of sentiment, sovereign pathos of expression, beauty of melody, of rhythm, of harmony, all combine to give his noble tragedies in music an irresistible emotional force," says Pierre Lalo, "and all is conveyed with sobriety and striking precision. Rameau knows better than anyone the value of brief and strong effects. No artist further emphasized passion with such succinctness, such distaste for overstatement. His work contains nothing that is overstressed, superfluous or inert; it is all action and all life. Neither the voice nor the orchestra betray dead weight or filling in. Every note, every color, every chord, every accent has its value, its necessity, its signification. This music, clear, rapid, proud, graceful without weakness, tragic without melodrama, says what it has to say quite simply; but says it with an accent so just and so penetrating that all moves directly to its conclusion, seizes at one time the mind and the heart."

The opposition of the Lullists to Rameau was only one of two major musical wars in which that master was involved. The second and even more virulent battle came from the proponents of the Italian tradition, and their spearhead was Pergolesi. In 1752, an Italian opera company presented Pergolesi's opera buffa, *La Serva padrona,* in Paris for the first time. The tremendous success of this little comic opera led to a cult in Paris proclaiming Pergolesi, and Italian methods, as the highest form of operatic art; and insisting that the classic French opera of Rameau, with its complexity, represented a step backwards. Among those who espoused the cause of the Italian opera were the Encyclopedists, among whom were Diderot and Rousseau. "The French airs are not airs at all," said Rousseau, "and the French recitative is not recitative." In *Le Neveu de Rameau,* Diderot wrote: "His theory of music which neither he nor anyone else will ever understand, and from which we have a number of operas where there is harmony, tag ends of songs, ideas that come apart, turmoils, flights, triumphs, upheavals, glorifications, murmurs, breath-taking victories, dance airs which never end and which, having buried the Florentine [Lully], will be buried by the Italian experts."

To propagandize his ideas about opera further, Rousseau wrote a little opera buffa of his own in the style of Pergolesi, calling it *Le Devin du village;* it was successfully produced in Paris in 1752.

But Rameau also had stout allies. The members of the Opéra orchestra (partly out of admiration for Rameau, partly out of nationalism) burned Rousseau in effigy. Voltaire exclaimed: "Rameau has made of music a new art." And the distinguished composer, André Campra (1660–1744) remarked prophetically: "This man will eclipse us all."

This war of words, of charges and countercharges, has since become known as "la guerre des bouffons." Its outcome was never really in doubt. Despite the opposition, Rameau's operas continued to flourish; and long before his death, the victory of his methods, ideals, and aesthetics was complete.

Jean-Philippe Rameau was born in Dijon, France, on September 25, 1683, the son of the organist of the Dijon Cathedral. As a boy, Rameau pursued music studies while receiving his academic education at the Jesuit College of Dijon. After a visit to Italy, where he first became acquainted with Italian opera, he assumed, in 1702, the post of organist at Clermont-Ferrand. In 1705, he settled in Paris, where he played the organ, studied musical theory with a passionate intensity, and in 1706, had published the first volume of his monumental *Pièces de clavecin.* He held various organ posts in Dijon and Lyons before assuming the job of church organist at Clermont-Ferrand, a position that he held for several years. There, in 1722, he issued *Le Traité de l'harmonie,* a theoretical treatise with which the modern science of harmony is established for the first time. A second volume, no less significant, appeared in Paris in 1726—*Le Nouveau système de musique théorique*. Meanwhile, in 1723, he returned to Paris, which he now made his home for the remainder of his life, and where, in 1726, he married Marie-Louise Mangot, a singer. In or about 1730, he acquired a powerful patron in Le Riche de la Poupelinière, who appointed him the music master of his household. Through the influence of la Poupelinière, and with Voltaire's encouragement, Rameau completed his first opera, *Hippolyte et Aricie,* produced at the Opéra on October 1, 1733. It was a failure, mainly due to the efforts of Lullists to discredit it. But they were ineffectual in stemming the tide of public approbation where Rameau's later operas were concerned, notably his ballet-opera *Les Indes galantes* in 1735, *Castor et Pollux* in 1737, *Dardanus* and *Les Fêtes d'Hébé* in 1739. In 1745, Rameau wrote *La Princesse de Navarre,* a comédie-ballet, to help celebrate the wedding of the Dauphin and the Infante Marie-Thérèse at Versailles. Soon after that, he was made composer of chamber music at court. Rameau died in Paris on September 12, 1764, having lived long enough to see the complete triumph of his operas and his ideals.

1706–1724. PIÈCES DE CLAVECIN, three sets of pieces for the harpsichord:

FIRST VOLUME: 1. Prelude. 2. Allemande. 3. Second Allemande. 4. Courante. 5. Gigue. 6. Sarabande. 7. Second Sarabande. 8. Vénitienne. 9. Gavotte. 10. Minuet.

SECOND VOLUME: 1. Menuet en rondeau. 2. Allemande. 3. Courante. 4. Gigue en rondeau. 5. Second Gigue en rondeau. 6. Le Rappel des oiseaux. 7. Rigaudon. 8. Second Rigaudon. 9. Double du deuxième rigaudon. 10. Musette en rondeau. 11. Tambourin. 12. La Villageoise. 13. Les Tendres plaintes. 14. Les Niais de Sologne. 15. Double de niais. 16. Second double de niais. 17. Les Soupirs. 18. La Joyeuse. 19. La Follette. 20. L'Entretien des muses. 21. Les Tourbillons. 22. Les Cyclopes. 23. Le Lardon. 24. La Boiteuse.

THIRD VOLUME (Nouvelle Suite de Pièces de Clavecin): 1. Allemande. 2. Courante. 3. Sarabande. 4. Les Trois mains. 5. Fanfarinette. 6. La Triomphante. 7. Gavotte. 8. Les Tricotets. 9. L'Indifférente. 10. Menuet. 11. Second Menuet. 12. La Poule. 13. Les Triolets. 14. Les Sauvages. 15. L'Enharmonique 16. L'Égyptienne. 17. La Dauphine.

Rameau published the first set of his pieces for harpsichord in 1706. A second set of twenty-four numbers followed in 1724. The date of a third set, comprising seventeen more compositions, is unknown.

Only Couperin, among Rameau's contemporaries, made a more historic contribution to the literature of French keyboard music than Rameau. Like Couperin, Rameau pieces are varied in style, mood, nuance, suggestion; they understand and cater to keyboard techniques. Many are dances (allemandes, courantes, gavottes, gigues, minuets, sarabandes). Some are descriptive pieces, others are mood pictures, still others reflections of emotional states. Some are outright realistic, and some are subtly suggestive.

Wilfrid Mellers explains the difference between Couperin and Rameau: "Rameau does not achieve in his keyboard music the close texture of Couperin's finest work. He is more harmonic, less linear in layout, more virtuoso and theatrical in treatment. It is more brilliant and more immediately emotional than Couperin's work; but it is not therefore more profound."

Then, while singling out some of the more distinguished or Rameau's pieces, Mellers adds: "Perhaps Rameau's very finest pieces, such as the superb A minor Allemande [no. 2 in the first set], and in a quieter vein, 'Les Tendres plaintes,' are an exception to this, having much of Couperin's dignity. But they are less characteristic of his work than an audaciously imaginative 'coloristic' piece like 'Le Rappel des oiseaux'; a grand Handelian piece like the Gavotte with variations, or the A major Sarabande [No. 7 in the first set]; or an expansive virtuoso piece such as 'Les Tourbillons,' 'Les Cyclopes' with its non-melodic Alberti bass, 'La Dauphine,' 'La Triomphante,' or the exciting rondeau, 'Les Niais de Sologne.' "

Besides those pieces mentioned above, these are of particular importance and interest: "La Poule," which Mellers calls a "genuine harpsichord piece in the classical Baroque tradition"; "Les Soupirs," on the one hand and "La Joyeuse" on the other, two expressive mood pictures; and the very popular "Tambourin."

1735. LES INDES GALANTES (THE INDIGO SUITORS), ballét-opera (ballét-héroïque) in prologue and four "entrées," with text by Louis Fuzelier. First performance: Paris Opéra, August 23, 1735.

Les Indes galantes is Rameau's third opera, coming just two years after he had made his bow in the theater with *Hippolyte et Aricie.* An elaborate spectacle involving storms, volcanos, festivals, and numerous ballet sequences, *Les Indes galantes* recounts four tales of love. Each takes place in a different and remote part of the world, and each is described in a different act, or "entrée." The first, called "Le Turc genereux" takes place in Turkey; the second, "Les Incas," in Peru; the third, "Les Fleurs," in Persia; and the last, "Les Sauvages," in a North American forest.

The overture opens with a stately introduction before progressing toward a lively fugal Allegro, whose subject and answer have broad intervallic leaps. The prologue (the only part of the opera using mythological subjects) presents Hebe, Love, and a chorus of shepherds in hymns, flag-waving and dancing. Here we find an outstanding vocal number in Love's beautiful air, "Ranimez vos flambeaux."

In the first "entrée," the Pasha Osman is in love with a French captive, Emilia, but he finally surrenders her to her lover, Valère, who has been washed upon the shores of Turkey. For this episode Rameau produced some remarkably effective storm music, equally picturesque music for a ballet of African slaves, and a dramatic chorus of terrified sailors.

The second "entrée" tells of the love affair between Phani, a member of the royal Incas race, and Don Carlos. Huascar, the high priest of the Sun, tries to frustrate them but fails. In this act, Rameau created some stunning realistic music descriptive of a sun-god festival and an eruption of a volcano, the latter with remarkable discords. In the third "entrée," on the other hand, it is the ballet music rather the descriptive pages that is most notable. The last act, in an American forest, involves an Indian girl, Zima, who is sought by a Frenchman and a Spanish nobleman but who prefers Adario, a native nobleman. Zima's air, "Dans ces bois l'amour vole" and an orchestral chaconne are of particular interest here.

"The opera-ballet, *Les Indes galantes,*" wrote Robert Stevenson in *Music before the Classic Era,* "contains some of his freshest music." For "beauty of line" Stevenson singles out Huascar's airs, "Clair flambeau du monde" and "Permettez, astre du jour." As an example "of entrancing color in orchestration" he cites the first of Zephyr's airs in the "entrée" entitled "Les Fleurs" and the accompaniment to the air, "Musettes, résonnez," which makes effective use of a bagpipe. "Huascar's self-immolation scene," continues Stevenson, "provides an example of what Rameau could do toward stirring up an orchestral typhoon. The use of the orchestra for massive tonal effects is also well illustrated in the passage sung by Zima. . . as she addresses her lover Adario in the last scene."

1737. CASTOR ET POLLUX (CASTOR AND POLLUX), tragedy with music, in five acts, with text by Pierre Joseph Justin Bernard. First performance: Paris Opéra, October 24, 1737.

The legend about the brothers, Castor and Pollux, comes out of Greek and Roman mythology. The death of Castor is mourned by the people of Sparta, and by his brother Pollux, and Pollux's beloved Telaire. Telaire prevails on Pollux to enlist the aid of the gods in bringing Castor back to life. The gods are willing, but only if Pollux stands ready to take Castor's place. Pollux is now torn between his sense of duty toward his brother and his love for Telaire. Duty wins out. Pollux descends into the infernal regions to substitute for his brother. For this act of self-sacrifice, Pollux is rewarded by being deified with his brother and placed in the heavens as a constellation.

The noble overture is in the style of Lully. A slow movement, characterized by dotted rhythms combined with arpeggio figures, leads into a rapid one in fugal style. The overture then blends into the prologue, which is for the most part remarkable for its choral writing. A prayer is sent up to Venus to return to earth and restore peace and happiness to the world. Cupid, in a song of unforgettable eloquence ("Plaisir, ramenez-vous, Venus, descends des cieux"), implores Venus to come down to earth. One of Rameau's characteristically effective descriptive pages for orchestra follows, as we trace Venus's descent in triplet quavers in the violins. The joy of the gods is then reflected in a series of dances—gavotte, minuet, tambourin.

The first act soars to the highest elevation of nobility in Telaire's moving air to Pollux, "Tristes apprêts" (probably the most celebrated single excerpt in the opera). But the funeral music for Castor is no less moving. In the second act, we get Pollux's deeply felt song, "Natur, amour," in which he is torn between love and duty. Here we find demonstrated Rameau's rare gift to make structure serve the purposes of the drama. The ternary form here utilized was favored by the Italians but generally avoided by Rameau. However, Rameau realized that the three-part structure was essential to emphasize Pollux's state of indecision: he must return to the problem that tortures him and with which his aria opens.

When Castor descends to the lower regions, and then visits the realm of the blessed spirits, we hear anticipations of Gluck's *Orfeo*. The vivid chorus of the demons, Castor's unforgettable song in the Elysian fields, and the dances of the infernal spirits can leave but small doubt where Gluck found both a model and an inspiration when he himself described Orfeo's visit to the underworld and to the heavenly fields.

Castor et Pollux ends in the kind of pageantry and display to which eighteenth-century operagoers were so partial. Here chorus and ballet play a prominent role. The repetition of the main theme of the overture (in the key of A major instead of G minor) points up the apotheosis of the brothers, and the mighty chaconne in the concluding ballet brings the opera to a striking culmination.

Writing a quarter of a century after Rameau's death, the venerable English historian, Charles Burney, found the dances in *Castor et Pollux* the parts that pleased him most. "The major minuet . . . is rich in harmony and graceful in melody. . . . In the chaconne, which is admirable, the measure is well marked and well accented. . . . More genius and invention appear in the dances of Rameau than elsewhere, because in them, there is a necessity for motion, measure, and symmetry of phrase. And it may with truth be said that nothing in Lully's operas was imitated or adopted by the rest of Europe but the style of his overtures, or in Rameau's but the dances."

A delightful orchestral suite was prepared by François Gevaert made up of some of these dances: Gavotte, Minuet, the first-act Tambourin, and the fourth-act Passepied. *Castor et Pollux* is Rameau's masterwork; it was also the most successful of his operas during his lifetime. It was mounted by the Opéra over two hundred and fifty times before 1785. It is still frequently given in Paris. In 1934, it was performed in an English translation in Oxford, England, and in 1935, it was acclaimed at the May Music Festival in Florence. There is no record of a performance in the United States.

1741. 5 PIÈCES DE CLAVECIN EN CONCERT, for harpsichord, violin (or flute), and viol (or second violin):

PREMIER CONCERT: I. La Coulicam. II. La Livri. III. Le Vésinet.

DEUXIÈME CONCERT: I. La Laborde. II. La Boucon. III. L'Agaçante. IV. Premier Menuet. V. Deuxième Menuet.

TROISIÈME CONCERT: I. La Poupelinière. II. La Timide. III. Deuxième Rondeau. IV. Premier Tambourin. V. Deuxième Tambourin en rondeau.

QUATRIÈME CONCERT: I. La Pantomine. II. L'Indiscrète. III. La Rameau.

CINQUIÈME CONCERT: I. La Forqueray. II. La Cupis. III. La Marais.

Rameau wrote five remarkable chamber-music works for the combination of harpsichord, violin (or flute), and viol (or second violin). The first, fourth, and fifth are in three movements; the second and third are in five. Some of these movements are in the dance forms of a minuet, rondeau, or tambourin. Some bear the names of people of whom it is a tonal portrait or to whom it is dedicated. The fifth *Concert* pays tribute to three distinguished French musicians: Antoine Forqueray (1671–1745), Jean-Baptiste Cupis (1711–1788), and Marin Marais (1656–1728). The fourth contains an autobiographical movement, gay music in dance style and rhythm. The third opens with homage to Rameau's patron, La Poupelinière. Some movements bear pictorial titles, providing clues to the descriptive purpose of the music. The second movement of the third *Concert* is called "La Timide," while the first two movements of the fourth are named "La Pantomime" and "L'Indiscrète."

All *Concerts*—the descriptive titles notwithstanding—are in the concertante style. Henri Prunières refers to some of them as "real classical concertos." The keyboard, explains Wilfrid Mellers, "is not a continuo part like that of Couperin's trio sonatas, not a piece of polyphonic writing like that of Bach's sonatas. The keyboard is treated as a virtuoso solo instrument in a way that suggests Haydn and Mozart's treatment of the combination of piano and strings."

The second *Concert,* in G major, is typical. The first two movements apparently pay tribute to two people. The first is elegant and cultured in style, while the other has a touch of melancholy. The third movement is a trifle called "Agaçante," or "Irritating." The harpsichord here engages the other instruments in light banter. The last two movements are graceful minuets.

FRANCESCO GEMINIANI 1687–1762

Geminiani took the torch of instrumental music from the hands of Corelli and kept the fires burning. He wrote concerti grossi and sonatas in which the structures, as previously used by Corelli, were enlarged and made more flexible; where the thematic material is more greatly varied; and where the orchestral colorations are enriched. Lawrence Gilman once noted two other important ways in which Geminiani differed from Corelli: in his "remarkable individuality in part writing (which foreshadows the forthcoming string quartet) and the importance given to the viola." Geminiani was also one of several early eighteenth-century masters to write orchestral compositions, other than concerti grossi, suite, or overture, with a recognizable symphonic texture and form.

Francesco Geminiani was born in Lucca, Italy, in 1687. He studied the violin first with Carlo Lonati in Milan, then with Corelli in Rome; he was also a pupil in composition of Alessandro Scarlatti. Geminiani achieved renown as a violin virtuoso by the time he came to England in 1714. There he prospered both as a concert performer and as a teacher. His first opus, a set of twelve violin sonatas, appeared in London in 1716. His second published work, issued some fifteen years after that, was a group of six concerti grossi. In 1733, Geminiani went to live in Dublin, where he opened up his own auditorium for public concerts, which for a number of years attracted large audiences. Three publications appeared between 1733 and 1739: a second set of six concerti grossi; a second volume of twelve violin sonatas; a set of six cello sonatas. In 1740, Geminiani returned to London, where for the next nine years he directed significant public concerts at Drury Lane. His opus 6 and opus 7 (twelve more concerti grossi) appeared in 1741 and 1746. From 1749 to 1755, he lived in Paris. He returned to Dublin in 1759, where he died on September 17, 1762. Besides his sonatas and concerti grossi, Geminiani produced symphonies, violin concertos, pieces for the harpsichord, and *The Art of Violin Playing,* the first published violin instruction book.

1733. CONCERTO GROSSO IN G MINOR, op. 3, no. 2. I. Spiritoso. II. Allegro. III. Andante. IV. Vivace.

The opus 3 set of concerti grossi is distinguished through their occasional exploitation of divided violas—an innovation in orchestral music in Geminiani's day. The first movement of the G minor Concerto has Handelian grandeur. A lively fugato follows. The slow movement emphasizes a soulful song that provides testimony to the composer's uncommon gift at melody. The finale is dominated by a lively dance tune with the character of an Italian tarantella.

—— SYMPHONY NO. 3 IN G MAJOR. I. Allegro. II. Andantino e grazioso. III. Allegro vivo.

Geminiani was one of the early masters of the symphony. The first movement of his Symphony in G major presents a robust theme for full orchestra, which eventually finds contrast in a secondary subject delicate in texture and feeling. This entire movement makes effective use of the concerto-grosso technique of alternating loud and soft passages, light and shade. In the slow movement, we find a spacious melody for muted strings accompanied by cembalo. There are two important themes in the finale, which has a semblance of a rondo form. Both are gentle and introspective.

GIUSEPPE TARTINI 1692–1770

Among Corelli's many successors in the art of playing the violin and of writing music for that instrument, Tartini was the most significant. He wrote some 150 violin concertos and a hundred violin sonatas in which the technique of violin performance made significant progress over that established by Corelli. At the same time, Tartini's thematic material reveals a deepening of thought and an enrichment of expression far beyond any realized by Corelli. Tartini's slow movements plumb emotional depths, and often betray an intensity and passion, never encountered in Corelli. Here is how one unidentified critic compared the two: "As a composer, Tartini combined the serenity and dignity of Corelli with an added grace and passion all his own, and his writing for the violin was technically more advanced and complicated than that of his predecessors. He contrived to infuse a variety of expression into his music lacking in the works of Corelli."

Giuseppe Tartini was born in Pirano, Istria, Italy, on April 8, 1692 to an affluent family. Though obviously musical from childhood he was first directed to theology, and after that to law. After attending the University of Padua for about three years he abandoned law for music, devoting himself passionately to the development of his violin technique. A secret marriage in 1713 to one of his pupils—Elisabetta Premazone—aroused the anger of her protector, Cardinal Giorgio Cornaro, who ordered Tartini's arrest. Tartini fled from Padua and found refuge in Assisi, where, still in 1713, he wrote his famous *Devil's Trill Sonata*. By 1726, he was able to return to Padua, where he established not only his reputation as one of the foremost violin virtuosos in Italy but also founded a violin school that achieved renown throughout Europe. He died in Padua on February 26, 1770.

1713–1734. SONATA IN G MINOR, "IL TRILLO DEL DIAVOLO" ("DEVIL'S TRILL SONATA"), for violin and piano. I. Larghetto. II. Grave. III. Allegro.

SONATA IN G MINOR, "DIDONE ABBANDONATA" ("DIDO ABANDONED"), for violin and piano, op. 1, no. 10. I. Andante. II. Presto. III. Allegro.

The unusual circumstances surrounding the composition of Tartini's most popular composition—the *Devil's Trill Sonata*—was described by the composer himself: "One night . . . I dreamed that I had made a compact with the devil, who promised to be at my service on all occasions. . . . Everything succeeded . . . . At last I thought I would offer my violin to the devil, in order to discover what kind of musician he was, when to my great astonishment I heard him play a solo so singularly beautiful and with such superior taste and precision that it surpassed all the music I had ever heard or conceived in the whole course of my life. I was so overcome with surprise and delight that I lost my power of breathing, and the violence of the sensation awoke me. Instantly I seized my violin in the hopes of remembering some portion of what I had heard, but in vain! The work which this dream suggested and which I wrote at the time is doubtless the best of my compositions. I call it the *Devil's Trill Sonata*."

The work, completed in 1713, is in three movements. The first is in two-part song form. A trill leads to the slow movement in which a stately melody unfolds. The finale is rhythmically spirited, its main melody graced by continual trills, the reason why the work acquired its name. Franz Liszt transcribed the sonata for piano. Many present-day violinists perform the work in an edition prepared by Fritz Kreisler.

The *Didone abbandonata Sonata* appears in Tartini's first opus, published in 1734. As the title reveals, the inspiration for this sonata came from the fourth book of Virgil's *The Aeneid,* which tells of the abandonment of Dido, Queen of Carthage, by Aeneas, the Trojan hero. Tartini, however, provided no specific program for his music. The first movement is bathed in melancholy and may be interpreted as Dido's grief. It is in the form of a theme and variations, the theme being a succinct two-measure phrase. The dramatic character of the second movement, and the rhythmically exciting music of the third may, if the listener so wishes, be explained as the Queen's aroused emotional states upon recovering from her grief. In the third movement, the main melody is a spirited dance tune.

—— CONCERTO IN D MINOR, for violin and orchestra. I. Allegro. II. Grave. III. Presto.

CONCERTO IN A MAJOR, for cello and orchestra. I. Allegro. II. Larghetto. III. Allegro assai.

The Violin Concerto in D minor is generally played in an edition prepared by Emilio Fante. The first movement opens with a two-part soulful melody for orchestra. The solo violin takes it over and embellishes upon it. In the slow movement, an aria-type melody soars from the violin over a continuo background. The vigorous finale is based entirely on a lively dance tune with which the movement opens.

The A major Cello Concerto has been edited for modern audiences by Oreste Ravenello. The program annotator for the Philadelphia Orchestra described the first movement as "brisk and cheerful, the solo instrument entering after a short introduction." The slow movement is "beautifully lyric and is written in the instrument's tenor range." The finale is "written with many embellishments (as are the first two movements) and presents figures in triplets." To the musicologist, Hans Joachim Moser, the embellishments in this finale suggest "a pretty ornament like the carved cupids of the Rococo period."

GIOVANNI BATTISTA PERGOLESI 1710–1736

To Pergolesi goes the distinction and the achievement of having been the first to establish the traditions that would govern the writing of opera buffa for more than a century. Pergolesi's *La*

Serva padrona is not the first comic opera ever written, as is sometimes loosely inferred or maintained. Comic characters had been used in serious operas long before Pergolesi, short comic scenes, "intermezzi," having been popular for many years. For a while these "intermezzi" were played during intermissions of serious operas to provide a change of pace and mood. These little comic scenes proved so popular that, in 1709, a special intimate theater was opened in Naples for them. Many important Neapolitan composers were now commissioned to write new "intermezzi." Among them were Nicola Logroscino (1698–1765), who is believed to have originated the "extended finale," with which opera-buffa composers closed each act.

Neapolitan composers had also written full-length comic operas before *La Serva padrona* had been produced. One of the most notable was *Il Trionfo dell' onore* in 1718 (see ALESSANDRO SCARLATTI). But comic opera is not necessarily opera buffa, and *Il Trionfo* was not an opera buffa.

Opera buffa was governed by certain conventions to which its composers adhered—and most of these conventions are found for the first time in *La Serva padrona*. Opera buffa liked to deal with everyday people in everyday settings, involved in everyday farcical episodes—in sharp contrast to opera seria, which favored mythological subjects, characters, and exploits. In opera buffa, scheming servants, cuckolds, deceived wives, were among the preferential stock of characters. A busybody is the deus ex machina to set the story moving; he is the conniver responsible for the deceptions, mock marriages, and mock legal practices in which the main characters become involved. Mistaken identity is a popular device for complicating the plot; disguises, a favorite piece of machinery to bring about the denouement. Musically, everything is reduced to simplicity. In place of the elaborately ornamented arias of opera seria, we find in opera buffa only melodious little tunes—wistful, poignant, or sentimental on the one hand, mocking or gay on the other. Chattering choruses, patter songs, rhythmically fleet ensemble numbers continually introduce notes of levity.

Thus Pergolesi's greatest contribution to music, in his all too brief life's span, was to bring into existence the first successful opera buffa in music history. But he completed a good deal of instrumental music as well: for orchestra, for harpsichord, for chamber-music combinations. (Many compositions long attributed to him, however, have recently proved to be the work of others.) In his instrumental music, Pergolesi sometimes helped anticipate some of the features of the later sonata. He also brought to his instrumental writing an elegant workmanship and an ingratiating lyricism, even while he lacked depth of invention or originality.

However, some of Pergolesi's most significant music, away from the theater, was for the church. In this area, we encounter compositions like the *Stabat Mater* and the *Salve Regina* in C minor, which are minor masterpieces.

Giovanni Battista Pergolesi was born in Jesi, near Ancona, Italy, on January 4, 1710. His musical training took place with Francesco Santi and

Francesco Mondini; for five years after that he attended the Conservatorio dei Poveri di Gesù Cristo, a pupil of Greco, Durante, and Domenico de Matteis. Pergolesi's first significant composition was *La Conversione di S. Guglielmo d'Aquitania,* performed in Naples in 1731. The following winter, he completed and had produced his first serious opera, *Salustia.* Into this work, he interpolated a little comic scene, or intermezzo—his first such piece of music. Another intermezzo, *Lo frate 'nnammorato',* was a huge success when introduced in 1732. Between 1732 and 1734, Pergolesi was the Maestro di Cappella for the Prince of Stigliano. While thus employed, he wrote the epoch-making opera buffa, *La Serva padrona,* produced in 1733. In 1734, Pergolesi was employed by the Duke of Maddaloni, and in 1735, his last opera, *Flaminio,* was produced in Naples. A victim of tuberculosis, Pergolesi went to Pozzuoli for a rest cure. Among his last works were the *Salve Regina* in C minor and the *Stabat Mater.* Pergolesi died in Pozzuoli on March 16, 1736, shortly before his twenty-sixth birthday.

1733. LA SERVA PADRONA (THE SERVANT-MISTRESS), opera buffa in one act (two parts), with text by G. A. Federico. First performance: Naples, August 28, 1733.

Few opera buffas ever accomplished so much with such limited resources. The entire cast comprises only three characters, and one of them is a mute. There is no chorus. Pergolesi's whole score is made up of four arias and two duets—an aria for each of the two principals and a duet for each of the two parts. Yet it is with this most sparing material that Pergolesi was able to realize not only the first opera buffa, but one that was a model of its kind. It contained, as Paul Bekker wrote, "the essence of the entire species. . . . Everything essential it had itself established beyond excelling."

Perhaps the most remarkable thing about *La Serva padrona* is the way in which Pergolesi was able to achieve a variety of mood and feeling within the highly constricted area in which he allowed himself to move. As Bekker said: "Nothing more can be said about the interplay of man and woman than bass and soprano tell each other and enact in their raving, dancing, and singing."

The action takes place in eighteenth-century Naples. Uberto is losing patience with his servant, Serpina, whom he finds to be domineering, hot-tempered, volatile, and capricious. The only way he can get out of her toils is to find himself a wife. He asks his valet, Vespone (a mute) to find him a woman. Since Serpina would very much like to be a candidate, she tries to arouse Uberto's jealousy by telling him of her intent to marry a soldier. In a tender air, "A Serpine penserete" she urges Uberto not to forget her once she leaves him for good. Vespone, acting as Serpina's ally, dresses up as a soldier and provides convincing proof that what Serpina has just told Uberto is true. For the first time, Uberto realizes that in actuality he loves Serpina, that he does not like to see her marry anybody else. Before he is fully aware of what is happening, he proposes to Serpina and is accepted. He soon discovers that he has been the victim of a deception. But as he exclaims in the jovial tune, "O gioia, o gioià" he is so delighted in having Serpina as a wife that he forgives her.

When introduced at the Teatro de S. Bartolomeo in Naples, *La Serva padrona* was a triumph. From there it went on to win the hearts of audiences throughout Italy, An Italian troupe introduced it to Paris in 1752, where it made such a cataclysmic impression that forthwith musical Paris was split into two warring camps: those who considered it the perfect opera, and those who preferred the more subtle and complex works of Rameau (see RAMEAU). Because he was convinced of the artistic validity of Italian opera as exemplified by *La Serva padrona,* the French philosopher, Jean Jacques Rousseau, wrote an opera buffa of his own, *Le Devin du village,* introduced at Fontainbleau in 1752, and at the Paris Opéra in 1753; it remained a favorite with French operagoers for many years. Thus French comic opera came into being, to be further cultivated by such masters as Pierre-Alexander Monsigny (1729–1817) and Grétry both of whom confessed that they had been stimulated into writing their comic operas by *La Serva padrona.* "My own music is but a continuation of his [Pergolesi]," maintained Grétry. In Italy, of course, the impact of *La Serva padrona* was overwhelming. The opera stimulated other composers to write opera buffas of their own—Baldassare Galuppi (1706–1785), Cimarosa, Paisiello, and finally the supreme master of that *genre,* Rossini.

The first American performance took place in Baltimore, Maryland, on June 12, 1790 (in Italian). Not until May 7, 1917 was this little opera heard in New York; at that time, it was heard in an English translation. The first presentation by the Metropolitan Opera took place on February 23, 1934.

1736. SALVE REGINA, in C minor, for soprano and strings.

Pergolesi wrote five Salve Reginas—the Salve Regina being an antiphon in praise of the Virgin Mary, its text set by many composers from Dunstable in the fifteenth century to Gabriel Fauré in the twentieth. The greatest of Pergolesi's works in this form is the fifth and last, written in the closing year of his life. The same kind of spiritual exaltation we encounter in his *Stabat Mater*—the music of a man who has seen the face of death—is found in this deeply moving work. Pergolesi speaks throughout not in anguish but in serenity, not in defiance but in supplication. In the concluding section, his prayer becomes touched with the same kind of radiance Mozart carried over into his Requiem, when he, too, knew he was not long of this earth.

The C minor *Salve Regina* has six sections, alternating slow and somewhat faster movements; but even the latter have deep religious conviction. The sections are: "Salve Regina" (Grave); "Ad te clamamus" (Andante); "Ad te suspiramus" (Largo); "Eia Ergo" (Andante); "Et Jesum Benedictum" (Andante amoroso); and "O Clemens, O Pia" (Largo assai).

1736. STABAT MATER, for soprano, contralto, chorus, and orchestra.

The Confraternity of San Luigi di Palazzo of Naples was accustomed to perform Alessandro Scarlatti's *Stabat Mater* every year. Feeling the need of a change, the Confraternity commissioned Pergolesi to write a new work for them on the same text, giving him an advance of only ten ducats. Pergolesi wrote his music while residing at the Capuchin monastery of Pozzuoli, and he completed his score just before his death. It was, therefore, his last work; and as had been the case with his *Salve Regina* (see above), he brought to his writing the otherworldly concept and vision of a man who did not have much longer to live.

Here Pergolesi is at turn operatic and religious. This fact long made the *Stabat Mater* a subject for criticism. In explanation, Alfred Einstein points out that Pergolesi's *Stabat Mater* is not essentially "a work for the church. It is not even an example of the Neapolitan church style, which—as Pergolesi's ten-part Masses with double chorus prove—is capable of rising to great heights of earnestness. Viewed subjectively, the *Stabat Mater* is nothing more than a Good Friday hymn of a single mortal to the mother of God, not intended for a church festival, but for the edification of a small circle; in a word, it is sacred chamber music."

There are thirteen sections with alternations of slow and fast movements and with ever-changing rhythmic and melodic patterns. The sections are: "Stabat Mater dolorsa" for chorus (Grave); "Cuius animam" for soprano (Andante amoroso); "O quam tristis," a duet (Larghetto); "Quae morebat" for alto (Allegro); "Quis est homo," a duet (Largo); "Pro peccatis" for chorus (Allegro); "Vidit suum" for soprano (Tempo giusto); "Eia, mater," a duet (Allegro moderato); "Fac ut ardeat," for chorus (Allegro); "Sancta mater," a duet (Tempo qiusto); "Fac ut portem Christi mortem," for alto (Largo); "Inflammatus et accensus," a duet (Allegro); "Quando corpus," a duet (Largo); and "Amen," for chorus (Presto assai).

CHRISTOPH WILLIBALD GLUCK 1714–1787

The Enlightenment that swept across Europe in the latter half of the eighteenth century—promoting simplicity, humanity, the heart—found its spokesmen in Rousseau, Diderot, and Voltaire, among others. Gluck belonged with these men in fomenting an intellectual revolution. In his greatest operas, he was the prophet of directness of speech, simplicity of means, dramatic truth, and forthright emotion. He was impatient with the Italian opera mores of his time, with opera's artifical, flowery, and euphuistic texts (mainly the work of Pietro Metastasio), and its florid melodies; with its synthetic plots and its glorification of singer over song; with its concern for pomp and circumstance rather than the demands of story and characters. In his epoch-making preface to his opera *Alceste,* Gluck clarified the new ideals of opera by which he was motivated: "I endeavored to reduce music to its proper function, that of seconding poetry by enforcing the expression of the sentiment, and the interest of the situations, without interrupting the action, or weakening it by superfluous ornament. My idea was that the relation of music to poetry was much the same as that of harmonious coloring and well-disposed light and shade to accurate drawing, which animates the figures without altering their outlines. I have, therefore, been very careful never to interrupt a singer in the heat of a dialogue in order to introduce a tedious ritornelle, nor to stop him in the middle of a piece, either for the purpose of displaying the flexibility of his voice on some favorable vowel, or that the orchestra might give him time to take breath before a long sustained note. . . . My idea was that the overture ought to indicate the subject and prepare the spectators for the character of the piece they are about to see; that the instruments ought to be introduced in proportion to the degree of interest and passion in the words; and that it was necessary above all to avoid making too great a disparity between the recitative and the air of a dialogue, so as not to break the sense of a period or awkwardly interrupt the movement and animation of a scene. I also thought that my chief endeavor should be to attain a grand simplicity, and consequently I have avoided making a parade of difficulties at the cost of clearness; I have set no value on novelty as such, unless it was naturally suggested by the situation and suited to the expression; in short, there was no rule which I did not consider myself bound to sacrifice for the sake of effect."

Before he launched upon these reforms, Gluck, too, had been faithful to Italian opera; he, too, had written operas to Metastasio's texts. Indeed, he completed over twenty Italian-type operas before finally beating out for himself a new path in *Orfeo ed Euridice* in 1762. Nevertheless, from the beginning he was impatient with set formulas, and had made tentative efforts to write for voice and orchestra in a manner more dramatic than that of his fellow-Italians. "He is somewhat mad," Metastasio observed in commenting upon Gluck's adventurous ways in writing Italian operas, adding that Gluck's writing was full of "noise and extravagance." To a remark such as this—and more directly as a reply to a more scathing denunciation of one of Gluck's expressive arias in *La Clemenza di Tito* (1752)—the venerable Francesco Durante said firmly: "I do not feel like deciding whether this passage is entirely in accordance with the rules of composition; but this I can tell you, that all of us, myself to begin with, would be very proud of having thought of and written such a passage."

Before his restlessness and impatience with the status quo in opera could be translated into a new procedure, Gluck had to meet and exchange ideas with two remarkable men in Vienna. One was the Italian poet, Raniere de' Calzabigi, a strong advocate of French culture, an admirer of Lully and Rameau. In discussing with Calzabigi the serious shortcomings of opera seria, Gluck soon came to the conviction that the main fault lay with Metastasio's vapid, lifeless, and flowery texts; a secondary fault rested with the composer's efforts to cater to the vanity of virtuoso singers. Calzabigi now became Gluck's ally, and the two of them were joined by a third man, no less passionately concerned over the sad state of opera—Count Giacomo Durazzo, assistant director of the court theaters, also a pronounced Francophile.

The three men joined forces to reform opera. Their first collaborative effort was a ballet in the French manner, *Don Juan,* performed in Vienna on October 17, 1761. Calzabigi's scenario was based on a play by Molière; Gluck wrote music that was a faithful realization of the text; and Durazzo saw to it that the ballet was produced, and produced properly.

Then the trio became increasingly ambitious by deciding once and for all to overthrow the influence of Metastasio and the Italian composers then dominating opera in Vienna. In 1762, they conceived and had produced *Orfeo ed Euridice,* a *new* kind of opera grounded in French traditions. After that, they brought to Vienna *Alceste* in 1767 and *Paride ed Elena* in 1770. It is with these three works that the new age of opera unfolds—the age of the musical drama that was to reach its culmination with Wagner.

The goal toward which Gluck was heading was the creation of an opera in which everything would serve the drama—ballet, music, production numbers; that which did not serve the drama had to be eliminated. Everything in an opera had to be reduced to essentials—the action and situations, scenes and the musical writing. The ornaments that had up to now cluttered the Italian aria had to be dispensed with. The conventional separation of recitativo secco and the aria had to be abandoned, the recitative serving to keep fluid the flow of music and action. Dramatic truth had to be sought out in vocal and orchestral writing. To increase the expressiveness of the orchestra, instruments thus far foreign to it had to be introduced, such as clarinets, trombones, cymbals; the harpsichord, up to now serving as accompaniment to the recitativo secco, had to be discarded once and for all. Above everything else, as Gluck had maintained, "simplicity and truth" had to be the "sole principles of the beautiful in works of art."

Christoph Willibald Ritter von Gluck was born in Erasbach, in Upper Palatinate, on July 2, 1714. During his boyhood, he received some music instruction in village schools. Then, for a while, he earned his living playing dance music and singing in church choirs. In 1736, he came to Vienna, where he was employed as chamber musician at Prince Lobkowitz's palace. One year later, he traveled in Italy, where he studied with Giovanni Battista Sammartini, absorbed the traditions of Italian opera, and had his own first opera, *Artaserse,* produced in Milan in 1741. Back in Vienna in 1748, his opera *Semiramide riconosciuta* reopened the Burgtheater on May 14, and was outstandingly successful. Two years later, he married Marianna Pergin; and in 1754, he was made Kapellmeister of the Vienna Court Theater. In this post, he wrote numerous operas, ballet scores, and music for various court entertainments.

In 1762, he completed and had produced the first opera with which he aspired to reform opera, *Orfeo ed Euridice*. Along the same lines, he wrote *Alceste* in 1767 and *Paride ed Elena* in 1770. In 1773, he came to Paris, where his opera, *Iphigénie en Aulide,* was successfully introduced on April 19, 1774. His success in Paris, which mounted with the French première of *Orfeo ed Euridice* on August 2, 1774, led his enemies to import to Paris one of Italy's most highly regarded and popular opera composers, Niccolò Piccini (1728–1800). As the climax to the rivalry between Gluck and Piccini, both composers were contracted to write an opera on the same subject (though to different librettos), *Iphigénie en Tauride.* Gluck's opera was heard first on May 18, 1779, and proved a triumph. Piccini's opera, which suffered an execrable performance, was poorly received. His triumph in France now complete, Gluck returned to Vienna. There he spent the last years of his life incapacitated by partial paralysis. He died in Vienna on November 15, 1787.

1762. ORFEO ED EURIDICE (ORPHEUS AND EURYDICE), opera in four acts, with text by Raniere de' Calzabigi, based on the Greek legend. First performance: Burgtheater, Vienna, October 5, 1762.

Orfeo ed Euridice has been described as the first cannon shot in Gluck's war against the formulas of text and music to which eighteenth-century Italian opera adhered so rigidly. The Greek legend of Orpheus and Eurydice had been favored by composers from the time opera was born in Florence. Gluck returned to it in an effort to re-create for his own time, and for Vienna, a musical drama in the style of the Greek tragedy. Calzabigi's libretto (in Italian) was the last word in simplicity, engaging only three characters, and reducing the action to basics. Spectacle, overpowering climaxes, pageantry, lavish scenes—all these, so dear to the hearts of eighteenth-century opera audiences—were eliminated. Where ballet and chorus were utilized (and they were used extensively), they were integrated into the play and were essential to it. What was all important was the tragedy itself, the way in which the two principle characters were affected by the cross-currents in the legend. What were stressed were deep-felt emotion and dramatic truth, not florid melodies for their own sake. "Both words and music," said Prof. Edward J. Dent, "are intensely concentrated on the story of Orpheus and Eurydice, and on every shade of feeling experienced by hero and heroine in the course of action."

After a brief overture (one of the less distinguished moments in the opera, and the least significant of Gluck's overtures to his musical dramas), the curtain rises showing nymphs and shepherds mourning the death of Eurydice. The threnody for chorus, punctuated by Orpheus's cry of "Euridice!" forthwith elevates the opera to eloquent heights. After the chorus has finished its plaint, and has performed a stylized dance around the tomb, Orpheus voices his terrible grief in "Chiamo il mio ben così," and bitterly denounces the gods for having robbed him of his beloved. The gods, moved by the intensity of Orpheus's sorrow, send Amor down to him with a message. Orpheus will be permitted to go down to the underworld and try to win over the Furies with his singing. If he succeeds, Eurydice will come back to earth but only on one condition: Orpheus must not look on Eurydice until he has brought her back safely.

Orpheus descends, appearing at the entrance of Tartarus. He hears the chant of the demoniac Furies, "Chi mai dell' Erebo," and witnesses their corybantic. Then, plucking the strings of his lute, Orpheus pleads to the furies to pity him, in one of the most deeply moving airs in the opera, "Deh placatevi con me!" At first, the Furies interrupt his song with vigorous, "No's!", but they soon become so moved by his song that they allow him to pass on. And now Orpheus comes to the Elysian fields, whose unearthly beauty is depicted in an orchestral episode of incomparable magic, highlighted by a beatific melody for the flute. Orpheus sings with wonder and awe of the sweetness and light in this kingdom, "Che puro ciel." The blessed spirits respond with a joyful chorus and lead him to his beloved Eurydice.

Orpheus begins to lead Eurydice out of Elysium. Because he refuses to look at her, Eurydice is convinced he loves her no longer. In vain does she beg him to cast a glance at her, and stubbornly Orpheus refuses to do so. But Eurydice is not to be denied. At last Orpheus can no longer remain deaf to her entreaties. He looks at her—and Eurydice falls dead in his arms. Once again, the terrible grief at his loss finds voice in magic song—undoubtedly the most celebrated air in the opera, "Che farò senza Euridice." Then Orpheus is about to kill himself, when Amor appears to tell him that the gods have taken pity and are once again ready to restore Eurydice to life. This joyous ending is celebrated with song and dance before the temple of Eros.

The music of *Orpheus* is more than two centuries old. Yet, as Lawrence Gilman once wrote, "how much in the score . . . remains impressive and affecting! It is not easy to forget that savage and terrible 'No!' of the chorus of the Furies that breaks in repeatedly upon the anguished supplications of Orpheus at the beginning of the second act. And at the other end of the gamut is the deathless beauty of the scene in the Elysian Fields. Is there anything more perfect in its kind than this beatific music, which gives us, with such exquisite certainty of touch, a sense of beauty and serenity of an ineffable world? How simple, yet how magical, are the means by which this music suggests the quivering of light and the flowing of quiet streams and the stirring of soft airs, in some unimaginable country of the dreaming mind! And did Gluck ever write a more entrancing melody than the oboe solo that introduces the air of Orpheus, 'Che puro ciel,' with its prophetic resemblance to the theme of the slow movement of Mozart's *Jupiter Symphony.*"

At its première in Vienna, *Orfeo ed Euridice* was a failure. An audience partial to Italian opera could hardly react favorably to what Johann Joachim Winckelman described as "noble simplicity and calm greatness." That audience was bored by the complete absence of decorated melodies, big scenes, pageants. It did not respond sysmpathetically to the extended use of the chorus, and the dramatic way in which Gluck wrote for it. The Viennese thought Gluck's orchestration was noisy, especially during the pictorial description of the Furies. They were confused by the way in which Gluck used passionate, expressive declamation, and by the breaking down of artificial barriers between recitativo secco and aria. They were bewildered by the fact that Gluck did not use a harpsichord to accompany these recitatives, substituting the orchestra instead.

At this première, the part of Orpheus was sung by a castrato. When *Orfeo ed Euridice* was given for the first time in Paris in 1774, however, the role was assumed by a tenor. It has also been sung by a baritone in Germany. The general practice now is to have the male part sung by a mezzo-soprano.

Orfeo ed Euridice was performed in America for the first time at the Winter Garden in New York, on May 25, 1863 (in English). The first time the opera appeared at the Metropolitan Opera—on December 30, 1891—it was used as a curtain raiser for *Cavalleria rusticana.* Unforgettable to those who heard them were the performances given by the Metropolitan Opera in the early 1900's with Toscanini conducting, Louise Homer appearing as Orpheus, and the role of Eurydice shared by Johanna Gadski and Alma Gluck.

1767. ALCESTE, opera in three acts, with text by Raniere de' Calzabigi, based on the tragedy of Euripides. First performance: Burgtheater, Vienna, December 26, 1767.

It took five years after *Orfeo ed Euridice* for Gluck and Calzabigi to fire a second shot against the powerful stronghold of Italian opera. That shot came with *Alceste.* Here the reforms first suggested in *Orfeo* were carried out with even greater courage and vision. In *Alceste,* far more than in *Orfeo,* Gluck was the dramatist to whom musical invention was of secondary importance. "The drama," René Leibowitz pointed out, "completely penetrated by the music is thus endowed with a musical architecture of monumental plasticity and unity." More than ever does the chorus become an integral part of the dramatic action—"sometimes active," explains Leibowitz, and "sometimes merely contemplative." More than ever are the recitatives "not only organically linked to the general flow of the music and the action, but they even become the vivifying breath of the whole structure."

Perhaps nothing points up Gluck's progress as a musical dramatist more than the overture to *Alceste.* In *Orfeo,* the overture had been of secondary interest, of minor musical and dramatic importance, adding nothing whatsoever to what follows. In *Alceste,* the overture becomes an "intrada"—an introduction—to set the mood for the coming drama. It leads right into the opening scene without a break and in its final bars becomes the platform on which to place the brief poignant outcry of the chorus. The overture is by itself a miniature drama. A short introduction, with the somber descending figure of its theme like Fate's implacable tread, precedes the main body. Two subjects are heard in the strings, both equally tragic in expression. The tragedy is intensified as these melodies are developed. Then the somber opening chords return as if to remind us that the force of Fate cannot be denied.

The text by Calzabigi is based on the famous tragedy of Euripides, though with minor modifications. King Admetus of Thessaly is on the brink of death. His people are grief-stricken, and so is his wife Alcestis, who raises her voice in a soulful prayer to Apollo ("Grands dieux du destin"). Slow and stately march music (which Mozart may have remembered when he wrote his own march for the Priests of Isis in *The Magic Flute*) brings on the High Priest and his retinue. Praying in the oracle of Apollo, the High Priest reveals that King Admetus can be saved if someone stands ready to take his place in death. His subjects flee in horror, leaving behind them only Alcestis. In the opera's most celebrated air, and one of the greatest Gluck ever wrote—the "Divinités du Styx"—she announces to the gods that she is prepared to die in place of her husband.

General rejoicing takes place with the tidings that the King has recovered. There are songs by the people, and dancing. When Alcestis joins in the festivities, she is compelled by the king's persistent questioning to reveal that she is about to give up her own life in exchange for his. Admetus is horrified at the news, since life for him is unthinkable without his wife. But there is nothing he can do about it; the bargain has been made. Alcestis makes preparation to descend into the lower world.

Once again the curtain rises on a people's mourning, this time for their queen. Hercules now arrives to announce he will do what he can to save the queen. At the gates of Hades, Admetus catches up with his wife, since he still hopes to replace her in death. When Thanatos (god of death) arrives, he gives Alcestis her final opportunity to change her mind. But when Alcestis cannot be swayed, the spirits of the underworld summon her within their gates. Just then Hercules engages the spirits in a bitter struggle. Apollo also arrives. When he learns of the devotion of Admetus and Alcestis for each other, he is moved to permit them to return to earth and continue there their happy lives together. The scene shifts back to the kingdom of Thessaly, where the people once again rejoice with singing and dancing.

"What a great artistic feat is here," once remarked Alfred Einstein, "and what an abundance of incidental beauty! The realistic proclamation of the oracle by the herald, the people's scene of lamentation before the palace, with the solos of Ismene and Evander, the mourning dumb-show, the orchestral interjections, Alcestis's resolve to sacrifice herself, her farewell from Admetus and her last request to him, weighed down as she is with the heaviness of death. Beauty enters with the overture . . . the first truly tragic introduction to an opera."

When first performed—in Vienna—*Alcestis* was a failure. It was too somber and too classical for Viennese tastes. One of the noblemen remarked at the première: "For nine days the Burgtheater has been closed, and on the tenth it opened with a Requiem." (Only at a later date, with subsequent revivals, did the Viennese learn to admire *Alceste*.) In Paris, where it was performed on April 23, 1776, it also met with a frigid reception. Jean Jacques Rousseau maintained: "I know of no opera in which the passions are less varied than in *Alceste;* almost everything turns on two sentiments, affliction and terror, and the prolonged enjoyment of these two sentiments must have cost the composer incredible pains to avoid the most lamentable monotony." Gluck was heartbroken that Paris, the home of Rameau, should have greeted his musical drama so coldly. After the première performance, he rushed out of the theater, exclaiming to a friend: "*Alceste* has fallen." "Yes," his friend replied softly, "fallen—from heaven." But Gluck did not for a moment doubt that *Alceste* was a completely successful realization of his theories. He said: "*Alceste* can only displease now when it is new. It has not had time yet; I say that it will please equally in two hundred years, if the French language does not change; and my reason for saying so is that I have built wholly on nature, which is never subject to changes of fashion."

What is probably the first American performance took place at Wellesley College in Wellesley, Massachusetts, in March 1938: On January 14, 1941, *Alceste* was performed for the first time by the Metropolitan Opera; and on March 4, 1952, it was given there again (this time in an English translation) starring Kirsten Flagstad in the title role, in her farewell opera appearance in the United States.

1774. IPHIGÉNIE EN AULIDE (IPHIGENIA IN AULIS), lyric tragedy in three acts, with text by du Roullet based on a drama of Racine, which in turn was derived from Euripides. First performance: Paris Opéra, April 19, 1774.

Gluck made one more effort after *Alceste* to woo the Viennese opera public with his reforms: *Paride ed Elena,* produced at the Burgtheater on November 3, 1770. That opera was also a failure. "The half-learned, the judges and legislators of art—a class of persons unfortunately too numerous, and at the same time of greater disadvantage to art than ignoramuses—rage against a method which, if established, would obviously endanger their criteria," wrote Gluck in revulsion. Then he added defiantly: "No obstacles will deter me from making new attempts to achieve my purposes. Sufficit mihi unus Plato per cuncto populo; I would rather have one Plato on my side than all the populace."

He decided to seek another battleground for his war against Italian opera:

Paris, where Rameau's own ideas on musical drama had by now taken root. In Vienna, Gluck had befriended du Roullet, an attaché at the French legation. Du Roullet prepared for Gluck the libretto of *Iphigénie en Aulide,* hoping that this would open the doors of the Paris Opéra for Gluck. When Gluck completed his score, du Roullet despatched a long letter of entreaty to the director of the Paris Opéra to mount the work. "This great man," wrote du Roullet, "has exhausted in this score all the powers of art. Simple and natural song, supported throughout by a genuine and interesting expression and enchanting melody; an inexhaustible variety of ideas and devices; the loftiest effects of harmony, whether in the portrayal of the terrible, the sublime, or the tender; a rapidly moving and at the same time noble and expressive recitative, similar to the best of the French recitatives; the greatest versatility in the dance pieces, which are of a quite new kind, full of the most alluring freshness; choruses, duets, terzets, quartets—all alike expressive, moving, and well-declaimed with a scrupulous regard to the prosody; in short, everything in this composition appears to the taste of the French."

The director of the Opéra hesitated to accept *Iphigénie*. But Gluck had a powerful ally in Marie Antoinette, who had been his pupil in Vienna. Because of Marie Antoinette's influence, *Iphigénie* was accepted, and Gluck was invited to Paris to help with the production. But things did not go smoothly. In Paris, as in Vienna, Gluck had enemies who preferred Italian ways. They did whatever they could to obstruct him. But for the personal intervention of Marie Antoinette, *Iphigénie* might never have been produced. At rehearsals, Gluck had to struggle against inefficient singers, poorly disciplined dancers and orchestra players, sheer incompetence on the part of the baritone who played Agamemnon, and the defiance and impudence of Sophie Arnould, darling of Paris, cast in the title role. Nevertheless, the performance was whipped into shape. At the première, the opera was poorly received; but at the second performance it was given a tremendous ovation. In short order, the opera became such a vogue in Paris that a hair-dress was called "à la Iphigénie."

Once again, as in *Alceste,* the opera opens not with a formal overture but with an introduction ("intrada") to establish the mood. This overture is one of the most exalted pieces of orchestral music of the eighteenth century. It opens with a somber section for strings, which Wagner described as an "invocation for deliverance from affliction"; its main subject appears in Agamemnon's stirring air, "Diane impitoyable," with which the opera opens. We then hear a heroic theme in full orchestra, said by Wagner to be an assertion of imperious demand. (This idea reappears in one of the choruses in the first act.) A more lyrical idea for the violin follows; to Wagner it represented Iphigenia. A fourth subject, for flutes and oboes alternating with strings, indicated to Wagner "painful, tormenting pity." The overture does not come to a close, but its last phrase joins the opening exclamation of Agamemnon in his "Diane impitoyable" air when the curtain rises. (For concert performances, Wagner prepared a formal ending for the overture, in which the opening somber theme is recalled over a background of a phrase from the first stirring subject; a last repetition of this stirring idea is given in the closing measures.)

Agamemnon is lamenting that he is compelled by the goddess Diana to sacrifice his daughter, Iphigenia. Only then will the Greeks, waylaid in Aulis, be permitted to proceed on to Troy. A group of Greeks come to Agamemnon insisting he make the sacrifice; upon Iphigenia's arrival, the king resigns himself sadly to his fate. But he still harbors the hope of saving his daughter by getting her to leave Aulis. The ruse he employs to gain her consent to this departure is to suggest that her beloved, Achilles, is unfaithful. Just then Achilles appears to reassure Iphigenia.

The second act opens with the festive celebration of the marriage of Iphigenia and Achilles. The people sing a paean, "Chantons, célébrons notre reine." Just as the wedding couple approaches the altar, Arcas announces that Agamemnon will kill his daughter then and there. In the ensuing confusion, Achilles expresses his determination to save his bride's life. The act ends with one of the most moving scenes in the opera. Agamemnon, torn between his duty to his people and his love for his daughter, finally resolves to save Iphigenia. He orders his wife Clytemnestra to take Iphigenia off to Mycenae.

In the third act, the Greek people are insistent on having Iphigenia sacrificed, and Achilles is just as insistent that he will first destroy Agamemnon rather then let Iphigenia die. Proudly, Iphigenia decides to meet her fate, bids farewell to her people and her beloved in "Adieu, conservez dans votre âme." To Ernest Newman this air is "one of the most perfect emotional utterances of the eighteenth century." After Iphigenia is led away, the people pray to Diana to accept the sacrifice. Suddenly, Achilles and his men arrive and join the Greeks in battle. But before it ends, Calchas announces that the gods have been appeased, that no sacrifice is necessary. As Iphigenia rejoins Achilles, the people give voice to their joy.

Where *Orfeo* (to a large degree) and *Alceste* (to a lesser one) had been a succession of pictorial scenes, *Iphigénie* is made up of a series of dramatic events. Consequently, Gluck's writing in *Iphigénie* is more dramatic and animated than in his earlier lyric dramas. The recitatives have greater impact; the arias are, more than ever, inextricable parts of a dramatic whole. But, as Lawrence Gilman remarked, what is perhaps most remarkable about Gluck's score is "the genius and fidelity with which it suggests in essence the character of Iphigenia as she lives in the great drama of Euripides. . . . We end up by remembering not the Iphigenia of Racine, but the wonderful prototype of whom Alexander Harvey painted so true and loving a portrait: 'She has simplicity,' he wrote, 'and yet she is complex.' She is timid and shrinking, but she is a heroine. She has strength and weakness, she is deep and she is shallow, she wants to live and she wants to die. All these contradictions she manifests swiftly, but the character is unified so cunningly . . . that we can say of Iphigenia that to the passion of Juliet she adds the sweetness of Viola, the wisdom of Portia, the madness of Ophelia, and the purity of Isabella."

The first time *Iphigénie en Aulide* was seen in the United States was on February 22, 1935, in Philadelphia.

1779. IPHIGÉNIE EN TAURIDE (IPHIGENIA IN TAURIS), lyric drama in four acts, with text by François Guillard, based on Euripides. First performance: Paris Opéra, May 18, 1779.

The victory of Gluck over Piccini in Paris—and the full vindication of Gluck's new concept of opera—were realized decisively with *Iphigénie en Tauride*. It is not hard to see why. *Iphigénie en Tauride* is Gluck's masterwork. The reforms first instituted in earlier operas were here refined, crystallized, and perfected. The ideals of lyric drama are completely realized. Once and for all, coloratura singing is banished to make way for dramatic melodies and declamations that lock and interlock into a single inextricable tonal design. Once and for all, the drama sweeps on to its final resolution unimpeded by extraneous episodes. Rarely before did Gluck penetrate so deeply into the psychological motivations and impulses of his characters: Orestes is the first great baritone figure in tragic opera, and Iphigenia is a many-dimensional portrait. The great emotional utterances in the drama find their musical equivalents in some of the most moving pages of lyricism encountered in eighteenth-century opera: Iphigenia's first-act air where she prognosticates the future tragedy awaiting her by describing a dream, "Cette nuit, j'ai revu le palais de mon père"; her deeply emotional episode that follows, "O toi qui prolongeas mes jours"; her mighty lament with which the second act closes, "O malheureuse Iphigénie"; and in the same second act, Orestes's poignant air, "Dieux! qui me poursuivez" followed by Pylades's haunting refrain, "Unis dès la plus tendre enfance." The writing for chorus and for ballet is on a no less lofty plane of inspiration. And a new dramatic subtlety and insight enters Gluck's orchestration to give him new dimension as a musical dramatist. The rising arpeggio figures in the orchestra endow Thanos's air, "De noirs pressentiments," with increased expressiveness; they have been described by Adolf Bernhard Marx as rising like the "tentacles of the underworld." And in Orestes's magnificent air, "Le calme rentre dans mon coeur" —in which his placid melody recounts that serenity is now his—the orchestra betrays that for all his protestations, Orestes is still a victim of torment.

The action in *Iphigénie en Tauride* continues where it had left off in *Iphigénie en Aulide*. The introduction is a tone poem alternating between the same calm and the storm that provide the ensuing drama with its sharp emotional contrasts. The final bar of the overture is joined to the despairing cry of Iphigenia and chorus, "Grand dieux!" as the curtain rises. Iphigenia, having been saved from doom, has been brought on a cloud to Tauris. There she serves as high priestess of the Scythian temple. When the enraged gods of Tauris demand a human sacrifice, King Thaos orders Iphigenia to kill one of two Greek strangers, recently come to her shores; they are Orestes and Pylades. Iphigenia is reluctant to do so, recalling her own Greek background. But in the end, she relents and designates one of the two strangers—Orestes—as the victim. After this grim decision has been made, she discovers to her horror that Orestes is her brother. Now Iphigenia insists that she join her brother in death. But a band of Greeks, headed by Pylades, attack the Scythians. The king is killed, and the Greeks prove triumphant. The goddess Diana now pardons Orestes and allows him to go back to Greece in triumph.

The first performance of *Iphigénie en Tauride* in the United States took place at the Metropolitan Opera on November 25, 1916 (in German). The version here used was an edition by Richard Strauss, with additional changes and interpolations by Artur Bodanzky, who conducted. The first time *Iphigénie en Tauride* was heard in New York in the French language was when the American Opera Society gave it a concert performance on February 15, 1955.

——— BALLET SUITE, a suite for orchestra, arranged by Felix Mottl from Gluck's music.

BALLET SUITE, a suite for orchestra, arranged by François Gevaert from Gluck's music.

Delightful sequences from various Gluck works have been lifted for two popular orchestral suites. The more familiar one is that arranged by Felix Mottl. The first movement borrows an episode from the ballet, *Don Juan,* produced in Vienna in 1761. After that come "Air Gai" and "Lento" from *Iphigénie en Aulide,* the "Dance of the Blessed Spirits" from *Orfeo ed Euridice,* and "Musette" and "Sicilienne" from *Armide* (1777).

Gevaert derived his material from just two Gluck operas. From *Iphigénie en Aulide* he extracted the "Air," "Danse," "Tambourin," and "Chaconne"; and from *Armide,* the "Musette."

JOHANN STAMITZ 1717–1757

The first modern symphony orchestra came into existence at the court of the Elector Palatine, Duke Carl Theodor, in the German city of Mannheim. It was led by Johann Stamitz. Under his direction, the orchestra achieved such discipline, precision, and flexible technique that the eighteenth-century music historian Burney referred to it as "an army of generals." Everybody who heard the Mannheim orchestra—Mozart included—marveled at the way in which the orchestra passed from pianissimo to fortissimo; produced tremolos, crescendos, diminuendos; realized stunning contrasts of light and shade; and achieved a singing tone in the violins and a beautiful texture in the winds. "No orchestra in the world," said Burney, has ever surpassed the Mannheim orchestra in execution. Its forte is thunder, its crescendo cataract, its diminuendo is a crystal stream babbling along in the distance, its piano, a breath of spring."

The presence of such a remarkable ensemble in Mannheim, of course, proved a powerful stimulant to the city's composers in writing music for orchestra. Such a group appeared, and made a historic contribution to orchestral music in general, and to the symphony in particular. Its leading figure was Johann Stamitz, whose most significant successor was his own son, Karl (1745–1801). Hugo Riemann maintained that the symphony was born in Mannheim. This is not strictly true, but there can be small doubt that remarkable progress was made in Mannheim to fix a symphonic structure and develop an orchestral style. "We can minimize neither the greatness of Stamitz as a composer nor the role of the school, which was not the invention but the stabilization of a new form and idiom, and the working out of its orchestral technique," says Paul Henry Lang. "Stamitz established . . . the clear disposition of the sections of the sonata."

Johann Wenzel Anton Stamitz was born in Deutsch Brod, Bohemia, on June 19, 1717. He received music instruction from his father and at a Jesuit school, revealing an outstanding gift both for the violin and for composition. In 1741, he joined the orchestra at the court of the Elector in Mannheim. Four years later he was made its concertmaster and director of chamber music. Through his efforts, and with the support and encouragement of the Elector, Stamitz succeeded in making his orchestra one of the finest in the world at that time. For these concerts—as well as for performances of chamber music at court—Stamitz produced a rich library of instrumental music. His first opus, trios for orchestra, was issued in 1750. After that, compositions came quick and fast. By the time he died, Stamitz had created about one hundred and seventy-five works, embracing symphonies, concertos (including the first clarinet concerto ever written), quartets, and some choral music. In 1754, he visited Paris for about a year, conducting concerts in various salons and at the establishment of Rameau's patron, La Poupèliniere. Stamitz died in Mannheim on March 27, 1757.

——— SYMPHONIES.

In all, Stamitz wrote almost seventy-five symphonies. He did not invent the symphony, but he certainly developed it, and set the stage for Haydn. Stamitz was one of the earliest composers to use a contrasting lyrical second theme in his Allegro movements, and to subject both themes to development. Thus the sonata form became more clearly defined than heretofore. Stamitz was also one of the first composers to expand the symphonic structure from three to four movements, adding a finale after the minuet (the minuet up to now having served as a last movement). He was just as significant a pioneer in orchestral style. He minimized the importance of the basso continuo, emphasized the role of melody and harmony, and evolved such an orchestral manner that one of his contemporaries said after listening to a Stamitz symphony, "one forgets that such a thing as voices exist."

Here is how Wilfrid Mellers described the Stamitz symphony in *The Sonata Principle:* "In his orchestration, he concentrates all his attention on getting the tune across. The harpsichord continuo . . . disappears; ostinato string figures and sustained notes on the horns now fill in the middle parts since melodic definition in any part except the top is unimportant." Mellers states further that "all the effects which in Rameau's operas had grown from theatrical exigencies (such as earthquakes) become an end in themselves." Thus Stamitz developed the use of crescendo, diminuendo, tremolo, change of dynamics, and marks of expression and nuance. "The bouncing upward arpeggio figures 'across the strings' (known as the Mannheim sky-rocket), the twiddling figurations (the Mannheim birdies), the long crescendo over a reiterated bass (the Mannheim steam-roller) became famous or notorious all over Europe."

The Stamitz symphony opens with an Allegro in classical sonata form. The movement is now divided into an exposition, a development, and a recapitulation while the two-theme structure is crystallized. A lyrical, tender, expressive slow movement follows. The third movement is a minuet, and the fourth, a sprightly finale. "The roots of Beethoven exist already . . . in the work of that astonishing Johann Stamitz," wrote Romain Rolland. Then he goes on to add what some regard as excessive enthusiasm: "I have no hesitation in saying that a Stamitz symphony, though less rich, less beautiful, less exuberant, is much more spontaneous than a Haydn or a Mozart symphony. It is made to its own measure; it creates its own forms; it does not submit to them."

CARL PHILIPP EMANUEL BACH 1714–1788

The works of Carl Philipp Emanuel Bach loom large, not only in the older age of polyphony, but in the newer one of homophony. While some of his music looks backwards, most of it is faced toward the future. Just as the classic symphony was first developed significantly by Johann Stamitz and the Mannheim school, so the classic piano sonata owes its early evolution to Carl Philipp Emanuel Bach. He perfected the three-movement piano structure, and clarified the sonata form. This accomplishment had a powerful effect on his immediate successors. "Whoever knows me well," said Haydn, who had committed Bach's piano sonatas to memory before trying to write some of his own, "will see how much I owe to Carl Philipp Emanuel Bach, and how I have understood and thoroughly studied him." Mozart said: "Those of us who can do what is right learned from him; whoever will not admit it is a *Lump*." Burney emphasized how strongly Haydn had been affected by Bach: "If Haydn ever looked up to any great master as a model it seems to have been Carl Philipp Emanuel Bach: the bold modulations, rests, pauses, free use of semitones, and unexpected flights of Haydn remind us frequently of Bach's early works more than that of any other composer."

Bach's influence penetrated even into Beethoven, who was the fulfillment of Bach's personalized, dramatic expression (*Empfindsamer Stil*) then new to instrumental music. It was for the sake of this new dramatic expression—and for the voicing of human feelings with greater authenticity and directness—that led Bach to introduce his bold harmonies, modulations, and progressions that so startled his contemporaries. At the same time he perfected the *galant* style of piano writing: an elegant manner which he above all others helped to make so important in eighteenth-century music. In short, as Paul Henry Lang remarked, "this great master stands out as a beacon in the eighteenth century, the rays of which illumined the course of everyone."

Carl Philipp Emanuel Bach was the second son of Johann Sebastian and Maria Barbara Bach. He was born in Weimar, Germany, on March 8, 1714. His celebrated father was his sole music teacher; at the same time young Bach pursued his academic training at the Thomasschule in Leipzig and at the University in Frankfort-on-the-Oder. In his twenty-fourth year, Carl Philipp Emanuel settled in Berlin, where he distinguished himself as a clavier performer and composer. Frederick the Great appointed him court Kapellmeister in 1740. Bach held this post with distinction for twenty-seven years. In Berlin, in 1744, Bach married Johanna Maria Dannemann, who bore him three children.

In 1767, Bach became the cantor of the Johanneum Church in Hamburg, as well as director of musical performances at several other churches in that city. His fame became so widespread that during the latter part of his life—and for some years thereafter—whenever the name of Bach was mentioned, it was Carl Philipp Emanuel who was being referred to, not Johann Sebastian. Carl Philipp Emanuel Bach died in Hamburg on December 14, 1788.

1749. MAGNIFICAT IN D MINOR, for solo voices, chorus, and orchestra.

Bach's most famous choral work was written a year before the death of his father, Johann Sebastian. The *Magnificat* carries more than one reminder of the polyphonic art and science in their full glory. Though there are orchestral effects, harmonic devices, and at times a homophonic lyricism that bespeaks the new age in music, most of the *Magnificat* is a reminder of the past.

The text comes from the Gospel according to St. Luke (1: 46–55). The work opens with "Magnificat anima mea Dominum," in which homophonic writing is combined with imitative passages. The violins provide a brilliant background for the chorus, as a subject first heard in the orchestral introduction is amplified. In "Quia respexit," the soprano offers a page of surpassing tenderness, while contrast comes with "Quia fecit," in which the tenor is heard in a florid melody over a striking orchestral accompaniment. A majestic choral episode, "Et misericordia," precedes "Fecit potentiam," in which the bass presents a melody of encompassing humanity. A duet for tenor and alto in the Italian style, "Deposuit potentes," and a somber alto solo, "Suscepit Israel," are the next two sections. In the penultimate section, "Gloria patre," God is praised in a majestic chorus, in which the music of the opening "Magnificat" is recalled. The work then comes to an exultant conclusion with a double fugue for chorus, "Sicut erat."

1773. SINFONIA NO. 3 IN C MAJOR, for string orchestra and continuo. I. Allegro assai. II. Adagio. III. Allegro assai.

Baron van Swieten, a powerful Viennese music patron and Mozart's friend, commissioned Bach to write a set of six sinfonias. The C major is the third in this group. These sinfonias are not in the style and structure of the classic symphony already formalized by Johann Stamitz, among others. Rather they are in the tripartate form of the Italian overture, with a slow section flanked by two fast ones.

The first movement of the C major Sinfonia is dramatic. A single subject is dominant, powerfully stated by the entire string section. Dramatization is achieved through unexpected key changes, surprising inversions, and a forceful rhythmic impulse that sweeps the music relentlessly to the closing measures. The opening measures then return to end the movement. The Adagio movement comes without a break to present a strongly felt melody in the upper strings over accompanying basses. Here expressiveness is heightened through rapid alternations of loud and soft passages. The spirited finale is in binary form, its main theme possessing the exuberance of a gigue.

1774–1787. SONATAS FOR PIANO:
Wuerttemberg Sonatas; Fuer Kenner und Liebhaber (*For Connoisseurs and Amateurs*).

The piano sonata is the area beyond all others in which Carl Philipp Emanual Bach proved most influential. It was he who was among the first to achieve a piano sonata in true classic form. From Bach to Haydn is just a short step.

Bach's sonatas are already in the three-movement structure found in Haydn. The opening movement is in a recognizable sonata form, with two main themes (though not necessarily of a contrasting nature), a development, and a recapitulation. The developments are still brief and tentative. The second movement is in singing *galant* style; frequently the slow movement is just a short transition into the finale. That finale is lively, sometimes in a structure suggesting the rondo with a recurring main theme; it is here that we find Bach in some of his most delightful and ingratiating thoughts.

Bach wrote and published his first set of six piano sonatas in 1742, dedicating them to the king of Prussia. These and the *Wuerttemberg Sonatas* that followed in 1774—so called because they were dedicated to the King of Wuerttemberg—still lean heavily on older traditions. In the *Wuerttemberg* set, the A minor Sonata, the first in the volume, is typical. (I. Moderato. II. Andante. III. Allegro assai). The opening movement has the character of an improvisation. The main theme, in broken chords, comes without preliminaries to be developed in a fantasia like manner. The stately slow movement boasts a free-flowing melody with the singing quality of an aria. It is only in the finale that the new age begins to assert itself—in music full of daring harmonic and dynamic effects, galanterie, and rhythmic vitality.

Bach comes to full maturity as a composer of piano sonatas with the six sets of works collectively entitled *For Connoisseurs and Amateurs,* published between 1779 and 1787. Not only is the classic structure now clearly articulated, but we find here page upon page in which a dramatic impulse charges the music with a feeling and expressiveness anticipating Beethoven. It is surely symbolic to find that the main theme in the first movement of the F minor Sonata, in this collection, should sound so much like the first theme in the first movement of Beethoven's first piano sonata. It is almost as if this were an acknowledgment on Beethoven's part that he is now ready to take over where Bach had left off.

Bach's piano sonatas are filled with a personal language new to piano literature: the beautifully realized galant style in the slow movement of the G major (the first in the second set); the exquisite blending of sentiment and galanterie in the slow movement of the G major (third sonata, first set); the bold harmony magically combined with rococo figurations in the slow movement of the D minor.

Wilfrid Mellers describes some of the ways in which Bach achieved his individual dramatic idiom. "Consider the first movement of the F minor Sonata. . . . The initial figure is a bounding Mannheim sky-rocket; and the interest of the music lies not in the themes, which as melody do not exist, but in the tonal conflict which is generated from them. The point of the movement is the dramatic crisis which occurs in the middle section—we can legitimately call it a development—on the surprising chord of F-flat major; a 'Neapolitan' relationship to the minor of the relative (A flat). Here the popular manner of Stamitz has not lost its vitality; but it has gained a personal urgency." Mellers further points out that the "surprises and explosive contrasts of the new style become significant only when they achieve a new kind of order; and this order, depending on oppositions of tonality and harmony, is inherently dramatic. The drama is no longer projected on to a stage; it is embodied in self-contained instrumental form."

——— CONCERTO IN D MAJOR, for orchestra, arranged by Maximilian Steinberg. I. Allegro moderato. II. Andante lento molto. III. Allegro.

Curiously, the orchestral work by Bach played most often is an adaptation —that made by Maximilian Steinberg of a composition in the style of a concerto grosso, originally scored for four violas. The Steinberg arrangement was made in 1909 at the behest of Serge Koussevitzky; it was introduced in St. Petersburg on October 23, 1909, Siloti conducting. Steinberg's orchestration calls for flute, two oboes, bassoon, horn, and strings.

The first movement is in a robust vein, making use of polyphonic resources. There are two main themes—the first virile, the second lyrical. The slow movement is a stirringly beautiful lyrical page, sensitive and of deep feeling. The spell is broken in the finale, which, like the opening movement, is of stout fiber, with occasional recourse to polyphony.

WILHELM FRIEDEMANN BACH 1710–1784

To Karl Geiringer, Wilhelm Friedemann Bach stands "closer to the work of his father than any of his great brothers." Carl Philipp Emanuel Bach put it even more forcefully. "He could replace our father better than all of us put together."

Much of Wilhelm Friedemann Bach's music is in the rococo style of the period. But like his brother Carl Philipp Emanuel, he sounded deeper notes than those of so many of his Baroque contemporaries. Indeed, like Carl Philipp Emanuel, Wilhelm Friedmann was a master of *Empfindsamer Stil,* with which Baroque music finally lost its stylization and objectivity and became personalized. Bach's subjective feelings expressed themselves in music often of the most compelling intensity. "He felt," says Geiringer, "an artistic responsibility toward the trends of his own time, and the violent effort he made to adjust his production to contemporary ideas led to a tragic intensity of expression foreshadowing nineteenth-century Romanticism. . . . His later works display passion and grief . . . a fervor and depth of feeling which few composers expressed in his time."

Had he been less lazy, less erratic emotionally, less intractable, and if, in his last years, had he been less bitter and less the victim of frustrations, Wilhelm Friedemann Bach might have ascended to a place in music not far below that occupied by his august father. As it is, Wilhelm Friedemann produced some works for the piano that carry the name of Bach with dignity. "The man's music," says Heinrich Lindlar, "is between the eras of Johann Sebastian and Beethoven, perhaps the most intense, tightly spun music composed in Germany."

Wilhelm Friedemann Bach, the oldest son of Johann Sebastian and Maria Barbara Bach, was born in Weimar on November 22, 1710. His music study took place with his father, and with J. G. Graun at Merseburg. His academic education was acquired at the University of Leipzig, from which he was graduated in 1729. In 1733, he became the organist of the St. Sophia Church in Dresden, and for an eighteen-year period, until 1764, he played the organ and conducted the musical performances at the Liebfrauen Church in Halle. In 1751, he married Dorothea Elisabeth Georgi. After 1764, he led a precarious existence, teaching, writing music for wealthy patrons, and giving concerts on the organ. His last years were embittered by frustrations and poverty. He died in Berlin on July 1, 1784.

1765. 12 POLONAISES, for piano: 1. C major. 2. C minor. 3. D major. 4. D minor. 5. E-flat major. 6. E-flat minor. 7. E major. 8. E minor. 9. F major. 10. F minor. 11. G major. 12. G minor.

After leaving his secure post in Halle in 1764, Wilhelm Friedemann Bach was reduced to earning his living as best he could. Not infrequently, he wrote music for the sole purpose of winning audiences and getting some badly needed money. The twelve polonaises were written under such regrettable circumstances—yet, for all that, they remain remarkable compositions. The polonaise, originally a Polish court dance with marked syncopations and accents on the half-beat, had long been a movement of the classical suite. But Wilhelm Friedemann was one of the first significant composers to use this dance form for piano music, thereby anticipating Chopin by almost half a century. Already, with Bach, the polonaise for the piano loses some of the courtly grace it had known in the classical suite and assumes the fiery national identity and dynamic rhythmic spirit that characterized Chopin's pieces in this form.

——— SONATA IN G MAJOR, for piano. I. Allegro. II. Lamento. III. Allegro.

The outer Allegro movements of this sonata follow Baroque traditions. They have robustness, vitality, a strong momentum; the vivacious thematic material is often subjected to contrapuntal treatment. But it is in the middle slow movement, designated by the composer as a "Lament," that the sonata parts company with other similar works of the period. This is music of an ardor and with a poetic feeling that seem to herald the approach of Romanticism. The simple, plangent melody—a controlled lamentation—rises from the treble over a bare accompaniment. Stripped of eighteenth-century ornamentations, this melody rises to a peak of emotion with loud and dramatic bass tones before reverting to its original elegiac mood.

JOHN CHRISTIAN BACH 1735–1782

There was little of Carl Philipp Emanuel Bach's varied invention, individuality and powerful creativity in the works of his half-brother, John Christian. But, for all that, John Christian's instrumental works are suave, facile, and workmanlike, and represent an important link between the Baroque and the classical eras. He inhabited, says Charles Sanford Terry, "the borderland between these two dispensations, the old and the new." Within such a borderland he wrote a great deal of choral music (Masses, Requiems, motets), and many operas. All this belonged to the older age. His music for orchestra, however, invaded the new era. Bach's instrumental compositions made a strong impression upon Mozart, who was influenced by them. Mozart was impressed by the sensitiveness and grace of Bach's style, his skilful use of contrasts, his indulgence in subtle nuances, and the elegance of his rococo writing.

Terry, who concedes that Bach's stature was by no means "gigantic," undoubtedly gives a just appraisal when he adds: "On the platform of his generation, Bach owes his honorable position, not to the inheritance of a great name, but to his own eclectic genius and indomitable industry."

Known as the "English Bach," by virtue of his long residence in London, John Christian was the youngest son of Johann Sebastian and Anna Magdalena. John Christian was born in Leipzig on September 5, 1735. He received his musical training from his half-brother, Carl Philipp Emanuel, and in Italy from Padre Martini. In Italy, Bach proved prolific as a composer of religious music and operas. He was invited to London in 1762 to write Italian operas. His introduction to English audiences took place at the King's Theater on February 19, 1763, with *Orione,* which proved so successful that it had a run of nearly three months. Another opera, *Zanaida,* produced on May 7, 1763, was even more successful. Bach was now appointed music master to the Queen, a post he held with outstanding distinction up to the time of his death. During this period, he married Cecilia Grassi, a singer; they had no children.

John Christian Bach died in London on January 1, 1782. His vast output included numerous operas, choral works, about fifty symphonies, thirty-one sinfonie concertante, thirty-seven concertos, thirty-eight piano sonatas, and various other orchestral and chamber-music compositions.

——— SYMPHONY IN G MINOR, op. 6, no. 6. I. Allegro. II. Andante più tosto adagio. III. Allegro molto.

The symphonic structure employed by John Christian Bach was in the three-part form of the Italian overture. Georges de Saint-Fox notes that the first movement reveals "clear-cut dualism between its ideas, the two themes being in opposition to each other, the one strong and rhythmic, the other slighter and cantabile. This movement is generally without a development and with a single re-entry of the second subject in the tonic." The slow movement usually achieves "a noble and expressive beauty." By contrast, the short and quick finale that follows "most often takes the form of a rondo with two contrasting episodes, with the rondo theme da capo." In his orchestration, Bach supports "this musical edifice essentially [with] two violins, in the Italian fashion, with the wind horns and oboes or flutes coloring the ensemble lightly and adequately."

The Symphony in G minor—scored for two oboes, two horns, strings, and harpsichord—is unusual for its time because of its tonality; the minor key was rarely used up to then. The first movement has for its central subject a brusque, rhythmic figure that gives the music an unrelenting momentum to which oboes provide occasional relief with lyric interpolations. The minor key continues in the second movement with a sober melody that has muscle as well as heart. In the finale, a gigue-like tune in 12/8 meter contributes rhythmic vitality, relaxed occasionally by fragmentary phrases for oboe duet. The symphony has an unusual ending—not the forceful and climactic close we might expect but a gentle whisper, the concluding measure being pianissimo.

1774–1777. SINFONIA IN E-FLAT MAJOR, op. 18, no. 1, for double orchestra. I. Allegro spiritoso. II. Andante. III. Allegro.

John Christian Bach often used the terms "sinfonia" and "overture" interchangeably. Six orchestral works now described as sinfonias were originally published in opus 18 as "grand overtures." The truth is that Bach here utilized the three-part structure of the Italian Overture, but with a spaciousness of design and an elaboration of thematic material that brings to these works a symphonic character.

The first movement of the E-flat major Sinfonia opens with a virile theme in unison. A few scale passages lead into the second subject—a lyrical episode for strings. In the ensuing development, antiphonal writing is utilized by the two orchestras. An arpeggio figure in the bassoon brings on a return of the second lyrical theme in both orchestras. The main ideas are then recapitulated before the movement ends with a gentle coda. In the slow movement, two groups of strings are used, the one presenting a soulful song, while the other offers figurations and ornaments. Before the movement ends, the two orchestras are united. In the finale, antiphonal writing is once again used extensively. This movement is in the form of a rondo. A gigue-like tune is heard in the first orchestra and recurs throughout the movement. The second orchestra introduces a new thought, which soon receives elaboration in both orchestras.

FRANZ JOSEPH HAYDN 1732–1809

Haydn changed the course of music history. What he accomplished during a long, industrious lifetime had decisive consequences. Nineteenth-century music would hardly have followed the course it did had Haydn not lived. While he did not invent the symphony, he was the first to realize its full structural and aesthetic potential, and to make it the most significant medium for all later instrumental composers. To the inchoate and elementary symphonic mold he had inherited from his predecessors, he brought a new expanse, a new richness of material, a new variety of expression, and a new subtlety of nuance. He extended and solidifed the sonata form; he brought new dimension to the slow movement through the perfection of the variation form; he introduced the minuet as the third movement, and perfected the rondo form for the finale. He gave new breadth and new scope to orchestration, to thematic development, to modulation; he continually injected novelty and surprise. He also carried over to the symphony an expressiveness—*Empfindsamkeit*—and a dramatic thrust which are already suggestive of Romanticism. The gamut of his style passed so easily from the jovial and the lighthearted to pathos that Mozart could say: "He alone has the secret of making me smile, and touching me to the bottom of my soul."

In addition to his monumental accomplishments as a composer of symphonies, he was virtually the creator of the string quartet. The string quartet was a neglected stepchild of music when he first came to it; Haydn's predecessors favored the chamber-music structure of the trio-sonata. But Haydn seized upon the string quartet as a medium uniquely suited to his personality and artistic needs. On it he lavished such love, devotion, and talent that forthwith the string quartet gained legitimacy in the family of musical forms. "It is not often," commented Otto Jahn, "that a composer hits so exactly upon the form suited to his conceptions; the quartet was Haydn's natural mode of expressing his feelings." He endowed it with individuality and personality; evoked from it a full measure of its inherent charm and talent. He elevated it to a lofty position among the great works of art."

With an extraordinary and, at times, unparalleled resiliency, Haydn allowed himself to profit from the work of three masters, at three different points of his life. First, it was Carl Philipp Emanuel Bach; Bach led him to the sonata, the galant style, and classicism. Then in Haydn's middle years, when he was a universally recognized master in his own right in full possession of a supreme technique and mature creative powers, he came upon Mozart. Through Mozart's example, he was now able to find in himself new strength, new resources, new approaches. Haydn did not hesitate to penetrate the world Mozart had suddenly opened for him, even though Mozart was so much younger and less famous than he. Then in his old age, largely due to Handel, Haydn abandoned the symphony and piano sonata for religious choral music. For the first time in his life, he tried writing an oratorio. He also completed half a dozen Masses, which once again carry him to the summit.

Still another indelible influence upon him was not a man but a musical style—that of the Croatian folk song. Haydn was one of the first—possibly *the* first—to allow his melodies to be patterned after folk tunes and dances. Right up to his final masterworks, he continued introducing such material into his major works, even into his sacred music.

"He could afford to study and follow models," comments Karl Geiringer, "for he was entirely sure of himself. Haydn, in body and mind one of the healthiest of all great composers, knew that whatever he tried, the firm, gentle, humorous, eternally young and optimistic core of his personality would remain unchanged." However much Haydn might be influenced, however much he experimented and changed, he never seemed to lose his personal identifying touch. From his first masterwork to his last, we encounter in his writing what Paul Henry Lang once described as "love of life, wholesomeness, clarity, purity of feeling, noble and profound sentiment, inexhaustible humor, and impeccable craftsmanship."

Haydn's speech, sums up Franz Bellinger, "like that of every genius, was not only that of his race, but of the world. He had the heart of a rustic poet unspoiled by a decayed civilization. Like Wordsworth, he used the speech of a whole nation, and lived to work out all that was in him. Although almost entirely self-taught, he mastered every scientific principle of musical composition known at his time. He was able to compose for the people without pandering to what was vicious or ignorant in their taste. He identified himself absolutely with secular music, and gave it a status equal to the music of the church. He took the idea of the symphony and quartet, while it was yet rather formless and chaotic, floating in the musical consciousness of the period as salt floats on the ocean, drew it from the surrounding medium, and crystallized it into an art form. . . . He rises above all his contemporaries, except Mozart, as a lighthouse rises above the waves of the sea. With Mozart and Beethoven, he formed the immortal trio whose individual work, each with its own quality and its own weight, are the completion and the sum of the first era of orchestral music."

Franz Joseph Haydn was born in Rohrau-on-the-Leitha, Lower Austria, on March 31, 1732. Haydn's father, a wheelwright, and his mother, a cook, were both musical. From earliest childhood, Haydn grew up in a home where musical performances were frequent events. When he was five, Haydn was taken under the wing of a cousin, Johann Matthias Frankh, a professional musician, who gave the boy a thorough training at his home in Hainburg. Two years later, Haydn became a choirboy at St. Stephen's Cathedral, where his musical education continued. In 1748, when his voice broke, he left the Cathedral to set up home for himself in Vienna and embark on a musical career. He earned his living by teaching, playing the harpsichord, and doing hack work. But all this time, he was also busily engaged in studying the harpsichord and the violin, and in memorizing the keyboard sonatas of Carl Philipp Emanuel Bach. For a brief period, he performed menial services for Niccolà Porpora (1686–1768), a renowned singing teacher and composer, in return for lessons. Through Porpora, Haydn met such distinguished musicians as Gluck and Karl von Dittersdorf (1739–1799). They stimulated him to intensify his efforts as a composer. Thus Haydn completed some instrumental music, a Mass, and *Der krumme Teufel,* a Singspiel produced in Vienna in 1752.

In 1755, Baron Karl Joseph von Fuernberg engaged Haydn as the conductor of his orchestra. While thus employed, Haydn wrote some nocturnes and divertimentos, as well as his earliest string quartets. From 1758 to 1761, Haydn served as musical director and chamber composer for Count Ferdinand Maximilian Morzin. This was the period in which Haydn produced his first symphonies. In 1760, Haydn married Maria Anna Keller, after her sister, with whom he had been in love, suddenly entered a convent. Maria Anna proved a shrew; her marriage to Haydn was so unhappy from the beginning that before long they agreed on a permanent separation.

In 1761, Haydn became second Kapellmeister for Prince Paul Anton Esterházy at his estate in Eisenstadt; five years after that, Haydn was elevated to the position of first Kapellmeister. Haydn remained in Esterházy's employ almost thirty years, directing at the palace performances of operas and instrumental music. For these concerts, he completed a fabulous repertory: some eighty symphonies; over forty string quartets; divertimenti; concertos; keyboard compositions; operas; and choral music. Though he rarely left the Esterházy estate, except for an occasional visit to Vienna, his music and his fame spread all over Europe. Recognized as the foremost composer of his age, he became the recipient of many gifts and honors from major musical organizations and from some of Europe's crowned heads.

In 1790, Haydn finally left the employ of the Esterházys and went to live in Vienna. On a contractual arrangement with Johann Peter Salomon, an impresario, Haydn paid two visits to London—the first time in 1791, then again in 1794. There he conducted orchestral concerts for which he wrote his famous "London" symphonies. Back in Vienna after his second London visit, Haydn completed his first oratorio, *The Creation*. In 1797, at the request of the government, he wrote the Austrian national anthem. After 1801, he lived in seclusion. One of his rare public appearances took place in 1808 with a performance of *The Creation*. Haydn died in Vienna on May 31, 1809.

1761. SYMPHONY NO. 7 IN C, "LE MIDI" ("THE AFTERNOON"). I. Adagio; Allegro. II. Adagio. III. Adagio. IV. Con moto. V. Allegro.

To describe Haydn as "the father of the symphony," as was the tendency of some older historians, is to do a disservice to those pioneers who preceded him: the Mannheim school, of which Johann Stamitz was the dean; in Italy, Giovanni Battista Sammartini (1701–1775); Franz Xaver Richter (1709–1789), a Viennese who completed some seventy symphonies. Nevertheless, it could hardly be denied that it was Haydn whose innovations and experiments finally established the structure and style of the classic symphony. It is only necessary to compare one of Haydn's earliest symphonies with one of his last, to realize how far the symphony had traveled and how close it comes to the age of the mature Mozart and the early Beethoven. From the elementary orchestra used by many of Haydn's predecessors (usually just a quartet of strings, supplemented by a few woodwind and an occasional intrusion of horns and trumpets), the Haydn orchestra of his later symphonies becomes a fully developed ensemble, rich in texture, capable of varied colors and nuances, with advanced technical resources: strings, oboes, bassoons, flutes, horns, trumpets, timpani, and on occasion, clarinets. From the simple and formal presentation of thematic material in Haydn's predecessors and early contemporaries, we get in his later works a new concept of thematic development, bold modulations, enlargement and flexibility of structural design. Where Haydn's forerunners had resorted only to a most elementary use of dynamics through crescendos and diminuendos, we find in Haydn a wealth of color, nuance, and effect, undreamed of in Mannheim and Vienna before him. Haydn liberated the symphony from its bondage to the basso continuo, thus allowing him a greater richness of harmony and a greater elasticity of rhythm and tempo.

Haydn's first symphony, in D major, came in or about 1759, while he was employed in Bohemia by Count von Morzin. It is in three movements (no minuet); it still utilizes the continuo; the wind instruments serve just to reinforce the sonority. Within five years, Haydn completed some thirty symphonies, many of which were little more than serenades or divertimenti. All the while, he was groping for a new approach to symphonic writing through trial and error and indefatigable experimentations.

Soon after getting his appointment as assistant Kapellmeister for Prince Paul Anton Esterházy in Eisenstadt, Haydn set about reorganizing its orchestra. He had the instruments repaired, and he instituted a rigorous schedule of rehearsals. In time, he evolved an excellent ensemble with which to work and for which to write. As he himself said, he could now "make experiments, observe what produced an effect and what weakened it, and was thus in a position to improve, to alter, to make additions or omissions, and be as bold as I pleased."

The first symphony Haydn wrote for his Eisenstadt concerts is also the first to be available in present-day currency. It is numbered "seven" because this is its place in the Breitkopf and Haertel catalog of Haydn's symphonies. This symphony in C is one of a trio of such works in which the composer tried to depict different periods of the day. The C major Symphony is *Le Midi,* or *The Afternoon;* the other two are *Le Matin,* or *The Morning,* and *Le Soir* or *The Evening.*

The scoring for *Le Midi* is for two flutes, two oboes, bassoon, two horns, first and second violin concertante, cello concertante, and strings. The use of the violin and cello concertante points up the fact that in writing his symphony Haydn was still remembering the older concerto-grosso form. But there was also a good practical reason for using three solo instruments: the orchestra in Eisenstadt boasted two violinists and a cellist of exceptional talent, and Haydn, in his first symphony for the Eisenstadt concerts, was eager to throw the limelight on them.

The Symphony in C, *Le Midi,* opens with a ten-measure slow introduction. A slow introduction was a device utilized before Haydn by Georg Matthias Monn (1717–1750), but one that Haydn was henceforth to employ frequently and with extraordinary effect. In the main section that follows, a brusque first theme is heard in the strings. A transition in solo strings leads into the second theme, in the cello. The development of these two subjects is simple and economical, the instrumentation occasionally reinforced by the wind. The movement ends with a brief coda; the coda is another of Haydn's important symphonic innovations.

A short Adagio movement is a preface to a larger and more extended slow movement, also an Adagio. Here two melodies are prominent. This movement ends with a cadenza for solo violin and solo cello. A minuet and trio follow. The minuet theme is presented by strings, woodwind, and horns, while that of the trio appears in the cello. The symphony ends with a sprightly Allegro, whose opening theme is given by the strings. In this finale, all the solo instruments are prominently featured.

1763. 6 STRING QUARTETS, op. 3: I. E major. II. C major. III. G major. IV. B-flat major. V. F major. VI. A major.

The development of the Haydn string quartet paralleled that of the Haydn symphony, with one difference: With the string quartet, Haydn had few precedents to guide him. Before Haydn, string quartets had been written by Tomasso Antonio Vitali (c. 1665–?) and Alessandro Scarlatti (which see) in the seventeenth century; by Giuseppe Tartini and Sammartini in the eighteenth. But these quartets were so primitive that they bear little relation to a Haydn string quartet. Then, with composers like Boccherini, Florian Leopold Gassmann (1729–1774) and Franz Xaver Richter, an awareness of the possibilities of string-quartet writing began to set in. But it was after them, with Haydn, that the artistic validity of this form became realized; that the four members of the ensemble gained independence and individuality.

Haydn wrote his first string quartet in or about 1755, when employed by Count Fuernberg. The first dozen works in this medium (published as opus 1 and opus 2) are not string quartets actually, but five-movement divertimenti in which the four instruments were treated like a chamber orchestra. Here, as Rosemary Hughes has explained, "the cello line is mainly foundation bass, and the viola frequently crosses it, as if Haydn were unconsciously reckoning on a phantom double bass an octave lower." So tenuous is the line separating the quartet from orchestral music in these early compositions, that when Haydn's opus 2 string quartets were issued in Paris they were described as "six Sinfonias," and two of these works had horn parts added. "It is the measure of Haydn's real achievement," continues Rosemary Hughes, "in 'making' the string quartet that, starting with this divertimento-like conception of the quartet of strings, he should have realized that it had other and profounder potentialities and brought them to fruition."

The six quartets in opus 3 are a transition from Haydn's earlier divertimenti-type quartets and the later fully realized compositions. Haydn completed these op. 3 works during his initial years as Prince Esterházy's second Kapellmeister. Of this set, the fifth quartet deserves special attention (I. Presto. II. Andante cantabile. III. Menuetto. IV. Scherzando). It is here that a chamber-music style, as distinguished from a chamber-orchestral style, is achieved. The most popular movement here is the second, a serenade sometimes heard separately, and frequently in an orchestral transcription. This movement consists of a graceful tune in the first violin, accompanied by pizzicati in the other strings. The first movement has two sunny melodies within a clearly realized sonata form. The third movement is a minuet whose main theme has a four-bar phrase answered by one of six. The finale is a rondo with two lively themes.

The most curious work in this set is the fourth, which has just two movements (I. Allegro moderato. II. Adagio; Presto). "Both," explains Donald Francis Tovey, "are sprawling, long-limbed sonata-form movements, with some half-a-dozen agreeable themes, and a perfunctory and primitive passage of goose-step on the dominant to serve for development. The second is really two-in-one. A brief Adagio is built out of a reflective subject. Then comes a mercurial change of mood and tempo, beginning with an irregular ten-bar theme. Both the Adagio and the ensuing Presto are repeated. In making the concluding phrase of the Presto subject reminiscent of that of the Adagio melody, Haydn was here making one of his earliest experiments in correlating his themes."

1765. CAPRICCIO IN G MAJOR, for piano, op. 43.

This little item was particularly close to the composer's heart. When he sent it off to his publisher, Artaria, he explained: "In a humorous mood, I have composed an entirely new capriccio for the piano; its good taste, singularity, and elaborate finish are sure to please both experts and amateurs." The work is based on a north-German folk song, "Ich wuenscht' es waere Nacht."

1768. DER APOTHEKER, or LO SPEZIALE (THE APOTHECARY), opera buffa in three acts, with text by Carlo Goldoni. First performance: Esterház, autumn of 1768.

The twentieth century has witnessed some notable revivals of Haydn's comic operas. One of the most distinguished of these rarely heard works is *The Apothecary*. Here Haydn reveals himself to be a true master of the opera-buffa style.

The Apothecary is an amusing sketch about the rivalry of Sempronio, a druggist, and his clerk, Mengono, for lovely Grilletta. Matters are complicated by the fact that Grilletta is also being sought by Volpino. Discovering Mengono and Grilletta kissing and flirting, Sempronio decides to consummate his own marriage to the girl without further delay. When he summons a notary to draw up the marriage contract, both Mengono and Volpino appear in disguise and try to insert their own names into the document. But Sempronio discovers the trick and sends them away. Volpino then arrives at Sempronio's shop in the guise of a Pasha in search of medicines. He proceeds to destroy all the medicine bottles on the shelves and threatens to kill the poor apothecary. Mengono comes in the nick of time to save his employer. Sempronio proves so grateful that he no longer stands in the way of Grilletta and Mengono in consummating their marriage.

Karl Geiringer is impressed by Haydn's gift at characterization. "The conceit of the narrow-minded Sempronio . . . is beautifully described in the first aria. . . . The bold impudence of Volpino is well expressed in his aria in E major in the second act." Haydn's lyricism achieves at times the cream of the jest and at times poignancy and enchantment, most notably in Mengono's air, "Sitzt einem hier im Kopf das Weh'," and Grilletta's song, "Wie Schleier se'e ichs nieder schweben." The second-act finale (where Sempronio's marriage contract is being drawn up by false notaries) is to Geiringer "one of the most effective numbers of ensemble music in the pre-Mozart opera buffa," with its "repeated changes of tempo, and the introduction of roguish, but also affectionate, mirth."

What is believed to have been the American première of this opera buffa took place in New York at the Neighborhood Playhouse on March 16, 1926. The opera was revived in New York City in 1959 and 1961.

1772–1774. SYMPHONY NO. 45 IN F-SHARP MINOR, "ABSCHIED" ("FAREWELL"). I. Allegro assai. II. Adagio. III. Menuetto. IV. Presto; Adagio.

SYMPHONY NO. 48 IN C MAJOR, "MARIA THERESA." I. Allegro. II. Adagio. III. Menuetto. IV. Allegro.

SYMPHONY NO. 55 IN E-FLAT MAJOR, "DIE SCHULMEISTER" ("THE SCHOOLMASTER"). I. Allegro di molto. II. Adagio, ma semplicimente. III. Menuetto. IV. Presto.

Beginning with 1768, Haydn began introducing a personal, at times even a romantic, element into the formal procedures and staid methods of his symphonic writing. With 1768, and the Symphony No. 39 in G minor, there begins for Haydn a period designated as his "Sturm und Drang." A heightened emotion, a new intensity, at times even a feverish or tragic expression, now intrude into his writing. This is the reason why the Symphony No. 44 in E minor (c. 1771) has been called *Tragic,* and the Symphony No. 49 in F minor (1768), *Passion.* This deepened feeling is continually in evidence in several significant symphonies completed between 1772 and 1774.

A pretty story is told about the writing of the F-sharp minor Symphony (1772), the reason why it has been named *Farewell.* Legend would have us believe that Haydn wrote the last movement to remind Prince Esterházy that a vacation was long overdue for the orchestra. In that finale, the instruments are made to drop out gradually one by one until, at the end, only two solo violins remain. Each musician in the orchestra—so continues the story—blew out his candle on the music stand and slipped silently off the platform, music and instrument under arm. This departure was intended as a gentle hint that he was ready to start his vacation. But one of Haydn's friends has a far different interpretation for this music. He saw in it a picturesque way for Haydn to try to dissuade his employer from proceeding with projected plans to disband the orchestra.

The new expressiveness (*Empfindsamkeit*) that marked Haydn's style during this period is found, not in the finale of this symphony, but in its second movement. Here we get a melody of unusual tenderness and melancholy in the violins. The first movement is in strict, and traditional, sonata form. The first theme in the violins, with contrasts in the wind, is followed by a second lyrical subject in strings and oboe. The third movement, a minuet, is endowed with flashes of wit through unusual rhythmic patterns.

The Symphony No. 48 in C major (1772) is called *Maria Theresa* because it was written, and first performed, to honor the visit of that Empress to Eisenstadt in 1773. "The Empress," reported the *Wiener Diarium,* "was taken to the Chinese pavilion whose mirror-covered walls reflected countless lampions and chandeliers flooding the room with light. On a platform sat the princely orchestra in gala uniform and played under Haydn's direction his new symphony." As befitting this occasion, the symphony has gaiety and sparkle, particularly in the first theme of the first movement for oboes and brasses, in the vivacity of the main melody of the minuet, and throughout the ebullient and effervescent finale.

Nobody knows why the Symphony No. 55 in E-flat major (1774) has come to be known as *The Schoolmaster*. Some suspect that the precise and measured way in which the muted melody of the Adagio proceeds in unison violins is a picture of as schoolmaster's disciplined way of life. The first movement has two contrasting subjects, the first lively, the second lyrical. The minuet differs from others in Haydn symphonies by its faster tempo and the enchanting effect achieved in the trio by a single cello providing an uninterrupted accompaniment in eighth notes. The finale, though mainly jovial, especially in the playful second subject in bassoon, ends in a striking contrast between serenity and a sudden forceful procession of four loud concluding chords.

1772. 6 "SUN " QUARTETS, op. 20: I. E-flat major. II. C major. III. G minor. IV. D major. V. F minor. VI. A major.

After almost forty string quartets, Haydn finally created a series of works in which the medium found its master. This set has come to be known as the *Sun Quartets,* for the rather prosaic reason that the publisher's trademark on an early Berlin edition carried the picture of the sun. With far better cause are these works also referred to as "*Die Grossen Quartette,*" or the *Great Quartets*. "Great they are," says W. W. Cobbett, "a sunrise over the domain of sonata style as well as quartets in particular. Every page of the six quartets of opus 20 is of historic and aesthetic importance; and though the total results will leave Haydn with a long road to travel, there is perhaps no single or sextuple opus in the history of instrumental music which has achieved so much or achieved it so quietly." Chamber-music style is realized here in all its individuality and purity. Here we confront that power of thematic invention, those relationships and that development that make the mature Haydn symphonies so significant. An altogether new expressive use of polyphonic devices in instrumental music is made here. Here, too, the four instruments are finally liberated to endow each his own personality. These six quartets are also remarkable for the chameleon changes of personality from one work to the next. The first quartet has such an intimate quality that it almost sounds like a conversation. The second has nobility. The third has been described as "brusque and angular." The fourth has that animation for which the word "Haydnish" is possibly the best description. The fifth has overtones of melancholy and is for the most part high-tensioned music. The sixth has rococo grace.

The fifth string quartet in F minor has been described as "the most nearly tragic work Haydn ever wrote" (I. Allegro moderato. II. Menuetto. III. Adagio. IV. Fuga e due soggetti.) The intensity of expression found throughout the work makes itself felt immediately in the haunting first theme of the opening Allegro moderato. Though the second movement, a minuet, offers temporary digression from the strongly felt emotion through its whimsical mood, the slow movement that follows plunges us even more deeply into the abyss of despair. The tragedy comes charged with dramatic impulses in the finale, a fugue based on two subjects.

1777. IL MONDO DELLA LUNA (THE WORLD OF THE MOON), opera buffa in three acts, with text by Carlo Goldoni. First performance: Esterház, August 3, 1777.

An eccentric wealthy Venetian, Buonafede, tries to keep his daughter Clarissa from having contacts with the outside world, and particularly with Leandro, with whom she is in love. A local astrologer, Dr. Ecclittico, decides to perpetrate a trick on the old man. He concocts a fake telescope through which he convinces Buonafede that the moon becomes clearly visible. Then he puts Buonafede to rest with a sleeping pill and transports him to his own garden. Upon awakening, Buonafede becomes convinced he is on the moon. So engrossed does he become with his lunar experiences that he willingly allows Clarissa to marry Leandro.

Some of the orchestral episodes in this little opera are as distinguished as the best vocal ones. A first-act interlude offers a picture of the moon; an orchestral passage in the first-act finale describes a voyage to the lunar regions; and a second-act prelude tells of ceremonies attending the arrival of the moon's sovereign. In addition, there is a brief orchestral number for each of the three times Buonafede studies the moon through his fake telescope. Among the more distinguished vocal pages are Leandro's beautiful air, "Und liegt auch zwischen dir und mir"; the ecstatic duet of Leandro and Clarissa, "Am Tor der himmlischen Freude"; and Clarissa's song, "Wind der mich faechelt warm."

The World of the Moon lay forgotten for almost two centuries after its première in Esterház. H. C. Robbins, the English musicologist, pieced the work together from fragments he found in different places in Europe. In 1959, the comic opera was heard for the first time since Haydn's own day at several European music festivals, including those at Holland and Aix-en-Provence.

1778. SYMPHONY NO. 67 IN F MAJOR. I. Presto. II. Adagio. III. Allegretto. IV. Allegro molto.

The F major Symphony is a much finer and more original work than its comparative neglect would suggest. The *Empfindsamkeit* of the slow movement, and of the extended middle Adagio section in the finale with its gentle melancholy, places this symphony with the most mature works of Haydn's middle period. Irving Kolodin further notes the presence of a 6/8 meter in the first movement (not usual with Haydn) that "encourages a particularly contrapuntal development, as the figures are used in overlapping relationships, and inverted. There is also much interweaving of instruments, the strings enforced by oboes, horns, and bassoons, and a considerable degree of virtuosity is required of the players, the strings in particular." The slow movement, in which the strings are throughout muted, is in the sonata form, one of its two main subjects being a soaring melody for strings. An innovation for the time is to have the violins play col legno (wood of the bow on the strings instead of the hair) in the concluding measures. In the first part of the minuet, "an angular, country-dance type figure prevails," explains Kolodin, "succeeded by a trio for solo first and solo second violin, in which the second violin is directed to tune the G string down to F, which effect persists as a drone bass throughout the section." There are three parts in the finale, the outer ones being spirited, and the middle one an unusual and highly impressive Adagio.

1780–1794. PIANO SONATAS:

No. 35 in C major. I. Allegro con brio. II. Adagio. III. Allegro.

No. 37 in D major. I. Allegro con brio. II. Largo e sostenuto. III. Presto ma non troppo.

No. 43 in A-flat major. I. Allegro moderato. II. Adagio. III. Presto.

No. 49 in E-flat major. I. Allegro ma non troppo. II. Adagio cantabile. III. Tempo di minuet.

No. 51 in D major. I. Andante. II. Presto.

The piano sonata, a form to which Haydn contributed some fifty works, was perhaps not quite the happy medium for his creativity that the symphony and the string quartet were. All the same, his greatest works in this genre rank with the best produced before Beethoven's time. To the piano sonata, Haydn brought a new concept of thematic presentation and enlargement, a mastery of structure, at times a daring in the use of tonalities and unexpected effects, and a wealth of expressiveness.

Building on the sonatas of Carl Philipp Emanuel Bach, Haydn developed the classic form by "improving so largely upon the earlier," says J. Cuthbert Hadeen, "that we could pass from his sonatas directly to those of Beethoven without the intervention of Mozart's as a connecting link. Beethoven's sonatas were certainly more influenced by Haydn's than by Mozart's. The masterpieces among Haydn's sonatas . . . astonish by their order, regularity, fluency, harmony and roundness, and by their splendid development into full and complete growth out of the sometimes apparently unimportant germs. . . . The changes which have been made in the classical sonata form since his day are merely changes of detail. To him is due the fixity of the form."

The first movement of the C major Sonata (1780) is perhaps the last word in elegant rococo writing. The D major Sonata (1789) is written in the grand manner of Beethoven. The A-flat major Sonata (1785) boasts a slow movement that is one of the most soul-searching Haydn ever wrote for the piano. The wonderful E-flat major Sonata (1790) shows new approaches in amplifying and changing thematic material. The D major Sonata (1792) is full of surprises, both in the development section of the first movement which sidesteps classical tradition, and in the off-beat accents and unexpected transitions in the finale.

1781. 6 "RUSSIAN" QUARTETS, op. 33: I. B minor. II. E-flat major, "The Joke." III. C major, "The Bird." IV. B-flat major. V. G major. VI. D major.

This set of chamber-music compositions is sometimes identified as *Russian* and sometimes as *Gli scherzi*. It is called *Russian* because all works were dedicated to the Grand Duke Paul of Russia, and *Gli scherzi* because Haydn here designated his minuet movements as scherzos or scherzandos.

Individual quartets also have their identifying nicknames. The E-flat major Quartet is known as "The Joke," due to its finale. Here Haydn interpolates unexpected rests in order—so goes the story—to catch flat-footed those ladies in the audience insisting on talking throughout the music. In the finale, elements of amusing byplay are introduced, especially in the coda, where a solemn subject is given a droll treatment. In the first movement of the C major Quartet, the main theme has grace notes that sound like the chirping of birds; their voices return again in the trio of the scherzando movement, in a duet for first and second violins. This is the reason why the C major Quartet has been dubbed *The Bird.*

Haydn himself boasted that his writing in these quartets was in a "new and graceful manner." "If there is nothing inherently 'new' about the opus 33 quartets," remarks Rosemary Hughes, "there is indeed something 'special'. . . . It is not merely that the part-writing has taken on a new ease, fluency, and grace; it is rather that texture has become one with organic structure, as the development of the themes takes possession of the entire fabric." Then Rosemary Hughes concludes: "From now on, texture holds no problems, and he is free to concentrate on those of structure and design. The results are immediately apparent. Whereas his instinct was formerly toward terseness, he now begins to expand. It is in the first movement of the last three quartets of op. 33 . . . that this new expansiveness appears; their recapitulation instead of being sharply telescoped, grows outwards in fresh contours and with new changes of key and further developments of the main themes."

1782. MARIAZELLERMESSE (MISSA CELLENSIS), for solo voices, chorus, and orchestra.

Haydn wrote his first Mass—the Missa Brevis in F major—in 1749–1750. When Haydn revised it late in life, he said: "What I particularly like about this little work is its tunefulness and a certain youthful fire." But a wide gulf separates Haydn's first Masses and those he wrote many years later. The earlier Masses resemble the secular cantata and the concerto grosso. The style is less in a religious vein and more in a rococo style, sometimes even with a suggestion of frivolity. There is little attempt on Haydn's part to convey the essence of the text in the music.

The *Mariazellermesse* in C major is the transition from these earlier rococo Masses to those grandiose fruits of Haydn's old age. He wrote it for the Monastery of Mariazell. This music, says Wilfrid Mellers, is "Mozartian" in its "theatrical manner," particularly in the powerful "Crucifixus," in which "Haydn can regard Christ not as a superhuman divinity but as a man suffering."

Karl Geiringer sees in this Mass "both elements of the old and the new style." He explains: "The 'Gratias' is a real coloratura aria for soprano, while the expressive 'Miserere nobis' in F minor is given to the quartet of solo voices. 'Et resurrexit,' as in a Missa Brevis, brings simultaneously in each separate voice a different section of the text, so that while the soprano sings 'Et Resurrexit,' the alto has the words of 'Et in Spiritum Sanctum,' the tenor 'Et Iterum Venturus,' and the bass, 'Qui cum Patre.' Nor does it inspire great confidence in Haydn's liturgical technique to discover that the 'Benedictus' uses an aria that was originally written for the comic opera, *Il Mondo della luna*. Yet there are passages in this score that show a deep understanding of the true meaning of the text. An excellent example is provided by the aria for tenor, 'Et Incarnatus Est.' Beginning in A minor, it modulates to C major at the words 'homo factus est' and reaches the melancholy C minor when the catastrophe of the 'Crucifixus' approaches. This 'Crucifixus,' sung by the chorus and gradually rising from the low bass register, is most impressive."

1783. CONCERTO NO. 2 IN D MAJOR, for cello and orchestra, op. 101. I. Allegro. II. Adagio. III. Allegro.

CONCERTO IN D MAJOR, for harpsichord and orchestra, op. 21. I. Vivace. II. Larghetto. III. Allegro assai.

The authenticity of Haydn's most famous cello concerto—the second, in D major—has long been questioned. It was suggested by some Haydn authorities that it is the work of Anton Kraft, first cellist of Haydn's orchestra at Esterház, even though the work is of a consistently high standard, bearing more than one of Haydn's fingerprints. However, all doubts about its author were permanently laid to rest when, in the 1950's, Haydn's manuscript was finally discovered. On its first page, there appears the inscription in unmistakable Haydn caligraphy: "Concerto for the violoncello—by Joseph Haydn." And at the end of the manuscript appears the words "In Praise of God" in Haydn's handwriting.

The first-movement orchestral introduction offers the main thematic material. The solo instrument repeats the broadly melodious first subject with some embellishments. The virtuosity of the soloist is highlighted in the development before the main melody is repeated. In the slow movement, the solo cello raises its voice in a spritual song before setting forth on two more subjects of contrasting mood. The finale is set spinning with a jovial tune that sounds like a folk song. It is heard in the solo cello. Three more lyrical episodes follow.

Haydn's most popular concerto for a keyboard instrument is the D major Harpsichord Concerto. After the orchestra has given the two principal themes of the first movement—the first, a lyrical subject for the strings, and the second, a melody for the strings supplemented by the woodwind—the solo instrument repeats and embroiders upon them. In the slow movement, a lyrical passage unfolds in the violins before it is given further extension by the harpsichord. The principal subject in the finale is Hungarian in its dash and abandon.

1784. DIE SIEBEN WORTE DES ERLOESERS AM KREUZE (THE SEVEN LAST WORDS OF THE SAVIOUR ON THE CROSS), for basso and orchestra.

In 1784, Haydn was commissioned by the canon of the Cadiz Cathedral in Spain to create an instrumental composition based on "The Seven Last Words of Our Saviour on the Cross." It was intended for performance during Lent. In the preface to his score, Haydn himself explained: "It was customary to produce an oratorio every year during Lent, the effect of the performance being not a little enhanced by the following circumstances. The walls, windows, and pillars of the church were hung with black cloth and only one large lamp hanging from the center of the roof broke the solemn obscurity. . . . After a short service, the bishop ascended the pulpit, pronounced the first of the seven words (or sentences) and delivered a discourse thereon. This ended, he left the pulpit and prostrated himself before the altar. The pause was filled by music. The bishop then in like manner pronounced the second word, then the third, and so on, the orchestra following on the conclusion of each discourse. My composition was subject to these conditions, and it was no easy matter to compose seven Adagios to last ten minutes each, and succeed one another without fatiguing the listeners.

The seven slow movements, or "sonatas," are preceded by a slow introduction, and concluded by a fast movement describing an earthquake. The seven "sonatas"—sometimes also referred to as "meditations"—are in the following keys: B-flat major, C minor and major, E major, F minor, A major, G minor and major, E-flat major. "They combine," says Wilfred Mellers, "a sublime lyrical serenity and intense tonal drama. The themes, however, are more Italianate than the Masonic hymns of Haydn's last years. Perhaps for this reason the music has a meditative ecstasy which makes it seem more Catholic in spirit than any music Haydn wrote."

1785–1786. 6 "PARIS" SYMPHONIES:

No. 82, C major, "L'Ours" ("The Bear"). I. Vivace assai. II. Allegretto. III. Menuetto. IV. Vivace assai.

No. 83, G minor, "La Poule" ("The Hen"). I. Allegro spiritoso. II. Andante. III. Menuetto. IV. Vivace.

No. 84, E-flat major. I. Largo; Allegro. II. Andante. III. Menuetto. IV. Vivace.

No. 85, B-flat major, "La Reine" ("The Queen"). I. Adagio; Vivace. II. Romanze; Allegretto. III. Menuetto. IV. Presto.

No. 86, D major. I. Adagio; Allegro spiritoso. II. Capriccio; Largo. III. Menuetto. IV. Allegro con spirito.

No. 87, A major. I. Vivace. II. Adagio. III. Menuetto. IV. Vivace.

In 1785, Haydn was commissioned to write six symphonies for performance by the Concerts de la Loge Olympique at the Salle des Gardes in the Tuileries in Paris. Technically, the most significant feature of these works is their abundance of thematic ideas, and the enlarged scope of the development sections.

The first of these symphonies is known as *The Bear*. In the finale, there are sounded growling bass notes that resemble a bear's roar. The name of *The Hen* is fixed to the second of these symphonies because of the unusual instrumental effect in the first movement: persistent notes in the oboe, punctuating the florid melody (second theme) of the movement, have the sound of a cackling hen. Karl Geiringer finds this symphony also unusual for the "dramatic quality" of the slow movement, and the "peculiar charm" of the finale, which is in the style of a siciliano.

The E-flat major Symphony, says Geiringer, boasts a first movement that "grows out of the main idea almost completely. Haydn postpones the entrance of the contrasting subject so long that it assumes the role of an epilogue instead of a subsidiary subject." The second movement is a theme and variations which "separates the theme in the major from its first variation by a rather dramatic passage in the minor." The vivacious finale features "sudden changes from the pianissimo of a few instruments to the forte of the whole orchestra," in anticipation of Haydn's later *Surprise Symphony*.

La Reine—the Symphony No. 85—was believed to have been a particular favorite of Queen Marie Antoinette. Here the second movement is a most delightful set of variations on the French tune, "La gentille et jeune Lisette" —"full of effects of tone color," says Geiringer, "while the melody and harmony of the theme undergo but little change."

To Geiringer, the Symphony No. 86 in B-flat major is "one of the greatest of this set." The slow movement "shows an affinity with both the sonata and rondo forms but without adopting either. Haydn called this interesting and surprisingly serious movement Capriccio. The Allegro spiritoso of the first movement and the final Allegro con spirito certainly deserve the designation 'spirited' as they are full of life and wit."

Geiringer singles out the minuet movement (particularly the haunting flute solo in its trio) as one of the most memorable parts of the A major symphony No. 87. But on the whole, he regards this as one "of the least serious of Haydn's mature symphonies."

1787. 6 "PRUSSIAN" QUARTETS, op. 50: I. B-flat major. II. C major. III. E-flat major. IV. F-sharp minor. V. F major. VI. D major.

Haydn had already proved himself the greatest composer of string-quartet music of his generation, when, in 1781, he met Mozart and became his friend and admirer. The new horizons that Mozart opened up in his own music, which extended so immeasurably the world Haydn himself had been exploring, made a profound impression on the master. Now fifty years old and acknowledged one of Europe's greatest composers, Haydn stood ready to profit from experiences which Mozart's music brought him. In consequence of these experiences, a fresh concept of form and style, a new independence of thought, an increasing intensity of feeling began to invade Haydn's string-quartet writing. The influence of Mozart upon Haydn became strikingly evident in the six *Prussian Quartets,* so named because they were dedicated to the King of Prussia. Structurally, these works reveal the composer's new interest in monothematic movements: movements in the sonata form in which the secondary subject (or group of subjects) is either derived from or is a variation of the first subject or group. The finest of these *Prussian Quartets* makes a most skilful use of this monothematic process.

To Donald Francis Tovey, the third of these quartets (E-flat major) is not only the aristocrat of this group but also one of the greatest of all Haydn chamber-music works (I. Allegro con brio. II. Andante più tosto. III. Allegretto. IV. Menuetto. V. Presto). Haydn here deviates from the traditional sonata form by presenting both main themes (the second intimately related to the first) at the very opening of the first movement. The exposition then consists of a working out of these ideas. The first, often treated contrapuntally, becomes Haydn's prime concern in the development, while the second helps to bring on the recapitulation. The coda repeats the opening material. The second movement is a set of variations on a stately melody first heard in cello, then carried on by the two violins. In the minuet, the minuet melody is heard not only in the opening section but also in the trio. The finale is structurally a compromise between the sonata and the rondo forms.

In the finale of the fourth string quartet in F-sharp minor, a monumental tragedy unfolds within the fugue form—an instance of Haydn's intensified *Empfindsamkeit* (I. Allegretto spiritoso. II. Andante. III. Menuetto. IV. Fuga: allegro moderato). The sixth quartet in D major is known as *The Frog* (I. Allegro. II. Poco adagio. III. Menuetto. Iv. Allegro con spirito). This is due to the groaning, frog-like croakings produced in the finale by having the same notes played alternately on neighboring instruments. In this quartet, Haydn's increased expressiveness becomes marked, first in the eloquent song of the second movement, a theme and variations, and then in the main subject of the minuet.

1787–1788. SYMPHONY NO. 88 IN G MAJOR, op. 56, no. 2. I. Adagio; Allegro. II. Largo. III. Menuetto. IV. Allegro con spirito.

SYMPHONY NO. 92 IN G MAJOR, "OXFORD," op. 66, no. 2. I. Allegro spiritoso. II. Adagio. III. Menuetto. IV. Presto.

TOY SYMPHONY. I. Allegro. II. Minuet. III. Finale.

The most popular of Haydn's symphonies before the set of twelve he wrote for London is that in G major (1787)—and with good reason. This is Haydn in full maturity, flooding the symphonic structure with richness of emotion and beauty of thematic material. This is Haydn refining and perfecting many of the experiments and innovations of earlier symphonies. The slow episode, which Haydn liked to use as a preface to his first movement, here has a courtly majesty. A soft but vivacious little subject for the violins, and a chromatic melody that has kinship to the first theme, are the main subjects of this movement. In the second movement, a wondrous song is heard in the cellos and oboes, accompanied by horn, bassoon, and strings. Several variations follow. Midway, strong chords, and a stirring tutti, in which drums and trumpets participate, introduce a change of mood. The minuet, which has the character of a peasant dance, is made continually exciting through subtle changes of rhythm. Now comes the finale, to some the high point of the whole symphony. A genial tune opens this movement in much the same way that it does other Haydn symphonies. But then, unexpectedly, a miraculous canonic passage is evolved. This in itself, says H. C. Robbins Landon, is not only "a tour de force," but also "the logical outcome of the foregoing material." A dramatic pause precedes and points up the exciting finish that follows.

During his first visit to London in 1791, Haydn was conferred an honorary degree by Oxford. To celebrate the occasion, three concerts were given, for which Haydn wrote a new symphony. The work, however, arrived too late for rehearsal. Consequently, an earlier work was chosen for performance—the Symphony in G major, henceforth known as the *Oxford* (1788). It begins with a stately preface for strings. At a climactic point, the woodwinds join in. The main body enters with a vigorous first theme in the strings, to which is also assigned the lyrical second subject. The development and recapitulation are along traditional lines. The coda embellishes upon the two subjects, the first theme being presented somewhat falteringly, while the second unfolds more fully, first in the oboe, then in flute and first violins. Descending scales precede the movement's powerful three concluding chords. The slow movement is in a reflective mood, dominated by a melody of religious character in the strings. The minuet is along familiar Haydn lines, the main theme being developed with dignity; a syncopated dance melody, answered by a run for first violins, is heard in the trio. The finale opens with a lively dance in the strings, the flute joining in when the tune is repeated. The second subject here is also spirited and rhythmic, but with a descending melody where the opening thought had been ascending. In the development, the first subject receives fugato treatment.

The *Toy Symphony* (1788) is a little curiosity long attributed to Haydn. It was introduced as a Haydn composition in Vienna in 1790 and today is often credited to the master. But recent research leans to the belief that this was the work of either Mozart's father or Haydn's brother, Michael. Those who regard Haydn as its composer maintain the master wrote it while visiting Berchtesgaden in Bavaria. There he came upon several toy instruments that so intrigued him that he decided to write a mock symphony for them. In its original version, the *Toy Symphony* used only three conventional instruments, two violins and a bass. All other instruments were toys and noisemakers: penny trumpet, quail call, rattle, cuckoo, screeching owl, whistle, a little drum, and a miniature triangle. The mood throughout the three movements is one of extreme levity. The music, both as to form and content, is so slight and undemanding that it proves ideal fare for children.

1789–1790. 12 "TOST" QUARTETS, op. 54, op. 55, op. 64: I. G major. II. C major. III. E major. IV. A major. V. F minor and major, "Razor". VI. B-flat major. VII. C major. VIII. B minor. IX. B-flat major. X. G major. XI. D major, "Lark". XII. E-flat major.

The three sets of string quartets, totaling twelve works in all (gathered in op. 54, op. 55 and op. 64) are collectively known as the *Tost Quartets*. This is because they were dedicated to a certain Johann Tost, about whom Haydn biographers seem to know very little. In these compositions, the monothematic technique that Haydn had deployed in earlier works is developed with increasing sophistication. At the same time, a new prominence is assigned to the first violin, as Haydn permits his lyricism to soar to new altitudes of eloquence. Continual surprises are introduced through unexpected fugato passages, unusual harmonies, progressions and modulations, unorthodox arrangement of the voices, and new approaches to the architectonic structure.

In the String Quartet in F minor and major, op. 55, no. 2, structural procedure of the classic variety is reversed by allowing a slow theme and variations to come as a first movement, and an Allegro in sonata form as the second. (I. Andante più tosto; Allegretto. II. Allegro. III. Menuetto. IV. Presto). A fanciful story is responsible for having this work dubbed *The Razor*. While shaving, Haydn was said to have shouted to a friend that he would gladly trade one of his string quartets for a good razor. When the friend later provided him with one, Haydn completed the bargain by turning over to him the Quartet in F minor.

The sobriquet of *The Lark* was earned for the D major Quartet, op. 64, no. 5, by its first movement, one of Haydn's purest and noblest inspirations. "From the earth-bound accompaniment of the lower parts," says Karl Geiringer, "the first violin soars up to heavenly heights." But the lyrical outpouring does not end with this inspired melody. "The rich expansion of the second subject which follows is a wholly unexpected development," wrote Rosemary Hughes, "and its climax is succeeded by the most surprising stroke of all, as the first subject sails calmly in once more and starts a brand new, and this time, a closely condensed recapitulation. The effect of spontaneity and spaciousness, combined with close unity thus achieved, is unique. Haydn never wrote another movement like it." (I. Allegro moderato. II. Adagio cantabile. III. Menuetto. IV. Vivace).

1789. FANTASIA IN C, for piano, op. 58.

This work is an earnest of the composer's gift at improvisation, for its material is developed ever so freely, with sudden changes of mood and almost spontaneous flights of inspiration within a pliable structure. In addition, the *Fantasia* is noteworthy for its unorthodox modulations, advanced keyboard techniques, and the way passages are distributed between the two hands for pianistic reasons. Noteworthy, too, is the striking effect produced by having the bass notes held until they die away.

1791–1795. 12 "LONDON" SYMPHONIES: I. No. 93 in D major, op. 83, no. 2. II. No. 94 in G major, "Paukenschlag" ("Surprise"), op. 80, no. 1. III. No. 95 in C minor, op. 77, no. 1. IV. No. 96 in D major, "Miracle," op. 77, no. 2. V. No. 97 in C major, op. 83, no. 1. VI. No. 98 in B-flat major, op. 82, no. 2. VII. No. 99 in E-flat major, op. 98, no. 3. VIII. No. 100 in G major, "Military," op. 90. IX. No. 101 in D major, "Clock," op. 95, no. 2. X. No. 102 in B-flat major, op. 98, no. 2. XI. No. 103 in E-flat major, "Paukenwirbel" ("Drum Roll"), op. 95, no. 1; XII. No. 104 in D major, "London," op. 98, no. 1.

The two sets of symphonies that Haydn wrote, one for each of his two visits to London in 1791 and 1794, represent the crown of that composer's symphonic output. These are the last of his hundred or so works in that form. In technical mastery, in maturity of thought, in profundity of feeling, in originality of means, these symphonies clearly outstrip all his previous efforts. "No other of Haydn's scores," maintains Karl Geiringer, "show such virtuosity of instrumentation or such delightful unorthodox treatment of musical forms and contrapuntal devices. . . . The whole nineteenth century, beginning with Beethoven and ending with Brahms, was able to draw rich inspiration from Haydn's last . . . symphonies."

In the first of these *London* symphonies, that in D major, the Largo movement, is particularly significant. The noble melody, first announced in the strings and then repeated in bassoons and violins, has the kind of spiritual exaltation we encounter in Haydn's *Creation* and last Masses. (I. Adagio; Allegro assai. II. Largo cantabile. III. Menuetto. IV. Presto ma non troppo.)

The second in this group is popularly known as the *Surprise.* (I. Adagio cantabile; Vivace assai. II. Andante. III. Menuetto. IV. Allegro di molto.) This comes from the fact that the second movement opens quietly with a sedate little tune for the strings (a melody Haydn later used as an air for Simon in *The Seasons*). After this theme has been repeated, once again gently, the full orchestra enters precipitously and unexpectedly with a resounding chord. This, in turn, is followed by a dramatic pause. The story goes—and it is a myth pure and simple—that the playful Haydn wanted to wake up his audiences, which, he felt, habitually fell asleep during the slow movements of symphonies. After the dramatic pause, the sedate melody receives four variations.

In this symphony, the first movement has the traditional slow opening. The main theme of the movement is a vivacious subject for the violins, which begins serenely enough but soon gains in vigor; the second theme is in a similarly light tone. The third movement is a two-section minuet; the last two measures of the minuet provide the material for the second section, which is presented canonically. The finale maintains a consistent note of jollity with two lively tunes that proceed at a vigorous pace.

Like the *Surprise,* the D major Symphony acquired its popular name—that of *Miracle*—from legend rather than fact. (I. Allegro. II. Andante. III. Menuetto. IV. Vivace assai.) This symphony was introduced at the Hanover Rooms in London on March 11, 1791. "When Haydn appeared in the orchestra," wrote A. K. Dies in 1810, "the curious audience in the parterre left their seats and pressed forward toward the orchestra with a view to seeing Haydn better at close range. The seats in the middle of the parterre were therefore, empty, and no sooner were they empty but a great chandelier plunged down, smashed, and threw the numerous company into great confusion. As soon as the first moment of shock was over, and those who had pressed forward realized the danger which they had so luckily escaped, and could find words to express the same, many persons showed their state of mind by shouting loudly: 'Miracle! Miracle!'" All this is a very pretty story. But at the concert of March 11, it was the Symphony No. 102 that opened the program and before whose playing the audience rushed to the stage; the *Miracle* was played in the second part, *after* the chandelier had fallen. Haydn himself, when questioned by Dies, did not remember the entire episode at all.

The *Miracle* opens with a slow sixteen-measure introduction. After that, the full orchestra presents the first theme loudly. A transition in woodwind and strings in unison brings on the melodious second theme in the violins. The second movement is made up of a charming rococo melody in the strings decorated by grace notes. The formal minuet is followed by the finale, in which the principal theme has the drive of a perpetuum mobile.

The Symphony No. 97 in C major (I. Adagio; Vivace. II. Adagio ma non troppo. III. Menuetto. IV. Presto assai.) has a sober thirteen-measure introduction. The main subject is then proclaimed loudly by full orchestra. After a sudden soft passage, a lilting melody is heard in the first violins, supported by other strings and bassoons. "The work out," says John N. Burk in his informative program notes for the Boston Symphony, "is compact, sinuous in a shifting chain of modulations." A melody with folk-song lack of pretension is the basis of the slow movement. It is presented first by the strings, "woven into triplets by the first violins," explains Burk, "transformed into the minor, and then delivered back into the major in a longer section in rippling sixteenth-notes." A lusty dance tune is loudly projected by the orchestra as the main theme of the minuet; to this vigor, the simple and delicate trio comes as a refreshing contrast. The finale is built from a major subject and two subsidiary ones. The first part of the major subject, says Burk, is "gently playful, its closing phrase a unison descent forte. In development, the hammered insistence of this phrase becomes convenient for driving home new keys. There are playful surprises, sudden explosions of an unrelated note which . . . would turn out to be justified by a modulation."

What is unusual about the Symphony No. 99 in E-flat major is the inclusion of two clarinets in the orchestration; the clarinet appeared in only six of Haydn's more than hundred symphonies. (I. Adagio; Vivace assai. II. Adagio. III. Menuetto. IV. Vivace.) Hugo Botsiber, one of Haydn's biographers, maintained that this one was Haydn's favorite among his symphonies. After an eighteen-measure slow introduction, the main body of the first movement opens with a vigorous idea for strings. The full orchestra repeats the melody before it receives a brief development. The lyrical second subject is then given by clarinet and first violins. The development opens with a passing reference to the first subject and continues with an elaboration of the second. The full orchestra, in a statement of the first theme, brings on the recapitulation in which the second subject appears in the first violins in an enlarged format. In the slow movement, a simple melody is presented by strings, the flute entering on the third and fourth measures. The woodwind later elaborates this thought. After a short pause, a new theme unfolds to terminate in a staccato chord. The minuet starts with a strongly accented descending subject for clarinet and strings in octaves. In the trio, oboe and strings are heard in a delightful tune. The finale begins vivaciously with a Croatian folk song in the strings. To the woodwind is assigned the second theme before the opening subject is recalled. The development follows traditional procedures. In the recapitulation, the first theme is merely suggested, but full play is given to the second one.

The title of *Military* assigned to the Symphony No. 100 in G major arises from the fact that this work features bugle calls, and that the percussion group calls for instruments associated by the eighteenth century with military music, such as the drums, cymbals, and triangle. Except for an unusual emphasis on the percussion in the second movement (otherwise devoted to a characteristically melodious Haydn tune in first violins and flute) there is nothing in the symphony to suggest the military life. (I. Adagio; Allegro. II. Allegretto. III. Menuetto. IV. Presto.)

But there is a sound reason for calling the Symphony No. 101 in D major, the *Clock*. (I. Adagio; Presto. II. Andante. III. Allegretto. IV. Vivace.) In the second movement, a flowing song for strings is accompanied by the even pulse of a staccato accompaniment that sounds like a ticking clock. In this symphony, the first movement has a sober introduction before the main section offers a sprightly ascending melody in first violins; the first violins are also called upon to introduce the lyrical second subject. In the trio of the minuet, we encounter unusual harmonic colorations when a drone bass gives the impression of dissonance. The finale highlights a broad string melody as a main subject; toward the end of the movement, it provides the basis for an effective fugal passage.

Donald Francis Tovey regarded the Symphony No. 102 in B-flat major as one of the three greatest instrumental compositions by Haydn. (I. Largo; Allegro. II. Adagio. III. Menuetto. IV. Presto.) The customary slow introduction in the first movement precedes the main section where the first theme is vigorously stated by the full orchestra. A sprightly figure in the violins is worked up climactically and sets the stage for the emergence of the melodious second theme. This material is developed dramatically. The recapitulation to Tovey resembles "a true Beethovenian coda of the ripest kind." The Adagio is made up almost entirely from a single elegant melody with overtones of sentimentality. (Haydn used this theme also for his Piano Trio in F-sharp.) The minuet is in a playful mood. In the finale, "syncopations, pianissimo staccatos, unexpected pauses, clashes of the full orchestra, sudden transitions of key, the playful use of parts of a motive combine," wrote Felix Borowski, "in making a picture of happiness and joyousness."

The Symphony No. 103 in E-flat (I. Allegro con spirito. II. Andante. III. Menuetto. IV. Allegro con spirito.) opens unorthodoxly with a roll of the timpani in the first measure. Later on in the movement this drum roll is repeated with droll effect. This is the reason why the symphony as a whole is often identified as the "symphony with the drum roll" ("Mit dem Paukenwirbel"). The second movement boasts a charming song, which is given variation treatment. After the minuet, the symphony concludes with a finale in which the main theme has dramatic thrust and the sensual feelings of a Hungarian gypsy dance.

Nobody knows why the Symphony No. 104 in D major is designated *London,* the name also used for the whole collection of a dozen symphonies. (I. Adagio; Allegro. II. Andante. III. Menuetto. IV. Allegro spiritoso.) The first-movement introduction features a fanfare-like theme for full orchestra. After a pause we get the main part of the movement, with the presentation of the main subject in the strings. In place of a second theme, Haydn recalls the main one in the dominant in flute and first violins. In the second movement, the soaring melody is treated with a freedom and a variety of nuance and color not often encountered in a classical symphony. The minuet combines graceful humor with peasant vigor, while the finale engages a rhythmic dance tune over a pedal point in cellos and horns. The latter subject, and a subsidiary one with greater harmonic than melodic interest, are worked out in the grand manner and often with contrapuntal dexterity.

1792–1795. SONGS, for voice and piano:

"My Mother Bids Me Bind My Hair" ("A Pastoral Song"); "She Never Told Her Love."

One of the consequences of Haydn's two visits to England was the completion of two sets of six songs each (or canzonettas) to English lyrics. Though

Haydn never regarded the song form as seriously as he did the symphony or string quartet, he did succeed in producing a handful that deserve high rank. In his English songs, his melodies are sometimes influenced by Italian opera, and sometimes by the German Singspiel. His piano introductions and accompaniments sometimes have such breadth that it is apparent Haydn was thinking more orchestrally than pianistically. In the first set of English songs we find one of Haydn's most celebrated vocal compositions, known as "A Pastoral Song," but most often called "My Mother Bids Me Bind My Hair." This text is by Mrs. John Hunter, to whom the entire set is dedicated. In the second group is the exquisite number, "She Never Told Her Love," text from Shakespeare's *Twelfth Night*.

1792. SINFONIE CONCERTANTE IN B-FLAT MAJOR, for violin, oboe, bassoon, cello, and orchestra, op. 84. I. Allegro. II. Andante. III. Allegro con spirito.

The sinfonie (or symphonie) concertante is a large work usually for several solo instruments and orchestra. It is a kind of cross between the symphony and the concerto; the individuality of the solo instruments is emphasized within a symphonic texture. One of the earliest successful uses of this form is found in Haydn's B-flat major Sinfonie concertante. Here is the way Nicolas Slonimsky described this work: "The first movement is of considerable length, and the composition of the principal subjects is detailed and complete. There is a flowery cadenza in the best rococo manner." In the second movement, the solo instruments are "given ample opportunity to display both the singing and technical quality of their genre," and the figurations "are brilliant and varied." The finale presents "an interesting departure from the instrumental character of a concerto in recitatives for solo violin that follow the melodic and harmonic procedures associated with opera. These recitatives, in Adagio, interrupt the spirited progress of the movement at frequent intervals. Other solo instruments contribute their fioriturас and little arias as well as rapid figurations. There is an effective interplay between the solo instruments and the orchestra. Once more a recitative of the violin intervenes, and the movement concludes in a brilliant finale."

1793. VARIATIONS IN F MINOR, for piano, op. 83.

This is one of Haydn's finest compositions for the piano, as well as one of the most original. "In the aspects of harmony and color," said Karl Geiringer, "[this work] anticipates the first beginnings of the romantic style." There are two themes, the first of which sounds like a funeral march. A D major trio follows. After two variations, the work ends with an extended improvisational coda.

1795. GYPSY RONDO, for piano trio, op. 73, no. 2.

The so-called *Gypsy Rondo*—familiar in various transcriptions, including one for violin and piano by Fritz Kreisler named *Hungarian Rondo*—is the finale of the Piano Trio No. 1 in G major. In the larger work it is designated as a rondo in the Hungarian style ("Rondo all' ongarese"). The movement is built from vigorous and rhythmic themes, all with a pronounced Hungarian identity.

1796–1802. MASSES, for solo voices, chorus, and orchestra: *Missa in Tempore Belli* (*Paukenmesse*); *Heiligmesse; Nelson Missa* (*Missa in Angustiis*); *Theresienmesse; Missa solennis* (*Schoepfungsmesse*); *Harmoniemesse.*

During the closing decade of his long life, Haydn wrote his greatest Masses. These six works stand sharply apart from earlier ones by Haydn in the same form, by virtue of their heightened dramatic interest and the deep religious conviction which sometimes touches mysticism, the enriched gift at tone painting, the consummate polyphonic technique, and the faithful way in which music interprets text. Each of Haydn's last Masses is a choral masterwork. So many new veins are tapped that it is hardly possible to know Haydn well without an intimate knowledge of these remarkable works. "The rococo perkiness is gone," says Wilfred Mellers. "Instead we have the dramatic power of Haydn the symphonist, reconciled with the monumental counterpart of the baroque; and thus translated into the relative impersonality of the liturgical style."

The *Missa in tempore belli,* or "Mass in Time of War," in C major (1796) is also sometimes referred to as the *Paukenmesse* because of the use of the tympani in the "Agnus Dei" section. Haydn wrote this work at a time when Napoleon's armies were penetrating the Styrian border. Haydn himself directed the première of the Mass in Eisenstadt, on September 13, 1796, for the name day of Princess Maria Josepha Hermengild, wife of Prince Esterházy. "The trumpet calls and kettledrums of the slow introduction to the 'Kyrie,'" Wilfred Mellers explains, "have the dramatic solemnity of one of Haydn's or even Beethoven's symphonic openings; and the 'Kyrie' theme is a symphonic rather than an operatic motive. The orchestra is handled with powerful independence throughout, in the same style as in the last symphonies; the choruses, on the other hand, have a contrapuntal grandeur which suggests Bach even more than Handel. A movement such as the 'Miserere nobis' is a liturgical act which is also a personal utterance. Haydn's true religion has brust through the facade of dogma." It should also be remarked that in the magnificent 'Credo," and particularly in the fugue, Haydn surpasses all his previous efforts at polyphony.

In the 'Sanctus' movement of the *Heiligmesse* (1796), Haydn uses a melody from the hymn, "Heilig, Heilig"; this is the reason why this work is named the way it is. Two years after the *Heiligmesse,* Haydn completed one of the most dramatic of his Masses, the *Nelsonmissa* in D minor. The trumpets of the "Benedictus" are believed to proclaim Nelson's victory at the Battle of the Nile. "Never except in *The Creation,*" writes an unidentified program annotator for the Haydn Society recordings, "did Haydn achieve the unflagging emotional intensity of the *Nelson Mass,* nor is there a single section that falls below the unique artistic perfection established during the first bars of the . . . grim menacing 'Kyrie' [where] an explosive rhythmic figure for trumpets and tympani . . . stalks through the whole section." This annotator singles out the slow movements of this Mass as the most distinguished in the entire work. "The bitter-sweet reflection of the soprano solo in the 'Et Incarnatus' is as unforgettable as the aching sorrow of Mozart's lyrical E-flat themes. . . . The 'Sanctus' is stately, dignified, and so heartfelt that there leaves no room for doubt about Haydn's religious attitude. . . . The 'Benedictus' . . . is so vividly portrayed, so moving, and, at the end, so wildly intense, so completely personal, that one feels a new grim Herculean Haydn has appeared."

The *Theresienmesse* in B-flat major (1799) was probably named for Empress Maria Theresa. This work, says Mellers, is "remarkable for the way in which elements of sonata and opera are absorbed into a dramatic fugue to the words 'Et vitam venturi.'" The *Missa solennis* in B-flat major (1801) is also known as the *Schoepfungsmesse,* since a melody from Haydn's *The Creation* ("The Dewy Morning") is here borrowed for the "Qui tollis" and the "Miserere."

Perhaps the greatest of the Masses is the last, the *Harmoniemesse* in B-flat major (1802), thus identified in view of its prominent utilization of wind instruments. Robert C. Marsh regards this Mass as "virtually a Haydn choral symphony . . . the final development of Haydn's contribution to symphonic form, the liturgical text being used as a means for adding soloists and chorus to the instrumental forces available." Marsh then adds: "There is no religiosity here, any more than in Beethoven's *Missa Solemnis*. They have a sense of splendor common to all noble works of art, but there is nothing doctrinal about it, and the force of the message is universal in scope." Wilfrid Mellers also compares this Haydn Mass to Beethoven's *Missa Solemnis* because of "the large scale sonata of the 'Kyrie' and the majestic use of the wind. . . . On the other hand, the counterpoint of the 'Qui tollis' comes closer to the spiritual essence of Bach than did any other composer of a later generation. He [Haydn] rebuilds the church in the spirit of the Enlightenment. . . . The serenity he attains may not be mystical; it certainly entails what one can call Belief."

1797. "Gott erhalte Franz den Kaiser," the Austrian national anthem for voice and piano.

The Austrian Minister of the Interior invited Haydn to write a patriotic hymn to arouse the national spirit of the Austrian people. Haydn complied with "Gott erhalte," which was sung in every Austrian theater on the Emperor's birthday, on February 12, 1797. "You have expressed," the Emperor told Haydn, "what is in every loyal heart and through your melody Austria will always be honored." Since 1797, Haydn's melody has been used not only as the Austrian national anthem, but also for the German ("Deutschland, Deutschland, ueber alles"). Haydn himself borrowed it for the slow movement of the String Quartet in C major, op. 76, no. 3, a work which consequently has become identified as the *Emperor Quartet*.

1798. THE CREATION (DIE SCHOEPFUNG), oratorio for solo voices, chorus, and orchestra.

During his two visits to London, Haydn had an opportunity to become reacquainted with several of Handel's oratorios, including the *Messiah.* They had a powerful impact on him. From this moment on, Haydn aspired to write an oratorio of his own, his first in that form, in which he could give voice to his profound religious feelings. All his life Haydn had worshiped God with humility. Many of his works began with the phrase, "In the name of God," and ended with "In praise of God." He drew his creative strength from the Almighty, whom he was always entreating for renewed powers, and thanking for work well done. "I rise early, and as soon as I am dressed, I fall on my knees and pray to God and the Holy Virgin that I may succeed again." One of his favorite mottos was: "Be good and industrious and serve God continually."

He was sparked into the writing of his first oratorio when Liddell's text of *The Creation* (adapted from parts of the *Genesis* and Milton's *Paradise Lost*) came into his hands. Liddell had written it with the hope of having Handel set it to music, but Handel had turned it down. Baron van Swieten then translated Liddell's words into German for Haydn's use. Sixty-six years old, his greatest symphonies and most of his great string quartets behind him, Haydn approached the writing of his first oratorio with a religious fervor and a passion he had rarely demonstrated up to now. "Daily I fell on my knees and begged God to vouchsafe me strength for the fortunate outcome of my work," he said. "I felt myself so penetrated with religious feeling that before I sat down to the piano, I prayed to God with earnestness that He would enable me to praise Him worthily." About one of the sections of *The Creation* he remarked simply: "It came from on high."

The Creation, a child of Haydn's old age, is remarkable, not only because it contains so many flashes of creative genius, but also because its finest pages represent some of the noblest music found in the post-Handel oratorio. Within this Baroque structure, we find advanced styles and techniques. The orchestral prelude (which Zelter once picturesquely described as the crown on God's head) contains tonal painting, modern harmonies and dynamics, and instrumental effects unheard of in 1798. This is a tone poem (more than half a century before Liszt devised the form) describing chaos being resolved into order, darkness into light. Several pages after that, we get a chorus of incomparable grandeur, "And the Spirit of God," in which, with compelling realism, several electrifying chords tell of the first burst of light in a dark world ("Let there be Light"). Realism is found later on, though sometimes somewhat more naïvely, in descriptions of thunder, lightning, rainfall, snowdrops. With drama and pictorialism, we also get lyricism of the highest inspiration: the eloquent song for basso, "Rolling in Foaming Billows," followed at once by one of the most celebrated soprano arias in all oratorio literature, the pastoral "In Verdure Clad." The first part of *The Creation* ends with a mighty chorus, "The Heavens are Telling," another of the score's celebrated pages.

The second part begins with the fifth day of Creation, in which animals come to life and are made to sound their voices in descriptive musical passages. In Gabriel's opening melody, "On Mighty Pens," bassoons and violins suggest the cooing of pigeons. In the recitative, "Be Fruitful All and Multiply," divided violins, cellos, and double basses suggest the earth's fruition. Uriel's aria, "In Native Worth," glows resplendently with the wonder of the creation of the first man and woman. Two choruses follow, the second containing a giant fugue.

In the third and last section, Haydn sings a hymn to the Creation through the voices of Adam (a basso) and Eve (a soprano). The orchestral introduction paints the dawn in three flutes accompanied by plucked strings. The duet of Adam and Eve with chorus, "By Thee With Bliss," is one of the longest and most consistently inspired sections in the entire oratorio. After that come the love duet of Adam and Eve, and the hymn of thanksgiving for vocal quartet and chorus, "Sing the Lord."

The first public performance took place in Vienna on March 19, 1799, the composer conducting. *The Creation* was the last piece of music its composer was destined to hear in public. On March 2, 1808, his seventy-sixth birthday was celebrated (a few days early) with a presentation of this choral masterwork. When Haydn was carried in and out of the auditorium in a chair, the audience (which included Beethoven) rose in homage, not only in token of their affection and admiration, but also in expression of permanent farewell.

1799. 6 "ERDOEDY" QUARTETS, op. 76: I. G major. II. D minor, "Quinten." III. C major, "Kaiser" ("Emperor"). IV. B-flat major, "Sunrise." V. D major. VI. E-flat major.

The six compositions in opus 76, dedicated to Count Erdoedy, are among Haydn's greatest string quartets. "If an appropriate motto were sought for this series," says Karl Geiringer, "the word Excelsior would have the first choice. Everything here is condensed and intensified, the expression more personal and direct."

Haydn's power of concentration can be observed in the first movement of the D minor Quartet (I. Allegro. II. Andante o piu tosto allegretto. III. Menuetto. IV. Vivace assai). It is built entirely from the opening theme, a figure of fifths, which gives the entire work the name of "Quinten." No other melodic material is introduced in that movement, yet power of invention and variety of expression are never lacking. This work is also notable for its integration. All four movements are in the same key, and a subtle thematic unity is maintained throughout. The slow movement is one of Haydn's lofty reflections. The minuet—dubbed "Hexen" or "Witches"—is a canon in which the two violins offer the main melody in octaves, with viola and cello entering a bar later in imitation, also in octaves.

The third quartet in this set, in C major, is named *Emperor*—Haydn having utilized in its slow movement the melody of his Austrian national anthem, "Gott erhalte Franz den Kaiser" (see above) as the starting point for four variations. In each variation a different instrument is allowed to linger over this noble melody. In the first movement we once again encounter Haydn's power at concentration. An impressive edifice is constructed from the simple material of the opening five-note motto. (I. Allegro. II. Poco adagio. III. Menuetto. IV. Presto.)

The fifth quartet in D major is most celebrated for its ethereal slow movement. This is why the whole work is sometimes called "The Largo Quartet." The first movement is in a simplified sonata form, utilizing only a single three-part melody. After the eloquent slow movement, there comes a minuet which has the character of a scherzo. Here the main theme is a two-note motive, which recurs in the trio with telling effect. The finale is in the sonata form, its first theme a vigorous Croatian dance tune.

1801. THE SEASONS (DIE JAHRESZEITEN), oratorio for solo voices, chorus, and orchestra.

Just as Haydn's first oratorio, *The Creation,* voices his deep religious beliefs, so his second and last oratorio, *The Seasons,* reflects his profound love of nature. James Thomson, author of the English poem *The Seasons* on which this oratorio is based, was one of England's first poets to deal with Nature in the lyrical manner of the later Romantics. His hymn to the four seasons, and his depiction of natural beauties, struck a responsive chord with Haydn, who tapped every creative vein he possessed in singing a hymn to the wonder of Nature with each changing season.

There are four separate units in the oratorio, each a self-sufficient cantata devoted to one of the seasons, beginning with Springtime. Each is introduced by an atmospheric, sometimes pictorial orchestral prelude, far ahead of its time in harmonic invention and orchestration. The first prelude describes Spring emerging from the severity of winter. An ebullient melody speaks for the vernal season, while the sensitive and transparent orchestration portrays the melting of winter's ice and snow.

The first section opens with an expressive recitative, followed by a bucolic chorus of peasants, "Come Gentle Spring." Simon's lovely song, "Happily the Farmer Goes to the Field," quotes a theme Haydn previously had used for the *Surprise* Symphony. Simon, Lucas, and Jane—together with the peasants—implore for rain. When the countryside is bathed, and the fields burst into bloom, Lucas, Jane, and the peasants offer a paean to Nature. Here the music re-creates the running brook, the frolic of lambs, the buzzing of bees, the flight of birds in the sky and fish in the sea. The Spring section concludes with a song of thanksgiving for the chorus.

There is a melancholy air to the prelude to Summer: the fears of nighttime are suggested and then dissipated by the morning light. Lucas now sings of summer's oppressive heat ("Nature, Exhausted Languished"). Following Jane's recitative, "O Welcome Now," and her aria, "O How Passing," a vivid presentation of a summer thunderstorm is given, with the chorus commenting,

"Hark! the Deep Tremendous Voice." Karl Geiringer considers this the greatest storm music Haydn ever wrote. The concluding trio with chorus is "Now Cease the Conflicts."

In Autumn, the orchestral introduction tells of the husbandman's content with the harvest. Lucas and Jane speak of their love in the lengthy coloratura air, "Leaves Fall, Fruit Falls." A realistic hunting scene begins with Simon's air, "Behold the Dewy Grass" and is climaxed by a stag hunt narrated by the chorus, "Hark, the Mountains Resound," with its daring key changes. The peasants celebrate in the final chorus, "Joyful, Joyful the Liquor Flows."

A sad, contemplative orchestral prelude precedes the final Winter section. The bleakness thus projected continues on into Jane's opening cavatina, "Light and Life Dejected Languish." Following Lucas's air, "The Traveler Stands Perplexed," we hear the celebrated chorus, "Song of the Weavers," in which the rhythm of the spinning wheel is simulated in the accompaniment. The sober mood of the opening sections recurs in Simon's aria, "Blind Mortal Regard the True Picture of Your Life," where Haydn uses the winter as a symbol for old age. But optimism and joy of life return in the magnificent closing page, "Let Us Never Tire of Doing Good," a vision of peace and happiness for those with faith in the Almighty and in the miracle of Nature. With a four-measure "Amen," *The Seasons* is brought to a resounding conclusion.

The public première of *The Seasons* took place in Vienna, at the Redoutensaal, on May 29, 1801. It was a triumph. But Haydn maintained that the oratorio had give him "the finishing stroke." His health deteriorated rapidly after he had put the final strokes of the pen on his manuscript. Though he lived on for several more years, he was too ill to work and produced little of any consequence.

WOLFGANG AMADEUS MOZART 1756–1791

The fabulous musical exploits of the child Mozart read like legends—but they are biographical facts. As a child of three and a half, he would spend hours picking out chords. At four, he gave remarkable demonstrations at the harpsichord. Three years later, he completed his first sonata. His first symphony was written when he was eight, his first comic opera when he was eleven, and his first opera seria at fourteen. By the time he reached full adolescence, there was seemingly nothing he could not do in music. "A phenomenon like that of Mozart," said Goethe, "remains an inexplicable thing."

Yet the fulfillment in his maturity of the promises made as a prodigy are more incredible still. There was no field of music that was not enriched and changed through him. No other composer since his time dedicated himself with such intensity, and with such equal creative power, to every branch and form of musical composition. At the same time, there was no facet, no nuance of human emotion that he did not carry over into his music. He was the apotheosis of techniques and structures developed before him; he was the inception of idioms, procedures, human and spiritual values crystallized after his death. He was at turns the master of the rococo, galant, Baroque, and classical styles; and he was the dawn of romanticism. In short, Mozart the fully mature composer—like Mozart the child prodigy—was what César Saerchinger once described as a "one-time phenomenon in the history of the human mind. . . . His creative vitality, measured in sheer accomplishment, has not been surpassed by any artist in history. . . . He has influenced the thought and culture of the past two centuries probably as much as any intellectual giant of our era."

If he was the most versatile of all composers, he was also the most universal —as universal as Shakespeare in literature. As Konrad Wolff said: "Both bring the scope of the universe in their dramas, but Mozart is universal also in the forms and types of work in which he expresses himself. He has created works of equal greatness in both the dramatic and undramatic field. His symphonies, concertos, chamber music, and church music are as essentially and directly an emanation of his genius as his operas." The basis of Mozart's universality, continues Wolff, is the unity of his language. "Within the same piece, he can risk all kinds of changes in mood without every endangering the unity of the composition. His slow movements, for instance, after much intensity and expressiveness, frequently end on a playful note. . . . The contrast is as sharp and as violent as anything that occurs in Beethoven's music, but unlike Beethoven, it appears so naturally in the composition that no duality is felt. . . . Edvard Grieg once wisely remarked that in Mozart's music 'even the most practised eye and ear cannot discover the subtlest point of connection.'"

One of the miracles of Mozart's music, continues Wolff, is that it "not only seems to be, but actually is, complete at any stage of our receptive capacities; and as these capacities increase after new inner experiences, we may find that these experiences, too, are included in Mozart's music. . . . In Mozart, we find human emotions as well as nature. His music speaks of God, of moral values . . . but it can also be used to suggest the ringing of wine glasses, or of sleigh bells."

Hugo Leichtentritt has maintained that if Mozart's music had been lost to us "the world would have lost something irreparable. Nowhere else—neither in Haydn, Beethoven, Schubert, Schumann, Wagner, nor in Brahms

—can this Mozartean flavor, this lyric expressiveness, this candid yet modest revelation of the soul, this divine grace, this animated amiability be found in any comparable degree. The genius of youth is embodied most gloriously in the touching yet luminous and joyful life and art of Wolfgang Amadeus Mozart."

Wolfgang Amadeus Mozart was born in Salzburg, Austria, on January 27, 1756. His father, Leopold, was second Kapellmeister at the court of the Archbishop. From earliest childhood, Mozart revealed the most extraordinary musical powers. For a number of years, beginning when he was six, Mozart appeared throughout Europe, inspiring awe, and gathering gifts and accolades wherever he went. His first four violin sonatas were published in Paris when he was eight; his first symphonies were performed in London when he was nine; his first two comic operas—*La Finta semplice* and *Bastien and Bastienne* —were completed when he was twelve; and when he was fourteen, he wrote, on commission, his first opera seria, *Mitridate, rè di Ponto,* produced in Milan on December 1770 during his first tour of Italy. While there, he gave one of the most remarkable evidences of his genius by writing down from memory, and after only two hearings, the entire score of Gregorio Allegri's *Miserere.*

The recipient of the most extravagant praises and honors away from Salzburg, Mozart knew little more than humiliation and frustration in his own native city. Between 1772 and 1774, while employed by the Archbishop of Salzburg, he was treated hardly better than a menial servant, subjected all the time to personal abuse. In an effort to escape from his misery, he embarked on travels to Germany and Paris between 1777 and 1778. But since he was no longer the electrifying prodigy but a fully mature musician—even if with uncommon powers—Mozart had lost the capacity to excite the admiration of his audiences. He was compelled to return to Salzburg and resume there both his drab and ill-paying post and his humdrum everyday existence.

The success of his opera *Idomeneo* in Munich, on January 29, 1781, convinced him of the necessity of leaving Salzburg for good and seeking an important post elsewhere. A heated exchange of angry words led to a permanent break between Mozart and the Salzburg Archbishop in 1782. Mozart now made his home in Vienna, where, on a commission from the Emperor, he wrote and had produced *The Abduction from the Seraglio* in 1782. Its success, and the promise of an important court appointment, gave him the confidence to get married—to Constance Weber on August 4, 1782.

But in Vienna, as in Salzburg, Mozart encountered only frustration and disappointments. To support himself, he gave lessons and concerts. All the while he kept waiting for the court appointment that did not come. But while waiting, he produced masterwork after masterwork in every conceivable medium.

When recognition came, it arrived not in Vienna but in Prague, where his *The Marriage of Figaro* proved a triumph in 1786. For Prague, he wrote *Don Giovanni,* and its première in 1787 was another success of the first magnitude.

Returning to Vienna with renewed confidence, Mozart was finally appointed to succeed Gluck as court composer and chamber musician. But since he was hired at a greatly reduced salary, this appointment did little to resolve his pressing financial problems. In the last two years of his life, he was reduced to begging friends for financial assistance. He was also sick in body and broken in spirit. But nothing could stem the tide of his production. Some of the greatest music he was to write came in his last year—beset though he was by worry, illness, depressions: the Requiem, *The Magic Flute,* the Ave Verum, the B-flat major Piano Concerto, and the E-flat major Piano Concerto. He died in Vienna on December 5, 1791, and was buried in a pauper's section of the St. Mark's Cathedral, with neither a tombstone nor a cross to mark the place of burial.

1764. SYMPHONY NO. 1 IN E-FLAT, K. 16. I. Allegro molto. II. Andante. III. Presto.

Mozart's first symphonies were influenced by those of John Christian Bach, with whom the boy Mozart came into contact upon visiting England in 1764. "This form," says Georges de Saint-Fox, "easy of comprehension, is marked by a charm both lively and distinguished and by an expression of sensual femininity that made a particular appeal to Mozart's intimate nature." The early Mozart symphonies, like those of John Christian Bach, were usually in the three-movement form of the Italian overture, with little development of themes. Violins are the foundation upon which the orchestral structure rests—with winds, horns, and oboes or flutes providing colorations and filling in the harmonies.

Mozart's first symphony, completed when he was only eight, was introduced at the Little Theater in Haymarket, in London, on February 21, 1765, during Mozart's first visit to England. The first theme of the opening movement is immediately given by the full orchestra. After the first eleven bars of this subject are repeated, a brief new thought enters with the first violins. Nine measures later, the lyrical second theme appears in strings. The development is terse, entirely devoted to the first theme. In the recapitulation, it is the second theme that is discussed. The second movement, which is only fifty measures in length, is based on a flowing cantabile subject with which it opens. The finale is introduced with a spirited sixteen-measure subject, repeated before the second melody is heard. Here the development consists of little more than a repetition of this material. This movement ends as it began, with the opening sprightly tune.

1767–1780. SONATAS FOR ORGAN AND ORCHESTRA:

E-flat major, K. 67; B-flat major, K. 68; B-flat major, K. 212; A major, K. 225; C major, K. 278; C major, K. 328; C major, K. 329; C major, K. 336.

All of Mozart's seventeen organ sonatas were written in Salzburg. The first two (E-flat major, K. 67 and B-flat major, K. 68) came early in 1767; the last four (all of them in C major, K. 278, 328, 329, 336) appeared between

1789 and 1780. These works were written on commission from the Archbishop of Salzburg, Hieronymus, and were performed for the first time by Anton Adlgasser, organist at Salzburg, whom Mozart succeeded in 1777. These sonatas differ from similar works by Mozart for other instruments in that they were all in a single movement. The sonata form, with two contrasting themes, is employed; both the developments and the recapitulations are spare and lean. An organ sonata usually requires no more than five minutes for performance. The first of these works, in E-flat major, is the only one in a slow tempo, corresponding in style and spirit to some of the short lyrical movements in Mozart's earlier chamber compositions. The earliest sonatas are scored for organ and strings, while some of the later ones include winds; an interesting feature in the orchestration of all these works is that they dispense with the viola. With the Sonata in A major, K. 225, completed in 1776, the structure becomes somewhat more extended, particularly in the working out of the themes. The two sonatas in C major, written in 1779, have the orchestration of some of Mozart's smaller symphonies (two oboes, two trumpets, drums, and strings for K. 278; two oboes, two horns, two trumpets, drums, and strings for K. 329).

1768–1769. BASTIEN UND BASTIENNE (BASTIEN AND BASTIENNE), K. 50, Singspiel in one act, with text by Friedrich Wilhelm Weiskern, based on Favart's *Les Amours de Bastien et Bastienne.* First performance: Vienna, October, 1768.

LA FINTA SEMPLICE (THE PRETENDING SIMPLETON), K. 51, opera buffa in three acts, with text by Marco Coltellini, based on a libretto by Carlo Goldoni. First performance: Salzburg, May 1, 1769.

Mozart's two earliest operas were completed when he was about twelve years old. That each is still able to bring modern audiences moments of amusement, and at times enchantment, speaks volumes for the composer's genius. In these two operas, Mozart was expected to write music for texts involving love intrigues, a philanderer, a woman hater, scheming bachelors, and so forth—all obviously well beyond the experiences of a child. Yet Mozart, with his God-given instinct, rose to the occasion with music filled with amusing characterizations, witty in its suggestions of intrigues and schemings, and in the more tender moments, of a lyrical beauty to melt a heart of stone. More than that, there are pages in *La Finta Semplice* where, as Nathan Broder once remarked, we can find touches "that point to the future master, like Cassandro's aria, 'Ella vuole ed io torrei' . . . or Rosina's 'Amoretti' which in spirit anticipates some of the lyric moments in *Così fan tutte;* or Cassandro's 'Ubriaco non son io' with the violins reeling around in their ritornel as drunk as the singer; or the pantomime bit in Act II, where the music, subdued and poetic, is on a much higher level than the silly scene being enacted." And in *Bastien and Bastienne,* there are other forceful anticipations of Mozart's later genius for laughter and mockery—in an air like that of Colas, "Diggi, Daggi, Schurry,

Murry," where the clichés, pretentions, and absurdities of Italian opera seria are burlesqued with broad musical strokes.

Bastien and Bastienne was written in 1768 in Vienna, on a commission from Dr. Anton Mesmer, a specialist in magnetic therapy from whose name we get the word "mesmerism." Mesmer had a little theater in his garden. It was for this place that he wanted Mozart to write an opera. For his text, Mozart selected the German adaptation of a parody of Jean Jacques Rousseau's famous little comic opera, *Le Devin du village,* which had been introduced in Fontainbleau, France, on October 18, 1752. This parody had been translated into German by Friedrich Wilhelm Weiskern. But in preparing his score, Mozart emphasized the pastoral qualities of the text instead of the burleque, the lyrical and tender sentiments rather than the humorous. *Bastien and Bastienne* is not opera buffa but Singspiel—the Singspiel being an early variety of German comic opera popular with the general public. This Singspiel has only three characters: the shepherdess, Bastienne; the young man, Bastien, with whom she is in love; and a magician, Colas. Bastienne, feeling she has lost Bastien's love, appeals to Colas for help. The magician then goes on to arouse Bastien's jealousy by informing him that the shepherdess has found a new lover. Bastien refuses to believe him, insists he must get the truth from Bastienne's lips. When the lovers meet again, they are so happy to see each other that they fall into each other's arms.

Mozart wrote sixteen numbers—arias, duets, and a trio. (In 1769, he added recitatives.) "Within this limited sphere," says Nathan Broder, "the boy writes some charming melodies. Many of them, as was to be the case whenever Mozart set German texts, have a folk-like flavor." Among the best of these melodies are Bastien's love song, "Meiner Liebsten schoene Wangen," and Bastienne's lament, "Wenn mein Bastien einst im Scherze."

La Finta semplice was commissioned by the Austrian Emperor for performance at a comic-opera theater in Vienna managed by Affligio. Mozart completed his opera in about four months, his score including twenty-one arias, three finales, one duet, and one chorus. But after he had turned over the finished product to Affligio, he encountered nothing but subterfuge, evasions, and procrastinations as far as the première was concerned. Many of the musicians affiliated with the theater deeply resented appearing in the work of a mere child. At last, Affligio warned Mozart's father that if he were stubborn about getting the boy's opera performed, it would be hissed off the stage. The opera was withdrawn; and its première took place in Mozart's home town of Salzburg in 1769.

The plot involves the machinations of Cassandro and Pilodoro, two brothers who are also bachelors, in preventing their sister from marrying an officer. Their sister, and her beloved, finally manage to outwit them.

There is no record of an American première of *La Finta semplice;* a complete recording was issued by Epic in 1960 in a Salzburg performance. What is believed to have been the first American production of *Bastien and Bastienne* took place in an English translation at the Empire Theater in New York, on October 26, 1916; this opera has also been recorded in its entirety.

1772–1773. SYMPHONY NO. 18 IN F MAJOR, K. 130. I. Allegro. II. Andantino grazioso. III. Menuetto. IV. Molto allegro.

SYMPHONY NO. 25 IN G MINOR, K. 183. I. Allegro con brio. II. Andante. III. Menuetto. IV. Allegro.

The F major Symphony, Mozart's eighteenth (1772), represents a huge step forward for the composer. The influence of Haydn has now begun to make itself felt. Grandeur, nobility, sobriety intrude into his writing, but without affecting the Italian sunshine which thus far had been flooding his melodies and harmonies. Mozart's musical thinking is enlarged through a more ambitious and more imaginative development of themes than heretofore. Georges de Saint-Fox calls the F major "the first of his great symphonies," adding that this is "a new world. . . . The whole of the symphony is steeped in the spirit of Italy, but this time it is Mozart alone who displays and bestows the acquired riches; bizarrerie and boldness in the minuets, tender delicacy in the Andantes, gaiety or whirlwind force in the finales, strength and power in the design."

The sonata form is followed more rigidly in the first movement than in earlier Mozart symphonies. The first subject, in the tonic, is heard at once; the second theme, in the dominant, follows soon after this. These ideas are developed and recapitulated along sonata-form procedures Mozart would henceforth pursue. The finale, in the sonata form, marks a new approach for Mozart. To Alfred Einstein, it is one of the earliest examples of the extended Mozart finales, so ambitious in structure and so rich in variety of material that it serves as a crown to the entire composition. Between the first and last movements come a slow movement in abbreviated song form, and a succinct minuet.

The mellowness of growing maturity, together with its sobriety, predominate in the G minor Symphony (1773), even in the minuet and finale movements, where Mozart usually allowed his ebullient boyish spirits to erupt. Without preliminaries, the first movement offers the main theme loudly in full orchestra, in unison and octaves. Passage work leads into the second theme, first given simply by the strings, then repeated with enriched instrumentation. The development consists of a fantasia on this material, the recapitulation presenting the two main themes in the tonic instead of the expected G major. A reminder of the opening of the fantasia, and a brief coda based on the first theme, bring the opening Allegro to its conclusion. The second-movement melody makes such effective use of imitation that William F. Apthorp here finds the influence of Johann Sebastian Bach, and specifically that of *The Well-Tempered Clavier*. The minuet begins with a sensitive twelve-measure theme, followed by another in a similar vein, twenty-four measures long. Both sections are repeated before the trio. The finale, in concise sonata form, opens with a soft first theme in strings, in unison and octaves, soon loudly repeated by the full orchestra. The second theme has a melancholy cast. As in the first movement, both ideas are elaborated upon in a free fantasia section, with emphasis on the contrapuntal technique.

1773. EXSULTATE, JUBILATE, K. 165, motet for soprano and orchestra.

While visiting Milan, in January of 1773, Mozart wrote a motet for Venanzio Rauzzini, a castrato who had appeared in Mozart's opera, *Lucio Silla,* produced one month earlier in Milan. This motet, says Dr. William B. Ober, "is an exceptionally fine example of church music which is Baroque in structure and feeling, but which foreshadows the rococo in the florid ornaments used to decorate the melodic line." The work has three parts, the most famous being the last, a Presto. This is exultant music, spun floridly around the single word, "Alleluia." The opening section is an Allegro, "Exsultate, jubilate." A recitative, "Fulget amica," is the transition to a slow section, an Andante with deep religious feeling, "Tu virginum corona." The brilliant concluding "Alleluia" serves as a highly effective contrast to the deeply expressive music that had preceded it.

1773. STRING QUARTET IN C MAJOR, K. 157. I. Allegro. II. Andante. III. Presto.

STRING QUARTET IN F MAJOR, K. 168. I. Allegro. II. Andante. III. Menuetto. IV. Allegro.

STRING QUARTET IN D MINOR, K. 173. I. Allegro ma molto moderato. II. Andantino grazioso. III. Menuetto. IV. Allegro.

Mozart was only fourteen when he wrote his first string quartet—that in G major, K. 80. He completed it in a single evening during his first visit to Italy. Actually this is not a string quartet but a divertimento; the influence of the Italian instrumental school—especially that of Sammartini—is obvious.

Between 1772 and 1773, during another visit to Italy, Mozart completed six more string quartets (K. 155–160). Here the movements are brief, the developments episodic. But Mozart was now beginning to introduce a personal note into his writing. To Abert, the mood of these six works is "partly dreamy, partly wild and passionate, but always subjective." The new vigor and the increasing emotional feeling can be found in the singing first theme of the C major String Quartet, K. 157, and in the pathos of its slow movement.

Six more quartets were completed by Mozart in Vienna in 1773 (K. 168–173). In the first of these, in F major, the opening movement is built from episodic material rather than from fully stated themes; the third bar of the first subject then becomes the source of the development section. Mozart made considerable use of polyphony in the ensuing movements. In the Andante, for muted strings, the four instruments enter canonically. The subject of the trio, in the minuet, is treated in imitation, while the finale presents a strict fugue on a single subject.

In the last of these six quartets, that in D major, a good deal of emotional disturbance can be detected. Abert describes the first movement as "painfully agitated, while Wyzewa and Saint-Fox find here a "desperate lamentation, answered by a plaint, no less agonized, of the first violin." The slow movement, in rondo form, provides momentary relief, but the restlessness of the first movement stirs anew in the minuet and becomes uninhibited in the finale, whose core is a fugue based on a descending chromatic subject. With each transformation of the theme, it acquires increasing dramatic and emotional intensity.

1774–1791. CONCERTOS FOR VARIOUS WIND INSTRUMENTS AND ORCHESTRA:

B-flat major, K. 191, for bassoon and orchestra. I. Allegro. II. Andante ma adagio. III. Tempo di menuetto.

C major, K. 299, for flute, harp, and orchestra. I. Allegro. II. Andantino. III. Allegro.

G major, K. 313, for flute and orchestra. I. Allegro maestoso. II. Adagio non troppo. III. Tempo di menuetto.

E-flat major, K. 447, for horn and orchestra. I. Allegro. II. Larghetto. III. Allegro.

A major, K. 622, for clarinet and orchestra. I. Allegro. II. Adagio. III. Allegro.

Mozart's various concertos for wind instruments and orchestra were, generally speaking, *pièces d'occasion,* functional music for specific performers or occasions. His profounder thoughts, his deeper emotions, and his more original approaches he reserved for his piano and violin concertos. The wind concertos are mainly show pieces for the performer; but since they are by Mozart, they are also compositions rich in grace and charm, and overflowing with infectious tunes.

The bassoon concerto in B-flat major was written in 1774 on a commission from Baron von Duernitz, an amateur performer. This is, for the most part, music in the galant style that distinguished so much of Mozart's writing when he was eighteen. But here we also confront nobility, as in the aristocratic slow movement, and flashes of good humor, as in parts of the first movement and the finale. Of the three concertos that Mozart wrote for bassoon, this is the one heard most often.

The C major Concerto for flute and harp came in 1778, written for one of Mozart's pupils, the daughter of the Duc de Guines. This work abounds with the kind of graceful melodies suited for the delicate-toned solo instruments; even transitional material provide precious lyrical thoughts. The work as a whole, says Abraham Veinus, has a consistently "quiet and relaxed tone." The "color relationships between the two solos are mainly of a sweet and subtle pastel variety." Nevertheless, the concerto as a whole is "remarkably rich in color and entrancingly subtle in its sonorities."

In 1778, Mozart wrote on commission two flute concertos for the Dutch musical amateur, De Jean: the first in G major, K. 313, and the second in D major, K. 314. Though Mozart did not favor the flute as a solo instrument, he nevertheless consigned to both of these works some of the most exquisite thematic ideas and sensitive colorations to be found in his wind concertos. Donald Francis Tovey is of the opinion that Mozart had tongue in cheek in writing the first movement of the G major Concerto. "He is in fact doing very much what Mendelssohn did in *A Midsummer Night's Dream* music," says Tovey, "when Pease-blossom, Cobweb and Mustard-seed make their bows to Bottom the Weaver to the accompaniment of a flourish of trumpets on two oboes, while two flutes execute a roll of drums." If this is so, then the tongue leaves cheek in the slow movement, where a soulful and romantic melody, in the style of a nocturne, seems to speak of the most tender sentiments.

There are four concertos for horn and orchestra by Mozart, all written for Ignaz Leutgeb, an amateur performer. The best is the third in E-flat major, written in 1788—1789 according to Georges Saint-Fox, though other authorities place it as early as 1783. The rondo movement is replete with amusing verbal remarks and asides written into the score in Mozart's own handwriting, many of them directed to Leutgeb—evidence that Mozart approached the writing of this music with lightness and vivacity. Elsewhere in the concerto, levities are dispensed with. In many of the pages, we come upon depth of feeling, strength of personality, originality of orchestration, and nobility. There is such poetic beauty to the slow movement that placing the concerto as late as 1788 or 1789 seems justified.

The clarinet concerto in A major, was completed in 1791 for Anton Stadler, just two months before Mozart's death. Except for the reflective slow movement, there is no hint of the suffering and anguish that Mozart experienced at the time and that he carried over into the writing of his Requiem. Indeed, the first movement is full of youthful vigor and ebullience, while in the finale the unpredictable Mozart introduces a note of buffoonery with material that earlier he had treated poignantly.

1774. SYMPHONY NO. 29 IN A MAJOR, K. 201. I. Allegro moderato. II. Andante. III. Menuetto. IV. Allegro con spirito.

SYMPHONY NO. 30 IN D MAJOR, K. 202. I. Molto allegro. II. Andantino con moto. III. Menuetto. IV. Presto.

In 1774, while engaged at the court of the Archbishop of Salzburg, Mozart completed four symphonies. Mozart here succumbs to the lure of the galant style then influencing so much of European music. The sobriety, the emotion, the expressiveness that occasionally characterize the F major and G minor symphonies of 1772–1773 (see above)—and that were to reassert themselves even more strongly in his later symphonies—here give way to light, elegant music intended more to entertain than to stir or inspire. Yet even when he sets out merely to please, rather than plumb profound depths of feeling, Mozart can produce masterworks, even if only minor ones.

Both main themes of the first movement of the A major Symphony are light and gay. The octave interval in both these subjects becomes for John N. Burk a kind of motto for the entire work. The development is brief and concise, only thirty measures in length, while the recapitulation is along formal lines. The short coda emphasizes the first theme. The slow movement presents a song in muted first violins. When it is repeated, second violins (also muted) provide intriguing figurations. A middle section serves as a fourteen-measure interlude before the opening song returns. A traditional minuet precedes the finale, whose main first theme is embellished with trills and grace notes.

In the D major Symphony, the two themes of the first movement are in sharp contrast. The first has a brisk march-like character, while the second is enchantingly lyrical. It is the second that interests the composer in his development. The slow movement (scored for strings alone) has the romantic character of some of the Andantes of Mozart's serenades. The minuet is more or less conventional, except for the intriguing use of syncopation in the trio. In its vitality, the finale has been compared by Alfred Einstein to a "Kehraus,"—a "Kehraus" being a concluding dance to whose strains guests begin to put on outer wraps before taking their leave.

1775. LA FINTA GIARDINIERA (THE PRETENDER GARDENER), K. 196, opera buffa in three acts, with text probably by Raniere de Calzabigi, revised by Marco Coltellini. First performance: Munich, January 13, 1775.

Mozart was nineteen when he wrote *La Finta giardiniera* for the Carnival of Munich in 1775, where it was introduced. We need only to read the criticism leveled at this work by some of Mozart's early biographers to realize how Mozart's opera-buffa writing—since his first attempt with *La Finta Semplice* seven years earlier—had become richer, deeper, and more subtle. Because he introduced dramatic strength into his music, these early critics felt that the opera was "more powerful and passionate than the situations demand"; because the comic pages do not carry their humor on the surface, the critics insisted Mozart had become "too subtle, elaborate, ingenious, and clever for the words." Such opinions notwithstanding, the score of *La Finta giardiniera* boasts riches not found in earlier Mozart comic operas—particularly in the touching emotion of arias like "Noi donne poverine" and "Geme la tortorella" and in a duet like "Dove mai son." The score as a whole, maintains W. J. Turner, is "entrancing . . . without reserve," boasting an "inimitable charm and gaiety, tenderness and fertility of invention." Apparently, the Munich audience attending the première was fully capable of appreciating the remarkable qualities of the new opera. As Mozart reported to his mother: "It is impossible for me to describe the tumult of applause."

The story is a slight one, involving disguises, love intrigues, and machinations by hired help. The love interest involves Marchesa Violante, who has been slighted by Count Belfiore so that he might marry the Podesta's niece. The niece is being pursued by Ramiro. A subsidiary love problem enmeshes the valet and the maid. The complications of these various affairs are happily resolved in the final act. The Marchesa and the Count, the niece and Ramiro, and the valet and the maid are all reconciled with one another.

After 1791, *La Finta giardiniera* went into complete discard, and was not heard again for a century. It was revived for the first time since Mozart's death at the Vienna Royal Opera on December 25, 1891. What is believed to have been the American première took place in New York City on January 18, 1927, when the opera was given in an English translation.

1775. CONCERTOS FOR VIOLIN AND ORCHESTRA:

G major, K. 216. I. Allegro. II. Adagio. III. Allegro.

D major, K. 218. I. Allegro. II. Andante cantabile. III. Andante grazioso; Allegro ma non troppo.

A major, "Turkish," K. 219. I. Allegro aperto. II. Adagio III. Tempo di menuetto.

Mozart completed five violin concertos in 1775, including the three most often played today. There were good reasons why Mozart devoted himself to the violin at this time. He wanted to justify his post of court Kapellmeister, one of whose main functions was playing the violin in the orchestra; he wanted to placate his father, who felt that writing for the violin would be the best way of winning the approval of the new Archibishop, Hieronymus von Colleredo; and Mozart wanted some new items for his own concerts.

Otto Jahn pointed out that all the Mozart violin concertos follow a more or less similar pattern. The first movement is usually the most elaborate, "more suggestive of the aria than is the corresponding movement of the symphonies. The passages grow out of the principal subjects, converting and adorning them. . . . The second movement is simple and rests essentially on the tuneful and artistic delivery of the cantilene. . . . Embellishments are not excluded, but they are kept in the background. . . . The last movement is, as a rule, in the form of a rondo in which the solo part moves more freely especially in the connecting middle passages."

Of the three most popular concertos, that in G major is the slightest in structure and musical content. The main two subjects of the first movement are offered by the orchestra, before the solo instrument takes over the material; the second subject modulates to the key of D major when it returns to the solo violin. The development and recapitulation follow expected procedures, with numerous virtuoso passages for the performer. A cadenza precedes the brief concluding coda. The song of the second movement begins in the strings and is then completed by the solo violin. In the concluding rondo, the first theme, a vigorous tune, is given by the strings, while the second subject is heard in the solo violin. Midway in the movement, a new episode appears, a slow and graceful dance melody in G minor shared by soloist and strings.

The fourth concerto, in D major, is Mozart's most famous for the violin.

A martial theme opens the first movement and is amplified before the solo violin appears with a tender and thoughtful melody. The development is mainly concerned with bravura writing for the violin. The movement's first subject, in a somewhat abbreviated version, brings on the recapitulation. A cadenza and an eight-bar orchestral tutti close the movement. There are two melodies in the slow movement. The first is heard in the orchestra without preliminaries, and is repeated by the violin; the second theme, in the dominant, is presented by the solo instrument over string chords. The concluding movement is a two-part rondo. A melody of courtly grace opens it in the solo violin, to receive a vigorous reply by the orchestra. A livelier tune then follows in the violin, accompanied by strings. After these ideas have been discussed in some detail, an entirely new episode, in gavotte rhythm, is introduced; its second part is an exchange between the solo violin and the orchestra's first violins, while oboes sustain a single note. The movement's graceful opening melody comes back after a brief cadenza.

The A major Concerto is not only full of a simple and ingenuous beauty but also of surprises. One of these comes at the very beginning of the work where the solo makes its first appearance, not with the main theme, but with what Donald Francis Tovey describes as a "sustained arioso in a very slow Adagio time with a running accompaniment. There is a childlike grandeur in this gesture, which almost overawes the sense of humor to which Mozart was undoubtedly appealing." A second surprise is found in the finale where unexpectedly the composer brings on a section with a Turkish-like tune, the reason why the concerto as a whole has acquired the sobriquet of "Turkish."

The two main subjects of the first movement are first heard in the orchestra. The violin arrives with the surprising six-bar reflective arioso before discussing the first subject. Somewhat later, after a transitional episode, the second theme is given. An orchestral tutti brings on the brief development and recapitulation; in the latter, the second theme is modulated from E major to A major. A cadenza precedes the terse seven-measure coda.

The main and soulful melody of the slow movement is heard first in the first violins. At the twenty-second measure, the solo violin repeats this theme before passing on to the second main subject. As in the first movement, an orchestral tutti precedes the succinct development, which is devoted primarily to the first theme. This melody, in the solo violin, also brings on the recapitulation, in which the second theme is stated in E major instead of B major. The movement ends with a cadenza.

The finale is a compromise between a minuet and a rondo—a rondo in structure, and a minuet in tempo. A minuet-like tune in solo violin, accompanied by strings, opens the movement. The theme is assumed by the orchestra in the eighth measure. A transitional passage leads into the movement's second theme, in E major. Midway in the movement, a new section is introduced, in which the violin offers an intriguing new melody in pseudo-Turkish style. The opening minuet-like tune, however, is soon recalled to end the concerto gracefully.

1775. MISSA BREVIS IN C, "SPATZENMESSE," K. 220.

The *Missa Brevis,* as that title indicates, is a short Mass. It was intended for church services less ceremonial than those requiring a full Mass. Shorter in structure and less elaborate in technique, it makes far less exacting demands on the listener than would a full-length Mass. Mozart wrote about ten Masses of this variety. The first—in G major, K. 49—came in 1768; the last—B-flat major, K. 275—was completed in 1776. In between, comes the so-called *Spatzenmesse,* which the composer wrote in Munich in January 1775, possibly on a commission from his Salzburg employer, the Archbishop Colloredo. "Spatzen" means "jest"; the "jest" in the C major *Missa Brevis* is found in the violin figures in the Allegro of the "Sanctus" section. Alfred Einstein even finds this work to be a parody of the Mass. He deduces that Mozart may well have written this music with tongue in cheek—a gesture of defiance to ecclesiastical authority in general and to his autocratic employer in particular.

1776–1777. CONCERT ARIAS, for voice and orchestra:

Ombra felice, K. 255, recitative and aria for alto and orchestra.

Ah, lo Previdi, K. 272, scena for soprano and orchestra.

Mozart wrote an entire library of concert arias—thirty-six for soprano, ten for tenor and bass, but only one for contralto. The last of these, *Ombra felice* (1776), is a recitative and aria based on a text from *Didone abbondonata,* an opera by Martellari. Mozart's concert aria describes Aeneas's poignant farewell to Dido. *Ah, lo previdi* (1777) is one of the most extended and dramatic of all Mozart's concert arias. The words (taken from Paisiello's opera, *Andromeda*) first tell of Andromeda's bitter accusation against Perseus for having destroyed her love with the same sword he had previously used to save her. This recitative is followed by a poignant aria, "Ah, t'invola agl' occhi miei." Andromeda banishes Perseus to live with wild beasts. A second recitative finds Andromeda plunged in the depths of sorrow as she realizes she cannot remove thoughts of the man she loves. The concert aria ends with an eloquent cavatina—Andromeda's address to Perseus, informing him she will join him at the banks of Lethe.

1776–1777. DIVERTIMENTI, for orchestra:

F major, K. 247, for strings and two horns. I. Allegro II. Andante grazioso. III. Menuetto. IV. Adagio. V. Menuetto. VI. Andante. VII. Allegro assai.

D major, K. 251, for oboe, two horns, and strings. I. Allegro molto. II. Menuetto. III. Andantino. IV. Menuetto. V. Allegro assai. VI. Marcia alla francese.

B-flat, major, K. 287, for two horns and strings. I. Allegro. II. Andante grazioso. III. Menuetto. IV. Adagio. V. Andante. VI. Allegro molto.

Mozart wrote two divertimenti for Countess Antonia Lodron, whose two daughters were his pupils in Salzburg. The first and lighter of these two works is that in F major, K. 247; it was writen to honor the Countess' birthday in June, 1776. The highlights of this charming composition are: the second movement, in which the main subject is a graceful melody, and out of which is derived the subsidiary material of the same movement; the haunting Andante; and the sprightly finale, which opens with a delicate tune shared by horns and violins.

The D major Divertimento was Mozart's birthday gift to his beloved sister, Marianne, in 1776. The entire work differs from other Mozart Divertimenti in its essentially French character. The first and last movements are marked "in the French style"; the solo instrument—the oboe (or hautbois) is primarily French; and to Alfred Einstein most of the themes have their prototypes in French chansons. The reason why Mozart leaned here so heavily on French influences was that he wished to remind his sister of their delightful visit together to France a decade earlier.

The B-flat major Divertimento came in 1777. Otto Jahn described this work as "grand in design and composition." The first violin "is treated as a solo instrument throughout, with a strong tendency to bravura, the remaining instruments cooperating in such a way as to display the creative spirit of an artist in every detail however delicate or subordinate."

Jahn has provided the following analysis: "In the very first thematically elaborate passage the solo passages for the violin occur, which it is the chief concern of the second part to elaborate. The second movement is an air with variations, in which all the instruments take part, but the violin more prominently, and with more of the executive bravura than any of the others. This is most apparent in the two minuets, but it is very decided also in the broadly conceived Adagio, where the second violin and tenor are muted, the cello plays pizzicato, while the first violin leads a melody richly adorned with figures and passages, and requiring the execution of a finished performer. . . . The concluding movement introduced by an Andante with a recitative for the first violin, not too long, and so worked out that the whole compass of the instrument is characteristically displayed. A long Molto allegro follows this introduction in 3/8 time. . . . The recitative recurs at the end, followed by a short and brilliant conclusion. The tone of the movement is not as cheerful as usual; it is full of impulsive haste and changeful humor, and its stronger accent betrays a certain intensity, even in the introductory recitative."

1776–1779. SERENADE NO. 6 IN D MAJOR, "SERENATA NOTTURNA," K. 239, for two small orchestras and drums. I. Maestoso. II. Menuetto. III. Allegretto.

SERENADE NO. 7 IN D MAJOR, "HAFFNER," K. 250. I. Allegro maestoso. II. Allegro molto. III. Andante. IV. Menuetto. V. Rondo. VI. Menuetto galante. VII. Andante. VIII. Menuetto. IX. Adagio. X. Allegro assai.

SERENADE NO. 9 IN D MAJOR, "POSTHORN," K. 320, for wind instruments. I. Adagio maestoso; Allegro con spirito. II. Concertante: andante grazioso. III. Allegretto. IV. Allegro ma non troppo. V. Andantino. VI. Menuetto. VII. Presto.

Most Mozart serenades were functional pieces written for specific events or upon the request of some patron or friend. However, research has failed to uncover why or for whom Mozart wrote the *Serenata Notturna* (1776). Wyzewa and de Saint-Fox, in their biography of Mozart, suggest it might have been intended as a New Year's gift for the composer's sister; or perhaps it was written for a child of Mozart's friends, the Lodrons.

The unusual feature of this Serenade is that it is scored for two orchestras. One is made up of two violins, viola, and double bass; the other, for two violins, viola, cello, and drums. For the most part, explain Wyzewa and de Saint Fox, "the role of the second orchestra is merely to double the first, save when it responds as an echo or fills up the intervals between phrases without bursts of the drums. The full effect of the Serenade can only be achieved if the two orchestras are placed sufficiently apart, as, for example, at opposite ends of a room, so that the exchanged dialogue may create an atmosphere of novelty."

The first movement opens with a two-measure march for both orchestras, forte. This is followed by two soft measures for the solo orchestra. Both orchestras then present a subject, and indulge in an exchange of phrases before basic material is recalled. The second movement is a three-part minuet, the main theme assigned to both orchestras; in the trio, the principal theme is heard only in the solo orchestra. The finale, a rondo, is unconventional in that an eloquent slow section comes midway in a movement otherwise consistently exuberant.

The seventh Serenade is known as the *Haffner* (not to be confused with the *Haffner* Symphony in D major, K. 385). This is because Mozart wrote it in 1776 for the wedding of Elizabeth, daughter of Sigmund Haffner, Salzburg's Burgomaster. To G. de Saint-Fox, this work marks "the climax, not to say the apotheosis, of the period . . . designated as galant. . . . It is really, in every sense of the word, a musical feast, in which Mozart gives rein to his fancy, creating almost new forms; where, too, rhythms to be used later in his *Don Giovanni* make their appearance before our delighted eyes." G. de Saint-Fox further finds in this music "the adoption of a new galant ideal" in the "abnormal length of the movements, their variety, their brilliance, the elaboration of detail entrusted to a big orchestra."

The inclusion of a posthorn in the wind orchestra gives the ninth Serenade its familiar sobriquet (1779). A posthorn, Percy Scholes explains, is a "straight or oblong-coiled (or circular coiled) brass instrument with no valves or other means of producing any notes but those of the harmonic series. Its name comes from its old-time use by the guards of the mail coaches to announce their arrival in the villages and towns on their route."

In the first movement a brief and emotional slow section precedes the short Allegro. All instruments of the wind orchestra, except the flutes, are used here. In the second movement, two flutes, two oboes, and bassoons are allowed to move freely in five independently moving parts; one of the interesting features of this section is a cadenza in five voices. The third-movement minuet and the fourth-movement Allegro are described by Otto Jahn as "light and sunshiny." But in the fifth-movement Andantino, a "serious melancholy" provides a dramatic change. The Minuet that follows, unlike the earlier one, dispenses with the flutes. Here we find two trios, the first for strings, the second with added oboes and a solo posthorn. The serenade ends with an electrifying presto.

1777. QUARTET IN D MAJOR, K. 285, for flute and strings. I. Allegro. II. Adagio. III. Rondo.

Mozart's three flute quartets were written for Monsieur de Jean, a Dutch amateur flutist who had commissioned them. The first, in D major, is a happy blend of the joyful spirit so often encountered in Mozart's earlier compositions. But we also find here a touch of pathos. The opening theme of the first movement, subjected to detailed elaboration in the development, and the main rondo theme of the last movement represent the ebullient Mozart; the wonderful slow movement, with its expansive melody for the flute over a pizzicato accompaniment, reflects the more serious Mozart.

1777–1778. SONATAS FOR PIANO:

A minor, K. 310. I. Allegro maestoso. II. Andante cantabile con espressione. III. Presto.

D major, K. 311. I. Allegro con spirito. II. Andante con espressione. III. Allegro.

A major, "Turkish," K. 331. I. Andante grazioso. II. Menuetto. III. Allegretto.

F major, K. 332. I. Allegro. II. Adagio. III. Allegro assai.

Mozart's eighteen sonatas for the piano are unquestionably of historic importance in solidifying the sonata form, and in extending the technique and dynamics of writing for the keyboard. As a medium through which Mozart expressed himself throughout his career—and with an instrument that was his favorite—the piano sonatas provide us with a wealth of enchanting moods and captivating thoughts and feelings always expressed with perfection and originality. In addition, in these sonatas we can detect valuable clues as to Mozart's changing states of heart and mind. Claudio Arrau, the distinguished concert pianist, is eminently justified in saying that Mozart's sonatas "tell the history of Mozart's life. From the first he begins to fill out the conventional patterns of his time with his life blood and as he grew and developed, lived and suffered, they became the mirror of his soul and mind. They are the internal evidence of his total being and tell us more than anything to be found even in his voluminous and extraordinary correspondence with his family."

Mozart produced his first set of piano sonatas in Salzburg in 1774. They comprise six works (K. 279–284), all of them in the galant style favored by that period, with elegance and polish preferable to expressiveness and depth. Yet even here we occasionally catch a glimpse of the later Mozart: in pages such as the Adagio of the F major Sonata, K. 280, in which we come face to face with the grandeur and sublimity of some of Mozart's later slow movements.

The A minor Sonata, K. 310 (1778), is Mozart's only such work in the minor mode. Ernest Hutcheson describes it as "a work of genius in which every movement is masterly . . . a gripping composition dramatically conceived and calling for an impassioned interpretation. Even the final Rondo has a touch of Weltschmerz."

The D major Sonata (1777) was described by Claudio Arrau as follows: "Both in the opening Allegro and concluding magnificent rondo, the first of a festive character in 6/8 time, there can be no mistake about the impression the playing of the famed Mannheim orchestra had made on him." The galant style of Mozart's earlier sonatas is here quickly being displaced by the passion and subjectivity of the later Beethoven.

The A major Sonata (1778) is one of the most popular by Mozart, and structurally one of the most unusual. Instead of a first movement in the sonata form, we encounter here a theme and variations. The theme is a fully stated two-part melody, which in its grace and elegance is obviously a child of the eighteenth century. Six simple variations follow. The usual slow movement is replaced by a minuet, whose charm and classic repose once again belong to the eighteenth century, though there is a romantic intrusion in the trio. The finale is so famous that it is sometimes played independently of the other movements, and can also be heard in numerous transcriptions. This is the so-called "Turkish March," its light and airy tune being in a style that eighteenth-century Vienna liked to identify as Turkish.

The first movement of the F major Sonata (1777) combines Beethovenian drama with Mozartian pleasantries. The slow movement has a soaring melody that might have come out of one of Mozart's operas, while the finale is music of extraordinary power, continually dramatized by unexpected modulations.

1778–1779. SONATAS FOR VIOLIN AND PIANO:

C major, K. 296. I. Allegro vivace. II. Andante sostenuto. III. Allegro.

B-flat major, K. 378. I. Allegro moderato. II. Andantino sostenuto e cantabile. III. Allegro.

With Mozart's forty-two violin sonatas, the modern violin sonata comes into its own. "It was the genius of Mozart," says Frank Walker, "which imparted life to the form, and he may be said to have brought the dramatic violin sonata to perfection, in the same way that Haydn developed the string quartet. Both accepted the hints of their predecessors and contemporaries but were finally reliant on the strength of their own genius. . . . In Mozart's works, we can observe his growth to the mastery of his medium, from timid beginnings to the first dramatic sonatas in the modern sense, which are played today on their own merits, irrespective of merely historic considerations."

Mozart published his first set of violin sonatas in Paris when he was only eight. These, and similar works that followed in the next dozen years, were influenced by and imitative of composers like John Christian Bach and Georg Christoph Wagenseil (1715–1777). Mozart begins to free himself from this dependence on other composers with a set of sonatas in 1768, in which Abert finds a "true Mozartian spirit" and an "extraordinary subjective note." But for all that, a good deal of the material in these works is of lesser inspiration.

It is with his twenty-fourth sonata, in C major, that Mozart comes to maturity within the violin-sonata medium. This is one of seven such works written during Mozart's stay in Mannheim between 1777 and 1778. The C major Sonata was completed in a single day (March 11, 1778) and was intended for one of Mozart's pupils. Here the two instruments are given equal attention by the composer; and the thematic material assigned to them is full of joyful vigor. The second movement is particularly lovely, though not yet as poetic as the slow movements of his later sonatas; the main melody is accompanied by a triplet variation of the Alberti bass.

The B-flat major Sonata, Mozart's twenty-sixth, was completed in Salzburg in 1779, soon after his return from a visit to Paris that had ended abruptly with the death of his mother. Alfred Einstein described the first movement as "very brilliant"; the finale, as "very characteristic of Salzburg . . . with its interlude before the return to the rondo theme"; and the slow movement as "deeply felt" looking backwards to John Christian Bach and forward to *The Abduction from the Seraglio*.

1778–1779. SINFONIA CONCERTANTE IN E-FLAT MAJOR, K. Anh. 9, for oboe, clarinet, horn, bassoon, and orchestra. I. Allegro. II. Adagio. III. Andantino con variozione.

SINFONIA CONCERTANTE IN E-FLAT MAJOR, K. 364, for violin and viola and orchestra. I. Allegro maestoso. II. Andante. III. Presto.

The Sinfonia concertante is a Baroque form that attempted to fuse the symphony with the concerto. While, like the concerto, it set off the virtuosity of the soloists, it also paid far greater attention to the orchestra than concertos were accustomed to do at that time.

The Sinfonia concertante in E-flat major, K. Anh. 9, is scored for four solo wind instruments and orchestra. It was written in 1778 while Mozart was visiting Paris. There he was encouraged to produce a work in concerto-grosso style for performances at a Concert spirituel, conducted by Joseph Le Gros.

Since Mozart had originally planned this work for four instrumentalists of the famous Mannheim Orchestra, it is not surprising to find a good deal of the Mannheim tradition in his writing—recognizable, as Alfred Einstein notes, in the "pomp and general scope, not only through the use of the 'Mannheim crescendo' but also by the exploitation of solo effects."

The first movement opens with a subject that Mozart liked well enough to use earlier in the E-flat major Symphony, K. 132 (1772), and that he remembered in 1785 in the first subject of the E-flat major Piano Concerto, K. 482. Two other important melodies follow. The orchestral introduction over, the woodwind quartet enters with the first of these themes, before proceeding to the other two. Solo instruments and orchestra then embellish upon this material. The solo choir sets the development into motion with a completely new thought. In this development, the solo clarinet and the solo oboe are given personal attention. The recapitulation and coda follow.

The Adagio spins a wondrous song, primarily in the four solo instruments. The finale consists of a charming tune with ten variations. In these variations, each of the four solo instruments is given an opportunity to express himself. After the tenth variation, comes a moving slow section followed by a vigorous coda.

The Sinfonia concertante for viola, violin, and orchestra is Mozart's masterwork in this form. He wrote it in 1779 soon after his return to Salzburg from travels in Germany and Paris. The first movement is built from two sets of principal themes. The first set, robust in style, is heard initially in the orchestra. Sixteen measures of violin trills, that reach a crescendo over shifting harmonies and a series of lower string E-flats, precede the second set. This is given by the two solo instruments. In the slow movement, Mozart achieves an intensity that borders on the tragic. The orchestra embarks upon an extended melody which the two instruments soon elaborate upon. Then a secondary song, no less sublime, is heard in the orchestra—violas entering in imitation a half-measure after the first violins, while the solo instruments provide figurations. In the finale, a lighthearted rondo, the gloom is dispelled. As in the opening movement, two sets of themes are heard. The first is heard in the orchestra, and the second in the solo instruments.

1778–1780. SYMPHONY NO. 31 IN D MAJOR, "PARIS," K. 297. I. Allegro assai. II. Andantino. III. Allegro.

SYMPHONY NO .34 IN C MAJOR, K. 338. I. Allegro vivace. II. Andante di molto. III. Allegro vivace.

Le Gros, director of the Concert spirituel in Paris, commissioned Mozart to write for him a symphony "in the Parisian style." The work, completed in 1778, was Mozart's attempt to conform to Parisian tastes. "I have been careful," he wrote a friend, "not to neglect *le première coup d'archet* [precise attack of a full orchestra]—and that is quite sufficient. What a fuss the oxen make of this trick!" He also explained: "I had noticed here [Paris] that the last movements always begin like the first, with a full tutti, and generally in unison, so I began mine with the two violins alone, and after eight bars made a forte. When they heard it begin *piano* every body said, 'Hush,' till the forte came, and then they all clapped like fury." However, the Parisian public thought his slow movement far too long, and in compliance with this criticism, Mozart shortened it. The *Paris* Symphony was scored for the largest orchestra Mozart had thus far utilized, and represents his first use of clarinets in a symphony.

The symphony begins with the "coup d'archet." The first subject follows with unison scale passages for strings, developed by full orchestra. The second theme, in the relative major key of A, is lighter in tone. After a repetition of this idea, we hear a staccato string passage, repeated four times in modulation, about which Mozart said: "I knew it was sure to please, so I brought it in again later: the audience was transported by it." In the development, interest is centered on the first theme, which is also given foreceful treatment in the coda.

Strings followed by the woodwind appear with the broad, solemn melody that opens the second movement. When the second subject is heard in the first violins, the mood becomes exalted, though occasionally dramatized by a loud upward unison passage. The vigor is soon dissipated with a variation of the second theme in a lighter vein, before the beautiful opening melody is repeated. A new variation of the second theme is then introduced by a sustained "D" in the flutes. The symphony has no third-movement, the slow movement being followed immediately by the finale. Its first subject is a soft, syncopated tune for first violins, followed eight measures later by a hardier melody for bassoons and strings. After an extended tutti, a fugato for strings serves as the second subject, and as material for the development. A return of the first sprightly subject permits the symphony to end vivaciously.

The Symphony No. 34 (1780) was the last Mozart wrote in Salzburg. The first movement is marked by what Otto Jahn calls a "constant propensity to fall into the minor key" and by a blend of "strength and decision with expression not so much of melancholy as of consolation." It opens dramatically with a majestic subject. This mood of sobriety continues after the fourth bar with a *piano* echo and expansion which to Donald Francis Tovey is "more like a serious dramatic question than any echoes in the *Paris* Symphony." The second subject, to Tovey, "marks the epoch of Mozart's full maturity of invention." Without repeating his exposition, Mozart proceeds to an episodic development. "Twelve impressively gloomy bars," writes Tovey, "lead to the dark key of A-flat where a dramatic passage proceeds, in plaintive dialogue between strings and wind, to the dominant C minor, where it remains in suspense just long enough to determine the right moment for the return of the first theme with a regular recapitulation."

The slow movement is scored for strings and bassoons (the latter doubling the basses); the violas are divided. "The movement," says Tovey, "is the richest slow movement Mozart had as yet produced, and he did not often surpass it in subtlety. It is eminently witty, and the attention is concentrated on its pure musical sense without any distractions of orchestral color." As had been the case with the *Paris* Symphony, there is no minuet here to separate the slow movement from the finale, whose principal idea is a lively dance tune in 6/8 time.

1778–1786. COMPOSITIONS FOR SOLO PIANO:
Variations on 'Ah. vous dirai-je maman,' K. 265; Fantasy and Fugue in C major, K. 394; Fantasia in D minor, K. 397; *Variations on 'Unser dummer Poebel meint,'* K. 455; Rondo in D major, K. 485.

One of Mozart's less pretentious piano pieces, whose simplicity has made it ideal fare for elementary piano students, is the *Variations on 'Ah. vous dirai-je, maman'* (1778). It is music of surpassing charm. The melody, based on a popular French tune, is the same one that children today sing to the alphabet. Twelve simple variations follow.

In the Fantasy and Fugue in C major (1782), Mozart is influenced by Johann Sebastian Bach, as he himself disclosed. "The reason for this fugue coming into the world," he wrote, "is that Baron van Swieten, to whom I go every Sunday, gave me all Handel's and Bach's works (after I had played them through for him) to take home with me. When Constance heard the fugues, she fell in love with them . . . and would not stop urging me until I composed a fugue for her." Though this music is rooted in Bach, it remains Mozartian in its appealing tenderness, and in its digressions into striking modulations.

There is even greater independence of structure and thought in the Fantasia in D minor. (1782). It opens with a bold arpeggio subject, which once again carries a reminder of the great Johann Sebastian Bach. A deeply emotional and introspective melody follows, which is dramatically interrupted by pauses. The sober mood is finally broken with a gay Allegretto section.

The *Variations on 'Unser dummer Poebel meint'* (1784) is one of Mozart's finest piano pieces in the variation form. The melody comes out of Gluck's opera, *La Rencontre imprévue,* but in the ensuing ten variations, the style is more perceptibly Mozart's than Gluck's. Eric Blom wrote: "Mozart let his fancy roam at will, holding it close to the model, but playing with his material with a sort of kittenish elegance." Of particular interest is the extended and poetic Adagio section, and the finale with its intriguing time changes from 3/8 to common.

The Rondo in D major (1786) is a movement independent of any sonata. The graceful line of its single melody is made exciting by its modulations.

1779. KROENUNGSMESSE (CORONATION MASS), K. 317, for solo voices, chorus, and orchestra.

Mozart wrote his *Coronation Mass* for the Maria Plain Church near Salzburg to commemorate the miraculous appearance there of the Virgin Mary. It is not clear, though, why this work acquired its name. Certainly it was not written for any secular coronation. Possibly the crowning of the effigy of the Virgin during the Maria Plain Church festivities might have had something to do with the title.

The opening "Kyrie" has two sections: a stately introduction interrupted by interpolations by the chorus (the choral episodes here separated by string arpeggios), and a section in quicker tempo assigned to the solo voices. This is followed by a dramatic "Gloria," toward whose conclusion there appears a remarkably effective descending figure by each of the solo voices in close imitation, followed at once by an equally telling outburst from chorus and orchestra. Throughout the next section there moves a restless ostinato figure in the string orchestra, a climax coming with "Et Incarnatus est," an eloquent Adagio for four solo voices accompanied by chromatic figures in the strings. An introspective slow section (Andante maestoso) in the "Sanctus" leads into the "Osanna in excelsis" (Allegro assai), which is dramatized by successive trills in the violins. The "Benedictus" ascends a lofty plane of eloquence, first in the strings, later in the four solo voices without chorus. The exalted mood is temporarily broken by an exultant "Osanna" but resumed in the concluding "Agnus Dei," which opens with a melody that reminds us of the beautiful "Dovo sono" aria from *The Marriage of Figaro*. The music sweeps on to a magnificent conclusion (Allegro con spirito) with material lifted from the opening "Kyrie."

1779. CONCERTO IN E-FLAT, K. 365, for two pianos and orchestra. I. Allegro. II. Andante. III. Allegro.

This is Mozart's only concerto for two pianos and orchestra—written for performance by himself and his sister. The starring role is equally divided between the two soloists, as Otto Jahn noted when he said: "The players emulate each other in the deliverance of the melodies and passages, sometimes together, sometimes in succession, often breaking off in rapid changes and interruptions; the melodies are sometimes simply stated, sometimes with variations so divided between the two instruments that neither can be said to have the advantage over the other."

The principal theme of the first movement, which enters without delay, is a robust melody with a descending octave. The secondary subject is, on the other hand, lyrical. It comes in violins and violas, with the horns joining in at the end of the phrase. A soulful song for the orchestra is the heart of the second movement, the two pianos here serving mainly to provide intriguing decorations. The finale, a rondo, is bright-faced and light-hearted, even though midway a somber passage introduces temporary sobriety.

1780. VESPERAE SOLENNES DE CONFESSORE, K. 339, for four voices, orchestra, and organ.

Though not so well known as the Requiem or the *Great Mass*, the *Vesperae Solennes de Confessor* is one of Mozart's most important compositions for the church. It is a setting of the Latin texts of five Psalms (110, 111, 112, 113, 117) and of the Hymn of the Virgin Mary from the Gospel according to St. Luke. Psalms 110 and 111 ("Dixit Dominus" and "Confiteor tibi") are treated robustly with music that has a ceremonial character; a lighter touch is used for the 112th Psalm ("Beatus vir"). Psalms 113 and 114—"Laudate Pueri" and "Laudate Dominum—contain some of the most awe-inspiring music in this work. The former receives fugal treatment, while the latter has such surpassing eloquence that it is often given apart from the rest of the composition. The work closes with a grandiose "Magnificat."

1781. IDOMENEO, RÈ DI CRETA (IDOMENEO, KING OF CRETE), K. 366, opera seria in three acts, with text by Giambattista Varesco, based on a libretto by Danchet for Campra's opera, *Idomenée*. First performance: Munich, January 29, 1781.

Idomeneo is Mozart's first significant serious opera, his first fully mature work for the stage in any style. He was commissioned to write it by the Elector of Bavaria, Carl Theodor, for performance during the Munich Carnival of 1781. The opera aroused considerable enthusiasm both at rehearsals and during the première.

Mozart here remains faithful to the traditions of opera seria. The action is allowed to move in the recitatives, most of which are of the secco variety. Recitatives, accompanied by orchestra, were used at climactic points in the story. Ensembles were avoided, since the composer wished to focus the full attention of the audience upon the solo singers, for whom he wrote elaborate arias, mostly in the da capo form. The influence of Gluck and French opera is discernible in the ballets. As Prof. Edwards J. Dent put it so well, *Idomeneo* is "French by deliberate intention, but Italian by natural instinct."

Though heard less rarely than Mozart's famous operatic masterworks, *Idomeneo* (when properly presented) is "one of Mozart's grandest and most ambitious works," as W. J. Turner called it, "and unique among his operas for brilliance of instrumentation, virtuosity, and dramatic intensity, and in the splendid use of chorus." Some of the arias have rare grandeur and nobility: that of Idamante in the first act, "Non ho colpa"; Idomeneo's air in the second act, "Vedrommi intorno"; and Ilia's aria in the third, "Zeffiretti lusinghieri." At least in one of the episodes, Mozart looks forward to Wagner (rather than backwards to Gluck); this is in the extended accompanied recitative in the last act in which arioso and secco passages alternate within an ambitious structure, dramatized by continual changes of tempo, orchestral color, and key.

The note of grandeur, with tragic overtones, that courses through the opera, is first sounded in the popular overture. Loud chords and ascending passages set the stage for a sensitive melody in the strings, decorated with trills. The forceful material of this opening is then expanded, the lower strings giving occasional intimations of impending doom.

The text is a variation of the Biblical story of Jephtha, transferred to Greek mythology. The King of Crete, returning from the Trojan wars, is menaced by a violent storm. In his terror, he promises Neptune to sacrifice the first living creature he meets upon coming home, if his life is spared. His wish is granted. The first person to great the king is his own son, Idamante. To save his son's life, the king plans to send him off to a distant kingdom. But just before Idamante boards ship, another tremendous storm is let loose—a sign to the King that the gods insist upon the fulfillment of the bargain. Idamante now stands ready to meet death; but Ilia, who is in love with him, begs him to allow her to die in his stead. Suddenly Neptune's voice announces Idomeneo's release from his vow, but only on the condition that he relinquish his throne to Idamante, and that the new king be allowed to marry Ilia. The solution is joyfully accepted by the king. The people sing the praises of Love, and pray for the peace and happiness of the new rulers.

1781. QUARTET IN F MAJOR, K. 370, for oboe and strings. I. Allegro. II. Adagio. III. Allegro ma non troppo.

This is one of several compositions written for the oboe virtuoso, Friedrich Ramm of Munich. Alfred Einstein described it as a "masterwork which in its combination of the concertante and chamber-music spirits can be compared only with Mozart's own later Clarinet Quintet." Einstein goes on to explain: "It is somewhat concertante and even supplies an opportunity for a small cadenza in the Adagio (in D minor); the rondo finale contains a device that is very rare in Mozart: while the three-stringed instruments proceed along their somewhat easygoing way in 6/8 time, the wind instrument has a cantilene and figurations in 4/4 time."

1781. SONATA IN G MAJOR-MINOR, K. 379, for violin and piano. I. Adagio; Allegro. II. Allegro. III. Andante cantabile.

During Mozart's first Viennese period, in 1781, he completed five violin sonatas, published in a set of six; the sixth being an earlier product to help fill out the volume. The second of this series, in G major-minor, is one of the most significant. It opens, in Frank Walker's analysis, "with a nobly spacious Adagio in the Italian manner, in which the accompanying arpeggios grow and are made magnificent, when the violin is silent. . . . The serenity of this lovely song is interrupted by a phrase moving toward G minor, intruded by the violin, and passed down from the treble to the bass of the piano until the significant . . . thrilling pause of the dominant is reached. . . . Then we are plunged into the passionate pleading of the wonderful G minor Allegro." The finale consists of a melody with five variations. "The statement of the first half of the air in G major brings back peace and serenity, though in the second half there is an excursion into the minor which will disturb the first variation —for piano alone—and, intensively, the two variations following. The fourth variation, in G minor, is calmer and of a haunting melancholy, and the fifth, in the major again, is a florid elaboration of the air with the violin pizzicato throughout. By the time this is over the mood is attuned to the repetition of the air in quickened time (Allegretto) and the coming of a happy assured coda."

1782. DIE ENTFUEHRUNG AUS DEM SERAIL (THE ABDUCTION FROM THE SERAGLIO), K. 384, comic opera in three acts, with text by Gottlieb Stephanie, based on a play by Christoph Bretzner. First performance: Burgtheater, Vienna, July 16, 1782.

The Abduction from the Seraglio is Singspiel raised to the "nth power" of its artistic potential. The Singspiel, an early form of German comic opera, was entertainment for the masses. The text was in the vernacular; tunes of popular or folk variety were interspersed among sequences of dialogue; the comedy was broad burlesque. Mozart had written Singspiel from his boyhood days on, beginning with *Bastien and Bastienne* (which see). While he was faithful to the popular demands of this medium and adhered to its traditions, he kept enriching its musical content until he achieved with *The Abduction* a comic art of the first significance. Since *The Abduction* is also the first important opera in the German language, it can be considered the beginnings of German comic opera.

One of the unusual things about this work is that one of its characters—Selim, the Pasha—never sings a note throughout the work, but has only a speaking part. Some Mozart commentators believe that Mozart was striving for an unusual effect. But Herbert Weinstock and Wallace Brockway, in their book on *The Opera,* are convinced that the only reason the Pasha fails to sing is because Mozart could not devise Pasha-like music for him, or, being able to devise such music, was convinced he could never find a singer able to interpret it adequately.

There was good practical reason why Mozart should have selected a Turkish setting and Turkish characters for his first mature opera for Vienna; also why he should have introduced Turkish-like effects into his musical writing. Vienna in the seventeenth and eighteenth centuries had a passion for all things Turkish—candy, coffee, and music with percussive effects and minor-mode melodies, which was considered Turkish. It is for this reason that Mozart introduced so-called Turkish music into his A major Piano Sonata and A major Violin Concerto (which see). And this is the reason why, in trying to win the favor of his public, Mozart should have produced a stage work with Turkish interest.

The Emperor himself commissioned Mozart to write the opera for the Burgtheater. But the path leading from commission to first performance was rugged. Antonio Salieri, the renowed Kapellmeister in Vienna, saw in Mozart a formidable rival who might endanger his own position at court. He used influence, power, prestige, and intrigue to keep the opera from getting performed. Delay followed delay; for a while, it seemed that the opera would never reach the stage. Then the Emperor himself interceded. All opposition to Mozart and his opera now crumbled. The première went exceptionally well. "The populace is quite crazy about this opera," reported Mozart. "The people will hear nothing else, and the theater is constantly filled to the doors." It became Mozart's most popular stage work in Vienna during his own lifetime, receiving forty-two performances in six years. Carl Maria von Weber said of it: "I venture to express the belief that in Mozart's *Seraglio* experience in artistic creation reached its maturity, after which only experience in life added to his creative powers."

The sprightly little overture is based on the breezy little tune in the strings with which it opens; this tune is endowed with alla turca colorations by an accompanying triangle. The curtain then rises on a square in front of the Pasha's palace in sixteenth-century Turkey. Within that palace, Constanza and Blonda are prisoners, having been kidnaped by pirates and sold to the Turkish ruler. Outside the palace, Belmonte, a Spanish nobleman in love with Constanza, is rhapsodic over the thought that he might soon be seeing his loved one again ("Hier soll' ich dich denn sehen"). As he is musing, he espies Osmin, the fat overseer of the women, who is singing a little ditty about the fickleness of women ("Wer ein Liebchen hat gefunden"). When Belmonte accosts him, the fat overseer rebuffs him rudely. Now Pedrillo, Belmonte's servant, taunts Osmin and sends him into a rage ("Solche hergelauf'ne Laffen"). When the Pasha comes upon the scene he is hailed by a chorus of janissaries ("Singt dem grossen Bassa Lieder"). The Pasha is accompanied by Constanza. Belmonte goes into hiding, but not before he expresses the intensity of his feeings at seeing Constanza again ("Konstanze! dich widerzusehen"). In vain does the Pasha try to gain her love. Constanza rejects him, since she loves somebody else and is ready to face death rather than be unfaithful ("Ach, ich liebte"). Angrily, the Pasha presents Constanza with an ultimatum: she must accept his love by the morrow or face the grim consequences. After Constanza departs with heavy heart, Pedrillo introduces Belmonte to the Pasha, who invites him into the palace.

In the palace garden, Blonde—Constanza's maid—is trying to elude Osmin's amorous advances. Constanza now appears. She is lamenting her unfortunate fate ("Traurigkeit ward mir zum Lose"). Her despair mounts when the Pasha comes to remind her that she has only one more day to decide to give her love to him. Enraged, Constanza insists she prefers torture or death ("Martern aller Arten"). Later on, Blonde is apprised by Pedrillo of a plot to effect Constanza's escape: Pedrillo and Belmonte plan to get the guards drunk. The thought of freedom overjoys Blonde ("Welche Wonne, welche Lust"). And now Pedrillo appears with a bottle or wine under his arm. Before long he has Osmin in a drunken stupor. Thus, at last, Belmonte and Constanza can meet again. The fervor of their love is voiced in the rapturous duet, "Wenn der Freude Thraenen fliessen."

Later, outside the palace, Belmonte—come to arrange Constanza's escape —serenades her ("Ich baue ganz auf deine Staerke"). Pedrillo, too, has a serenade for the lady of his love—Blonde ("Im Mohrenland gefangen war").

But before the escape can be realized, Constanza and Blonde are apprehended and brought for judgment to the Pasha. The Pasha takes both women severely to task for flouting his wishes. But he forgives them, grants them their freedom, and allows them to rejoin their sweethearts. The magnanimity of the Pasha is hailed in the closing chorus, "Nie werd' ich deine Huld verkennen."

What Eric Blom said of the finale applies to the opera as a whole: "It is a structure and a collection of tunes of such fascinating grace that one would like to call back every phrase of it to hug it over and over again. But it just flows on happily and will not wait to be loved. That is the worst of music—and the best: it will not be possessed. However, to such a score as that of *The Abduction* you can at least go back for another spell of enticement, and you will never fail to find it fresh."

The first performance in the United States was in the Italian language, in Brooklyn, New York, on February 16, 1860. Two years later, the opera was seen in German at the German Opera House in New York. Its first appearance in the repertory of the Metropolitan Opera was on December 18, 1946, in an English translation.

1782. QUINTET IN E-FLAT, K. 407, for horn and strings. I. Allegro. II. Andante. III. Allegro.

Like a good many of his other chamber-music works employing wind instruments, the E-flat Quintet was written for a specific performer—in this instance, Ignatz Leutgeb, a horn player. Alfred Einstein explains that this composition is a "rudimentary concerto with chamber-music accompaniment and even includes opportunities for cadenzas. Except for the deeply felt slow movement, this music offers Mozart in some of his more satirical attitudes. In this instance he is poking fun at the limitations of the horn, especially in the finale with its mocking fanfare."

1782–1784. CONCERTOS FOR PIANO AND ORCHESTRA:

C major, K. 415. I. Allegro. II. Andante. III. Allegro.

E-flat major, K. 449. I. Allegro vivace. II. Andantino. III. Allegro ma non troppo.

B-flat major, K. 450. I. Allegro. II. Andante. III. Allegro.

G major, K. 453. I. Allegro. II. Andante. III. Allegretto.

F major, K. 459. I. Allegro. II. Allegretto. III. Allegro assai.

Mozart directed his supreme effort and his purest inspiration to the piano-concerto medium. He cultivated the form throughout his career, and with such success that a high percentage of his twenty and more concertos are among his most treasurable achievements. The structure is advanced far beyond that of his predecessors; the orchestra becomes fully emancipated; the solo instrument is recruited, not merely for exhibitions of virtuosity, but also for the expression of either profundity or gaiety. No wonder, then, that Alfred Einstein spoke of Mozart's piano concertos as "the peak of all his instrumental achievement, at least in the orchestral domain. . . . Mozart's concerto form is a vessel of a far richer, finer and more sublime content [than that developed by Beethoven]. . . . Mozart's piano concertos . . . leave the door open to the expression of the darkest and brightest, the most serious and the gayest, the deepest feeling. . . . [They] pressed forward from the galant world into the symphonic: [they] lift the listener to a higher level."

Mozart's first five piano concertos, written between 1765 and 1767, were actually adaptations of sonatas, or movements of sonatas, by other composers, including John Christian Bach. The first concerto containing his own material exclusively is that in D major, K. 175. completed in 1773. This was the first of six concertos for piano written in Salzburg, between 1773 and 1779.

The C major Concerto, K. 415, belongs to Mozart's early Vienna period, having been written between 1782 and 1783. Here is how Wanda Landowska describes it: "The first movement . . . is a type of alla marcia which advances in canonic imitations. Tranquil at first, it augments little by little and overflows into the same triplet motif which marks the opening of the *Jupiter* Symphony. . . . The Andante is a tender and lyrical dialogue between the soloist and strings, the latter supported from time to time by oboes, bassoons, and horns. But it is above all, the finale, a frolicsome dance in 6/8, which merits our fullest attention. . . . At the end of the Rondo, Mozart introduced, against the murmuring of the strings, a popular folk song, ingratiating and fresh in mood."

Mozart wrote six piano concertos in the single year of 1784. Each is significant, even if only the four greatest come in for discussion here. To Eric Blom, the E-flat major reveals "a distinctly new manner," since the lightness and gaiety of earlier concertos are often supplemented or replaced by sobriety or even suggestions of tragedy. Blom adds: "There is something dark and melancholy about this Concerto. . . . Although the first movement is marked Allegretto vivace, it never shows the least vivacity of spirit. It moves along in large steps of wide intervals, with frequent turns into minor keys, and the 3/4 time has a restless effect that is unusual." The second movement features an extended cantilena in two strophes, repeated or decorated by the piano. The finale, a rondo, makes frequent excursions into the minor key to carry on the often lugubrious atmosphere first evoked in the opening movement and then touched upon every so gently in the second.

In the B-flat Concerto, K. 450, the orchestra presents the leading thematic material of the first movement before the piano appears with scale passages and sixteenth-notes. The piano then discourses eloquently on the major themes. The first is a pleasing rococo tune that might have stepped out of a Mozart Serenade. In the recapitulation, we get a résumé of material first offered in the orchestral prelude and in the first exposition by the piano. The second movement consists of a mobile E-flat melody in two strophes, two variations, and a coda. In the finale, a rondo, Mozart introduces a flute into the orchestration of his tutti to provide increased brilliance of color.

Donald Francis Tovey considers the G major Concerto "one of Mozart's richest and wittiest. "C. M. Girdlestone is reminded by it of "celestial fields where the flocks of gods go grazing." The work opens softly with a march-like melody in first violins. This is the movement's main theme. A forceful tutti brings on the second theme, its first part assigned to the strings, and the second to the woodwind. At the end of this orchestral episode, the piano arrives with the main theme. After some passage work, it devotes itself to the second subject. Additional passage work in the piano and an orchestral tutti later bring on the development section; in the recapitulation, the two main themes return in ever newer and fresher formats. A cadenza (by Mozart himself) precedes the coda. The slow movement is the gem in this diadem. The strings progress for five measures with a haunting thought, stop momentarily on the dominant, then permit the woodwind to carry on. After the introduction of new material, in which soft and loud passages alternate, the piano appears with a restatement of the four measures with which the movement opened. It then proceeds to a new melody in G major. This and subsequent material, often shared by piano and woodwind, creates a religious and, at moments, a tragic atmosphere. In the finale, a rondo, the main theme is given at once to the strings, and a subsidiary one later to the piano. The main theme then receives five variations. The concerto ends with a brilliant presto.

The F major Concerto opens with a sensitive, graceful melody for the strings. A canonic passage for flute and bassoon under piano figurations follow. We now hear a beautifully lyric thought, first shared by strings and wind, then repeated by the piano. These ideas are spaciously extended in the development, and altered in the recapitulation. A piano cadenza and a brief coda end the movement. In the Allegretto, there are two entrancing thoughts, the first an expressive melody that opens the movement, and the second, even lighter in texture, heard in the oboe. The finale, a rondo, is one of Mozart's most entertaining and vivacious movements in which his remarkable contrapuntal skill is frequently exploited.

1782–1783. SYMPHONY NO. 35 IN D MAJOR, "HAFFNER," K. 385. I. Allegro con spirito. II. Andante. III. Menuetto. IV. Presto.

SYMPHONY NO. 36 IN C MAJOR, "LINZ," K. 425. I. Adagio; Allegro spiritoso. II. Poco adagio. III. Menuetto. IV. Presto.

The *Haffner* Symphony (not to be confused with the earlier *Haffner* Serenade) is Mozart's most popular before the trio of masterworks he later produced in 1788. Like the Serenade, the symphony was named for the Burgomaster of Salzburg, Sigmund Haffner. In this instance, the work gets its name because the Burgomaster had commissioned it for a party celebrating the ennoblement of his son. One of the unusual features of this work is the fact that the first movement has only a single theme—a dynamic subject that leaps an octave. In place of a second theme, this idea is repeated in a changed key. Counter melodies in the violin soon provide renewed interest in this melody. The slow movement is a simple and direct statement of a romantic song, followed by an even more sensitive passage. The minuet starts off robustly, but in the trio a pastoral mood is introduced. The symphony comes to a whirlwind finish, Mozart instructing that the finale be played throughout as quickly as possible. The strings offer both themes, which eventually get skilful contrapuntal treatment. A breathless momentum is carried on to the closing measure.

The Symphony No. 36 is generally known as the *Linz*. Whether this is the work Mozart wrote for a concert in Linz in October of 1783 is open to question. Some authorities maintain that the work played at Linz was the one in G, K. 444.

The symphony opens with an extended introduction, a practice often found in Haydn, but rarely in Mozart. The main part of the movement goes into motion with an exuberant march-like melody for strings—a four-measure subject receiving a six-measure reply. The second subject, has even greater vivacity. The beautiful slow movement (in sonata form) offers at once a broadly flowing, touching melody. This is followed by a minuet which, to Georges de Saint-Fox, is more suitable for dancing than for symphonic listening; even in the trio, he says, "its charming, soft light is maintained; the way the theme of this trio is taken up in imitation is unrivalled in any similar passage of Mozart." Georges de Saint-Fox detects the shadow of Haydn hovering over the finale—particularly in the "treatment of the development section and the rapid passages preceding the ends of both parts." But he also hastens to add that "the variety of emotions and the undercurrent of passionate uneasiness give it so Mozartian a quality as soon as the composer gets into his subject that the very intention of following a model is effaced, and all previous suggestions become subject to an inner world of his own."

1782–1785. 6 STRING QUARTETS, "HAYDN":

G major, K. 387. I. Allegro vivace assai. II. Allegretto. III. Andante cantabile. IV. Molto allegro.

D minor, K. 421. I. Allegro moderato. II. Andante. III. Allegretto. IV. Allegretto ma non troppo.

E-flat major, K. 428. I. Allegro ma non troppo. II. Andante con moto. III. Allegro. IV. Allegro vivace.

B-flat major, "Hunt," K. 458. I. Allegro vivace assai. II. Menuetto. III. Adagio. IV. Allegro assai.

A major, K. 464. I. Allegro. II. Andante. III. Menuetto. IV. Allegro non troppo.

C major, "Dissonant," K. 465. I. Adagio; Allegro. II. Andante cantabile. III. Menuetto. IV. Allegro molto.

Nine years elapsed after the writing of the String Quartet in D minor, K. 173, before Mozart returned to this medium. When he did, late in 1782, it was not because of a commission, or to satisfy some performer or group of performers, but out of artistic compulsion. He had become acquainted with

Haydn's Quartets, op. 33, in 1782. They opened up for him altogether new vistas, which he was eager to explore for himself. He wanted to begin where Haydn had left off, to proceed in the new directions only pointed out by Haydn.

It was with the full awareness of the greatness of the op. 33 Quartets, and of his indebtedness to their composer, that Mozart dedicated to Haydn the string quartets he completed between 1782 and 1785. These six quartets open a new world. Nothing Mozart had written before this reveals such freedom of structure and style, such an unorthodox technique, iconoclasm, varied invention, and high flights of inspiration. No wonder, then, that when Haydn first heard this music he shook his head with incredulity. He did not always understand what Mozart was trying to say with his striking innovations, but he recognized the power, magic, and greatness of this music. "I tell you before God and as an honest man," he is reported to have told Mozart's father, "that your son is the greatest composer I know, either personally or by name." The impact of these quartets on Haydn was decisive: he himself would now have to write quartets differently and with more daring than heretofore.

Homer Ulrich points out the salient difference between these six Mozart string quartets and those written by Haydn. In Mozart, he remarks, there is an abundance of chromaticism, which is lacking in Haydn—"the half poignant, half resigned tone of Mozart's late works is due in no small part to the use of short chromatic lines." A second point of difference is "the element of subtlety." Ulrich explains that Haydn's music "is a reflection of a mind that was serene and strong in religious faith." But Mozart gave us music "in which unrest, a degree of pessimism, and some concern over the prospect of death are reflected, however faintly." Even in his minuets, Mozart could be "aloof, dignified, and reflective," while in his finales "the humor and liveliness are seen as though from a distance." A third distinction between Mozart and Haydn lies in the "formal aspect" and most notably in "the recapitulation of the sonata-form movements." Haydn often did the unexpected. But where with Mozart the expected usually takes place, it does so "in ever new and interesting ways. . . . The transitions between development and recapitulation and the transitions between the main themes best show his genius and marvelous subtlety."

The G major Quartet (1782) is in many of its pages a miracle of polyphonic writing. In the first movement, which has a happy face throughout, the four instruments have an independence of movement and a personal identity new to quartet writing. The main theme is heard at once, its second half exchanged between violin and viola. The second subject is heard in the lower strings; when it is taken over by the violin, the cello offers interesting syncopations as a background. A single measure of the opening theme brings on the development, which has an improvisatory character. The second movement minuet, unusually long for Mozart, begins in a classical style. But its G minor trio suddenly penetrates into the lowest depths of despair. The quiet exaltation of the slow movement is instantly established by a forceful open "C" in the cello. The first violin then presents the sober main melody. But is is the finale which —technically and structurally at any rate—is the most remarkable in the work, a successful attempt to fuse the forms of sonata and fugue. It is made up of two thematic groups. The first consists of two fugal subjects; the other, of two homogeneous themes. Toward the end of the movement, a marriage of polyphony and homophony is achieved by putting the first fugal subject over a homophonic accompaniment.

In the first movement of the D minor Quartet (1783) we continually confront bold modulations and daring enharmonic changes. The mood is prevailingly sober, sometimes even melancholy. The first subject is a descending theme for the lower strings; the second an ascending one, also in lower strings. A striking change of key from E-flat major to A minor brings on the development. The melancholia deepens in the slow movement with the poignant main melody, heard at the beginning and the end of the movement. There is even a tragic overtone to the minuet, though a lighter note is introduced into the trio with delightful pizzicato effects. A spirited, somewhat agitated siciliano melody opens the finale (an idea Mozart borrowed from the finale of Haydn's Quartet, op. 33, no. 5). Four variations follow, the first three in the upper instruments. The quartet ends with an emotionally disturbed coda.

There is serenity and quiet beauty in the first movement of the E-flat major Quartet (1783). Unison strings are heard in the gentle and moody first subject. A feeling of unrest is introduced by the second theme through its rhythmic vitality. A recall of the first theme precedes the free development section. The recapitulation and coda than proceed ailong formal lines. The slow movement, with its long and sustained melodic line, breaks new ground through an extensive use of chromatic progressions in the major mode, and its frequent use of discords to heighten and intensify the mood. A somber feeling is introduced into the otherwise graceful minuet in the trio section, while the finale—a compromise between the rondo and sonata forms—is for the most part an outburst of energy and good humor.

The B-flat major Quartet (1784) is known as the *Hunt* because a horn call in the first movement is created by a musical figure known as "horn fifths." It appears at the opening, in the violins. The suggestion of a hunt is carried out in the subjects that follow immediately in violins and viola. The rhythmic vitality of the remainder of the movement, keeps alive the picture of the hunting scene to the end, and mainly through a detailed treatment of the opening hunt theme. The charming minuet is along conventional lines, and is followed by an eloquent slow movement, which passes from the sobriety of its first theme to the tragedy of the second. A folk melody in the first violin brings on the finale, to be succeeded by a vivacious melody, once again in the first violin.

In the A major Quartet (1785), homogeneity is achieved by the intimate kinship among the principal subjects of all four movements. The opening theme of the minuet is the second half of the first-movement opening idea in altered form; and it is quoted in the opening measure of the slow movement. The main melody of the finale carries echoes of the first theme of the first movement. Viennese Gemuetlichkeit prevails in the first movement, whose initial theme sounds like an Austrian waltz. The energetic second theme makes effective use of pauses after each phrase. Mozart designed the minuet as his second movement, but it is sometimes customary today to place it in the third slot. The main minuet theme is built from two ascending measures in unison succeeded by two descending measures. This material is then amplified contrapuntally. The trio is unusual in that it is in the dominant key. The slow movement opens with a stately melody, which then receives six variations in which all the instruments take turns at leadership. The most notable of these variations is the sixth, which begins with a vigorous march-like figure, that receives attention in the coda. There is only a single main theme in the finale, which is in sonata form. This is a descending subject first heard in the viola. What might appear as the second theme, in E major, is just a slight variation of this melody. The contrapuntal skill Mozart brought to this movement made such an impression on Beethoven that he copied out the music note for note.

In the opening of the C major Quartet (1785), there appear chromatics that create cross relations, and an obscurity of a definite key which produces dissonant effects far in advance of Mozart's day. Not until the ensuing Allegro is the key of C major established. For this reason, the work as a whole has come to be known as the *Dissonant*. Both themes of the first movement are sensitive melodies, the second characterized by a repeated suspension and round triplets. In the second movement, Mozart's lyricism embarks upon one of its wondrous flights. Occasionally, it is dramatized by abrupt and subtle changes of meter. The vigor of the minuet, with its passionate trio, is succeeded by the robust and vivacious finale. An unusual aspect of the coda in this movement is the fact that Mozart here utilizes a motive he had previously borrowed for a set of piano variations on a theme of Gluck, as well as a succession of trills he later employed for one of the scenes in *Così fan tutte*.

1783. MASS IN C MINOR, "THE GREAT," K. 427, for solo voices, chorus, and orchestra.

While Constance, then Mozart's sweetheart but later his wife, lay ill in bed, the composer made a vow that, should she recover and should she become his bride, he would write a huge Mass in gratitude. Constance *did* recover; and on August 4, 1782, she did become his wife. Providence having seemingly fulfilled all the necessary requirements, Mozart proceeded to keep his promise. He began to work on his Mass early in 1783. By the time he brought his wife to Salzburg to meet his father, in August 1783, he had completed the "Kyrie," "Gloria," "Sanctus," and "Benedictus."

For some mysterious reason, Mozart never did complete the Mass. The sketches of the first part of the "Credo" and the "Et Incarnatus est" were committed to paper; the second half of the "Credo" and the "Agnus Dei" were never even sketched out. When Mozart presented his new Mass at St. Peter's Church in Salzburg on August 25, 1783, he used material from earlier church music to fill out the composition. It is possible that Mozart felt that through this performance he was fulfilling his vow and that he was no longer honor bound to write the rest of the Mass. It is also possible that a cetrain amount of disenchantment had begun to set in about his marriage with Constance which resulted in a diminished enthusiasm for a work she had inspired. Whatever the reason, the "Great Mass" remained unfinished. In 1899, Alois Schmitt and Ernest Lewicki tried rounding out the work with excerpts from earlier Mozart church music. The result was none too happy, since there was a wide disparity of style, approach, and quality between the music Mozart actually wrote for his Mass and that which was interpolated.

Unfinished though it is, the "Great" Mass is a masterwork. The opening "Kyrie" is in three sections, the first and third for chorus, and the middle part ("Christe eleison") for soprano and chorus. This is followed by a seven-part "Gloria," the highlights of which are a moving Adagio passage for chorus ("Gratias agimus"), a beatifically serene duet for soprano and contralto ("Domine deus") and the concluding fugue for chorus ("Cum sancto spiritu"). The first half of the "Credo" is a declamatory section for full chorus. After that we get the "Et Incarnatus est," a sublime arioso for soprano accompanied by flute, oboe, and bassoon. "It is," explains William B. Ober, "an expression of adoration—placed deliberately at the midpoint of the Creed—which is as pure and pious as a Van Eyck representation of the Virgin. It is an impassionate outpouring of religious fervor, not in an unrefined or untrammeled manner, nor in the uncontrolled rhapsodic style of the nineteenth-century Romantics, but in a style which is so wholly appropriate to the feeling expressed that the listener is scarcely aware of any formal element. The "Sanctus" for chorus is only seventeen measures long, but despite its brevity generates considerable power. An equally dramatic double fugue for chorus, "Osanna," follows. The Mass, as Mozart wrote it, ends with the eloquent "Benedictus," for soprano, contralto, tenor, and bass.

1783–1788. ADAGIO AND FUGUE IN C MINOR, K. 546, for strings.

This composition was written at two different periods. In 1783, Mozart completed a four-voiced fugue for two pianos (K. 426), which Marcia Davenport once described as "one of the most beautiful of all his noble works for the piano," and which Beethoven esteemed highly enough to score for orchestra. Apparently, Mozart himself was partial to it. Five years later, he added to it an introductory Adagio, and rewrote it for strings. "The effect of the C minor Fugue," says Otto Jahn, "rests neither on the sound effects of the piano, nor on those of the stringed instruments. It is so broadly conceived, so earnestly and with such ruthless severity carried out, that the external means of expression falls into the background before the energetic enunciation of the laws of form, obeyed consciously but without servility. Quite otherwise is the case with the Adagio which, written originally for strings, is expressly adapted to their peculiarities of sound effect. The harmonic treatment, and more especially the enharmonic changes, are of extraordinary beauty and depth, and occasionally show remarkable effects of suspense and climax. Most admirable is the art with which the character of the movement as an introduction is maintained, and the defiant style of the following fugue clearly indicates, at the same time, that the mind is tuned to a pitch of longing and melancholy which makes the entry of the categorical fugue a positive relief and stimulant."

1784–1786. COMPOSITIONS FOR PIANO:

Fantasia in C minor, K. 475.

Sonata in C minor, K. 457. I. Allegro. II. Adagio. III. Molto allegro.

The Fantasia and Sonata in C minor together is one of Mozart's most monumental works for solo piano. They were written a year apart, for one of Mozart's pupils. The Sonata was completed in 1784, and the Fantasia a year after that. Both works have the same kind of dramatic quality and intensity of feeling, the same subtle and ever changing moods. They were originally published in one volume because Mozart intended them to be played together. It is greatly to be regretted that his wishes are not always carried out. Georges de Saint Fox regards the Fantasia as a "gigantic entrance arch" leading into the sonata. The Fantasia opens and closes dramatically, and in between come various passages of rapidly contrasting emotions, and at times of lofty melodic inspiration. Tragic statements predominate in the first movement of the Sonata, which opens with a staccato subject to which an expressive reply is forthcoming. The tensions are built up throughout the development and recapitulation, until the coda comes, in Abert's description, to bring down the curtain slowly to end the tragedy. The slow movement brings repose with a gentle melody of singing character, in its middle section reminiscent of and probably the inspiration for the Adagio cantabile section in Beethoven's sonata pathétiques. But the drama continues into the mighty finale, despite a highly sensitive lyrical middle section. Repeated syncopations contribute a feeling of unrest throughout the movement.

1784–1787. SONATAS FOR VIOLIN AND PIANO:

B-flat major, K. 454. I. Largo; Allegro. II. Andante. III. Allegretto.

E-flat major, K. 481 I. Allegro molto. II. Adagio. III. Allegretto.

A major, K. 526. I. Allegro molto. II. Andante. III. Presto.

Mozart wrote the B-flat major Violin Sonata for Regina Strinasacchi, a Mantuan violinist, scheduled to appear with Mozart in a concert in that city on April 24, 1784. On the day preceding that performance, Mozart had not yet written down the piano part, but had completed just the violin music. Strinasacchi, consequently, had to play without rehearsal, and Mozart had to improvise the piano accompaniment as she played. Despite this, the performance seems to have gone well. This sonata opens with a brief and noble slow introduction. The main part of the first movement presents a soaring melody for the violin. The slow movement is a song in which the two instruments are equally important. The finale is infectious music abounding with rhythmic vitality and with interesting contrasts of light and shade.

The E-flat major Sonata (1785) has a spaciousness of design and freedom of melodic treatment that led some writers to suggest it has the scope of a concerto. The first movement contrasts a vigorous first subject with a more lyrical second one, over a pedal point. The writing in the development is along dramatic lines, with occasional suggestions of the tragic. The slow movement is in the form of a rondo. Here a stately melody is followed by a number of variations with unusual modulations. A sprightly tune that opens the finale receives five variations in which the main musical content is assigned more often to the piano than to the violin.

The A major Sonata (1787), the penultimate of Mozart's works in this category, is, in the opinion of some authorites, the greatest of the composer's violins sonatas. It begins with a syncopated subject, unusual for its irregular accents and rhythms. A concertante transition in the piano leads into the lively second theme, presented by the violin. The first subject is the one discussed in the development. The second movement starts with a dialogue in which a subject in the piano is followed by an answering phrase in the violin. The second subject appears against this theme, first in the violin, then in the piano. As in the preceding movement, the first theme dominates the development. The finale, a rondo, has two sections, each with two themes. A new reflective idea is heard after a return of the opening subject. The sonata ends with an elaborate coda, marked by brilliant figurations.

1785. CONCERTOS FOR PIANO AND ORCHESTRA:

D minor, K. 466. I. Allegro. II. Romanza. III. Allegro assai.

C major, K. 467. I. Allegro maestoso. II. Andante. III. Allegro vivace assai.

E-flat major, K. 482. I. Allegro. II. Andante. III. Allegro.

Even before the D minor Concerto was dry on paper, its first performance took place. Mozart completed it on February 10, 1785. Only a few hours after that, he himself introduced the concerto in Vienna. As Mozart's father informed Marianne (Mozart's sister), the composer did not even have the time to play through the rondo after having committed it to paper. The first movement opens with a theatrical syncopated subject in violins and violas, over throbbing ascending triplets in cellos and basses; those triplets play an important part throughout the movement. This first subject is built up passionately, through occasional eruptions of storm, before the second theme, in F major, appears; this is an exchange between oboes and bassoons on the one hand, and in flutes on the other. Now the solo instrument arrives with a completely new melody. Its serenity momentarily descends on the preceding disturbance like a benediction. But fifteen measures later, the syncopation and heart throb of the opening break the spell. The second subject of the orchestral exposition returns as a dialogue between piano and orchestra. This material is worked out, with the addition of some new thoughts (including a haunting theme for piano, to which the violins contribute descending figures). The orchestra then brings on the recapitulation, and the movement ends with a brief coda.

The second movement is a romantic song, first in the solo piano, then nine measures later in the orchestra. After this has been fully presented, a new section unfolds, which offers a theme in G minor for the woodwind, with graceful decorations by the piano. The earlier song returns before the movement ends with its coda.

In the finale, the piano appears without delay with the first principal theme. In the thirteenth measure, the orchestra takes over and embarks on a fifty-measure episode. A transition in the piano leads into the second theme, first given by the orchestra, and then in piano. The first theme is the composer's chief concern in the development, while in the recapitulation, he pays attention to the transitional material for piano heard between the first and second themes. A brief orchestral passage brings on the cadenza, after which the two main themes of the movement are recalled.

The C major Concerto came only four weeks after that in D minor. If there are turbulence and passion in the earlier work, there is the calm after the storm in the later one. The shadows of melancholia may sometimes darken the surfaces of this music, but in the main, it is the voice of a man who, at least temporarily, is at peace with himself. The orchestra first offers a solemn march-like theme. After a brief interlude for oboe, bassoon, and flute, the second theme (in G minor) arrives with three forceful notes of the tonic chord. The entry of the piano at this point, says Peter Hugh Reed, "has been called one of the magical moments in music, and likened to a beam of light shooting from banked clouds in a lovely sunset. But the sunset mood created at the end of the orchestral tutti is deceiving, for the music continues to radiate light and is consistently brilliant." The development and recapitulation are of such symphonic scope, so rich in invention and variation, that C. M. Girdlestone does not hesitate to describe the whole first movement as "Olympian" and to put it in the class of the *Jupiter* Symphony.

The three-part slow movement is one of the most exalted in all concerto literature. An extended melody of surpassing beauty is given by the orchestra; it is built from four motives. Then the piano repeats this material, while adding some ideas of its own. After that, the piano and orchestra share the spotlight in varying this melody. Throughout the movement a sublime serenity is maintained, the expression of a "misty and sadly impassioned spirit," as Girdlestone described it.

The finale is a rondo, whose main theme is a jovial chromatic subject in piano and orchestra. After the orchestra embarks on an extended interlude, a new theme in G major is introduced by the woodwind. The movement's principal theme, on its return, is shared by piano and orchestra, who then digress to a new thought in F major. A cadenza precedes the concluding coda.

Before the year of 1785 was over, Mozart completed still another important piano concerto, that in E-flat major. He himself introduced it in Vienna on December 23 of that same year. To Arthur Hutchings, this work is the "Venus" of Mozart's piano concertos. Strong chords, to which horns and bassoon offer a gentle reply, open the extended orchestral preface that spans seventy-six measures; its most significant thought is a delightful tune for violins, flutes, and horns. When the piano enters, it engages a new melody, which the orchestra interrupts with forceful chords. Passage work for the piano precedes the second theme, an ascending melody in B-flat minor in the piano, soon taken over by strings and winds to elaborate figurations by the solo instrument. After a spacious development, the first orchestral theme brings on the recapitulation. Here the second theme is assigned to the solo piano in the key of E-flat major just before the concluding coda.

Muted strings embark on an expansive melody in the second movement. After the piano intrudes with an elaboration of this subject at the thirty-third measure, the orchestra appears with a new section. The piano then comes in with a poignant descending theme (derived from the first subject) accompanied by bassoon. The finale opens with a vivacious tune in piano accompanied by strings. After an orchestral tutti, the piano is heard in the second theme in B-flat major. A cadenza precedes a section whose melody in the woodwind has a dancelike character, almost like a minuet. A second cadenza then sets the stage for the return of the two main subjects, while a third cadenza precedes the final recall of the first theme.

1785–1786. PIANO QUARTETS.:
G minor, K. 478. I. Allegro. II. Andante. III. Allegro.
E-flat major, K. 493. I. Allegro. II. Larghetto. III. Allegretto.

Mozart's two piano quartets are the first works for this combination of instruments. The G minor came first in 1785, followed by the E-flat major a year after. The first movement of the G minor begins with a terse and vigorous theme in all four instruments, to which the unaccompanied piano gives response. This idea is repeated, then succeeded by plaintive material with piano answering statements by the three instruments. A new subject, with melancholy overtones, is now introduced by the piano, and repeated canonically by the strings. The development is spacious in design and dramatic in character, until a gentle recall of the second theme by the violin restores placidity. A repetition of the development leads into the concluding coda.

There are two important melodies in the slow movement, both heard first in the piano, both deeply moving in emotion. But gaiety prevails in the concluding rondo, which is set into motion with a jaunty tune for the piano, followed by a vivacious theme for strings. In this movement, the piano embarks on several brilliant virtuoso passages.

In the first movement of the E-flat major Quartet, there are three thematic groups. Not until the second group is presented do we get the main subject. In the development, this main theme is elaborated upon by the strings, the piano providing a harmonic base. There are two equal sections in the development, separated by a repetition of the main theme in unison. This theme is also the basis of a brief coda. The second movement, a Romanza, is dominated by a pensive melody exchanged by the three strings and piano. Serenity also prevails in the extended coda. The finale, a rondo, allows Mozart to give free expression to his ebullient nature, though midway a reflective passage arrives in the relative minor.

1785–1797. SONGS, for voice and piano.:

"Das Veilchen," K. 476; "Das Lied der Trennung," K. 519; "Als Luise die Briefe ihres ungetreuen," K. 520; "Abendempfindung," K. 523; "An Chloe," K. 524.

Of Mozart's five geatest songs, one, "Das Veilchen" (poem by Goethe), came in 1785; three, in 1787, "An Chloe," "Als Luise die Briefe ihres ungetreuen" and "Abendempfindung"; one in Mozart's last year, 1797, "Das Lied der Trennung." "Many of the songs," says Eric Blom, "are simple strophic ditties, but the more developed ones, even the best among them, are the outcome of a dramatic, sometimes frankly theatrical impulse, not a purely lyrical one." Blom describes "Das Veilchen" as "an exquisite and perfectly shaped little thing in its way" but still possessing an "operatic touch in that recitative-like passage which is so wonderfully welded into the whole." To Blom, the song of Luisa (burning the letters of her faithless lover) is "plainly a dramatic scene in miniature, contrived very briefly with one or two grand gestures that seem to come from the later and greater of the two piano Fantasias in C minor." Blom finds that "An Chloe" is "in the vein of the concert-like arias interpolated into the operas, only on a less grown-up scale, so to speak," while "Das Lied der Trennung" he describes as "a strophic song with large aria extensions . . . a passionate lament in F minor that might very well come from any of Mozart's heroines in a lovelorn mood." Blom considers "Abendempfindung" the greatest of all Mozart songs, "the most purely a song as distinct from an aria . . . the more marvelous in its avoidance of all that is theatrical because the rather vapid words by Campe contain a far-fetched reference to 'a curtain falling on the gaudy scene of life.'"

1786. SONATA IN F MAJOR, K. 497, for piano four hands. I. Adagio; Allegro. II. Andante. III. Allegro.

This is the most significant of Mozart's sonatas for piano four hands.

Indeed, Donald Francis Tovey places it among the best of all Mozart's instrumental compositions. The opening is unusual in that it is an extended section of rare introspective beauty before the more usual Allegro unfolds. The slow movement, in sonata form, makes extensive use of polyphonic resources, but not at a sacrifice of deep emotion. Vigor and vitality abound in the concluding rondo movement.

1786. LE NOZZE DI FIGARO (THE MARRIAGE OF FIGARO), K. 492, opera buffa in four acts with text by Lorenzo da Ponte, based on *Le Mariage de Figaro* by Beaumarchais. First performance: Burgtheater, Vienna, May 1, 1786.

In the Spring of 1783, Mozart met Lorenzo da Ponte, who had come to Vienna a few years earlier and had been appointed theater poet. Da Ponte promised to write a libretto for Mozart, a prospect that pleased the composer no end since, as he confided to his father, he wanted "to show what I can do in Italian opera." But he had serious doubts that Da Ponte would keep his word. After all, Da Ponte was a Salieri appointee and a Salieri librettist—and Salieri was Mozart's arch-enemy. Possible due to such doubts, Mozart did not again broach the subject of collaboration to Da Ponte for another two years. When he did, he suggested the Beaumarchais comedy, *Le Mariage de Figaro* as a possible source for a libretto. This was a startling selection, indeed. The Beaumarchais play was such a vigorous attack on aristocracy and the existing social order that Napoleon described it as "the revolution already in action." It was hardly likely that the Austrian Emperor would look with favor on such a subject for an opera.

In his *Memoirs,* Da Ponte describes what happened: "The proposal pleased me very well, and I promised to do as he wished. But there was a great difficulty to overcome. Only a few days before, the Emperor had forbidden the company at the German theater to act this same comedy, as it was, he said, too outspoken for a polite audience. How could one suggest it to him for an opera?. . . . I . . . proposed that words and music should be written secretly and that we should await a favorable opportunity to show it to the theatrical managers or to the Emperor, which I boldly undertook to do. . . . So I set to work, and as I wrote the words he composed the music for them. In six weeks all was ready. As Mozart's good luck would have it, they were in need of a new work at the theater. So I seized the opportunity and without saying anything to anybody, I went to the Emperor himself and offered him *Figaro.*"

As Da Ponte had expected, the Emperor disapproved of Beaumarchais' play. But then he gave his approval after Da Ponte promised to delete the poet's offensive passages of social criticism and to emphasize the comic elements. The poet "hastened to Mozart and had not finished telling him the good news, when one of the Emperor's lackeys came with a note requesting him to go to the palace at once with the score. He obeyed the royal command and had various pieces performed before the Emperor, who liked them wonderfully well and was, without exaggeration, amazed by them."

Though Salieri and his friends did whatever they could to sabotage the impending première of *The Marriage of Figaro,* they were powerless. All those who participated in the performance were thoroughly enchanted by Mozart's music by the time of the second rehearsal. "The performers on the stage and those in the orchestra," recalled Michael Kelly, Mozart's friend, "vociferated, 'Bravo, Maestro, Viva, viva grande Mozart!' I thought the orchestra would never cease applauding, beating the bows of their violins against the music desks." At the première, the audience proved so enthusiastic that almost every aria had to be encored. The Emperor sprang to his feet to express his delight.

Such a triumph was not to be tolerated by Mozart's enemies. They worked out a subtle bit of strategy whereby *The Marriage of Figaro* could be thrown into a shade. Hurriedly, they mounted a catchy little comic opera filled with popular tunes as competition for Mozart. The opera was *Un cosa rara* by Vicente Martin y Soler (1754–1806)—one of the first to feature a waltz. This maneuver worked. In falling in love with *Una cosa rara,* the fickle Viennese operagoers deserted *The Marriage of Figaro*. It left the boards after only nine performances.

But the opera did not go into permanent discard. In 1786, it was produced in Prague to achieve what was probably the greatest triumph Mozart personally experienced. The city went *Figaro*-mad. "Here, no one hums, sings, or whistles anything but airs . . . of *Figaro,*" reported Mozart. "No other opera draws . . . but *Figaro.*" On January 20, 1787, when Mozart directed an orchestral concert in Prague, the audience kept shouting "*Figaro,*" until he went to the piano and improvised a dozen variations on the aria, "Non più andrai."

Mozart, who had raised the Singspiel to an art form in *The Abduction from the Seraglio* (which see), created in *The Marriage of Figaro* what Eric Blom has described as "the perfect opera buffa . . . in its final stage of perfection . . . as great as a whole as it is captivating in detail. . . . It is doubtful if any opera buffa ever written matches it for humanity and compassion." Wallace Brockway and Herbert Weinstock said: "It carried the profound internal reality of its own made world and has the razor-sharp edge of seriousness that the mature satire of Beaumarchais deserves."

The brief overture busily engages a bustling little melody before the curtain rises. We are in quarters assigned to Figaro, valet of Count Almaviva, in seventeenth-century Spain. Figaro, about to get married to the Countess' maid, Susanna, is worried that his new apartment is so close to the Count's bedroom; he knows full well that the Count has tried to make love to Susanna. However, Figaro sweeps cares away with the belief he knows how to handle his master ("Se vuol ballare"). But something else begins to bother him. He had once borrowed money from the elderly Marcellina with the promise he would marry her if he did not return the debt. Marcellina has just come to demand he stick to his bargain, the money never having been returned. With the appearance of Susanna, the two rivals for Figaro reveal their mutual dislike for each other ("Via resti servita"). Marcellina leaves in a rage. Now Cherubino, the Count's page, comes to complain he is about to lose his post because he has flirted with Barberina, the gardener's daughter. Cherubino entreats Susanna to intercede for him with the Count. When the Count appears—he has come to arrange a rendezvous with Susanna—Cherubino hides behind a huge chair. Discovered by the irate Count, Cherubino is punished by being forced to enlist in the regiment. Figaro mockingly teaches Cherubino how to behave as a soldier ("Non più andrai").

In the second act, the Countess is in her boudoir, despairing over her husband's infidelity ("Porgi amor"). She cooks up a plan with Figaro and Susanna to win back the Count's love—by making him suspect she has a lover. They arrange for the Count to come upon a letter intended for the Countess; they also plan to dress Cherubino as Susanna and let him keep Susanna's imminent rendezvous with the Count. When Cherubino enters, he is musing over the meaning and the pangs of love ("Voi che sapete"). Hurriedly, he is dressed up in Susanna's clothes, then sent hiding into a closet when the Count makes a precipitous appearance. While the Count's back is turned, Cherubino effects his escape through the window, thus allowing Susanna to take his place in the closet and to be found there by the suspicious Count. The Count becomes contrite and apologetic. But his supicions once again are inflamed when the gardener brings him the news that somebody has just jumped out of the boudoir window and dropped a piece of paper in the flower bed. The paper is evidence incriminating Cherubino, since it is his army's commission. But Figaro comes to Cherubino's defense by saying it was he who had dropped from the window and had lost Cherubino's commission. At this point, Marcellina appears to demand from the Count that Figaro keep his bargain and marry her.

In a richly decorated hall in the palace, in the third act, Susanna consents to a rendezvous with the Count ("Crudel, perchè finora"); but she has already arranged with the Countess to have the latter take her place at this meeting. Complicated negotiations ensue between Marcellina and her lawyer, and Figaro and the Count. During this exchange, it is learned that Figaro is actually Marcellina's long lost son. Thus he is no longer honor bound to marry her. Left to herself, the Countess recalls nostalgically the time when the Count once was so deeply in love with her ("Dove sono"). She then dictates to Susanna a letter in which time and place are set for the Count's forthcoming secret tryst ("Che soave zeffiretto"). The scene then shifts to the wedding hall where the marriage of Figaro and Susanna takes place. After Susanna has slipped the Count an invitation to meet her in the garden, he invites everybody to a gala party.

Later the same evening, the Countess and Susanna appear in the garden, each disguised as the other. Figaro, now suspicious that Susanna is planning to meet the Count, goes into hiding to catch her unawares. He is more than ever convinced of Susanna's infidelity when he hears her call out to her lover to join her ("Deh vieni, non tardar"). Now Cherubino comes upon the scene, mistakes Susanna for the Countess, and is caught by the Count in the process of trying to steal a kiss. For his part, the Count is fooled into believing that the Countess is Susanna. When he proceeds to make passionate advances, the Countess reveals her true identity. But she is ready to forget and forgive if the Count promises to mend his ways. Everybody now is in the proper frame of mind to celebrate Figaro's marriage.

The probable first performance of *The Marriage of Figaro* in the United States took place in New York on May 10, 1824 in an English translation. The first Italian-speaking production came to New York on November 23, 1858. When the Metropolitan Opera mounted the opera for the first time—on January 31, 1894—it enjoyed a stellar cast with Emma Eames as the Countess, Nordica as Susanna, and Edouard de Reszke as the Count.

1786. CONCERTOS FOR PIANO AND ORCHESTRA.:
A major, K. 488. I. Allegro. II. Andante. III. Presto.
C minor, K. 491. I. Allegro. II. Larghetto. III. Allegretto.

Two of Mozart's supreme achievements in the piano-concerto medium came within the single month of March, 1786. In commenting on the first movement of the A major Concerto, Einstein maintains the composer never wrote another "so simple in structure, so 'normal' in thematic relations between tutti and solo, or so clear in thematic invention." The main theme is given at once, first in the strings, then in the woodwind. The second subject follows in the first violins, after which bassoons and flutes take it over. The second movement, says Einstein, contains "the soul of the work." Here we find "in veiled form that passion which the Andante of the preceding Concerto (E-flat major, K. 482), had revealed. . . . The resignation and the hopelessness are the same." The solo instrument announces a pastoral melody in the key of F-sharp minor. The subdued mood is sustained with a subsidiary idea in violins and clarinet, continued by woodwind and strings. In the concluding rondo, Einstein continues, Mozart is "a true magician. This Presto seems to introduce a breath of fresh air and a ray of sunshine into a dark and musty room. The gaiety of this uninterrupted stream of melody and rhythm is irresistible."

The C minor, K. 491, is the second of Mozart's piano concertos in the minor the mode (the other being the D minor). Like its companion, the C minor is characterized by passion, conflict, and at times tragedy. These dark moods are uncovered in writing that is bolder and more provocative with personal approaches than is discernible in other Mozart concertos. As John N. Burk explained, in place of the "usual diatonic opening subject" we here get a "tortuous, chromatic succession of phrases with upward skips of diminished sevenths." There is a temporary respite from adventurous writing in the gentle melody for the woodwind. But, continues Burk, "the first theme sweeps it away" and then the piano is heard in a new C minor melody to add "to the excitement with agitating scale passages." The development and recapitulation both emphasize and intensify the pathos of the earlier material. A cadenza then leads into an extended coda.

Agitation makes way for serenity in the Larghetto, which is in the form of a rondo. The finale—variations on two themes—reverts to sobriety and gloom. The second subject, says Burk, sets the stage for "astonishing chromatic development—a chromaticism which serves for thematic individualization and transition."

1786. STRING QUARTET IN D MAJOR, K. 499. I. Allegretto. II. Allegretto. III. Adagio. IV. Allegro.

The D major Quartet stands alone as a bridge from the six "Haydn" Quartets in 1782–1785, and the three "Prussian" Quartets which followed it in 1789–1790. "It is," explains Homer Ulrich, "a gracious work, clear and direct in its first movement, strong in its minuet, and deeply moving in its Adagio." In the last movement Ulrich finds "melancholy" but "even there it is manfully concealed under the outward signs of brightness: D major tonality, bustling vitality in the themes, incisive pauses between phrases."

1786. SYMPHONY No. 38 IN D MAJOR, "PRAGUE," K. 504. I. Adagio; Allegro. II. Andante. III. Presto.

In the winter of 1786–1787, Prague had gone wild over Mozart and *The Marriage of Figaro*. Two all-Mozart concerts were arranged. At the first of these, Mozart introduced a new symphony, that in D major. It met with such enthusiasm that to quiet the audience Mozart had to sit down at the piano and entertain it with improvisations.

This work is unusual for several reasons. It is one of the few by Mozart to use an extended slow introduction to the first movement; it dispenses with a minuet; and it calls for one of the largest orchestral ensembles Mozart ever used (flutes, oboes, bassoons, horns, trumpets in pairs, as well as strings and timpani).

"After the eloquent tension of the slow introduction" wrote Alfred Einstein in his analysis, "there comes a movement saturated with polyphony. . . . The thematic material stated in the first thirty-five measures seems quite heterogeneous, and yet it forms a wonderful unity. . . . For the development section he reserves a feature of increased intensity: canonic treatment. This development section is one of the greatest, most serious, most aggressive in all Mozart's works. In it, characteristically, the second theme cannot take part, but must remain untouched."

The slow movement, to Einstein, is no "mere intermezzo between two animated movements" but "has its own inner animation, and it embodies the most complete combination of singing and polyphonic character." The finale "is one of those rare D major movements of Mozart's which, despite all their appearance of cheerfulness, and despite their genuine perfection and feeling of completeness, leave a wound in the soul: beauty is wedded to death."

1786–1787. 2 CONCERT ARIAS.:

"Ch'io mi scordi di te," K. 505, scena for soprano, piano and orchestra.

"Bella mia fiamma, addio!", K. 528, for soprano and orchestra.

"Ch'io mi scordi" (1786)—describing the tragedy of a deserted lover bidding his faithless sweetheart farewell—was used some months earlier by the composer for a revision of the second act of the opera *Idomeneo*. There the aria (sung by Idamante) begins on the tenor vocal line but unexpectedly proceeds to the soprano clef. In his three-part scena (Recitative, Rondo, and Allegretto) Mozart wrote the entire piece for soprano. Still another change was effected. Where the earlier aria used a violin solo, the latter called for a solo piano. The change of instrument is explained by Mozart's ardent feelings for the singer Nancy Storace. Since she was singing at the première, Mozart wanted a piano part so that he might participate in her performance.

A pretty tale surrounds the writing of "Bella mia fiamma" in 1787. Mme. Duschek, impatient for an aria that Mozart had long promised her, locked him in a room and refused to release him until he had written it. Mozart replied by saying he would write that aria on condition she would sing it at sight without errors. He went on to write a scena with all sorts of tricky intonations. The text describes the farewell to his beloved of a hero about to meet a sacrificial death. The scene has three parts: Recitative, Aria (Andante), and Allegro.

1787. STRING QUINTETS.:

C major, K. 515. I. Allegro. I.. Allegretto. III. Andante. IV. Allegro.

G minor, K. 516. I. Allegro. II. Menuetto. III. Adagio ma non troppo. IV. Adagio; Allegro.

Mozart wrote five quintets for two violins, two violas, and cello, the first (B-flat major, K. 174) in 1773. The second, in C major, came four years later. An extended first theme in the opening movement is heard in an exchange between cello and first violin, accompanied by repeated eighth notes in the three middle instruments. This idea is repeated three times. After a short pause, the arpeggio figure which opens the first theme returns in the violin, to which the cello offers a reply. After some elaboration, a transition passage in the first violin over sustained chords introduces the second theme. The spacious exposition extends for one hundred and fifty-one measures, coming to an end on a sustained pedal point. The development, which is comparatively brief, makes use of fugal passages.

The second movement is a stately minuet whose main melody is heard in the two violins, and repeated by second viola and cello. The trio has a poetic character. A wonderful serenity pervades the pages of the Andante. It begins with an eight-measure theme for the two violins, followed by a poignant passage for the viola. Violin and viola then engage in a gentle, introspective dialogue. The finale is in a happy mood, its vivacious main theme heard at once in the first violin, while the second theme is distributed among the five instruments.

The G minor Quintet was completed less than a month after the C major. W. W. Cobbett described it as "the most passionate piece of music that Mozart wrote in this, his favorite key. . . . It is a piece filled with the resignation of despair, a struggle with destiny." Alfred Einstein compares this music with a scene in the Garden of Gethsemane, "the chalice, with its bitter potion must be emptied, and the disciples asleep. The drama of the first movement comes to a compelling climax with two closing vigorous chords which set the stage for the minuet that follows." Here we get not classic grace, but the agitation of irregular rhythms. To Einstein, the third movement is a Prayer "of a lonely one surrounded on all sides by the walls of a deep chasm." The finale opens with a slow introduction described by Sydney Grew as "one of the most earnestly expressive passages in the whole of Mozart." The ensuing Allegro makes a pretense at gaiety, but, as Grew adds, it is soon "forced to embody something of restlessness and distress. . . It is excited . . . the issue is defeat."

1787. EIN MUSIKALISCHER SPASS (A MUSICAL JOKE), K. 522, for strings and two horns. I. Allegro. II. Menuetto. III. Adagio cantabile. IV. Presto.

EINE KLEINE NACHTMUSIK (A LITTLE NIGHT MUSIC), K. 525, serenade for strings. I. Allegro. II. Andante. III. Allegretto. IV. Allegro.

It was believed for a long time that *A Musical Joke* was poking fun at the inept performances of village musicians through its discords, unrelated melodies, gawky ornaments, and so forth. This is the reason why in some early editions the work bears the name *Die Dorfmusikanten* (*The Village Musicians*). However, Mozart's barbs were aimed at a far more deserving target: the ignorance and blundering of self-styled composers who believe themselves ready and able to write ambitious symphonies. In the Adagio cantabile, says G. de Saint-Fox, "the long and ungainly fioriture seem to suggest an over-ambitious violinist, but also reveal to us a composer who is prey to the worst sentimentality, endeavoring to interpret it by scrappy bits of tune and excessive digressions." The Presto is "the most remarkable of all. . . . It is a hotch-potch of unrelated themes, with no logical order in it." The work ends appropriately with a grating discord.

Mozart's lovable *Eine kleine Nachtmusik* was one of the first light efforts (serenades, divertimenti, and so forth) he had produced in some five years. Some musicologists believe that the work originally had five movements; that a minuet, intended between the first and second movements has been lost. Simple, direct, and unsophisticated, *Eine kleine Nachtmusik* stands at the very opposite pole of the dramatic and profound *Don Giovanni,* which Mozart wrote in the self-same year of 1787. Nevertheless, it is so full of Mozartean grace and charm that it has become the most popular of his orchestral serenades.

The first movement opens with a brisk march-like tune in G major, which soon makes room for a more lyrical and sensitive subject in D major. There is only the slightest development, and this concerns itself mainly with the first theme. The second movement is a "romanza," an atmospheric song which finds contrast in a vigorous C minor section. A traditional minuet is followed by a vivacious rondo; the opening theme is repeated five times, though sometimes in different tonalities.

1787. DON GIOVANNI (DON JUAN), K. 527, "dramma giocoso" in two acts, with text by Lorenzo da Ponte, based on Giuseppe Bertati's play of the same name. First performance: Prague, October 28, 1787.

If there is any city that can be said to have appreciated Mozart during his lifetime the way he deserved, that place was not Salzburg nor Vienna but Prague. It was Prague that went wild over *The Marriage of Figaro* in 1786 and gave its composer the homage due a master. And it was Prague that soon after that commissioned Mozart and Da Ponte to write *Don Giovanni.* The commission came from Pasquale Bondini, director of Italian Opera. Mozart and Da Ponte, whose first successful collaboration had been *The Marriage of Figaro* one year earlier, decided on the subject of Don Juan, a theme that Gluck had previously used for a ballet and Giuseppe Gazzaniga (1743–1818) for an opera produced in Venice early in 1787.

In calling on Mozart and Da Ponte for a new opera, Bondini hoped to get another work as gay, vivacious, satirical, and full of intrigue as *The Marriage of Figaro*. What he finally got was something far different—a "gay drama" as the authors designated it; a work in which drama and even tragedy rubbed elbows with comedy. Through the years, arguments have been long and heated as to whether Don Giovanni is an opera buffa or a musical drama. Certainly there are many delightful buffa touches in both text and music: Don Giovanni's Italian-like serenade, "Deh, vieni, alla finestra," for example, or Leporello's celebrated "catalogue aria," "Madamina! il catalogo è questo," as well as characters like Masetto and Zerlina, for whom Mozart produced music with the most deft touch. But the opera is also darkened by profound shadows: the piercing expression of Donna Anna's grief at the death of her father in the first act; Don Giovanni's doom in the last. To Tchaikovsky, the scenes dominated by Donna Anna are "rendered by Mozart with such compelling truth that they can be compared in depth of expression only with the best scenes in Shakespeare's tragedies." Bernard Shaw regarded the character of Don Giovanni as "the first Byronic hero in music." Perhaps the best answer to the question as to whether *Don Giovanni* is a comedy or a tragedy was provided by Alfred Einstein when he wrote: "The work presents no riddle: It is an opera buffa with seria roles—for instance, those of Donna Anna and Don Ottavio—and buffa roles. . . Where material like this is concerned, in which, as in Faust, such dark, primeval, demonic forces are inextricably combined, analysis can never be complete. The work is sui generis, incomparable and enigmatic from the evening of its first performance to the present day."

If there is any doubt that Mozart himself intended stressing the dramatic and tragic elements in the Da Ponte text, it must be hastily dispelled by the overture (which he wrote in a single evening). It opens with somber chords for the trombone repeated three times. These are the same chords Mozart chose for the scene in the opera where the Statue appears before Don Giovanni. Unusual modulations in the violins and subdued rolls of the drums accentuate an ominous atmosphere. In the ensuing Allegro, three main thoughts are presented, none repeated in the opera itself. The first is given by the violins over a tremolo in violas and cellos; the second is introduced by full chords in the orchestra and consists of a tender melody for oboe and clarinet; the third, equally expressive, is offered by all the strings and woodwind. In the free development these ideas are enlarged. Strings and woodwind introduce a coda that leads directly into the opera's first scene—the courtyard of the Commandant's palace in seventeenth-century Seville.

Leporello, Don Giovanni's servant, is upset because his master keeps him busy night and day ("Notte e giorno"). Don Giovanni emerges from the palace, followed by Donna Anna, who is angrily trying to uncover his identity, Don Giovanni having come concealed by a huge cloak. Her outcries bring the Commendatore on the scene. He soon gets embroiled in a duel with Giovanni in which he gets killed. When Donna Anna realizes her father is dead, she voices her terrible grief in a heart-rending recitative. Her lover, Don Ottavio, tries in vain to console her, but she repulses him ("Fuggi, crudele, fuggi"). Don Ottavio and Donna Anna now vow to avenge the murder.

The scene shifts to a road outside the city, early the next morning. Don Giovanni reveals to Leporello that there is a new woman he is eager to pursue. Just then a veiled lady appears. She is Donna Elvira, bitter over a recent seduction by a man who then deserted her ("Ah! Chi mi dice mai!"). When Don Giovanni tries to console her, he discovers that she is the woman whom he had seduced and deserted, and that he is the man she is condemning. Elvira soon recognizes Don Giovanni. At first, he tries convincing her that there was good reason why he left her so precipitously. Then he slips away. Leporello now lightly comments that Elvira is only one name on a long list of those betrayed by Giovanni, in the so-called "catalogue song"—"Madamina, il catalago è questo." Having listened to Leporello's mockery, Elvira becomes determined to punish Giovanni.

In a village green near a tavern, later the same morning peasants are gaily singing and dancing. Among them are Masetto and Zerlina, two peasants about to get married to each other ("Giovinette, che fate all' amore"). Into this happy scene intrude Don Giovanni and Leporello. Giovanni invites all those present to come to his nearby palace for refreshment. He sees to it, however, that Zerlina stays behind, so that he can make advances to her. At first she eludes him, but then succumbs to his charm ("Là ci darem la mano"). He is about to lead Zerlina off, when Elvira appears and prevents this imminent escapade by passionately revealing the kind of man Giovanni really is ("Ah! fuggi il traditor"). Donna Anna and Ottavio are also at hand. At first, they do not recognize Giovanni as the one they are pursuing. But after Giovanni has effected his escape, Anna discloses to Ottavio that the man they just permitted to flee is the one who had killed her father. Though Ottavio has always regarded Giovanni as a friend and nobleman, he stands ready to fulfil his vow to destroy him. He then brings to mind the image of the woman he loves, the only one able to bring him peace and happiness ("Dalla sua pace").

Later the same afternoon, a feast is taking place in Don Giovanni's palace. Leporello and Giovanni are in the garden, the former describing how he has helped the peasants. Giovanni orders Leporello to arrange a still bigger festival ("Finch' han dal vino"). When Zerlina and Masetto enter, the latter upbraids Zerlina for having flirted with Giovanni. Zerlina coyly and coquettishly begs for forgiveness ("Batti, batti, o bel Masetto"). After Giovanni invites Zerlina and Masetto into the palace, three masked figures appear. They are Donna Anna, Donna Elvira, and Don Ottavio come for vengeance. Giovanni, knowing nothing of their mission, and mistaking them for invited guests, urges them to partake of the festivities inside. Praying softly for help ("Protegga, il giusto cielo") Donna Anna, Donna Elvira, and Don Ottavio enter the palace.

Inside the palace, a ball is taking place. The guests are participating in a minuet, whose music is one of the most universally popular of all Mozart's instrumental compositions. Other dances follow. In one of these, Giovanni seizes Zerlina and dances with her out of the ballroom. When her cries attract the attention of the guests, Giovanni returns with sword in hand, accusing Leporello of having forced his attention on poor Zerlina. But Anna, Elvira, and Ottavio know he is lying. They join with others in violently denouncing the roué ("Traditore! traditore!"). Giovanni seizes Leporello, fights off Ottavio with his sword, and manages to escape unharmed.

In the first scene of the second act, Don Giovanni is determined to win Zerlina. For this purpose, he disguises himself as Leporello and serenades her ("Deh, vieni, alla finestra"). When Masetto appears, he prepares to give Giovanni a sound thrashing, but fails to recognize him in Leporello's cloak. Caught off guard, it is Masetto who gets the whipping from Giovanni. Hearing Masetto's groans. Zerlina comes to soothe him with her caresses ("Vedrai carino").

Disguised as Giovanni, Leporello now comes to the garden of the Commendatore's palace, where he confronts Ottavio, Anna, Elvira, and Zerlina. He escapes physical punishment by revealing his true identity, and by his protests that whatever evil has been done was on Giovanni's orders ("Ah, pietà! Signori miei"). Now more than ever is Ottavio determined to destroy Giovanni, while expressing his love for Donna Anna ("Il mio tesoro").

In the scene that follows, Giovanni appears in a cemetery, near a life-sized statue of the Commendatore. With mocking tones, he invites the statue to have dinner with him in the palace; to his horror the statue nods acceptance.

In Donna Anna's palace, Ottavio is trying to console the woman he loves. Insisting that Giovanni will soon be brought to justice, Ottavio pleads for Anna to marry him. But Anna protests she cannot think of happiness for herself until her father's murder has been punished ("Non mi dir, bell'idol mio").

In his banquet hall, Giovanni is partaking of an elaborate feast while an orchestra is serenading him. (One of the pieces it is playing is the "Non più andrai" from Mozart's *The Marriage of Figaro*!) Donna Elvira soon comes to plead with Giovanni to reform, but Giovanni replies only with laughter. She leaves in despair, but returns screaming: she has seen an apparition. It is the statue of the Commendatore come to life, arriving to keep his dinner appointment with Giovanni. Giovanni, though amazed, is not intimidated. When the Commendatore orders Giovanni to repent, the roué stoutly refuses. Flames now leap up to snatch Giovanni to his doom, as unearthly demons describe the tortures awaiting him in the world below.

A brief epilogue follows (sometimes omitted in present-day performances). Anna, Elvira, Zerlina, Ottavio, Masetto, and Leporello all come to a road near a cemetery. Leporello describes what has happened to Giovanni, while the others rejoice that evil has been destroyed.

At the première in Prague, *Don Giovanni* was a triumph. "Connoisseurs and artists say that nothing like this has been given in Prague," commented a contemporary journal. "Mozart himself conducted and when he appeared in the orchestra he was hailed by triple acclamation." Nor did the enthusiasm of Prague for this opera die down quickly. Within a century, *Don Giovanni* was heard over five hundred times. It also proved highly successful in Germany where, during Mozart's lifetime, it was given in about fifteen theaters. In Vienna, however, it was seen only fifteen times when first produced, then discarded until after Mozart's death.

Don Giovanni received its American première in a performance by Manuel Garcia and his Italian company at the Park Theater in New York on May 23, 1826. The Metropolitan Opera produced it during the first season of its existence, on November 29, 1883.

1787–1791. COMPOSITIONS FOR SOLO PIANO:

Minuet in D major, K. 355; Rondo in A minor, K. 511; Adagio in B minor, K. 540; Variations on "*Ein Weib ist das herrlichste Ding*," K. 613.

These four solo pieces, among the last produced by Mozart for the piano, are among his most remarkable of the shorter forms. Here is how Claudio Arrau described them: "The Minuet in D major (1790) is no ordinary minuet. Anyone who sees it as that fails to see what lies in it. It is at once the distillation and the quintessence of the minuet, the very portrait of a whole cultural period as seen through a dance. But more than a dance, it is like a courtly procession rising from the grave." "Nor," continues Arrau, "is the A minor Rondo (1787) just one more rondo movement. "It flows like a river of heavy-hearted sadness, and, like the great Adagio, is virtually a summation in itself of the whole spiritual content of Mozart's life." About the B minor Adagio (1788), Arrau has said that "by itself [it would] establish Mozart as one of the most profound of tragic composers. In its anguish and intensity, it harks back to the Fantasia in C minor of three years before, and indeed it is more like a free fantasy of suffering rumination than like an Adagio of a sonata." The eight variations on a theme by Schack, *Ein Weib ist das herrlichste Ding* (1791), is Mozart's last composition for the piano. Arrau also regards it as one most often misunderstood. "Variations notwithstanding, the resignation and weariness of the end is clearly here. . . . Instead of gaiety and brilliance there is cold, gray emanation about it from the very beginning. The first eight introductory bars to the theme are curiously repeated in every variation. . . . The poignant minor sixth variation is like an apotheosis of himself, with its quotation from the music of *The Magic Flute*—still to come. The last variation, more hopeful and sans 'introduction' is followed by a strange kind of fantasia coda, and remote. It is Mozart's farewell to the piano."

1788. PIANO TRIO IN E MAJOR, K. 542. I. Allegro. II. Andante grazioso. III. Allegro.

Within the space of three months in 1788, Mozart completed three piano trios, of which the E major is the first and the most significant. The piano enters with twelve measures of the first theme, in the opening movement. After that the subject is repeated by the three instruments. Following amplification of this material, a short transition leads to the second subject, which is also in twelve measures. The exposition ends with a chromatic version of the first melody. This receives fugato treatment in the development, with a new melody superimposed. The slow movement, in rondo form, opens with a simple statement that soon evolves into an eloquent solo for the violin, daring for its rhythms and modulations. The concluding rondo now introduces brilliance through virtuoso passages, both for the piano and for the violin; this takes the place of a second subject.

1788–1791. COUNTRY DANCES, and GERMAN DANCES, for orchestra:

COUNTRY DANCES: "Das Donnerwetter," K. 534; "La Bataille," K. 535; "Der Sieg vom Helden Koburg," K. 587.

GERMAN DANCES: "Der Kanarienvogel," K. 571; "Der Leiermann," K. 602; "Die Schlittenfahrt," K. 605.

Most of the more than a hundred *Country* and *German* Dances for orchestra came toward the end of Mozart's life. His friend, Michael Kelly, described how passionately Mozart loved to dance. He was not the only Viennese with such a weakness. With the establishment of a public ballroom in Vienna, in the second half of the eighteenth century, dancing became the major diversion of the middle classes. The *Country* Dance, or *Contredanse,* is sometimes regarded as the first modern dance, the predecessor of the quadrille. The *German* Dance—originally *Deutscher* or *Teuscher*—was a transition from the early Austrian peasant dance, the *Laendler,* to the later waltz. Both forms used lively tunes carefully divided into eight-measure phrases, frequently repeated over and over again. The rhythm is robust, with accent on the first beat, and emphasis on the bass note.

As a lover of the dance, Mozart was not above writing music for it. His *Country* and *German* dances overflow with the most infectious tunes and, at times, with the most extraordinary orchestration. Among the most popular of these dances are those in which Mozart is programmatic. Two of the better-known *Country* Dances use dynamics and harmonic colorations to describe battle scenes: *The Battle,* K. 535 (1788) and *The Battle of the Hero Koburg,* K. 587 (1789). A third familiar *Country* Dance—K. 534 (1788)—makes effective use of the timpani to simulate thunderclaps, in a piece entitled *The Thunder Storm.* Among the most frequently heard *German* Dances are *The Canary,* K. 571 (1789), in which flutes are made to imitate the chirping of the bird; *The Hurdy Gurdy,* K. 602 (1791), with its realistic reproduction of the sounds of that instrument; and *The Sleigh Ride,* K. 605 (1791), in whose trio, the tones "A-F-E-C" imitate the ringing of sleigh bells.

1788. CONCERTO IN D MAJOR, "CORONATION," K. 537, for piano and orchestra. I. Allegro. II. Larghetto. III. Allegretto.

The name of "Coronation" was assigned to this piano concerto because this is the work Mozart played during the coronation ceremonies of Emperor Leopold II at Frankfort-on-the-Main, on October 9, 1790, three years after its composition. Alfred Einstein regards this as the proper kind of music for a festive event. Both themes of the first movement are airy and melodious, and both are introduced in the opening orchestral preface. The piano makes its entrance with the first of these subjects, after which the orchestra recalls parts of the second. Following brilliant passage work for the solo instrument, a new lyrical idea emerges. The slow movement has three parts. In the first, the piano is heard in a simple, pleasing melody that is soon restated by the orchestra. After a countersubject is heard, the second section is introduced by the piano. The movement ends with a return of the first section and its first melody. The finale is a vivacious rondo, whose principal theme is immediately stated by the piano, followed by some subsidiary ideas; the most important of the latter is a flowing, expressive melody for the piano.

1788. SYMPHONY NO. 39 IN E-FLAT MAJOR, K. 543. I. Adagio; Allegro. II. Andante. III. Allegretto. IV. Allegro.

SYMPHONY NO. 40 IN G MINOR, K. 550. I. Molto allegro. II. Andante. III. Allegretto. IV. Allegro assai.

SYMPHONY NO. 41 IN C MAJOR, "JUPITER," K. 551. I. Allegro vivace. II. Andante cantabile. III. Allegretto. IV. Molto allegro.

That Mozart could have produced three such mighty symphonies within the space of just about six weeks offers the most eloquent possible testimony that there was certainly no let-up in his prodigious creativity during his last years—nor any drying up of his incomparable inspiration. Each of these three symphonies is so different in style and character that here again we are made forcefully aware of the variety of Mozart's style.

Donald Francis Tovey suggests that the E-flat Symphony "has always been known as the locus classicus for euphony; the G minor, accurately defines the range of passion comprehended in terms of Mozart's art; and the C major ends his symphonic career with the joyful majesty of a Greek god." Prof. Tovey adds: "Within these three types each individual movement is no less distinctive, while, of course, the contrasts within the individual symphony are expressly designed for vividness and coherence. Even in the treatment of the orchestra . . . each symphony has its own special coloring; and that coloring is none the less vivid in that it is most easily defined by stating what instruments of the normal orchestra are absent." The E-flat Symphony is scored without oboes; the G minor, without clarinets, trumpets, or timpani (though subsequently Mozart added the clarinets); the C major, without clarinets.

Mozart's unbelievable detachment from the world around him when he was writing is demonstrated in the E-flat major Symphony. At the time he was putting it down on paper, he was in the depths of despair, oppressed by debts, by the failure to get a secure post, and by fears for the future. Yet none of this intrudes into his music, which is consistently gay or serene, at peace with the world or in love with it.

The symphony opens with a stately introduction in which chords and runs in the strings alternate with melodic passages for strings. The Allegro opens with a suave lyrical melody for violins—the horns, bassoons, and other woodwind entering in imitation. The full orchestra is soon heard in a subsidiary thought before the second theme unfolds gracefully in the strings. A brief development, which pays attention to the second theme, is worked up into a climax before the recapitulation recalls the material of the exposition, and a short coda brings on a forceful conclusion.

In the second movement, a melody with the serenity of a benediction rises from the strings. After the woodwind join in, a second beautiful subject is heard, again in the strings. In the minuet, the opening vigorous dance tune is given by the violins over chords in the rest of the orchestra. The strings enter with a graceful reply. A flowing song that has the earmarks of a folk tune, given by the clarinet, is the main thought of the trio.

The finale abounds with vitality, beginning with a lightning subject for violins alone, with the rest of the orchestra soon participating. The second subject, for first violins, is equally vivacious, making its own contribution to the effervescent mood.

There is no introduction to the first movement of the G minor Symphony. It begins at once with its principal melody, a somewhat restless melody in the violins, which becomes increasingly agitated and dramatic as it is taken over by the full orchestra. But lyrical repose soon sets in with the graceful and somewhat melancholy melody in B-flat major, divided by strings and woodwind. After a change of key to F-sharp minor, and a return of the opening theme, the development section discusses the first melody with the most remarkable harmonic and polyphonic invention, while exploring all the emotion of which it is capable. In the recapitulation, the poignancy of the second theme is intensified through transposition to the key of G minor.

There is an even more pronounced suggestion of melancholy in the second movement, which begins with a tender melody with repeated notes. It is first heard in the strings, then echoed by the horns. (It is more than probable that Beethoven remembered this tune when he wrote the main theme of the second movement of his First Symphony.) A figure used to trim a restatement of this melody by the basses becomes part of the structure of the second theme, in which we can also detect an echo of the opening tender subject. The development concerns itself mainly with the first theme, while the second one makes its initial return in the recapitulation.

A robust, almost military sounding minuet leads into a lyrical trio in which the timbres of the various choirs are contrasted. An ascending subject in the strings, to which full orchestra replies, endows the finale with a nervous energy that persists throughout the movement. The second theme, in B-flat major, is first heard in violins and violas, then repeated by clarinet and bassoon. The opening phrase of the first theme is given an elaborate polyphonic treatment in the development. In the recapitulation, new depths of feeling are explored.

The name *Jupiter* was given to the C major Symphony—Mozart's last—not by the composer, but probably by the English pianist-composer, J. B. Cramer, in 1821. But Philip Hale finds nothing in this music to remind him of Jupiter. "The music," says, "is not of an Olympian mood. It is intensely human in its loveliness and gaiety." The principal subject of the first movement, arriving without anticipation, combines strength with tenderness. The strength is found in the first two measures for full orchestra; the tenderness, in an answering two-measure phrase in the strings. The martial music, however, takes over and is built up forcefully. Then the second subject comes to change the mood to one of gaiety, with a charming little tune in

G major for strings. The monumental one-hundred-measure development is brought on after a change of key from G major to E-flat major. The varied feelings suggested by the two contrasting themes are here exploited to the full. The recapitulation is brought on by a return of the strong opening theme; here the second subject is modulated to the key of C major. The coda derives naturally from the closing material of the recapitulation.

Muted strings offer the elegant melody of the slow movement, in which there are overtones of tragedy. The feeling grows increasingly intense with sforzando chords in the wind before the opening melody is repeated with new colors and fresh nuances.

But the Mozartian lightness of touch returns in the minuet with the soft and graceful melody for the first violins. The main idea in the trio is exchanged between wind and strings.

If the C major Symphony deserves the description of "Jovian" it is for its finale. The movement opens sedately with a tranquil subject, the first four notes of which were used by Mozart several times earlier, both in church and instrumental compositions. At the nineteenth measure, a descending passage for strings and woodwind leads into a brief fugal presentation of the opening subject. An episode in G major for first violins, imitated by the basses, precedes the presentation of the second theme—a quiet subject for strings in G major with interpolations by the winds. A recall of the first theme brings on the development in which considerable use is made of fugato writing. A passage for two bassoons brings on the recapitulation, where earlier thematic material is presented in a modified version. The main subject of the movement, once again treated fugally, then becomes the source of an extended coda.

1788. DIVERTIMENTO IN E-FLAT MAJOR, K. 563, for violin, viola, and cello. I. Allegro. II. Adagio. III. Allegro IV. Andante. V. Allegretto. VI. Allegro.

Mozart wrote only a single work for string trio. Though this is a chamber music combination that through the years yielded only a scattered few works of genuine distinction, Mozart's Divertimento is important music. The first movement, built mainly from a single theme evolved from the chord of E-flat (the opening motive) is in a grand design. A poignant slow movement in sonata form follows, its main thought growing from an ascending motive given by the cello in the opening measure. A delightful minuet in a comparatively fast tempo stands between this Adagio and an Andante in which a folk-like tune is given the variation treatment. The fifth movement is a slow minuet, both trios being in the style of a *German Dance*. Between each of these trios, the stately melody of the minuet is recalled. The finale is an exuberant rondo, abundant with vitality which is temporarily halted by a haunting melody with the tender quality of a lullaby.

1788–1789. SONATAS FOR PIANO:
F major, K. 533. I. Allegro. II. Andante. III. Rondo.
B-flat major, K. 570. I. Allegro. II. Adagio. III. Allegretto.
D major, K. 576. I. Allegro. II. Adagio. III. Allegretto.

In 1786, Mozart wrote a Rondo for piano solo for one of his pupils (K. 494). Two years after that, he completed an Allegro and an Andante for solo piano. In order to settle a debt with his publisher, Hoffmeister, he despatched the three pieces to him, having meanwhile revised the rondo. In 1790, Hoffmeister issued the three movements as a single sonata. Curiously enough, the sonata is all of one piece stylistically, so much so that it sometimes becomes difficult to remember that the finale (with its F minor three-part trio) was written at a different period from the earlier movements and had never been intended as their companion. The entire sonata is characterized by rich polyphonic writing, harmonic boldness, and striking chromaticisms. The deep emotion uncovered in the slow movement achieves an even greater passion in parts of the finale.

The B-flat major and the D major were Mozart's last piano sonatas. They are, says Claudio Arrau, "a spiritual summing up as it were. Mozart strips his pianistic fabric to almost bare, naked outlines, and with their tone of abstract remoteness and lonely farewell, makes a last plunge into the aching roots of being in this world." The first movement of the B-flat Sonata—structurally, one of Mozart's most compact—fluctuates in mood and feeling, but the impression it finally leaves is that of quiet and gentle resignation. But the tragic overtones that vibrate in so much of Mozart's music of this period is found in the sublime slow movement, a three-part structure.

Tragedy also penetrates the slow movement of Mozart's last piano sonata, in D major, which he completed in 1789—especially in its middle part, a poignant and richly harmonized melody that pierces the heart with a single direct thrust. The first movement contrasts a vigorous, almost optimistic, subject by which the movement is dominated, with a tender one heard toward the end of the exposition section. There are three main themes in the finale. These are later handled with extraordinary contrapuntal skill. The first of these becomes the basis of the concluding coda.

1789. CLARINET QUINTET IN A MAJOR, K. 581, for clarinet and strings. I. Allegro. II. Larghetto. III. Menuetto. IV. Allegretto con variazioni.

Like the Clarinet Concerto, the quintet was written for Anton Stadler, a clarinetist who was known to have outrageously exploited Mozart's friendship and generosity. Unlike the concerto, the clarinet is not given solo preference in the Quintet. In the first movement, it does not assume any of the major material until the forty-ninth measure—being used up to that time mainly to provide graceful ornamentation to material presented by other instruments. This movement opens with a strong theme—descending in the violins, ascending in viola and cello. The clarinet enters in the sixth bar with figurations. The second theme, which has a lyric character, appears in the first violin with plucked strings providing an accompaniment. The theme is then repeated by the clarinet, and from this point on, that instrument begins assuming greater significance. Then in the second movement, the clarinet takes over to project a romantic song over a muted string accompaniment. The third-movement minuet has two trios. The first is for strings alone, and the second is highlighted by a waltz tune for the clarinet. In the finale, an unpretentious subject is subjected to variations; these variations are light and buoyant, with the exception of the fifth, a beautiful Adagio shared by violin and clarinet.

1789–1790. 3 STRING QUARTETS, "PRUSSIAN":

D major, "Cello," K. 575. I. Allegretto. II. Andante. III. Allegretto. IV. Allegretto.

B-flat major, K. 589. I. Allegro. II. Larghetto. III. Moderato. IV. Allegro assai.

F major, K. 590. I. Allegro moderato. II. Andante. III. Allegretto. IV. Allegro.

In the Spring of 1789, Mozart visited Potsdam and Berlin, where he frequently attended the private concerts of the King of Prussia; at some of these, the king himself participated at the cello. The King then commissioned Mozart to write for him several chamber-music works. Bearing in mind the king's favorite instrument, Mozart completed three string quartets, emphasizing the role of the cello. That instrument plays such a prominent part in the first of these quartets that it has since become known as the "Cello" Quartet. These three works—collectively known as the *Prussian* because of the commission—were Mozart's last string quartets.

In the first movement of the D major Quartet (1789) considerable interest centers about a brief phrase that ends the opening theme. It returns after the appearance of the second theme (which is distributed among the four instruments) and is subjected to considerable attention in the development. The main melody of the second movement is a variant of Mozart's song, "Das Veilchen" (which see). After the trio, the finale enters with a serene song for the cello accompanied by the viola; placidity and warmth of feeling characterize the movement as a whole.

The B-flat major and F major Quartets came in 1790. The first movement of the B-flat major has considerable rhythmic interest. The way the instruments are pitted against one another from time to time suggests a concerto-grosso style. A beautiful melody rises from the cello in the second movement, decorated by figures in the upper strings. The minuet is brilliant; its extended trio features the violin in an improvisation. The finale emphasizes contrapuntal writing within the rondo structure. The two-part opening theme is repeated. After a brief transition, new material in the dominant is introduced. The development is marked by unusual modulations. The second subject, omitted in the recapitulation, is briefly discussed in the coda.

Mozart's last string quartet, in F major, is more consistently good-humored, more consistently optimistic, than its two neighbors. Healthy animal spirits erupt in the opening descending theme, while the last two notes of the second subject (assigned to the cello) become uninhibited it their effervescence when shared by first violin and cello towards the beginning of the development. The rest of the development concerns itself with the opening theme. In the recapitulation, the viola replaces the cello in recalling the second theme, and the coda reviews the former dialogue between first violin and cello.

The second movement has a somewhat faster pace than most of Mozart's slow movements. Its melodic material is found mainly in the lower voices of viola and cello, around which the two violins weave subtle trimmings. The minuet is one of the few places in these *Prussian* Quartets in which the cello is not emphasized. The finale opens with a dance theme that dominates the entire movement; at times it is subjected to "perpetual motion" treatment.

1790. COSÌ FAN TUTTE (WOMEN ARE LIKE THAT, or SO DO THEY ALL), opera buffa in two acts, with text by Lorenzo da Ponte. First performance: Burgtheater, Vienna, January 26, 1790.

The third and last time Mozart collaborated with Lorenzo da Ponte they produced an opera buffa that accepted this form of musical theater on its own terms. The plot was so contrived as to make use of most of the devices of opera buffa: the busybody who sets the plot spinning; characters appearing in disguises; love intrigues that get hopelessly involved and then get magically unraveled; the happy ending, in which all things turn out as they should in the best of possible worlds. From the opening measure of the overture to the concluding sextet of the last act, levity, gaiety, broad humor, satire, and burlesque are given free rein in pointing up woman's capacity for infidelity. But as an unidentified commentator reported in a Berlin music magazine in 1805, "that this evidence of the infidelity of all women was regarded merely as a jest is precisely the delicate charm of the whole opera, and that this infidelity, on the other hand, is let off so easily is proof of the playful sense of beauty on the part of the composer. Everything is only masquerade, playfulness, jest, dallying, and irony."

Notwithstanding the trivialities of the story and the unbelievable behavior of the heroines, da Ponte's text was able to draw out of Mozart one of his most wonderful and varied scores—a continual flow of inspiration, both in the arias and the ensemble numbers, all marked by Mozart's incomparable craftsmanship. Nathan Broder points out how effectively "a mock serious piece, aping the style of the lamenting or heroic aria of the opera seria, underscores the gentle irony of the work." He concluded by saying: "It is difficult to see why *Così fan tutte* has not always been accepted, and especially in our times, for what it is—a musical lark that is one of the gems of opera buffa."

The effervescent wit of the opera shines through the delightful overture from its opening measures, with its mock sentimental little tune for the oboe that comes after the introductory chords. This is followed by a satirical descending subject in low strings, which recurs in the opera in the third scene of the second act, where all three male characters remark that "all women are like that." The principal section of the overture now is set into quicksilver motion with a rapid theme that courses gracefully through the strings, and then the woodwind.

In eighteenth-century Naples, two soldiers, Ferrando and Guglielmo, are boasting that their respective sweethearts, Dorabella and Fiordiligi, are faithful to them. Don Alfonso, an elderly bachelor, is convinced that no woman alive can be trusted. To prove his point, he offers the two soldiers a wager that, given the proper opportunity, their sweethearts would quickly succumb to temptation. The soldiers readily accept the bet.

The scene shifts to the garden of a villa where the sisters, Dorabella and Fiordiligi, reveal the extent of their love for Ferrando and Guglielmo ("Ah guarda, sorella"). Don Alfonso now enters with a fabricated story that Ferrando and Guglielmo must soon rejoin their troops. Indeed, the two soldiers soon come to bid their sweethearts a poignant farewell ("Al fato dan legge"). When they finally leave—and after Despina has had a chance to discuss the tribulations of a servant's life in "Che vita maledetta"—Dorabella bemoans her sad fate ("Smanie, implacabili"). Despina is incapable of sympathizing with her mistress' woe, since in her opinion, no man is worthy of woman's unselfish love ("In uomini, in soldati").

The plot to test the moral fiber of the heroines is now set into motion. Ferrando and Guglielmo, disguised as Albanian noblemen, arrive. Without delay they begin to woo Dorabella and Fiordiligi passionately. At first, the women are cold to these advances, Fiordiligi insisting she will always be true to her beloved Guglielmo ("Come scoglio"). For a moment, then, it seems as if the two soldiers have won their wager, a fact that sends Ferrando into a sentimental mood over his beloved ("Un' aura amorosa"). But the "Albanian noblemen" continue to press their suit most ardently. Being once again repelled, they tell the girls that rather than face life without them, they have chosen death by poison. Despina, masquerading as a doctor, rushes in to whisper various incantations over the "dying" soldiers ("Questo è quel pezzo"), and to remove the poison from their bodies with a magnet. The cure works. The "noblemen" are again healthy, ready to resume their wooing. After Despina has convinced her mistresses that there is really no great harm in indulging in some mild flirtation ("Una donna a quindici anni"), both Dorabella and Fiordiligi become more interested in their visitors, especially after an eloquent serenade ("Secondate, aurette amiche"). Guglielmo now goes off with Dorabella, and whispers tender love words into her receptive ears ("Il core vi dono"). Fiordiligi, after a bit of resistance, also confesses to Ferrando that his exquisite song of love ("Per pietà, ben mio, perdona") has touched her heart.

The two romances now develop rapidly; both couples are beginning to talk of marriage. Despina, this time disguised as a notary, comes with a marriage contract. Suddenly a roll of drums announces the return of the troops from Naples; Ferrando and Guglielmo have come home. In the confusion that follows, the "Albanians" make a hurried retreat. They soon return wearing their own soldier's uniform. The sight of the marriage contract sends Ferrando and Guglielmo into a mock rage, and the women into actual penitence. Finally, the soldiers break down and reveal the whole plot to their women, who, in turn, promise to remain faithful to their own men for the rest of their lives. Everybody agrees that no one but Don Alfonso is a villain, while Don Alfonso muses that everything that has happened has been for the best ("V'ingannai, ma fu l'inganno").

When introduced in Vienna, *Così fan tutte* was only moderately successful. The death of Joseph II, on February 20, 1790, closed all the theaters in Vienna for a two-month period of mourning. *Così fan tutte* had been given only five performances by that time. When the theaters reopened, *Così* was restored to the repertory; but it was given only five times more. Strange to say, the American première apparently had to wait until March 24, 1922, when the opera was produced at the Metropolitan Opera House.

1790–1791. STRING QUINTETS:

D major, K. 593. I. Larghetto; Allegro. II. Adagio. III. Allegretto. IV. Allegro.

E-flat major, K. 614. I. Allegro di molto. II. Andante. III. Allegretto. IV. Allegro.

In the first movement of Mozart's fourth string quintet (1790), the sobriety of the slow introduction is sharply contrasted with the spirited good humor of the ensuing Allegro. In that slow opening, effective use is made of a cello phrase, which is built up with great intensity of feeling. The main subject in the first group of themes, in the Allegro, is a rhythmic passage that begins in quarter-notes, quickens into eighth-note triplets, and ends up in dotted rhythm. Mozart uses this subject again in the second group of themes. The opening slow introduction is recalled toward the end of the movement, a practice highly unusual with Mozart. The coda, in quick time, makes use of the first phrase of the initial theme.

The cello phrase that proved so important in the first-movement introduction is again suggested in the Adagio. This movement opens with a stately melody, which returns after an elaborate development section. The minuet exploits canonic writing, but its trio is an unpretentious section, constructed from a single arpeggio figure in the violin. In the finale, the sonata form and the fugue are skilfully merged. A dance-like tune in two parts opens this movement, whose second subject receives fugal treatment. In the development, we get an extended fugato on a new subject that is related to the first theme. A climactic point is reached in the recapitulation in which all the basic material is woven together in triple counterpoint.

Mozart's last quintet (1791) was completed about eight months before his death. Each movement, except the Andante, is opened by the first violins with the same three notes: B-flat, A-flat, and G. The first movement is dominated by its initial subject, a hunt-theme shared by the two violas and two violins. The slow movement offers us a romantic melody, which is then heard with two variants before a highly expressive section in the subdominant unfolds. In the coda, the basic melody is heard in still another varied form. The minuet opens gracefully, but the trio is energized by the vital rhythms of a peasant dance over a consistent pedal point. Contrapuntal writing is emphasized in the finale. The vivacious first theme is presented in imitation as the second theme, and an extended fugato appears in the development.

1791. CONCERTO IN B-FLAT MAJOR, K. 595, for piano and orchestra. I. Allegro. II. Larghetto. III. Allegro.

This is Mozart's last piano concerto, and it was the work with which he made his final appearance as a pianist, in Vienna on March 4, 1791. A single introductory measure brings on the gentle main theme of the first movement in the first violins, with woodwind and horns occasionally intruding with a loud exclamation. The second theme is also assigned to the first violins. After this extended orchestral exposition (which spans seventy-three measures), the piano appears with a flowery presentation of the first theme. Passage work serves as a transition to a restatement of the second theme in the piano, in the key of F major. In the development, piano and orchestra elaborate upon the first theme, which also serves to bring on the recapitulation. In the latter, the piano offers the second theme in the key of B-flat major, with a commentary by the woodwind after each alternate measure. A cadenza precedes the brief coda.

The main melody of the Larghetto is sung by the piano, the orchestra repeating the subject at the ninth measure. A second important melody comes after an orchestral tutti, a lyrical passage for the piano in E-flat major, accompanied softly by the strings.

In the concluding rondo, the piano introduces, and the orchestra continues with, a vivacious dance tune. A new idea in the piano comes after a twenty-five-measure orchestral passage. Brilliant virtuoso passages precede the return of the first subject in the piano, after which all earlier material is given a brilliant and at times ebullient working out.

1791. DIE ZAUBERFLOETE (THE MAGIC FLUTE), K. 620, comic opera in two acts, with text by Emanuel Schikaneder. First performance: Theater auf der Wieden, Vienna, September 30, 1791.

That Mozart should have been able to produce the vivacity and buffoonery of *The Magic Flute* at a time when he was tormented by illness, debts, and the fear of death, speaks volumes for his inordinate capacity to meet a creative problem on its own terms, and allow nothing extraneous to intrude.

In 1789, Emanuel Schikaneder—actor, stage director, and poet—organized a company to present popular and spectacular productions at the Theater auf der Wieden. He asked Mozart to write for him a Singspiel, and he himself provided the libretto. The long held belief that Schikaneder was in desperate financial straits at the time—from which he hoped to extricate himself with a successful Mozart opera—is not true. Schikaneder was doing very well with his new theater when he commissioned Mozart. If any proof is needed on this score it is provided by the fact that Schikaneder spent about five thousand florins to mount the Mozart comic opera as lavishly as possible.

Mozart completed the last pages of his opera (the overture and the "March of the Priests") on September 28, 1791. The première of the opera took place two days later, Mozart himself conducting. It proved a huge success. Even Mozart's arch enemy, Antonio Salieri, was enchanted. During the next two weeks, hundreds had to be turned away from the theater at each performance, many of them having arrived hours before curtain time with the hope of gaining admission. During its first decade, *The Magic Flute* was heard two hundred and thirty-three times in Schikaneder's theater. The opera made the impresario a wealthy man, but regrettably, Mozart himself did not live long enough to profit from this success. The popularity of the opera spread quickly out of Vienna, fanning out in all directions. By 1800, sixty-five German towns had produced it. In 1801, it was given successfully in Moscow and Paris; by 1816, it had been seen by London, Stockholm, Copenhagen, and Milan. The American première took place at the Park Theater in New York on April 17, 1833, in an English translation. The first presentation at the Metropolitan Opera was in Italian, on March 30, 1900.

Schikaneder, a Mason, filled his fairy tale with all kinds of Masonic references and symbols; and so did Mozart, a fellow Mason. Nathan Broder points to one notable example of such symbolism. The mystic number of three is stressed throughout the opera. The work begins and ends in E-flat major (three flats); the overture opens with three chords; the characters include Three Ladies and Three Spirits; there are three doors for Tamino to knock upon; the serpent is cut into three parts. The Masonic influence is also felt in the selection of Egypt as a setting. However, Tamino, the hero, was intended to personify the Austrian Emperor, while his beloved Pamina represented the Austrian people.

The curious way in which, midstream in the libretto, Schikaneder transforms Sarastro from an evil magician into the personification of the highest ideals of Masonry—and, by the same token, changes the Queen of the Night from a good spirit to an evil one—has long disturbed Mozart's biographers and critics. The general belief was held for a long time that a competing opera on the same subject forced Schikaneder to turn his own text topsy-turvy.

But this is no longer accepted as valid. What is more probable is that in setting the text, Mozart felt the need for the introduction of deeper values—the concept of the brotherhood of man, for example—and Schikaneder stood ready to follow Mozart's suggestions. These deeper values are consistently uncovered in Mozart's music, especially in the two famous arias of Sarastro, about which Bernard Shaw once said that it is the only music he knows worthy of coming from the lips of God. The tomfoolery of some of its scenes notwithstanding—and in spite of the confusion in the development of the plot—*The Magic Flute* remains one of the most majestic operas ever written.

With three solemn chords (which in the opera precede Sarastro's aria, "O Isis und Osiris," and the "March of the Priests") the overture embarks on a noble introductory section. The main section devotes itself to a sprightly melody that is given fugal treatment before it is elaborated upon.

The prince Tamino, hero of the opera, appears against a bleak landscape. He is fleeing from a serpent, which the three attendants of the Queen of the Night destroy. Papageno, a birdcatcher, comes upon the scene and describes the nature of his trade in a little ditty that sounds like a folk song ("Der Vogelfaenger bin ich ja"). Tamino erroneously believes that it is Papageno who saved his life from the serpent, and Papageno, flattered by this attention, does nothing to disenchant him. Because of this indiscretion, Papageno is punished by the three attendants of the Queen of the Night: his lips are sealed with a padlock. The attendants now turn their attention to Tamino by showing him a portrait of Pamina, daughter of the Queen of the Night. Tamino is rhapsodic over her beauty ("Dies Bildnis ist bezaubernd schoen"). Now the Queen of the Night arises from the depths to tell Tamino that Pamina is a prisoner of the evil magician, Sarastro. She promises to give Pamina to Tamino in marriage if he stands ready to rescue her ("Zum Leiden bin ich auserkoren"). To help him in this mission, the Queen presents Tamino with a magic flute, which when played upon will keep him from harm. At the same time, she unlocks Papageno's lips and assigns him to accompany Tamino, providing him with magic chimes for protection.

In Sarastro's palace, Pamina is guarded by a Moor, Monostatos. Tamino and Papageno penetrate the palace. When Monostatos has caught a glimpse of Papageno, he flees in horror, convinced he has seen the devil. Thus left unguarded, Pamina can be told by Papageno that the handsome prince, Tamino, will soon liberate her. Pamina and Papageno joyfully sing the praises of love ("Bei Maennern, welche Liebe fuehlen").

Tamino now comes to a grove outside the Temple of Isis. There he discovers that, far from being an evil magician, Sarastro is a priest of high ideals and purpose; that there is sound reason for him to hold Pamina a captive. At this point, Monostatos comes in dragging Papageno and Pamina, having caught them trying to effect their escape. Preceded by three stately chords, Sarastro appears. He dictates to Tamino and Pamina the tests they must perform to prove their devotion and courage.

In the second act, Sarastro and his High Priests file in to the stately music of "The March of the Priests." Sarastro entreats his priests to permit Tamino to become a member of their holy order, and that he be permitted to marry Pamina. The Priests consent. Sarastro now prays to the gods to help the lovers undergo their trials successfully ("O Isis und Osiris").

The first of these ordeals prohibits Tamino from speaking to Pamina, whatever the provocation; at the same time, Papageno must remain silent in the presence of the bride chosen for him by Sarastro. Papageno, however, succumbs to temptation. When he starts to talk to an old woman come to bring him a drink of water, he is sent rushing away in terror by a clap of thunder. Tamino, however, proves successful. Believing that her beloved prince has turned cold to her, Pamina voices her poignant grief in "Ach, ich fuehl's." Her mother, the Queen of the Night, advises her to kill Sarastro ("Der Hoelle Rache"), a suggestion that horrifies her. When she later begs Sarastro to forgive her mother, the priest informs her that there is no room in this holy temple for either hate or vengeance ("In diesen heil'gen Hallen").

But Tamino and Papageno must now undergo further tests. After Sarastro has led Tamino off, Papageno, weary and thirsty, comes upon a jug of wine, from which he takes his fill. Now tipsy, Papageno longs for a wife to love ("Ein Maedchen oder Weibchen"), a wish that is fulfilled with the arrival of an old, haggard woman. Papageno is ordered to take her as wife, a fate he contemplates with no little anguish, until the old woman sheds her disguises and reveals herself to be a young and beautiful bird-girl called Papagena. Ecstatically, Papageno wants to take her in his arms, but is warned by a voice that first he was to submit to some ordeals.

Still convinced she has been spurned by Tamino, Pamina wants to take her own life. The Queen of the Night returns to reassure her that she has been mistaken. Tamino, in turn, is soon able to dispel Pamina's last doubts. Hand in hand, they go bravely through the trials of fire and water, protected by the magic flute played by Tamino.

For his own part, Papageno is also distraught, thinking he has lost Papagena. In despair, he decides to hang himself. But he delays long enough for the Queen of the Night to come and remind him of the powers of his magic chimes. With the sounding of the first notes, Papagena appears.

But the Queen of the Night is still determined to destroy Sarastro and abduct Pamina. She gathers the powers of evil in a gloomy grove to formulate the necessary plans. Thunder and lightning drive the evildoers into the deepest caverns of the earth. Tamino and Pamina are now brought before the High Priests and Sarastro, to be initiated into the mysteries of the holy order.

1791 LA CLEMENZA DI TITO (THE CLEMENCY OF TITUS), K. 621, opera in two acts, with text by Caterino Mazzola, adapted from a libretto by Metastasio. First performance: Prague, September 6, 1791.

Mozart was commissioned by Prague to write an opera for the festivities attending the coronation of the King of Bohemia on September 6, 1791. The authorities chose Mozart's subject for him—an operatic portrait of the Roman Emperor, Titus, which cast a favorable light on monarchy in general. Metastasio had written a libretto that had been set by a number of composers, including Gluck. This text was revised for Mozart by Mazzola. Many solo arias were deleted to be replaced by duets, trios, and ensemble numbers so greatly favored by the audiences in the late eighteenth century. Despite these revisions, the Metastasio text remains basically an opera seria along conventional lines. Thus, in his last opera, Mozart was reverting to the now outmoded style of his youth, in which he had produced *Idomeneo*.

Yet, as Prof. Edward J. Dent points out, there is a radical difference between Mozart's opera and those by earlier composers using the same libretto. "The arias, which ought to be long and stately, he cuts down to the shortest proportions; he invents a new form for them, based on Gluck's French operas, with a slow introduction and a quick movement to follow. . . . He takes his time only in the two great arias which have now become favorite concert pieces. . . . In the concerted numbers, Mozart allows his dramatic genius more freedom, and we meet with modulations and other complexities which may well have bewildered the Empress." Prof. Dent then selects the first-act finale as the finest movement in the whole opera. "This finale has great importance because it is the first in which Mozart has combined both solo voices and chorus, too, in a great ensemble."

The central thread of the Mozart libretto is the desire of Emperor Titus to marry Berenice, daughter of Agrippa I of Judea; and the plan of Vitellia, in love with him, to destroy Titus. She enlists the aid of Sextus, who is interested in her, to foment a conspiracy against the Emperor. Sextus sets fire to the capitol, in which the Emperor is believed to have been a fatal victim. But somebody else, wearing Titus's mantle has been killed, and Titus has been saved. Sextus is tried by the Senate and condemned to death. But the all-merciful Titus forgives both Sextus and Vitellia.

Prague, which previously had been so hospitable to other Mozart operas, at first rejected *Tito*. At the coronation ceremonies it was a complete failure. But when it later returned to the same city, the audiences seemed more favorably disposed to it. Nevertheless, it has never really become a favorite of operagoers and is given infrequently. Its première in London, in 1806, was the first Mozart opera heard in that city. The American stage première had to wait one hundred and fifty years, taking place at the Berkshire Music Festival in Tanglewood on August 4, 1952.

1791. AVE VERUM CORPUS, K. 618, motet for chorus and orchestra.
REQUIEM IN D MINOR, K. 626, for solo voices, chorus, and orchestra.

Mozart completed the *Ave Verum* on June 17, 1791. It is probably the simplest of all his church compositions, both in the structure and in the easy flow of the melodic line. But it is also one of his noblest pages. This is music in which the composer leaves behind the anguish he was then suffering to find solace in religion. This is the music of a man who has seen the heavens open and has had a glimpse of ultimate serenity.

There are pages in Mozart's last composition, the Requiem, with the same kind of spiritual exaltation and tranquillity; there is also, in other parts, a good deal of agitation, conflict, and tragedy. The dramatic circumstances surrounding the writing of this, Mozart's swan song, has been frequently described. The story reads like the fabrication of a romantic biographer, yet it is grounded in fact. Its telling helps to throw illumination on the music itself, to explain its deeply personal character.

In July of 1791, a half-year before Mozart's death, a tall, thin stranger dressed in gray visited him with an anonymous letter commissioning a requiem. There were two stipulations. Mozart was to complete the work in the shortest time possible; and he was to make no attempt to uncover the identity of the man buying the music. The strange way in which this offer was made, and the peculiar appearance of the person bringing him the commission, made a profound impression. Suffering as he was at that time from physical disorders that were soon to prove fatal, and from mental anguish brought on by debts and frustrations, Mozart soon became obsessed with the thought that this messenger was a visitor from the other world come to urge him to write his own requiem before it was too late. When, some time later, the stranger returned to inquire how the Requiem was progressing, Mozart became more convinced than ever that his time was running short, that the writing of the Requiem represented for him a race with death.

Actually, this commission has a simple explanation, though Mozart never learned it. The stranger was the steward of Count Franz von Walsegg, a nobleman with ambitions to become a composer. He adopted the simple expedient of commissioning composers to write works for him at a decent price which he then palmed off as his own. The recent death of the Count's wife was the immediate impetus to send the Count to Mozart for a requiem which the Count wanted performed as his own tribute to her memory.

But unaware of all this, Mozart—who felt he was producing death music for himself—worked with a passion and an intensity that often had to ignore physical pain and mental torment. He knew death was close at hand; he was determined to complete his work before then. In this, as in so many other ways in the past, he was frustrated. He managed to finish only twelve of the fifteen sections. To his pupil, Franz Xaver Suessmayr, he gave explicit instructions and detailed sketches on how the other three parts were to be written. Apparently, Mozart's ideas were followed meticulously; there is no sign of creative deterioration in the last there parts. As Beethoven said, when asked if Suessmayr had written the last part of the Requiem: "If Suessmayr wrote it, then he is a Mozart."

How close the Requiem was to Mozart's heart was proved just before his death. On December 4, 1791, he gathered some of his friends around him to join him in singing the "Lacrymosa." Midway, he burst into tears. All the rest of that day and evening he was still thinking of his Requiem, even though he was already stricken by partial paralysis. Even after he bid his family farewell, he tried to sing parts of his last work. A few hours later he was dead.

For these reasons, the Requiem is one of the most personal of Mozart's creations. In it Mozart plunges to the very depths of his tortured soul, and then rises to a state of spiritual exaltation rarely encountered in his other church music. The "strained, nerve-wracked quality" that Eric Blom finds in so much of the Requiem, makes its presence strongly felt in the first section, the "Introitus"—a prayer for eternal rest. This opening, says Blom, "with its restless syncopations and suspensions, is in its way as unhappily agitated below the surface of slow and subdued notes as any incident in Wagner's *Tristan und Isolde* three-quarters of a century later." A climax is reached with the "Kyrie eleison" and the "Christe eleison," a mighty double fugue characterized by chromatic figurations. In the second part—the turbulent "Dies Irae"—man contemplates his own sins in the face of the final judgment. Here, says Dyneley Hussey, we have "the counterpart . . . of those strange pictures of the Last Judgment, which still awe the spectators by the crude violence of their horrors. . . . So the 'Dies Irae' appeared to Mozart an opportunity for a splendid and terrible musical design. . . . But there entered another factor—the delusions under which Mozart labored concerning the work on which he was engaged. For once, a note of hysterical passion sounded in his music. . . . It is this note of hysteria which makes the Requiem one of the most painful works to contemplate."

The "Tuba mirum" is introduced by an elementary subject for tenor trumpet. The solo quartet of voices first describes the terrors of Judgment Day, and then—in "Cum vix iustus sit securus"—joins in supplication, in melting tones of the most tender beauty. The overpowering chorus, "Rex tremendae"—with the interpolations of dramatic exclamations of "Rex" and "Rex tremendae majestatis"—is followed by the more placid and suppliant measures of the "Recordare" for vocal quartet. Here the Saviour is presented as all-merciful. Then the storm and stress of the "Confutatis" for chorus, with its rapid changes from major to minor, bring up the disturbed image of the damned, while a gentler section offers an eloquent supplication for redemption. Drama and agitation give way to the surpassing grief of the "Lacrymosa," whose melody, says Eric Blom, "is almost too limpid for choral singing." This is one of the peaks of the score, music that speaks for the day of mourning with a pathos that pierces the heart like a scalpel. The terror of Judgment Day is brought back in the "Domine Jesu," whose drama is accentuated through repeated use of short phrases, and which is swept to a climax with a brief fugue on the words "Ne absorbeat eas Tartarus."

The majestic stride of the "Sanctus" sweeps toward a monumental eight-part fugue for double chorus. At long last, the other-worldly radiance of the "Benedictus"—in which the subject of the preceding fugue becomes transfigured—brings a lasting peace to the weary spirit, and the heart is once and for all appeased of all anguish. Now comes the concluding "Agnus Dei," a sublime melody for the soprano, later repeated by chorus and orchestra in unison. "It is altogether typically Mozartian in feeling," says Dyneley Hussey, in recalling that Suessmayr was supposed to have written this music, "and the figure of the violin accompaniment is so characteristic and original that it is almost impossible to accept it as a brilliant imitiaton." The Requiem comes to a conclusion on a elegiac note, with a brief recollection of the first section's opening subject and with a choral fugue.

DOMENICO CIMAROSA 1749–1801

Of the seventy-six operas completed by Cimarosa, only one survives—the opera buffa, *Il Matrimonio segreto*. Here his touch was light and gay; the writing of vocal ensembles had nimbleness and flexibility; his sentiment proved touching, just as his patter songs revealed a fine sense for the comic. In all this, he reminds us of the Mozart who wrote *The Marriage of Figaro* and *Così fan tutte*.

Cimarosa wrote a considerable amount of instrumental music, of which only a handful of concertos and sonatas for the harpsichord are now occasionally revived. His instrumental compositions are slight in structure and content, but their gracious melodies and harmonies fall pleasantly on the ear. Material from Cimarosa's instrumental music was used by two twentieth-century composers for delightful concert works: by Arthur Benjamin for a Concerto for Oboe and Orchestra, and by Gian Francesco Malipiero for the orchestral suite, *Cimarosiana*.

Domenico Cimarosa was born in Aversa, near Naples, Italy, on December 17, 1749. For about eleven years, he attended the renowned Santa Maria di Loreto Conservatory in Naples, where he came under the influence of Niccolò Piccini (1728–1800), distinguished composer of opera buffa. Cimarosa's first opera was *Le Stravaganze del conte,* produced in Naples in 1772. During the next quarter of a century, Cimarosa completed more than seventy operas. His first emphatic success came in 1773 with *La Finta parigina,* while with *Giannina e Bernardone*, produced in 1781, his fame spread all over Europe.

Between 1787 and 1791, Cimarosa was court composer for Catherine II in St. Petersburg. In this post, he wrote several more operas besides some church music and a ballet. In 1791, he succeeded Antonio Salieri as court

Kapellmeister for Leopold II in Vienna. His masterwork, *Il Matrimonio segreto,* was written for Vienna, and introduced at the Burgtheater in 1792. In 1798, Cimarosa returned to Naples to become Kapellmeister at court and music teacher to the royal children. When the French republican army entered Naples, and the Bourbons fled to Sicily, Cimarosa became involved in revolutionary activities. Upon the return of the Bourbons to Naples, Cimarosa was put into prison for several days. He was then allowed to leave Naples. He proceeded to Venice, where he died on January 11, 1801.

1792. IL MATRIMONIO SEGRETO (THE SECRET, or CLANDESTINE, MARRIAGE), opera buffa in two acts, with text by Giovanni Bertati, based on *The Clandestine Marriage,* a play by George Colman and David Garrick. First performance: Burgtheater, Vienna, February 7, 1792.

Il Matrimonio segreto was one of the most successful opera buffas in the eighteenth century. It is still being revived; it has been recorded in its entirety; and it holds its place solidly as a classic of Italian comic opera. One reason for its endurance rests with its libretto—livelier and fresher than most of those encountered in eighteenth-century opera.

Geronimo, a wealthy but avaricious merchant of Bologna, strongly opposes the marriage of his lovely daughter Carolina to Paolino. The young couple, therefore, is forced to marry secretly. In an effort to win the old man's favor, Paolino tries arranging a marriage between Geronimo's older daughter, Elisetta, and a desirable Englishman, Count Robinson. But things get out of hand when Elisetta falls in love with Paolino, and Count Robinson is attracted to Carolina. In desperation, Paolino and Carolina run away, but are intercepted. In the end, Geronimo learns that Paolino and Carolina are married. He reconciles himself to this fact, while Elisetta and Count Robinson discover that they are in love with each other after all.

But it is Cimarosa's music that gives this merry tale its sparkle and vitality. Cimarosa's lyricism reaches heights of expressiveness in Carolina's poignant song upon discovering her father plans sending her to a convent ("E possono mai nascere") and in Paolino's passionate avowal to Carolina, "Ah! no, che tu così morir." Cimarosa also proves himself a master of buffa style in Geronimo's arias, "Udite, tutti, udite" and "Un matrimonio nobile." The opera, moreover, boasts an overture that is Mozartian in transparency and deftness. Three chords lead to a chattering theme that moves along briskly until a change of mood is invoked with a lyrical second subject. The orchestral writing, both here and in the opera itself, is always handled with uncommon good taste, just as the ensemble writing is consistently brilliant. From beginning to end, then, the music is in the tradition of Mozart, as Francis Toye remarked, gay, fluent, natural, captivating. "There is, of course, never a trace of underlying Mozartian pathos, but the youthful high spirits are not unworthy of comparison with Mozart." No wonder, then, that Verdi regarded this as a model of what opera buffa should be.

Francis Toye prefers to describe *Il Matrimonio* as a "comic opera" rather than "opera buffa." He explains: "The opera buffa form knew no sentiment, whereas the lovers in Cimarosa's opera remain human beings . . . and indulge in some delicate and pretty emotion."

Il Matrimonio was such a huge success that, by 1793, it was seen throughout all of Italy. It was first produced in the United States, in New York, in 1834 (presented in English), and it was mounted by the Metropolitan Opera on February 25, 1937. The opera was selected to open the La Piccola Scala in Milan in 1955.

——— CONCERTO FOR OBOE AND ORCHESTRA, adapted by Arthur Benjamin. I. Introduzione: larghetto. II. Allegro. III. Siciliana. IV. Allegro giusto.

Cimarosa never wrote an oboe concerto. The present work—popular on programs and on records—was adapted by Arthur Benjamin from four harpsichord sonatas by Cimarosa: A minor (No. 23), C major (No. 24), C minor (No. 29) and G major (No. 31). The work, strictly speaking, is more of a suite than a concerto. Each movement contains one basic theme, which is presented with the classic forthrightness of Cimarosa's time. The prevailing mood of the fast movements is gaiety, while the slow sections have the singing character of Italian arias, all in the style of Cimarosa's best comic operas.

The first movement opens with a melody for the solo instrument, softly accompanied by strings. After a brief passage for oboe alone, this melody returns as a dialogue between oboe and first violins. Two soft chords lead into the second movement, which has two sections. The main theme, in strings, has classic grace. A pastoral-like "Siciliana" follows. The concerto ends with a lovely Allegro in which the solo instrument and orchestra have happy exchanges.

LUIGI BOCCHERINI 1743–1805

Boccherini was one of the most prolific composers of his time. His works include over one hundred string quartets, another hundred and twenty-five string quintets, sixty string trios, twenty-seven violin sonatas, two symphonies, four cello concertos, and sundry other items. The fact that he was also a major creative figure in eighteenth-century music is sometimes overlooked through the unhappy circumstance that he was a contemporary of giants like Haydn and Mozart. Their tremendous shadows tend to obscure Boccherini to contemporary view. But with Haydn and Mozart, Boccherini was a significant pioneer in clarifying and solidifying the sonata form; in writing for string instruments in combination; in developing the personality of the cello within the string quartet. He was also the first composer to venture into formerly untouched areas, such as the string quintet and string sextet. "What constitutes an epoch-making characteristic of Boccherini's work," writes Robert Sondheimer, "is the skilful manner in which he continues to vary his forms of expression within the smallest framework. . . . In this respect none of Boccherini's contemporaries can compare with him."

It is truly ironical that a composer who wrote as much as Boccherini did—and often so well—should be known to so many music lovers almost exclusively through a charming trifle: the minuet from his String Quintet in E major, op. 13, no. 5. In its elegance and grace, this piece is, of course, a classic example of minuet music. But Boccherini's finest quartets and symphonies—and the B-flat major Cello Concerto—are worthier examples of his gifts, and point to a master well worth exploring in depth. "So long as men take delight in pure melody," once said W. H. Hadow, "in transparent style, in fancy alert, sensitive and sincere, so long is his place in the history of music assured."

Luigi Boccherini was born in Lucca, Italy, on February 19, 1743. He received instruction in music from his father and from Abbate Vannucci, after which he won acclaim as a cello virtuoso. In 1768, he came to Paris, where he was lionized and where his first published works appeared, a set of six string quartets and two sets of string trios. In 1769, he settled in Madrid. There he enjoyed the patronage of Infante Don Luis, the king's brother, who engaged him as chamber musician and virtuoso. When Don Luis died in 1785, Boccherini moved on to Berlin. From then until 1797, he was chamber musician for Frederick William II of Prussia. When that monarch died, Boccherini returned to Madrid. His fame and personal fortunes now went into sharp decline. His last years were spent in appalling poverty. He died in Madrid on May 28, 1805.

c. 1780. STRING QUARTETS:

G minor, op. 33, no. 5. I. Allegro comodo. II. Andantino. III. Menuetto. IV. Allegro giusto.

A major, op. 33, no. 6. I. Allegro. II. Andantino lentarello. III. Menuetto con moto. IV. Presto assai.

In the almost one hundred string quartets by Boccherini, we find clarity of structure, freshness and variety of thematic material, and skill in the writing for the four instruments. All this brings to these quartets artistic as well as historic importance. Noteworthy in particular is the way in which Boccherini gives new importance to the viola and cello. Indeed, as Robert Sondheimer noted, "the technique of string instruments which progressed during the eighteenth century from almost primitive simplicity to all-embracing brilliance was led on to its final stages by Boccherini."

In the G minor and A major Quartets, of the op. 33 set, rococo grace and charm predominate. The first movement of the G minor Quartet is almost entirely built around a soaring, effusive melody. The Andantino that follows is particularly noteworthy, not only for its lyricism, but also for the way in which the main melody is distributed among the four instruments. One instrument begins the theme then passes it on to a colleague. The four instruments are equal partners in the presentation of basic material. In the slow movement of the A major Quartet, classic objectivity is abandoned for a profound emotion; and in the trio of the minuet movement, the cello acquires an independence and a personality not often encountered in the chamber-music writing of this period.

c. 1780. CONCERTO IN B-FLAT MAJOR, for cello and orchestra, op. 34. I. Allegro moderato. II. Adagio. III. Allegro.

The only work by Boccherini to appear regularly in our symphony halls is this concerto, a favorite of cello virtuosos everywhere. As heard today, however, the concerto is given most often in an edition prepared by Friedrich Gruetzmacher in 1900; Gruetzmacher also contributed the first-movement cadenza. The first movement is in classic sonata form. All the thematic material is found in the opening orchestral introduction. The solo instrument then takes the main melodies over and repeats them with embellishments. The second movement is a song for the solo instrument in which the virtuoso can give play to beauty of tone and sensitivity of phrasing. The finale is in rondo form. It opens with a sprightly theme in the upper register of the solo instrument; this theme recurs throughout the movement.

1787. SYMPHONY IN A MAJOR. I. Allegro assai. II. Allegro. III. Andante. IV. Allegro ma non troppo presto.

Only one or two of Boccherini's twenty symphonies are today occasionally performed. That in A major was written when the composer worked for the king of Prussia. The symphony presents the main theme at once in full orchestra. A forceful transition leads to the second theme, softly given by flute and first violins. In the development, this second subject is heard in the woodwind in varied shapes and forms. After that, the first theme is discussed at length. A gentle passage for flute and strings leads into the recapitulation. The second and third movements depart from symphonic tradition by changing places. The second is a charming minuet, and the third highlights a soulful melody for oboe and solo viola, accompanied by strings. Other sections of the orchestra take this dance tune over in imitation, before the second subject arrives. The development section is introduced by bassoon and violins. Several soft, expressive measures for the violins, followed by three loud chords, bring the symphony to its conclusion.

——— SCUOLA DI BALLO (SCHOOL OF DANCING), ballet suite for orchestra arranged from Boccherini's music by Jean Françaix. I. Leçon; Menuet. II. Larghetto; Rondo; Dispute. III. Presto; Pastorale; Danse allemande. IV. Scène du notaire; Finale.

The *Scuola di Ballo is* a ballet, book and choreography by Léonide Massine. It was introduced in Monte Carlo by the Ballet Russe in 1933. Its score, the work of the twentieth-century French composer, Jean Françaix, is derived from material lifted from rarely heard Boccherini compositions—several quintets and the Sinfonia No. 2 in B-flat. The wealth of treasurable melodies that unexplored regions of Boccherini can yield is proved by his ballet score. It is a veritable cornucopia of delightful tunes. As for the ballet, the scenario concerns itself with the efforts of a dancing master to palm off on an impresario one of his backward, instead of star, pupils. An unidentified program annotator points out some of the salient features of the score: "An occasional stern note in the 'Leçon' and strong chords in the 'Menuet' suggest the teacher. The violin and bassoon play a duet which very clearly pictures the inept pupil. Further atmosphere is furnished by a guitar-like accompaniment heard on the harp from time to time. One is soon acquainted with the characters who appear in the various sections. The Larghetto closely resembles a movement in one of Haydn's symphonies, which suggests a tempting line of speculation."

GIOVANNI BATTISTA VIOTTI 1755–1824

Though Viotti is today generally represented on concert programs by a single work—the melodious A minor Violin Concerto No. 22—he produced a good deal of other fine instrumental music. In a productive lifetime, he completed twenty-eight other violin concertos, and a considerable amount of chamber music. As a composer for the violin, he was a significant representative of the eighteenth-century school of violin performance and composition founded by Corelli and developed by Tartini. Viotti had the gift of song, workmanship of a high order, and rich orchestral and harmonic resources not usually found in eighteenth-century violin music.

Viotti's chamber music is for the most part terra incognita. Yet two string quartets which the Society of Forgotten Music resurrected and recorded reveal a rich invention, and a chamber-music style of great refinement and charm. Vernon Duke considers them worthy of a place "in the very first rank of eighteenth-century chamber music."

Giovanni Battista Viotti was born in Fontanetto da Po, Italy, on May 12, 1755. After studying the violin with Pugnani, Viotti embarked on a successful virtuoso career that brought him all over Europe. In 1788, he was appointed court musician to Marie Antoinette, and in 1788, he was made co-manager of the Théâtre de Monsieur in Paris, where he was responsible for outstanding opera performances. He left Paris in 1792, came to London and for several years was a violin soloist at the Salomon concerts and conductor of Italian operas. Involved in political intrigue, he was compelled to leave England in 1798, but in 1801, was permitted to return. After a disastrous adventure in the wine business, Viotti returned to Paris. From 1819 to 1822, he was director of Italian Opera in that city. He paid his last visit to London in 1822. By that time, his health and his fame were on the downgrade. He died in London on March 3, 1824.

c. 1795. CONCERTO NO. 22 IN A MINOR, for violin and orchestra. I. Moderato. II. Adagio. III. Agitato assai.

One can see why this violin concerto has survived: its lyricism is elegant, its style aristocratic. Brahms regarded it with particular enthusiasm. "It is a splendid work," he said, "of remarkable fineness of invention. Everything is thought out and worked out in masterly fashion and with imaginative power."

The concerto opens with a brief orchestral introduction. Then the solo violin enters with a deeply moving melody. A brief transition leads into an equally appealing lyrical thought, once again in the solo instrument. The heart of the second movement is another melody of surpassing elegance and poetic feeling; and once again, it is presented by the solo instrument (after a ten-measure orchestral introduction). The finale, in rondo form, offers two lively ideas in the solo violin.

1818. STRING QUARTETS:

B-flat major. I. Larghetto; Tempo giusto. II. Andante. III. Menuetto: più tosto presto. IV. Allegretto.

G major. I. Larghetto; Allegro comodo. II. Menuetto; Comodo. III. Andantino. IV. Allegretto vivace.

These two string quartets appeared in a volume entitled *Trois Quatuors concertants,* issued in Paris in 1818. They were rescued from undeserved obscurity by the Society for Forgotten Music, which recorded them on SFM Records. In his program notes, Vernon Duke notes that the music in both quartets is "full of sparkling gaiety, vigor, and bright Italian sunshine." Mr. Duke adds: "In these two quartets (he wrote seven books of them!) Viotti displays a lighthearted songfulness, some of the rich tunes sounding as though they belonged in opera, and a preference for metric variety. . . . The Menuetto of the B-flat major Quartet is perhaps the most unusual and personal conception of the traditional dance form, with which Viotti's music has little in common. The oddly shifting accents and the constant suggestion of syncopation make this episode specially memorable."

LUDWIG VAN BEETHOVEN 1770–1827

Of few composers can it be said that through them, and them alone, the art of music became completely transformed. Beethoven is such a composer. He represented a break with all the old concepts of what music should be and with the methods by which these concepts should be realized. Beauty of sound, balance and symmetry of structure, attractive lyricism for its own sake, even the expression of deeply felt emotion—all this was no longer that toward which Beethoven directed his means. He not only had to speak that which was in his heart; he also had to give voice to the beliefs and ideals that governed his life. He was a son of the Enlightenment. The new ideas of freedom and the rights of man sweeping across Europe, with Voltaire and Rousseau as their leading voices, sound loud and clear in Beethoven's music. The world was aflame with the spirit of Revolution, its fires kindled in France. The "I"—the creative personality—was asserting itself more strongly than ever. "I *must* write," Beethoven said, "for what weighs on my heart, I *must* express." Everywhere in Europe, wherever genius spoke, such words were now being heard.

What Paul Bekker described as "the poetic idea" and "the spiritual and intellectual creed" governed Beethoven's musical thinking. Music had to be a reflection of his experiences and of his inner life—of his Titanic struggle with destiny; his religious adoration of Nature; his passionate love of freedom; his glorification of the human spirit; his apotheosis of Joy; his search for ultimate serenity of heart and mind. These and similar extra-musical concepts are "spiritualized and transcended," says Bekker, "and expressed upon a higher plane of abstraction through the power of music. Instrumental tone is used to reflect and interpret the occurrences of a world far removed from actuality, a world, however, which is an abstract representation of an actual region of the intellectual and emotional life, and is consequently subject to the motions and laws of prototypes." Bekker sums up the total of Beethoven's message as "freedom, artistic freedom, political freedom, personal freedom of will, of art, of faith, freedom of the individual in all aspects of life."

The tempests that raged within him and demanded release through music made him impatient with rules or traditions. The concepts he tried to put in musical dress were too vast to be confined within the circumscribed limits of classical structures or textbook regulations. The boundary lines of classicism had to give way to acquire new spaciousness and flexibility. New methods had to be devised in writing for voices and instruments. New progressions and modulations, unorthodox tonalities and harmonies had to be introduced to increase the expressiveness of music. As Beethoven himself once remarked bitterly, when told by a violinist he had difficulty in negotiating the technique in one of the *Rasoumovsky* Quartets: "Does he really suppose I think of his puling little fiddle when the spirit speaks to me and I compose something?"

The division of Beethoven's creative life into three epochs is a convenient one that still serves to point up and demarcate the master's evolution. The first period, roughly up to 1800, was that of apprenticeship, of comparative conformance to classical tradition. The influence of Haydn and Mozart are predominant. This is the period that Vincent d'Indy described as that of "imitation," even though time and again Beethoven's own personality restlessly began to assert itself. The second period is the one in which, as Beethoven explained, "I am making a fresh start." This is the period that covers his symphonies from the third through the eighth, the concertos, *Fidelio,* piano sonatas such as the *Waldstein* and the *Appassionata,* and quartets such as the *Rasoumovsky* trilogy. The poetic idea begins to dictate the character of the music. Beethoven's writing becomes "externalized," as Vincent d'Indy put it. In this music, we find a new orientation to the world around Beethoven, a reflection of the changes taking place, a conflict with society and the status quo, a necessity to communicate ideas and ideals, a seeking out of new techniques, idioms, forms. Then, beginning roughly with 1817, came the third and last period, which Vincent d'Indy described as "reflective." Alfred Frankenstein explains further: "The spirit of the music is remote from external conflict. It floats high in a mysterious realm of its own and it involves a series of unprecedented invention in the domain of musical structure. In contrast to the second period where he expands traditional form, the Beethoven of the final period creates totally new forms."

But in all three periods, Beethoven speaks a language "no one has spoken before," as Dannreuther wrote, "and treats of things no one has dreamed of before; yet it seems as though he were speaking of matters long familiar, in one's mother tongue; as though he touched upon emotions one had lived through in some former existence." Or, in the words of Paul Bekker, "in Beethoven a composer arose who completely understood the possibilities of the art and ruled its form with the absolute confidence of an infallible despot. He knew the secret forces of his spiritual kingdom. He worked with unremitting critical consideration, tireless experiment, a constantly increasing consciousness of his own enormous power. He was artist enough to enforce his will. . . . The might of his inspiration made light of the rules of etiquette. The last secrets of a soul, of an elemental stormy personality, are revealed without reserve. The impulse to self-revelation came from within, not from without. He made himself the subject of artistic exposition, choosing as his medium an art magically expressive of all thoughts and feelings of mankind—wordless instrumental music."

Ludwig van Beethoven was born in Bonn, Germany, on December 16, 1770. Though his childhood was spent in poverty under the despotic rule of a drunkard father who wanted to make him into another Mozart, the child Beethoven made remarkable progress in music. Under the sympathetic guidance of the court organist, Christian Gottlob Neefe, with whom he began to study in 1781, Beethoven developed into an outstanding musician. At fourteen, he became Neefe's assistant as court organist; at fifteen, he took over his teacher's job as cembalist at the Opera. Encouraged by Neefe, Beethoven visited Vienna in 1787, where he deeply impressed Mozart with his powers at improvisation. Upon his return home, Beethoven was employed at court, and gave private lessons. His gifts made a deep impression on some of Bonn's leading families, some of whom became his patrons; these included the Waldsteins and the Breunings. His powers were also remarked and praised by Haydn when that master passed through Bonn.

In November 1792, Beethoven made Vienna his permanent home. For a while, he tried studying with Haydn, but their temperaments, personalities, and outlook on music clashed violently. Later, Beethoven was a pupil of Albrechtsberger and Salieri. In March 1795, he made his first public appearance in Vienna, to be described by one critic as a "giant of pianoforte players." His Viennese debut as composer followed on April 20, 1800, with the première of his first symphony.

He had already made his mark as one of Vienna's leading musicians—both in the concert halls and in the palaces of nobility—when in 1801, he became aware for the first time that he was losing his hearing. This tragedy sent him into the deepest of despair, to which he gave voice in 1802 in a remarkable document called the Heiligenstadt Testament. He withdrew from the society of friends, and found refuge in his music, in which, as he said, he was now making "a fresh start." "I live only in my music," he wrote, "and I have scarcely begun one thing when I start another. . . . With whom need I fear to measure my strength?" One masterwork followed another—the mighty epics of his second creative period with which music was carried to the threshhold of Romanticism.

As he grew in creative power and self-assurance, and as he separated himself more and more from the world of sound, he became increasingly irritable, unreasonable in his demands on friends, given to rages and suspicions. A little incident would be enough for him to break a friendship of many years' standing. Yet many of his friends and wealthy patrons were remarkably tolerant to his moods and tempers, recognizing him as a giant, and ever ready to help him in every way they could.

Between 1812 and 1818, there came a lull in his titanic production. Then, as if he had renewed his strength, he entered upon a new and perhaps the most remarkable phase of his creativity, by opening up horizons completely new to music. He now completed the last quartets and piano sonatas, the Ninth Symphony, the *Missa solemnis*. But he was fulfilling himself as an artist and not as a man. He remained terribly lonely, not only because he was deaf, but also because he never found a woman willing to share his life. Through the years, he had loved many women, but usually those who were out of reach, either because they were too young or on too high a social plane. He suffered continually the pangs of unrequited love, a fact that was revealed with striking force in a letter found after his death in a secret drawer in his desk. It was addressed to his "immortal beloved" and proved a passionate, flaming, unrestrained outpouring, the expression of the deepest suffering because he never had a woman he could call his own. Whether this remarkable letter was addressed to any one woman—or, as is now generally believed, to all women in general—is not known.

Beethoven's last public appearance took place on May 7, 1824, at the première of his Ninth Symphony. In 1826, he contracted pneumonia, which soon developed into dropsy and jaundice. He signed his will on March 23, 1827, and received his last sacrament one day later. Death came on March 26 from cirrhosis of the liver, as an autopsy later revealed. His funeral took place on March 29. Thousands lined the streets to pay him final homage. Schubert was one of the torchbearers at the funeral, and the famous Austrian poet, Grillparzer, delivered the eulogy at the cemetery gate.

1792–1796. SEXTET IN E-FLAT MAJOR, for two clarinets, two bassoons, and two horns, op. 71. I. Adagio; Allegro. II. Adagio. III. Menuetto. IV. Allegretto.

OCTET IN E-FLAT MAJOR, for two oboes, two clarinets, two bassoons, and two horns, op. 103. I. Allegro. II. Andante. III. Menuetto. IV. Presto.

Beethoven did not regard his early Sextet (1796) too highly. He wrote: "[It] belongs to my earlier work and was, moreover, written in a single night—there is nothing more to be said but that it is the work of an author who has done at least a few things better." The Octet, which preceded it by four years, apparently appealed more to him, since he adapted it in 1796 into the String Quintet, op. 4. In either instance, both the Sextet and the Octet are more distinguished by Mozartian charm than by Beethovenian vigor and independence.

The Sextet opens with several slow measures before the presentation in the clarinet of the first main theme, which is as vivacious as a dance tune; the second theme comes in the bassoon. The entire movement is ebullient, but the movement that follows is thoroughly romantic throughout. The main theme of the minuet is a hunt-like subject for horns, to which other instruments give reply; in the trio, the clarinets are heard in a little canon. The finale, a rondo, opens with a march-like melody which, later on, alternates with several infectious melodic ideas.

Sam Morgenstern thus described the wind Octet: "In the first movement, the oboe spins out an utterly charming theme, the rhythm of which permeates, in one instrument or another, the entire movement. . . . The second theme in the bassoon finishes with a curt little bow from the clarinets." In the slow movement, a sensual melody for the oboe "might be an arioso out of an early Italian opera. When the bassoon repeats the theme, the operatic feeling is intensified. . . . The solo oboe carries on its bel canto in the second section of the movement in the minor key, accompanied in a guitar-like staccato by the second oboe. The bassoons answer in identical fahion. . . . In the last section of this three-part song form the entire ensemble joins to bring the movement to a lovely pianissimo close." The minuet, to Morgenstern, foreshadows not only the later Beethoven scherzo, but specifically the scherzo of the Ninth Symphony. Its trio consists of a charming dialogue between clarinets and horns. The finale is "witty, gay, and mischievous. . . . The instruments tumble over each other in sprightly runs, arpeggios, and syncopated chords."

1795–1798. CONCERTOS FOR PIANO AND ORCHESTRA:

No. 1, C major, op. 15. I. Allegro con brio. II. Largo. III. Allegro scherzando.

No. 2, B-flat major, op. 19. I. Allegro con brio. II. Adagio. III. Molto allegro.

Beethoven's so-called Second Piano Concerto preceded the one now designated as the First. The Second was completed in 1795 and was introduced at the Burgtheater in Vienna on March 20, 1795, with Beethoven himself as the soloist (his first public appearance in Vienna). The C major Concerto was finished in 1798 and introduced the same year in Prague, Beethoven once again serving as soloist. However, the B-flat major Concerto was revised by Beethoven in 1798 and published in 1801, a short time *after* the C major Concerto had been issued. Its later publication is the reason why the B-flat major is now numbered as Beethoven's second concerto.

Both concertos are Mozartian in their acceptance of classical structure and in the rococo grace of their thematic material. Yet John N. Burk takes pains to point out the stirrings of the later Beethoven in the C major Concerto: in the "characteristic rising scales" and "twists of modulation"; in the way in which the "incandescence is raised" and the "line broadened"; in the "freer" use of the orchestra, "as in the Largo, where the second strain (given to the orchestra and designed for it) finds an impassioned pulse"; in the "delightful irregularity of phrase, first set forth in a light staccato by the piano" in the first theme in the concluding rondo. In the orchestration, adds Burk, "the horns are used already with a special sense . . . and in the slow movement the clarinet stands out as it had not before. The orchestra is not yet liberated, but it is perceptibly finding itself."

The orchestral introduction to the first movement of the C major Concerto presents both principal themes along classic lines. The first is characterized by an octave leap; it is heard first in the strings, then repeated by full orchestra. The second is a descending melody stated quietly (and in the usual key of E-flat major). This orchestral preface ends with the first four notes of the first theme. The piano enters with a kind of improvisation before it elaborates upon the first theme; it turns its attention to the second theme, following its recall by the orchestra. The development features some more improvisations by the piano. Chords in the piano, imitated by the horns, leads into the recapitulation, which opens with a forceful statement of the opening theme. A cadenza precedes the concluding tutti.

In the second movement, a broad, stately melody is heard in the piano, and repeated by the orchestra. The concluding rondo offers for its main theme a lively subject for the piano. After an orchestral episode, and a brief piano passage, the second main thought is assigned to oboe and first violins, and then is taken over by the piano. Before long, still a third theme is offered—a staccato subject for the piano, accompanied by flute and bassoon.

The B-flat major Concerto, in Rosa Newmarch's description, opens "with a vigorous tutti presenting the first subject, several subordinate themes being touched upon before the solo instrument enters with a more elaborate statement of the leading subject. . . . An ascending passage in sixteenth-notes for the piano, and a passing reference to the opening figure of the movement, brings us to the announcement of the second subject by the first violins and bassoons in octaves." This material is fancifully elaborated upon in the development, the solo instrument engaging scale and virtuoso passages. After the piano has brought the first theme back, the orchestra pronounces the first part of this theme and the piano the second part to bring on the Recapitulation. The movement ends with a brief six-measure tutti.

In the second movement, the violins "give out the quiet and melancholy theme which is afterwards repeated by the piano with some embellishments, and a gracefully tributary theme is added. . . . A chain of trills for the piano leads to a restatement of the subject by the orchestra. The free passages for the soloist at the close of the movement . . . will be noticed, after which a short tutti brings the movement to a pianissimo close."

The finale is a rondo in which a forceful theme is heard at once in the piano; the idea is then repeated by the orchestra. The second subject is given by the piano in chords. "Later on some bravura work leads to a return of the first subject, which is treated first by the soloist and subsequently by the orchestra. A short tutti conducts us to the third theme of the rondo, a syncopated subject, given to the piano with accompaniment for strings."

1795–1825. COMPOSITIONS FOR SOLO PIANO:

6 Minuets, op. 167; 6 Écossaises in E-flat major; *Fuer Elise,* bagatelle in A minor, op. 173; *Rondo a capriccio* in G major, op. 129

One of the most famous minuets ever written is found in a set of six that

Beethoven wrote early in his career, in 1795. It is in the key of G major, and is the second in the group.

The "Écossaise" is a dance in 2/4 or 4/4 time, believed to be of Scottish origin. It retains its Scottish identity in its transformation for the piano. Beethoven wrote seven such Écossaises, all of them in the key of E-flat major; they came between 1823 and 1825. An eighth Écossaise, in G major, is of an unknown date.

Beethoven was the first composer to give significance to the piano form of the "bagatelle." He wrote twenty-seven such pieces. As its name implies, the bagatelle is a musical trifle, unpretentious in purpose, simple in technique. The most celebrated (particularly to young piano students) is that in A minor, written in 1810 and named *Fuer Elise*. It has been suggested by some Beethoven scholars that this item was really dedicated to Therese and not Elise—Therese being Malfatti, with whom Beethoven was then in love and for whom he wrote this music bearing in mind her limitations as a performer. These scholars also suggest that some inept copyist was responsible for changing the name on the title page.

The *Rondo a capriccio* in G major (1823) is a curiosity because of an enigmatic inscription placed at the head of the composition: "Anger at the loss of a penny, vented in caprice." The agitated measures of this music, rich in mockery, can readily evoke the image of the master going into a fury at the loss of a penny—then suddenly made to realize the absurdity of losing his temper over such a trifle.

1796–1816. SONGS, for voice and piano:

"Adelaide," op. 46; "In Questa tomba oscura."

An die ferne Geliebte, song cycle: 1. Auf dem Huegel sitz ich. 2. Wo die Berge so blau. 3. Leichte Segler. 4. Dieses Wolken in den Hoehen. 5. Es kehret der Maien. 6. Nimm sie hin denn, diese Lieder.

Beethoven is not generally considered when the song comes up for discussion. Yet he was an influential song composer. It is false to assume that Beethoven regarded the song form as a stepchild. The mere fact that he wrote eighty Lieder, and over a hundred other kinds of songs (including adaptations of Irish, Welsh, and Scottish airs) emphasizes his interest in this medium. Nor is it correct to say that his writing for the voice is awkward. This may be true at times in such monumental works as the Ninth Symphony or the *Missa solemnis,* where he is driven to make the voice suggest visions beyond music's boundaries. But when he wrote songs, he was always conscious of the limitations and potentials of the voice, and catered to them.

Two of his most popular single songs, "Adelaide" (1796) and "In questa tomba oscura" (1807), are operatic in style and design. Both are far more expansive in structure than most art songs, being conceived in terms of an aria or arietta. "Adelaide," text by Matthison which the poet described as "a lyrical fantasia," is ten pages in length, with six large divisions. Though coming early in Beethoven's career, this song has much that is original, both in the construction of the melody and in the piano accompaniment. James Husst Hall remarks the magical variety with which Beethoven treats musically the recurrence of the name of the beloved; he also sees the Allegro molto section as similar to an extended coda in one of Beethoven's sonatas. "The brusque change of meter, the answerings of voice and piano, the relentless drive toward the climax, and the whispered cadence—all were prompted by the lyric and dramatic suggestions of the text which Beethoven so spaciously interpreted."

"In questa tomba oscura"—text by G. Carpani—is of a character completely different from that of "Adelaide." It is moody, atmospheric, at times lugubrious, where "Adelaide" is lyrical and warm. In the poem, a tortured soul yearns for the tranquillity of death, and entreats a faithless beloved not to disturb his eternal rest with her tears. The opening is somber; the middle part, dramatic and emotionally agitated; and the closing, funeral.

Beethoven's foremost achievement within the song form is the cycle, *An die ferne Geliebte,* or *To the Distant Beloved,* text by A. Jeitteles (1816). It is here that Beethoven, like his contemporary Schubert, becomes a significant creator of the Lied. This is the first significant cycle in song history. In his attempt to create a unity out of the six separate parts, Beethoven repeats the melody of the opening song toward the end of the cycle. Noteworthy, too, is the prominence of the piano, especially in joining one verse to the next, and in the expressiveness of the harmony. There is much here that looks into the future. Philip Radcliffe has noted that the unusual modulations between the first and second, and the second and third songs foreshadow Beethoven's last period; that the opening of the sixth song anticipates Mendelssohn and Schumann.

In the first song, the poet atop a mountain looks down into the valley where his beloved lives. In the second, he speaks of his passionate desire to be with her. In the third and fourth, he calls upon the clouds, the brook, the breezes to carry to her his tender message. In the fifth, he contrasts the joy of birds to his own pain in being separated from the woman he loves. In the last, the poet humbly submits his verses to his beloved.

1796. AH, PERFIDO!, scena and aria for soprano and orchestra, op. 65.

It is now believed that Beethoven wrote this concert scena and aria for Countess Clari, a musical amateur to whom the work is dedicated. Its first performance was given by Mme. Josephine Duschek, a distinguished singer, in Leipzig on November 21, 1796. The work is a miniature drama, beginning with a recitative filled with emotion and electric in feeling ("Ah, unfaithful deceiver! Cruel traitor! Dost thou leave me now?"). The aria that follows is a poignant outpouring of tender grief. ("Say not the words of farewell, I implore thee. How shall I live without thee?"). It is not known who is the author of the text.

1798. SONATAS FOR PIANO:

D major, op. 10, no. 3. I. Presto. II. Largo e mesto. III. Allegro. IV. Presto.

C minor, "Pathétique," op. 13. I. Grave; Allegro molto e con brio. II. Adagio cantabile. III. Allegro.

Beethoven's first piano sonatas were written in 1795. Three works (F minor, A major, C major) were assembled then in opus 2 and dedicated to Haydn. This dedication is possibly not only a gesture of homage to master but also a confession of creative indebtedness. All three sonatas are basically Haydnesque in structure and style—though the slow movement of the A major Sonata, marked Largo appassionato suggests the later Beethoven in the intensity of its speech.

One year later, Beethoven produced his fourth piano sonata—in E-flat, op. 7, designated by the composer as "grand." Here the increased brilliance of the fast movements, the growing expansivness of the developments, and the brooding melancholy of the slow movement (Largo con gran espressione) carry Beethoven further toward self-fulfillment within the piano-sonata medium.

That fulfillment becomes realized for the first time in two sonatas completed in 1798. In the D major—Beethoven's seventh—the Largo e mesto movement (Beethoven's first slow movement in the minor key) is filled with the anguish that comes from profound inner probing. "The whole of Beethoven is already there," wrote Romain Rolland. "What maturity of soul! If not so precocious as Mozart in the art of smooth harmonious speech, how much more precocious he was in his interior life, in knowledge and mastery of himself, of his passions, and his dream!" This, to Rolland, is a "sovereign meditation" in which "the full grandeur of Beethoven's soul is for the first time revealed."

The subdued tragedy of such a slow movement becomes passionate, at times even agonized in the "grand" Sonata in C minor, which Beethoven himself dubbed as the *Pathétique*. The anguish of the opening C minor introduction, with its chromatic shifting chords, prefaces a frenetic Allegro movement in which a Herculean struggle seems to take place. Again and again, the lugubrious opening voices torment—first, as a preface to the development; then again, just before the coda. But the tragedy makes way for an almost religious serenity in the slow movement. And the finale tries to banish sorrow with its rhythmic impetuosity, but not without introducing moments of reflection, as in the gentle passage that precedes the concluding outburst of uncontrolled rebellion.

1800. 6 STRING QUARTETS, "LOBKOWITZ," op. 18:

No. 1, F major. I. Allegro con brio. II. Adagio affetuoso ed appassionato. III. Allegro molto. IV. Allegro.

No. 2, G major. I. Allegro. II. Adagio cantabile; Allegro. III. Allegro.

IV. Allegro molto quasi presto.

No. 3, D major. I. Allegro. II. Andante con moto. III. Allegro. IV. Presto.

No. 4, C minor. I. Allegro ma non tanto. II. Andante scherzoso quasi allegretto. III. Allegretto. IV. Allegro.

No. 5, A major. I. Allegro. II. Menuetto. III. Andante cantabile. IV. Allegro.

No. 6, B-flat major. I. Allegro con brio. II. Adagio ma non troppo. III. Allegro. IV. La Malinconia: adagio; Allegretto quasi allegro.

All the string quartets Beethoven produced in his first creative period are tied up in a single package—in opus 18, dedicated to Prince Lobkowitz. Though thoroughly grounded in the classical soil of Haydn and Mozart, these six quartets continually betray new attitudes, techniques and nuances of expression. Beethoven's later strength and independence reveal themselves again and again: in his impatience with a confining classical structure; in his gift for taking a generating motive and building it up into a huge design; in the frequent brusqueness of his speech. However, for the time being, innovation and experiment are generally subservient to the exuberance and tranquil grace that belong to an old order.

One of the unusual features of the first of these six quartets is the way in which, in the first movement, a simple two-bar motive is subjected to extensive elaboration. Marliave has pointed out that this motive appears over a hundred times in the movement, passing from instrument to instrument, changing its personality all the time. A subsidiary subject, a tripping figure divided among the four strings, provides contrast. It is believed that the second movement was inspired by the tomb scene is Shakespeare's *Romeo and Juliet*. Donald Francis Tovey speaks of this music as one of "the great early tragic slow movements." In the Scherzo, the trio section is particularly notable, its main theme in staccato octaves and drone bass. Beethovenian impetuosity characterizes the finale.

The courtly grace of the opening theme of the second quartet is responsible for giving the entire work the name of *The Compliments*. But there is no suggestion of old-world refinements in the succeeding two subjects that make up the movement, the second a soft staccato passage in D major, and the other a spirited theme opening in B minor and ending in D major. What is most unusual about the slow movement is that, while it begins and ends with a stately melody, its middle part is an electrifying Allegro.

The third string quartet is believed to have been the first to get written —probably the reason why it adhered most closely to the past procedures and styles of Haydn and Mozart. A certain amount of individuality can be detected in the closing measures of the second movement, and in the uninhibited vigor of the concluding presto.

The fourth quartet is the only one in the set in a minor mode. The opening theme of the first movement breaks with precedence through its passionate intensity. The second subject is derived from the fifth and sixth measures of the first. Another unexpected structural feature of this work is the fact that it has no slow movement, utilizing both a minuet and a scherzo.

What stands out particularly in the fifth quartet is its third movement. This is a set of variations on a delightfully simple theme, which Tovey described as "exquisite." He adds: "The ostentatious naïveté of the tonic and dominant bass is in keeping with the wit of the melody, which goes down and up a hexachord with a nursery rhyme kind of wit. Meanwhile, the viola has its own opinions, which it tells sleepily, like the tale of the Dormouse in the Hatter's tea party in *Alice in Wonderland*."

The sixth quartet has one of the most tragic pages found in the entire set—a brief slow introduction to the finale entitled by Beethoven "Melancholy." He insisted that it be played "with the greatest of delicacy." Many writers refer to this passage as the real beginnings of Romanticism in music. But the fast movement that follows rejects sorrow to embark on a convivial mood. The first movement, with its light-footed first subject in the first violin, has grace, while the second subject has lightness of heart. The Scherzo is energized by its effective syncopations.

1800. SEPTET IN E-FLAT MAJOR, for violin, viola, horn, clarinet, bassoon, cello, and double bass, op. 20. I. Adagio; Allegro con brio. II. Adagio cantabile. III. Tempo di menuetto. IV. Tema con variazioni. V. Allegro molto e vivace. VI. Adante con moto; Presto.

One can well understand Beethoven's impatience with the popularity of his Septet. While coming as late as 1800, it is decidedly early Beethoven in its emphasis on pleasing lyricism and its lack of deeper emotional or dramatic values. It is almost consistently sunny in mood, except for the dark-hued Andante con moto that precedes the concluding Presto. In the second movement, each of the wind instruments has a solo, while the trio of the fifth-movement Scherzo boasts a delightful solo for the viola. The melodic attractions of the fourth movement, a theme and variations, and the contrasts of tonality in the finale are also of interest.

1800. CONCERTO NO. 3 IN C MINOR, for piano and orchestra, op. 37. I. Allegro con brio. II. Largo. III. Allegro.

Though completed in 1800, this concerto was not introduced until April 5, 1803, when the composer performed it at the Theater-an-der-Wien. Neither audience nor critics responded favorably. Perhaps a good deal of their disappointment came from the fact that they expected a formal and classical work in the style of the composer's two earlier concertos. But the Third Concerto was beginning to veer sharply toward new directions. It brought a new independence of thought and motion to the solo instrument; it extended the symphonic breadth of the orchestra; it introduced striking enharmonic passages for the piano.

The robust first theme of the first movement, in unison strings, is Beethovenian in its fire and energy. Fifty measures later, the first violins and clarinets offer the second subject, which has an expressive lyric character. The orchestral preface concludes with a brief codetta, based on the first theme. With three C minor scale passages in the piano and a forceful reminder of the first theme, the second subject recurs in the piano for eight measures, after which it is taken over by the orchestra. The orchestra then embarks on an episode that leads into the development where much is made of the first four measures of the opening theme. With a vigorous statement by the orchestra, followed ten measures later by the piano, the recapitulation is introduced. A brief orchestral tutti based on the first theme, and a piano cadenza, bring on the concluding coda.

The slow movement (scored in the exclusively orchestral parts only for flutes, bassoons, horns, and strings) is primarily concerned with an aristocratic song, heard first in the piano, and after that in muted strings. Following a cadenza, a serene coda based on this melody brings the movement to its conclusion.

The piano enters with a lively principal subject to open the rondo. When the orchestra repeats it, the piano accompanies it with broken chords. After an orchestral tutti, the piano introduces the second subject, in the key of E-flat major. Some passage work now brings on a repetition of the first vivacious theme, after which it is treated in imitation. A return in the piano of the second subject in the key of C major and a cadenza provide a vigorous conclusion.

1800. OVERTURE TO DIE GESCHOEPFE DES PROMETHEUS (THE CREATURES OF PROMETHEUS), op. 43.

Beethoven's first dramatic work was music for a ballet commissioned by Salvatore Vigno (celebrated dancer and choreographer) to honor Empress Maria Theresa. Beethoven's score comprises sixteen numbers. About all that remains fresh in the repertory are the overture; a Contredanse in the concluding Allegretto (its melody in E-flat subsequently used by the composer in the finale of the *Eroica* Symphony); and a shepherd's dance designated as a Pastorale (Allegro). The ballet itself was allegorical, based on the legend of Prometheus.

Despite the seriousness of the subject, Beethoven's overture is comparatively light in style and mood. Several strong chords bring on a thoughtful sixteen-measure strain. Once this introduction (Adagio) is disposed of, levity prevails, beginning with a vivacious tune in the strings, staccato and pianissimo (Allegro molto con brio). This is followed by a gentle syncopated subject for flutes and oboes that receives contrapuntal treatment. The overture ends with a lively coda.

1800–1802. SYMPHONY NO. 1 IN C MAJOR, op. 21. I. Adagio molto; Allegro con brio. II. Andante cantabile con molto. III. Allegro molto e vivace. IV. Adagio; Allegro molto e vivace.

SYMPHONY NO. 2 IN D MAJOR, op. 36. I. Adagio molto; Allegro con brio. II. Larghetto. III. Allegro. IV. Allegro molto.

Undertaking his first symphony, Beethoven already was a composer in full command of his technique and one restless to explore new areas of self-expression. The iconcolast was beginning to break down the obstructions in the way of his emancipation. The very opening of the first symphony (1800) represented a new world. It begins seemingly in the key of F, then passes on to the key of G, before finally coming to its C major tonality. This unorthodox harmonic procedure provoked a howl of protest from Beethoven's critics. The way in which he used the brass instruments and timpani in his orchestration also came in for severe criticism. Some said that the work sounded as if it had been written for a brass band; others called Beethoven a musical ignoramus, a "poorly tutored student."

Yet for all these unorthodoxies, which led one of Beethoven's critics to describe the symphony as "a caricature of Haydn pushed to absurdity," the work represents Beethoven still clinging to the coattails of Haydn. A twelve-measure introduction, with its ambiguous tonality, precedes the main Allegro section, which opens with a vigorous C major theme in the strings. A transitional passage leads into the gentle second subject, shared by oboe and flute. In the development, the first two measures of the first subject are discussed. Like the recapitulation that follows, it proceeds along conventional lines. The movement ends with an extended coda.

A mobile melody (reminiscent of Mozart) opens the slow movement. The second violins present it softly; cellos and violas, and later on basses and first violins, enter in imitation. The equally placid second subject is in the key of C major. It begins in the strings and is then carried on by the woodwind and second violins over a contrapuntal background by the first violins.

Already the minuet movement has a scherzo-like quality, particularly in the robustness of its sharply accented and syncopated opening theme in first violins. The trio features a dialogue between strings and wind. In the slow introduction to the finale, the violins are heard in an ascending subject, which, like the steps of a ladder, comes to rest at the top rung to provide access to the first main theme—a vivacious tune for strings. The wind provide a transition to the graceful second subject in the violins. Only the first theme is discussed in the development. The recapitulation opens with a forceful presentation of the main melody in full orchestra, while the second subject is then given a more subdued treatment in the woodwind. The symphony ends with a coda, in which the first theme is further developed.

The Second Symphony came two years later. It cannot be said that the critics were any more favorably disposed to Beethoven's second venture into symphonic writing. The unprepared modulations and the sudden alternation of dynamics were regarded as quixotic. A Leipzig critic described the work as "a repulsive monster, a wounded tail-lashing serpent, dealing wild and furious blows as it stiffens into its death agony at the end."

Though written at a time when Beethoven first realized he was going deaf, the Symphony gives few clues of the composer's torment. It is mostly music with a sunny disposition, elegant in classical design, and generally serene in mood. Yet it represented an important advance over the First Symphony; even more than the First Symphony had done, it pointed up the fact that Beethoven was breaking loose from tradition.

The Symphony opens with a thirty-three measure slow introduction of extraordinary eloquence. Then comes the spirited Allegro con brio, which opens with a moody thought in cellos and basses that gains vigor and brightens in color as it passes on to the higher instruments. The second theme brightens this picture further. The woodwind introduce the development section. Here the main theme is treated vigorously, often in imitative passages in woodwind and strings. In the recapitulation, the material returns considerably changed in structure and orchestration. The coda devotes itself to the main theme.

The slow movement is a wonderfully serene two-part song with religious overtones. It is first heard in the strings, then in the wind. With the third movement, Beethoven dispenses with the minuet and exchanges it for the more vigorous Scherzo. The main theme is built from a three-note motive that is repeated continually by different sections of the orchestra. The melody of the trio resembles a country dance. It is heard in oboe and bassoons, which play it twice. The joyful outburst of the first theme of the finale, in the violins, established the mood of the entire movement. It is continually alive with contrasts of dynamics and an irresistible rhythmic drive.

1801. SONATAS FOR PIANO:

A-flat major, op. 26. I. Tema con variazioni: andante. II. Allegro molto. III. Marcia funèbre sulla morte d'un eroe. IV. Allegro.

C-sharp minor, "Moonlight," op. 27, no. 2. I. Adagio sostenuto. II. Allegretto. III. Presto agitato.

D major, "Pastoral," op. 28. I. Allegro. II. Andante. III. Allegro vivace. IV. Allegro ma non troppo.

In 1803, Beethoven would include a funeral march for the first time in a symphony. Five years after that, in still another of his symphonies, he would speak his great love of Nature. He anticipated both such developments in his piano sonatas. The A-flat major Sonata has for its third movement a somber funeral march (the first time a thing like this happened in such a work). The death music, with the slow and solemn tread of its first part, and simulations of drum rolls and cannon shots in the second, has been transcribed for orchestra and for brass band.

The D major Sonata is so alive with the rapture of Nature in its first and last movements that the publisher Cranz gave it the sobriquet of *Pastoral,* which has stuck. But the listener would be hard put to find anything bucolic or pastoral in the grave accents of the Andante, or in the frivolity of the Scherzo, with its waltz-like main theme.

In between the A-flat major Sonata with its funeral march, and the D major Sonata with its pastoral movements, stands what is probably Beethoven's most popular piano sonata—the so-called *Moonlight* Sonata. The name "Moonlight" was conceived by a German critic, Ludwig Rellstab, who interpreted the tranquil music of the first movement as moonlight playing on the waters of Lake Lucerne. By virtue of its romantic name, a number of legends have arisen about the writing of the *Moonlight* Sonata—all of them equally absurd. Beethoven himself, designated his sonata as "quasi una fantasia." This is because the classic structure of the sonata has been side-stepped. In place of the usual sonata-form first movement, we get an unconventional slow movement. Besides, the thematic material in this sonata is frequently elaborated upon in the free manner of a fantasia. The poetic main melody of the first movement—come without preliminaries over triplets in the bass—was probably the composer's expression of love for the Countess Giulietta Guicciardi, to whom the work is dedicated. Beethoven insisted that this melody be played "throughout with the greatest of delicacy." The Allegretto and finale that follow without a break pass from a scherzo-like delicacy of the second movement to the emotional storms of the finale. The coda of this finale is one of the composer's most passionate utterances for the piano.

1801–1802. 12 CONTRETAENZE (CONTREDANSES), op. 141.: I. C major. II. A major. III. D major. IV. B-flat major. V. E-flat major. VI. C major. VII. E-flat major. VIII. C major. IX. A major. X. C major. XI. G major. XII. E-flat major.

Like Haydn and Mozart before him, Beethoven was not above writing light, tuneful dance music. This lighter repertory consists of minuets, Laendler, contredanses, German dances, and waltzes. Characteristic of these excursions into trivia, are the dozen *Contredanses* produced between 1801 and 1802. As this writer explained in *Lighter Classics of Music,* these are not 'country dances' as the "Contretanz," or "Contredanse," is sometimes erroneously translated. The Contredanse is the predecessor of the waltz. Like the waltz, it is in three sections, the third repeating the first, while the middle part is usually a contrasting trio. . . . This is earthy music, overflowing with melodies of folk-song vigor and vitalized by infectious peasant rhythms." One of the most celebrated of these dances is the seventh, in E-flat major, because Beethoven used this same melody in the finale of his *Eroica* Symphony and in his score for the ballet *Prometheus*.

In the same lively, unpretentious, and earthy style are the delightful German Dances (Deutsche Taenze), a set of twelve completed in 1795. "The form, style, and spirit of the German Dance," this writer has explained, "are so similar to the Contredanse that many Austrian and German composers used the terms interchangeably."

1801–1803. SONATAS FOR VIOLIN AND PIANO:

F major, "Spring," op. 24. I. Allegro. II. Adagio molto espressivo. III. Allegro molto. IV. Allegro ma non troppo.

A major, op. 30, no. 1. I. Allegro. II. Adagio. III. Allegretto con variazioni.

C minor, op. 30, no. 2. I. Allegro con brio. II. Adagio cantabile. III. Allegro. IV. Allegro.

G major, op. 30, no. 3. I. Allegro assai. II. Tempo di menuetto. III. Allegro vivace.

A major, "Kreutzer," op. 47. I. Adagio sostenuto; Presto. II. Andante con variazioni. III. Presto.

Some of Beethoven's violin sonatas were described on publication as works "for piano with the accompaniment of the violin." This apparently carries on the eighteenth-century tradition of relegating the violin to a secondary role in duo sonatas, which to a large degree governed even Mozart in his earlier works for this medium. But one would be hard put to find in Beethoven sonatas—at least in those beginning with the fifth, in F major—any attempt to assign to either of the two instruments a subsidiary role in the musical scheme. Here the two instruments are equal partners; here each is an individualist in his own right. Paul Bekker is of the opinion that Beethoven wrote most of his violin sonatas, not from inner compulsion, but to cater to the performing needs of specific virtuosos. Says Bekker: "The necessity to balance imaginative and structural elements, giving full value to the character of each instrument and allowing a display of virtuosity from each performer, demanded from the first a spirit of compromise which made high poetic flights impossible." To Bekker, these sonatas "are examples of the concert piece, aiming principally at brilliant outward effect."

Yet there are many pages in Beethoven's best violin sonatas that bear the stamp of the master. The ebullient spirit projected so consistently in the F major Sonata (1801) has earned it the name of *Spring*. The first movement is sunny throughout, with frequent suggestions of humor. The slow movement is a simple cantilena-like theme which, Vincent d'Indy maintains, might have come out of a Mozart opera. A gay staccato tune is the main idea in the third-movement Scherzo, while the final rondo is an outpouring of irrepressible good spirits.

Of the three violin sonatas grouped as opus 30 (1802), the first, in A major, is perhaps the least attractive, though the lyricism of the Adagio is undoubtedly most appealing. Much more consistently interesting is the second Sonata, in C minor. As so often happens with Beethoven's compositions in that key, violent struggle predominates in the first movement: in the militant first theme with its agitated accompaniment; again in the staccato second subject in E-flat major. The storm subsides in the next two movements. The second is a gentle song shared by the two instruments, and the third has a remarkable placidity for a scherzo movement—a placidity that remains undisturbed in the canonic trio. The drama of the first movement returns in the finale. It opens with ominous staccato figures and brooding chords. The turmoil reaches a climax with a tempestuous concluding presto.

No less vigorous and forthright is the opening theme of the Sonata in G major, heard in both instruments. Transitional material leads into the second subject, which is built out of three chords in the piano and a descending theme in the violin. Additional melodic ideas, most of them lighthearted, follow, but a good deal of attention is paid to the opening measure, which recurs in varied alterations. It is the exposition that dominates this movement, the development lasting only twenty-five measures, and the recapitulation greatly condensed. For his second movement, Beethoven makes a curious compromise between the sedateness of a minuet and the expressiveness of a slow movement. The first theme is given to the piano, and repeated by the violin. Two elementary melodic thoughts appear in the trio, their basic rhythm derived from the opening bar of the minuet melody. The finale, in rondo form, is mainly spirited, with many brilliant passages for the violin.

Beethoven's Sonata in A major (1803) is his most celebrated. It is known as the *Kreutzer* because it was dedicated to the famous violinist, Rudolph Kreutzer. However, Kreutzer refused to perform it, finding it "outrageously unintelligible"; and the première presentation went to a young mulatto violinist named Bridgetower, who was accompanied by Beethoven. The sonata is the only one to which Beethoven appended an introductory slow section to the first movement. The calm thus projected is completely shattered in the ensuing Presto. This is high-tensioned music, which grows in turbulence as the movement progresses. This movement, and the the finale, have such a dramatic character that they inspired Tolstoy to conceive his celebrated story of passion and jealousy, *The Kreutzer Sonata* (also adapted for the stage). The middle movement provides a point of repose with a graceful melody and its forthright variations.

1802. SONATA IN D MINOR, for piano, op. 31, no. 2. I. Largo; Allegro. II. Adagio. III. Allegretto.

The theatrical and tempestuous personality of this sonata places it squarely in Beethoven's "Sturm und Drang" second period. When Beethoven's friend and first biographer, Schindler, asked the composer for the meaning of this music he was told, "read Shakespeare's *Tempest.*" It may well have been that Beethoven was misguided by the title of Shakespeare's play to believe that it was a stormy and passionate drama—for there is very little in Beethoven's music that has any kinship to spirits or Ariel. The opening Largo, of the first movement, is only a measure and a quarter in length. It is the peace before the storm, a storm that erupts vehemently in the Allegro. Peace permeates the second movement, which is in binary form, and whose main melody is built from a three-note figure. The agitation of the first movement, however, returns in the finale, with its exciting successions of triplets and sextuplets. The four-note figure, from which the main theme of the finale is evolved, has been said to have been suggested by the rhythm of a horse's canter.

1802. CHRISTUS AM OELBERGE (CHRIST ON THE MOUNT OF OLIVES), oratorio for solo voices, chorus, and orchestra, op. 85.

Having made a successful invasion of the stage with the ballet, *The Creatures of Prometheus* (which see), Beethoven was ready to embark upon his first dramatic vocal composition. *Christ on the Mount of Olives* is Beethoven's only attempt at writing an oratorio. The text by Franz Xaver Huber was prepared for the composer in two weeks' time, with Beethoven's assistance. It did not please Beethoven at all. When the score was published in 1811, he wrote to his publishers: "Here and there the text must remain as in the original. I know that the text is extremely bad, but after one has conceived a unit out of even a bad text, it is difficult to avoid spoiling it by individual changes. . . . And he is a bad composer who does not know how to try to make the best possible things out of a bad text." As for the score, Beethoven worked on it virtually up to performance time, which took place at the Theater-an-der-Wien on April 5, 1803.

The three solo voices (soprano, tenor, and bass) portray the Seraph, Jesus, and Peter. The text carries Jesus from the agony in the garden and the time He learns about His fate from the Seraph, to the moment when he gives himself up uncomplainingly to the soldiers.

The following commentary was prepared by Felix Borowski: "The score opens with an Adagio introduction for instruments which is of very dramatic character. The first number is a recitative and aria for tenor, sung by Jesus ('All My Soul Within Me Shudders'), and is simple and touching in expression. The Seraph follows with a scene and aria ('Praise the Redeemer's Goodness'), concluding with a jubilant obbligato with chorus ('O Triumph, all Ye Ransomed!'). The next number is an elaborate duet between Jesus and Seraph ('On Me then Fall Thy Heavy Judgment'). In a short recitative passage, Jesus welcomes death; and then ensues one of the most powerful numbers in the work, the chorus of soldiers in march time ('We Surely Here Shall Find Him'), interspersed with the cries of the people demanding His death, and the lamentation of the Apostles. At the conclusion of the tumult a dialogue ensues between Jesus and Peter ('Not Unchastized Shall this Audacious Band'), which leads up to a trio between Jesus, Peter, and the Seraph, with chorus ('O Sons of Men with Gladness'). The closing number, a chorus of angels ('Hallelujah, God's Almighty Son') is introduced with a short but massive symphony leading to a jubilant burst of 'Hallelujah,' which finally resolves itself into a glorious fugue. In all choral music it is difficult to find a choral number which can surpass it in majesty or power."

1802–1803. 2 ROMANCES, for violin and orchestra:
No. 1, G major, op. 40; No. 2, F major, op. 50.

Beethoven's two *Romances* for violin and orchestra—the G major written in 1803, and the F major in 1802—are instrumental songs in a lyrical, romantic style. They follow a single pattern. Each is set into motion by the solo violin appearing with the main melody: in the G major, the violin is heard as a solo;

in the F major, it is accompanied by the orchestra. Each then progresses along its melodic course, with occasional digression into figurations; in each the violin and orchestra finally engage in a quiet exchange. Each is in a slow tempo, each in a single movement. Beethoven gave no indication of the tempo for the G major Romance, but the F major is marked Adagio cantabile.

1804. PIANO SONATAS:

C major, "Waldstein," op. 53. I. Allegro con brio. II. Adagio molto. III. Allegretto moderato.

F major, op. 54. I. In tempo d'un menuetto. II. Allegretto.

F minor, "Appassionata," op. 57. I. Allegro assai. II. Andante con moto. III. Allegro ma non troppo.

The *Waldstein* and *Appassionata* Sonatas are the twin peaks in the piano-sonata literature of Beethoven's middle period. Both are mighty dramas in which Herculean conflicts alternate with contemplative moods. The *Waldstein* (so-called because it was dedicated to Count Waldstein) opens tempestuously. The music is then driven by a demoniac force until a resting point arrives with a hymn-like melody. Originally, Beethoven wrote an involved and ornamented slow movement for this sonata. But he soon felt it was completely out of character with the epic stature of the work and published it separately as *Andante Favori* in F major, op. 170. In its place, Beethoven wrote a three-part song that pierces the deepest recesses of the heart. This serves as the eloquent preface to the "jubilant radiance," as John N. Burk described it, of the concluding rondo, "which gleams forth with such complete enchantment. The pianissimo movement is the most exciting of an exciting sonata."

The two-movement F major Sonata is a lyric poem. The first movement is in the style of a minuet; here staccato octaves and sixths in contrary motion replace the trio usually found in minuets. The second and final movement have the breathless character of a perpetual motion.

The *Appassionata*—a name affixed to the F minor Sonata by the publisher Cranz—was once described by Lenz as a "volcanic eruption which rends the earth and shuts out the sky with a shower of projectiles." To Romain Rolland this is the most characteristic of all Beethoven piano sonatas—the sonata that evokes the image of the composer "with the massive jaws firmly set, the upturned eyes, the visage lined by suffering, the head of a Titan." To Rolland, this sonata also "holds the palm amongst all sonatas written for the clavier" because of its "deep passionate note which sounds ceaselessly throughout the first movement and the immense vitality of the finale, [and] the calm beauty of the Andante with its variations."

The first movement grows out of a germinal theme—an F minor arpeggio, the first three notes of the opening motive. This became the source of a monumental struggle, with resignation following briefly in a chorale-like melody. The second subject, in the major, is in octaves over a rolling accompaniment.

The movement as a whole represents the same kind of Titanic struggle with Fate we later confront in the first movement of the Fifth Symphony. Indeed, a four-note motif, similar to the one in the Fifth Symphony, strides irresistibly through the early part of the first movement of the piano sonata. The middle movement consists of a beatific melody in simple chords in the lower register, and its variations. The theme returns after the variations are over. Then violent chords break the spell and become the thunder to warn us of an impending typhoon, which bursts with uncontrolled fury in the finale. Toward the end of the sonata, comes a hymn-like section in the minor mode, sounding like the welcome voice of deliverance. "The spirit has freed itself," explains Ernst von Eiterlein, "and at last the struggle ceases in solemn minor strains."

1804. SYMPHONY NO. 3 IN E-FLAT MAJOR, "EROICA," op. 55. I. Allegro con brio. II. Marcia funebre: adagio assai. III. Allegro vivace. IV. Allegro molto.

Only a single year separates the Second and Third Symphonies, but it is as if they were written in different centuries. For all its restless stirrings and innovations, the Second is still an offspring of classicism. But with the first two staccato chords of the *Eroica,* the old symphonic order is destroyed. The *Eroica,* as Paul Henry Lang has said, is "one of the incomprehensible deeds in arts and letters, the greatest single step made by an individual composer in the history of the symphony and the history of music in general."

The *Eroica* is Beethoven's first symphony to come to life, not because the composer had musical material that needed symphonic treatment, but from extra-musical considerations--the compulsion to speak through music of his democratic ideals. Beethoven originally planned the symphony as homage to Napoleon, when Napoleon appeared to be a champion of equality and freedom. But when it turned out that Napoleon, too, was motivated by a lust for power and personal aggrandizement, Beethoven removed Napoleon's name from his manuscript and replaced it with the word "Eroica." The symphony was now a tribute to "the memory of a great man"—but not a conqueror on the field of battle nor a monarch in Schoenbrunn, but Plato's philosopher-turned-king, who kept alight the torch of freedom and respected the dignity of the common man. As Richard Wagner wrote in 1852: "The designation 'heroic' is to be taken in its widest sense. . . . If we broadly connote by 'hero' ('Held') the whole, the full-fledged man, in whom are present all the purely human feelings—of love, of grief, of force—in their highest fullness and strength, then we shall rightly grasp the subject which the artist lets appeal to us in the speaking accents of his tone work."

Everything about the *Eroica* is new: its discords, displaced accents, and unusual modulations; its extended orchestration; its monumental developments built from germinal ideas; its interpolation of a funeral march within a symphonic structure; the unity of purpose in the four movements; its deeply poetic content. It is no wonder, then, that the work was badly misunderstood when first heard: at a private concert at Prince Lobkowitz's place in Vienna in December, 1804; at the first public performance at the Theater-an-der-Wien on April 7, 1805. Beethoven's pupil, Ries, thought that the entry of the horn in the recapitulation in the first movement represented a blunder on the part of the performer. He told Beethoven so—and almost received a sound box on his ear. Some described the music as "a tremendously expanded, daring and wild fantasia"; some said it "loses itself in lawlessness" and that "the principle of unity is almost wholly lost sight of." An unidentified reporter for the *Freimuethige* described the reaction of one large segment of the public by saying: "By means of strange modulations and violent transitions, by combining the most heterogeneous elements . . . a certain undesirable originality may be achieved without much trouble. . . . The inordinate length of this longest and perhaps most difficult of all symphonies, wearies even the cognoscenti and is unendurable to the mere music lover." But Beethoven never doubted the importance of his symphony. Even after he had completed five more masterworks in this form, he regarded the *Eroica* as his favorite.

Two loud staccato chords in full orchestra precede the first main theme—one of extraordinary simplicity, since it is based on the tones of the tonic triad. It rises from the cellos, passes on to the violins, then to the woodwind, and ends up on a long-held C-sharp. A powerful tension is meanwhile being generated, relief coming through a tender exchange between woodwind and strings. But this relief is temporary. A strong descending figure in the violins recalls the earlier struggle and intensifies it. Once again, tensions are relaxed, this time through an exquisite passage (harmonic rather than melodic) beginning with the woodwind and carried on by the violins. And once again, the struggle continues and mounts until it is climaxed by a series of piercing discords. The emotions thus spent, resignation comes with a poignant melody in the woodwind. The exposition now over, the development proceeds along monumental lines. It extends for two hundred and fifty measures, as earlier material is altered rhythmically and harmonically. Richard Wagner saw in this mighty drama "the violence of the destroyer, and in its braggart strength we think we see a wrecker of the world before us, a Titan wrestling with the gods." A horn now recalls the first two measures of the first theme, in the tonic chord over a tremolo on A-flat and B-flat in the strings. (This is the discord that made Ries think the horn player was performing the wrong notes.) The recapitulation, far from repeating the exposition, not only subjects earlier material to new variation but even introduces fresh thematic ideas. And still the structure keeps expanding! The coda is one hundred and forty measures long, with new light being directed on old ideas. The over-all note here is one of triumph. "It is," said Romain Rolland, "the Grand Army of the soul that will not step until it has trampled the whole earth."

And now, for his second movement, Beethoven creates one of the greatest threnodies in music, a funeral march for his hero. The march music is first heard in violins over throbbing basses. After the oboe repeats the melody, over marked rhythms in strings, a plaintive song rises from the strings. The march melody is repeated and developed before the trio section introduces introspection. Oboe and flute, soon joined by other woodwinds, are heard in the main subject followed by a subsidiary hymn-like chant in the violins. And now the march music comes back to be built up into a mighty fugue. The march returns for the last time in the coda—the melody broken up just as the voice breaks when affected by grief.

An energetic, fleet-footed pianissimo theme sets the Scherzo movement into action. In the middle trio, a hunting theme for horn is prominent. Of the finale that follows, Wagner said: "The closing section is the harvest, the lucid counterpart, and commentary of the first. Just as we saw all human feelings in infinitely varied utterance, so here this manifold variety invites us to one harmonious close, embracing all the feelings in itself and taking on a graceful plasticity of shape." The finale opens stormily, with a passionate outburst. Plucked strings then offer a melody (which Beethoven had previously used in his *Prometheus* music). Variations of this melody follow, climaxed by a fugato. The woodwind now emerge with an exultant hymn of triumph. The main theme is then developed with overpowering effect. A breathless presto sweeps the music to its final denouement, which arrives with a series of crushing chords.

1805. CONCERTO IN C MAJOR, for piano, violin, cello, and orchestra, op. 56. I. Allegro. II. Largo. III. Rondo alla polacca.

Though a product of Beethoven's middle period, the "triple" concerto reaches back stylistically, not only to the early Beethoven of the first two-piano concertos, but even further into the past. For in the C major Concerto, Beethoven reverts to the old concerto-grosso structure. He uses his three solo instruments as the concertino, and the orchestra as the ripieno. The orchestra presents the basic two themes of the first movement—the first in cellos and basses, and the lyrical second one in the first violins. When the three solo instruments enter, they restate these themes, then proceed with decorations and elaborations. The development and recapitulation are in the classic design. In the slow movement, a song is heard in solo cello, accompanied by the piano. It is repeated by clarinets and bassoons before it is amplified by orchestra and solo instruments. The concluding Rondo follows without a pause. A lively tune in the style of a polonaise is first presented by the solo cello, after which it is discussed vivaciously by the other solo instruments and the orchestra.

1805–1807. LEONORE OVERTURES NOS. 1, 2, and 3, for orchestra, op. 138, op. 72a, and op. 72b. *See:* FIDELIO (below).

1805. FIDELIO, opera in two acts, with text by Josef von Sonnleithner and Friedrich Treitschke, based on Jean-Nicolas Bouilly's, *Lénore, ou l'amour conjugal.* First performance: Theater-an-der-Wien, Vienna, November 20, 1805.

Henry E. Krehbiel once described *Fidelio* as Beethoven's "child of sorrow." None of Beethoven's works cost him so much effort and grief, both in conception and production. Beethoven was essentially an instrumental composer. He found it difficult to adjust his musical thinking to the requirements of the stage. He filled notebook after notebook with his sketches, rewriting continually. He sketched out eighteen different version of Leonore's aria, "Komm, Hoffnung," and of Florestan's aria, "In des Lebens Fruehlingstagen"; he made ten revisions of the chorus, "Wer ein solches Weib errungen." He prepared four different overtures. For the return of the opera to Vienna in 1806, he rewrote the opera completely; and he revised it once again for the revival in 1814. "Of all my children, "he told Schindler, "this is the one that cost me the worst birth pangs, the one that brought me the most sorrow; and for that reason it is the one most dear to me."

He never again wrote another opera; he never again found a text to stir him the way *Fidelio* had done. It was not a very good libretto, to be sure. Too much of it is old-fashioned and contrived, too much taxes an audience's credulity. But the story of Leonore's devoted and faithful love to her husband, and her success in delivering him, moved Beethoven profoundly. All his life he, too, had been searching for a Leonore. More significantly, Florestan—unjustly imprisoned by a tyrant—represented to him the oppressed and the subjugated of the world; and Leonore who effects her husband's freedom, became the symbol of liberty. Thus Beethoven soared to the heights when the symbol of the play obsessed him: in Leonore's fiery and defiant challenge to oppressors in "Abscheulicher! wo eilst du hin?"; in the poignant chorus of the prisoners, as they emerge from the dungeon to the sunlight singing a paean to freedom, "O welche Lust"; in Florestan's gloom-ridden soliloquy about his sad fate in his lonely cell, "Gott! welch ein Dunkel hier"; in the concluding song of joy at the reunion of husband and wife and the hymn to Leonore—or if you will to liberty—in "O namelose Freude" and "Wer ein solches Weib errungen."

"The music," said Marcia Davenport, "transcends any love story, any temporal experience. It is the mightiest of strivings toward the divine aims of an immortal spirit imprisoned for one lifetime in a very faulty man. The symbolism of this, almost supernaturally clear in *Fidelio,* is Beethoven's brooding obsession with imprisonment, released at last by overwhelming outpourings of joy in the triumph of freedom."

In 1803, Emanuel Schikaneder asked Beethoven to write an opera for the Theater-an-der-Wien, of which he had recently become manager. This is the same Schikaneder who, a decade earlier, had commissioned Mozart to write *The Magic Flute*. As it turned out, before Beethoven could get to work on his opera, Schikaneder sold out his interest in the Theater-an-der-Wien to the Court Theater. The new director, Baron von Braun, now once again approached Beethoven about writing an opera—suggesting the popular play of

Bouilly, *Lénore, ou l'amour conjugal,* which had been adapted into German by Josef von Sonnleithner, secretary of the Court Theater. Beethoven now went to work with a will; he completed his score by early autumn of 1805.

The première on November 20, 1805, was a disaster. Napoleon's troops were occupying Vienna. The audience—made up mostly of soldiers—found little in the opera to please it. The opera seemed too long, too dull, and too static; in addition the performance had been slipshod. "The melody in this opera," wrote a critic, "is tormented and lacks the expressive passion and strikingly irresistible charm which captures our imagination in the works of Mozart and Cherubini. And if the score can claim a few lovely pages, it is still far from being a perfect—or even a welcome—work."

Fidelio played to empty houses for the next two performances and then was dropped. Beethoven now subjected his opera to drastic rewriting. The three acts were reduced to two; a new overture (the monumental *Leonore No. 3*) was written; certain numbers were curtailed, others completely deleted The new version was heard on March 29, 1806, and seemed to find favor. But Beethoven soon became involved with Baron von Braun in a bitter dispute over box-office receipts and angrily withdrew his opera after it had been given only five times.

The opera was not heard again for another eight years. In 1814, the court officials decided to revive it. Once again, a general overhauling took place, both in text and music; once again, Beethoven prepared a new overture. The revival took place at the Kaernthnerthor Theater on May 23, 1814. This time the opera had been carefully prepared and was performed brilliantly. The opera proved a tremendous success—at long last. It now started to make the rounds of the leading opera houses of Germany and Austria. It was a triumph in Berlin in 1815, and again in 1823 in Dresden, when it was conducted by Carl Maria von Weber. In 1829, it was heard for the first time in Paris, and in 1832, in London. The first American presentation took place in New York on September 9, 1839 (in English). When first prouduced at the Metropolitan Opera in New York—on November 19, 1884—the original German-language text was used.

Beethoven wrote four different overtures for *Fidelio,* three entitled *Leonore,* and the fourth, *Fidelio.* The overture used for the 1805 world première was the *Leonore Overture No. 2; Leonore Overture No. 3,* as we have seen, was written for the 1806 revival. *Leonore No. 1* is a simplification and condensation of No. 3, completed in 1807 for a projected production of *Fidelio* in Prague, which never materialized. The so-called *Fidelio Overture* was the one Beethoven wrote for the Vienna revival of the opera in 1814. It is now the general practice to use the *Fidelio Overture* at the beginning of the opera, and to interpolate the *Leonore Overture No. 3* between the first and second scenes of the second act.

The *Fidelio Overture* begins vigorously. A unison Allegro for strings and winds is followed by an Adagio for horns and clarinet. This is repeated, after which the slow horn theme is developed and used as transition to the main body of the overture. Second horns now present the main theme. It is answered by the clarinet, and developed by the full orchestra. The second subject follows in the strings. This and the opening material are developed. The overture concludes with a presto section built from a phrase from the first main theme.

The action of the play takes place in eighteenth-century Seville. The curtain rises on a courtyard in a prison fortress. Florestan, a Spanish nobleman, has been imprisoned by his political enemy, Pizarro; he is being left to die in his dungeon cell. Though Pizarro has spread the report that Florestan is dead, Leonore, Florestan's wife, refuses to believe the news. Determined to save her husband, she assumes the disguise of a man, takes on the name of Fidelio, and finds employment with the jailer, Rocco.

Jacquino, one of Rocco's assistants, is in love with the jailer's daughter, Marcellina. As the opera begins, he is imploring Marcellina to marry him. When he is summoned by Rocco, Marcellina reveals she is in love with Fidelio ("O waer ich schon mit dir vereint"). After Rocco, Jacquino, and Fidelio appear, they join Marcellina in voicing their respective reactions to the complicated love situation. This is the celebrated canonic quartet, "Mir ist so wunderbar," one of the most remarkable ensemble numbers in opera. Rocco is in favor of a match between Fidelio and Marcellina, but points up the importance of money in any marriage ("Hat man nicht auch Gold daneben"). Leonore now manages to win Rocco's consent to join him in making his rounds of the prison.

Martial music brings Pizarro on the scene. He has come with the news that the Prime Minister will soon inspect the prison. This means that Florestan must be done away with quickly ("Ha! welch ein Augenblick"). Leonore, having overheard the plot, voices her horror in the moving aria, "Abscheulicher! wo eilst du hin?" But terror gives way to confidence that her great love will effect her husband's rescue ("Komm, Hoffnung"). In an attempt to catch a glimpse of her husband, Leonore prevails on Rocco to permit the prisoners to leave their cells and come out into the courtyard. As they stumble out into the light of day, they chant a hymn of joy at being able once again to see sun and sky; vigorously they sound their determination to be free again ("O welche Lust"). Pizarro angrily orders the prisoners to their dungeons. Meanwhile Rocco has brought Fidelio the tidings that Pizarro will permit Fidelio to come into Florestan's cell to help dig a grave for the doomed prisoner.

The first scene of the second act takes place in Florestan's cell. Chained to the wall, he laments his tragic fate while recalling happier days with his beloved Leonore ("In des Lebens Fruehlingstagen"). Rocco and Leonore now enter. Leonore is shocked to see how aged and shriveled Florestan has become, but with supreme effort she controls her emotion lest Rocco grow suspicious. Now the jailer and Fidelio set about the business of digging Florestan's grave. At an arranged signal from Rocco, Pizarro rushes in with dagger in hand, ready to murder his enemy and thus erase all evidence of his own perfidy. Fidelio intervenes with pistol in hand, threatening to kill Pizarro if he makes a move towards Florestan. Just then a trumpet call announces the arrival of the Prime Minister. Leonore, Florestan, and Rocco exclaim with joy; Pizarro gives vent to his anger. When Pizarro leaves to welcome the Prime Minister, Florestan and Leonore rush to each other ("O namenlose Freude!"); Leonore conducts her husband out of prison.

During the change of scene, the orchestra performs the *Leonore Overture No. 3.* This is Beethoven's symphonic concept of the main episodes in the opera. The solemn slow introduction begins with loud chords in full orchestra followed by scale passages. We now hear in clarinet and bassoon a quotation from Florestan's gloomy aria, "In des Lebens Fruehlingstagen." This theme is developed dramatically finally erupting into a violent exclamation for the full orchestra. The main body of the overture now appears quietly, its first theme given by first violins and cellos. A strong and elaborate development follows before the second subject is heard, first in the horns and after that in first violins and flutes. Another dynamic climax is built up, at whose peak offstage trumpet fanfares tell of the arrival of the Prime Minister. Strings present Leonore's poignant song of thanksgiving for her husband's deliverance. A flute solo brings on a return of both main themes and their further development. Then the coda describes Leonore's unbounded joy that her husband's life has been saved.

The second scene is in the public square. The people hail the Prime Minister ("Heil sei dem Tag!"). Then the Prime Minister announces he has come to right all wrongs, to bring tyranny to an end. Rocco now leads Florestan and Leonore to the Prime Minister, when he reveals the full extent of Pizarro's treachery. Florestan gains his freedom. The people sing the praises of Leonore for her courage and devotion ("Wer ein solches Weib errungen"). Husband and wife speak ecstatically of the joy of reunion.

1806. CONCERTO NO. 4 IN G MAJOR, for piano and orchestra, op. 58. I. Allegro moderato. II. Andante con moto. III. Vivace.

Sir George Grove once referred to this Fourth Piano Concerto as the "Cinderella" of Beethoven's concertos. This is because it suffered neglect for many years, until Mendelssohn revived it successfully in Leipzig in 1836. Perhaps the reason why the concerto went into discard after Beethoven had introduced it in Vienna in 1807 is because, both in structure and style, it is so different from earlier concertos by Mozart and Beethoven. Here, in the Fourth Concerto, we see the full emancipation of the concerto from virtuosity and pyrotechnical display. No longer is the piano the hero of all the proceedings; it must now share the stage with the orchestra. Both are partners in the presentation of some of the loftiest concepts and some of the noblest utterances found in concerto literature.

The new paths traveled by the Fourth Concerto are apparent in the very opening. In place of an extended orchestral preface, in which main themes are introduced, we find the piano in a gentle presentation of the first five measures of the first theme. The orchestra completes the melody, then elaborates it. The second subject, another sensitive melody, this time in the minor key with unusual modulations, is given by the strings. Still a third motive is introduced loudly before the piano returns to discuss all this material. The spacious development concerns itself mainly with the first theme, whose opening motive provides the basic material for the recapitulation. Cadenza and coda follow.

There is perhaps nothing in all concerto literature to match the kind of philosophic dialogue that takes place in the second movement for some seventy measures. The strings enter with a loud recitative. To this the piano gives reply with a comment of surpassing tenderness. The give and take between the comparatively stormy strings and the meditative piano continues, until midway in the movement the piano gives voice to an exultant monologue. It then lapses back into its earlier introspection. There is no pause between the magical discourse of the second movement and the vivacity of the concluding rondo. The latter begins with an energetic tune in the strings, which is soon continued by the piano. The second theme, in the upper register of the piano, is lyrical. But the prevailing mood of the movement remains uninhibited in its vigor. Following a cadenza, a presto section gives an electrifying presentation of the rondo theme in full orchestra, beginning pianissimo and growing in dynamics up to a fortissimo. Arpeggios in piano treble, and a dramatic crescendo, then provide an exciting conclusion.

1806. 3 STRING QUARTETS, "RASOUMOVSKY," op. 59:

No. 1, F major. I. Allegro. II. Allegretto vivace e sempre scherzando. III. Adagio molto e mesto. IV. Allegro.

No. 2, E minor. I. Allegro. II. Molto adagio. III. Allegretto. IV. Presto.

No. 3, C major. I. Andante con moto; Allegro vivace. II. Andante con moto quasi allegretto. III. Grazioso. IV. Allegro molto.

In 1805, Beethoven was commissioned by Count Andreas Rasoumovsky, Russian Ambassador to Austria, to write three string quartets. Beethoven completed them in rapid succession during the summer of 1806. This marked his return to string-quartet writing since the opus 18 set, completed six years earlier. In picking up the string quartet medium, so long abandoned, Beethoven was now ready to bring to it new methods and aesthetics. "The current is broad and deep," remarks John N. Burk, "vigorously independent, calling forth the full tonal capacity of four stringed instruments when his thoughts tend to symphonic proportions. His manipulatory power, enormously increased, welds and tightens, liberates, builds. The fancy takes any sort of flight it wills and is richly various." Burk sums up as follows: "The three quartets, op. 59, are in their way the subtlest, the most viable and deeply personal expression of what is called Beethoven's second period."

Keeping in mind that his patron was Russian, Beethoven introduced Russian thematic material in two of the three quartets; and since Rasoumovsky was an amateur cellist, Beethoven so extended the cello role in the first of these quartets that it is sometimes identified as the *Cello* Quartet. In that first quartet, all four movements are in the sonata form, the last of which makes use of a "thème Russe," a folk song. This finale is preceded by one of those tragic and sublime slow movements that are frequently encountered in the later Beethoven —two main melodies combined to give expression to a pathos beyond solace.

In the second of these *Rasoumovsky Quartets* we are once again brought into the presence of a second movement of surpassing eloquence. Not tragedy is spoken here but what Vincent d'Indy once described as "deep religious calm." It has been said that this music came to Beethoven as he contemplated the beauty of a starry night in Baden, near Vienna. A peace that is close to a benediction pervades the entire movement. The Russian element is emphasized in the trio section of the Scherzo. This is the same tune that Mussorgsky later utilized in the Coronation scene in *Boris Godunov*.

The third string quartet is the most dramatic of the set. It is so consistently aggressive and virile that it has been given the nickname of *Heroic*. Power dominates both the first movement and the finale, the latter of which highlights a tumultous fugue. This fugue, says Homer Ulrich, is the "culmination" and the "crowning glory" of the entire opus 59. "Its confidence, its unrestrained joy, its dramatic climaxes, and its sheer joie de vivre make it one of the most exciting pieces in the literature." The middle movements have a lighter texture and a brighter spirit. Here the slow movement is gentle and reflective. And in place of a vigorous Scherzo, this quartet has a delicate Allegretto with some of the personality of a minuet.

1806. SYMPHONY NO. 4 IN B-FLAT MAJOR, op. 60. I. Adagio; Allegro vivace. II. Adagio. III. Allegro vivace. IV. Allegro ma non troppo.

The Fourth Symphony is a gentle, at times, even a joyful idyl, of "a heavenly sweetness," as Berlioz described it. The first movement slow introduction features a descending subject for strings, to which the wind instruments provide the background of a long sustained B-flat. A vigorous chord, repeated six times, prefaces the Allegro vivace, whose first theme is a lively tune for the first violins, answered by the woodwind over a staccato accompaniment. Transitional material leads into the second subject, in F major, an exchange among bassoon, oboe, and flute. A long crescendo brings on a new idea treated canonically by clarinet and bassoon. The extended development is devoted mainly to the lively first subject. A timpani roll, a fleet figure in the strings, and a crescendo precede the recapitulation, in which the first theme is given by the full orchestra, and the second theme appears in the key of B-flat major.

Berlioz said of the second movement: "You are seized, from the first measure, by an emotion which at the end becomes overwhelming in its intensity." The opening melody is a sublime song for the first violins, repeated by the woodwind. A second exalted melody follows in the clarinet. In the development, an ingenious working out of the introductory measure of the opening song takes place. The principal theme is heard in a slight variation in the recapitulation, and later becomes the heart of the coda.

For his third movement, Beethoven temporarily returns to the minuet; this movement, however, has all the dynamic character and vibrant pulse of a scherzo. Vigor, even brusqueness, prevails in the opening section, to which a gentle melody for woodwind and horns in the trio provides contrast. The effervescent spirit of the opening movement recurs in the happy finale. A rapid and vivacious theme in the strings, with sixteenth-note figures, starts the merriment. It continues on through the development, recapitulation, and coda, in all of which the first bustling subject is given prominence.

1806. CONCERTO IN D MAJOR, for violin and orchestra, op. 61. I. Allegro ma non troppo. II. Larghetto. III. Allegro.

Beethoven wrote his only violin concerto for Franz Clement. Since Beethoven worked on the score up to the zero hour of performance, Clement had to read most of the music at sight. The performance, consequently—on December 23, 1806—did not go well, the reason possibly why the new concerto was poorly received. After this, concert performances of the concerto were few and far between—until Joseph Joachim played it so consistently that it found a permanent place in the repertory. Since Joachim's time, of course, the Beethoven Violin Concerto has been accepted as one of the greatest ever written.

Four strokes of the timpani (a rhythmic figure that persists throughout the movement) sets the stage for an expansive orchestral introduction in which both main themes are set forth. The first comes in oboe, clarinets, and bassoons after the fourth timpani stroke. The haunting second subject appears in the woodwind and horns. Without a formal conclusion of this orchestral episode, the solo violin enters with an ascending passage in octaves, which leads into a statement of the first theme. The working out of this subject and the second theme is detailed and imaginative, the solo violin often providing filigree decorations to the presentation of the main themes in the orchestra. Before the recapitulation arrives loudly in full orchestra, a tranquil section unfolds in solo violin. A cadenza, and a recall of the second theme bring the movement to a close.

The wondrous melody of the second movement is heard first in muted strings. It is then repeated in turn by clarinet, bassoon, and strings, as the solo violin provides delicate embroidery. A new melody is then sung by the violin, before the first subject is recalled in pizzicato strings and the second theme is heard again in the solo violin.

The rondo opens with a lively melody on the G string of the solo violin, lightly accompanied by the cellos. This idea is repeated by the solo instrument two octaves higher, and after that by full orchestra. A kind of hunting subject for horns ornamented by the solo violin, proves to be a transition to the second theme, which the full orchestra states loudly for two measures, and which the solo violin then completes. In the recapitulation, the first theme is again heard in the solo violin over a cello accompaniment, after which there is a brief recall of the second theme and the hunting call. A loud orchestral tutti precedes the cadenza. A final recollection of the opening theme becomes the concluding statement of the movement, and of the concerto.

In August 1808, Beethoven arranged the violin concerto for piano and orchestra. In this transcription, Beethoven prepared a new cadenza, with timpani obbligato, for the first movement, and a fresh transition from the slow movement (here designated as an Andante) to the rondo.

1807. CORIOLON OVERTURE, for orchestra, op. 62.

The drama for which Beethoven wrote one of his powerful concert overtures is not the famous tragedy of Shakespeare, but an unfamiliar one by Heinrich Joseph von Collin, first produced in Vienna in 1802. This drama has been described as "philosophic." Coriolanus is the Roman patrician who, after his victory over the Volscians, becomes consul. His hatred and contempt for the people bring on a revolt. Coriolanus is banished. He now turns traitor by assuming the command of the Volscian army in an attack on Rome. But when his mother and son both come to plead with him, he relents and is ready to accept an honorable truce. In the end, he is killed by the Volscians for treason.

The overture opens with three loud unison C's in the strings, each interrupted by a staccato chord for full orchestra. This music portrays the fierce pride of Coriolanus. The first main theme—an agitated subject for strings built up with overpowering strength—now brings the picture of the hero in action. The second subject is a poetic melody in E-flat for the first violins, believed to represent Coriolanus's mother. A two-note figure that ends this theme becomes the core of a dynamic development. In the recapitulation, the first theme is heard in the key of F minor and the second in C major. The second theme dominates the coda, which ends with the forceful unison chords that opened the overture and which now tell of Coriolanus's death.

1807–1808. SYMPHONY NO. 5 IN C MINOR, op. 67. I. Allegro con brio. II. Andante con moto. III. Allegro vivace. IV. Allegro.

SYMPHONY NO. 6 IN F MAJOR, "PASTORAL," op. 68. I. Allegro ma non troppo. II. Andante molto molto. III. Allegro. IV. Allegro. V. Allegretto.

The power generated by the opening of the first movement of the Fifth Symphony (1807)—the relentless surge of the opening eight-note motive—has lent itself to varied extra-musical interpretations. The most familiar is the one suggested by Beethoven's friend and biographer, Schindler: "Thus fate knocks at the door." Building on this statement, program annotators have found in this music a Herculean struggle between the composer and a destiny that made him deaf—with an occasional respite in resignation. However, many Beethoven authorities seriously doubt if Beethoven had any intention whatsoever of portraying here his own personal drama; they insist that the concept of the first movement is an exclusively musical one. Be that as it may, the "struggle against fate" idea continues to survive, continues to serve as an interpretation of this most popular of all symphonic movements. The truth is that this music happens to lend itself ever so neatly to such a program. The four hammer blows of the opening measures—out of which the whole movement evolves—sound like the knocks on a door by some implacable fate, a knock that grows increasingly insistent as the theme is allowed to grow in dynamics and tempo. And the melodious second theme, shared by strings and woodwind (the four notes still heard in the background) is indeed like the voice of peaceful resignation.

Ferdinand Ries and Czerny both maintained that the four-note motive came to Beethoven while he was listening to the chirping of a goldfinch. In our own time, during World War II, this subject was used in Europe as a sign of victory by the forces of freedom: the three short notes followed by the lone one resembles the three dots and dash that in the Morse code stand for "V" or "Victory."

The second movement is in the form of theme and variations; however, we have here not one but two themes. The first is given at once in cellos and violas, to be continued by woodwind and strings. The second comes in clarinets and bassoons, accompanied by triplets in violas and plucked strings in the bass. Two variations on the first theme follow. A duet between clarinet and bassoon, with other woodwind in imitation, precedes a strong restatement of the second melody in full orchestra. After this comes a third variation and a coda.

A subject in the basses—described by Sir George Grove as "mysterious and almost uncanny"—opens the third-movement Scherzo. This is followed by a triumphant statement in the horns. The trio, in the key of C major, opens with a busy figure in the double basses, the first time in symphonic music that this cumbersome fellow has received such attention. The trio ends with an extended diminuendo leading into a repetition of the opening theme, now given staccato. The movement ends in the same kind of ominous mystery with which it began—with insistent beats of the timpani over a long sustained C in the strings. An extended crescendo now leads directly into the finale, which erupts with a robust and triumphant march melody in full orchestra. Following a transitional figure in woodwind and horns, a second subject, in G major, is heard. This is a triplet figure in the first violins over a triplet accompaniment in second violins and violas. The development concerns itself with this triplet figure. Before the recapitulation appears, there is a quiet recall of part of the main theme of the preceding Scherzo. Then the principal melody of the finale is vigorously projected, followed by the second theme now heard in C major. The coda, with which the symphony comes to a majestic close, is long and extended, dramatized by the quickening of the tempo and increase of the dynamics.

If there is some doubt about Beethoven's programmatic intentions in the Fifth Symphony, there is none whatsoever regarding the symphony that followed it, the *Pastoral* (1808). Beethoven's own title was "Sinfonie Pastorale, mehr Ausdruck der Empfindug als Malerei" ("Pastoral Symphony, more expression of feeling than painting"). To provide still further clues to his purpose in writing this music, Beethoven headed each of the movements with a programmatic title. The first is called "Awakening of Joyful Feelings upon Arrival in the Country." It is in the key of F major, which Beethoven often used for his more cheerful music. The opening effervescent theme for strings, over a sustained pedal point in violas and cellos, might very well reflect Beethoven's own joy in the presence of Nature. This theme is repeated continuously throughout the movement, though often in altered form. There is no second subject as such; there is not even a formal development, but only a further repetition of fragments of this theme. "I believe," said Sir George Grove, "that the delicious, natural, May-day, out-of-doors feeling of this movement arises in a great measure from this kind of repetition."

In the second movement, "The Brook," the flow of the water is re-created in a running rippling figure of falling thirds in triplets. This appears in second violins and violas. Before long, the bucolic scene becomes alive with the song of cuckoos, nightingales, and quails, reproduced by the woodwind. This is followed by a rustic picture, "The Village Festival," which opens with a gay peasant dance. The trio here starts off with a pleasant tune for the oboe; but before long, this music becomes an amusing caricature of village bands, and particularly of an inept bassoon player who concentrates on three notes. A tremolo in lower strings is the transition to the fourth movement, "The Storm," which is allowed to grow and gather its strength until it finally erupts with full fury. Suddenly the elements grow calm, a descending scale in the oboe suggests a rainbow, and the piping of a shepherd brings on the last movement, "The Shepherd's Song." Clarinets, followed by the horns and the violins, intone a radiant song of thanksgiving for the storm's end and the return of tranquillity. The hymn is given with renewed fervor, then lapses into the same kind of peace with which the countryside is now blessed.

1807. MASS IN C MAJOR, for solo voices, chorus, and orchestra, op. 86.

The C major Mass was commissioned by Prince Nicholas Esterházy, at whose place it was introduced on September 13, 1807. "I believe," Beethoven informed his publishers, "that I have treated the text as seldom it has been treated before." By this Beethoven probably meant that, though he wrote the music for a church service, he was emphasizing dramatic over religious values. "In all musical literature," explains Karl Geiringer, "we will find few examples of a Mass in which dramatic expression and spiritual depth are so firmly welded into one perfect unit. There are visions in this Mass whose powerful grandeur and fervent soulfulness clearly point to the composer of the Fifth Symphony and of *Fidelio*. The desire to form a connection with tradition, to be sure, is clearly felt in Beethoven's evident determination to uphold the musical continuity between the different sections."

The C major is the first and lesser of Beethoven's two Masses, the other being the monumental *Missa solemnis* (which see). Comparing the two works, Paul Bekker wrote: "The earlier work appeals to a devout congregation assembled to worship. In the *Missa solemnis,* all consideration for, all immediate reference to, ritual is abandoned. The tremendous length of the individual sections, and the consequent duration of the work as a whole, would make an accompanying ecclesiastical ceremony seem a mere irreverent interruption."

The C major Mass is in the usual five sections, beginning with the three-part "Kyrie." After that come a three-part "Gloria," a three part "Credo," the "Sanctus," and the "Agnus Dei." "Like most of Beethoven's middle period works, the Mass is affirmative," wrote Harold C. Schonberg, "a direct emotional outpouring rather than the mystic, tortured, ineffable spirit of the last works."

Beethoven is believed to have borrowed a figure for his "Credo" from the inept playing of village musicians which he heard while walking in the country. Another amusing item is the fact that this Mass boasts one of the longest tempo markings known (it appears over the "Kyrie"): Andante con moto assai vivace quasi allegretto ma non troppo. Of greater importance—to be sure—is that there are no solo passages for individual singers throughout the work, the solo quartet being used as a unit. Also, Beethoven achieves a unity of concept for the entire Mass by repeating at the end the theme of the opening "Kyrie."

1808. 2 PIANO TRIOS, op. 70:

D major, "Geister." I. Allegro vivace e con brio. II. Largo assai. III. Presto.

E-flat major. I. Poco sostenuto; Allegro ma non troppo. II. Allegretto. III. Allegretto ma non troppo. IV. Allegro.

Beethoven's first trios for the combination of piano, violin, and cello appeared in 1795 with a set of three works, opus 1 (E-flat, G major, C minor). Eight years later, Beethoven returned to the piano-trio medium to produce two works assembled in opus 70. This is Beethoven in full maturity.

The first movement of the D major Trio offers us the vigorous and strongly assertive Beethoven. The opening theme is a powerful statement for all three instruments in octaves. But before long a haunting lyrical passage in the cello contributes melodic interest. In the development, in which a good deal of virtuoso writing can be found, Beethoven combines the second bar of the second theme with the first bar of the first with extraordinary effect. The melancholy slow movement is the reason that the trio as a whole has been named "Spirit." The tremolo piano chords that repeatedly recur create a feeling of mystery and despair. As the movement progresses, the music gains in gloom to become one of the most pessimistic utterances of Beethoven's middle period. This slow movement is the most important in the work, which concludes with a presto movement that helps dispel all melancholy.

Where the *Geister* Trio is in three movements, the E-flat major is in the traditional four. The first movement opens with a slow introduction (an unusual practice for piano trios). The second movement features two themes and variations. Then comes a scherzo-like movement with a buoyant dance tune in the first part and a melody in the trio given antiphonally by strings and piano. The bright, engaging mood of this movement spills over into the sprightly finale.

1808. FANTASY IN C MINOR, for piano, chorus, and orchestra, op. 80. I. Adagio. II. Allegro; Meno allegro; Allegretto ma non troppo.

Beethoven wrote this unusual work as the dessert for a Gargantuan musical feast he planned for a Vienna concert on December 22, 1808. All the works he then presented were new to Vienna, including the *Pastoral* Symphony, the concert aria, "Ah, Perfido!," four parts of the Mass in C, the Fourth Piano Concerto, the Fifth Symphony, a piano solo and, to top it all off, the C minor Fantasy as the grand finale. Indeed, he had hardly put down the last notes of the Fantasy before rehearsals began.

To Beethoven students, the Fantasy has special interest because to a slight degree it is the prototype of the finale of the Ninth Symphony. The Fantasy opens with an extended Adagio fantasia for solo piano. The second section starts with an Allegro in which the opening subject is quietly stated by the basses, then developed canonically by the violins. A new theme is now heard in oboes and horns, then taken over by the piano over a horn accompaniment; this material was borrowed by the composer from one of his own songs, "Seufzer eines Ungeliebten," op. 254 (1795). This subject is varied. A brief episode for piano brings on the development of this melody with changes of tempo. A new thought in the piano brings on an exchange between piano and basses, until the major subject of the work is heard in the wind. At this point, the solo voices take over the melody, accompanied by the piano. The work comes to a magnificent end with a final projection of the melody by full chorus and orchestra—a setting of a poem by Kuffner in praise of music, "Schmeichelnd hold."

1809. SONATA IN A MAJOR, for cello and piano, op. 69. I. Allegro ma non tanto. II. Allegro molto. III. Adagio cantabile; Allegro vivace.

Beethoven wrote five cello sonatas. The first two, op. 5 (F major and G minor) were early creations, having been written in 1795. The last two came in 1815, op. 102 (C major and D major). In between stands the greatest of these cello sonatas. In the first movement, the cello steps forward boldly with a mellow unaccompanied melody. Throughout the movement, the rich mellow voice of the cello is catered to with fullsome thematic material, though more vigorous ideas are not avoided. The Scherzo that follows opens with what John N. Burk describes as "the merest wisp of a tune," whose last two notes "continue in a dreaming ostinato and furnish the trio." The finale begins with one of Beethoven's most deeply moving melodies. This takes the place of the more usual slow movement and serves as a fitting preface to the light-textured music that comes after that. In the sonata form, the Allegro part of the finale is based on two capricious themes, both receiving spacious development.

1809. CONCERTO NO. 5 IN E-FLAT MAJOR, "EMPEROR," for piano and orchestra, op. 73. I. Allegro. II. Adagio un poco mosso. III. Allegro.

Beethoven's last piano concerto is the noblest of them all, its over-all majesty leading an unidentified publisher to name it the *Emperor*. It opens with a powerful tonic chord out of which the piano emerges with a rhapsodic recitative. This alternation of orchestral harmonies and piano declamation is repeated twice more to establish at once what John N. Burk described as "music of sweeping and imperious grandeur unknown to any concerto written up to 1812, and beside which the dignity of emperors or archdukes loses all consequence." Now there comes a one-hundred-measure section for orchestra in which both main themes are presented. The first is proud and assertive; the second, in the unusual key of E-flat minor, combines vitality with sensitivity. After the orchestra has worked these ideas out, the piano arrives with a repetition of the exposition, but with alterations. "The solo piano," Burk explains, "traverses elaborate figurations which, however, never obscure the thematic outlines, but unfailingly intensify it and enhance the development." Following that development—an epic in its own right—a stirring climax and a brief pause precede the cadenza which Beethoven himself wrote. The recapitulation and coda come after that.

There is only one theme in the slow movement. It is a stately melody with the quality of a hymn, heard in the higher strings over a pizzicato bass. The piano reflects on this subject in an improvisational manner, then restates it over plucked strings. Toward the end of the movement, the melody is repeated, this time by the orchestra, as the piano provides embellishments. Two measures before the end of the movement, a vital rhythmic subject suddenly emerges to give a hint of the main theme of the concluding rondo, which follows without pause. The opening of this finale is good-humored and energetic. This mood is carried on by a quotation of a few bars of a popular folk tune (the Grossvatertanz), which Schumann also used in some of his piano music. With the piano in the forefront, the movement proceeds to a dynamic conclusion with many brilliant passages and effects.

1809–1810. STRING QUARTETS:

E-flat major, "Harp," op. 74. I. Poco adagio; Allegro. II. Adagio ma non troppo. III. Presto. IV. Allegretto con variazioni.

F minor, "Serious," op. 95. I. Allegro con brio. II. Allegretto ma non troppo. III. Allegro assai vivace ma serioso. IV. Larghetto espressivo; Allegretto agitato.

The E-flat major and the F minor String Quartets are the last such works of Beethoven's middle period. The first of these (1809) is known as the *Harp* due to the pizzicato arpeggios for the four instruments in the first movement, an effect that sounds like the strummings on a harp. This quartet opens with a slow and dreamy introduction, "sotte voce." The movement then abounds with rich sonorities, except for the harp-like subject, and features a brilliant cadenza for the solo violin. Homer Ulrich finds that the two middle movements are the main points of interest. "The romantic and intensely beautiful Adagio, with its expressive, exquisitely ornamented melodies, realizes the perfect balance between sentiment and restraint." The Scherzo is described by Ulrich as "diabolical, full of hammering figures and breathless scale passages. . . . Its concentration and rhythmic drive are unmatched even in Beethoven." The finale starts off with a graceful, flowing melody which is then given six variations.

There is such sobriety, such solemnity in most of the F minor Quartet (1810) that it is now known as the *Serious*. A brusque, harsh opening statement in the opening Allegro, loud and in unison, projects a grimness that seems to dominate the entire movement. An Allegretto replaces the more usual slow movement; but gloom is not absent by any means. "Heavy, descending short notes from the cello foretell trouble," writes John N. Burk. "A mournful theme suggests a wailing phrase to the viola, the instrument which is to suffuse each movement with its special dark coloring." Burk also notes a device that Beethoven continually exploits: "the melodic half-tone lapse from the sixth degree of the minor scale to the fifth, a veritable accent of lamentation." Even the scherzo, with its sharp and incisive opening, maintains the earlier darkness, particularly in the mournful melody in the trio. But in the finale, the heavy clouds are scattered first by the storm of struggle and then by sunshine of victory over despair. A bright new melody in the coda proclaims this joyful victory.

1809. SONATA IN E-FLAT MAJOR, "DAS LEBEWOHL, DIE ABWESENHEIT, DAS WIEDERSEHN," ("LES ADIEUX, L'ABSENCE, LE RETOUR"), for piano, op. 81a. I. Adagio; Allegro. II. Andante espressivo (In gehender Bewegung, doch mit viel Ausdruck). III. Vivacissimamente (Im lebhaftesten Zeitmasse).

The last piano sonata of Beethoven's middle period is one of two to which he himself affixed a descriptive title (the other being the earlier *Pathétique*). It is also the only programmatic sonata. When the French invading troops approached Vienna, Beethoven's patron and friend, the Archduke Rudolph, made hasty retreat out of the city. Beethoven, who preferred staying on in Vienna, wrote his sonata as a personal testament to Rudolph, "written from the heart," as he himself noted in his dedication. In this sonata, Beethoven spoke his sorrow at bidding his friend farewell; he also anticipated the joy of reunion.

In the introduction to the first movement, over the three-note theme with which it opens, Beethoven scrawled the word "Le-be-wohl," or "Farewell." This motto, Romain Rolland explains, "is the generating idea, the essence of the whole sonata. Whether written in clear notes or obscured subtly, this leading motive lies at the bottom of every phrase." The first movement is permeated with sadness and tenderness. This mood grows more poignant and desolate in the slow movement, with its expressive recitative-like passages. A shattering chord releases the energy and the unbridled joy of the concluding Vivacissimamente.

In the second and third movements, Beethoven uses German tempo markings for the first time (together with Italian).

1809. OVERTURE AND INCIDENTAL MUSIC TO EGMONT, op. 84: 1. "Die Trommel geruehret." 2. Entr'acte I. 3. Entr'acte II. 4. "Freudvoll und leidvoll." 5. Entr'acte III. 6. En'tracte IV. 7. Claerchen's Death. 8. Melodrama. 9. Siegesymphonie.

There were two good reasons why the writing of *Egmont* should have been for Beethoven a labor of love. The first was his veneration of Goethe, who wrote *Egmont*. The second was that the subject of his drama is a passionate espousal of liberty and a bitter denunciation of tyranny—something close to Beethoven's heart. When, therefore, the Burgtheater in Vienna asked Beethoven to write incidental music for a revival of the Goethe drama, the composer responsed enthusiastically.

The setting of the Goethe drama is sixteenth-century Netherlands. There Count Egmont becomes the leader in a revolt against Spanish despotism. When the Duke of Alba is despatched to the Low Countries to suppress any signs of rebellion, Egmont becomes the champion of independence, for which he pays with his life.

The overture, one of Beethoven's most sublime, is a tone poem in which the essence of the drama has been fixed. Strongly accented chords in F minor create an ominous opening, which some like to interpret as the weight of Spanish oppression. Into this foreboding atmosphere, lyric phrases intrude, but without providing relief from tension. Then the main section (Allegro) erupts dramatically, describing a rapidly developing rebellion. A gentler episode for the woodwind tells of Claerchen's love for Egmont. The development section is brief, then the main melodies are recalled. The earlier foreboding is once and for all dissipated by an exultant and joyous proclamation in F major by the full orchestra, the voice of victory for the forces of freedom.

Of the remaining eight numbers in Beethoven's incidental music, the most celebrated, besides the Overture, is Claerchen's song in Act I, scene three, "Die Trommel geruehret," with its stirring martial character. The ringing tones of this music find a companion in the opening military music of the second orchestral Entr'acte, between the second and third acts. A gentler mood is evoked with the haunting strains of Claerchen's song in Act III, second scene, though even here there is at times a suggestion of agitation ("Freudvoll und Leidvolle"). The third Entr'acte—following the love scene of Claerchen and Egmont—begins with a tender preface to Claerchen's song to Egmont. After a three measure transition in solo oboe, the music changes character and becomes rhythmically vigorous, suggesting the arrival of the Duke of Alba and his Spanish troops to quell the rebellion. The exquisite and moving music of "Claerchen's Death" is heard while the curtain in the fifth act remains raised upon an empty stage. "Melodrama" is a highly atmospheric orchestral episode that accompanies Egmont's prison scene in which he cries out for sleep to ease his torment.

1811. PIANO TRIO IN B-FLAT MAJOR, "ARCHDUKE," op. 97. I. Allegro moderato. II. Allegro. III. Andante cantabile ma però con moto. IV. Allegro moderato.

Beethoven's last piano trio is his greatest in this medium. It is known as the *Archduke* by virtue of its dedication to Beethoven's friend and patron, the Archduke Rudolph. A spacious melody for the piano, "dolce," which opens the first movement is its most important subject. A subsidiary theme, also for the piano (it bears resemblance to the main theme in the first movement of the Fourth Piano Concerto) fails to detract interest from that opening melody. Beethoven places his Scherzo in the second-movement slot. It is lively and mischievous, with a vivacious tune for the strings in the first part, and two themes (one of them fugato) in the trio. The third movement opens with an extended song of a decidedly religious nature, and continues on with five variations; in each, the melody undergoes radical transformation, but with the harmony only slightly altered. After a recitative-like coda, the final movement, a rondo, comes without break. This music, says Roger Fiske, "is something of an oddity, different in mood from any other music. The main tune trips along with a gaiety that is somehow not real, while the principal episode is definitely uncouth; perhaps it is one of Beethoven's jokes."

1812. SYMPHONY NO. 7 IN A MAJOR, op. 92. I. Poco sostenuto; Vivace. II. Allegretto. III. Prèsto; Assai meno presto. IV. Allegro con brio.

SYMPHONY NO. 8 IN F MAJOR, op. 93. I. Allegro vivace e con brio. II. Allegretto scherzando. III. Tempo di minuetto. IV. Allegro vivace.

Four years elapsed after the writing of the *Pastoral* before Beethoven set to work on a new symphony. In 1812, he completed not one but two symphonies.

Wagner's interpretation of the Seventh Symphony as the "apotheosis of the dance" is familiar, but it should not be taken too literally. Actually, the symphony is the apotheosis of rhythm. In each of the four movements,

Beethoven uses a single rhythmic figure and builds it up with Titanic strength and accumulative power,—most especially in the first, third, and fourth movements.

Beethoven had dispensed with a slow introduction to the first movements of the Fifth and Sixth Symphonies; he reverts to it in the Seventh. Here it is based on an ascending passage for first violins and a delicate little melody for oboe. The note of "E" repeated consistently, with increasing volume, leads into the main theme of the Vivace. This is a free-flowing melody for the flute. There is no contrasting second subject; the rest of the movement is but a rhythmic treatment of the main theme, the rhythm all the while gaining in force and kinaesthetic drive. In the coda, a five-note phrase in cellos and double-basses provides a dynamic background for the relentless sweep by the rest of the orchestra toward a climax. This coda generates such inexorable power that Weber, on hearing it, remarked that Beethoven was now "quite ripe for the madhouse."

The rhythmic force, while held in check, still makes its presence felt in the second-movement Allegretto. Following an opening chord, cellos and basses are heard in a simple march tune. When it is repeated in second violins, it is placed contrapuntally above a new melody in violas and cellos. A fugato passage brings on a passing storm, which subsides into a haunting song for clarinets and bassoons, accompanied by violin triplets. A suggestion rather than a complete restatement of the opening march tune brings the movement to an end.

In the third movement the full orchestra erupts with a windswept subject. Alternations of loud and soft passages provide an ever-changing landscape. In the middle trio, a religious kind of melody is chanted by clarinets, bassoons, and horns; it is said to have been derived from a pilgrim's hymn familiar in Lower Austria.

In the finale, the demoniac forces are let loose. The uncontrolled energy of the opening theme has, says Sir George Grove, "a vein of rough, hard, personal boisterousness," and the same kind of feeling "which inspired the strange jests, puns and nicknames that abound in his [Beethoven's] letters." The music now moves from one climax to the next, never relenting in its motor energy. "The force that reigns throughout this movement," says Grove, "is literally prodigious, and reminds one of Carlyle's hero, Ram Dass, who had a 'fire enough in his belly to burn up the entire world.'"

The Eighth Symphony is like a graceful basilica standing beside the two cathedrals of the Seventh and the Ninth. Its dimension is smaller than that of either of these two monuments; its writing is more concise. The Eighth Symphony is full of the same kind of "unbuttoned" joviality, good humor, and impishness in which Beethoven liked to indulge in his lighter moments. "In the Eighth," said Wagner, "the power is not so sublime, though it is still more strange and characteristic of the man, mingling farce and Herculean vigor with the games and caprices of a child." Beethoven himself cherished this symphony, referred to it affectionately as the "little one," and insisted that, though it did not make much of an impression when first performed, it was "much better" than many of his larger works.

The first movement presents the principal theme without introduction. It is an ebullient subject heard in full orchestra; clarinet and other woodwind offer a gentle reply. A brief pause precedes the second theme, a lilting tune in D minor for first and second violins. The first five notes of the first theme, and an octave figure ending the first division of the movement, are the material for the development section. This main subject, now given by basses and bassoons, brings on the recapitulation. The coda comes after a restatement of the second theme, while the first five notes of the first theme bring the movement to a peaceful conclusion.

This symphony has no slow movement. Its place is taken by a delightful scherzando. Delicate staccato chords in the winds lead into an exquisite tune shared by first violins and basses. It has been said that the even beat of the chords with which this movement opens, and which persists as a discreet background to the main melody, was intended to imitate the metronome, which Beethoven's friend Maelzel had recently invented. The consistent lightness of mood of this scherzando continues on into the next movement, a Minuet, with a stately first melody and a graceful lyric line as the basic thought of the middle trio. But it is in the finale, in free rondo form, that Beethoven is most impish and boisterous. The jovial first theme is heard at once quietly in the strings, then repeated loudly by the orchestra. A lovely refrain in the first violins—the second subject—provides a change of mood. The woodwind repeat this thought. This material is developed and recapitulated with lightning changes of dynamics and tempo, and with the arresting intrusion of unexpected pauses, which help to maintain a vivacious spirit right up to and through the breezy coda.

1812. SONATA IN G MAJOR, for violin and piano, op. 96. I. Allegro moderato. II. Adagio espressivo. III. Allegro. IV. Poco allegretto.

Beethoven's tenth and last violin sonata was written for the French virtuoso Pierre Rode, who introduced it in Vienna in 1812, with the Archduke Rudolph at the piano. This is one of the composer's warmest, and most intimate, creations in the violin-sonata form. The delicate opening theme dominates the first movement and, however altered, never seems to abandon either lightness of touch or grace. The slow movement has a subdued and restrained beauty, its heart a supple and mobile melody. The Scherzo, says John N. Burk, "never touches the ground" while the finale "is simplicity itself . . . its course . . . held back before the close by a long Adagio episode which without literal reminiscence strives to reestablish the mood of the slow movement."

1815. 2 SONATAS FOR CELLO AND PIANO, op. 102:

C major. I. Andante; Allegro vivace. II. Adagio; Tempo d'andante; Allegro vivace.

D major. I. Allegro con brio. II. Adagio con molto sentimento d'affetto. III. Allegro fugato.

Beethoven's last two cello sonatas (which came six years after the one in A major) "set us squarely in the so-called third period of Beethoven's development," wrote Mark Brunswick. "The style of these two sonatas combines intensity with the greatest possible suppleness and economy to give the effect of complete relaxation in the midst of extreme effort. Beethoven has abandoned the expansiveness of the A major Sonata. He has renounced some of the external grandeur which he himself had almost invented in music. . . . He now takes his technique so for granted that he can skip over all non-essentials, following the course of his mind with greater precision and expressiveness than ever before."

Both sonatas are described in the title as "free." Free and unusual is their structure! The C major is in only two movements, with a slow introduction for each. The D major ends with a fugue. Free, too, is the way in which the thematic material grows and changes in the first movement of the C major, almost in a rhapsodic manner. In the second movement, the first-movement Andante melody recurs unexpectedly between the opening Adagio and the concluding Allegro. In the D major Sonata, we find the only fully developed slow movement in any of the Beethoven cello sonatas. "The melody as it stands," says John N. Burk, "is sparingly used; the cello sings it only once. But the melodic invention is abundant and marvelously expressed in the duet which it maintains with the piano. The whole movement is ethereally light, at once tender and remote."

1816–1822. THE LAST PIANO SONATAS:

A major, op. 101. I. Allegretto ma non troppo: Etwas lebhaft, und mit der innigsten Empfindung. II. Vivace alla marcia: Lebhaft, marschmaessig. III. Adagio, ma non troppo, con affetto: Langsam und sehnsuchtsvoll; Allegro: Geschwind, doch nicht zu sehr, und mit Entschlossenheit.

B-flat major, "Hammerklavier," op. 106. I. Allegro. II. Assai vivace. III. Adagio sostenuto. IV. Largo; Allegro risoluto.

E major, op. 109. I. Vivace, ma non troppo. II. Prestissimo. III. Andante molto cantabile ed espressivo.

A-flat major, op. 110. I. Moderato cantabile molto espressivo. II. Allegro molto. III. Adagio ma non troppo; Fuga: allegro ma non troppo.

C minor, op. 111. I. Maestoso; Allegro con brio ed appassionato. II. Arietta: adagio molto semplice e cantabile.

In his last five sonatas (Numbers twenty-eight through thirty-two) Beethoven strikes a new course for piano music. Here (as in his last string quartets) we encounter spiritual concepts and mysticism, probings into regions never before ventured into by music. Here, too, structure must give way and crumble before the hurricane of Beethoven's tempestuous moods. His revelations demand dynamics, sonorities, and colors the piano had never been known to give: Beethoven was now writing for the Hammerklavier, with its percussive action, and not for the clavier with its more delicate tones produced by plucked strings. These sonatas also call for a new orientation to melody, harmony, thematic growth, and polyphony.

The A major Sonata (1816) is chameleon-like in its changing emotions. The first movement is gentle and reflective, unified by the use of a single basic theme and a consistent rhythm. Vigor enters the second movement with a march-like subject introduced by two strong chords. The vitality thus generated continues on into the trio, which makes use of canonic imitations; but the coda reverts to the poetic atmosphere of the first movement. From this point on, the music ascends to a lofty elevation of thought and feeling with a brief fourteen-measure Adagio. Beethoven intended this to be the preface to the mighty drama of the finale, whose opening subject is later built up into a four-voiced fugue.

Beethoven designed all five of his last piano sonatas for the "Hammerklavier," but only one of these is specifically entitled *Hammerklavier*. This is the one in B-flat major (1818), the colossus among Beethoven's sonatas. On none of his other works in this medium did he expend so much time, thought, effort, and concentration. None is more spacious in design, more meaningful in thought, more epical in concept and more demanding on pianistic technique. This is almost a symphony for the piano—a fact well recognized by Felix Weingartner when he orchestrated it. Herculean strength and surpassing tenderness take turns in the opening movement. Stout-fisted chords thunder out defiance in the opening measures, but soon get a sensitive reply. But it is struggle that is uppermost in this cyclonic music, its material evolved from the germinal theme found in the opening two measures. The Scherzo passes from levity to anguish and back to levity again. Now comes the Adagio (the longest one Beethoven ever wrote) whose quivering nerves are laid bare by discords, shifting tonalities, sudden leaps from the highest treble to the lowest bass. "The pain that tears the heart no longer has the word here," said Hans von Buelow, "but—as it were—tearless resignation rigid as death." To this Robert Haven Schauffler adds: "In this superhuman passage . . . Beethoven triumphantly stands the test of the supreme artist—even in death we are in beauty. . . . Half-way through the immensity of this movement something happens. We have been too long under an intense strain. Though the movement is in strict form and every note has its unimpeachable reason for being, the listener is so weary by the time he reaches the middle, that from there on much of the music sounds to him as though Beethoven, plunged into the depths of an amorphous daydream, had remained too long submerged."

This sonata ends with a giant three-voice fugue built from a ten-measure subject. J. W. N. Sullivan described this fugue as "the expression of the final refusal of annihilation, even if no hope and no object be left in life." Preceded by a low fantasia-like section with a nebulous tonality (which comes to a peak with high trills) this fugue becomes not just musical architecture but human experience. A succession of searing trills point up a grief too terrible to be borne. A singing D major melodic episode marked "sempre dolce e cantabile" brings balm to the troubled heart; and the cascade of trills and chords with which the movement ends proclaims victory of the spirit over the flesh.

Like the *Moonlight* Sonata of an earlier period, the Sonata in E major (1820) was designated by the composer "quasi una fantasia." The first movement flexibly alternates fast and slow passages in a fantasia structure. A Vivace section, with its prelude-like character, is heard at the beginning, in the middle and at the end of the movement. This Vivace alternates with a poetic, moody Adagio episode. The ensuing Prestissimo is a substitute for the more usual Scherzo and provides a graceful prelude to the finale. In that closing movement, a theme of surpassing beauty is subjected to six variations. Both theme and variations are in a slow tempo, the first time that Beethoven ended a sonata with an Andante.

The Sonata in A-flat major (1821) is one of the most lyrical in this group. While the main melodic interest can be found in the soulful Arioso dolente, there is almost a continuous flow of the melodic line in the opening movement. The Scherzo, however, has the kind of whimsical fancy we more usually associate with Schumann. And in the finale, Beethoven once again utilizes the fugue to provide the entire composition with a crown.

Beethoven's last piano sonata, in C minor, (1822) is in only two movements. A majestic introduction serves as a prelude to a fugal section that unfolds in the ensuing Allegro. This is music of storm and stress. Its principal theme, in octave unison, erupts like a thunderbolt. But in the last sonata movement he was destined to write for the piano, Beethoven finds true serenity. This second (and concluding) movement is an Arietta with variations. These variations, says Romain Rolland, "lap around it [the melody] tenderly, like waves caressing the sands on a beautiful calm day. The first variation gently stirs the rhythm of the theme. The second doubles the movement, and the third redoubles, and yet the peaceful calm is not disturbed. Into the coda steals one of those beautiful pensive movements in the minor key. This emerges into the return of the theme, scintillating with heavenly radiance. Thus Beethoven closes his sonatas in a heavenly peace."

1823. THIRTY-THREE VARIATIONS IN C MAJOR ON A WALTZ BY DIABELLI, op. 120.

This was Beethoven's last work for the piano, and it is one of his mightiest. To Hans von Buelow these *Variations* is a "mikrokosmos of Beethoven's genius." He added that "the whole image of the world of tone is outlined here, the whole evolution of musical thought and sound fantasy from the most contained contemplation to the most abandoned humor—an unbelievably rich variety." The melody by Diabelli (which Beethoven once described as a "cobbler's patch") is an insignificant little waltz tune. Diabelli invited a number of composers to write variations for it, Schubert included. Beethoven preferred doing not just one variation but thirty-three. Variety of tempo, key, mood, ever changing moods, alterations of harmony and rhythm, all make possible the exploration of a whole gamut of emotion, a whole world of human experience. The last variation opens significantly in the tempo of a minuet. It is almost as if Beethoven wanted to recall for the last time the age of Haydn and Mozart that had nurtured him. Then the minuet is abandoned for the remote and objective kind of music Beethoven himself had conceived for his last sonatas. This step from the minuet to Beethoven's last piano style represented to Schumann Beethoven's farewell to his audience; and, since Beethoven never again wrote for the keyboard, it was also his farewell to the piano.

1823. MISSA SOLEMNIS IN D MAJOR, for solo voices, chorus, and orchestra, op. 123.

Beethoven planned the *Missa solemnis* as a festive *pièce d'occasion* for the installation of the Archduke Rudolph as the Archbishop of Olmuetz in 1820. As befitting such an event, Beethoven decided upon a religious work, a Mass, and started to work on it in 1819. His purpose, he explained, was "to arouse religious emotions in singers and auditors alike, and to render this emotion lasting." Notwithstanding his intentions, Beethoven did not produce a religious work, but the personal testament and credo of a man whose religion was Nature, and who worshiped the spirit of man and the creative process. As Lawrence Gilman said: "Beethoven paid scant attention to the rubrics, to the institutional traditions and properties, to liturgical formulas. His passionate and dramatizing imagination had not gone far in its dealing with the text when it overleaped all bounds and went its own way. For Beethoven had fixed his mind and heart less on the churchly rubrics than on the immemorial human realities that lie behind and below and above the missal text—upon the pitiful and everlasting soul of man, suffering, fearing, longing, pleasing, hoping, worshiping, praying."

In the London *Sunday Times,* Ernest Newman explained: "He dramatized his religious text as no one had done before or has done since. It is equally true that in the text of the Mass the mature Beethoven found an outlet for the dramatic part of him which he was unable to find in opera after *Fidelio,* because he could never light upon a theater subject that appealed to him. The unusual dimensions of the Mass are due, strictly speaking, not so much to the choruses, colossal as these are, as to Beethoven's minute exploration of the emotional possibilities of what may be called the more personal sections of the text. It is after he has finished with his great choral movements, with their mountainous wave on wave of polyphony that . . . he abandons himself to his heart's content to the personal and dramatic forms of expression that give the Mass its unique quality; it is now that we get the long and searching meditation upon the 'Benedictus,' the moving 'Agnus Dei' with its startled cry of 'Agnus Dei qui tollis peccata mundi' interpolated between the two developments of 'Dona nobis pacem,' its realistic treatment of the emotional motive of the longing for 'peace in our time, O Lord,' with its plain hinting at the drums and trumpets of war and, according to the old Vienna tradition . . . the beating of the wings of the dove in the orchestra interlude that precedes the final 'Dona nobis pacem.'"

When the spirit seized him, and he had to put down on paper the visions that tortured him, Beethoven was seized by what he once described as "raptus." This happened to him when he wrote the *Missa solemnis*. "In the living room, behind a locked door," described his friend Schindler, "we heard the master singing, howling, stamping. After we had been listening a long time to this almost awful scene, and were about to go away, the door opened and Beethoven stood before us with distorted features, calculated to excite fears. . . . Never, it may be said, did so great an art work see its creation under more adverse circumstances."

The project kept growing under his fingertips, assuming monumental proportions. Thus by the time the Archduke Rudolph was installed in 1820, the *Missa Solemnis* was not ready, and music by Haydn and Hummel had to be substituted. In fact, it took Beethoven three more years to complete his giant work.

Over the opening "Kyrie," Beethoven wrote: "It comes from the heart—may it go to the heart." A majestic orchestral introduction precedes the arrival of the chorus in the "Kyrie eleison"—the outburst coming like a flash of blinding sun. The emotion is heightened with a modulation from D to F-sharp, and with the acceleration of the tempo. "Against the melodic figure of the 'Eleison,'" Rosa Newmarch explains, "the cry of 'Christe' is constantly reiterated. At first only the solo quartet carries on the contrapuntal treatment, but presently the chorus joins in with grand effect." Then the opening "Kyrie" music is repeated, extended, amplified.

The second section is the resplendent "Gloria in excelsis," an overpowering chorus in praise of the Lord. The music rises to a peak of exultation and ends up in a stirring fugal section. An orchestral interlude of deeply felt emotion brings on the solo quartet in the "Gratias agimus," the voices entering in imitation, beginning with the tenor, and continuing with the contralto, soprano, and bass. A mighty climax is reached with the word "Omnipotens," in which the trombones join, but the second ends in a subdued choral episode. The woodwind (Larghetto) now bring on the solo quartet and chorus in the "Qui tollis"—a poignant plea for mercy. This is followed by the dramatic "Quoniam tu solus sanctus" with which the "Gloria" section ends after bringing back a brief recollection of the opening "Gloria" theme.

The magnificent "Credo," says Rosa Newmarch, "has been compared in structure to a cathedral having three aisles, the center one leading to the high altar of sacrifice: 'Et homo factus est.'" The trombones present the main

"Credo" subject, which is then repeated by the basses, and after that developed in imitation. Eloquence is achieved in the "Crucifixus," while joy erupts in the choral "Et Resurrexit" that follows it. The "Credo" concludes with a monumental fugue on the word "Amen."

A touching orchestral prelude (Adagio) introduces the main melody of the "Sanctus." One by one the voices of the solo quartet appear, joining upon the word "Dominus." This material is repeated, the last six measures "intoned softly against an accompaniment which adds greatly to their effect: the quivering figures for strings, the soft roll of drums, the occasional entry of trombones . . . all combine to give a somber and mysterious color in complete accordance with the impressive character of the text." The sopranos in the chorus are now heard in the fugue subject ("Pleni sunt coeli"). This section ends with a rousing "Osanna."

An instrumental, thirty-two measure Praeludium introduces the beatific "Benedictus" for quartet and chorus, while a solo violin provides an ethereal background. The Mass ends no less sublimely, with the "Agnus Dei," whose opening theme is given by the bass. The solo contralto takes this melody over, followed by the solo tenor; then all the voices are finally joined. Now comes the section over which Beethoven wrote: "A prayer for inward and outward peace." "He begins," says Rosa Newmarch, "with the prayer for inward peace, 'Dona nobis pacem,' the chorus dealing with the first theme. Soon we come to the use of double counterpoint, the second violins having a moving accompaniment in semiquaver figures. . . . The prayer for eternal peace now has its turn. In an Allegro assai (B-flat) distant drums and trumpets suggest the advance of a hostile army. The strings keep up an agitated tremolo against which the contralto solo (followed by the tenor) softly and timidly gives out in recitative the words 'Agnus dei, qui tollis,' while the chorus breaks in with 'Miserere nobis.'" The last part of the "Agnus Dei," and the Mass as a whole, concludes Rosa Newmarch, has "few parallels in religious music [for] power and benignity. . . . The key is now the clear and radiant one of D major, and the 'Dona nobis' has taken on an aspect of restful confidence; earthly fears are calmed, and the Mass ends in an atmosphere of spiritual serenity."

1823. SYMPHONY NO. 9 IN D MINOR, "CHORAL," for solo voices, chorus, and orchestra, op. 125. I. Allegro ma non troppo, un poco maestoso. II. Molto vivace. III. Adagio molto e cantabile. IV. Allegro assai.

Beethoven's last symphony took many years to germinate. As early as 1792, he had been attracted to Schiller's *Ode to Joy.* His Piano Fantasy of 1800 (which see) contains a melodic germ of the "ode to joy" theme of the Ninth Symphony. Sketches for this last symphony are found in his notebooks two years before he started to work in earnest, in 1817. Then other projects compelled him to put the symphony aside. He returned to it in 1822. Only when the work was in an advanced stage did Beethoven finally decide that this was the place for the "ode to joy." But Beethoven apparently had misgivings about a choral ending. Even in 1823, he was still thinking of using an instrumental, instead of a choral, last movement; and both Czerny and Sonnleithner maintain that after the symphony had already been performed with chorus, Beethoven was still pondering whether he should not abandon the choral parts and write new instrumental ones.

The finale—the first time Beethoven introduced the human voice into a symphony—was the last will and testament of a man who all his life had clung to the ideal of brotherhood of man, who was ready to sing a culminating paean to Joy at the fulfillment of that ideal. A good deal of controversy has long persisted regarding this choral movement. Some regard it as the inevitable culminating peak of the entire symphony—the essence of Beethoven's poetic, social, and philosophic ideas; the mightiest hymn to joy ever conceived. Wagner extolled the "pure and lasting humanity of this music." Donald Francis Tovey pointed out that "there is no part of Beethoven's Choral Symphony which does not become the clearer to us for assuming that choral finale is right; and there is hardly a point that does not become difficult and obscure as soon as we fall into the habit which assumes that the chorale finale is wrong." Others (perhaps made too painfully aware of Beethoven's cumbersome writing for the voices) feel that these choral pages are anti-climactic. Here is how Philip Hale put it: "The music of the first three movements is not the less sublime or beautiful because it has no program, because it has no text for singers. With the exception of a few stupendous passages in the finale, where Beethoven is among the stars, the finale falls below the movements that precede it. . . . The theme of Joy is not in itself one of Beethoven's most fortunate inventions, and there are pages both for singers and for the orchestra that disconcert even if they do not seem to the hearer abnormal and impotent." But where Hale had found the Joy theme one of Beethoven's lesser conceptions, Sir George Grove maintained that a "nobler and more enduring tune does not exist," while Wagner found that "Beethoven has emancipated his melody from all influence of fashion and variations of taste, and has raised it into a type of pure and lasting humanity."

The symphony opens with the merest suggestion of a theme founded on the D minor triad, played tremolo by the first violins. Slowly, inevitably—like an embryo being given birth—the theme grows for sixteen measures until it emerges full grown in unison orchestra. The subject is treated with agitation. The struggle goes on and on, then subsides as a gentle and reflective melody is shared by flute and clarinet. But the struggle must resume; one idea after another, some of them no more than fragments while others are fully stated, come in successive waves. To Wagner this music represented a Titanic battle "conceived in the greatest grandeur of the soul, contending for happiness against the oppression of that inimical power which places itself between us and the joys of earth." A heart-rending descending melody for the first violins may suggest temporary defeat. And before the movement closes, there is even a somber threnody for the woodwind. But the human spirit must prevail. The movement comes to a triumphant end with the opening theme exclaimed proudly by the full orchestra over thundering rolls of the timpani.

Beethoven changes the usual order of the symphony by placing the Scherzo before the slow movement. The joyous Scherzo melody appears staccato in the second violins after a twelve-measure introduction. Other instruments join in fugally. The spirit of merriment penetrates right into the trio, with its tripping melody for oboes and clarinets.

The gaiety over, Beethoven embarks in his slow movement on one of the most exalted and serene reflections in all symphonic literature. First, we hear a melody of ethereal beauty in the first violins. Then second violins and violas contribute a second subject in which the former serenity is transformed into other-worldly radiance. As one variation follows the next, the music becomes, as Robert Haven Schauffler said of it, "one of the holiest, purest outpourings of exaltation in the whole domain of mystical music."

This sublimity is shattered by a piercing chord and a shriek from the entire orchestra. The stage is being set for the Ode to Joy. But what should be its basic melody? The principal theme of each of the preceding movements is briefly recalled, and just as quickly dismissed. Joy unconfined calls for a nobler statement than any of these. That nobler statement is now heard in cellos and basses. The violas join in, then the violins take over, and finally the full orchestra adopts it. After the hymn to joy has been varied, a turbulent presto section brings on a recitative for solo baritone: "Oh, Friends, no more these sounds continue. Let us raise a song of sympathy and gladness. Oh, Joy, let us praise thee!" The song now emerges loud and clear and rapturous in the solo baritone (accompanied by oboes and clarinets). Chorus and vocal quartet take it over. As the hymn is repeated and varied, new strains are introduced—sometimes martial, sometimes dramatic, sometimes religious. In the final prestissimo for chorus, the joy becomes unconfined.

Beethoven sold the exclusive performance rights for a year and a half to the London Philharmonic Society for fifty pounds. Though Beethoven kept the money, he did not stick to his bargain. The première of the Ninth Symphony took place not in London but in Vienna, on May 7, 1824. Michael Umlauf conducted, Beethoven sat among the orchestra players in full sight of the audience, indicating to the conductor tempo changes with brisk movements of the hand. The response to the new symphony was electrifying. The excitement during the Scherzo was so great that midway the audience applauded and drowned out the music. After the finale, the audience rose to thunder its approval. Totally deaf, and deeply engrossed, Beethoven was not aware of this tumult until the contralto soloist, Frau Unger, came to him and gently led him to the edge of the stage to acknowledge the ovation. "His turning around," Mme. Unger later recalled, "and the sudden conviction thereby forced on everybody that he had not done so before because he could not hear what was going on, acted like an electric shock on all those present, and a volcanic explosion of sympathy and admiration followed, which was repeated again and again, and seemed as if it would never end."

1824–1826. THE LAST STRING QUARTETS:

E-flat major, op. 127. I. Maestoso; Allegro. II. Adagio ma non troppo e molto cantabile. III. Scherzando vivace. IV. Allegro.

B-flat major, op. 130. I. Adagio ma non troppo; Allegro. II. Presto. III. Andante con moto ma non troppo poco scherzando. IV. Alla danza tedesca: allegro assai. V. Cavatina: adagio molto espressivo. VI. Allegro.

C-sharp minor, op. 131. I. Adagio ma non troppo e molto espressivo. II. Allegro molto vivace. III. Allegro moderato. IV. Andante ma non troppo e molto cantabile. V. Presto. VI. Adagio quasi un poco andante. VII. Allegro.

A minor, op. 132. I. Assai sostenuto; Allegro. II. Allegro ma non tanto. III. Molto adagio. IV. Alla marcia assai vivace; Allegro appassionato.

F major, op. 135. I. Allegretto. II. Vivace. III. Lento assai cantate e tranquillo. IV. Grave ma non troppo tratto; Allegro.

Grosse Fuge, in B-flat major, op. 133.

The last five Beethoven string quartets are the most remarkable not only among his own creations but also in all string-quartet literature. Here we confront a new manner of voice treatment, a new approach to structure, a new concept of lyricism and thematic development together with the most daring progressions, modulations, and discords. All this helps to create an emotional state, a kind of spiritualization, music had never known before this. Beethoven seeks to make music the means by which ever deeper, ever profounder concepts are projected. It is music that at times seems to transcend human experience, seeks to attain what J. W. N. Sullivan once called "a state of consciousness surpassing our own where our problems do not exist and to which our highest aspirations . . . provide no key." To Aldous Huxley, this music has realized "the miraculous paradox of eternal life and eternal repose." Beauty of sound is displaced by harsh statements and brusque accents. The formal presentation of themes and their development must make way for a new process where one theme, or the fragment of a theme, follows another in quick succession and with unprecedented fluidity; now this material is altered, now it is interrupted, now it is varied, now it is just suggested in a whisper or in a passing breath. The impact of this onrush of ideas and states of consciousness once and for all breaks down old structural barriers to permit musical thought full freedom of movement.

Each of these last quartets, says A. Hyatt King "coordinates an aspect of some transcendent, mystical vision which is expressed, as Wagner put it, in a serenity that passes beyond beauty. Chamber music here attains its apotheosis . . . [explores] wholly new regions of consciousness . . . [discovers] new synthesis of spiritual experience." What we have here is no longer the emotional gamut of earlier Beethoven quartets but, as Homer Ulrich notes, "the spiritualized equivalents of these moods." He adds: "The subjective, merely human emotions have been transformed into their objective, almost disembodied counterparts. Great strength becomes inexorable force; charm becomes austere beauty; extreme joy becomes divine abandon."

The first of these final quartets—that in E-flat major (1824)—has a majestic six-bar slow introduction before proceeding to an Allegro movement that is mainly serene and pastoral. From such an idyllic state we pass on to the slow movement, with its spirituality and mysticism. A sublime melody is followed by five variations, some of which make extensive use of polyphonic resources. In its various transformations, the melody continually acquires a new identity, a new way of life. This slow movement is one of the longest in any Beethoven quartet; and so is the Scherzo that follows. The Scherzo opens nervously, a feeling of unrest that continues on in the trio. The finale, however, provides occasional respite from agitation through its excursions into warm lyricism and at times subjective approaches.

The need for more *Lebensraum* compelled Beethoven to expand the string-quartet structure into six movements in the B-flat major Quartet (1825). To the usual four-movement form he added a German-like movement, and a second slow movement. That slow episode, a Cavatina that lasts only sixty measures, appears between the third movement Andante and the finale. It begins in an ethereal vein, but quickly gains in intensity and passion until it reaches a C-flat major passage; after that, when the tonality changes to the relative A-flat minor, the feeling is "anguished," a word which the composer himself placed over the passage. Beethoven followed this stirring, soulful, and at times tortured Cavatina with a monumental fugue as a finale. But the publishers regarded this music as too complicated and abstruse, and convinced Beethoven to write a new finale. The one with which Beethoven finally replaced the fugue is Beethoven's last piece of music. "It was," says John N. Burk, "a swan song, smiling and fulsome, a final proof that heavy sickness, misery and drab surroundings could not encroach upon the serene spirit and the firm hand." The fugue was published separately as opus 133, and is commented upon below.

An even larger structure was needed by Beethoven for his C-sharp minor Quartet (1826)—seven movements. The work opens with an introductory slow fugue that has an awesome grandeur and is filled with brooding mysticism. The Allegro movement that follows represents to Paul Bekker "the return to life, to joyful thought and emotion, an incarnatus est in the human rather than religious sense." The third-movement Andante is merely a transition to the slow movement, a theme and variations. The ensuing quicksilver music of the Presto is, in reality, a Scherzo. There now comes a brief twenty-eight measure slow section, Adagio, surely one of the most profound revelations in all Beethoven. The quartet ends triumphantly, with the joyful music of a finale in sonata form.

The most remarkable movement in the A minor Quartet (1825) is the third, Molto adagio. Over it Beethoven appended the following comment: "A sacred thanksgiving of a Convalescent to the Divinity, in the Lydian Mode." Beethoven had fallen seriously ill in the spring of 1825. This movement spoke his gratitude for his full recovery. This other-worldly music opens with a chorale-like prayer and continues with a more dynamic section (Andante), over which Beethoven inscribed, "with a feeling of renewed strength." The chorale is heard three times, and its contrasting Andante, twice, suggesting *in toto* a five-part song form. The closing measures of this movement, marked "with the most intimate feeling," sound a note of sublimity without equal in quartet literature.

Beethoven's last string quartet, in F major, (1826) has caused some speculation. Over the slow theme of the finale (Grave), Beethoven scrawled the question, "Must it be?" And over the first theme of the fast section that follows, he added a second inscription, the answer, "It must be." Annotators and biographers have suggested various explanations for these two curious annotations. The most logical is that Beethoven was fully aware that he was writing his last string quartet. He is posing his question, and receiving his answer from an implacable fate. This interpretation is strengthened by the fact that at the end of the manuscript the words "last quartet" were prominently written out in the composer's hand. But there is no intimation of tragedy in this the composer's farewell to string-quartet music. There is a quiet, gentle feeling of repose throughout the slow movement. In the first movement, there is a healthy rhythmic stride that even suggests optimism; the thematic material is consistently dynamic, fragments of which are worked out powerfully, often in a polyphonic design. The Vivace that follows is, as Homer Ulrich said of it, "an impulsive, syncopated piece with a powerful, and relentless trio."

The *Grosse Fuge* which Beethoven had written as the finale to the B-flat Quartet but which he published separately, is one of the most monumental dramas ever contained within a fugal structure. It opens with a brief "Overture" (Allegro), in which the motto theme is introduced. A variation of this theme (Meno mosso e moderato) precedes the unfolding of the fugue proper, the subject passing in turn from the first violin, to the second violin, to the viola, to the cello. This fugue—with a variant of the motto theme placed in opposition to the main subject—is carried to a climax. After a sensitive interlude, a dance-like melody (a variant of the fugue motive) is interpolated. The fugal writing is then resumed, to be built up with shattering emotional effect. The agonized sounds are relieved by a return of the dance melody. The main themes are then transfigured into a *Siegensymphonie,* a Symphony of Victory.

The rich polyphonic texture and sonorities of the *Grosse Fuge* make it particularly effective in performances by a string or chamber orchestra.

LUIGI CHERUBINI 1760–1842

During the past half-century, the world of music has come to value Cherubini for compositions other than the familiar overtures to *Anacreon* and *The Water Carrier*. Arturo Toscanini's passionate espousal of Cherubini's Mass in C minor helped to establish that work permanently in the repertory of great choral music; and Cherubini's little Symphony in D introduced a good deal of grace and charm into the symphony hall as long as Toscanini was around to perform it for us. But even greater recognition has now come to Cherubini's operas. Revivals of the long neglected *Medea* at La Scala and San Francisco (as well as a complete recording) have proved once and for all that this is a classic well able to bring a rich aesthetic experience to opera lovers. Other long forgotten Cherubini operas (some of which were not even remembered by name) have shown us, in resurrection, that they also have much to recommend. When *L'Hôtellerie portugaise,* or *The Portuguese Inn* (1798) was given its first performance in America by the San Francisco Opera in 1954, Alfred Frankenstein wrote: "The music as a whole recalls Mozart, with touches of Rossinian earthiness and irony." And when *Elisa* (1794) was revived in 1960 at the Florence May Music Festival, Francis Toye reported that it contained "magnificent music. . . . It is all so beautifully done; the composition is so masterly; and the scoring and the writing for chorus especially, are so effective."

Because he had enjoyed such a rich career, first as a professor at, and then as director of, the Paris Conservatory, Cherubini was too long thought of merely as an academician with nose buried in the text book. But the more we become acquainted with his works, the more do we begin to realize not only how much fine music he wrote, but also how strongly he had influenced his successors. If some of Beethoven's themes sound like Cherubini's, this is no coincidence. Beethoven had the highest admiration for Cherubini and knew his music well. Rossini's famous crescendos had their origin in Cherubini. Weber and Wagner were two other composers who had been nurtured on Cherubini's scores.

Drawing deeply from past resources in Italian opera, Cherubini nevertheless allowed himself to be influenced by Rameau, Gluck, and Haydn. Faithful though he was to older traditions, Cherubini succeeded in bringing to his operas an enriched orchestration and harmony, a mastery in writing for the voice, and a dramatic impulse that brought the musical theater a step or two nearer to Weber, Rossini, and Verdi.

Luigi Cherubini was born in Florence, Italy, on September 14, 1760. The son of a Florentine musician, Cherubini received music instruction from several teachers including his father, Alessandro Felici, and J. Castrucci. Between his twelfth and seventeenth years, he produced a considerable amount of church music that pointed up his remarkable creative gift. Then, after an additional period of study with Giuseppe Sarti in Venice, he completed his first opera, *Quinto Fabio*—a failure when produced in Alessandria in 1780. This did not deter Cherubini from writing several more operas during the next few years. The most important was *Alessandro nell' Indie,* introduced in Mantua in 1784. Between 1784 and 1786, he lived in London, where he wrote four new operas for King's Theater; and for a year, he served as composer to the king. In 1788, he established permanent residence in Paris. Stimulated by the operas of Rameau and Gluck, Cherubini now began to extend his own horizons by emphasizing dramatic values. His new approach to opera became apparent with *Lodoïska,* an immense success when mounted at the Théâtre Feydeau in Paris on July 18, 1791. *Médée* followed in 1797, and *Les Deux Journées* (*The Water Carrier*) in 1800.

Meanwhile, Cherubini distinguished himself in other areas of music besides composition. He made successful appearances as conductor at the Italian Opera and at the Théâtre de Monsieur. In 1795 (the year in which he married Cécile Tourette), he was made Inspector of the then newly founded Conservatory in Paris.

In 1805, Cherubini paid a visit to Vienna, where several of his operas were produced. In 1816, he was made professor of composition at the Paris Conservatory; and in 1821, he rose to the post of director.

After 1809, Cherubini devoted himself more assiduously to church music than to opera; it was during this period, in 1816, that he completed his remarkable Mass in C. Cherubini went into retirement in or about 1840, and died in Paris on March 15, 1842.

1797. MÉDÉE (MEDEA), opera in three acts, with text by François Benoit Hoffman, based on the tragedy of Corneille. First performance: Paris, March 13, 1797.

It was many years before *Medea* received the recognition it deserves. When first produced, at the Théâtre Feydeau in Paris in 1797, it was more or less of a failure. Performances that followed in Vienna and Rome managed to bring a certain measure of appreciation from discriminating musicians (most notably from Beethoven, who did not hesitate to place both composer and opera on a pedestal), but the general public remained aloof. Then *Medea* lapsed into total neglect, from which it did not emerge for many a year. Indeed, the Italian première (at La Scala) did not take place until 1909. And the first performance in America had to wait a century and a half after the opera's première, and even then—in 1956 in New York—it was given only a concert presentation. Since then, however, a number of highly successful revivals have helped to put the opera in proper perspective. These included a performance at La Scala in 1953, with Maria Meneghini Callas in the title role and Leonard Bernstein conducting; and the first American-staged presentation, in 1958, by the San Francisco Opera. Alfred Frankenstein could now speak about the "broad, noble, grandly scaled score with its reflections of Gluck and its intimations of Beethoven"; and Howard Taubman could describe it as an "extraordinary work, which might have enriched the musical scene [but which] has been overlooked."

One of the reasons why *Medea* has suffered such long neglect was the difficulty in adequately filling the title role. The tortured and anguished Medea, crazed by her passion for vengeance, makes such exacting vocal and histrionic demands that singers for the part are not readily available. Fortunately, a number of artists in our time have been able to fill the bill very well, including Callas and Eileen Farrell. But casting difficulties is not the only force working against a general appreciation for *Medea*. Regrettably, the opera suffers from a static and dull libretto; most of the lesser characters are wax images rather than human beings; many a scene is nothing more than spectacle that finally wearies the eye and dulls the senses.

But the nobility and grandeur which Cherubini so often carried into his score more than compensate for the dramatic weakness of the opera: the magnificent overture; Jason's aria, "Or che piu non vedro," and that of Medea, "Deo tuoi figli la madre"; the first act duet of Jason and Medea; the march music and the bridal scene in the second act; the third-act storm music. The character of Medea is developed—even more in the music than in the text—with a compelling power. As Henry Chorley wrote: "From the time when Medea appears on the scene in the midst of the tumult of the elements, she is never again allowed to leave the stage, the remainder of the opera consisting of two scenes for her, both on the grandest scale; the first with her children, the second as the triumphal Nemesis dealing destruction around her."

About the overture—with its Beethoven-like majesty and at times even anticipations of Beethovenian thematic material—Sir George Grove wrote: "The intention of the overture—doubtless designed to reflect the story, though quite independent of the opera itself—every hearer must best interpret for himself. Though a most effective composition, and as an orchestral piece of music full of beauties, it appears to the writer to belong more to the region of pure music . . . than to those more romantic picturesque compositions of which Beethoven gave the world the earliest examples in *Coriolon* and *Leonore*."

The text stresses some of the more lurid aspects of the Greek legend (as retold by Corneille). Jason, eager to marry the daughter of the King of Corinth, threatens to murder his wife, Medea. She is given a twenty-four hour stay in which to make provisions for her children. Crazed by the desire for vengeance, Medea uses this time to murder, not only Jason's bride, but also the King of Corinth, and even her own two children. After prophecying an ignominious end for Jason, she speeds off to Athens on her chariot.

In its original version, *Medea* used spoken dialogue. But in the nineteenth century, Franz Lachner transformed all the dialogue into recitatives, a version now generally used when the opera is produced.

1800. DER WASSERTRAEGER, or LES DEUX JOURNÉES (THE WATER CARRIER), opera in three acts, with text by Jean Nicolas Bouilly. First performance: Paris, January 16, 1800.

Bouilly's text for *The Water Carrier* was an early effort to exploit the "rescue subject" to which so many opera librettists at the time were so partial, and of which Beethoven's *Fidelio* is a classic example. In *The Water Carrier,* the rescue involves Count Armand and his wife, who have fallen into disfavor with Cardinal Mazarin. Antonio, son of Michele, the water carrier, arranges for their escape. He conceals the Count and his wife in a water barrel for transport to safety. But the wagon is apprehended by the Cardinal's soldiers, who bring the Count and Countess back to Paris. There the Count learns he has been forgiven and that he will be permitted to resume his former high station without interference.

The Water Carrier is the most human of all Cherubini's operas, and its characters the most believable. This is one of the reasons why this opera has been Cherubini's most sustained success, not only in France, but also in Germany, England, and Italy. Another reason for this success has been the opera's effective arias. The most remarkable of these is Antonio's beautiful romance, "Un pauvre petit Savoyard," the prototype of later romances and ballads, and the one Wagner studied and imitated in writing "Senta's Ballad" in *The Flying Dutchman*. Two outstanding choral episodes are also strong assets to the opera: the soldier's chorus with which the second act opens, and the third-act bridal chorus, with its wholesome folk-song interest.

But the greatest single attraction of the opera, and the one that gives music lovers the greatest pleasure today, is the overture on which Beethoven lavished so much admiration. It begins with a slow introduction that has an almost ominous character as if foretelling imminent tragedy. A climax brings on the main part of the overture, where two themes are presented characterizing the Count and the Countess. The Count is represented by the first subject in the strings (later given fortissimo by full orchestra); the Countess, by an expressive thought in bassoons and violas. Passage work in flute, first violins, and clarinets is the transition to a free development section.

1803. OVERTURE TO ANACREON, for orchestra.

Anacreon was Cherubini's twentieth opera. When first produced—at the Paris Opéra on October 4, 1803—it was a fiasco. The fault lay with the librettist, who produced such a silly story that the audience frequently burst into guffaws. The principal character is the sixth-century lyrical poet of Greece, who was partial both to the grape and to the opposite sex.

The opera is forgotten, but its overture remains one of Cherubini's masterworks. The slow introduction begins with ten measures of chords for full orchestra. A dialogue between two horns and woodwind follows, progressing toward a climactic chord. The principal section is now at hand, beginning with a brisk four-measure theme for violins that is discussed in some detail. An extended crescendo (a forerunner of an effect later mastered and popularized by Rossini) contributes dramatic interest. (In this crescendo, an English horn appears significantly for the first time in symphonic music.) A change of key to F major brings on a turbulent section, where earlier material is recalled and developed. The opening theme is then recalled by the violins to lead into a forceful coda.

1813. SYMPHONY IN D MAJOR. I. Largo; Allegro. II. Larghetto cantabile. III. Allegro molto. IV. Allegro assai.

Cherubini wrote this delightful symphony for the Royal Philharmonic Orchestra of London which introduced it. For many years after that, it lay forgotten. Arturo Toscanini resuscitated it both in Italy and in the United States. A melodious slow introduction precedes the first movement, which, in place of the usual binary form, is made up of a series of successive motives. The slow movement (its instrumentation emphasizing the bassoon) has a pleasing melody that falls easily on the ear without particularly penetrating the heart. The third movement originally was a minuet; but in 1827, Cherubini rewrote it as a scherzo. The first part is interesting for its inversions and imitations; the trio is scored mainly for the woodwind. The finale, in rondo form, presents a number of ebullient subjects which help maintain a light-hearted attitude throughout the movement.

1816. MASS IN C MINOR, for mixed chorus and orchestra.

This Mass is regarded by many musicologists as Cherubini's most consistently inspired masterwork. Political considerations played a major part both in the writing and in the first performance. Cherubini, a Royalist at heart, wrote this music in memory of the recently executed Louis XVI. The first performance at the St. Denis Church in 1816 was a solemn occasion full of political overtones.

This is one of the shortest of Cherubini's Masses. Frederick J. Crowest has described it as follows: "The 'Kyrie' . . . is a chaste movement, more noteworthy for the purity of the vocal writing, and the clever blending of the voices, than for any great orchestral effects or startling harmonies. It ends peacefully enough and leads to a 'Gloria,' herein the same sentiment and coloring are hardly dispelled. The music moves leisurely on, there is no lashing of huge tone waves, no heaving of mighty forces of wind and strings. . . . There is however a suggestion of pent-up strength in the opening bars of the fine 'Credo.' The deliberate scale passage in G major, the key of the movement (Allegro maestoso), followed by the voices on the words 'Patrem omnipotentem' is bold to a degree and gives a swing and freedom to the music which are maintained up to the exquisite 'Incarnatus' movement, the latter led off slowly by first and second sopranos and altos in a beautiful passage of three-part voice writing. The 'Crucifixus' is subdued and solemn in character—indeed, it is so shrouded that the bright and triumphant tones of the 'Et Resurrexit' are welcome theologically and musically. The close of the 'Credo' is original and very striking, the intermingled soli and chorus on the word 'Amen' being skilful and effective in the extreme. The 'Sanctus,' 'O Salutaris' and 'Agnus Dei'—worthy parts of this beautiful Mass—are thoroughly characteristic of their composer, being clear in outline, pure in harmony, fresh and life-giving in melodic vigor and strength."

FRANZ SCHUBERT 1797–1828

Schubert venerated Beethoven above all other composers; and it was Beethoven who influenced him the most. The deepening of the poetic content in music, and the seeking out of new ways to extend music's expressiveness, motivated Schubert from his very beginnings. One of the reasons why his structure and modulation are so clumsy in the early works was because he was trying to emulate Beethoven without possessing the necessary know-how. As time went by, Schubert learned full well how to make his means serve his ends. Within the extended sonata form inherited from Beethoven, Schubert carried over some of Beethoven's subtle harmonic devices, unusual progressions, unexpected modulations, and intensity of lyricism.

But Schubert, of course, had to charter his own course. Because he did so—because he did not emulate Beethoven in developing and varying his thematic material but preferred developments in which the themes were continually repeated with key changes—Schubert has often been accused of lacking a sound technique in the larger forms. Nothing could be further from the truth. He did possess an extraordinary technique, and particularly in his last works; but it was his own technique, not Beethoven's. "The principal charge against Schubert for a century," wrote Hugo Leichtentritt, "is that his working-out sections are excessively long, loosely constructed, too little organic in the sense of Bach and Beethoven. . . . These apparent faults are faults only if Schubert's works are considered from the point of view appropriate to Bach and Beethoven. . . . Schubert's exposition and working-out section in the sonata form follow their own law which is not identical with Beethoven's law. . . . The reason for this departure from the classical model lies in the nature of the Romantic imagination, less inclined toward the plastic and architectural tendencies of classical music, but rather desirous of breaking away from the predominance of the tonic and dominant keys, and of bringing it quickly the brighter and richer colors of harmony."

Schubert's point of departure was ever and always melody. Since he was probably the greatest melodist of all time, he could mold lyricism at will for every possible emotion or effect—in the larger forms as well as in his songs. In the symphonies, sonatas, and quartets he could compound one beautiful melody on another with the most incredible profusion. All the while, he builds up his expositions and recapitulations—introducing magical surprises through ever changing tonalities, freshly conceived harmonies, and impressive polyphony. His innovations are always within the scope of the sonata form. These include—as pointed out in *The Outline of Music* edited by Sir Malcolm Sargent—"the enlargement and architectural use of tonality, the codettas that have their own key, the irregular recapitulations and the expositions that develop their own themes as they present them. . . . They accord with the principle of opposed tonalities. . . . The world of Schubert's tonality is that of the modern composer, who regards any tonality as a center to which all the related keys are more or less concerned."

Schubert produced masterworks in all the larger forms of music except opera. He was essentially no pioneer. He created no new musical language, invented no new forms, crystallized no new systems. But, as Marcel Schneider said, "if his attainment does not embrace the inception of new form or utterance, his own unique contribution to music lies in his approach to the inner music of the imagination, its transformation at his hands, as he raised it to new heights, new significance, in works that are creations of the absolute, the mirror of the emotions, the image of another world—an achievement, at his death, of genius not unfulfilled."

Sir George Grove put it another way when he wrote: "He did nothing to extend the formal limits of symphony or sonata, but he endowed them with a magic, a romance, a sweet naturalness which no one yet approached."

Yet there were two areas in which Schubert was *sui generis*. One was the art song, the other, miniatures for the piano. "When he began," Hugo Leichtentritt explains, "German song was merely a narrow side line in music, in which the great masters of the art disdained to promenade and which was peopled only by smaller musicians of second and third rank." In Schubert's hands, the art song became "full of dramatic fire, poetry, and pathos," Sir George Grove continues, "set to no simple Volkslieder, but to long complex poems, the best poetry of the greatest poets, and an absolute reflection of every change and breath of sentiment in that poetry; with an accompaniment of the utmost force, fitness, and variety—such songs were his and his alone. . . . There is nothing to detract from his just claim to be the creator of the German song as we know it, and the direct progenitor of those priceless treasures in which Schumann, Mendelssohn and Brahms have followed his example."

His excursions into the shorter piano forms—notably the Intermezzo and the Moment musical—meant a good deal "for the instrumental art of the entire nineteenth century," as Hugo Leichtentritt claimed. Here Schubert creates a literature of Romantic piano music whose impact on Schumann and Chopin and Mendelssohn was immediate and profound.

Franz Peter Schubert, son of a schoolmaster, was born in Vienna, Austria, on January 31, 1797. He received his first music instruction from his father, and from the organist and choirmaster of the local parish church, Michael Holzer. Revealing extraordinary ability from the beginning, Schubert was entered in 1808 in the so-called "Konvict" School which trained singers for the court; as student, he was made a member of the Vienna court choir. Under the instruction of Antonio Salieri and Ruzicka, Schubert made remarkable strides. In 1810, he completed a fantasy for piano duet; in 1811, his first art song, "Hagars Klage," was written; and by 1813, he had produced several orchestral overtures and his first symphony.

When, in 1814, his voice broke, he had to leave the "Konvict." He now prepared himself for a career as schoolteacher, a post he filled in his father's school from 1814 to 1816. He detested his work and his pupils. All his free time—and many of his working hours—were absorbed by composition. In 1814, he completed an opera, a Mass, two string quartets, piano pieces, and songs. The Mass was his first work to get performed, heard at the local parish church in Liechtenthal on October 16, 1814. The songs included his first masterwork, "Gretchen am Spinnrade." The year of 1815 proved even more productive, yielding about one hundred and fifty songs (including "Der Erlkoenig"), two symphonies, two Masses, four piano sonatas, and a string quartet.

In 1816, he decided to give up teaching and concentrate exclusively on music. He went to live with one of his friends, Franz von Schober, while other friends provided him with the wherewithall to keep body and soul together. This circle—which included the singer Johann Michael Vogl, the poet Johann Mayrhofer, and Joseph von Spaun, among others—gave him the appreciation and understanding the world outside denied him. Through merry social evenings (called "Schubertiaden") they introduced into his life most of the little joys and pleasures he was destined to experience. It was through their bounty that his first publication was made possible, a volume of songs that included "Der Erlkoenig," published in 1821. His friends also did what they could to bring about performances for his works. But these proved few and far between and, when realized, were dismal failures. Two operettas were produced in 1820—*Die Zwillingsbrueder* in 1820, and *Die Zauberharfe* a year later; in 1821, his music to *Rosamunde* was played. None of these was able to lift him out of his poverty or obscurity.

Yet he kept on working, kept on producing masterworks in prodigious quantities. Not even the deterioration of his health, beginning with 1823, nor ever mounting frustrations and depressions could stem the tide of creativity. He remained a pauper until the end of his days. Few in Vienna were aware of his real musical stature. Finally, on March 26, 1828, there took place in Vienna a concert of his works. It was received with outstanding enthusiasm and for the first time promised him a change in fortune. But it was too late. He died in Vienna on November 19, 1828, and (at his own request) was buried in a grave near Beethoven's.

It took many years for the world to realize the extent of his achievements. The manuscripts of most of his works, including many masterpieces, were gathering dust in the homes of relatives and friends. Not until they were resuscitated—through the painstaking efforts of musicians like Robert Schumann, George Grove, and Arthur Sullivan—did it become evident how much he had written during his brief life span, and how much of it was music of the first significance.

1813–1814. STRING QUARTETS:

E-flat major, op. 125. I. Allegro moderato. II. Adagio. III. Prestissimo. IV. Allegro.

B-flat major, op. 168. I. Allegro ma non troppo. II. Andante sostenuto. III. Allegretto. IV. Presto.

Schubert's first string quartet—he completed fifteen in all—came when he was fifteen years old; the last appeared in 1826. Only three were written after his nineteenth year, when he was approaching full maturity as an instrumental composer; each is treasurable.

Among the earlier quartets, the E-flat major (1813) and the B-flat major (1814) are the most interesting. There is so much in the E-flat major Quartet to suggest Schubert's later powers that some authorities place this work as late as 1817. Certainly, many of the traits we associate with Schubert can be uncovered here: the way in which he uses his four stringed instruments as voices, and writes soaring melodies for them that are almost vocal; his partiality for setting one pair of stringed instruments against the other; the spontaneity of his writing, even when it was most subtle.

The two middle movements are pure Schubert, particularly the exalted song of the Adagio and the Laendler-like Prestissimo that follows. In the first movement, there are three main and equally important themes, all in the tonic; a subsidiary idea is in B-flat. The finale is filled with the vivacity we associate with Schubert in his happier hours.

The B-flat major Quartet, written in eight days, overflows with youthful exuberance. The first movement opens with the main theme in first violin. A brief fugato ensues, with viola entering, followed by the two violins. This melody is restated by the solo cello, and imitated by the first violin. A virile second subject and broad Schubertian melody in the minor are then subjected to extensive repetition and variation. The development is brief, concerned mainly with changes in harmony. In the recapitulation, there is a striking freedom and subtlety of tonality to open up new vistas of beauty for the melodic material.

The slow movement in the sonata form (but without development) is the most beautiful in the entire work. After a fourteen-measure introduction, we hear two radiant melodies. The minuet returns meekly to Haydn, but the finale, as J. A. Westrup has noted, "is so prophetic as to suggest the Scherzo of the great C major Symphony. . . . The repeated crotchets are very characteristic."

1813–1815. SYMPHONY NO. 1 IN D MAJOR. I. Adagio; Allegro vivace. II. Andante. III. Menuetto. IV. Allegro.

SYMPHONY NO. 2 IN B-FLAT MAJOR. I. Largo; Allegro vivace. II. Andante. III. Allegro vivace. IV. Presto vivace.

SYMPHONY NO. 3 IN D MAJOR. I. Adagio maestoso; Allegro con brio. II. Allegretto. III. Vivace. IV. Presto; Vivace.

The boy Schubert, writing his first Lieder, plunged headlong and fearlessly into a brave new world of his own making. But the boy Schubert writing his first symphony, was somebody satisfied with the musical environment into which he was born. All three symphonies, written between Schubert's sixteenth and eighteenth years, are faithful to the Viennese classical school. They penetrate no emotional depths. They are satisfied to be consistently charming, even if unoriginal.

Except for the lyrical second theme of the first movement, and the youthful verve and excitement of the finale, the first symphony in D major (1813) is consistently Haydnesque. There is no denying the sweetness and grace of the slow movement of the second symphony, with its five simple variations, even while conceding that there is nothing new here (1815). But it is only in the finale that the classical formality and derivative speech give way to a personal point of view. Albert Roussel once noted that here we find the most interesting pages in the entire work. "The first bar of the opening theme . . . afterward gives opportunity towards the middle of the movement for a development of rather Beethovenian character, but original and daring and evidently contemporaneous with the writing of the 'Erlkoenig.' It is also noteworthy that the second theme of this movement in E-flat is repeated at the end in G minor."

Though the Third Symphony was begun only one month after the second had been completed, a bolder invention begins to intrude into Schubert's symphonic style. The chromaticism of the slow introduction to the first movement, whose main theme is related to the principal subject of the fast section that follows, gives us a glimpse into the future Romantic symphony. And the way in which the wind instruments, later in the same movement, indulge in an improvised conversation is a foretaste of the mature Schubert. Schubertian, too, are the two melodies of the romantic slow movement; while the minuet has the peasant exuberance of some of Schubert's best Laendler. The conversational exchange that had distinguished the first movement returns in the finale where the ideas, as Walter Dahms noted, flit "hither and yon with extraordinary vitality and lightness of motion."

1814–1828. INDIVIDUAL SONGS, for voice and piano:

"Die Allmacht," op. 79, no. 2; "An die Leier," op. 56, no. 2; "An die Musik," op. 88, no. 4; "Auf dem Wasser zu singen," op. 72; "Ave Maria," op. 52, no. 6; "Du bist die Ruh,"' op. 59, no. 3; "Der Erlkoenig," op. 1; "Die Forelle," op. 32; "Fruehlingsglaube," op. 20, no. 2; "Ganymed," op. 19, no. 3; "Geheimes," op. 14, no. 2; "Gretchen am Spinnrade," op. 2;

"Gruppe aus dem Tartarus," op. 24, no. 1; "Hark, Hark, the Lark"; "Heidenroeslein," op. 3, no. 3; "Der Hirt auf dem Felsen" (with clarinet), op. 129; "Im Abendroth"; "Im Fruehling"; "Die junge Nonne," op. 43, no. 1; "Der juengling an der Quelle"; "Die Liebe hat gelogen," op. 23, no. 1; "Litanei"; "Der Musensohn," op. 92, no. 1; "Nacht und Traeume," op. 43, no. 2; "Sei mir gegruesst," op. 20, no. 1; "Seligkeit"; "Der Tod und das Maedchen," op. 7, no. 3; "Dem Unendlichen"; "Der Wanderer," op. 4, no. 1; "Wanderers Nachtlied," op. 4, no. 3; "Who is Sylvia?" op. 106, no. 4; "Wiegenlied," op. 98, no. 2.

With his first published songs—"Der Erlkoenig" was opus 1—Schubert emerged at once the mature, fully developed genius, come full grown like Minerva from the head of Jupiter. With little precedent to guide him, and virtually no experience, the seventeen-year-old Schubert produced, between 1813 and 1814, two numbers with which the Lied, or art song, becomes fully realized. Schubert did not invent the Lied. Haydn and Mozart had written art songs, though in a simple strophic structure. Beethoven's finest songs have a strong suggestion of the Schubertian Lied in their atmosphere and expressiveness. Schubert, indeed, profited from the songwriting efforts of several now forgotten composers who preceded him, among them being Carl Friedrich Zelter (1758–1832) and Johann Rudolf Zumsteeg (1760–1802). The influence of Zumsteeg on Schubert, for example, becomes evident when we realize that the first song Schubert ever wrote—*Hagars Klage* in 1811—not only has the same text that Zumsteeg had used, but even imitates Zumsteeg's song in details.

Within the framework of their times, songs like "Gretchen am Spinnrade" and "Der Erlkoenig" are truly miraculous creations. A new concept of songwriting is here being realized. The beauty of the melody is of subsidiary importance to the needs of the text. A good many of the methods and techniques of the later and mature Schubert can already be detected here. His boldness in modulation for expressive effects is found in the third line of "Gretchen," where, as Donald Francis Tovey remarks, he shifts from "D minor to C major and straight back again without repeating C as the dominant of F. This modulation is here entirely Schubert's own." Schubert's gift at musical realism is also already fully developed—in the discords and the concluding declamation of "Der Erlkoenig"; in the simulation of a whirring spinning wheel in the piano accompaniment of "Gretchen," now in continuous motion, now the movement interrupted, and now beginning slowly to regain momentum. The genius for crystallizing a profound emotion with the simplest of means is found again and again—for example, the use of the interval of a fourth, followed by a sudden pause, to point up Margaret's ecstatic feelings when she recalls her lover's kiss. And finally, the art of *Durchkomponieren*—allowing the music chameleon-like to change shape and style continually to meet the demands of the word—becomes a basic tool of Lied creation, both in "Der Erlkoenig" and in "Gretchen," each more of a miniature human drama than a song.

Finding the proper musical dress for a poem was no casual operation for Schubert, even though many of his songs were produced with remarkable speed. Sir George Grove noted how Schubert "identified himself with the poem and the poet's mood. . . . He goes through his poem and confines himself to enforcing the expression as music alone can do to poetry. The music changes with the words as a landscape does when sun and cloud pass over it. And in this Schubert anticipated Wagner, since the words to which he writes are as much the absolute basis of his songs as Wagner's are of his librettos." So profound was Schubert's understanding of a text, so incredible his gift at finding its musical equivalent, that some of the contemporaries whose words he set were amazed to find that they had not fully understood the meaning of their own poems until they had heard Schubert's melody.

In his more than six hundred songs, Schubert became "the pioneer and pilot of a new art," as Rudolf Felber has written, "whose foundations and typical characteristics he established and whose whole . . . growth he fertilized."

Schubert's incomparable inventiveness as a writer of melodies has been the subject of many treatises. His lyricism ran the gamut from the ingenuous and folk-song simplicity of "Heidenroeslein" to the stark and austere declamation of "An die Leier"; from the effervescence of "Hark, Hark, the Lark" to the radiance of "An die Musik"; from the romantic ardor of "Who Is Sylvia?" to the storm and stress of "Der Tod und das Maedchen." But elements other than melody were at his command, to be summoned in pointing up a mood, or projecting an atmosphere, or intensifying an emotion. Rhythm suggests the quicksilver movement of fish in water in "Die Forelle" and the awesome terror of death's call to the maiden in "Der Tod und das Maedchen." Unrelated harmonies and discords carry us into the lower depths in "Gruppe aus dem Tartarus." Syncopated piano figures translate the stirring breezes in treetops into musical sound in "Wanderers Nachtlied," while rippling arpeggios simulate the play of the water in "Auf dem Wasser zu singen." Modulations and crescendos are recruited to bring up the majestic image of the Almighty in "Die Allmacht." The simplest harmonies—just a few tonic, subdominant, and dominant chords—can create the wonder and beauty of the world at sunset in "Im Abendroth." Chromaticism and enharmonic changes achieve a wondrous sublimity in "Litanei." A restless drifting from one tonality to another (Schubert's particular gift) brings touches of magic to the famous "Hark, Hark, the Lark" and "Der Mussensohn."

"Whatever he has to say," sums up Marcel Schneider, "he always says naturally and aptly, unforced in manner and feeling. He is adept at combining dramatic power with simplicity. . . . In all his music he maintains restraint and a 'sweet reasonableness'; he suggests suffering rather than conveys it, his smile is always a trifle inscrutable. Schubert expresses the essential enigma of our human nature and state, an ambiguity not to be conveyed by shouting, clamor and gesticulation or dogmatic assertion. The search for truth begins with self-searching, and Schubert pursues it scrupulously and ardently, with discretion and a sense of mysticism, as a solitary who seeks artistic revelation no less than the soul's perfection. . . . It is this which gives his songs their emotional force and their ultimate beauty, unique to Schubert."

Marcel Schneider further points out that what endows Schubert's Lieder with their remarkable beauty and expressive power are his "daring, piquant individuality of harmonies," a faculty to "create an atmosphere by altering one note, a change unexpected yet somehow anticipated," a remarkable "economy of means" and the creation of contrast "between the simple flowing melodic line and the complexity of the accompaniment." Amplifying on Schubert's accompaniments—where lies one of the basic components of his genius in song—Schneider adds: "The accompaniment somtimes becomes almost independent, having always a strongly marked individuality; Schubert conceives it symbolically, giving it a role of equal importance with the voice, treating it sometimes decoratively, as in 'Die Forelle,' sometimes as abstract, as 'Die junge Nonne,' more often both at once as in 'Der Erlkoenig.'"

Schubert, remarks Hugo Leichtentritt, came at a time when "the astounding rise of German lyric poetry called for a musician of his caliber. Goethe's matchless poetry was like Moses' staff in its effect on Schubert; at its touch a lyric stream, thus far hidden and enclosed, gushed forth. . . . He explored and conquered musically the entire field of classical and pre-classical German lyric poetry. It was not only Goethe and Schiller who inspired him to songs of incomparable beauty and expressiveness; Ossian, Klopstock, Claudius, Wilhelm Mueller, Platen, Rueckert, Heine and dozens of minor poets also helped to quench his insatiable thirst. And what a variety of lyric types! There is a continuation of the plain, folk-song like form used by . . . Zumsteeg . . . and Zelter. There is dithyrambic ode, religious ecstasy, fantastic ballad, dramatic scene; there is pathos, romantic effusion, magnificent landscape painting, vehement passion, idyllic loveliness; there is an endless variety of emotional moods, a wealth of vision combined with a power of form and artistic treatment that has never been equalled in the domain of song."

1815. MASS IN G MAJOR, for solo voices, chorus, and orchestra.

Schubert wrote six Masses, the first (F major) when he was seventeen. The G major Mass—a far more impressive work—came less than a year after that, completed within a period of five days in March of 1815 and first performed in the Liechtenthal parish church that year. Schubert's earliest Masses were influenced by Haydn, but we find in them a welcome infusion of Romanticism. The style is more homophonic than polyphonic, more secular than religious. The opening "Kyrie" of the G major Mass, and the "Gloria" that follows are brilliant and vigorous; searing melodies and deep feeling characterize the "Benedictus" and the closing "Agnus Dei," the latter of particular interest for its chromatic harmonies that serve as the base for the poignant melody for soprano solo. This Mass ends with a jubilant "Dona nobis pacem."

1816. SYMPHONY NO. 4 IN C MINOR, "TRAGIC." I. Adagio molto; Allegro vivace. II. Andante. III. Allegro vivace. IV. Allegro.

SYMPHONY NO. 5 IN B-FLAT MAJOR. I. Allegro. II. Andante con moto. III. Allegro molto. IV. Allegro vivace.

Between the writing of his third and fourth symphonies, Schubert became acquainted with Beethoven's music. The Fourth Symphony betrays the influence of this experience. The four-note rhythm pervading practically the whole work is not remote from the one dominating the first movement of Beethoven's Fifth Symphony. And the tragedy that Schubert was infilterating into some of his writing was his attempt to produce another *Eroica.*

There are some unusual passages in the first movement, beyond the gravity of expression of the slow preface which gives the entire symphony the name of *Tragic.* The second theme is in the unusual key of A-flat (instead of the expected E-flat), and the coda marks still another excursion into unorthodox tonality, that of G minor. The Minuet movement offers unusual chromaticism and novel syncopations, while the finale has some strikingly original harmonies of true romantic character, just before the end of the exposition, and preceding the close of the symphony. The most popular movement, however, is the second with its buoyant Schubertian melodies.

The fifth symphony is the finest Schubert thus far had written, and today the most popular except for the later *Unfinished* and the "great" C major. The ambition to be Beethovenian is temporarily forgotten. Schubert returns here to the classical structure and style of Haydn and Mozart—but with a difference. "Not only has he here completely mastered the classical style," says Mosco Carner, "but what is more important, he now fuses the traditional idiom with a remarkable individual expression, and the result is a work in which Haydn's wit and Mozart's gracefulness and light touch combine in perfect union with the composer's happy flow of melody and exuberant expression."

The first movement opens with a four-bar introduction leading into the happy first theme, in the strings. In a similarly jovial mood, we find the second subject, also in strings. Youthful ardor and romanticism spill over in the development with an efflorescence of lovely tunes. The slow movement presents a Schubertian song tinged with melancholy. It is given by the strings, and is enriched both harmonically and in orchestral color through the addition of woodwind. A melody of even greater tenderness is then shared by strings and woodwind. We now find an extended section, a dialogue between strings and woodwind, marked by chromaticism and striking rhythms. Now the beautiful second melody returns, while the first subject is given fresh treatment in the coda. Vivacity and vigor predominate in both the energetic Minuet and the finale; in the latter, two lively subjects are both given first by the strings.

1816–1824. DANCES, for solo piano:
Deutsche (German Dances)*; Laendler;* Waltzes.
Valses sentimentales, op. 50; *Valses nobles,* op. 77.

Some of Schubert's happiest hours were spent at his friends' homes, drinking wine, dancing, perpetrating pranks, and performing music. These soirées came to be known as "Schubert Evenings"—or "Schubertiaden"—since Schubert was their focal point of interest. For these and similar events, Schubert produced a library of dance music, all permeated with the carefree spirit of the Vienna café-house. Of Schubert's waltzes for the piano, the most famous is the second in opus 9 (written between 1816 and 1821) which some publisher gave the misnomer of *Mourning* (*Trauer*). There is, however, nothing to suggest a funereal atmosphere in the sensitive little tune which some have erroneously credited to Beethoven and which became popular in the United States in Sigmund Romberg's operetta *Blossom Time*.

Most of the waltzes, Laendler, and German Dances reveal their peasant origin in their vigorous rhythmic thrust and in the ingenuous folk-song type of melodies. "Many composers," said Robert Haven Schauffler, "have lit their miner's lamps and delved with delight in these rich subterranean deposits. The excellent parodist, Robert Schumann, knew them well, for he fooled Toepken into believing that the original D minor form of Number 8 in *Papillons* was a Schubert dance. Numbers 3, 4, and 8 of these same *Laendler,* op. 171 (1823) and Numbers 6, 7, 9 of the *German Dances,* op. 33 (in or about 1824), sound also as if they were *Papillons;* while Numbers 2 and 10 of op. 33 could have had more than a little to do with the origins of *Carnaval.* To my ear, the last of the *Valses nobles,* op. 77, might well have inspired the 'March of the Davidsbuendler Against the Philistines,' which is the finale of Schumann's amusing suite. And Number 4 of the *Last Waltzes,* op. 127 (1815–1824) has a trio that opens with a transparent paraphrase of the Grossvatertanz which is used both in *Papillons* and *Carnaval.*"

The *Valses sentimentales* (1825) and the *Valses nobles* (1827) represent a pioneer effort to combine several different waltz melodies into a single integrated composition—a form soon to come to full flower in Vienna with Joseph Lanner and Johann Strauss II. In 1910, Maurice Ravel was inspired by these Schubert waltzes to write his own *Valses nobles et sentimentales,* in two versions, one for the piano, and the other for orchestra.

1817. SONATA (OR DUO) IN A MAJOR, for piano and violin, op. 162. I. Allegro moderato. II. Presto. III. Andantino. IV. Allegro vivace.

Schubert wrote four violin sonatas. Three are found in opus 137 and were completed in 1816. The fourth came one year later. In the opening movement, four measures in the bass precede the appearance of the violin with a radiant melody. The movement retains its lyrical character throughout, though a certain amount of unrest comes through discords. The energetic and compact Scherzo movement is followed by an Andantino remarkable for unusual modulations and colorations in the piano. The finale opens with a lively tune which is followed by a second vivacious subject with the style and rhythm of a waltz.

1818. SYMPHONY NO. 6 IN C MAJOR. I. Adagio; Allegro. II. Andante. III. Presto. IV. Allegro moderato.

Schubert's Sixth Symphony is identified as the "Little" to distinguish it from the larger and greater C major Symphony that came one decade later. But it is "little" in other ways, too—in fact, it is one of the least interesting of all of Schubert's symphonies. Nor does fresh lyrical invention compensate for an over-all monotony of style.

The first movement emphasizes the woodwind. After a slow introduction, it presents the first two main themes. The lyrical interest of these ideas is maintained throughout the exposition and development. Most of the dramatic content of this movement is found only in the coda. In the second movement, a graceful melody is given by the strings and repeated by the woodwind. Several formal variations follow. In the third-movement Scherzo, woodwind and strings alternate in presenting the thematic material, which is mainly energetic; but a calm, even sober, mood intrudes into the trio. There are two main subjects in the finale. The first is capricious, the second in a perpetual-motion style.

1819. QUINTET IN A MAJOR, "DIE FORELLE," op. 114, for piano, violin, viola, cello, and double bass. I. Allegro vivace. II. Andante. III. Presto. IV. Andantino. V. Allegro giusto.

The A major Quintet is one of the earliest significant works for piano and four string instruments. Quintets by Mozart and Beethoven which preceded it were for piano and winds. The A major is also the only important quintet in the entire repertory one of whose members is a double bass.

This is one of Schubert's most lovable chamber-music compositions, due to its haunting melodies and its consistently light spirit. Willi Kahl suggests that the beautiful countryside of Steyr is a "secret collaborator in this quintet." (Schubert wrote the work in Steyr after making a walking trip through Upper Austria.) But Eric Blom insists that "those happy strains of wandering and roaming—the finale . . . is a good instance—do not suggest remote and solitary landscapes; there is always a feeling of town sociability behind them."

An arpeggio passage in the first movement brings on the first enchanting theme in the strings. This is discussed at some length before the piano contributes a second haunting melody. In the development, maintains M. J. E. Brown, "Schubert's skill is so spontaneously charming that it goes—as it it should of course—unnoticed. . . . It . . . builds up its powerful climaxes on the thematic ideas . . . against a throbbing background of upper strings."

There is a touch of nostalgia in the second movement, particularly in the opening melody, initially heard in the piano, then repeated by the violin. Two other wistful tunes follow rapidly, the first in viola and cello (accompanied by decorative passages in the piano); and the second, a rhythmic idea in the piano. The third movement Scherzo and the finale are based on Austrian and Hungarian folk melodies. In between these two dance movements comes the Andante. Here Schubert's song, "Die Forelle" (or "The Trout"), is stated by violin. Five variations follow, in two of which (the third and the fourth) the double bass plays a prominent role.

1819. SONATA IN A MAJOR, for piano, op. 120. I. Allegro moderato. II. Andante. III. Allegro.

Schubert's piano sonatas number more than twenty. The earliest ones, while continually sprouting the attractive foliage and blossoms of lovely melodies, represent for the most part a weeded garden. These sonatas are generally weak in structure and conventional in the working out of the material. The first of Schubert's piano sonatas that is consistently interesting is the A major—a comparatively small work requiring about fifteen minutes for performance. Within this slight frame, Schubert carried a number of melodies of the highest inspiration. The first comes as the initial theme of the opening movement; it is really a fully developed song, spread over nineteen measures. The second can be found in the slow movement, an inspired melody that bears a slight resemblance to the minuet from Mozart's *Don Giovanni.* There are a number of infectious tunes in the finale. These include a first subject that reminds Robert Haven Schauffler of a music box; several other themes have the vitality of Viennese dances.

1820. QUARTET IN C MINOR, "SATZ."

This is a curiosity since it consists only of a single movement (Allegro assai). Since sketches were made for a second movement, there is reason to believe that Schubert intended this music as the first movement of a full-length quartet. Why he never wrote the other movements has never been explained.

Though in a single movement, the *Quartetsatz* is among Schubert's most significant chamber-music compositions. "It is," says William Mann, "an Allegro assai of hectic dramatic power, wide-ranging in its ideas, at times almost Wagnerian. The design is audacious and, in effect, thrilling, for although the Wagnerian storm opening influences the transition subject in A-flat and the second subject in G major, it is not recapitulated exactly until after those melodies, in what proves to be the coda; so that the recapitulation seems to start with the transition subject in B-flat major (the dominant of the relative major)."

1822. THE WANDERER FANTASY, in C major, for piano solo, op. 15. (Transcribed for piano and orchestra by Franz Liszt.)

This fantasy comes by its title by virtue of the fact that it uses one of Schubert's celebrated songs, "Der Wanderer" (1819). Schubert's own version of this fantasy is for solo piano; but the work is now perhaps best known in a transcription made by Liszt for piano and orchestra. Four movements are played without interruption (I. Allegro con fuoco ma non troppo. II. Adagio. III. Presto. IV. Allegro). In the first, in sonata form without a recapitulation, the main subject is given by the orchestra; it is derived from the song rhythmically. A short cadenza precedes the statement of a new melody (dolce con grazia). In the second movement, the song is heard richly harmonized, followed by several variations. A scherzo movement comes next, first with a vigorous idea in piano and orchestra, and later with a waltz tune in the piano. The finale is an extended coda in fugal style.

1822. SYMPHONY NO. 8 IN B MINOR, "UNFINISHED." I. Allegro moderato. II. Andante con moto.

One of the few honors to come to Schubert during his lifetime was an honorary membership to a musical society in Graz in 1822. As a token of his gratitude, Schubert wrote for, and despatched to, the society an eighth symphony in B minor. That musical society rehearsed the work but never performed it. Then the manuscript was thrown into discard on a shelf at the Graz home of Schubert's friend, Anselm Huettenbrenner. There it lay forgotten for many years. In 1860, thirty-two years after Schubert's death, Huettenbrenner apprised Johann Herbeck, conductor of the Gesellschaft der Musikfreunde in Vienna, of the existence of the symphony and of its outstanding merit, and urged him to perform it. It took Herbeck five years to investigate this matter further. Finally, on December 17, 1865, Herbeck directed the world première of the B minor Symphony in Vienna. At this performance the music was played exactly as Schubert had left it, with two complete movements and nine measures of a projected Scherzo.

The enigma of why Schubert never completed the B minor Symphony, the *Unfinished,* has never been solved. The nine measures of the Scherzo movement reveal that Schubert had planned more movements than two. The fact that a composer like Schubert, who always wrote with fluency and was never at a loss for ideas, should stop after nine measures of a third movement; that he should be ready and willing to send an uncompleted work as a gift to the Graz musical society—all this offers rich material for speculation. It is the opinion of some that Schubert actually did complete two more movements and that they were lost; but this is extremely doubtful, since Huettenbrenner's manuscript did have the nine measures of the Scherzo followed by empty pages. Nor can we seriously believe that Schubert's inspiration had failed him. It had never done so before, and it was never to do so again. What is probably closest to the truth is that Schubert must have sensed that the two movements represented a complete work of art by itself—so perfect in concept and projection that any movements added to them would have been anticlimactic.

It does the B minor Symphony a disservice to call it "Unfinished." It is a completely realized masterwork. The Allegro opens with a brooding subject in basses and cellos; this is the germinal idea of the whole movement. The violins enter with a soft running passage, over which oboe and clarinet present a poignant melody. This subject soon grows in intensity as wind instruments join in. The mood now grows agitated. Suddenly, syncopated chords in violas and clarinets usher in and accompany one of the most beautiful thoughts in all symphonic literature—a song for the cellos, which gains in tenderness when it is repeated by the violins. The serenity of this rapturous page is shattered by brusque chords. Agitation returns, occasionally and intermittently relieved by a brief recall of the second theme. The drama is heightened in the development, while in the recapitulation lyricism is stressed. In the coda, the opening subject of the movement is carried to an effective climax.

The second movement is a sustained, uninterrupted rapture. A melody of otherworldly radiance is heard in violins over a descending piano accompaniment by the bass. A stronger thought intrudes with the trombones and woodwind, but this strength is soon dissipated by the return of the exquisite opening melody. Now we hear a second inspired melody, this time in clarinet over syncopated strings. Then, for a while, the full orchestra interjects a strong commentary, but even this does not break the spell. The magic continues on into the coda, where the first melody is heard for the last time, softly and poignantly, and once again over a descending pizzicato accompaniment.

1823. OVERTURE AND INCIDENTAL MUSIC TO ROSAMUNDE, op. 26: I. Entr'acte in B minor. II. Ballet in B minor. III. Entr'acte No. 2 in D major and Romanza. IV. Geister Chor (Male chorus). V. Entr'acte No. 3 in B-flat major. VI. Hirtenmelodie (Shepherd's Melody). VII. Hirtenchor (Shepherd's Chorus). VIII. Jaegerchor (Hunter's Chorus). IX. Ballet No. 2 in G major.

On December 20, 1823, the Theater-an-der-Wien presented *Rosamunde,* a romantic play by Wilhelmine von Chézy (the librettist of Weber's *Euryanthe*). It was compounded of a good deal of nonsense, impossible situations, and confusion. The play lasted only two nights.

Considering the kind of fiasco *Rosamunde* suffered, Schubert's music did well. The overture had to be repeated. "In the last act," Moriz von Schwind reported, "there came a chorus of shepherds and huntsmen so beautiful and natural that I don't recall hearing the like. It was encored, and I believe it will give the chorus in Weber's *Euryanthe* the coup de grâce. An aria, though horribly sung by Mme. Vogel, and a short pastorale were applauded."

However, once the play expired, Schubert's music went into a prolonged discard. For forty-five years it gathered dust. Then, in 1868, George Grove and Arthur Sullivan came to Vienna to seek out forgotten Schubert manuscripts. They came upon a veritable treasure trove: five symphonies, some sixty songs, and the entire *Rosamunde* score."

The most frequently played parts of this music are the Overture, the Ballet Music in G major, and the second Entr'acte in B-flat major.

The *Rosamunde* Overture we hear today was not written for the play at all. The one heard in 1823 was a composition Schubert had done three years earlier for the operetta, *Die Zauberharfe*. Schubert *did* write a *Rosamunde* Overture later, published as a piano duet. But, to add to the confusion, this once again was no new piece of music but an overture he had written in 1822 for the operetta, *Alfonso und Estrella*.

The *Die Zauberharfe* Overture—now universally known as *Rosamunde*—has a stately introduction, its main subject a lovely refrain for oboe and clarinet. The Allegro section arrives with a lively melody for violins. A brief development precedes the presentation of the hauntingly lyrical second subject in the woodwind.

The G major Ballet Music (Andantino)—the ninth number in the score—is a light, graceful Viennese dance become familiar to us through various transcriptions. The B-flat major En'tracte (Andantino) is the fifth number. This is the melody that Schubert loved so dearly that he used it in the slow movement of his A minor String Quartet and in his B-flat major Impromptu for piano.

1823. SONATA IN A MINOR, for piano, op. 143. I. Allegro giusto. II. Andante. III. Allegro vivace.

This is one of the later piano sonatas that consistently bears the stamp of greatness. The first theme of the first movement is a poignant melody in soft unison octaves. Some supercharged emotion erupts and dies away before the simple second subject, in repeated chords and notable for the use of suspension, is heard. The development has such grandeur that Ralph Bates has felt the need of an orchestra for proper projection. The main melody of the lyrical slow movement has two sections, each interrupted by a brief comment. A subsidiary melody carries on the melodic interest, and is discussed in some detail in the closing part of the movement. The finale is a rondo in which a three-part idea is three times repeated. This music finds Schubert in one of his prankish moods.

1823–1827. SONG CYCLES, for voice and piano:

DIE SCHOENE MUELLERIN (THE LOVELY MILLER MAID): 1. Das Wandern. 2. Wohin? 3. Halt! 4. Danksagung an den Bach. 5. Am Feierabend. 6. Der Neugierige. 7. Ungeduld. 8. Morgengruss. 9. Des Muellers Blumen. 10. Traenenregen. 11. Mein! 12. Pause. 13. Mit dem gruenen Lautenbande. 14. Der Jaeger. 15. Eifersucht und Stolz. 16. Die liebe Farbe. 17. Die boese Farbe. 18. Trock'ne Blumen. 19. Der Mueller und der Bach. 20. Des Baches Wiegenlied.

DIE WINTERREISE (WINTER'S JOURNEY): 1. Gute Nacht. 2. Die Wetterfahne. 3. Gefror'ne Traenen. 4. Erstarrung. 5. Der Lindenbaum. 6. Wasserflut. 7. Auf dem Flusse. 8. Rueckblick. 9. Irrlicht. 10. Rast. 11. Fruehlingstraum. 12. Einsamkeit. 13. Die Post. 14. Der greise Kopf. 15. Die Kraehe. 16. Letzte Hoffnung. 17. Im Dorfe. 18. Der stuermische Morgen. 19. Taeuschung. 20. Der Wegweiser. 21. Das Wirsthaus. 22. Mut. 23. Die Nebensonne. 24. Der Leiermann.

The song cycle—the stringing together of a number of songs into a unified concept, both in text and music—was born with Beethoven's *An die ferne Geliebte* (which see). But it was with the two Schubert cycles, *Die schoene Muellerin* (1823) and *Die Winterreise* (1827), that the song cycle achieves artistic fulfillment. Here we no longer get just a succession of songs tied together by some unifying thread; we are in the presence of a miniature drama, in which the effect is cumulative.

Both Schubert cycles are based on poem cycles by Wilhelm Mueller,

Schubert's contemporary. "It is easy to see," says Alec Robertson, "why these two sequences of poems appealed so much to Schubert. Here was another chance to paint again in music the romantic scene he loved so well. He was not so much a townsman now that he did not seize upon any opportunity to escape imaginatively into the country his purse could ill afford to visit in person. Apart from that, the poems were of the immediately suggestive kind."

The two cycles are antipodes. *Die schoene Muellerin* is for the most part (and particularly in its first half) bucolic. *Die Winterreise* is consistently tragic. Alec Robertson points out that in both cycles a journey takes place—the same kind of journey. It is, he explains, "a journey from spring to winter divided by a spiritual death from which the traveler, escapist though he be, has to awaken to face again the unfriendly world. In this winter world, broken by a dream of May, two suns had set, the suns of love and hope, which had faded into spring, and down the road of life, where a signpost points, another begins to set, the sun of life itself."

The first ten poems of *Die schoene Muellerin* describe the miller, his lovely daughter, his apprentice, and the rustic courtship of daughter and apprentice. The first four numbers are in the major mode. In the first, "Wandering," we learn of the apprentice's delight in wandering. He hears a streamlet gurgling from its rocky bed in "Whither," halts by a brook and an old mill in "Halt," and thanks the brooklet for all its kindess in "Thanks to the Brook." A minor-mode number, "The Evening Song," suggests the joy and peace that comes with the respite following a day's labors. The miller's apprentice is now fired with dreams and ambitions to prove his worth to his employer and his lovely daughter. Now come four more songs in the major. In "The Question," the apprentice returns to the brook to inquire if the miller's daughter loves him. In "Impatience" he becomes restless when the brook offers no reply. He addresses a tender message to the miller's daughter in "Morning Greeting," while in "The Miller's Flowers" he gathers blue blossoms from the banks of a brook to present her. "Teardrops" begins in a nebulous tonality to end up in the minor: the miller's daughter and the apprentice are together at the brooklet, only to be driven off by a sudden downpour. Three major-mode songs now follow. In an outburst of joy, the apprentice exclaims that the girl he loves is his in "Mine," then in "Pause," he stops for a moment to hang his lute on the wall. From the instrument, he removes a green band with which to tie his beloved's hair in "With the Green Lute Band." For the next half dozen songs, the minor mode prevails. A hunter comes on the scene in "The Hunter" to become the apprentice's rival for the love of the maid. The apprentice comes to the brook to enlist its help in "Jealousy and Pride," entreating it to scold the maid but to ignore his grief. In "The Favorite Color," he vows that from this time on he will always wear green, and become a hunter stalking death. To flee from his grief he will roam the world, as he explains in "The Hated Color." But he can find no peace; everywhere he goes he sees green. The flowers he gave his beloved are now withered; in "Withered Flowers," he suggests that they will henceforth lie on his grave. He pays a last visit to the brook in "The Miller and the Brook" but finds little consolation in its babbling. In the last song, in a major key, ("The Brook's Lullaby") he intones a gentle lullaby and finds repose at last in its peaceful waters, which lull him to sleep.

The funereal atmosphere in the closing songs of *Die schoene Muellerin* deepens and permeates the whole of the *Winterreise* cycle. "The overwhelming grief of the hero of this Winter's Journey," remarks Edgar Istel, "to this day grips us with incomparable power, quite contrary to the pretty love-sorrow in the previous cycle, whose griefs now impress us as being somewhat negligible. In *Der Winterreise* the poet discovers cosmic interconnections, tremendous metaphysical vistas to which Schubert's genius first lends power in adequate tones. Positively overpowering to begin with is the manner in which Schubert, in the very first song, 'Good Night,' established the fundamental mood."

The writing of this song cycle cost Schubert no little anguish, for the music came from the depths of his despair. Recalling how Schubert sang the cycle to his friends soon after he had completed it, Josef von Spaun wrote: "We who were near and dear to him knew how much the creatures of his mind took out of him, and in what anguish they were born. . . . I hold it beyond question that the excitement in which he composed his finest songs, in particular the *Winterreise,* brought about his untimely death." Schubert himself told his friends when he played and sang these songs for them: "I will play for you a cycle of terrifying songs; they have affected me more than has ever been the case with any of my other songs."

The story line of the *Winterreise* is somewhat more nebulous than that in *Die schoene Muellerin*. In mid-winter a wanderer sets forth on his journey. As he leaves behind him the town where his beloved had deserted him, he recalls his lost happiness, and looks forward to a death which does not come.

"*Die Winterreise,*" wrote Walter Dahms, "shows a step further on the road which Schubert took in *Die schoene Muellerin*. One finds here full mastery of artistic methods, an almost unheard-of expressiveness in depicting shades of mood, and indeed—this must be emphasized—by the simplest means. . . . Such tones as sound here had never yet been heard with lyric poetry. . . . It was a strange world in which no one had before set foot. Some of the songs nearly touch the boundaries of the pathological. The intensity of their expression of pain has risen to madness. No further rise would be possible."

H. C. Colles provides the following description of the best of these songs. "From the first, 'Gute Nacht' ('Good Night'), to the last, 'Der Leiermann' ('The Organ Grinder'), they are pervaded by the idea of loneliness, and the very persistence of the idea in spite of the great variety of ways in which it is illustrated makes the cycle rather monotonous for complete performance. Almost every one of its songs, however, is a masterpiece in itself. Among the most typical are 'Die Wetterfahne' ('The Weather Vane') in which the undulating melody pictures the turning about of the vane in the wind; 'Der Lindenbaum' ('The Linden Tree'), one of Schubert's loveliest melodies with a beautiful rustling accompaniment which should be compared to 'Freuhlingstraum' ('A Dream of Spring'); 'Die Post' ('The Post') with its vigorous illustration of the post-boy's horn; and lastly, 'Der Leiermann,' in which the old organ-grinder's tune drones wearily through the whole song."

1823–1828. 6 MOMENTS MUSICAUX, op. 94: I. C major. II. A-flat major. III. F minor, "Air Russe." IV. C-sharp minor. V. F minor. VI. A-flat major.

The *Moment musical* was a form of piano music devised by Schubert: a short composition in song form, highly lyrical, but often with the character of an improvisation. The most famous of his *Moments musicaux* is the third in F minor, thoroughly Viennese in its effervescence and joy. It is also popular in various transcriptions including one for violin and piano by Fritz Kreisler.

To Robert Haven Schauffler, the *Moments musicaux* reveal the "Ariel side" of Schubert. "We find it," he says, "in the exquisite first theme of Number 1, in the tender, intimate loveliness of Number 2, which begins in the D-flat delicacies that make a sort of Trio in Number 4, and in the consecrated harmonies of Number 6. Contrasting moods also abound, as where Number 1, in changing to G major, modulates from Schubert to the future Schumann. . . . Number 4 begins with an adumbration of the Chopin of the Études, and Number 5 looks down long years to the Brahms of the E-flat Rhapsody."

1823. SONATA IN A MINOR, for cello and piano. (Transcribed by Gaspar Cassado as Concerto in A minor, for cello and orchestra.) I. Allegro moderato. II. Adagio. III. Allegretto.

In 1823, Johann Georg Stauffer invented a six-string fretted instrument called an "arpeggione." It was similar in shape to a guitar, but like a cello, it was held between the knees and played with a bow. For this unique (and now obsolete) instrument, Schubert wrote the A minor Sonata, which today is played by cello and piano. In the first movement, the piano is the first to offer the opening melodic subject, the cello joining in the tenth measure. A brief transition and a change of key lead into the lyrical second subject, this time in the cello. Both themes are in Schubert's finest lyric vein. So is the wondrous melody that unfolds in the slow movement, in the key of E major. A subdued mood is first introduced in the finale (a rondo), by an A major theme for the cello. But a happy spirit finally asserts itself through the second subject, built from vivacious semiquavers. Additional attractive melodic material in this movement includes an E major melody and an infectious pizzicato passage for the cello.

1824. GRAND DUO (or SONATA) IN C MAJOR, for piano duet, op. 140. I. Allegro moderato. II. Andante con moto. III. Scherzo. IV. Allegro ma non troppo.

There has been considerable speculation about this composition. The writing for the keyboard here has such symphonic breadth and character that the suspicion has been raised that this is just the piano arrangement of a symphony. Such a symphony was reputedly written by Schubert during a visit to Bad Gastein in the Austrian Salzkammergut, but has never been found. It is mentioned in some letters by the composer's friends. The orchestral, at times even Beethovenian, character of the *Grand Duo* has encouraged several musicians to adapt it as a symphony, the most notable of these versions being that of Joseph Joachim.

This is Donald Francis Tovey's analysis of the Joachim orchestration: "The first movement begins with a quiet theme that soon develops in a crescendo interrupted by a bright pianissimo modulation. . . . The main theme of the second subject is in the same rhythm as the first. . . . The development is spacious but not inordinately long, though it manages to find room for features that recur in the usual Schubertian way. This is notably the case with a grandiose outburst of the full orchestra on the rhythm of the first theme. The recapitulation may sound regular; but, in fact, the earlier part of the second subject is totally reharmonized, being mostly in the tonic minor. . . . The coda is broad and impressive, making, before its quiet end, a noble climax to a movement [which is] . . . one of Schubert's most perfect achievements on a large scale."

In the second movement "the opening is pure enough Schubert and so is the ensuing first modulation to the distant key of E, with the energetic theme associated with it. . . . But when the orthodox dominant emerges from these remoter keys Schubert's surrender is delightfully complete."

Tovey describes the Scherzo as a "grotesque." "The theme is in the bass and its fluttering prelude becomes the subject of a lively dialogue before the end. . . . The trio is another inspiration of unique originality, consisting of a melody in F minor in whole-bar notes as uniform as any canto fermo for a counterpoint exercise. The bass moves note against note below, and a syncopated throbbing middle part completes the harmony with the least possible deviation from monotony."

The finale, concludes Tovey, "though full of poetry and grand climaxes, is inveterately comic, as its cheeky second subject shows."

1824. OCTET IN F MAJOR, for two violins, viola, cello, double bass, clarinet, bassoon, and horn, op. 166. I. Adagio; Andante con poco mosso. II. Allegro vivace. III. Andante. IV. Allegretto. V. Andante molto; Allegro.

This Octet is Schubert's only significant chamber-music work for more than five instruments. It is generally believed that Schubert wrote it at the request of Count Ferdinand Troyer, at whose home it was played for the first time in 1824. Troyer had requested a work similar in content and style to the popular Septet in E-flat, op. 20, by Beethoven. Schubert digressed only slightly from the patterns established in the Beethoven Septet. He added a second violin to Beethoven's instrumentation, and he alternated the positions of the Minuet and Scherzo movements. But in basics, the two works are similar. Both have slow introductions to preface the first and last movements; both have an Andante utilizing the theme and variations structure; both have the over-all character of a divertimento.

The Octet is gay, popular, light-hearted music. Only in the finale, as J. A. Westrup notes, does a heavy gray cloud obscure the sunshine that burned so hot and clear in the earlier movements. "It is not difficult to see in the somber opening an echo of the plaintive cry, 'Schoene welt, wo bist du?' ('Beautiful world, where art thou?') . . . and this passionate outburst recurs later in the movement, as though the burden of grief were too heavy to be lightly shaken off."

But all is gaiety in the preceding four movements with a "sufficient diversity . . . to avoid the danger of tedium, and almost everywhere Schubert's imagination fans sparks into flames." A high spot in these earlier movements is, as Westrup singles out, "the Allegro of the first movement [which] grows out of the initial up-beat: a dotted quaver and semiquaver; observe how to this rhythm the horn sings its lingering farewell in the coda."

The weakness of the work to Westrup lies in the fourth movement, a set of formal variations to a theme lifted by Schubert from his early operetta, *Die Freunde von Salamanka* (1815). "The theme itself is not particularly distinguished [and] the real weakness of the movement is in the variations themselves. Their manner of relying for the most part on artificial embellishment is outmoded. Only in the sixth variation—in A-flat major—do we escape from the itch for acrobatics."

1824–1826. 3 STRING QUARTETS:

A minor, op. 29. I. Allegro ma non troppo. II. Andante. III. Allegro. IV. Allegro moderato.

D minor, "Der Tod und das Maedchen" ("Death and the Maiden"). I. Allegro. II. Andante con moto. III. Allegro molto. IV. Presto.

G major, op. 161. I Allegro molto moderato. II. Andante un poco moto. III. Allegro vivace. IV. Allegro assai.

Only one of Schubert's last four string quartets was published during his lifetime. This one also happens to be one of the greatest he ever wrote, that in A minor (1824). It begins in an elegiac mood, with a soft sweet melody in the first violin over an accompanying swaying figure in the second violin. The second subject, introduced after a brief and vigorous transition, is also an expression of melancholia. The first theme becomes the basis of the development, now harmonically enriched and its emotion heightened and intensified by magical modulations.

Schubert was partial to the melody of this slow movement. He used it in his incidental music to *Rosamunde* and as an Impromptu for piano. Surely this is one of the most sublime subjects in all quartet literature, the very essence of Schubert's melodic genius. H. L. Mencken once maintained that this music was the only proof he needed for the existence of God.

A single phrase in the cello, repeated by the other strings, brings on the minuet. (Schubert used this same motive in 1820 in his song, "Die Goetter Griechenlands.") It is possible that he repeats it here to recall the lugubrious words of Schiller on which the song was based: "Where art thou, beautiful world?" Out of this germ grows music with a somber cast, not generally encountered in a minuet. The gray colors are continued in the trio, with its tender passage for the cello. Grief is banished and optimism returns with the spirited music of the finale, some of whose themes and rhythms are derived from Hungarian folk music.

The D minor Quartet, written in 1826, and published posthumously, is called "Death and the Maiden," because this song appears in part in the slow movement. Death is the theme not only of this Andante, but also of the other three movements. The opening of the first movement is like a gesture of defiance to death: a powerful five-note rhythmic phrase. (Cobbett described this as a struggle with death.) This is built up before the fiery first theme of the movement erupts with full force. If this represents struggle, then resignation or submission can be found in the gentle beauty of the second subject in violins, the viola and cello providing a rhythmic accompaniment. This material is treated in the development with extraordinary contrapuntal skill, while the first theme is the material out of which two codas are derived.

The second movement is a theme and variations. The theme is the second half of the Schubert Lied, "Der Tod und das Maedchen," in which Death gives solemn reply to the frantic pleading of the maiden. The movement then continues on its melancholy way through five variations of this theme.

Despite the vigor in the opening of the Scherzo, the tragic overtones of the second movement are readily detected, and most particularly in the trio. The finale is set spinning with a whirling tarantella-like melody. But even here, the suggestion of death is not absent. In the second subject, for the four instruments, we can detect echoes of another of Schubert's songs about death, "Der Erlkoenig."

Though less famous than the *Death and the Maiden* Quartet, that in G major (1826)—Schubert's last string quartet—is hardly less remarkable. "The chief characteristics of this music," explains Robert Haven Schauffler, "are a forward looking modernity, surpassing even that of the D minor, the rhapsodic quality of certain themes, much of Schubert's characteristic wavering between major and minor, the antiphonal play of the upper against the lower strings, a more marked orchestral quality, a tendency toward horizontal counterpoint rather than vertical harmony, and a diffuseness that stretches the work to an inordinate length."

The quartet opens with a conflict in tonality that establishes a questioning attitude. The music of this introduction is rhythmically nervous, before it finally settles on the key of the tonic. Now we get a poignant song in short phrases from the first violin (then repeated by the cello). The second subject is subsequently assigned in turn to each of the four instruments. In the development, the first theme is discussed with power and imagination. The recapitulation repeats the exposition except that the alternation of major and minor is reversed.

Except for two stormy interludes, the slow movement is dominated by a melody in E minor of heavenly calm; it is heard in the cello. In its dynamic thrusts and rhythmic vitality, the Scherzo anticipates the one in the great C major symphony. The main subject of the trio is a Laendler-like tune with a bagpipe drone. Like the *Death and the Maiden* Quartet, the G major first presents in its finale a whirling subject in a tarantella style and rhythm. The strongly accented second subject is also virile, helping to maintain the momentum generated in earlier measures.

1825. SONATA IN D MAJOR, for piano, op. 53. I. Allegro vivace. II. Con moto. III. Scherzo. IV. Allegro moderato.

Schubert completed three piano sonatas in 1825; that in D major is the finest. The first movement has a powerful rhythmic surge, beginning with a strong first theme. After a repetition of the whole exposition section, the development gives even more forceful play to the rhythmic element. The slow movement has an effective melody made up of short phrases. The Scherzo is vigorous and exuberant—a romantic effusion, where so many other Schubert Scherzos are just peasant dances. The finale, which offers three important themes, alternates light and passionate moods. This movement has been transcribed for violin and piano by Carl Friedberg.

1827. IMPROMPTUS, for piano:

Op. 90: I. C minor. II. E-flat major. III. G major. IV. A-flat major.

Op. 142: I. F minor. II. A-flat major. III. B-flat major. IV. F minor.

It is doubtful if Schubert himself designated these eight pieces as "impromptus." The general belief is that this was done for the composer by some enterprising publisher. However, the association of "impromptu" with these remarkable pieces has brought the impromptu structure significance in piano literature—the impromptu being a short composition for the piano in an extended song form, with the feeling of an improvisation.

The most famous of Schubert's Impromptus is the third in the opus 142 set, in B-flat major. This is a melody of haunting loveliness which Schubert liked so well that he used it in his incidental music to *Rosamunde* and in the slow movement of his A minor String Quartet. This Impromptu presents this melody with five brief variations.

The C minor Impromptu, op. 90, no. 1, is unusual in structure. It opens with a declamation but soon progresses to a double set of variations on alternate lyrical themes. The second in the opus 90 set, E-flat major, is episodic in structure, and makes a brilliant use of a fleet rippling figure which passes dramatically from E-flat major to B minor. The third Impromptu, in G major, is distinguished by its exalted lyricism; while the fourth in A-flat major is structurally a Scherzo with a contrasting trio—the scherzo glistening with arpeggio figures, the melody of the trio, passionate.

Schumann found an affinity in style, form, and key among the first, second, and fourth Impromptus of the opus 142 set. He was tempted to believe that Schubert originally had intended them as movements of a sonata. The first is one of the longest and most complex of all the Schubert Impromptus, and has a prevailing somber character. The second, on the other hand, is light and airy,—a minuet with trio in form. The fourth is essentially a bravura piece more appealing for brilliant runs, figures, and scale passages than for its lyrical content.

1827. PIANO TRIOS:

B-flat major, op. 99. I. Allegro moderato. II. Andante un poco mosso. III. Allegro. IV. Allegro vivace.

E-flat major, op. 100. I. Allegro. II. Andante con moto. III. Allegro moderato. IV. Allegro moderato.

These are Schubert's only piano trios, and both are masterworks. M. J. E. Brown describes the first movement of the B-flat major Trio as follows: "The main theme, a buoyantly lyrical and strongly characterized melody is played at the outset, and followed by a complex modulatory episode based on a fragment from it. . . . Then comes its second presentation, not more elaborate this time, but differently instrumented, a famous touch of Schubertian charm. . . . . [In] the development . . . the melody is given forte in the minor key, builds up imitatively to a big climax and then yields to the second contrasting subject played in a soft, dolce, episode style. . . . Toward the end of the development . . . there is a remarkable 'false start' to the recapitulation."

The second movement offers a soaring Schubert melody, first in the cello, then in the violin, and finally in the piano; a second subject in thirty-second-notes provides contrast. In the Scherzo, the first part is notable for its thythmic pulse, while the trio has melodic interest. A lively dance tune followed by a unison passage opens the finale, which is consistently vivacious. J. A. Westrup likened the coda to a "comic opera finale."

Schumann placed the E-flat major Trio with Schubert's "most individual" works. He regarded it as "more active, masculine, and dramatic" than its B-flat major companion. To Schumann, the first movement combined "profound indignation with heart-felt longing." A bold theme, with three instruments in unison, and an equally vigorous statement that later is transformed into a strong second subject, is the basic thematic material of the exposition. But the most fascinating theme in the movement comes in the development, a poignant melody that first is varied in different tonalities and then is brought to a climax. The second movement has the solemn character of a funeral march. A lugubrious melody is heard in the cello over a march-like rhythm in the piano. Schumann said that in this music can be found "sights that would rise and spread until they swell into the heart's anguish." The opening of the Scherzo is canonic. By way of change from the soft strains of the first part, comes a forceful trio with strong chords on the downbeat. The finale is structurally the most ambitious movement in the entire work. There are three melodic groups. In the first, a gentle folk tune is contrasted with a Laendler melody. The piano plays a major role in the second group. In the third, the funeral-like music of the second movement is recalled. All this material is developed at length, after which all three groups are repeated. The solemn march music of the second movement, somewhat condensed, precedes the virile closing measures.

1828. FANTASY IN F MINOR, for piano duet, op. 103.

The last of four Fantasies for piano by Schubert is one of his finest keyboard creations. Schubert's first biographer, Kreissle, called it "remarkable for the wealth and beauty of melody, its startling modulations, and a certain moderation in the treatment of various themes. Schubert has written no second work in this style to be compared with it in the delicate fancies here explained." The work is in four clearly defined contrasting movements, but played without interruption (I. Allegro molto moderato. II. Largo. III. Scherzo. IV. Allegro vivace). The main melody of the first movement, one of Schubert's loftiest, is repeated several times throughout the work, including the coda in the finale; thus the work has an over-all integration. To Alfred Einstein, the deeply moving Adagio is "a declaration of love." After the elegiac moods of the first two movements, the gaiety of the Scherzo provides relief.

1828. 3 SONATAS, for piano, posthumous:

C minor. I. Allegro. II. Adagio. III. Menuetto: allegro. IV. Allegro.

A major. I. Allegro. II. Andantino. III. Allegro vivace. IV. Allegretto.

B-flat major. I. Molto moderato. II. Andante sostenuto. III. Allegro vivace con delicatezza. IV. Allegro ma non troppo.

The shadow of Beethoven hovers over most of Schubert's piano sonatas. But only in his last three sonatas can Schubert be said to be truly Beethovenian: in the powerful thrust of his themes; in the epical stature of his developments; in the enlargement of the sonata structure; and most of all, in the attainment of an expressiveness that reaches above and beyond melodic appeal.

The first of these posthumous sonatas, that in C minor, is the most uneven in quality and at the same time most Beethovenian. "The principal theme of the Allegro not only resembles that of the Thirty-Two Variations in C minor [by Beethoven]," maintains Kathleen Dale, "but is hurled forth in Beethoven's own peremptory manner. The succeeding figures of the agitated semiquavers recall those of the *Pathétique,* and later, curious pianissimo chromatic passages . . . seemed to have strayed from one of Beethoven's last sonatas. The refrain of the Adagio rondo and the melody of the Menuetto are typical Beethovenian cantabiles, though rhythmical shape of the latter (three, four and five bars) proclaims it Schubert's own. In the 6/8 finale, the player's thoughts are divided between the rondo before him and the presto finale of Beethoven's op. 31, no. 3, the two movements having many features in common: the galloping triplets, the quick alternations of major and minor arpeggio figures, the sforzando explosions and the cross-hand passages. But while the Beethoven finale is concise, Schubert's is inclined to be diffused. All the same, it is breathlessly thrilling to play."

The drama and majesty of the Sonatas in A major and B-flat major also have Beethovenian echoes. But here, much more than in the C minor, the voice is recognizably Schubert's, though richer and deeper than that found in earlier sonatas. The first movement of the A major enters with a sober, contemplative subject, instead of the stormy one that set the C minor into action. This subject is discussed at length, with the imposition of some attractive subsidiary material, before the second theme arrives in the dominant key of E. This second subject is one of Schubert's most inspired lyrical flights. The development has the character of an improvisation. It is for the most part an epic enlargement of a simple idea first heard in the codetta of the exposition. In the coda, the movement's first theme gains monumental strength.

If the first movement is a drama in miniature, the second is a lyrical poem. Its main melody combines lyricism with emotion. The dramatic element of the first movement recurs in the Scherzo, and most particularly in the dynamic trio. The finale—structurally a compromise between the sonata form and the rondo—contains many exalted lyrical passages. The sonata gains unification toward the end of this finale with a return of the opening subject of the first movement.

Many musicologists consider the B-flat major Sonata—Schubert's last—as his greatest. "Lyrical charm," explains Kathleen Dale, "is here combined with structural grandeur, serene meditation with urgent progression, and tonal daring with harmonic sureness, while pianistic treatment is consistently expressive." The first movement starts off with an expansive and eloquent melody that concludes with a low trill in an air of mystery. This mystery deepens with the second subject, which begins in the key of F-sharp minor and then lapses into F. The slow movement is a continual ascent towards sublimity, the starting point being a poetic thirteen-measure melody with religious echoes. The Scherzo is remarkable for the variety of its harmony and the exciting alternations of major and minor. The finale is once again Beethovenian in its storm and stress; it opens on a dramatic note in a foreign key.

1828. SYMPHONY NO. 7 or 9 IN C MAJOR, "GREAT." I. Andante; Allegro ma non troppo. II. Andante con moto. III. Allegro vivace. IV. Allegro vivace.

The so-called "Great" Symphony in C major was Schubert's last. Ninth in order of composition, but seventh in publication, it is the composer's vastest symphonic creation, a work not only of "heavenly length," as Schumann described it, but of monumental power, profound emotional content, great complexity and individuality. "Bright, fascinating and original throughout," Mendelssohn said of it, "it stands at quite the head of his [Schubert's] instrumental works.

There is an extended, seventy-seven measure introduction to the first movement which establishes a nobility new to Schubert. Its main subject is a majestic melody for the horns, which the woodwind later take over. A crescendo brings on the Allegro section with a vigorous theme, the first two measures in the strings, the next two in the woodwind. A more delicate staccato theme follows in oboes and bassoons to receive detailed attention. With a triumphant melody for full orchestra the exposition comes to an end. The development is the most elaborate of any in Schubert's symphonies, its immense power generated by repetitions rather than variations. A new wonderful thought comes here into play, an awesome melody for the horns. The recapitulation opens with a restatement of the two main themes of the exposition, the second now appearing in C minor. A final, strong return of the melody of the opening introduction brings the movement to a proud conclusion.

Seven measures of introduction in the second movement precede the principal melody in the oboe over string accompaniment. The clarinet joins in, then goes off on its own to vary the melody and extend it. A forceful statement by the full orchestra, and a change of key to F major, brings on an idyllic second subject in the strings. When this material is repeated and amplified, new exquisite ideas are introduced. The most significant are a stately melody for the trumpet and a poignant refrain for cello over plucked strings (the oboe providing a countermelody). The coda is based on the beautiful first melody.

The Scherzo opens with a peasant-like dance tune in strings in octaves, with an answering phrase in woodwind and horns. Two subsidiary thoughts are introduced later on. The first is a waltz tune for strings, with cellos offering a countertheme; the second is a suave melody for the flute. A repeated "E" in the horns leads into the trio, its main subject presented by wind with string accompaniment.

A two-measure loud call in full orchestra, followed by a soft triplet figure in reply, sets the whirlwind of the finale into action. In the main part, the oboes present a mobile melody; this is the main theme. Four "D's" in the horns lead into the second subject, another fine melody, for the woodwind. Demoniac forces are now released and canalized into a monumental crescendo that sweeps over a hundred measures.

1828. STRING QUINTET IN C MAJOR, for two violins, viola, and two cellos, op. 163. I. Allegro ma non troppo. II. Adagio. III. Presto. IV. Allegretto.

It would be difficult to find a greater contrast between two chamber-music works than that we confront in Schubert's two quintets. The earlier one in A major, *Die Forelle*, is a reflection of sheer joy and contentment. The C major Quintet, nine years later, is one of the most pessimistic documents in all chamber music. On the threshold of death, sick in body and spirit, Schubert searched deeply into his heart and could find only darkness. We need but to listen to the C major Quintet to perceive the extent of Schubert's despair in his closing months.

In using two cellos for a quintet, Schubert had been anticipated by Boccherini. But this unusual combination of five string instruments has fallen into disuse since Schubert's time.

Melancholia hovers over the opening measures of the first movement. At the thirty-third measure, there comes a strongly accented loud section serving as a transition to the second subject. This is a melody that reaches into the depths of tragedy. First we hear the somber voices of the two cellos; as the theme is repeated in a higher register by the other instruments, the darkness of mood deepens. There is new and no less solemn material in the coda that concludes the exposition, material unfolding with increasing emotion in the development that follows. The recapitulation begins with the movement's lugubrious opening subject in the violas over an ascending pizzicato figure in the violins. This is followed by the elegiac strains of the second theme. A last reminder of this latter subject brings the movement to a poignant conclusion.

The second movement is a tragic song for the three middle voices over throbbing pizzicati in the second cello, and with the first violin contributing a gentle commentary. An outburst of grief precedes the development in which, Marcel Schneider notes, "Schubert's grandeur of inspiration, his depths of feeling are such that he has no need of recourse to technical subtleties. The instruments play often in unison, there are many repeats: only one interlude of agitation occurs to trouble the atmosphere of . . . intangible sadness that suffuses the whole."

The Scherzo, to Schneider, "has a fully realized orchestral texture: hunting calls, folk songs pass in the rich fabric of sound, conspiring together in tempestuous mobility. And then with the trio, there follows one of Schubert's most electrifying contrasts. Instead of a Presto in C major, there is an Andante sostenuto in D-flat major in a different rhythm, strange music, 'languorous and funereal,' said Gerard de Nerval, "with the instruments used in their darker registers."

Then at long last—release from grief, victory over despair! This comes at once in the finale, with the opening spirited theme in a popular dance style. It is as though, says Schneider, "after a long retirement into the depths of his soul, having laid bare its secrets, he wanted to leave us with the impression of his everyday self, as though the sufferings, longings and heavenly visions of his solitary hours had given place to the ordinary everyday man."

1828. MASS IN E-FLAT MAJOR, for solo voices, chorus, and orchestra.

Schubert's sixth and last Mass was finished just four months before his death. Ralph Bates has written that the Mass to Schubert was "a great musical form of a kind that might secure performance. If his work in that form is often filled with deep feeling, it is for the reason that its imagery, its solemnity and drama awakened the profound mysticism in him, as it does in most of us, a mysticism that probably he mistakenly thought the better part of religion."

The E-flat Major Mass is the longest, most ambitious, and in many ways the most consistently inspired of Schubert's works in this genre. Brahms was so taken with this music that on one occasion he set himself the task of transcribing the orchestral accompaniment for the piano.

Mystery and unrest is evoked in the first part of the the "Kyrie," but with the entrance of "Christe eleison," the statement grows forceful and dramatic. Toward the end of this section, with an extended "Eleison," the music reaches toward the tragic. To Robert Haven Schauffler, there is little in liturgical music to match "the brilliant 'Gloria,' suddenly bursting from behind the clouds of the 'Kyrie.' And after all the exuberance, how effective is the soft ending of the 'Glorificamus, laudamus te.'" The "Miserere" works up "to one of the most thrilling of choral climaxes"—a powerful fugue to the words "Cum Sancto Spiritu," followed by the no less dynamic "Amen." The "Credo" is notable for its contrapuntal imitations. "In the last pages before the somewhat Schubertian trio, 'Et Incarnatus Est,' Ariel gives forth such ethereal strains as to remind one how few of his last days separated this Mass from the String Quartet. Schubert might have written the profoundly moving choral portions of the 'Crucifixus' with his heart's blood. . . . The 'Benedictus,' too, is the music of heaven. . . Here, in ever increasing beauty, solo quartet alternates with choir, hymnlike passages with fugued passages. But in the 'Agnus Dei,' the greatest movement in any of the Masses, we are suddenly brought back to the realization of the poor sick composer's wretched plight; for it starts with the bass theme which opens the song of unutterable woe, 'Der Doppelgaenger.' Touching in its tender simplicity and in the moving antiphonal accents of solo quartet and choir, the 'Dona nobis pacem' has the quality of those Lieder in which Schubert caught the inner essence of folk song."

1828. SCHWANENGESANG (SWAN SONG), song cycle for voice and piano: 1. Liebesbotschaft. 2. Kriegers Ahnung. 3. Fruehlingssehnsucht. 4. Staendchen. 5. Aufenthalt. 6. In der Ferne. 7. Abschied. 8, Der Atlas. 9. Ihr Bild. 10. Des Fischermaedchen. 11. Die Stadt. 12. Am Meer. 13. Der Doppelgaenger. 14. Die Taubenpost.

Strictly speaking, the *Schwanengesang* is not a song cycle (though often described as such), since it was not written with a unifying theme in mind. As a matter of fact, the composer was not the one who gathered these fourteen songs into a single package; this was done for him by his publisher, Haslinger, from various Lieder completed in the last year of Schubert's life. The first seven of these songs have texts by Rellstab, the next six by Heine, and the fourteenth again by Rellstab.

The most celebrated number in this set is the ever popular "Staendchen" or "Serenade," one of the greatest love songs ever written. But hardly less distinguished are many other songs in this collection. "Liebesbotschaft" boasts an echo effect which, as Alec Robertson remarks, "one has grown to love in Schubert" and which is here "subtilized and presented in a new way." In "Aufenthalt" and "Abschied" we find a raging storm, "this is the last time we shall meet with 'Erlkoenig' triplets, and the stream rushes by, the drum-like bars tell us, in no unfriendly manner." "Abschied," continues Robertson, "is as human and warm as 'Aufenthalt' is sinister and cold. The horse's hoofs clattering over the cobbles carry the reluctant traveler past the sights he loved so well. . . . In spite of the jolly tone of the music, it is full of nostalgia."

In the Heine group, "Der Atlas" is unforgettable for "the terrible groan of Atlas . . . intensified by the bass doubling the vocal part, and his stricken cries at the end of each verse." Quite different is "Ihr Bild," in which "the smiling thirds turn to tears [with] wonderful art." "Das Fischermaedchen," is "delightfully fresh and buoyant." "Die Stadt" opens the door "into post-Wagnerian era of impressionism"; and "Am Meer" is Schubert's "greatest picture of the sea." In "Der Doppelgaenger," the "ghostly chiming" of the piano accompaniment "strikes into the depths of our very hearts. It is as relentless in its motion as time."

H. C. Colles considers "Der Doppelgaenger" the most tragic of all Schubert songs. Here is his description: "A man stands in the silent street before a house where once his beloved lived. He is conscious of another figure standing there. Suddenly the moon lights up the face of the other and, horror-struck, he recognizes—himself. It is his double which haunts the empty scene of his past love and present grief. Schubert's music has the simplicity which only the most inspired things can afford to have. It is inexplicable; one cannot say why these four chords are so relentlessly haunting, though the fact that each contains only two notes contributes to their strangely hollow effect. The song has little positive melody, but every note is in place as an expression both of the prevalent feeling and of the particular details of the short poem."

LOUIS SPOHR 1784–1859

The twentieth century remembers Louis Spohr as an eminent concert violinist; as a conductor who became a pioneer in demonstrating the feasibility of using a baton; as the author of a violin method upon which many a student has been raised. Only incidentally do we also recall that he was a composer. Yet Spohr was one of the most prolific of the early German Romantics. His output included operas and oratorios; nine symphonies, fifteen violin concertos, and four concert overtures; thirty-four string quartets, seven string quintets, five piano trios; and a great amount of other chamber, choral and orchestral music. In the nineteenth century his fame as composer circled the globe. In Germany's leading opera houses at that time Spohr's opera *Jessonda* was second in popularity only to Weber's *Der Freischuetz*. Spohr's concertos, chamber music and orchestral compositions were extensively played and universally admired. Today about all that brings Spohr's name to a concert program are two violin concertos; occasionally, his overture to *Jessonda;* much less frequently, the Nonet in F major and his fourth symphony, *Die Weihe der Toene* (*The Consecration of Tone*).

Spohr frequently struck new paths for music. He was the first composer to write a nonet; he was one of the first to produce a single-movement integrated concerto; he was an early master in creating literal program music; he was one of the first composers to lift the oratorio out of the Baroque era and to place it into the Romantic. He was always seeking out new and novel formats and instrumental combinations: He wrote a concerto for string quartet and orchestra, a symphony for two orchestras, and a sonatina for voice and piano.

Louis, or Ludwig, Spohr was born in Brunswick, Germany, on April 5, 1784. He received a thorough training in the violin, but his only study in musical theory took place when he was twelve, when he was given lessons in counterpoint. In 1799 Spohr became a violinist in the ducal orchestra in Brunswick. The Duke of Brunswick became so interested in him that he arranged for Spohr to study with Franz Eck and to travel in Russia. Between 1800 and 1804, Spohr completed his first ambitious compositions, including three violin concertos and two string quartets. In 1804 he toured Germany as violinist and established his reputation solidly. One year later he became the concertmaster of the ducal orchestra in Gotha. Between 1812 and 1815 he served as the conductor of the Theater-an-der-Wien in Vienna and from 1815 to 1817 he made extensive tours as concert violinist. Meanwhile in 1816 his fame as composer achieved new dimensions with the world première of his opera *Faust* in Prague, conducted by Carl Maria von Weber. In 1820, Spohr paid his first visit to London, an occasion upon which he made performing history by directing an orchestra with a baton. After returning to Germany, Spohr held the post of court Kapellmeister to the Elector of Hesse-Cassel for thirty-five years. Spohr died in Cassel on October 22, 1859.

1816. CONCERTO NO. 8 IN A MINOR ("GESANGSZENE"), for violin and orchestra, op. 47. I. Allegro molto. II. Adagio. III. Andante; Allegro molto.

Spohr completed fifteen violin concertos. Henry Chorley, England's distinguished music critic in the nineteenth century, found them to be a "blessed thing for the great and noble school of violin players in Germany . . . a fact no more to be denied than that Mozart helped opera a step forward, Beethoven the orchestra, and Clementi the piano." Chorley then went on to praise the Spohr concertos for their "verve, brightness and contrast." But to a present-day authority like Abraham Veinus "there is nothing eternal about the Spohr concertos. They represent him in the parliament of composers as a local conservative who knew a few set speeches and delivered them well."

Spohr's eighth violin concerto is a curiosity. He wrote it for his concert appearances in Italy. Bearing in mind the partiality of Italian music lovers for opera, he planned an instrumental concerto of operatic character—an operatic scena translated into a composition for violin and orchestra, with the violin replacing the voice. At the same time, Spohr dispensed with the formal presentation and development of thematic material usually found in concertos, replacing them with alternations of recitatives and aria-type melodies.

The first movement opens with an orchestral introduction which makes prominent use of a song-like theme. The violin enters with a recitative, then embarks on bravura passages. The slow movement is in three-part song form. First the orchestra is heard in the main theme which soon receives decorative treatment from the solo violin. After that comes a rhapsodic section followed by a return of the opening melody. A dramatic recitative for the violin is a transition to the concerto's finale. Here a slow introductory section offers a stately melody, first in the orchestra, then in solo violin. The violin is then heard in an aria-like episode. A return of the finale's opening idea, a cadenza for the solo violin, and a dramatic final statement by the orchestra bring the concerto to its conclusion.

1820. CONCERTO NO. 9 IN D MINOR, for violin and orchestra, op. 55. I. Allegro. II. Adagio. III. Rondo.

If Spohr's eighth concerto is the most unusual of his compositions for violin and orchestra, the ninth has proved the most durable. The orchestral introduction offers the main thematic material for a first movement which the composer himself described as "serious but impassioned." The solo violin repeats the two main themes. The development then permits the soloist to embark on flights of virtuosity. The middle movement, characterized by the composer as "mild and serene," also has two principal thoughts; both are lyrical and contemplative. In the finale, a rondo, the virtuosity of the performer is fully exploited in a movement described by the composer as "agitated and imperious."

OVERTURE TO JESSONDA.

Jessonda is not even a familiar name to most music lovers today. One century ago it was one of the most widely performed and admired operas in

Germany. The heroine is the young widow of an aged rajah in Malabar. After the rajah's death, she is required by law to be burned with him. She is, however, rescued by the man with whom she had been in love long before she had married—Tristan d'Acunha, general of the now invading Portuguese army. Tristan bears her off to Portugal, and to a happiness so long denied her.

The opera (text by Eduard Heinrich Gehe based on Lemierre's tragedy, *La Veuve de Malabar*) was introduced in Cassel on July 28, 1823, at a festival performance honoring the birthday of Spohr's employer, the Elector. Demonstrations of any kind were not permitted on such occasions. Nevertheless the audience could not contain itself, and thundered its enthusiasm after each act.

A lengthy introduction in the overture uses material from the first-act opening chorus. A change of tempo brings on the woodwind with an excerpt from a soldier's chorus from the second act. In the main body of the overture, the principal theme in the first violins is derived from Jessonda's beautiful aria in the opera's closing scene. The second theme also comes from the same aria, and is given by the horn. This material is worked out, and is followed by the merest suggestion of a recapitulation.

GIOACCHINO ROSSINI 1792–1868

If Rossini had not been born a genius he would have become a hack. He wrote too much, and too quickly. For nineteen years, he averaged two operas a year, and some years saw a yield of four operas. At the same time, his artistic conscience left a good deal to be desired. He was satisfied with second-rate material when the first-rate took too much pains. He was ever seeking out the easiest solutions to his creative problems. He would shift material from one opera to another whether it fit or not, and at times he stood ready to incorporate the work of other composers into his own. He accepted and set music to librettos that should have been dumped before a single note was committed to paper. He would not hesitate to write manufactured music to specific order, whether to fit the needs of a singer or to cater to the less noble tastes of the general public.

Yet when the spirit moved him, he was capable of creating an unblemished masterwork like *The Barber of Seville,* which to some authorities is still the finest comic opera ever written. He could fill his other operas, serious as well as comic, with treasurable pages that rank with the finest creations of the Italian musical theater. He had a gift for melody and comic relief second to none. Few before or since wrote so naturally, so effortlessly and so inevitably for the voice, whether for solos or ensembles.

He was one of the most influential figures opera has known. Up until his last work, *William Tell,* he possessed the inquisitiveness, restlessness, and adventurousness of a real innovator. In *William Tell,* for example, he anticipated the Leitmotiv technique, as well as other significant dramatic and stylistic approaches, of Wagner—a fact fully acknowledged by Wagner himself. Rossini set the stage for the Meyerbeer melodramatic opera. Francis Toye goes on to point out that in *Moïse* and *Semiramide,* Rossini influenced the early Verdi, especially in the choruses Verdi wrote for *Nabucco* and *I Lombardi.* Even the later Verdi was not untouched by Rossini, since Toye regards Falstaff as "a pendant for *The Barber.*" Toye also sees *La Gazza ladra* of Rossini as the ancestor to the realistic school of Mascagni and Puccini, and recalls the impact Rossini had on Schubert.

Many of Rossini's innovations had far-reaching significance. He continually introduced new instruments into his orchestration to increase its articulateness, extend its dramatic range, and enrich its palette. He was forever experimenting with richer harmonic resources. He was one of the first composers to dispense with the cembalo as an accompanying instrument for recitatives and to use the strings instead. He was also one of the first, if not the first, to write out the florid passages, which up to now singers had been improvising. He perfected the "Rossini crescendo" and used it with the most telling effect. He was one of the earliest masters to alternate slow (cavatina) and fast (cabaletto) passages, henceforth a favorite device of Italian opera composers. "Rossini," sums up Ernest Newman, "altered the form and spirit of Italian opera in a way that must have been disconcerting to the conservative minds of his own day. . . . He broke away, bit by bit, from a good deal of the older formalism of structure."

Gioacchino Rossini was born in Pesaro, Italy, on February 29, 1792. When he was twelve, his family settled in Bologna. There he attended the Conservatory, a pupil of Padre Mattei. In 1808, his first ambitious composition, a cantata, was performed at the Conservatory. Less than two years after that, on November 3, 1810, Rossini's first opera, which he completed in three days' time, was heard in Venice. He wrote a number of operas before achieving his first success, which came in 1812 with *La Pietra del paragone,* performed at La Scala in Milan. In 1813, he completed two significant operas which already made him one of the most highly esteemed opera composers in Italy: *Tancredi,* a serious opera, given in Venice on February 6, and *L'Italiana in Algeri,* an opera buffa, heard in the same city on May 22. With *The Barber of Seville,* first produced in Rome in 1815, he stood without a rival in Italian opera.

Now becoming increasingly prolific, Rossini wrote sixteen operas in the six-year period between 1815 and 1821, in both the serious and comic styles. The most important were *La Cenerentola* and *La Gazza ladra* in 1817, and *Mosè in Egitto* in 1818. In 1822, he married Isabella Colbran, the noted Spanish singer. Soon after that, he left Italy for the first time, to create a furor during his visits to Vienna and London. In 1824, he settled permanently in Paris, where for two years he was the manager of the Théâtre Italien. Under the provisions of a generous contract given him by Charles X, he wrote his last and most ambitious opera in 1829, *William Tell.*

After 1829, and for the next thirty-nine years, Rossini wrote some church music and piano pieces—but no more operas. Considering that when he did *William Tell* he was at the very peak of both his fame and his creative potential, this "great renunciation" is surely without parallel in all art. Nobody can say for sure why Rossini renounced the stage. The composer himself proved either evasive or whimsical when posed the question. The argument, however, that Rossini was inordinately lazy—that since he was now a wealthy man he could well indulge this inertia—holds little conviction. A man who had produced as much as Rossini did, and over such a long period of time, could hardly have been lazy; and besides, long before 1829, he had the wherewithal to indulge himself in any way he wished, had he so been disposed.

Other explanations, also, have a hollow ring. It is hardly possible, as some have said, that Rossini renounced opera because the audiences in Paris had rejected *William Tell.* For one thing, *William Tell* was no failure. For another, in his time, Rossini had been rejected many times, and always he emerged from defeats with a new resounding victory. Nor is it possible, as has been suggested, that Rossini's envy of Meyerbeer's soaring star after 1833 was responsible for the silence. Rossini had never feared competition, even when he had been in a far more vulnerable position. As it was, with his popularity circling the world, it is ridiculous to believe that he feared Meyerbeer's immense successes. Not even Meyerbeer would have been able to nudge Rossini from his imperial place in opera.

The only solution to this problem that seems to make any sense is that Rossini's health suffered serious decline, and that he was victimized by a neurasthenia that tortured him no end. Due to such declining physical powers, he may not have been able to summon those inner resources required for the writing of operas.

Despite his poor health and shattered nerves, Rossini continued to live the good life. In August 1846 (ten months after the death of his first wife), he married Olympe Pélissier. Their establishment in Paris was the favored rendezvous of leading cultural and social figures in that city. Less than two months before his death, Rossini was still entertaining guests in the grand manner. He died in Passy, on the outskirts of Paris, on November 13, 1868. Though originally buried in Père Lachaise in Paris, his remains were subsequently removed to the Santa Croce Church in Florence.

1813. L'ITALIANA IN ALGERI (THE ITALIAN WOMAN IN ALGIERS), opera buffa in two acts, with text by Angelo Anelli. First performance: Teatro San Benedetto, Venice, May 22, 1813.

This was Rossini's first major success in the field in which he proved himself a master—opera buffa. He was only twenty at the time, and the score had taken him less than a month to produce. Venetian audiences were beside themselves with delight, and so were the critics. As Stendhal noted, Rossini's music here was tailor-made for pleasure-loving Venetians; it combined infectious comedy and broad burlesque with the most affecting lyricism and touching sentiment. "The outstanding feature of *L'Italiana,*" remarks Francis Toye, "is the impression it gives, as an entity, of spontaneity, freshness, and, above all, gaiety."

The Oriental setting was something Italian opera lovers were particularly partial to. In this case it was Algiers in the eighteenth century. The Bey, weary of his favorite, Elvira, decides to marry her off to the Italian slave, Lindoro. Lindoro, however, is in love with the Italian lady, Isabella, who is making the long voyage from Italy to join him. Near the shores of Algiers, her ship is wrecked. Isabella is saved by Ali, who senses she might be the ideal candidate to replace Elvira in the Bey's favor. The Bey is delighted with her. But Isabella, true to Lindoro, plans to elope with him. They work out an elaborate scheme to dupe the Bey. They inform him they are the members of a secret society named Pappataci. The Bey can join it if he is willing to perform the initiation rites, which consist of drinking intoxicating liquor in immense quantity. When the Bey gets drunk, Lindoro and Isabella effect their escape. Recovering from his stupor, the Bey consoles himself by taking Elvira back.

The overture, a genuine Rossini gem, features a haunting melody for oboe in the opening slow section. A characteristic Rossini crescendo leads into the main Allegro, where two vivacious tunes are presented by the woodwind. Another crescendo, more dramatic than the first, sweeps the overture to a stirring end.

After that, the score moves nimbly from comedy to tenderness, from sensitive emotion to farce. "The succession of so many numbers tripping along, one after another," says Toye, "in so sprightly and impertinent a fashion is [the opera's] especial charm." The finest comic episodes are found in the first act finale (with the burlesque hymn of praise to the Bey) and the initiation scene to the Pappataci, with its sparkling trio. The most memorable lyrical passages include two outstanding arias: one by Lindoro, "Languir per una bella" and the other by Isabella (with quartet) in which she describes her love for Lindoro, "Per lui che adoro."

The first American presentation took place at the Richmond Hill Theater in New York on November 5, 1832. On December 5, 1919, *L'Italiana in Algeri* was produced at the Metropolitan Opera.

1815. IL BARBIERE DI SIVIGLIA (THE BARBER OF SEVILLE), opera buffa in two acts, with text by Cesare Sterbini, based on *Le Barbier de*

Séville and *Le Mariage de Figaro* by Beaumarchais. First performance: Teatro Argentino, Rome, February 20, 1816.

Rossini's masterwork is possibly both the most famous and the best comic opera ever written. Rising to one of the finest librettos he ever set, Rossini created a score, which, for richness and variety of style, for poignancy and gaiety, for abundance of musical riches, is without equal in the literature. "It will be played as long as opera exists," said Beethoven prophetically. Berlioz, Brahms, Wagner were some other masters who spoke of it with the highest of possible praise. Among present-day musicologists there is Ernest Newman to refer to it as an "immortal work . . . the finest flower of the older Italian musical comedy." And Francis Toye said: "Every situation, almost every idea seems to have suggested to him one musical train of thought after another, nearly all equally felicitous." Yet—wonder of wonders!—this miracle was written within the space of thirteen days.

The effervescent little overture completely captures the vivacious spirit of the opera, and puts the audience at once in the proper frame of mind and spirit for the appreciation of the delights to come. For this reason, it must come as a shock to learn that this overture was not written specifically for *The Barber;* that Rossini had used it previously for several other operas, serious as well as comic.

A slow introduction offers a suave melody for the violins. After four vigorous chords, the Allegro arrives with a pert, dashing tune for strings and piccolo. The second theme, hardly less infectious, follows in oboe and clarinet. A Rossini crescendo brings on the development of these ideas; the overture ends with a lively coda.

The curtain rises on seventeenth-century Seville. Count Almaviva is in love with Rosina, ward of Bartolo. Since Bartolo would like Rosina for himself, he discourages all suitors. Almaviva, therefore, must assume the disguise of a poor student named Lindoro in order to further his suit. As Lindoro, he serenades Rosina with the romantic air, "Ecco ridente in cielo," then gives voice to his passionate emotions in "Se il mio nome." The barber Figaro now makes his appearance. He is a jack-of-all-trades as he explains in one of the most famous patter songs in comic opera, "Largo al factotum." Figaro then suggests to Almaviva that he disguise himself as a soldier and, feigning inebriation, seek shelter in Rosina's household.

Within that household, Rosina is reading a letter sent her by Lindoro, "Una voce poco fa," probably the best-known coloratura aria in the opera. Her guardian, Bartolo, is suspicious about the strange people lurking around in the neighborhood. This leads him to comment on the malicious force of slander, "La Calunnia." Almaviva now stalks in drunk, dressed up as a soldier. Once inside, he furtively makes contact with Rosina, identifies himself as Lindoro, and exchanges written messages with her. Before long, Bartolo recognizes something suspicious in the air. When he threatens to call the police, Almaviva is forced to reveal who he really is.

But Almaviva is not discouraged from trying to contact his beloved.

Now appearing as a music teacher—substituting for the ailing Basilio—he returns. "Pace e gioia sia con voi," he says in a greeting to Rosina and Bartolo. The suspicious Bartolo insists upon remaining in the room while the singing lesson takes place. In spite of this, Rosina and Almaviva manage to plan elopement, even while going through the vocal exercises. Bartolo's doubts begin to mount. Finally, he summons a notary to draw up a marriage contract between himself and his ward. But the notary has been bribed to substitute the name of Almaviva for that of Bartolo. After the wedding ceremony, Bartolo's ruffled feelings at being duped are assuaged when he learns he can keep Rosina's wealth for himself.

Incredible to believe, the première of *Le Barber* in Rome was a fiasco. Many things were responsible. The admirers of the beloved Italian opera composer, Giovanni Paisiello (1740–1816) deeply resented having a young upstart write an opera on a subject previously used so successfully by their own man; Paisiello's *The Barber of Seville* had established itself as one of the most successful opera buffas of its age, following its world première in St. Petersburgh on September 26, 1782. Rossini, apparently, had had some misgivings of his own. He had written Paisiello inquiring if that master had any objections about a new setting of *The Barber*. Since it was habitual at that time for different composers to use the same text, Paisiello proved completely agreeable. As an added precaution against being accused of competing with Paisiello, Rossini at first decided to call his opera *Almaviva*—and this is the title that was used at the première. But all such considerations did not stop Paisiello's admirers from doing everything they could to create a scandal in the theater.

The performance did not work on Rossini's behalf. One thing after another went wrong. Don Basilio fell through a trap door at one point; at another, a cat ambled lazily across the stage. In addition, the singers had been poorly rehearsed, and the production sloppily staged. Stimulated by the laughter and boos of Paisiello's followers, the audience went into an uproar. Rossini, who conducted the performance, fled from the theater.

For the second presentation, Rossini effected several significant changes, including the introduction of Almaviva's serenade, "Ecco ridente." For some reason or other, Paisiello's admirers were no longer at hand to cause a scandal. With the performances greatly improved upon, the audience expressed its enthusiasm in no uncertain terms. At the third performance, there was a resounding ovation for Rossini.

On August 19, 1816, when the opera was seen in Bologna, the title of *Almaviva* was permanently discarded for *The Barber of Seville*. Five years after its Rome première, the opera went on a triumphant tour of Italy.

The Barber of Seville was the first opera to get sung in Italian in New York. This took place on November 29, 1825. But its American première had taken place a few years earlier—at the Park Theater in New York on May 3, 1819, given in English. The first Metropolitan Opera presentation took place in that company's first season, on November 23, 1883.

As produced today, the opera differs in several ways from that seen in Rossini's time. Rossini originally wrote the role of Rosina for a mezzo-soprano. Since 1826, when Henrietta Sontag appeared in the role, it has been more usual to assign the part to a soprano. The second-act aria Rossini wrote for Bartolo, "A un dottor," is now replaced by the more singable, "Manca un foglio," the work of a composer by the name of Romani. The music Rossini created for the famous "lesson scene" is lost. Prima donnas have long made it a practice to interpolate here any one of several popular numbers or arias by other composers, including John Howard Payne's "Home Sweet Home," Arditi's "Il Bacio," or Alabiev's "The Nightingale."

1817. LA CENERENTOLA (CINDERELLA), opera buffa in two acts, with text by Jacopo Ferretti, based on the fairy tale of Perrault. First performance: Teatro Valle, Rome, January 25, 1817.

The librettists here took liberties with the famous Cinderella story of Perrault. Fairy elements were eliminated. There is no fairy godmother in the opera, her place being taken by Alidoro, a kindly philosopher. Cinderella becomes a charming young lady, interested in Parisian and Viennese fashions, while suffering abuse at the hands of her two stepsisters and stepfather. Alidoro comes to their household disguised as a beggar. The two stepsisters drive him off, but Cinderella generously turns over to him her own meal. This makes such an impression on the philosopher that he arranges for Cinderella to attend the Prince's ball. The Prince is seeking a wife. Since he wants somebody to love him for himself alone, he comes to the ball disguised as a valet, while his valet poses as the Prince. The pseudo-Prince tries to make love to Cinderella but is rebuffed. However, Cinderella is attracted to the real prince, who she believes is a humble valet. The Prince now presents her with a bracelet by which he can identify her and claim her as his bride a few days later.

La Cenerentola is one of Rossini's finest comic operas—consistently lyrical, gay, and effervescent. The overture is one Rossini had previously used for another opera, *La Gazzetta* (1816). In lightness of touch and infectiousness of spirit, it is completely in tune with the *Cinderella* text. An extended slow section opens with soft phrases in lower strings and woodwind, separated by vigorous chords. The principal subject in this introduction is a romantic episode for the woodwind. Four chords bring on the main section in which two graceful melodies are presented, the first in strings, the other in woodwind. A Rossini crescendo, and brio passages, inject dramatic interest. An extended crescendo sweeps toward an exciting conclusion.

The opera opens and closes with an attractive aria for the heroine: "Una volta c'era un re" at the beginning, and "Ah prence, io cado ai vostri piè" at the conclusion; the latter is Cinderella's plea to the Prince to forgive her stepfather and stepsisters. In an attractive buffa style, we find the first-act air, "Miei rampoli" of Don Magnifico (Cinderella's father), a complaint at being roused from sleep by continual noisemaking.

The opera was introduced to the United States by the Manuel Garcia company at the Park Theater in New York on June 27, 1826. On that occasion, Mme. Malibran assumed the title role. The opera lay in discard for many years. Remarkable revivals in London (in 1934, with Conchita Supervia) and in New York (in 1953, by the New York City Opera) have helped to restore the work into the comic-opera repertory.

1817. LA GAZZA LADRA (THE THIEVING MAGPIE), opera buffa in two acts, with text by Giovanni Cherardini, based on *La Pie voleuse* by d'Aubigny and Caigniez. First performance: La Scala, Milan, May 31, 1817.

Rossini, ever sensitive to audience tastes, wrote *La Gazza ladra* to woo back the Milanese public, which had recently rejected two of his operas. Since Milan had recently come to favor German operas, Rossini here paid greater attention than heretofore to harmony and orchestration. Since a prayer had recently inspired an ovation at La Scala in another opera, Rossini introduced a prayer of his own. Most important of all, Rossini decided to blend all the elements opera lovers favored into a single work combining comedy and tragedy, gaiety and sentimentality, powerful drama and lightness of mood. His incomparable sense for comedy revealed itself in the portrayal of the lecherous Podesta, and in the Podesta's cumbersome efforts to win the love of Ninetta. Rossini's feeling for drama can be found in the Judgment Scene, while his flair for tenderness and sentiment appear in arias like "Di piacer mi balza il cor," and "Deh, tu reggi in tal momento," sung by Ninetta, and in Fernando's second-act aria, "Accusata di furto."

The text is based on a slight episode. Ninetta, a servant girl, is falsely accused of having stolen a silver spoon. She is unable to plead innocence, for to do so she would have to incriminate her father, an army deserter. In the end, the discovery is made that the silver was stolen and secreted by a pet magpie. Ninetta is exonerated. She can now pursue her love affair with Fernando.

The popular overture starts off with a roll of two snare drums. This is the preface to a vigorous march tune in the entire orchestra. Five loud chords lead into the main section. This begins with a soaring melody taken from a third-act duet, which is elaborated upon. A Rossini crescendo brings on a stormy passage. A transition in bassoon, horns, and trombones leads into the recapitulation in which the first theme is recalled by strings, and the second by clarinets.

The first American performance took place in Philadelphia in October, 1827 (in a French translation). An Italian language production followed in New York on November 16, 1833, and an English one in the same city on January 14, 1839.

1823. SEMIRAMIDE, opera seria in two acts, with text by Gaetano Rossi, based on a drama by Voltaire. First performance: Teatro la Fenice, Venice, February 3, 1823.

Among Rossini's serious operas, *Semiramide* is second only to *William Tell* in importance and musical interest. This is the last of the thirty or so operas Rossini wrote in Italy.

The heroine is Semiramis, queen of Babylon, who murders her husband with the aid of her lover, Assur. But subsequently, she falls in love with a handsome young warrior without knowing that he is her son, Arsace. Assur plans Arsace's death, but Semiramis—now realizing who Arsace really is—intercepts Assur's dagger and is killed. After Arsace has disposed of Assur, he ascends the Babylonian throne and marries Azema.

The overture, a masterpiece, is one of the few by Rossini in which he uses material from the opera itself. An Allegro vivace section passes from pianissimo to fortissimo before the presentation of the principal theme—a stately melody for four horns, which comes from the "oath quintet" to the Queen in the first act. After this thought is developed with fanciful figurations by the woodwind over plucked strings, a short woodwind passage brings on the main part of the overture. A melody for the strings, the first theme, is derived from the orchestral preface to the opera's final scene. This is followed by a vigorous subject for the woodwind. An effective crescendo is the bridge to a restatement of both subjects, while a second crescendo leads into the vigorous close.

There are two outstanding ensemble pieces in the opera, among the greatest by Rossini. One is the duet of Arsace and Semiramide, "Ebbene, a te fericsi"; the other is "Qual mesto gemito," in the first act finale, which is said to have influenced Verdi when he wrote the "Miserere" in *Il Trovatore*. Both Semiramide and Arsace have extraordinary arias, the former with "Bel raggio lusinghier" and the latter with "Ah! quel giorno."

Semiramide was first presented in the United States in New Orleans on May 1, 1837. Adelina Patti later scored successfully in this opera; first in 1883, at the Academy of Music in New York, and then, during the Spring Season of 1887, at the Metropolitan Opera. After being produced again in 1893–1894, the opera was dropped from the Metropolitan Opera repertory. *Semiramide* was successfully revived in New York early in 1964 (after a sixty-nine year absence) in a concert performance by the American Opera Society, with Joan Sutherland in the title role.

1829. GUILLAUME TELL (WILLIAM TELL), romantic opera in four acts, with text by Étienne de Jouy, Hippolyte Bis, and Armand Marrast, based on a drama by Schiller. First performance: Paris Opéra, August 3, 1829.

Almost as if conscious that this was to be his swan song in the theater, Rossini fashioned *William Tell* along lines more spacious and ambitious than those of any of his earlier operas. If performed in its entirely, *William Tell* would take six hours. It makes extraordinary demands on scenic designer and stage director with its grandiose scenes of pageantry. And to the writing of his music, Rossini brought, not only all the science and artistry of which he was capable, but also an idealism and integrity not often confronted in his earlier work. He brought to *William Tell* a new dramatic power, psychological insight, gift at character delineation, a nobility of emotion and loftiness of sentiment. This does not mean that *William Tell* is without serious shortcomings. It has too many stretches of monotony, too many lapses from inspiration. But, the faults notwithstanding, *William Tell* is Rossini's greatest serious opera, one with which he might have entered upon an altogether new phase in his career had he chosen to write more operas. As it is, *William Tell* marks a new day for French grand opera, besides anticipating techniques and methods later realized by Wagner.

The overture, surely one of the most popular ever written by an Italian, already gives us a clue to Rossini's extended horizon. Heretofore, he had often been content to expropriate an overture from an earlier work without qualms of conscience; otherwise he produced one hastily to a stereotype. For *William Tell* he deserted old procedures for a piece of music that is more of a tone poem than an overture. This, said Berlioz, is a "work of immense talent which resembles genius so closely as to be mistaken for it." There are four parts. In the first, an eloquent subject for cellos and basses brings up the picture of a sunrise over the Swiss mountains. In the second, a storm gathers to unleash its strength in exciting brio passages. After the storm passes, an atmosphere of tranquillity is introduced with the celebrated "Ranz des vaches" melody for the English horn. A trumpet heralds the approach of the Swiss army. The fourth and concluding section contains the celebrated march music which for so many years was familiar to young American radio listeners as the identifying theme of the "Lone Ranger" program.

The hero in the opera is, of course, the legendary fourteenth-century patriot who gives the opera its name. William Tell is fired with the ambition to overthrow the despotic rule of the Austrians, headed by the tyrant, Gessler. He enlists the aid of Arnold, son of Melcthal, a Swiss patriarch, in spite of the fact that Arnold is in love with Gessler's daughter, Matthilde. A celebration, during which shepherds perform a colorful folk dance (Passo a sei) is interrupted by the appearance of the shepherd Leuthold. He is in flight, and is being pursued by Austrian troops. William Tell stands ready to row Leuthhold across the lake to safety. When Gessler's soldiers realize their victim has eluded them, they seize old Melcthal as a hostage, and set fire to the fishermen's huts.

In a forest, Matthilde is musing about her great love for Arnold in the beautiful cavatina, "Sombre forêt." When Arnold appears, the lovers embrace passionately; for the moment, Arnold stands ready to forget his patriotic ideals. But when William Tell brings him the news that Melcthal has been killed by Gessler, Arnold abandons all doubts. He vows to avenge himself by driving the tyrants out of Switzerland.

Arnold comes to a ruined chapel near Gessler's palace to bid Matthilde farewell ("Pour notre amour"). In return, Matthilde swears to remain true to her love until her death. The scene shifts to a market place. The Swiss are in festive mood, celebrating with folk songs and dances. The tyrant, Gessler, has placed his hat on the top of a pole, and insists that the people bow to it as a token of submission. When William Tell refuses to do so, he is seized by the guards. Gessler now orders Tell to shoot an apple off the head of his son. Before taking aim, Tell intones a prayer ("Sois immobile"), then shoots, and hits the mark squarely. Bitterly, William Tell informs Gessler that had his son been killed in this test, Tell would have reserved a second arrow for Gessler. Tell is arrested, and Tell's son is taken into custody by Matthilde.

In the first scene of the fourth act, Arnold is in front of his home, now in ashes. Poignantly, in "Asile héreditaire" he recalls the happiness of youth. Then, in the second scene, Matthilde has come to the shores of Lake Lucerne to inform William Tell's wife, Hedwig, that the hero is in prison. As a storm erupts, William Tell—having escaped from incarceration—arrives with a band of patriots. He kills Gessler with an arrow. The Swiss people are at last free. Matthilde and Arnold, and William Tell and his family, are happily reunited. The Swiss sing a song of praise to their newly won emancipation.

When first produced, *William Tell* was highly praised by the French critics, and the work enjoyed a substantial success. It was seen at the Opéra over a hundred times during the first five years. By 1868 (the year of Rossini's death), it had been given over five hundred performances there. Most of the time, because of its excessive length, the opera was seen in truncated versions; and at times, it was represented only by a single act.

William Tell was seen for the first time in the United States on September 19, 1831, when it was given in New York in an English translation. A French language production followed in New York on June 16, 1845. During the second season of the Metropolitan Opera, *William Tell* entered its repertory—on November 28, 1884.

1832. STABAT MATER, for solo voices, chorus, and orchestra.

After 1829, Rossini canalized his creativity mainly into church music. In 1832, he was invited to write a religious composition for a church in Madrid. He complied with the first six sections of a Stabat Mater. Then laid low by lumbago, Rossini asked his friend Tadolini (the singing master at the Théâtre Italien) to do the remaining four parts. This curiosity was despatched to Madrid without anyone realizing that it was not entirely Rossini's. But in 1841, when a publisher planned to issue the score, Rossini bought back the rights to the music. He now discarded what Tadolini had written and replaced it with his own sections. On January 7, 1842, the Stabat Mater, now entirely Rossini's, was heard at the Théâtre Italien and was a triumph. Heine thought that it was better than Mendelssohn's *St. Paul,* while some French critics regarded it as superior even to Haydn's *Creation*. Soon after this première, Donizetti directed a performance in Bologna that created such excitement that the audience stormed to Rossini's apartment, demanding he appear on the balcony and acknowledge an ovation.

The Stabat Mater is music of the first order, combining the most extraordinary skill at writing for the voices, with exalted melodies and sentiments. It opens with a choral section, "Stabat Mater." This is followed by a tenor aria, "Cuius anima"; a duet for two sopranos, "Qui est homo"; an aria for bass, "Pro peccatis"; a chorus, "Eia mater"; a quartet, "Sancta mater"; a cavatina for soprano, "Fac ut portem"; an aria for soprano with chorus, "Inflammatus et accensus"; a vocal quartet, "Quando corpus morietur"; and the concluding chorus, "Amen."

1863. PETITE MESSE SOLENNELLE, for soloists, chorus, and orchestra.

With his customary bent for whimsy, Rossini described this work as "the last mortal sin of my old age." He then added: "Dear God. This poor little Mass is completed. Have I for once written real sacred music or merely damned bad music? I was born for opera buffa as Thou knowest! Little skill, but some heart; that about sums it up. So blessed be Thou, and grant me paradise."

But this remarkable Mass is not "little" in dimension. Nor is there any levity in its music, which is, throughout, reverent and noble. Indeed, this is Rossini's most consistently inspired choral work—an eloquent testimony that there was nothing wrong in his creative resources, imagination, or technical skill, even in old age. Meyerbeer, who attended the première on March 14, 1868, was beside himself with delight. He called the fugue, "Cum sancto spiritu," the "finest composition of its kind ever written." He further exclaimed: "In two months he has created a whole world. He is the Jupiter of our time and holds us all in the hollow of his hand."

The musical writing is far more ecclesiastical than might be expected from Rossini. Page after page rises to lofty peaks of religious sublimity. Francis Toye writes: "The beauties of melodies such as the bass solo, 'Quoniam,' and the soprano solo, 'O Salutaris'; the exquisite part-writing in the 'Gratias'; the finale ensemble of the 'Agnus Dei' should be obvious to everybody." Then while going on to praise the surpassing merits of "Et Resurrexit" and the "Et vitam venturi" fugue from the "Credo," Toye singles out the "Gloria" as "the gem of the whole work." He also concurs with Meyerbeer that the "Cum sancto spiritu" fugue is an "outstanding example of Rossini's genius."

——LA BOUTIQUE FANTASQUE (THE FANTASTIC TOYSHOP), ballet in one act, with music by Rossini, arranged and orchestrated by Ottorino Respighi. Choreography by Massine. First performance: Alhambra Theater, London, June 5, 1919.

SOIRÉES MUSICALES (MUSICAL EVENINGS), suite for orchestra, based on music by Rossini, arranged and adapted by Benjamin Britten. I. March. II. Canzonetta. III. Tyrolese. IV. Bolero. V. Tarantella.

MATINÉES MUSICALES (MUSICAL AFTERNOONS), suite for orchestra, based on music by Rossini, arranged and adapted by Benjamin Britten. I. March. II. Nocturne. III. Waltz. IV. Pantomime. V. Moto perpetuo.

During the years of Rossini's abstinence from operatic composition, he wrote some one hundred and eighty pieces for the piano, collected under the single title *Péchés de vieillesse* (*Sins of Old Age*). Some of these trifles were arranged and orchestrated by Respighi for the ballet score, *La Boutique fantasque,* produced by the Ballet Russe of Diaghilev. The setting for the ballet is a toy shop in southern France, where dolls from all parts of the world become animated. Headed by the shopkeeper, they perform dances for delighted customers. Rossini's pieces (which bear such descriptive, Satie-like titles as *Four Hors d'oevures, or Radishes, Anchovies, Gherkins and Butter Themes in Variation,* or *Castor Oil,* or *Abortive Polka*) are neatly transfigured by Respighi into a tarantella, barcarolle, can-can, mazurka, Russian dance, and so forth.

Rossini's piano pieces (with additional samplings from *William Tell*) are the source from which Benjamin Britten drew for his two five-movement orchestral suites—the *Soirées musicales* in 1936 and the *Matinées musicales* in 1941. The music of both these suites, combined with the overture to *La Cenerentola,* was subsequently used for a ballet entitled *Divertimento;* the two suites were also used for the ballet *Fantaisie italienne,* produced in Brussels in 1948.

GAETANO DONIZETTI 1797–1848

Donizetti's sixty and more operas fall conveniently into three groups. His first thirty-two works belong to the years of apprenticeship, when he imitated Rossini. Here Donizetti apes Rossini's style, borrows his little mannerisms, assumes his idiosyncrasies. In the process, Donizetti's own personality was obliterated. But these thirty-two apprentice works were no waste motion. Copying Rossini's methods and techniques taught Donizetti how to write gracefully and at times brilliantly for the voice; how to make a melody soar spaciously; how to achieve a buffa style that was both vivacious and spontaneous.

The second group begins with *Anna Bolena,* in 1830, the opera with which Donizetti first won renown in Europe. During his own lifetime, and for some years thereafter, *Anna Bolena* was esteemed as Donizetti's masterwork. Today, it is rarely heard; and if it is at all remembered, it is mainly because one of its melodies was the same one which Sir Henry Rowley Bishop (1786–1855) used for John Howard Payne's words in "Home Sweet Home."

Having cut his umbilical cord to Rossini with *Anna Bolena,* Donizetti was ready to set off on his own, to become Rossini's logical successor. In this second period, we find Donizetti's first significant opera buffa, *L'Elisir d'amore,* and his greatest opera seria, *Lucia di Lammermoor*. But whether his writing was comic or tragic, here he is Rossini's alter ego no longer. In his virtuoso coloratura arias, in his mastery of writing for ensembles, in his flair for theatrical effects, in the dexterity of his comedy, and most of all in the sovereign beauty of his lyricism, Donizetti is now his own lord and master.

It is in his lyricism, in bel canto, that Donizetti borrows no man's language. As Donald Jay Grout said: "He had a Midas gift of turning everything into the kind of melody which people could remember and sing. His tunes have a robust swing, with catchy rhythms, reinforced by frequent sforzandos on the offbeats. Every cavatina ends with a cadenza and every cabaletta bristles with coloratura passages." Donizetti, also, fashioned a declamation "of an outstanding or significant phrase by a couple, or half a dozen, or a whole stageful, of singers all in unison or octaves—an effect electrifying in its brilliance and the very apotheosis of the idea of melody as the crown of music."

The third and final group of Donizetti's operas begins with *La Fille du régiment* and includes *La Favorita* and *Don Pasquale*. This is Donizetti's French period in which an Italian master adapts his thinking and writing to French tastes. A kind of Meyerbeer splendor and grandeur now characterize Donizetti's tragic operas, and a French sparkle and sophistication are discernible in his comedies.

Gaetano Donizetti, the son of a weaver, was born in Bergamo, Italy, on November 29, 1797. He attended first the Bergamo School of Music, then the Liceo Filarmonico in Bologna. After completing music study, he entered the army. While still in uniform, he completed *Enrico di Borgogna,* produced in Venice in 1818. The success of *Zoraide di Granata,* heard in Rome in 1822, was responsible for exempting him from all further military duties and allowed him to concentrate on writing operas. He became remarkably prolific. Between 1822 and 1829, he completed twenty-three operas. During this period, in 1823, he married Virginia Vasselli, whose death fourteen years later plunged him into permanent grief.

Anna Bolena, in 1830, spread Donizetti's fame throughout Europe. It was followed by the first two of Donizetti's operas to remain in the repertory up until the present day, *L'Elisir d'amore* and *Lucia di Lammermoor*. In 1837, he was appointed director of the Naples Conservatory, but he did not hold this post long. Upset by the interference of censors in the production of *Poliuto,* Donizetti left Italy in 1839 and established residence in Paris. There he completed *La Fille du régiment, La Favorite,* and *Don Pasquale*. In 1842, Donizetti visited Vienna, where he received the titles of Court Composer and Master of the Imperial Chapel from the Austrian Emperor. After returning to Italy in 1844, he wrote and had produced in Naples his last opera, *Caterina Cornaro.*

A victim of a paralytic stroke in 1845, Donizetti died in the city of his birth on April 8, 1848.

1832. L'ELISIR D'AMORE (THE ELIXIR OF LOVE), opera buffa in two acts, with text by Felice Romani, based on Eugène Scribe's libretto, *Le Philtre.* First performance: Teatro della Canobbiana, Milan, May 12, 1832.

Like Rossini, Donizetti was equally gifted in both comic and serious operas. He had to complete thirty-seven operas before he wrote the first that has survived—the opera buffa, *L'Elisir d'amore.* It came with his customary speed and despatch. In discussing the project with his librettist, Donizetti permitted him only one week in which to complete the text. He matched this furious writing pace by doing the whole score in fourteen days. But there is not much in this tuneful and lovable score to betray the carelessness or superficiality of haste. For it includes one of the most beautiful and the most popular arias Donizetti ever wrote, "Una furtiva lagrima" (one of Caruso's prime favorites), and with it such other soulful and eloquent airs by Nemorino as "Quanto è bella" and "Adina credimi." In a buffa style, his inspiration yielded a veritable gem in "Udite, Udite" with which the quack, Dr. Dulcamara, introduces himself.

The power of elixirs was a subject close to the hearts of opera buffo writers. Its super-salesman in the Donizetti opera is Dr. Dulcamara. One man above others is interested in his ware—Nemorino, the young farmer in love with the beautiful and wealthy Adina. Since he has a serious rival in Belcore, an army sergeant—and since Adina seems incapable of choosing between them—Nemorino purchases from Dulcamara a potion able to inspire love. But what the wily old fox has sold Nemorino is just cheap wine. Nevertheless, Nemorino is convinced that this "potion" has magic powers, and he sings to it a hymn, "Dell' elisir mirabile." He is now determined to use it on Adina, who by this time has announced her intention of marrying Belcore. But Dulcamara will not sell Nemorino any more elixirs, since the young man can no longer raise the price. In despair, Nemorino enlists in the army to take advantage of a bonus given all recruits. With that money he is able to buy the elixir. But since the elixir needs time to work its magic on Adina, Nemorino entreats her to delay her marriage to Belcore. During the delay, word arrives that Nemorino has inherited a fortune from his uncle—news that sends the village girls swarming around him, and throws Adina into an envious rage. Nemorino placates her with the poignant romance, "Una furtiva lagrima." Now determined to marry Nemorino, Adina arranges for his release from the army. Nemorino is now convinced that the elixir truly has remarkable powers.

L'Elisir was first seen in the United States on June 18, 1838, produced in an English translation at the Park Theater in New York. It had to wait almost a century before entering the repertory of the Metropolitan Opera—January 23, 1904. The main reason it was then given was that Enrico Caruso had joined the company in 1903, and *L'Elisir* was one of his favorite operas.

1835. LUCIA DI LAMMERMOOR, opera in three acts, with libretto by Salvatore Cammarano, based on Sir Walter Scott's *The Bride of Lammermoor.* First performance: San Carlo, Naples, September 26, 1835.

Lucia was Donizetti's forty-second opera; and it is the first of his serious works that is performed regularly today in the world's foremost opera houses. Cammarano's text passes through the whole gamut of tragedy—madness, death, suicide, treachery, deception—so much so, that at times it almost appears like a parody of Italian operas. Indeed, a good case might be built that the libretto of *Lucia* is one of the poorest among surviving Italian operas. The plot taxes an audience's tolerance with its impossible-to-believe situations and developments, besides being synthetic from beginning to end.

But Donizetti's music is something else again. It boasts one of the most brilliant coloratura roles in all Italian opera, sought after by the world's foremost sopranos, beginning with Fanny Persiana (for whom the opera was written) and continuing on with Patti, Jenny Lind, Sembrich, Melba, Tetrazzini, Galli-Curci, Lily Pons, and Joan Sutherland. It contains one of the most celebrated ensemble numbers in the sextet "Chi mi frena," and a no less popular coloratura aria in the "Mad Scene." The other pages in this remarkable score are hardly less distinguished. The music that follows right after the Sextet, and carries the act to an end, was regarded by Herbert F. Peyser as "among the great episodes in Italian opera. The "Tomb Scene" is extraordinary for its atmospheric writing. For sheer loveliness of melody and intensity of feeling, we have Lucia's first-act entrance cavatina, "Regnava nel silenzio," followed by her sprightly air, "Quando rapita." For particularly effective choral writing, one can point to two choruses in the opening scene ("Percorrete le spiagge vicine" and "Come vinti,") and the chorus in the wedding scene, "Per te d'immenso giubilo."

The setting is Scotland; the time, the end of the seventeenth century. Lucia and Edgardo, master of Ravenswood, are in love. But Lucia's brother, Lord Ashton, is opposed to their union, and becomes Edgardo's mortal enemy. In a park near her castle, Lucia makes her entry by describing an apparition that has been haunting her, that of a young woman murdered by one of the Ravenswoods. But her mood soon becomes perceptibly more cheerful, as she begins to think of Edgardo. He soon arrives, bearing sorrowful news: He must leave at once for France. The lovers bid each other a tender farewell in "Verrano a te sull' aure."

In his ruthless effort to break up all ties binding his sister to Edgardo, and to relieve his own financial distress, Lord Ashton decides to get Lucia to marry Arturo Bucklaw. He forges letters proving Edgardo has abandoned Lucia for good; thus he connives to get Lucia to consent to a loveless union with Arturo. Preparations are now made for the signing of a marriage contract. Soon a stranger appears; he is soon recognized as Edgardo At this strange development, six leading characters give voice to their inmost emotions in the celebrated sextet: Edgardo, Lucia, Enrico, the chaplain Raimondo, Lucia's companion (Alisa), and Arturo Bucklaw. When Edgardo discovers that Lucia has consented to marry Arturo, he curses the house of Lammermoor and flees.

And now the castle becomes festive with the wedding ceremony. Horrible tidings shatter the joy: Lucia has lost her mind. Suddenly she enters, dressed in a long, white gown, and walking as if in a trance. She raves that Edgardo is about to become her husband. Poignantly, she begs that a flower be placed on her grave, that no tears be shed when she is gone. Then she swoons in the arms of her companion, Alisa.

But Edgardo, unaware of these tragic developments, longs for death, as he laments man's duplicity (the Tomb Scene). A row of mourners file by. It is from them that Edgardo learns that Lucia is mad. He rushes to the house of Lammermoor to be with the woman he loves. But before he can get there, the tolling of bells announces that Lucia is dead. Now for the first time made aware that all this while Lucia has been true to him, Edgardo loses the will to live and stabs himself.

The American première took place in New Orleans on December 28, 1841. When Adelina Patti made her formal debut in opera, she chose the role of Lucia—at the Academy of Music in New York on November 24, 1859. And when Marcella Sembrich made her American debut on October 24, 1883, she, too, was seen and heard as Lucia. That performance of *Lucia* was the second offering of the newly opened Metropolitan Opera, given two days after its doors opened for the first time with *Faust*.

1840. LA FILLE DU RÉGIMENT (THE DAUGHTER OF THE REGIMENT), opéra-comique in two acts, with text by Jean-François Alfred Bayard and Jules Henri Vernoy de Saint-Georges. First performance: Opéra-Comique, Paris, February 11, 1840.

La Fille du régiment carries its martial tunes and patriotic airs like the waving banners and flags of an army on parade. It is understandable why a work like this always has had particular appeal for the French people. Many an episode is calculated here to stir French blood: the rousing paean to war and victory by the French troops, "Rataplan, Rataplan"; Marie's patriotic salute to her regiment in "Chacun le sait"; the stirring hymn to France which closes the opera, "Salut à la France." Once in a while interpolations have been made into the opera to heighten its French national spirit. During World War II, for example (shortly after the Nazis occupied Paris), Lily Pons draped a French flag around her body and gave a rousing rendition of the "Marseillaise" at the Metropolitan Opera.

But, of course, the popularity of this opera is not confined to France alone. In Italy, as *La Figlia del reggimento,* and in the United States, Donizetti's melodious and theatrical opéra-comique has found many staunch advocates.

For the composer's rare gift at melody was not exclusively confined to robust, strong-muscled airs. A welcome change of feeling is invoked with several musical highlights in which the sentimental or romantic elements are pronounced. Some of these grow naturally out of the love interest involving Marie and Tonio: "Depuis l'instant òu dans mes bras," "Tous les trois réunis," and "Quand le destin au milieu."

The "daughter of the regiment" is Marie—a canteen manager of the 21st French Regiment during the French invasion of the Tyrols in or about 1815. Since the soldiers are all deeply devoted to her, they rally to the defense of Tonio (with whom Marie is in love) when that Tyrolean peasant is accused of being a spy; they even take him in as a recruit. Despair seizes the French when they discover that Marie must soon leave them. Countess of Berkenfeld, having learned that Marie is her niece, insists she come to live with her at her castle. Marie poignantly bids the French farewell in "Il faut partir." Despite the luxury with which the Countess surrounds her, Marie is plunged into the deepest sorrow. She misses the French troops, but most of all, she misses Tonio. Besides, the Countess has insisted she marry a Duke in whom she has no interest. But her misery is dispelled with the arrival of her French regiment into the Berkenfeld castle, particularly since Tonio is with them. And it is through the intercession of her friends that the Countess (who now confesses that Marie is her daughter and not her niece) becomes convinced that Marie must be allowed to marry Tonio.

The first American performance took place in New Orleans on March 6, 1843. After that, an English production was seen in New York City in 1844, and a German one in the same city in 1854. When the opera was produced during the early part of the Civil War (with Clara Louise Kellogg as Marie), Union zouaves were made to appear in the cast. And when *La Fille* was mounted at the Metropolitan Opera during World War I, Frieda Hempel, as Marie, introduced into the Donizetti score the popular English war ballad, "Keep the Home Fires Burning."

1840. LA FAVORITE, opera in four acts, with libretto by Alphonse Royer and Gustave Vaëz, based on *Le Comte du Commingues* by Baculard-d'Arnaud. First performance: Paris Opéra, December 2, 1840.

Perhaps nothing proves more convincingly Donizetti's capacity to turn from light to melodramatic subjects with equal skill and success than the fact that in the single year of 1840 he was able to produce two such operas as *La Fille du régiment* and *La Favorite*.

Based on a seemingly historical subject set in fourteenth-century Castille, *La Favorite* was decked out with all those trappings favored by Parisian operagoers: processions, ceremonials, ballets, stage-crowded scenes. It has music in kind: big arias—Leonora's third-act tour de force, "O Mio Fernando" (the most famous aria in the opera) and Fernando's two beautiful romances, "Una vergine" and "Spirto gentil"; big choruses—the compelling chant of the monks, "Splendon più belle."; big scenes—the massive ending of the third act, which Wallace Brockway and Herbert Weinstock described as "an artistic statement of a harrowing situation brought to a violent climax."

Fernando, a novice monk, has fallen in love with a mysterious woman of unknown identity, who keeps passing by his window. Ejected from the monastery, Fernando goes in search of the woman of his dreams. He comes to the island of Leon, where Leonora de Guzman, the king's favorite, summons him. He forthwith recognizes her as the woman he is seeking. But Leonora, fully aware that Fernando would have no use for her once he learns she is the king's mistress, sends him off with a parchment giving him an officer's commission in the army. Convinced that Leonora is out his reach, Fernando plies his soldier's trade recklessly, and emerges a hero. In recognition of his services, the king offers him any reward he seeks. Still unaware that Leonora is the king's mistress, he asks for her hand in marriage. The king is willing to comply, since it would help him solve a personal problem—over his head there has long dangled the threat of losing his throne for having abandoned his wife. Only after he has married Leonora, does Fernando learn of her illicit affair with the king. This news shatters him, and sends him back to the monastery in search of peace of mind. Leonora seeks him out there, disguised as a novice, and dies in his arms. Fernando is now ready to renounce the world and become a monk.

The American première took place in New Orleans on February 9, 1843. When *La Favorite* was presented at the Metropolitan Opera for the first time, on November 29, 1895, W. J. Henderson complained about the "undramatic conditions which arise from the old-fashioned way of writing operas." And though individual pages of the score appealed to him, and represented "the finest vocal graces of the old school," he was firmly of the belief that, since Verdi and Wagner, there was "little room for such works."

1843. DON PASQUALE, opera buffa in three acts, with text by Giacomo Ruffini and the composer, based on Angelo Anelli's *Ser Merc' Antonio.* First performance: Théâtre des Italiens, Paris, January 3, 1843.

If any one opera lifts Donizetti into the select company of operatic geniuses that work is *Don Pasquale.* Nowhere is his invention so consistently sparkling, fresh, and exciting; nowhere is his touch so sure; nowhere are his characterizations so subtle; nowhere is his lyricism so varied.

When first produced, Don Pasquale enjoyed one of the most distinguished casts assembled in Paris for a single opera. Lablache was Pasquale, to become at once one of the foremost interpreters of the role in his time. Tamburini was Maltesta; Grisi, was Norina; and Mario was Ernesto. At that time, the characters in the opera were dressed in contemporary nineteenth-century clothes. But since operagoers preferred costumed plays, the opera has since been shifted in time a century earlier, allowing for a more picturesque dress.

The main cahracter is a wily old bachelor, Don Pasquale, who opposes the marriage of his nephew Ernesto to the charming widow, Norina. Pasquale himself is looking for a wife, and at the suggestion of his friend and physician, Dr. Malatesta, consents to meet the doctor's sister, Soforina. Actually, there is no such person; the doctor plans to present Norina in disguise. As Soforina, Norina wins over old Pasquale so completely that immediately he proposes marriage. A mock ceremony supposedly joins the old man and Norina in matrimony. Then Norina proceeds to become a shrew who makes old Pasquale's life miserable with her tempers and whims. In despair, Pasquale summons Dr. Malatesta to extricate him from this emergency. When he finally discovers how he had been duped, Pasquale is so delighted to find he is still single, and that the shrew is not really his wife, that he gives his blessings to Norina and Ernesto for their marriage.

The aristocratic lyricism for which Donizetti is so famous is found in Norina's first-act aria, "So anch'io la virtù magica"; in Ernesto's lament, "Sogno soave e casto"; and in his fervent serenade to Norina, "Com' è gentil." This is bel canto writing at its noblest. The comic episodes are buffa writing *in excelsis:* Norina and Malatesta's conspiracy to dupe Pasquale ("Vado, carro"); Malatesta's description to Pasquale of his lovely sister ("Bella siccome un angelo"); the vivacious finale to the second act, opening with "Son tradito" and ending with the sparkling "Bravo, bravo Don Pasquale."

The overture is the most familiar by the composer. A spacious melody for the cellos is introduced by descending chords. It leads, in turn, to a vivacious tune for strings. After a dramatic interlude, the woodwinds and strings present another saucy idea to maintain a mood of levity.

Don Pasquale was first seen in the United States at the Park Theater in New York on March 9, 1846.

VINCENZO BELLINI 1801–1835

Bellini's strong suit was his gift for melody; his most gratifying medium, the voice. His weakness lay in his harmony and orchestration, and in accepting so meekly the concessions forced upon him by the Italian opera of his day. But the strength far overpowers the weaknesses. In Bellini's operas, we find bel canto at its purest and noblest. So remarkable was Bellini's lyricism that he could traverse a wide gamut of emotion and drama exclusively with his wonderful melodies. His song, Ildebrando Pizzetti once wrote, "gushes with the essence of an emotion that brings the drama to a resolution like a fire which is ignited after it emits hot sparks. And this song, gushing forth, becomes a stream, a river, finally an ocean that rolls away to the distance towards an immense horizon."

"Like the folk song," explains Cecil Gray about Bellini's lyricism, "it instinctively rejects harmonic elaborateness as foreign to its nature. . . . In the same way that a jewel is displayed to better advantage in a simple setting than in none at all, but is overshadowed by the brilliance of an elaborate one, so a melody of Bellini requires a certain degree of accompaniment which never is allowed to become so obtrusive as to distract our attention from the melody, or to impress itself too strongly on our consciousness."

Vincenzo Bellini was born in Catania, Sicily, on November 3, 1801. Both his grandfather and father had served as organists of the Catania Cathedral. They gave the boy Bellini his first music lessons. Music study after that continued at the Collegio San Sebastiano in Naples. While still a student there, Bellini completed two Masses, and his first opera—*Adelson e Salvina,* produced successfully at the Conservatory on January 12, 1825. On the strength of this opera, the eminent impresario, Domenico Barbaja, commissioned Bellini to write *Bianca e Fernando* for the San Carlo in Naples, which presented it on May 30, 1826. During the next few years, Bellini wrote several more operas that were seen at La Scala in Milan, and in Parma and Venice. The most important of these was *I Capuletti e i Montecchi,* in 1830, based on Shakespeare's *Romeo and Juliet.* His first masterwork, *La Sonnambula,* and his greatest opera, *Norma,* were both produced in 1831, placing him with the leading opera composers in Italy. In 1833, Bellini visited London and Paris. His last opera, *I Puritani,* was seen in Paris in 1835. Bellini died in Puteaux, near Paris, on September 23, 1835; he had not yet reached his thirty-fourth birthday. Forty years after his death his remains were removed to Catania.

1831. LA SONNAMBULA (THE SLEEP WALKER), opera in two acts, with text by Felice Romani. First performance: Teatro Carcano, Milan, March 6, 1831.

Bellini was only twenty when he wrote *La Sonnambula.* It was his seventh opera, but the first still performed. Romani's libretto was beautifully suited to Bellini's uncommon gift at recitatives and to the sensitivity of his melody. The story concerns the sleepwalking habits of the heroine, Amina, in a nineteenth-century Swiss village. Her betrothal to the prosperous young farmer, Elvino, is being celebrated ("Viva Amina"), as the opera begins. Only the proprietess of the inn, Lisa, is disconsolate, since she is in love with Elvino. Any attempt by Alexis to soothe her proves futile. When Amina appears, she voices her happiness in "Come per me sereno." Soon after the marriage contract is drawn, a stranger appears and muses about his childhood in these very surroundings ("Vi ravviso, o luoghi ameni"). He rents a room in Lisa's inn where later that night, walking in her sleep, Amina enters his room through a window. This leads Elvino to suspect that his beloved is carrying on an affair with the stranger—who turns out to be Count Rodolfo, master of the local castle. Unable to explain her presence in the Count's room, Amina arouses the anger of the townspeople, who denounce her in no uncertain terms. But a few of Amina's friends are determined to prove her innocence; at the same time Amina is trying to convince Elvino she has been faithful to him. Elvino turns a deaf ear. Indeed, as reprisal, he announces his readiness to marry Lisa. But he finally becomes convinced of Amina's virtue when with his own eyes he sees her sleepwalking out of her boudoir window. As she descends to ground, she sings of her unwavering love for Elvino ("Ah, non credea mirarti"). Then she awakens with a start to express her unbounded joy in being reconciled with her beloved, in one of the opera's most brilliant coloratura airs, "Ah! non giunge."

Profiting from a remarkable cast that included Giuditta Pasta as Amina, Rubini as Elvino, and Mariani as Rodolfo, *La Sonnambula* was a striking success at its première. By 1850, it had been given triumphantly in twelve countries, including the United States, where it was introduced on July 29, 1850, in Chicago. From the première performance on, the role of Amina has been a favorite of the world's greatest coloratura sopranos, including Mme. Malibran, Jenny Lind, Patti (who made her impressive debuts both in Paris and London in this role), Tetrazzini, Sembrich, Galli-Curci, Rosa Ponselle, Callas, and Sutherland.

1831. NORMA, opera in two acts, with text by Felice Romani, based on a tragedy by Louis-Alexandre Soumet. First performance: La Scala, Milan, December 26, 1831.

Only ten months after the première of *La Sonnambula,* Bellini's greatest opera, *Norma,* was given its first performance. Wagner did not overstate the case when five years after this première he said that Bellini here "climbed to the summit of his power." Wagner then explained the source of his enthusiasm. "The action, bare of all theatrical coups and dazzling effects, reminds one of the dignity of Greek tragedy. . . . Can you tell me a picture of the soul better executed than that of the wild prophetess, whom we see endure all phases of passion on to the final resignation of a heroic death? Is not everything we feel with her true and great?. . . . Those who can hear in *Norma* only the usual Italian tinkle are not worthy of serious consideration. This music is noble and great, simple and grandiose in style. The very fact that there is style in this music makes it important for our time, a time of experiments and of lack of form."

Bellini had good cause for optimism about the outcome of the première of his new opera. In Romani's libretto he had one of the most powerful of any he had thus far set to music; and he knew full well that for it he had created one of his most consistently inspired scores. In addition, a notable cast had been meticulously rehearsed for the production, including Pasta as the Druidess, Giulia Grisi as Adalgisa, and Donzelli as Pollione. Besides all this, *La Sonnambula* had just extended Bellini's fame to the point where that opera's immediate successor would inevitably be awaited with a good deal of anticipation and excitement. Yet, as Bellini himself reported, the première was a fiasco; the audience hissed the composer.

It did not take *Norma* long to become popular. Indeed, already at the second presentation, a warmer reaction began to set in. During the next forty or so performances at the La Scala that season, enthusiasm kept mounting all the time. Then the opera began to win friends outside of Italy. In 1833, it was successfully produced in Vienna and London. On January 11, 1841, it was seen in the United States—simultaneously in two theaters in Philadelphia. In the same year of 1841, it became the first opera performed in Italian in Constantinople; and in 1843, it became the first Italian language opera seen in Bucharest. Within a quarter of a century following the world première, *Norma* had been seen in most of the capitals of the world. And by the beginning of the twentieth century, it had been given in thirty-five countries, in sixteen different languages.

As a lyric-heroic work dramatizing the conflict of love and duty, *Norma* was the kind of opera to which the nineteenth century was particularly partial. The notes of high tragedy and nobility that sound throughout the score are heard at once in the magnificent overture. Majestic chords for full orchestra introduce a lyrical episode. A rhythmic melody is then heard in flutes and violins, followed by another strongly accented subject, this time in strings. Both ideas—intended to reveal first Norma's courage, then her anger and defiance—are spaciously discussed; particular importance is assigned to the second theme.

The curtain rises on a Druid forest at night, in Gaul, during the Roman occupation in or about 50 *B. C.* The Druids, headed by their High Priest, Oroveso, are invoking the aid of the gods in overcoming the Roman oppressors ("Dell' aura tua profetica"). When the Druids leave, Pollione, a Roman proconsul, reveals to Flavio, the centurion, that Norma, high priestess of the Temple of Esus, has borne him two sons. But Pollione is now in love with Adalgisa, a virgin of the Temple ("Meco all' altar di venere"). A gong brings the Druids back to the scene. Norma ascends the altar steps to urge her people not to revolt, promising that Rome would be destroyed by its own decadence. She then prays to the Moon goddess for peace in one of the most moving arias in all Italian opera, "Casta diva." She further entreats the gods to rescue her from her guilty love affair with Pollione. When Pollione returns, she tries to be aloof. But her emotions are too strong for her. She rushes into his arms, promising to escape with him to Rome.

Then Adalgisa, also tormented by her passion for Pollione and by her guilt in desecrating her holy vows, comes to Norma to confide to her her terrible secret. But she does not reveal the identity of the man she loves. Norma is sympathetic ("Ah si, fa core e abbraccia") after Adalgisa has explained she must leave the Temple forever. Norma's sympathy, however soon turns to rage when for the first time she discovers that she and Adalgisa are rivals for the same man.

In a fit of despair, Norma decides to kill not only herself, but also her children and Pollione. But she cannot summon the strength to murder those she loves. Instead, she compromises on suicide. When she begs Adalgisa to take care of her children ("Deh! con te li prendi"), Adalgisa pleads with Norma not to destroy herself ("Mira o Norma"). In fact, Adalgisa stands ready to give up Pollione for good.

In the woods, near the Temple, where the Gallic warriors and the Druids have gathered to wage war on the Romans, Pollione stoutly refuses to give up Adalgisa for Norma. Norma meanwhile rallies her people for battle ("Guerra! le Galliche selve!"). Later, in a private session with Pollione, she threatens him with a dagger. Even in the face of death, Pollione refuses to give up Adalgisa. Norma now decides to reveal to her people the extent of her crime and to demand punishment. For the last time, she speaks of her great love for Pollione, prophesying they would be reunited in death ("Qual cor tradisti"). She then plunges to her doom in a flaming pyre, to be immediately followed by Pollione.

1835. I PURITANI DI SCOZIA (THE PURITANS OF SCOTLAND), opera in three acts, with text by Count Carlo Pepoli, based on *Têtes rondes et cavaliers,* a play by François Ancelot and Xavier Boniface Saintine. First performance: Théâtre Italien, Paris, January 25, 1835.

In 1833, Bellini paid a visit to Paris, where Rossini encouraged him to write an opera for the Théâtre Italien. Bellini complied with *I Puritani,* which he not only flooded with his incomparable lyricism (most particularly in his arias for tenor), but which he also filled with dramatic impact and psychological insight. *I Puritani* was fated to be Bellini's last opera. Eight months after its brilliant première in Paris (with a star-studded cast that included Grisi, Rubini, Tamburini, and Lablache), Bellini was dead. *I Puritani* soon made the rounds of the music world, with particularly successful presentations at La Scala and in London in 1835, Berlin and Vienna in 1836, and at Palmo's Opera House in New York on February 3, 1844.

Some confusion exists about the title, which indicates that the Puritans come from Scotland. The librettist, however, placed the locale of his text "near Plymouth." What happened is that the librettist quixotically decided to locate Plymouth not in England but in Scotland. The story is set in the seventeenth century during the struggle between the Puritans and the Cavaliers. The parents of Elvira consent to have her marry the royalist, Cavalier Lord Arthur Talbot, even though she is already betrothed to the Puritan, Sir Richard Forth. Elvira speaks her happiness in the radiant aria, "Son vergin vezzosa." Lord Arthur Talbot comes to Elvira's apartment bearing gifts, including a wedding veil. When he learns that Queen Henrietta, widow of

Charles I, is imprisoned nearby, and threatened with execution, he becomes determined to save her. Throwing the wedding veil over the Queen, he is able to secrete her out of the castle. Elvira is led to suspect that Lord Arthur Talbot has a mistress. Her grief drives her to insanity in one of the opera's most dramatic incidents, Elvira's "Mad Scene" ("Qui la voce soave"). The Puritans vow vengeance.

In the Puritan camp, Talbot is condemned to die for having saved the Queen. Offstage, the still mad Elvira recalls her love for Talbot in "A una fonta afflitto." Fleeing from his enemies, Talbot comes to Elvira to protest his innocence, and his undying devotion. His sincerity helps restore Elvira's sanity. But her mind totters once again on the brink of madness when Talbot is seized by the Puritans, imprisoned and sentenced to death. Then with the defeat of the royalists by the Puritans, all prisoners are pardoned, Talbot included. This turn of events helps to restore permanently Elvira's sanity and happiness.

GIACOMO MEYERBEER 1791–1864

Though it had its antecedents in works like *La Muette de Portici* by Daniel-François-Ésprit Auber (1782–1871), French grand, or melodramatic, opera, appears in full panoply for the first time with Meyerbeer. After the early 1830's, French grand operas are the recognizable offspring of *Robert le diable, Les Huguenots,* and *Le Prophète.* Meyerbeer's way of building up a monumental climax, of introducing large scenes, of featuring many-splendored choruses and ballets, of highlighting processionals and ceremonials—in short, Meyerbeer's weakness for overemphasis and overstatement—became the bone and sinew of the French tradition in grand opera.

While he was alive, Meyerbeer dominated French opera as completely as Rossini had previously done in Italy. Meyerbeer was undoubtedly the most successful composer of operas in France of his time. If he had been willing to influence audiences, instead of being influenced by them, he might also have become one of opera's immortals. He had a true dramatic instinct and gift. His skill for writing for voices was extraordinary. His inspiration, when he did not try or could not control it, soared to summits. Unlike Rossini, he was a most fastidious workman and continually revised his material. Unfortunately, however, all this revision and re-editing and rewriting was not impelled by the artistic necessity to achieve the ultimate truth in art, but merely to arrive at the surest and most efficacious manner of winning the enthusiasm of audiences. It is for this reason that so much in his operas is hollow, artificial, contrived, of mere surface appeal. And it is for the same reason that his operas today do not carry the same kind of excitement they did a century ago.

Few musical historians have balanced the weaknesses and strength of Meyerbeer more accurately than C. Hubert Parry. "Musically," Parry says of Meyerbeer's operas, "[they are] a huge pile of commonplaces, infinitely ingenious and barren. There is but little cohesion to the situations in style and expression. No doubt, Meyerbeer had a great sense of general effect. The music glitters and roars and warbles in well-disposed contrasts, but the inner life is wanting. It is the same with his treatment of characters. They metaphorically strut and pose and gesticulate, but express next to nothing; they get into frenzies, but are for the most part incapable of human passion. The element of wholesome musical sincerity is wanting in him, but the power of astonishing and bewildering is almost unlimited. His cleverness is equal to any emergency. . . . He studied his audience carefully, developed his machinery with infinite pains, carried out his aims, and succeeded in the way he desired."

But Parry does not neglect to point out that Meyerbeer "thoroughly understood the theater and he took infinite pains to carry out every detail which served theatrical effect. He tried and tested his orchestral experiments again and again with tireless patience. . . . He was so painfully anxious that his effects should tell, that his existence at the time when any new work was in preparation of performance is described as perfect martrydom."

In the final analysis, for all his partiality for pomp and circumstance, for all his studied attempts to please his public, Meyerbeer's importance in the history of opera cannot be dismissed. Franz Liszt regarded him as a "new epoch in operatic writing" and Hugo Riemann maintained that "history will point to Meyerbeer's music as one of the most important steps to Wagner's art."

Giacomo Meyerbeer was born Jakob Liebmann Beer, in Berlin, Germany, on September 5, 1791. He changed his name to Meyerbeer after a wealthy relative named Meyer left him a legacy that made him financially independent for life. And he Italianized his first name to Giacomo after he had begun to write operas in the Italian style and to seek the support of Italian operagoers. From boyhood on, he studied music with private teachers including Anselm Weber and Abbé Vogler. An oratorio of his—*Gott und die Natur*—was performed in Berlin in 1811. One year later, his first opera, *Jephthas Geluebde,* was produced in Munich. For a while, he followed a successful career as piano virtuoso. Finally, convinced that his future lay in writing operas, he went to Italy in 1815 to study Italian operatic traditions at first hand. His first important opera in the Italian style was *Romilda e Costanza,* produced in Padua in 1817. He continued writing Italian operas for the next few years, scoring a huge success with *Il Crociato in Egitto* in Venice in 1824. Between 1824 and 1830, he wrote no more operas. This silence is partially explained by his marriage in 1827 to his cousin, Minna Mosson, and the death of two of his children. During this period, Meyerbeer devoted himself to a study of French methods and techniques of opera as developed by Lully and Rameau.

In 1830, Meyerbeer settled in Paris, where he adopted a new approach to opera by combining Italian concepts of lyricism and vocal writing with French declamation and German interest in orchestration and harmony. These elements, combined with his own flair for the theatrical, made his first French grand opera—*Robert le diable*—a sensation when produced in Paris in 1831. With *Les Huguenots* in 1836 and *Le Prophète* in 1849, he assumed leadership in French opera. Meanwhile, in 1842, he was appointed in Berlin general musical director by Emperor Friedrich Wilhelm IV. Meyerbeer's last opera, *L'Africaine,* absorbed his energies for about a quarter of a century. He was still working on detailed revisions when he died in Paris on May 2, 1864, a year before *L'Africaine* received its world première.

1831. ROBERT LE DIABLE, grand opera in five acts, with text by Eugène Scribe and Germain Delavigne. First performance: Paris Opéra, November 21, 1831.

French spectacle opera was fully realized for the first time with *Robert le diable.* This was Meyerbeer's tenth work for the stage (all earlier ones had been in the Italian tradition), but the first in which his own mission in opera became fulfilled. The action takes place in Palermo, in the thirteenth century, where Robert, Duke of Normandy, is the son of a mortal woman and a devil disguised as a man named Bertram. Robert is in love with Isabella, daughter of the king of Sicily. He calls on his foster sister, Alice, to intercede for him with Isabella. When she fails, Robert enlists Bertram's diabolical powers in return for his soul. Bearing a magic cypress branch, Robert is able to invade Isabella's boudoir to abduct her. But her tender pleas soften him in this resolve. With the help of Bertram he effects his escape. Now stricken by pangs of remorse, Robert denounces his devil father, who is claimed by the spirits of the underworld.

"The music," say Wallace Brockway and Herbert Weinstock, "was suited to both the frenziedly romantic libretto . . . and Ciceri's settings. That is, it was grandiose, searchingly characteristic, highfalutin' and grotesque—on the edge of the Gothic." They find that the score "teems with those easy melodies Meyerbeer had learned to write in Venice—graceful, fluent, singable." The most celebrated were two of Alice's arias, "Robert, toi que j'aime" and the romance, "Vanne, disse." The most effective ensemble pages embrace the chorus of the Sicilian knights, "Sorte amica" in the first act, and the chorus of the demons in the third act, "Demoni fatale." The sensation-seeking

Meyerbeer can be discerned in the third act ballet in which nuns rise from the dead to participate in a voluptous ballet.

The Opéra realized a fortune from *Robert le diable,* which became one of the most successful operas of its time; within a quarter of a century, it had earned from it some four million francs. In London, the opera proved less successful—at least until 1847, when Jenny Lind made her debut in that city as Alice. The first performance in the United States was at the Park Theatre in New York, on April 7, 1834, in an English translation. It appeared in the repertory of the Metropolitan Opera on November 19, 1883, only three months after that company had been founded. After three performances that season the opera disappeared permanently from the Metropolitan Opera repertory.

1836. LES HUGUENOTS, grand opera in five acts, with text by Eugène Scribe and Émile Deschamps. First performance: Paris Opéra, February 29, 1836.

A century ago, extravagant and effusive praises were lavished upon *Les Huguenots*. Wagner considered it a peak in operatic literature. Verdi remembered *Les Huguenots* well when some thirty years later he wrote *Aïda,* especially his aria "Le causa e santa." Berlioz said: "The effervescence of the emotions excited by this masterpiece makes one wish to be a great man in order to place one's glory and genius at Meyerbeer's feet."

In more recent years, *Les Huguenots* has aroused denunciation (when it is not completely ignored). Actually, if *Les Huguenots* is not as good as Meyerbeer's contemporaries thought it was, it is neither as poor as some of its severest critics today would have us believe. It remains a stirring spectacle for eye and ear, with many musical pages of grandeur and majesty. Today, as Teodoro Celli noted, "it is [still] an opera that is largely alive, that seizes upon the audience and rouses it to enthusiasm." Its incomparable fourth act remains "one of the century's inspired and dramatic conceptions."

The text is based on the religious fanaticism in France in 1572, when Catholics massacred their rival Huguenots. Throughout the opera Meyerbeer quotes the strain of the famous Lutheran chorale, "Ein' feste Burg," which symbolizes militant Protestantism. The theme is heard first in the short orchestral prelude to the first act (where the composer achieves a striking theatrical effect through rapid changes in dynamics; he also quickens the tempo towards the end of this prelude to make it blend in with the music of the opening scene).

The first scene takes place at the home of Count de Nevers. He has summoned Catholics and Huguenots in an attempt to effect a reconciliation between them. Raoul de Nangis, a Huguenot nobleman, describes how that very morning he had saved a lady from danger, but her identity he has been unable to discover ("Plus blanche que la blanche ermine"). This romance, one of the opera's most beautiful arias, has an unusual accompaniment—an obbligato by the obsolete instrument, the viola d'amore. Marcel, one of Raoul's old servants, an uncompromising Protestant, tries to save his master from perdition. He sings a snatch of Luther's hymn, "Ein' feste Burg," a stark contrast to the gay and romantic melodies previously heard. Then, on invitation from Raoul, Marcel breaks into a more joyous ditty—accompanied by a refrain "piff, paff, piff, paff"—in which is reflected his hatred for the Catholics—"Pour les couvents c'est fini" ("Chanson Huguenote"). Marcel hardly has finished the ditty when a veiled lady arrives, seeking an audience with the Count de Nevers. Raoul immediately recognizes her as the woman he had that day rescued. But he is not aware that she is the Count's betrothed come to beg him to release her from her vows, since she has fallen in love with her rescuer, Raoul. When she departs, a page salutes the noblemen in the stirring "Nobles, seigneurs, salut" and invites Raoul to come to him blindfolded on an unspecified mission.

The music of the first act is mainly for male voices; that of the second act emphasizes the female. Marguerite de Valois, betrothed to Henry IV, is in the castle garden singing of the beauty of the Touraine countryside, "O beau pays de la Touraine." Valentine, daughter of Count de St. Bris—who turns out to be the woman whom Raoul had saved and with whom he is in love—pays Marguerite a visit in order to inform her she is now free to love Raoul, the Count having released her. This pleases Marguerite, for she sees in the union of Raoul and Valentine a way of cementing the schism between Catholics and Huguenots. Now Raoul is brought in blindfolded to be informed that soon he will marry Valentine. But when Raoul catches a glimpse of Valentine, he denounces her viciously, being convinced she is the mistress of Count de Nevers. Valentine's father, Count de St. Bris, arrives with groups of Catholics and Huguenots. Raoul's insult to Valentine charges the atmosphere and threatens a serious conflict between the two religious groups.

The third act is set in the Pré-aux-clercs, the meadow that runs down to the banks of the Seine in Paris. The place is crowded with Huguenot soldiers, singing the praise of their calling in "Rataplan." Valentine is in church. There she overhears a plot hatched by the Catholics to slay Raoul. She pleads with Marcel to warn his master of the danger, but Raoul is too involved in a duel with the Count de St. Bris to take warning. The duel is interrupted by an outbreak of fighting between the Catholics and Huguenots. With the arrival of the Queen, the fighting temporarily ends. Raoul now learns from her how gravely he has misjudged Valentine.

In a room in Count de Nevers' castle, Valentine is grieving over the loss of Raoul ("Parmi les pleurs"). But Raoul, at the risk of his life, has come to her. While in her room, he overhears a plot to massacre the Huguenots. Three monks bless the Catholics on this mission in the "Benediction of the Swords" ("Glaives pieux, saintes epées"). Raoul now emerges from hiding, exchanges tender sentiments with Valetine ("Oh ciel, òu courez-vous") and entreats her to flee with him. The ringing of church bells reminds Raoul of his duty to his fellow Huguenots. Passionately he renounces love and rushes into the street where the massacre has begun.

In the fifth act, Valentine has followed Raoul into the street, during the massacre, to tell him she loves him enough to become a Protestant. With Marcel as their priest, they get married in a nearby church. The Catholics break in, fire at the Huguenots, and kill both Raoul and Valentine.

Les Huguenots was first performed in the United States in New Orleans on April 29, 1839. The first presentation at the Metropolitan Opera took place during its first season, on March 19, 1884.

1849. LE PROPHÈTE (THE PROPHET), grand opera in five acts, with text by Eugène Scribe. First performance: Paris Opéra, April 19, 1849.

Scribe's text was based on a historical episode—the uprising of the Anabaptists in Holland during the sixteenth century. This dramatic incident inspired some of Meyerbeer's most spectacular scenes, and with them some of his most memorable music: the Coronation March; Fides's immortal aria, "Ah, mon fils!"; the eloquent cantique of John of Leyden (with chorus), "Roi du ciel."

In *Les Huguenots* the Luther chorale, "Ein' feste Burg," had served as a recurrent motif; in *Le Prophète* a similar service is performed by the unison chant, "Ad nos, ad salutram," first sung in the opening of the first act by three Anabaptists. They instigate a revolt among peasants which is soon quelled by Count Oberthal and his guards. Bertha—in love with the innkeeper, John of Leyden—begs the Count to permit her to marry the man she loves; since the Count has designs of his own on Bertha, the request is turned down. Instead, he imprisons her, together with John's mother, Fides.

In John's inn, in a suburb of Leyden, the three Anabaptists remark how strongly he resembles a painting of David in the Muenster Cathedral. For this reason they urge him to become the leader of their movement. Though John once dreamed he is the object of veneration from people in front of the cathedral, he turns down the request; his prime aim is to marry Bertha, for whom he expresses his sentiments in the pastorale, "Pour Bertha". Bertha, having escaped from her prison cell, comes to John. She is followed by the Count, who threatens John that if he does not surrender Bertha, John's mother, Fides, would be killed. Faced with such a grim alternative, John prefers to give Bertha up to the Count. Fides, released from prison, comes to John with overflowing gratitude ("Ah, mon fils!"). John now becomes convinced he must become the Anabaptist leader. To insure his success, he has the Anabaptists leave behind the impression that he has been killed.

The revolt under his leadership prospers. The third act takes place in the camp of the Anabaptists outside Muenster, where a skating sequence takes place during a ballet scene. Several prisoners are brought in, one of whom is the Count. The Anabaptists plan to kill him, but John insists on sparing his life, since he wants Bertha, and Bertha alone, to pass sentence on him.

Then the Anabaptist forces, sounding a hymn to victory, launch a major attack on Muenster. There Bertha, once again having escaped from prison, is a refugee. Told that John is dead, Bertha is convinced that the Anabaptists are guilty of the crime and vows to destroy their prophet and leader. At the Muenster Cathedral, John is being crowned. There, Fides recognizes her son and rushes to him. John's followers insist she has been mistaken, that their leader is no human but of divine origin. When John himself joins vigorously in this great lie, Fides cries out in pain that she no longer has a son. Accused of being a fraud, Fides is imprisoned by John's men. John comes to her cell to effect a reconciliation. But when Bertha learns that John and the prophet are one, she is determined to carry out her vow. She plunges a dagger into the prophet's breast, then sets fire to the place, in which Fides meets her doom.

"In *Le Prophète*," says R. A. Streatfeild, "Meyerbeer chose a subject which, if less rich in dramatic possibility than that of *Les Huguenots*, has a far deeper psychological interest. Unfortunately, Scribe, with all his cleverness, was quite the worst man in the world to treat the story of John of Leyden. In the libretto that he constructed for Meyerbeer's benefit, the psychological interest is conspicuous only by its absence, and the character of the young leader of the Anabaptists is degraded to the level of the merest puppet. Meyerbeer's music, fine as much of it is, suffers chiefly from the character of the libretto. The latter is merely a stringing together of conveniently effective scenes, and the music could hardly fail to be disjointed and scrappy. Meyerbeer has little or no feeling for characterizations, so the opportunities for really dramatic effect, which lay in the character of John of Leyden, have been almost entirely neglected."

Following its première in Paris, *Le Prophète* proved so popular that by the end of the nineteenth century it had been given over five hundred times by the Opéra alone. The American première took place in New Orleans on April 2, 1850. The first performance at the Metropolitan Opera took place during that company's first season, on March 21, 1884.

1864. L'AFRICAINE (THE AFRICAN MAID), grand opera in five acts, with text by Eugène Scribe. First performance: Paris Opéra, April 28, 1865.

L'Africaine was Meyerbeer's last opera; and upon it he expended more care, pain, and fastidious self-criticism than on any of his earlier operas. He began writing it as far back as 1838. Over twenty-five years later, just before his death, he was still revising it. In this opera, notes Donald Jay Grout, we can find in evidence "a higher degree of artistic integrity and a more consistent and continuous musical style" than in any other Meyerbeer opera. "Its score remains an example of the composer's mature style, purged of many earlier excesses, rich in melodic beauties, and containing some interesting harmonic refinements; its musical exoticism was not without influence on Verdi when he undertook the composition of *Aïda* five years later."

Its central character is Vasco da Gama, the famed explorer; the time is the fifteenth century; the setting, Lisbon and Madagascar. At the palace of the Portugal king, Inez, daughter of Don Diego, is concerned over the prolonged absence of Vasco da Gama. In "Adieu mon doux rivage" she recalls tenderly how they had parted. The councilors now file into the chamber and acclaim the Grand Inquisitor ("Dieu que le monde révère"). Suddenly Vasco da Gama appears, to inform the councilors of his recent expedition to a strange land ("J'ai vu, noble seigneurs") and to present two slaves whom he has brought back with him—Selika and Nelusko. He asks for a ship so that he might return and claim this land for Portugal. When the councilors refuse, Vasco denounces them and is imprisoned. There he is patiently attended by his slave, Selika, who lulls him to sleep ("Sur mes genoux"). Nelusko, jealous of Selika's concern for Vasco, tries in vain to kill the explorer. He declares his unwavering allegiance to Selika, whom he hails as queen of their realm ("Fille des rois"). Meanwhile, Inez has purchased Vasco's freedom by marrying Don Pedro, president of the council. Pedro convinces the councilors to allow him to set forth on the expedition in place of Vasco.

Don Pedro sets sail with Inez, Selika, and Nelusko, as the sailors sing a rousing chantey, "Debout! matelots!" Nelusko, determined to frustrate Pedro, heads the ship towards a reef, As he does so he sings about a monarch of the sea who sends ships to their doom ("Adamastor, roi des vagues"). Another ship comes to view: Vasco has come to warn Pedro of the danger facing him. But Pedro, suspicious, binds Vasco to a mast. Vasco is saved by the faithful Selika. The ship then is wrecked, and most of its survivors are killed by Selika's tribesmen.

Selika takes Vasco back with her to the island of Madagascar, of which she is queen. The fourth act opens with an atmospheric prelude, a *Marche indienne* (*Indian March*). After the rise of the curtain, Vasco is inspired by the beauty of the place to sing a rhapsody, "O Paradiso" (the opera's most celebrated aria). The tribesmen are determined to kill Vasco, but once again Selika manages to save him—this time by maintaining she has secretly been married to him. In gratitude, Vasco tells Selika how much he loves her ("O transport, o douce extase"). But when Vasco hears the voice of Inez from afar, he knows it is Inez he really loves. Magnanimously, Selika puts Vasco and Inez aboard ship for their voyage home. Selika then confides to the sea the extent of her misery in "D'ici je vois la mer immense" before poisoning herself with the sap of a deadly manchineel tree. Nelusko, faithful to the end, joins her in death. An invisible chorus points up the moral that all are equal in the face of death in "C'est ici le séjour."

The American première of *L'Africaine* took place at the Academy of Music in New York on December 1, 1865. The first performance at the Metropolitan Opera was given on December 7, 1888. Enrico Caruso, who was partial to the role of Vasco, appeared for the first time at the Metropolitan Opera in *L'Africaine* on January 11, 1907.

CARL MARIA VON WEBER 1786–1826

One day after the première of *Der Freischuetz*, the German Romantic, E. T. A. Hoffmann, placed a wreath on Weber's brow. It was a symbolic gesture proclaiming him spokesman for the new Romantic movement then sweeping over all of Europe. In Weber, the young German Romantics had found a standard-bearer for their ideal to free the imagination; to allow it to roam freely in the worlds of dreams, fantasies, superstitions, and supernatural mysteries; to evoke the past; to affirm the German spirit.

Romantic opera—as Alfred Einstein has explained—provided "a world of marvels [through] legend and superstition. . . filling the air and exerting horrifying or beneficent influences upon human destinies. All Nature's secret forces took on an individual life and were more or less personified." Measured in terms like these, Carl Maria von Weber may very well be singled out as opera's first important Romantic, and his opera, *Der Freischuetz*, as the beginnings of German national opera. Here, as elsewhere, Weber used texts rich with German backgrounds, experiences, and landscapes. His music echoed with the vibrations of the Volkslied (German folk song).

Far and beyond his contribution in creating German Romantic opera is Weber's influence in transforming opera into musical drama. He suggested strongly the Leitmotif technique. He enriched musical characterizations. He used orchestra with extraordinary effect, both for describing natural phenomena and other stage action and for atmosphere and symbolism. He carried to the writing of male choruses a new depth. He transformed the formal opera overture into a tone poem. He even dreamed of achieving within opera a unity of the arts—"an art work," as he explained, "complete in itself, in which all the parts and details of the related and involved arts, mingling together, disappear, and, in a sense, submerging themselves, create a new world." Understanding both the nature and the extent of Weber's conceptions and innovations, we begin to appreciate how cataclysmic was his influence on Wagner. "What modern music owes to him," remarks R. A. Streatfeild, "may be summed up in a word. Without Weber, Wagner would have been impossible."

Weber's prodigious achievements in opera have tended to obscure his importance in other areas of Romantic music. He was a pioneer in the writing of large concert works with detailed programs: His *Konzertstueck,* for piano and orchestra, preceded Berlioz's *Symphonie fantastique* by seven years. He was one of the first composers of shorter pieces for the piano—setting the stage for Schubert, Schumann and Chopin. He preceded Johann Strauss II in producing concert waltzes within ambitious structures. And he was one of the earliest composers to free himself from the binary structure, to which the classicists had been so faithful, thereby providing his musical ideas with a larger canvas.

Carl Maria won Weber was born in Eutin, Germany, on November 18, 1786. As the son of the musical director of a traveling theatrical group, Weber was forced to travel about a good deal during his childhood, even though he was sickly, the victim of a chronic limp. But his music study was not neglected. His first teacher was his stepbrother. After that he received his musical training with Michael Haydn in Salzburg, J. N. Kalcher in Munich, and Abbé Vogler in Vienna. His first opus—a set of six fughettas for the piano—appeared when he was twelve. At thirteen, he wrote an opera; and soon after his fourteenth birthday, another opera, *Das Waldmaedchen,* was produced in Freiberg. Success came between 1810 and 1811, with performances of two more operas—*Silvana* in Frankfort-on-the-Main and *Abu Hassan* in Munich.

In 1813, Weber was appointed musical director of the German Opera in Prague. Four years after that, he was made musical director for life of the Dresden Opera, which, under his guidance, became one of the foremost musical theaters in Europe. In that same year of 1817, he married Caroline Brandt, a singer.

Weber's work with German-language operas in Dresden stimulated him into writing a German national opera. It was *Der Freischuetz,* a triumph when produced in Berlin 1821. Weber completed only two more operas after that, *Euryanthe* in 1823, and *Oberon* in 1826. The work of preparing the last-named opera for the stage and conducting its première proved too taxing for his delicate health. Weber died in London on June 5, 1826.

1818. JUBEL OUVERTUERE (JUBEL OVERTURE), for orchestra, op. 59.

This stirring music was written for the fiftieth anniversary of the rule of Friedrich August of Saxony; and it was performed as part of the festivities attending the anniversary of his ascension on September 20, 1818. A solemn Adagio precedes the main body of the overture, in which a theme is vigorously presented by the full orchestra. A transition leads to a lighter idea for woodwind and horns; this receives attention in the development. After the first theme is repeated, the music sweeps to a climax at whose peak the English anthem, "God Save the King," is proclaimed by the wind, accompanied by strings.

1819. AUFFORDERUNG ZUM TANZ (INVITATION TO THE DANCE), rondo brilliant in D-flat major, for piano, op. 65. (Transcribed for orchestra by Hector Berlioz).

By writing this rondo brilliant, Weber became the first composer to write a waltz-sequence: an integrated composition comprising several waltz tunes preceded by an introduction, and concluded by a coda or epilogue. The waltz-sequence subsequently became a structure favored by Johann Strauss II, who carried it to its most sophisticated development.

It is as an orchestral work that this music is best known—in transcriptions by Berlioz and by Felix Weingartner. The Berlioz version, the one most often heard today, was done in 1841 for a Paris production of Weber's *Der Freischuetz*, where it was used as ballet music.

In the introduction, a suave melody shared by cello and woodwind suggests a young man's invitation to a lady to the dance. and her acceptance. We now get a series of lilting waltzes, as the couple spin along merrily. The epilogue repeats the dialogue of the introduction: the gentleman is thanking the lady for having danced with him.

1821. DER FREISCHUETZ (THE FREE SHOOTER), romantic opera in three acts, with text by Friedrich Kind, based on a tale in the *Gespensterbuch* edited by Apel and Laun. First performance: Berlin, June 18, 1821.

Though German national opera begins with *Der Freischuetz*—and though it proceeds toward Wagner—its antecedent was the old German Singspiel. Spoken dialogue both in Der *Freischuetz* and in the old Singspiel separates the set formal musical numbers. In both, the popular element is strongly accented. As William Foster Apthorp noted: "He brought . . . the popular element into serious opera, and the form itself closer to the hearts of the German people. . . . In Weber's melody, no matter how broad in style or elaborately ornamented, you get all the romantic, out-of-door freshness of the Swabian folk song, and the peculiarly Teutonic sentimentality in its best expression; one might almost say he wrote in dialect." Among the episodes deeply rooted in popular or folk styles and idioms are the choruses of the hunters and the bridesmaids; the first-act waltzes; the drinking songs; an aria like the one Max sings early in the first act, "Durch die Waelder."

But if the pronounced popular and folk elements relate *Der Freischuetz* to the Singspiel, other characteristics identify it with the later Wagnerian music drama. "He effected," says Apthorp, "a sort of interweaving of the scena with the aria that did much to relax the strictness of conventional form and rendered the form more scenically plastic. The so-called incantation [or Wolf Glen] scene . . . even reaches out toward the Wagnerian music drama. . . . In this scene Weber shows all his romantic deviltry; probably no other composer in the whole list supped with the Devil with so short a spoon. Upon the whole, the supernatural was an element very congenial to him; few composers have treated it so to the manner born, with so little of the melodramatic as he."

The famous overture, a concert hall fixture, utilizes some of the opera's thematic material. But unlike most opera overtures of the time, this is no mere potpourri. This is an integrated, skilfully constructed symphonic poem offering a summation of the opera's high points. In the eight introductory measures, a slow and stately melody is given by four horns, first accompanied quietly by the strings, then by an ominous tremolo, which recurs in the opera to identify the demon, Samiel. The main body of the overture arrives with a loud, disturbed subject in full orchestra; this is material lifted from the Wolf Glen scene. The second principal theme is heard soon afterwards. The first part of this melody is given by clarinet over tremolo strings; this is taken from Max's second-act recitative. The other part of the melody is assigned to violins and clarinet over a syncopated accompaniment—part of Agathe's celebrated scena, "Leise, Leise." This second theme is carried to a climax, after which both subjects are developed dramatically. After the recapitulation, the coda concerns itself with material from the finale of the opera.

The action takes place in Bohemia soon after the Thirty Years' War. The curtain rises on the court of an inn near a forest. A shooting match is taking place. Max, a young forester, is defeated by the peasant Kilian. This disturbs him no end, for if he cannot win the match on the morrow, he will also lose Agathe, daughter of Prince Ottokar. Max expresses his fears and anxieties in the bucolic air, "Durch die Waelder." Caspar, another forester—he has sold his soul to the demon Samiel—offers Max a solution. He can provide Max with magic bullets that never miss aim. He even arranges to meet Max in the Wolf's Glen in the nearby forest, the haunt of Samiel, where these bullets can be cast.

In the second act, Agathe looks out of her boudoir window, contemplating the beauty of the night in "Leise, Leise," the most popular aria from the opera. Max comes to visit her, and to inform her he must be off to the Wolf's Glen. His pretext for going is that he has shot a stag there and must bring it back. Since Agathe knows the place is haunted, she begs him not to go. The scene now shifts to this mysterious, forbidding place. It is crowded with apparitions; the air reverberates with incantations. As the fearful specters surround them, Caspar and Max cast seven magic bullets, six to hit their mark, and the seventh to be directed by Samiel.

And now it is Agathe's wedding day. Dressed in her bridal clothes, she entreats heaven's protection in "Und ob die Wolke sie verhuellt." She is filled with terror. Her dread mounts when her bridal flowers turn out to be a funeral wreath. Her friend Aennchen tries to comfort her. Then the bridesmaids appear with their chant, "Wir winden dir den Jungfernkranz."

At the shooting range, the huntsmen raise their voices in praise of their profession: "Was gleicht wohl auf Erden." The contest now begins. Max has used up his six magic bullets during a hunt that very morning. He must rely on the seventh one. The target is a passing dove, which begs him not to shoot since the dove is Agathe transfigured. But it is too late; the trigger has been pulled. The bullet, however, is deflected and kills Caspar. Max now comes forth with the confession on how he had made a deal with Samiel through Caspar. The Prince forgives him, but also abolishes all future shooting matches. Max expresses his gratitude in "Die Zukunft soll mein Herz bewahren." All the others now sing a hymn of thanksgiving, "Ja! lasst uns zum Himmel die Blicke erheben."

Though some musicians who attended the première of *Der Freischuetz* were critical of it—and especially of the Wolf Glen scene—the work was a success of the first magnitude. "The curtain fell," recalled Weber's son, "but not a soul left the house. Thunders of applause and thousands of voices summoned the composer before the enraptured audience. At last he appeared . . . . Amid the deafening shouting, flowers and verses were flung from all directions. The success of *Der Freischuetz* had been immense, unparalleled."

From Berlin, *Der Freischuetz* went on to conquer the rest of Europe. It was heard in Vienna on February 10, 1822. In London, where it was heard in an English translation in 1824, it proved so popular that it had to be given simultaneously in three different theaters. On March 2, 1825, the American première took place in New York, once again in an English translation.

"The heart of *Der Freischuetz*," Hans Pfitzner wrote, "is the indescribably inward and sensitive feeling for Nature that suffuses it. The chief character of the opera, one might say, is the German forest in its multifarious aspects. . . . Compared with the manifestations of Nature herself, the characters of the piece are hardly more than decorative figures in a landscape."

1821. KONZERTSTUECK (CONCERT PIECE) IN F MINOR AND MAJOR, for piano and orchestra, op. 79. I. Larghetto affettuoso. II. Allegro passionato. III. Tempo di marcia. IV. Presto giocoso.

The final strokes of the pen were put on the manuscript of the *Konzertstueck* on the day *Der Freischuetz* received its world première in Berlin. Weber had actually planned this large work for piano and orchestra some six years earlier, but had abandoned it. But in Berlin he decided to give a concert in the way of bidding his public farewell; for this performance he wanted to present a new piece of music. This concert took place on June 25, 1821, and proved so successful that Weber had to repeat it four days later.

In this *Concert Piece* we have an early example of the programmatic concerto. The four movements are played without interruption, representing a single and unified design. In the first movement, "the lady sits all alone on her balcony gazing far into the distance. Her knight has gone to the Holy Land. Years have passed by. Battles have been fought. Is he still alive? Will she ever see him again?" The most significant musical subject in this section is a poetic refrain for the woodwind with which the composition opens.

In the second movement, a romantic episode, "her excited imagination calls up a vision of her husband lying wounded and forsaken on the battlefield. Can she not fly to him and die by his side? She falls unconscious."

A slow transition, in which the bassoon is prominent, leads to vigorous march music—the third movement. "But, hark! What notes are those in the distance? Over there in the forest something flashes in the sunlight nearer and nearer. Knights and squires with the cross of Crusaders, banners waving, acclamations of the people. And there it is—he!"

The *Concert Piece* ends jubilantly. "She sinks into his arms. Love is triumphant. Happiness without end. The very woods and waves sing the song of love; a thousand voices proclaim his victory."

1823. EURYANTHE, romantic opera in three acts, with text by Wilhelmine von Chézy. First performance: Kaernthnerthor Theater, Vienna, October 25, 1823.

Not long after *Der Freischuetz* made Weber the most celebrated opera composer in Germany, he received a commission from Domenico Barbaja, the distinguished impresario, to write a new opera for one of his theaters in Vienna. Recalling with no little hurt that some critics had depreciated the significance of *Der Freischuetz* because it had spoken dialogue in place of recitatives, Weber now planned an opera entirely set to music, meeting the most exacting demands of his critics. Wilhelmine von Chézy prepared the libretto, drawing her material from a thirteenth-century tale by Gilbert de Montreuil. But her text was such a compound of nonsense and confusion that not even Weber's genius could endow it with significance as a stage work.

The main action, set in the twelfth century, revolves around the efforts of Euryanthe of Savoy to prove her fidelity to her husband. Adolar, Count of Nevers. Eglantine, also in love with Adolar, tries to bring about her rival's destruction by proving to Adolar that Euryanthe has been unfaithful. She convinces him to the point where at first he wants to kill Euryanthe, but then permits her to remain alive in a thick forest. In time, Adolar begins to suspect that Euryanthe has been victimized by Eglantine's treachery. When the rumor that Euryanthe is dead proves false, the lovers are reunited. Eglantine meets her due at the hands of Count Lysiar, whom she is about to marry, and who stabs her fatally when he discovers that all this time she has been in love with Adolar.

When first heard—Henrietta Sontag, aged seventeen, appeared in the title role to begin her remarkable career—*Euryanthe* was a total failure. In America, its première is believed to have taken place at the Wallack Theater in New York in 1863. The Metropolitan Opera mounted it on December 23, 1887. Whether in Europe or America, *Euryanthe* is rarely given today.

But its magnificent overture (written in three days) is a durable symphonic masterwork. A brilliant, fiery opening leads into the sonorous first theme—a subject for the winds derived from a first-act aria of Adolar. A stormy development rises to a piercing B-flat chord for full orchestra. A transition by the violins leads into the lyrical second theme, given by the first violins over string harmonies; this material also comes from an aria by Adolar, this time in the second act. The brilliant opening is temporarily recalled to break the spell. After a new climax, a sudden silence ensues. Now comes an eloquent

Largo for muted strings in which we get anticipations of Wagner's *Lohengrin* Prelude. A fugal episode, and a restatement of the two main themes bring the overture to its conclusion.

Perhaps the most memorable vocal episode in the opera is Adolar's hymn to the beauty and virtue of Euryanthe, "Unter bluehenden Mandelbaeumen."

1826. OBERON, opera in three acts, with text by James Robinson Planché, based on the French romance, *Huon de Bordeaux*. First performance: Covent Garden, London, April 12, 1826.

The success of *Der Freischuetz* in London brought Weber a commission for a new opera for Covent Garden. James Robinson Planché provided the English text for a spectacular fairy opera in twenty-one scenes calling for an immense cast and lavish sets. Weber, already suffering from consumption which would soon take his life, came to England to supervise the rehearsals and conduct the première performance. This grueling grind proved fatal. Less than a month after the triumphant première, Weber died in his sleep in London.

In its best pages, the opera reaches the summit. It is at its best in the overture; in Rezia's magnificent scena, "Ocean, Thou Mighty Monster"; and in Huon's romantic song, "From Boyhood Trained." But as a whole, the opera lacks sustained interest and suffers from a deplorable libretto. For these reasons, it is rarely produced. It was given in the United States for the first time at the Park Theater in New York on October 9, 1828, and at the Metropolitan Opera (in an English translation) on December 28, 1918.

The overture is a magical excursion into the kingdom of fairies and elves, continually touched with the mystery and wonder of the woodlands. The horn call of Oberon, to which muted strings offer a reply, evokes at once the fanciful Romantic world of romance and dreams. Flashing figures in flute and clarinet, which in the first scene of the first act accompany the Chorus of Elves, contribute to the eeriness of the setting. After a brief solo for the cello, the introductory section ends with a dramatic fortissimo chord in full orchestra. The main part of the overture now presents its main subject—the agitated material that is heard accompanying the finale of the second-act quartet, "Over the Dark Blue Waters." The opening horn call is now again heard, this time as the preface to a haunting song for solo clarinet derived from Huon's first-act aria; the melody is soon taken over by the strings. This is followed by a reminder in the violins of Rezia's wonderful aria, "Ocean, Thou Mighty Monster." After the two principal themes are elaborated, a new thought—a bit of march music—is suddenly introduced. The overture ends with an exultant statement of the Rezia melody.

The first act takes place in Oberon's bower. Having quarelled with Titania, Oberon vows never again to be reconciled with the fairy queen until he has found a pair of lovers whose constancy can be proved beyond all doubt. With the help of Puck, a pair of lovers is found for the test. He is Sir Huon of

Bordeaux, a member of Charlemagne's court; she, Rezia, daughter of Haroun el Rashid of Bagdad. Each sees the other in a vision. Huon proceeds on a journey to Bagdad to find Rezia, equipped with a magic horn able to summon elves and fairies for support. But Rezia is compelled by her father to marry Babekan. When, on the day of her wedding, Huon arrives, Rezia rushes into his arms. Babekan attacks Huon and is killed in the brawl. Sounding his horn, Huon calls for assistance from Oberon, who carries the pair off by ship to Greece. Puck and his fellow spirits induce a mighty storm, which sends the ship reeling to a desert island. Pirates capture Rezia and sell her to the Emir of Tunis. Huon follows her there, is discovered by the Emir, and is ordered to die in a pyre. Once again Huon sounds his magic horn. Oberon now announces that the trials of Huon and Rezia are at an end. They have proved their love and constancy. He bears them back in trumph to the court of Charlemagne.

ADOLPHE ADAM 1803–1856

With serious opera in France a monopoly then controlled by the Académie de Musique (or L'Opéra), a new form had to be evolved by competing theaters. That new form was opéra-comique, lighter in style, simpler in structure and more direct in its appeal than were the productions at the Académie; spoken dialogue replaced recitatives. This new musico-dramatic species was seen for the first time in 1715 at the Foire St. Germain. At that time, opéra-comique used comic or satirical texts exclusively, but it was not long before more serious subjects were tapped, though still used in a tuneful and palatable form.

The father of opéra-comique was François Boieldieu (1775–1834), If there is any single work with which opéra-comique can be said to have emerged with its recognizable identity it is Boieldieu's *Le Calife de Bagdad,* produced in Paris on September 16, 1800. Boieldieu's *Chef d'oeuvre,* and his greatest success, followed fifteen years later with *La Dame Blanche,* introduced in Paris on December 10, 1825.

Adolphe Adam continued where Boieldieu had left off. Adam had studied the piano with Boieldieu at the Paris Conservatory, an association which directed him towards the opéra-comique. As his transition from pupil to professional musician, Adam wrote an overture for Boieldieu's *La Dame Blanche* using some of the basic melodies from that work. Adam's first opéra-comique, *Pierre et Catherine* in 1829, put into practice the lessons he had learned from his teacher, lessons which he would henceforth put to good use in the creation of such later opéra-comiques as *Danilowa* in 1830, *Le Chalet* in 1834, and his masterwork, *Le Postillon de Longjumeau* in 1836. From Boieldieu he learned how to apply a light touch to the writing of melodies; how to build up a comic effect; how to write for combinations of voices. But however much Adam may have been influenced by his teacher, he was no carbon copy of Boieldieu. Arthur Pougin, Adam's biographer, has pointed out how Adam brought to the opéra-comique "a truly personal style, touched at the same time with grace and coquetry, with sentiment of emotion and gaiety and comic verve." And Sterling MacKinlay found in Adam's best works "flowing melodiousness, rhythmical piquancy of style, precision of declamatory phrasing, and charming effects of graceful, though sketchy, instrumentation."

Despite his significance in the field of opéra-comique, we remember Adam today primarily for his remarkable score to one of the most celebrated ballets in the repertory—*Giselle*.

Adolphe-Charles Adam was born in Paris on July 24, 1803. In 1817 he entered the Paris Conservatory where he studied the organ with Benoist and piano with Boieldieu. His interest in opéra-comique aroused through his personal associations with Boieldieu, Adam completed his first work in that genre in 1828. It was *Pierre et Catherine,* a one-act operetta produced at the Opéra-Comique in Paris on February 9, 1829. His third operetta, *Le Chalet*—seen at the Opéra-Comique on September 25, 1834—was a triumph whose popularity proved endurable: Before the century ended it had been given almost fifteen hundred performances in Paris alone. His fame thus solidified, Adam went on to produce two masterworks, the opéra-comique *Le Postillon de Longjumeau* in 1836, and the ballet *Giselle,* in 1841. In 1844 he became a member of the Institut, and in 1849 he was appointed professor of composition at the Paris Conservatory. He died in Paris on May 3, 1856.

1836. LE POSTILLON DE LONGJUMEAU (THE POSTILLION OF LONGJUMEAU), opéra-comique in three acts with text by Adolphe de Leuven and Léon L. Brunswick. First performance: Opéra-Comique, Paris, October 13, 1836.

The hero of this opéra-comique is the postillion Chappelou, employed by Madame de Latour at her estate in Longjumeau in the middle of the eighteenth century. While repairing a wheel on the carriage of Marquis de Corcy, Chappelou bursts into song. Impressed by the beauty of his voice, the Marquis offers to promote Chappelou's career in music. The postillion accepts this offer eagerly, even though it means he must leave his recently married wife, Madeleine. Under the assumed name of St. Phar, Chappelou eventually achieves renown in music; and as St. Phar he meets the wealthy Madame de La Tour, who is actually Madeleine under a different name. Without realizing that she is his deserted wife, Chappelou falls in love with her. The discovery that Madame de La Tour and Madeleine are one and the same person —and the readiness of his wife to forget and forgive—brings everlasting joy to the now-famous singer, just as it brings distress to the Marquis who is himself in love with Madeleine.

There is one vocal excerpt in this score that stands out prominently and which has never lost its popularity. It is Chappelou's first-act postillion song, "Mes amis, écoutez l'histoire." More lyrical and expressive is Chappelou's second-act romance, "Assis au pied d'un hêtre" and Madeleine's beautiful second-act song, "Je vais donc le revoir."

The American première of this opéra-comique took place at the Park Theater in New York on March 30, 1840. In the United States, Theodore Wachtel became celebrated for his interpretation of the role of Chappelou, in which he appeared over a thousand times. He was particularly famous for his rendition of the postillion song to which he would provide an exciting rhythmic accompaniment by cracking a whip.

1841. GISELLE, fantastic ballet in two acts, with book by Vernoy de Saint-Georges, Théophile Gautier and Jean Coralli. First performance: Paris Opéra, June 28, 1841.

Giselle is a masterwork in Romantic ballet, a vehicle that has attracted the foremost ballerinas of past and present from Carlotta Grisi, who created the role, through Pavlova, Karsavina, Markova and Danilova, to Margot Fonteyn, Galina Ulanova, and Moira Shearer. Its story, which George Balanchine described as "ideal for ballet," originated with Heine's *De L'Allemagne*. This tale describes how elves in white, or "wilis," died the day before their wedding; how they left their graves in bridal dress to dance from midnight to dawn; how any man confronting such an elf was doomed to dance himself to death. Théophile Gautier and Vernoy de Saint-Georges adapted this story for Carlotta Grisi, the famous dancer; Jean Coralli planned the choreography. In the ballet scenario, Giselle becomes a peasant girl who, betrayed by Albrecht, Duke of Silesia, commits suicide. The Queen of the Wilis touches her grave with a magic branch which transforms the corpse into a wili. Albrecht comes upon her when he visits Giselle's grave. Thus he is compelled to dance until he dies.

The scenic designer, Alexander Benois, has explained why this ballet has such a permanent appeal to lovers of the dance. "It is mainly due to its simplicity and clearness of plot, to the amazingly impetuous spontaneity with which the drama is developed. There is barely time to collect one's thoughts before the heroine, who but a moment ago charmed everybody with her vitality, is lying stiff and cold and dead at the feet of the lover who deceived her. . . . It is deeply moving, and the magic of a true poet . . . consists in making us accept without question any absurdities he may choose to offer us. . . . No one is inclined to criticize while under the spell of this strange idyl."

But a good measure of the success of *Giselle* comes from Adam's remarkable score. Théophile Gautier wrote to Heine one week after the première of the ballet: "Adam's music is superior to the usual run of ballet music, it abounds in tunes and orchestral effects; it even includes a touching attention for lovers of difficult music, a very well produced fugue. The second act solves the musical problem of graceful fantasy and is full of melody."

In his book *Lighter Classics of Music* this writer has said: "A master of expressive and dramatized melodies, Adam here created a score filled with the most ingratiating tunes and spirited rhythms, all beautifully adjusted to the sensitive moods of this delicate fantasy."

The twentieth-century English composer, Constant Lambert, used four appealing excerpts from this score for a suite that has often been performed and recorded: Giselle's Dance; the Mad Scene; the second-act Pas de Deux; and the Closing Scene.

Giselle was seen for the first time in the United States at the Howard Atheneum in Boston on January 1, 1846. At that time the title role was danced by Mary Ann Lee, who is described by Lillian Moore as "the first American dancer to attain nationwide fame as an exponent of the classic ballet."

1852. OVERTURE TO SI J'ÉTAIS ROI.

Si j'étais roi is an opéra-comique which was first produced at the Théâtre Lyrique in Paris on September 4, 1852. Its setting is an old Arabian village where Zephoris, a humble fisherman, rescues Nemea, cousin of King Oman, from drowning. Neither Zephoris nor Nemea know each other's identity; nevertheless they are in love with one another. When he finally discovers she is of royal blood, Zephoris despairs of winning her. But Nemea manages to overcome all obstacles to gain King Oman's consent to her marriage. Zephoris, now made a commander of the king's troops, emerges a hero in battle.

The popular overture is particularly appealing for its oriental melodies and colors. A dignified introduction for full orchestra is followed by a sprightly little exotic tune for first violins accompanied by pizzicati cellos. A secondary thought is then presented by flutes and clarinets. This basic material is built up to a climax, which then serves as a preface to a robust song for the violins. A change of mood comes with a delicate subject for solo flute and oboes. All these ideas are then worked out with considerable power and dramatic interest.

DANIEL FRANÇOIS AUBER 1782–1871

Daniel François Auber is the third member of a triumvirate that ruled over opéra-comique in the early nineteenth century, the other two being François Boieldieu and Adolphe Adam. In Auber, as in Adam, wit, grace and charm are ominpresent. But Auber also manages to sound richer and deeper strains than did either Boieldieu or Adam. Auber's *La Muette de Portici* is so forceful in its invention, so original in procedures, so ambitious in structural dimensions, and so dramatic in concept that the line which separates it from serious opera is indeed nebulous. As a matter of fact, some historians regard *La Muette de Portici* as a significant precursor of French grand opera. Auber's *Fra Diavolo* and *Le Domino noir* are, to be sure, of smaller dimension and lighter of texture. But here, too, the creative impulse is powerful. When someone once remarked to Rossini that Auber's lighter opera is "petty music," the Italian master countered with: "Petty music, perhaps, but the petty music of a *great* musician." Richard Wagner went even further in singing Auber's praises. "His music is at once elegant and popular, fluent and precise, graceful and bold, bending with marvelous facility to every turn of his caprice. . . . He mastered vocal music with a keen vivacity, multiplied its rhythms to infinity, and gave the ensemble pieces an *entrain,* a characteristic briskness scarcely known before his time."

Daniel François Auber was born in Caen, Normandy, on January 29, 1782. He began to study music systematically only after he had completed his first comic opera *L'Erreur d'un Moment* in 1806. That study took place for a number of years with Cherubini. Successive failures with his operas brought on a period of such discouragement that for six years he stopped writing for the stage. But in 1820 he scored a brilliant success with *La Bergère Châtelaine,* and in 1821 he realized a triumph with *Emma.*

A meeting in 1823 with Eugène Scribe, eminent poet and dramatist, opened for Auber new horizons. The two men decided to form an artistic partnership during which, through the years, Scribe provided Auber with librettos for thirty-seven operas. Their first major collaboration took place with *La Muette de Portici* in 1828. This was followed by *Fra Diavolo* in 1830, *Le Domino Noir* in 1837, and *Les Diamants de la Couronne* in 1841.

A succession of honors, beginning with an appointment to the French Academy in 1829, pointed to Auber's high place in French music. From 1842 until the end of his life he was the director of the Paris Conservatory. In 1857 he was made Maître de Chapelle by Napoleon III. Auber continued writing operas until the end of his life, the last one (*Rêve d'amour*) completed when he was eighty-seven. Auber died in Paris on May 12, 1871.

1828. LA MUETTE DE PORTICI, or MASANIELLO (THE MUTE FROM PORTICI), opéra-comique in five acts with text by Eugène Scribe and Germain Delavigne. First performance: Paris Opéra, February 29, 1828.

La Muette de Portici is more a serious romantic opera than an opéra-comique; this is true of both the text and the music. The music is consistently unconventional and original, beginning with the unorthodox diminished seventh chord that opens the overture. Wagner stood in admiration at Auber's "bold effects in instrumentation, particularly in the treatment of strings; the drastic groupings of the choral masses which here take on an important role in the action; the original harmonies; and the happy strokes of dramatic characterization."

The text is based on the historic revolt in Naples in 1647 against Spanish despotism. Fenella, a mute, has been seduced and imprisoned by Alfonso, son of the Spanish Viceroy in Naples. After she manages to escape, her brother, Masaniello, became the leader in a revolt against despotic Spanish rule. Masaniello becomes the fatal victim in the battle that follows. Distraught, Fenella goes to her death by jumping into the sea.

The story of this revolt had an overpowering impact on early nineteenth-century audiences. It helped make combustible the revolutionary fires that ignited Paris in July of 1830. In Brussels—immediately after the opera had received its première there on August 25, 1830—it instigated so many riots among Belgian patriots that the Dutch were forced to withdraw from Belgium.

The American première took place (in the French language) in New York on August 15, 1831. An English-speaking production followed at the Park Theatre in New York on November 28 of the same year.

The unusual discord that opens the overture precedes a section of storm and stress in full orchestra. The storm subsides to allow a haunting melody to unfold in clarinets and bassoons in octaves. The principal section of the overture now introduces a main theme, divided between strings and woodwind. A secondary subject is assigned to the woodwind and violins. This material is then dramatized, the turbulence continuing in the concluding coda in which the percussion instruments play a prominent role.

The most important vocal numbers are in an operatic mold. The most celebrated include Masaniello's cavatina, "Du pauvre seul ami fidèle"; and the duet of Masaniello and Fenella known as the "Slumber Song" ("Air du Sommeil"). Both are heard in the fourth act.

1830. FRA DIAVOLO, or L'HÔTELLERIE DE TERRACINE (FRA DIAVOLO, or THE INN OF TERRACINE), opéra-comique in three acts with text by Eugène Scribe. First performance: Opéra-Comique, Paris, January 28, 1830.

Fra Diavolo is its composer's most celebrated and most successful opéra-comique. By World War I, it had received over a thousand performances in Paris alone. It has been frequently revived in the United States, where it was seen for the first time on October 17, 1831, in New York. Hollywood made it into a motion-picture farce starring Laurel and Hardy.

The brisk overture opens with a drum roll. This is the preface for a robust march melody. This march tune is taken over by various sections of the orchestra before being built up into a dramatic climax. We then hear a series of lilting melodies (all of them taken from the first act) which are elaborated upon.

Fra Diavolo is an Italian bandit chief who has terrorized the countryside; a lucrative reward is promised to his captors. Fra Diavolo comes to Matteo's tavern in a Terracine village, disguised as the Marquis of San Marco. An aroused English lord soon learns that he has been robbed, and that his wife is being pursued by the newly arrived "Marquis." Fra Diavolo and his two henchmen are later compelled to go into hiding in the bedroom of the innkeeper's daughter, Zerlina. Unaware that there is anybody in her room, Zerlina gives voice to her joy in being loved by Lorenzo, an officer. Her rhapsodic song, "Quel bonheur" is the most celebrated aria in the opera. After she has fallen asleep, Fra Diavolo sneaks out of her room to invade the chambers of the English lord, whom he has come to rob further. But a commotion ensues in which the entire household is awakened. To avoid suspicion, Fra Diavolo as the Marquis, explains he has just come from Zerlina's room where he has enjoyed a rendezvous. This piece of news arouses Lorenzo who challenges the "Marquis" to a duel. Fra Diavolo effects his escape and finds refuge with his men in a nearby forest. There he is apprehended by Lorenzo and his men and is killed.

Besides the overture and Zerlina's ecstatic aria, the most memorable pages in this score include Zerlina's second-act song, "Voyez sur cette roche"; Diavolo's barcarolle, "Agnès la jouvencelle"; and Lorenzo's romance, "Pour toujours disait-elle."

NICCOLÒ PAGANINI 1782–1840

The first modern violin virtuoso appears with Paganini. Of diabolical appearance, with long bony fingers and a cadaverous face, Paganini inspired wonder, adulation, and fear. His incredible virtuosity tempted some to believe he was in league with infernal powers. People crossed themselves if they passed him. Others maintained he was Cagliastro. Poems and plays were inspired by him. Food and delicacies were named after him. Women fawned over him. Most important, even the most discriminating musicians exhausted superlatives in describing his performances. Meyerbeer said: "Where our power of thought end, there Paganini's begins." Schumann—whose early piano pieces reflect Paganini's influence—maintained: "Paganini is the turning point in the history of virtuosity." Liszt exclaimed: "What a violinist, what an artist!" Rossini confessed he had cried only three times in his life, the third time when he heard Paganini play.

The same technical fireworks that electrified and dazzled all those coming into contact with Paganini's playing, abound in the music he created for his instrument. It unfolds new worlds of sound and technical means for the violin. Breathtaking pyrotechnics are found in such shorter pieces as the celebrated *La Streghe* (*Witches' Dance*), or *Moto perpetuo* (*Perpetual Motion*) or the variations he produced for melodies like Rossini's "Di tanti palpiti" and "God Save the King." But elswhere—and most obviously in his Twenty-Four Caprices—Paganini's music is remarkable, not only as technical exercises, but for the soundest musical values and the richest and most varied kind of invention. "His melodies are broad Italian melodies," said Berlioz, "but full of passionate ardor found in the best pages of dramatic composers of his country. His harmonies are always clear, simple, and of extraordinary sonority." Schumann wrote: "His compositions contain many pure and precious qualities." And the noted Berlin critic of Paganini's day, Rellstab, remarked: "I never knew that music contained such sounds. He spoke, he wept, he sang, and yet compared with his Adagio, all virtuosity is as nothing."

Niccolò Paganini was born in Genoa, Italy, on October 27, 1782. His father, ambitious to make the boy a prodigy, engaged first Servetto then Giacomo Costa to teach the boy composition and the violin. Paganini revealed his uncommon gifts early. At eight, he wrote an excellent piano sonata, and before he was ten, he had made an impressive debut as a violinist. A year and a half after that, he created a sensation in a public recital with one of his own compositions, a set of variations. After additional study in Leghorn with Ferdinando Paer, and Alessandro Rolla, Paganini, aged fourteen, embarked on his first tours of Italy, reaping triumph after triumph. For several years, beginning with 1800 or so, he withdrew from the limelight to live with a wealthy Tuscan lady, for whom he wrote several guitar compositions. All this while, he worked slavishly to develop his violin technique. In 1805, he emerged from this retirement to become the conductor of the Lucca Opera and musical director at court. He also returned to the concert stage, re-establishing his imperial position among the virtuosos of his generation. Up until 1828, Paganini confined his concert work to Italy. But in that year, he gave performances for the first time in Vienna, Paris, and London. Wherever he came, he was met with the most extravagant adulation by critics, professional musicians, and the general public. He amassed considerable wealth, most of which he lost through investments in a gambling casino in Paris. His health impaired by these severe financial reverses, Paganini left in 1839 for a rest cure in Nice, where he died on May 27, 1840.

1811. CONCERTO NO. 1 IN D MAJOR, for violin and orchestra, op. 6. I. Allegro maestoso. II. Adagio. III. Allegro spiritoso.

Paganini published two violin concertos. The second (B minor, op. 7) is today remembered primarily for its second movement, often performed independently of the other parts. It is the "Ronde à la clochette," which Liszt transcribed for piano and renamed *La Campanella.*

The first concerto has often been played in editions by either Wilhelmj or Fritz Kreisler. In either of these versions only the first movement is given, and that in a shortened form and with a changed orchestration. But more and more concert violinists are now disposed to present this concerto in toto, precisely as Paganini wrote it. The results have been rewarding. There is a good deal of attractive music in both the second and third movements.

The key signature poses something of a problem. The concerto is designated D major, but Paganini wrote his music in E-flat major. It seems that the virtuoso was in the habit of tuning his violin half a tone higher to make the sounds more brilliant to the ear, and at the same time to make fingering more grateful to the fingers.

An extended orchestral introduction offers us the main themes of the first movement. The most important of these is a soaring melody for the violins. The solo instrument strives with virtuoso passages before engaging this beautiful melody. Lyrical and bravura writing alternate continually within the traditional sonata form. It is believed that Paganini's inspiration for the slow movement was a stage performance by Demarini in which he implored God to save his life. So moved was the composer by this scene that he sought to set it to music. A short orchestral prelude brings on the soloist with an intense, passionate melody. To William Gardiner, the tones here are "more than human" and seem to be "wrung from the deepest anguish of a broken heart." The finale is in rondo form, characterized by dashing virtuosity, with notable passages in double harmonics; the movement is dominated by its opening vivacious thought.

1820. TWENTY-FOUR CAPRICES, for unaccompanied violin, op. 1: 1. E major, "Arpeggio." 2. B minor. 3. E minor. 4. E-flat major. 5. A minor. 6. G minor, "Tremolo." 7. A minor. 8. E-flat major. 9. E major, "La Chasse." 10. G minor. 11. C major. 12. A-flat major. 13. B-flat major, "Le Rire du diable." 14. E-flat major, "Militaire." 15. G major. 16. G minor. 17. E-flat major, "Andantino capriccioso." 18. C major. 19. E-flat major. 20. D major. 21. A major. 22. F major. 23. E-flat major. 24. A minor.

The whole range of Paganini's fabulous technical endowments as a violinist is encompassed in his twenty-four caprices, or studies. Violinists the world over have mastered this music as a basic part of their training. Performers have been playing them to the vast delight of audiences who find joy in their intrinsic musical merit. Arpeggios, tremolos, double and triple stops, harmonics, left-hand pizzicati, octave passages—there is hardly a technical device of modern-day violin performance that is not exploited in these brilliant pieces. But these compositions are not just a showcase for a performer's digital and bow dexterity. They are no less rewarding experiences musically. This has been proved by the fact that Schumann and Liszt both thought enough of them to transcribe them for the piano. Georges Enesco and Fritz Kreisler each provided these Caprices with a piano accompaniment.

The most important, the most frequently played Caprices are the following: the fifth in A minor; the ninth, called *The Chase* because double-stop passages simulate hunting horn calls; the thirteenth, *The Devil's Laugh,* in which a mocking melody simulates diabolical laughter; the fourteenth, which has a martial character; the seventeenth, for its graceful lyricism; the twentieth; and most famous of all, the twenty-fourth, a theme and variations. The theme of this last Caprice was taken by Brahms for his *Variations on a Theme by Paganini* for solo piano (which see) and by Serge Rachmaninoff for his *Rhapsody on a Theme of Paganini,* for piano and orchestra. The contemporary German composer, Boris Blacher, wrote a set of orchestral variations on this same melody.

KARL LOEWE 1796–1869

In the early history of the Romantic song, the Lied, Karl Loewe occupies a place not far below that of Schubert. Both Loewe and Schubert had been influenced by a now completely forgotten pioneer of song, Johann Zumsteeg (1760–1802), creator of the German ballad. This was a sophisticated development of the English ballad—a setting for voice and piano of an extended poem usually combining narrative with dialogue. Schubert and Loewe—they were contemporaries—took the ballad form from Zumsteeg and transformed it into a vital art form. Neither Schubert nor Loewe was aware of the other's work. Each went his own way as a ballad composer, filling that mold with a lavish wealth of melodic beauty and emotion, with poetic insight and dramatic force. At the same time, each brought an importance to piano accompaniment the song had never known. As Donald Jay Grout has said: "The influence of the ballad . . . worked to expand the concept of the Lied, both in its form and in the range and force of its emotional content." Loewe's ballads, therefore, played a significant role in the evolution of the German art song.

Johann Karl Gottfried Loewe was born in Lobejun, near Halle, Germany, on November 30, 1796. In 1807, he became a chorister in the chapel of Coethen. From 1809 to 1812, he received instruction in singing and theory at the Franke Institut in Halle. In that latter year of 1812, he wrote his first two songs, "Klothar" and "Das Gebet des Herrn." In 1813, he enrolled in the University of Halle as a student of theology; at the same time, he continued his musical training at the Singakademie. His first masterworks—the ballads "Der Erlkoenig" and "Edward"—came in 1818. Three years later, he became director of the municipality of Stettin and organist of the St. Jacobus Church. His livelihood assured, he married his youthful sweetheart, Julie von Jacob, on September 7, 1821. This marriage ended abruptly a year and a half later with his wife's tragic death. Loewe married a second time in 1824, his new wife having been one of his pupils, Augusta Lange.

His reputation as a composer was established in the 1820's. In the years that followed, he also became known for his oratorios and operas. In 1834, he was decorated with a gold medal by the Crown Prince of Germany, after the successful première in Berlin of his opera, *Die drei Wuensche;* in 1837, he was elected to the Academy of Berlin. Between 1837 and 1857, he made many tours of Europe in song recitals. Deterioration of his health in the early 1860's made him give up both his concert work and his organ post at Stettin. Loewe went into retirement in 1866, and died in Kiel on April 20, 1869.

1818–1824. BALLADS, for voice and piano, op. 1:
"Edward"; "Der Erlkoenig"; "Der Wirtin Toechterlein."

It speaks volumes for the genius of Loewe that his setting of Goethe's "Der Erlkoenig" is not dwarfed by Schubert's. Indeed, no less an authority of Schubert' music than Donald Francis Tovey regards Loewe's musical interpretation of the Goethe text superior in some ways to Schubert's—"more in touch with modern methods." Schubert's song came in 1815, Loewe's three years later. "Der Erlkoenig" (together with "Edward") represents Loewe's first effort at writing ballads; and with this first effort he realized full maturity as a songwriter.

Tovey provides the following interesting comparison between the two "Erlkoenig" versions, those of Schubert and Loewe: "Loewe brings out the rationalistic vein of Goethe's ballad by setting the Erlking's words to a mere ghostly bugle call which never leaves the notes of its one chord. Schubert uses melodies as pretty as the Erlking's promises. In other words, Loewe's point of view is that of the father assuring the fever-stricken child that the Erlking, with his laughter and his whisperings, are nothing but the marsh mists and the wind in the trees; while Schubert, like the child, remains unconvinced by the explanation. His terror is the child's; Loewe's terror is the father's."

The fidelity with which the music catches all the hidden or subtle nuances of the text—and the power of imagination with which Loewe develops his musical material—is also found in other Loewe ballads. "Edward," written in the same year as the "Erlkoenig" is a setting of a poem by Herder. In "Der Wirtin Toechterlein," poem by Uhland, also in opus 1, is suffused with so much emotion that it is easy to believe it was written when the composer was suffering grief at the death of his young wife, Julie.

———SONGS, for voice and piano:

"Das Erkennen," op. 65, no. 2; "Fridericus Rex," op. 61, no. 1; "Der heilige Franziskus," op. 75, no. 3; "Heinrich der Vogler," op. 56, no. 1; "Der Noeck," op. 129, no. 2; "Odins Meerestritt," op. 118; "Prinz Eugen, der edle Ritter," op. 92; "Suesses Begraebnis," op. 62, no. 4; "Tom der Reimer," op. 135; "Die Uhr," op. 123, no. 3.

Loewe's songs and ballads fill seventeen published volumes. In commenting on some of the best of these (a representation of which is listed above), Franz Gehring wrote: "Their melodic simplicity and squareness are akin to the artless tunes by minor composers which are misguidedly regarded as folk songs in German-speaking countries. . . . They are greatly superior to what used to be known as 'ballads' in England and quite different from these: truly narrative songs of a kind Loewe may be said to represent most consistently."

ROBERT FRANZ 1815–1892

The domain of Robert Franz was limited—that of the Lied, or art song—but here he was an undisputed master. Except for some choral music (chorales, part songs, a liturgy, and a few other similar items), Franz's entire production consists of some three hundred and fifty Lieder. In the development of the song, Franz stands midway between Schubert and Schumann on the one side, and Brahms and Hugo Wolf, on the other. Though the figures flanking him are of giant stature, his own is not completely dwarfed by comparison. He is one of music's greatest songwriters.

It is not difficult to see why, when he published his first opus in 1843, Franz made Schumann, Mendelssohn, and Liszt sit up and take notice. In this collection, we find numbers like "O saeh ich auf der Haide dort," "Die Lotosblume," and "Schlummerlied" in which, as Henry T. Finck once wrote, "expressions of personal feeling [are contained] in simple, well-balanced musical forms, undisfigured by dramatic episodes, obtrusive climaxes, or any of those other devices of less fastidious songwriters." Though with later songs Robert Franz developed his technical skill by making his structure concise and inexorable in its logic, and though he continually deepened the emotional content of his lyricism, he never lost the simplicity and directness of his first songs. W. F. Apthorp has shown that Franz always succeeded in uniting the "purely lyric element one finds in such splendor in Schubert [with] the wondrously subtle and mobile expressiveness of every varying shade of emotion that characterized Schumann, fusing these two elements so that their union was absolutely . . . complete."

Robert Franz was born in Halle, Germany, on June 28, 1815. Though his parents objected to his interest in music, he managed to acquire a knowledge of piano and organ secretly. When he finally gained his parents' consent for musical study, he became a pupil of Heinrich Schneider in Dessau. Back in Halle in 1837, he continued his training by himself for a number of years. His first published work, a set of twelve songs in 1843, attracted the attention of several notable musicians, including Schumann and Mendelssohn. This publication, and this attention, led to his appointment as organist of the Ulrichskirche in Halle and as the conductor of the Singakademie. Subsequently, he filled the post of music director at the Halle University. In 1868, he had to give up his various posts because of nervous disorders and deafness. He was rescued from abject poverty through the generosity of Liszt and Joachim (among others), who helped raise $25,000 for him. In the last years of his life, Franz devoted himself to the editing and arranging of music by Bach, Handel, Mozart, and Schubert, among others. Franz died in Halle on October 24, 1892.

1843–1868. SONGS, for mezzo-soprano and piano:

"Es hat die Rose sich beklagt," op. 42, no. 5; "Im Rhein, im heiligen Strome," op. 18, no. 2; "Die Lotosblume," op. 1, no. 3; "Marie am Fenster," op. 18, no. 1; "Mutter, O Sing mich zur Ruh," op. 10, no. 3; "O saeh ich auf der Haide dort," op. 1, no. 5; "Schilflieder," op. 2; "Schlummerlied," op. 1, no. 10; "Stille Sicherheit," op. 10, no. 2; "Widmung," op. 14, no. 1; "Wonne der Wehmuth," op. 33, no. 1.

Franz wrote about three hundred songs, always confining himself to the range of the mezzo-soprano. From the earliest efforts, he revealed a personal approach to lyricism. He was not interested in passion or drama. He avoided any suggestion of realistic tone painting. He wanted his songs to bring, as he himself once explained, "peace and reconciliation," to emphasize, "the ethical side." His writing, consequently, is generally subdued (he rarely permits the voice full sonority). He aspired to be as simple as possible, generally utilizing the strophic structure and building up his melodies from one or two phrases. His accent is on tenderness and surface beauty. He allowed others to seek out in their music the deeper implications of any given text.

Henry T. Finck explains: "He cared primarily not for luxuriance of decoration, but for structural symmetry and harmony; not for an emotionality bordering on hysteria, but for the calm expression of sincere, simple feeling; not for utter revelation but for a dignified presentation of what was artistically worthy presentation, against a background of reticence and reserve. . . . In simplicity and graciousness of melody, in musicianly part-writing and in legitimately expressive harmony, Franz is preeminent."

JACQUES HALÉVY 1799–1862

Different opera composers in France reacted in different ways to Meyerbeer's success in writing spectacular operas. Some were tempted to speak his language and imitate his methods. They managed to deflect some of Meyerbeer's popularity to themselves, but in the process they finally lost not only their own artistic identity but even their public. In such a group do we find Halévy. By 1835, he had not yet been seriously affected by Meyerbeer—though unquestionably he was acquainted and impressed with *Robert le diable*. And so, by 1835, he proved himself a master both in comic and serious operas by virtue of a refined and sensitive lyricism and a French grace that led Wagner (no less) to assign him a "leading position in our lyric theater." While still true to himself, borrowing no man's vestments, Halévy could produce *La Juive* in serious opera, and *L'Éclair* in the comic field. Then *Les Huguenots,* in 1836, elevated Meyerbeer as the undisputed god of French opera. Halévy became one of those who tried to hold on to their audiences and their fame by writing the way Meyerbeer did. Of the almost twenty-five operas Halévy completed after *La Juive,* only a scattered handful made any sort of an impression on his contemporaries—*La Reine de Chypre* in 1841, *Les Mousquetaires de la reine* in 1846, and *La Tempésta* in 1850. And none of these have survived.

Jacques Halévy, son of a celebrated Hebrew poet and synagogue cantor, was born in Paris on May 27, 1799. He attended the Paris Conservatory, where for five years he was a pupil of Cherubini and where, in 1819, he won the Prix de Rome. He started writing operas during his three-year residence in Italy; but not until 1827 was one of them produced—*L'Artisan,* a one-act comedy introduced at the Théâtre Feydeau. From 1827 to 1830, Halévy was cembalist at the Paris Opéra, and from 1830 on, he served for several years as "chef du chant." In 1827, he was also appointed professor of harmony and accompaniment at the Paris Conservatory, taking over the classes in counterpoint and fugue in 1830, and advanced composition in 1840. One of his pupils, Georges Bizet, married his daughter in 1869.

Halévy's success in French opera was permanently solidifed in 1835 with *La Juive* and *L'Éclair*. They brought him several honors. He was made Chevalier of the Legion of Honor and in 1836, he became a member of the Académie, of which he was made Secretary for life in 1854. He never again reached the high quality maintained in his two masterworks; nor did any of his subsequent operas equal their success. A victim of consumption, Halévy went for a rest cure to Nice in 1861. He died there on March 17, 1862. His body was brought back to Paris for burial in the Montmartre cemetery.

1835. LA JUIVE (THE JEWESS), opera in five acts, with text by Eugène Scribe. First performance; Paris Opéra, February 23, 1835.

Two influences helped make *La Juive* the masterwork it is. The first is an exceptionally fine libretto by Scribe, whose action, as Ernest Newman has said, "is admirably planned for progressive theatrical effect," and whose characters are "entirely credible." The other influence was Halevy's background as the son of a Hebrew poet and cantor. The impressive and stately character of the Jewish goldsmith, Eleazar; the persecution of the Jewish race; the tragic fate of Eleazar and Rachel as a result of anti-Semitic hatred—all this stirred Halévy and inflamed his musical imagination. Without ever trying to write Jewish music as such—not even in the devout and deeply moving Passover Scene—Halévy produced a score rich in compassion and humanity, in tender sympathy for his persecuted race.

The action takes place in Constance, in Baden, during the historic council of 1414. The first-act curtain rises upon a square in front of the town cathedral. Eleazar is at work at his bench, his hammering interruping the hymns with which the people are celebrating Prince Leopold's victory over the Hussites. He and his daughter are dragged out of their home by an angry mob. They are, however, saved from prison or death through Cardinal Brogny's intervention, the Cardinal entreating his people to substitute tolerance for hate ("Si la rigueur ou la vengeance"). After Eleazar and Rachel go free, and the square is emptied, Prince Leopold arrives, disguised as Samuel, a Jewish painter. This is the way he hopes to win Rachel's heart, with whom he has fallen in love. As Samuel, the Prince is invited to Eleazar's house to be a guest at the Passover feast. The old Jew intones prayers to the Lord—first to beg for divine guidance ("O Dieu, Dieu de nos pères"); then to pray for the destruction of Israel's enemies ("Dieu, que ma voix tremblante"). During these ceremonies, Leopold's true identity is revealed. Eleazar is at first horrified to learn that Rachel is in love with a Christian, and is ready to elope with him. Then seeing how strong the attachment is between the two young people, he sadly consents to their marriage. But Leopold had never intended to marry Rachel. He rushes out of Eleazar's home shouting he can never be joined in matrimony to a Jewess. Heartbroken, Rachel comes to his palace to denounce Leopold. She reveals to the startled assemblage that Leopold has made love to her. For this offense Leopold is excommunicated, while Eleazar and Rachel are sent to prison. There Cardinal Brogny offers to free them if they embrace Christianity, something both refuse to do. In torment, Eleazar realizes that fate has compelled him to sacrifice Rachel, whom he loved so dearly, and whom he had raised with such tenderness. This poignant lament, "Rachel, quand du Seigneur," is not only the most famous aria in the opera, but one of the most celebrated in French lyric theater.

Just before they are to meet their death, Eleazar entreats Rachel to save her own life by embracing Christianity. Proudly, courageously, Rachel refuses. When she is thrown into a cauldron of boiling oil, Eleazar turns in anguish to the Cardinal and reveals the secret that Rachel is really the Cardinal's daughter, whom he had saved from a burning house many years ago and raised as his own daughter. The confession made, Eleazar goes off to meet death with head high.

La Juive first came to the United States with a performance in New Orleans on January 13, 1844. The opera was so popular that one year later, upon coming to New York, it was played in five languages (including Yiddish). The opera entered the Metropolitan Opera repertory on January 16, 1885; on November 22, 1919, Caruso appeared for the first time at the Metropolitan Opera as Eleazar, one of his most celebrated roles. Caruso sang in *La Juive* for the last time on December 24, 1921; and this was also the last time he was seen on any stage.

HECTOR BERLIOZ 1803–1869

"Beethoven is dead," Paganini wrote to Berlioz in 1838 after hearing *Harold in Italy,* "and Berlioz alone can revive him." Paganini was merely echoing Berlioz's own belief that he was Beethoven's successor. Like Beethoven, he consciously broke down the barriers of symphonic music to gain greater flexibility and spaciousness; like Beethoven, he was subjective; like Beethoven, he sought to make tones the voice of human and poetic experiences. But Beethoven was the transition from classicism to romanticism, while Berlioz was the full-grown child of the Romantic movement—music's Delacroix or Victor Hugo, as he has often been described.

Berlioz was a Romantic in life and deed as well as music. He wrote as he lived (and vice versa)—passionately, intensely, turbulently, egotistically, neurotically. He made frequent flights into a world where reality and fantasy were confused. Like the poet Alfred de Vigny, his supreme concern was the "moi," and music was always for him a personal testament in which he could speak his ever changing emotions and moods. The program he was setting—and he always had to have a literary source to stimulate the creative process—was just a convenient means with which to reveal himself ever more intimately. The poet in the *Symphonie fantastique,* Harold, Benvenuto Cellini, and Juliet's Romeo are all Berlioz when he set them to music. Since he was a Romantic with a pronounced literary bent, he used all the technical resources at his command (and they were truly immense) to present his detailed program literally, colorfully, and pictorially. In the process, he had to revise old classical methods and structures, while devising new styles and techniques.

He was one of music's most daring innovators and iconoclasts. The *Symphonie fantastique* (written only three years after Beethoven's death!) is the father of the Liszt tone poem. In its excursion into fantasy and the grotesque, it invades an area new to musical expression. Its idée fixe is the forerunner of the Wagnerian Leitmotiv.

Berlioz emancipated rhythm from its traditional adherence to two, four, and eight beats by introducing new irregular patterns and effects, which many of his contemporaries regarded as eccentric, but which today we realize released new sources of dynamism. He made a new science of orchestration by ever seeking out new colors and effects through the introduction of instruments never before found in traditional orchestras; also, by increasing the size of the orchestra to Gargantuan proportions and experimenting with unusual combinations. In this last department, orchestration, he was —as Hugo Leichtentritt said—an "inventive genius of the first order. Berlioz's art of orchestral coloring is an achievement comparable to Chopin's chromatic harmony, a fundamental achievement on which the art of Wagner, Liszt, Richard Strauss and Debussy is based."

Arthur Ware Locke says in summation: "Practically every important tendency in the Romantic movement is represented in Berlioz's music. The picturesqueness and sense of local and historical color, conspicuous in the writings of Chateaubriand and Sir Walter Scott, are found in . . . *Benvenuto Cellini* and *Harold in Italy*. Such movements as the "Witches' Sabbath" have all the unrestraint of the satanic school of Byron. The *Symphonie fantastique* reveals the wild melancholy which is so characteristic of most of the French Romantic poets. The purely lyrical quality is less evident in Berlioz than in Liszt. Berlioz had an essentially dramatic genius and the lyric entered merely as a contributing element to his dramatic scheme. *Roméo et Juliette* shows the intrinsic character of Berlioz's music, not its startling originality, but its subtle quality of poetic suggestiveness, the truest sign of genuine Romanticism."

The son of a physician, Hector Berlioz—born in La Côte-Saint-André, Isère, France, on December 11, 1803—was first intended for medicine. In 1821, he came to Paris to pursue medical studies, but abandoned them three years later to enter the Paris Conservatory. On July 10, 1825, his first abmitious composition was heard; it was the *Messe solennelle,* calling for the services of one hundred and fifty performers. This was followed by a cantata, *La Mort d'Orphée* (with which Berlioz made an unsuccessful bid for the Prix de Rome in 1827) and two concert overtures, *Waverley* and *Les Francs-juges,* performed at the Paris Conservatory in 1828.

It was at this time that Berlioz became romantically involved with the actress Harriet Smithson. He saw her in 1827 in a performance of *Hamlet,* and from his seat in the audience he fell in love with her. Though he deluged her with letters and other forms of attention, she avoided him completely. Berlioz then arranged a concert of his works for May 26, 1828, hoping thereby to arouse her interest in him. She refused to attend. In despair, he wrote a mammoth orchestral work, the *Symphonie fantastique,* identifying himself in it as the morbid poet, and his beloved Harriet as a shameless courtesan. The symphony, and the concert in which it was introduced, were both ignored by her.

In 1830, Berlioz won the Prix de Rome. He was not happy in Italy, and therefore terminated his Roman stay before the required three-year period was over. Back in Paris in 1832, he resumed his stormy, feverish efforts to woo and win Harriet Smithson. It was only now that a first personal meeting between them was arranged. Following a turbulent courtship, Berlioz and Harriet were married on October 3, 1833. It was not a happy marriage to begin with, a continual clash of temperaments and personalities. After the birth of a son, they parted permanently. But Berlioz's second marriage—to Marie Recio—did not take place until after Harriet died in 1854.

A repetition of the *Symphonie fantastique* in Paris in 1832 brought Berlioz his first major success. During the next decade, he completed several more masterworks, with which he gained the admiration of such notable contemporaries as Paganini, Wagner, Liszt, and Schumann. The most significant of these works were *Harold in Italy* in 1834 and *Romeo and Juliet* in 1839. The decade that followed saw the completion of some other ambitious and provocative compositions: the *Roman Carnival Overture;* the dramatic legend, *The Damnation of Faust;* the *Te Deum.*

Beginning with 1842, Berlioz made several tours of Europe as conductor of his works. In 1852, and again in 1855, he participated in a Berlioz Week in Weimar at the invitation of Liszt; and in 1856 he was elected a member of the French Institut. From 1852 until his death, he served as librarian of the Paris Conservatory. An unhappy second marriage, and the death of his beloved son in 1867—combined with the ravages of a nervous ailment—combined to darken Berlioz's last years. He died in Paris on March 8, 1869.

1830. SYMPHONIE FANTASTIQUE (FANTASTIC SYMPHONY), op. 14. I. Dreams, Passions. II. The Ball. III. Scene in the Country. IV. The March to the Gallows. V. Dreams of the Witches' Sabbath.

Berlioz did not wait long to depart sharply from all symphonic structures and procedures established by Haydn, Mozart, Beethoven, and Schubert. He did so with his very first symphony, when he was only twenty-seven. That symphony, the *Fantastic,* represented a new world of sound for 1830. Never before had a composer made all the resources of symphonic music so subservient to a detailed and literal program; never before had a composer made such a journey into the fantastic, the macabre, and the psychological; never before had a composer brought such expansiveness and elasticity to the symphony structure nor such immense harmonic and instrumental equipment; never before had a symphony been the medium for such turbulence of emotion. Innovation was the rule rather than the exception: in the unorthodox interpolation of a waltz movement into a symphony; in the desertion of orthodox thematic development procedures and substituting for them the use of a unifying theme (here called the "idée fixe"), a recurring motto, though often disguised and transfigured.

The writing of this symphony was closely bound up with Berlioz's stormy romance with Harriet Smithson. Her failure to take notice of him was the stimulus he needed for a work into which he could flood his overwhelming emotions; in which he himself would be the protagonist; and which might prove such a shock in Paris that it might finally compel Harriet to take notice of him. But while deep at work on this project, Berlioz received some disquieting tidings about Harriet that fanned his jealousy to white heat. This led him to transform the heroine of his symphony into a reprehensible courtesan, who drives the poet to an attempt at suicide through opium.

Nevertheless, he still harbored the hope that his symphony might arouse Harriet's curiosity and make her more partial to him. The première at the Conservatory, on December 5, 1830, attracted a notable audience that included Liszt, Spontini, and Meyerbeer. But though Harriet was in the city, she did not attend. Had she done so she would have witnessed a truly remarkable demonstration for the young composer. Parts of the work caused a sensation, and one of them, "The March to the Gallows," had to be repeated. The conservative elements might be puzzled and upset by what they heard, but there was a healthy representation of young Romantics to hail this remarkable work as the music of the future.

Originally entitled *Episode in the Life of an Artist,* the *Fantastic Symphony* was based on De Quincy's *Confessions of an English Opium Eater,* then recently translated into French by de Musset. Berlioz himself provided a detailed program for his music in his published score. It reads in part: "A young musician of morbid sensibility and ardent imagination poisons himself with opium, in a fit of amorous despair. The narcotic dose, too weak to result in death, plunges him into a heavy sleep accompanied by the strangest visions, during which his sensations, sentiments, and recollections are translated in his sick brain into musical thoughts and images. The beloved woman herself has become for him like a melody, like a fixed idea, which he finds and hears everywhere."

The five movements then trace the hero as he falls in love; meets his beloved at a ball; thinks of her as he wanders through the country; dreams in a nightmare that he has killed her and must go to the gallows; and attends the rites of a Witches' Sabbath.

The first movement (Largo; Allegro e appassionato assai) opens with a slow and passionate subject in the violins, introduced by a solo horn over a violin obbligato. The motto theme is heard for the first time in the ensuing Allegro, a haunting refrain for first violins and flutes; it identifies Harriet Smithson. Even as her image acquires a variety of aspects, so the motto theme undergoes transformations, at times becoming feverish and passionate. The movement ends with the motto theme become a devout statement.

In the ball scene (Allegro non troppo), a waltz melody unfolds gracefully. After the motto theme is recalled by flute and oboe, the waltz becomes brilliant and vigorous. The third part of the symphony portrays country scenes, and is consequently pastoral (Adagio). An unaccompanied duet for English horn and oboe proceeds to a delicate subject for flute and first violins, which carries within itself the germ of the motto. Three more ideas are later introduced. The first is for the woodwind after the preceding delicate subject has been built climactically; the second is for cellos and basses, following a brief recollection of the movement's opening idea; and the third is a solo for the clarinet over pizzicato strings.

The fourth movement (Allegretto non troppo) is grotesque march music. The artist dreams that, having killed the woman he loves, he must be executed. The motto theme is here interpolated by solo clarinet.

The finale (Larghetto; Allegro) finds the artist at a Witches' Sabbath, surrounded by monsters and magicians. Tremolo chords for divided strings lead to the motto, first given a vigorous treatment by the clarinets, then taken over by the other woodwind. Bells bring on a section in which the strains of the "Dies Irae" are mockingly offered by tubas and bassoons. A demoniac dance is given fugally. After that, a tremendous climax is built up, at whose peak we once again hear the "Dies Irae," this time combined with the feverish refrain of the witches' dance.

1831. KING LEAR, overture for orchestra, op. 4.

This work was written during a feverish period in Berlioz's early life. While in Italy, as the winner of the Prix de Rome, he had received the news that a young woman to whom he had become betrothed after his first rejection by Harriet Smithson—a Mlle. Moke—had married another man. Bent on vengeance, Berlioz disguised himself as a lady's maid and set out for Paris intending to kill the young couple, and with vague ideas of committing suicide after that. But in Nice, he had a sudden change of heart. He decided to accept the situation and make the most of it. "And so I drink deep draughts of the sunny, balmy air of Nice, and life and joy return to me, and I dream of music and the future. . . . I wrote the overture to *King Lear*. I sing. I believe in God. Convalescence!"

Though inspired by Shakespeare, the music makes no attempt to trace the action of the drama. A dramatic recitative in the lower strings is soon repeated by muted violins. This sets the stage for a lofty statement by oboe to which first violins provide figurations. After a feverish restatement of the opening recitative, the Allegro section engages an agitated subject to which a beautiful melody in oboe provides contrast. The working out of both ideas is a spacious one, with considerable emphasis on dramatic values. The coda is similarly theatrical and stormy.

1831. LE CORSAIRE (THE CORSAIR), overture for orchestra, op. 21.

Berlioz's point of departure here was Byron's *The Corsair*. He had the Byron poem with him when, in 1831, he paid a visit to St. Peter's Cathedral in Rome. "There at my leisure I sat drinking in that burning poetry. I followed the Corsair in his desperate adventures; I adored that inexorable yet tender nature—pitiless yet generous—a strange combination of apparently contradictory feelings; love of woman, hatred of his kind." He completed his overture early in 1831, but thirteen years later revised it extensively.

Donald Francis Tovey says that this music is "as salt a sea piece as has ever been written." Tonal images of the sea are evoked in the opening stormy passage. A highly expressive melody (Adagio sostenuto) describes the parting of Conrad and Medora in Byron's dramatic poem. In the main part of the overture, we get a vigorous melody into which, as Tovey says, "the breezy elements settle." This is the heart of the overture. "I have not the slightest idea," comments Tovey further, "of what Byronic subjects, other than generalized brilliance, are [here] represented."

1837. OVERTURE TO BENVENUTO CELLINI, for orchestra, op. 23.

The ambition to write an opera about Benvenuto Cellini first occurred to Berlioz in 1831 during a visit to Florence, where he saw the famous Perseus statue. His interest in Cellini thus aroused, Berlioz began to seek out information, both about the sculptor and the Renaissance. A reading of Cellini's Memoirs convinced him that Cellini was an attractive character for an opera. He started work on that opera in 1834, and completed it three years later—the text prepared for him by Léon de Wailly and Auguste Barbier. The main interest in the plot lay in the fashioning of the Perseus statue and in the romance of Cellini and Teresa.

Benvenuto Cellini, Berlioz's first full-length opera, was a fiasco when introduced at the Paris Opéra on September 10, 1838. The audience almost started a riot. The opera was given only three times after that, always to half-empty auditoriums. Then it went into virtual discard until 1913, when it was revived in Paris. So disheartened was Berlioz by the unhappy fate of his first opera that it took him a quarter of a century to summon the courage to write another major work for the stage.

In the overture, the spirited opening subject (Allegro deciso con impeto) was intended to portray Cellini. After twenty-two measures, there comes a brief pause. A Larghetto episode presents a recollection of the third-act air, "A tous péchés," in pizzicato basses. After that, we hear a melody for woodwind recalling the Harlequin air from the carnival scene. The vigorous Allegro has for its principal subject a beautiful melody derived from the love duet of Cellini and Teresa. This is given for the first time by the woodwind over a syncopated accompaniment. A loud transition brings on the second theme, first in the woodwind, then in violins and violas. In the development, the opening subject and the first melody of the Larghetto are given detailed attention.

1834. HAROLD EN ITALIE (HAROLD IN ITALY), symphony for orchestra with solo viola, op. 16. I. Harold in the Mountains. Scenes of Melancholy, Happiness, and Joy. II. March of the Pilgrims Singing their Evening Prayers. III. Serenade of a Mountaineer of the Abruzzi to his Mistress. IV. Orgy of Brigands. Recall of Preceding Scenes.

Among those impressed by the *Symphonie fantastique* (which see) was the fabulous violin virtuoso, Paganini. A few weeks after he had heard it for the first time, Paganini commissioned Berlioz to write for him a work featuring the viola prominently—the viola being an instrument in which Paganini had just become interested. Paganini expected a meretricious work exploiting technical feats. But what Berlioz planned for him was a work stressing Romantic and poetical values. When Paganini saw the sketches of the first movement, he told Berlioz that this music did not serve his purpose and lost all interest in it. Freed of the commission, Berlioz could now proceed in his own direction without inhibitions. As he himself explained, he now "wove round the viola a series of scenes drawn from my memories of wanderings in the Abruzzi, which I called *Childe Harold,* as there seemed to me about the whole symphony a poetic melancholy worthy of Byron's hero." The symphony has, however, only the remotest relationship to the Byron poem. Most of the program describing the poet's wanderings about the Italian countryside was the composer's own invention.

Though at its première, on November 23, 1834—at the Paris Conservatory—the symphony was poorly performed, the audience reaction was most enthusiastic; the "March of the Pilgrims" section had to be repeated. Paganini did not hear the work until December 16, 1838. At that time, he was so impressed by the power and originality of the music that he presented the composer with a handsome gift of twenty thousand francs.

The Adagio with which the symphony opens is a brooding, contrapuntal description of "scenes of melancholy." The Harold theme (which recurs throughout the work) is now given, first by the woodwind, then by the violins in conjunction with clarinets. A passage in triplets leads into the Allegro, in which "scenes of happiness and joy" are evoked. Here the main subject is presented by solo viola, in a dialogue with the orchestra. A brief development and recapitulation bring on an extended coda in which the solo viola theme of the introduction, and the two main themes of the Allegro, receive fugal treatment.

The second movement (Allegretto) presents a parade of pilgrims as seen from a distant vantage point. The march tune, initially presented by the violins, grows in sonority, then dies down to a whisper over the sound of a convent bell.

An Allegro assai replaces the traditional scherzo of the classical symphony. A grotesque-like tune appears in piccolo and oboe over a drone bass. Now comes the serenade of the Abruzzi mountaineer to his mistress—a romantic melody in English horn. During the course of the serenade, the Harold theme is recalled.

The finale (Allegro frenetico) is in Heine's description "a furious orgy where wine, blood, joy, rage all combined parade their intoxication—where the rhythm sometimes seems to stumble along, sometimes to rush on in fury, and the bars seem to vomit forth curses and to answer prayer with blasphemies. . . . There was something positively supernatural and terrifying in its frantic life and spirit, and the violins, basses, trombones, drums and cymbals all sang and bounded and roared with diabolical order and concord, while from the solo viola, the dreamy Harold, some trembling notes of his evening hymn were still heard in the distance as he fled in terror."

1837. GRAND MESSE DES MORTS, requiem for solo voices, chorus, and orchestra, op. 5.

The Minister of the Interior in the cabinet of Louis Philippe commissioned Berlioz to write a work honoring the dead of the 1830 Revolution, for performance at a special service. Political intrigues and machinations prevented the completed requiem from being given for the purpose for which it was intended. It was, however, heard as a memorial service at the funeral of General Damremont, hero of the Algerian campaign of October, 1837. This première took place at the Invalides in Paris on December 5, 1837. Mammoth musical forces had to be gathered for this concert. There were some four hundred voices in the chorus, a hundred and ten performers in the orchestra. In addition, the work called for small brass choirs, ranging in size from eight to fourteen instruments, stationed (as the score specified) "at the four corners of the choral and instrumental mass" to sound the calls of the Last Judgment.

"If I were threatened with the burning of all my works except one," Berlioz once confessed, "it is for the Requiem that I would ask for mercy." It is not hard to see why Berlioz was so partial to this work. It contains some of his most awesome, grandiose, and even terrifying musical pronouncements. In ten sections, the Requiem skilfully combines the noble and the sublime with the theatrical and the grotesque, Berlioz himself once described this music as "overwhelming . . . of a horrifying grandeur."

The majestic introduction—built from three melodic episodes—has the character of a stately dirge in the opening "Requiem." This is followed by the awe-inspiring "Dies Irae," perhaps the most remarkable part of the entire work. It is here, following a dramatic pause, that we hear for the first time the four small brass choirs pronouncing Judgment Day. A brief episode in basses, repeated three times in different keys, brings on the "Tuba mirum," whose overpowering effect was once described by Alfred de Vigny as "beautiful, queer, wild, convulsive, sorrowful music." Its theatrical effect is intensified by the thundering sounds of the timpani. In "Quid sum miser," there is a momentary recess from the tensions. But drama returns in the "Rex Tremendae" with its titanic chords and overwhelming dynamics. A six-part unaccompanied chorus, "Quaerens me," precedes the extended "Lacrymosa," which abounds with rhythmic virtuosity and unusual effects, but never at a sacrifice of deep feeling. The "Offertorium," once described as "a chorus of souls in purgatory," is unusual in that it is built from a two-note phrase that is never varied. The "Hostias et Preces," for tenor and basses, is also out of the ordinary, particularly in an instrumentation that calls for three flutes and eight trombones for accompaniment. The poetic "Sanctus"—a tenor solo, with responses by sopranos and altos—ends in a fugue. The Requiem concludes with an "Agnus Dei" for male voices, in which the strains of the opening Requiem are remembered, followed by a gentle "Amen."

1839. ROMÉO ET JULIETTE, dramatic symphony for solo voices, chorus, and orchestra, op. 17, Part One: I. Introduction: Combat, Tumult, Intervention of the Prince. II. Prologue. Part Two: I. Romeo Alone. II. Starlight Night. III. Queen Mab or the Fairy of Dreams. Part Three: I. Juliet's Funeral. II. Romeo in the Family Vault of the Capulets. III. Finale.

Under the influence of his unsatisfied passion for Harriet Smithson, Berlioz attended in 1827 (and was overwhelmed by) a performance of *Romeo and Juliet* in which Harriet played the heroine. He was quoted as having said at the time: "I will marry that woman, and I will write my greatest symphony on that play." He did both.

How deeply Berlioz was affected by Shakespeare's tragedy was proved by the following lines he contributed to a French journal in or about 1827. "Shakespeare's Romeo! God, what a subject. Made for music! . . . the brilliant ball at Capulet's house . . . the fierce fighting in the streets of Verona . . . that inexpressible night scene at Juliet's balcony. . . . The piquant buffooneries of the gay, irresponsible Mercutio . . . then the frightful catastrophe—voluptuous sighs giving way to the death rattle . . . and to close it all, the solemn vow of the two hostile families too late, over the dead bodies of their children, to sink forever the hates which had provoked such torrents of blood and tears. . . . And my own tears ran down my cheeks as I thought of it."

The unexpected, munificent gift of twenty thousand francs which Paganini presented Berlioz in 1838 was the wherewithal enabling Berlioz to devote himself completely to his symphony. He wrote it between January and September of 1838; he himself directed the première performance—at the Paris Conservatory —on November 24, 1838, scoring a major success.

Berlioz wrote: "Although voices are frequently employed, this is not a concert opera, a cantata, but a symphony with chorus. If song occurs in the beginning, it is for the purpose of preparing the mind of the hearer for the dramatic scenes, in which sentiments and passions should be expressed by the orchestra. It is moreover to introduce gradually in the musical development choral masses whose too sudden appearance would do harm to the unity of the composition. Thus the prologue, in which . . . the chorus exposes the action, is sung by only fourteen voices. Later is heard, behind the scenes, the male chorus of the Capulets; but in the funeral ceremonies women and men take part. At the beginning of the finale, the two choruses of Capulets and Montagues appear with Friar Lawrence; and at the end the three choruses are united."

The symphony is made up of three large sections, which, in turn, are split up into twelve smaller segments. In the first section, the feud of the Capulets and Montagues is described. The introduction is a brisk fugato followed by a stern declaration by the trombones and tuba. The hostility of the Capulets and Montagues is arrested by a stern demand for peace on the part of the Prince. We next get a choral recitative for sixteen voices, a contralto solo, and a recitative and scherzetto for tenor solo with small chorus.

In the second large section, Romeo invades the hall of the Capulets during a ball. There he sees and falls in love with Juliet. The opening (Andante malinconico e sostenuto) tells of Romeo's loneliness and sadness. The distant sounds of music and dancing can be heard. An effective Larghetto espressivo continues to describe Romeo's somber mood. Now the music gains in sonority and intensity as Romeo makes his way into the festive ballroom.

The middle part of this section is perhaps the jewel of the entire symphony —the love music for the balcony scene. "This music," says Arthur Ware Locke, "shows the most sensitive sympathy with the situation it portrays. There is the magic of moonlight darkness in the low tones of the strings; there is the mystery of the scarcely visible background of the garden, the quivering of nature that penetrates the whole romantic picture. The long sustained tones of the clarinet and the English horn intensify the mood of passionate longing." After this love music comes a popular excerpt: the delicate, exquisite "Queen Mab Scherzo," in which Mercutio describes how the queen of the fairies visits him during his sleep."

The symphony ends with the lovers' tragic end. A fugal march tells about Juliet's funeral procession. The chorus takes up this funeral melody. After Romeo has entered the Capulet vault, the symphony comes to a resounding conclusion with a dramatic episode for two simultaneous choruses. Capulets and Montagues swear on a cross to be friends forevermore.

1844. LE CARNAVAL ROMAIN (ROMAN CARNIVAL OVERTURE), for orchestra, op. 9.

Berlioz's original intent was to use this music as a symphonic introduction to the second act of his opera *Benvenuto Cellini*. When that opera was given in Paris in 1838, the *Roman Carnival* had not yet been written. Berlioz did not get around to completing this music until 1844; but by then he had decided to issue it as a separate orchestral composition, completely independent of the opera. As such, it was introduced in Paris on February 3, 1844, when it received such an ovation that it had to be repeated.

The heart of the overture is an exciting saltarello melody appearing in the second act of the opera as background music for an Italian dance. In the overture's introduction, the saltarello tune is suggested without preliminaries. It is followed by a meditative melody for the English horn (taken from Cellini's first-act love song, "O Teresa"). With a quickening of the tempo, and some chromatic passages in the woodwind, we reach the Allegro vivace, where the saltarello becomes the principal subject. This theme is discussed at great length, with occasional reminders of the "O Teresa" motive.

1846. LA DAMNATION DE FAUST (THE DAMNATION OF FAUST), dramatic legend for solo voices, chorus, and orchestra, op. 24. I. In the Plains of Hungary. II. In Northern Germany. Faust's Study. Auerbach's Cellar. The Banks of the Elbe. III. Marguerite's Room. IV. Marguerite's Room. Forest and Caverns. The Trip to the Abyss. Hell. Heaven.

Goethe's *Faust* had attracted Berlioz as early as 1827, when he read Gérard de Nerval's recently issued French translation. "I could not put it down," Berlioz later recalled. "I read it constantly, at my meals, in the theater, in the streets, everywhere." Inevitably, he was led to canalize such enthusiasms into music. He wrote eight scenes, which he published in April, 1829.

A little more than fifteen years after that, while traveling about in Eastern Europe, Berlioz's interest in *Faust* was revived. He now became fired with the ambition to complete the huge project. Preparing most of the text himself (though some parts were prepared for him by Almire Gaudonnière) Berlioz finally completed his dramatic legend on October 19, 1846.

Berlioz explained in the preface to his score, that this work was not "based on the principal idea of Goethe's *Faust,* in which illustrious poem Faust is saved. . . . The author . . . is indebted to Goethe only for a certain number of scenes which entered into his original plan—scenes whose charm was irresistible." Only four characters were used: Faust, Mephistopholes, Marguerite, Brander. Much of Goethe's philosophical and metaphysical concepts were deleted, only those parts lifted from Goethe that Berlioz felt could be treated musically. One or two sections (such as the ride to Hell) was Berlioz's own invention. Berlioz, finally, doomed Faust to perdition, where Goethe had brought him salvation.

Berlioz intended *The Damnation of Faust* for concert performance. This is the way it was given for the first time—at the Opéra-Comique on December 6, 1846, the composer conducting. This presentation was a sorry failure. The hall was three-quarters empty, and the handful that did attend reacted frigidly. "Nothing in all my career has wounded me as this did," Berlioz later confessed.

On June 19, 1847, Berlioz directed another concert performance, this time in Berlin; and in 1848, he gave parts of the work in London. In both places, the reaction was more appreciative. But full recognition of the originality and importance of this masterwork came only after the composer's death, with a revival in Paris in 1877, in two different performances by two different conductors. "At that time," says Adolphe Boschot, "it began its prodigious and triumphal career. No other concert work ever enjoyed such numerous multiplied and constant successes." Because this work has such a pronounced dramatic quality, it has also been staged as an opera. The first time this happened was on February 18, 1903, in Monte Carlo.

Berlioz frankly revealed that he brought his hero to Hungary because he wished "to bring to the ear a piece of instrumental music whose theme was Hungarian." That piece of music is the celebrated *Rakóczy* or *Hungarian March*. It opens with a brass fanfare. The vigorous, sweeping march melody is first heard quietly in the woodwind. Slowly it gains in sonority until it is thundered by the full orchestra. The basic theme was borrowed by the composer from an old Hungarian folk melody.

The *Rakóczy March* is not the only part of the legend popular with present-day concert audiences. Three other excerpts are frequently given. The *Invocation* in the third part (Allegro moderato) is the music with which Mephisto summons the evil spirits and the will-o'-the-wisps to encircle Marguerite's house. This is followed by the *Dance of the Will-o'-the-Wisps* (Moderato), a delicate minuet for woodwind and brass, with trio. The *Dance of the Sylphs* (Allegro: mouvement de valse) from the second part is an elegant waltz for violins, describing the dancing of spirits and gnomes in Faust's feverish dreams.

1849. TE DEUM, for chorus and orchestra, op. 22.

The *Te Deum* took many years to achieve its definitive form. Berlioz began planning it in 1832 to celebrate the victorious return of French troops from Italy. He did not get around to putting the final touches on his manuscript until 1849. Six years after that, he himself directed its première, at the Saint-Eustache Church in Paris, on April 30, 1855.

Like so many of Berlioz's major works, the *Te Deum* is a giant project, enlisting the services of almost a thousand performers at its première. Originally, this work required two choirs of a hundred voices each, and a third chorus of six hundred children. Berlioz subsequently revised the score for a more modest choral group, one comprising one hundred and thirty voices; this is the version that is given today.

For all its size—and for all its daring modulations and unusual instrumental and vocal resources—the *Te Deum* remains a deeply religious work, a majestic and devout hymn to God. There are eight parts, all "bathed in an atmosphere where religious sentiment and poetic sentiment are balanced," says Henri Barraud. It opens with a fugal section filled, says Barraud "with fervor and solemnity but without exuberance." The climax of the work as a whole comes with the seventh section, "Judex crederis," music of the most compelling power and surging drama.

1854. L'ENFANCE DU CHRIST (THE CHILDHOOD OF CHRIST), oratorio for solo voices, chorus, and orchestra, op. 25. I. Herod's Dream. II. The Flight into Egypt. III. The Arrival at Saïs.

In the fall of 1850, Berlioz directed *La Fuite en Egypt* (*The Flight into Egypt*), which he identified as a "mystery by Pierre Ducre." He maintained that this work had been written in 1679. When some critics remarked acidly that Berlioz could have taken a lesson or two from this remarkable composition in the writing of devout and sincere music, Berlioz confessed that both the music and text of *La Fuite en Egypt* were his own, and that there never existed a composer by the name of Pierre Ducre.

Four years after that, Berlioz added two choral sections to flank his *Flight into Egypt,* designing the whole work as a "dramatic trilogy." In the first part, he described Herod's command to massacre the children of Judea, and the angel's warning to Joseph and Mary. In the middle part—subtitled *The Shepherds Assemble before the Manger of Bethlehem*—the Holy Family is warned by a host of angels to flee into Egypt, and the shepherds assemble to bid them farewell. *The Arrival at Saïs* recounts how the Roman citizens of the Egyptian city of Saïs reject Joseph, Mary, and Jesus, and how the Holy family is finally welcomed by the Ishmaelites.

F. Bonavia says that *L'Enfance du Christ* shows "but one facet of Berlioz's genius but it shows that facet in the best possible light. . . . [It] is both revolutionary and reactionary. It is revolutionary in that Berlioz's scheme differs entirely from that of his predecessors. It does not include, like the oratorios of Mendelssohn, arias, display pieces for solo singers, and numerous choral occasions. But it retains a recitative which is not quite the 'recitativo secco' of the old masters, but is still further from the intensely dramatic and elaborate recitative of his successors. . . . They have an individuality all their own. They share the general character of the oratorio, which is essentially gentle, introspective, and tender. One has the impression that Berlioz was here expressing the feelings and emotions of his own childhood recalled after many years of harsh experience."

The first performance of the complete oratorio was given in Paris on December 10, 1854. It proved such a success that it had to be repeated on Christmas Eve of the same year and again the following January 28. Berlioz conducted it during the next few years in Hanover, Baden, and Bordeaux. In the last-named city, the audience was so moved that, at the end of the performance, it rushed to the composer to crown him with a laurel wreath. A still later performance in Strasbourg (in a hall built especially for this occasion) an audience of eight thousand continually interrupted the music with outbursts of enthusiasm.

1859. LES TROYENS (THE TROJANS), opera in five acts—but divided into two operas: I. La Prise de Troie; II. Les Troyens à Carthage. Text by the composer based on Virgil's *The Aeneid.* First performance of the complete opera: Karlsruhe, Germany, December 6, 1890.

For many years Berlioz had been haunted by a dream to set Virgil's *Aeneid* to music as an opera. He wanted to make it a vast epic along Shakespearean lines. But intensive and concentrated work on it did not begin until 1856, after a visit to the Princess Sayn-Wittgenstein, who encouraged him to undertake the project. It now took Berlioz two years to complete the assignment—a monumental undertaking requiring five hours for complete performance. The Théâtre Lyrique in Paris wanted to produce an excerpt, regarding the whole opera too huge and difficult for a single presentation. It was then that Berlioz decided to make two operas out of one. The second opera was accepted by the Théâtre Lyrique, with considerable deletions. Despite the fact that this work was finally given in a version different from that originally conceived by the composer—and though the performance was far from adequate—it was so well received that it was given twenty times during a six-week period. The two operas were never given as a unit, or in their entirety, during Berlioz's lifetime. When finally heard—in Karlsruhe, in 1890—a German translation was used. The first performance in French of *La Prise de Troie*—and its première in France—took place in Nice in February 1891; this was followed by a production at the Paris Opéra on November 16, 1899.

A remarkable revival of the complete opera took place at Covent Garden in London on June 6, 1957, given in an English translation by Edward J. Dent. Rafael Kubelik conducted; John Gielgud was the producer, and the cast included Blanche Thebom and John Vickers. A concert performance was given in New York on December 29, 1959, which many believe to be the American première of the complete opera.

The first opera, *The Capture of Troy,* treats the legend of the wooden horse and Troy's conquest. The spirit of Hector then sends Aeneas to Italy to found a new kingdom. The second opera, *The Trojans in Carthage,* is based on the same love story involving Dido and Aeneas that Henry Purcell had used many years earlier for his classic, *Dido and Aeneas* (which see).

Aeneas, writes Desmond Shawe-Taylor, "is an admirably virile and vigorous portrait of a man of action. It is not too much to say that Berlioz has given flesh and blood to a personage who remains frigid in Virgil. He is always good at depicting impetuosity and impatience, which he had so much of himself. Nor are we left in any doubt of the reality of the love between the Trojan hero and the Queen of Carthage: opera has little to parallel the great sequence of numbers in the garden scene—the quintet, the septet with chorus, and finally the Shakespearean love duet, 'In Such a Night as This.' . . . The opera makes an immense scheme, a grand nineteenth-century 'machine,' and its very grandeur and scope seem to appeal to a public that has long accepted an uncut *Ring of the Nibelungs* as a regular fixture in the musical calendar."

To Ernest Newman, *The Trojans* is "a truly stupendous work, and until a man has seen and heard it he can hardly lay claim to much more than a rudimentary knowledge of the composer—certainly the dramatic composer. . . . Really to understand the mighty work demands a great deal more from the spectator-listener than just sitting in the theater and letting himself be moved by what he sees and hears. One requires not only to know the score inside out but to be intimately acquainted with the first four books of *The Aeneid*—for Berlioz has done many things the clue to which [in Virgil] it has been impossible for him to work logically into the tissue of his stage action. The first thing to be grasped is that the whole purpose of the opera is expressed in the title. Its main subject is not, as many people imagine, the love of Dido and Aeneas but the *Trojans*—the long drawn-out working out by the rival gods and goddesses of the irreconcilable destinies of Troy and Carthage and Augustan Rome."

Orchestral excerpts from the opera are often given at symphony concerts. The *Royal Hunt and Storm* comes from the second section of the opera. A theme for horns suggests a hunt in progress. The music then describes a storm during which, in a thick forest, fauns and satyrs perform a corybantic. When lightning uproots a huge tree, they seize the burning branches and disappear. The tumult dies down, and all is serene. The *Trojan March* comes in both the first and second parts of the opera. In the first part, it appears as a triumphal march; in the second, it becomes a dirge, telling of the return of the Trojans to Carthage.

1862. BÉATRICE ET BÉNÉDICT, opéra-comique in two acts, with text by the composer, based on Shakespeare's *Much Ado About Nothing*. First performance: Baden-Baden, Germany, August 9, 1862.

Berlioz's last work came when he was sorely pressed by domestic problems, besides suffering physically from intestinal neuralgia. Yet there is nothing in this music to betray such unhappy circumstances. The score is vivacious and lighthearted, touched by laughter and mockery, sparkling for its travesty and parody. Berlioz wrote it, on a commission from the director of the Baden-Baden Casino, for a new theater in the resort town. There it was introduced under Berlioz's own direction with outstanding success. But poor Berlioz was too ill to enjoy his victory.

In adapting Shakespeare for an opera, Berlioz emphasized comedy over romance. He made only passing reference to the main Shakespeare romance between Claudio and Hero; on the other hand, he accented the love of Beatrice and Benedick. In the opera, the play opens with the return from war of Claudio and Benedick; they are awaited by their respective sweethearts, Hero and Beatrice. After that, the love affair of Beatrice and Benedick runs a tortuous course, since both are self-willed, hot-tempered, reluctant to reveal the true state of their feelings for each other. When their friends contrive to have each overhear the other in a confession of love, all turns out well.

One of the most beautiful vocal pages in the score is Beatrice's air, "Dieu, viens-je d'entendre." A strong lyric element is also pronounced in the nocturne that closes the first act, and in Hero's aria, "Je vais le voir." Comedy and travesty become pronounced in the "Wedding Cantata" and in the madrigal, "Mourez tendres époux," which Berlioz wrote for Somarona, a character of his own invention.

The overture, scored for small orchestra, is also of exceptional interest. A vivacious theme for strings and woodwind (derived from the second act duet of Beatrice and Benedick) appears in the introduction. A second section, in slow tempo, brings a romantic subject for horn and clarinets with which, in the opera, Beatrice finally recognizes that she is in love. The main part of the overture (Allegro) makes use of the introduction subject and a new haunting tune for violins over woodwind harmonies. The overture ends with a coda, accenting comedy.

The United States did not hear a performance of *Beatrice and Benedick* until March 21, 1960, when it was given in a concert version by the Little Orchestra Society, Thomas Scherman conducting; the performance took place in Carnegie Hall, New York.

MIKHAIL GLINKA 1804–1857

Glinka was Russia's first significant composer; the first to win recognition outside his own country; the first whose works are still a part of our listening experiences. However impressive these achievements may be—and they would have been enough to assure him a permanent place in music history—they are dwarfed by his surpassing accomplishments as a musical nationalist. Drawing his stimulation and inspiration from Russia's greatest poet, Pushkin, Glinka became the first important composer to realize a national style based on folk songs, dances, and old church music. He was the first to draw his strength and materials from Russian backgrounds, history, and poetry.

He was a young man of twenty-six, touring Europe in 1830, when homesickness or nostalgia or the perspective of distance fired him for the first time with the ambition to create a *Russian* musical art. He recognized the immeasurable wealth hidden deep within the storehouse of Russian folk songs; he started to avail himself of these treasures. And so, he wrote a *Capriccio on Russian Themes* for piano duet, and two movements of a symphony on Russian melodies worked out "in the German manner." Both are the works of an apprentice. He also experimented with writing melodies of his own, but in the style and idiom of Russian folk songs. (Two of these he later used in his first opera, *A Life for the Tsar.*) He dreamed about writing a national Russian opera. "My most earnest desire," he wrote to a friend, "is to compose music which would make all my beloved fellow countrymen feel quite at home, and lead no one to allege that I strutted about in borrowed plumes."

Once back in Russia, he marched with unfaltering step toward his self-imposed goal. He wrote two national operas, both of them of epochal importance in Russian music; also sundry other works grounded in Russian backgrounds and folk music. He accomplished his mission with such success that Russia's greatest composers after that felt impelled to draw their nourishment from his music; all seemed to find their own direction from the signposts in Glinka's compositions. Tchaikovsky (to whom *A Life for the Tsar* had been one of the overwhelming musical experiences of his youth) called Glinka "the arch patriarch of all Russian music." Rimsky-Korsakov said: "My greatest liking was reserved for Glinka." Balakirev modeled his own aims and ideals after Glinka. Anton Rubinstein spoke of Glinka and Beethoven in the same breath. Stravinsky learned to love Glinka's music "to distraction" during his formative years. Indeed, it would be difficult to find a single major creative figure in Russia who had not been decisively influenced by Glinka. As Victor I. Seroff wrote: "Just as the Russian writers used to say that they all came from Gogol's *The Cloak,* so the Russian composers could say they have all come from Glinka's *A Life for the Tsar.*"

But when we speak of Glinka as the father of Russian musical nationalism, we have not exhausted his contributions. There are other ways in which he stood apart from other composers of his day. He was the first foreign composer anywhere to write important music about Spain—half a century before Chabrier's *España.* He was such a master of orchestration (the "founder of an entirely new school," says Gerald Abraham) that even Rimsky-Korsakov (himself a master in this field) could exclaim: "I studied his handling of the natural-scale brass instruments. . . . How subtle everything is with him and yet how simple and natural at the same time." Glinka experimented with the whole-tone scale and with discords a half a century before Debussy and the twentieth-century modernists. "All things considered—his passive character, his training and his surroundings, Glinka the composer remains an inexplicable natural phenomenon of a kind almost unique in the history of music," in the words of Gerald Abraham.

Mikhail Ivanovich Glinka was born in Novospasskoi, Smolensk, Russia, on June 1, 1804 to a wealthy family. As a boy he attended private school, where he excelled in sciences and languages. At the same time, he studied the piano with Carl Meyer and John Field, and the violin with Boehm. Glinka wrote his first composition when he was eighteen—five waltzes for the piano.

After a period of rest, following a nervous ailment, Glinka devoted himself to the study of orchestration and harmony by himself. He took to memorizing one musical masterwork after another. But music as a career was far from his mind. From 1824 to 1828, he worked in the Ministry of Communications. In 1830, however, he reached the decision to try and become a composer. For about three years, he lived on the Continent, studying with Francesco Basili and absorbing the traditions of Italian opera; in 1833, he was a composition pupil of Dehn in Berlin.

Back in Russia, he married Maria Petrovna Ivanova, on May 8, 1835. It was an unhappy relationship from the beginning, for Maria was a shrew and a coquette, who made him consistently miserable. But this did not keep him from composition. Between 1834 and 1836, he worked on *A Life for the Tsar,* with which Russian nationalism first comes into being. The success of this opera, at its première in 1836, brought him the post of choral director of the Imperial Chapel. His second opera, *Ruslan and Ludmilla,* and his orchestral fantasy, *Kamarinskaya,* brought his nationalist style to full maturity.

In the closing years of his life, Glinka traveled about a good deal. An extended visit to Spain, beginning with 1845, led to the writing of two outstanding orchestral works in a Spanish idiom, the *Jota aragonesa* and *Night in Madrid.* He was on a visit to Berlin in 1856 to make a firsthand study of Western church music, when he was stricken by his last fatal illness. He died in Berlin on February 15, 1857. A few months after his death, his remains were disinterred and transferred to the cemetery of the Alexander Nevsky Monastery in St. Petersburg.

1836. A LIFE FOR THE TSAR (IVAN SUSSANIN), opera in five acts, with text by Baron Georg von Rozen. First performance: St. Petersburg, December 9, 1836.

Upon returning to Russia in 1834, following his travels on the Continent, Glinka joined a group of Russian artists, writers, and intellectuals; they included Gogol, Pushkin, and Zhukovsky. He confessed to them his hope of creating a national Russian opera. Zhukovsky suggested a subject from Russian history, the seventeenth-century peasant hero, Ivan Sussanin. Zhukovsky originally planned to write Glinka's libretto but, after beginning to put material down on paper, he was distracted by other activities. Baron Georg von Rozen, secretary to the Czarevich, took over for Zhukovsky. Once the text was completed, it took Glinka two years to write his score.

The action of the opera takes place during the Russo-Polish conflict of 1633, soon after the boy Michael Feodorvich became the first of the Romanovs to ascend the throne. The Poles enter into a conspiracy to overthrow the young king for somebody of their own choice. To achieve this, a Polish army is despatched to Moscow, ostensibly on a peace mission, but actually to kill the young Czar. En route they come upon Ivan Sussanin's hut. They hire Ivan as their guide. When he discovers their evil designs, Ivan sends his adopted son, Vanya, to warn the Czar. At the same time, he deflects the Polish troops from Moscow by getting them lost in a forest, a maneuver that costs him his life.

Glinka originally called his opera after the name of his hero. But when Czar Nicholas I expressed enthusiasm for the opera during a rehearsal, Glinka decided to dedicate the work to him; at the same time he retitled it *A Life for the Tsar*. Under that name it was seen on December 9, 1836 before a brilliant audience, including the Czar, his court, and leading members of Russian nobility. The latter (ever partial to foreign culture and disdainful of anything Russian) looked with disfavor on Glinka's use of popular Russian elements in his score; they described it as "coachman's music." But the Czar was beside himself with delight; he presented the composer with a precious ring. The public at large took the opera to its heart. *A Life for the Tsar* had an impressive initial run of thirty-two performances.

For all its pronounced nationalism, *A Life for the Tsar* is an eclectic opera. Meeting the demands of his text, Glinka introduced Polish ingredients into his score—such as the mazurka and polonaise that are heard in the second act as a climax to a festive celebration in the ancient castle of Sigismund III of Poland. There are many arias that are carry-overs from Glinka's experiences in Italy in 1830, and their Italian identity is unmistakable. But all such foreign intrusions notwithstanding, *A Life for the Tsar* remains basically a Russian opera. Most of its finest material sprang from the soil of Russian folk song and dance and of Russian church music.

"The thematic material," wrote Rosa Newmarch, "is partly drawn from national sources, not so much directly as modeled on the folk-song pattern. The crude folk stuff is treated in a very different way to that which prevailed in early national operas. Glinka does not interpolate a whole popular song—often harmonized in a very ordinary manner—into his opera. . . . With Glinka, the material passes through the melting pot of his genius, and flows out again in the form of a plastic national idiom. The treatment of his theme is also in accordance with national tradition; thus in the patriotic chorus in the first act, 'In the Storm and Threatening Tempest,' we have an introduction for male chorus, led by a precentor (Zapievets), a special feature of folk singing in Great Russia. Another chorus has a pizzicato accompaniment in imitation of the national instrument, the balalaika. Many of Glinka's themes are built upon the medieval church modes which lie at the foundation of the majority of national songs."

The overture's dignified introduction highlights a theme for oboe. In the main part, a vigorous theme undergoes transformation and elaboration before the second main subject appears in the clarinet.

Two of the most impressive scenes in the opera are assigned to the hero, Ivan. "The first," Rosa Newmarch explains, "occurs when the Poles insist on his acting as their guide and he resolves to lay down his life for the Czar. Here the orchestra plays an important part, suggesting the agitations which rend the soul of the hero; now it reflects his superhuman courage, and again those inevitable, but passing, fears and regrets without which his deed would lose half of its heroism. Sussanin's second great moment occurs when the Poles, worn out by hunger and fatigue, fall asleep around their campfire and the peasant hero, watching for the tardy winter sunshine which will bring death to him and safety to the young Czar, sings in a mood of intense exaltation, the aria, 'Thou Comes Dawn!' a touching and natural outburst of emotion that never fails to stir a Russian audience to its emotional depths."

Some of Glinka's most effective national music is assigned to the chorus: the Bridal Chorus; the choruses based on the *Slavsia,* the old Russian song of glory; the paean to Russia that opens the final act; the exultant hymn to the Czar and to Ivan which closes the opera. Of that closing chorus, Camille Bellaigue has written: "Every element of national beauty is pressed into service here. The people, their ruler, and God himself are present. Not one degree in all the sacred hierarchy is lacking; not one feature of the ideal, not one ray from the apotheosis of the fatherland."

In the Soviet Union, performances of *A Life for the Tsar,* carry Glinka's original title of *Ivan Sussanin,* ever since the opera was successfully revived in Moscow on February 27, 1939.

1842. RUSLAN AND LUDMILLA, opera in five acts, with text by Shirkov, Gedeonov, the composer, and others, based on a poem by Pushkin. First performance: St. Petersburg, December 9, 1842.

Where the main interest of *A Life for the Tsar* lay in its patriotic ardor—and in the hymns of glory to land and ruler—the appeal of *Ruslan* is more subtle and elusive. For *Ruslan* is a delicate fantasy with a fairy-tale charm which does not overpower its audience but rather beguiles it. The Italian manners that still clung to *A Life for the Tsar* are left behind. *Ruslan* is thoroughly Russian; its musical idiom combines those pronounced Russian elements of folk song and dance with traits of Orientalism that appear in Russian music perhaps for the first time. Orientalism would henceforth determine much of the writing of later Russian nationalist composers.

The play is set in pagan times. Ludmilla, daughter of a prince from Kiev, is being sought by three suitors, one of whom is Ruslan, with whom Ludmilla is really in love; the other two are Ratmir and Farlaf. But since the wizard Chernomor wants Ludmilla for himself, he abducts her. The Prince despatches all three suitors to rescue Ludmilla, promising her hand to the one who is successful. Ruslan enlists the help of another wizard, the benevolent Finn, who provides Ruslan with a magic sword. With that weapon Ruslan is finally able to free Ludmilla. On their journey back to Kiev, the pair encounters one of the other suitors, who puts both of them into a profound slumber. He then takes Ludmilla back with him to the Prince, claiming his reward. Ruslan, however, emerges from his sleep in time to get to Kiev and reveal the tale of treachery to the Prince. The opera ends with a magnificent ceremony celebrating the marriage of Ruslan and Ludmilla.

The delightful overture, a perennial favorite at symphony concerts, opens with several robust chords. An ebullient, vivacious tune in violins, violas, and woodwind follows. The contrasting theme is in the style of a Russian folk song, presented by violas, cellos, and bassoon.

"*Ruslan and Ludmilla,*" says Richard Anthony Leonard, "was the composer's masterpiece as a pioneer work of nationalism and it created almost at one stroke the essential style of modern Russian music." In evolving the language that later nationalists in Russia would use, Glinka was solving a central problem. "Russia's folk music," continues Leonard, "and her ancient church music was based on old modal scales which Western music had centuries ago abandoned for the major-minor and their principles of tonality. The problem was to reconcile and join the two systems, and this extended beyond melody and harmony into the basic principles of tonal relationship and form."

These are some of the highlights of the opera: The archaic song of the Bard, "There is a Desert Country"; Ludmilla's poignant farewell to her father, the cavatina, "Soon I Must Leave Thee"; Farlaf's delightful rondo in buffa style, "The Happy Day is Done"; Ruslan's emotional air, "O Say, Ye Fields"; the famous "Persian Chorus" for unison women's voices, based on a genuine Persian tune, "The Evening Shadow"; Gorislava's romance and cavatina, "O My Ratmir"; Ratmir's air, "The Wondrous Dream of Love"; and in the final act the "Chorus of the Flowers," the march of Chernomor (with its startling discords), and the brilliantly orchestrated oriental dances.

When first produced, *Ruslan and Ludmilla* was a failure; too many people in the audience (including the Czar himself) had expected another *A Life for the Tsar* and were disappointed. In the minority were those who recognized the full measure of this opera. To Stassov, it represented "the mature expression of Glinka's inspiration." And to César Cui, it was "a work of the first rank" in which Glinka "marked out new paths and opened up horizons undreamed of before his time."

In 1859 (two years after Glinka's death), *Ruslan and Ludmilla* was acclaimed for the first time. A revival in Russia in 1892 was a triumph.

1845–1848. JOTA ARAGONESA, caprice-brilliant for orchestra.
NIGHT IN MADRID, a Spanish overture for orchestra.
KAMARINSKAYA, fantasy for orchestra.

In 1845, Glinka visited Spain and was completely captivated by the appeal of Spanish folk songs and dances. He planned to do a service for Spanish folk music by trying to create amibitious compositions with Spanish components. "Original focal melodies," he wrote to a friend, "will supply me with excellent source material, the more since this field has not been previously exploited." He listened to and studied Spanish music wherever he went, putting down all sorts of fetching ideas into a little notebook.

His aim was to write a number of concert pieces for the orchestra designated as "fantaisies pittoresques"—more popular in over-all appeal than the symphonic fare audiences were getting at the time.

The first of these "fantaisies" was the *Jota aragonesa,* based on a jota melody Glinka had picked up in Valladolid from a guitarist. This sinuous type melody, which appears at the beginning of the composition, is treated to several fanciful variations.

A Night in Madrid, Glinka's second "fantaisie", written in 1848, was made up of two Spanish melodies in the style of a seguidille: a rapid dance in triple time accompanied by guitar or castanets.

Kamarinskaya was also written in 1848. This orchestral fantasy developed two folk songs heard by Glinka at a Russian wedding in Warsaw: "Over the Hills, the High Hills," a marriage song, and a dance-song, "Kamarinskaya." "They suddenly awoke my inspiration," Glinka explained in his autobiography, "and instead of composing the piece for piano as I first intended, I wrote it for orchestra under the title *Wedding Song and Dance.* I can honestly say that I was guided in the composition of the work solely by my inward musical feelings, never giving a thought to what takes place at rustic weddings, nor to the revels of our orthodox people, nor to the belated drunkards who go knocking at the doors of huts to be let in. . . . Nevertheless, a critic assures me that at the rehearsal of *Kamarinskaya,* the Emperor told him that in the last section of the work (where the first horn holds a pedal on F sharp, and then the trumpet on C) there was a realistic representation of the tipsy peasant hammering on their cottage doors. This idea seemed to me vastly amusing, as it would never have occurred to me in my life."

The marriage song, "Over the Hills, the High Hills" is heard in the eleventh measure. It is repeated, then merged with a countersubject. At this point, the dance melody, "Kamarinskaya" is presented by the first violins and worked out with force and brilliance of color. The fantasy ends in a fiery hopak-like coda.

FELIX MENDELSSOHN 1809–1847

It has become a cliché to compare the tranquillity and well-being of Mendelssohn's life with those of his music. Surely he was buffeted by fewer inner or outer storms than any other composer. He was born rich. From the beginning, he was encouraged to cultivate his immense talent. He met success early and saw it develop, as the years passed, to heights achieved by few other musicians of his time. He was so attractive physically, and so personable, that he inspired affection as easily as admiration. He fulfilled himself as a composer and conductor.

His music, like his life, is singularly free of struggle, torment, frustration, or passion. He never aspired for the new kinds of musical expressions groped after by Berlioz or Schumann, his fellow Romantics. He did not seek out new forms, being thoroughly satisfied to dwell within such classical structures as the symphony, the concerto, the string quartet, and the oratorio. He was often faithful to the classic sonata form. He did not particularly try to make music a medium for the projection of extra-musical experiences, ideas, or sensations. He was at times programmatic, in that he gave some of his compositions descriptive titles providing a hint as to the intent of the music. But the music itself is hardly more than a subtle suggestion or impression of the program rather than a vividly realistic picture; the program, as Donald Jay Grout put it so well, "is no more than a faint mist about the structure, lending charm to the view but not obscuring the outlines."

Though he was no revolutionist, no innovator, he nevertheless succeeded in creating his own language. His greatest strength lay in the variety and richness of his lyricism; in the clarity and inexorable logic of his thinking; in the supreme mastery of his technique. He was, as Wagner once said of him, a "landscape painter of the first order" who could re-create more than one kind of scene with the most telling effect. Mendelssohn was also the incomparable musical interpreter of the fairy kingdom. To the Scherzo, he brought a grace, delicacy, tranparency, and fleetness of motion that made it a particularly grateful medium with which to evoke the fanciful world of fairies, elves, and forest spirits. As Hugo Leichtentritt once said, Mendelssohn's Scherzos have "a delightfully fantastic play of the most delicate tones, suggestive of a dance of spirits that floats in the air like clouds, soaring lightly in most graceful undulations, hardly touching the ground with their nimble feet, wrapped in veils, like clouds of smoke mounting toward the sky."

Only on infrequent occasions did Mendelssohn try to achieve either depth or drama in his music. He knew his limitations and for the most part was satisfied to produce that kind of cultured, well-mannered, refined, and exquisitely fashioned music of which he, more than his other fellow Romanticists, possessed the secret. The human equation was not for him. "His personality is tenuous, overrarefied," wrote Daniel Gregory Mason. "He seems more like a faun than a man. And hence it comes about that when, leaving his world of fairies, elves, visionary landscapes, and ethereal joys and sorrows, he tried to sound a fuller note of human pain and passion, he is felt to be out of his element. His style is too fluent, too insinuating, and inoffensive, to embody tragic emotion. It lacked the rugged force, the virile energy, the occasional harshness and discordance even, of the natural human voice; its reading of life, in which there is ugliness, crudity and violence, as well as beauty, is too fastidiously expurgated."

Because his world was circumscribed, Mendelssohn—for all the enchantment he brought to his writing—rarely soars to the heights achieved by other masters of music. But as Frederic H. Cowen maintains, "he came within measurable distance of them. . . . His high level of excellence is undeniable."

Felix Mendelssohn was born in Hamburg, Germany, on February 3, 1809. He was the son of a banker, and the grandson of the famous philosopher, Moses Mendelssohn. When the immediate family was converted from Judiasm to Protestanism, the name of "Bartholdy" was affixed to that of Mendelssohn to distinguish themselves from the rest of the family who had remained Jewish. Extraordinarily precocious, Felix received his early musical training from Ludwig Berger and Karl Friedrich Zelter. Mendelssohn was nine when he made his debut as concert pianist, and at ten, one of his compositions was played by the Singakademie in Berlin. By 1821, he had written numerous works, including symphonies and operas. His first masterworks—the Octet for strings, and the *Overture to A Midsummer Night's Dream*—came between 1825 and 1826, when he was still in his teens. An opera, *Die Hochzeit des Camacho,* was produced in Berlin on April 29, 1827.

Having been a profound admirer of Bach's music from boyhood days on, Mendelssohn conducted the first performance of the *Passion According to St. Matthew* since Bach's own day, in Berlin, on March 11, 1829. This concert was so successful that it helped set into motion a revival of Bach's music, which, when completed, lifted that master from his long obscurity and neglect to a position of first importance in the world's music.

Early in 1829, Mendelssohn paid the first of many visits to England, where he directed performances of several of his works. After traveling about in Europe between 1829 and 1832, Mendelssohn returned to London for a second visit to introduce there his *Fingal's Cave Overture,* the G minor Piano Concerto, and *Capriccio brilliante,* and also to publish the first volume of his *Songs Without Words*. Between 1835 and 1840, Mendelssohn was the conductor of the Gewandhaus Orchestra in Leipzig, initiating a new era, both in the history of conducting and in that of the celebrated orchestra. While retaining this post, he completed some of his most significant compositions. Among them were the oratorio *St. Paul,* the first piano trio, the *Ruy Blas* overture, and six preludes and fugues for piano. During this period, he also got married—to Cécile Jeanrenaud, on March 28, 1837; they had five children.

When an Academy of the Arts was planned in Berlin, Mendelssohn was invited in 1841 by the Emperor to become its head. Mendelssohn held this post only a short time, exchanging it for the honorary appointment of General Music Director in Berlin. Since the latter did not call for his presence in Berlin, he returned to Leipzig to resume his former activities as conductor, and where, in 1843, he helped found the Leipzig Conservatory.

In 1847, Mendelssohn paid his tenth and last visit to London. His ever delicate health now broke, partly under the impact of the news that his beloved sister, Fanny, had died. Mendelssohn died in Leipzig on November 4, 1847.

1825. OCTET IN E-FLAT MAJOR, for strings, op. 20. I. Allegro moderato. II. Andante. III. Allegro leggierissimo. IV. Presto.

Mendelssohn's Octet is one of the earliest such works. As the production of a mere boy, it is no less remarkable than the *Overture to A Midsummer Night's*

Dream—especially in the third movement to which it bears such an affinity and which it antedates. "The sea of sound that rages through this octet," says William Altmann, "is very powerful, achieving indeed quite an orchestral tone at times, though there is no lack of delicate passages." All four movements are in the sonata form. The first presents a strong subject accompanied by tremolos and syncopations. A fanfare-like episode and a semiquaver figure bring on the second lyrical theme. In the development, Mendelssohn already proved his mastery in altering his thematic material, while in the recapitulation he provides some intriguing variants of earlier themes. The slow movement is in the rhythm of a siciliano. A melancholy song here finds contrast in a comparatively cheerful middle part. The Scherzo movement is the masterpiece in this octet, in the delicate, magical fairyland mood that Mendelssohn projected so wonderfully in his *A Midsummer Night's Dream Overture,* and in the Scherzo from that suite. The composer is believed here to have been inspired by a passage from Goethe's *Faust:* "Trails of cloud and mist brighten from above; breezes in the foliage and wind in the reeds—everything is scattered." "The whole piece," Mendelssohn's sister, Fanny, goes on to explain, "should be played staccato and pianissimo: The peculiar tremulous shuddering, the light flashing mordents, all is new, strange, and yet so interesting, so intimate that one feels near the world of ghosts, lightly borne aloft; yes, one might take in hand a broomstick, to follow better the aerial crowd. At the end, the first violin flutters upwards, light as a feather—and all vanishes away."

In 1829, Mendelssohn himself orchestrated the Scherzo. He was in London at that time, conducting the English première of his so-called First Symphony in C minor, written in 1824. Dissatisfied with its minuet movement, he decided to use as replacement an orchestrated version of his Scherzo from the youthful Octet. The orchestral adaptation was received with such enthusiasm that, as Ignaz Moscheles wrote, it "was obstinately encored against his wish."

The finale of the Octet opens with a fugue, its subject appearing in the low notes of cello and second violin. The Scherzo theme is then repeated in the original key. Now the momentum grows to carry the movement to a brilliant conclusion, capped by a melodious coda.

1826. OVERTURE TO A MIDSUMMER NIGHT'S DREAM, for orchestra, op. 21.

The miracle of this overture is not only that it is such a perfect realization of the play on which it is based but that it should have posed its composer as a fully developed, original voice in music when he was only seventeen. With no precedent to guide him, and at the same time while parting company with the composers of the past who had influenced him, the boy Mendelssohn created for himself a world of fantasy—a world of fairies, elves, and spirits of the forest—with the most delicate touch, sensitive instrumentation and harmony, and an uninhibited imagination all his own. This was musical Romanticism in full flower. This was a new age—ushered in by a child.

Mendelssohn originally wrote the overture for two pianos. He later orchestrated it. The latter version received its world première in Stettin, Germany, in February 1827, Karl Loewe conducting.

The supernatural world is immediately evoked with four sensitive chords in the woodwind. A fifth chord, pianissimo, precedes a fleet staccato passage for divided violins, suggesting fairies and elves at play. After a subsidiary passage for full orchestra, we get the lyrical second theme in the woodwind, carried on soon thereafter by other sections of the orchestra. In rapid succession after that come a song for the horn suggesting the mystery of the forest; a spacious melody shared by woodwind and strings; a rustic dance for the strings. Throughout the overture, the orchestral texture remains diaphanous, and the mood elfin. The magic spell is never broken. The overture ends as it began, with four delicate chords.

Seventeen years after writing the overture, Mendelssohn added to it twelve numbers as incidental music to Shakespeare's play (which see).

1829. STRING QUARTET NO. 1 IN E-FLAT MAJOR, op. 12. I. Adagio; Allegro non tardente. II. Canzonetta. III. Andante espressivo. IV. Molto allegro e vivace.

Mendelssohn wrote six string quartets; curiously, the first, written when he was twenty-four, has proved the most popular. A sober seven-measure introduction precedes the main section of the first movement. Its first subject is a spacious and emotional melody, while the second is in a calmer vein. Later on in the movement a new thought is introduced: a sorrowful song for the second violin over viola quavers. The second movement is a canzonetta in which effective use is made of staccato and pizzicato passages; in the trio, there is a charming exchange between the two violins over a pedal note in the two lower instruments. The slow movement has been described as a "noble song of thanksgiving." The music begins quietly, but as it progresses it grows in passion. The finale arrives without a break with two strong chords in the four instruments. The first theme receives a strong build up, but the second theme is a serene melody. In the development, a stormy atmosphere is interrupted by a return of the beautiful sorrowful song of the first movement, this time in viola. After a restatement of the main theme of the finale, the movement ebbs away quietly.

1829. RONDO CAPRICCIOSO, for solo piano, op. 14.

CAPRICCIO BRILLIANT IN B MINOR, for piano and orchestra, op. 22.

The *Rondo capriccioso* is one of Mendelssohn's finest compositions for the piano. Its second half is in the gossamer and fanciful style of the Scherzo in the Octet and *A Midsummer Night's Dream Overture*. The first part, however, is in a sentimental and lyrical vein (Andante), in which a broad and expressive melody predominates. The sprightly and light-footed rondo capriccioso that follows seems to depict a dance of woodland sprites.

Like the *Rondo capriccioso,* the *Capriccio brilliant* has two sections. The first is a slow introduction in the key of the tonic, in which a sustained melody is accompanied by detached chords. The second part is fast (Allegro con fuoco), beginning with a vivacious melody that soon finds contrast in a sentimental one.

1830–1835. LIEDER OHNE WORTE (SONGS WITHOUT WORDS), eight books of pieces for solo piano:

op. 19: 1. E major. 2. A minor. 3. A major, "Jaegerlied." 4. A major. 5. F-sharp minor. 6. G minor, "Venezianisches Gondellied."

op. 30: 1. E-flat major. 2. B-flat minor. 3. E major. 4. B minor. 5. D major, 6. F-sharp minor, "Venezianisches Gondellied."

Op. 38: 1. E-flat major. 2. C minor. 3. E major. 4. A major. 5. A minor. 6. A-flat major, "Duetto."

Op. 53: 1. A-flat major. 2. E-flat major. 3. G minor. 4. F major. 5. A minor, "Volkslied." 6. A major.

Op. 62: 1. G major. 2. B-flat major. 3. E. minor, "Trauermarsch." 4. G major. 5. A minor, "Venezianisches Gondellied." 6. A major, "Fruehlingslied."

Op. 67: 1. E-flat major. 2. F-sharp minor. 3. B-flat major. 4. C major, "Spinnerlied." 5. B minor. 6. E major.

Op. 85: 1. F major. 2. A minor. 3. E-flat major. 4. D major. 5. A major. 6. B-flat major.

Op. 102. 1. E minor. 2. D major. 3. C major. 4. G minor. 5. A major. "Kinderstueck." 6. C major.

Some of Mendelssohn's most popular piano pieces—the *Spring Song,* for example—are found in this collection of forty-eight pieces. The happy term "song without words" was coined by Mendelssohn for a piano composition so lyric in style that it is, in essence, a song for that instrument. Mendelssohn's "songs without words" are graceful and charming pieces; but, compared with his more significant piano works, are essentially trifles, frequently written at a single sitting, and some published posthumously without the benefit of the composer's revisions. It should be noted that while each composition bears a descriptive title, these were not concocted by the composer but by his various publishers; the exceptions are the various *Venetian Boat Songs* and the *Duetto.*

The best of the "songs" are sentimental, descriptive, atmospheric, at times fanciful morsels, fresh in melodic and harmonic material, appealing for the easy and natural flow of the musical thought. Here are some of the most celebrated: *Hunting Song,* in A major, op. 19, no. 3; three *Venetian Gondola Songs,* in G minor, op. 19, no. 6, F-sharp minor, op. 30, no. 6, and A minor, op. 62, no. 5; *Duetto,* in A-flat major, op. 38, no. 6, a poignant love song; *May Breezes* and *Spring Song,* in G major and A major respectively, op. 62, nos. 1 and 6; and *Elegy* in D major, op. 85, no. 4.

In a general discussion of Mendelssohn's style and pianism in the *Songs Without Words,* Wilfrid Mellers wrote: "There is no pianistic feature that suggests the pressure of a new experience. . . . The tunes are habitually Andante, neither fast nor slow; neither operatic nor folk like. . . . In harmony and modulation [there is] . . . no breach with classical precedent." Mellers further points out "how far Mendelssohn is from Chopin and Schumann" by revealing that "the most successful pieces in the *Songs Without Words* tend to be those which approximate the sonata form."

1830. SYMPHONY NO. 5 IN D MAJOR, "REFORMATION," op. 107. I. Andante; Allegro con fuoco. II. Allegro vivace. III. Andante; Andante con moto; Allegro vivace; Allegro maestoso.

There is a good deal of confusion about Mendelssohn's symphonies. What today is accepted as his "first" symphony—that in C minor, op. 11 (1824)—was by no means the composer's first attempt at writing such a work. He had previously done a dozen symphonies for string orchestra; since these are juvenalia, essentially, they are not included in the listings of the composer's symphonic production. Of the five symphonies that are listed, only the last three are consistently played. The fifth of these, the *Reformation,* was actually written before the third (*Scotch*) and the fourth (*Italian*), but published after them. For this reason, in any chronological discussion of Mendelssohn's symphonies, the fifth, which was completed in 1830, must be discussed before the fourth (1833); and both of these must be treated before the third (1842).

Mendelssohn's Reformation Symphony came in 1830, written for a projected celebration in Germany of the tercentenary of the Augsburg Protestant Confession (the Lutheran creed as proposed in 1530 to the Diet of Augsburg). Bearing in mind the purpose of his symphony, Mendelssohn incorporated into the introduction of the first movement the "Dresden Amen" (which Wagner also used later in *Parsifal*); this was a hymn heard in the churches of Dresden according to Lutheran and Catholic liturgies. Some believe that Mendelssohn used this motive to symbolize the Roman Catholic Church; others feel he wanted to point up the divine spirit. Another religious element in this symphony is the quotation of Luther's famous chorale, "Ein' feste Burg," in the introduction to the finale.

The *Reformation Symphony* is actually in three movements, though its subdivisions would tend to indicate five. In the first movement, a soft, solemn phrase in lower strings and a proud statement by the brass and woodwind precede the presentation of the "Dresden Amen," quietly played by the strings. The fast section of the movement arrives with a forceful theme for full orchestra (except for trombones). This theme is developed dramatically, but the atmosphere soon becomes serene with the appearance of the lyrical second subject in the strings. After the first theme reappears in the development, the turmoil is revived, reaching a peak with a recollection of the "Dresden Amen." This portion of the symphony has often been interpreted as a struggle between two opposing forces, the church emerging triumphant over the secular.

The second movement is in reality a Scherzo, with two graceful subjects.

The first is heard in the initial section in woodwind and lower strings; the second emerges in the trio, in oboes over pizzicati bass.

The third movement starts off with a soaring song of liturgical cast in first violins. A second division in this movement is dominated by a quotation of the chorale, "Ein' feste Burg," in the flute. A quick syncopated figure in strings—the background for a repetition of the chorale melody in clarinet—introduces the third part of the movement. The full orchestra comes in with an exultant proclamation for the fourth and concluding section. A new idea is then given fugal treatment, followed by a second important idea in the wind, repeated by strings. The chorale melody in full orchestra brings the symphony to a triumphant conclusion.

1831. CONCERTO NO. 1 IN G MINOR, for piano and orchestra, op. 25. I. Molto allegro con fuoco. II. Andante. III. Molto allegro e vivace.

Mendelssohn completed two piano concertos; the first in G minor is the more celebrated. There are seven crescendo measures in the first movement before the piano appears with a dramatic octave passage. This leads into a stormy and romantic subject, the first important theme. When the orchestra takes it over, the piano provides the lyrical second subject over a staccato eighth-note accompaniment. The development of this material is free and rhapsodic. A fanfare in horn and trumpets brings on the second movement—a beautiful romanza for violas, cellos, double basses, bassoons, and horns. The piano restates this melody with some embellishments. Another fanfare brings on the finale, a rondo. The robust main theme is given by the solo piano. It later receives bravura treatment. The finale ends quietly with a recall of the sensitive lyrical second theme of the first movement.

1832–1833. CONCERT OVERTURES, for orchestra:
FINGAL'S CAVE (or HEBRIDES), op. 26.
MEERESSTILLE UND GLUECKLICHE FAHRT (CALM SEA AND PROSPEROUS VOYAGE), op. 27.
DIE SCHOENE MELUSINA (FAIR MELUSINA), op. 32.

Fingal's Cave (1832) was one of the works inspired by Mendelssohn's visit to Scotland in 1829. While going on foot through the Scottish Highland, he came upon the caverns of Staffa, which made such an impression upon him that then and there he wrote down twenty-one measures of music which he later used for his concert overture. The first version of the overture, completed in 1830, displeased him. The final version was played for the first time in London in 1832. Wagner later called it "one of the most beautiful pieces we possess. Wonderful imagination and delicate feeling are here presented with consummate art. Note the extraordinary beauty of the passage where the oboes rise above the other instruments with a plaintive wail, like sea winds over the sea."

The principal subject is heard without any preliminaries—in lower strings and bassoons. It portrays vividly the roll of the waves toward the mouth of the cave. After this subject has received extended treatment, the second theme, brighter in texture and mood, is presented by the clarinet. The development pays attention to the first theme, which once again receives prominence in the coda.

Two poems by Goethe provided the composer with the material for *Meeresstille und Glueckliche Fahrt.* The first, "Meeresstille" describes the stillness of the sea and the fear it strikes in the heart of the anxious mariner. In the second, "Glueckliche Fahrt," the mariner "looks alive" as the fog lifts, the sky becomes clear, the water becomes restful, and land looms in the distance. The motto theme of the overture is heard in the introductory Adagio in the basses. This is followed by a picture of the calm sea with full harmonies in the strings over accompanying winds. The sea voyage is launched by a melody for flute and wind over pizzicati strings. In the second section (Molto allegro vivace; Allegro maestoso), a beautiful melody for the cellos is prominent. The safe arrival is suggested in the coda (Allegro maestoso), the last three measures of which carry the boat safe to harbor.

The twentieth-century British composer, Sir Edward Elgar, quoted a theme from this overture in his *Enigma Variations* (thirteenth variation).

Die schoene Melusina (1833) started out as an overture which Mendelssohn wrote for an opera by another composer—Conradin Kreutzer. "I disliked it exceedingly, and the whole opera quite as much," Mendelssohn confessed to his sister, Fanny. He rewrote the overture, selecting that "portion of the subject which pleased me (exactly corresponding with the legend)." After completing the revision, Mendelssohn added with contentment: "I think [it] will be the best thing that I have done so far."

The legend that served as Mendelssohn's program relates how Melusina—in some versions a mermaid, in others, a fairy—extracts a promise from her husband, Count Raymond: he will permit her a complete day of seclusion once a week. On that day she undergoes transformation into a mermaid (or fairy), her punishment for having had her father entombed in a mountain. The husband's curiosity leads him to spy on his wife. Thus he witnesses her transformation. With a piercing cry, Melusina deserts her human form—and her husband—forever.

The graceful, undulating Melusina theme is heard in the clarinet as the overture opens. With a change of key, the music grows forceful; a strong subject identifying Count Raymond is given by the strings. The second main theme is a melody in the violins, over chords in strings and clarinet. In the development, a new thought is heard in the oboe. The coda is mainly concerned with the Melusina theme.

1833. SYMPHONY NO. 4 IN A MAJOR-MINOR, "ITALIAN," op. 90. I. Allegro vivace. II. Andante con moto. III. Con moto moderato. IV. Presto.

The *Italian* is identified as Mendelssohn's fourth symphony because that is its place among his published works. But in the date of composition, it comes between the so-called fifth, the *Reformation* (which see) and the third, the *Scotch* (which see).

During his twenty-first and twenty-second years, Mendelssohn traveled through Italy. The experience overwhelmed him; he poured out his excitement in one letter after another. Then he sought an outlet for his supercharged emotions through music, specifically through a symphony. He had no wish to write a programmatic work about Italy, its landscapes, or its people; all he wanted to do was to have his music reflect his own emotional responses.

The main subject of the first movement appears in the violins in the second measure. In its optimism and vitality it seems to echo Mendelssohn's ebullient spirits as he visits Italy for the first time. After this theme is enlarged and transformed, a second subject, much more sober and sedate, is presented by clarinets and bassoons. The development is initiated with an imitative episode in the strings; the two main themes then come in for detailed discussion.

The opening two bars of the slow movement were once described by Sir George Grove as "the cry of a muezzin from his minaret." But there is nothing in Mendelssohn's letters to suggest he had any such idea in mind; nor is there any justification in referring to this movement as a "pilgrim's march," as some annotators have done. The main melody is heard in oboe, clarinet, and violas. The violins then take it over, with flutes providing a contrapuntal embellishment. A second theme is later given by the clarinets.

The third movement is in the three-part structure of a scherzo or minuet. In the first section, the main thought consists of a delicate melody for the first violins. The middle trio features a sensitive passage for bassoons and horns.

It is only in the finale that there is a direct and intimate relationship between the music and the country that inspired it. This movement is a saltarello, a lively Italian folk dance, in which three main ideas are projected. All of them are equally lively. The first comes in the flutes after six introductory measures; and the second and third are shared by the first and second violins.

1834–1837. SONGS, for voice and piano:

"An die Entfernte," op. 71, no. 3; "Auf Fluegeln des Gesanges," op. 34, no. 2; "Gruss," op. 19a, no. 5; "Jagdlied," op. 84, no. 3; Lieblingsplaetzchen," op. 99, no. 3; "Nachtlied," op. 71, no. 6; "O Jugend," op. 57, no. 4; "Schilflied," op. 71, no. 4; "Volkslied," op. 47, no. 4.

Mendelssohn's most famous song is "On Wings of Song" ("Auf Fluegeln des Gesanges"), poem by Heine (1834). The same aristocratic lyricism and sensitive emotion that made this song so popular (both in its original version, and in various instrumental compositions) can be found in other important Mendelssohn songs.

"His songs," says Sir George Grove, "may be said to have introduced the

German Lied to England, and to have led the way for the deeper strains of Schumann, Schubert, and Brahms in English houses and concert auditoriums. No doubt the songs of those composers do touch lower depths of the hearer than Mendelssohn's do; but the clearness and directness of his music, the spontaneity of his melody, and a certain pure charm pervading the whole, have given a place of importance with the great public to some of his songs, such as 'Auf Fluegeln des Gesanges.' Others, such as 'Nachtlied' (1847) and 'Volkslied' (1839) and the 'Schilflied' (1847) are deeply pathetic; others, as the 'Lieblingsplaetzchen' (1841) are at the same time extremely original; others, as 'O Jugend' and 'Jagdlied' (1834) and 'An die Entfernte' (1847), the soul of gaiety. He was very fastidious in his choice of words, and often marks his sense of the climax by varying the last stanza in the accompaniment or otherwise, a practice which he was perhaps the first to adopt."

1835. ST. PAUL, oratorio for solo voices, chorus, and orchestra, op. 36.

Mendelssohn's first published choral work was the *Psalm* 115, op. 31 (1830). In 1833, he conceived the idea of writing his first oratorio, centering it around St. Paul, and concentrating on the martrydom of St. Stephen and on the conversion and later career of St. Paul. Mendelssohn prepared his own text from the Bible, consulting Pastor Julius Schubring on the arrangement and selection of the material. *St. Paul* was a huge success when it was played for the first time—at the Lower Rhine Festival in Duesseldorf, on May 22, 1836.

There are two sections. The first is essentially dramatic; the second is lyrical and contemplative. The overture opens with the Protestant chorale, "Wachet auf," in clarinets, bassoons, and lower strings. This is followed by an anticipation of the scene of Saul's conversion ("Saul, Saul Why Persecutest Me?"). The main part of the overture has for its main subject a fugal episode depicting the struggle of the convert's soul. A repetition of the chorale in the winds serves as the second theme. The fugal idea is expanded in the development. The overture ends with a loud restatement of the chorale melody, pointing up the victory of faith.

The oratorio opens with an elaborate chorus, "Lord! Thou Alone Art God." The martrydom of Stephen is then detailed, highlighted by Stephen's eloquent air, "Men, Brethren, and Fathers." After a shout by the chorus, "Take Him Away," the soprano sounds a warning in "Jerusalem Thou That Killest the Prophets." The stoning of St. Stephen is narrated in a poignant tenor recitative, which is succeeded by the lament for Stephen by the chorus, "Happy and Blest Are They." Saul now appears with the fiery air, "Consume Them All." There now comes a beautiful alto arioso, "But the Lord is Mindful of His Own" and a description of the conversion. Saul's effective prayer, "O God Have Mercy Upon Us," precedes a jubilant chorus with which this part ends, "Oh, Great Is the Depth of the Riches of Wisdom."

The second part opens with a five-part fugal chorus, "The Nations Are

Now the Lord's." Several effective choruses follow, including the contemplative "How Lovely are the Messengers" and the passionate, "Is This Who in Jerusalem?". After the chorale, "O Thou, the True and Only Light," a tenor recitative tells of the departure of Paul and Barnabas. The scene of the sacrifice at Lystra contributes two powerful choruses in "The Gods Themselves as Mortals" and "Oh, Be Gracious Ye Immortals." The Jews voice their wrath in "This Is Jehovah's Temple" and Paul takes pathetic leave of his brethren in "Be Thou Faithful Unto Death." The oratorio ends with two mighty choral episodes, "See What Love Hath the Father" and "Now Only Unto Him."

1836–1837. 6 PRELUDES AND FUGUES, for solo piano, op. 35: I. E minor-major. II. D major. III. B minor. IV. A-flat major. V. F minor. VI. B-flat major.

It is poetic justice to find some of the finest fugal writing in the Romantic period coming from Mendelssohn, who played such a decisive role in reviving Bach's music. But as Robert Schumann said, Mendelssohn adapted the structure and technique of the fugue to nineteenth-century taste. Amplifying on this point, Ernest Hutcheson said: "In the scholarly A major Fugue of the *Characterstuecke,* op. 7, he has trodden closely in Bach's footsteps. Now he goes farther, modernizing his counterpoint, diverging at times into a harmonic style, and handling the form with a new flow and freedom."

The best known of the six preludes and fugues is the first in E minor-major (1836). The prelude is in Mendelssohn's characteristic lyrical and elegant manner. The fugue begins softly, then, as Hutcheson has written, works up "through a long crescendo and accelerando to its climax, then breaking with superb effect into a majestic choral, finally subsiding to a serene return of the fugue theme and a pianissimo close."

The third prelude in B minor is a "delightful staccato etude"; the prelude and fugue in A-flat major are soul mates in that both are "continuously legato and cantabile"; and the prelude and fugue in F minor has a "sad and lovely" prelude contrasted with a "highly temperamental fugue."

1839. PIANO TRIO NO. 1 IN D MINOR, op. 49. I. Molto allegro e agitato. II. Andante con molto tranquillo. III. Scherzo. IV. Allegro assai appassionato.

The D minor is the more familiar of Mendelssohn's two piano trios, with enough charm and aesthetic appeal to maintain its popularity in the repertory. The first movement has both main subjects introduced by the cello. Structurally, this movement has special interest because in the recapitulation a new and unexpected development of the two major themes takes place. The second movement, says Andrew Porter, "is like one of the sweeter *Songs Without Words.*" The main melody has two parts, each introduced by a piano solo before being repeated by the violin. "There succeeds," says Porter, "a variant in B-flat minor, and then the tune returns tricked out in new finery." A single theme dominates the Scherzo movement, which has no trio. A gypsy-like tune in the violin brings on the finale. There are two other main thoughts, the second being a melody "in the same dactyllic rhythm as the first," and the third in B-flat "a first cousin to that of the E major *Song Without Words,* op. 33, no. 3, "with faster tempo but with the melody "underlain by similar religioso harmonies."

1839. RUY BLAS, concert overture for orchestra, op. 95.

In 1839, Mendelssohn was invited by the Theatrical Pension Fund in Leipzig to write an overture and romance for Victor Hugo's *Ruy Blas,* to be performed for charity. Though Mendelssohn regarded Hugo's play as "detestable and beneath contempt," he complied. The overture was played for the first time (on March 11, 1839) as the musical introduction to the play. It begins with four bars of stately music in brass and woodwind. After the principal theme has been foreshadowed in the strings, it is given by first violins and flutes. The introductory slow measures are then repeated, followed by a suggestion of the second theme, staccato in clarinet, bassoon, and cellos. All themes are then developed. The overture ends with an energetic coda.

1841. VARIATIONS SÉRIEUSES IN D MINOR, for piano, op. 54.

One of Mendelssohn's most significant works for the piano, the *Variations sérieuses* comprises a poignant melody rich in feeling, followed by eighteen variations. They traverse the gamut of emotion from levity to tragedy. Some of the finest variations are in slow tempo, plumbing profound sentiments or evoking exquisitely sensitive moods.

1842. SYMPHONY NO. 3 IN A MINOR-MAJOR, "SCOTCH," op. 56. I. Andante con moto; Allegro un poco agitato. II. Vivace non troppo. III. Adagio. IV. Allegro vivacissimo; Allegro maestoso assai.

Though the *Scotch* Symphony bears the number "3" among Mendelssohn's symphonies, it was written after the *Italian* and the *Reformation,* which by virtue of their later publications are numbered four and five respectively.

Like the *Fingal's Cave* Overture, the third symphony was the result of Mendelssohn's tour through Scotland during the spring of 1829. While visiting the old chapel at the Palace of Holyrood, he conceived the melody that would serve as the slow introduction to the first movement. Beyond this, Walter Dahms explains, "the landscape gave him his mood—the melancholy, the fog, the sea and the rocky coasts, the reserve and the dreaming of the people." But Mendelssohn carried the project of the *Scotch* Symphony around a long time before he could bring it to full realization. The final notes were put down in 1842, over a dozen years after that visit to Scotland.

The symphony has a unified concept. In fact, the first published score instructs that the symphony be played throughout without a single interruption.

The following analysis is by Walter Dahms: "The slow introduction of the first movement suggests that we are in the land of melancholy. . . . Then begins the mournful wailing of the principal theme. The strings announce it, the winds repeat, strengthen and raise it to a passionate outburst of the whole orchestra. . . . The excitement subsides . . . softly, with unending sadness, sobbing and suffused in tears, the second theme is heard. There is no contrast. It is in the same fundamental mood of melancholy. Inevitably the closing subject grips us to end the exposition. The development opens with the first motive of the main theme. Restlessly it pursues its course throughout the orchestra. The winds recall the noble melodic motive of a sub-theme which forms a counterpoint. . . . In gentle consolation, the second theme is heard in E major. . . . The recapitulation begins in A minor. There are no more surprises. The introductory Andante ends the movement harmoniously.

"The Scherzo follows the first movement. . . . This is a joyous piece, youthful, abandoned, high-spirited. Effervescently the principal theme is tossed from instrument to instrument. The second theme is of a somewhat precious character. It contends often with the principal theme in order to give the contrast that is necessary, in the absence of a Trio. . . . A short transition leads to the Adagio, in which the dream becomes a reality. The violins sing a melody of singular intimacy, beauty, and sweetness, a miracle of inspiration and form. Thrice in the course of the movement more energetic accents appear, but the gentler mood always supervenes.

"The last movement is filled with living, growing power. Yet the thematic material does not conflict with the whole tendency of the symphony. The poetic idea is retained in the storming of passion. Here the composer establishes a Scottish identity with a breezy melody in thirds and sixths, presented by the violins against chords in violas, bassoons, and horns. The second main idea is a lyrical passage by the woodwind over an organ point in first violins. A third theme, heard in full orchestra, has a martial character. It comes towards the end of the movement and has occasionally been identified as 'the gathering of the Scottish clans.'"

1843. A MIDSUMMER NIGHT'S DREAM, incidental music for voice, chorus, and orchestra, op. 61: I. Scherzo. II. "Over the Hill, Over Dale" and Fairy March. III. "Ye Spotted Snakes." IV. Melodrama. V. Intermezzo. VI. Melodrama. VII. Nocturne. VIII. Andante. IX. Wedding March. X. Allegro commodo and Marcia funèbre. XI. Dance of the Clowns. XII. Finale.

Seventeen years after he had written his remarkable Overture to *A Midsummer Night's Dream,* Mendelssohn was commissioned by King Frederick William of Prussia to write additional music for this same Shakespeare play, whose production was scheduled to open a new theater in Potsdam. Mendelssohn complied with twelve new numbers. The play, with Mendelssohn's music, was produced at Potsdam on October 18, 1843.

The first number in Mendelssohn's incidental music was the Scherzo. In its elf-like grace and mercurial style, it maintains the delicate mood and sensitive mobility of the youthful overture. This is an orchestral interlude between the first and second acts of the play, prefacing the scene where the audience penetrates Shakespeare's fairyland —the world of Puck, Oberon, and Titania. The two main melodies of the Scherzo appear in woodwind and unison strings. Thematic material from the Scherzo accompanying the stage action is repeated in the second number, followed by a fairy's march. The third number is a song for solo voice and chorus, "Ye Spotted Snakes." After some additional background music, there appears an Intermezzo following the second act. This music (Allegro appassionato) precedes the action in which Puck, through error, causes Lysander to fall in love with the wrong woman, Helene. Lysander's betrothed, Hermia, meanwhile is alone, lost and terrified in the forest. The next portion is an orchestral background for Titania's love scene with Bottom. This is followed by one of the most famous episodes in this score—the *Nocturne*, heard just before the third-act curtain. This is a romantic song for the horn, to which Puck, having restored Bottom to his real shape and form, sprinkles juice on Lysander's sleeping eyes to set things right again. The next musical selection is some more background music. Now comes the world famous *Wedding March,* second only in popularity to that of Wagner for wedding ceremonies. A trumpet fanfare introduces the dignified march music. There are two lyrical trio sections, between and after which the wedding march music is repeated. The three concluding parts are additional background music, a brief funeral march, a dance of clowns (Bergomask), and the finale to the concluding act.

1844. CONCERTO IN E MINOR, for violin and orchestra, op. 64. I. Allegro molto appassionato. II. Andante. III. Allegretto non troppo; Allegro molto vivace.

It took a number of years for Mendelssohn's only violin concerto to crystallize. The idea to do a concerto for the violinist, Ferdinand David, first occurred to Mendelssohn in 1838. But the entire work was not on paper until September 16, 1844. Even then, it had to undergo considerable revision, often with David's advice and criticism. The concerto in its final and definitive form was given in Leipzig on March 13, 1845, with Ferdinand David as soloist, and Niels Gade conducting.

It was Mendelssohn's original intention to have the three movements played without interruption. A single introductory measure precedes the entrance of the solo violin with the passionate first subject of the opening Allegro. The orchestra assumes this idea. A transitional passage in triplets for the solo instrument brings the soaring second theme, in clarinets and flutes over a sustained low G in violin. The violin repeats this melody, at which point the development section devotes itself to the first theme. The development culminates with the violin cadenza. Arpeggios in the solo instrument bring on the recapitulation.

There are eight measures of introduction before the solo violin is heard in the main melody of the slow movement. This is a lofty song, which midway in the movement finds contrast in an agitated section. But the song returns to conclude the movement as eloquently as it had begun. A fourteen-bar transition separates this slow movement from the finale. The violin engages a brilliant theme. Following some passage work in the solo instrument, the orchestra appears with the loud second theme. This is worked out in detail before a third important subject is heard in the solo violin. In the recapitulation, this third subject is placed contrapuntally in the orchestra against the first theme, restated by the solo violin. A forceful recall of the second theme precedes a brilliant coda.

1846. ELIJAH, oratorio for solo voices, chorus, and orchestra, op. 70.

Mendelssohn had hardly completed the writing of his first oratorio, *St. Paul,* in 1836, when the idea of a new oratorio began to haunt him, a work about Elijah. He once again called upon Pastor Julius Schubring to help him prepare a text. "I figured to myself Elijah as a grand, mighty prophet, such as we might again require in our own day," Mendelssohn told Schubring, "energetic and zealous, but also stern, wrathful and gloomy; a striking contrast to the court henchmen and popular rabble—in fact, in opposition to the whole world, and yet borne on angels' wings." Mendelssohn further explained the kind of music he was planning for such a subject. "I am particularly anxious to do justice to the *dramatic* element, and, as you say, no epic narrative must be introduced. If I might make one observation it is that I would fain see the dramatic element more prominent, as well as more vividly and sharply defined —appeal and rejoinder, question and answer, sudden interruptions, and so forth. Not that it disturbs me, for example, to have Elijah first speak of the assembling of the people and then forthwith address them; all such liberties are the natural privileges of oratorio representation. But I should like the representation itself to be as spirited as possible."

In another communication to Schubring, Mendelssohn reaffirmed his wish to make the oratorio as dramatic as possible. "In such a character as that of Elijah, like every one in the Old Testament, except perhaps Moses, it seems to me that the dramatic should predominate—the personages should be introduced as acting and speaking with fervor; not, in Heaven's name, to become mere musical pictures, but as inhabitants of a positive, practical world, such as we see in every chapter of the Old Testament."

For almost a decade, *Elijah* remained an unfulfilled dream. Then in 1845, the Committee of the Birmingham Music Festival invited Mendelssohn to direct its concerts the following season, and to prepare for this event a new oratorio or some other suitable composition. Mendelssohn declined to appear as conductor for all the performances, but accepted the offer for a new work.

Mendelssohn now went to work on *Elijah* for the Birmingham Festival, completing the first part and some material for the second by May 1846. By mid-July of the same year, *Elijah* was ready for rehearsals. The world première took place on August 26, 1846, the composer conducting. "The reception he met from the assembled thousands . . . was absolutely overwhelming," Julius Benedict reported. Four choruses and four arias had to be encored. "No work of mine," Mendelssohn wrote his brother, "ever went so admirably at the first performance, or was received with such enthusiasm both by musicians and the public as this. I never in my life heard a better performance—no, nor so good, and almost doubt if I can ever hear one like it again." Since then, *Elijah* has become a prime favorite with English audiences, second in popularity among the world's great oratorios only to Handel's *Messiah*.

Elijah has two sections. The first describes how the prophet brings on a drought in Israel to punish the people for deserting God for Baal. After performing the miracle of raising a widow's son from the dead, Elijah challenges the prophets of Baal to a contest to determine who the true God is. Elijah emerges victorious in this test and thus brings about doom to the false prophets. In the second part, Elijah is hounded by enemies out to destroy him. But under the protection of the Lord, he triumphs over them, and in the end is carried aloft to heaven in a flaming chariot.

Already in the opening of the oratorio we encounter the dramatic element Mendelssohn sought to emphasize throughout the work. Elijah announces in a stern recitative that the drought will be inflicted on the people. Only then do we get the overture, which in its dirge-like mood reflects the people's anguish. The overture ended, the people voice their terror in the first dramatic chorus, "Help, Lord! Wilt Thou Destroy Us?" The stirring duets, choruses, and recitatives that follow carry the drama on with telling theatrical effect. Climactic points are reached with the raising from the dead of the widow's son, which ends with the chorus "Blessed Are the Men that Are Free"; and in Elijah's pronouncement of doom to the priest of Baal, the recitative "O, Thou Who Makest Thine Angels Spirits", followed by the aria, "Is Not His Word like Fire?"

Lyricism is not completely sacrificed for the drama. It is found in such affecting arias as that of Obadiah, "If With All Your Hearts"; also in the prophet's prayer, "Lord God of Abraham," which is immediately followed by the poignant chorale, "Cast Thy Burden Upon the Lord." The first part concludes with the people's hymn of praise and joy, "Thanks Be to God!"

The second part opens with a brilliant soprano aria, "Hear Ye Israel," and soars to heights with Elijah's plea for death, "It is Enough." Other high moments are achieved by the angel's radiant aria, "Oh, Rest in the Lord," the tenor aria "Then Shall the Righteous Shine Forth as the Sun," and the exultant chorus, "Oh! Come, Every One that Thirsteth." The oratorio ends with a mighty choral outburst, "And then Shall Your Light Break Forth."

ROBERT SCHUMANN 1810–1856

The Romantic movement, set into motion by Berlioz, Weber, and Schubert, comes to full fruition with Robert Schumann. Like other Romantics, Schumann's romanticism expressed itself in a love for whimsy, the fantastic, the grotesque, and the imaginative. It found voice in his rapturous utterances, in his chameleon-like changes of images and moods, in his vivid imagery, and in his rhythmic impetuosity. But most of all, Schumann's romanticism reveals itself in the way literature affected his thinking and creativity. On few composers of his time did the written word carry such an impact. From boyhood on, he steeped himself in Romantic literature. His early idols were Jean Paul Richter, Byron, E. T. A. Hoffmann; later on, Heine and Eichendorff joined the circle of his favorites. Indeed, literature and music formed the dichotomy of Schumann's early life. For a while, he thought of becoming a poet rather than a musician. He ended up as one of the most poetic musicians of the Romantic era, his musical resources continually nourished and enriched by literary materials. "The poetic quality he seeks to achieve," says Hugo Leichtentritt, "is that ideal aspect, that elevation above the commonplace, that escape into a world of fantasy which is the desire and final aim of the romantic soul." But not Nature, nor landscapes, nor fairyland interested Schumann they way they did Weber and Mendelssohn. Schumann's concern was for what Leichtentritt describes as "the poetic exaltation, youthful exuberance, and soulful lyricism of romantic art. In short, he is concerned not so much with the frame, the outer aspects of this romantic feeling, as with its inner aspects."

At first Schumann directed himself exclusively to the piano, to miniatures, and to collections of miniatures within a larger framework. It is in his piano music that Schumann is at his greatest, most daring, and most original. It is in his piano music that the Romantic movement in music finds fulfillment. "Their exuberant quality," writes Daniel Gregory Mason of Schumann's piano masterworks, "their prodigal wealth of melodic invention, their rhythmic vigor and harmonic luxuriance, their absolutely novel pianistic effects, their curious undercurrent of fanciful imagery and extra-musical allusion, the peculiarly personal, even perverse idiom in which they are couched, all conspire to make them unique even among their author's works, and in some respects more happily representative of him than the later productions in which he was more influenced by conventional or borrowed ideals. In them we have the wild-flavored first fruits of his genius, fresh with all the aroma and bloom of unsophisticated youth."

Schumann was the only one of the great composers to cultivate one area fully before proceeding to the next. The piano occupied him virtually to the exclusion of all other media through 1839. Then he turned to the Lied. Here the poet in him and the musician found common ground. To the art song, Schumann brought Schubert's extraordinary gift for melody, poetic expression, nuance of feeling, and aptitude for word setting. But as Robert Haven Schauffler pointed out, he surpassed Schubert in "harmonic richness and subtlety, in atmospheric opulence, psychological verisimiltude, knowledge of poetry, and in the *Innigkeit* and fervor of his love Lieder."

The year of 1840 was basically Schumann's song period. Then having had his fill of whimsy, fantasy, and musical anagrams that had occupied his interests when writing for the piano—and with the extra-musical and poetical insights that dominated his songwriting—he veered toward a more objective beauty, a greater impersonality of expression and a more absolute approach to musical style and structure. "The whole elaborate machinery of allusion to extra-musical interests are forgotten," says Daniel Gregory Mason, "and the interest of the music itself becomes all in all." In 1841, Schumann became interested in the orchestra, producing his first symphony, the *Overture, Scherzo and Finale,* the first movement of the A minor Piano Concerto, and the first draft of the D minor Symphony. In 1842, he became involved with chamber music, completing three string quartets, the E-flat major Piano Quintet, and the E-flat major Piano Quartet.

Though he was less happy, less at ease in the larger structures, Schumann nevertheless filled his most significant chamber and orchestral compositions with the same kind of poetic beauty, flights of musical fancy, romantic ardor and intensity that place his piano music and songs in a class by themselves. For all his shortcomings as an orchestrator—shortcomings that led many musicians, including Mahler, to revise his symphonies—Schumann was, as George Szell once said of him, the founder of "the Romantic symphony, the inventor of not just lovely tunes, but of interesting novel designs of harmony and formal structure which have influenced and stimulated great composers after him."

Whatever his medium, Schumann was, as Szell said, "the greatest purely Romantic composer" and his music was "the exponent of the more affecting traits of German character, nobly representative of a people of *Dichter und Denker*. . . . The originality of his musical thought and design, his imagination and his warmth, his tenderness and his fire, his solemnity, and also his frolicsome boisterousness, the infinite variety of characters populating his musical stage, have secured Schumann a place in the heart of every sensitive musician and music lover."

Robert Schumann was born in Zwickau, Saxony, on June 8, 1810, the son of a bookseller. Composition began when he was seven, piano study a year or so later. By the time he was eleven, Schumann had completed several choral and orchestral compositions. Nevertheless, he was directed to law. After attending the Zwickau High School from 1820 to 1828, he entered the University of Leipzig in 1828; and in 1829, continued the study of law in Heidelberg. In the latter city, he started to absorb himself intensively with music study. By 1830, he had become convinced he wanted to be a musician rather than lawyer. Returning to Leipzig, he became a piano student of Friedrich Wieck, working under him with complete dedication and passionate intensity. He dreamed of becoming a virtuoso second to none. In an attempt to extend the flexibility of the fourth finger of his right hand he deviced a means of suspending it in a sling while employing the other fingers. This only led to a paralysis of the right hand in 1832, shattering all hopes of a concert career. He now decided to direct his musical interests into creative channels. After studying composition with Heinrich Dorn, he completed his first mature works for the piano in 1832, the *Abegg Variations, Papillons,* and the *Paganini Etudes.* He devoted himself to piano music for the next eight years, producing some of the his greatest music, masterworks that opened a new epoch for piano literature: *Carnaval, Kreisleriana, Études symphoniques, Fantaisiestuecke,* and the C major Fantasy.

Even though deeply involved in creativity, he found the enthusiasm and energy to embark on other musical endeavors. In 1833, he helped organize a group of idealistic young musicians into the Davidsbuendler, its aim to destroy Philistinism in music and promote the highest ideals in music. One year later, he founded a music journal, the first important one in Germany—the *Neue Zeitschrift fuer Musik,* which he edited until 1844. Here Schumann revealed himself to be a penetrating music critic, a valiant fighter on behalf of new music and young composers. It was through these columns that the genius of Brahms and Chopin was first recognized. Later on, in 1843, he also distinguished himself as a teacher, becoming a professor of piano and composition at the then newly organized Conservatory of Music in Leipzig.

In 1836, Schumann fell in love with the sixteen-year-old daughter of his former teacher, Friedrich Wieck—Clara, herself a remarkable pianist. Since Wieck wanted nothing to interfere with her career, and since he did not want her to marry a musician, Wieck did everything in his power to keep the lovers apart. For four years, Robert Schumann and Clara had to seek each other out through hurried and secret meetings, through furtive exchanges of correspondence. Then Schumann went to the law courts to establish his legal right to marry the woman of his choice. The suit proved successful: Clara and Robert Schumann were married on September 12, 1840.

Schumann's marital happiness inspired an unprecedented fertility in composition. In 1840, he wrote almost one hundred and fifty songs, many of them expressing his love and tenderness for his wife. In 1841, he turned to orchestral music for the first time; and in 1842, to chamber music.

The deterioration of his health, combined with increasing manifestations of nervous disorders, compelled him in 1844 to give up all activities except composing. For a number of years, he lived in retirement in Dresden. Then, in 1850, he took on the post of general music director of the city of Duesseldorf. But the further deterioration of his physical and mental resources compelled him to resign in 1853. After an unsuccessful attempt to commit suicide by drowning, Schumann was confined to an insane asylum in Endenich, near Bonn, Germany. He died there on July 29, 1856.

1830–1833. COMPOSITIONS FOR SOLO PIANO:
Abegg Variations (*Thème sur le nom Abegg*), variations in F major, op. 1.
Papillons (*Butterflies*), op. 2.
Études after Caprices by Paganini, op. 3.
Six Intermezzi, op. 4.

Impromptus on a Theme by Clara Wieck, op. 5
Toccata, op. 7

The *Abegg Variations* (1830) was Schumann's first published composition. Here he already began to indulge his love for musical anagrams. Meta Abegg, who gave the work its title, was a young lady whom the composer met at a ball. He wrote this composition for, and dedicated it to, her. The opening theme is derived from the letters in her name, consisting as it does of the notes "A," "B" (German for B-flat), "E," "G," and "G." The musical interest is derived from the fact that this piece is a rare example for its time of variations based on an original melody rather than some popular tune, operatic aria, or a subject by some other composer. Noteworthy, too, is the dynamic writing in the finale, consisting of cross-accents, syncopations, and rapidly changing rhythms.

Papillons, Schumann's second opus (1832) consists of a dozen little pieces. Schumann's inspiration came from Jean Paul Richter's *Flegeljahre*. The gentle opening melody, with its rise and descent, was repeated by the composer in the finale. (Several years later Schumann used it again, in the "Florestan" section of *Carnaval.*) Several pieces now describe a carnival or ball, once again in anticipation of *Carnaval*. The eighth and tenth pieces are rooted in Austrian and German peasant dances, while the eleventh is a polonaise. The finale uses the famous seventeenth-century dance tune, the Grossvatertanz (which Schumann would borrow for *Carnaval*).

In his opus 3 (1832), Schumann makes a literal, but nevertheless brilliant, transcription for piano of six Paganini caprices for solo violin. The six Intermezzi, op. 4 (1832), utilize the song form, each being based on two melodic ideas, the first repeated after the second. The *Impromptus on a Theme by Clara Wieck,* op. 5 (1833), is based on a charming little tune by Schumann's beloved Clara, preceded by a ground bass. The Toccata, op. 7, was originally conceived in 1830, but revised three years later. This is brilliant virtuoso music within the sonata form. The basic subject is a short four-note figure developed in thirds, sixths, and broken chords, building up a powerful momentum all the while.

1834. ÉTUDES SYMPHONIQUES (SYMPHONIC ETUDES), for piano, op. 13.

In 1834, Schumann looked over a composition by Baron von Fricken. (He was the father of Ernestine, with whom Schumann was briefly in love and who appears in *Carnaval* as "Estrella.") The work was a theme and variations for flute. The theme so impressed Schumann that he decided to use it in a major work, the starting point of his own variations. These variations, of which there are nine, were conceived by Schumann as a series of etudes. The variations are followed by two intermezzi and a finale.

The theme appears at once—a stately descending melody in chords. In most of the etudes that follow, it reappears in varied forms and guises. Often the transformation is so radical that the physiognomy of the basic melody is not always recognizable. Variants of the theme are found in the first two etudes. In the first, the theme, assigned to the bass, is virile and incisive; in the second, it expands into a broadly poetic song. The third is in the nature of a technical exercise. In the fourth and fifth, canonic technique is utilized; while in the sixth, the basic melody returns for full presentation. A completely new lyrical thought, with no relation to the basic melody, is heard in the seventh etude. The eighth, by contrast, once again assumes the bravura of an etude. In the ninth, the theme is suggested in rapid scherzando chords. Fuller staccato chords appear in the first of the two intermezzi, while the theme is provided an expressive countermelody in the second. The composition ends with stirring march music. This subject comes from an opera air by Heinrich Marschner. The air is "Du stolze England," and the opera is *Der Templar und die Judin,* based on Sir Walter Scott's *Ivanhoe.* The reason why Schumann suddenly interpolates this Marschner melody is because the work as a whole was dedicated to the distinguished English musician, William Sterndale Bennett, and Bennett was an admirer of Marschner's operas.

1835. CARNAVAL (CARNIVAL), for piano, op. 9: 1. Préambule. 2. Pierrot. 3. Arlequin. 4. Valse noble. 5. Eusebius. 6. Florestan. 7. Coquette. 8. Réplique. Sphinxes. 9. Papillons. 10. A.S.C.H.—S.C.H.A. (Lettres dansantes). 11. Chiarina. 12. Chopin. 13. Estrella. 14. Reconnaissance. 15. Pantalon et Colombine. 16. Valse allemande. 17. Intermezzo: Paganini. 18. Aveu. 19. Promenade. 20. Pause. 21. Marche des Davidsbuendler contre les Philistins.

Early in 1834, Schumann fell in love with Ernestine von Fricken, born in the Bohemian town of Asch. The lady, and her native town, play an important role in *Carnival.* The work is a large, unified structure built out of little segments, played without interruption. Some of these pieces are descriptive; some are nostalgic; some are autobiographical; and some are witty or whimsical. All of them are intended to portray a gay carnival. In 1832, Schumann had described a carnival in *Papillons,* op. 2 (which see). Schumann regarded *Carnival* as "a fuller *Papillons.*"

"Little scenes composed for the piano on four notes" is a subtitle that appears in the published score. The "four notes" are "A-flat" (in German "As"), E-flat (in German "Es"), C, and B-natural (in German, "H"). Putting these four notes together we can spell the town of Asch. These four letters assumed still greater significance to the composer when he discovered they were the only ones in his own names capable of being translated into musical notes.

In *Carnival,* Schumann built three musical motives out of the four notes, in three different combinations: A-flat, E-flat, C, and B-natural, spelling "Asch"; in reverse, E-flat, C, B-natural and A-flat, giving the musical letters in Schumann's name in proper sequence; and a three-note variant of "Asch," A-flat, C, B-natural. All three motives are given in a brief section that Schumann identified as "Sphinxes" and that is inserted between the eighth and ninth pieces. (This part is usually omitted in performances today.) All but three or four of the other movements are constructed from these three motives.

Even though the titles of the individual movements (as well as the name of the composition as a whole) were added by the composer only *after* he had written the music, they provide a valuable clue to their programmatic content. The opening piece is a preamble, a brilliant, gay picture of a carnival. "Pierrot" and "Arlequin" are two clowns long popular in European masquerades, the second and third episodes describe them vividly. A sentimental waltz tune in "Valse noble" is followed by two self-portraits in "Eusebius" and "Florestan." These are two imaginary characters invented by Schumann to identify two opposing facets of his personality: his dreamy, introspective self (Eusebius) and his stormy, temperamental personality (Florestan). In "Coquette" a flirtatious girl is described, while in "Réplique" a receptive male responds to her coquetry. After "Sphinxes," there comes a quicksilver movement depicting the flight of butterflies. (This movement must not be confused with the earlier *Papillons,* op. 2.) A brief atmospheric episode, "Lettres dansantes," is followed by "Chiarina," a poignant character study of the little girl who would some day become Schumann's wife. A tribute to Chopin, in a Chopin-like style, characterizes that master. The mood becomes romanticized in "Estrella," in which Schumann pays tribute to his lady love, Ernestine von Fricken. After the joy of reunion has been exuberantly painted in "Reconnaissance," Schumann presents two more portraits, this time of characters famous in Italian comedy—Pantalon and Colombine. Dance music predominates in "Valse allemande"; virtuoso music, in a brief homage to Paganini. A beautiful melody unfolds in "Aveu"; a slow waltz is prominent in "Promenade"; and stormy music surges into a powerful climax in "Pause." The final section is the march of the Davidsbuendler against the Philistines. The Davidsbuendler, or League of David, is an imaginary music society created by Schumann to promote modern music and combat musical Philistinism. In this vigorous march music, Schumann proclaims the victory of idealism and truth over materialism and chicanery. A briet quotation from the famous German folk dance, the Grossvatertanz, is here interpolated to represent the Philistines.

On June 4, 1910, the Ballet Russe in Paris presented *Carnival* as a ballet. The choreography was by Michel Fokine. It has since acquired a permanent place in ballet repertory. The orchestration was the work of four famous Russian composers: Rimsky-Korsakov, Liadov, Glazunov, and Nicolas Tcherepnine. Occasionally, this orchestral version is given at symphony concerts.

1836. FANTASY IN C MAJOR, for piano, op. 17.

The plan to erect a monument to Beethoven in Bonn, Germany, led Schumann to plan a major piano work, the proceeds to be used for the fund. Schumann's first thought was a "grand sonata" to be entitled *Ruins, Trophies,*

Palms. The project to raise money for the memorial collapsed, to remain neglected for almost a decade. But this did not keep Schumann from proceeding with his composition. He soon decided to abandon the sonata structure and descriptive titles, and to call his work simply a "Fantasy." To Clara Wieck, then his sweetheart but later his wife, he explained in 1838: "I do not think I ever wrote anything more impassioned than the first movement. It is a profound lament about you. You can understand the Fantasy only if you transport yourself back to the unhappy summer of 1836 when I resigned you. Now I have no reason to compose in so miserable and melancholy a way." Schumann even suggested that a theme in the first section was intended to represent Clara.

When the Fantasy was published in 1839, it was dedicated not to Clara but to Franz Liszt. Atop the score Schumann fixed a poetic motto by Schlegel which read: "Through all the tones resounding through earth's many-hued dream a soft tone threads its way for him who secretly listens."

The Fantasy has three sections played without interruption. The composer indicated that the first part was to be played with "passion and fantasy throughout." A throbbing phrase over a flowing accompaniment persists throughout this first section. This is built up with considerable stress, though slower sections introduce volatile changes of mood, sometimes of a peaceful nature, sometimes in the plangent tones of a lamentation. The second part (Moderato con energia) is march music with monumental sonorities, striking modulations, and even discords. "The march," Clara explained after seeing the manuscript, "is like a triumphal pageant of warriors returning from battle and at the A-flat major I imagine young maidens from the village, attired in white and crowning with laurel the kneeling heroes." The third and concluding part (Lento sostenuto; Un poco più mosso) is a dreamy nocturne which sustains a poetic, and at times even an elegiac, atmosphere almost to the end. Momentarily, a climax is built up, but almost at once the fever subsides and the composition ends in quiet revery.

1837. DAVIDSBUENDLERTAENZE (DANCES OF THE LEAGUE OF DAVID), suite for piano, op. 6.

The "Davidsbund" in the title, of course, refers to the imaginary music society Schumann created to combat sham and artifice in music and to promote the highest ideals. The second half of the title, the "Dances," is a misnomer. The eighteen pieces in this set are not dances at all, but a series of dialogues between the two characters whom Schumann devised to represent his gentle and dreamy personality (Eusebius) and his passionate and stormy one (Florestan). Indeed, in the original edition of this work, Schumann emphasized the roles of Eusebius and Florestan by setting the notes "F" (for Florestan) and "E" (for Eusebius) at the end of each piece. These characters are also found in two verbal notations in the score. Following the eighth number, Schumann wrote: "Herewith Florestan made an end, and his lips quivered painfully." After Number 18, he added, "quite superfluously Eusebius remarked as follows: but all the time great bliss spoke from his eyes."

A motto appears at the head of the score reading: "Delight is linked with pain, forever and ever. In Joy, remain devout. In Woe, never lose courage."

The so-called "dances" pass from gaiety to sorrow, from introspection to an outpouring of love. "The alternation of humor and revery," said Robert Haven Schauffler, "of high spirits and quiet dreams of love was identified in Schumann's mind with the festive doings on the eve before a wedding, which the Germans call a *Polterabend*." Schumann himself explained that these pieces represented "many marriage thoughts. They originated in the most joyful excitement that I can ever recall. . . . If ever I was happy at the piano, it was while composing these."

The *Davidsbuendlertaenze* ends with the striking of a clock to mark the end of festivities. In the last "dance," the clock striking is represented by twelve low C's signifying midnight.

1837. FANTAISIESTUECKE (FANTASY PIECES), for piano, op. 12. 1: Des Abends. 2. Aufschwung. 3. Warum? 4. Grillen. 5. In der Nacht. 6. Fabel. 7. Traumeswirren. 8. Ende von Lied.

Schumann identified the two facets of his personality as Eusebius (the dreamy self) and Florestan (the passionate self). He intended the eight pieces of the *Fantaisiestuecke* to reflect this dual personality. In the first four pieces, Eusebius alternates with Florestan; in the last four, they are blended together in each of the numbers. It is interesting to note that Schumann wrote the titles for the respective sections *after* he had completed the music.

The first piece, "Evening," is a gentle picture of dusk. By contrast, "Flight of Fancy" is stormy music. The gentle questioning, and the inconclusive answer, in "Why?" precedes the caprice of "Whims." There is passion together with nocturnal calm in "In the Night," which Schumann intended as an interpretation of the story of Hero and Leander. Rich veins of humor are tapped in "Fable," together with placid narrative. A stirring rhythmic drive sweeps through the pages of "Tangled Dreams." The last number, "Song's End," was described by Schumann as a mingling of wedding and funeral bells. "At the time," he wrote Clara, "I thought: well in the end it all resolves itself into a jolly wedding. But at the close, my painful anxiety about you returned."

1838. KINDERSCENEN (SCENES FROM CHILDHOOD), suite for piano, op. 15: I. Von fremden Laendern und Menschen. II. Curiose Geschichte. III. Hasche-Mann. IV. Bittendes Kind. V. Glueckes Genug. VI. Wichtige Begebenheit. VII. Traeumerie. VIII. Am Camin. IX. Ritter von Steckenpferd. X. Fast zu ernst. XI. Fuerchtenmachen. XII. Kind im Einschlummern. XIII. Der Dichter spricht.

Because Clara Schumann once told her beloved Schumann that in many ways he was just like a child, the composer decided to tap this creative vein by producing a suite about childhood. These pieces are not *for* children. Schumann would produce such a composition a decade later in *Album fuer die Jugend.* On the contrary—these are sophisticated and mature descriptive works about a child's world seen through the eyes of an adult. Schumann described them as "peaceful, tender, and happy." On another occasion he remarked: "In my compositions I myself have grown gayer, mellower, more melodious. Perhaps you have already found this out in the *Kinderscenen.*"

In the first piece, "From Strange Countries," a broad and expressive melody is superimposed on broken chords. "Curious Stories" places one subject in dotted rhythm against a second with flowing quavers. "Blind Man's Buff" has rhythmic vitality and dramatic sforzandos. "Questioning Child" makes effective use of an unresolved dominant seventh for its ending. "Quite Happy" is also unusual in technique, this time in tonality, which lapses from D major to F major. "Important Event" introduces a sober episode. "Dreaming", or "Traeumerie," is undoubtedly the most popular piece in this set, familiar in various transcriptions. It is a revery as gentle as the twilight hour. "At the Log Fire" is primarily a mood picture. This is followed by the picturesque "The Rocking Horse Knight" and the syncopations and off-beat melody of "Almost Too Serious." "Frightening" brings us into the child's world of evil spirits and hobgoblins through sforzandos and rapid changes of tempo. In "Child Falling Asleep," the nebulous zone between waking and sleeping is suggested by the sudden change of key from E minor to E major. The closing measures suggest the gradual closing of the eyes. In the concluding part, "The Poet Speaks," Schumann addresses himself directly to the child with a recitative-like melody; he is here sharing his own fancies and dreams with his little audience.

1838. KREISLERIANA, for piano, op. 16.

Kapellmeister Johannes Kreisler was a character created by E. T. A. Hoffmann in his fantastic tales. Kreisler was, in Schumann's description, an "eccentric, wild, clever conductor" who became involved in mad adventures and strange hallucinations. The tales impressed Schuman, ever partial as he was to the bizarre, the fantastic, and the grotesque. In addition, he identified himself with Kreisler. For the latter reason, *Kreisleriana* perhaps gives us a deeper and profounder insight into the composer's complex and many-sided personality than do most of his other works. This music, as Robert Haven Schauffler notes, bring us "close to this sudden and startling manic-depressive alternations and contrasts; desperate, brooding, melancholy, wild exaltation, a frantic soul straining to free itself, the joy of a delighted child, the querulousness of a spoiled boy who cannot brook contradiction.

Kreisleriana is made up of eight fantasies. Each is a self-sufficient piece by itself; however, each bears such an intimate spiritual and emotional relationship to the others that it can be best understood within the over-all context. By utilizing the rhythms from the third and sixth pieces in the last one, Schumann was able to realize unity of design. The fantasies alternate the passionate moods of Florestan (Nos. 1, 3, 5, 7) with the poetic nature of Eusebius (Nos. 2, 4, 6). "In its romantic meaning," explains André Boucourechliev, "the world is closer to 'nightmare' and 'hallucination' than to 'fantasy.' There was already the agitation of a feverish foreboding in the very first of the eight pieces. A calmer melodic episode followed, full of inward quality, interrupted by two short interludes; the violence of the one, and the volatile rapidity of the other, vanished on the return of the melodic *motif*." The third fantasy has powerful rhythmic drive, while the fourth is pervaded by a soothing calm. Then," continues Boucourechliev, "after the changing rhythms, brought together with such violence, followed the glorious melody in the sixth piece, one of the most Schumannesque, and one of the most amazing in the whole of piano literature. The theme of the last piece glided into it like a warning. The desperate character which the lyrical pages of *Kreisleriana* assumed, in obsessive rhythms of the third, the eighth, and also the seventh pieces, in which there palpitated the 'savage love' of which Schumann had spoken, revealed, in one of its key works, what was most accomplished and most tragic in German Romanticism."

1838. NOVELLETTEN, for piano, op. 21.

The "Novellette" is a Schumann concoction. It is a short romantic piece that seems to be telling a story; the form is fluid and flexible. Schumann wrote eight such pieces that, he explained, are "closely connected" and were written "with great enjoyment and are on the whole light and superficial, excepting one or two sections where I go deeper."

Kathleen Dale explains: "These pieces are resplendent with a multitude of brilliant ideas presented in bold and effective pianistic terms." The most popular is the first, which offers a strong march-like melody in the initial section, and an opulent melody in the trio part. The most ambitious of these pieces is the last—so spacious in structure that it assumes the character of a suite. This composition consists of two scherzos, each with two trios. We encounter here two lyrical passages, one with the personality of a ballade, and the other of a Lied.

Other Novelletten of particular interest are the third and sixth, both of them excursions into vivacity and the fantastic; the fourth, which Schumann said was "in the spirit of a ball" and which highlights delightful waltz music; and the seventh, a spirited scherzo. The ninth number in *Bunteblaetter,* op. 99, is also a Novellette.

1838. SONATA NO. 2 IN G MINOR, for piano, op. 22. I. So rasch wie moeglich. II. Andantino. III. Sehr rash und markiert. IV. Presto.

Schumann wrote three piano sonatas. The first, in F-sharp minor, op. 11, was completed in 1835; the third, in F minor, op. 14, was written between 1835 and 1836. Between them comes the most popular of this group, the G minor Sonata. This work was done in 1833; but in 1838, Schumann replaced the final movement with a new one.

The first-movement opening presents a tempestuous subject, which the composer said had to be played "as fast as possible." (It is amusing to note that later on, in the coda, Schumann indicates a tempo "faster still" and after that "still faster.") If this first theme represents Florestan, then the second subject is Eusebius in its flight to a dream world. The slow movement —an intimate revelation—is a conversion to the piano of one of the composer's early unpublished songs, "Im Herbste," written in 1828. The third-movement Scherzo has a four-measure introduction. This is followed by an unusual theme in which three phrases are each in a different beat. The finale begins tempestuously, contains a second subject no less passionate, and ends with an electrifying "quasi cadenza, prestissimo."

1839. COMPOSITIONS FOR SOLO PIANO:

Arabeske in C major, op. 18.

Humoreske in B-flat major, op. 20.

Faschingsschwank aus Wien (*Carnival Jest from Vienna*), op. 26. I. Allegro. II. Romanze. III. Scherzino. IV. Intermezzo. V. Finale.

Three Romances, op. 28. I. B-flat minor. II. F-sharp major. III. B major.

Schumann regarded the Arabeske condescendingly, saying that he wrote it as a salon piece to please the Viennese ladies. Nevertheless, it is one of Schumann's most popular short pieces for the piano. Its tender main melody is followed by two contrasting secondary themes, each in a different key. The coda maintains interest through the introduction of fresh material.

The *Humoreske* is more original. Here Schumann departs radically from the usual concept of a "Humoresque," as a slight, whimsical piece of music. Schumann's is neither slight nor whimsical. "This live-long week," he wrote to Clara, "I've sat at the piano and composed and written and laughed and cried altogether. All this you will find beautifully depicted in my opus 20." The prevailing mood, as this quotation suggests, is melancholia. In place of the circumscribed structure usually encountered in Humoresques, Schumann used a five-movement frame, played without interruption. None of these five pieces were given descriptive titles. Structurally, notes Kathleen Dale, the *Humoreske* is "invested with the attributes of a rondo form in that one or two of the sections recur in part or in whole, albeit at regular intervals.

Faschingsschwank aus Wien, described by Schumann as a "jest," was an attempt to record his impressions of a Viennese carnival, which he had enjoyed during a visit to Vienna in 1838. The work has five sections played without interruption. The bustle of the carnival is reproduced in the first part; this section is made up of folk melodies and rhythms. One of the reasons why Schumann looked upon this work as a "jest" is the fact that he interpolated into this first part a few bars of the French national anthem, the "Marseillaise," which at that time was forbidden to be played in Austria. A romantic episode is then succeeded by a scherzo filled with electrifying virtuoso passages. An intermezzo comes next, with a poetic melody soaring above a triplet accompaniment. The work ends with a finale, whose dynamic rhythms, incandescent harmonies, and sweeping passages reveal that the carnival is at its peak of excitement and abandon.

Schumann regarded his three piano Romances highly, placing them in the same exalted class as the *Kreisleriana,* the *Fantaisiestuecke,* and the Novelletten. Here is how Robert Haven Schauffler described these compositions: "The first is full of Schumannian quality. The start shows what he could do with extreme melodic simplicity. The second is the justly popular favorite. . . . The luscious 'cello melody,' embedded in a harp-like filigree, and tenderly answered as if by the voices of violins, makes a piece of an *Innigkeit* unusual even for Schumann. . . . The third Romance, with its two intermezzi, is longer and more elaborate, but less deeply satisfying than its brothers."

1840. INDIVIDUAL SONGS, for voice and piano:

"Die beiden Grenadiere," op. 49, no. 1; "Du bist wie eine Blume," op. 25, no. 24; "Der Himmel hat eine Traene geweinet," op. 37, no. 1; "Liebeslied," op. 51, no. 5; "Die Lotosblume," op. 25, no. 7; "Der Nussbaum," op. 25, no. 3; "Sehnsucht," op. 35, no. 5; "Stille Traenen," op. 35, no. 10; "Wanderlust," op. 35, no. 3; "Widmung," op. 25, no. 1.

Despite Schumann's lifelong passion for literature—and his particularly sensitive response to German Romantic poetry—he did not turn to writing songs until after a decade of creative activity; not before he had produced his remarkable literature for the piano. Under the stimulus of his emotional fulfillment through his marriage to Clara, Schumann sought a medium through which to pour the feelings of an overflowing heart, and he found it in song. "Clara," he exclaimed once he began uniting his musical genius to his love of poetry, "what a joy it is to write for the voice, a joy I have lacked too long!" And later he added: "I should like to sing myself to death like a nightingale."

Of the two hundred and fifty or so songs he produced, almost half were written in the year of his marriage (1840), and the majority of these are love songs. Though he wrote songs later in life, he never quite equaled the spontaneity, ardor, imagination, invention, and variety of the songs of 1840. Some of these are strophic, others are through-composed. At times the feeling is sensual and passionate, as in "Widmung." At times the mood is calm and the feeling remote, as in "Liebeslied," where the serene vocal line hovers gently over deep sonorities in the piano. Sometimes an indefinable sadness is introduced, as in "Stille Traenen" and "Sehnsucht." There are times when the tone painting becomes literal—the music imitating the whirring of a spinning wheel, the movement of a boat in Venetian waters, the roll of wagon wheels.

There are songs in which a simply projected melody for the voice is enough to catch the essence of a poem: "Du bist wie eine Blume" (possibly the most exquisite setting this Heine poem ever received) and "Wanderlust." There are other songs in which the lyrical line must be shared by voice and piano for proper effect, as in "Der Nussbaum." And there are songs in which the accompaniment assumes first importance in projecting the mood or emotion, as in "Der Himmel hat eine Traene geweinet." Some songs gain their effect through subtle key or harmonic changes. In "Die Lotosblume" we confront a magical transition from C major to A-flat midway, while throughout the rest of the song the serene melody moves gracefully over rapid changes in the harmony.

C. Hubert Parry emphasizes that Schumann always "looked to the poet's conception to guide his own inspiration." He continues: "Everything available was made to minister to the purpose of intensifying the design, thought, and meter of the poet by the music. The piano part and the voice part had well-balanced functions. The voice did all that was possible in the way of melodious declamation, and the accompaniment supplied color, character, rhythm and all that must necessarily fall to its share, in the most perfect manner possible. Moreover, Schumann, by nature a poet himself, seized the purpose and spirit of the poems he set with an astonishingly powerful grip, and conveyed infinite shades and varieties of meaning in forms which are almost always perfect works of art in detail and in entirety. He expressed with equal success pathos, passion, bitterness, humor, joy, exultation, and even gaiety and sarcasm."

"The Two Grenadiers" is not only Schumann's most celebrated dramatic ballad, but one of his most popular songs in any style. It opens with a 4/4 martial strain, lapses into a tragic statement when the soldier hears the sorrowful news of Napoleon's defeat, and finally rises to a compelling climax with a quotation from the "Marseillaise."

1840. SONG CYCLES, for voice and piano:

LIEDERKREIS, op. 24: 1. Morgens steh' ich auf. 2. Es treibt mich hin. 3. Ich wandelte unter den Baeumen. 4. Lieb, Liebchen. 5. Schoene Wege meiner Leiden. 6. Warte, warte, wilder Schiffsmann. 7. Berg und Burgen schau'n herunter. 8. Anfangs wollt' ich fast verzagen. 9. Mit Myrthen und Rosen.

FRAUENLIEBE UND LEBEN, op. 42: 1. Seit ich ihn gesehen. 2. Er, der herrlichste von allen. 3. Ich kann's nicht fassen. 4. Du Ring an meinem Finger. 5. Helft mir, ihr Schwestern. 6. Suesser Freund. 7. An meinem Herzen. 8. Nun hast du mir den ersten Schmerz getan.

DICHTERLIEBE, op. 48: 1. Im wunderschoenen Monat Mai. 2. Aus meinen Traenen. 3. Die Rose, die Lilie. 4. Wenn ich in deine Augen seh'. 5. Ich will meine Seele. 6. Im Rhein, im heiligen Strome. 7. Ich grolle nicht. 8. Und wuessten's die Blumen. 9. Das ist ein Floeten und Geigen. 10. Hoer' ich das Liedchen klagen. 11. Ein Jungling liebt ein Maedchen. 12. Am leuchtenden Sommermorgen. 13. Ich hab' im Traum geweinet. 14. Allnaechtlich in Traume. 15. Aus alten Maerchen winkt es. 16. Die alten, boesen Lieder.

Some of Schumann's greatest songs can be found in his three monumental song cycles, each devoted to a single poet. The *Liederkreis* and *Dichterliebe* are settings of poems by Heine; *Frauenliebe und Leben,* of poems by Chamisso.

"Heine," says Martin Cooper, "was the ideal poet for Schumann, not only because a certain spiritual affinity existed between them, showing itself in the deliberate cultivation of sharply contrasted emotional moods within a single lyric; but also because of the conciseness and point of his style."

The *Liederkreis,* op. 24, is Schumann's first significant production within the song form and, as André Boucourechliev wrote, "allows us to follow Schumann's first footsteps in his new musical world." His personal style, continued Boucourechliev, is already apparent in the third song of this cycle, "Ich wandelte unter den Baumen." "The song began with a prelude rich in polyphony, and with the curve of the first vocal phrase was revealed that convergence of the voice and piano, equal but independent, which is the hallmark of Schumann's Lieder." Boucourechliev singles out the other distinguished numbers in this cycle of love songs. "In 'Warte, warte wilder Schiffsmann' he made full use of his dramatic sense of contrast and accent, and an echo of this song of farewell persisted, groaning, into its long postlude. In the last song of the cycle, 'Mit Myrthen und Rosen,' Schumann grappled with a larger and already complex form which he mastered thoroughly: the vocal compass was wide, a strong breath was needed and the voice led the piano, which resumed the opening rhythm of the cycle in a long postlude, thus affirming its unity."

The *Dichterliebe* comprises sixteen songs, "unique in their astonishing diversity of inspiration, composition and atmosphere," says Boucourcheliev. It opens with one of Schumann's most exquisite love songs, "Im wunderschoenen Monat Mai," which ends on an imperfect cadence, probably the first time this has been known to happen in song literature. (This is also true of "Und wuessten's die Blumen".) "Aus meinem Traenen" is in a dreamy mood, and "Die Rose, die Lilie" is built from a single elementary motif. There is a good deal of *Innigkeit*—warm, intimate, meditative sentiment, so often encountered in Schumann's greatest songs—in "Wenn ich in deine Augen seh." "Ich will meine Seele" is in the style of a gentle revery while "Im Rhein, im heiligen Strome" is one of Schumann's most exquisite mood pictures. The seventh song in this cycle is probably the best known, "Ich grolle nicht." It was described by Boucourechliev as "one of Schumann's most completely romantic songs which imparted to Heine's text, itself hovering on the brink of irony, a feeling that was dramatic in the extreme." By contrast comes "Und wuessten's die Blumen," its music "without depth of register, as if without roots, a continuous rustling, a transparency where the murmuring voice afforded the only perceptible outline."

"Das ist ein Floeten und Geigen" is remarkable for the way in which the piano accompaniment develops its own melodic line, a freedom and independence which we also encounter in the accompaniment of "Hoer' ich das Liedchen klagen." One of Heine's most celebrated poems, "Ein Jungling liebt ein Maedchen," with its ironic overtones, finds an appropriate musical equivalent in the eleventh song. In "Am leuchtenden Sommermorgen," the expressive epilogue anticipates the poetic content of the last song in the cycle. In "Ich hab' im Traum geweinet" the melodic line assumes a declamatory character while in "Allnaechtlich in Traume," it becomes highly personal and intimate. The drama of "Aus alten Maerchen winkt es" is succeeded by the concluding song, "Die alten boesen Lieder," which was described by Boucourcheliev as follows: "Its deep register attracted the voice like a lover, and all the melodic lines converged towards it."

Chamisso's poems, which are the literary source of *Frauenleben und Liebe,* are a sentimental tribute to woman as wife and mother; they are an idealization of domestic love. The poet, aged forty, wrote the verses as a tribute to his eighteen-year old bride, the poems a description of the girl's reaction to her husband. It is, of course, not too difficult to comprehend why Schumann, so soon after his marriage, should have been affected by these poems, whose standards, truthfully, are none too high; also why Schumann should have been able to translate Chamisso's words into music of such passion and ardor. Through these mediocre verses Schumann was idealizing his own beloved Clara, and providing an outlet for his joy in finally becoming her husband.

The most famous number in this set is the second, "Er, der herrlichste von allen" whose "jubilant sweep is the perfect feminine counterpart to 'Widmung,'" says Robert Haven Schauffler.

1841, SYMPHONY NO. 1 IN B-LAT, "SPRING," op. 38. I. Andante un poco maestoso; Allegro molto vivace. II. Larghetto. III. Molto vivace. IV. Allegro animato e grazioso.

In 1840, Schumann began to direct his creativity from piano and vocal music toward the orchestra. One year later came his first symphony, written in such white heat that the whole work was sketched out in four days. The winter of 1840 was drawing to a close and, as Schumann explained, he was filled "with that longing for Spring which since the most ancient times has taken possession of men and arises anew with each year." However, in writing a symphony about Spring he had no intention, as he said, to resort to "illustration or painting; but that the season in which the symphony was conceived influenced its creation and made it what it is, I fully believe."

The following lines from a poem by Boettiger were uppermost in Schumann's mind when he wrote some of the music: "O turn, O turn thy course, the valley blooms with Spring." The symphony consequently is a paean to Spring. For a while he even played with the idea of providing a descriptive title to each of the four movements: "Dawn of Spring," "Evening," "Joyful

Playing," "Full Spring." The symphony was also an expression of the joy in Schumann's heart during the first Spring he could share with his wife.

A slow horn and trumpet call, "as if from on high," opens the first movement, to become the heart of the first-movement introduction. When the tempo is accelerated, a derivative of this call becomes the movement's first principal theme. Horn octaves provide a transition to the second subject, heard in clarinets and bassoons. The exposition ends with a new thought, an ascending staccato motive. In the development, these thoughts are elaborated while a new idea—a beautiful song for oboe—is introduced as a countertheme to the movement's first main theme in the strings.

The slow movement is a radiant hymn to Springtime. A wondrous melody is given by divided strings, passes on to the cellos, and after that to oboe and horns. Just before this movement ends, the spell is broken. A phrase is introduced to anticipate the strongly accented first theme of the third-movement Scherzo. A gentler and more poetic melody provides contrast. The Scherzo has two trios, the first beginning with a succession of chords before it embarks upon a light, dancing tune; the second is built from an ascending figure in the basses.

The joy of Springtime—and the joy in Schumann's heart—erupt into an exultant melody for full orchestra in the finale. A dance tune follows in the violins. But this exuberance must finally yield to moments of poignant regret. A sustained melody brings on a reflective mood, as the composer sadly contemplates the passing of Spring.

1841. OVERTURE, SCHERZO AND FINALE, for orchestra, op. 52.

Schumann originally entitled this orchestral tryptique a Suite, then a Symphonette. He finally decided on *Overture, Scherzo and Finale*. In reality, the work is a little symphony without a slow movement. "The whole," the composer explained, "has a light friendly character. I wrote it in a really gay mood."

The overture, in E major, has a slow introduction in the tonic minor. The principal section opens with a vigorous subject in the first violins, followed by a more lyrical idea in oboe and clarinet accompanied by strings. Before the coda, the full orchestra is heard in still another subject. In the Scherzo in C-sharp minor, as Felix Borowski explains, "the tripping dotted rhythm in 6/8 time prevails throughout, and is relieved in the trio by a graceful phrase in 2/4 time. Both scherzo and trio are repeated." In the finale, the first violins present a vigorous theme over viola triplets. After the exposition is repeated, a new theme is introduced which, says Borowski, "by its obstinate and uncompromising rhythm is in strong contrast to the former."

1841. SYMPHONY NO. 4 IN D MINOR, op. 120. I. Ziemlich langsam; Lebhaft. II. Ziemlich langsam. III. Lebhaft. IV. Langsam; Lebhaft.

Though the Fourth was the last of Schumann's symphonies to get published, it was the second to be written. Its première took place in Leipzig in 1841. A decade later Schumann reorchestrated it.

Donald Francis Tovey regarded the Fourth Symphony as "perhaps Schumann's highest achievement for originality of form and concentration of material." It is an unusual work in that, as the composer specified, the four movements are to be played without a break. He further unified the work by repeating some of the basic material throughout. This is the reason why W. J. Henderson once described the Fourth Symphony as the first tone poem ever written, in which "there is no break between two successive emotional states."

The first-movement introduction is of particular importance to the overall design. An arpeggio figure heard at once is a motto theme that unifies the whole symphony. The second violins, violas, and bassoons present a solemn melody. It is repeated with growing sonority, after which the first violins arrive with a figure anticipating the main theme that follows. An ascending figure in first violins, flutes, and oboes leads into the "lively" section, the main theme now given by first violins. The rhythm of this melody is used in what can be regarded as the second subject, a lyrical passage for first violins. The whole first part is now repeated, after which the main theme is elaborated. The development is along free lines, and there is no recapitulation beyond a further restatement of the first theme.

To Philip Hale, the middle two movements "breathe a romantic spirit that Schumann himself never surpassed as expressions of gentle, dreamy melancholy." The second-movement Romanza consists mainly of a beautiful Italian song for oboes and cellos over plucked strings. Here we also get a hurried recall of the melody from the first-movement introduction. The energetic Scherzo begins with a vigorous theme in first violins, imitated by the violas. A lyrical subject comes by way of contrast in the trio; here, too, we can detect an echo of earlier material, this time the main melody of the slow movement. The finale is prefaced by a slow section in which the main theme of the first movement is repeated by first violins over tremolo second violins and violas. The main section of the movement arrives after a sustained loud chord. A march-like subject is introduced, the lower strings reminding us all the time of the main theme of the first movement. This is followed by the lyrical second subject in the first violins, its second half supported by flute and oboe. The development is a free fantasia, in which fugal treatment is given to a figure from the first theme. The recapitulation concerns itself primarily with a modification of the second theme. In the coda, we get a completely new idea—in violas, bassoons, and clarinets. The symphony surges with renewed power and intensified brilliance to a dynamic conclusion.

1842. STRING QUARTET IN A MAJOR, op. 41, no. 3. I. Andante espressivo; Allegro molto moderato. II. Assai agitato; Un poco adagio. III. Adagio molto. IV. Allegro molto vivace.

In 1842, Schumann turned to chamber music. His first significant exercises in this area came with three string quartets, written within the period of a few weeks: No. 1, A minor; No. 2, F major; No. 3, A major. These may not be among Schumann's masterworks, in the class, say, of the A minor Piano Quintet (which see); but there is much in them that is attractive to the discerning ear. What is particularly interesting in the first quartet is its free modulatory scheme. The work as a whole is designated as A minor, yet the key of F major is found in the first two movements; and the quartet ends in the key of A major. The contrapuntal skill that we encounter in the introduction to, and the development section of, the first movement is also a rewarding feature of the first movement of the second quartet. Nobility of thought and what Robert Haven Schauffler describes as a kind of "mystic exaltation" characterize the slow movements of each of these two quartets.

But it is the third of these quartets that has proved most popular with audiences. A curious technical feature here is that Schumann emphasizes certain specific intervals in his themes in each of the four movements: fifths and fourths in the first movement; fourths, in the second; sevenths, in the third; descending sixths, in the fourth.

A moody introduction places stress on the interval of the falling fifth in the first movement, an interval that is also basic to the structure of the first theme, heard in the first violin. A chordal transition leads into the highly expressive melody of the second subject; it is presented in the cello over gentle staccato figures in the first violin. The interval of the falling fifth is prominent throughout the development and in the coda; indeed, this interval provides the very last notes of the movement, in the cello.

Though the second movement is more or less in the theme-and-variations form, the variations themselves bear little relationship to the stormy subject on which they are supposedly based. In this theme, the interval of the fourth is exploited. The third movement, an Adagio, has a poignant melody dominated by the interval of the seventh. The second theme contributes to the gray melancholy thus far projected. Both development and recapitulation are short. The coda is concerned with the second subject.

The finale, a free rondo, dispenses at once with melancholia by presenting a spirited, rhythmic subject in the first violin. An equally energetic second theme is heard in the viola before being repeated by the other instruments. An interesting episode in gavotte rhythm (designated by the composer as a "quasi trio") provides contrapuntal interest midway in the movement.

1842. PIANO QUINTET IN E-FLAT MAJOR, op. 44. I. Allegro brillante. II. Un poco largamente. III. Molto vivace. IV. Allegro ma non troppo.

PIANO QUARTET IN E-FLAT MAJOR, op. 47. I. Allegro ma non troppo. II. Molto vivace. III. Andante cantabile. IV. Finale.

Schumann's E-flat major Piano Quintet is the first significant work for piano and strings; it is still one of the best, and one of the most popular. It opens with a bold statement, immediately followed by a tender one; the latter is the principal subject of the first movement. The second theme is anticipated in the transitional passage before emerging full-grown. It is a moving elegy shared by cello and viola.

The elegiac character of this second theme from the opening Allegro pervades the slow movement, in which a march-like subject of funereal character is presented by the first violin after a three-measure piano introduction. Lyrical and dramatic episodes are introduced between repetitions of this funeral-march music; one of these is a plangent melody for the violin.

The first subject of the third-movement Scherzo is constructed from a vigorous ascending scale passage in E-flat. There are two trios. In the first, the lyricism has a moody character; in the second, the melody of the first trio is inverted over a quick sixteenth-note figuration.

The finale offers a powerful theme (sempre marcato) as its first thought. Tension is built up. Then it finds release in a fugue, its subjects derived from the main themes of the first and fourth movements.

The E-flat Piano Quartet belongs in the aristocratic class of the E-flat Piano Quintet. Joan Chissell provides the following description: "The sonata-form argument of the first movement is spaciously conceived, and is marked by powerful climaxes, notably at the junction of the masterly development section and recapitulation. The G minor Scherzo, extended by a second trio, derives a great deal of charm from a recurrent staccato phrase used to link each section; and the ternary form slow movement brings a nostalgically romantic main theme of rising and falling sevenths as well as an arresting key change from B-flat to G-flat for its middle section. The finale's main theme is anticipated at the end of the slow movement in a link for which the cellist has to lower his bottom string to B-flat.

1845. CONCERTO IN A MINOR, for piano and orchestra, p. 54. I. Allegro affettuoso. II. Andante grazioso. III. Allegro vivace.

The springtime of Schumann's life, following his marriage to Clara, saw the first flowering of his only piano concerto. At that time—the summer of 1841—it consisted only of a single movement, a Fantasy in A minor, which Clara Schumann introduced that year in Leipzig. Four years later, Schumann decided to expand it into a full-length concerto. He retained the Fantasy as a first movement, adding two others.

The A minor Concerto is one of the mightiest of Schumann's achievements, and one of the most brilliant jewels in the diadem of Romantic piano literature. "It is a spontaneous expression of the joy of living," says Herbert Bedford, "full of exquisite movements, with many an inspired instance of sheer beauty of sound obtained by the simplest means. . . . It is packed with genial happiness in a degree that few composers have been capable of achieving."

To Frederick Niecks, the first movement "gives expression to all the heroic moods in him [Schumann]—loftiness, dignity, and pride, with intervening patches of darker color and intenser pathos." In the second movement

Schumann is "satisfied with more reticent qualities." And in the finale "all is impetuous, joyous—note the whirligig of quavers with breathless syncopations in the accompaniment."

A single strong chord in the orchestra and descending chords in the piano serve as the preface to the romantic first subject of the first movement; it is given by the woodwind. The piano repeats it; then with the help of the orchestra, embellishes upon it. The second subject is a variation on and a further development of this same subject. The development section is a free fantasia with dramatic changes of tempo, rhythm, and tonality. A further elaboration and variation of the thematic material is encountered in the spacious cadenza. The coda makes an energetic recall of the first theme.

The second movement is a poetic Intermezzo. The first main staccato subject is shared by piano and strings. This is followed by an expansive song for cellos, accompanied by piano arpeggios. A recall of the first theme of the opening movement serves as a transition to the finale, which enters without a break. The piano is heard in a brilliant syncopated theme. Another syncopated subject serves as the second theme, offered by the strings and woodwind to filigree trimmings by the piano. A free fantasia section opens with a fugato based on the brilliant first subject. A return of the two main themes, and an elaborate coda based on the first one, follow. The concerto ends in a triumphant mood, with brilliant runs in the piano and resounding chords in the orchestra.

1846. SYMPHONY NO. 2 IN C MAJOR, op. 61. I. Sostenuto assai; Allegro ma non troppo. II. Allegro vivace. III. Adagio espressivo. IV. Allegro molto vivace.

While working on his second symphony Schumann was harassed by nervous disorders. Only when he reached the end of the work did he feel, as he confessed, "a lot better." "But," he added, "apart from that it [the symphony] is a souvenir of a dark period. In February 1846, while working on the orchestration, the ringing and roaring in his head compelled him to stop work and go off for a rest cure; at the seacoast resort of Nordeney he was able, at last, to complete his symphony.

Though it bears the number "2," the C major Symphony was actually Schumann's third, having been completed five years after the D minor, now identified as the fourth (which see).

Describing his symphony, Schumann explained to a friend that "it appears more or less clad in armor. It is music of light and shade, sunshine and shadow." The fanfare with which the symphony begins is a motto that recurs later in the symphony. It is the core of a slow introduction. A forceful, angry statement by the full orchestra is the main theme of the principal section. This marks the beginning of a short-lived struggle. A second subject, gentle and resigned, concludes the exposition. But conflict rather than repose are emphasized in the development. A long pedal point in the bass brings a return of the strong first theme, now effectively accompanied by the wind. In the coda, the motto recurs in the trumpets.

There is little suggestion of turmoil in the second-movement Scherzo, whose bright humor is instantly projected with a sprightly tune in sixteenths for the violins. There are two contrasting trios, the first, a lively melody in triplets shared by woodwind and strings; the second, slow and stately, has a religious character. The movement ends with a recall of the motto theme.

The lyricism of the slow movement is tinged with melancholy. The strings are heard in a poignant melody, in which oboes and clarinets join. A second episode—this time for strings, horn, and trumpet—maintains the lugubrious mood. The opening melody is then repeated.

The finale is more optimistic. The spirited opening subject bears a striking resemblance to the opening melody in the first movement of Mendelssohn's *Italian Symphony*. The second theme, though derived from the melody of the Adagio, is a further expression of youthful vitality. A third melody is one of Schumann's loftiest lyrical inventions. A climax is reached with a final statement of the motto theme.

1847. PIANO TRIO NO. 1 IN D MAJOR, op. 63. I. Mit Energie und Leidenschaft. II. Lebhaft, doch nicht so rasch. III. Langsam, mit imiger Empfindung. IV. Mit Feuer.

The first and finest of Schumann's three piano trios was written as a birthday gift for Clara. "The first movement," remarked Clara, "is to my mind one of the loveliest I know." That first movement, adds Robert Haven Schauffler, "belongs to the brooder rather than to the gay enthusiast." Of particular interest is an episode in the development section, with its rich and unusual tone coloring, produced by having the strings play "sul ponticello," while the piano is heard in high treble "una corda" and staccato. "The rich *Kreisleriana* gloom," says Robert Haven Schauffler of this movement, "provides a foil for the vivacious Scherzo. While the noble but morbidly melancholy introspection of the slow movement is a perfect prelude to the jubilant young cavortings of the finale."

1847. OVERTURE TO GENOVEVA, for orchestra, op. 81.

Schumann wrote only one completed opera. It was *Genoveva,* inspired by a reading of Hebbel's drama of the same name. The opera was introduced at the Leipzig Municipal Theater on June 25, 1850. After a number of performances in various German cities the opera went into discard. One of its rare revivals in recent times took place at the Florence May Music Festival in 1951.

The libretto was the work of Robert Reineck (with alterations by the composer), based on dramas by Ludwig Tieck and Friedrich Hebbel. The setting is France during Charles Martel's campaign against the Saracens. Siegfried, the Palatinate Count, entrusts his wife Genoveva to the care of his friend, Golo, while he himself sets forth with the crusades. Golo, in love with Genoveva, plots her destruction when she rejects him. He brings news to Siegfried, at camp, of Genoveva's infidelity. Siegfried plots to kill her, but before this happens, her innocence is proved. Genoveva and Siegfried are reconciled, and Golo is punished by the fates by falling off a precipice.

The overture was completed in four days. A slow introduction presents a passionate subject for the violins that identifies Golo. The cellos invoke an atmosphere charged with foreboding, suggesting the danger facing the heroine. A hunt-like theme for horns, which oboes and flutes take over, precedes the free development. Here the conflicts and emotional stresses besetting Genoveva are depicted. The coda is based on the hunt subject; it is brought to conclusion with a sober exclamation by trombones.

1848. ALBUM FUER DIE JUGEND (ALBUM FOR THE YOUNG), suite for piano, op. 68: 1. Melodie. 2. Soldatenmarsch. 3. Traellerliedchen. 4. Ein Choral. 5. Stueckchen. 6. Armes Waisenkind. 7. Jaegerliedchen. 8. Wilder Reiter. 9. Volksliedchen. 10. Froehlicher Landmann. 11. Sicilianisch. 12. Knecht Ruprecht. 13. Mai, lieber Mai. 14. Kleine Studie. 15. Fruehlingsgesang. 16. Erster Verlust. 17. Kleiner Morgenwanderer. 18. Schnitterliedchen. 19. Fuer Erwachsenere. 20. Laendliches Lied. 21. **. 22. Rundgesang. 23. Reiterstueck. 24. Ernteliedchen. 25. Nachklaenge aus dem Theater. 26. **. 27. Canonisches Liedchen. 28. Errinerung. 29. Fremder Mann. 30. **. 31. Kriegslied. 32. Sheherazade. 33. "Weinlesezeit—Froehliche Zeit!". 34. Thema. 35. Mignon. 36. Lied italienischer Marinari. 37. Matrosenlied. 38. Winterzeit I. 39. Winterzeit II. 40, Kleine Fuge. 41. Nordisches Lied. 42. Figuierter Choral. 43. Sylvesterlied.

This is the second set of pieces by Schumann inspired by childhood and children. It differs from the first—*Kinderscenen,* completed a decade earlier (which see). It comprises pieces of music written *for* children ,where the earlier work was *about* children for an adult audience. Thus where the *Kinderscenen* was sophisticated and mature, the *Album fuer die Jugend* consists of little unpretentious numbers, describing all sorts of things of interest to the young—games, stories, moods, fancies, thoughts. And since this music was intended to be played by children, the technique is elementary, the approach simple and direct, the style almost ingenuous.

Among the more popular items in this suite are the following: the opening "Melody," and the "Soldier's March" that follows it; No. 7, "Little Hunting Song"; No. 8, "Wild Horseman," which was made into an American popular song; No. 9, "Little Folk Song"; No. 10, "The Happy Farmer" or "The Merry Peasant"; No. 12, "Knight Ruprecht"; No. 19, "Little Romance"; No. 25, "Echoes from the Theater"; No. 27, "Canonic Song," whose melody is familiar to present-day American children as "Three Blind Mice"; No. 28, "In Memory," an affecting piece created in memory of Mendelssohn on the day of his death; No. 31, "War Song"; No. 37, "Sailor's Song"; No. 41, "Northern Song."

1849. OVERTURE TO MANFRED, for orchestra, op. 115.

Schumann, a passionate admirer of Byron, was stirred to the roots of his being by *Manfred.* Schumann's biographer, Wasielewski described how, while reading parts of *Manfred* to friends, Schumann "burst into tears and was so overcome he could go on no further." Wasielewski also explains why this dramatic poem had such an impact on the composer. "For what is this Bryonic Manfred but a restless, wandering, distracted man, tormented by fearful thoughts, and the mad soul-destroying intercourse with spirits—which must of course be taken symbolically—was also the culminating point of Schumann's last illness."

In setting *Manfred,* Schumann completed not only his famous overture, but also a less familiar entr'acte, Melodrama, solos, and choruses—indeed, music for most of the poem's principal episodes and incidents. The entire score was completed by spring of 1849. The overture was introduced in Leipzig in 1852, and the entire score in Weimar two months later.

This is Paul Graf Waldersee's illuminating analysis of the overture, one of Schumann's most powerful and moving short compositions for orchestra. It is, said Waldersee, "a deeply earnest picture of the soul, which describes in the most affecting manner the torture and conflict of the human heart, gradually dying out, in allusion to the liberation wrought by death. . . . The rhythmic precipitancy in the first measure . . . transports us at once into a state of excited expectation. After a short, slow introduction the development begins in passionate tempo, the portrayal of the restless and tormented mood. It is the syncope, employed continually in the motive, that indicates the conflict of the soul. This storms itself out, and then appears the expression of a melancholy, milder mood. Mysteriously, in the pianissimo, three trumpets are introduced in isolated chords: a warning from another world. But the evil spirits cannot be reduced in silence; with increased intensity of passion the struggle begins anew. The battle rages hotly, but in the pauses of the fight resound voices of reconciliation. At last the strength is exhausted, the pulse beats slower, the unrest is assuaged, the music gradually dies away. A slow movement, nearly related to the introduction, leads to the conclusion."

1850. SYMPHONY NO. 3 IN E-FLAT MAJOR, "RHENISH," op. 97. I. Lebhaft. II. Sehr maessig. III. Nicht schnell. IV. Feierlich. V. Lebhaft.

Though the *Rhenish* is numbered the third among Schumann's four symphonies, it was actually the last to get written. Schumann began working on it in November of 1850, two months after he had come to the Rhine city of Duesseldorf to serve as its musical director. The sights and the life along the Rhine—particularly a ceremony at the Cologne Cathedral where the Archbishop was elevated to rank of Cardinal—made a profound impression on the composer. He recorded some of these impressions in his third symphony, the only one of the four that is descriptive. As he informed his publisher, Schumann hoped his music "perhaps mirrors here and there something of Rhenish life."

It is not difficult to find reflected in the opening measures of the first movement Schumann's excitement and joy at first coming to the Rhineland. Here we get a buoyant syncopated subject, full of élan. It is presented by the full orchestra. The happy feelings thus released are permitted full freedom of expression, until the second subject, in G minor, in oboe and clarinet, introduces some melancholy overtones. But in the vast two-hundred-measure introduction, the two subjects are worked out exuberantly. The ebullient first theme, stated loudly again in full orchestra, brings on a vigorous recapitulation and an equally energetic coda.

The main melody of the second-movement Scherzo, presented by cellos, violas, and bassoons, was derived from a German folk song, "Rheinweinland." This theme is continued by the violins, soon to be freely altered into a light staccato subject in sixteenth-notes. The principal subject of the trio is given by horns and other winds over a pedal C.

A Romanza movement follows, scored throughout for woodwind, strings, and two horns. A graceful melody flows easily from clarinets and bassoons, the violas providing a sixteenth-note accompaniment. The violins carry this melody along, then digress into a new lyrical thought with the aid of flutes. A third theme engages bassoons and violins over an accompanying cello figure.

The fourth movement was inspired by the ceremony Schumann witnessed in the Cologne Cathedral. Originally, Schumann wrote at the head of this movement: "In the character of an accompaniment to a solemn ceremony." Subsequently, he deleted this programmatic note with the explanation: "One should not show his heart to the people, for the general impression of a work of art is more effective." Three trombones are here added to the orchestral fabric to endow a greater majesty to the music. These trombones join with horns and bassoons to present a religious melody; violins provide a pizzicato accompaniment. Later on, this melody is elaborated upon contrapuntally. A change of key brings on a fanfare in brass and woodwind to which strings, flutes, and oboes provide a gentle reply. The fanfare then helps to bring the movement to its conclusion.

The finale can be interpreted as a Rhineland festival. Woodwind, horns, and strings are heard in a vigorous melody. This gets a contrast from a delicate theme in first violins and oboes. This material is then developed with brilliant colors and powerful rhythmic drive. Just before the end of the symphony, the music of the Cathedral scene is recalled—an exalted mood carried over into the concluding coda.

1850. CONCERTO IN A MINOR, for cello and orchestra, op. 129. I. Nicht zu schnell. II. Langsam. III. Sehr lebhaft.

The Cello Concerto in A minor was one of the first major works completed by Schumann after assuming the post of musical director of Duesseldorf. The writing went quickly. Sketches consumed only six days. Eight days later, the concerto was completed. In her diary, Clara Schumann noted that the work "pleased me very much. It seems to me to be written in true violoncello style." But Schumann himself was not quite so satisfied with it. Though he had planned the première of the concerto in 1852, that performance never took place; and the concerto was never played during the composer's lifetime. Nor did Schumann submit the work to a publisher until four years after he had completed it.

On the published score Schumann described the work as a concerto "for violoncello with the accompaniment of the orchestra," thus emphasizing the importance of the solo instrument, and the subisidiary role of the orchestra. The three movements are played without a break. A few introductory measures for the orchestra bring on the solo instrument in an ample and impressive melody. Passage work and an orchestral tutti lead into the second theme, also in the solo instrument. An episode in triplets prefaces the development, in which the cello is frequently permitted to exercise his virtuosity with brilliant pyrotechnical passages.

In the second movement, a spacious Schumannesque song is heard in the solo cello over a discreet orchestral accompaniment. A livelier passage takes a hurried backward glance into the first movement. Then an accelerando passage becomes the transition into the finale, in which the solo instrument offers an energetic subject, interrupted by abrupt chordal interpolations by the orchestra. A more lyrical passages arrives as the second theme. Following the cadenza, the tempo quickens and a vigorous coda comes as a forceful conclusion to the concerto.

FRÉDÉRIC CHOPIN 1810–1849

No other great composer imposed upon himself the restrictions and limitations that Chopin did. There is not one opera, not one symphony, nor one quartet among Chopin's more than one hundred and seventy compositions. Except for two concertos, three piano sonatas, and a cello sonata, he confined himself to the smaller structures; all but a meager handful of his compositions are not for piano solo, and even these exceptions have to make use of a piano. Yet, in spite of the narrow bound aries to which he confined his creativity, Chopin remains one of music's lord and masters—one of the most original and influential geniuses, not only in the Romantic movement, but even in the entire history of music. Indeed, in some ways he was unique. He is the only great composer whose entire output maintains a consistently high level of artistic achievement. His integrity was of the highest; he always subjected his works to the most painstaking editing and revision; and he would not permit anything of his to be published that he felt was not his best. For these reasons, perhaps, and because of his extraordinary endowments, he is also the only great composer who, a generation after his death, has practically everything he wrote (with a few minor exceptions) alive and significant in the repertory. Finally, Chopin is perhaps the only one of music's supreme masters who functioned for the most part in a world of his own making. Except for minor influences—the late Beethoven, John Field (1782–1837), and Johann Nepomuk Hummel (1778–1837)—there is little in Chopin's style, methods, and piano technique that is derived from others. On the other hand, there is little in piano music since his time that was not affected by him. Chopin revolutionized piano technique; he introduced dynamics and sonorities, a brilliance and daring of virtuoso writing, piano idioms and a rhetoric that were his and his alone. His music is so thoroughly pianistic that it cannot be conceived in terms of any other instrument. He created an epoch in piano music. Indeed, it is not too much to say that modern piano music and modern piano technique began with Chopin.

He was essentially a miniaturist—his larger works, such as his piano sonatas and concertos were often hardly more than the sum of several shorter ones—but a miniaturist with an elegance and perfection of structure, an originality of musical thought, and a personal style that place these morsels into a category all their own. He was a supreme melodist; the opulence of his lyricism was invariably trimmed with those exquisite embellishments and figurations that he brought to piano music from bel canto. His concepts of harmony, progressions, voice leading, tonality were so advanced that in his own day Chopin was regarded as a revolutionary. His excursions into discords led some of the outstanding critics of Chopin's time—including Chorley and Rellstab—to consider him an eccentric. Liszt could point to Chopin's use of "bold dissonance and strange harmonies" while noting that Chopin was "one of those original beings . . . adrift from all bondage." Chopin's fresh and new harmonic language influenced Liszt and Wagner almost as much as his revolutionary approach to keyboard technique affected subsequent composers of piano music.

Two aspects of Chopin's art deserve special attention. One is his partiality to dance forms: the mazurka, polonaise, waltz. This preference, Paul Henry Lang explains, "was not merely for their stimulating notion and freshness." Lang here found "deep-seated symbolic meaning," explaining that "the lonely artist who lived his whole life in the turmoil of society enlivened and populated with these dances the solitude of his creative fancy."

The other aspect of Chopin's art is its pronounced Polish nationalism. This did not consist in quotations of folk songs or dances, but rather in carrying over into his writing the heart, pulse, and soul of his land and people. "I should like to be to my people," Chopin once said, "what Uhland is to the Germans." The influence of Poland remains pronounced even where the materials are Chopin's own. This national influence, explains W. H. Hadow, is revealed in three different ways: in the fact that more than a quarter of Chopin's literature is devoted to dance forms, and notably Polish dance forms; that Chopin used tonalities of Polish folk music; and that he borrowed from Polish folk art the primitive practice of "founding a whole paragraph either on a single phrase repeated in similar shapes, or on two phrases in alternation."

Frédéric François Chopin was born in Zelasowa Wola, Poland, on February 22, 1810. He began to study the piano when he was six, with Albert Zywny; one year later, he published his first piece of music (a polonaise) and made his concert debut. Between 1823 and 1826, he attended the Warsaw High School. During this period, his music study continued privately with Joseph Elsner, director of the Warsaw Conservatory. Following his graduation with honors in 1829, Chopin visited Vienna. There he gave two outstandingly successful concerts, playing some of his own compositions. After a brief return to Warsaw, where he suffered the pangs of unrequited love as well as boredom with his everyday life, Chopin decided to leave his native land. Just before his departure, in November of 1830, his teacher and friend, Elsner, presented him with a silver urn containing some Polish earth. "May you never forget your native land wherever you may go, nor cease to love it with a warm and faithful heart," Elsner said. Chopin never did forget Poland; but never again was he to set foot on Polish soil.

His first stop was Vienna, where he stayed six months. There he received news that Poland had revolted against Russian domination. His first impulse was to rush home and help in the fight. But reconsidering this decision, he expressed his patriotic ardor through music. When, in Stuttgart, he discovered that Warsaw had fallen to the Russians, he canalized his powerful emotion into the music of the *Revolutionary Étude*.

From Vienna he went on to Paris, henceforth his permanent home. There he made his first public appearance on February 26, 1832. This performance did not go well, and for a while Chopin deserted the concert hall. Instead, he concentrated on the Parisian salon, introducing there many of his new compositions. He soon became the darling of the social and intellectual élite of the city. He was able to achieve a huge success through the publication of his music, and to command a high price for his services as a teacher of the piano.

In 1837, Liszt introduced Chopin to George Sand, the famous novelist. At first, Chopin was repelled by her masculinity, her unattractive physical appearance, her lax moral standards, and her offensive mannerisms and frankness. But with additional association, he became completely fascinated by her brilliant mind and dynamic personality. Her strength of character and will filled a vital need in one so sensitive and delicate as he. Though they were opposites—or perhaps because of it—they began to seek each other out until they became well-nigh inseparable.

This liaison stimulated Chopin into writing some of his greatest music. But it also proved emotionally disturbing. They spent the winter of 1838 on the island of Majorca, but what had been hoped would be an idyllic holiday turned into a nightmare, completely undermining Chopin's delicate health. The weather and food were miserable; the townspeople were so antagonistic that Sand and Chopin were reduced to living like hermits. Nevertheless, Chopin did manage to complete one of his greatest works, the twenty-four preludes.

After returning to France, Chopin's health improved, and he was able to produce some of his most ambitious works, including the B-flat minor Sonata, the F minor Fantaisie, as well as ballades and impromptus. But tuberculosis seriously undermined his health again; and a permanent rupture with George Sand in 1847 broke his spirit.

Chopin made his last public appearance on February 16, 1848—in Paris. Though his strength was gone, he toured England and Scotland. Returning to Paris, he became an invalid and a recluse, forced to live on the bounty of his friends. He died in Paris on October 17, 1849, and was buried in the cemetery of Père Lachaise.

1817–1846. POLONAISES, for solo piano:

Op. 26: 1. C-sharp minor; 2. E-flat major, "Serbian" or "Revolt."

Op. 40: 1. A major, "Militaire"; C minor.

Op. 44: F-sharp minor.

Op. 53: A-flat major, "Heroic."

Op. 61: A-flat major, "Fantaisie."

Op. 71: D minor; B-flat major; F minor.

Introduction and Polonaise, for cello and piano, op. 3.

Andante spianato and Grande Polonaise brillante in E-flat, for piano and orchestra (also for solo piano), op. 22.

In the polonaise, Chopin found a grateful medium through which to speak his intense, passionate Polish nationalism. Olin Downes spoke of the "grand lines and striding phrase lengths of the polonaises, with their bardic evocations of the past, and battles heroically lost, and deathless ancestral glory. Everything is cut here to the grand pattern, whether it is the explosive outburst of the first polonaise in C-sharp minor (1834–1835), or the trumpet calls and visions of the advancing hosts of the famous A-flat Polonaise, the so-called *Heroic* (1824), or that great fresco of battle with the mournful interpolation of the mazurka dances by ghosts in the Polonaise in F-sharp minor (1840–1841)."

The two polonaises in opus 25 (1838) are particularly famous. The first, in C-sharp minor, is more lyrical, though often achieving considerable grandeur. The second, known as *Serbian* or *Revolt,* begins in a reflective and melancholy vein. But the storm of revolt soon erupts. Toward the end of the piece it is dispelled, with the return of an introspective unharmonized voice.

The A major Polonaise (1838) is also extremely popular. The virile character of its massive chords and the strength and power of its main subject are the reasons this music has come to be known as *Military*. In a more pensive and brooding style is the Polonaise in C minor (1839). It opens powerfully enough, but before long there unfolds a most graceful melody with exquisite decorations.

There is no interrelationship between the *Andante spianato* and the Polonaise that follows, for piano and orchestra. The *Andante spianato* is in an idyllic mood, "a landscape in soft bright sunlight," as Arthur Hedley once described it. "The trio, marked semplice, brings no darker contrast before the return of the rippling G major stream." In *Introduction and Polonaise,* the dance movement that Chopin tacked on to the atmospheric music that preceded it, is not of the high quality of his other polonaises and appears anticlimactic; however, it has such ambitious and spacious design that it has received the title of *Grand.*

1825–1849. MAZURKAS, for solo piano:
Op. 6: 1. F-sharp minor; 2. C-sharp minor; 3. E major; 4. E-flat minor.
Op. 7: 1. B-flat; 2. A minor; 3. F minor; 4. A-flat; 5. C major.
Op. 17: 1. B-flat; 2. E minor; 3. A-flat; 4. A minor.
Op. 24: 1. G minor; 2. C major; 3. A-flat; 4. B-flat minor.
Op. 30: 1. C minor; 2. B minor; 3. D-flat; 4. C-sharp minor.
Op. 33: 1. G-sharp minor; 2. D major; 3. C major; 4. B minor.
Op. 41: 1. C-sharp minor; 2. E minor; 3. B major; 4. A-flat.
Op. 50: 1. G major; 2. A-flat; 3. C-sharp minor.
Op. 56: 1. B major; 2. C major. 3. C minor.
Op. 59: 1. A minor; 2. A-flat; 3. F-sharp minor.
Op. 63: 1. B major; 2. F minor; 3. C-sharp minor.
Op. 67: 1. G major; 2. G minor; 3. C major; 4. A minor.
Op. 68: 1. C major; 2. A minor; 3. F major; 4. F minor.
No opus numbers: 1. A minor; 2. A minor; 3 B-flat major; 4. G major.

The mazurka was the second of the Polish dance forms that the ex-patriate Chopin could flood with his patriotic ardor (the first being the polonaise). The Mazurka was a two-part or four-part dance form in triple time, accent usually coming on the second beat. Generally speaking, Chopin's mazurkas have a flexible, improvisational structure, and are varied both as to rhythm and emotional content. The more than fifty such pieces produced by Chopin traverse a wide gamut, from sobriety to fiery passion; from irony to pensive introspection; from tenderness to martial strength. From the Polish folk dance, Chopin lifted, not only its basic rhythms, accentuations, and structures, but also its medieval Church modes to which it was partial, and its tendency to build up complete sections from a simple phrase or from two simple alternating phrases.

"There never have been," says Olin Downes, "such revelations of all the mazurka can mean and say to us as the pieces which Chopin composed in this form. In not a measure does he lose sight of the fundamental musical elements. Nor does he in a single measure merely repeat himself or fail to strike every emotional chord that this, the most popular of all the national dances, permits. Each mazurka has the concision and concentration necessitated by seldom more than one to three minutes of music. In this space, short motives, often of disparate character, may be bound together in a manner which seems almost like an improvisation, yet achieves a remarkable unity. Among the means that Chopin employs here to achieve his swift transitions are the enharmonic modulations and the chromaticism which he so subtly developed, in pages prophetic of a whole period."

"The latent and unknown poetry which was only indicated in the original Polish mazurkas," wrote Franz Liszt, "was divined, developed and brought to light by Chopin. Preserving their rhythm, he ennobled their melody, enlarged their proportions; and—in order to paint more fully in these productions, which he loved to hear us call 'pictures from the easel,' the innumerable and widely differing emotions which agitate the heart during the progress of this dance . . . he wrought into their tissues harmonic lights and shadows, as new in themselves as were the subjects to which he adapted them."

Unusual modalities provide some of the mazurkas with their fascinating exotic personality—as in the B-flat, op. 7, no. 1 (1830–1831), which is built from the gypsy mode using two strong notes; the C major, op. 24, no 2 (1834–1835), derived from the Hippolydian mode; and the C-sharp minor, op. 41, no. 1 (1838) based on the Dorian mode.

Many other mazurkas are noteworthy for either melodic or harmonic interest. In the E minor, op. 17, no. 2, and the A-flat, op. 17, no. 3 (1832–1833) the lyricism has such a melancholy tinge that these pieces may well be regarded as elegies. The G-sharp minor, op. 33, no. 1 (1837–1838) has the simplicity of a folk song. There is a contagiously happy spirit about the B minor, op. 33, no. 4 (1837–1838), created through effective accentuations and the subtle way in which the composer uses the 3/4 rhythm. Rhythmic fascination, together with a richness of harmonic language, provides the attraction for the A-flat, op. 17, no. 3 (1832–1833) and the B major, op. 41, no. 3 (1839). The Mazurka in A-flat, op. 50, no. 2 (1841) alternates from its opening sensitivity to a sturdier episode with the virility of a peasant dance. (Pauline Viardot made a vocal adaptation of this composition.) The A minor Mazurka, op. 17, no. 4 (1825) indulges in effective tone painting, while that in B-flat minor, op. 24, no 4 (1834–1835) gives way to uninhibited romanticism. The C-sharp minor, op. 63, no. 3 (1846)—some authorities regard this as perhaps the greatest mazurka of them all—was described by Arthur Hedley as a "dance fantasy with symphonic elements." The A minor, op. 68, no. 2 (1846), sometimes called *The Nightingale,* has roots in the soil of Bohemian folk music.

The last two compositions Chopin was destined to write were the Mazurkas in G minor, op. 67, no. 2, and the F minor, op. 68, no. 4, both in 1849. At that time he was so ill he was unable to copy the music or to try it out on the piano.

1829–1830. CONCERTOS FOR PIANO AND ORCHESTRA:
No. 1, E minor, op. 11. I. Allegro maestoso. II. Larghetto. III. Vivace.
No. 2, F minor, op. 21. I. Maestoso. II. Larghetto. III. Allegro vivace.

Both of Chopin's two piano concertos—his most significant works involving an orchestra—came early in his career. The F minor—designated as the "second" because of its later publication—was completed in 1829; one year later Chopin wrote the E minor Concerto, today numbered as the "first."

Because of its earlier composition, the so-called Second Concerto will engage our attention first. The opening Allegro has a double exposition. The first is for the orchestra, the initial forceful theme presented by the strings; while the more lyrical second theme is heard first in the oboe, then in the first violins. The second exposition is assigned to the piano. Here the first subject is the same that had been heard in the orchestral exposition, but after that the piano embarks on a new episode, and some passage work. The second subject now occupies the piano. In the development, the piano elaborates upon the first four notes of the initial subject with the wind providing elaborations and amplifications. The second subject, however, is completely avoided. An orchestral tutti brings on the recapitulation, in which the first theme is briefly suggested before the second one becomes an extended statement. A forceful orchestral tutti brings this movement to a close.

The haunting nocturne of the second movement was inspired by Chopin's frustrated love for Constantia Gladkowska, a pupil at the Warsaw Conservatory. "Six months have elapsed," he wrote to a friend in 1829, "and I have not yet exchanged a syllable with her of whom I dream every night. While my thoughts were with her I composed the Adagio of my concerto." This soulful melody appears in the piano (molto con delicatezza) after a six measure introduction. It is then repeated with some ornamentations. A narrative for solo instrument, accompanied by strings, introduces a sterner mood. But the poetic song soon returns in the piano to sustain a dream world right through the closing coda. The spirited finale starts off with a vital mazurka-like tune in the piano; the second subject also has a lively dance character. This movement abounds with rhythmic energy and brilliant virtuosity. A solo for horn leads into the concluding coda, in which once again use is made of brilliant passages for the piano.

In the E minor Concerto, a rhapsodic introduction for the orchestra presents the first theme of the opening movement—a stately subject for first violins, accompanied by the rest of the orchestra. When the piano arrives, it presents this theme, then goes off into intriguing arabesques and arpeggios. A slight pause precedes the statement of the second subject in the piano—a gentle and touching melody. A crescendo now leads into an orchestral tutti to conclude the exposition. In the development, the first theme receives elaboration as the piano embarks on brilliant passages. A climax for full orchestra precedes the recapitulation. In the short coda, the first theme is given in the bass—first loudly, then softly. The movement ends with three energetic chords.

After several introductory bars for the strings, the piano engages a dreamy melody in the second-movement Romanza. Chopin described this music as "calm and of a partly melancholy character. It is intended to convey the impression which one receives when the eye rests on a beloved landscape that calls up in one's soul beautiful memories—for instance, on a fine moonlight, spring night."

The concerto closes with an energetic rondo movement. Its first subject is a spirited theme begun by the strings and answered softly by the woodwind. The piano appears with a dance tune, which before long is taken over by the orchestra. Following a transition in the orchestra, the piano thunders a powerful statement, while strings provide delicate figures. When the first main theme returns, it appears in a contrasting tonality. The first section is repeated with variations, followed by a recall of the second theme. Vigorous scale passages, which gain in strength and sonority, carry the concerto to its dramatic conclusion.

1829–1836. ÉTUDES, for piano:

Op. 10: 1. C major, "Arpeggio"; 2. A minor; 3. E major; 4. C-sharp minor; 5. G-flat, "Black Key"; 6. E-flat minor; 7. C major; 8. F major; 9. F minor; 10. A-flat major; 11. E-flat major; 12. C minor, "Revolutionary."

Op. 25: 1. A-flat major, "Aeolian Harp"; 2. F minor, "Les Abeilles"; 3. F major; 4. A minor; 5. E minor; 6. G-sharp minor; 7. C-sharp minor; 8. D-flat major, 9. G-flat major, "Butterfly"; 10. B minor; 11. A minor, "Winter Wind"; 12. C minor.

Nouvelles études: 1. F minor; 2. A-flat; 3. D-flat.

Études for the piano had, of course, been written before Chopin's time, notably by Karl Czerny (1791–1857), Johann Baptist Cramer (1771–1858), and Muzio Clementi (1752–1832). However, the études of these masters are of pedagogical interest, serving several generations of piano students in perfecting technique. But with Chopin, the piano étude acquired a new character, and a new artistic status. "I have composed a study in my own manner," Chopin wrote a friend on October 20, 1829. Thus without fanfare, he announced the creation of a form of piano literature that he revolutionized single-handedly. Chopin's études might provide a means of mastering piano technique. But at the same time it was filled with all the fancy and magic and invention of which he was capable. Consequently, Chopin's pieces have come to be known as "concert études," a genre he can be said to have invented;

and these concert études have enriched the experiences of music lovers the world over.

The first set of études, gathered in opus 10, were completed between 1829 and 1832. Already in the first étude, known as the *Arpeggio,* we are brought face to face with a new system of piano writing. "To take a dispersed harmony and transform it into an epical study, to raise the chord of the tenth to heroic stature—only Chopin could have accomplished such a miracle," wrote Frederick Niecks. The second étude has a chromatic character that anticipates the dreamy nocturnal quality of some of Chopin's later etudes. To Niecks, the third étude "combines classical chasteness of contour with the fragrance of romanticism." The fourth is sparkling and vital music that, says James Gibbons Huneker, "bubbles with life and spurts with flame." The fifth étude, called the *Black Key* because it was written exclusively for the black keys, is described by Huneker as "graceful, delicately witty, a trifle naughty and roguish." The sixth sounds like a nocturne, while the seventh has a toccata-like propulsion. The eighth is distinguished for its rich sonority. The ninth presents a melody that to Huneker is "morbid, almost irritatingly so, and yet not without a certain accent of grandeur." The tenth has a salon character with its aristocratic grace. Of the eleventh, Huneker said: "Its novel design, delicate arabesques—as if the guitar had been endowed with a soul—and the richness and originality of its harmonic scheme gives us pause to ask if Chopin's technical invention is not almost boundless." The concluding number in opus ten is perhaps the most popular—the *Revolutionary,* so named because of its elemental power and military personality. It was written in 1831, when the composer heard the news that the Russians had taken Warsaw. Here is how Huneker described this music: "Out of the mad and tempestuous storm of passages for the left hand the melody arises aloft, now passionate and now profoundly majestic, until thrills of awe stream over the listener, and the image is evoked of Zeus hurling thunderbolts at the world.

The twelve études in opus 25 were completed between 1832 and 1836. Here are some of the more notable pieces in this set. The first, *Aeolian Harp,* was described by Schumann as an "undulation of the A-flat major chord . . . exquisitely entangled in the harmony." The second, the *Abeilles*—named that way because it seems to bring up the image of bees in flight—was "charming, dreamy and soft as the song of the sleeping child," in Schumann's description. The seventh is a work gently touched by sadness. This music, says Stephen Heller, "engenders the sweetest sadness, the most enviable torments." Hans von Buelow looked upon this piece as a nocturne-like duet for "flute and cello." The eighth is a study in sixths. The popular ninth étude in G-flat,—given the sobriquet of *Butterfly* for the swift and graceful flight of the melody—is a study in sixths. The tenth is a study in octaves. The eleventh, named *Winter Wind,* is tempestuous music, which Frederick Niecks referred to as "real pandemonium" in which "hell prevails." A middle B major section provides a lyrical respite from the storm.

Of the three études published posthumously, the first in F minor has the greatest interest. The theme is rich-textured and emotional, hovering over four eight-notes in the bass.

1829–1847. WALTZES, for piano:
Op. 18: 1. E-flat, "Grande valse brillante."
Op. 34: 1. A-flat major; 2. A minor; 3. F major, "Cat Waltz."
Op. 42: A-flat major.
Op. 64: 1. D-flat major, "Minute"; 2. C-sharp minor; 3. A-flat major.
Op. 69: 1. A-flat major; 2. B minor.
Op. 70: 1. G-flat major; 2. F minor; 3. D-flat major.
No opus number: E minor; E major.

Haydn, Mozart, Beethoven, Schubert, Weber, all preceded Chopin in the writing of concert waltzes for the piano. But Chopin's waltzes have little structural or stylistic affinity with those of his predecessors. Chopin's have greater elegance and refinement, and project magical moods not found in earlier concert waltz music for piano, which always tends to remember that the waltz was a peasant dance. Camille Bourniquel had this in mind when he regarded Chopin's waltzes more like caprices or impromptus, in spite of their infectious three-quarter time.

One of Chopin's waltzes is so pictorial that it has acquired a silly programmatic interpretation: The leaping appoggiaturas of the Waltz in F major, op. 34, no. 3 (1838) has suggested to some the flight of a cat across the keyboard. Some also like to interpret the D-flat major Waltz, op. 64, no. 1 (1847) as a dog chasing its own tail; but this piece is undoubtedly more often identified as *Minute*—the descriptive word being the French for "little" and not the sixty seconds of time supposedly required to play the piece. Some waltzes have the rhythmic pulse that can inspire dancing—that in A-flat, op. 42 (1840), for example; and that in B minor, op. 69, no 2 (1829), about which Schumann said "so throbbing a life flows in them that they seem to have been improvised in the ballroom."

Other waltzes, in the description of James Gibbons Huneker, "dance for the soul and not for the body." These include that in C-sharp minor, op. 64, no 2 (1847); and two pieces in which Chopin spoke his frustrations in love, the D-flat, op. 70, no. 3 (1829) and the A-flat major, op. 69, no. 1 (1835).

1831–1847. NOCTURNES, for piano:
Op. 9: 1. B-flat minor; 2. E-flat major; 3. B major.
Op. 15: 1. F major; 2. F-sharp major; 3. G minor.
Op. 27: 1. C-sharp minor; 2. D-flat major.
Op. 32: 1. B major; 2. A-flat major.
Op. 37: 1. G minor; 2. G major.

Op. 48: 1. C minor; 2. F-sharp minor.
Op. 55: 1. F minor; 2. E-flat major.
Op. 62: 1. B major; 2. E major.
Op. 72: E minor.
Posthumous: C-sharp minor.

The nocturne for the piano was the creation of John Field, who wrote eighteen dreamy, sentimental night pieces. From Field, Chopin inherited not only the medium but also the style; but to them, he contributed a richness of poetic thought, an eloquent expressiveness and a subtlety of atmosphere not found in Field. It was Chopin, and not Field, who made the nocturne a significant form of piano literature. "He ennobled the form originated by Field," says James Gibbons Huneker, "giving it dramatic breadth, passion, even grandeur. Set against Field's naïve and idyllic specimens, the efforts of Chopin are often too bejeweled, far too lugubrious, too tropical—Asiatic is a better word; and they have the exotic savor of the heated conservatory, not the fresh scene of the flowers grown in the open by the less poetic John Field. . . . Chopin loved the night and its starry mysteries; his Nocturnes are truly night pieces, some wearing an agitated, remorseful countenance; others seen in the profile only; while many are like whisperings at dusk—Verlaine moods."

It is just such a "Verlaine mood," and "whisperings at dusk" that we find in what is Chopin's most famous nocturne, that in E-flat major, op. 9, no. 2 (1831), which has also become a favorite in various transcriptions. A song of night, calm and romantic, is here given the most fanciful embellishments. To the celebrated Nocturne in C-sharp minor, op. 27, no. 1 (1835), the composer provided the following somber program note, a clue to the meaning of his solemn melody which he builds up to a dramatic climax: "A calm night at Venice, where after a murder the corpse is thrown into the sea while the moon shines serenely on." Equally perfect in design, and equally revelatory of Chopin the poet, is the second nocturne in the same opus, in D-flat major. "No brooding air of mystery is in this music," says Arthur Hedley. "It is serenely lyrical, not without a touch of sentimentality—the temptation of thirds and sixths is hard to resist—but not languishing. The coda provides a further example of Chopin's gift for producing new sounding effects by essentially simple means. In this case, straightforward chromatic movement over the fundamental D-flat is turned into something 'rich and strange' by the way in which the parts are laid out on the keyboard."

Almost as popular as the E-flat major Nocturne is that in A-flat major, op. 32, no. 2 (1837), which has also been adapted into various transcriptions. Here, too, as in the E-flat, a sentimental melodic line is built up into a romantic song. The companion in opus 32, the Nocturne in B major, opens in a soft and pensive mood and ends in agitation with what James Gibbons Huneker said was "like the drum beat of tragedy."

One of the nocturnes with a tragic personality, and one of the masterworks in this form, is that in C minor, op. 48, no. 1 (1841), with its declamatory lyric line, and its noble interlude that is built up into a dramatic climax.

Among the other nocturnes favored by audiences are those in G minor, op. 15, no. 3 (1831–1833) and E-flat major, op. 55, no. 2 (1843), both sounding like improvisations; the G minor was written after the composer had seen a performance of *Hamlet*. The G major Nocturne, op. 37, no. 2 (1838–1839) reminds Ernest Hutcheson of a barcarolle; it has "the undulation of a boat song, both in the rippling double notes of the main subject and in the swaying motion of the alternating theme." The Nocturne in F minor, op. 55, no. 1 (1843) is an exquisite miniature; Chopin here repeats the germinal thought of his main melody about a dozen times, each time with variation. The B major and E major, of op. 62 (1846), are noteworthy for their delicacy of style as well as poignancy of lyricism.

1832–1834. 4 SCHERZOS, for piano: I. B minor, op. 20. II. B-flat minor, op. 31. III. C-sharp minor, op. 39. IV. E major, op. 54.

In Chopin's scherzos we do not detect any of the humorous overtones the classicists so often brought to this form, nor the strong impetuous drive of Beethoven, nor the fairy-like capers of Mendelssohn. Chopin's scherzos are strong-fibered; they are dramatic; at times they are somber. His first scherzo (1832), written when he was twenty-five, already demonstrates a new kind of personality that the scherzo would reveal with him. Richard Anthony Leonard explains: "It opens with two shocking chords—and then a blast of passion is let loose. No music Chopin had then written . . . had ever twisted euphony which was supposed to be music into spiritual warfare so violent." The second scherzo (1837) is "much more pleasing melodically and its emotions are constrained to more reasonable bounds." The third scherzo (1839) was written during Chopin's unhappy visit to Majorca. Niecks describes this music as "fretful and fiercely scornful," while James Gibbons Huneker said "it is a somber and fantastic pile of architecture, and about it hovers despairing and perpetual night." The fourth scherzo (1842) is heard far less frequently than the other three. It is more tranquil, more contained in emotion, more rambling in structure.

1834–1842. IMPROMPTUS, for piano: I. A-flat major, op. 29. II. F-sharp major, op. 36. III. G-flat major, op. 51. IV. C-sharp minor, "Fantaisie impromptu," op. 66.

The impromptu for piano, which first achieved significance with Schubert, was enriched by Chopin with a remarkable quartet of compositions. The most celebrated are the first in A-flat (1837) and the fourth, named *Fantaisie impromptu* (1834). The A-flat Impromptu, which has the character of an improvisation, contrasts introspective passages with stormy ones. This is the composition with which, in George du Maurier's novel, Svengali would hypnotize Trilby into singing. The *Fantaisie Impromptu,* written upon the stimulation of a similar composition by Ignaz Moscheles (1794–1870), opens with a vigorous section; we soon hear a poetic song, which the Tin Pan Alley tunesmith, Harry Carroll, lifted for his song hit, "I'm Always Chasing Rainbows."

The second Impromptu, in F-sharp, alternates between a pastoral mood and a vigorous march-like subject; a remarkable modulation into the key of F major has often been discussed. The third Impromptu in G-flat is the least favored of this group; the composer himself regarded it condescendingly, maintaining he wrote it principally to please a friend.

1835–1841. 4 BALLADES, for piano. I. G minor, op. 23. II. F major, op. 38. III. A-flat major, op. 47. IV. F minor, op. 52.

The ballade for piano is a Chopin invention—a composition with such a pronounced narrative character that it appears to be telling a story while remaining absolute music. All four of Chopin's compositions in this form were inspired by poems of the celebrated Polish patriot and writer, Adam Mickiewicz. The first ballade (1835) finds its literary source in the battle of the Christian Knights against the pagan Lithuanians, as detailed in *Konrad Valenrod.* This ballade is the largest in structure and the most complex in style, "the most daring and spirited of Chopin's compositions," in Schumann's opinion. The second ballade (1839) got its stimulation from *Le Lac de Willis.* This music is remarkable for its striking contrasts of mood and emotion, the music fluctuating from the tender to the passionate, and from the serene to the tempestuous. The third ballade (1841) is the one heard most frequently. This music was derived from *Undine* and is most notable for its delicate and haunting lyricism. The fourth ballade (1842) is regarded by many Chopin authorities as the greatest one in this form—rich in melodic invention and varied in harmonic treatment; James Gibbons Huneker spoke of its "irresistible witchery."

1836–1839. 24 PRELUDES, for piano, op. 28: 1. C major. 2. A minor. 3. G major. 4. E minor. 5. D major. 6. B minor. 7. A major. 8. F-sharp minor. 9. E major. 10. C-sharp minor. 11. B major. 12. G-sharp minor. 13. F-sharp minor. 14. E-flat minor. 15. D-flat major, "Raindrop." 16. B-flat minor. 17. A-flat major. 18. F minor. 19. E-flat major. 20. C minor. 21. B-flat major. 22. G minor. 23. F major. 24. D minor.

Chopin brought artistic significance to the piano form of the prelude. In his hands it became a short composition without a set form, suggesting a temporary mood or emotion, and one which, at the end of the composition, leaves the listener with an inconclusive feeling that much more could be said.

The twenty-four preludes in opus 28 are each in a different major or minor key, beginning with C major and A minor and ending with F major and D minor. Most reflect the torment, anguish, and physical suffering to which the composer was subjected in Majorca, where so much of this music was written. "Many of them," George Sand wrote, "call up to the mind's eyes visions of dead monks and the souls of their funeral chants, which obsessed him [Chopin]. Others are suave and melancholy; these would come to him in his hours of sunshine and health, amid the sound of children's laughter beneath his window, the distant thrum of the guitar, and the song of the birds among the damp leafage; or at the sight of pale little roses blooming above the snow. Others again are dreary and sad and wringing the heart while charming the ear."

In his discussion of the preludes, Frederick Niecks said: "This heterogeneous collection of pieces reminds me of nothing so much as of an artist's portfolio filled with drawings in all stages of advancement—finished and unfinished, complete and incomplete compositions, sketches and mere memoranda, all mixed indiscriminately together. The finished works were either too small or too slight to be sent into the world separately, and the right mood for developing, completing and giving the last touch to the rest was gone, and could not be found again. Schumann, after expressing his admiration for these preludes, as well he might, adds: 'This book contains morbid, feverish and repellent matter.' I do not think that there is much that could justly be called repellent; but the morbidity and feverishness of a considerable portion must be admitted."

Niecks singles out the following Preludes for special consideration: "The E minor Prelude, No. 4, is a little poem; the exquisitely sweet languid pensiveness defies description. (This was played at Chopin's funeral services at the Madeleine Church in Paris). . . . No. 6, in B minor, we have no doubt, was the one of which George Sand said it occurred to Chopin one evening while the rain was falling and that it 'precipitates the soul into a frightful depression.' How wonderfully the contending rhythms of the accompaniment, and the fitful jerky course of the melody depict in the F-sharp minor Prelude, No. 8, a state of anxiety and agitation! The premature conclusion of that bright vivacious thing—B major, No. 11—fills one with regret. Of that beautiful melodious Prelude in F-sharp major, No. 13, the più lento and the peculiar closing bars are especially noteworthy. No. 14—E-flat minor—invites a comparison with the finale of the B-flat minor Sonata. In the middle section of the following number (D-flat major), one of the larger numbers, familiarly known as the *Raindrop* Prelude, rises before one's mind the cloistered court of the monastery at Valdemosa, and a procession of monks chanting lugubrious prayers and carrying in the dark hours of night their departed brother to his last resting place. . . . The C-sharp minor portion of No. 15 affects one like an oppressive dream; the re-entrance of the opening D-flat major, which dispels the dreadful nightmare, comes upon one with the smiling freshness of a dear, familiar nature—only after these horrors of the imagination can its serene beauty be fully appreciated. No. 17 in A-flat major, another developed piece, strikes one as akin to Mendelssohn's *Songs Without Words*. I must not omit to mention No. 21, in B-flat major, one of the finest of the collection, with its calming cantilena, and the palpitating quaver figures."

In addition to the twenty-four preludes in opus 28, Chopin wrote and had published two other pieces in this form: C-sharp major, issued in op. 45 (1841), and A-flat major, published posthumously in 1918. Discussing the finer of these two preludes—the one in C-sharp major—Niecks says: "This composition deserves its name better than almost any of the twenty-four; still I would rather call it an 'improvisata.' It seems unpremeditated, a heedless outpouring when sitting at the piano in a lonely, dreary hour, perhaps in the twilight. The quaver figure rises aspiringly and the sustained parts swell out proudly. The piquant cadenza forestalls in the progression of diminished chords favorite effects of some of our modern composers. The modulation from C-sharp minor to D major and back again (after the cadenza) is very striking and. . . beautiful."

1839–1844. SONATAS FOR PIANO:

No. 2, B-flat minor, op. 35. I. Allegro. II. Scherzo. III. Grave; Doppio movimento. IV. Presto.

No. 3, B minor, op. 58. I. Allegro maestoso. II. Largo. III. Allegro vivace. IV. Presto non tanto.

The B-flat minor (1839) is frequently referred to as the *Funeral March* Sonata because of the third movement, certainly the most celebrated elegy in all instrumental music. But the pall of death is spread over the other movements as well. The abrupt and incisive first theme in the opening Allegro—which comes after four somber measures of introduction and an agitated rhythmic passage—carries a feeling of terror; and the lyrical second theme is suffused with pathos. For his second movement, Chopin uses the scherzo form, which opens so nervously that M. Poirée sees in its impulsive movement a picture of "terrifying pursuit and headlong flight." There is foreboding as well as breathless movement in the first part of the Scherzo, which soon finds contrast of mood and material in the sentimental trio. And now comes the monumental Funeral March. The solemn tread of the mourners can be found in the opening funeral melody, the tolling of bells simulated in the bass. The trio is a tender elegy, a gentle recollection, as it were, of one now gone. Sorrow gives way to torment in the short three-page finale, about which Schumann said: "This great movement is perhaps the boldest page which has ever been written in the whole of music. Death appears here in all the cruel realism of its brute force, which destroys and ruins all things."

The third and last of Chopin's piano sonatas (1844) came six years after the second. This is a much less integrated work than its predecessor, one with a far less unified concept. The parts, indeed, are better than the whole. "Leaving aside the questions of fitness and unity, however," writes Arthur Hedley, "one must agree that in this sonata Chopin surpassed himself in the wealth of ideas of the first order. Its four movements contain some of the finest music ever written for the piano. Color, grace, passion, revery—all are here at the command of a composer who had reached the heights of his power."

To Donald N. Ferguson, the first movement—though filled with impressive thematic material—is "more diffuse than one would expect after the conciseness of opus 25 [the second piano sonata]. . . . Beethoven might have been able to strike developmental fire out of the principal subject. Chopin can only manipulate it. The second subject is no more poetic than the weakest of the Nocturnes, so that the chief interest lies in the connecting passages, which are often exciting in themselves, but contribute little to the whole thought." A light, graceful Scherzo movement preceded a Largo which, while not a funeral march, is nevertheless so somber and deeply felt that it sounds like a threnody. The most forceful, original, and effectively conceived movement of the entire work is the finale, in rondo form. Says Herbert Weinstock: "In subject matter, in handling, in scope, and in sheer sonorous beauty, it is one of the major musical achievements after Beethoven."

1843–1846. BERCEUSE IN D-FLAT MAJOR, for piano, op. 57.
BARCAROLLE IN F-SHARP MINOR, for piano, op. 60.

Chopin's only cradle song (1843) is one of his most sensitive and poignant compositions. The frequently and subtly ornamented melody has the caressing tenderness of a lullaby. It is set against a swaying rhythm suggesting a rocking cradle—"a transparent veil cast over the theme" is the way Louis Aguettant described it. At the close of the composition, the melody dies away, suggesting that our child has fallen asleep.

Like the Berceuse, the F-sharp minor Barcarolle (1846) is one of its kind among Chopin's works. To James Gibbons Huneker, the work represents a lament "for the splendors, now vanished, of Venice, the Queen." To Karl Tausig, the music brings up the picture of a love scene in a gondola. "This is expressed in thirds and sixths and the dualism of the two notes—or persons—is maintained throughout. All is two-voiced, or two-souled! In the modulation in C-sharp major (dolce sfogato) there are, it is evident, kisses and embraces. When after several bars of introduction the theme enters, lightly rocking in the bass, it is utilized as an accompaniment on which the cantilena in two parts is laid. And we have a continuous and tender dialogue."

—— LES SYLPHIDES, ballet in one act, with choreography by Michel Fokine. The music is by Chopin, orchestrated by Glazunov, Liadov, Nicholas Tcherepnine, and Stravinsky. First performance: Paris, June 2, 1909.

Les Sylphides is a masterwork of classic ballet, one of the supreme achievements of Diaghilev's Ballet Russe. When introduced, the principal dancers included Pavlova, Karsavina, and Nijinsky. This ballet is known as "ballet blanc." There is no plot. "Here instead of characters," George Balanchine has explained, "with definite personalities and narrative, we have simply dancers in long white dresses and a danseur in white and black velvet, whose movements to music invoke the romantic imagination to a story of its own." Balanchine then adds: "It is the music, and the care with which the classic dance embodies it, that tells us the story of these magical creatures who dance in the light of the moon."

The music comes from various Chopin compositions, dressed in orchestral garb. The overture is the A major Prelude, op. 28, no. 7. The curtain then rises on an ancient ruin in the woods. Girls are grouped in a tableau. The Nocturne in A-flat, op. 32, no. 2, inspires some of them to dance; they are soon joined by the principals. Then one of the girls finds an outlet for her joy in a dance to the music of the Waltz in G-flat, op. 70, no. 1. Two mazurkas follow—the D major, op. 33, no. 2, and the C major, op. 67, no. 3. After a repetition of the opening A major Prelude, dances are performed to the following Chopin compositions: Waltz in A-flat, op. 69, no. 1; Waltz in C-sharp minor, op. 64, no. 2; and the *Grande valse brillante,* op. 18. The A major Prelude is repeated between the A-flat and C-sharp minor Waltzes.

FRANZ LISZT 1811–1886

It is truly regrettable that Liszt should be known to so many through his weakest music. *Les Préludes, Liebestraum,* the *Second Hungarian Rhapsody,* the two piano concertos, *La Campanella*—all this is the work of a composer who too often preferred the sentimental, the obvious, the garish, the trite, and the theatrical to the profound or the subtle. This is the Liszt of the salon, whose charm and manner made women swoon. This is Liszt the virtuoso, who never hesitated to use showmanship and dramatics to sell himself (and his magnificent pianism) to audiences.

But there was another and a far different Liszt—the profoundly religious and spiritual man, as opposed to the sensualist in search of carnal delights; the high-principled conductor at Weimar, who always functioned on the highest levels of his art and who fought so courageously to bring recognition to his contemporaries; the pianist whose interpretations of the great literature were often revelations, as opposed to his virtuoso efforts to woo public adulation with trickery and pyrotechnics. In his compositions, too, we can seek out and find a profounder Liszt than the one who wrote *Liebestraum*. This is the author of the Piano Sonata, the *Faust Symphony,* the *Funérailles,* the best pages of *Anneés de pèlerinage*. It is here that Liszt becomes one of the great influences in, as well as contributor to, Romantic composition. He was not only the composer who created the tone (or symphonic) poem, and popularized the rhapsody form; he was also the composer whose piano techniques, methods, and approaches—even notation—influenced every piano composer who followed him. The influence of Liszt on Wagner's development was something Wagner himself recognized; and the impact of Liszt on the music of the late nineteenth and early twentieth century was equally decisive. Liszt anticipated impressionism by half a century, and his nationalism predated the "Russian Five." His harmonic procedures, his excursions into discords, paved the way for some of the revolutionary practices of our time.

But in his greatest works Liszt was not only an influence but also (as Cecil Gray said of him) an inspired creator "of some of the greatest and most original masterpieces of the nineteenth century. . . . The real, fundamental Liszt is not the brilliant and facile rhetorician that he is invariably made out to be, delighting principally in grandiose sonorities and triumphant apotheoses; the essence of his art, on the contrary, consists in a sadness, a melancholy, a disillusion, a despair, of depth and intensity unequalled perhaps in all music."

His music, continues Philip Hale, "was a religion. He was one of the very few composers that stood at ease in the presence of the mighty and were not snobbish towards the unfortunate, the misunderstood, the unappreciated. As a man in the world of his art he is therefore to be ranked with Handel and Hector Berlioz."

Franz Liszt was born in Raiding, Hungary, on October 22, 1811. He began to study the piano when he was six, making such progress that, by the time he was nine, he was able to make successful public appearances. Several important noblemen created a substantial fund to finance his education. In 1821, Liszt came to Vienna, where he studied the piano with Czerny and theory with Salieri. In 1823, Liszt gave a sensational concert in Vienna. This was followed by appearances in Germany. Liszt then proceeded on to Paris for the purpose of entering the Conservatory. Denied admission because he was a foreigner, Liszt studied composition instead with Paer and Reicha; but he took no more piano lessons. Between 1824 and 1827, he concertized extensively in France, England, and Switzerland with outstanding success. Then he settled in Paris, where he became a favorite of the salons, and moved in and was influenced by the highest intellectual circles. For a while, he deserted music with the intention of finding a new career, first in religion, then in philosophy and literature. But Paganini's sensational performances in 1831 was one of several influences to bring Liszt back to music. He now aspired to become the Paganini of the piano—the greatest piano virtuoso of his generation. For two years, he concentrated on developing his piano technique. From this period of study, he emerged in 1833 to give concerts again. From this time on, his performances as well as his electrifying personality made him the most glamorous, idolized, and highly regarded virtuoso of his generation. It may well be said that it was with Liszt, during this period, that the modern piano virtuoso of the grand manner and style emerged.

His career on the concert stage was interrupted for a number of years when he formed an intimate relationship with Marie Countess d'Agoult. Out of this illicit union came three children; one of them was Cosima, destined to become, first the wife of Hans von Buelow, and then the wife of Richard Wagner.

When the relationship between Liszt and Countess d'Agoult ended in 1839, Liszt returned to the concert platform to earn new triumphs. Then in 1848, he was appointed Kapellmeister to the Grand Duke of Weimar. During the eleven years Liszt held this post as director of orchestral concerts and operas, he gave brilliant performances, not only of the standard literature, but also of the music of his contemporaries. His many significant premières included that of Wagner's *Lohengrin* in 1850. Liszt was also the first one in Germany to present the major works of Berlioz.

In Weimar, he established an intimate association with Princess Carolyne von Sayn-Wittgenstein, who left her husband to join him. Her influence upon Liszt was profound. She reawakened in him his one-time religious ardor and, in his music, she directed him toward the creation of ambitious compositions. Until now, Liszt had written mainly for the piano. The inspiration and guidance of the Princess led Liszt to undertake such vast projects as the *Faust* and *Dante* symphonies, and to conceive the symphonic poem.

Liszt left Weimar in 1859 to spend most of his time in Rome. There he achieved minor orders and became an abbé of the Third Order of St. Francis of Assisi. In 1866, when his daughter Cosima deserted her husband, von Buelow, to live with Wagner, Liszt broke off all personal contact with that master. Wagner and Liszt became reconciled in 1873 when Liszt came to Bayreuth to attend ceremonies for the laying of the cornerstone of Wagner's festival theater. But Cosima never forgave her father and refused to allow him to attend Wagner's funeral.

Liszt's last years were devoted mainly to composition and to teaching the piano to select pupils. He died on July 31, 1886, in Bayreuth, where he had come to attend the Bayreuth Festival.

1836–1877. ANNÉES DE PÈLERINAGE (YEARS OF PILGRIMAGE), three sets of tone pictures for piano:

Première année—Suisse: 1. Chapelle de Guillaume Tell; 2. Au lac du Wallenstadt; 3. Pastorale; 4. Au bord d'une source; 5. Orage; 6. Vallée d'Obermann; 7. Eglogue; 8. Le Mal du pays; 9. Les Cloches de Genève.

Deuxième année—Italie: 1. Sposalizio; 2. Il Pensieroso; 3. Canzonetta del Salvator Rosa; 4. Sonetto 47 del Petrarca; 5. Sonetto 104 del Petrarca; 6. Sonetto 123 del Petrarca; 7. Après une lecture du Dante.

Troisième année: 1. Angelus: Prière aux anges gardiens; 2. Aux cyprès de la Villa d'Este, thrénodie (3–4); 3. Aux cyprès de la Villa d'Este, thrénodie (4–4); 4. Les Jeux d'eaux à la Villa d'Este; 5. Sunt Lacrymae rerum, en mode hongrois; 6. Marche funèbre; 7. Sursum corda.

From his extensive travels all over Europe, Liszt drew the material for a monumental cycle of piano pieces. The first set, inspired by Switzerland, consists of nine compositions completed between 1835 and 1836. Poems by Byron stimulated "Eglogue" and "Les Cloches de Genève," the latter quoting in the published score an epigram from *Childe Harold.* The most famous number in this set is "Au bord d'une source," an impressionistic picture of a spring of water, and the emotions it inspires in a poet.

The Italian set was completed between 1838 and 1839. The first number is an impression of Raphael's painting in the Milan Brera; a bell theme is here combined with a hymn-like passage. The second number is an impression of Michelangelo's statue of Lorenzo di Medici in Florence. The third is a setting of a poem by Salvator Rosa, the music in a popular Italian style, harmonized richly. The next three pieces, all settings of Petrarch's sonnets, were also adapted as songs. The concluding number, designated as "Fantasia quasi sonata," was inspired by Victor Hugo's poem.

The third set—completed in 1877—is made up of random pieces first published separately. Though generally inferior to the other two sets, this one includes a remarkable composition in "Les Jeux d'eaux à la Villa d'Este," a successful realization of impressionist writing in anticipation of Debussy.

1838–1863. ÉTUDES, for piano:

Études d'exécution transcendante d'après Paganini: 1. G minor; 2. E-flat major; 3. A-flat minor "La Campanella"; 4. E major; 5. E major; 6. A minor.

Études de concert (*Caprices poètiques*)*:* 1. A-flat major "Il Lamento"; 2. F minor "La Leggierezza"; 3. D-flat major "Un Sospiro".

Études d'exécution transcendante: 1. Preludio; 2. A minor; 3. Paysage. 4. Mazeppa; 5. Feux-follets; 6. Vision; 7. Eroica; 8. Wilde Jagd; 9. Ricordanza; 10. F minor; 11. Harmonies du soir; 12. Chasse-neige.

Études de concert: 1. Waldesrauschen; 2. Gnomenreigen.

The Liszt études for the piano are not merely brilliant exercises opening new vistas for piano technique and new facets of piano style. They are also remarkable for the variety of their musical content. The études are dramatic, or sentimental, or lyrical, or atmospheric. To Busoni, Liszt's études reflect the composer's personality "in his manifold lights and poses."

The six *Études d'exécution transcendante* (1838) are, with a single exception, based on Paganini's violin caprices (which see). The most famous number in this Liszt set happens to be that exception—the third étude in A-flat, *La Campanella.* This dazzling pyrotechnical piece, simulating the tolling of bells, is a transcription of the finale (Ronde à la clochette) of Paganini's Concerto in

B minor, for violin and orchestra. The first étude, is based on Paganini's sixth caprice (*Tremolo*); the second, on the seventeenth (*Octave*); the fourth, on the first (*Arpeggio*); the fifth, on the ninth (*La Chasse*); and the sixth, a theme and variations, is evolved from Paganini's celebrated twenty-fourth caprice.

The three études—sometimes called *Études de concert,* and sometimes, *Caprices poètiques* (1848)—have the following subtitles: *Il Lamento, La Leggierezza,* and *Il Sospiro*. "They all depend," comments Ernest Hutcheson, "on musical effect rather than technical display."

The *Études d'exécution transcendante* (1851) is a compilation of a dozen pieces. The most famous are the fourth and fifth, *Mazeppa* and *Feux-follets*. "What a difference between the tremendous bravura of *Mazeppa* and the delicate refinement of *Feux-follets,*" says Hutcheson. "This entrancing will-o'-the-wisp is the priceless gem of the étude literature."

The two *Études de concert* (1863)—the *Waldesrauschen* and the *Gnomenreigen* —are among the most frequently heard of Liszt's études. The first is sensitive and delicate; it was inspired by a poem of the Queen Elizabeth of Rumania (using the pen name of Carmen Sylva). The other is dramatic.

1842–1860. SONGS, for voice and piano:

"Anfangs wollt' ich fast verzagen"; "Die drei Zigeuner"; "Du bist wie eine Blume"; "Es muss ein Wunderbares sein"; "Kling leise, mein Lied"; "O Lieb', so lang du lieben kannst"; "O quand je dors"; "Vergiftet sind meine Lieder."

Tre sonetti di Petrarca: 1. "Pace non trovo"; 2. "Benedetto sia 'l giorno"; 3. "I vidi in terra angelici costumi."

Liszt wrote about seventy songs in all. They were settings of French, German, Italian, Hungarian, and English poems. In his finest French song, "O quand je dors", poem by Hugo (1844), Liszt reveals an extraordinarily sensitive lyricism; while in his excellent three sonnets of Petrarch (1861), he demonstrates an equally uncommon gift at bel canto. But Liszt is perhaps at his most forceful and original in his German songs. At times these are starkly dramatic, often more declamatory than lyrical; and they boast an extraordinary harmonic invention. Wilfred Mellers points out that in "Anfangs wollt' ich fast verzagen," to Heine's poem (1856), the effect is achieved through breaking up the lyrical phrases "under the stress of feeling" and through summing up the bitterness of the poem "in the unexpected, inverted resolution from major to minor." In "Vergiftet sind meine Lieder," poem once again by Heine (1842), Liszt "dispenses with lyricism altogether; the dissonant appoggiaturas of the opening and the ninths of the climax are as violent as *Tristan* and much starker."

1846–1885. HUNGARIAN RHAPSODIES, for piano: I. E major. II. C-sharp minor. III. B-flat major. IV. E-flat major. V. E minor. VI. D-flat major. VII. D minor. VIII. F-sharp minor. IX. E-flat major. X. E major. XI. A minor. XII. C-sharp minor. XIII. A minor. XIV. F minor. XV. A minor. XVI. A minor. XVII. D minor. XVIII. F-sharp minor. XIX. D minor.

The rhapsody, as a form of piano music was created by Václav Tomasek (1774–1850). But it first became prominent with Liszt through his *Hungarian Rhapsodies*. With Liszt, the rhapsody became a free, pliable form in which popular melodies were elaborated in a rhapsodic manner. Rapid changes of mood from the slow and the sensual (*lassan*) to the pulsating and the dramatic (*frissan*) take place, together with electrifying alternation of contrasting moods, and rapid changes of tempo, rhythm, and dynamics. Liszt, who spent many years of research into Hungarian folk music, had collated the fruits of these efforts into ten volumes. His rhapsodies—overflowing with authentic Hungarian or gypsy melodies and dance rhythms—represents one of the earlies successful attempts to realize a musical nationalism.

The most famous of these rhapsodies—and probably the most famous of all Liszt's compositions—is the second in C-sharp minor (1847). In style, structure, and musical content it is characteristic of all the works in this genre. It opens with a slow, sedate melody—the *lassan*. A cadenza leads into the energetic, bubbling *frissan* melody. This material is built up with enormous dramatic effect and with a mounting feeling of excitement through expanding sonorities and uninhibited rhythmic impulses. A stirring climax is reached with a loud restatement of the gay *frissan* tune. Toward the end of the rhapsody, a completely new—and plaintive—thought is suddenly introduced. After a brief pause, a stirring coda helps to unleash once again the former unbridled energy.

The following rhapsodies are also very popular: the ninth, known as the *Carnaval de Pesth;* the twelfth; the fourteenth, which the composer adapted into the *Hungarian Fantasy* for piano and orchestra (which see); the fifteenth, named *Rakóczy March* (not to be confused with the composition of the same name by Berlioz).

Liszt and Franz Doppler transcribed six of the rhapsodies for orchestra (2, 5, 6, 9, 12, 14). Karl Muller Berghaus made an excellent orchestral transcription of the second; Hans Kindler, of the sixth.

1849. CONCERTOS FOR PIANO AND ORCHESTRA:

No. 1, E-flat major. I. Allegro maestoso. II. Quasi adagio; Allegretto vivace. III. Allegro animato; Allegro marziale animato.

No. 2, A major.

The most famous of Liszt's several piano concertos—the first in E-flat major—was played for the first time anywhere in Weimar in 1855. Two years later, when heard in Vienna, Eduard Hanslick—who was violently opposed to Liszt's progressive ideas and to his espousal of the Wagnerian dogma—seized upon the rather insignificant fact that Liszt was using a triangle in the orchestra of the third movement. With this feeble ammunition for his attack, Hanslick heaped such scorn and contempt upon the work that for a long time it was identified as "the triangle concerto." It was also due to Hanslick's vituperation that this concerto was not again heard in Vienna until 1869, when it was received most enthusiastically. Liszt himself justified the unorthodox use of a triangle by saying he was seeking "the effect of contrast."

Though the concerto is in several movements, it is unified in concept, and is played without interruption. Liszt side-stepped the traditional concerto form by treating his structure with the greatest of liberty, and by dispensing with formal developments of his thematic material. The first principal theme is heard immediately—a forceful statement for strings over chords by the winds. The piano arrives in the fifth measure. After a cadenza, and some elaboration of the opening theme, the Adagio movement is introduced with a subject for muted cellos and double basses amplified by the solo piano. Solo flute, and a passage for the clarinet, both over trills in the piano, lead into a scherzo passage. It is here that we hear the controversial but inoffensive triangle—in the very opening. A third main theme is presented. This is a brisk martial subject for strings, prefaced by a long trill on the piano accompanied by the triangle. This part of the concerto ends with a piano cadenza in which the concerto's opening theme is again suggested. Octave passages in the piano bring on the Allegretto animato, where the initial subject of the first movement and the closing part of the Adagio are recalled. The fourth movement, in Liszt's own description "corresponds to the second movement Adagio. It is merely an urgent recapitulation of the earlier subject matter, with quickened livelier rhythm, and contains no new motive. . . . The trombones and basses take up the second part of the motive of the Adagio. The piano figure that follows is no other than the reproduction of the motive that was given in the Adagio by flute and clarinet, just as the concluding passage is a variant and working up in the major of the motive of the Scherzo, until finally the first motive on the dominant pedal B flat, with a trill accompaniment, comes in and concludes the whole."

It is not easy to pinpoint exactly when the second Liszt piano concerto was written. Liszt began to work on it in 1839, completed the first draft between 1840 and 1845, and revised it in 1849. He subsequently rewrote parts several times.

To emphasize the symphonic character of this work, Liszt identified it on his manuscript as a "concerto symphonique." It is in a single-movement structure, romantic in style throughout, and dominated by the melodious subject that is forthwith heard in the woodwind (Adagio sostenuto assai). This theme becomes transformed when the piano enters at the thirteenth measure. A new pensive thought is introduced by the horn, accompanied by the piano; it is soon taken over by oboe and solo cello. Following a cadenza for the piano, a quickening of the tempo and a crescendo bring on a new section (Allegro agitato assai). This is stormy music, built up into a powerful climax. A new cadenza for the piano and another change in tempo (Allegro moderato) bring in the solo cello with a new suggestion of the concerto's first theme. Still another cadenza introduces the Allegro deciso section in which earlier material is freely treated. Then the important first theme is loudly given in a march rhythm by piano and orchestra before a brilliant coda concludes the concerto.

1849. TOTENTANZ (DANSE MACABRE), fantasy for piano and orchestra.

During a visit to Pisa, Liszt was attracted to a fresco in the Campo Santo —*The Triumph of Death,* attributed by some to Andrea Orcagna, and by others to the Lorenzettis. This picture impelled him to write a large work for piano and orchestra embodying the "Dies Irae." The fantasy has no set program. It opens with piano and timpani dramatically setting the stage for the first appearance of the awesome "Dies Irae" melody in woodwind, brass, and strings. After a brief piano cadenza, the theme is repeated by the orchestra and then by the solo piano. The tense, even diabolic, atmosphere increases as the "Dies Irae" melody is subjected to several variations. Here the piano is often heard in dazzling virtuoso passages, while the orchestra accentuates the macabre mood. The last variation, with its demoniac glissandi in the piano, carries the mood to the edge of terror.

1849–1850. COMPOSITIONS FOR SOLO PIANO:

Funérailles; Liebestraum No. 2, in A-flat; *Consolation No. 3* in D-flat major.

Funérailles (1849) is one of the most eloquent threnodies in solo piano literature. It is the seventh number in *Harmonies poètiques et religieuses.* Some Liszt biographers and critics are of the opinion that the composer was inspired by Chopin's death to write this music. The work is dated October, 1849, and Chopin died on October 17 of that year. Others believe that Liszt here intended to honor the memory of several friends fallen in the recent revolutions.

A slow and percussive introduction provides a dramatic preface for the eloquent funeral march music that follows. A plangent melody in the relative major (lagrimoso) plunges even more deeply into grief. A new march-like episode is then built up climactically before the funeral-march theme is triumphantly recalled, and the Lagrimoso melody is plaintively repeated. The composition ends with an agitated coda.

Liszt wrote three sentimental nocturnes for the piano, all of them in 1850, all of them based on his songs, and all of them entitled *Love's Dream* (*Liebestraum*). But whenever *Liebestraum* is mentioned, it is the third in A-flat that is being referred to. With the second *Hungarian Rhapsody,* it is Liszt's most popular instrumental composition. The second *Liebestraum,* with its tender melody over an arpeggio accompaniment, is based on the Liszt song, "O Lieb, so lang du lieben kannst."

Liszt wrote six *Consolations* in 1850. Each is a brief mood picture in either a sentimental, passionate, or religious vein. In the third (Lento placido) a serene atmosphere is projected through a flowing, singable melody.

1851–1854. TONE POEMS, for orchestra:
"*Mazeppa; Tasso: Lamento e Trionfo (Tasso: Lament and Triumph); Les Préludes; Orpheus*.

Liszt wrote his first tone poem in 1848–1849. It was *Ce qu'on entend sur la montagne,* based on Victor Hugo. The tone or symphonic poem is a musical structure devised by Liszt to carry into orchestral music some of Wagner's dramatic implications and aesthetic ideals. In Liszt's hands it became a fluid structure in which the thematic material is developed freely along dramatic lines. A program—a story, painting, poem, or idea—is realistically translated into musical terms.

Mazeppa (1851) is also based on a poem by Victor Hugo; and its musical material is partly derived from one of the etudes in Liszt's *Études d'exécution transcendante*. Mazeppa is an Asiatic chieftain. He is tied to an untamed horse which drags him for three days across the Ukrainian plains until the animal collapses with exhaustion and Mazeppa lies dead on the horse's back. Liszt's music follows the Hugo text literally. A brief descending phrase in the winds, and a discordant crash, prefaces a heroic ascending subject for trombones, cellos, and double basses; this subject represents Mazeppa. It is developed dramatically and at times with considerable agitation. Then the ride across the plains is realistically described with powerful dynamics and brilliant sonorities. The Mazeppa theme returns and is amplified, followed by a proud martial subject over viola and cello tremolos proclaiming Mazeppa a conqueror. The tone poem ends first with a return of the Mazeppa theme, then with a tranquil episode depicting birds encircling the dead hero and horse.

Tasso originated in 1840 as a piano composition. Three years later Liszt orchestrated it and used it as a prelude for a performance of Goethe's *Tasso* in Weimar. An elaborate revision of this music into the mold of the tone poem took place some years after that.

Though it started out as a prelude for the Goethe drama, and though the program of Tasso's triumph was derived from it, Liszt took pains to explain that his stimulation in writing *Tasso* came from reading Byron. He was, he said, influenced by "the respectful compassion of Byron for the . . . great man whom he evoked." In further amplification, Liszt provided his music with the following programmatic interpretation: "Tasso loved and suffered at Ferrara; he was avenged at Rome; his glory still lives in the people's songs of Venice. These three points are inseparably connected with his memory. To express them in music, we first invoked the mighty shadow of the hero as it is now appearing, haunting the lagoons of Venice; we have caught a glimpse of his proud, sad face at the feats in Ferrara; and we have followed him to Rome, the Eternal City, which crowned him with the crown of glory and glorified in him the martyr and the poet."

The tone poem opens with the "Lamento" (Lento), its theme heard in lower strings before being built up effectively. After a change of tempo to Allegro strepitoso, a modification of this theme leads into the Tasso motive, in cellos and double basses. This is followed by the poignant strain of Tasso's suffering; it is given by the bass clarinet accompanied by harp and strings. This melody, the main one in the tone poem, was taken by Liszt from a song of Venetian gondoliers. A minuet-like movement (Allegretto moso con grazia) now describes Tasso's life at the court of Ferrara; its principal theme is presented by two solo cellos. The closing section is the "Trionfo" (Allegro con brio), which is an extension and a grandiose restatement of the opening subject.

Les Préludes (1854) is Liszt's most popular tone poem. For his program, the composer went to Lamartine's *Méditations poètiques,* an excerpt from which is found in the published score. "What is our life but a series of Preludes to that unknown song of which death strikes the first solemn note? Love is the enchanted dawn of every life; but where is the destiny in which the first pleasures of happiness are not interrupted by some storm, whose deadly breath dissipates its fair illusions, whose fatal thunderbolt consumes its altar? And where is the soul which, cruelly wounded, does not seek, at the coming of one of these storms, to calm its memories in the tranquil life of the country? Man, however, cannot long resign himself to the kindly tedium which has at first charmed him in the companionship of nature, and when 'the trumpet has sounded the signal of alarms,' he hastens to the post of peril, whatever may be the strife which calls him to the ranks, in order to regain in combat the full consciousness of himself and the complete command of his powers."

Two plucked notes in the strings invoke a solemn subject in the double basses. This is the principal theme of the tone poem. Some elaboration follows, together with a sonorous repetition of the theme in brass and basses, and a meditative version of the same melody in cellos. A new subject, portraying the "happiness of love" is then presented by horns, strings, and harp. This material is built up into an overpowering climax, after which a new variation of the principal theme is presented. The music now becomes storm-ridden, dramatized by chromaticisms and diminished sevenths. When the storm is over, the oboe introduces a pastoral atmosphere with a nostalgic recollection of our main theme. A country dance is soon suggested by the horn, and the love melody is recalled. Once again unrest sets in. The music again becomes increasingly agitated before the tone poem rises to a dynamic climax in the coda. A variation of the main theme brings the work to a majestic conclusion.

Orpheus (1854) had its origin while Liszt was rehearsing Gluck's *Orfeo ed Euridice* in Weimar. He was moved by the legend to create a tone poem on the same subject. He saw Orpheus as symbolizing art, which he felt "must exert the power of melody, its vibrant chords, its gentle luminosity, to combat the elements hidden in every individual in all society. Orpheus mourns for Eurydice. Eurydice, that symbol of the Ideal, assailed by evil and suffering, whom he is allowed to rescue from the monsters of Erebus, but whom he is unable to lead out into the light of day."

Orpheus's lyre is suggested by harp arpeggios in the opening measures. These serve as an accompaniment to the first principal theme personifying Eurydice, an expressive melody in horns and cellos. A Lento section contributes effective passages for English horn and oboe over harp and pizzicati strings. A transition in the solo violin then brings on a dramatic development of this material, its climax representing the victory of Art over sensuality and the savagery of human nature. Strong figures in the bass speak for the evil forces in the world, while a glorious melody symbolizes Orpheus and Art. The earlier transition theme in the solo violin returns in the English horn in the coda to end the tone poem quietly and mysteriously.

1853. SONATA IN B MINOR, for piano.

The B minor Sonata, one of Liszt's masterworks, was described by Wagner as "beyond all conception beautiful, great, lovely; deep and noble; sublime even as thyself." It is more like a fantasia or tone poem than a sonata—diffuse in form, rhapsodic in style, free in the treatment of the thematic material. There is only a single movement. The main thematic material can be found in the introductory passage. One theme is a powerful statement in octaves; another, is an even more epical and extended thought; a third is a marcato passage for the bass. This material is developed with immense power, and at times, with extraordinary eloquence. A strong religious note is injected with a chorale. The concluding section, a Prestissimo, recalls all the basic themes. James Gibbons Huneker has written about this section as follows: "Nothing more exciting is there in the literature of the piano. Then follow a few bars of that very Beethoven-like Andante, a moving return of the early themes, and silently the first Lento descends to the subterranean depths whence it emerged; then a true Liszt chord-sequence and a stillness in B major."

1856–1857. A SYMPHONY TO DANTE'S DIVINE COMEDY, for solo voice, chorus, and orchestra. I. Inferno. II. Purgatorio.

A FAUST SYMPHONY in "three character pictures," for tenor, male chorus, and orchestra. I. Faust. II. Marguerite. III. Mephistopheles.

Though Liszt called the *Dante* (1856) a symphony, it is in reality two descriptive tone poems. He first planned this work in 1847, but devoted himself to it intensively between 1855 and 1856. An ominous introductory phrase in the bass instruments, and a recitative describing the inscription over hell's door in the *Divine Comedy,* bring on a stirring subject for trombones and horns sounding the celebrated Dante warning: "Leave hope behind, all ye who enter here." There follows a gruesome tonal presentation of hell's torments in chromatic sequences, discords, and brilliant sonorities. A brief lull precedes a quieter section. This is an exchange between bass clarinet and English horn telling about the sad fate of Paolo and Francesca da Rimini. But the shrieks and unholy sounds of hell return to bring the first movement to a demoniac conclusion.

The second movement opens serenely with a religious, chorale-like melody describing the joys of Heaven. A monumental fugue, and a return of the opening chorale, bring on the concluding episode. This is a mighty, classical Magnificat for solo voice, chorus, and orchestra. Liszt wrote two different finales for his symphony. One was an ecstatic, exultant sequence culminating in a Hallelujah; the other was in the subdued and peaceful mood with which the symphony opened.

In making a symphonic setting of Goethe's *Faust,* Liszt decided to devote each of his three movements to one of three principal characters. The result is a suite rather than a symphony, a suite comprising three tone poems. It is generally believed that Liszt's admiration for Berlioz's *The Damnation of Faust* was the force sending him to make his own setting of the Goethe drama. He started work in 1854, and completed the symphony three years later. The world première in Weimar, on September 5, 1857, was by way of celebrating the dedication of a Goethe-Schiller monument and a statue to the poet Wielad, in Weimar.

The first movement (Allegro) is a portrait of the disturbed and tormented philosopher, Faust. The solemn opening theme, in cellos and double basses, emphasizes Faust's frustrations, together with his yearning for his lost youth. The orchestra builds up this theme into an expression of revolt. Then a subject in the bassoons suggests the theme of "fatalism." Strings and woodwind now provide a transition to the main part of the movement, where two expressive ideas are projected. The first is introduced by horns and clarinets, and the second by trumpet. In this part, Faust's doubts and torments are dissipated. His romantic nature is reawakened and his passionate feelings are aroused through his recollection of Marguerite. But the inner struggle is not over. A chromatic transition in plucked strings brings on another period of agitation. Then a brass fanfare brings back the theme of fatalism. Faust plunges more deeply than ever into the melancholy mood that had enveloped him earlier.

The tenderness, the passionate love suggested in the first movement is given free rein in the Andante. After a brief introduction by clarinet and flute, the oboe sings a tender melody supported by viola arpeggios. This is Marguerite's song of love, permeated with purity and innocence. The strings bring on a new melody which soon is taken over by the flute. The music becomes increasingly sensual as Marguerite becomes more and more aware of her overwhelming physical desires. The mood is further dramatized by a recall of the first-movement subject identifying Faust. But the sweetness and innocence of Marguerite are in the end victorious.

In the third-movement Scherzo, portraying Mephistopheles, Liszt indulges his bent for irony and sardonic moods. A chromatic subject in cellos and basses, interrupted by exclamations from woodwind and cymbals, immediately introduces Mephistopheles. Thematic material of the first movement reappears, but burlesqued and caricatured. A sudden recall of the Marguerite melody from the second movement helps to dispel the evil forces—but only temporarily. A demoniac accelerando erupts into a wild demonstration in which the Faust theme is a hopeless victim. Once again the Marguerite melody is heard to speak for womanly virtue and the selflessness of true love. Then the majestic strains of an organ bring in a "chorus mysticus" for tenor and male chorus. They intone the solemn closing lines of Goethe's *Faust,* extolling Woman and Love. Thus the symphony ends on a positive and triumphant note.

1860. HUNGARIAN FANTASY, for piano and orchestra.

This is the composer's own adaptation of the *Hungarian Rhapsody* No. 14 which he had written eight years earlier. A slow, dignified introduction for the orchestra and a piano cadenza bring on the main body of the Fantasy. It spills over with sensual Hungarian melodies, fiery rhythms, and contrasting moods.

1861. MEPHISTO WALTZ (THE DANCE AT THE VILLAGE INN), for orchestra.

Liszt completed two short works for orchestra, based on Nikolaus Lenau's *Faust.* The first—*Midnight Procession*—is rarely given. The second—*Mephisto Waltz*—is, however, a concert favorite, its passion, sensuality, and dramatics never failing to create an emotional impact. James Gibbons Huneker described its "languorous syncopated melody" as "one of the most voluptuous episodes outside of the *Tristan* score."

The following programmatic note, lifted from Lenau, is found in the published score: "There is a wedding feast in progress in the village inn, with music, dancing, carousing. Mephistopheles and Faust pass by, and Mephistopheles induces Faust to enter and take part in the festivities. Mephistopheles snatches the instrument from the hands of a lethargic fiddler and draws from it indescribably seductive and intoxicating strains. The amorous Faust whirls about with a full-blooded village beauty in a wild dance; they waltz in mad abandonment out of the room, into the open, away into the woods. The sounds of the fiddle grow softer and softer, and the nightingale warbles his love-laden song."

The dance at the inn, the first principal motive, is heard first as a rhythmic and strongly accented subject for the cellos. The seductive strains of Mephistopheles's violin playing is the second main theme of the work; it is initially presented as a passionate song for strings.

1862–1883. COMPOSITIONS FOR SOLO PIANO:
Variations on Weinen, Klagen, Sorgen, Zagen.
Two Legends: I. St. François d'Assise prédication aux oiseaux. II. St. François de Paule marchant sur les flots.
Nuages gris; La lugubre gondole; Sinistre.
Two Ballades: I. D-flat major. II. B minor.

Weinen, Klagen, Sorgen, Zagen is a cantata by Johann Sebastian Bach. From its first movement Liszt expropriated the ground bass supporting the main melody, building around it a series of variations (1862). The subject is a four-bar phrase of eight descending chromatic steps. Its first appearance is in four groups, each comprising two chords. After that, the theme is heard in its entirety. The variations are improvisations in which the lofty character of Bach is never lost sight of, even though the writing frequently has a virtuoso character. In the coda, Liszt quotes Bach's chorale, "Was Gott tut dass is wohlgetan." Liszt originally wrote these variations for organ, but in 1870, he transcribed them for the piano; he also made an orchestral adaptation.

In 1866, Liszt completed two *Legends* for the piano, each descriptive and programmatic. In the first—St. *Francis' Sermon to the Birds*—a broad, religious melody represents the sermon, while the chirpings of the birds are suggested rather than directly imitated. In the second—*St. Francis Walking on the Waves*—Liszt was inspired by a drawing by E. J. von Steinle showing St. Francis crossing the Straits of Messina. Liszt's writing here is more literally programmatic than in the first legend, especially in the way in which he imitates in his music the flow and ebb of the waters.

Nuages gris, La lugubre gondole, and *Sinistre* are among Liszt's last compositions for the piano (1881–1882). To Cecil Gray, it is here that we encounter "the essential Liszt," here that we confront his "true greatness," here that Liszt is "original, unique unsurpassed." Gray adds: "In all these works with which he concluded his creative career, one finds quite a disconcerting bareness of idiom and a complete sacrifice of every means of effect to the purposes of expression. The conceptions, moreover, to which expression is given in these later works, are almost invariably of a gloomy and tragic order. . . . No composer has ever ventured further into the City of Dreadful Night of which the poet Thomson sings; none has expressed with greater poignancy 'that all is vanity and nothingness.'"

To Hans von Buelow, Liszt's last two ballades (1883) are superior to those by Chopin for their "dramatic power" of structure, subtlety of melodic line and the "wonderful compelling technique." The first ballade contrasts a singing lyrical thought with a march-like subject. The second opens mournfully, with a figure in the bass that sounds like a dirge; after that, a stormy, martial melody is highlighted.

RICHARD WAGNER 1813–1883

The ambition to create musical drama, as opposed to formal operas, had been the ideal of musicians almost from the beginnings of opera itself. Monteverdi, Rameau, and Gluck were some of the early pioneers trying to achieve a fusion, not only of drama and music, but also of these two elements with ballet, scenery, costuming, and staging. Thus, speaking strictly, Wagner was not the father of the music drama. But he did come closer to the realization of this goal by writing his own poetical dramas, setting forth his ideas about costuming and scenic designs and staging clearly and explicitly, and bringing into being a theater where his advanced thinking about music and the stage could be realized. He also came closer than anyone before him to the musico-dramatic dream by devising all kinds of new musical techniques and idioms able to meet the most exacting and precise needs of his dramatic and poetic concepts. He built a gargantuan orchestra of his own—increasing its number and variety and even devising such new members as the so-called Wagner tubas. He endowed that orchestra with new nuances, dynamics, and colors; and he assigned to it a significance within his musico-dramatic scheme without precedence. He invented a new harmonic language: suspended ninth chords; six-four chords in protracted cadences; chromatic harmonies evoking a new kind of dissonance through continual modulations until all sense of a consistent tonality was lost. He devised a new procedure by once and for all discarding the distinction between recitative and aria, and evolving a continual flow of melody, the variety of subtlety of which impelled him to invent new vocal and instrumental resources. He introduced a new and complex treatment of the leading motive technique. He used hundreds and hundreds of motives—one for every possible mood, situation, character, or emotion. Some were melodies, and some fragments. All were built up in their infinite permutations and combinations into a gigantic symphonic fabric without precedent or parallel.

His theories on the musical drama were propounded in such treatises as *The Art Work of the Future* and *Opera and Drama.* William Foster Apthorp has stripped these ideas of their "dialectic trappings" and straightened out their "metaphysical convolutions" to provide the essence of Wagner's proposed revolution. "In any sort of Drama, whether musical or otherwise, the play's the thing; and in the Music Drama, the music must lend itself unreservedly and continuously to intensifying the emotional expression of the text, and to giving an illustrative coloring to the dramatic action. In the end—aye, and even down to the minute details—it is the theory of the old Florentine Camerata, and nothing else under the sun. As to the practical means by which music can best fulfil this its allotted mission, two points in Wagner's theory are noteworthy; the first fundamental, the second more adventitious. The first point is that music must abandon all those forms which were developed, not so much from its own intrinsic nature, as from its first application to human uses—that is, from the Dance—and assume only such plastic forms as spring naturally and freely from the nature of the dramatic subject it seeks to illustrate. The second point is what is known as the Leitmotiv. . . . Almost the whole web of the music is woven out of the Leitmotiven; they come either singly and in succession, or else simultaneously and interwoven. There is no melodic constituent of the music that is not a Leitmotiv. This gives the music, if not greater dramatic force, at least an unflagging dramatic suggestiveness. . . . Not the least merits of Wagner's . . . manner is its wondrous flexibility and adaptability. It can lend itself to every conceivable kind of drama, from the most exalted tragedy to the broadest farce. In its more colloquial phase it becomes the first German substitute for the Italian recitative quasi-parlando ever discovered, a fit musical vehicle for homely dialogue. Nor does it lose caste amid the grandest and most elaborate musical developments. It is at once thoroughly dramatic and thoroughly musical."

How well did Wagner realize his musico-dramatic ideals, his synthesis of the arts? H. C. Colles provides the following answer, pro and con: "In the first place, his union of all the arts was limited by the fact that his genius was infinitely greater as a musician than as a poet or dramatist. A master of tone, he was only a very skilful workman with words, and he was unable ultimately to control the third element in his scheme, gesture, which necessarily rested with the interpreters. Moreover, his overmastering conviction of the moral importance of his ideas made him insist upon explaining himself at every crucial point, and explanation is fatal to drama. He never outgrew this habit. . . . Explanations . . . are constant in *The Ring* where the whole of the complex story has an allegorical meaning; in *Die Meistersinger* they give way to a tendency to harangue the multitudes on the principles of artistic criticism; in *Tristan,* save for King Mark's dialogue, they are much less insistent, and this fact, together with the simplicity of the story, brings the work nearest to the ideal union which he had asserted ought to be found. . . . One might expend many pages in examining the planning of the orchestral commentary, the power with which it bursts into the most vivid prismatic coloring or retires to form a gently suggestive background to the voices. Enough has been said to show that if we answer the question whether the Wagnerian synthesis of the arts was a success with a negative, it is simply because Wagner's powers as a musician were so much greater than those as a poet or dramatist that his musical splendor swamps all other considerations."

The poet and the dramatist, then, frequently leave much to be desired—in the obscure mysticism of the poetry; the immobility of so much of the dramatic action; the repetitiousness of the story material through interminable monologues. But the musician is never found wanting. With the most extraordinary technical equipment, invention, and imagination, Wagner the composer never failed his text. Every climactic episode finds appropriate music to lift the drama to incomparable heights of grandeur and majesty—whether it be the pomp and circumstance that closes *Die Meistersinger;* the passion and sensuality that envelop Tristan and Isolde in their incomparable second-act love music; the tender compassion of Wotan's farewell to Bruennhilde in *Die Walkuere;* the cataclysmic drama that brings the Ring cycle to its catastrophic conclusion in the Immolation scene. Where drama and poetry may fail, there music steps in unfalteringly to create an art with few equals in the musical theater.

No musician had more virulent enemies, or was subject to more violent attacks, than Wagner. Eduard Hanslick described the music dramas as "formlessness elevated to a principle, a systematized non-music, a melodic nerve fever written out on the five lines of the staff." Other critics described him as a "madman," a "corrupter of art," a "disease who contaminates everything he touches—he has made music sick." And no musician ever had more dedicated, more self-effacing, and more passionate disciples than Wagner—musicians like Hans von Buelow (whose wife Wagner stole), Franz Liszt, Ludwig II of Bavaria. These and others like them regarded him truly as a prophet of the new music, of "the art of the future."

But whatever may be his shortcomings in the fulfillment of his artistic destiny, Wagner remains one of the greatest revolutionaries music has known, one of the greatest musical dramatists of all time, and one of the most significant creative figures in the entire history of art. "In the whole range of opera," once said W. H. Hadow, "there will be found no greater name than that of Wagner. He has clothed it with a new life, he has taught it to deliver a new message, and the echoes of his voice will last, not only in his own works, but in the days to come."

"For vastness of artistic concept," this writer has summed up in a book on modern music, "for newness of musical language, for independence of musical thought, Wagner dominated the closing nineteenth century like a Colossus. He might be hated or worshiped; but to ignore him was impossible. The spell of Wagner was inescapable; it was felt by every composer who followed him. There were those who tried to write as he did (and not necessarily for the stage). In following in his giant footsteps, these men carried German Romanticism to a point beyond which it could go no further. Then there were those who reacted violently against his superstructure, grandiloquence, determination to make music express ideas and concepts beyond the boundaries of tones. Such composers, breaking with Wagner, helped to swing the musical pendulum to the extreme that opposed German Romanticism."

Wilhelm Richard Wagner was born in Leipzig, Germany, on May 22, 1813. There is good reason to believe that he was the illegitimate son of Johanna Wagner and an actor named Ludwig Geyer. In any event, while Richard was still an infant, his mother married Geyer. For about five years, from 1822 to 1827, Richard attended the Kreuzschule in Dresden, where he demonstrated a strong gift for classical literature. Piano study began in 1825; theoretical study was at first pursued from texts, without the benefit of teachers, and later on in Leipzig with C. G. Mueller. Despite his hapazard musical training, Wagner was able to complete a string quartet, piano sonata, and an orchestral overture, the last of which was publicly performed in Leipzig in 1830. Meanwhile, between 1828 and 1830, he continued his academic education at the Nikolaischule in Leipzig; and in 1831, he entered the University of Leipzig for the study of law. Being an irresponsible student at the university, he soon deserted all thoughts of law to concentrate on music. After some additional instruction from Theodor Weinlig, Wagner wrote two ambitious orchestral works, an overture and a symphony, both of which were performed. He was also beginning to think in terms of the theater, completing a libretto and some musical episodes for *Die Hochzeit,* an opera he never finished.

While working as a chorusmaster at the Wuerzburg Opera, Wagner wrote his first complete opera—*Die Feen,* his own libretto based on a play by Gozzi. From this time on, and until the end of his life, he would serve as his own librettist. Between 1834 and 1836, he served as conductor of the Magdeburg Opera. During this period, he wrote his second opera, *Das Liebesverbot,* based on Shakespeare's *Measure for Measure.* Its première at Magdeburg on March 29, 1836 was a fiasco and was largely responsible for sending the company to bankruptcy. In 1836, he became conductor of the Koenigsberg Opera. While holding this post, he married Minna Planer, an actress, on November 24, 1836. One year later found him in Riga as conductor of its Opera and of orchestral concerts. In Riga, Wagner completed libretto and music for two acts of *Rienzi.*

Heavily involved in debts, and threatened with prison, Wagner and his wife escaped stealthily from Riga, arriving in Paris in September of 1839. His letters of introduction from Meyerbeer failed to open for him the doors of the Opéra, where he hoped to get *Rienzi* produced. The next three years were spent in abject poverty; not even the hack work to which he was reduced was able to bring him a livelihood. For a few weeks in 1840, he was even confined to debtor's prison. Despite these harrowing hardships and frustrations, Wagner remained creatively productive. He completed an orchestral work, *A Faust Overture,* and began working on the opera, *The Flying Dutchman.*

A change of fortune came with the triumphant première of *Rienzi* at the Dresden Opera on October 20, 1842. The acclaim enjoyed by this opera and by its immediate successor—*The Flying Dutchman,* produced on January 2, 1843—led to an appointment as musical director of the Dresden Opera. For the next six years, Wagner helped create a new epoch for the Dresden Opera through his painstakingly prepared and musicianly performances; these included the world première of his own opera, *Tannhaeuser,* on October 19, 1845. By 1848, he was putting the final strokes of his pen on still another opera, *Lohengrin.*

Involved in the revolutionary movement in Germany in 1848–1849, and threatened by arrest, Wagner fled from Saxony and went into exile. He soon found a new home in Zurich, where he started to formulate his ideas about opera and the "music of the future" in a series of pamphlets and treatises. Meanwhile, in Weimar, Franz Liszt helped mount and conducted the world première of *Lohengrin,* on August 28, 1850. Wagner, a political refugee, could not attend these successful performances.

Despite the fact that with *Lohengrin* he had become one of Germany's most highly esteemed opera composers, Wagner now began to concentrate on revolutionizing the musical theater. A monumental project now engaged him with which he hoped to realize his new ideas about opera and perfect his new methods and techniques. This giant project was *The Ring of the Nibelungs,* a cycle of four dramas that took him a quarter of a century to complete. From time to time he interrupted his labors on the *Ring* to complete two other music dramas—*Tristan and Isolde* in 1859, and his only comedy opera, *Die Meistersinger* in 1867.

While working on the *Ring* and on *Tristan,* Wagner lived in a villa, "The Asyl," provided him by the generous merchant, Otto Wesendonck. Despite the friendship and generosity of his patron, Wagner carried on an illicit affair with Wesendonck's wife, Mathilde, under the influence of which he not only wrote much of *Tristan* but also five songs for voice and orchestra on texts by Mathilde Wesendonck. This love affair with his patron's wife created a permanent break between Wagner and his wife, Minna. She died in Dresden in 1866.

An amnesty in 1860 finally allowed Wagner to return to Germany. Four years later, King Ludwig II of Bavaria became Wagner's patron, ready to throw his influence and enormous financial resources to promote Wagner's dramas. Thus in Munich the first of Wagner's musical dramas reached the stage —*Tristan and Isolde,* on June 10, 1865. It was followed by *Die Meistersinger* on June 21, 1868; *Das Rheingold* on September 22, 1869; and *Die Walkuere* on June 26, 1870.

During this period Wagner fell in love with Cosima, daughter of Liszt and wife of Hans von Buelow. An illegitimate daughter was born to Wagner and Cosima, named Isolde. After the birth of a second illegitimate daughter, Cosima deserted her own husband for good and set up house with Wagner at Triebschen, on Lake Lucerne. A son, Siegfried, was born in 1869. Only then —on August 25, 1870—were Wagner and Cosima married.

Through the machinations of his enemies, Wagner finally lost the support of King Ludwig. This, however, did not keep Wagner from conceiving, and trying to realize, a Gargantuan dream: a festival theater of his own where his dramas could be produced strictly according to his own specifications, and under ideal performing conditions. Once the idea seized him, it gave him neither peace nor rest. Provided a site from the Bavarian city of Bayreuth, Wagner built himself there a permanent home in 1874, Villa Wahnfried. Then he set about to raise the money he needed for the erection of a festival theater —through public subscriptions; through gifts by societies founded for the purpose; through his own concerts. On August 13, 1876, the festival theater opened with *Das Rheingold,* the first presentation of the *Ring* cycle being played in its entirety for the first time. That first festival attracted world interest. From then on, Bayrueth has remained a shrine of Wagnerian music drama.

Wagner's last drama, *Parsifal,* was given in Bayreuth on July 26, 1882. While on vacation in Venice, Wagner was stricken by a fatal heart attack. He died in Venice on February 13, 1883, and was buried in the garden of Villa Wahnfried in Bayreuth.

1840. EIN FAUST OUVERTURE (A FAUST OVERTURE), for orchestra.

While suffering in Paris severe personal deprivations and disappointments, Wagner planned a *Faust Symphony* based on Goethe. This project was abandoned when he became absorbed with the writing of *The Flying Dutchman.* A first movement, which he managed to complete, was now adapted into an orchestral overture which he first thought of calling *Faust in Solitude* or *The Solitary Faust.* When Wagner sent the manuscript to Liszt, the latter found much in it to criticize, and suggested some changes. Wagner agreed with Liszt's evaluation, but confessed he had lost interest in the work and for this reason was not enthusiastic about rewriting it. But in 1854, he returned to this manuscript and made extensive revisions; he now called his composition *A Faust Overture.*

A Faust Overture is one of two of Wagner's purely symphonic works heard today (the other being the *Siegfried Idyl*). There is much in this overture to hint at Wagner's later development as a musical dramatist and orchestrator. Over the published score there appears a brief quotation from Goethe's Faust beginning with the lines: "The God who abides in my breast, Can stir my soul through all its depths."

The overture is in classical structure, and is almost consistently gloomy. In a somber slow introduction (Assai sostenuto) double basses and tuba offer the opening phrase of a first theme over soft rumblings in the drums. After the cellos arrive with a more vigorous statement, the first theme unfolds in the violins. In this part of the overture, the aged Faust is contemplating his lost youth with despair. A vigorous staccato chord sets the stage for the main part of the overture. Over bassoons and horns, the violins are heard in the principal subject. The second theme in F major is later given by the flute. Both themes are freely developed. A repetition of the material of the exposition in classical form and a coda bring this solemn work to its conclusion.

1840. OVERTURE TO RIENZI, for orchestra.

From Wagner's first three operas only the *Rienzi Overture* (and one or two vocal episodes from that opera) can provide sustaining interest to present-day music lovers. The opera *Rienzi* is now rarely given, and with good reason. Written for the most part while Wagner was living in Paris—and suffering neglect and poverty—*Rienzi* was a conscious attempt to win fame. It is theatrical, contrived, old-fashioned—and for the most part, uninspired. Only too well aware how highly the French regarded Meyerbeer, Wagner set out to write a French opera in Meyerbeer's style. He selected a drama full of pomp and circumstance: a novel by Bulwer-Lytton which he himself fashioned into a libretto. Set in fourteenth-century Rome, the story involved intrigues, battles, the rivalry of two powerful factions, the panoply of nobility and high Church officials, revolution. Rienzi leads a people's insurrection and becomes ruler of Rome. But in the end, his enemies conspire to bring about his doom and to burn the Capitol.

Wagner, apparently, knew his audience. *Rienzi*—introduced at the Dresden Opera on October 20, 1842 with a magnificent cast and in a lavish production —proved such a triumph that it spread Wagner's fame for the first time throughout Europe. By Christmas time of 1842, it had been given six times in Dresden, after which it settled into the permanent repertory. The first American performance took place at the Academy of Music in New York on March 4, 1878; the first presentation at the Metropolitan Opera was given during its third season, on February 3, 1886.

The still popular overture derives its thematic material from the opera itself and points to some of the main episodes in the drama. A sustained note, "A" on the trumpet, first growing then diminishing in volume, opens a slow introduction (Molto sostenuto e maestoso). In this opera, this trumpet call is the signal for revolt. Before long, a stately melody is heard in violins and cellos—Rienzi's third-act prayer. After stormy episodes, the opening trumpet call is brought back over tremolo strings. The introduction now over, the full orchestra loudly proclaims the first theme. It comes from the people's cry for freedom, "Gegruesst sei hoher Tag!" with which the first act closes. A reference to the battle hymn of Rienzi's forces, "Sancto spirito cavaliere," in the brass, and a transitional episode in the cellos, precede the second theme, which is a full statement of the Rienzi prayer in the violins. The exposition concludes with a new theme lifted from the stretto of the second-act finale. In the development, the Rienzi battle motive is worked out freely and elaborately, and the recapitulation is a condensation of the exposition with emphasis on agitated passages. The battle hymn is recalled in the powerful coda.

1843. DER FLIEGENDE HOLLAENDER (THE FLYING DUTCHMAN), opera in three acts, with text by the composer, based on an old legend as adapted by Heine in *Memoiren des Herrn von Schnabelewopski.* First performance: Dresden Opera, January 2, 1843.

Fleeing from the threat of debtor's prison in Riga, Wagner and his wife boarded the ship *Thetis,* sailing the Baltic Sea from Pillau to London. He was en route to Paris, where he hoped to advance his career. It was during this voyage that the plans were first germinated for an opera based on the legend of the Flying Dutchman. Battered by terrible storms, the *Thetis* was driven off course several times. It was in danger of being destroyed on a reef, and at one time had to seek a temporary haven in a Norwegian fjord. The thunder and lightning, the lashing of the rain, the howling of the winds, the floundering of the ship, the feverish activity and cries of the sailors—all this made an indelible impression on Wagner. He began identifying himself with the Dutch sea captain whose story he had read in Heine's *Memoiren.* As a refugee, he saw himself fated to wander in misery until he could find peace in a permanent home, and happiness through the redemption of a woman's love. He saw a parallel between the storms of the seas and those besetting his own life. He looked upon the raging waters as symbolic of the devil haunting and crushing him.

Once he reached Paris, he discussed with Heine his plan to transform the legend into an opera. When he had completed his libretto, Wagner tried interesting the Paris Opéra in his project, but the directors showed no interest except to buy the libretto for another composer. Wagner's pressing need for funds made him agree to the bargain. For the time being he turned his efforts to another opera, *Rienzi.* Meanwhile the Paris Opéra commissioned Pierre Louis Dietsch to write music for Wagner's libretto of *The Flying Dutchman.* That opera was produced in 1842 and proved a total failure.

Though he had sold his libretto, Wagner had no real intention of abandoning *The Flying Dutchman.* With *Rienzi* finally out of the way, he decided to write his own music for the *Flying Dutchman* text. So seized was Wagner with the subject that he completed the entire score (except for the overture) in seven months. Even before he had begun the actual writing of the music, he already conceived both the words and melody of Senta's Ballad, which was to become the focal point of the opera. Then the idea for the Sailors' Chorus and Spinning Song came to him. "Everything went easily, fluently," he later revealed. "I actually shouted for joy, as I felt through my whole being that I was still an artist."

The enormous success of *Rienzi* made a performance of *The Flying Dutchman* at the Dresden Opera a foregone conclusion. The new opera, however, failed to duplicate the success of its predecessor. The audience was disappointed that Wagner for the most part had abandoned the sensationalism and spectacle they had so admired in *Rienzi. The Flying Dutchman* was an opera in the Meyerbeer manner no longer. Wagner had resumed his national identity by returning to Weber. Now for the first time he was beginning to show concern for dramatic values, for characterization, for interpreting the inner conflicts of his principals, for authenticity of background and for contrasts of mood and feeling. He even had begun to experiment with a Leitmotiv technique, though of course still tentatively.

Only four performances of the opera were initially given in Dresden. Not until it was revived in 1865 did Dresden operagoers come to realize how much richer, subtler, and deeper *The Flying Dutchman* was than *Rienzi*. *The Flying Dutchman* now became a favorite in Dresden, and it stayed that way.

The Flying Dutchman was the first Wagner opera given in England—presented in Italian at the Drury Lane in London on July 23, 1870. In the United States, its première took place at the Academy of Music in Philadelphia on November 8, 1876 (again in Italian). When the opera was performed for the first time at the Metropolitan Opera (November 27, 1889) it was sung in German.

The familiar overture opens with a forceful theme thrust by horns and bassoons over tremolo strings and chords in the woodwind. This is the motive of the Flying Dutchman. It receives agitated treatment, as a storm erupts with full fury. When it finally abates, a quieter episode brings up a suggestion of Senta's Ballad, soon to become the overture's first main theme. Now comes the principal section of the overture (Allegro con brio), which is dominated by the melody of Senta's Ballad, sometimes punctuated with the recall of the Flying Dutchman motive. Once again, a tempest is let loose. A quotation from the Sailors' Chorus, "Steuermann, lass' die Wacht!" is followed by recollections of both the Senta Ballad and the Flying Dutchman motive. The overture ends with a gentle reflection on the Senta melody.

The legend of the Dutchman relates that, because he has challenged heaven and hell, he must sail the seven seas until he is redeemed by the love of a faithful woman. To help him find such a woman, he is allowed to set foot on soil once every seven years.

When the curtain rises, we are in eighteenth-century Norway. The ship of Daland, a Norwegian sea captain, has found a haven in the bay of a fishing village. The Steersman, on watch, entertains himself with a love ballad ("Mit Gewitter und Sturm"). A vessel named *The Flying Dutchman* comes floundering through wind and rain to anchor next to the Norwegian ship. Its captain is a Dutchman who tells of his restless voyage through many dangers, and how he ever seeks for escape in death ("Wie oft in Meeres tiefsten Schlund"); after that he relates to Daland his many trials at sea ("Durch Sturm und boesen Wind"). Impressed by the jewels the Dutchman has shown him, Daland offers him the hospitality of his home; he even stands ready to turn his daughter, Senta, over in marriage.

The second act transpires in Daland's living room. Senta and a group of girls are spinning ("Summ' und brumm'"). But Senta soon grows weary of this chant. She offers a song of her own, a ballad about the Flying Dutchman, and the hope that she might become the instrument for his redemption (Senta's Ballad: "Traft ihr das Schiff im Meere an"). When Erik, Senta's betrothed, appears, she rejects him coldly. In vain does Erik plead with her to forget her fancies. He recounts a dream in which he saw a mysterious vessel come to shore, followed by the Dutchman walking arm in arm with Senta's father ("Auf hohem Felsen lag' ich traeumend"). After Erik leaves, his dreams become a reality with the appearance of the Dutchman and Daland. Senta becomes transfixed with joy when she hears her father say that the stranger wants to marry her ("Moegst du, mein Kind"). After Daland leaves her alone with the Dutchman, the latter speaks of his happiness in finally finding a woman of his dreams ("Wie aus der Ferne laengst vergang'ner Zeiten"). Upon Daland's return, Senta announces her willingness to marry the Dutchman.

A brief orchestral prelude precedes the third act, its main subjects being motives from Senta's Ballad and the Sailors' Chorus. Aboard Daland's ship in the bay, sailors are singing a rousing chantey ("Steuermann! lass' die Wacht"). Soon the storm rises again and begins to gather its strength. From their formerly gay tune, the sailors pass on to a more sober one in which they defy the elements and the failure of their captain to gain redemption. Senta is now seen being pursued by Erik, the latter pleading that she recall their one-time happy days together ("Willst jenes Tag's du nicht dich mehr entsinnen"). The Dutchman overhears Erik. Realizing that Senta had been untrue to Erik, and that she might just as easily betray him as well, the Dutchman orders his ship to set sail. In vain does Senta try to convince him of her eternal faithfulness. The Dutchman boards his ship after confessing to the startled villagers that he is indeed the accursed Dutchman. When the *Flying Dutchman* begins to leave harbor, Senta rushes atop a cliff exclaiming she will be true to the man she loves till death ("Hier steh' ich teur dir bis zum Tod"). She then plunges into the waters. Through this sacrifice, Senta has won redemption for the Dutchman. In an eternal embrace, he and Senta rise slowly from the sea.

1845. TANNHAEUSER, opera in three acts, with text by the composer. First performance: Dresden Opera, October 19, 1845.

Tannhaeuser, like *The Flying Dutchman,* is still a romantic opera that clings to the older traditions. It relies for its musical effect on individual numbers. The stage interest is focused on a big ballet (the Bacchanale), processionals (the March and Entrance of the Guests), choral episodes (the Pilgrims' Chorus and the Chorus of the Guests), and, most of all, in big vocal numbers (Elisabeth's greeting to her guests, her prayer, Tannhaeuser's hymn to Venus, and his Rome narrative, and Wolfram's "Ode to the Evening Star").

But such is Wagner's dramatic skill and intuition that, unlike so many of the older French and Italian operas, *Tannhaeuser* is distinguished, not only for its parts, but also for the sum of its parts. For one thing, Wagner profited from one of the best librettos he had thus far set, and one of the best found in operatic literature up to this point. Its dramatic climaxes have, with few exceptions, a logical motivation; his characters have dimension; the story is filled with human interest, compassion, pathos. For another, Wagner already reveals himself as a *musical* dramatist second to none. Despite the prominence of individual episodes, Wagner succeeds (as Deems Taylor once pointed out) in keeping "the action going, and at its best it has symphonic sweep and power." Deems Taylor then singles out two scenes that he considers particularly significant. The first is the dialogue of Venus and Tannhaeuser just after the Bacchanale. "It contains some music that its composer never surpassed." The other is Tannhaeuser's narrative describing his journey to Rome. "Both these scenes in their day were almost unheard of. They are not recitatives, they are not set numbers. They are early examples of the endless 'song speech' that Wagner devised to keep the flow of his drama continuous—the long breathed arioso, supported by an eloquent orchestra that was destined, together with the leading motive system, to create the gigantic vocal symphonic poems that we know as *Tristan, Die Meistersinger, Parsifal,* and the *Ring*."

Wagner had already become a student of medieval Germany and German legends when he came upon material about the Wartburg through E. T. A. Hoffmann and Tieck. This happened in Paris between 1839 and 1842. From this point on, he went on to explore all the information he could find about the minstrel knights of Thuringia and their song contests. When he made a trip from Paris to Dresden that carried him through the Thuringian valley, he saw at once his third-act setting.

His libretto was completed in Dresden in May of 1843, his score by the end of 1844, and the orchestration by April 1845. He originally planned to call his opera *Der Venusberg,* but his publisher convinced him such a title might encourage objectionable allusions. When the score was published, it bore the full name of *Tannhaeuser and the Song Contest at the Wartburg.*

The Dresden Opera mounted *Tannhaeuser* handsomely on October 19, 1845; it had even gone to the trouble of ordering sets from Paris. But for all that, the new opera was not too well received. Some of the singers failed to meet the challenge of the music. But this represented only a fraction of the trouble. Many in the audience failed to keep pace with the composer's progress from the showy spectacle of *Rienzi* to the vibrant drama of *Tannhaeuser;* many resented a text which they interpreted as a glorification of Catholicism; many condemned the opera for its pornography and sensuality.

At the second performance, the auditorium was almost empty. But for some inexplicable reason, the third performance played to a full and appreciative house. Succeeding performances saw a continual mounting of enthusiasm and interest until the opera's permanent success became assured. By 1861, it had been seen in thirteen German cities.

However, its first appearance in Paris (given in French) provoked a scandal. To comply with French partiality for ballets, Wagner introduced his famous and elaborate Bacchanale, something he had not originally intended for his opera. Dictated by the needs of his text, Wagner insisted on placing this sequence at the beginning of the opera. Members of the fashionable Jockey Club in Paris, who habitually came late to operas, resented missing the ballet, and were further infuriated by Wagner's stubborn refusal to put it into a later act. They came en masse for the first performance, on March 13, 1861, to create a disturbance. At the second presentation, they intensified their demonstrations. The third performance disintegrated into confusion. *Tannhaeuser* now had to be removed from the repertory, and was not heard again in Paris until 1887.

America heard *Tannhaeuser* for the first time at the Stadt Theater in New York on April 4, 1859; this was the first Wagnerian opera seen in the United States. It came to the Metropolitan Opera for the first time in 1884 to inaugurate that company's second season. At both the Stadt Theater and the Metropolitan the original Dresden version was used. It has since become the practice to utilize the Paris version.

The theme of redemption through a woman's love that threads through *The Flying Dutchman* returns in *Tannhaeuser*. (It would recur in later Wagnerian music dramas.) But the greatest emphasis in this drama, as W. J. Henderson explains, is in the "struggle of the pure and the impure, the lusts and aspirations of man's nature. It is essentially the tragedy of man. We may try as we please to exalt the importance of Elisabeth as a dramatic character, but the truth is that she is merely the embodiment of a force. Tannhaeuser is typical of his sex, beset on the one hand by the desire of the flesh, which satiates and maddens, and courted on the other by the undying loveliness of chaste and holy love."

The overture is the most ambitious—and the most successful—that Wagner had thus far produced in capturing the essence of the drama through the use of basic melodies from the opera. First we hear the Pilgrim's Chorus, chanted by clarinets, bassoons, and horns. There follows in strings the somber melody representing Tannhaeuser's repentance. Both subjects are repeated before some of the sensual music of the Venusberg scene erupts in strings. At its peak, we get Tannhaeuser's exultant hymn to Venus in full orchestra. The overture ends with a recall of the Pilgrim's Chorus.

As the curtain rises we get a view of the Hill of Venus in the thirteenth century. Tannhaeuser, a minstrel knight, having escaped from the world, is reveling in sensual pleasures and delights with Venus. Bacchantes are performing a dance—the famous Bacchanale—in whose music Wagner has brought all the delirium, lasciviousness and sensuality of carnal love. The emotions are built up to a point of frenzy, then allowed to subside in languor. Tannhaeuser now sings his hymn to Venus ("Dir toene Lob"). But he is beginning to grow weary of physical pleasures, yearns to get back to his own world. At first, Venus tries to revive his old fires ("Geliebter, komm!"). Failing to do so, she becomes enraged, insisting that his fellow knights will never forgive him, or take him back in their fold. But Tannhaeuser puts his trust in the Virgin Mary. At the mention of Her name, the scene dissipates into mist and Venus disappears.

The scene changes to a valley over which looms the castle of the Wartburg. A passing shepherd intones a pastoral tune hailing the Goddess of Spring

("Frau Holda kam aus dem Berg hervor"). He is followed by a band of pilgrims, chanting a religious hymn ("Pilgrim's Chorus") as they make their way toward Rome. Tannhaeuser falls to his knees in prayer. Minstrel-knights now come upon the scene, one of whom is Tannhaeuser's life-long friend, Wolfram. Wolfram informs Tannhaeuser how Elisabeth has been grieving over him, how eagerly she would welcome him back to the Wartburg ("Als du im kuehnem Sange"). This is all that Tannhaeuser needs to convince him to return to his comrades ("Ha, jetzt erkenne ich sie wieder"). Joyously the minstrel-knights set off for the Wartburg ("Er kehrt zurueck den wir verloren").

In the Castle of the Wartburg, Elisabeth—rapturous at the news that Tannhaeuser has returned—sings a paean to the Hall of the Minstrels ("Dich teure Halle"). Then Wolfram leads Tannhaeuser to her. When she questions him about his absence, Tannhaeuser is evasive, but this does not prevent an ecstatic reunion ("Gepriesen sei die Stunde"). Now the minstrel-knights file into the hall to the dignified strains of march music. Nobles, ladies, attendants raise their voices in song ("Freudig begruessen wir die edle Halle"). A song contest is about to take place, the subject being "Love," the winner to get Elisabeth's hand in marriage. Wolfram is the first contestant. He rhapsodizes pure and unselfish love in "Blick' ich umher." Tannhaeuser comes next. Seized by an emotion he cannot control, and in a rapture, he extols the kind of carnal love he had experienced on the Venusberg ("Dir Goettin der Liebe"). Horrified, the ladies rush out of the hall, while several knights attack Tannhaeuser with drawn swords. But Elisabeth intervenes to save him. She pleads for his right to gain salvation from heavenly powers ("Zurueck von ihn!") and promises to pray for his redemption. Penitent, Tannhaeuser stands ready to do whatever is demanded of him. The Landgrave pronounces sentence: Tannhaeuser is to be banished; he must join the pilgrims to Rome and gain absolution from the Pope. As if inspired, Tannhaeuser kisses the hem of Elisabeth's gown, then goes forth to join the pilgrims.

The prelude to the third act is named *Tannhaeuser's Pilgrimage* in the score. The lugubrious subject with which it opens is the motive of Tannhaeuser's Penitence. It is followed by a tender melody representing Elisabeth's intercession on his behalf. The violas maintain the melancholy mood with a description of Tannhaeuser's suffering. Later material includes a reminder of the Pilgrim's Chorus and the motive of Heavenly Grace, the latter first heard in brass, then in strings. The quiet and resigned ending suggests Tannhaeuser's ultimate salvation.

Several months have elapsed. Elisabeth is waiting for Tannhaeuser's return in the valley. When a group of pilgrims passes by, Elisabeth searches eagerly for the knight, but he is not with them. Poignantly she prays to the Holy Virgin to forgive Tannhaeuser's sins ("Allmaecht'ge Jungfrau"). When she leaves, Wolfram enters, entreating the evening star to guide and protect Elisabeth ("O du mein holder Abendstern"). Suddenly Tannhauser stumbles in wearily. In an extended narrative, he tells Wolfram of his experiences. The Pope has refused him absolution until the staff in his hand sprouts leaves ("In brunst im Herzen"). Broken in spirit, Tannhaeuser now intends to return to Venus. Wolfram tries to restrain Tannhaeuser, first through entreaty, then through force. Only the mention of Elisabeth's name keeps Tannhaeuser from Venus. A funeral procession now draws near, bearing the dead body of Elisabeth. Broken by weariness and heartbreak, Tannhauser falls dead on the bier. Then a band of pilgrims from Rome come to chant of a miracle that had taken place in the Holy City: the Pope's staff had sprouted leaves. Tannhaeuser has been redeemed.

1848. LOHENGRIN, opera in three acts, with text by the composer, based on medieval legends. First performance: Weimar, August 28, 1850.

While *Lohengrin* still clings to older traditions, it is also the first of Wagner's operas to provide a forecast of the future. The past is found in its heroic, romantic style; in its extended use of the chorus; in some of the duets and arias; in the scenes of pageantry. But in *Lohengrin,* far more than in *Tannhaeuser,* there is a unity of all the elements of opera; there is greater use made of the Leitmotiv technique; there is a higher degree of virtuosity in the handling of the orchestra. Most important of all, perhaps, there is a conscious attempt to arrive at melodic continuity with no demarcation between recitative and aria. As Wagner himself explained: "Nowhere in *Lohengrin* have I written the word recitative over a vocal passage. The singers are not to know that there are any recitatives in it. On the contrary, I have been at pains to determine and indicate the spoken accent of the words with such sharpness and certainty that the singer has only to sing in the tempo prescribed, giving to each its note value, to have the speaking expression completely in control."

Though the idea for *Lohengrin* had been hatched as early as 1839 or 1840, during Wagner's stay in Paris, it was not until 1845 that he began to think seriously about the project. On a holiday in Marienbad in Bohemia, in July of that year, Wagner browsed through a book detailing the legend of Lohengrin. "The result," he explained, "was an ever-increasing and distressing state of excitement. Lohengrin . . . suddenly stood fully formed before me, down to the smallest detail of dramatic construction." However, not until March of 1847 was he able to complete the opera; the orchestration came a year after that.

As a political fugitive and exile, Wagner could not expect the Dresden Opera to produce his new opera. He, therefore, despatched the score to Liszt in Weimar. That Liszt should have been willing to perform *Lohengrin* in view of Wagner's disrepute at the time speaks volumes for his courage. Liszt directed the première on August 28, 1850. The audience did not at first react favorably, finding the work too long, and in some respects, too new in style and approach. The opera, however, did make the rounds of the German opera houses. In short order, it became so popular that a decade after the première, Wagner (still in exile) could remark acidly that he was probably the only German who had never seen *Lohengrin* performed. Wagner's first sight and sound of the opera came in Vienna on May 15, 1861.

The first performance in the United States took place at the Stadt Theater in New York on April 3, 1871. Three years later, the Academy of Music presented it in Italian. The Metropolitan mounted it on November 23, 1883, during its very first season. Then as now, *Lohengrin* was a particular favorite with Americans.

Perhaps the crowning glory of the opera is its first-act prelude, an altogether new concept in operatic overtures. Here we find a tone poem synthesizing the spiritual mood of the opera. Its material, as Lawrence Gilman noted, is developed "with a concentrated power and a splendor of genius that are never equalled in the opera itself." Wagner himself explained that this music was intended to describe a heavenly vision in which angels bear aloft the Holy Grail. The entire prelude is built from a single motive, that of the Holy Grail, heard first quietly in the upper register of the violins, then in the other instruments. A crescendo is built up, its apex a statement of the Holy Grail theme in trumpets and trombones. A decrescendo follows. The prelude ebbs away softly and serenely in the strings.

On the banks of the Scheldt River, near Antwerp, in the tenth century, King Henry is summoning the people of Brabant to defend their kingdom. He greets his people ("Gott gruess euch"), then informs them of the threats posed externally by the Hungarians, and internally by dissension and strife. Telramund explains the reason for civil strife: the people suspect Elsa of having murdered her brother in order to gain power. A herald now summons Elsa before the king to speak for herself. As in a trance, she describes a dream in which a knight emerged as her protector ("Einsam in trueben Tagen"). Telramund presses charges against her, threatening to challenge anybody who doubts his word. When the king inquires from Elsa who her champion will be, she replies ecstatically that it is the warrior of her dreams who will defend her, and that in compensation, she will become his bride ("Des Ritters will ich wahren"). When Elsa's champion fails to appear, she falls to her knees in prayer ("Du trugest zu ihm meine Klage"). Suddenly a swan-drawn boat comes to view, and Lohengrin is its passenger. After he is hailed by the throng ("Gegruesst, du gottgesandter Held"), he bids his swan farewell ("Nun sei bedankt, mein lieber Schwan"). Lohengrin now addresses the king, then Elsa, offering himself to her as her champion and husband—but only on the condition she promise never to seek out his identity or the place of his origin. Having extracted that promise, he takes Elsa in his arms ("Elsa, ich liebe dich").

The combat is about to begin. Following a solemn prayer by the king ("Mein Herr und Gott"), the trumpets sound the call to battle. Lohengrin defeats Telramund decisively, but magnanimously spares his life. The crowd hails the victor, while Elsa pledges eternal faithfulness to her future husband ("O faend ich Jubelweisen").

Telramund and his wife Ortrud are in disgrace. In the second act, in an Antwerp fortress, they are plotting to avenge themselves ("Der Rache Werk"). They contrive to get Elsa to break her promise and make Lohengrin reveal whence he came. When Elsa appears on the balcony, she is radiant with happiness ("Euch Lueften die mein Klagen"). She is sympathetic to Ortrud's sad fate, pronounces forgiveness, and promises to gain clemency for her from Lohengrin. Ortrud now warns Elsa not to put all her faith and trust in love. But Elsa remains convinced that faith is the root of all true love ("Lass mich dich lehren").

At the approach of dawn, trumpet calls from the tower announce that it is Elsa's wedding day. The square becomes filled with knights and courtiers in a festive mood ("In Frueh'n versammelt uns der Ruf"). A king's herald pronounces Telramund a traitor. When Telramund appears, he tries to incite the crowd against the king; but before he can succeed, the bridal procession begins, and the populace turns its attention to the bride ("Heil dir, Elsa von Brabant"). Just as Elsa mounts the cathedral steps, she is accosted by Ortrud, come to accuse Lohengrin of being a magician using supernatural powers to conquer Telramund. This is the reason, Ortrud exclaims, why Lohengrin refuses to reveal his identity. Elsa angrily denounces her, and defiantly reaffirms her faith in her champion. With the appearance of the king and Lohengrin, the latter takes Elsa into his arms and orders Ortrud to leave. In the face of Telramund's repeated accusations, Lohengrin is forced to affirm his innocence; nevertheless, he still cannot reveal who he is. The populace now begins to express its suspicions ("Welch ein Geheimnis muss der Held bewahren"). Even Elsa is wavering. But she soon gains control of herself, falls in shame at Lohengrin's feet, affirming that her love has overcome all doubts ("Mein Ritter, der mir Heil gebracht"). With Lohengrin at her side, Elsa helps lead the procession into the cathedral.

The third-act prelude sets the mood of festivity attending Elsa's wedding. A joyous subject leaps from the full orchestra, followed by a secondary jubilant theme in cellos, horns, and bassoons in unison, and a march-like melody in the wind.

The curtain rises upon the bridal procession, progressing to the strains of the world-famous "Wedding March" ("Treulich gefuehrt"). After the assemblage has scattered, Elsa and Lohengrin, now alone, embrace and reaffirm their devotion and love ("Das suesse Lied verhallt"). But the radiance subsides as Elsa becomes tormented by questions about Lohengrin. In vain does she entreat her husband to reveal his name and place of origin. Suddenly, Telramund and four of his henchmen burst into the room to attack Lohengrin. In the ensuing struggle, Telramund is killed. Elsa goes into a faint and is gently lifted by Lohengrin and carried to a couch. As he does so, Lohengrin remarks sadly that happiness is no longer possible for him ("Weh! Nun ist all unser Glueck dahin").

The curtain is lowered to suggest a change of scene and time. At the banks of the Scheldt, King Henry urges his followers to prepare for battle ("Wie fuehl ich stolz mein Herz entbrannt"). The people proclaim Lohengrin their leader. But Lohengrin replies in solemn tones that he is unable to lead the people to battle, since he has just killed Telramund and must be punished. Though the people reaffirm their allegiance, Lohengrin goes on to lament Elsa's treachery that now compels him to reveal that which must have remained a secret. In a moving narrative ("In fernem Land"), he discloses he is a knight of the Holy Grail, the son of Parsifal, come from Monsalvat to destroy evil. Now that this secret is known, he must leave Brabant forever and return to Monsalvat. Then he embraces Elsa, and with infinite tenderness and sorrow, upbraids her for having betrayed his trust· ("O Elsa, was hast du mir angethan?").

Lohengrin's swan has come to bear him away. Before he leaves, Lohengrin deposits with Elsa his sword, horn, and ring as protection. Suddenly Ortrud bursts in upon the scene to reveal that through her own evil powers Elsa's brother, Gottfried, had been transformed into Lohengrin's swan; that had Elsa but kept faith with her husband, her brother would now have been able to return to human form. But Lohengrin is able to break Ortrud's spell by removing a chain from the swan's neck. The swan disappears below the waters. In its place there arises the form of Gottfried, whom Lohengrin conducts toward the people ("Seht da den Herzog von Brabant"). Lohengrin now departs in his boat. The crowd raises a mighty lamentation, while Gottfried takes Elsa in his arms to console her in her terrible grief.

1857–1858. FUENF GEDICHTE VON MATHILDE WESENDONCK (FIVE WESENDONCK SONGS), for voice and orchestra. I. Der Engel. II. Stehe still. III. Im Treibhaus. IV. Schmerzen. V. Traeume.

In 1857, Wagner accepted the generous hospitality of the wealthy merchant, Otto Wesendonck, by moving into a little garden house (the "Asyl") adjoining the Wesendonck mansion. Wagner proceeded to reward his patron by falling in love and carrying on an affair with Otto's wife, Mathilde. Out of this passionate interlude came the text and some of the music for *Tristan and Isolde;* also the ardent *Five Songs* to Mathilde's poems.

There is an intimate relationship between this song cycle and *Tristan.* Two of its songs—and incidentally the best and the most popular—are "studies" for *Tristan,* including some material from that music drama. "Traeume," or "Dreams" (now often heard in orchestral transcription) takes its melody from the love duet from the second act. But where in the music drama the theme is used with passionate intensity, in the song it becomes a moody nocturne. On the occasion of Mathilde's birthday, on December 23, 1857, Wagner performed the song under her window, directing an orchestra of eighteen musicians.

"Im Treibhaus," or "In the Greenhouse," makes use of the motive of the "wounded Tristan" in the instrumental opening, Later on, in the song proper, the motive of "Tristan's longing" is presented with minor alterations.

1854–1872. DER RING DES NIBELUNGEN (THE RING OF THE NIBELUNGS), a cycle of four music dramas which the composer designated as a tetralogy, the first drama serving as the prelude: I. Das Rheingold (The Rhinegold). II. Die Walkuere (The Valkyries). III. Siegfried. IV. Goetterdaemmerung (The Twilight of the Gods). The text of all four dramas is by the composer, based on sagas from Germany, Scandinavia, and Iceland, but mainly from the *Nibelungenlied.* First performance of the complete cycle: Bayreuth, Germany, August 13, 14, 16, 17, 1876.

The *Ring of the Nibelungs* is possibly the most ambitious artistic project undertaken by one man. It absorbed Wagner's dreams and energies for a quarter of a century.

He first became interested in the sagas of Germany, Scandinavia, and Iceland while working on *Lohengrin.* In 1848, Wagner completed the poetical text for a single work called *Siegfried's Death.* Since this one drama seemed insufficient to unfold Siegfried's story—leaving open necessary information about Siegfried's background and youth—Wagner felt impelled to write a second text with the basic episodes preceding the events of *Siegfried's Death.* He called the new poem, *Young Siegfried,* completing it in 1851. And still he felt the need for a good deal of preliminary information to clarify the events of these two plays. Now renaming his first text *The Twilight of the Gods,* and the second one, *Siegfried,* he proceeded to write the poem of *The Valkyries* in 1852, and finally *The Rhinegold* as an over-all preface. Thus the four dramas were written in reverse order from the way they are now presented. The text completed—and published privately in 1853—Wagner could now consider the Herculean assignment of doing the music. This was written in proper sequence. *The Rhinegold* was completed in 1853, *The Valkyries* in 1856, *Siegfried* in 1869, and *The Twilight of the Gods,* in 1872.

Wagner was a sufficiently practical showman and musician to recognize the gargantuan difficulties standing in the way of a production of his cycle. The drama needed four evenings for performance; it called for gigantic musical and theatrical forces; it required stage methods and paraphernalia far in advance of the theater of Wagner's day; and its musical idiom and technique were often beyond the capabilities of singers and instrumentalists. Wagner seriously doubted if the *Ring* would ever be performed in his own lifetime. For this reason, he interrupted this labor to complete two other musical dramas more adaptable to the stage—*Tristan und Isolde* and *Die Meistersinger.* But never did he lose faith in the ultimate importance and victory of his *Ring;* never did he doubt that he was producing a towering masterwork; never did he allow himself to suspect that the *Ring* would not be the successful realization of all his ideas and ideals of opera. Ultimately, if not in his own time, Wagner knew with unwavering conviction, the *Ring* would find both the stage and the musicians to cope with its problems. The fact that he himself would probably never see the giant creation mounted, did not deter him from devoting a quarter of a century of his life and energies toward putting his mighty concepts down on paper.

The central theme of the entire *Ring,* as Ernest Newman has pointed out, is "Wotan's love for power. "That lust led him in the *The Rhinegold* to build Valhalla; it is symbolized in the ring Alberich fashions from gold stolen from the Rhine maidens." It is, of course, not difficult to seek out the symbolism of this theme, nor to recognize here Wagner's own social thinking. The lust for power, or gold, leads to destruction of men and gods. And Siegfried, the fearless hero who gains the ring only to meet his doom through it, is the embodiment of Nietzsche's Superman, come to redeem the world from avarice, fear, and hate. "Wagner's way," as Kurt Pahlen explains, "led from Nietzsche's Superman to Schopenhauer's abysmal pessimism, but he clothed everything in a symbolism and an ideology of his own. Every detail in this work is profoundly symbolic: the rape of the Rhinegold, the dwarf's curse of love, the giants' quarrel over the treasure. Equally symbolic is the act of Wotan who had fathered Siegmund and Sieglinde and then permitted them to commit the double crime of incest and adultery: symbolic, too, the long controversy between Wotan and his wife Fricka, the guardian of matrimony; and the god's final decision, reached after grave pondering, that Siegmund must die, even though the Valkyrie Bruennhilde for the first time tries to disobey his explicit command."

Both *The Rhinegold* and *The Valkyries* were given performances before the *Ring* cycle was heard in its entirety. *The Rhinegold* was produced for the first time at the Munich Opera on September 22, 1869; *The Valkyries* in the same city and opera house on June 26, 1870. But Wagner, creator of grand visions, was not satisfied merely to get the individual dramas played. He harbored the dream of a special theater of his own, where his dramas could be produced according to his own concepts of staging, under auspices and conditions most favorable for audience receptiveness, and in musical presentations that met his most exacting requirements. Once this idea seized him, he pursued it with all his customary passion, and his indomitable refusal to accept defeat. He found some patrons ready to provide a part of the subsidy, and he convinced the town of Bayreuth in Bavaria to provide a site. He then toured Europe conducting concerts to raise some of the vast sums needed for the building of a festival theater. Time and again, it looked as if the whole gigantic scheme would collapse; only Wagner's Herculean will to succeed kept the framework of his adventure all in one piece. Finally, a theater was built to Wagner's specifications, and there on August 13, 1876 there took place a performance of *The Rhinegold* to begin the first complete presentation anywhere of the *Ring* cycle. World interest was focused on the event. Some of Europe's foremost musicians were in attendance, including Grieg, Tchaikovsky, Gounod, and

Saint-Saëns; so were nobility and royalty. Correspondents from all parts of the world came to report what they heard and saw. The facilities of hotels and restaurants were overtaxed; shops were cluttered with Wagner souvenirs.

The reaction to the *Ring* was mixed. Wagner disciples were ecstatic. "Nothing like it, nothing approaching it, has ever been produced in any tongue, anywhere, at any time," said Hans von Buelow. Tchaikovsky reported: "From the point of view of artistic ideals, it is destined one way or another to have an enormous historic significance. . . . What happened in Bayreuth will be well remembered by our grandchildren and our great-grandchildren." But a good many critics thought that Wagner's aims were too pretentious, and that the *Ring* cycle as a whole left much to be desired.

The first time the complete *Ring* cycle was given in the United States was at the Metropolitan Opera in 1889; but by that time, all four dramas had already been heard individually. The American première of *The Rhinegold* had taken place on January 4, 1889 at the Metropolitan Opera. *The Valkyries* was introduced at the Academy of Music in New York on April 2, 1877. Both *Siegfried* and *The Twilight of the Gods* received their American premières at the Metropolitan Opera, on November 9, 1887, and January 25, 1888, respectively.

The Rhinegold

The Rhinegold, designated by Wagner as a prelude (or *Vorabend*) is in a single act, divided into four scenes. The orchestral prelude, extending for one hundred and thirty-six measures, is based on the chord of E-flat. A slow and extended phrase is heard in bassoons and horns. The phrase then expands slowly, quickens, until the music simulates the flow of the Rhine River.

The first scene shows three Rhine maidens swimming at the bottom of the river, guarding their magic gold. Alberich, a misshapen dwarf, tries to seize now one and now another of the maidens, but they elude him, mock his efforts, and send him off cursing. The Rhine maidens now explain the power of their gold: he who fashions it into a ring can rule the world, but only if he stands ready to renounce love. Alberich finally seizes the gold from the maidens and escapes. The maidens cry out in dismay. Darkness descends.

As light slowly begins to penetrate the darkness, we see a mountain top where Wotan, ruler of the gods, and his wife, Fricka, contemplate the stately palace that the giants Fasolt and Fafner have just built for them. Fricka reminds Wotan that the price demanded by the giants is Fricka's sister, Freia; bitterly she upbraids her husband for having made such a callous bargain. Freia now comes to beg Wotan to protect her from the giants. But Wotan puts the blame for this situation on the fire god, Loge, insisting that Loge had advised him some subterfuge could eventually be found to placate the giants. Loge explains apologetically that he has scoured the world to seek out some treasure that the giants might be willing to accept instead of Freia, but has failed. The giants, however, are willing to compromise. They will renounce Freia if Wotan can turn over to them the Rhine gold that Alberich possesses. When Wotan refuses, the giants seize Freia and drag her off. The gods are horrified. Loge warns that with the loss of Freia, the gods will lose their immortality. All this sends Wotan into action. He decides to descend into the lower depths, seek out Alberich, and try to convince him to turn over the gold.

In Nibelheim, Alberich's caverns, Mime—brother of Alberich—has fashioned a helmet called Tarnhelm; when worn it allows a person to assume any form he desires. Upon the arrival of Wotan and Loge, Mime tells them about the powers of the Tarnhelm and reveals that Alberich has fashioned a ring from the Rhine gold. Alberich soon boasts to the gods how, with the ring and the Tarnhelm, he can rule the world. Craftily, Wotan induces Alberich to try out the magic of the Tarnhelm by transforming himself into a toad. Thus Wotan is able to capture Alberich and drag him back to the abode of the gods.

The price Wotan demands from Alberich for his freedom is his Tarnhelm and the Ring. Grudgingly, Alberich meets the price. At the same time, he pronounces a curse that will bring disaster to anyone come into possession of the Ring. When the giants come to exchange Freia for their ransom, they demand the Tarnhelm and the Ring as part of the bargain. From the bowels of the earth, Erda, earth goddess, rises to warn Wotan not to relinquish it ("Weiche, Wotan, weiche!"). But Wotan is helpless. As he hurls the ring contemptuously at the giants, Fafner and Fasolt go into a mad scramble for it. Fasolt is killed. Thus Alberich's terrible curse already is being realized. But Wotan prefers to disregard the warning. Freia has been redeemed. The gods are ready to occupy the magnificent new home which Wotan has named Valhalla. As the storm clouds are dissipated and a rainbow spans the sky, the gods begin their ascent toward their new abode—to the stately music of "The Entrance of the Gods into Valhalla." First comes the motive of "Donner," the thunder-god who had dissipated the storm. This is followed by the radiant motive of the "Rainbow" and then by the majestic theme of Valhalla.

The Valkyries

The preliminaries of an explanatory prelude disposed of, the saga of Siegfried and the redemption of the Ring can begin to unfold. Between the curtain fall of *The Rhinegold* and its rise for *The Valkyries,* a good deal has happened. The giant Fafner has used the Tarnhelm to transform himself into a dragon, the better to guard his coveted Ring. Wotan realizes that only a hero can wrest the Ring from the dragon. To create such a hero, he comes down to earth and gives birth to the Walsung twins—Siegmund and Sieglinde. While they are still children, their house burns to the ground, their mother dies in the flames, and they themselves are separated.

The first act orchestral prelude describes a raging storm. A rushing subject in the lower strings, set against a repeated "D" in violins and violas, suggests the driving rain. Discords interject the flashes of lightning. Then the tuba pronounces the motive of Donner, the thunder-god.

Siegmund, a refugee from this storm, finds shelter in the forest home of Hunding and Sieglinde. In a state of exhaustion, Siegmund sinks to the ground in front of a welcome fire. There Sieglinde finds him and brings him refreshment. Siegmund reveals that his sword and shield have been destroyed in a struggle with hostile tribesmen. Misfortune, he says, dogs his footsteps. For this reason he must leave this household immediately. Sieglinde prevails on him to remain as a guest. When her husband Hunding appears, he invites Siegmund to partake of a meal, at which Siegmund reveals his identity. He is a member of the Walsung tribe; his mother died in a disastrous fire; he himself has been separated from his sister and must be a wanderer. Hunding recognizes Siegmund as an enemy. Nevertheless, since he is the host, he is ready to provide Siegmund safety but only for that night. Left alone, Siegmund bewails the fact that he should be unarmed in the face of an enemy, that he has been unable to find the sword his father had promised him ("Ein Schwert verhiess mir der Vater"). Meanwhile, having administered a sleeping potion to her husband, Sieglinde slips back to explain to Siegmund how she had been forced to marry Hunding; how a one-eyed stranger had plunged a sword, called Nothung, into a tree within that very house, prophesying that a warrior-hero would some day extricate it. Exultantly, Siegmund announces that he is the one destined to remove the sword, and thus free Sieglinde from Hunding. Just then the door swings open and bathes the room with a Spring moonlight. As Sieglinde and Siegmund look at each other, they realize at once they are in love. A rapturous duet follows. Siegmund sings a glowing love song ("Winterstuerme wichen dem Wonnemond") to which Sieglinde replies with rapture ("Du bist der Lenz"). Now they know for a certainty what all the while they had suspected: they are twin brother and sister, children of Wotan, so long separated; also, that their father had been the one to plant the sword into the trunk of the tree. With an apostrophe to the sword ("Nothung! So nenn' ich dich Schwert"), Siegmund releases it. Arm in arm, Siegmund and Sieglinde flee into the forest.

Atop a mountain, in the second act, Bruenhilde, daughter of Wotan, is sounding a battle cry ("Ho-jo-to-ho"). She is summoning her sister Valkyries to come to Siegmund's help. This arouses Fricka's anger, for Fricka is the guardian of the household, and Hunding's home has been violated. Wotan, for his part, maintains that Siegmund must be protected for the mission he is destined to accomplish ("Der alte Sturm"). But Fricka is immovable. In the end, Wotan promises to punish Siegmund, a fact that makes Bruennhilde distraught. Sadly, Wotan explains to his daughter that the Ring is now fulfilling Alberich's curse, and that doom confronts the gods. But he is now helpless. When Brunnhilde continues to plead for the safety and protection of Siegmund and Sieglinde, Wotan explodes into fury. In the face of his promise to Fricka, there is nothing he can do for them.

In the valley below, Bruennhilde confronts the fleeing lovers ("Siegmund, sich' auf mich!"). She reveals that Siegmund must die, that Wotan has withdrawn from the sword its magic powers. When Siegmund cries out that he will kill both himself and his beloved rather than be parted from her, Bruennhilde helplessly decides to do what she can for him, in spite of her father's commands. The sound of a horn announces the arrival of Hunding, whom Siegmund soon engages in mortal combat. Bruennhilde tries to come to Siegmund's aid, but Wotan intervenes. As Siegmund is killed by Hunding, Bruennhilde recoils in horror. Wotan then destroys Hunding and vows to punish Bruennhilde for having defied him. Meanwhile, Bruennhilde takes Sieglinde off to safety.

The dramatic prelude to the third act portrays the flight of the Valkyries on their steeds—in one of the most dramatic and realistic pieces of music ever written about locomotion, "The Ride of the Valkyries." An introductory stormy episode suggests an oncoming storm. Strong rhythmic figures simulate the gallop of the horses. The motives of the Valkyries, Bruennhilde and her battle cry follow in rapid succession. This prelude ends with a chromatic episode describing the disappearance of the Valkyries.

Bruennhilde has brought Sieglinde to a mountain retreat, where she begs her sister Valkyries for help. This they refuse to do, fearing Wotan's anger. Sadly, Bruennhilde sends Sieglinde off to bear a child destined to become a hero; she also gives Sieglinde the broken pieces of Siegmund's sword. With tempestuous music betraying the extent of Wotan's wrath, the god arrives to deprive Bruennhilde of her right to be a Valkyrie. Falling to her knees, Bruennhilde begs for forgiveness. Poignantly she asks if she is deserving of such a terrible punishment ("War es so schmaelich"). Wotan, moved by grief, and overwhelmed by his love for his daughter, decides to temper his punishment with mercy. He will put his daughter into a deep slumber surrounded by a protecting ring of flame. Only a hero would then have the courage to penetrate the fire and save her. Such a hero would come some day to become her husband. And now Wotan bids Bruennhilde a sorrowful farewell ("Leb' wohl, du kuehnes, herrliches Kind"). Tenderly he places her on a rock, covers her with her shield, and commands Loge to raise a circle of fire around her ("Magic Fire Scene"). Leaping figures in the woodwind reproduce the flicker of the flames. The motives of Bruennhilde's Slumber and Fate are introduced and built up dramatically, reaching toward the majestic pronouncement in the brass of the Siegfried motive. Then the fire theme and a suggestion of Bruennhilde's slumber motive are recalled. Taking one last look at his daughter, Wotan sadly takes leave.

Siegfried

The hero of the *Ring* cycle, Siegfried, is already in his manhood. He is the offspring of Siegmund and Sieglinde. Mime, the dwarf, had found Sieglinde wandering in the forests and had taken her into his cave for refuge.

There she dies giving birth to Siegfried, who then is raised by the dwarf.

A short, vigorous prelude offers the motive of Mime, simulates the sound of the hammer on an anvil, and concludes with a suggestion of the Sword motive. The curtain rises on Mime's cave. The dwarf is trying to mend Nothung, the sword left by Sieglinde to her son. Mime knows that, when repaired, the sword in Siegfried's hands could be the instrument to destroy Fafner and gain the Ring. But the job is beyond him, as he soon realizes ("Zwangvolle Plage!"). Leading a bear by a rope, Siegfried appears. First he makes sport of Mime, whom he detests. Then he angrily seizes the dwarf to try to get from him information about his own origins, convinced as he is that Mime is not his father. In terror, Mime tells Siegfried the story of Sieglinde and Siegmund and how Mime had raised him in the forest, and of the broken sword Sieglinde had left for Siegfried. Siegfried orders Mime to mend the broken pieces, leaving the cave to let Mime complete this chore. While he is gone, Wotan—disguised as the Wanderer—comes to engage Mime in a test of wits. He offers to answer any question Mime poses, and in return he wants to ask Mime to answer some questions of his own. To the query as to who will repair Nothung, Mime has no reply. The game over, Wotan explains that only he who is without fear can achieve the task, and takes his leave. Upon Siegfried's return, he decides to forge the sword into a single blade himself ("Nothung! Nothung!"). While he is doing this, the wily Mime prepares a poison with which he hopes to kill Siegfried once the Ring has been acquired. At last the task is done: Nothung is as good as new. With a giant blow of the sword, Siegfried splits the forge in two.

A dark, brooding prelude precedes the second act; it is built from the motives of Fafner, the Ring, the Curse, and Destruction. In his forest cave, Fafner, in the guise of a dragon, is guarding his precious hoard. Alberich is outside, hoping in some way to get the Ring. Wotan, as the Wanderer, comes to try to get Alberich to convince Fafner to give up the prize and avoid destruction; but Fafner is intransigent. When Wotan mocks Alberich for his failure, the Nibelung leaves in a huff, vowing some day to avenge himself against the god. Now Siegfried and Mime are at hand, the hero come to engage Fafner in combat. But first stretching lazily under a tree, Siegfried becomes enchanted by the beauty of the surrounding forests, and by the overhead song of the birds ("Forest Murmurs"). The murmuring orchestra re-creates the whispering of the leaves through which emerges the wondrous melody of the forest bird in the woodwind. Suddenly comes the sound of Siegfried's horn call. He is ready for action. Rushing into the cave, he engages Fafner in a life and death struggle and kills him. When a few drops of Fafner's blood burn his fingers, Siegfried instinctively puts them in his mouth. The taste of blood endows the hero with the power to understand the language of the forest bird. Through this song, Siegfried learns about the Tarnhelm and the Ring awaiting him in the cave. While he sets off to get the treasure, Alberich and Mime appear, bickering and arguing with one another as to which one is the rightful owner of Fafner's treasures. Emerging from the cave, Siegfried receives another message from the forest bird—about Mime's deceitful plan to kill him. When, therefore, Mime hands Siegfried the poisonous drink, Siegfried fells him with a single blow of his sword. Then once again he stretches under a tree. Now the forest bird reveals that on a distant rock Bruennhilde lies asleep. She will be awakened and claimed only by a man who has never known fear. With a triumphant cry, Siegfried leaps to his feet and asks the bird to lead him to his bride.

A stormy prelude precedes the third act. In a wild glen, Wotan, as the Wanderer, calls to Erda, the earth goddess. He tells her he no longer fears the destruction of the gods, since he has found a savior in Siegfried. When Erda sinks back into the ground, Wotan awaits the arrival of Siegfried to ask questions about Mime, the death of the dragon, and the history of Nothung. At first, Siegfried is patient with his replies, but he soon wearies of the colloquy and tries to brush his way past Wotan. When the god stands in his way, Siegfried brandishes his sword and shatters Wotan's shield. Siegfried now proceeds in his quest for Bruennhilde, blowing his horn as he goes. The strains of the Fire Music leap in the orchestra as he approaches the rock on which Bruennhilde lies asleep. Fearlessly, he penetrates the flames and awakens her from her slumber with a tender kiss. Bruennhilde welcomes him ecstatically ("Siegfried seliger Held"). For the first time, Siegfried experiences the rapture of love. He sweeps her to his arms. An exultant love duet ("Leuchtende Liebe! lachender Tod!") brings the drama to an end.

The Twilight of the Gods

In the prologue, we are back at the rock where Siegfried had awakened Bruennhilde. It is night now. Three Norns are spinning the fate of the world. As they do so, they detail episodes involving Wotan. When the threads break in their hands, they realize, with a cry of despair, that the twilight of the gods is at hand.

As dawn breaks, Siegfried and Bruennhilde appear. She is leading her horse, Grane, while he is dressed in battle armor, for she is sending him off for new exploits and triumphs ("Zu neuen Thaten, theurer Helde!"). At the same time, she is apprehensive that she might lose him. As a pledge of love, Siegfried presents her with the Ring in exchange for Grane. Then sounding his horn call, Siegfried sets forth on a journey down the Rhine.

The curtain falls to the strains of the celebrated orchestral episode known as "Siegfried's Rhine Journey." A descending passage for full orchestra precedes two important motives, that of "Decision to Love" in strings and clarinet, and the majestic Siegfried theme in the horns. An elaborate and complicated orchestral fabric now offers one motive after another in a kind of tonal summation of all that has thus far transpired. First, we get the "Magic Fire" music in strings; then the "Rhine" motive in the brass; after that the

"Ring" motive in woodwind and strings; and then the "Power of the Ring" in oboes. In the last twenty-one measures, the music provides the listener with a brief forward look at some of the action soon to transpire.

The actual first act of this drama takes place in the hall of the Gibichungs, ruled over by Gunther. Hagen, his half-brother, is concerned over the future of his race: neither Gunther nor Gunther's half-sister, Gutrune are married. Hagen suggests Bruennhilde as a possible wife for Gunther, even though he knows she belongs to Siegfried. When Gunther becomes upset over a proposition that he feels cannot be realized, Hagen unfolds a plan. Siegfried is soon due to arrive in their castle. Through the powers of a magic potion, Hagen plans to make Siegfried forget Bruennhilde; at the same time, the hero will fall in love with Gutrune. Thus the field will be clear for Gunther to gain Bruennhilde.

The sound of Siegfried's horn announces the arrival of the hero. He is welcomed warmly, and he willingly accepts a drink of friendship offered him by Gutrune. The potion brings on complete forgetfulness. Siegfried now is receptive to Gutrune's beauty. He is even ready to set forth with Gunther on the mission to capture Bruennhilde, in return for which he will get Gutrune's hand in marrage. Pleading eternal brotherhood ("Bluehenden Lebens labendes Blut"), Gunther and Siegfried set forth to find Bruennhilde.

Back at the rock, Bruennhilde is looking with delight on the Ring Siegfried had given her. Waltraute, a sister Valkyrie, appears with a stern warning ("Seit er von dir geschieden"). Doom faces man and gods unless Bruennhilde is willing to surrender the Ring. When Bruennhilde refuses, Waltraute leaves in despair. From a distance, Bruennhilde espies the approach of her beloved Siegfried. But love turns to horror when she sees approaching not Siegfried but Gunther: through the power of the Tarnhelm, Siegfried had transformed himself into the Gibichung king. He tears the Ring from her finger, seizes her, and proclaims her his bride.

In the second act, in the hall of the Gibichungs, Alberich is telling Hagen of the Ring's curse ("Schlaefst du, Hagen"), and warns him it must be captured at all costs. Once Alberich is gone, Siegfried comes to announce that Gunther and his bride Bruennhilde are about to arrive; at the same time he claims Gutrune as his bride. With a loud call, Hagen summons his vassals, who first hail Siegfried as hero, then welcome Gunther home. No sooner does Bruennhilde see Siegfried, and notices the Ring on his finger, when she becomes convinced he has deserted her for Gutrune. Siegfried vows on his spear that never has he been married to Bruennhilde ("Helle Wehr"). This so inflames the former Valkyrie that on the same spear she swears to destroy Siegfried. In this, Hagen and Gunther become her confederates. She reveals that the only part of Siegfried's body vulnerable to attack is his back. With this information, Hagen and Gunther, determined to gain possession of the Ring, plan to murder Siegfried the following day during a hunting party.

In the first scene of the third act, the Rhine maidens are swimming about in the river. Siegfried, temporarily separated from the hunting party, greets them. They urge him to return the Ring to the Rhine. When he refuses, they warn him that on that very day he will be doomed. The hunting party, headed by Gunther and Hagen, catches up with Siegfried. Gunther offers Siegfried a draught capable of restoring memory. Suddenly Siegfried remembers Bruennhilde. As two ravens fly overhead to distract Siegfried's attention, Hagen plunges his spear into the hero's back. Mortally wounded, Siegfried addresses his beloved Bruennhilde in an exalted farewell ("Bruennhilde, heilige Braut!"). Then he dies. The vassals lift his body and carry him off in a solemn procession, on a darkened stage, to the accompaniment of the sublime Funeral Music. This orchestral interlude (which serves for a change of scene) is not a funeral march but, as Albert Lavignac once remarked, a "funeral oration without words." Numerous motives from the various dramas are woven like so many colored strands into a most remarkable tonal fabric describing the life and achievements of our hero. Here is how Herbert F. Peyser describes this music: "Kettledrum beats precede a scale figure of sixteenth-notes which, soon associated with four mighty chords, forms the solemn, crushing Death motive, whose majestic recurrence unifies, like a refrain, the whole shattering march. We are given a kind of review of the dead man's life as seen from the perspective of his bier. The orchestra now becomes the sole actor in the tragedy, first evokes the unhappy Volsungs, who were Siegfried's parents. The motive of the Volsung race and of its heroism is followed by the poignant phrase associated with Sieglinde's compassion, and this with the melody representing the love of the fated pair. A grandiose transition, combining the Volsung theme and the figure of mourning, leads over to the main body of the funeral music. . . . In bright C major the theme of the Sword flashes by. . . . The awesome Death motive succeeds the symbol of the gleaming weapon; then comes the Siegfried theme, twice over, the second time with its frank ending, followed by that of Siegfried the Hero, a grandiose expansion of Siegfried's jubilant horn call. Alternating with these the crashing Death motive now lends to the music a colossal impact and an immensity more than life-sized. . . . Toward the close . . . we hear, twice over, the tender phrase of Bruennhilde's Womanhood, leading to the gloomy chords of Bondage and the Power of the Ring as well as a recall in funereal minor of the phrase of Siegfried the Hero. At this point, in the stage performance, the scene opens to show us the Hall of the Gibichungs."

With horror, Gutrune watches the vassals bring in Siegfried's body. When Hagen informs her that the hero was killed by a boar, she falls into a faint; but then, after recovering, she accuses Gunther of being the murderer. It is then that Gunther reveals Hagen to be the guilty man. A violent struggle involves Hagen and Gunther for the possession of the Ring, in which Gunther becomes the fatal victim. In trying to tear the Ring from Siegfried's finger,

Hagen is frozen in his tracks by the slow rise of the hero's hand, as if in warning. Bruennhilde now steps forward to tell the terrified people they are unworthy to mourn a hero like Siegfried, and to insist that Gutrune had never been Siegfried's wife. Bruennhilde orders the building of a funeral pyre. While this is being done, she gives voice to her terrible sorrow and to her undying love for Siegfried ("Wie Sonne lauter strahlt mir sein Licht"). Once the pyre is set aflame, Bruennhilde mounts her horse, hails Siegfried, and bravely rides to death in the leaping fires ("Starke Scheite schichtet mir dort"). As the flames begin to die down, the Rhine rises. The Rhine maidens seize Hagen and carry him to his death in the waters. One of them, Flosshilde, holds the Ring aloft. The waters subside; Valhalla crumbles. The twilight of the gods has come, and now there is only darkness.

1859. TRISTAN UND ISOLDE, a music drama in three acts, with text by the composer. First performance: Munich Opera, June 10, 1865.

Lohengrin was Wagner's last "opera"; *Tristan and Isolde,* his first "music drama." After *Lohengrin* had been produced, Wagner crystallized, wrote, and published his theories about opera and "the art of the future." He also began to plan his monumental *Ring of the Nibelungs*. This giant project absorbed him for a quarter of a century. As a respite from this taxing, all-consuming labor —and to get something produced in the foreseeable, instead of remote, future—he went to work on a music drama more modest in aim and structure than the *Ring*. In 1857, he seized upon the story of the love and death of Tristram, the Cornish knight, and the Irish princess, Iseult, which he found in the Arthurian legends. His recent emotional involvement with Mathilde Wesendonck made him particularly receptive to such a passionate love story.

There are two schools of thought regarding Wagner's inspiration for this his most passionate and sensual creation, his ecstatic paean to physical love. Some maintain it was the result of his affair with Mathilde. Ernest Newman, however, is of another opinion. He feels the reason why Wagner fell in love with Mathilde was because he was writing an opera about love, and thus was in the proper emotional frame to embark on an illicit relationship.

In any event, Wagner continually had Mathilde in mind in writing his opera. "That I wrote *Tristan,*" he once confessed to her, "I thank you from the bottom of my soul and in all eternity." He would send notes to her describing what he was writing. In sending her the Prelude and a new finale, he commented: "You will sense ivy and grapevine once more in this music." And when he finished the second act, he wrote to Mathilde: "My child, *Tristan,* will be terrific. The last act is overwhelming tragedy. This *Tristan* is a veritable alternating fever, with profoundest grief and disgrace intermittently followed by a most unheard of joy and jubilation."

When first he planned the writing of *Tristan,* Wagner had in mind a "practicable work," tailored to meet the tastes of opera audiences everywhere, so that it might bring him some badly needed revenue. "My idea," he wrote his publisher in 1857, "is to make things attractive and easy. The warm interest of my subject, its happy adaptation to a melodious flow in musical treatment, the effective leading roles, which should rapidly take their places among the most inviting parts open to our sopranos and tenors—all this satisfies me that, without having especially sought it, I have gone the right way to secure a remarkable popular success." But once Wagner steeped himself in his opera, the work acquired a far different character from the one he had planned. He embodied into it all his new concepts, aesthetic and artistic goals. He gave his imagination freedom of movement. He instantly forgot the tastes of his public and even the technical equipment of singers and orchestra players. When he finally completed *Tristan,* it no longer was a modest opera catering to popular taste, but a musical drama of monumental design, completely revolutionary in concept and idiom. Indeed, there are many Wagner authorities who regard *Tristan and Isolde* as the most successful realization of its composer's theories and, from many dramatic and musical points of view, his finest work for the stage.

"*Tristan,*" says Lawrence Gilman, "is unique not only among Wagner's works but among all outgivings of the musical mind, because it is devoted, with an exclusiveness and concentration and intensity beyond comparison, to the rendering of essential experience. Wagner is concerned here not with epic paragons, or elemental beings of fire and of the depths, or gods and goddesses, or a cosmos in distress, or some brilliant and crowded chapter out of a romantic past, but with the inner life of life itself. In this score he is at the summit of his genius. These passionate transvaluations of love and death have called forth the greatest that he could give; and he has steeped this miraculous music in a beauty that is outside of time."

Its world première was scheduled for Vienna, but there were delays upon delays stretching into months, then years. First, the leading tenor fell ill; then he maintained that by the time he had studied the second act, he had forgotten the first. Many singers complained that the music was unsingable, and just as many of the orchestra men thought it was unplayable. In addition, an anti-Wagner faction was beginning to show its strength in Vienna. Finally, after fifty-four rehearsals, the management of the Vienna Royal Opera came to the conclusion that the opera was "impossible" and abandoned it.

Having surrendered all hopes of getting *Tristan* performed, Wagner turned to the writing of a new musical drama, *Die Meistersinger*. Not until he had found a patron in King Ludwig II of Bavaria was his hope for a production of *Tristan* revived. That première finally took place in Munich on June 10, 1865, Hans von Buelow conducting. Considering that Wagner's enemies in Munich were working toward creating a fiasco, and considering the work's advanced ideas and idioms, the success of *Tristan* was remarkable. "There were enthusiastic calls after every act," reported Ludwig Schnorr von Carolsfeld, who appeared as Tristan, "and after the last, we had the pleasure of bringing Wagner into our midst before the applauding audience."

Tristan also achieved a huge success when first it was heard in the United States—at the Metropolitan Opera on December 1, 1886. The critics and audience were equally enthusiastic; the opera had to be given seven times that season. A decade later, *Tristan* became something of a vogue at the Metropolitan, due largely to the efforts of a brilliant cast that included the two de Reszke brothers and Lillian Nordica.

The first-act prelude opens with the slow and languorous "motive of longing" in the cellos; oboes soon contribute a phrase connoting "desire." The tonality is vague, the harmonies chromatic. This opening phrase, extending for three measures, is repeated twice. Then strings and woodwind seem to cry out in torment, and the orchestra adds its own exclamation with a loud chord. At this point, the cellos raise their voice in an eloquent love song, its theme derived from the motive of Tristan's "love-glance." As other parts of the orchestra provide a luscious contrapuntal background, the melody gains in intensity and passion. The fever subsides with the return of the motives of "longing" and "desire." But an ominous mood prevails with the quiet rumblings of the timpani as the curtain rises.

In legendary times, Tristan's ship is bearing Isolde, the Irish princess, to Cornwall. There she is to become the bride of King Mark. The strains of a chantey are sounded by one of the sailors ("Westwaerts schweift der Blick"). We now catch a glimpse of Isolde. Bitter that Tristan has been avoiding her during the voyage, she asks her lady-in-waiting, Brangaene, to bring him to her. Tristan refuses to come, his pretext being that he must steer the ship. This changes Isolde's bitterness to anger. To Brangaene, she describes how Tristan first came to Ireland; how he had killed her betrothed, Morold; how she had saved Tristan's life after he had been wounded; and how Tristan decided to bring Isolde to Cornwall to become King Mark's wife ("Wie lachend sie mir Lieder singen"). Brangaene tries to soothe Isolde by reminding her that she is about to become a queen. But Isolde is not assuaged. She can only think of the torment of having to live near Tristan, with whom she has secretly fallen in love. The only way out for her is in death. To Brangaene's horror, Isolde orders her to prepare a death potion. Suddenly, Tristan appears, to be denounced by Isolde for having killed Morold. Gallantly, heroically, Tristan offers Isolde his sword, but she spurns this opportunity to avenge herself. Instead, she invites Tristan to partake with her a cup of peace. The ringing tones of a sailors' chorus warn that the shores of Cornwall are approaching. Tristan takes the cup offered him. It contains a love potion which Brangaene had concocted in place of the poison. After Tristan has drained the cup, he and Isolde exchange meaningful glances. Each cries out the other's name in ecstasy, then rush into a passionate embrace. With the ship arriving at Cornwall, the sailors loudly acclaim King Mark.

The brief second-act prelude touches upon the flowering of the love and the growing agitation of Tristan and Isolde. The scene is a garden before

Isolde's chamber. Isolde, though married to King Mark, is more deeply in love with Tristan than ever. Brangaene is troubled. She warns Isolde that Melot, King Mark's courtier, is planning her destruction; that King Mark's imminent departure for a hunting expedition is just a ruse. Isolde is deaf to all warnings. She orders Brangaene to extinguish her torch as a signal to Tristan. She herself frantically waves her scarf to hurry him on. When Tristan appears, they rush irresistibly to each other. The duet that follows, and for which the orchestra provides a sensual frame, is perhaps the most ecstatic love music ever written ("O sink' hernieder Nacht der Liebe"). From atop the tower, Brangaene issues a warning ("Habet acht"), but the lovers are aware of nothing but their passion, the orchestra all the while rising to a new pitch of eroticism. Suddenly, Brangaene's scream of terror breaks the spell. Tristan's trusty henchman, Kurwenal, rushes in to warn the lovers that King Mark is arriving in the company of Melot and some huntsmen. Poignantly, the king reproaches Tristan for having betrayed him. Tristan confesses his guilt, then asks Isolde to follow him wherever he will go. Melot rushes at Tristan with drawn sword. Making no effort to defend himself, Tristan is seriously wounded.

The ailing Tristan has been brought to his castle in Brittany, where he is being attended to by Kurwenal. The third-act prelude provides a gloomy picture of the garden scene overlooking the sea, where Tristan is lying gravely ill. A somber subject is heard in the low register. Then an ascending passage for the violins brings on a second mournful theme in horn and cellos. As the curtain rises, we hear a shepherd playing a haunting refrain on a reed pipe. Revived to consciousness, Tristan is told by Kurwenal how he was brought here; at the same time, Kurwenal assures him that Isolde will soon come to him. Feverishly, Tristan entreats Kurwenal to scan the horizon for a sight of Isolde's ship. As Tristan becomes increasingly delirious, and Kurwenal more and more solicitous, the pipings of the shepherd grow light and gay. Looking over the ramparts, Kurwenal announces the ship's approach. It is, indeed, Isolde. Painfully, Tristan rises to his feet and falls into her arms, whispering her name with his final breath. Isolde is grief-stricken to see her beloved fall dead. Now a second ship arrives. It bears King Mark, come to forgive Tristan and bless his union with Isolde. But when Mark approaches, Kurwenal, mistaking his mission, attacks him, and is fatally wounded by Melot. Isolde now bids Tristan a permanent, poignant farewell ("Mild und leise wie er laechelt"). Then she falls dead over his inert body. Death has finally reunited the lovers.

1867. DIE MEISTERSINGER VON NUERENBERG (THE MASTERSINGERS OF NUREMBERG), opera in three acts, with text by the composer. First performance: Munich Opera, June 21, 1868.

Only in work could Wagner find a refuge from the harrowing disappointments and frustrations attending the projected but never realized world première of *Tristan and Isolde* in Vienna. The *Ring* was progressing; but that gargantuan project was many years from completion. Wagner now needed another immediate and possibly producible project to consume his creative passion—another work like *Tristan,* more modest in scope than the *Ring.* "I asked myself what I should do next," Wagner said. "Then suddenly my wonderful *Meistersinger* cropped up, and all in a moment I felt once more master of my Fate."

He had nursed the idea of writing a second opera around a song contest soon after he had finished *Tannhaeuser.* He had even decided then to build his text around the sixteenth-century craft guild, the Mastersingers—middle-class poets and musicians producing their art according to set rules and strict discipline. Now in 1862, in search of new operatic material, he returned to an idea first hatched in 1845. With his customary intensity, he threw himself into the completion of the text, reading it at the house of his publishers in Mainz in February 1862. In May of the same year, he suddenly came upon the idea for his third-act prelude; he became more convinced than ever that "this is my most perfect masterpiece." He completed the score in 1867.

In *The Mastersingers,* as in *Tristan,* Wagner side-stepped the supernatural world of gods and goddesses. But where tragedy and passion had obsessed him in *Tristan,* in *Meistersinger* he was concerned with a human comedy—a work that was gentle, serene, tender; a work with philosophic overtones and mellow wisdom; a work continually spiced with comic or satiric episodes. "The raging, uncontrollable passions, the eroticism and sensuality of the love of Tristan and Isolde gives way to the sweet and simple emotion governing Walther and Eva," wrote W. J. Henderson. "Not defeat and death confront the lovers of the *Meistersinger,* but fulfillment. Not personal destruction confronts the hero through his entrance into the song contest, as had happened in *Tannhaeuser,* but a victory of ideals. . . . In short, Wagner's outlook on life and people is positive in the *Meistersinger* as he details the emotions and conflicts of everyday people."

Though built mainly along the new musico-dramatic lines crystallized after *Lohengrin, Die Meistersinger* is in many important ways a throwback to old operatic values. Wagner was too consummate an artist, too much the man of the theater, not to meet characters and plot on their own terms. Some of the main musical episodes in *Die Meistersinger* come in set numbers: Walther's "Prize Song," for example, and the wonderful third-act quintet. The pomp and ceremony attending the song contest in the third act, the choral hymn of praise to Sachs, the dance of the apprentices, all belong more fittingly in opera than in music drama. Wagner's emphasis on diatonic rather than chromatic harmony, the importance he places on melody and the voice, his reliance on material borrowed from old German chorales, and street and lute songs—all this points up an operatic method. Even the orchestral preface to the first act is more of a traditional opera overture than the atmospheric prelude he had produced for *Tristan.*

For Wagner, the text of *Meistersinger* had deep personal significance. He identified himself with Walther, who defied the Beckmessers of the world by producing a musical art that shattered rules and traditions; he was Walther who, in the end, emerged victor over his enemies. As for the character of Beckmesser, he was none other than Eduard Hanslick under a different name being reduced to ridicule—Hanslick, of course, being the powerful Viennese critic who was devastatingly critical of Wagner; in fact, Wagner originally thought of naming this character Hans Lick.

Die Meistersinger was first produced in Munich on June 21, 1868, Hans von Buelow conducting. It was an outstanding success—Wagner's enemies notwithstanding. "Of all Wagner operas," says Alfred Loewenberg, "*Die Meistersinger* was the one which made its way most quietly and steadily, and without that note of sensation and hostility so characteristic of the earlier (and later) operas." The first production in the United States took place at the Metropolitan Opera on January 4, 1886.

The first-act Prelude, made up of some principal motives from the opera, is what Ernest Newman describes as a "potpourri feuilleton form of the *Tannhaeuser* Overture." First, we get the "Mastersingers" motive, a regal march for orchestra in full chords. After that, a gentler episode is given by the woodwind; this is the theme of "awakening love." A second march tune, this time in the brass, is based on the motive of the "Banner of the Mastersingers." A detailed and powerful workout of the second march tune precedes the presentation by the violins of a lyrical passage utilizing the "love possessed" motive, but which in actuality is Walther's "Prize Song." This episode gives way to an agitated section, which reaches a climax with the five basic motives of the prelude woven into a polyphonic texture. The overture ends with a loud restatement of the opening Mastersingers theme.

The first act takes place at the St. Katharine Church in Nuremberg. The services are concluded with a chorale. Eva, accompanied by her nurse Magdalene, is about to leave when she is stopped by Walther von Stolzing, a knight. He is in love with Eva. But Eva explains that her hand in marriage can go only to him who proves victorious in a forthcoming Mastersingers contest. David, an apprentice in love with Magdalene, provides additional information: a preliminary song trial would precede the competition for all those interested in joining the guild. Magdalene urges Walther to enter the trial, and David is recruited to teach Walther some of the rules governing the writing of the songs, a lesson the knight finds confusing. Now the Mastersingers file into the hall, headed by Pogner, Eva's father. He delivers an extended monologue explaining the terms of the competition ("Das schoene Fest"). Then he announces Walther as a contestant. The knight explains he has learned the art of song from an old minstrel, and from Nature itself ("Am stillen Herd"). Then he decides to sing of love. With Beckmesser assigned the chore of marking down mistakes, Walther proceeds to sing an ardent song ("Fangent an!

So rief der Lenz in den Wald"). He breaks so many rules that Beckmesser's slate is filled with marks. The other Mastersingers agree that Walther has failed. Only Hans Sachs, the cobbler-philosopher, is sympathetic. When Sachs is drowned out by disapproving shouts, Walther rushes angrily out of the hall. The Mastersingers now vote against Walther, then leave the hall.

In the second act, in a street, David has come to tell Magdalene of Walther's failure, only to be mocked by his fellow apprentices for his interest in Eva's nurse. They disperse when Hans Sachs comes out of his shop to begin work at his bench. As he labors, he muses about the beauty and originality of Walther's song ("Wie duftet doch der Flieder"). His revery is interrupted by the arrival of Eva who is coquettish with the old man ("Gut'n Abend, Meister"). Sachs, in reality, loves Eva, but is too wise not to realize she is out of reach. He is deeply touched to hear her say she would not at all be heartbroken were he, Sachs, to win the contest. But he knows how much Eva is in love with Walther. After Sachs has re-entered his shop, Walther arrives with a plan to elope with Eva. Their conversation is interrupted by the appearance of the watchman announcing all is well, then by Beckmesser come to serenade Eva. As Beckmesser proceeds with his love ballad ("Den Tag seh' ich erscheinen"), he is rudely interrupted by Hans Sach's loud hammering at his bench, and by his lusty singing as he works ("Jerum! Jerum!"). Soon Sachs is through with his job. Proudly, he maintains that a shoe, like a song, must be fashioned with care ("Mit den Schuhen ward ich fertig schier"). The din created by Beckmesser's serenading, and Hans Sachs's loud activity at cobbling, attract attention. The townspeople look out of their windows to see what is happening. Among them is Magdalene, whom Beckmesser mistakes for Eva, and to whom he addresses an ardent love song. David, seeing Beckmesser serenading Magdalene, administers him a sound thrashing. In the ensuing confusion, Eva and Walther make their escape. The hubbub dies down; the streets return to their nocturnal quiet. The returning watchman is back to announce the hour ("Hoert ihr Leut' und lasst euch sagen").

The third-act prelude is intended as a portrait of Hans Sachs. A brooding, reflective melody associated with Sachs (which returns in the third act in Sachs's monologue, "Wahn, Wahn") begins in unaccompanied cellos, then is continued fugato in the other strings. This is followed by a chorale for brass —the greeting to Sachs just before the song contest—and a quotation from the "Prize Song." The Prelude ends in a solemn mood, the opening reflective melody assigned first to orchestra, then just to the strings.

The first of two scenes in the third act is in Hans Sachs's shop. David has come to tell his master that he has delivered a pair of shoes to Beckmesser and to apologize for his behavior of the evening before ("Ach, Meister, woll't Ihr mir verzeih'n"). Sachs readily forgives him, then asks him to sing a hymn to St. John in honor of his festival day ("Am Jordan Sankt Johannes stand"). After David leaves, Sachs soliloquizes about the sad state of the world, of the dissensions and hatreds that poison the air of Nuremberg ("Wahn, Wahn").

Hardly has he finished, when Walther comes to tell Sachs of a wonderful dream during which a magic melody came to him. He begins to sing a part of the "Prize Song," which so impresses Sachs that he starts to put the tune down on paper, while urging Walther to enter it into the contest. Later, after Sachs and Walther have gone out of the shop, Beckmesser arrives. Seeing a paper with a melody on it, he seizes it, thinking it is something Sachs has written and which he, Beckmesser, can use in the contest. But when Sachs returns and discovers what Beckmesser has done, he magnanimously offers the melody to him as a gift. Beckmesser withdraws with delight. Now Eva enters, followed by Walther, Magdalene, and David. In a magnificent quintet ("Selig wie die Sonne"), Walther describes his dream to Eva; Magdalene, Eva, David, and Sachs express their individual reactions to recent events and how they have affected their respective lives.

And now the day of the contest is at hand. All Nuremberg has come to an open meadow outside the town in a festive mood. Apprentices dance merrily ("Dance of the Apprentices"). Then the various guilds arrive in a colorful procession. The crowd hails Sachs ("Wach' auf, es nahet gen den Tag"), and Sachs responds ("Euch wird es leicht"). The contest can now begin. Beckmesser, the first to perform, makes a ridiculous spectacle of himself. Walther comes forward with his "Prize Song" ("Morgenlich leuchtend im rosigen Schein"). The crowd is deeply moved. There can be no question but that Walther has come out victorious. But when the golden chain of the Masters Guild is conferred on Walther, he spurns it. Hans Sachs, however, entreats him to reconsider, pointing out that though rules may at times appear inflexible, yet by virtue of such discipline has German art prevailed ("Verachtet mir die Meister nicht"). This time it is Sachs who offers the Master Guild chain, which Walther now accepts with humility. A mighty paean is sounded for Sachs ("Heil Sachs! Hans Sachs!").

1870. A SIEGFRIED IDYL, for chamber orchestra.

During the first year of his marriage to Cosima, Wagner planned an unusual birthday for her. He completed an orchestral work, and had it copied and rehearsed in utmost secrecy. Then at half-past seven in the morning of Christmas Day of 1870, he assembled fifteen musicians at his home at Triebschen, in Switzerland. He lined them on the stairs leading to Cosima's bedroom. Standing at the foot of the stairs, Wagner led them in a performance of what is one of the most poignant, most eloquent lullabies ever written, music of surpassing tenderness and serenity. That piece was played a number of times that day. Its first public presentation took place in Mannheim on December 20, 1871, Wagner conducting.

As may have been expected, Cosima treasured the gift. Eight years after it was written she begrudged the fact that Wagner was allowing it to be published. "The Idyl is going off today," she confided to her diary. "My secret treasure is becoming common property. May the joy it will give mankind be commensurate with the sacrifice that I am making."

Several verses appeared in the published score; the last two lines reflect the spirit in which Wagner wrote this music. "Now, by thy grace in tones shall be revealed, Our dear unspoken bliss, till now concealed."

All the themes, save one, are taken from the music drama, *Siegfried.* The exception is the German cradle song of folk origin, "Schlaf' mein Kind, schlaf' ein." There was good reason for Wagner to use this tune as a tribute to his wife. Their son, Siegfried, whose presence brought such a glow to the household, was then six months old. "Just as Wagner named his first born after a hero long associated with his creative career," explains Ernest Newman, "in writing the *Idyl* he would have readily linked the child, Siegfried, then the center of his parents' delight, with every fond association of Triebchen."

The *Idyl* opens with a gentle melody for strings—Bruennhilde's awakening music. This is followed by the cradlesong. After that, the flute presents Bruennhilde's slumber motive. This is followed by the love music that ends *Siegfried* and motives suggesting the Siegfried horn theme and the forest song of the bird.

1882. PARSIFAL, a "stage-consecrating festival drama" in three acts, with text by the composer, based on a medieval legend and a poem by Wolfram von Eschenbach. First performance: Bayreuth, Germany, July 26, 1882.

It is significant to point out that Wagner did not describe his last stage work either as an "opera" or a "music drama," but as a "stage-consecrating festival drama." In short, he thought of it, not as theater, but as a sacred service. For this reason, he wanted its performances confined exclusively to Bayreuth. As Kufferath remarked, Wagner here was not producing a work "for an entertainment" nor for "a ministering of the senses." To Wagner, *Parsifal* was "akin to the theater of the ancient Greeks, or that of the Middle Ages in certain Mysteries, becoming again a place where the teachings of religions, of philosophy, of national traditions and ideals were consecrated." To this explanation, Lawrence Gilman provides a footnote: "But—and herein lies the grandeur and elevation of Wagner's aesthetic conception—his emphasis is not upon morals or dogma, but upon the communicating and exalting influence of the work of art itself, which is conceived as an ideal representation of the essential impulses and aspirations of life."

The ambition to write a religious drama haunted Wagner for many years. The first stimulus was the reading of Wolfram von Eschenbach's thirteenth-century poem. Wagner himself pinpointed the very moment when a vague ambition became a concrete project. In the Spring of 1857, while residing at the "Asyl" on the Wesendonck estate near Zurich, he looked out of his window. "The garden was breaking into leaf," he recorded in his autobiography, "the birds were singing, and at last, on the roof of my little house, I could rejoice in the fruitful quiet I had so long thirsted for. I was filled with it, when suddenly it came to me that this was Good Friday, and I remembered the great message it had once brought me as I was reading Wolfram's *Parzival*. . . . That ideal figure now came into my mind with overwhelming force, and setting out from the Good Friday idea, I quickly conceived an entire drama, the main features of which I immediately and very briefly noted down in three-act form."

Nevertheless, not until August of 1865 did he complete the first sketch of his text, and not until 1877 did this text achieve enough of a definite form to get published. He completed the music in the Spring of 1879, and the orchestration in 1882.

Where in several other operas and music dramas Wagner had dwelt on the subject of salvation through love, in *Parsifal,* his last drama, salvation is achieved through suffering, renunciation, and compassion. It is almost as if in this last drama—and at the dusk of his life—Wagner was finally substituting spiritual values for physical ones. His points of departure are the story of the redemption of the Holy Grail and the terrible suffering of Amfortas.

There are pages in *Parsifal* that are among the most sublime and the most exalted Wagner—or, for that matter, anybody else ever wrote for the stage. It is for such moments that many Wagnerians regard *Parsifal* as the summit of Wagner's art, one of the noblest musical dramas ever conceived. Others are conscious of the extended and repetitious monologues, the static action, the stock characterizations, the inconsistencies of plot. And being conscious of these faults, they place *Parsifal* far below *Tristan* and the *Ring* as a realization of Wagner's artistic aims. Possibly the truth lies somewhere between these two opposing opinions. *Parsifal* may not be the ultimate in Wagnerian musical theater, but it is a stirring and eloquent religious spectacle. What is lacking in the text is compensated for in the music, which attains a spirituality and explores an expressiveness unique unto itself. "The score of *Parsifal* as a whole," sums up Lawrence Gilman, "is rife with marvels; but perhaps the greatest of these is the sense of an embracing compassionateness with which this music at its noblest is filled, as if the old master in the evening of his tempestuous life had wanted to show us, as he unveiled for the last time the glowing Chalice of his miraculous art, that the innermost secret of all loveliness is its benison of profound appeasement."

The world première took place at Bayreuth on July 26, 1882. This was a subscription performance; the first public presentation took place four days after that. Wagner personally attended to all the details of the production. It was a Herculean assignment that probably shortened his life. In any event, as conducted by Hermann Levi, the music drama was magnificently performed, and generated considerable enthusiasm. It was given sixteen times that season.

At the last of these performances, Hermann Levi fell ill and Wagner himself took over.

There is reason to believe that Wagner was ready to retreat from his original decision to confine *Parsifal* to Bayreuth. Toward the end of 1882, he was discussing with the impresario, Angelo Neumann, arrangements for a tour of *Parsifal*. Wagner, however, died before these negotations were concluded. After Wagner's death, Cosima was relentless in her insistence that *Parsifal* be denied stage performances outside Bayreuth. Presentations in oratorio form were permitted. One of these, directed by Walter Damrosch in New York City on March 4, 1886, represented the first American hearing of the drama.

The first stage presentation outside Bayreuth took place at the Metropolitan Opera in New York in Christmas Eve of 1903. Despite vigorous protests, and a legal suit originating from Bayreuth, the Metropolitan proceeded with the announced plans to give *Parsifal* in New York. Interest in the music drama was kept alive by violent controversy, the Metropolitan Opera being attacked severely on moral, ethical, musical, and religious grounds. Then, having been given the green light by the courts, the Metropolitan presented *Parsifal* to a sold-out house. Eleven more performances after that were also sold out. (A special *Parsifal* train was run from Chicago to New York.) On the whole, the praise and the enthusiasm drowned out the denunciations.

The first-act Prelude (for which the composer provided the heading of *Love—Faith: Hope*), projects the atmosphere of mysticism and spirituality which characterizes the whole music drama. The opening phrase in woodwind and strings is the motive of the "Last Supper." Some elaboration of this precedes the presentation of the majestic second theme in the brass, derived from the "Grail" motive; this is a version of the famous liturgical "Dresden Amen." Next comes the vigorous "Faith" motive in horns and trombones. Amplification of this material follows, before a new idea is introduced: the "Lance" motive, come from the four notes of the "Last Supper" motive. The prelude ends with a powerful restatement of the "Faith" motive.

The first of the two scenes in the opening act takes place in a forest near Monsalvat, in the Spanish Pyrenees, during the Middle Ages. Gurnemanz, a knight of the Grail, instructs his squires how to help the ailing Amfortas bathe his wounds in the lake. He then reveals that only one remedy will heal the sick man. But before he can disclose what this remedy is, Kundry—a servant of the knights who is half sorceress and half woman—brings oil to soothe Amfortas's pain. Now Amfortas is being carried in on a litter. In terrible pain, Amfortas explains that the only person capable of saving him is an "innocent fool." Once Amfortas leaves for the lake, Gurnemanz embarks on an extended monologue to explain the source of Amfortas's wound ("O wunden, wundervoller, heiliger Speer"). He describes how Klingsor, the magician, bent on gaining possession of the Holy Grail and the spear that had pierced Christ's body, enticed Amfortas into a magic garden. There he seized

Amfortas's Spear, and with it wounded him grievously. Amfortas has been suffering ever since. Only he who regains the Spear and touches Amfortas's wound with it can heal the sick man; and the man to perform this must be an "innocent fool" made wise through pity, compassion, and understanding.

Just as Gurnemanz completes his monologue, a cry is heard. A wild swan is seen falling dead to the ground, the victim of an arrow. Parsifal, the man who had killed the bird, is dragged to Gurnemanz. Upon questioning, Parsifal reveals that the forest is his home, and that his mother is "Heart's Sorrow." As Parsifal rambles on with his story, he shows himself to be the "innocent fool" able to save Amfortas. Gently, Amfortas takes Parsifal by the hand to lead him to the Hall of the Holy Grail.

The setting changes to the accompaniment of the music of the "Transformation Scene." The background of tolling bells contributes solemnity to a stately march melody. Gurnemanz leads Parsifal into the Hall where the knights soon file in, singing as they seat themselves ("Zum letzten Liebesmahle"). And now Amfortas is brought in and laid on a couch. A boys' chorus chants a litany ("Den suendigen Welten"). Soon the voice of Titurel is heard; the one-time king of the Grail advises Amfortas to expiate his guilt by performing the Communion. Amfortas, however, insists he is unworthy of performing so sacred a duty ("Lasst ihn unenthuellt"). Esquires uncover the golden shrine and the crystal cup, and place them before Amfortas. When the chalice lights up magically, Amfortas lifts it high and places it on the table. Now the knights sing of the Last Supper ("Blut und Leib der heil'gen Gabe"), as Parsifal looks on dumbfounded and uncomprehending. After the knights and Amfortas leave, Parsifal confesses his ignorance by remaining silent. Angered, Gurnemanz drives Parsifal out of the Hall.

A short prelude to the second act suggests the supernatural world of Klingsor. The thematic material is derived mainly from the motives of "Enchantment" and "Kundry." From a tower atop his castle, Klingsor is calling to Kundry, commanding her to seduce Parsifal, whom Klingsor recognizes as a threat to his power. Kundry is horrified at this assignment, but she must follow his bidding. The tower suddenly vanishes, and in its place a magic garden comes to view. Parsifal is here, enthralled by the beauty of the place and enchanted by the seductive dance performed for him by flower-maidens ("Flower Maidens Scene"). Parsifal resists their enticements. Now Kundry appears—no longer the hag she had been up to now, but a beautiful woman. She has come to tell Parsifal about his mother and the circumstances of his youth ("Ich sah das Kind an seiner Mutter Brust"). With increasing tenderness, Kundry kisses Parsifal. Savagely, he thrusts her away. He has suddenly remembered Amfortas's suffering ("Amfortas! Die Wunde"); he also recalls the Communion scene, and now knows that he has been appointed to redeem the Grail. When Kundry resumes her efforts to seduce him, he realizes for the first time that it was in just such a garden that Amfortas was wounded. Once again he rejects Kundry. Now Kundry tries to win him over with pity, by relating how she has become the victim of a curse from which she can be saved by a redeemer ("Seit Ewigkeiten harre ich deiner"). Poignantly, she begs Parsifal to be that man, but Parsifal remains unmoved. In rage, Kundry calls on Klingsor for help. The magician hurls the magic Spear at Parsifal. Protected as he is by mysterious powers, Parsifal sees the Spear remain suspended in mid-air. Seizing it, he makes a sign of the cross and pronounces Klingsor's doom. At his words, Klingsor's castle falls to ruins.

The third-act prelude is bleak and melancholy; it suggests the utter despair of the knights. The motive of "Desolation" is heard first, followed by the motives of "Kundry," "Straying," "Spear," "Enchantment," "Grail," and the "Perfect Fool." The curtain rises on a meadow near Monsalvat. Years have passed; Gurnemanz is now an old man. He hears groans nearby and discovers they come from Kundry, dressed in the tattered garb of a penitent. Gurnemanz tells her that the knights of the Grail no longer need her services. While going to a spring to fetch water, Kundry sees Parsifal approaching. He is wearing black armor, and holds a Spear in hand. Parsifal relates how he has been wandering in search of the Grail, and how he has been involved in battle ("Der Irrnis und der Leiden Pfade"). In return, Gurnemanz describes the sad plight of the knights and the continuing suffering of Amfortas; also that Titurel is dead, and he himself has become a hermit. All this news sends Parsifal into a faint. When he recovers, he begs to be led to the Hall of the Knights for Titurel's last rites. He is now anointed with oil and baptized with spring water, as Kundry dries his feet with her hair. Suddenly, Parsifal is made aware how radiant the countryside has suddenly become. Gurnemanz tells him that it is Good Friday. From the orchestra comes what Lawrence Gilman described as "the most exalted and magnificent" page in all Wagner, the music of the *Charfreitagszauber,* or the *Good Friday Spell.* "As Parsifal turns and gazes on the tranquil loveliness of the fields and woods and meadows, the music . . . begins with the enamoring melody that is sung by the oboe in B major . . . over a murmuring of the muted strings and sustained harmonies of the horns and woodwind: music of ineffable tenderness, yet penetrated with a subtle emotion of remembered pain, as if the music were shadowed by the recollection of some assuaged but unforgettable grief."

Tolling bells now call the knights to prayer. Gurnemanz, Parsifal, and Kundry ascend to Monsalvat. The scene shifts to the great hall where knights are carrying in Titurel's bier. A second procession follows in which Amfortas is brought to the throne. The people sound a mighty lamentation. With terrible grief and pain, Amfortas vows never again to uncover the Grail; he begs the people to end his suffering with death. The assemblage recoils in horror. Parsifal now steps forward and lightly touches Amfortas's wound with his Spear, effecting a cure ("Nur eine Waffe taugt"). Parsifal then kneels in prayer before the Grail, which burns with a holy light. A beam points toward Parsifal as a dove circles his head. Kundry, absolved of her sins, falls dead at Parsifal's feet. Humbly, Amfortas and Gurnemanz bow before Parsifal as he lifts the holy chalice in consecration.

GIUSEPPE VERDI 1813–1901

Between them, Wagner and Verdi completely dominated the world of opera during the second half of the nineteenth century. Verdi brought Italian opera to its apotheosis, just as Wagner did to German opera. Each was motivated by the same ideal of creating a musical art form with dramatic truth and artistic validity; a form in which music was servant to the text; in which every other element was basic to the whole; and which dispensed with peripheral attractions and stultifying procedures. Verdi did this in the Italian way, by emphasizing vocal melody over symphonic methods, through the charm and grace of deeply-felt emotion, and through the humanity and compassion of his lyricism. As Hugo Leichtentritt explains: "The essential difference between Wagner and Verdi is the difference between German and Italian temperament, language, and expression. Verdi invariably makes the vocal part the essence of his music. This difference in the center of gravity in the art of Wagner and Verdi explains all the differences in style which are the logical outcome of this fundamental attitude. Though Wagner occasionally knew how to produce magnificent vocal effects, and significant and finely wrought symphonic workmanship had hardly any secrets for Verdi when he found reason for employing it, on the whole the orchestral basis in Wagner and the vocal preponderance in Verdi remain the true sources of invention and style."

Verdi is sometimes described as the pragmatic composer—as opposed to Wagner, the theorist and revolutionary. It is quite true that Verdi had sound theatrical instincts, a respect for the box office, and an eye on his audience. But like Wagner, he was a revolutionary, who sought out new horizons for Italian opera.

The early Verdi, like the Italians who preceded him, was of course mainly concerned with song, bel canto, stage effects. But already in his third opera *Nabucco,* in 1842, rebellion against earlier procedures begins to stir restlessly within him. Here the melody might be derived from Rossini and Bellini, and the stage effects from Gasparo Spontini (1774—1851). But the dramatist in Verdi begins to challenge the musician.

Even more daring in its emphasis on dramatic values over musical ones is *Macbeth,* another early Verdi opera (1847). *Macbeth,* as Paul Henry Lang pointed out in a review of that opera in the New York *Herald Tribune,* was a parting of the ways with the methods of the old opera seria. "Suddenly the Florence opera, where it was produced, was confronted with the demands, musical, dramatic, and technical that were unknown to the age. For this is real music drama, and one admires the assured competence with which the young composer . . . is able to fill his hearers' minds with an eerie, strongly charged psychological atmosphere."

The celebrated operas of Verdi's famous middle period, beginning with *Rigoletto* and ending with *Aïda,* are overcrowded with incomparable arias and ensemble numbers, with some of the most wonderful bel canto and coloratura numbers found in Italian opera. Nevertheless, these operas represent a significant forward advance for Italian musical drama in their dramatic strength, penetrating characterizations, remarkable ability to project atmosphere and mood. Here, as Hugo Leichtentritt points out, "he is not like his predecessors primarily intent on melodic beauty and sweetness, on brilliant vocal virtuosity, but on sharply characteristic, even realistic vocal treatment and invention. . . . He is the tragedian par excellence."

The supreme dramatist comes fully into his own with his last two operas—the one a tragedy, the other a comedy. Undoubtedly Verdi had assimilated lessons taught him by the Wagnerian music drama. But neither *Otello* nor *Falstaff* are Wagnerian. They are both pure Italian and pure Verdi—still aristocratic in their lyricism, still compelling in their humanity, still seductive in their charm. The musical dramatist and the singer of unforgettable songs are now one and indivisible, even as music and text are one. "These rich and beautiful creations," says Dyneley Hussey, "merit no less than *Tristan* and *Die Meistersinger* the title of music drama. For they are dramas—great tragedy and human comedy—presented through music."

Giuseppe Verdi was born in Le Roncole, Italy, on October 10, 1813. A local musician and the organist of the nearby town of Busseto gave young Verdi his first formal musical training. In 1832, a fund was raised to send him to the Milan Conservatory. Denied admission because he was both too old and too poorly trained, Verdi studied privately for a while with Vincenzo Lavigna. Then, in 1833, he settled in Busseto, where he conducted a symphony orchestra, married Margherita Barezzi in 1836, and completed his first surviving opera. *Oberto*. That opera, introduced at La Scala on November 17, 1839, proved so successful that the young composer received commissions for three new stage works. One of these—the comic opera, *Un giorno di regno* in 1840—was a fiasco. But *Nabucco,* produced in 1842, was a sensation and instantly made its composer one of the most idolized opera composers of his time.

That first creative period ended in 1849 with *Luisa Miller,* and included such highly successful and significant works as *I Lombardi* in 1843, *Ernani* in 1844, and *Macbeth* in 1847. Verdi's second creative period, which saw the writing and production of his most popular works, began in 1851 with *Rigoletto. La Traviata* and *Il Trovatore* both followed in 1853, *Simon Boccanegra* in 1857, *Un Ballo in maschera* in 1859, *La Forza del destino* in 1862, *Don Carlo* in 1867, and *Aïda* in 1871.

Verdi's first wife died in 1840. In 1859, he married again—his new wife being Giuseppina Strepponi, who had appeared in the première of *Nabucco.* They lived during the summers on a huge farm in Sant' Agata, where Verdi enjoyed a simple, peasant existence. Winters were spent in a palatial home in Genoa. An attempt was made to draw Verdi into politics, when Cavour instituted the first Italian parliament. Verdi was elected deputy. But he disliked politics and soon withdrew. When, in 1874, he was appointed Senator by the King, this was an honorary office making no demands on him.

For about fifteen years after *Aida,* Verdi wrote no more operas. Only a handful of other compositions came during this interim, including his only string quartet, and his magnificent *Manzoni Requiem.* Then he was drawn out of his prolonged retirement from the stage by Boïto's remarkable libretto based on Shakespeare's *Othello.* With *Otello* in 1887 and *Falstaff* in 1893, Verdi scaled new heights, with which Italian opera reached the summit.

With the death of his beloved wife Giuseppina in 1897, Verdi lost the will to live. Physical disintegration now took place, resulting first in the failure of sight and hearing, and after that in paralysis. Verdi's death took place in Milan on January 27, 1901, and was the occasion for national mourning. He was buried in the oratory of the Musicians Home in Milan, which he had helped to found and for whose support he had made ample provisions.

1842. NABUCCO (NEBUCHADNEZZER), opera in four acts, with text by Temistocle Solera. First performance: La Scala, Milan, March 9, 1842.

Nabucco was Verdi's third opera. The first had been a success, and the second a fiasco. But *Nabucco* was a triumph. After the première, audience, singers, and musicians gave the composer a resounding ovation. So great was the furor that for a moment Verdi thought it was inspired by hostility. The next day, the stirring "Hebrew Chorus" (which had to be repeated on opening night) seemed to be on everybody's lips. Donizetti left the opera house muttering: "Oh that *Nabucco*—beautiful, beautiful, beautiful!" The public forthwith made a vogue out of Verdi. Ties, hats, sauces were named after him. The critics were equally enthusiastic. Felice Romani wrote in *Figaro* that "Verdi had imbued his opera with an austere, grandiose atmosphere," adding that the music "has an emotional quality all its own that profoundly affects the spectators and on occasion arouses them to enthusiastic applause."

The libretto was old-vintage opera, full of those spectacular scenes and ceremonies so dear to Italian audiences at that time. It was a pretty silly text, full of coincidences, accidents, obscure motivations. But the music was something else. As Harold C. Schonberg wrote in *The New York Times* in reviewing the revival of *Nabucco* at the Metropolitan Opera in 1960: "Never before had a composer of such power and passion come on the scene. Instead of the sweet melodies of Bellini and the buffa of Rossini was heard an elemental voice that obviously was going to sweep aside all convention."

An elaborate story involving love, madness, suicide, political intrigues, takes place within the grandiose halls and temples and palaces of Babylon and Jerusalem. Fenena, daughter of Nabucco, is a hostage of the Jews in Jerusalem. She has fallen in love with her guard, Ismaele, nephew of the King of Judah. Babylonian troops, headed by Nabucco, descend on Jerusalem and conquer it. Abigaille—who thinks she is Fenena's sister, and consequently a princess—is also in love with Ismaele. She promises him his freedom if he will look with favor on her. This he refuses to do. Once freed, Fenena becomes regent of Babylon, while Nabucco is off to the wars. During his absence, Abigaille comes upon a document proving she is not a princess at all, but a former slave. Driven by her envy of Fenena, Abigaille plots her destruction. Meanwhile, Fenena has become a convert to Judaism, and has freed the Hebrew captives. Gathering around her a band of followers, Abigaille sets forth to overthrow Fenena's rule; but the precipitous return of Nabucco prevents further developments. Proudly, Nabucco places a crown on his own head, daring anyone to remove it. When a flash of lightning sends the crown toppling, Nabucco loses his sanity. Abigaille picks it up and proclaims herself the new regent. She makes a prisoner of the now insane Nabucco and plans to massacre the Hebrews and execute Fenena. The Jews lament their sad fate in one of the most glorious pages in early Verdi, the chorus, "Va, pensiero" From his prison window, Nabucco sees Fenena being led to her death. In a moving prayer, he entreats Jehovah to forgive him for his sins and save his daughter. His prayer is answered when loyal troops come to his rescue. By this time, Nabucco has recovered his sanity. He and his men save Fenena, proclaim their allegiance to Jehovah, and are hailed by the people. Distressed by these developments, Abigaille takes poison.

The first performance of *Nabucco* in America took place at the Astor Place Opera House on April 4, 1848. The opera was rarely given after that. When it was revived by the Metropolitan Opera on October 24, 1960, for the season's opening attraction, it was the first time that this opera was seen in that auditorium, and the first revival in America in about a century. The reason for the neglect of *Nabucco* is twofold. The absurd libretto makes an appreciation of the opera's sound musical values difficult. In addition, casting a soprano for the role of Abigaille is a problem not readily solved (this role had been written for the remarkable voice of Giuseppina Strepponi, who years later became Verdi's wife). Harold C. Schonberg explains: "The opera stands or falls on the role of Abigaille. . . . The chances are that no living singer could handle the writing as Verdi composed it."

1843. I LOMBARDI ALLA PRIMA CROCIATA (THE LOMBARDS IN THE FIRST CRUSADE), opera in four acts, with text by Temistocle Solera, based on a poem by Tommaso Grossi. First performance; La Scala, Milan, February 11, 1843.

I Lombardi, like *Nabucco,* was seriously burdened by an overcomplicated and frequently confused libretto. But once again, as in *Nabucco,* there are enough appealing musical episodes to rescue the opera from total oblivion: the powerful contrasts in the three first-act choruses that follow one another in rapid succession—those of the nuns, the conspirators, and the demand for revenge; the haunting prayer of Giselda, also in the first act, "Salve Maria," which Rossini admired so greatly and which Francis Toye finds anticipates the "Ave Maria" of *Otello;* the remarkable trio, "Qui posa il fianco," with its eloquent violin obbligato, that comes as a climax to the third act; the powerful chorus of the Crusaders in the fourth act, "O Signore, dal tetto natio." As Francis Toye sums it up: "The surprising thing about *I Lombardi* is not that it abounds in absurdities and crudities, but that it contains so much fine music."

The première at La Scala involved Verdi in the first of his many conflicts with censors. Civil authorities saw here an attempt to influence Pope Gregory XVI to help bring about a unification of Italy; ecclesiastics objected to the use of holy sites as settings for some of the action. Verdi remained immovable to their efforts to get him to change the opera, and in the end Verdi won out.

The first-night audience responded enthusiastically to the new opera. The critics were much less appreciative. When the opera was given in Venice in 1844, it was a fiasco. Subsequent performances in Europe and the United States were also initially unsuccessful. The American première took place at Palmo's Opera House in New York on March 3, 1847; this was the first time a Verdi opera was heard in the city.

In 1847, the opera was given in Paris in a French translation and under a new title, *Jerusalem.* Here and now was one of the rare occasions in which the opera proved highly successful.

The story is set in Milan during the time of the Crusades. It involves the rivalry of two brothers, Arvino and Pagano, for the love of Viclinda. Since Arvino is the lucky man to win Viclinda's hand in marriage, Pagano plots against his brother; for this, he is sent into exile. But Arvino soon grants Pagano clemency and permits him to come home. Pagano, still bent on vengeance, assembles a band of ruffians with whom he plots to kill Arvino. By mistake, he kills his own father instead. Overcome by shame, grief, and guilt, Pagano becomes a hermit in the mountains. Meanwhile, Arvino's daughter, Giselda, has fallen in love with the infidel Oronte. They plot to elope but are stopped by Arvino. Fatally wounded, Oronte turns Christian just before his death. Then, in an attack by Arvino and the Crusaders on Jerusalem, Pagano is mortally wounded. With his dying breath, he begs for and receives his brother's forgiveness.

1844. ERNANI, opera in four acts, with text by Francesco Maria Piave, based on Victor Hugo's drama, *Hernani.* First performance: Teatro la Fenice, Venice, March 9, 1844.

Ernani was the opera with which Verdi first gained international recognition; it is also the opera from his first creative period most likely to get revived. It makes a forthright appeal to the senses through melodramatic scenes, supercharged emotion, romance and passion. The first act aria of Elvira, "Ernani, involami," and the third-act chorus "O sommo Carlo" are deservedly famous. But there are other musical moments of a high order and a telling impact that are no less remarkable: the opening drinking chorus, "Evviva! Beviam!"; the unaccompanied first-act chorus, "Vedi come il buon vegliardo"; Don Carlo's two soaring arias, in the second act "Lo vedremo, veglio audace", and in the third, "Oh! de' verd'anni miei"; and the magnificent trio that closes the opera, "Solingo, errante e misero." Of technical interest is the fact that in this opera, Verdi experiments with a Leitmotiv—at a time when he could not possibly have known anything about Wagner's operas; the theme of Ernani's horn, suggested in the orchestral prelude, is repeated in the second and fourth acts.

As had happened before with *I Lombardi,* and would happen again with later operas, *Ernani* involved Verdi with censors and government officials. The main point of contention was the fact that the text was regarded as an attack on crowned authority. Several changes had to be made before the officials were placated. But Verdi was intransigent when the director of the La Fenice theater objected to the appearance of a horn player on the stage (something the composer regarded as basic to the drama); also, when the prima donna wanted the closing trio to be rewritten as a brilliant soprano aria.

The production of the première did not go off well, mainly because the prima donna and leading tenor were in poor voice. But the opera, nonetheless, was well received. "More or less every piece was applauded," wrote Verdi to Countess Appiani. "There were three calls after the first act, one after the second, three after the third, and three or four at the end of the opera." The critic of the *Gazzetta di Venezia* said: "The music made such an impression that . . . people came out of the theater already humming the tunes. . . . Maestro Verdi has an abundant and felicitous imagination, only equalled by his good taste."

From Venice, *Ernani* went on to most of Italy's leading opera houses. It became the first Verdi opera heard in London, produced there in 1845. In 1846, it was seen in Paris. On April 15, 1847, it was given for the first time in the United States, at the Park Theater in New York. Before the year of 1847 had ended, *Ernani* was made the opening attraction at the newly opened Astor Place Opera House in New York. The first of many presentations at the Metropolitan Opera took place on January 28, 1903.

1847. MACBETH, opera in four acts, with text by the composer and Francesco Maria Piave, with additional verse by Andrea Maffei, based on the tragedy of Shakespeare. First performance: Teatro della Pergola, Florence, March 14, 1847.

Macbeth is the transition from Verdi's first (and apprentice) creative period to his fruitful second one. In *Macbeth,* Verdi makes significant progress in freeing himself from any limitations and restrictions imposed upon him by his singers and audiences, and in emphasizing dramatic interest. "I believe," Verdi said when he wrote *Macbeth,* "it is time to abandon the customary formulas and the usual methods." To Felice Varesi, who assumed the title role, he said: "I would rather you served the poet better than the composer."

Like the best of Verdi's early operas, Macbeth combines superior and inferior music. The choruses of the witches and the assassins might leave much to be desired—a carry-over of older and less desirable operatic materials. But other pages reveal a new Verdi, ready to cross the threshold of greatness. Lady Macbeth's unforgettable aria, "La luce langue," is one such episode. "With its tremulous accompaniment," explains Dyneley Hussey, "it is a sensitive expression of dawning doubt in Lady Macbeth's mind." Another significant moment comes with her drinking song, "the exact expression of a neurotic temperament unsure of itself." A third remarkable incident is the duet of Macbeth and Lady Macbeth, "Fatal, mia donna," in which song gives way to dramatic declamation, unique in Italian opera of that day. But most significant of all is the sleepwalking scene—"Una macchia è qui tutt'ora"—for which Frank Walker says "there is absolutely no precedent in Italian opera. In characterization and atmosphere, in freedom of form, in dramatic truth, it stands alone." Dyneley Hussey adds: "Here . . . the composer rises to the level of the poet and gives the full equivalent in music of the spoken word."

Verdi knew what he was accomplishing in *Macbeth.* The opera always had a special place in his heart. Through the years, he kept on trying to improve it, frequently making drastic and elaborate revisions. The most significant changes were made for the production in French at the Théâtre Italien in Paris in 1865, when Verdi added the "La luce langue" aria, the third-act duet of Lady Macbeth and Macbeth, and some ballet music.

Macbeth was written on commission for the Teatro della Pergola in Florence. He chose the Shakespeare tragedy, not because he was particularly enamored of it, but because of the fortuitous circumstance that a good tenor was not available in Florence. This fact dictated the writing of an opera in which the central male character could be a baritone, and in which a tenor could assume a negligible role. *Macbeth* seemed the most likely candidate. At the Florence première, *Macbeth* did not make an impression; but at the second presentation, the atmosphere changed radically. "From the reserve of the first evening," reported the *Gazzetta Musicale,* "the public passed suddenly to wild applause. So much so, that all the numbers, even those that had been received with indifference on the first night, were greeted with enthusiasm."

The first performance in the United States took place at Niblo's Gardens in New York on April 24, 1850. The first production at the Metropolitan Opera followed more than a century later—on February 5, 1959, when Maria Meneghini Callas was starred as Lady Macbeth.

The libretto makes Lady Macbeth the dominating character, reducing Macbeth from the ambitious and noble soldier he had been in Shakespeare to a villain more in line with operatic convention. The first scene opens with the witches' chorus as they prophesy that Macbeth would soon become Thane of Cawdor and King of Scotland, with Banquo the father of kings to come. A messenger from King Duncan appears with the information that Cawdor had been executed as traitor, that Macbeth is his successor. Their prophecy fulfilled, the witches sing and dance triumphantly.

At the Castle of Cawdor, Lady Macbeth is reading a letter in which Macbeth describes the witches' prophecy. Soon Macbeth himself appears, ready to be an ally in his wife's scheme to seize the Scottish throne by killing Duncan. At an agreed signal, Macbeth performs the murder late at night. The crime is discovered by Macduff who, with Banquo's help, arouses the entire household.

In the second act, Macbeth rules Scotland. In his castle, he is troubled by his conscience; his wife's efforts to pacify him are to no avail. Suspicious of Banquo, Lady Macbeth spurs Macbeth on to arrange for the death of both Banquo and Banquo's son; then she exults at her royal status in "La luce langue." Banquo's son, however, manages to elude the killers.

During a palace banquet, at which Lady Macbeth toasts her guests, Banquo's ghost appears. Lady Macbeth tries to calm Macbeth's obvious agitation by repeating her toast; failing, she accuses him bitterly of cowardice.

Determined to have one more glimpse into the future, Macbeth seeks out the witches in their cave. In an elaborate pantomime, the witches invoke Hecate, then dance around their cauldron. Various apparitions appear before Macbeth, including kings and Banquo. Horrified, he falls into a swoon. Recovering, he joins Lady Macbeth in a vow to exterminate all enemies.

The fourth act opens in a deserted place near Birnam Wood. Scottish exiles are lamenting the tyranny suffered by their people ("Patria oppressa"), while Macduff is mourning the death of his wife and children at the hands of Macbeth ("Ahi la paterna mano!"). An English army, headed by Malcolm, sings a patriotic hymn just before it battles with Macbeth's forces.

Back in her castle, Lady Macbeth, haunted by fears, walks in her sleep, bewailing the fact she cannot rid her hands of blood stains ("Una macchia è qui tutt' oro"). In a different part of the palace, where Macbeth has been musing over his tragic plight ("Pietà, rispetto amore"), the king is informed of Lady Macbeth's death.

A brief orchestral interlude marks a change of scene to the battlefield, where Macbeth is killed. The liberated Scottish people hail their new king, Malcolm.

1849. LUISA MILLER, opera in three acts, with text by Salvatore Cammarano, based on *Kabale und Liebe* by Schiller. First performance: San Carlo, Naples, December 8, 1849.

Luisa Miller is the last of the transitional operas bridging Verdi's first two creative periods. It is one of the most intimate operas of this important phase of Verdi's development, one of the best integrated, and the one that most often maintains a consistently high standard of text and music.

The overture is based on a single melody, which is developed with extraordinary polyphonic skill while suggesting varying moods and emotional states.

In the seventeenth century, a peasant village in the Tyrols is celebrating Luisa Miller's birthday. Luisa is impatiently awaiting the arrival of a stranger with whom she has fallen in love ("Lo vidi, e'l primo palpito il cor sentì d'amore"). He is Rodolfo, son of Count Walter. When he appears, he brings her flowers. But Luisa's father doubts Rodolfo's honorable intentions, his suspicions fed by Wurm, who wants Luisa for himself. Determined to win her, Wurm betrays to Count Walter that an attachment exists between Rodolfo and Luisa, a fact that infuriates the nobleman, since he wants his son to marry the wealthy widow, Federica. After Rodolfo is ordered by his father to forget Luisa, the young lover implores Federica to release him, much to that lady's anger. Managing to slip away from a hunt, Rodolfo comes to Luisa to reassure her of his undying love. The Count breaks in on them, orders the arrest of both father and daughter. But on the threat of disclosing how his father came to power, Rodolfo manages to get his release. To Francis Toye, this finale provides the finest music of the act—the Adagio (in which Rodolfo speaks of his determination to marry Luisa); the Largo, "with its fine crescendo, worked on a constant bass figure" (where he threatens to betray the Count's secret); and the concerted number before the concluding Allegro, all combining "to make music of a high order."

Despite Rodolfo's efforts, Luisa's father is arrested. In the first scene of the second act, he is led in chains, charged with a conspiracy punishable by death. Count Walter and Wurm also conspire to destroy Luisa, by concocting a letter in which she denies loving Rodolfo and confesses her true love is Wurm. On the promise that her father will be freed, Luisa is made to sign a note in which she promises to marry Wurm. Before Rodolfo learns of his beloved's "treachery," he rhapsodizes over the beauty of the night in one of the most beautiful arias in the opera, "Quando le sere al placido." Then, learning what Luisa has promised to do, he retaliates by offering to marry Federica.

Luisa, aware of Rodolfo's imminent marriage, is writing a farewell letter to him in the third act. But at the request of her father, she tears it up. Soon Rodolfo comes to her room to ask her to share a poisonous drink with him, which she does. Dying, Rodolfo slays Wurm with his last ounce of strength.

Luisa Miller was written for the San Carlo Opera in Naples. The various difficulties and tribulations confronting Verdi during the presentation of this opera would surely provide rich material for a comic opera. In turns, Verdi and his opera had to put up with a cholera epidemic; a financially floundering opera house; an offer by a local journalist to review the opera favorabiy for a bribe. But in the end, all turned out well, and the première was a triumph. The first production in the United States took place at Castle Garden in New York on July 20, 1854; the first presentation at the Metropolitan Opera came on December 21, 1929. *Luisa Miller* has never been particularly appealing to American audiences. After four performances in the 1929–1930 season at the Metropolitan, and a single performance one season later, *Luisa Miller* was never again given by that company.

1851. RIGOLETTO, opera in three acts, with text by Francesco Maria Piave, based on *Le Roi s'amuse,* a drama by Victor Hugo. First performance: Teatro la Fenice, Venice, March 11, 1851.

Rigoletto was the first opera in Verdi's extraordinarily productive second period. To Francis Toye, this opera remains "even today among the finest manifestations of Verdi's genius. In unity of dramatic conception, in delineation of character, this music excels not only all the operas that preceded it, but most of the operas that succeeded it. If there was ever a case of sheer inspiration, *Rigoletto* constitutes such a one."

Today we regard *Rigoletto* as Italian opera in excelsis, with its procession of unforgettable arias, and its wonderful quartet. Yet in *Rigoletto,* Verdi's prime concern was to subordinate the set numbers to dramatic interest. He did not want to glorify the voice nor to spin wondrous melodies half so much as to catch in his music the nuances and echoes of his characters and plot. Ensemble numbers like the quartet and arias like "Caro nome," "Quest' o quella," "La donna è mobile," and "Pari siamo" seem to indicate that Verdi's artistic aim fell short of its target—so prominently do these and similar episodes stand out from their context, and so often are they heard apart from the opera as a whole. But when *Rigoletto* is properly produced and properly sung, we realize how successful Verdi was in making these numbers germane to the drama; they spring from character and dramatic episodes naturally and effortlessly. "The effect of 'La donna è mobile,'" explains Dyneley Hussey, "is made not by its rather facile melodic charm, but by its context. The contrast of its airy gaiety with the setting of Sparafucile's tavern produces a powerful sense of tragic irony and is carried to the extreme limit when Rigoletto hears the careless strain as he drags away the supposed body of the Duke." The other popular numbers are just as basic to the story. "The Duke's 'Quest' o quella,'" adds Hussey, "is not a set aria, but the end of a conversation and the beginning of a ballet." "Pari siamo" provides us with a penetrating insight into Rigoletto's personality. The popular Quartet gives side lights of the emotional states of the four participants. "You have here," explains William F. Apthorp, "Gilda's horror and despair, Rigoletto's rage, the Duke's cavalierly wooing, Maddalena's laughing coquetry; and each and all of these simultaneously contrasted emotions are reflected in the music with a truth and vividness, with a dramatic force, that are simply incomparable."

Though Verdi placed greater stress on dramatic than on lyrical values, he knew when he had a good melody, and recognized when it had popular appeal. So sure was he of the impact of "La donna è mobile"—and so fearful was he that the tune might become famous even before the opera was heard—that he refused to turn the music over to the tenor up to the time of the dress rehearsal. "It is so easy to remember," Verdi warned the singer, "that anybody could steal it from your lips; and then goodbye—they would be singing it all over the streets of Venice before the performance." Verdi did not overestimate the contagious effect of his song. At the première, the audience went wild over it; and the following day, it seemed that everybody in Venice was either singing or whistling it. But "La donna è mobile" was only one of many things that audience and critics found to like in *Rigoletto*. "An opera like this," reported the *Gazzetta di Venezia,* "cannot be judged after one evening. Yesterday we were, so to say, overwhelmed by the novelty of it all . . . novelty in the music, in the style, in the very form of the numbers. . . . The opera had a most complete success and the composer was acclaimed, applauded, and called after almost every number, two of which had to be repeated."

Rigoletto first came to the United States in a performance at the Academy of Music in New York on February 19, 1855; the first production at the Metropolitan Opera was seen on November 17, 1883, during the first month of that institution's opening. It was in this opera that Enrico Caruso made his American debut—at the Metropolitan Opera on November 23, 1903.

A short, atmospheric overture to the first act is dominated by the theme of "the Curse" heard in the brass. The curtain rises on the Duke's palace in Mantua in the sixteenth century. In an aside, the Duke of Mantua is telling a courtier about an attractive girl he had seen at Mass. She lives in a remote part of the city and her identity is not known to him. This leads him to comment on some of the attractive women in the ballroom and to discuss specifically the beautiful wife of Count Ceprano. But where women are concerned, the Duke is a cynic, as he reveals in the air "Quest' o quella." Then the guests participate in a graceful minuet; the Duke dances with the Countess Ceprano. Rigoletto, the Duke's deformed jester, notes and comments sarcastically on the obvious signs of jealousy betrayed by Count Ceprano. Rigoletto himself comes in for some amused comment by the courtiers, who make sly references that he is concealing a young and attractive sweetheart. The Duke now takes Rigoletto into his confidence by inquiring what would be the best way of getting rid of Count Ceprano, so that he, the Duke, might continue his affair with the Countess. Rigoletto's callous cynicism arouses Ceprano's fury and the bitterness of the courtiers, all of whom speak their mind in "Vendetta del pazzo." Rigoletto's only response is the quiet and arrogant assurance that no harm whatsoever can come to him. The situation is further dramatized by the precipitous arrival of Count Monterone, come to accuse the Duke of having ruined his daughter. The Duke orders the Count's arrest. Rigoletto's amused and sardonic reaction to all this elicits from the Count a violent curse, from which the hunchback recoils in horror.

In a deserted street near Rigoletto's home, in the second act, the jester is stopped by Sparafucile, a hired assassin. He informs Rigoletto his services are for hire. When Rigoletto inquires the price for killing a nobleman, the assassin describes not only his terms but his methods. After Sparafucile leaves, Rigoletto muses bitterly over the fate that had made him a deformed man and had placed him in an unpleasant job among contemptible courtiers ("Pari siamo"). His soliloquy over, he is greeted by his daughter Gilda. She presses him to tell her about her dead mother, and he complies in "Deh! non parlare al misero." He also warns her to be wary of strangers. A sound in the streets sends Rigoletto to investigate its source. As he does so, the Duke—disguised as a student—slips into Rigoletto's yard and goes into hiding. When he sees Rigoletto leaving, the Duke makes his presence known to Gilda, and tenderly affirms his love for her ("È il sol dell' anima"). Gilda is receptive to his ardent love-making. He bids her a fond farewell. Gilda speaks of her suddenly awakened love in the brilliant coloratura aria, "Caro nome." After Gilda has re-entered her house, a group of masked courtiers, headed by Count Ceprano, come to avenge themselves on Rigoletto. When they see the hunchback, they tell him they have come to abduct Ceprano's wife for the Duke and ask Rigoletto to join in this adventure. He does so willingly, and consents to wear a mask. He, therefore, does not realize that he is a partner to the crime of abducting Gilda, an escapade in which the courtiers participate with considerable delight, since they are of the belief that Gilda is Rigoletto's mistress ("Zitti, zitti, moviamo e vendetta"). When they drag Gilda away, Rigoletto tears the mask from his face and immediately realizes what has happened. He is also made aware that Monterone's curse has already begun to work its evil.

The action shifts back to the Duke's palace in the second act. The Duke is upset: having returned to Rigoletto's home he found Gilda has disappeared ("Parmi veder le lagrime"). The courtiers try to dispel his unhappy mood by recounting to him how they had abducted Rigoletto's "mistress" and had brought her to the palace. The Duke realizes at once that the "mistress" they are talking about is Gilda. He rushes out to greet her. Meanwhile, Rigoletto, disheveled and troubled, has come to seek his daughter. He denounces the courtiers bitterly ("Cortigiani, vil razza dannata"). At the same time he reveals that the person abducted was his daughter. Gilda now comes in to reveal to her father how deeply she loves the Duke. This distresses Rigoletto no end and he vows to avenge himself.

In the third act, the Duke—disguised as a soldier—regales himself at Sparafucile's inn. He makes sport of woman's fickleness in "La donna è mobile," then flirts with Maddalena, Sparafucile's sister. Outside the inn, Rigoletto has Gilda watch this scene through a window in an effort to disenchant her about her lover. The celebrated quartet now voices Gilda's bitterness over the Duke's infidelity, Rigoletto's fury, and the flirtatious byplay of the Duke and Maddalena ("Bella figlia dell' amore"). Then Rigoletto sends Gilda away. He arranges with Sparafucile for the murder of the Duke, the body to be delivered to him at midnight in a sack. When Maddalena uncovers this plot, she prevails on her brother to spare the Duke's life, to find another victim, and to turn the corpse over to Rigoletto. The victim that Sparafucile chooses is someone he thinks is a total stranger. In reality, it is Gilda, returned in a disguise. A violent storm erupts, a harbinger of coming disaster. The body is put hurriedly into a sack and delivered to Rigoletto. When Rigoletto suddenly hears the Duke's gay voice singing once again "La donna è mobile," he realizes he has been duped. He tears open to sack only to find Gilda inside, breathing her last. Poignantly, he takes her in his arms and bids her a last farewell, "Lassù in cielo". Realizing that Monterone's curse has been fulfilled, Rigoletto falls sobbing over Gilda's dead body.

1853. IL TROVATORE (THE TROUBADOURS), opera in four acts, with text by Salvatore Cammarano, based on *El Trovador,* a play by Antonio García Gutiérrez. First performance: Teatro Apollo, Rome, January 19, 1853.

If—as some Verdi authorities have maintained—*Il Trovatore* is the hardiest, most durable, and most popular of all Verdi operas, it certainly derives none of its strength and appeal from its libretto. The play piles plot upon subplot, introduces one character more unbelievable than the next. Improbability is compounded on improbability. The sum total is a text that reads like a travesty of opera librettos. Yet this is the play that sparked Verdi into writing one of his most opulent scores. There are probably more outstanding arias and ensemble numbers in *Il Trovatore* than in any other Italian opera. As Herbert F. Peyser wrote: "A discussion of *Il Trovatore* resolves itself into a chronicle of 'song hits,' spirited, impetuous, vehement, tender, dashing, elegiac, trashy."

The setting is Biscay and Aragon in the middle-fifteenth century. A short orchestral introduction serves, as Peyser says, "to call the audience to attention rather than to perform a dramatic function." It begins with a roll of the timpani repeated twice, followed by "falling and rising arpeggiated triplets, sharply accented, with intervening fanfares."

The first act is given the title of *The Duel.* The first of its two scenes takes place at the palace at Aliaferia where Ferrando, captain of the guards, is explaining to the Queen's soldiers how Count di Luna and his brother had been separated for many years: a gypsy, burned as a witch by the Count's father, was avenged by her daughter who had the Count's younger brother kidnapped and consigned him to flames. Count di Luna, however, refusing to believe his brother is dead, is indefatigable in his efforts to find him. Meanwhile, the ghost of the dead gypsy continues to haunt the Count's palace ("Di due figli").

The second scene finds Leonora, lady-in-waiting to the Queen, in the palace garden. She confides to her attendant, Inez, that a mysterious troubadour has been serenading her, and that she is in love with him ("Tacea la notte placida"). After the two ladies leave, Count di Luna comes to tell Leonora how much he loves her. Suddenly he hears the strains of the troubadour's serenade ("Deserto sulla terra"). Leonora, rushing back into the garden, mistakes the Count for the unknown troubadour and runs into his arms. But she realizes her mistake when from the shadows the troubadour's angry voice denounces her for infidelity. The troubadour now makes his identity known. He is Manrico, officer in the service of the Prince of Biscay. Tenderly, Leonora tries to convince Manrico that her love was intended for him alone. This so angers the Count that he challenges Manrico to a duel.

The second act—*The Gypsy*—opens in a gypsy camp in Biscay. Gypsies are working at a forge, singing an anvil chorus as they labor ("Vedi le fosche"). Nearby, Azucena, the gypsy, is in a dark mood; she recalls the bitter past in which her mother had been burned as a witch ("Stride la vampa"). Several gypsies try to console her, but she brushes them aside, and urges Manrico to avenge this foul murder ("Mi vendica"). The gypsies leave the scene to the brisk rhythm of the "Anvil Chorus." Azucena goes on to explain to Manrico how she had abducted Count di Luna's younger brother, and how, through a tragic error, she had thrown her own child into the flames in place of the Count's brother. This creates doubts in Manrico about his own origin; for all the while, he had believed Azucena was his mother. But the gypsy is insistent on considering Manrico her son, since she has found him dying on a battlefield and had brought him back to life. Manrico now reveals to Azucena that in his recent duel with Count di Luna a mysterious force kept him from killing his enemy ("Mal reggendo all'aspro assalto"). This arouses Azucena to fury. She orders Manrico to destroy the Count once and for all if ever again they meet in combat. A horn call brings in Ruiz; he is a soldier in Manrico's service. Ruiz comes with the news that the fortress of Castellor has fallen, and that Manrico must return to his troops. He also brings tidings about Leonora. Believing Manrico dead, she is planning to enter a convent.

With Leonora in a convent near Castellor, Count di Luna and his men have come there to abduct her. He first speaks of his anguished love for Leonora ("Il balen del suo sorriso"). Then he informs his men that life without her is unthinkable ("Per me ora fatale"). The chanting of nuns inside the convent reveals that Leonora is about to renounce love and the outside world. Leonora, Inez, and some of the nuns soon emerge. Leonora is seized by the Count's men, but before they can abduct her, Manrico and his followers intervene. Ecstatically, Leonora realizes that the man she loves is still alive ("E deggio e posso crederlo"). A fierce encounter follows between the men of Count di Luna and those of Manrico, during which Manrico is able to effect his escape with Leonora.

The third act—*The Gypsy's Son*—brings us at first to the military encampment of Count di Luna. The Count is planning an attack on Castellor to which

Manrico has brought Leonora. The Count's soldiers sing a vigorous hymn to war and victory ("Squilli, echeggi la tromba"). The Count bitterly reflects over the fact that Leonora is with Manrico and is determined to kill his rival. His reflections are interrupted when Ferrando comes to say that guards have seized Azucena, whom they suspect of being a spy. Subjected to questioning, the gypsy reveals the story of her past ("Giorni poveri vivea"). She then informs the Count that she is Manrico's mother. Her story convinces the Count that she is the one responsible for his brother's death; he also recognizes the bargaining value of having Manrico's mother in his power. He orders that Azucena die at the stake.

At the fortress of Castellor, Manrico and Leonora—about to get married—promise each other eternal love ("Ah, si, ben mio"). Their joy is short-lived. Ruiz brings the sorrowful information that Azucena is about to be executed. Manrico vows to save Azucena's life ("Di quella pira"). He bids Leonora farewell, as his soldiers exclaim their allegiance to him.

Manrico has been captured and is confined to a cell in the palace of Aliaferia. The fourth act—*The Torture*—brings Leonora, in disguise, to the battlements of the prison. She hopes to catch a glimpse of her beloved in the nearby prison tower. Poignantly, she prays that her overwhelming love may sustain him through his suffering ("D'amor sull' ali rosee"). A bell tolls. Voices from within the palace lament the doom of the prisoners in the celebrated *Miserere* ("Ah! che la morte"). This solemn music impels Leonora to make a last effort to save Manrico's life ("Tu vedrai che amore in terra"). When Count di Luna appears, she trades herself and her love in return for Manrico's life. When the bargain is accepted, she is ecstatic ("Vivrà! Contende il giubilo").

In the final scene, Azucena and Manrico are in a dungeon cell. Each tries to console the other. Some day, they say, they hope to return to their home in the mountains where once they had been so happy ("Ai nostri monti"). Azucena then falls asleep. Leonora now arrives to tell Manrico he is free. But when Leonora refuses to go off with him, Manrico learns about the price she had paid for his liberty. Bitterly, Manrico denounces her, but his anger turns to horror when he sees Leonora collapse at his feet. She has taken poison, and is dying. Taking her in his arms, Manrico pleads for forgiveness. When Count di Luna arrives, and sees Leonora dying, he orders Manrico's immediate execution. Manrico is led off, after having bid his mother farewell ("Ah, madre, addio"). Azucena is forced to watch Manrico's death from the prison window. Half-crazed, Azucena now reveals to the Count that he has just killed his younger brother ("Egli era tuo fratello"), that her gypsy mother has finally been avenged.

Few operas were ever introduced to their public under such unfavorable auspices as *Il Trovatore*. The Tiber had overflowed that day; the first-night audience had to wade through rivers of water and mud to get to the theater. Such unpleasant circumstances notwithstanding, the new opera was a triumph. "The music transported us to heaven," reported the Roman correspondent of the *Gazzetta Musicale*. "It could not be otherwise, because this is, without exaggeration, heavenly music." Soon after the première, three companies had to be formed in Venice to give simultaneous performances to meet the great demand for this new opera. Before two years had gone by, the opera had been heard in Paris, London, and New York. The American première took place at the Academy of Music in New York on May 2, 1855. A quarter of a century later, *Il Trovatore* became the third opera presented during the initial season of the Metropolitan Opera—on October 26, 1883. Another quarter of a century after that—on February 26, 1908—Enrico Caruso assumed there the role of Manrico for the first time.

1853. LA TRAVIATA (THE LOST ONE), opera in four acts, with text by Francesco Maria Piave, based on Alexandre Dumas's tragedy, *La Dame aux camélias*. First performance: Teatro la Fenice, Venice, March 6, 1853.

The sweetness and sentimentality, the grace and charm of *La Traviata* have made it one of Verdi's most popular operas—a perennial favorite the world over. These qualities make it somewhat difficult for us to realize today what a revolution this opera represented in its own time. As originally conceived by Verdi, the characters appeared in contemporary dress—something opera had not done before this, preferring the costumes of a bygone era. This novelty had to be dispensed with before *La Traviata* became popular, but other innovations, basic to the work, remained: the realism of text and music, which anticipates the later "Verismo" movement; the sympathetic portrayal of a courtesan, and the tender presentation of an undisguised illicit relationship; the almost chamber-music simplicity and intimacy of structure and style, with principal interest focused, not on big scenes or mighty climaxes, but on personal human relationships; the increasing subtlety of the musical characterizations in some of the main arias; most of all, the capacity of the music to convey the changing emotional states of the characters with such deft and telling strokes.

Here, even more than in his earlier operas, Verdi is a musical dramatist, ready to cater to character and situation rather than singer and song. Significant evidence of Verdi's growing dramatic powers is demonstrated in the first act with the "Un di felice" duet of Alfredo and Violetta. Dyneley Hussey explains: "Beneath its deceptive simplicity lies a depth of psychological understanding that gives us a measure of Verdi's ability as a dramatic composer. The contrast between the tender melody given to Alfredo and the cynical brilliance of Violetta's reply is obvious enough, but not on that account less admirable as a piece of character drawing. . . . The one musical theme develops into the other with a complete naturalness and inevitability that is as convincing as the arrival of the second subject is the true complement to the first in a great classical symphony."

The celebrated arias of Violetta that follow—"Ah, fors è lui" and "Sempre libera"—are more than just a brilliant tour de force for the soprano. They probe deeply into the personality of Violetta and into her inmost responses to Alfredo. "In the first air," William S. Ashbrook explains, "to a charmingly introspective melody, she attempts to analyze her new emotion. . . . Then in a magnificently florid recitative, she declares it is folly for a woman of her kind to think of a serious attachment." The "Sempre libera" that follows without interruption is Violetta's determination to stay a courtesan forever. "In the melody he has provided for this aria, Verdi has crowded all the brilliance and emptiness of her way of life."

William S. Ashbrook points to other penetrating dramatic subtleties in the score, but only one or two more examples need be cited. In the second act, he singles out the duet of the elder Germont and Violetta, the high point of which is the passage "Dite alla giovane" in which Violetta consents to give up her love for good. "This episode is simplicity itself—a scalewise melody in E-flat major. Germont's responses, "Piangi, piangi," demonstrate in a masterly way, by their contrary motion, the poignantly different positions of the characters." In the third act, Verdi utilizes "a relentess *idée fixe* for the scene of Alfredo's gambling with the Baron . . . [reiterating] a certain feverish figure."

Most Verdi authorities regard the fourth act as the greatest. To Francis Toye, it is "the poetry of the music in general that is chiefly remarkable." Toye then points out that the value of this act lies, not in its techniques, but "in the inspiration of the musical ideas themselves; the pathos of 'Addio del passato'; the wistfulness of 'Parigi, o cara'; the emotional quality of the final pages."

Verdi wasted no time in striking new paths for Italian opera. The first-act prelude is not a potpourri of familiar airs from the opera but a brief, atmospheric tone poem setting a tragic mood. It begins slowly and quietly with a haunting subject in divided strings. (In the opera this theme suggests Violetta's sickness.) The exquisite singing melody that follows in the strings is material later used to depict Violetta's love for Alfredo.

The curtain rises on a drawing room in Violetta's house in Paris in the mid-nineteenth century. (Some productions today like to set the time back into the early eighteenth century.) Violetta Valery, a courtesan, though ill, is entertaining her friends at a brilliant party. One of her guests is Alfredo Germont, who is encouraged to sing a drinking tune in praise of youth, love, and life ("Libiamo, libiamo"). Violetta than invites her guests to dance in the adjoining ballroom. Suddenly, she is stricken by a fainting spell, but takes hold of herself to assure her friends that nothing is seriously wrong with her. When the guests leave, Alfredo expresses deep concern to Violetta over her frail health. He betrays how long and how deeply he has been in love with her, to which she responds she is unworthy of such devotion ("Un di felice"). When the guests file in to say good night to their hostess, Alfredo takes leave. Finally left alone, Violetta muses over Alfredo's love for her and reveals her own interest in him ("Ah, fors è lui"). But in the end, she is in command over her emotions, insisting that her life must be free and uninhibited ("Sempre libera").

Despite such intentions, Violetta and Alfredo have become lovers. In the second act, they are living in Violetta's country home near Paris. Alfredo is delighted to have learned from her the meaning of true love ("De' miei bollenti spiriti"). But this joy vanishes when Violetta's maid, Annina, discloses that her mistress has been selling her jewels to support them. Humiliated and enraged, Alfredo decides to go to Paris to raise funds. While he is gone, Violetta is visited by Alfredo's father, come to denounce her. Violetta pleads with him: her great love for Alfredo has wiped out her former indiscretions; for the sake of that love she stood ready to sell all her jewelry. The elder Germont is moved by her sincerity, but is intransigent in his determination to see the affair ended. He discloses that his daughter is about to marry a man of high social position, who is becoming upset over the scandals involving the name of Germont. For the sake of his daughter, it is necessary for Violetta to give Alfredo up for good. At first, Violetta insists she cannot make such a sacrifice ("Non sapete quale affetto"). But as the elder Germont presses his arguments, she is made to realize that eventually this illicit affair must destroy Alfredo. She now promises the old man to devise some plan to end the liaison. When he leaves, she writes Alfredo a farewell letter, but before she has had time to seal it, Alfredo has returned. Concocting a convenient excuse for the necessity of going to Paris, she bids Alfredo goodbye with a passion that mystifies him. Once she is gone, he comes upon her letter. Heartsick, he interprets it as an act of desertion. His father returns to console him with reminders of Alfredo's happy boyhood in their native Provence ("Di Provenza il mar"), but Alfredo is by turns desolate and enraged.

In the third act, a lively party is taking place at Flora Bervoix's house in Paris. The place is alive with song, gambling, fortune-telling and mild flirtations. A colorful spectacle depicts Spanish matadors and picadors. Alfredo makes an appearance. He dismisses all questions about Violetta, and soon becames successfully engaged in gambling. Before long Violetta also arrives, accompanied by Baron Duphol. At first, Alfredo ignores her, concentrating on the gaming tables, where he is a heavy winner, and where Baron Duphol becomes one of his victims. Not until the room has been emptied, do Violetta and Alfredo meet face to face. She begs him to leave, feeling that trouble is brewing for Alfredo as a result of the Baron's heavy losses. At last, Alfredo promises to go, if Violetta consents to leave with him. This Violetta is unwilling to do. This is a sign to Alfredo that she is now so deeply involved with the Baron that she can no longer be interested in him. Contemptuously, Alfredo calls to the guests to return to the room. He throws all his winnings at Violetta, crying he is paying her back in full for whatever money she spent on him in the past. This behavior shocks the guests, including Alfredo's father. But Alfredo, oblivious to the furor he has caused, bewails the fact that he has lost forever the woman he loves. Violetta notes sadly that some day Alfredo will be made to realize that she has always loved him and that she has made her greatest possible sacrifice for his sake.

By the time the fourth act begins, Violetta has been stricken by tuberculosis and is seriously ill. The tender, sensitive theme of Violetta's sickness opens the fourth-act prelude; the ebbing away of Violetta's life is suggested by a series of broken descending phrases. Violetta is in her bedroom, attended by Annina and the doctor. The latter assures her she will rally, but Violetta knows her end cannot be far off. When Annina and the doctor leave her to herself, Violetta reads a letter sent her by Alfredo's father. The elder Germont informs her that the Baron and Alfredo have fought a duel in which the Baron was slightly wounded; that Alfredo would return to her now that the father stands ready to sanction the reconciliation. But Violetta knows the hour is late. She bids the world farewell ("Addio del passato"). Hardly has she finished, when Alfredo bursts into the room, envelops her in his arms, and begs for forgiveness. Having discovered the truth about Violetta's renunciation, he wants them to resume their former life together. He promises to bear her off to their home in Paris where once they had been so happy ("Parigi, o cara"). Violetta responds joyfully. She even tries to leave bed and dress for the trip. But when she collapses, both she and Alfredo know they are spinning a hopeless dream. As a farewell gift, Violetta presents Alfredo with a miniature of herself. Then she falls back dead, as Alfredo is grief-stricken.

In 1853, it hardly seemed possible that *La Traviata* would ever survive more than a handful of performances. The première in Venice was a fiasco, for which a combination of unhappy circumstances was responsible. The casting (over which Verdi had fretted from the beginning) was unfortunate. The leading soprano was a huge woman who hardly looked the part of a consumptive; there were times in the fourth act when the audience went into gales of laughter. The principal tenor was hoarse; the baritone thought the role beneath him and acted and sang accordingly. The staging also left much to be desired. In addition to all this, the novelty of seeing characters wear the dress of 1853 rubbed the audience the wrong way. Some critics, however, were perceptive enough to recognize the real worth of the opera. "Let us summon up the courage to say," wrote the Venetian correspondent of the *Gazzetta Musicale,* "that *La Traviata,* too, is a worthy product of that inexhaustible genius which has given to Europe *Nabucco, Ernani, Rigoletto,* and so on. Let us say that the music is marvelously effective and throws the dramatic evolution of the passions into terrible relief."

The management of La Fenice withdrew the opera from its repertory after the second performance. But *La Traviata* did not have to wait long for vindication. With some revisions by the composer—and with the drama set back two centuries to allow costuming and proper staging—*La Traviata* was revived at the San Benedetto Theater in Venice on May 6, 1854, when it was a triumph. From there, it went on to win the hearts of operagoers the world over.

The first American presentation took place at the Academy of Music in New York on December 3, 1856. A quarter of a century later, the opera was mounted at the Metropolitan Opera (the sixth presentation of the company's first season), on November 5, 1883.

1855. I VÊSPRI SICILIANI, or LÊS VEPRES SICILIENNES (SICILIAN VESPERS), opera in five acts, with text by Eugène Scribe and Charles Duveyrier. First performance: Paris Opéra, June 13, 1855.

I Vespri siciliani was the result of a commission from the Paris Opéra. For this reason, Verdi selected a text by the eminent French librettist, Scribe, and his collaborator, Charles Duveyrier (a libretto they had originally written for a Donizetti opera, *Le Duc d'alba*). To fulfil his obligations, Verdi came to Paris in October 1853, and finished most of his score by October 1854. Preparations for the rehearsals were quickly set into motion. But suddenly the soprano cast for the leading female role disappeared—into thin air, it seemed. The rehearsals had to be temporarily cancelled. Then she returned, as mysteriously as she had left; she had been on a secret honeymoon. The opera could finally be mounted. Its première attracted a brilliant audience that proved unresponsive. The critics, however, were of another mind. The *Débats* said that Verdi "has carried further the respect for dramatic properties and dramatic truth; his writing for the orchestra shows colors and accents previously unknown in Italian music."

The first American presentation took place on November 7, 1859, in New York. The opera has never proved a favorite in the United States and is rarely revived.

The tuneful overture, made up of some of the opera's principal melodies, remains a concert favorite. A vigorous first theme describes the massacre of the French garrison. A quiet and sensitive lyrical episode over tremolos follows; this is derived from the farewell of the hero and heroine just before their deaths. A robust third subject comes from the duet of Montforte and Arrigo. To Francis Toye, this overture represents "better than the opera itself, the gloom, the fury, and the pathos of the dramatic idea."

The second-act ballet music is still another popular orchestra episode. Among the memorable vocal pages are Elena's bolero, "Mercè, diletti amiche" and Arrigo's air, "La brezza aleggia," both heard in the fifth act; and, in the second act, Procida's nostalgic hymn, "O tu, Palermo."

The story gravitates around the efforts of thirteenth-century Sicilians to rise in revolt against the occupying French. Elena, a Sicilian of noble birth, is in love with the commoner, Arrigo. Complications develop when it is learned that he is, in reality, the son of Montforte, the French governor in Sicily, and that consequently he is a political foe of Elena. The governor, however, consents to the marriage of the two lovers. During the wedding ceremonies, Elena uses the wedding bells as a signal for the Sicilians to rise and massacre the French.

1857. SIMON BOCCANEGRA, opera in three acts and prologue, with text by Francesco Maria Piave, based on a play by Antonio García Gutiérrez. First performance: Teatro la Fenice, Venice, March 12, 1857.

Like *Il Trovatore, Simon Boccanegra* suffers from a thoroughly confused libretto. But unlike *Il Trovatore,* Verdi's score for this opera (good as it is) has never been able to give it widespread public appeal. A whole bill of particulars might be drawn up against Piave's text; but about Verdi's music, there is little division of opinion. Dyneley Hussey says: "The score . . . represents Verdi at the full maturity of his powers. . . . There is hardly a page of it that is not first-rate. As a whole the score produces an effect of somber magnificence, like some richly woven tapestry in which there is a preponderance of dark and expressive color." Hussey also sees *Simon Boccanegra* as a further move on the part of the composer away from "the lyrical style of his earlier works toward a more heroic type of opera."

The action takes place in the fourteenth century, when Genoa was a republic. A short, somber orchestral prelude blends right into the dialogue of the prologue. Here we learn about a conspiracy headed by Paolo and Pietro to make Simon Boccanegra, one-time pirate, into the Doge of Genoa. We also discover that Boccanegra has had an illicit love affair with Maria, daughter of the powerful nobleman, Fiesco. Fiesco wants the daughter born from this affair, but Simon cannot comply; the child has wandered off after the death of her nurse. The prologue ends as the people hail Simon as their new ruler.

Twenty-five years have passed. A descriptive orchestral prelude describes the break of dawn as the curtain rises on the first act. Simon Boccanegra, coming from a hunt, finds refuge at the home of Grimaldi. There he recognizes Amelia Grimaldi as his long-lost daughter. Amelia is betrothed to the Genoese nobleman, Gabriele Adorno. Paolo, who had been responsible for Simon's rise to power, falls in love with Amelia, seeks her hand in marriage and is rebuffed. Embittered, Paolo joins with Pietro in bringing about Boccanegra's destruction. They kidnap Amelia, and accuse Simon of having perpetrated this foul deed. Unaware that Simon is Amelia's father, Gabriele tries to kill Simon in reprisal. Amelia's escape, and her intervention, help save Simon's life. Once again, Gabriele attempts to kill Simon, this time during a tender scene between father and daughter; once again, Amelia saves her father's life. Only then does Gabriele discover the relationship between Simon and Amelia. Forgiven, Gabriele stands ready to protect the Doge from all his enemies. Nevertheless, Paolo manages to poison Simon. With his last breath, Simon blesses the imminent union of Amelia and Gabriele.

The most celebrated excerpt is Fiesco's air in the prologue, "Il lacerato spirito," sung contrapuntally off stage to the choral strains of a "Miserere." Other distinguished pages include Amelia's first-act refrain, "Come in quest' ora brua," and the extended finale to that act; Gabriele's expressive second-act aria, "O Inferno," and the effective trio in the same act, "Perdon, perdon, Amelia"; the third-act ensemble number, "Piango su voi."

When the opera was introduced in Venice, the press had kind words for it, but the audiences rejected it, finding the libretto too incomprehensible and too lugubrious. But though the opera failed to gain public favor—or because of it—Verdi always held a warm affection for this work. "Whatever friends or enemies may say," he wrote to his publisher after the opera had been pronounced a failure at La Scala in 1859, "*Boccanegra* is not inferior to many of my other operas that have been more lucky, but perhaps it needs a higher standard of performance and a public ready to listen." In 1881, Verdi revised the opera, enlisting the services of Arrigo Boïto to make important changes in the text. This new version (the one now given) was produced at La Scala on March 24, 1881. But even with the changes, the opera never really became a favorite with audiences. It had to wait until 1932—on January 28—to get heard in the United States, when it was given by the Metropolitan Opera.

1859. UN BALLO IN MASCHERA (A MASKED BALL), opera in three acts, with text by Antonio Somma, based on Eugène Scribe's libretto for *Gustavus III,* an opera by Auber. First performance: Teatro Apollo, Rome, February 17, 1859.

The Masked Ball is Verdi's only opera to use America as a setting. The choice of seventeenth-century Boston was made, not by prearrangement with the librettist seeking a fresh or unusual background, but an opportunistic measure to placate censors. Originally, the Scribe libretto, adapted by Somma, was set in Sweden in 1792; its main plot concerned the assassination of Gustavus III at a court ball. But the San Carlo, for whom *A Masked Ball* was written under contract, was timid about producing a work highlighting a conspiracy against a reigning monarch that ended in assassination. It suggested a change of time, locale, and characters. A compromise was reached by shifting the story to fourteenth-century Florence. This arrangement upset Verdi, since he was convinced Scribe's text would suffer by this change. But he accepted this decision, nevertheless, and left for Naples to supervise the production.

But the struggle with censors was not over. An attempted assassination of Napoleon III in Paris made the authorities in Naples more sensitive than ever to Verdi's opera. They now insisted upon far-reaching revisions that would have reduced the opera to absurdity. Verdi refused these demands, insisted upon a release from his contract, and was threatened with a heavy fine and prison. Immediately, a political storm erupted, with Verdi as its center. Neapolitans of all classes rallied behind the composer, seeing him as a symbol for Italian independence to which Napoleon III had been opposed. Public furor compelled the Neapolitan authorities to retreat. Verdi was allowed to take his opera elsewhere. He brought it to Rome, where the censors allowed it to get performed if the setting were transferred to some far-off place, and if the names of characters were changed. Thus King Gustavus III became the governor of Boston, Massachusetts. Only two characters stayed the way they had been with Scribe: Oscar (patterned after Gainsborough's "Blue Boy") and Amelia. Verdi approved all these changes. At last the opera was produced and enjoyed a major success.

An analysis published in the *Gazzetta Musicale* soon after the première is still of value. "In *Un Ballo in maschera* the music is everything—words, action, sentiment, passion, and character. Taking its inspiration from the moods of the characters and the movement of the action, the music in this case exercises such complete domination that in comparison and in relation with it the poetry becomes less than an accessory. Here we can say in truth that the notes begin their discourse where the poetry stops; anger, entreaty, jealousy, love are felt and heard above, if not quite apart, from the words in which they are expressed."

Because of the glaring contradiction between the brilliance of an eighteenth-century court and the austerity of colonial New England, it is often the custom today to mount *Un Ballo in maschera* in a Swedish setting. In eighteenth-century Sweden, the then king Riccardo is being hailed by his subjects. Provided with a list of guests for a prospective ball, he notices the name of Amelia, wife of his secretary Renato. He sings an ardent love song to and about her ("La rivedrò nell' estasi"). When the courtiers leave, the king is warned by Renato of mounting rebellion in his kingdom ("All vita che t'arride"). Then a judge comes to announce exile for Ulrica, a fortune teller accused of being a witch; the case for Ulrica is eloquently pleaded by the page, Oscar ("Volta la terrea"). Determined to seek out the truth for himself, the king decides to visit Ulrica in her cave in disguise. There Ulrica is performing an incantation ("Rè dell' abisso affretati"). From a hiding place in the cave, the king overhears Amelia begging Ulrica for a potion capable of relieving her of her overwhelming passion for the king. Ulrica advises her to seek out at midnight a magic herb near a gallows ("Della città all' occaso"). When she departs, the king emerges to ask Ulrica to read his fortune in the barcarolle "Di' tu se fedele." To the horror of the courtiers, she prophecies he will be murdered by the first man to shake his hand. Riccardo takes this prophecy lightly ("È scherzo od è follia"). Suddenly, Renato appears and, delighted at seeing the King, shakes his hand. This is further reassurance to the king, since he is convinced no harm can come to him from so devoted a secretary. The king then reveals his true identity and throws a purse at Ulrica.

In a deserted heath near a gallows, Amelia is seeking the magic herb Ulrica had described ("Ma dall' arido"). A clock strikes twelve. Out of the shadows comes Riccardo. She begs the king to leave before he is discovered, but he is deaf to her entreaties. Then, giving way to their feelings, they fall into each others' arms and sing of their overwhelming love ("O qual soave brivido"). They are interrupted by Renato, come to warn the king of assassins. Having covered her face, Amelia is not recognized by her husband. But when the assassins rush in to attack the king, Amelia's veil falls. It is then that Renato realizes his wife has had a rendezvous with the King, who manages to escape unharmed.

In his study, Renato, blind with rage, accuses Amelia of having been unfaithful. Nothing she can say convinces him she is innocent. Finally, she implores him to permit her to go away, and to say goodbye to her son ("Morrò, ma prima in grazia"). After she leaves, Renato looks at a portrait of the king and vows to avenge himself ("Eri tu che macchiavi"). The conspirators arrive to plan with Renato for the murder of their king. In drawing lots, Renato is the one chosen to perform the deed.

Within the palace, the king is signing a document sending Renato and his family into exile; thus he hopes to free himself of his unhappy love for Amelia. He laments this separation ("Ma se m'è forza perderti"). The curtains now part to reveal a magnificent ballroom. Despite warnings, the king joins his guests. After he bids Amelia farewell ("T'amo, si t'amo, e in lagrime"), he is fatally stabbed by Renato. While dying, the king reassures Renato of Amelia's innocence and begs his courtiers to spare Renato's life.

The first American production took place at the Academy of Music in New York on February 11, 1861. On December 11, 1889, it was seen for the first time at the Metropolitan Opera, when it was given in the German language.

1862. LA FORZA DEL DESTINO (THE FORCE OF DESTINY), opera in four acts, with text by Francesco Maria Piave, based on *Don Álvaro, o La Fuerza del Sino* by Ángel Pérez de Saavedra. First performance: Imperial Opera, St. Petersburg, November 10, 1862.

Up to World War I, *La Forza del destino* was little known outside Italy. Then, on November 15, 1918, the Metropolitan Opera gave its first presentation of this opera (Rosa Ponselle making her debut here). American opera lovers were now made aware of how much musical interest there was in this neglected work. James Gibbons Huneker found it crammed full of "robust melodies, rousing choruses, sighing ditties." *La Forza del destino* now stayed in the Metropolitan repertory for the next fourteen years. Meanwhile, the opera was for the first time beginning to win audiences throughout central Europe. Today if *La Forza* is less popular than *Il Trovatore, La Traviata,* or *Rigoletto,* it is certainly regarded much more highly than many other operas of Verdi's second period.

Much has been written about the unevenness of both score and text. "The truth is," maintains Herbert F. Peyser, "that the virtues and jostling weaknesses . . . have the same origin as those which in greater or lesser degree beset every Verdi opera after *La Traviata* and before *Aïda*. . . . There are new and considerable advances in technique (incidentally, *La Forza* is probably the first opera which Verdi orchestrated in advance of the rehearsals and not during their progress), a richer, more expressive vein of melody, finer workmanship and warmer harmony, side by side with throwbacks into the earlier manner."

This opera was written on commission from the Imperial Opera in St. Petersburg, where it received its first performance in 1862 with extraordinary success. Verdi himself, however, was dissatisfied with the opera. He later had Antonio Ghislanzoni revise the libretto; he himself shortened the score and made a number of other changes. The new version was given for the first time in Milan on February 27, 1869; this is the way the opera is generally produced today. The revised opera was produced for the first time in the United States at the Academy of Music in New York in 1881—sixteen years after the first American presentation in New York of the original version (February 24, 1865).

The overture offers significant material from the opera. It opens with a trumpet passage. A gentle air in the minor key then leads into Leonora's famous second-act prayer, "Madre pietosa," given by the strings. A brief pastoral episode—used in the third act to describe the Italian countryside—precedes a forceful recall of Leonora's prayer in full orchestra.

In eighteenth-century Seville, at the home of the Marquis of Calatrava, Leonora laments that her proud family will never sanction her marriage to Don Alvaro ("Me pellegrina ed orfana"). She conspires to elope with him, but when this plot is uncovered by Leonora's father, Don Alvaro gallantly assumes all the blame and asks that he be punished. To emphasize his submission, he tosses his pistol at Leonora's father. It explodes and wounds the Marquis fatally, who just before dying curses his daughter.

After her father's death, Leonora loses all trace of her beloved, Alvaro. She has come to seek him out in an inn at Hornachuelos, disguised as a man. There she espies her brother, Don Carlo, who has sworn to kill both her and Alvaro. Making her escape unnoticed, she arrives at the town monastery. There she prays to the Virgin for help ("Madre pietosa Vergine"). Padre Guardiano offers her a refuge in a nearby mountain cave. The monks pray that a curse befall anybody attempting to harm her. Then, joined by Leonora, they chant a prayer to the Virgin ("La Vergine degli angeli").

In the third act, the action passes on to Italy, where Don Alvaro, under an assumed identity, is fighting the Germans with the Spanish army. He thinks Leonora is dead, and remembers her with tenderness ("O tu che in seno"). His reveries are disturbed by outcries from a wounded soldier, who turns out to be Leonora's brother, Carlo. After Alvaro saves Carlo's life, the two men pledge eternal friendship, neither having recognized the other. A bugle summons the soldiers to battle, in which Don Alvaro is seriously wounded. Since he feels death is near, Alvaro entreats Carlo to destroy some letters that Alvaro has been guarding ("Solenne in quest' ora"). Going through these documents, Carlo comes upon Leonora's picture. Instantly, he realizes who Alvaro is, and is determined to kill him ("Egli è salvo"). Don Alvaro, having recovered from his wounds, now recognizes Carlo as his enemy. In vain does he try to convince Carlo that he is innocent of the Marquis' death. But Carlo will not listen, and instead challenges Alvaro to a duel in which Carlo is gravely wounded. Realizing with despair that once again he has brought tragedy to one near and dear to Leonora, Alvaro decides to accept holy vows and seek redemption in religion.

Five years elapse. Alvaro is now Father Raphael, a member of the Hornachuelos monastery. Having recovered, Carlo has followed Alvaro to the monastery ("Invano, Alvaro"), and once again demands satisfaction through a duel. Alvaro now refuses to fight, insisting that only God can bring retribution. But as Carlo grows increasingly venomous, Alvaro loses compassion, seizes a sword and rushes at Carlo.

In her cave, Leonora is praying for relief from tormenting dreams and memories ("Pace, pace mio Dio"). She hears the clash of swords. Fatally wounded in the duel, Carlo now begs Alvaro for absolution for his sins. Since Alvaro no longer regards himself as a holy man, he refuses. Instead, he calls out to the mountain "hermit" to pray for the dying man. It is only then that Alvaro recognizes the hermit as Leonora, and Leonora realizes that the stricken man is her brother. As she bends over him, the dying Carlo plunges a dagger into her bosom. Expiring, Leonora urges Alvaro to seek salvation in religion. When Alvaro curses his fate, Padre Guardiano commands him to ask God for forgiveness ("Non imprecare, umiliati").

1867. DON CARLO, opera in four acts, with text by François-Joseph Méry and Camille du Locle, based on a drama by Schiller. First performance: Paris Opéra, March 11, 1867.

When *Don Carlo* received its world première at the Opéra, which had commissioned it, the critics remarked the influence of Wagner and Meyerbeer. This was probably the first time Verdi was accused of trying to walk in Wagner's footsteps, an accusation that was untrue, and that Verdi resented. But the Meyerbeer charge carried greater weight. Verdi could not resist the temptation of producing a work in the grand manner favored by Parisian operagoers—with a text in which incident is piled upon incident; which boasts spectacular scenes and ballets; and is supercharged with emotion and dramatics. These are qualities that Meyerbeer had helped to make a tradition in French opera. But the elements that made the operas of Verdi's second period so distinguished are not absent in *Don Carlo*—dramatic expressiveness, lyrical beauty, deep psychological probings. Indeed, the marriage of Meyerbeer and Verdi represents an important phase in Verdi's development. Francis Toye is convinced if Verdi had not written *Don Carlo,* he probably would never have done *Aïda*. He even finds things in Don Carlo to point to *Otello* and *Falstaff*. "Without the orchestral and harmonic experiments, to say nothing of the conscientious endeavor to blend more intimately words and music characteristic of the best pages of the score, Verdi could hardly have risen to the heights of *Aïda, Otello* and *Falstaff*."

Though discriminating critics found much to admire in *Don Carlo,* the world première in Paris was far from a success. The principal singers, distinguished though they were, had an off night. Empress Eugénie, upset by a heretical remark made by one of the characters, turned her back to the stage at the end of the act as a sign of disapproval—a gesture that was noticed and seconded by many in the audience. Italians were at the time not very popular in France, and some of France's musicians resented paying tribute to a foreign composer.

Don Carlo had to wait a long time to gain audience approbation. Introduced in London in 1867, it did not get its first revival there until 1933; on both occasions it was received poorly. Not until 1958, when it was given a brilliant production in its original five-act version, was the opera hailed in London. The first American presentation took place at the Academy of Music in New York on April 12, 1877; the first revival in America after that came forty three years later, at the Metropolitan Opera.

The story is set in sixteenth-century France and Spain. Don Carlo, son of Philip II of Spain, is in love with Elizabeth de Valois. He comes to her in the forests of Fontainebleau in disguise, bearing a gift; he insists he is a messenger from Don Carlo, but she soon recognizes him and responds to him passionately. However, for reasons of State, Elizabeth must marry Carlo's father, Philip II. In the second act, set in the convent of St. Just, Carlo is unable to forget his love for his stepmother. His friend Rodrigo convinces him to leave the country for good and get from his father a commission for the Netherlands. Since Philip II is unsympathetic to Carlo's request, the young man comes to Elizabeth to plead his case for him. Thus thrown together again, Elizabeth and Carlo find their passion for each other has been reawakened.

The Princess Eboli is also in love with Carlo. They meet in the palace garden during a masked ball when Carlo mistakes her for Elizabeth and makes love to her. Aware that Carlo's passionate words are intended for Elizabeth, the Princess Eboli denounces him and threatens to expose him to the king. The latter, tormented by jealousy, is unable to sleep as he ponders his problems ("Dormirò sol nel manto"). When the Grand Inquisitor arrives to demand Carlo's arrest, because of his overt espousal of the cause of Flemish freedom, the King gives his assent. Having thus been the instrument of Carlo's ruin, the Princess Eboli gives voice to her anguish in one of the most celebrated arias in the opera, "O don fatale." Meanwhile, Rodrigo—condemned to death for his part in the insurrection—bids farewell to the world in "O Carlo, ascolta."

In the closing scene, in the cloisters of St. Just Convent, Don Carlos, having been released from prison, is having a secret rendezvous with Elizabeth at the tomb of Charles V. There he is found by the king, who orders his officers to seize him. Suddenly, a monk, dressed like the Emperor Charles V, rises from the tomb. Believing this to be an apparition, the terrified officers permit the monk to lead Carlo to safety within the monastery.

1871. AÏDA, opera in four acts, with text by Antonio Ghislanzoni, based on a plot by François Auguste Mariette. First performance: Cairo, Egypt, December 24, 1871.

With *Aïda,* Verdi's second period comes to a magnificent conclusion. Here, sound dramatic values, human interest, penetrating characterizations, deep-felt emotion, and surpassingly effective lyricism are skilfully combined with pageantry, ballet, large choral sequences, spectacle, and exoticism. "Aïda," explains Donald Jay Grout, "is Italian opera made heroic, grand opera infused with true human passion, a masterwork of two representative nineteenth-century styles." In *Aïda,* we confront a new sensitivity to and richness in harmonic and orchestral colorations, a marked advance in the use of recurring motives, a developed skill in fusing drama with music. If *Aïda* is a wonderful spectacle for the eye, it is at the same time a significant musico-dramatic conception. It offers the final confirmation—if such be needed—that if Verdi never wrote another opera, he still would have been the greatest composer for the stage produced by Italy, and one of the greatest from any country.

Aïda was commissioned by the Khedive of Cairo for a new opera house in Cairo built to help celebrate the opening of the Suez Canal. However, both the theater and the canal had to be opened in 1869 without the benefit of *Aïda.* Numerous delays were responsible. The libretto took longer than had been expected; the scenery and costumes, designed and executed in Paris, could not be transported to Egypt because of the Franco-Prussian War.

Not until Christmas Eve of 1871 was *Aïda* finally produced with all the munificence and splendor that seemingly limitless financial resources could purchase. As George R. Marek described it in *A Front Seat at the Opera:* "The backdrops were authentic copies of Egyptian buildings. Amneris's diadem of pure gold was ornamented by symbols found on the monuments at Nubia. Radames's helmet and shield were of solid silver. The materials covering the throne were copies of pieces in the Louvre. The King's costume was blue with a white velvet tunic covered with gold and jeweled design. . . . There were native Arab trumpeters, a military band from Cairo and three hundred people for the triumphal march."

A brilliant audience attended, some of them come from the far corners of the world. The Khedive and his entire harem occupied three boxes. The enthusiasm could not be controlled. It spilled over after every important number and compelled the conductor, Bottestini, to bark at the audience: "That isn't done!"

Verdi did not attend the première. He detested gala, highly publicized productions, and he was afraid of ocean travel. But he received a full report from Cairo, and it disgusted him. He said that *Aïda,* as seen there, "was no longer art but a trade, a pleasure party, a hunt, anything that can be run after, to which it is desired to give, if not success, at least notoriety." He personally saw to it that there be no duplication of such shenanigans when *Aïda* was given its first Italian presentation—at La Scala in Milan on February 8, 1872. He supervised all details of the performance, and attended every rehearsal. This performance was outstandingly successful.

Aïda was not received with equal enthusiasm when it was first given in the United States. This presentation took place at the Academy of Music in New York on November 25, 1873. To the critic of the *New York Times,* the work was "clearly the offspring of an almost Wagnerian system," while the critic of the *Herald* felt that most of the effect of the opera came from its scenery. When *Aïda* was given for the first time at the Metropolitan Opera, on November 12, 1886, it was heard in German.

It was with *Aïda* that the nineteen-year old Arturo Toscanini made his spectacular debut as a conductor—on June 25, 1886 in Rio de Janeiro. Then and there he stepped in to substitute for the regular conductor and, performing entirely from memory, directed an extraordinary performance. It was with *Aïda* that Toscanini made his American debut—at the Metropolitan Opera on November 16, 1908. And, to round out the circle, *Aïda* was the last piece of music he was destined to perform—a recording made in 1954.

The story is set in ancient Egypt during the reign of the Pharaohs—in Memphis and Thebes. The first act orchestral introduction, which Ernest Newman regards as "the finest operatic prelude ever written by Verdi," opens with an elegiac melody for the violins, used in the opera to identify Aïda. A brief development leads into the solemn motive of the priests of Isis. "Just as it is getting into stride as it were," explains Newman, "it is swept aside by the Aïda motive which, after being put through some exquisite metamorphoses, soars to a triumphant climax and then dies away in the heights."

The curtain rises on a hall in the palace at Memphis. Ramfis, the High Priest, reveals to Radames, captain of the Egyptian guards, that the Ethiopian army is advancing on Egypt; that the goddess Isis has picked an Egyptian warrior to lead the defenders. Radames's ambition is to become that hero; he wants to place the fruit of that victory at the feet of the woman he loves—Aïda, an Ethiopian slave held captive by Amneris, daughter of the king of Egypt ("Celeste Aïda"). In reality, Aïda is the daughter of the Ethiopian king, though this fact is not known in the Egyptian court. When Radames completes his radiant hymn to Aïda, Amneris appears. She is in love with Radames but suspects that his heart is elsewhere. Her suspicion falls upon Aïda, whose arrival leads Amneris to question her on the cause for her sadness ("Vieni, o diletta, appressati"). Aïda explains she is troubled by dangers besetting her native land. A trumpet fanfare brings on the king, come to appoint Radames commander of the Egyptian army. The king calls on his people to rally behind their new leader ("Su! del Nilo al sacro lido!"). Then, left to herself, Aïda prays for Radames's victorious return ("Ritorna vincitor!"), even though his success must inevitably spell doom for her own people.

Ramfis and his priestesses are at the temple of Vulcan praying for their country's victory ("Possente, Phtha!"). A ritual dance follows. Radames now comes to get a blessing on his sword and armor. When the High Priest invokes the aid of the gods, ("Nume, custode e vindici") Radames repeats the prayer; and the assembled priests and priestesses raise a mighty supplication to the god Phtha ("Immenso Phtha").

In the first scene of the second act, Amneris is being dressed by her servants in silks and jewels in preparation for the festival attending the return of the victorious Egyptian army. Moorish slave boys perform a dance. Female slaves sing of the delights of love ("Chi mai fra gli inni e i plausi"). Reclining on her couch, Amneris begins to dream about the imminent return of Radames ("Vieni, amor mio"). When Aïda appears, Amneris dismisses all the other slaves; she is eager to seek out Aïda's inmost feelings about Radames. Amneris invents the fiction that Radames has been killed, a ruse that betrays what Aïda really feels about the hero. Then, confessing she had lied, Amneris proudly maintains that only she, of royal blood, could win Radames's love, and not a humble slave like Aïda. Aïda pleads for mercy. The sound of trumpets and the shouts of the people announce that the victory celebration is about to begin.

Outside the city walls, the King and his retinue appear, followed by Amneris, Aïda, and other slaves. The people sing a hymn to victory ("Gloria all' Egitto"), and the priests sound a prayer of thanksgiving ("Della vittoria agli' arbitri"). The Egyptian army, headed by Radames, enters in a magnificent procession—to the strains of the celebrated "March." Dancing girls perform a ballet symbolizing victory. The people hail Radames, as Amneris places a laurel wreath on his brow. Now the captive Ethiopians are brought in. At their head is their king, Amonasro, who entreats the Egyptian king to be lenient with his people ("Ma tu, o Rè, tu possente"), a plea in which both Radames and Aïda join. The High Priest also intercedes for the captives and gains their freedom. Only king Amonasro is held as a hostage. The Egyptian King now rewards Radames by offering him the hand of Amneris. The people once again lift their voices in praise of their gods and their country.

In the third act, at the banks of the Nile, the priests pray to Isis in a nearby temple. Ramfis brings Amneris here to invoke divine blessings for her impending marriage to Radames. After they enter the temple, Aïda enters and nostalgically recalls her beloved homeland ("O patria mia"). Her father now comes to take her to task for having fallen in love with an enemy, Radames. He prevails on her to gain from Radames the name of a secret pass to be used by Egyptian forces; this information would prove valuable to the Ethiopians about to stage a mass attack against Egypt. With broken heart, Aïda promises to help her father. When Radames arrives, the Ethiopian king goes into hiding. Radames is overjoyed to see Aida again, and promises to flee with her out of Egypt ("Fuggiam gli ardori inospiti"). By subtly asking for the pass they must take to insure the safety of their flight, Aïda gains the information Amonasro needs to wage war on Egypt. The Ethiopian king springs from his hiding place, reveals himself, and announces his intention to command his troops in an attack on Egypt. Radames now realizes that he has become a traitor to his land and people ("Io son disonorato"). After he is denounced by Amneris, he meekly hands over his sword to Ramfis as a sign of surrender. Meanwhile, Aïda and her father make their escape.

Somewhat later, within the palace, Amneris is torn between her love for Radames and her jealousy. Sending for Radames, she entreats him to confess his guilt to the High Priest, and to beg for mercy; she stands ready to intercede for him, if only he will give up Aïda ("Già i sacredoti adunansi"). This

Radames refuses to do, preferring death to a life without Aïda. After Radames returns to his cell, Amneris laments that she has become the instrument for her beloved's destruction ("Ohimè! morir mi sento"). From a distance she hears priests calling upon the gods to see that justice is done ("Spirito del Nume sovra noi discendi"). The High Priest states the case against Radames. Three times Radames is called upon to defend himself, and three times he refuses. Finally, sentence is pronounced: Radames is to be buried alive ("Radames, è deciso il tuo fato"). The priests are satisfied that a traitor has been punished, as Amneris voices her anguish.

In the closing scene, in the temple of Vulcan, Radames, within his tomb, bemoans the fact that never again will he see Aïda ("La fatal pietra"). Suddenly Aïda emerges from the shadows. She had slipped unnoticed into the tomb before it had been sealed, and is ready to meet death with Radames ("Presago il core della tua condanna"). Above them, in the temple, a ritual dance is being performed; priests are chanting a somber elegy. Within the tomb, Radames and Aïda bid the world farewell ("O terra, addio"); outside, Amneris begs the gods for peace ("Pace t'imploro"), while the priests are invoking the blessings of the god Phtha.

1873. STRING QUARTET IN E MINOR. I. Allegro. II. Andantino. III. Prestissimo. IV. Scherzo fuga: allegro assai mosso.

During the period when the première of *Aïda* was being continually postponed, Verdi turned to the writing of his one and only chamber-music composition, a string quartet. He completed it in 1873, then thought so little of it that he discouraged both publication and performances. Nevertheless, Francis Toye finds much here to admire. The first theme of the opening Allegro bears a resemblance to a figure identifying Amneris in *Aïda*. This, with a contrasting and charming second theme "provides the most satisfactory music in a movement that is otherwise inclined to degenerate into something of a scramble," says Toye. The second movement is the frame for a delightful minuet-like tune of "wistful grace and unaffected simplicity." The third movement is monotonous to Toye, due to the "abundance of fast passages." But the finale, built from a single theme, is "treated and developed with marked ingenuity," suggesting "the rapid chatter of the women in Falstaff." Toye adds: "There is a good deal of individuality, not only in the subject itself but in several details of its handling, notably when the first violin holds a long E against the bustle of other instruments, as well as in the effective coda marked Poco più presto."

1874. THE MANZONI REQUIEM, for solo voices, chorus, and orchestra.

For about fifteen years after *Aïda,* Verdi wrote no more operas—and little else. But he did complete his only masterwork not intended for the stage, and the only one of his non-dramatic works still extensively performed—the Requiem Mass.

The *Manzoni Requiem* had its genesis in a project conceived by Verdi in 1868 to commemorate Rossini's death. At that time, Verdi planned a Requiem whose thirteen sections would be the work of thirteen different composers. His own contribution was the concluding part, "Libera me." This omnibus venture apparently did not turn out well, and was never performed.

A professor of composition at the Milan Conservatory, deeply impressed by the "Libera me," tried to get Verdi to write a complete Requiem by himself. But Verdi was not interested. "I have no love for useless things," he told the professor. "Requiem Masses exist in plenty, plenty, plenty! It is useless to add one more to their number."

But a number of years later, Verdi found the proper stimulus for the writing of a Requiem in the death of his friend Alessandro Manzoni—poet, patriot, novelist, author of the famous *I Promessi sposi.* Verdi now sought a way of honoring the memory of this great Italian, and his beloved friend. He wrote the city authorities in Milan offering to do a Requiem in memory of Manzoni for performance at one of the city churches on the anniversary of Manzoni's death, "It is a heartfelt impulse," he explained, "or rather necessity which prompts me to do honor as best I can to that Great One whom I so admired as a writer and venerated as a man, and as a model of patriotism." The Milan authorities eagerly gave Verdi the green light, offering to defray all expenses.

It took Verdi about a year to write his Requiem. He used his "Libera me" as the concluding section; but all the other parts were new. Then on the first anniversary of Manzoni's death—on May 22, 1874—Verdi directed the world première of his Requiem at the San Marco Church in Milan. It was a sensation. Before long it was played at La Scala, an occasion upon which Verdi was presented with a silver crown on a silken cushion. The next few times it was performed at La Scala, many of its sections had to be repeated. Soon all Italy heard and acclaimed the work. Often the performances were unauthorized, and on several occasions the most unorthodox forces were used. In Bologna, four pianos served as the accompanying orchestra; while in Ferrara, the local military band was used. Verdi had to go to court to stop such desecrations. In 1875, he himself toured Europe conducting the Requiem.

Verdi described his music as a "tribute of respectful affection, the expression of my sorrow." But elegiac moods are combined with deeply felt religious feelings, and with many stirring theatrical pages. The theatrical, almost operatic, quality of some of the passages has been the subject of criticism, to which Rosa Newmarch gives an apt response: "Those who feel that sacred music cannot be sacred unless it is darkly mystical and strictly liturgical, may experience a sense of shock and disapproval while listening to the natural flow of dramatic, impassioned and many-tinted emotions which Verdi permits himself in this Mass for the Dead. . . . In the Requiem he has created a work which moves in an atmosphere of tense emotion. Not contemplation but action is its ruling motive. Grief, awe, terrors of Death and Judgment, are all depicted here in forcible strokes. But hope and aspiring love are not entirely left out of the picture."

In his *Encyclopedia of Concert Music,* this author described the Requiem as follows: "It opens in an elegiac vein with 'Requiem aeternam,' a gentle plea for eternal rest, which reaches a climax with a fugue. But after that the work as a whole is more dramatic than lyrical, achieving great sweeps of power in parts of the 'Dies Irae' and 'Tuba Mirum.' The dramatic element becomes even more pronounced in the exchange between basses and tenor in 'Rex Tremendae,' while a more lyrical and at times operatic element is introduced in the poignant 'Recordare' for soprano and mezzo-soprano, the 'Ingemisco' for tenor solo, the 'Confutatis' for bass solo, and the moving 'Lacrimosa' for quartet and chorus. But a religious atmosphere is restored with the 'Sanctus,' a monumental eight-part fugue for double choir which is succeeded by the 'Benedictus' in which a more tranquil treatment is given to the chief subject in the preceding fugue. The 'Agnus Dei' is one of the peaks of this score, beginning with an exalted melody for soprano which is later repeated by chorus and orchestra in unison. Then comes the 'Lux aeterna,' a graceful trio for mezzo-soprano, tenor, and bass. In the concluding section, 'Libera me,' parts of the opening are recalled. After a powerful fugal chorus, the work ends in the same restrained and elegiac vein in which it began."

1887. OTELLO, opera in four acts, with text by Arrigo Boïto, based on the Shakespeare tragedy. First performance: La Scala, Milan, February 5, 1887.

During the almost fifteen-year hiatus that separates *Aïda* from *Otello,* Verdi often spoke of doing an opera. The subject of King Lear had obsessed him for many years. He also aspired to do a comic opera—perhaps to redeem the fiasco suffered by his only adventure into comedy, *Un giorno di regno* in 1840. But as the years passed, the probability that he would ever write a successor to *Aïda* became increasingly remote. He felt he was too old; he was afraid of failure at this stage of his life. He looked upon *Aïda* as the summit of his achievements and he preferred his career to end on the heights. Most of all, he felt that the kind of operas that had won him greatness had been eclipsed by the Wagnerian music drama. He admired Wagner; but he also realized that Wagnerian methods and aesthetics were not for him.

Undoubtedly, he would never again have written an opera if Arrigo Boïto had not brought him a dramatically arresting and eloquent libretto based on Shakespeare's *Othello.* Even so, it took Verdi several years to start to work in earnest—in 1885, or almost six years after he had first become interested in the idea. But once pen was in hand, the music started flowing. His score was completed by 1886. Almost immediately, plans were made for a grandiose première. A brilliant cast was assembled, including Francesco

Tamagno as Othello and Victor Maurel as Iago (each to become world famous for his interpretation of his role). The baton went to Franco Faccio. But the wary Verdi, still uncertain about the merits of his opera, reserved the right to withdraw it any time during the rehearsals.

That première, on February 5, 1887, generated phenomenal excitement. There were some who opposed having Verdi set a subject that Rossini had done before him and that was then still alive in the repertory. But most looked forward to Verdi's first opera after so many years of silence with feverish anticipation. That first-night audience could hardly contain its enthusiasm. In the first act—both after the fire chorus and Iago's drinking song—it shouted for the composer to come to the stage—and when he did, recorded Monaldi, "one immense simultaneous shout made the theater rock." When the opera ended, the composer received twenty curtain calls. Then his admirers dragged his carriage to his hotel, where for the rest of that night they kept shouting under his window, "Viva, Verdi."

By the end of 1888, *Otello* had been acclaimed in fifteen Italian cities. It had also been heard in Mexico City, St. Petersburg, Budapest, Prague, Hamburg, Amsterdam, Vienna, and New York. The American première took place at the Academy of Music in New York on April 16, 1888. On March 24, 1890, the opera came to the Metropolitan Opera.

Otello is the realization of Verdi's lifelong musico-dramatic ideals. Inspired by Wagner, and meeting the exacting specifications of Boïto's remarkable libretto, Verdi produced the most powerful and the best integrated tragedy of his career. *Otello* is a mighty musical drama, in which the music always serves the best interests of play and characters. Though there are unforgettable musical episodes, they are blended into a continuous, indivisible texture. But the design and the methods are always Verdi's, not Wagner's. The melody is Verdi melody at its aristocratic best. It might perhaps be less lyrical than that in Verdi's best earlier operas but, as Wallace Brockway and Herbert Weinstock point out, it reveals "seriatim the facets of character. . . . The man who composed *Otello* was more interested in the subtleties of psychological verisimilitude than even the man who had composed *Aïda*. The chief characters in *Otello* reveal themselves constantly until the moment of their usually violent ends: it is literally true, for example, that Othello discloses the last creative fact about himself with his last breath."

There is no orchestral prelude as such. A violent storm is unleashed in the opening measures. At the fourth measure, the curtain rises—but the storm continues to rage with an intensity rarely equalled in opera, with arpeggios, chromatics, and discords. Here and now we already confront a *new* Verdi, the supreme musical dramatist.

Othello, the new governor of Cyprus, steps out of the eye of the storm to be greeted by his people for his recent victory over the Turkish fleet. Othello responds with a twelve-measure "Exultate." In the background, Iago and Rodrigo are engaged in earnest conversation. Iago resents that Othello has chosen Cassio as his lieutenant; and Rodrigo is in despair because he is in love with Othello's beautiful wife, Desdemona. Iago tries to convince Rodrigo to be patient, since Desdemona is sure to grow tired of her husband. Now the people build a festive fire and sing its praises ("Fuoco di gioia"), while the soldiers are indulging in drinks. Iago toasts the beauty of Desdemona. Cassio joins in enthusiastically, a fact that further arouses Rodrigo's jealousy. Rodrigo now becomes Iago's ally in trying to destroy Cassio. With Iago bursting into a rousing drinking song ("Inaffia l'ugola"), Cassio is pressed into joining the revelry.

Under the influence of liquor, Cassio becomes noisy and argumentative. Before long he provokes a fight with Rodrigo, then one with Montanto, former governor of Cyprus. A riot breaks out, bringing Othello back to the scene to restore order. Angrily Othello dismisses Cassio as his lieutenant. Then when the crowd has dispersed, Othello and Desdemona join in a haunting love duet ("Gìa nella notte densa").

In the second act, in Othello's palace, Iago advises Cassio to plead his case with Desdemona and have her intercede for him with Othello. When Cassio leaves, Iago expresses his contempt for him in particular, and for all human beings in general, in his famous aria, "Credo in un Dio crudel". Upon Othello's appearance, Iago subtly and skilfully fans the Moor's suspicions by dropping hints about Desdemona and Cassio, and then warning the Moor not to succumb to the poison of jealousy. At this point, Desdemona comes upon the scene, surrounded by women and children singing her praises ("Dove guardi splendono"). Upon seeing Othello, she comes to him with a plea to restore Cassio to his former office. The more she presses this request, the more does Othello's anxiety grow. In a fit of anger, he seizes a handkerchief, with which Desdemona had tried to wipe his brow, and throws it angrily to the ground. It is retrieved by Iago's wife, Emilia, who turns it over to Iago, who is wily enough to realize that he now has in his possession a piece of property capable of destroying Othello. Meanwhile, Othello, oppressed by suspicions and fears, bids farewell to his tranquillity and to his hopes for success ("Ora e per sempre addio"). Iago makes a pretense of soothing him, but all the while he stealthily throws more oil on Othello's inner fires. When Othello attacks him, Iago insists he has seen Desdemona's handkerchief in Cassio's hand. Since this handkerchief had been Othello's first gift to Desdemona, this piece of news makes him frantic. He falls on his knees and vows to seek vengeance ("Si, pel ciel marmoreo giuro!").

In the great hall of the castle—in the third act—Iago is ready to give Othello further proof of Desdemona's guilt, if the Moor hides nearby and watches developments. Upon Desdemona's appearance, Othello tries to trap her into betraying herself, but she insists that both she and Cassio are innocent of any wrongdoing ("Dio ti giocondi"). She is unable to understand the cause for Othello's rage, and more pitifully than before, she protests that Othello is the only man she loves ("Esterrefatta fisso lo sguardo tuo tremendo"). Then

Othello asks for the handkerchief he had once given her as a gift. When she goes to fetch it, Othello bewails the fact that all his illusions have now been shattered ("Dio! mi potevi scagliar"). Upon Cassio's approach, Iago again urges Othello to conceal himself behind a column. Then Iago spurs Cassio on to boast about one of his love affairs, which Othello believes involves Desdemona. When Cassio brings out for Iago Desdemona's handkerchief, which he has somehow found in his room, Othello can have doubts no longer. Now he is determined to kill Desdemona, while Iago himself is ready to take care of Cassio. In gratitude, Othello raises Iago to the rank of lieutenant. At this point, an ambassador arrives to summon Othello back to Venice and to turn over the governorship of Cyprus to Cassio. Come to bid Desdemona farewell, Othello loses control of himself and savagely throws her to the ground. Heartbroken, Desdemona realizes she has lost Othello's love for good ("A terra, sì nel livido fango"). For his part, Othello is so completely overwhelmed by his emotions that he falls into a dead faint.

The fourth act—and one which many Verdi authorities regard as the finest in the opera—takes place in Desdemona's bedroom. A brief orchestral preface, in which an English horn is prominent, creates a foreboding atmosphere. Emilia is preparing Desdemona for bed. Desdemona recalls a song about her mother's maid she had learned in childhood, the "Willow Song" ("Mia madre aveva una povera ancella"). Then, when Emilia leaves, she prays to the Madonna ("Ave Maria"). After she goes to bed, Othello enters by a secret door. Once again he subjects her to questioning, and once again she affirms her innocence, insisting he call Cassio to confirm this fact. When Othello tells her that Cassio is dead, Desdemona's sudden grief sends him into a blind fury. He chokes her. Emilia bursts into the room with the news that Cassio is still alive; that he has murdered Rodrigo; that just before his death, Rodrigo had confessed the part he played in Iago's plot against Othello and Desdemona. Now aware that Iago had invented the whole story of Desdemona's infidelity, Othello kills himself with his dagger ("Niun mi tema").

1893. FALSTAFF, opera in three acts, with text by Arrigo Boïto, based on Shakespeare's *The Merry Wives of Windsor* and *Henry IV*. First performance: La Scala, Milan, February 9, 1893.

Verdi had good cause to believe that with *Otello* he had had his last say in opera. He had returned to the stage after many years with a masterwork; he had proved that in old age his creative powers had been renewed and revivified, had grown stronger and mellower. If he wrote no more, he was ending his long and productive career in triumph.

Apparently, the recollection that his only comic opera—*Un giorno di regno,* a half a century earlier—had been a dismal failure rankled deep within him. His ambition to write a successful comic opera had been reduced to embers, nevertheless, it still glowed hot with him. Then Boïto came forward again with another remarkable libretto, *Falstaff,* once again derived from Shakespeare.

"You have longed for a good subject for a comic opera all your life," Boïto wrote Verdi. "There is only one way of ending your career better than with *Otello,* that is to end it with *Falstaff.*"

Verdi doubted if he had the strength to bring to a new opera. But a persuasive Boïto, the encouragement of Verdi's wife, and his own dreams of doing a comic opera, all prevailed in the end. He went to work, just "to pass the time," he explained to his publisher, "nothing else." He spent two hours a day, every day, for two years. Then his score was completed—and Verdi knew it was good.

As Pitts Sanborn once wrote: "As a comedy in music, *Falstaff* ranks with the very greatest of the species. . . . Musically *Falstaff* is the comic counterpart of *Otello.* Here the style blends the traditional element of the opera buffa, from the half-spoken 'dry' recitative to the scintillant ensemble, in a thoroughly fused current of tone. It has been deemed astonishing that a man just short of eighty should create a work so overbrimming with youthful vivacity and humorous zest, but no less remarkable, if not so astonishing, in view of Verdi's untiring quest of perfection, is the excelling workmanship, from the broad outlines to the finest detail, that distinguishes this masterpiece."

"*Falstaff* is the very incarnation of youth and high spirits," adds R. A. Streatfeild. "He has combined a schoolboy's sense of fun with the grace and science of a Mozart. The part-writing is often exceedingly elaborate, but the most complicated concerted pieces flow on as naturally as a ballad. The glorious final fugue is an epitome of the entire work. It is really a marvel of contrapuntal ingenuity, yet it is so full of bewitching melody and healthy animal spirits that an uncultivated hearer would probably think it is nothing but an ordinary jovial finale. In the last act, Verdi strikes a deeper note. He has caught the very charm and mystery of the sleeping forest with exquisite art. There is an unearthly beauty about this scene, which is new to students of Verdi. In the fairy music, too, he reveals yet another side of his genius. Nothing so delicate nor so rich in imaginative beauty has been written since the days of Weber."

The première of *Falstaff* attracted music lovers from all parts of Europe; some had even come from the United States. The enthusiasm was loud and sustained. But it is hardly likely that that first-night audience fully appreciated both the subtlety and the inspiration of the new opera. Monaldi, for example, confessed that "after the fairy music and the exquisite romance for the tenor, the music, though graceful and elegant, no longer pleased." He regarded the closing fugue as "too long and in no-wise beautiful," and insisted that the interest "definitely waned in the third act."

By the end of 1893, the opera had been seen through most of Italy, as well as in Vienna, Berlin, Prague, Stuttgart, and several cities in South America. It came in a French translation to Paris in 1894, and in the same year to London. On February 4, 1895 it was seen at the Metropolitan Opera.

The first scene takes place in a room in Garter Inn, in fifteenth-century Windsor, England. Falstaff is imbibing wine in the company of his two disreputable henchmen, Bardolph and Pistol. He has just written love letters to two respectable married women—Mistress Page and Mistress Ford—hoping to arrange a rendezvous with one of them. Dr. Caius breaks in on him with the accusation that Falstaff has broken into his house and done injury to his horse. Falstaff does not deny his guilt. Bardolph contrives to get the good physician drunk and to steal his purse. Then, when Dr, Caius recovers sufficiently to make his departure, he vows never again to partake wine with such scoundrels. To this, Bardolph and Pistol reply with a canonic "Amen."

Falstaff now orders more wine and rhapsodizes over the beauty of Ford's wife ("O amor! sguardo di stella"). He then asks his henchmen to deliver his notes, which, fearing the consequences, they refuse to do. Cursing them as cowards, Falstaff turns his letters over to the page. He then goes into one of his most celebrated monologues, a soliloquy on honor ("L'Onore, ladri").

The second scene is in the garden of Ford's house. Mistress Ford and Mistress Page are discussing Falstaff's love letters, recognizing the humor implicit in Falstaff's advances, and determined to subject him to deserving ridicule. Ford also plans to avenge himself, having been advised by Pistol of Falstaff's interest in Mistress Ford. Dame Quickly is despatched to the inn to invite Falstaff to a rendezvous with Mistress Page; at the same time, Ford arranges to meet Falstaff under an assumed name. While this intrigue is being hatched, young Fenton and Ford's daughter, Nanette, speak of their love for one another in two expressive duets—"Labbra di foco" and "Torno all' assalto."

In the second act, we are back at Garter Inn. Once again Falstaff is with his cronies. Dame Quickly arrives to set the time for Falstaff's rendezvous with Mistress Ford. Now more than ever is Falstaff convinced of his appeal to women ("Va, vecchio John"). His soliloquy is interrupted by the appearance of "Signor Fontana," who is none other than Ford under an assumed name. He has come to bribe Falstaff to plead his cause with Mistress Ford with whom, he says, he is in love. This leads Falstaff to sing the praises of love in a delightful madrigal ("L'amor che non ci dà mai tregue"). He then promises "Signor Fontata" to be of service, revealing that he himself has a rendezvous planned with the same lady. This piece of news arouses Ford's jealousy. When Falstaff goes off to change his clothes, Ford denounces all women for their faithlessness in the celebrated monologue, "È sogno? O realtà?" Then the two men go off arm in arm.

Back at Ford's home, Dame Quickly has come to reveal to the two women that arrangements for meeting Falstaff have been made ("Giunta all' albergo"). Mistress Ford comments gaily on the farce they are about to stage ("Gaie comari di Windsor"). Now Falstaff appears to plead for himself with Mistress Ford, showering her with flattery ("Degna d'un Re") and insisting that though he is now old and fat that once he was young and handsome

("Quand'ero paggio del Duca di Norfolk"). When Dame Quickly comes to say that Mistress Page is about to appear, Falstaff hides behind a screen, where he overhears Mistress Page telling her friend that Ford is suspicious about her extra-marital activities and is coming home in a rage. Hardly has she spoken her warning, when Ford bursts into the room in search of Falstaff. When he fails to find him he leaves in a huff. Hurriedly, the two women hide Falstaff in a basket of laundry, which they drop unceremoniously out of the window into the river below.

Outside Garter Inn, in the final act, Falstaff is sad and disullusioned. He laments the callousness of the world, and tries to soothe his pain with wine ("Mondo, ladro"). Dame Quickly brings him solace with the news that Mistress Ford wants to make amends for what has happened by meeting him secretly in Windsor Park at midnight; she also suggests that Falstaff come disguised as the Black Huntsman. The other conspirators also map out a plot to reduce Falstaff to the ridiculous. At the same time, Ford promises Dr. Caius that he—and not Fenton—will get Nanette's hand in marriage.

It is midnight at Windsor Park. Fenton, disguised as Oberon, sings a serenade to his lady love ("Dal labbro il canto estasiato vola"). Nanette soon joins him, while the other conspirators lurk in hiding. Now Falstaff, disguised as the Huntsman, appears. Hearing eerie noises, he is convinced supernatural forces are surrounding him; he entreats the gods for protection ("Questa è la quercia"). His fears vanish when he sees and tries to make love to Mistress Ford, but his efforts are frustrated when he hears Mistress Page's voice from a distance. Nanette, dressed up as Titania, summons her fairy allies ("Sul fil d'un soffio etesio"). Terrified to see fairies and elves jump out of the forest blackness, Falstaff falls to the ground and is administered a sound thrashing ("Pizzica, pizzica"). Soon the conspirators weary of torturing poor Falstaff. Ford now reluctantly gives his consent to the marriage of his daughter Nanette and Fenton, much to the delight of all those present. The assemblage joins in a brilliant closing fugue in which they remark that all the world's a stage and all the people in it merely players ("Tutto nel mondo è burla").

ARRIGO BOÏTO 1842–1918

Boïto was a man of many gifts. He was a penetrating music critic about whom Victor Hugo said: "Critics like you are the philosophers of art. You are one of the talents of the new Italy." He was a brilliant poet and librettist. His texts for Verdi's *Otello* and *Falstaff* (and to a lesser degree to Ponchielli's *La Gioconda*) represent some of the finest dramatic writing in opera. Finally as a composer he produced a masterwork, though a blemished one, in *Mefistofele.* That work and an unfinished opera, *Nerone,* represent the sum total of his achievements as composer. Here, as in his criticisms, he attacked passionately the clichés and formulas to which the Italian opera of his time was usually reduced, and he sought to emphasize the significance of drama over music in the lyric theater. This was the reason that he was labelled as Wagnerian. But as H. C. Colles points out, "the musical source of his reforming zeal was not Wagner himself but Wagner's great examplar, Beethoven. . . . In *Mefistofele* Boïto made a serious attempt to convey in his music something of the philosophy underlying the Faust drama of Goethe. He succeeded sufficiently, at any rate in the prologue, to be ranged with the German masters, Schumann, Wagner and Liszt, who had essayed a similar task."

Impressive though *Mefistofele* and *Nerone* are at their best, it cannot be doubted that Boïto was greater as critic, poet, and dramatist than as composer. Colles summed it up well when he said: "His influence on the art of his country would have been virtually the same had he never produced the two operas which now represent him."

Arrigo Boïto was born in Padua, Italy, on February 24, 1842. While attending the Milan Conservatory he collaborated with Franco Faccio in the writing of two cantatas which were performed and which created such a good impression that both composers were provided subsidies by the Italian government for foreign travel. For two years, Boïto wandered about France, Germany, Belgium, and England, where he came into contact with the new music of these countries. Back in Italy, he set out to reform the Italian musical scene by writing numerous articles and criticisms in which the status quo in Italian music was attacked, and in which he deplored the way in which Italians neglected the masterworks of German music. He soon set out to put theory into practice by writing both the text and the score of *Mefistofele,* introduced at La Scala in Milan in 1868. He spent many years writing a second opera, *Nerone,* which he did not live to complete. (*Nerone* was introduced posthumously on May 2, 1924 at La Scala, Toscanini conducting. Toscanini also had revised the opera and contributed some of the finishing touches it needed.) While engaged on *Nerone,* Boïto provided Verdi with the librettos for that master's last two operas, *Otello* and *Falstaff.* In addition to all this, Boïto translated several of Wagner's music dramas into Italian; wrote a volume of poetry which appeared under the pen name of Tobia Gorrio; and published several novels. In 1892 he was made Inspector-General of the Milan Conservatory, and in 1912 the King of Italy appointed him Senator. His health deteriorated after he had made a taxing voyage to the war front during World War I. He died in a nursing home in Milan on June 10, 1918.

1868. MEFISTOFELE, opera in prologue, four acts, and epilogue, with text by the composer based on Goethe's *Faust*. First performance: La Scala, Milan, March 5, 1868.

Of the three famous dramatico-musical settings of Goethe's *Faust* (those by Gounod, Berlioz, and Boïto), *Mefistofele* is the one that proved most true to the spirit and intent of Goethe. Since Boïto had a trenchant intellect and possessed a strong bent for mysticism, he tried to translate in terms of musical sound and theater some of Goethe's philosophic concepts and symbolism. Boïto aspired to penetrate deeply into the cerebrations and inner conflicts of his characters. For the most part, *Mefistofele* becomes a kind of intellectual process just as Gounod's *Faust* is primarily a sentimental one. And where Gounod's style had been of a single fabric, that of Boïto was a cloth of many colors. His writing was a curious mixture of German dramatic procedures and polyphony; of old conventions with startling innovations in harmony and melody. Yet the Italian in him produced several magnificent lyrical pages, and this is the main reason why in time the opera became such a favorite with Italian audiences.

Boïto aspired to embrace Goethe's whole epic, where Gounod has used only the first part. In the prologue, Mephistopholes appears before the heavenly hosts who challenge him to test his powers against Faust. The first act is set in Frankfort-on-the-Main. It is Easter Sunday. Faust, mingling with the festival holiday crowd, espies a somber individual clad in monk's dress—Mephistopholes in disguise. Later on in his study, Faust, in a contemplative mood, extols virtue in "Dai campi, dai prati." Mephistopholes appears, introduce himself in "Son lo spirito che nega," and makes a pact whereby Faust exchanges his soul for a taste on earth of true happiness.

Disguised as a young cavalier named Henry, Faust comes to Marguerite's garden. There with Mephistopholes' help, and with the assistance of a sleeping potion administered to Marguerite's mother, Faust woos and makes love to Marguerite. Mephistopholes then brings Faust to a valley for a glimpse at a Witches' Sabbath. Suddenly Faust is disturbed by a vision in which Marguerite appears in chains.

Marguerite, having lost her sanity, has murdered both her mother and the child she has borne to Faust. In the third act she is in prison where she is contemplating her imminent execution in "L'Altre notte." Faust comes to plead with her that she escape with him. But in the dramatic duet, "Lonatonò, lontanò," she rejects his plan and voices her horror of Faust.

Mephistopholes now conducts Faust to the River Perreus for the spectacle of Walpurgis Night ("La Notte del sabba"). There Faust addresses and makes love to the goddess Helen ("Forma Ideal").

In the epilogue Faust is back in his study brooding over his experiences ("Il real fu dolore"). He ultimately finds redemption. As he dies, the heavenly spirits sing a hymn to his passing.

Partly because it was both complex and cerebral, partly because it was so long (requiring six hours for performance), partly because there was so little action, but mainly because Boïto's enemies had come to destroy his reputation, the première of *Mefistofele* was a fiasco. In fact there was a riot in the theater during the performance. When similar demonstrations erupted at the next two presentations, the police stepped in and forebade any more performances of the opera.

Boïto now revised his opera extensively. He shortened it; simplified some of the musical structure; introduced some new material, including the effective duet, "Lontanò, lontanò"; changed Faust from a baritone to a tenor. The new version, given in Bologna on October 4, 1875, was a huge success. From then on *Mefistofele* acquired a permanent place in the Italian repertory. It has been given over five thousand performances in Italy. Less than five years after its successful appearance in the new version, *Mefistofele* was heard outside Italy for the first time, when it was given in London on July 6, 1880. On November 16, 1880 the opera was introduced in the United States—in Boston, in an English translation. An Italian-language production took place at the Academy of Music in New York on November 24, 1880. By the time the Metropolitan Opera came into existence in 1883, the opera had found so much favor in the United States that it was included in the repertory of that company during its initial season.

OTTO NICOLAI 1810–1849

John S. Weissman pointed to two important influences on Nicolai. The first was the polyphonic music of the old Italian masters from whom Nicolai acquired both an interest and a skill in writing counterpoint. The other was Mozart, a standard for the writing of beautifully constructed flowing melodies, for the attainment of an elegance of style, for the curiosity in seeking out novel effects in orchestration. Italian polyphony endows much of Nicolai's church music with its character and style. Mozart's echoes can be detected in Nicolai's orchestral and chamber music. In the only work by which Nicolai is today remembered and for which he is honored—the comic opera *The Merry Wives of Windsor*—the influences of polyphony and Mozart are recognizable, together with a third not mentioned by Weissman, that of Italian opera.

Otto Nicolai was born in Koenigsberg, Germany, on June 9, 1810. After intensive study of music in Berlin with Zelter, Berger and other masters,

Nicolai completed in 1830 several impressive vocal and choral compositions. In 1833, he visited Italy, where he was given an appointment as organist at the chapel of the Prussian Ambassador in Rome. It was during this period that Nicolai became vitally interested in, and affected by, the polyphonic music of the old Italian masters, and by the operas of such then contemporaries as Bellini and Donizetti.

In 1837, Nicolai became conductor of the Kaernthnerthor Theater in Vienna. One year after that he wrote his first opera, *Rosmonda d'Inghilterra,* introduced that year in Turin. Several more operas followed. The most successful was *Il Templario,* based on Sir Walter Scott's *Ivanhoe,* first performed in Turin on February 11, 1840. In 1841, Nicolai assumed the post of principal conductor at the Vienna Royal Opera, holding it with great distinction for the next half dozen years. During this period he helped to found, and for a number of years conducted, the Vienna Philharmonic Orchestra. In 1847, Nicolai became the principal Kapellmeister of the Berlin Royal Opera. It was there that his last opera, and his masterwork, received its first performance in 1849—*The Merry Wives of Windsor.* Nicolai directed only four performances of his opera before being stricken by a fatal apoplectic stroke. He died in Berlin on May 11, 1849, and was buried in the churchyard of the Dorotheenstadt in Berlin. On the day of his death his appointment to the Berlin Academy was announced.

1849. THE MERRY WIVES OF WINDSOR (DIE LUSTIGEN WEIBER VON WINDSOR), comic opera in three acts with text by Salomon Hermann Mosenthal based on the Shakespeare comedy of the same name. First performance: Royal Opera, Berlin, March 9, 1849.

The Merry Wives of Windsor is one of the most celebrated and one of the most important German comic operas of the nineteenth century. But its enduring qualities were not at first recognized. Nicolai wrote it for Vienna in 1844, but the Royal Opera there rejected it; it was not to get performed for another five years. Meanwhile, Nicolai had become the Kapellmeister of the Berlin Royal Opera. It was on royal invitation that he finally mounted and conducted his last and greatest opera—and none too soon. Only two months later he died.

The new opera was received magnificently in Berlin—and wherever else it was given immediately after that. Vienna produced it on February 12, 1852 with formidable success. The opera came for the first time to the United States on March 16, 1863, in Philadelphia. It was heard in New York in 1864, and in London later the same year.

The text is for the most part faithful to Shakespeare. The rotund lecher, Falstaff, has been sending identical love notes to Mrs. Ford and Mrs. Page. The good women decide to punish him by having him come to Mrs. Ford's house apparently for a rendezvous. As part of the plan, Mrs. Page interrupts them by announcing the immediate appearance of Mr. Ford. Falstaff must be secreted in a basket of dirty wash from which he is unceremoniously dumped out of the window into the Thames River. Notwithstanding this unfortunate experience, Falstaff boasts to his cronies in the town inn that Mrs. Ford is interested in him. This leads Mr. Ford, in disguise, to hire Falstaff to woo Mrs. Ford for him. A second rendezvous is now arranged for Falstaff and Mrs. Ford, once again to be disturbed by the precipitous arrival of Mr. Ford. Now Falstaff is hurriedly disguised in women's clothes, in spite of which he is discovered by Mr. Ford who administers to him a sound thrashing. Still the two wives are not satisfied that Falstaff has been properly punished. They invite him to Herne's Oak where their friends, dressed up as woodsprites and elves, frighten the fat man out of his wits. When they feel Falstaff has been sufficiently chastized they reveal their true identities and finally forgive him.

The overture is a classic in salon music. A slow introduction presents a soaring tune over a high C in the violins. After various sections of the orchestra have had the opportunity to discuss this subject, and treat it in imitation, the main body of the overture unfolds. Here two principal themes are heard. Both of them are lively, and the second (in the violins in octaves) is intended to portray Mrs. Page. In the development, a vigorous F minor passage suggests Falstaff. This development is consistently sprightly, and so is the concluding coda.

Melodies from this overture recur in the concluding Herne's Oak scene—in various choral passages and dance episodes. In this act we also get perhaps the most celebrated vocal number in the entire score, Mrs. Page's "The Ballad of Herne the Huntsman." Other outstanding vocal episodes include Fenton's beautiful serenade to his sweetheart, Anne (daughter of Mrs. Page) in the second act, "Horch, die Lerche Singt im Hain"; and Falstaff's vivacious second-act drinking song, "Als Bueblein klein," long a favorite of German bassos.

FRIEDRICH VON FLOTOW 1812–1883

Flotow wrote about thirty operas. Only one (*Martha*) has a permanent place in the repertory, and only one other (*Alessandro Stradella*) is occasionally revived. The truth of the matter is that Flotow had neither excessive originality nor daring, neither depth nor subtlety, neither a gift for characterization nor dramatic power. What he did own was a most pleasing lyricism, a lightness of touch in ensemble writing, and an ingratiating manner. As Louis Biancolli remarked when *Martha* was revived in New York: "Only a heart of stone could resist its bland charms." In short, though Flotow did nothing to change the course of operatic history, nor to endow the opera house with an individuality, he did manage to infuse a welcome warmth and glow into the theater. Unforgettable, for example, is the comedy of the two assassins in *Alessandro Stradella,* and the radiant third-act song of Stradella, "Jungfrau Maria." Unforgettable, too, is the consistently pleasing sentiment and loveliness of melody of *Martha.*

Friedrich von Flotow, a descendant of a Prussian noble family that traced its geneology back to the thirteenth century, was born in Teutendorf, in Mecklenburg-Schwerin, on April 26, 1812. His musical training took place first with private teachers and then at the Paris Conservatory. His first opera, *Pierre et Catherine,* was produced in 1835. Meanwhile he had made Paris his permanent home, and for its theaters he wrote a number of operas including *Rob Roy* in 1836 (based on Sir Walter Scott), and *Le Comte de Saint-Mégrin* with which he realized his first success in 1838. *Alessandro Stradella* was his first important work; it was introduced in Hamburg on December 30, 1844. Three years after that came his masterwork *Martha.* The première of his opera *Sophia Catharina* in Berlin in 1850 brought him the decoration of the Cross of St. John. From 1856 to 1863 Flotow served as Intendant of the Court Theater in Schwerin. He died of an apoplectic stroke in Darmstadt on January 24, 1883.

1847. MARTHA, or DER MARKT VON RICHMOND (MARTHA, or THE MARKET AT RICHMOND), opera in four acts with text by W. Friedrich (pseudonym for Friedrich Wilhelm Riese) based on a scenario by Jules Henri Vernoy de Saint-Georges. First performance: Kaernthnerthor Theater, Vienna, November 25, 1847.

It is not unusual to remember an opera by a single aria. While *Martha* has a good many wonderful melodies, it is known mainly through two of them. One of these is "The Last Rose of Summer," which Flotow expropriated from an old Irish tune, "The Groves of Blarney," a setting of a poem by Thomas Moore. Flotow introduced this melody into the second act for his principal female character, Lady Harriet, when Lionel asks her to sing for him. It is then repeated several more times, including at the close of the opera where Lady Harriet and Lionel express their delight in becoming reconciled after their differences.

The second of the melodies by which *Martha* is most often remembered by music lovers is "M'Appari," This is a broad and stately melody in the Italian style of Flotow's own invention. It appears in the third act to express Lionel's longing for Lady Harriet. "M'Appari" was one of Enrico Caruso's favorite arias, and his rendition invariably inspired an overwhelming demonstration in the opera house.

Naturally, the continued popularity of *Martha* in opera houses the world over is due to factors other than two lovable arias. The entire score (beginning with the tuneful and frequently played overture, made up of basic melodies from the opera) is a rich soil out of which numerous delectable blossoms spring. Particularly noteworthy are the delightfully coquettish "Good Night" quartet of the four principals ("Schlafe wohl!"); the drinking song of Plunkett and the farmers ("Lasst mich euch fragen"); and the quintet with chorus, "Mag der Himmel euch vergeben."

In England, during the reign of Queen Anne, Lady Harriet and her maid Nancy seek adventure at the Richmond Fair. They disguise themselves as peasant girls, posing as Martha and Julia respectively. There they meet two charming young men. One is a farmer by the name of Plunkett; the other is his foster brother, Lionel. Finding the girls appealing, the men decide to hire them as servants on a one-year agreement. It is not long before Lionel falls in love with "Martha," and Plunkett with "Julia." But the girls soon grow weary of the game. They escape and resume their former stations in life. One day, Plunkett sees "Julia" at a hunting park, and Lionel comes upon "Martha." When the men insist that these ladies live up to their agreement and finish out the year in their service, the ladies refuse to do so. In fact, Lady Harriet gets Lionel arrested. Disillusioned, Lionel vows to have no further traffic with Lady Harriet, even after she has come with the confession that she is in love with him. With Plunkett and Nancy as allies, Lady Harriet devises a scheme to win back Lionel's love. A replica of Richmond Park is set up, to which Lionel is invited. There Lady Harriet appears dressed up once again as Martha. The ruse works. Lionel takes Lady Harriet into his arms.

Martha is sometimes identifed as a French opera written by a German composer and often produced in the Italian language. The "German composer" and the "Italian language" in this identification are easy to understand. But *Martha* as a "French opera" deserves some clarification. In 1844, with the collaboration of two French composers, and to a Frenchman's text, Flotow produced music for a French ballet entitled *Lady Henrietta,* which was produced at the Opéra. This was the original source from which *Martha* sprang. Flotow subsequently revised and enlarged the score; at the same time he had an opera libretto prepared for him by Friedrich Wilhelm Riese, with the ballet scenario as a point of departure.

The American première of *Martha* took place at Niblo Gardens in New York on November 1, 1852. Ann Bishop (former wife of the composer of "Home Sweet Home") appeared in the title role. On that occasion the opera was given in English. When first seen at the Metropolitan Opera—on March 14, 1884—the Italian language was used. *Martha* became particularly popular at the Metropolitan Opera during the first part of the twentieth century, because Caruso was partial to the role of Lionel. When the Metropolitan

Opera revived *Martha* in 1961, a new English translation was prepared for this occasion.

AMBROISE THOMAS 1811–1896

Of the twenty operas by Thomas, all that remains is an overture from one of them (*Raymond*), a second opera that is only infrequently revived outside France (*Hamlet*), and a third that is a blemished masterwork. Thomas's talent was a modest one. He was more lyrical than dramatic, more charming and graceful than passionate or profound. When the text made demands on him he could not meet, his spontaneity and effervescence were smothered, and all he could produce was lifeless tissue. But when his librettists provided him with a mold into which he could easily slip attractive vocal numbers, period pieces, and ingratiating episodes, he could be attractive. His instincts were not always sound, nor his taste immaculate. It is difficult to understand how a composer of his gifts could write Ophelia's mad scene in three-quarter time; introduce a drinking song in *Hamlet;* or have a coquette like Philine, whose youth is behind her, present such a seductive number as the polonaise, "Je suis Titania." But in themselves, numbers such as these—or one like "O vin, dissipe la tristesse" in *Hamlet* —are so alluring that the temptation is great to forgive the composer for their incongruity within the context of the opera. Of Thomas, it can be said what one unidentified writer remarked about *Mignon.* He is "for hearts susceptible to honest emotions and for a public of average assimilative powers which enjoys melodies easy to remember."

Ambroise Thomas was born in Metz, France, on August 5, 1811. He attended the Paris Conservatory, where he won first prizes in piano playing and harmony and, in 1832, the Prix de Rome. His first opera, was *La Double échelle* in 1837; his first successes were *Mina* in 1843 and *Le Caïd* in 1849. In 1851, he was elected to the Académie. *Mignon* in 1866, made him one of the most successful French opera composers of his time, and his success was enhanced by *Hamlet* in 1868. In 1871, he became the director of the Paris Conservatory, where he instituted major reforms. His last opera, *Françoise de Rimini,* was introduced in Paris on April 14, 1882. He became the first opera composer to live long enough to attend the thousandth performance of one of his operas. This took place on May 13, 1894, when the Opéra-Comique gave a gala presentation of *Mignon*. On that occasion he was presented by the French government the grand cordon of the Legion of Honor. Thomas died in Paris on February 12, 1896.

1851. OVERTURE TO RAYMOND, for orchestra.

Raymond is a rather silly operatic adaptation of the story of the Man with the Iron Mask. It was produced in Paris on June 5, 1851, was a dismal failure, and was relegated to oblivion. Its overture, however, has become one of the most popular in French opera. It opens energetically with vigorous chords punctuating the spirited music. A transitional passage, in which a solo cello is prominent, creates a calm atmosphere that continues on into the first major theme, a delicate tune for violins accompanied by other strings, pizzicati. This is followed by an appealing melody for the woodwind. There is still a third important subject, a spirited march melody that grows in volume until a climax has been reached. Temporarily a contrast of mood is introduced through a gentle idea in the strings. But the vigor and excitement previously created by the march tune is restored. The march melody brings the overture to its final resolution.

1866. MIGNON, opéra-comique in three acts, with text by Michel Carré and Jules Barbier based on Goethe's novel, *Wilhelm Meisters Lehrjahre*. First performance: Opéra-Comique, Paris, November 17, 1866.

If the librettists had been faithful to Goethe's philosophic, contemplative, and dramatic intentions, it is hardly likely that *Mignon* would have become one of the best loved and frequently heard operas of the French lyric theater. Thomas's limited creative powers never would have coped with the demands made on him by Goethe. But the librettists expurgated the profound, the eloquent, and the penetrating in the Goethe romance to leave only the obvious and melodramatic. By a reverse alchemy, gold had been transmuted into base metal. What Carré and Barbier turned over to Thomas was a contrived and conventional play, into which Thomas could introduce appealing interludes and numbers. It is these charming musical inventions, rather than the opera as a whole, that continues to delight operagoers today. Mignon's first-act recollection of her home is one of the lovelist melodies in the whole score —"Connais-tu le pays?" Other excerpts are equally enchanting: the duet of Mignon and Lothario with its exquisite accompaniment, "Légères hirondelles"; the orchestral gavotte that separates the first two acts; Frederick's rondo-gavotte, "Me voici dans son boudoir"; Philine's electrifying polonaise, "Je suis Titania"; Mignon's "Styrienne" with its suggestions of Alpine yodels. Indeed, the parts are far better than the whole. But it should be remembered in Thomas's defense that he was producing an opéra-comique and not a grand opera or a musical drama. In its original version, *Mignon* used spoken dialogue in place of recitatives. (The composer himself transformed the dialogue into recitatives to meet the demands of larger opera houses.) He conformed to the well-accepted techniques and ritual of opéra-comique by interrupting the dialogue at different points for set and formal pieces like arias, duets, trios, choruses, and so forth.

The popular overture is built from two familiar melodies of the opera. It opens with a haunting phrase which appears during Lothario's lullaby. A few chromatic measures and a harp cadenza lead to Mignon's air, "Connais-tu, le pays?" It is heard in solo horn. No sooner does this melody die down, when Philine's polonaise, "Je suis Titania," is heard. A sudden chord brings on the coda, where a vigorous dance tune (heard again in the third act) is featured prominently.

The curtain rises on a countryside inn in eighteenth-century Germany. Wilhelm Meister, a traveling student is present; so is Lothario, a deranged minstrel, in search of a daughter he had lost many years ago. A band of gypsies arrives to entertain the guests. One of them is Mignon, who refuses to obey the gypsy leader when he orders her to dance. Wilhelm Meister saves Mignon from a thrashing. Then when he asks her to tell him about herself she reveals she has come from a far-off land, and that she has been adopted by the gypsies ("Connais-tu le pays?"). Meister is so touched by her story that he purchases her freedom and hires her as his servant. Mignon now tells Lothario that the land of her childhood is a place of sunshine and swallows ("Légères hirondelles"). Meanwhile, Meister meets and is attracted to the actress, Philine, and readily accepts her invitation to come to a party at Baron Rosenberg's castle.

The orchestra offers a graceful classic gavotte as an entr'acte between the first and second acts. Laerte, an actor, has come to visit Philine in her boudoir in the castle. In a delightful madrigal, he confesses how her charm has won his heart ("Belle, ayez pitié de nous"). Wilhelm Meister and Mignon soon appear. The latter now realizes she is in love with her master but recognizes that he favors Philine. Meister and Philine soon leave Mignon to herself. She tries on one of Philine's dress, and while doing so recalls her onetime tenderness for a gypsy lad in the Styrienne, "Je connais un pauvre enfant." She is interrupted by the appearance of Frederick, the Baron's nephew. In love with Philine, he gets involved with Meister in a quarrel over her. Mignon separates them. Wilhelm Meister, noticing she is dressed in one of Philine's gowns, dismisses her from his service.

Within the castle, Philine and her fellow performers are putting on a production of *A Midsummer Night's Dream*. Wandering around outside the castle, Mignon is distraught at having lost Meister; she contemplates suicide. Meeting up with Lothario, she expresses the desperate wish that the castle might burn down to the ground and thus destroy Philine. When the performance is over, and the audience files out, Philine is surrounded by ardent admirers, to whom she responds coquettishly with the coloratura polonaise, "Je suis Titania." Philine then asks Mignon to go into the castle and bring her a bouquet she had left there. While Mignon is inside the castle, it bursts into flames: demented Lothario had taken Mignon at her word and had set the place afire. When Meister learns Mignon is inside, he rushes through the flames to rescue her.

In the last act, the setting changes to Italy, Lothario having brought Mignon to the sunny land she has been singing about. She is sick in body and spirit; Lothario is tending her gently, singing a lullaby as he rocks her to sleep ("De son coeur j'ai calmé"). Wilhelm Meister is also at hand, for by now he realizes how much he loves Mignon. Meanwhile, in the familiar setting of Italy, Lothario regains his sanity. He now remembers he is a nobleman, and that Mignon is his long lost daughter. This revelation—and the knowledge that Wilhelm Meister is hers at last—helps revive Mignon's strength.

When first performed, *Mignon* was a success of the first magnitude. It remained a strong favorite in Paris; by the time of World War I it had received over two thousand performances at the Opéra-Comique. The opera was given for the first time in the United States on November 22, 1871. The opera entered the repertory of the Metropolitan Opera during its first season, on October 31, 1883. A half-century later, the Metropolitan Opera gave *Mignon* as its first commercially sponsored radio program.

1868. HAMLET, opera in five acts, with text by Michel Carré and Jules Barbier, based on the Shakespeare tragedy. First performance: Paris Opéra, March 9, 1868.

Hamlet followed *Mignon.* It enjoyed an immediate success, and in France it has remained in the repertory. But elsewhere it has not done so well. The mutilations and desecrations perpetrated by the librettists on Shakespeare were not easily tolerated by English-speaking countries. Then, Thomas's score fails to sustain interest through the five acts; and at times it is at complete odds with Shakespeare's conception. The Grecian-like fatality of the drama, and the psychological torments of the hero, are nowhere found in the score. Instead, we find a rousing drinking song, pretty ballet music for villagers celebrating Spring, and a charming little aria like "Comme un pâle fleur"—none of which have an affinity with Shakespeare. Harder still for audiences outside France to accept is an aria like "Partagez vous mes fleurs," which is in three-quarter time, even though it represents Ophelia's mad scene; or the fact that the title role is assigned to a baritone instead of a tenor.

Yet taken by themselves these and other excerpts are sufficiently appealing to keep the opera alive. America first heard *Hamlet* during the Spring season of the first year of the Metropolitan Opera, on March 10, 1884; at that time, it was given in Italian. It was played seven times in 1887 then disappeared from the Metropolitan stage. Other American companies, however, have from time to time restored it into their repertories.

The opera opens with the marriage of Claudius, King of Denmark, and Hamlet's mother Gertrude. Hamlet is upset to have his mother marry so soon after his father's death. From his father's ghost, Hamlet discovers that the king's murder had been contrived by Gertrude and Claudius. The ghost then urges Hamlet to avenge that death.

Hamlet evolves a plan to trap his mother and stepfather into revealing their guilt. He has a group of strolling players enact the murder during a celebration in the castle. The reactions of Hamlet's mother and Claudius to the play is the proof Hamlet needs. He also discovers that Polonius, father of Ophelia, has been a partner to the crime. Later, in her room, the Queen tries to pacify Hamlet, urging him to marry Ophelia. But Hamlet replies hotly that he will never marry the daughter of one of his father's murderers. This rejection causes Ophelia to lose her mind and commit suicide. Then spurred on by his father's ghost, Hamlet kills Claudius and proclaims himself king of Denmark.

JACQUES OFFENBACH 1819 1880

Offenbach was the creator and the leading exponent of French comic opera (opéra-bouffe). The opéra-bouffe was a happy combination of Italian opera buffa and the French vaudeville-comedies popular in the eighteenth century. In Offenbach, the opéra-bouffe became a mirror to the foibles, mores, and social weaknesses of the Second Empire. Whether his texts dealt with Helen of Troy in ancient Sparta, the Olympian gods, Bluebeard of legend, a mythical kingdom called Gerolstein, or the Paris of Offenbach's own day, they put a scalpel to the flesh of French society and politics, laying bare the quivering nerves of Second-Empire frivolities, which placed so strong an accent on pleasures, illicit or otherwise. Offenbach's comic operas represented a stinging satirical commentary on the pretentions of court life, the laxity of moral codes, the hollowness of formal religious practises, the despotism of military life, the pompousness of petty princelings —in short, all those things that made the Second Empire what it was. And in a work like *La Belle Hélène,* Offenbach did not merely reflect a period; he also prognosticated its collapse through decay.

A lyricism of a freshness and a spontaneity not readily matched, a gift for laughter, a natural bent for turning a musical phrase for ironic or satiric purposes, and a style that was consistently light and gay were some of the qualities that made Offenbach the foremost light composer in France. Some of these qualities can also be found in his only serious opera, his swan song, *The Tales of Hoffmann.* For all its excursions into fantasy, theatricalism and even tragedy, many of the finest pages vibrate with the overtones of the opéra-bouffe.

Jacques Offenbach was born in Cologne, Germany, on June 20, 1819. He was the son of a synagogue cantor whose original name had been Eberst, but who adopted for himself that of the town of Offenbach, where he had lived. Jacques attended the Paris Conservatory for a single year, specializing in the cello. He then played that instrument in the orchestra of the Opéra-Comique, and in 1849, he became the conductor of the Théâtre Français. His first success came in 1850 with a song, "Chanson de Fortunio," which was interpolated into a play by De Musset. His first operetta to get produced was *Pepito* at the Théâtre des Varietés, in 1853. Two years later he opened up his own theater for the presentation of comic operas—the Bouffes Parisiens—inaugurating it with his own opéra-bouffe, *Les Deux aveugles,* on July 5, 1855. It was here that his first triumph, *Orphée aux enfers,* was produced, in 1858. Offenbach wrote about forty comic operas for his theater, which had to close down in 1862. In 1864, he opened a new theater in Paris, the Théâtre des Varietés, where some of his masterworks were introduced; among these were *La Belle Hélène* in 1864, *Barbe-bleu* in 1866, *La Vie parisienne* in 1866, *La Grande Duchesse de Gérolstein* in 1867, *La Périchole* in 1868. In 1873, he assumed the direction of the Théâtre de la Gaité, which went into bankruptcy. To help pay off his creditors, Offenbach made a successful tour of the United States in 1877. The last of his operettas to get produced during his lifetime was *La Fille du tambour-major* in 1879. During the closing years of his life, Offenbach was absorbed with the writing of his only serious opera, *The Tales of Hoffmann.* He regarded it as his chef d'oeuvre, but he did not live to see it performed. He died in Paris on October 4, 1880.

1858. ORPHÉE AUX ENFERS, or ORPHEUS IN DER UNTERWELT (ORPHEUS IN HADES), opéra-bouffe in four acts, with text by Hector Crémieux and Ludovic Halévy. First performance: Bouffes-Parisiens, Paris, October 21, 1858.

It is a paradox fit for Olympian gods that the only reason *Orphée aux enfers* became the composer's initial triumph, and made his name a household one in Paris, was a devastating review. At its première, and immediately afterwards, *Orphée* had all the appearances of a failure. Some disliked the fact that it satirized Olympian gods; others thought the subject and its treatment a bore; still others were shocked by its immoral suggestions and the interpolation of a cancan after a minuet. *Orphée* struggled on for about a month and a half, just about making ends meet. Its closing seemed imminent. Then Jules Janin hurled a savage attack at it in the *Journal des débats,* regarding it "a profanation of holy and glorious antiquity, in a spirit of irreverence that borders on blasphemy." Offenbach and his librettists made a heated reply in *Le Figaro.* Paris, which ever thrives on such controversies, now became embroiled in a bitter exchange between those who attacked the opera and those who were tolerant to it. Suddenly, the receipts at the box office mounted. People wanted to see this provocative show for themselves and form their own estimate. Some left the theater enchanted, and spread the word accordingly. Offenbach's tunes from this operetta suddenly were being heard everywhere. Lines from the text were being quoted; situations in the play were hotly discussed. *Orphée* began selling out for each performance, and continued to do so for the rest of the two hundred and more presentations. But for the fact that the cast was in a state of exhaustion, and insisted upon closing the play, *Orphée* could have run profitably for many months more.

Orphée was given for the first time in the United States at the Stadt Theater in New York in 1861, in a German translation. A French production followed in New York on January 17, 1867.

The overture is a classic in light music. It opens in a gay, infectious vein before the first theme is offered by the strings. After that comes the main subject of the overture. It is one of Offenbach's most celebrated melodies. The solo violin plays it before the full orchestra repeats it with resplendent harmonies.

In the first act, in a countryside adjacent to Thebes, Orpheus and his wife Eurydice have grown bored with each other. In a famous air, "Ah, Seigneur, ah quel supplice," she begs heaven for deliverance from her husband. But Orpheus insists that they cannot part since he cannot afford to offend Public Opinion. When Orpheus leaves, Aristeus enters and introduces himself ("Moi, je suis Aristée"); he is actually Pluto in disguise, carrying on an affair with Eurydice. Having been bitten by a snake, Eurydice sings an invocation to death ("La mort m'apparait souriante"). Then Pluto leads her to the Underworld. Learning of his wife's death, Orpheus is overjoyed; he is now free to pursue the lovely Maquilla. But his happiness is brief. Public Opinion compels him to ascend to Olympus and demand from Jupiter that Pluto return Eurydice to earth.

The second act takes place on Mount Olympus. Jupiter is in an ugly mood; his affair with Diana is causing talk among mortals. Furthermore, he is tired of Mount Olympus, with its continual diet of nectar and ambrosia. When Jupiter is told about Pluto's rape of Eurydice, he sends Mercury to investigate and bring back a report. Then Pluto is summoned; he is severely upbraided by Jupiter. The other gods side with Pluto, remembering as they do Jupiter's own indiscretions. At this point, Public Opinion drags Orpheus before Jupiter. To placate Public Opinion, the god not only insists that Eurydice return to Orpheus, but announces that he himself will descend to the Underworld to see that his command is carried out. The gods and goddesses beg Jupiter to be allowed to accompany him. His consent causes them to celebrate with a boisterous galop.

In the first scene of the third act, Eurydice is being guarded in her cell by John Styx. He entertains her with a gay autobiographical song, "Quand j'étais roi de Boétie." With the arrival of the gods and goddesses, Jupiter tells Pluto he will be tried in court. The trial takes place in the next scene. One of the witnesses—Cerebrus, the dog who guards the gates of hell—insists Pluto had come down to the Underworld unaccompanied. Jupiter accuses Cerebrus of bias, an act that so angers the dog that he bites the god's hand. This causes Jupiter to hurl a thunderbolt, which makes all those present disappear. In Pluto's study, Jupiter later transforms himself into a flea and invades Eurydice's cell. As he buzzes around her, he becomes entranced by her beauty; Eurydice, in turn, is enchanted by the insect. They then engage in a delightful "flea duet," "Il m'a semblé sur mon epaule." Jupiter reassumes his godly form and makes arrangements to take Eurydice away with him.

As the fourth-act curtain rises, a bacchanalian revel engages the gods and goddesses in Hades. Eurydice, now disguised as a Bacchante, sings a spirited hymn to Bacchus, "Evohé, Bacchus m'inspire." This is followed first by a staid minuet and then by an abandoned cancan. Jupiter and Eurydice now try to make their escape but are stopped by Pluto. Upon Orpheus's appearance, in the company of Public Opinion, Jupiter informs him he can take Eurydice back to earth, but only on the condition that he does not look at her until he has passed the gates of Hades. Before Eurydice and Orpheus have progressed many steps, Jupiter hurls a thunderbolt which startles Orpheus. Instinctively he looks back on Eurydice. Thus his wife is lost to him forever, a development that pleases both partners.

There were many things in the comic opera to startle and shock. There was parody here—as when Offenbach gave a tongue-in-the-cheek version of Gluck's unforgettable lament of Orpheus in *Orfeo ed Euridice*. There was satire here—the poignant songs of Cupid and Venus are accompanied by the discordant sounds of snoring gods. There were electrifying contrasts too—the juxtaposition of a classic minuet with a cancan, for example.

Though the cancan was not new in 1858, it is due to this opera that it began to enjoy a new and phenomenal vogue in Paris. As a contemporary writer, unidentified, remarked at that time: "This famous dance . . . has carried away our entire generation as would a tempestuous whirlwind."

1864. LA BELLE HÉLÈNE (BEAUTIFUL HELEN), opéra-bouffe in three acts, with text by Henri Meilhac and Ludovic Halévy. First performance: Théâtre des Varietés, Paris, December 17, 1864.

Having struck oil with *Orphée aux enfers,* Offenbach decided to drill again in mythological fields; and once again he came up with a gusher. Curiously, the production history of *La Belle Hélène* is virtually a carbon copy of that of *Orphée*. Despite the fact that it boasted Hortense Schneider, the glamorous Parisian star, in the title role, *La Belle Hélène* was received coldly by critics and audiences, and virtually for the same reasons they had at first rejected *Orphée*. They thought the text was a desecration of antiquity, and they did not like the mixture of a classical setting and characters with nineteenth-century frivolities. And once again, as had happened with *Orphée,* the attack of critics stimulated the curiosity and interest of Parisian theatergoers. Since *La Belle Hélène* was filled with some of Offenbach's most infectious tunes and provocative attitudes, it was not long before *La Belle Hélène* caught on; and it has remained a strong favorite in the opéra-bouffe repertory. Its American première took place in New York on December 3, 1867, in German; in French, it was given in New York on March 26, 1868.

In the first act, Helen comes to a public square in ancient Sparta, where worshipers are celebrating the Feast of Adonis, and sings a hymn to love in the celebrated air, "Amours divins." She discovers that at a recent beauty contest, Paris awarded first prize to Venus; in return, Venus promised him the love of Helen, wife of the Spartan king, Menelaus, reputed to be the most beautiful woman in the world. Disguised as a shepherd, Paris soon comes seeking Helen, his excuse for coming to Sparta being that he wants to participate in a World Competition of Wit and Intellect ("Au mont Ida"). When Calchas, the High Priest, arranges a meeting between Paris and Helen, they immediately fall in love with each other. Paris is the winner in the World Competition. Asked by Calchas if he is content, Paris replies that he seeks only one development: that Helen's husband, Menelaus, be sent away. Upon consulting the oracle, Colchas learns that Jupiter has ordered Menelaus to depart for the mountains of Crete—thus leaving Helen and Paris free to enjoy their love.

But in the second act, Helen is tortured by a guilty conscience, and thus far has kept Paris at arm's length. She invokes the help of Venus in "Dis moi Venus." Impatient for Helen's love, Paris enlists Colchas's aid. The High Priest prays to the gods that Helen might at least see Paris in her dreams. And so, one night, after Helen has fallen asleep, Paris, disguised as a slave, comes into her bedroom and makes love to her. Convinced that she is dreaming, Helen has no inhibitions about responding to Paris's passion ("Oui, c'est un rêve"). They are in each other's arms when Menelaus makes an unexpected appearance. Paris escapes, while Helen upbraids her husband for being so foolhardy as to return without warning.

The court is enjoying a summer holiday at the beach of Nauplia in the third act. Menelaus is still upset over Helen's infidelity. Meanwhile, in Sparta, an epidemic of divorces has broken out; Calchas interprets this as punishment meted out by Venus for the way in which Sparta has treated Paris. Then Paris returns—disguised this time as the Grand Augur, come bearing a message from Venus suggesting a solution to the problem involving Paris and Helen. Venus insists that Menelaus must give up Helen, and that Paris and Helen must go off together for Troy. In a rage, Menelaus throws himself into the sea, but is rescued by Calchas. Then Agamemnon musters an army to embark on the Trojan War.

1868. LA PÉRICHOLE, opéra-bouffe in three acts, with text by Henri Meilhac and Ludovic Halévy, based on Merimée's play, *Le Carrosse du Saint-Sacrement*. First performance: Théâtre des Variétés, Paris, October 6, 1868.

The revival of *La Périchole* at the Metropolitan Opera on December 21, 1956, in an English translation—and the subsequent recording of this performance—brought home to many Americans the delights of a comic opera that long had been a favorite in Europe. One of Offenbach's most beautiful melodies comes out of this work—La Périchole's letter song to Paquillo, "O mon chèr amant, je te jure." There is a healthy stock of other wonderful melodies in this score. And the text is filled with colorful backgrounds and characters. *La Périchole* is not satiric in the vein of *Orphée aux enfers* or *La Belle Hélène,* but is much more in the glamorous tradition of operetta.

The action takes place in eighteenth-century Peru. A holiday crowd is celebrating the Viceroy's birthday in a public square. Two strolling performers entertain the crowd. One is La Périchole, a gypsy street singer, and the other, her partner, Paquillo. The two are in love and want to get married, but they cannot raise the price for a marriage license. After the crowd has dispersed, La Périchole attracts the Viceroy, who is incognito. He invites her to dinner, after which he persuades her to live in his palace as lady-in-waiting. Weary of poverty, La Périchole consents. Peruvian law dictates that no unmarried woman can live in the Viceroy's palace. For this reason, the Viceroy must hunt up a stand-in to marry La Périchole. Meanwhile, she has written a poignant farewell letter to Paquillo ("O mon chèr amant, je te jure"). This letter has plunged Paquillo into despair. Consequently, when one of the Viceroy's men proposes that he marry a girl selected as a lady-in-waiting, Paquillo is willing. The Viceroy consoles Paquillo with wine. Though inebriated, Paquillo cannot forget La Périchole ("Je dois vous prévenir"). But, without further ado, the marriage ceremony takes place in the palace. La Périchole is fully aware that she is marrying Paquillo, but Paquillo has no idea who his bride is.

The following morning in the palace, Paquillo is in a bewildered state. He knows he has married somebody, but does not know whom. After singing the praises of womankind ("Et la maintenant") he finally discovers that it is La Périchole who is the lady-in-waiting that now is his bride. In an outburst of anger he denounces her. La Périchole tries to calm him down as she laments man's stupidity ("Que veulent dire ces colères"). But Paquillo is inconsolable. He presents La Périchole to the Viceroy as a woman with the most false heart in the world. Because of this he is arrested.

The first scene of the third act finds Paquillo in his cell brooding over his unhappiness ("On me proposait d'être infâme"). Here La Périchole comes to visit him, to convince him she still loves him, and to try to make plans for his escape ("Tu n'es pas beau"). They are aided by an old prisoner. La Périchole and Paquillo flee and go into hiding in an inn in the public square, where the Viceroy catches up with them. Then seeing how happy the pair is with one another, he gives them their freedom and blesses their union.

The first performance of *La Périchole* in the United States was at Pike's Opera House in New York on January 4, 1869. Between that year and 1925, the comic opera was seen and heard, not only in its original French version, but also in numerous translations (including German, Russian, and even Yiddish). The revival by the Metropolitan Opera in 1956 was the first time that this work was given in English in this country.

1880. LES CONTES D'HOFFMANN (TALES OF HOFFMANN), opera with prologue, three acts, and epilogue, with text by Jules Barbier and Michel Carré, based on stories by E. T. A. Hoffmann. First performance: Opéra-Comique, Paris, February 10, 1881.

The comedian who dreams of playing Hamlet finds his counterpart in the composer of comic operas who wants to write a grand opera. Offenbach finally realized this ambition with his very last creation. In doing so, he achieved a masterwork, if a minor one, whose popularity has never waned.

The Tales of Hoffmann was for its composer an all-consuming labor of love. He was seriously ill, aware he did not have much longer to live. To complete his opera and to see it performed was a force that kept him working in white heat up until the last day of his life. When he turned over the still unfinished score to the Opéra-Comique, he told its director to begin rehearsals without delay. "Make haste, make haste," he said. "I am in a hurry and have only one wish in the world—that of witnessing the performance." But production problems brought about so many postponements that the première did not take place until four months after Offenbach's death. When the opera was finally given, the recitatives and most of the orchestration had to be done by Ernest Guiraud.

The première was such a success that the opera was given over a hundred times during that first season. The American première took place at the Fifth Avenue Theater in New York on October 16, 1882. However, not until the work was revived by the Manhattan Opera in 1907, did *The Tales of Hoffmann* become popular in America. The Metropolitan Opera gave it for the first time in 1913.

The fantastic tales of E. T. A. Hoffmann provided the librettists with the material for an eerie text set in a half-real world, dominated by evil geniuses who control the destinies of the hero in his strange love affairs. Each act is concerned with one of these romances. Offenbach originally hoped to have one baritone for the evil geniuses, and one soprano for all the heroines, but this is rarely done today. Lawrence Tibbett appeared in all the leading baritone roles at the Metropolitan Opera in 1937, and Martial Singher twenty years later, also at the Metropolitan. Bruce Dargavel did a similar service in the English motion-picture adaptation conducted by Sir Thomas Beecham. At the world première of the opera, Adele Isaac appeared in the three principal soprano parts, a tour de force that has since been rarely repeated.

Only a few measures of orchestral music precede the prologue, set in Luther's tavern in nineteenth-century Nuremberg. The councilor, Lindorf, is jealous of the poet, Hoffmann, because the latter has received a note from Stella, an actress, arranging for a rendezvous. After students sing a toast to Stella, Hoffmann appears. He is despondent, and tries to dispel his gloom by singing a ballad about a hunchbacked jester ("Il était une fois à la cour d'Eisenach"). Later on, slightly inebriated, Hoffmann confides to his friends he is through with love forever. He then proceeds to tell them about three tragic episodes in his life.

The first involves Olympia, and that story unfolds in the opening act. Spalanzani, a scientist, has with the help of Coppelius constructed a mechanical doll called Olympia, which is almost human in appearance. Hoffmann, seeing it from a distance, falls in love with it, as he confesses to his friend Nicklausse. The latter takes the news lightly, then tells his friend a strange tale of love engaging a mechnical doll and a mechanical bird ("Une poupée aux yeux d'émail"). Spalanzani and a number of other guests come to see Olympia. The doll proves enchanting as she sings a little tune, "Les Oiseaux dans la charmille." When the guests leave, Hoffmann pours out his emotions to the doll. While touching her hand, he releases a spring that sends Olympia spinning out of the room. Hoffmann follows her, apologizes, then dances a hectic waltz with her. Coppelius now comes into the room in a fury. Spalanzani had purchased Coppelius's interest in Olympia with false currency. In an uncontrolled rage, Coppelius smashes Olympia into fragments. Only then does Hoffmann discover he has been in love with an inanimate object.

A dainty minuet serves as an orchestral entr'acte between the first two acts. Hoffmann is now in a Venetian palace where a party is taking place. Offstage voices are heard: those of Giulietta and Nicklausse in a rapturous hymn to the night and to the ecstasy of love—the world-famous Barcarolle ("Belle nuit, o nuit d'amour"). Offenbach did not write this melody directly for *The Tales of Hoffmann:* he had used it previously (1864) as a ghost song in his opera-ballet, *Die Rheinnixen.*

When Giulietta enters the palace, Hoffmann sings to her the praises of earthier pleasures ("Amis, l'amour tendre et rêveur"). Hoffmann, however, does not know that he is in the power of a magician, Dapertutto, nor that Schlemil is his rival for Giulietta. Dapertutto possesses a diamond ring that he feels can win the heart of any woman ("Scintille, diamant"). Giulietta wants that ring and is ready to barter Hoffmann's reflection for it. When Giulietta implores Hoffmann to leave his reflection in her mirror, the poet is delighted. Just then, Schlemil appears, involves Hoffmann in a duel, and is killed. When Giulietta abandons Hoffmann to go off in a gondola with a new lover, Hoffmann once again becomes sadly disillusioned.

In the third act, in a room in Crespel's house in Munich, Hoffmann is in love with Antonia Crespel. She is pining over a lost lover ("Elle a fui, la tourterelle"), then falls into a faint. Her father rushes to her help, then scolds her for singing; being the victim of consumption, Antonia must not subject herself to strain. When Hoffmann appears, love interest soon develops between him and Antonia ("J'ai le bonheur dans l'âme"). Antonia now insists on singing for him, and collapses in the effort. The evil power of Dr. Miracle soon evokes the ghost of Antonia's mother, come to plead with her to sing once more. Antonia responds—and dies in her father's arms.

Back in Luther's tavern, in the epilogue, Hoffmann has concluded his tales of woe. Nicklausse explains that the three women described by the poet are really one and the same person—the actress Stella. After the students sing the praises of wine, they leave Hoffmann to himself. The Muse enters to tell Hoffmann he must stop being a man and must begin being a poet. Hoffmann stands ready to give himself up completely to the Muse. Then

Stella comes into the tavern. For Hoffmann, she has only a flower, which she tosses lightly at his feet. The curtain falls as the students engage in a boisterous chorus.

"The music that Offenbach has written for the kaleidoscopic succession of fantastic incidents . . . is as amazing, as diverse, as colorful as the episodes it enlivens," wrote Herbert F. Peyser. "Some of it might have come straight out of the operettas which made their creator a world figure. Some of it is sensuously charming, some astonishingly dramatic, some sweetly nostalgic, some out and out macabre. Parts of the prologue might emanate from almost any of Offenbach's light operas—the drinking songs of the carousing students, for example. . . . The Olympia act is a masterpiece of perhaps involuntary satire, which pictures to the life the artifice, the sham, the spuriousness and hollow show of the Second Empire. . . . In a number of ways, the third episode is much the most affecting. There is something exquisitely pathetic in Antonia and her fatal longing to sing."

—— GAÎETÉ PARISIENNE, ballet in one act, with choreography by Léonide Massine and book by Comte Étienne de Beaumont; music derived from the works of Offenbach, adapted by Manuel Rosenthal. First performance: Théâtre du Monte Carlo, April 5, 1938.

Manuel Rosenthal extracted a number of choice morsels from various Offenbach opéra-bouffes (including *Orphée aux enfers, La Périchole,* and *La Vie parisienne*). He used them in an infectious score for one of the most successful productions of the Ballet Russe de Monte Carlo, Alexandra Danilova appearing in the part of the Glove Seller. The ballet setting is a fashionable Parisian restaurant a century ago; the main characters include the coquettish Glove Seller, sought after by a Peruvian and by a Baron. With the Baron, she engages in two exciting waltzes, the latter intended to reflect the romantic attachment between the pair. The ballet ends with an exciting cancan. Lovers pair off; only the Peruvian is left alone, his memories of a delightful evening his only company. In dance, sets, costuming and music, *La Gaîeté parisienne* provides a picture of the life and mores of the Second Empire.

FRANZ VON SUPPÉ 1819–1895

Suppé was the father of the Austrian operetta which was to reach its summit with Johann Strauss II. Like so many of his

German compatriots, Suppé was a profound admirer of Offenbach. In entering the popular German-speaking theater as composer, Suppé sought to carry the techniques and aims of opéra-bouffe into Germany and Austria. Actually he succeeded in creating a genre all his own: the operetta, which placed more stress on humor and less on satire; more on tenderness and sentimentality and less on burlesque; and in which the waltz became the favorite dance form. Suppé was endowed with vivacity and gaiety, sparkle and effervescence. These qualities made his melodies, and especially his waltzes, ideal for the popular theater. But he also managed to bring to his writing such sound musicianship, such a skill in the writing of ensemble and choral numbers, such a fine gift for orchestration and such an original harmony that his best operettas—though obviously slanted for popular appeal—are not out of place in the opera house.

Franz von Suppé was born in Spalato, Dalmatia (then a part of the Austro-Hungarian empire) on April 18, 1819. When he was thirteen he wrote music for a little play, and a Mass which was performed in a church in Zara. While attending the University of Padua for academic studies, he received music instruction from Cigala and Ferrari. His musical education ended at the Vienna Conservatory.

While serving as the conductor of the Josephstadtheater in Vienna he wrote music for a play produced there in 1841; this was his bow as a professional composer. It was some time before he came into his own as a composer. Meanwhile he directed theater orchestras in Pressburg, Baden, and at the famous Theater-an-der-Wien in Vienna. On August 24, 1846, his first operetta, *Dichter und Bauer* (*Poet and Peasant*) was produced in Vienna; its overture has become a staple in the repertory of salon or semi-classical music. This operetta was followed by *Das Maedchen vom Lande,* which enjoyed considerable success at the Theater-an-der-Wien in 1847.

During the next two decades, Suppé made his mark as one of Austria's most successful and highly esteemed operetta composers with *Zehn Maedchen und Kein Mann* in 1862, *Franz Schubert* in 1864, *Die Schoene Galathee* in 1865, and *Leichte Cavallerie* (*Light Cavalry*) in 1866.

From 1862 to 1865 Suppé was the conductor at the Karlstheater in Vienna, where some of his most famous operettas were introduced. These included *Fatinitza* in 1876, *Boccaccio* in 1879, and *Donna Juanita* in 1880. From 1865 on he served as principal conductor of the Leopoldstadt Theater, also in Vienna. Suppé died in Vienna on May 21, 1895.

1846–1866. OVERTURES FOR ORCHESTRA:
Poet and Peasant (*Dichter und Bauer*).
Light Cavalry (*Leichte Cavallerie*).
Morning, Noon and Night in Vienna (*Ein Morgen, Ein Mittag, Ein Abend in Wien*).

Of all the music he had written before he first became famous with *Beautiful Galatea,* only the overture to *Poet and Peasant* (1846) is remembered. It is one of the most celebrated pieces of music in semi-classical literature; it is found in the repertory of salon, "pop," café-house orchestras the world over. It has been adapted for about sixty different instrumental combinations.

The overture opens with a stately introduction that leads into a mobile melody for the strings. A dramatic and stormy episode follows. We now hear the main subject of the overture, a soaring melody in 3/8 time.

The *Light Cavalry* Overture (1866) is almost as popular as *Poet and Peasant.* This is consistently martial music which begins with strong chords and horn calls. Vigorous and sprightly tunes for the violins, and later for the woodwind, precede the celebrated theme by which the overture is always remembered (and which is often quoted to describe the gallop of the cavalry). This is a military melody with a vigorous rhythm. A delicate passage serves as a transition to a broad Hungarian-like song. Then the vigorous military melody and the opening horn calls bring the overture to its robust conclusion.

Morning, Noon and Night is the most famous of Suppé's concert overtures. Dramatic chords in full orchestra precede a wonderful melody in solo cello accompanied by plucked strings. The enchantment is broken with a dramatic interlude. We next hear the two main themes of the overture, both in an ebullient, Gemuetlich style, and both first presented by the strings.

1865. BEAUTIFUL GALATEA (DIE SCHOENE GALATHEE), operetta in one act with text by Leopold K. Ditmar Kohn von Kohlenegg (using the pseudonym of Poly Henrion). First performance: Berlin, June 30, 1865.

With *Die Schoene Galathee* the operetta becomes crystallized. But it is still derivative from Offenbach—particularly in the way text and characters are used to burlesque Greek mythology and the music is continually spiced with satirical condiments.

The overture opens with mock austerity and dignity, first with a sedate melody for horns and woodwind, then with an almost religious kind of song for the strings. The main subject of the overture, however, is in a lighter vein. Characteristic of all the great Austrian operettas of a later day, this main theme is a sweeping waltz. It is given by the strings over a harmonic background by the woodwind, and then is restated by the full orchestra.

The curtain rises on a Grecian landscape where an archaeological expedition is taking place. An ancient Grecian statue of Galatea is unearthed; it had been created by the ancient Greek sculptor, Pygmalion. Professor Agyris proceeds to tell his enchanted audience the story of the statue. As he talks, the scene shifts to ancient Greece, to Midas's art gallery, where Pygmalion's statue of Galatea is about to be exhibited. But Pygmalion has fallen in love with his artwork, and refuses to part with it. When Ganymede, Pygmalion's male servant, arrives ("Eine reizende Frau zu gewinnen"), he is bribed by

Midas to use his influence to get Pygmalion to sell the statue. Ganymede brings Midas to Pygmalion's studio where the art dealer is enraptured by the statue of Galatea. When Pygmalion discovers Midas in front of the statue, he angrily throws him out of the studio. Then, alone, he prays to Venus to give life to the statue so that he might love it as he would a woman. His prayer is answered. Galatea descends from her pedestal, speaking of the beauty of life and the world ("Schoen ist es zu leben"). Passionately, Pygmalion takes her into his arms and kisses her. Galatea voices her rapture in one of the most celebrated numbers in the operetta, the waltz "Einmal moecht ich so verliebt sein."

Ganymede is still determined to get the statue for Midas. Not knowing that Galatea has now become a living being, Ganymede sneaks into the studio where he comes upon Galatea and is completely taken by her charm and beauty. For her part, Galatea finds Ganymede most attractive, and begins to flirt with him. She insists to Pygmalion that he invite Ganymede to a supper party, where she continues to be coquettish with Ganymede, in the celebrated "kiss duet" ("Ach mich zieht's zu dir"). Pygmalion, upset by this development, prays to Venus to restore Galatea back to stone. When this is accomplished, Pygmalion no longer is hesitant about selling his statue to Midas.

In the epilogue we find Professor Agyris back in modern Greece, bringing his story to a close.

Beautiful Galatea was given its first American performance in New York on September 6, 1867; it was produced in German. The first time the work was heard in English was in New York on September 14, 1882. The operetta was successfully revived at the Central City Opera House in Colorado on July 12, 1951, with a modernized English text by Phyllis Mead.

1879. BOCCACCIO, operetta in three acts, with text by F. Zell and Richard Genée. First performance: Karlstheater, Vienna, February 1, 1879.

Though written for the popular stage, *Boccaccio* has proved of sufficient artistic importance to get performances in major opera houses. The Metropolitan produced it on January 2, 1931, with Maria Jeritza; this was the first time that this company had mounted a Suppé operetta.

The librettists drew their text from an episode in the life of Boccaccio as described in the Boccaccio biography, *L'Amoroso Fiametta*. The setting is Florence in 1331. In the city piazza, a bookseller is hawking Boccaccio's novels. Boccaccio is a favorite with the women, but the men detest him because of the way he has ridiculed them in his books. When Boccaccio himself arrives, he tells several admiring students that his material for his stories comes from life itself ("Das ist doch jedem Klar"). Hardly has he finished his recital when Fiametta appears. She is the illegitimate daughter of the Duke of Tuscany, raised from childhood by Lambertuccio, a grocer. She is filled with dreams of a young man who has caught her fancy, and over whom she rhapsodizes in the radiant song, "Hab' ich nur deine Liebe." Boccaccio, disguised as a beggar, approaches her. Despite his disguise, Fiametta recognizes him and is delighted to be the object his affection. After she goes off to church, some of the townspeople mistake Pietro, the Prince of Palermo, for Boccaccio and vent their rage against the author by administering a sound flogging to the Prince. The Prince has come to Florence on orders from his father for the purpose of marrying Fiametta; meanwhile he wants to have a good time, and this is the reason why he is in disguise. Good-naturedly, the Prince forgives his attackers, who now direct their anger against Boccaccio's books, which they destroy as Boccaccio himself watches with considerable amusement.

In the second act, Boccaccio comes in the guise of a peasant to Lambertuccio's house to woo Fiametta. Fiametta, now in love with him, refuses to go off with the Duke of Tuscany, when the latter finally comes to claim his own daughter; but she grows somewhat more amenable to the Duke's request, when Boccaccio promises her he will follow her wherever she may go.

The third act finds the Duke giving a huge reception in honor of the forthcoming marriage of Pietro to Fiametta. Pietro, however, does not love Fiametta. When Boccaccio appears, Pietro is more than ready to turn Fiametta over to him. Left alone, the lovers express their tenderness and eternal devotion in the duet, "Florenz hat schoene Frauen." When the townspeople come to the Duke to demand that Boccaccio be banished from the realm, the Duke delays his decision until he has had a chance to witness a little play the author had written for this reception. The play turns out to be a comedy pointing up the folly of having two people marry who do not love each other. The Duke fully understands the implications of Boccaccio's message, and responds to it generously. He appoints Boccaccio Poet Laureate, and decrees that he be sentenced to "life imprisonment" as the husband of Fiametta.

The first performance in the United States took place at the Chestnut Street Theater in Philadelphia on April 15, 1880 (in English). A modernized, revised version of *Boccaccio*—prepared by Alfred Rott, Friedrich Schreyvogel, Anton Paulig and Rudolf Kattnig—was successfully produced at the Volksoper in Vienna in 1951.

JOHANN STRAUSS II 1825–1899

Johann Strauss II was a popular composer who wrote dance music and operettas for mass consumption. But because he was a genius, his popular music rises to the level of art. His waltzes and operettas are today frequently played in serious concert halls and in opera houses. The interest of his music lies mainly in its remarkable melodies and the rhythmic invention; the harmony and instrumentation are in immaculate taste; the spirit is always ebullient and effervescent. This music is the voice of its times. Hapsburg Austria was ruled autocratically by Francis I, who employed an army of spies and informers to relay to him any signs of subversion. To be on the safe side, Austrians avoided politics and all other serious talk, seeking their pleasures in café-house gossip, light theater and music, romance, and most of all in dancing. This frivolity, this lighthearted attitude toward living, this indefatigable search for pleasure, echo in the measures of Johann Strauss's music. Hapsburg Austria died during World War I. But there are some Austrian historians who feel that it really died in 1899 with Johann Strauss II. The year of Johann Strauss's death was the end of an old century; it was also the end of an epoch that survives for us in Strauss's music.

Johann Strauss II was born in Vienna, Austria, on October 25, 1825. He was the son of the first Johann Strauss, in his own right a famous café-house conductor and composer of light music. Because the father opposed a musical career for the boy, the second Strauss had to begin music study in secret. Meanwhile he attended the public and technical schools in Vienna. When his father deserted his family in 1840, the younger Strauss could continue his music study in earnest. Violin lessons were taken with Kohlmann and theory with Joseph Drechsler. On October 15, 1844, the second Strauss made his café-house debut at Dommayer's Casino in a suburb of Vienna when he played his first waltzes. He created a sensation, beginning a reign over Vienna's café-houses, both as conductor and composer, that lasted as long as he lived. He became the music idol, not only of Vienna, but of the entire world. In 1854, he began conducting concerts in St. Petersburg; in 1867, he made a triumphant appearance at the World Exhibition in Paris; soon after that, he was heard at Covent Garden in London; and in 1872, he visited the United States for a series of mammoth concerts.

Meanwhile, he was writing waltzes, polkas, quadrilles, and so forth, that won the hearts of the world. Some of his greatest waltzes were written during his happy union with Henrietta Treffz, his first wife, whom he married on August 27, 1862. It was also on her urging that he finally turned to the stage. His first opera *Indigo,* produced on February 10, 1871, was a failure, and so was its successer, *Der Karneval in Rom,* in 1873. But with *Die Fledermaus,* in 1874, Strauss won immortality in the theater.

After Henrietta's death, Johann Strauss married twice more. His second wife was Angelika Dietrich, whom he divorced after five years. His third and last wife, Adele Deutsch, outlived him by several decades.

The fiftieth anniversary of Strauss's career was celebrated in 1894 with a festival week in Vienna. On May 22, 1899, Strauss made his last public appearance by directing *Die Fledermaus*. He died in Vienna less than a month after that, on June 3, the victim of bronchitis.

—— CONCERT WALTZES, for orchestra:

Acceleration (*Acceleration*), op. 234; *Artist's Life* (*Kuenstlerleben*), op. 316; *The Blue Danube* (*An der schoenen blauen Donau*), op. 314; *Emperor Waltz* (*Kaiserwalz*), op. 437; *Morning Journals* (*Morgenblaetter*), op. 279; *Roses from the South* (*Rosen aus dem Sueden*), op. 388; *Tales from the Vienna Woods* (*G'schichten aus dem Wiener Wald*), op. 325; *Vienna Blood* (*Wiener Blut*), op. 354; *Voices of Spring* (*Fruehlingsstimmen*), op. 410; *Wine, Woman and Song* (*Wein, Weib und Gesang*), op. 333.

The Viennese waltz started out as a "sweaty" ("Schwitzenden") peasant dance that captured the enthusiasm of the Viennese masses. One out of every four was dancing the waltz by the end of the eighteenth century, even though in some quarters it was regarded as obscene. But even while the waltz was capturing the hearts, and stimulating the feet, of the Viennese people, it was also beginning to penetrate the concert hall. Haydn, Mozart, Beethoven wrote delightful waltzes intended for listening rather than dancing. To Franz Schubert, in some of his fascinating waltzes for the piano, goes the distinction of being among the first to combine several waltzes into a single integrated work. Carl Maria von Weber made a remarkably effective use of this extended format in his *Invitation to the Dance* (which see).

Joseph Lanner (1834–1855) and the first Johann Strauss (1804–1849) wrote waltzes for orchestra. But it was Johann Strauss, the son, who perfected the structure of the waltz sequence and made it pliable and expansive. At the same time, he filled it with such creative imagination, such variety of moods and feelings, and such a wealth of lyricism, harmony, and orchestral colors that his greatest waltzes have been played by the world's foremost symphony orchestras, directed by its greatest conductors. "Just as Schubert had created the Lied out of the rudiments of simple folk songs," says Paul Bechert, "so Strauss had made out of the waltz an art form in the highest sense."

The Johann Strauss waltz invariably begins with an extended introduction, so symphonic in breadth and so ingenious in working out melodic fragments that it sometimes assumes the character of a miniature tone poem. Then comes a parade of waltz melodies, one blending naturally into another, so that a single fabric emerges from the many cloths. So wondrous was Strauss's melodic invention, and so varied are his tunes in mood and atmosphere, that the eminent musicologist Paul Bekker was once led to insist that a Strauss waltz boasts more melodies "than a symphony of Beethoven, and the aggregate of Straussian melodies is surely greater than the aggregate of Beethoven's." It is, therefore, appropriate to find some German critics describing the Strauss waltz as "symphonies for dancing."

After these waltzes have run their course—the usual number of waltzes in a single work is five—there comes a coda that is a kind of summation, a last recollection of some of the basic waltz tunes.

Strauss wrote his first waltz in 1844—the *Gunstweber*—introducing it at the same time that he was making his bow as conductor. It created such a furor that Strauss had to repeat it three times. Thus Strauss began his career as waltz composer with a triumph. As the years passed—and as he grew in technical skill and maturity—the triumphs kept mounting, until there was not a place in the civilized world that did not know and love the Strauss waltzes.

Strauss's most famous waltz—and possibly the most famous waltz ever written—is *The Blue Danube*. He wrote it for chorus and orchestra at the request of the Vienna Male Singing Society in 1867, using a poem by Karl Beck. When played for the first time, on February 15, 1867, the waltz was a sensation. Almost at once, it began to circle the globe. Strauss himself conducted it in 1872, when he made his American debut; for this performance, he led an orchestra of a thousand instruments and a chorus of a thousand voices.

The *Acceleration* gets its name (and derives its effect) through the use of accelerando in the main waltz. In *Artist's Life,* much of its kinaesthetic appeal comes from the alternation of soft and loud passages in the transition between the eloquent introduction and the ebullient first waltz melody. *Emperor Waltz* was written in 1888 to help celebrate the fortieth anniversary of the reign of Franz Joseph I. Its main waltz, a majestic melody, speaks for the grandeur of the Austrian Empire and the dignity of its monarch. *Morning Journals* owes its inspiration to a set of waltzes by Offenbach called *Evening Journals;* Strauss wrote this composition for the same press club in Vienna for which Offenbach had previously produced his own waltz music. *Roses from the South* is a collation of some of the best tunes from the Strauss operetta *Das Spitzentuch der Koenigen,* or *The Queen's Lace Handkerchief* (1880). *Tales from the Vienna Woods* was inspired by the beautiful forests skirting Vienna, which Beethoven loved so dearly; thus it is something of a tone picture of Nature. *Vienna Blood,* is, at turns, introspective and sensual, giving a somewhat different picture of Viennese life from that found in other waltzes. *Voices of Spring* rhapsodizes the vernal season and, like *Tales from the Vienna Woods,* betrays the composer's deep love of Nature. *Wine, Woman and Song* boasts one of the most spacious introductions found in any Strauss waltz, extending for ninety-one measures; by itself, and without its ensuing waltzes, it is a little orchestral masterpiece.

1874. DIE FLEDERMAUS (THE BAT), operetta in three acts, with text by Karl Haffner and R. Genée, based on *Le Réveillon* by Henri Meilhac and Ludovic Halévy, in turn derived from *Das Gefaengnis* by Roderich Benedix. First performance: Theater-an-der-Wien, Vienna, April 5, 1874.

Die Fledermaus is possibly the most famous operetta ever written; in addition it was certainly the one that exerted the strongest influence on all German-language operettas that followed.

Its historic career began on a lame foot. The shadow of an economic crisis that had ravaged Austria in 1873 was still darkening the life and spirits of the Viennese in 1874. *Die Fledermaus*—with its froth and frivolity—was out of tune with the times. Therefore, when it was first produced, the public did not take to it; the work was dropped after only sixteen performances.

Then later the same year, *Die Fledermaus* was produced in Berlin under more favorable conditions. It was a major success, with a run of about a hundred performances. By the time *Die Fledermaus* returned to Vienna late in 1874, the economic and social conditions there had improved. In a more optimistic frame of mind, the Viennese were again ready to enjoy the good things of life. It now took *Die Fledermaus* to its heart. In short order, *Die Fledermaus* started a march of triumph throughout the German-speaking world: within six months of its Viennese première, it was seen in over one hundred and thirty theaters in Germany alone. It was also acclaimed in other countries. The first American performance took place at the Thalia Theater in New York in 1874; a performance in English came a decade later at the Casino Theater.

Because of the great freshness, distinction, and originality of the score, *Die Fledermaus* was successfully introduced into the repertories of most of the world's great opera houses. It came to the august Vienna Royal Opera in 1894, Gustav Mahler conducting. The Metropolitan Opera produced it for the first time on February 16, 1905, with a cast headed by Marcella Sembrich. When *Die Fledermaus* was revived by the Metropolitan Opera during the 1950–1951 season, it was heard in a new English adaptation by Howard Dietz, with Garson Kanin serving as stage director. A decade earlier, under the name of *Roselinda, Die Fledermaus* enjoyed a run of over five hundred performances on Broadway.

Bruno Walter was one of many celebrated conductors to regard *Die Fledermaus* as a classic. This operetta, he said, has "beauty without heaviness, levity without vulgarity, gaiety without frivolity, and a strange mixture of exuberant musical richness (somewhat resembling Schubert) and a popular simplicity."

A waltz is the spine of the famous overture which is constructed from melodies from the opera. The first important subject is a strain for woodwind, a fragment of Rosalinda's lament, "So muss allein ich bleiben." This is followed by some material from the prison scene. At last, the great second-act waltz unfolds in the strings. The overture ends with a brief forewarning in strings of Baron von Eisenstein's first-act farewell to his wife.

The setting is Vienna in the second half of the nineteenth century. Baron Gabriel von Eisenstein, guilty of a minor offense, must go to prison for several days. His friend, Dr. Falke—determined to avenge himself on Eisenstein for having been the butt of a practical joke—convinces him to delay his appearance at the prison long enough to attend a gala ball that night at Prince Orlofsky's palace. After the Baron bids his wife, Rosalinda, a tearful farewell ("O je, O je, wie ruehrt mich dies"), Rosalinda's lover, Alfred, comes to share supper with her. He addresses to her a jovial drinking song ("Trinke,

Liebchen, trinke"). They are interrupted by the precipitous arrival of the Governor of the prison come to make his arrest. He naturally mistakes Alfred for the Baron and carts him off to jail.

In the second act, Prince Orlofsky is giving a mammoth ball. Among his guests are Rosalinda and her maid, Adele, both in disguise and masked. Adele is introduced to von Eistenstein, who in turn has assumed the name of "Marquis Renard." When von Eisenstein remarks that Adele looks like some lady-in-waiting he knows, she mockingly inquires if a lady-in-waiting ever possessed her figure, profile, and dress. This is the popular "laughing song" ("Mein Herr Marquis"). Later on, von Eisenstein is presented to a "Hungarian Countess"—who is none other than his own wife, Rosalinda. By way of self-introduction, she sings a passionate csardas, "Klaenge der Heimat," about which Ernest Newman said: "No genuine Hungarian music could sing more movingly of the pain of separation from the beloved homeland or of the fires in the Hungarian breast that drive them to the dance." Before long, Eisenstein begins to flirt with her without realizing who she is. During this exchange of pleasantries, she manages to steal from his pocket his watch, as evidence of this encounter. Later on, during supper, the Baron—momentarily forgetting that he is passing himself off as Marquis Renard—recounts the prank he once had perpetrated on his friend, Dr. Falke. Everybody is amused. The proceedings grow mellow with the drinking of champagne, to which the guests sing a rhapsodic hymn while swearing eternal brotherhood ("Bruederlein, Bruederlein und Schwesterlein"). A ballet now takes place. (It is now customary to use the music of *The Blue Danube* for this dance sequence.) Then all the guests join in dancing a waltz to one of Strauss's greatest melodies. When the festivties end, Baron von Eisenstein goes off to begin his prison sentence.

The third act takes place in prison. There the Baron learns to his horror that his wife has a lover. Upon Rosalinda's arrival to effect Alfred's release, the Baron accuses her of infidelity, and is in turn taken to task for having been so flirtatious at Prince Orlofsky's ball. Then Falke clears up the whole matter by explaining he was the party responsible for everything that has happened.

1885. DER ZIGEUENERBARON (THE GYPSY BARON), operetta in three acts, with text by Ignaz Schnitzer, based on *Saffi,* by Maurus Jókai. First performance: Theater-an-der-Wien, Vienna, October 24, 1885.

One of the more treasurable musical moments in *Die Fledermaus* had been a csardas, in which Strauss proved that he was as adept in writing Hungarian dance music as in writing the waltz. Once again he proved his gift with Hungarian-type sensual, throbbing melodies and rhythms in *The Gypsy Baron,* the second of his operetta masterworks, and the one other of his operettas with so much artistic significance that it is sometimes produced in the world's leading opera houses.

If (because of characters and setting) a good deal of Strauss's writing is spiced with Hungarian paprika, the more delicate Austrian flavors are not overpowered. Since an Austrian operetta without a big waltz is as unthinkable as a house without windows, *The Gypsy Baron* is not without a three-quarter time classic. Indeed, here we find one of the composer's most rapturous waltzes, the so called *Treasure or Schatz* Waltz, sung in the second act as a trio by Saffi, Sandor, and Kalman. The score boasts still one other remarkable waltz—the one Sandor sings with chorus when he makes his first entrance, "Ja, das alles auf Ehr."

The Gypsy Baron came, a dozen years after *Die Fledermaus*, to become Strauss's second most popular operetta. Its première was a gala event, for it was part of a general celebration in Vienna for the composer's sixtieth birthday. The new operetta received a thunderous ovation. It remained such a favorite with Viennese audiences that by World War I it had been played over a thousand times in that city.

The first American presentation took place at the Casino Theater in New York on February 15, 1886, in English. It then enjoyed the modest run of eighty-six performances; but upon its first return to New York, soon afterwards, the operetta was seen for more than five hundred consecutive presentations, a formidable figure for that time. It was produced at the Metropolitan Opera for the first time on February 15, 1906. A successful revival took place at the Metropolitan Opera during the 1959–1960 season, when it was given in a new English translation. Cyril Ritchard was the stage director, Walter Slezak played the part of Kalman, and Alexandra Danilova was featured in the third act ballet.

The celebrated overture opens with a vigorous section, in which we hear the Magyar-type music that accompanies the arrival of the gypsy clan in the first act. This is followed by Saffi's beautiful gypsy air, "So elend und treu." A climax comes with a powerful presentation of the *Treasure* Waltz from the second act.

The operetta opens in a gypsy encampment in Hungary, near the castle of Sandor Barinkay; the time is the end of the eighteenth century. Sandor has just returned home. He greets country and people with "Als flotter Geist," which is followed at once by the ecstatic waltz tune, "Ja, das alles auf Ehr." Sandor has come seeking a bride. His selection falls on Arsena, daughter of Kalman, a wealthy pig farmer. This is part of a prophecy made by Czipra that Sandor would soon find a bride; the other part of that prophecy concerns the finding of a treasure in Sandor's now devastated castle. The neighborhood gypsies, headed by Czipra, welcome Sandor jubilantly. One of them, the lovely Saffi, praises the loyalty of her clan in "So elend und treu."

Arsena rejects Sandor's attentions and advances, for she is in love with Ottakar. Sandor, however, consoles himself with Saffi, and it is Saffi whom he finally selects as a bride. With one-half of Czipra's prophecy now fulfilled, Sandor proceeds to look for the hidden treasure. He finds it at last in the tower of his castle. This discovery is joyously announced by Sandor, Saffi, and Kalman in "Ha, seht, es winkt," better known as the *Treasure* or *Schatz* Waltz.

But complications soon set in. Sandor and Saffi are accused of being lovers without the benefit of clergy and are threatened with arrest. Sternly, the Guardian of Public Morals demands to know who had married them. Sandor and Saffi reply, in the so-called "Bullfinch Song" ("Wer uns getraut?") that the ceremony had been performed by a bullfinch. Czipra soon comes forth with the evidence that Saffi had been born to nobility. The gypsies rejoice to hear the news, but Sandor is disconsolate, for Saffi's royal blood keeps her out of his reach. In despair, he turns over his treasure to his country, and joins the Hussars in a war that has just erupted between Hungary and Spain.

In the third act, the victorious Hungarian army is returning to Vienna after its victory over the Spaniards. Sandor is with them; he is hailed as a conquering hero. His treasure is returned to him by a grateful country, and the title of Baron is conferred on him. Proudly, Sandor announces that, since he is now a Baron, he would prefer being a "Gypsy Baron." Now that he is Saffi's social equal, his romance with her can proceed without further obstacles.

CÉSAR FRANCK 1822–1890

In music, as in life, Franck operated on an exalted plane. He was a simple and humble man, indifferent to self-aggrandizement, oblivious to the lures and rewards of success. He never reached for honors, nor did he ever stoop to conquer. He had only a single ambition—to maintain his music on the highest possible standards, never to be deflected from the highest purposes of his art. He accepted the indifference or hostility of the public or of critics quietly and stoically. Since he was a man of unbounded generosity and goodness, he never blamed anybody for the fiascos attending so many performances of his compositions. And he seemed incapable of envying those of his colleagues who were more fortunate than he, just as they were less gifted. At the same time, he demonstrated unlimited gratitude and affection for that small band of disciples who gathered around him, recognized his genius, and drew both their strength and their guidance from him. To one of these—Vincent d'Indy—Franck was "the highest minded and noblest musician that the nineteenth century has produced in France."

The man's personality is his music. In it we confront the serenity of his spirit, his deep religious convictions, his idealism, his innate mysticism. He took from others that which served him: the Leitmotiv technique of Wagner; Bach's polyphony; Liszt's piano techniques; the variation style of Schumann. But these were just the means to an end: the projection of a poetic beauty and the realization of a spiritual illumination in music that, for the most part, is singularly devoid of turmoil and conflict and becomes the kind of revelation we find in the late Beethoven. Franck's art, said Vincent d'Indy, has "clear truth and luminous serenity. His light was entirely spiritual, excluding the least touch of violent color."

Even in essentials and details, his individuality asserted itself: in the way he liked to reduce melodic lines to fragments; in his partiality for improvisation; in his rapid modulations and shifting techniques. He even evolved his own structural method, now known as the "cyclic form." Here "generative phrases," or melodic fragments, grow into fully developed melodies; in the larger forms, unification is achieved through the repetition in later movements of thematic material from earlier ones. Here is how Edward Lockspeiser described this method. "The principle of this form is that there should be one or more themes common to each of the movements of the work. These themes are frequently transformed in regards to dynamics, rhythm, or harmony, yet they are recognizably the same. They are Leitmotiv of a kind, the recurrence of which creates a mysterious association of ideas. . . . He allows them to germinate like the themes of the Beethoven variations. A unity of purpose, almost a philosophical unity, is thus proclaimed."

Franck took longer than almost any other master in music to realize his musical personality and to arrive at full maturity. His first significant work, *Rédemption,* came when he was fifty; before then he had produced little that is truly Franckian. His oratorio, *Les Béatitudes,* was not completed until he was fifty-seven. And the works by which he is most honored today—the Symphony, the Piano Quartet, the *Variations symphoniques,* the *Three Chorales* for organ—all came within the last five years of his life. This comparatively late development was the main reason why, virtually up to his last year, Franck was generally regarded in Paris as an organist rather than as a composer; why it took the public and the critics so long to recognize his true creative stature. But the acclaim accorded his Piano Quartet in 1890 was evidence that his genius was finally being recognized. It is altogether likely that had he lived beyond his sixty-eighth year, he would have come to be generally regarded with the same kind of veneration and appreciation his small clique of pupils and disciples bestowed on him.

César Franck was born in Liège, Belgium, on December 10, 1822. As a child he attended the Liège Conservatory and made several appearances as prodigy pianist. He came to Paris in 1835. There, for about eight years, he attended the Paris Conservatory, winning prizes for piano, organ, counterpoint, and fugue. On March 17, 1843, a concert of his works was given in Paris, but it did little to advance his reputation. His first ambitious work, the oratorio *Ruth,* was performed at the Paris Conservatory in 1846. In 1848, he married Mlle. Desmousseux, the daughter of a famous actress, and settled down to an industrious but humble existence. He earned his living giving lessons; his composition was generally relegated to the summer holiday season. In 1851, he was appointed organist of the St. Jean-St. François au Marais Church in Paris. In 1853, he was made Maître de Chapelle at Ste. Clotilde; and from 1858 until his death, he was its first organist. In 1872, he was made professor of the organ at the Paris Conservatory. He was an organ virtuoso of uncommon gifts, who attracted to Ste. Clotilde the great of the music world to listen to his performances. He was also an inspiring teacher, through whose influence an entire generation of young French composers were directed toward absolute music grounded in Bach's polyphonic methods, as opposed to the then new school of dramatic composers traveling under the leadership of Wagner and Liszt. Among Franck's most devoted followers and students were Gabriel Pierné (1863–1937), Vincent d'Indy (1851–1931), and Ernest Chausson. All the while, he labored long and hard on his own music, most of which received inadequate performances when introduced, and none of which brought him the recognition he deserved. When success finally came, it arrived in the last year of his life with the première of his String Quartet. Franck died in Paris on November 8, 1890.

1872. RÉDEMPTION, symphonic poem, for soprano solo, chorus, and orchestra.

Franck's lifelong association with the church as organist and his deep-rooted piety inevitably led him to write major religious works. The most significant were *Rédemption*—which the composer described as a "symphonic poem"—and the oratorio, *Les Béatitudes* (see 1879). Franck was working on *Les Béatitudes* when he received from Édouard Blau the text of *Rédemption.* It made such a deep impression on him that he temporarily put aside his oratorio and "threw himself into the musical realization of the poem," says Vincent d'Indy, "with such ardor that in spite of the small amount of time he could devote to the task, the work was finished in six months." The première took place at the Odéon on April 10, 1873, Édouard Colonne conducting. It was a sorry affair. The rehearsals had gone poorly, since the parts had been copied so badly that numerous mistakes had to be rectified then and there, putting the men of the orchestra into a violent temper. Poorly performed, the *Rédemption* was also poorly received.

After this performance, Franck prepared a second version of his symphonic poem, completing it in 1874; he now introduced a male chorus, and wrote a new symphonic interlude (*Morceau symphonique*) that is sometimes heard today by itself.

The *Rédemption* is in three sections. In the first, angels announce the coming of Christ; male voices join in a mighty Christmas hymn. The middle part is the symphonic piece for which Franck provided the following description. "The ages pass. The joy of the world, which is transformed and made radiant by the words of Christ." In the third part, angels weep over the fall of man, and an archangel announces the coming of redemption through prayer. *Rédemption* concludes with the repentant voices of a male chorus singing a hymn to charity.

"The subject," explains Vincent d'Indy, "which . . . is not lacking in grandeur, sets forth the material and the spiritual redemption; the first effected by Christ's coming upon earth, the second won through the future ages by means of prayer. This conception was quite in harmony with Franck's ideas, who willingly discoursed on this subject, emphasizing his discourse with warmth and enthusiasm."

1876. LES ÉOLIDES, tone poem for orchestra.

Franck wrote five tone (or symphonic) poems. The first was *Ce qu'on entend sur la montagne,* based on a poem by Victor Hugo. His first significant work for orchestra was *Les Éolides,* the second of his tone poems, based on a poem by Leconte de Lisle. Aeolus, according to mythology, was keeper of the winds on the Aeolian islands, where he lived with his wife, six sons, and six daughters. Leconte de Lisle's poem reads as follows: "O floating breezes of the skies, sweet breaths of fair spring, that caress the hills and plains with freakish kisses. Virgins, daughters of Aeolus, lovers of peace, eternal nature awakens to your songs; and the dryad seated amid the thick foliage sheds the tears of the scarlet dawn upon the mosses."

The basic material of Franck's tone poem (Allegretto vivo) is a figure appearing in the clarinet in the seventeenth measure. It is soon repeated by the oboe. A more expansive and somewhat more plaintive lyrical thought unfolds first in the clarinet (molto espressivo), then in first violins. The tone poem is then concerned with a working out of this material, frequently with passion. But at the end, serenity is restored with a last recollection of the final phrase of the clarinet subject.

1879. PIANO QUINTET IN F MINOR. I. Molto moderato quasi lento; Allegro. II. Lento con molto sentimento. III. Allegro con troppo ma con fuoco.

With the Piano Quintet Franck returned to chamber music, after an absence of thirty-five years, to produce an unqualified masterwork. Léon Vallas is of the opinion that some of the passionate moods in this music reflect Franck's feelings at the time for one of his pupils, the lovely Augusta Holmes. Indeed, says Vallas, there reverberate in this quintet "erotic suggestions" that seem to have shocked some of it earliest listeners, including Saint-Saëns, to whom the work is dedicated. Present-day audiences may find little here that is erotic, but there is no denying the music's emotional impact.

Structurally, this work is distinguished by its unity. All three movements (the usual third-movement Scherzo is dispensed with) are in the sonata form. The first and third movements utilize an opening introduction and a closing coda. In line with Franck's cyclic method, a single theme recurs in all the movements. It is heard first in the opening movement as a tender, intense melody for the first violin. It returns at a climactic point in the middle of the second movement, and it is the basic material of the extended coda in the finale.

1879. LES BÉATITUDES (THE BEATITUDES), oratorio for solo voices, chorus, and orchestra.

It took Franck a decade to complete his setting of the Sermon on the Mount, generally regarded as his foremost religious composition. Its writing was for him a labor of religious dedication, and to it he brought some of his most sublime and spiritual concepts. "One would have to go back to the very first classical masters," said Ernest Chausson, "to find so powerful an expression of the soul's despair, its appeal to divine justice, its striving after the ideal, after holiness." Leland Hall points out that here Franck "has almost created a new art form [in which] the dramatic element is almost wholly lacking." He added: "Here more than anywhere else Franck's peculiar gift of harmony has full force in the expression of religious rapture and the mysticism of the devout and childlike believer."

Les Béatitudes opens with a prologue in which a tenor solo presents the air, "Dark Brooded Fear Over the Land," followed by celestial voices chanting, "Oh, Blessed Be He!" Eight Beatitudes follow.

The first is "Blessed are the poor in spirit, for theirs is the kingdom of Heaven." Here a terrestial chorus introduces the powerful utterance of "All the Wealth of the Earth," to which the celestial chorus responds softly, "When Our Hearts Are Oppressed." Christ is then heard in the radiant air, "Blessed Be," accompanied by a celestial chorus.

The second Beatitude—"Blessed are the meek, for they shall inherit the earth"—opens with an oboe passage over tremolo strings. The terrestial chorus begins with "The Earth is Dark," followed by the celestial chorus, "Poor Human Souls" and the tender strains of Christ, "Oh Blessed are the Meek."

The third Beatitude—"Blessed are they that mourn, for they shall be comforted"—contains an opening chorus that Felix Borowski describes as "the strongest" in the entire work, "Grief Over All Creatures." "It is followed," says Borowski, "by a mother's lament over the empty cradle; the wail of the orphan over its wretched state; the sorrow of husband and wife over separation; and the slave's prayer for liberty. As the different voices unite in a farewell, the gentle voice of Christ is heard again, "Blessed are the Mourners,' followed by an inspiring celestial chorus, 'Oh, Blessed Forever.'"

The fourth Beatitude is "Blessed are they which do hunger and thirst after righteousness, for they shall be filled." A prelude with mystical connotations brings on the tenor solo, "Wher'er We Stray," followed by Christ's voice in "Oh, Happy He."

The fifth Beatitude—"Blessed are the merciful, for they shall obtain mercy"—starts off with a "beautiful string quartet," Borowski explains, "followed by an expressive tenor solo, 'Like Beaten Corn Sheaves.' In almost-furious accord, rises the appeal of the slaves, 'King All Glorious,' ever increasing in power and rising to a tremendous climax. The remainder of the Beatitude is in striking contrast. First, is heard the voice of Christ in 'Vengeance belongeth,' followed by the celestial chorus for soprano and tenors in unison, 'Ever Blessed are They,' which is one of the sweetest passages in the work. This in turn is followed by the song of the Angel of Forgiveness, 'Holy Love, Sweet Pardon,' a repetition of the celestial chorus closing the number."

The sixth Beatitude—"Blessed are the pure in heart for they shall see God"—has a masterly orchestral prelude to precede the chorus of heathen women, "The Gods from Us Their Faces Turning." This leads into the chorus of Jewish women, "Thou Who Once to Our Sires Appeared." There then come a descriptive quartet for the four Pharisees, "Great God! From Early Youth"; the song of the Angel of Death, "I Gather in Each Soul Immortal"; the celestial chorus, "Earthly Knowledge"; the voice of Christ, "Oh, Blessed are the Pure"; and the closing chorus, "Then Purge from Your Hearts."

Felix Borowski regards the seventh Beatitude—"Blessed are the peacemakers, for they shall be called children of God"—as "one of the most dramatic sections in the work. It opens with a bitter and vehemently declamatory air by Satan, 'Tis I Whose Baneful Spell.' The effect grows more and more passionate and furious as one after the other choruses of tyrants, pagan priests, and multitude enter. To them succeeds the tender voice of Christ, 'Blessed Are They,' followed by a remorseful wail from Satan, 'Ah, that Voice' and the famous quintet of the Peacemakers, 'Evil Cannot Stay.'"

The concluding Beatitude is "Blessed are they that are persecuted for righteousness' sake, for theirs is the kingdom of Heaven." This part is initiated by Satan with "Not Yet Defeated," followed by the Chorus of the Just, "Hear Us, Justice Eternal." An angry denunciation by Satan gives way to the song of the Mater Dolorosa, "Stricken with Sorrow." After Satan muses over his fate in "Mine the Doom," Christ is heard in "Oh Ye Righteous!" The oratorio ends with Christ's gentle song, "Oh Come, Ye of My Father Beloved," and the rousing chorus of the celestial in an exultant Hosanna.

Eager to impress prominent French musicians with a work he himself regarded so highly, Franck arranged a private performance of parts of the *Beatitudes* at his home. Few came, and most of those who were present slipped out of the room while the performance was in progress. (Truth to tell, the rendition was unsatisfactory. Having sprained his hand, Franck was forced to assign the piano accompaniment to a pupil.) The first public presentation took place almost fifteen years later at a Concert Colonne in Paris in 1893 (three years after Franck's death). It was a triumph, full justification of the composer's own faith and belief in his masterwork.

1882. LE CHASSEUR MAUDIT (THE ACCURSED HUNTSMAN), tone poem for orchestra.

Le Chasseur maudit is based on a ballad by Gottfried August Buerger, which in turn came from an old legend. The published score explains the program as follows: "It is Sunday morning. In the distance are heard the joyous pealing of bells and the sacred chanting of worshipers. What desecration! The wild Count of the Rhine sounds his hunting horn! The chase goes on over grain fields, moors, and prairies. 'Hold on, Count, I pray thee; listen to the pious chants!' 'No!' and the rider rushes on like a whirlwind. Suddenly, the count is alone. His horse cannot move, nor his horn any longer give forth a sound. A grim, pitiless voice curses him: 'Desecrator!' it says, 'be thou forever pursued by the Evil One!' The flames blaze up on all sides. The Count, mad with terror and pursued by a pack of demons, flees ever faster and faster—across the abysses by day and through the sky by night."

The tone poem has four uninterrupted sections. In the first, a hunting theme for horns describes the preparation for the chase, which is then depicted vividly in the second part. In this second section we hear the cellos in a solemn melody; this is the warning the huntsman fails to heed. The third part finds the huntsman alone, his horse failing to move, his horn incapable of sound. A sober melody is given, first by the bass tuba, and then by the brass choir. The tone poem ends with an agitated picture of the huntsman fleeing through the air, pursued by demons, tortured by leaping flames.

1884–1887. COMPOSITIONS FOR SOLO PIANO:
Prelude, Chorale and Fugue; Prelude, Aria and Finale.

Franck's conscious effort to bring about a renascence of French piano music was not confined exclusively to works for piano and orchestra. In 1884, he wrote the *Prelude, Chorale and Fugue,* for solo piano, following it in 1887, with *Prelude, Aria and Finale*. In both, we find a blending of French Romanticism, Franck's mysticism, and Bach's polyphony. In the *Prelude, Chorale and Fugue* there are two main themes in the prelude. The first is stately and religious; the second is more earthy and vigorous. A contemplative chorale follows, which, in turn, leads into a fugue whose subject is descending chromatic theme.

The *Prelude, Aria and Finale* appears to Léon Vallas as a "veritable sonata in a single movement, new in form." The spacious and extended chorale-like Andante of the Prelude, says Vallas, is in the traditional Allegro movement. The slow movement of the sonata form can be found in the beautiful Aria. The finale, in line with Franck's cyclic procedure, recalls the thematic material of the earlier two movements.

1884. LES DJINNS, tone poem for piano and orchestra.

A "Djinn" is a good or evil genie, a child of fire able to assume any form he wishes. He is found in Arabian mythology. Victor Hugo wrote about him in the poem *Les Orientales,* which Franck used as the source of his tone poem. Hugo's poem traces the aerial flight of Djinns over a city in the dead of the night. Rosa Newmarch explains: "César Franck observes this kind of tidal development of sonority in his musical picture."

The tone poem first gives us a picture of night in pianissimo harmonies of woodwind and cellos, and in detached pizzicato chords in strings. A mournful theme enters in the strings and wind in the thirteenth measure, suggesting the "breath of night." After that, as if from afar, the main theme of the tone poem is heard in the bassoon. This is followed by a new thought (molto marcato) in the violins, It is developed with considerable force. The piano is now heard in some virtuoso passages before it engages a plaintive theme that is soon subjected to considerable elaboration. And now the piano contributes a new thought. After some discussion of earlier material, a huge climax is built up; at its peak, the trombones present a new subject, fortissimo and in octaves. After the agitation subsides, the piano returns with a lyrical passage supported by muted strings. From this point on, the mood is subdued. In the coda, the opening theme is recalled. The tone poem ends with florid passages in the piano over quiet chords in the strings.

1885. VARIATIONS SYMPHONIQUES (SYMPHONIC VARIATIONS), for piano and orchestra.

Increasingly aware of the serious absence of major works for piano and orchestra in France, Franck made a conscious effort to fill the gap. He was not thinking in terms of a concerto. He sought a more flexible structure in which the piano was an equal partner with the orchestra. His first experiment in this area was with *Les Djinns* (see above). He followed this with the *Variations symphoniques*. Here Franck tried to revive for the late nineteenth century the variation structure of such earlier masters as Handel, Bach, and Beethoven. Franck, however, achieved a work that departed sharply from the older concepts of variation. In fact, the *Variations symphoniques* is more like a fantasia than variations on a given theme. It is in three sections, the variation technique being deployed in the middle part. In the first section, the introduction, the theme is at best only suggested. In the finale, it is used contrapuntally in the bass in two passages.

Here is Donald Francis Tovey's analysis: "The introduction states with dramatic roughness a figure which is dimly suggestive of the variation theme. The piano, however, answers with something really much more important. These two themes are worked up in a dialogue in Franck's delightful ruminating style. Soon the time changes to 3/4, with the strings (pizzicato, with staccato wind over a roll of kettledrums) giving out two phrases of the variation theme as it is going to be. The piano, however, intervenes with a sustained and impassioned speech. When the orchestra re-enters, the dialogue is resumed in ominously dramatic tones. After a fierce climax, it calms down and at last the piano is free to give out the variation theme in the shape of a quiet melody."

In the middle section, there are six variations to the main. The first is a dialogue between piano and orchestra; the second is assigned to the cello; the third is presented by the piano, accompanied by pizzicato chords in the strings. In the fourth, there is a loud statement of the theme in various keys; in the fifth, the mood becomes more subdued and restrained, with the piano providing the accompaniment. The sixth, says Tovey, "sails in slowly in F-sharp major [with a] beautiful meandering counterpoint . . . throughout the piano part, while the theme in the cellos forms the bass for the first eight bars."

When the mode changes to minor "below the flowing arpeggios of the piano, the cellos spell out a wonderful dream on the theme of the piano's original entry. There is no more thought now of variations: the rest of the work is concerned with the building up of a brilliant finale on the other theme."

1886. SONATA IN A MAJOR, for violin and piano. I. Allegretto ben moderato. II. Allegro. III. Ben moderato. IV. Allegretto poco mosso.

There is probably no finer violin sonata in all French music than that in A major by Franck. It was written for Eugène Ysaÿe, the distinguished Belgian virtuoso, who introduced it in 1886. The first movement is in modified sonata form, dispensing with a development. A reflective first theme is heard in the violin after a short piano introduction. The contemplative movement is maintained in the second theme, which the piano is the first to present. But as this material is extended, agitation sets in, soon to dissolve to permit the movement to conclude peacefully. The second movement is, on the other hand, turbulent. A fiery first theme is heard in the piano. This is followed by a vehement second subject in the violin. Separating these two basic thoughts is an idea reminding us of a theme in the first movement. The third movement was described by its composer as a "recitative-fantasia." A short exchange between piano and violin includes a thought from the first movement. These themes are elaborated in a rhapsodic manner. The finale opens with a serene melody stated canonically by the two instruments. After a climax, the third-movement theme is recalled by the piano. A restatement of the canonic melody now brings back material from the second and third movements, the third-movement subject being given passionately by the violin. The canonic melody brings the sonata to its conclusion.

1888. PSYCHÉ, tone poem (or suite) for orchestra. I. Psyche's Sleep. II. Psyche Borne Away by the Zephyrs. III. The Garden of Eros. IV. Psyche and Eros.

In 1887–1888, Franck completed a "symphony for chorus and orchestra" based on a text by Sicard and Fourcaud, which, in turn, came out of Apuleius's *The Golden Ass*. Franck then revamped the work into a four-movement tone poem, or suite, played without interruption—the version in which the work is now given.

In the first movement (Lento), the "sleep motive" is heard in the clarinet, accompanied by strings. It is then assigned to oboes and flutes, and then again to strings. The theme of "longing" follows in the strings, soon to be succeeded by the motives of "love" and "sleep." In the second part (Allegro vivo), there are two main subjects. The first is given by muted strings, with clarinets and flutes suggesting zephyrs; the second characterizes Psyche. In the third part (Poco animato), the "Eros" theme is presented by woodwind, horns, and violin trills, combined with the subject of the zephyrs. This material is given passionate treatment before it is allowed to relax. In the concluding part (Allegretto modéré), the happiness of the lovers is depicted in a succession of skilfully combined motives.

1888. SYMPHONY IN D MINOR, for orchestra. I. Lento; Allegro non troppo. II. Allegretto. III. Allegro non troppo.

The misunderstandings and the hostility attending Franck's career, virtually up to its end, were present when his only symphony was introduced in Paris on February 17, 1889. The Paris Conservatory Orchestra was so antagonistic to the music that for a while it refused to play any of it. One of the directors of the Conservatory was contemptuous about the use of an English horn. "Who ever heard of writing for the English horn in a symphony?" he inquired belligerently. Gounod described the symphony as "the affirmation of incompetence pushed to dogmatic lengths." The audience itself was either puzzled or apathetic. And what was Franck's reaction to this fiasco? One of his pupils described him as "radiant" when he emerged from the hall. His only comment was: "It sounded well, just as I thought it would." Not a single word of disappointment at the unfavorable reception given his masterwork, not a single regret!

Today, it is difficult to understand why a work that wears its attractions so openly should at first have been so violently attacked. The inexorable logic of its structure, its compelling dramatic effects, its overwhelming emotional appeal are all calculated to make an immediate appeal to the listener.

The symphony opens with a spacious theme in lower strings, with woodwinds and violins supplying answering phrases. It is built up powerfully, with string tremolos adding to the excitement, until the main section emerges dramatically with a virile first theme; this subject is actually a variation of the previously presented slow motive. Three other important thoughts follow. One is a tender, yearning passage for the strings, which receives canonic treatment; another is a powerful expression of faith and hope, in full orchestra; and the third is a plaintive subject, for solo horn and woodwind. In the development, power is generated in the working out of the themes through strong sonorities and striking modulations. In the closing part of this development, as well as in the coda, the slow stately opening melody is repeated canonically with considerable vigor.

The middle movement opens with a wonderful melody for the English horn. It is continued by clarinet and later by unison horns over a contrapuntal subject in violas and cellos. Another soulful, poetic melody follows; it is stated by the violins. After a fragmentary recollecton of the opening song, a scherzo section is introduced with muted triplets in strings. This leads into a third expressive melody, first in clarinet, then in strings over a triplet rhythm. This last idea is discussed at some length before the movement ends placidly with a single arpeggio in harp.

The finale arives with a robust, optimistic melody, first in cellos, then in full orchestra. Another vigorous thought is then given by the brass. At this point, the movement becomes a summation of what has transpired earlier in the symphony. First we recall the first theme of the second movement (again in the English horn). After some disturbance, which reaches its peak with a resounding repetition of the finale's opening subject, the first theme of the second movement becomes a song of joy in the brass over tremolo strings. After this, the third theme of the first movement and the slow stately opening phrases of that movement are repeated. The symphony ends with a triumphant recollection of the joyous tune that had opened the finale.

1889. STRING QUARTET IN D MAJOR. I. Allegro molto moderato. II. Allegro molto. III. Adagio ma non troppo. IV. Allegro molto.

When success finally came to Franck, it appeared in his last years during the première of his only string quartet; this happened at a concert of the Société Nationale in Paris on April 19, 1890. The audience was so enthusiastic that a second performance had to be arranged for the following month. Julien Tiersot maintained in *Le Ménéstral* that Franck here continued where Beethoven had left off in his last quartets.

The first movement has been described as a Lied, since it is basically a fully extended song; the fugal treatment this melody receives later in the movement reminds us of the mysticism in Beethoven's last quartets. This movement is followed by a Mendelssohn kind of a Scherzo, light in touch, diaphonous in texture. The main melody of the first movement is referred to in passing. The slow movement is one of the most majestic pages by Franck. This is an episode in five sections, all intense in feeling and exalted in mood. The finale opens with an introduction in which themes from earlier movements are reviewed. The first main theme in the principal section of this finale is a transformation of the main subject of the first movement, while the second theme is an enlargement of some of the first movement's transitional material. In the coda, themes from the three preceding movements are again recalled. Then the quartet ends with a final reminder of the noble song of the slow movement.

1890. TROIS CHORALS (THREE CHORALES), for organ. I. E major. II. B minor. III. A minor.

The organ had become a neglected stepchild of French music in the nineteenth century. It was restored to its one-time high status by Franck. A remarkable organist himself, whose improvisations were legendary, Franck brought to his organ music the same kind of lofty concepts, religious feelings, and mysticism that characterized his major works in other areas. What is regarded as Franck's masterwork for this instrument came in the closing year of his life, the *Three Chorales*. "Such is their beauty," says Léon Vallas, "such is their range, that one can well regard them as a kind of musical testament, or as the cliché would have it, as Franck's swan song."

The first chorale in E major presents an introduction in which all the thematic material, including the basic chorale, is stated. What follows is a majestic enlargement of this material. The second chorale, in B minor, is made up of a series of chromatic variations on a stately chorale melody which, says Vallas, "passes through a series of sonorities before achieving its final state of calm." The third chorale, in A minor, opens with a dramatic prelude as a preface to a chromatic chorale melody. This chorale melody is restated after a repetition of the opening prelude. Built up into a powerful crescendo, the chorale is recalled in forceful chords while the prelude provides a background of arpeggios. The opening material then contributes the sedate and somber chordal material to conclude the composition.

CHARLES GOUNOD 1818–1893

The genius of Gounod has two faces—the sacred and the profane. In his operas, he is often sensual, voluptuous, earthy. In his religious choral works and songs, he is the mystic. At the same time, Gounod often intrudes a solemn religiosity into his operas, just as he sometimes introduces incongruous operatic dramatics into his religious writing. This juxtaposition of the sacred and the profane is one of the characteristics identifying Gounod's music. There are others: the emotion and variety of his lyric gift, the mastery of his orchestration, the refinement of his style.

In the theater and the church, using the voice as his basic medium, Gounod was a master who created "a musical language of his own," as Arthur Hervey wrote, "one of extraordinary sweetness, of wondrous fascination, the soft eloquence of which seemed to penetrate into the inmost recesses of the heart." With his melodic grace and expressiveness, his sure instinct for effect, and the comparatively wide range of his eclectic style, Gounod helped to inaugurate a new era in the French musical theater. Maurice Ravel was aware of Gounod's historic importance when he said: "The musical renewal which took place with us toward 1880 has no more weightier precursor than Gounod."

Charles François Gounod was born in Paris, France, on June 18, 1818. After completing academic studies at the Lycée St. Louis in 1836, he attended the Paris Conservatory, a pupil of Halévy, Paër, and Lesueur. In 1839, he received the Prix de Rome. During his three years in Rome, he immersed himself in church music, an influence that led him to write a Mass, performed in Rome. He also completed a Requiem, conducting its première in Vienna during a visit there. Upon returning to Paris, he served as organist and precentor at the Missions Étrangères. For a while he thought of entering the Church, and with this aim in view, he studied theology for two years. But he discarded this plan to devote himself to the writing of music for the stage. His first opera, *Sapho,* was produced in Paris on April 16, 1851, and was a modest success. He wrote several more operas while filling the post of conductor of the Orphéon Choral Society between 1852 and 1860; the most significant of these works was the comic opera, *Le Médecin malgré lui,* introduced on January 15, 1858. World fame came with *Faust,* following its first performance in 1859. Among his later operas, the most successful were *Philémon et Baucis* in 1860, *La Reine de Saba* in 1862, *Mireille* in 1864, and *Roméo et Juliette* in 1867. During the Franco-Prussian War, Gounod visited London, where he directed the Royal Philharmonic and founded and conducted an important choral group. He was back in Paris in 1875, where he wrote and had produced several more operas, including *Polyeucte* in 1878. After 1880, he deserted the stage to concentrate on sacred music. He died in Paris on October 18, 1893.

1855–1882. SONGS, for voice and piano:

"Ave Maria"; "Jésus de Nazareth"; "Où voulez-vous aller?"; "Quand tu chantes" ("Serenade"); "There Is a Green Hill Far Away."

Gounod was a prolific song writer. His earliest ones, to poems by Lamartine, came in 1841; his last, to texts by La Fontaine and Jean Rameau, were written in his final year. He created love songs, religious melodies, atmospheric numbers, and sensitive mood pictures. He set French, Italian, and English texts. He was always the melodist, who emphasized the lyric element over all others, whose prime interest lay more in the vocal line than in the accompaniment.

His most famous song is the "Ave Maria," which he officially named "Meditation on Bach's Prelude in C major." This is because he used intact the first piano prelude from Bach's *Well-Tempered Clavier,* Book I, as the accompaniment for his own deeply moving religious melody. Yet accompaniment and melody seem to be of one piece, beautifully suited to one another. The "Ave Maria" has been transcribed for various solo instruments and piano, for orchestra, and also for chorus.

1859. FAUST, opera in five acts, with text by Jules Barbier and Michel Carré, based on Goethe's poetical drama. First performance: Théâtre Lyrique, Paris, March 19, 1859.

Gounod's *Faust* is most assuredly not Goethe's *Faust*. The librettists reduced a philosophical drama into something closely resembling a "soap opera." But had they been more true to Goethe, Gounod would hardly have been able to summon those creative resources needed for such a challenge. He had the gift of touching sentiment, affecting lyricism, theatricalism; depth and penetration were, however, not part of his equipment. As it is, the opera *Faust* might not be a mighty dramatic epic. But it is grand opera with all those trimmings that operagoers cherish; it is surely one of the most popular French operas ever written. Here will be found something for every taste: wonderful arias ranging from the sentimental to the sardonic, from the religious and the solemn to the jocose, from the spiritual to the erotic. Here we encounter rousing choruses, brilliant ceremonials, eye-filling production numbers and ballets. Here, also, are moving love scenes and tragic episodes to stir the heart; here passions are released to arouse the senses. For these reasons, R. A. Streatfeild regarded it "as the inauguration of a new era in French opera."

It has sometimes been said that *Faust,* when first produced, was a failure. This is not the case at all. It had fifty-seven performances during its initial season, and Gounod himself noted that "it has thus far been my greatest success in the theater." Even so, *Faust* did not at first give indication that it would some day become a favorite the world over. When first produced, *Faust* was an opéra-comique, that is, it had spoken dialogue. But in April 1860, dialogue was replaced by recitatives. In 1862, the Paris Opéra put on a magnificent production of *Faust* with recitatives, featuring Christine Nilsson and Jean-Baptiste Fauré in the principal roles. It is on this occasion that *Faust* graduated from a modest success into a triumph. It became one of the most frequently played and most highly regarded operas in France, heard in Paris on the average of once every nine days during the next quarter of a century; by 1934, it had been given two thousand times.

Faust came to London in 1863, with two different productions within a three-week period. It became an instantaneous favorite, not only with the general public, but also with royalty. Just before her death Queen Victoria asked to have some of the scenes played for her. What is believed to have been the American première took place at the Academy of Music in New York on November 25, 1863. By the time the Metropolitan Opera was founded, *Faust* had become so popular in America that it was selected to open that new opera house on October 22, 1883.

The orchestral introduction opens in a melancholy mood. Ernest Newman regard this as "the most truly Faustian-like music in the whole opera." A fugato and harp scales lead into a quotation of Valentin's aria, "Avant de quitter ces lieux."

The curtain rises on Faust's study. The venerable Faust embarks upon a monologue in which he expresses weariness with life and envy of youth ("Rien!. . . En vain, j'interroge"). When Mephistopheles invades his study with the lure of gold or glory, Faust confesses what he wants most of all is the return of his youth ("Je veux la jeunesse"). By evoking for Faust the image of Marguerite at her spinning wheel, Mephistopheles can lure Faust into making a bargain with him whereby he is ready to trade his soul for a return of youth. Mephistopheles now offers Faust a potion which, when drunk, transforms him into a dashing and handsome young man.

In the second act, students, soldiers, burghers are celebrating a fair in the village square ("Vin ou bière"). Valentin appears, handling a medallion he is sure will protect him now that he is leaving for the wars ("O sainte médaille"). But he is depressed by the fact that he is leaving behind his sister Marguerite without protection ("Avant de quitter ces lieux"). When Siebel reassures him he stands ready to be the girl's protector, Valentin is in more of a mood to join the festivities. Wagner, one of the students, raises his voice in a little ditty about a rat ("Un rat plus poltron"). He is interrupted by the arrival of Mephistopheles, who soon launches into a cynical tirade about man's greed for gold ("Le Veau d'or"). Then he delights the crowd with exhibitions of magic. When the devil proposes a toast to Marguerite, Valentin becomes so angered that he rushes at him with his sword, which snaps in half. Aware for the first time that they are in the presence of a supernatural power, the soldiers cross their swords into a cross-like design ("De l'enfer qui vient émousser"). The tensions, however, are soon relieved. Once again the burghers fill the square to dance to and sing an infectious waltz ("Ainsi que la brise légère"). Now Marguerite is seen; she is on her way to church. Faust accosts her, tells her of his high regard for her, and offers to escort her ("O belle enfant! Je t'aime"). When Marguerite declines the invitation, Mephistopheles becomes cynical. The crowd continues with its gay dancing.

The brief orchestral introduction to the third act describes a balmy summer evening. Siebel comes to Marguerite's garden bearing her flowers ("Faites-lui mes aveux"), but the flowers wither in her hand. Siebel disappears upon the appearance of Mephistopheles and Faust. Faust comments on the beauty of the place ("Salut! demeure chaste et pure"). His revery ends when Mephistopheles places a casket of jewels at Marguerite's door. After they withdraw, Marguerite comes out of the cottage, dreaming about the young, handsome man who had stopped her at the public square. Sitting at her spinning wheel she chants a ballad about the King of Thule ("Il était un roi de Thulé"), but recollections of Faust continually intrude into her song. Suddenly, she sees the casket of jewels. Trying them on, she inspects herself gaily in a mirror, as she bursts into her celebrated "jewel song" ("Ah! Je ris de me voir"). Her friend, Martha, is also pleased at the way the jewels enhance Marguerite's beauty. Now, with the return of Mephistopheles and Faust, the devil engages Martha's attention so that Faust can be left alone with Marguerite. The devil calls upon the night to enshroud the lovers ("O Nuit, étends sur eux ton ombre"). Faust and Marguerite, now fully aware of each other's love, give voice to their rapture in "Quoi! je t'implore en vain!" Later on, after they have separated, Faust sees Marguerite leaning out of her cottage window, ecstatic because she knows Faust loves her ("Il m'aime, quel trouble en mon coeur").

The first scene in the fourth act is sometimes omitted in present-day productions. Here the whole town has by now discovered that Marguerite and Faust are lovers. Marguerite is at her spinning wheel again, lamenting the fact that Faust has deserted her ("Elles se cachaient!"). Siebel comes to console her, to assure her of his own undying devotion. Expressing her gratitude, Marguerite tells him she will pray to God "for my child and my love."

Marguerite now comes to the cathedral to pray for her lover and her unborn child. There Mephistopheles jeers at her, and tells her she is forever doomed.

Outside the cathedral, the ringing voices of soldiers announce their victorious return from war ("Gloire immortelle"). Valentin, too, has come home. Eagerly he questions Siebel about Marguerite. Siebel's evasive answers arouse Valentin's suspicions. Rushing to Marguerite's cottage, he finds there Mephistopheles and Faust. The devil is singing a mock serenade under Marguerite's window ("Vous qui faites l'endormie"). Valentin challenges Faust to a duel in which, through Mephistopheles's magic, Valentin is fatally wounded. With his last breaths, Valentin curses his sister. The townspeople kneel in prayer for the salvation of Valentin's soul.

The first scene of the fifth act is generally omitted today. Here Faust and Mephistopheles attend the revels of Walpurgis Night, where Faust sees a vision of Marguerite. It is for this scene that Gounod wrote the ballet music that has become so popular out of its context. More usually, the fifth act takes place entirely in prison, to which Marguerite has been committed for having killed her child. Faust comes to beg Marguerite to escape. At the sound of his voice, she is delirious with joy ("Sa main, sa douce main"). But she refuses to save herself. Instead, she prays to the angel hosts to lift her soul heavenwards ("Anges purs, anges radieux!"). Then seeing Faust as evil, she rejects him. With Mephistopheles telling the dying Marguerite her soul is damned, the angels sing of her redemption ("Sauvée!").

1864. MIREILLE, opera in five acts, with text by Michel Carré, based on *Mirèlo,* a Provençal poem by Frédéric Mistral. First performance: Theatre Lyrique, Paris, March 19, 1864.

In writing music for a text based on a Provençal poem, Gounod chose to be descriptive rather than dramatic, suggestive rather than obvious in his emotional appeal, atmospheric in place of sentimental, tragic, or religious. The charms of *Mireille,* therefore, are more subtle and elusive than those of *Faust*. For this reason, *Mireille* has been less popular; but in some ways, it is one of Gounod's most charming operas. "Gounod's music," says R.A. Streatfeild, "seems to have borrowed the warm coloring of the Provençal poet's romance. *Mireille* glows with the life and sunlight of the south. There is little attempt at dramatic force in it, and the one scene in which the note of pathos is attempted is perhaps the least successful in the whole opera. But the lighter portions are irresistible."

The popular overture has a slow introduction whose main subject is presented by the woodwind. In the body of the overture, the first theme is heard in the strings. A transitional passage in first violins, with accentuations by a triangle, leads into a melodious theme for first violins. The second subject receives a good deal of attention in the development. A crescendo bring on the recapitulation, and the overture ends with a forceful coda.

In the province of Millaine, in legendary times, village girls are working on a plantation. Taven, a sorceress, is jeered; nevertheless, the girls want her to prognosticate the outcome of their love affairs. One of these girls is Mireille, in love with a humble basket-maker, Vincent. Since Mireille's father wants her to marry the drover, Ourrias, Taven can see only trouble ahead for her. Mireille, however, does not take this seriously. She reveals a happy spirit in the waltz, "Légère hirondelle," and in her duet with Vincent, "Vincinette, votre âge."

In the second act, a festival is taking place in an arena in Arles. Mireille and Vincent are among those participating in a gay farandole ("La brise est douce et parfumée"). In "Mon coeur ne peut changer" Mireille reiterates to Vincent her deep love, but Ourrias is pressing her to marry him. Upon asking Mireille's father for Mireille's hand, Vincent is rejected. Mireille faints, and is carried off by Vincent.

In the next act, the paths of Ourrias and Vincent cross in the Valley of Hell, where both have come to consult Taven. A violent quarrel erupts between the two rivals. Vincent is struck a serious blow. Thinking he has killed Vincent, Ourrias goes off in a barge down the river Rhone. The boat capsizes and sends Ourrias to his death.

When Mireille learns Vincent has been hurt, she seeks solace in church. En route, at the desert of Crau, she meets and addresses a a shepherd ("Le jour se lève"), who warns her to be careful of ill effects from the sun. Mireille manages to reach the church where she collapses. Now her father is ready to sanction her marriage to Vincent, but it is too late. Mireille dies, and Vincent, at her side, is grief-stricken.

Much of the initial success of *Mireille* was due to the brilliant performance of Marie Miolan-Carvalho, who created title role. Eight months after the world première, two acts of this opera were given in German in Philadelphia. The entire opera was produced in the United States in the 1880's, the exact date and place not known. The Metropolitan Opera presented it on February 28, 1919.

Gounod prepared a version that ends happily with the heroine's recovery and her marriage to Vincent. This was produced for the first time at the Opéra-Comique in 1899, but is rarely seen today.

1867. ROMÉO ET JULIETTE, opera in five acts, with text by Jules Barbier and Michel Carré, based on the Shakespeare tragedy. First performance: Théâtre Lyrique, Paris, April 27, 1867.

Though *Romeo and Juliet* ranks second to *Faust* in popularity among Gounod's dozen operas, it is by no means a consistent masterwork. Herbert F. Peyser notes that the libretto is little more than a "succession of love duets, now tender, now sorrowful," while Gounod's score is mainly "a series of sentimental numbers couched in a lyrical vein which had been worked out with much more freshness and originality in *Faust*." Ernest Newman puts a finger on the shortcomings of *Romeo and Juliet* by insisting that the Shakespeare tragedy is not good material for an opera. He explains: "There is very little in the play that lends itself readily to the purposes of opera. For even in opera one looks for some development of character. . . . and the lovers of Verona do not develop." If, however, *Romeo and Juliet* has admirers in the opera house, it is for its many moments of eloquent lyricism: for Juliet's ever popular waltz; Romeo's garden-scene cavatina; the lovers' duet in the tomb.

The opera is prefaced by an "overture-prologue" which requires an unaccompanied chorus. A dramatic phrase in octaves over a tremolo, followed by a rushing passage in sixteenths, help build up an ominous mood. A twelve-bar fugato then leads into the choral episode (the musical equivalent of Shakespeare's "two households both alike in dignity"). The orchestra then resumes with a plaintive section pointing up the tragedy of the two doomed lovers.

A masked ball is taking place at the palace of the Capulets to celebrate Juliet's birthday. When Juliet appears, the guests extol her beauty in "Ah, qu'elle est belle," after which Juliet allows her ebullient spirits to overflow in "Ecoutez! Ecoutez!" Romeo, Mercutio, and some of their fellow Montagues now appear. Romeo tells of a dream that has been haunting him; Mercutio relates the ballad of Queen Mab. When Juliet is again seen, she sings the waltz that is probably the most famous single aria in the opera. Here she explains that she has time enough to think yet of marriage, that first she wants to taste life's sweetness ("Je veux vivre dans ce rêve"). Romeo approaches her cautiously. Their immediate interest in each other is reflected in the duet, "Ange adorable." Tybalt, noticing this interest, vows to destroy Romeo. But for the moment the festivities and the dancing continue.

A barcarolle-like introduction—gentle and caressing—prefaces the second act. Mercutio and his friends are discussing Romeo's infatuation for Juliet. When they leave, Romeo confirms their suspicions by singing a cavatina to Juliet, in which he compares her to the brilliant sun ("Ah! lève-toi soleil!"). This is followed by the passionate love duet of Romeo and Juliet ("O nuit divine"). When Romeo leaves, Juliet confesses to her friend Gertrude how much she loves Romeo. Gertrude advises her to meet Romeo in Friar Lawrence's cell to marry him there in utter secrecy.

The first scene of the third act is in Friar Lawrence's cell. Monks are sounding a religious chant. The music passes from the spiritual to the turbulent when Romeo appears, followed by Juliet and Gertrude. After the marriage ceremony, Gertrude advises Romeo and Juliet to separate. The scene shifts to a public square in front of the Capulet palace. Stephano, looking for his master, Romeo, is singing a pleasant little ditty ("Que fais-tu, blanche tourterelle"). He provokes the Capulets until a fight breaks out between them and the Montagues. Mercutio is killed by Tybalt, and Tybalt in turn is dealt a death blow by Romeo. The Duke of Verona banishes Romeo from the kingdom.

Romeo, nevertheless, manages to steal into Juliet's room to bid her farewell. The melancholy strains of the fourth-act introduction repeat a subject from the first-act prelude. The first scene here is dominated by exquisite love music ("Nuit d'hyménée"). The night passes; the sound of the morning lark sends Romeo off. Juliet's father now appears to announce that Juliet must marry Paris without delay. After he departs, Friar Lawrence gives Juliet a powerful drug that will put her into a deep sleep simulating death. His plan is to bring the sleeping Juliet into the family tomb to await her husband, and then to flee with him out of the country. Soon Juliet is seen walking to the chapel, but suddenly she falls lifeless.

Somber harmonies symbolizing death introduce the fifth act. Romeo, who does not know of Friar Lawrence's plan, enters the tomb, weary and haggard. Seeing Juliet outstretched, he is sure she is dead. Grief-stricken, he takes poison. But before it can take effect, Juliet awakens from her deep slumber. The joy of seeing each other again is reflected in another ecstatic duet, "Salut, tombeau." But the poison soon destroys Romeo. Aware that her beloved is dead, Juliet stabs herself with a dagger.

Romeo and Juliet, when first given in 1867, was an immense success. It was first seen in the United States at the Academy of Music in New York on November 15, 1867. It came to the Metropolitan Opera on the opening night of the 1891–1892 season, with a distinguished cast including Jean and Édouard de Reszke and Emma Eames.

1873. MARCHE FUNÈBRE D'UNE MARIONNETTE (FUNERAL MARCH OF A MARIONETTE), for orchestra

Gounod planned writing a piano work, *Suite burlesque;* and one of its movements was a *Funeral March of a Marionette*. He never completed that composition. Instead, he orchestrated the *Funeral March*—since become one of his most popular concert works. The death of the marionette has come about through a duel. The music describes the funeral procession. The solemnity is relieved with a sprightly section in which the mourners stop off at an inn for refreshment. Then the march continues. The somber closing measures suggest that even for marionettes life can be ephemeral.

1881–1884. ORATORIOS, for solo voices, chorus, and orchestra: *La Rédemption; Mors et vita*.

Gounod's last opera, *Le Tribut de Zamora,* was completed in 1880 and produced at the Opéra on April 1, 1881. After 1880, the composer devoted himself to large sacred works to which he carried his deep-rooted mysticism and his profound religious feelings. As a result of extended stays in London, where he conducted orchestral and choral concerts, Gounod became interested in the oratorio. He decided to produce several such works for English consumption

La Rédemption was written in 1881 and introduced at the Birmingham Festival in 1882. This is Gounod's first important oratorio. *Mors et vita*—completed in 1884 and given at the Birmingham Festival a year later—is his finest one. Martin Cooper says: "The *Redemption* came as a new inspiration to the generation of English church composers who were well grounded in *Messiah* and *Elijah*. . . . and asked for nothing better than a restatement of oratorio ideals and principles in a rather modern form." In structure and style, however, Gounod was not touched by modern influences. "There were some strange harkings back to the aesthetic of an earlier generation bred in the love and holy fear of Meyerbeer," points out Cooper, "but the 'March au calvaire,' with its little cocky, precise, rhythms would not shock a generation for whom opera and oratorio were most beautiful when they most closely resembled each other." In his choral writing, some of which scales the sublime, Gounod "left a mark on the music of the Anglican rite which half a century barely succeeded in removing."

Gounod prepared his own texts for both *La Rédemption* and *Mors et vita*. "Musically," says Cooper, "*Mors et vita* is more dramatic and more concentrated than *Redemption*. The influence of Verdi is unmistakable in several places, as, for example, the tenor solo of the 'Ingemisco' and the introduction to the 'Inter oves locum praesta.'" But there is also an affinity in this music between Gounod and César Franck. "Franck repeated almost exactly the 'happiness of the blessed motif' in the second subject of the first movement of his symphony. This mental affinity between the two composers is sometimes so marked that one is tempted to think that at least a portion of Franck's music is little more than Wagnerized Gounod, though Franck had little use for Gounod's music."

ÉDOUARD LALO 1823–1892

Lalo was partial to esoteric subjects. His most celebrated work is of a Spanish identity—the *Symphonie espagnole,* for violin and orchestra. But he also produced a *Norwegian Rhapsody,* a Russian concerto (for violin), a ballet with an Oriental setting (*Namouna*), an oriental fantasy (for piano and orchestra), and an opera and songs of Breton interest. But whatever the subject, the influence of Wagner is evident. Indeed, it is with Lalo that Wagner made his first important inroads into French opera. "He remains," Martin Cooper says of Lalo, "one of the most important links between the pre-Wagnerian music of the 1860's and 1870's and the wholehearted Wagnerians of the late 1880's and 1890's."

Édouard Lalo was born in Lille, France, on January 27, 1823. After attending the Lille Conervatory, he entered the Paris Conservatory in 1839, where he studied with Habeneck, Schulhoff, and Crèvecoeur. In 1855, he joined the then recently organized Armingaud-Jacquard Quartet as violist. Meanwhile in 1848–1849, he issued his first opus, a number of songs, besides completing some chamber music. His failure to gain recognition led him to abandon composition for a number of years. But, after his marriage to Mlle. Bernier de Maligny in 1865, he completed a three-act opera, *Fiesque,* which received third prize in a competition sponsored by the Théâtre Lyrique. *Fiesque* was never produced; but its ballet music, renamed *Divertissement,* made a strong impression when introduced in Paris in 1872. The success of his Violin Concerto in 1874, and his *Symphonie espangole* in 1875—both introduced by Pablo de Sarasate—helped to enhance his reputation. It became permanently solidifed with the ballet *Namouna,* presented at the Opéra in 1882, and the opera, *Le Roi d'Ys,* produced at the Opéra-Comique on May 7, 1888. In 1888, Lalo was made an officer of the Legion of Honor. Subsequently he received the Prix Monbinne from the Académie des Beaux-Arts. He died in Paris on April 22, 1892.

1874. SYMPHONIE ESPANGOLE (SPANISH SYMPHONY), for violin and orchestra, op. 21. I. Allegro non troppo. II. Scherzando; Allegro molto. III. Intermezzo. IV. Andante. V. Allegro.

Stimulated by the success of his Violin Concerto, which Pablo de Sarasate introduced in Paris in 1874, the composer went to work on a new large composition for that eminent violin virtuoso. Keeping in mind Sarasate's nationality, Lalo completed a work with a pronounced Spanish identity. He called it a "symphony"—possibly to emphasize the importance of the orchestra—but in actuality, it is a five-movement suite for violin and orchestra. Sarasate introduced it in Paris on February 7, 1875, and from then on it became the composer's most frequently played concert work.

The first theme, in the opening Allegro, has two sections. The first is a vigorous statement for the orchestra (followed by the solo violin), and the second is a melody in triplets for the violin accompanied by plucked strings. A second subject later is heard in the solo instrument. In the development, this second theme is fancifully embellished with triplet figures in the violin. The first theme, which brings on the recapitulation, is also the basis of the coda.

In the second movement, a short orchestral preface emphasizing string pizzicato leads to a spacious waltz in the solo instrument. A middle section is marked by effective changes of tempo and tonality, after which the earlier part is repeated.

The third-movement Intermezzo, which boasts a romantic melody for the violin, is generally omitted today The fourth movement offers a sustained lyrical passage for the wind, repeated by the strings. The violin appears with a soulful subject, which soon gives way to a florid passage. The tranquil atmosphere thus far sustained carries over into the coda.

The finale, a rondo, opens with a figure in the orchestra repeated thirteen times with varying dynamics. Then the solo instrument is heard in a lively saltarello-type subject. This and a more expressive idea (poco piu lento), also for the violin, is the main material of the finale, which ends with a brilliant coda.

—

1876. OVERTURE TO LE ROI D'YS, for orchestra.

There is an eleven year hiatus between the writing of the overture and the completion of the opera for which it was intended. The opera, Lalo's most distinguished work for the stage, was introduced at the Opéra-Comique in Paris on May 7, 1888. (America heard it for the first time on January 5, 1922, in a presentation by the Metropolitan Opera.) The overture, however, received its first performance on November 12, 1876, in Paris.

Édouard Blau's libretto was based on the old Breton legend about the submerged city of Ys; this was also the source of Debussy's piano prelude, *La Cathédrale engloutie*. The principal characters are the two daughters of the king of Ys, Margared and Rozenn. They are rivals for the love of Mylio, a knight at court. When Mylio favors Rozenn, her sister is driven by her jealousy (and by the determination of her father to marry her off to a neighboring prince) to turn against her own people. She opens a dike and inundates the city. Distraught by her own treachery, Margared plunges to her death in the flood. Through a miracle, the waters recede and the city is saved.

The overture is built entirely from material used in the opera. First, we hear Mylio's stirring first act air, "Si le ciel est plein de flammes" in the clarinet. Trumpet fanfares lead to the main part of the overture. The first main theme (in cello) is a passionate subject lifted from Rozenn's second-act song, "Lorsque je t'ai vu." This passage describes Margared's intense jealousy. Another trumpet figure brings in a more placid thought, through which Rozenn is introduced. This material comes from her air, "En silence, pourquoi souffrir." After the two themes are developed, the overture ends with a dramatic restatement of the Mylio subject.

1876. CONCERTO IN D MINOR, for cello and orchestra. I. Prelude: lento; allegro maestoso. II. Intermezzo: andante con moto. III. Andante; Allegro vivace.

Lalo dedicated his cello concerto to Adolphe Fischer who introduced it in Paris in 1877. It begins with a twenty-two measure Lento introduction. In the principal part of the movement, two important themes are given by the solo cello. There are also two main subjects in the second-movement Intermezzo. After twelve introductory bars, the first is heard in cello. Then, with a change of tempo and key, the second is once again introduced by the solo instrument. The finale is a brilliantly conceived rondo. The first stately theme appears after a short orchestral introduction. The tempo then quickens and for the rest of the movement the mood is lively and the material energetic.

1879. RAPSODIE NORVÉGIENNE (NORWEGIAN RHAPSODY), for orchestra.

In 1875, Lalo wrote a *Fantasie norvégienne* for violin and orchestra for Pablo de Sarasate. This format displeased the composer, who later recast it as an exclusively orchestral composition; he now renamed it *Norwegian Rhapsody*. It has two sections. In the first (Andantino), a folk-song type of melody is heard in the strings, followed by some more vigorous material (Allegretto). The second part is introduced by a loud statement in trumpets, followed by a Presto section energized by vital dance rhythms.

LÉO DELIBES 1836–1891

Even while we concede that *Lakmé* is one of the finest creations of the nineteenth-century French lyric theater, we must acknowledge that Delibes's most significant contribution came through his music for ballet. Important ballet music had, of course, been written before Delibes's time—by masters like Lully, Rameau, and Gluck—but usually within the context of an opera. Occasionally, a significant composer turned his hand toward writing music for a ballet as an independent unit, as Gluck did with *Don Juan.* But for the most part, the writing of ballet music, outside the opera, was an assignment for hacks; and the music was generally contrived exclusively to meet the demands of the choreographer. But Delibes became one of the first composers to direct the full resources of his talent and imagination into original music for the dance; to write music which, while completely idiomatic for the dance, can stand apart from the ballet and afford delight in the concert hall. Thus Delibes became the predecessor of Tchaikovsky, whose admiration for *Coppélia* and *Sylvia* led him to write scores for Russian ballets. And from Tchaikovsky, the road leads directly into the twentieth century, whose composers often used ballet as the medium for some of their most ambitious and remarkable scores. Herbert Weinstock put it this way: "It was precisely *Swan Lake,* nonetheless, with *Coppélia* and *Sylvia,* that did most eventually to sweep the trashy tinklings of fifth-rate composers from the pit of ballets and substitute for them the possibility of *Daphnis et Chloé* and *Le Sacre du printemps.*"

Léo Delibes was born in St. Germain du Val, Sarthe, France, on February 21, 1836. After attending the Paris Conservatory—where he was a pupil of Bazin, Benoist, and Le Couppey, among others—he became the organist of the St. Pierre de Chaillot Church in 1853. In 1855, his first operetta—*Deux sous de charbons*—was produced in Paris. From 1862 to 1871, he was the first organist of the St. Jean-St. François Church in Paris. In 1863, he was made accompanist, and in 1865, second chorusmaster, of the Paris Opéra. On commisssion, he wrote his first ballet, *La Source,* produced at the Opéra on November 12, 1866. His first masterwork, the ballet *Coppélia,* came to the Opéra in 1870, followed by *Sylvia* in 1876. Meanwhile, Delibes scored his first success in opera with the opéra-comique, *Le Roi l'a dit,* given at the Opéra-Comique on May 24, 1873. His most significant opera, *Lakmé,* came to the same theater in 1883.

In 1877, Delibes was made Chevalier of the Legion of Honor. Four years later, he was appointed professor of composition at the Paris Conservatory; and in 1884, he was elected to the Institut. He died in Paris on January 16, 1891.

1870. COPPÉLIA, ou LA FILLE AUX YEUX D'ÉMAIL (COPPELIA, OR THE GIRL WITH THE ENAMEL EYES), ballet in three acts, with book by C. Nuitter and A. Saint-Léon, based on *Der Sandmann,* a story by E. T. A. Hoffmann. Choreography by A. Saint-Léon. First performance: Paris Opéra, May 25, 1870.

Coppélia was the first ballet to be built around the subject of a doll come to life. In a Galician town in the seventeenth century, Coppelius, an eccentric inventor, creates the doll Coppelia. Swanilda does not know that Coppelia is a doll, having seen her only from the street at her window. She tries to attract Coppelia's attention by dancing for her (Valse lente). Swanilda is convinced that Franz, with whom she is in love, has become interested in Coppelia. When he appears, she goes into hiding and sees him wave towards the doll, a gesture that convinces her that her suspicions are well founded. Swanilda then comes out of hiding to reprimand Franz, but is prevented from doing so by the precipitous arrival of the villagers, who perform a gay mazurka. The Burgomaster then announces that a festival will take place on the morrow celebrating the presentation of a new bell to the town; any couple desiring to get married on that day will receive a handsome gift of money. When the Burgomaster inquires from Swanilda if, perchance, she will take advantage of this offer by marrying Franz, she yields to a superstition that maintains that a stalk of wheat placed to the ear can reveal secrets. Putting such a stalk to her ear, Swanilda believes she hears that Franz has been unfaithful to her. In a fit of anger, she breaks the stalk and participates in a Polish dance. After this, all the villagers do a fiery czardas.

In the second act, Swanilda invades Coppelius's house. For the first time, she discovers that her rival is a doll. Upon Coppelius's return, she hides the doll in a closet, dons the doll's clothes and performs several dances, including the famous "Valse de la poupée". Coppelius becomes convinced his doll has come to life. But he soon learns that this is Swanilda performing. Swanilda and Franz now announce their intention of getting married during the festival celebration.

Coppélia made history on counts other than that it was the first ballet about a doll become human. It was the first to introduce into ballet such East European folk dances as the mazurka and the czardas, a practice later ballet composers would follow. Most important of all, *Coppélia* was one of the first ballets, outside of opera, whose score is so rich in melodic, harmonic, and rhythmic invention, and orchestrated with such mastery, that it can be heard with a good deal of pleasure without the trappings of dancing. The following orchestral episodes from this score are most often played whenever a *Coppélia* suite is heard at orchestral concerts: Prelude, Mazurka, Valse lente, Intermezzo, Czardas, Valse de la poupée, Bolero, Gigue, and Thème slav varié.

The American première of *Coppélia* took place at the Metropolitan Opera on March 11, 1887. But the success of this ballet dates from February 28, 1910, when Anna Pavlova, as Swanilda, made her American debut. "It is safe to say," reported Carl van Vechten of her performance, "that such dancing has not been seen on the local stage during the present generation."

1876. SYLVIA, ou LA NYMPHE DE DIANE (SYLVIA, or THE NYMPH OF DIANA), ballet in three acts, with book by Jules Barbier and

Baron de Reinach. Choreography by Louis Merante. First performance: Paris Opéra, June 14, 1876.

Sylvia is a beautiful huntress who comes upon the scene in the company of nymphs. They perform a dance in front of the statue of Eros describing a hunt ("Les Chasseresses"). With the background of a gentle, bucolic Intermezzo, some of the nymphs recline on the turf; others plunge into the nearby stream. Then, to the music of Valse lente, Sylvia swings rhythmically on the bough of a tree. But the black huntsman, Orion, captures and abducts her. And Amyntas, a shepherd in love with her, goes in pursuit to a wooded landscape on the seacoast. He is in abject misery since he cannot find her. There a festival to Bacchus is held ("Cortège de Bacchus"). A barcarolle, highlighted by a saxophone solo, gives warning of a ship's approach. It is bringing Eros, disguised as a pirate, and some veiled slaves. When the slaves disembark, one of them dances the "Pizzicato Polka" for Amyntas. Then she lifts her veil to reveal that she is Sylvia.

When first presented, *Sylvia* was a triumph. Following as it did the success of *Coppélia,* it permanently established Delibes as the foremost composer of ballet music in France. "Monsieur Delibes," reported the critic for *L'Opinion,* "has written a score which reveals the hand of a master symphonist. The picturesque choice of themes, the expressive variety of melodies, the attractive improvisation of the harmonies, and the highly colored orchestration make this ballet an exquisite work." Tchaikovsky esteemed this music more highly than *Goetterdaemmerung*!

The following episodes from the ballet score are usually assembled into a suite: "Les Chasseresses," Intermezzo, Valse lente, "Pizzicato Polka," "Cortège de Bacchus" ("Marche et Bacchanale").

1880. LAKMÉ, opéra-comique in three acts, with text by Edmond Gondinet and Philippe Gille, based on Pierre Loti's *Le Mariage de Loti.* First performance: Opéra-Comique, Paris, April 14, 1883.

The source of Gondinet's effective libretto was the thinly disguised autobiographical story of Pierre Loti, in which the famous author describes his romance with the native girl, Rarahu, in Tahiti. What most fascinated both Gondinet and Delibes in this Loti tale was the exotic settings and the colorful characters. With the help of Gille, Gondinent prepared an opera libretto for Delibes, transferring the setting from Tahiti to India so that they could introduce into the story the dramatic religious conflict between the Brahmans and the English. One other important change was made in the story. Rarahu died from overindulgence of alchohol. Delibes suggested a far more poetic end for her by having her consume a poisonous flower. (The fact that Delibes selected a plant, the datura stramonium, which was not at all lethal, didn't bother the composer. "For me," he told his librettists, "the datura is poison. If it isn't there, there can be no opera.")

The opera opens in the garden of an Indian temple, in the nineteenth century. The Brahmans are determined to chase the English out of India. Lakmé, daughter of the Brahman priest, Nilakantha, is heard in prayer ("Blanche Dourga"). A number of English sightseers invade the holy garden, even though foreigners are forbidden access on the penalty of death. One of them is Gerald, a British officer. The moment he sees Lakmé, he falls in love with her. She, too, is emotionally affected. She begs him to leave the grounds before he is discovered by the priests. As Gerald makes his escape, Nilakantha has caught a glimpse of him, but without recognizing who he is. The priest is determined to uncover his identity and kill him for having desecrated the temple. In an effort to find out who the culprit is, Nilakantha brings Lakmé to the public square and orders her to sing; he is convinced that the offender will have to reveal himself in one way or another when he hears her. She sings the haunting, exotic "Bell Song" ("De la fille du paria"). As Nilakantha suspected, Gerald, is so moved by the beauty of song and singer that he betrays himself. Nilakantha stabs Gerald and flees. Lakmé drags Gerald into a nearby forest to nurse him back to health. His friend, Frederic, finds him there and urges him to return to his regiment. The sound of martial music convinces Gerald he must sacrifice love for duty. Realizing she is about to lose Gerald, Lakmé eats a lethal flower. Her father appears and orders his men to kill Gerald. But Lakmé saves his life by telling her father she has placated the gods with her own death.

Three different styles are found in Delibes's score. One is French, used for the love music of Lakmé and Gerald; the most notable example is Lakmé's unforgettable first act aria, "Pourquoi dans les grands bois." The second style is predominantly English, to identify the British characters. The third, and most important, is the Oriental: the "Bell Song" and the prayer to Dourga; the oriental dances that precede the "Bell Song; the music for the Hindu ceremonials. "This music," says Philip L. Miller, "is rich in the formulas for Eastern color. . . . Rather square in contour, these melodies have a modal flavor and a peculiar sustained quality which must have seemed the very essence of Orientalism when first heard, and which to this day give to them an exotic attractiveness."

The high point of the opera—the pivot on which the opera rotates—is Lakmé's "Bell Song." Here is how Herbert F. Peyser described it: "The song begins with a kind of oriental, wordless call, a summons to the Hindu throng to assemble. Then follows an admirable recitative, supported by sustained chords and a few measures of staccato figures. Almost imperceptibly, the recitative, with its ornate and exotic cadenzas, merges into the aria proper, an Allegro moderato, in which the florid cadenzas, imitating the bell effects in the orchestra, grow quite naturally out of the melodic character of the air, instead of being dragged in gratuitously, like so many coloratura passages in opera."

Lakmé was first produced in the United States, at the Academy of Music in New York on March 1, 1886; it was given in English. It entered the repertory of the Metropolitan Opera on April 2, 1890, when Adelina Patti assumed the title role.

GEORGES BIZET 1838–1875

Georges Bizet was one of the first composers in France to step away from the spectacular brand of theater represented by Meyerbeer toward one that was restrained, refined, atmospheric, and contemporary. "Bizet had it in him to be the greatest musical dramatist of his age," says Winton Dean. "Where Wagner's characters were legendary, Meyerbeer's historical . . . Bizet's in his two greatest works were of his own century and of the common people. He steered a course equally remote from the disguised symphonist Wagner and the meretricious eclectic Meyerbeer."

But Bizet was not merely an opera composer. Some of his best writing is found in concert music. Here, as in the theater, Bizet has a lyrical gift that is both personal and beguiling; a strong rhythmic vitality; unusual powers at orchestration and harmony; youth and verve in his style; and a strong feeling for the exotic.

Georges Bizet was born in Paris, France, on October 25, 1838. The son of professional musicians, he was entered in the Paris Conservatory when he was ten. For the next few years, he studied with Marmontel, Benoist, Halévy, and Zimmerman, among others, winning prizes in piano, organ, and fugue. While still a Conservatory student, he completed a one-act opera, *Le Docteur miracle,* submitted in a competition sponsored by Offenbach. He shared first prize with Charles Lecocq (1832–1918), his own opera being produced at the Bouffes Parisiens on April 9, 1857. In that same year of 1857, he received the Prix de Rome. While in Italy, he wrote two operas and several orchestral compositions. Returning to Paris, he completed his first significant work for the stage, the opera *Les Pêcheurs de perles,* produced at the Théâtre Lyrique on September 30, 1863. (This is the opera that contains the famous tenor aria, "Je crois entendre encore.") This and the next three operas failed to make much of an impression. Meanwhile, in 1869, he married Genèvieve Halévy, daughter of his professor of composition at the Conservatory. Bizet's first contact with success came with the premiere of *L'Arlesienne Suite No. 1,* in 1872. Less than three years after that, his masterwork, *Carmen,* was produced at the Opéra-Comique. Bizet died only three months after that première, his death probably caused by a cancerous condition of the throat. He died in Bougival, near Paris, on June 3, 1875.

1855. SYMPHONY IN C MAJOR. I. Allegro vivo. II. Adagio. III. Allegro vivace. IV. Allegro vivace.

Over seventy-five years separate the writing and the première of Bizet's only symphony. Bizet completed it when he was only seventeen. Then he apparently forgot it, and so did everybody else. There was no mention of it in any of his letters; his early biographers were unaware of its existence. The work found a permanent resting place in the archives of the Paris Conservatory, where it was discovered by D. C. Parker. Parker interested the conductor, Felix Weingartner, into resuscitating it. When Weingartner directed the première, in Basel, Switzerland, on February 25, 1935, the work proved a joyful discovery. Mozartean classicism was beautifully married to Schubertian lyricism; here and there were intriguing touches, now of Rossini, now of Mendelssohn. Derivative though it undoubtedly was, the symphony proved to be music of winning charm, flooded with the warm sun of the Mediterranean.

In the first movement the two lyrical subjects are presented according to classical design. Two unaccompanied horns bring on the development; a crescendo leads into the recapitulation. The slow movement begins with an eight-bar introduction before a mournful song for oboe is given over a plucked-string accompaniment. A second soulful melody contributes to the romantic mood. The third movement is a Scherzo, in which the main subject of the first part returns in a transformed state in the trio, in clarinet and bassoon over a ground bass. A moto perpetuo subject in sixteenths, Mendelssohnian in grace, sets the finale into motion. A march-like subject introduces a lyrical passage in the violins. These ideas are then discussed with good humor.

This music was used for a four-movement classic ballet, *Symphony in C,* with choreography by George Balanchine. It was introduced in Paris on July 28, 1947. No scenery was used, only a blue background; the dancers wore classic ballet costumes. As Balanchine explained further: "*Symphony in C* is not based on a story, but on the music to which it is danced. . . . There is a different dance scheme and development for each of the four movements. Each movement has its own characteristic ballerina, première danseur, and corps de ballet."

1867. DANSE BOHÉMIENNE, for orchestra.

On December 26, 1867, Bizet's opera, *La Jolie Fille de Perth* (text by Vernoy de Saint-Georges and Jules Adenis, based on Sir Walter Scott) was introduced by and well received at the Théâtre Lyrique. The critics singled out the second act for special praise, *Le Ménéstral* describing it as "a masterpiece from beginning to end." Out of that second act, Ernest Reyer selected the *Bohemian Dance* as the jewel. Since then, it has become a favorite of semi-classical concerts; many impresarios like to interpolate it into *Carmen* as a ballet sequence. The "Bohemian dance" tune is a sinuous melody for the flute, first heard to a harp accompaniment. Then the strings take the melody over. It becomes increasingly rhythmic, dramatic, and abandoned, as other sections of the orchestra participate joyously.

1871. JEUX D'ENFANTS (CHILDREN'S GAMES), suite for orchestra, op. 22. I. Trompette et tambour. II. La Poupée. III. La Toupie. IV. Petit mari, petite femme. V. Le Bal.

In 1871, Bizet wrote a set of piano pieces for four hands about childhood, and for children. This work is made up of twelve short pieces. The composer orchestrated five of them and assembled them into a now popular *Little Suite*. The first number is a little march, "Trumpeter and Drummer," bringing us a picture of parading soldiers. A tender lullaby for muted strings follows in "The Doll." The third part, "The Top," is an impromptu, violins imitating the sound of a spinning top while the woodwind present a lively dance tune. This is followed by "Little Husband, Little Wife," a dialogue between first violins and cellos. The suite ends with a vigorous galop for full orchestra entitled "The Ball."

1872. L'ARLÉSIENNE (THE WOMAN OF ARLES), two suites for orchestra:

No. 1: I. Prelude. II. Minuet. III. Adagietto. IV. Carillon.

No. 2: I. Pastorale. II. Intermezzo. III. Minuet. IV. Farandole.

On October 1, 1872, the Théâtre du Vaudeville in Paris offered Daudet's Provençal drama, *L'Arlésienne,* with incidental music by Bizet comprising twenty-seven numbers. Bizet's contribution to the evening's entertainment was not highly regarded. Francisque Sarcey, distinguished critic, dismissed the score as "in no respect integral to the work." The first night audience was hardly more appreciative, drowning out much of the music with chatter, coughing, and other noises. To Daudet, Bizet complained: "They're not even listening!"

Later the same year, Bizet took four numbers, rescored them for full orchestra, and presented them as a symphonic suite. When played at the Châtelet in November 10, 1872, the music aroused such enthusiasm that the Minuet movement had to be encored. The suite was repeated in 1873, twice in 1875, and once again in 1876. It became Bizet's first substantial success; and to this day, it is his most popular work for orchestra.

The Prelude is a stout march tune based on an old French Christmas song. It is varied a number of times, then followed by a pastoral episode for clarinets, and a sensual song for strings to brass and woodwind accompaniment. In the second movement, a minuet, the subject is sharply accented and vigorous rather than graceful; but a more lyrical interlude occurs in the trio section.

The Adagietto is a gentle melody for muted strings. The suite ends with a "Carillon," depicting a peasant celebration during the Feast of St. Eloi. A three-note bell chime is imitated by the horns to become the background for a dance melody, first presented by strings, then by other sections of the orchestra. After a short subdued interlude, the dance tune returns, once again accompanied by the bell-like sounds of the horns.

After Bizet's death, his friend Ernest Guiraud arranged four more numbers from the incidental music to *L'Arlésienne* into Suite No. 2. This one, however, has never proved as popular as the first. The most familiar numbers are the second and the fourth. The second is an Intermezzo with such religious feeling that it has been adapted into a famous religious song with a liturgical text in Latin—"Agnus Dei." The fourth is a vivacious Provençal dance.

1873. LA PATRIE, dramatic overture for orchestra, op. 19.

In 1873, Pasdeloup, conductor of the Concerts populaires in Paris, commissioned three French composers to write new symphonic works. Bizet was one of them; he complied with *La Patrie,* introduced in 1874. In writing this music, says Charles Pigot, Bizet had in mind "the misfortune of his vanquished country and the anguish by the Terrible Year. . . . Then, by a poetic license . . . he invoked the great and agonized spirit of Poland, still conquered . . . . It is this profound feeling, this dark and dolorous despair of the vanquished and this indelible love of the child for the wounded and violated mother which have been expressed . . . with nervous ferocity and with incomparable brilliance and vigor."

The overture opens with a strongly rhythmed march in full orchestra. After being repeated more softly, a stately melody is presented by the violins and woodwind, accompanied by double basses. A climax comes in full orchestra, then a momentary pause. Two more subjects are now introduced. The first is in violas and cellos accompanied by brass and double basses. The second appears in violas, clarinet, and English horn over muted violin arpeggios. The opening march music is recalled and dramatized, and the other themes are reviewed with enriched harmonies and instrumentation.

1875. CARMEN, lyric opera in four acts, with text by Henri Meilhac and Ludovic Halévy, based on Prosper Mérimée's story. First performance: Opéra-Comique, Paris, March 3, 1875.

Any discussion of *Carmen* makes it necessary to separate fact from fiction. While it is quite true that at the première *Carmen* gave little indication of becoming one of the most popular operas ever written, it was not, on the other hand, the kind of dismal failure some writers have made it out to be; nor is it true that Bizet's disappointment over the fate of his masterwork brought on a fatal heart attack. As a matter of fact, all things considered, *Carmen* did very well. It had thirty-seven performances in its first season—a particularly respectable figure when we take into account that the opera came late in the season. And apparently it had enough of a draw to encourage the management to restore it to the repertory of the following year. Choudens, the publisher, paid the impressive sum of twenty-five thousand francs for the score—which would hardly have been likely if the opera had been a fiasco. While the opera was severely criticized in many quarters, and on several different counts, it is also true that several influential critics and musicians spoke loud and clear in its favor. Vincent d'Indy described it as a masterwork. The critic of *Le Courier de Paris* said it was "one of those works which redound to the credit of a composer."

There was much both in libretto and music to shock and provoke attack in 1875. The realism of the play, the lurid characterization of the heroine, the sight of working girls smoking, the immoral suggestions in the story—all this was disturbing to a nineteenth-century audience. Bizet's music was regarded by some as too Wagnerian for French tastes; other denounced him for his use of Spanish melodies and rhythms, and for his efforts in other episodes to imitate a Spanish style.

But those very things that were denounced in 1873 are those that lift *Carmen* to the status of a masterwork, with few rivals in French opera. The text has a dramatic power new to opera, and mainly due to its naturalism and the authenticity of its character delineations. What Bizet's contemporaries regarded as Wagnerian in Bizet's writing was the dramatic truth of his vocal line, the richness and variety of his orchestral and harmonic invention, and the integration of music and play. The Spanish flavors with which Bizet so generously spiced his writing contribute no end to the authenticity of the background and setting. *Carmen* rings true both as drama and as music.

It must be remembered that Bizet wrote *Carmen* as an opéra-comique. The musical episodes were originally separated by spoken dialogue, which endows the work with a greater directness and simplicity; this is the way it is still performed at the Opéra-Comique in Paris. In most of the other of the world's theaters, *Carmen* is given with recitatives provided it by Ernest Guiraud. The elaborate ballet sequences which endow *Carmen* with operatic dimensions are also interpolations not intended by the composer.

The pictorial prelude to the first act is a summation of the action that follows. A festive melody for full orchestra brings up the picture of a holiday in Seville, with preparations made for a bull fight. A modulation, and several abrupt chords, introduce Escamillo's "Toreador Song"; it is heard first quietly in the strings, then more loudly in the orchestra. Quivering strings now suggest the fatal fascination Carmen exerts on men. The atmosphere becomes ominous; a powerful chord for full orchestra prognosticates tragedy.

The curtain rises on a public square in Seville in or about 1820. Soldiers are loitering about; a change of guard takes place; street urchins imitate the formal military procedures. Don José, a member of the guard, and his command captain, Zuniga, talk about the charms of the cigarette girls who work in the nearby factory. Recess hour brings them out into the square for a smoke. One of them is the seductive Carmen. She makes flirtatious overtures to Don José with the alluring strains of a Habanera ("L'amour est un oiseau rebelle"). This is a melody Bizet lifted bodily from Sebastian Yradier's song, "El Arreglito," in the mistaken belief it was a folk song. When she finishes her singing, Carmen tosses a flower at him. He picks it up furtively and conceals it in a pocket near his heart. The noonday respite now over, Carmen and the other girls return into the factory. Micaëla, Don José's sweetheart, arrives to bring him greetings from his mother ("Parle moi de ma mère"). With Don José, she recalls childhood days ("Ma mère, je la vois"). A hubbub within the factory breaks in upon this tender scene. The girls rush out with the news that Carmen has stabbed one of them. Carmen is seized and, with her hands tied, is put in Don José's custody. Seductively, Carmen suggests to Don José that they will soon meet in the disreputable tavern of Lillas Pastia for song, dance, and love-making ("Près des remparts de Séville"). Now completely under Carmen's spell, Don José frees her hands and allows her to make her escape.

The second-act prelude is based on the soldier's song, which Don José sings offstage in praise of the dragoons of Alcala. In the inn of Lillas Pastia, gypsy girls, Carmen, and Captain Zuniga are celebrating ("Chanson bohème"). Carmen learns from the Captain that Don José, put in prison for having allowed her to escape, is about to be released. The famous toreador, Escamillo, enters to the idolatrous acclaim of his admirers. He describes the excitement of a bullfighter's life in the popular "Toreador Song" ("Votre toast"). Escamillo and Carmen are ineluctably drawn to each other. After Escamillo leaves, smugglers contact Carmen, trying to get her to work for them. The off-stage singing of Don José sends them scurrying off. Carmen welcomes him warmly, sings to and dances for him, makes him more than ever the victim of her beauty. But a distant trumpet call reminds him he is still a dragoon. When he makes a move to fulfil his duty, Carmen taunts him until he passionately tears from his pocket the flower that she had once thrown at him, and that he has saved; at the same time he protests his great love in the "Flower Song" ("La fleur que tu m'avais jetée"). Captain Zuniga orders him to return to his barracks. José attacks his commanding officer, an act of disobedience that puts an end to his military career. José must now join Carmen and the smugglers in their illicit operations.

The third-act prelude is a gentle intermezzo for flute solo. The setting is the lair of the smugglers in a mountain pass. In a rousing chorus, they explain how they must be ever on the alert ("Écoute, écoute, compagnons"). Don José remembers mother and home nostalgically. His mood provokes Carmen to advise him bitterly that he should leave her for good. This suggestion so upsets José that he threatens to kill her if she ever makes it again. Gypsy girls now begin to tell fortunes with cards. In her "Card Song," Carmen foresees disaster ("En vain pour éviter"). After smugglers leave to carry their contraband goods through the pass, Micaëla comes in search of her beloved. Frightened, she entreats heaven for protection ("Je dis que rien ne m'épouvante"). A shot sends her into hiding. It has come from Don José's gun at the approach of a stranger, who turns out to be Escamillo. Recognizing each other as rivals for Carmen's love, they rush at one another with drawn daggers. Tragedy is averted by the return of the smugglers. Before Escamillo leaves, he invites the smugglers to be guests at his next bullfight in Seville. And now Don José must take his leave, too, for Micaëla has informed him his mother is dying.

It is the day of the bullfight. The fourth-act prelude speaks of the gay festivities attending the event. Its brilliant main melody is an adaptation of an actual Andalusian folk song and dance. Into the lively square, Escamillo and Carmen make their appearance. As she is about to enter the arena, Carmen is warned by her gypsy friends that Don José is nearby. Indeed, he soon makes his entry—ragged and disheveled. He pleads for Carmen's love and is contemptuously rejected. The sound of cheering within the arena arouses Don José's fury. When Carmen tries to brush him aside, Don José kills her with a dagger. The triumphant Escamillo emerges from his fight to find Don José weeping bitterly over Carmen's dead body.

The triumphant march of *Carmen* around the world started soon after its world première. In less than four years, it had been successfully produced in London, Vienna, Brussels, Naples, Florence, Mainz, St. Petersburg, and New York. The American première took place at the Academy of Music on October 23, 1878. It entered the repertory of the Metropolitan Opera during the first season of that company, in 1883.

When the centenary of Bizet's birth was celebrated in Paris in 1938, the Opéra-Comique gave the 2,271st presentation of *Carmen*. By 1959, it had been played there more than three thousand times.

ANTON BRUCKNER 1824–1896

Bruckner stood at the head of those composers who realized their creative destinies through Wagner. Bruckner was a man as simple as a peasant and as naïve as a child. He was also a profoundly religious man who worshiped not one but two deities, the other being Wagner. Up to 1863, he served God in his music with humility and reverence—in his Masses, psalms, the D minor Requiem, the B-flat major Magnificat, and numerous shorter sacred works for chorus. Then in 1863, he heard *Tannhaeuser,* his first experience with a Wagner opera—and he had found a new deity. He made a pilgrimage to Munich in 1865 to attend the première of *Tristan und Isolde*. After that, he was the most devoted of all Wagner followers. Following the première of *Parsifal* in Bayreuth, Bruckner sank to his knees, kissed Wagner's hand and exclaimed: "Master, I worship you!"

Wagner's impact led him to write symphonies with pronounced Wagnerian accents in harmony and orchestration. Bruckner sought to carry over to his symphonic writing (since he harbored no ambition for the stage) some of the grandeur, sublimity, symbolism and epical designs of the Wagnerian music drama. Even in his mature three Masses (D minor, E minor, and F minor), where he remained a man of God, he introduced many of Wagner's stylistic mannerisms.

Some regard Bruckner's nine symphonies as the most significant contribution to the literature in the period between Beethoven and Brahms. These people find here a nobility of thought, visions, and a mystic revelation of which no composer since Beethoven had been capable. Others, however, have an opposing view. They recognize not only how derivative Bruckner was from Wagner, but also how prolix he was, how bombastic, discursive, rhetorical, and at times prosaic. The controversy between these two factions is undoubtedly less bitter today than it was yesterday—but a residue still persists. A medium course, however, is now adopted by most discriminating music lovers. If there are weaknesses in Bruckner, and they are pronounced, they do not obscure the majesty and radiance of his speech whenever he was touched by inspiration.

The program annotator for the Cincinati Symphony Orchestra neatly balances the strength and weakness of Bruckner as follows: "His spirit embraced the world—therefore, he must perpetually be building microcosms, symphonic planetary systems. In the gravity of his melodies, their broad diatonic strength, is to be heard the noble simplicity of the man. There is something Gothic in his art, like a cathedral. The arches rise to such imposing heights before branching into the groined dimness above. A monumental unity pervades the edifice, despite the lack of unity in design and in detail—a defect discernible in many of the Gothic cathedrals of France, due to the centuries their construction occupied. . . . Though it has not the Shakespearean variety of Beethoven's symphonies, it [Bruckner's music] achieves a true greatness of spirit and of expression. Bruckner belonged to the heroic age, he was born out of his time. He should have been a contemporary of Palestrina, or of Bach. . . Bruckner's music can only be the possession of the few, for few possess the humility and the spiritual sensitiveness to feel it, to respond to that which the composer himself felt. These are the reasons why Bruckner is the idol of the mystics, the rallying point of many for whom much great music is meaningless because of its secular character."

H. C. Robbins Landon finds in Bruckner's orchestral works "the mighty procession" of Austrian musical culture, a kind of summing up of all that had transpired in Austrian symphonic music before Bruckner. He explains: "In the Bruckner orchestral works, there are powerful echoes of the great symphonic tradition: of Austrian Baroque, with gigantic fugues, proud trumpets, and rattling kettledrums; of Haydn's late Masses, which were miraculous fusions of the late Viennese classical style and the older contrapuntal forms; of the doom-ridden tremolos in the first movement of Beethoven's Ninth—an atmosphere to which Bruckner, trancelike, returns again and again. There are also traces of Schubert's lyricism, and many of Bruckner's second subjects bear the stamp of music's greatest song writer. In the scherzos, we have a continuation of the famous Austrian dance tradition, one that flourished in the German Dances and Minuets which Haydn, Mozart and Beethoven wrote (and were not ashamed of writing) for court balls and also for less formal occasions; this tradition turned into the early waltz (Josef Lanner) and, of course, the Strauss dynasty. In the orchestration of Bruckner's symphonies, there is always a strong undercurrent of a mighty organ. . . . Finally, his orchestration and his harmonic language owe a strong debt to Wagner."

Anton Bruckner was born in Ansfelden, in Upper Austria, on September 4, 1824. He received music instruction at the secular music school at St. Florian, where he stayed almost four years. He then completed a ten-month course of study to prepare for teaching. He held several teaching posts before he became, in 1848, organist at the Foundation of the St. Augustine monks. There his remarkable virtuosity at the organ attracted much attention. Soon after this appointment, he completed his first ambitious work, the Requiem in D minor.

After some additional music study in Vienna with Simeon Sechter and Otto Kitzler, Bruckner became the organist of the Linz Cathedral in 1856, holding this post for about a dozen years. In 1860, he began commuting regularly between Linz and Vienna. In the Austrian capital, he became musical director of a choral group. A seven-voice Ave Maria and the Mass in D were heard at the Linz Cathedral in 1861 and 1864 respctively. Having meanwhile made his first contact with Wagner's music, he now began veering toward new directions in his composition. His first mature symphony, in C minor, was completed in 1866.

In 1868, Bruckner established permanent residence in Vienna. There he taught theory and organ at the Vienna Conservatory (rising to full professorship in 1871) and played the organ at the court chapel. All the while, he worked industriously on composition. He was continually subjected to the most intense abuse and the most devastating criticisms from the anti-Wagner faction in Vienna; also from colleagues who regarded him as a boor and a sycophant. But in 1881, with the first performance of his Fourth Symphony in Vienna, he was acclaimed for the first time. From then on, his successes kept mounting. In 1891, the year in which he resigned from the Conservatory, he received an honorary doctorate from the University of Vienna. Soon after that, Emperor Franz Joseph bestowed on him an imperial insignia. Bruckner was working on his ninth symphony when he died in Vienna on October 11, 1896.

1864–1868. MASS IN D MINOR, for soprano, chorus, and orchestra.

MASS IN E MINOR, for eight-part chorus and wind instruments.

MASS IN F MINOR ("GRAND MASS"), for solo voices, chorus, and orchestra.

Next to the symphony, the most gratifying medium for Bruckner was the Mass, in which he spoke of his love for God with directness, and in which his innate mysticism was reflected. Bruckner completed his first Mass in 1864, two years before he produced his first mature symphony. It was the Mass in D minor in which he already revealed an originality of harmonic thought, and his later tendency towards ambiguous tonalities. His second Mass, in E minor, was completed in 1866. Here, as Donald Jay Grout notes, we find "the happiest fusion of neo-medieval and Romantic elements."

The F minor Mass, in 1868, was both in structure and content the most significant of Bruckner's works in this form; for this reason, it has come to be known as the "Grand Mass." This, Bruckner's last Mass, is "relatively simple, compact, and direct," wrote Paul Affelder, "free of most of the excessive weight and endless modulations found in the symphonies. The work is in six main sections, without any set numbers, all solos and ensembles being incorporated into the main body of each section. Though the score calls for four vocal soloists, chorus, and full orchestra, there are many places where Bruckner achieves an almost chamber music effect through the use of one or two soloists and a handful of instruments. One of the most beautiful of these is the 'Et Incarnatus est,' a solo for tenor with solo violin and viola obbligato."

Hans F. Redlich has explained that Bruckner's Masses—particularly that in F minor—are "conditioned by the militant faith of the Roman Catholic counter-Reformation, and fertilized by the potent traditions of devotional music from Palestrina . . . to Fux and Caldara." He further points out that the Masses provide us with a key to the understanding of Bruckner's symphonies "with their colossal dimensions and sudden contrasts of mood in their 'Gloria' and 'Credo' sections"; that the F minor Mass is a work of "Beethovenian dimensions . . . establishing a type of 'symphonic Mass' with an impressive blend of orchestra and chorus."

1873. SYMPHONY NO. 3 IN D MINOR ("WAGNER"). I. Maessig bewegt. II. Adagio quasi andante. III. Ziemlich schnell. IV. Allegro.

Bruckner's first symphony had been a dismal failure when introduced in Linz on May 9, 1868. Critics found it too complicated, too pretentious, too exacting on performer and listener. In an effort to make his second symphony, in C minor, (1872) more palatable and more easily assimilable,

Bruckner introduced pauses throughout the work to provide periods of respite; for this reason, this symphony was nicknamed in Vienna the *Pausensymphonie*. But Bruckner's strategy was ineffectual. The Vienna Philharmonic turned it down as "unplayable," and when Bruckner paid for its first performance, on October 26, 1873, in Vienna, most of the critics were still hostile, Eduard Hanslick describing it as "insatiable rhetoric."

Bruckner's third symphony was dedicated to Wagner, with the master's permission and gratitude. Because the symphony thus carried Wagner's name on it, and because Wagner spoke so favorably of it, the anti-Wagner faction saw to it that disaster met the work at every turn. Accepted by the Vienna Philharmonic, the symphony was dropped after the first rehearsal; the men in the orchestra refused to play it. One of the directors of the Vienna Conservatory maintained it deserved a place in a trash basket. When the symphony was finally heard—performed at a concert of the Gesellschaft der Musikfreunde in Vienna on December 16, 1877, the composer conducting—the work suffered a humiliating defeat. Many in the audience burst into guffaws, jeers, and shouts of indignation. The symphony had not progressed very far when some of the audience began to leave the auditorium. By the final movement only twenty-five people were left! One of those was young Gustav Mahler, who rushed up to the stage after the performance to congratulate Bruckner. "Let me be," Bruckner said gruffly, the tears streaming down his cheeks, "the people don't want to know anything of me."

Except for the way in which Bruckner used his brass instruments, and for an occasional melodic fragment, there is not much in this music to remind us of Wagner. In the first movement, the initial subject is divided into two sections. The first, in horn over tremolo strings, serves as an introduction; the second is given fortissimo by the entire orchestra. Twenty-four measures later, the second theme appears, divided between first violins and violas. The three-note motive with which this second subject opens, receives considerable attention in the development section. On the other hand, the extended coda devotes itself to the horn motive that opened the symphony. In the slow movement, cellos unfold a spacious melody after a two-measure introduction. Subsidiary thoughts appear later. These include a chorale-like passage for the strings, and a passing thought for violas accompanied by pizzicato strings. A huge climax is evolved after these ideas have been developed; but the movement ends in a passive vein.

In the Scherzo, a fanfare for horns serves as the principal theme, while the main subject of the trio is in the style of an Austrian peasant dance. The finale enters with a solemn introduction over an organ point in lowest strings. This idea is then thundered by the full orchestra, and developed with tremendous effect. The tempest subsides. Several soft rumbles in the kettledrums and a brief pause precede the second subject, which is an expressive melody for flute and clarinet in octaves.

1874. SYMPHONY NO. 4 IN E-FLAT MAJOR ("ROMANTIC"). I. Ruhig bewegt. II. Andante. III. Bewegt. IV. Maessig.

The Fourth Symphony brought its composer his first taste of success, though Bruckner had to wait for it a number of years after completing the work. When the eminent Viennese conductor, Hans Richter, saw the score, he was so taken with it that he was determined to introduce it at one of the concerts of the Vienna Philharmonic, which had turned down all of Bruckner's earlier symphonies. This took place on February 20, 1881, and proved a huge success. The audience was so enthusiastic that the composer had to be called to the stage repeatedly to take his bows.

This is the only symphony to which the composer gave a descriptive title, that of *Romantic;* but he did so two years after he had completed his score. "The term 'romantic,'" comments H. C. Colles, "is of such general significance that one wonders at it having been appropriated by one rather than by all his nine." Yet, Werner Wolff explains, "the word . . . had been used for this symphony in its most popular sense, meaning imaginative, unrestrained, nebulous and mysterious. Nostalgic revery is also called 'romantic,' at times, and this meaning, too, has been applied to the Fourth."

The romantic element that predominates throughout the symphony is not its sole unifying factor. In all the movements, except the slow one, there recurs the interval of a descending fifth; it is heard for the first time in the opening horn theme over tremolo strings. In all four movements, we find a consistent use of the so-called "Bruckner rhythm" (two quarter-notes followed by a triplet of quarter-notes in 4/4 time). This rhythm can first be recognized in the second theme of the first movement, which is stated by the full orchestra.

The romanticism of the symphony becomes most pronounced in the second movement, in the bucolic song for the cellos heard after two measures of muted chords for violins and violas. A chorale-like episode is the bridge to a second eloquent melody, in violas accompanied by plucked strings. The volume is increased, with a brass fanfare and sweeping string figures appearing at its peak. Then the emotion subsides. An expressive melody for strings fades away, and the movement ends with the ebbing sounds of plucked strings, and the rumble of kettledrums.

The main theme in the Scherzo is a hunting call for horn. The trio devotes itself mainly to the ebullient spirit and rhythms of an Austrian peasant dance. The finale is for the most part a summation of earlier material, though several new ideas are also introduced. Among the latter are an extended subject for woodwind and horns, with which the movement opens; a dramatic statement by full orchestra; and a delicate theme for flute and clarinets in octaves over a countertheme in the violas.

1881. SYMPHONY NO. 6 IN A MAJOR. I. Maestoso. II. Adagio; Sehr feierlich. III. Scherzo: ruhig bewegt. IV. Finale: bewegt doch nicht zu schnell.

Only two movements of this symphony (the middle ones) were performed in Bruckner's lifetime—on February 11, 1883, in Vienna. When Gustav Mahler directed all four movements with the Vienna Philharmonic on February 26, 1899, he gave the work with many cuts and revisions. The symphony as Bruckner wrote it was played for the first time in Vienna on December 13, 1901.

The following analysis was prepared by G. Werner Wolff: "The violins start with a clear-cut leggiero rhythm; violoncelli and double basses join in at the third measure with the really tonal principal theme. . . . The secondary melody, of lyric character, is a long chant in the violins, which have an ecstatic leap of the ascending ninth in the fifth measure. . . . There is a third motive, one measure long. It is quickly surrendered and gives way to a soft episode, the bridge to the working-out section. . . . The orchestration gains new features in the important part given to trombones and tuba. The coda, based on the subdominant, displays full radiance."

Of the Adagio movement, Wolff says: "The opening theme is as simple as it is consummate in form and expression . . . . The next theme, in the first violins, has a grave expression and classical air. The development is so concise in extent that one is almost tempted to look at this movement as following a scheme other than the sonata scheme. The recapitulation rather resembles a variation . . . and the coda once more displays Bruckner's unexcelled art in obtaining exquisite tonal effects by the simplest means."

The Scherzo, Wolff explains, "is not a typical Bruckner Scherzo at all. Its texture is woven of fine threads which could not stand any weight. Its most characteristic feature is a lack of main theme. At the beginning, instead of a main theme, we meet three contrasting motives, drawn together from the start. They stay united throughout the movement. . . . In the trio, the pizzicato of the strings, alternating with the horns, provides . . . a special fragrance. Woodwinds surprisingly quote the principal theme of the first movement of the Fifth Symphony."

Wolff finds an affinity between the finale and the Second Symphony. "The opening theme in the violins has the same unrest. . . . A short rhythmical 'signal' preannounces the nearing first theme. It is very decidedly set forth by the four horns in unison. This fanfare is proferred four times, and each time it is followed by heavily accented chords in the trumpets and trombones . . . The two-voiced melody is carried on mainly by the strings. After the next climax, a dotted rhythm in the oboes and clarinets appears unexpectedly, giving way to a new outbrust of the whole orchestra. Here we witness the appearance of a unique feature in Bruckner's creation: the trombones are given contrapuntal phrases which have an outspoken 'recitative' character . . . . A general rest stops this interesting development suddenly. . . . The recapitulation contains some measures in which the symmetry of periods interferes with the unfolding of natural power. . . . The coda is marked by continuous reiteration of the principal theme, to which a theme from the first movement is added."

1883. SYMPHONY NO. 7 IN E MAJOR. I. Allegro moderato. II. Adagio: sehr feierlich und langsam. III. Scherzo: sehr schnell. IV. Finale: Bewegt, doch nicht schnell.

Bruckner's Seventh Symphony brought the composer his greatest success during his lifetime, and remained after his death his most universally admired and frequently played composition. When Artur Nikisch conducted its first performance in Leipzig on December 30, 1884, the work received a fifteen-minute ovation. By 1886, the symphony had been heard and acclaimed in Hamburg, Cologne, Vienna, Graz, and Chicago; one year later, it was given in Berlin, Dresden, Budapest, and London.

The Seventh Symphony is even more intimately associated with Wagner than the Third, which had been dedicated to him. Indeed, the slow movement of the Seventh is often considered a lament for Wagner's death. Actually, Bruckner began sketching this movement a year before Wagner died; even so, the shadow of Wagner's death hovers over it, the movement having been completed on April 21, 1883, nine weeks after Wagner's passing. The use of "Wagner tubas" (something new for Bruckner) further points up the fact that this music and Wagner were inextricably bound up in Bruckner's mind.

This Adagio is surely one of the most eloquent dirges in symphonic music, finding Bruckner at the height of his inspiration and at the threshold of immortality. The main melody is presented at once by a choir of tubas, doubled by violas, divided cellos, and basses. A new section appears after the thirty-seventh measure. This features a poignant melody for the violins. This material is carried to a climax that becomes a monumental outpouring of grief. Then the opening dirge returns in the tubas, soon to be reinforced by the horns. The elegy ends with a last quiet reflection on this melody. "Here," says Lawrence Gilman of this movement, "the voice of Bruckner's grieving, of his tenderness, of his exalting praise, speaks out of this nobly musing and impassioned elegy with subjugating eloquence of beauty."

In the first movement, the principal theme is immediately given by cellos and first horn over violin tremolos. After a dramatic climax and a diminuendo, the second contrasting subject appears in oboes and clarinets. The third movement is a Scherzo, which opens with a gentle though strongly rhythmed figure in the strings, over which the trumpet soon offers the principal subject. The trio is brought on by soft rolls of the timpani, following which the violins engage the main melody.

In the finale, the initial subject in the violins bears a close resemblance to the opening theme of the first movement. The second main thought in this finale is a melody of religious character in first violins, accompanied by plucked strings in cellos and double basses. A vigorous restatement of both melodies carries the symphony to a triumphant conclusion.

1884–1892. TE DEUM IN C MAJOR, for soprano, chorus, and orchestra. PSALM CL, for soprano, chorus, and orchestra.

The *Te Deum* (1884) and the *Psalm 150* (1892) are Bruckner's two last major sacred works—and among his most significant. The former was introduced in an intimate performance mainly for the composer's friends (two pianos serving in place of an orchestra) on May 2, 1885, in Vienna. The *Psalm* was heard for the first time on November 13, 1892, also in Vienna.

In these two works, Bruckner is, in Neville Cardus's description "God intoxicated." Cardus continues: "He is lost to the world in worship. He does not supplicate. . . . And it is a wholesome intoxication. No fumes, no incense. There is no awareness of evil . . . nothing demoniac. His Catholicism is Austrian and as likeable and humane as Haydn's."

Edward Downes finds a kinship between these two works, eight years apart. "Both are expressions of ecstatic rejoicing, both use tremendous sonorous resources building to overwhelming dynamic climaxes. In both compositions the artistic intensity of the climaxes is given added richness and impetus through the contrapuntal devices of a double fugue."

1885. SYMPHONY NO. 8 IN C MINOR. I. Allegro moderato. II. Scherzo: allegro moderato; Langsam. III. Adagio: Feierlich langsam, doch nicht schleppend. IV. Finale: feierlich, nicht schnell.

The Eighth Symphony established Bruckner's success on an even firmer foundation than did the Seventh Symphony. The première in Vienna, on December 18, 1892, was a success of formidable proportions. Among the the wreaths showered on the composer after the performance was one by the Emperor (who later also contributed fifteen hundred florins toward the publication of the work). The Wagner Verein also sent a wreath, and Johann Strauss II a congratulatory telegram. Even Bruckner's arch-enemy, the critic Eduard Hanslick, who found much in the symphony to condemn, had to admit the concert was a triumph. "How was the symphony received?" he wrote. "Boisterous rejoicings, wavings of handkerchiefs from those standing, innumerable recalls, laurel wreaths."

In the first movement, explains Philip Hale, "the first and chief motive is given to violas, violoncellos, and double basses. It is announced pianissimo; it is decisively rhythmed, and its rhythm and its upward leap of a sixth are important factors in the developments. . . . The first violins have the expressive and questioning second theme. Woodwind instruments answer the question. The rhythm of the second theme, a rhythm that is characteristically Brucknerian, is used in counterpoint to a new cantilena sung by horn and first violins. . . . The working-out section . . . is at first free. . . . The first theme, now a lamentation, is given to the first oboe. The clarinet answers in another tonality. After bold modulations the second theme is repeated. . . . Grief soon loses its voice. The violins sigh the chief motive thrice pianissimo. Only the last portion of the theme is then heard, and it dies away in the violas."

In the second-movement Scherzo, "the chief theme (violas and violoncellos) has a rough humor, while the violins have a contrasting figure of a whispering and mysterious nature. . . . The Trio begins Langsam (slow), softly and delicately (first violins). . . . The whole section breathes smiling happiness."

The Adagio is one of the longest movements encountered in any symphony. "It begins, 'solemn, slow, but not dragging,' in D-flat major. The first violins sing (on the G string) a long and intimate song to the accompaniment of the second violins and lower strings. . . . The second theme is sung by the violoncellos and they lead to the serenely quiet song of the tubas. . . . Then appears suddenly, and in a decided manner, the rhythm for horns of the 'Siegfried motive' in the *Ring*. . . . There is a return to the prevailing tempo. The mood is milder. . . . The coda brings in a peaceful close."

In the Finale, there are three motives to the chief theme. "Joyful fanfares sound in D-flat. The whole is repeated, and there is a modulation from A-flat to E-flat. Then appears sonorously the conclusion of the whole theme in the prevailing tonality of C minor. Out of the counterpoint arises a lamenting strain for oboes. There is a pause. The melodious and religious second theme is sung in slower tempo. . . . The third theme, woodwind and strings, is practically a double theme, and the lower voice has more importance later. . . . A blend of the two preceding themes leads to a new melody for violins. . . . The repetition section opens powerfully. . . . The coda begins quietly, but it soon becomes intense. In the triumphant ending, in C major, chief themes of the four movements are heard exulting."

1894. SYMPHONY NO. 9 IN D MINOR. I. Feierlich misterioso II. Scherzo: bewegt, lebhaft. III. Adagio.

Bruckner lived to write only three movements of a ninth symphony, but he is believed to have confided to friends that if he did not survive to write the finale, his *Te Deum* (which see) could serve as a fitting conclusion. This is the way the Ninth Symphony was heard when introduced in Vienna on February 11, 1903, Ferdinand Loewe conducting. In addition to following Bruckner's instructions about interpolating the *Te Deum,* Loewe made drastic revisions in and did an elaborate editing of the other three movements. True Brucknerites regard Loewe's version as a desecration. Bruckner's original version was not heard until April 2, 1932, in Munich.

There is a sixty-two measure introduction to the first movement. Horns appear with the main subject over a string tremolo. A subsidiary idea for the woodwind, opening with a downward octave leap, gives a clue to the personality of the movement's main subject. This is soon given loudly and dramatically by the full orchestra. After a change of key from D minor to A major, a lyrical passage is heard in the strings. Muted violas and violins follow with a second beautiful thought. A horn theme brings on the second section of the movement, which consists of a fantasia and a recapitulation. The chief subject introduces the coda.

The second-movement Scherzo opens with a pizzicato theme for first violins. A roll of the kettledrums leads into the trio in which two new ideas are projected—the first in muted first violins, and the second in strings and oboes. The Adagio is in sonata form. A melody of somber cast is presented by the strings, supported by the brass. After a climax, first and second violins in unison give the second theme. These ideas are amplified in a section that culminates with a powerful statement of the first phrase of the main theme by the full orchestra. A pause precedes the concluding tranquil section. Momentarily, a phrase from the Adagio of Bruckner's Eighth Symphony (like some heavenly utterance) is recalled by tubas. Pianissimo chords for the brass end the symphony on an elegiac note.

JOHANNES BRAHMS 1833–1897

It is not difficult to understand why the pro-Wagner faction in Vienna should have directed their venom against Brahms, his admirers, and followers. The Wagnerians were promoting "the art of the future"—the new art form of the musical drama with its progressive techniques and aesthetics. In Brahms, they saw a composer who seemed to live in the past: who wrote eighteenth-century Serenades for orchestra; resuscitated the concerto-grosso structure in his Double Concerto; went back to the Baroque era in writing a passacaglia for the last movement of his Fourth Symphony and a fugue for his *Handel Variations* for piano; whose choral music, especially *A German Requiem,* followed the traditions of the sixteenth century; whose partiality for the variation form was a carry-over from the classical age: whose melodies were often grounded in the German folk song.

More damaging still, in the eyes of the true Wagnerite, was the fact that Brahms was ever faithful to the principles of a pure and objective art devoid of literary programs in the Liszt manner; true to the ideals of absolute music as opposed to the dramatic art of Wagner. Yet the truth of the matter is, as is stated in the *Outline of Music* edited by Sir Malcom Sargent: "The music of Brahms did not, as it were, refute or disprove the music of Liszt, nor vice versa; the two men supplemented each other. The art of each was a facet of music considered as a wide reality."

It is quite true that in his preference for classical structures, and his occasional deployment of a contrapuntal technique, Brahms belonged in the past. Brahms was no pioneer, no revolutionary. "He was," says H. C. Colles, "like Bach, merely the most weighty wielder of the forces which his times had inherited. . . . He had held to an ideal of his own, which in many respects ran counter to the ideals of his most powerful contemporaries; but he had entirely justified that ideal . . . because he had proved that to be true to it was the only way for him to say what was in him to say."

He combined a partiality for tradition and classicism and absolute music with a heart and spirit that belonged to the Romantic years. He succeeded in creating a fusion between past formal procedures and the released emotions and exalted poetic speech of his own times. In Brahms, classicism and Romanticism meet and become one.

Despite the frequent complexity of his technique, despite the subtlety of his intellectual processes, despite his formidable gift at structure, rhythm, and counterpoint, his point of departure was invariably the song. In song he found the voice of every shade of emotion he wished to express. It was toward the song that, in his instrumental works, his most effective climaxes reach; it was in the song that his profoundest thoughts and feelings, and his subtlest moods and thoughts were captured.

James Gibbons Huneker wrote: "A classicist and a romanticist, he [Brahms] led music in her proper channels by showing that a phenomenal sense of form and a mastery of polyphony second only to Bach are not incompatible with progress, with a faculty of uttering new things in a new way. . . . Brahms reminds one of those medieval architects whose life was a prayer in marble; who slowly and assiduously erected cathedrals, the mighty abutments of which flanked majestically upon mother earth, and whose thin, high pinnacles pierced the blue; whose domes hung suspended between heaven and earth, and in whose nave an army could worship, while in the forest of arches music came and went like the voices of many waters. . . . Whatever he wrought, he wrought in bronze and for time, not for the hour. He restored to music its feeling for form. He was the greatest symphonist in the constructive sense since Beethoven. . . . His nobility of utterance, his remarkable eloquence and ingenuity in treatment make you forget his shortcomings in color. . . . Brahms is the first composer since Beethoven to sound the note of the sublime. . . . A pure musician, a maker of absolute music, a man of poetic ideals is Brahms, without thrusting himself forward in the contemporary canvas. Not Berlioz, not Wagner, but the plodding genius Brahms was elected by destiny to receive upon his shoulders the mantle dropped by Beethoven as he ascended the slope to Parnassus, and the shoulders were broad enough to bear the imposing weight."

Johannes Brahms, the son of a double bass player, was born in Hamburg, Germany, on May 7, 1833. From his father he received his first instruction in music. After that, he studied the piano with Otto Cossel and Eduard Marxsen. Remarkably gifted, the young Brahms made fast strides. When he was fourteen, he gave a public concert, his program including his own variations on a folk song. After that, because of his family's poverty, he had to earn his living playing the piano in disreputable taverns—an experience believed to have adversely and permanently affected his emotional development and his relationship with women. He also taught the piano and did hack work. At the same time, he was developing himself as a pianist, and making serious foray into composition with songs, piano pieces, and his first piano trio.

In 1853, Brahms became piano accompanist for the Hungarian violinist, Eduard Reményi, with whom he toured Germany. It was through Reményi that Brahms first became interested in Hungarian and gypsy folk music, an influence that stayed with him to the end of his life. It was also through Reményi that Brahms first met and became friendly with Robert and Clara Schumann. Schumann emerged as Brahms's first powerful advocate. In an article for the *Neue Zeitschrift fuer Musik,* on October 28, 1853, Schumann pronounced Brahms a genius of German music. Schumann also used his influence to get some of Brahms's works published, including a number of songs, and three piano sonatas. The bond between Brahms and Schumann remained close up to the time of Schumann's death in 1856; after that, Brahms remained one of Clara Schumann's most devoted friends.

From 1857 to 1860, Brahms was part-time music master to Prince of Lippe-Detmold. During this period, he completed two orchestral serenades and his first piano concerto. From 1860 to 1863, Brahms led a chorus in Hamburg; and from 1863 to 1864, he directed the concerts of the Singakademie in Vienna. All the while his creativity was gaining in assurance and strength. The two piano quartets, between 1861 and 1862, the *Handel Variations* for piano in 1861, the B-flat major Sextet in 1862, and the F minor Piano Quintet in 1864, all pointed up a mastery of technique and maturity and individuality of style that led Joseph Hellmesberger, the distinguished Viennese musician, to describe him at that time as "Beethoven's heir."

After 1863, Brahms made his home in Vienna, the base from which he set forth on numerous trips. For several years, he helped support himself by teaching the piano. But expanding creative powers went hand in hand with financial success and public acclaim. *A German Requiem* and his *Hungarian Dances* went a long way to establish his popularity; his *Variations on a Theme by Haydn* and his first symphony put him in the front rank of orchestral composers of his generation. He now became the recipient of significant appointments and honors. From 1871 until 1874, he was the director of the Gesellschaft der Musikfreunde in Vienna. He received an honorary doctorate from the University of Breslau in 1879, was made Knight of the Prussian Ordre pour le mérite in 1886, was given the honorary freedom of the city of Hamburg in 1889, and in 1890, was conferred the Order of Leopold by the Emperor of Austria.

Though he loved several women, one of whom was Clara Schumann, he never married. Most of his mature years were spent in a simple three-room apartment in Vienna, while summer vacations were taken in nearby mountain resorts. While attending Clara Schumann's funeral in 1896, he contracted a cold which aggravated a sickness from which he had for several years been suffering, cancer of the liver. He attended his last concert on March 7, 1897 (a performance of his Fourth Symphony). Less than a month after that, on April 3, he died in Vienna.

1853. SONATA NO. 3 IN F MINOR, for piano, op. 5. I. Allegro maestoso. II. Andante. III. Scherzo. IV. Intermezzo. V. Allegro moderato ma rubato.

All three of Brahms's piano sonatas were the fruits of his youth, and only the third is a portent of future powers. Percy Grainger described the first movement as a "heaven-storming affair: bold, overpowering, austere and, for a youthful work, remarkably learned." A vigorous first theme and a melodious second one make up the basic thematic material, which is developed imaginatively and at times with immense power. The second movement suggests a serene moonlit landscape. "All is serene," says Grainger, "and every note sings until the sweetness of it almost cloys." The composer provided a clue to the mood and purpose of his music by appending over this music a brief quotation by C. O. Sternau: "The twilight glimmers, by moonbeams lighted; two hearts are here in love united, and locked in blessed embrace." In the Scherzo, this sentimental mood is shattered by vigorous music vitalized by discords. Breaking with tradition, Brahms interpolated a short fourth-movement Intermezzo into the sonata structure, which he gave the title of *Retrospect.* This is music of such solemn character that it is sometimes described as a funeral march. A tempestuous finale is characterized by forceful sonorities and skilful polyphony, with a lyrical second theme contributing emotional relief. The sonata ends with two extended codas.

1854. PIANO TRIO IN B MAJOR, op. 8. I. Allegro con brio. II. Allegro molto. III. Adagio. IV. Allegro.

The B major Trio is a fascinating curiosity. It was Brahms's first chamber music work, completed before he was twenty-one, and at a time when he had written nothing except the piano sonatas. It is full of youthful exuberance, of a heady spirit lending itself to discursiveness and emotional overindulgence. Brahms himself later described this music as "wild." Yet apparently there was something vital in this work—an incandescent spark that refused to burn out—which led Brahms to return to it thirty-six years later. Using some of his original material, Brahms rewrote three of the movements completely in 1890, changing a youthful conception into a work of his full maturity. In the revised version, the exuberance and emotional excesses are curbed; the rambling form is tightened and made more logical; the writing becomes concentrated. Brahms retained the basic opening material of each of the three movements, but produced new material for his secondary subjects. Only the

Scherzo movement did he allow to stay as it originally was, except for minor editing.

In the revised version, the first movement opens with a rhapsodic ascending melody first in piano alone, then four measures later in the cello. To counteract the youthful romanticism of this subject, Brahms produced in his revision a new second subject for the piano, this time a descending melody. It is more austere and objective than the first. The contrast between the ascent of the first theme and the descent of the second is further emphasized in the development; in the coda the two subjects are combined.

In the Scherzo, a vigorous staccato tune is given by the cello. A different mood appears in the trio, with a melody that sounds like a stately folk song.

A chorale-like episode for the piano is the first idea in the meditative slow movement. Before long, the violin and cello join in unaccompanied. Two extended episodes—which Brahms had originally written for this movement—were deleted to make way for an effective and concentrated middle section. Here the quiet revery of the opening remains unruffled.

The finale is consistently vigorous, even brusque, beginning with a robust theme for the cello, and continuing with a loud and forceful second subject.

1854. COMPOSITIONS FOR SOLO PIANO:
Variations on a Theme by Robert Schumann, op. 9.

4 Ballades, op. 10: I. D minor, "Edward." II. D major. III. B minor. IV. B major.

Soon after Schumann had been committed to an asylum, Brahms wrote a work in his honor originally entitled *Little Variations on a Theme of His, dedicated to Her*. The "his" was Robert Schumann; the "her," Schumann's wife, Clara. The theme was taken from Schumann's *Albumblatt,* op. 99, no. 1. It served for Brahms as the inspiration for a series of miniatures of varied feelings and moods. After Brahms had dispatched the work to Schumann, the latter was still lucid enough of mind to reply with appropriate comments: "How tender, how original in its masterly expression, how ingenious every one of them. . . . The third, the fourth, the fifth, and the sixth with its retrogression in the second part. The following Andante, how tender; the eighth, with its beautiful second part. Then the ninth, how beautiful in form; the tenth, how full of art, how tender; how individual and delicate, the eleventh, and how ingeniously the twelfth joins it! Then the thirteenth, with its sweet metaphysical tones, and the next Andante, with its witty and artistic canon in seconds, and the fifteenth in G-flat major, and the sixteenth beautifully and blessedly ending in F-sharp major."

Brahms took over the ballade form from Chopin. The first of the Brahms ballades is a setting of the famous Scottish poem, "Edward." This is music of tremendous power and at times with tragic accents. The second ballade is more contemplative, its main interest being melodic rather than rhythmic, and its principal subject a tender melody built from a three-note motive (F-A-F). The third, an intermezzo, was described by Peter Latham as a "picturesque elfin piece . . . highly effective when played with sufficient lightness of touch." In the fourth ballade we are "dreaming Schumann's dreams again, listening to those characteristic inner voices."

Almost half a century after opus 10, Brahms wrote a fifth ballade. It was in the key of G minor and included in opus 118 (which see).

1858. CONCERTO NO. 1 IN D MINOR, for piano and orchestra, op. 15. I. Maestoso. II. Adagio. III. Allegro non troppo.

In 1854, Brahms completed a four-movement sonata for two pianos which Clara Schumann described as "powerful, quite original, noble and clearer than anything before." Brahms's friend, Julius Otto Grimm, however, felt the need for an orchestra. Brahms took Grimm's advice by readapting the first two movements as movements of a piano concerto; discarding the third-movement Scherzo (some of whose material he would later use for *A German Requiem*), Brahms prepared a completely new finale. The concerto—Brahms's first large-scale composition—was heard for the first time in Hanover in 1859, with Brahms at the piano, and Joachim conducting. It was a failure; hissing was clearly audible from parts of the auditorium. Clara Schumann, however, was most enthusiastic. "Almost all of it sounds beautiful," she wrote a friend, "some parts more beautiful than even Johannes himself had imagined or expected. The whole thing is wonderful; so rich, so full of feeling and at times so well proportioned."

In its power and passion, in the treatment of the piano as an equal of the orchestra, and in the breadth and scope of its architectonic structure, Brahms's First Piano Concerto continues where Beethoven's piano concertos had left off. "Never before," said Walter Niemann, "not even in Beethoven, has any instrumental concerto struck such a wild note of passion and revolt, indeed of demoniac terror, as this first movement." Its first theme is an outburst in strings over a timpani roll. The piano appears after a diminuendo, continuing the material first heard in that orchestral preface. The piano alone then introduces the second theme, a chorale-like subject in F major, which the strings carry on. A vigorous episode in piano brings on the development section, which engages much of the material first heard in the orchestral introduction. A crescendo and four loud chords precede the recapitulation, which opens with the main theme in solo piano. A brilliant coda follows.

In his manuscript, Brahms fixed over the slow movement the line, "Benedictus qui venit in nomine Domine." For this reason, it is believed this movement was inspired by Schumann's death. There are three sections. In the first, we hear an eloquent melody in strings and bassoon; it is later taken over by the piano. A contrasting middle section is followed by a repetition of the first, with some modifications and changes.

The finale is a rondo, its first theme, an energetic subject in unaccompanied piano. The piano also presents a second theme in F major. A brief working out of this material precedes the recall of the first subject, in the piano, accompanied by plucked lower strings. The strings later appear with a new melody in B-flat major, which receives fugato treatment. Elaboration of these melodies, a cadenza, and an extended coda comprise the rest of the rondo.

1859–1889. SONGS, for voice and piano:

"Am Sonntag Morgen," op. 49, no. 1; "An die Nachtigall," op. 46, no. 4; "Auf dem Kirchhofe," op. 105, no. 4; "Dein blaues Auge," op. 59, no. 8; "Feldeinsamkeit," op. 86, no. 2; "Der Gang zum Liebchen," op. 48, no. 1; "Immer leiser wird mein Schlummer," op. 105, no. 2; "Der Jaeger," op. 95, no. 4; "Das Maedchen spricht," op. 107, no. 3; "Die Mainacht," op. 43, no. 2; "Meine Liebe ist gruen," op. 63, no. 5; "Minnelied," op. 71, no. 5; "Nicht mehr zu dir zu gehen," op. 32, no. 2; "O wuesst ich doch den Weg zurueck," op. 63, no. 8; "Sapphische Ode," op. 94, no. 4; "Der Schmied," op. 19, no. 4; "Staendchen," op. 106, no. 1; "Therese," op. 86, no. 1; "Der Tod, das ist die kuehle Nacht," op. 96, no. 1; "Vergebliches Staendchen," op. 84, no. 4; "Von ewiger Liebe," op, 43, no. 1; "Wie bist du, meine Koenigen," op, 32, no. 9; "Wiegenlied," op. 49, no. 4:

Brahms is in the company of the greatest creators of the Lied. Standing as he does between Schubert and Schumann on the one hand, and Hugo Wolf on the other, he emphasizes in some of his songs the lyric line, while in others, the dramatic one. Many of Brahms's songs are melodic gems in the class of Schubert—the highly popular "Wiegenlied," for example (1868). Many have a folk-song simplicity and wholesomeness, as the familiar "Vergebliches Staendchen" (1881). Many are endowed with Schumannesque expressiveness of accompaniment, as "Die Mainacht" (1868), where the piano seems to move independently of the vocal line, gaining all the while in tenderness and emotion.

On the other hand, numerous Lieder look ahead to Hugo Wolf, in the declamatory character of the melodic line, in their attempt to unfold a miniature drama, and in the richness of harmonic and rhythmic language. Frequently Brahms's writing becomes unvocal as he gives preference to drama over lyricism. More effective for their dramatic force than for loveliness of melody or sensitivity of mood are songs like "Von ewiger Liebe" (1868) and "Der Tod, das ist die kuehle Nacht" (1886).

"It is astonishing," notes the famous singer Elisabeth Schumann, in *German Song,* "how . . . a firm grasp of classical style goes hand in hand with some of the most finely drawn characterizations and psychological insight; even more than in the others it is strikingly evident in 'Nicht mehr zu dir zu gehen (1864), with its almost neurasthenic suggestion." Elisabeth Schumann also remarks how, even in his dramatic songs, Brahms "remains true to his romantic self. Text which are too realistic or which, like ballads, recount actual happening did not appeal to him. Even among the lyric poems he selected those in which the romantic mood does not unduly stress any expression of intimate feeling. . . Brahms was no lover of what has come to be called 'tone-painting,' and in most of his songs, as in other music, shunned the imitation of bird song or other sounds of Nature. Only once or twice in the merry or humorous songs, which he regarded rather as jests, did he swerve from that principle. . . . In the charming song, 'Therese,' (1878), the humming of a shell held to the ear . . . [is] convincingly presented."

Elisabeth Schumann feels that Brahms's love of Nature carries him to the loftiest heights in his songs. "Many of his most splendid songs bear witness to this. As one instance, 'Feldeinsamkeit,' (1878) is a magical evocation of idyllic peace and a spirit merged in Nature's own. No one has expressed that in nobler music than Brahms."

"It was Brahms's sense of detail, warmed by his great melodic gift," wrote Philip Radcliffe, "that enabled him to continue in the classical tradition with such success; the emotional range and the literary sensitiveness of his songs may have been limited, but their musical value is of the highest, and few songwriters have maintained so consistent a standard."

1859. SERENADE NO. 2 IN A MAJOR, for wind instruments, violas, cellos, and basses, op. 16. I. Allegro moderato. II. Vivace. III. Adagio non troppo. IV. Quasi menuetto. V. Allegro.

Brahms's first Serenade, in D major, op. 11 (1858) is early Brahms, and for the most part immature Brahms. Though the second Serenade came only two years after that, we here confront the fully ripened artist, since Brahms returned to this music in 1875 for extensive revisions. Brahms was particularly partial to this work. He told Joachim: "I have seldom written music with such delight."

Both serenades are efforts to revive a form that had flourished with Haydn and Mozart. Where Brahms's first Serenade is an obvious reversal to the old Viennese and rococo styles, and maintains its classical posture, the second is Brahmsian in its subdued tone colors (made all the more somber through the elimination of violins in the scoring), the gravity of its thematic content, and the romanticism of its feelings. In the first movement, clarinets and bassoons present the first theme. After a brief development, the clarinets arrive with a livelier subject in thirds. The second-movement Scherzo is the most Brahmsian in this work, particularly in its use of cross-rhythms. Two characteristic Brahms themes make up the fabric of the opening section; a third, in the trio, is given in unison by clarinets and bassoons over a persistent scherzo rhythm.

The slow third movement, which Donald Francis Tovey regards as "one of the most elaborate things Brahms ever wrote," is structurally a chaconne. The ground bass shifts from key to key. The flute and clarinet are heard in a tender melody over a slow rhythm in the strings. After a middle intermezzo episode, highlighting a poignant passage for the winds, the opening dreamy melody returns.

The fourth movement, a minuet, is sometimes omitted from present-day performances. Here we encounter a restrained humor in the halting and broken rhythms. The good humor persists into the finale, a rondo, whose first theme is offered by the clarinets, with the oboe replying in triplets. The second subject appears canonically in clarinets and bassoons. A piccolo is here added to the orchestration. Tovey says it "is used with a recklessness about which Brahms does not seem to have felt squeamish."

1861–1862. PIANO QUARTETS:

G minor, op. 25. I. Allegro. II. Intermezzo. III. Andante con moto. IV. Rondo alla zingarese.

A major, op. 26. I. Allegro non troppo. II. Poco adagio. III. Poco allegro. IV. Allegro.

Brahms made his debut as composer in Vienna with these two piano quartets, the first completed in 1861, the other, one year later. These are Brahms's first significant chamber-music works. Nevertheless, when both quartets were introduced—by three members of the Hellmesberger Quartet with Brahms at the piano—most in the audience, and some of the critics, were more interested in Brahms's pianism than in his music. The first piano quartet was even found to be "gloomy, obscure, and ill developed."

To Donald Francis Tovey, the first movement of the G minor Quartet is "one of the most original and impressive tragic compositions since the first movement of Beethoven's Ninth Symphony." He goes on to say: "The association of the two themes . . . one in G minor, the other in B-flat, produces an astonishing dramatic result when, after the development section, the recapitulation begins, not with the first of the pair, but with the second in the sunniest G major. Still more astonishing is the transformation of the whole latter half of the enormous processing of triumphant and tender 'second-subject' themes in D major into tragic pathos in G minor; an operation on a scale unprecedented in classical music."

The second movement is an intermezzo, which usurps a place sometimes assumed by a Scherzo. This is one of the first movements in Brahms's characteristic intermezzo style. Niemann described this movement as "full of troubled excitement, throbbing as though with the incessant breaking of an agonized heart, at the same time capricious and bleak." The slow movement, written in memory of Robert Schumann, is the first of Brahms's richly poetic and romantic utterances, beginning with a broad melody and finding contrast in a middle animated section with a march-like subject. Hungarian gypsy melodies and rhythms endow the finale with its dashing vigor and arresting colors.

Brahms himself was more partial to his second piano quartet. Structurally, it differs from the first in that fragmentary motives are used in place of fully developed melodies. In the first movement, there is a departure from the norm in the development section which features three variations on the main subject. Toward the end of this movement, the thematic material is built up with such passion that Donald Francis Tovey describes this music as Wagnerian. The slow movement—in free rondo form—is a brooding nocturne whose "long drawn-out sweetness," says Peter Latham, is leavened by "a mysterious passage with arpeggios for the piano." The scherzo is made up of two themes, while the trio employs some effective canonic writing. The powerful rhythmic momentum and the robustness of thematic material characterizing the finale of the first piano quartet can also be found in the closing movement of the A major. But here, as Karl Geiringer remarks, "the Hungarian fire . . . is quenched by a touch of the Viennese spirit."

1861–1863. SOLO COMPOSITIONS FOR PIANO:

Variations on a Theme by Handel, op. 24; *Variations on a Theme by Paganini,* op. 35.

With Brahms, the technique of writing variations achieves new subtlety and complexity. He is not satisfied merely to change his basic melody by adding figurations, or making alterations in tempo, rhythm, or melodic line the way the classicists did. Brahms frequently takes a rhythmic pattern or the turn of a phrase in his melody as the starting point from which to embark on extended creative wanderings. It is often difficult to discover the original melodic idea in these radical transformations and transfigurations.

The *Handel Variations* (1861) comprise twenty-four variations capped off by a magnificent fugue. The melody that is subjected to Brahms's imaginative transformations comes out of Handel's Suite in B-flat. "What Brahms has done with this straightforward tune," explains William Murdoch, "is almost beyond comprehension. New technical inventions abound; changes of fancy, mood and rhythm. Every page teems with original ideas, yet all these devices are logically produced."

The *Paganini Variations* (1863) are based on the familiar melody from the twenty-fourth Caprice. There are thirty-five variations in all (gathered in two sets); Brahms described these as "etudes." This is a brilliant tour de force for the piano. "All Brahms's skill in writing pianistically difficult passages—runs in thirds, sixths, and octaves, passages with both hands in rhythmically contrary motion, glissandi and tremendous stretches—is here brought into play in order to exhibit the pianist's virtuosity," writes Karl Geiringer. But of greater musical than technical interest are the eleventh variation from the first set, and the fourth and twelfth variations in the second. Many concert performers today prefer deleting some of the variations with weaker musical content, and combine the best numbers from each of the two sets into a single one.

1862. STRING SEXTET IN B-FLAT MAJOR, op. 18. I. Allegro ma non troppo. II. Andante ma moderato. III. Allegro molto. IV. Poco allegretto.

Brahms was the first significant composer to write a string sextet (two each of violins, violas, and cellos). He completed two such compositions. With the first of these, in B-flat major—written in the composer's twenty-ninth year—he made a significant stride away from apprenticeship towards maturity. There may be pages here betraying the influence of Haydn, Mozart, Beethoven, and Schubert. But as Daniel Gregory Mason suggested, "the change in point of view is more striking than the influences it makes room for." A pronounced individuality is asserted in at least two of the three principal themes of the first movement, all with the personality of a waltz, and one (A major) suggesting the Laendler style of Schubert. The first dance subject is heard at once in first cello. A triplet figure in the first violin leads to the second waltz-like theme, in the violins, first viola, and cello, over plucked strings in the other instruments. The first cello presents the third melody. Besides the individuality of the thematic writing, a new sense of solidity is found in the structure of this movement. "Here," explains Mason, "the transitions are so flowing that we pass easily back and forth and our final impression is no less satisfying for its unity than for its variety."

The second movement opens with a simple two-part melody for the viola. Each part is repeated. Six variations follow, with the melody returning in the cello before the concluding coda.

There is both energy and good humor in the Scherzo. It begins with a refrain for first cello, then progresses to a lyrical subject in first violin and viola. Though the two main subjects of the rondo finale are lyrical and tender, some of the effervescence of the Scherzo is carried over. The first subject in this finale is presented by the cello, and the second by first violin and first viola.

1864. PIANO QUINTET IN F MINOR, op. 34. I. Allegro non troppo. II. Andante un poco adagio. III. Allegro. IV. Poco sostenuto.

Though coming comparatively early in Brahms's career, the Piano Quintet is one of his supreme achievements in chamber music. Brahms experimented a long time before the work assumed a format he wanted. Originally, he wrote it as a string quintet (with two cellos). Then he rewrote it as a sonata for two pianos. Clara Schumann now convinced him of the need for strings. Brahms went ahead and revamped the music into its final shape, as a piano quintet.

Though the first movement is comparatively short (about three hundred measures in all), it is made up of no less than five themes. The most prominent is a somewhat melancholy refrain for piano and strings, and a broad expressive melody for strings over piano figures. A homogeneous texture is usually achieved by setting the stage for a new subject in the cadence of a preceding one, the most effective of these "preparations" taking place just before the recapitulation. The movement as a whole has breadth and strength, to which the simple eloquent slow movement comes as a striking contrast. Here a melody of Schubertian sweetness and poignancy hovers gently over a light rhythm. Daniel Gregory Mason likens this music to a "meadow brook, now forgetting its current in eddies and pools, now passing more strongly into a cadence—at the end broadening into the coda as into a tranquil basin of brown pebbles and golden sands." The Herculean power of the first movement returns in the Scherzo. Its three themes are sharply contrasted in rhythm and tonality; an opulent melody unfolds in the trio section. The finale is the longest and most complex of the four movements. It opens with a somewhat brooding introduction, but the light and vivacious opening theme for the cello, accompanied by sixteenth-notes in the piano, dispels the clouds once and for all. With a second syncopated subject and a boisterous working-out of both themes, the music remains consistently optimistic, heading relentlessly toward a monumental climax.

1865. STRING SEXTET IN G MAJOR ("AGATHE"), op. 36. I. Allegro non troppo. II. Allegro non troppo; presto giocoso; Tempo primo. III. Poco adagio. IV. Poco allegro.

Donald Francis Tovey considers the G major Sextet as "the most ethereal of all Brahms's larger works." It is also one of his most romantic, and with good cause. It was written as the aftermath of a love affair with Agathe von Siebold; this is the reason why this work is sometimes identified as the *Agathe Sextet*. The young lady appears in the first movement in the principal theme —in a motive spelling out her name by using the notes of A, G, A, H (H being the German for B-natural), and E. This first movement, in the description of Eugene Goossens, "opens after two introductory measures of viola figuration with a wistful first subject which undergoes a lengthy preliminary exposition. . . . A deliciously suave second subject, in the dominant, is later announced by the . . . violins, duly followed by a long development section. Much use is made of the introductory viola figure, imparting a flowing character to the entire movement, which ends with three energetic chords."

The second movement is a Scherzo, whose opening theme is a simple melody in upper strings. This is followed by a triplet figure which is prominent throughout the movement. The trio is a presto section, which Goossens describes as "rollicking." This part consists of a theme and five variations, all of them in E minor. This music "proceeds in an unbroken flowing line until the sudden appearance of an animated fugato section, ushered in . . . forte. This eventually merges into a return of the opening tranquil mood, but this time woven in a mesh of elaborate figuration which rises to an intense climax and falls away to a remote ending."

A precipitous subject in sixteenth-notes sets the finale into motion. This is the material out of which most of the movement is constructed. A secondary theme has passion and intensity. "These two contrasting subjects build up an ingenious movement of considerable animation," Goossens explains. "A coda, much faster in tempo than what has preceded it, brings the work to a brilliant conclusion."

1865. WALTZES, for solo piano (also for piano four hands), op. 39: 1. B major. 2. E major. 3. C-sharp minor. 4. E minor. 5. E major. 6. C-sharp major. 7. C-sharp minor. 8. B-flat major. 9. D minor. 10. G major. 11. B minor 12 E major. 13. B major. 14. G-sharp minor. 15. A-flat major. 16. C-sharp minor.

Brahms admired the popular waltzes of Johann Strauss. It is a familiar anecdote how, one day, autographing Mme. Strauss's fan he quoted a few measures from *The Blue Danube* adding, "unfortunately—not by me." However, the sixteen waltzes in opus 39—originally for piano four hands, then transcribed by the composer for piano solo—are more Schubertian than Straussian. The composer himself conceded this by saying that these pieces were "innocent waltzes in Schubertian form." Most of the waltzes are Viennese in their charm and Gemuetlichkeit. Some have the warm blood of Hungarian gypsy music. The last waltz is thoughtful and moody in double counterpoint.

The most celebrated piece in the set is the graceful waltz in A-flat major, the fifteenth in the group, which David Hochstein transcribed for violin and piano (in A major).

Eduard Hanslick, to whom these waltzes were dedicated, described them as follows: "What bewitching, lovely strains! Naturally, nobody would look for real dance music, but for waltz melodies and rhythms handled in free artistic forms. . . . In spite of this, no artificial affectation jars on us in them, no overrefined detail to blur the impression of the whole—a simple ingenuousness informs them all, to an extent which we should hardly have expected. The waltzes . . . make no sort of pretentions to size; they are all short and have neither introduction nor finale. The characteristics of the individual dances sometimes approximate the lilting Viennese waltz. . . Towards the end of the book we hear, as it were, the clank of spurs, first softly, and as though tentatively, then with growing fire and resolution—without question we are now on Hungarian soil. . . . This Magyar temperament breaks forth with vehement energy; the accompaniment is no longer the peaceful ground bass of Strauss's orchestra, but the passionate clang of cymbals. . . . Reverting to the mood of the Austrian Laendler, he closes with a short and enchantingly seductive piece; a gracefully lulling air above an expressive middle part, which appears without modification in the second section as the higher part, while what was before the principal melody becomes the inner part."

1865. TRIO IN E-FLAT MAJOR, for horn, violin, and piano, op. 40. I. Andante. II. Scherzo. III. Adagio mesto. IV. Allegro con brio.

Brahms's only horn trio is elegiac music for which the mellow, at times lugubrious, voice of the French horn is particularly suited. Brahms is believed to have written this work as a memorial to his mother. It opens unorthodoxly with a rhapsodic slow movement in place of an Allegro in sonata form. An emotional melody is three times repeated; between each repetition there comes a stormy episode. After the spirited Scherzo, which also has suggestions of melancholy, there appears one of the most deeply felt pages Brahms wrote during this period; it is probably here that Brahms expresses his grief at his mother's passing. The main subject is based on an old German chorale, "Wer nur den lieben Gott lasst walten." This slow movement is directly linked with the finale. "Like an exquisite promise in the quiet solemnity of the Adagio messo," says Karl Geiringer, "the idea introduced in [the slow movement] soon reveals itself as an allusion to the main theme of the finale. Brahms might have done this in an effort to create a more organic union between the somber first, second and third movements and the finale, which is full of the joy of life."

1868. EIN DEUTSCHES REQUIEM (A GERMAN REQUIEM), for soprano and baritone solos, chorus, and orchestra, op. 45.

It took Brahms eleven years to complete this, his greatest choral work, and the most celebrated requiem in the German language. The plan to write a requiem first took root with him with Robert Schumann's death in 1856. For the time being, Brahms produced little more then sketches; at the same time, he completed a movement for a projected symphony that never materialized. This material was incorporated years later into the second section of his Requiem. Then in 1865, upon the death of his mother, Brahms once again felt the emotional and artistic need to sublimate his grief in memorial music. Returning to his projected Requiem of a decade before, he now completed all the parts except the fifth section by 1866; that fifth section came two years after that.

Three movements from the Requiem were given for the first time anywhere on December 1, 1867, in Vienna. In a performance that left much to be desired, this performance was hissed. When on April 10, 1868, all but the fifth movement (still to be written) was heard under Brahms's direction in Bremen, the success was unmistakable. "Never had the enthusiasm been so great," reported Albert Dietrich. "The effect . . . was simply overwhelming and it at once became clear to the audience that *A German Requiem* ranked among the loftiest music ever given to the world." The first complete performance that included the fifth section also proved a triumph. This took place in Leipzig on February 18, 1869.

Brahms's Requiem is called *German* because the composer used a German text instead of the traditional Latin one from Catholic liturgy encountered in other famous Requiems. Brahms prepared his own text, drawing his material from the Lutheran Bible. Where other famous Requiems are solemn Masses for the dead, fluctuating between sorrow and terror, Brahms's is slanted not towards the dead but towards the living. It has challenge and defiance, and with them gentle solace and peaceful resignation, at times even hope. Though inspired by the death of two people closest to Brahms, this is not music of sorrow. It has, as Rosa Newmarch points out, a "more universal intention." Brahms wanted the work to "bring comfort to all, irrespective of creed and race."

The opening chorus, "Blessed are They that Mourn" (Poco andante, e con espressione), is permeated with serenity. A fourteen-measure orchestral introduction (the colors darkened through the absence of violins) leads to the opening chorus, which enters calmly, then engages the orchestration in an exalted dialogue. The second section, "All Flesh Is As the Grass" (Moderato, in modo di marcia), begins with a march-like subject in triple time over a kettledrum throb. The mood brightens with the words "Now Therefore Be Patient," but the solemn march-like music soon returns. Here the final episode, "The Redeemed of the Lord Shall Return," is an outburst of triumphant feelings. This section, however, ends quietly, as the opening phrase is repeated in the winds over a double pedal, and the chorus intones the words, "Joy Everlasting."

The third section, "Lord Make Us to Know Mine End" (Andante moderato), is for solo baritone, chorus, and orchestra. The baritone presents a poignant plea for guidance—the only part of the Requiem that is touched with sorrow—to receive a choral reply in the form of a forceful fugue.

The fourth part, "How Lovely Is Thy Dwelling Place" (Con moto moderato), is one of the best loved in the entire work. It opens and closes with a sublime meditation; midway, there is heard a fugal interlude.

The fifth section, "Ye Now Are Sorrowful" (Andante), maintains this elevated character. A gentle orchestral prelude is followed by the comforting strains of a soprano solo and the equally reassuring words of the chorus.

There follows a section for baritone solo, chorus, and orchestra, "Here On Earth We Have No Continuing City" (Andante; Allegro). First comes the forceful prophecy of the coming Resurrection, in the baritone; then a monumental double fugue in praise of God to the words "Worthy Art Thou to Be Praised."

The Requiem concludes on a note of exaltation with "Blessed Are the Dead" (Feierlich). "Towards the close of this number," Rosa Newmarch explains, "the music is logically linked up with the opening chorus by the reappearance of its basic theme, and the codas of the first and last movements, with the peaceful and conciliatory tones of the harp, and the softly fading triplet figures, are identical."

1869–1880. HUNGARIAN DANCES, four books for piano duet (first two books also for piano solo): 1. G minor. 2. D minor. 3 F major. 4. F minor. 5. F-sharp minor. 6. D-flat major. 7. A major. 8. A minor. 9. E minor. 10. E major. 11. C major. 12. D minor. 13. D major. 14. D minor. 15. B-flat major. 16. F minor. 17. F-sharp minor. 18. D major. 19. B minor. 20. E minor. 21. E minor.

Brahms first became acquainted with Hungarian folk songs and dances through Eduard Reményi, the Hungarian violinst, with whom he toured as accompanist in 1853. Brahms never lost his pleasure in these sensual melodies and exciting rhythms. We frequently encounter them even in his major works.

In 1869, Brahms published two volumes of Hungarian Dances for piano duet, each book containing five pieces. Three years later he adapted them for piano solo. It is with this publication that Brahms realized his greatest success up to that time. The melodies were all borrowed; but they became so revitalized in Brahms's fresh and imaginative treatment that this music sounds as much Hungarian as it does Brahms-like. Indeed, in spite of the immense public acclaim given to this publication, Brahms was severely condemned by some musicians and newspapers for "plagiarism." This was in spite of the fact that Brahms had done everything humanly possible to make it clear he was an adaptor. The phrase "arranged for the piano" appeared prominently on the title page. In addition, Brahms refused to assign them an opus number to avoid possible confusion with his own compositions. He told his publisher, Simrock, that he was presenting these dances to the world "as genuine gypsy children which I did not beget but merely brought up with bread and milk."

Brahms produced two more volumes of *Hungarian Dances,* this time for piano duet alone, in 1880. In addition, Brahms orchestrated three dances from his first book (Nos. 1, 3, and 10.) All the other dances from the four books were orchestrated by others: Nos. 2, 4, and 7 by Andreas Hallén; Nos. 7 through 21, by Dvořák; the remainder by Albert Parlow. Some of these dances have been transcribed for orchestra by Walter Goehr, and Leopold Stokowski; Joseph Joachim arranged them for violin and piano.

The fifth dance, in F-sharp minor, is undoubtedly the most celebrated of the set, with its passionate gypsy tune over a strongly asserted rhythm. A similar kind of vivacity and abandon can be found in the familiar seventh dance, in A major. A more languorous, sensual mood is confronted in the first dance, in G minor, and the sixth, in D-flat major; and a lighter and more graceful style appears in the nineteenth dance, in B minor, and the twenty-first, in E minor. "He has maintained and preserved the essential, individual features of gypsy music in his musical idiom: the dances sound like original Hungarian folk music," wrote Walter Niemann. He added: "They are pure nature music, full of unfettered, vagrant roving spirit, and a chaotic ferment, drawn straight from the deepest wellsprings of music by children of Nature."

1869–1871. LIEBESLIEDER WALTZES, for vocal quartet and two pianos, op. 52.

ALTO RHAPSODY, for alto voice, male chorus, and orchestra, op. 53.

SCHICKSALSLIED (SONG OF FATE), for chorus and orchestra, op. 54.

TRIUMPHLIED (SONG OF TRIUMPH), for chorus and orchestra, op. 55.

It would be difficult to find in the catalog of any other composer an instance where two compositions, one written right after the other, are so different in mood and purpose as the *Liebeslieder* waltzes and the *Alto Rhapsody*. The waltzes (verses by Daumer) are light and infectious, as carefree as youth; here is reflected Brahms's admiration for the waltz music of Schubert and Johann Strauss. Strange to say, this airy, graceful, and joyous music came from a man who, in 1869, was beset by mental anguish. For a time, Brahms had harbored a secret passion for Clara Schumann's daughter, Julie. When Julie became engaged to another man, Brahms was plunged into despair. This despondency, so completely denied in the waltzes, apparently was canalized in to the *Alto Rhapsody,* a setting of three of eleven verses from Goethe's somber poems about solitude, the *Harzreise im Winter*. This poem was the aftermath of Goethe's wanderings in the Harz mountains, in whose bleak surroundings he found a visual image of his own torment. Brahms, too, unspeakably lonely after the loss of Julie, reacted personally and vibrantly to the Goethe poems. "It shook me by the deeply felt grief of its words and music," commented Clara Schumann. The utter despair of a lonely man is found in the first two verses, where the alto is accompanied by orchestra. But in the third verse, where the chorus participates, accompanied by horns, hope displaces gloom; and just before the end of the work, hopes gives way to a radiance proclaiming the victory of the human spirit over the anguished heart.

Five years after completing his *Liebeslieder* waltzes, Brahms prepared a similar set of pieces for vocal quartet and piano duet—the *Neue Liebeslieder,* op. 65.

The success of *A German Requiem* provided Brahms with the stimulus for writing other choral compositions. Though none is of the size or scope of the Requiem, some are among the composer's ripest fruits. Two came three years after the Requiem; one of these, the *Song of Fate,* is sometimes described as Brahms's "little Requiem." Albert Dietrich, Brahms's friend, has left a record of how this music came to be born. Brahms and Dietrich were on a trip to the naval port of Wilhelmshaven, during the summer of 1868. "On the way, our friend, who had hitherto been so lively, became silent and grave. He told us that early in the morning . . . he had found Hoelderlin's poems in the bookshelf, and had been profoundly impressed by the *Schicksalslied.* Later on, after we had wandered about and inspected all the interesting things, while we rested on the shore, we discovered Brahms in the far distance sitting alone by the sea and writing. He was making the first sketch of the *Song of Fate.*"

The *Song of Fate,* like the Requiem before it, deals with "the eternal contrast between life and death," Walter Niemann explains, "between the cruel sufferings of struggling mankind and the gods enjoying celestial peace and bliss, between the uncertain and the transitory on the one hand and the eternal on the other." An eloquent prelude in E-flat major (in which Max Kalbeck sees a picture of the sea with its boundless horizon) precedes the first section. Here the beatific existence of the Olympian gods is described. A turbulent C minor section re-creates the turmoil of the earth. With the change of tonality to C major, Brahms passes back to the Olympian serenity of his opening prelude and chorus.

The *Song of Triumph,* dedicated to Emperor Wilhelm I, was probably written with Bismarck in mind. It commemorated the victory of Germany in the Franco-Prussian War. Text came from the nineteenth chapter of the Book of Revelation. There are three sections, beginning, says Felix Borowski, with a "prelude of a solemn but animated and exultant character, in the closing measures of which both choirs unite in jubilant shouts of 'Hallelujah, Praise Be the Lord!' The theme of this movement is the German national hymn, 'Heil dir im Siegerkranz,' which is worked up with consummate skill. The first part closes with a climax of power and contrapuntal effect hardly to be found elsewhere outside the choruses of Handel."

The second part, "Glory Be to God," is similar in spirit to the first. "After the opening ascription, a short fugue intervenes, leading to a fresh melody alternately song by both choruses." A short orchestral flourish opens the concluding section. This is followed by the baritone solo, "And Behold then the Heavens Opened Wide," to which the chorus replies spiritedly, "And Yonder a Snow-White Horse." Additional material is then exchanged by baritone and chorus, leading into the final overpowering "Halleuljah," by choruses, orchestra, and organ.

1873. VARIATIONS ON A THEME BY HAYDN, for orchestra, op. 56-a (also for two pianos, op. 56-b).

In 1870, Brahms's biographer, Pohl, showed the composer an unpublished Divertimento that Haydn had written for an outdoor performance in or about 1782. In the second movement, Haydn quoted an old hymn, "Chorale St. Antoni," the precise source of which has never been identified. The chorale melody impressed Brahms enough to have him jot it down in a notebook. Three years later, he decided to use it as the basis of a series of variations. A version for two pianos became Brahms's last work for the keyboard in an extended structure. A version for orchestra was his first symphonic work in fourteen years and his first masterwork for the orchestra. It is not known which came first, though it is reasonable to assume that the two-piano version may have been written as a preliminary exercise to the more ambitious orchestral adaptation.

The chorale melody is heard immediately in oboes and bassoons, cellos and double basoons providing a pizzicato accompaniment. Eight variations follow. In the first (Poco più animato), the theme is suggested by the winds, while strings provide a delicate embroidery. The second (Più vivace) gives a freer treatment to the theme in clarinets and bassoons. The third is in a romantic vein (Con moto), the theme given a gentle and fluid treatment by oboes and bassoons, over a contrapuntal background of lower strings. Later on, violins and violas take over, with flutes and bassoons now providing embellishments in sixteenth-notes. In the fourth (Andante con moto), oboes and horns in octaves give a lyrical treatment to the theme over a moving figure in violas. When the melody is taken over by strings, the moving figure is assumed by flutes and clarinets. A light-textured Scherzo, with the melody sensitively suggested first by woodwind then by strings, makes up the fifth variation (Vivace); while in the sixth (Vivace), pizzicato strings give a hint of the theme following a hunting tune in horns. The seventh variation (Grazioso) is a haunting siciliano for flute and violas over a descending scale accompaniment in first violins. The last variation (Presto non troppo) is a delicate episode for muted strings. The finale is built from a five measure ground bass, repeated twelve times in different harmonies. A climax is reached with the main chorale melody given a fortissimo statement by brass, over runs in woodwind and strings.

1874. PIANO QUARTET IN C MINOR, op. 60. I. Allegro non troppo. II. Scherzo. III. Andante. IV. Finale.

The third of Brahms's piano quartets, and the one least consistently interesting, is a product of two creative periods. The opening and slow movements were written in 1855. They were put aside until the winter 1873, when Brahms revised them and added a recently completed Scherzo and finale. The first movement is described by Peter Latham as "somber grandeur." It opens bleakly with double octaves in the piano, a restless phrase in the strings, and an agitated subject. A lyrical interlude comes with the second subject, an eight-bar melody that receives four variations. The prevailing gloom of the first movement persists into the passionate Scherzo. Here, in place of a trio, we get a short episode in major tonality. The glory of the work is the slow movement, in which the cello is heard in a rhapsodic song in the high register. Richard Specht believes that here Brahms is renouncing his love for Clara Schumann. The finale, returning to the dark key of C minor, is once again turbulent and gloomy at turns; it is predominantly contrapuntal in style.

1874–1875. 3 STRING QUARTETS:

C minor, op. 51, no. 1. I. Allegro. II. Poco adagio. III. Allegro molto moderato e comodo. IV. Allegro.

A minor, op. 51, no. 2. I. Allegro ma non troppo. II. Andante moderato. III. Moderato; Allegretto vivace. IV. Allegro non assai.

B-flat major, "Hunt," op. 67. I. Vivace. II. Andante. III. Allegretto non troppo. IV. Poco allegretto con variazioni.

All three Brahms string quartets come within a period of less than two years, the first two in 1874, the third in 1875. Brahms had long been experimenting with the string-quartet form before he completed one that satisfied him sufficiently to allow him to publish it. The first quartet, in C minor, is a masterwork, with an economy, structural mastery, and integration not often encountered in Brahms's earlier chamber music.

In this first quartet, the initial eight notes of the opening theme are a recurrent motive. It becomes a part of the main themes of the slow movement and the finale. The quartet is integrated in other ways as well. In three of the four movements, a rising motive is used in opposition to a falling one; and in the opening of the first two movements, there is a marked similarity in the rhythmic pattern.

Unity is also achieved in this first quartet by the sameness of mood in three of the four movements: a solemnity that often touches the lugubrious, and an agitation that swells into passion. The severity of the first theme in C minor, in the opening movement, finds welcome relief in the lyricism of the second E-flat subject. The exposition is along a monumental design, covering some eighty measures; the two main themes are not only stated here but are also developed. An even more epical development section ensues, with struggle and passion predominating. In the second movement, a Romanza, the opening idyllic subject is permitted to grow into the poignant melancholia of the second theme, a passage in triplets in viola and second violin. Only in the third movement is the gloom dispelled, particularly in an infectious subject for viola, which is repeated with stunning effect later on by second violin and cello, over plucked strings in first violin and viola. But strong emotion reasserts itself in the opening unison theme of the finale, and restlessness stirs in the second subject, which makes use of the same notes found in the first theme (F, G, A-flat).

The Quartet in A minor sounds an even more elegiac strain, particularly in the first movement with its haunting, yearning, opening melody in the violin. The atmosphere darkens further in the slow movement, where a poignant melody in an upper range is set over a moving bass. Temporary release from emotional duress comes with a light exchange between violin and cello in imitation. The third movement is a minuet, in which lyrical episodes alternate with vigorous ones. In the finale, a rondo with two themes, amiability gives way to unrestricted vigor; Viennese Gemuetlichkeit is superseded by Hungarian sensuality.

In marked contrast to these two quartets is the third, in which joyous feelings are allowed to spill over. The work opens at once in a jovial vein with a spirited melody that sounds like a hunting fanfare; this is the reason why this quartet has been named the *Hunt*. Much of the gaiety of this movement comes from its continually contrasting rhythms. In the slow movement, no profound emotion is projected; it consists mainly of a graceful song over syncopated chords. The viola becomes the dominant performer in the scherzo-like third movement, the other three instruments being muted. Perhaps the finest movement of all is the finale, "the nucleus of the whole work," Karl Geiringer calls it. First we get a simple melody that sounds like a folk song. Eight variations follow, with occasional reminders of material from earlier movements. Between the sixth and seventh variations, a lively episode is introduced, recalling the first-movement hunt tune; some transitional material from that first movement is repeated in the eighth variation. The finale ends with a vigorous coda, in which the basic theme of the seventh variation is combined with the main folk-song tune on which all the variations were based.

1876. SYMPHONY NO. 1 IN C MINOR, op. 68. I. Un poco sostenuto; Allegro. II. Andante sostenuto. III. Un poco allegretto e grazioso. IV. Adagio più andante; Allegro non troppo con brio.

Brahms began making sketches for a first symphony in 1862. Not until fourteen years later was the work completed. The thought of invading a province over which Beethoven had ruled with such majesty was a terrifying one. "You will never know," he once remarked, "how the likes of us feel when we hear the tramp of a giant like Beethoven behind us." And even after he had finished a first movement, he insisted: "I will never write a symphony."

But he *did* write a symphony, at last, when he was forty-three, in full command of his technique, his creative personality fully evolved. That work is probably the greatest first symphony ever written. Hans von Buelow went further. He called it the "Tenth Symphony" to indicate that Brahms was Beethoven's symphonic heir. He also coined the descriptive phrase, "the three B's," to link Brahms's name with those of Bach and Beethoven.

Brahms originally intended to use the key of D minor for his first symphony (a performance of Beethoven's Ninth Symphony in D minor having shaken him to his roots in 1854). But it was in C minor that the symphony was finally written, the same tonality Beethoven had used for the Fifth. This key, says Walter Niemann, meant to Brahms "hard, pitiless struggle, demoniac, supernatural shapes, sinister defiance, steely energy, dramatic intensity of passion, darkly fantastic, grisly humor." The "pitiless struggle" and the "dramatic intensity of passion" are some of the qualities that make Beethoven's Fifth and Brahms's First brothers.

The conflict of the first movement (like that in Beethoven's Fifth) is of titanic proportions. But before it starts, we get a thirty-seven measure introduction of an eloquence with few counterparts in symphonic literature. Higher and higher ascend the strings over a throbbing background of "C's" in the kettledrums and with the woodwind proceeding in contrary motion. A secondary syncopated subject follows in woodwind and plucked strings. Then the main part of the movement erupts dramatically with a descending three-note phrase, which becomes the kernel of the first theme. The heroic struggle that follows, as this motive is enlarged, is finally allowed to subside when a quiet and subdued feeling of resignation sets in with a poignant melody for the woodwind. The development section brings back the conflict and extends it to Herculean dimensions; in few symphonies is drama projected on such a giant stage. The full orchestra is used almost constantly—nothing less can give voice to Brahms's torrential moods. The recapitulation is along more or less orthodox lines, leading into a forceful coda, in which the mood of the introduction is recalled.

The storm of the first movement yields to the peaceful benediction of the second. Strings and bassoons raise their voices in a beatific song. Another idyllic melody follows in the oboe. But now the feelings become intense and sensual, as strings soar over a strong, firm rhythm. A new theme, shared by oboes and clarinets, transforms passion into serenity. It is with such a feeling that the movement ends, the second theme brought back by horn and solo violin.

The third movement is not a Scherzo in Beethoven's robust style, but light and playful music that is almost elfin. First comes a graceful tune in clarinet over a pizzicato accompaniment; then a stronger subject in woodwinds, with strings offering a reply.

The finale has the same epic quality as the first movement. It opens with a dramatic thrust: chromatic chords in the wind and a forceful outcry in strings. The tempo quickens, and the sonority increases over a compelling rhythm in kettledrums. The horns enter with a radiant thought over tremolo strings. The flutes repeat it. Then a hymn erupts in strings, a hymn of joy, which bears such a striking resemblance to the ode in the finale of Beethoven's Ninth Symphony that we cannot forget the impact that symphony had made on Brahms. It is the opinion of some musicologists that this similarity is not coincidental but planned, that Brahms wished to carry on Beethoven's message of man's brotherhood. Now the music gains in dramatic strength and rises toward an overwhelming climax. The return of the beautiful horn theme, and a tender idea for strings over a basso ostinato, bring temporary calm. But it is a calm before another storm, at the peak of whose fury there is sounded the horn melody, loud and triumphant, in full orchestra. Thus the struggle has ended with the victory of the human spirit, and with an exultant expression of joy.

1877. SYMPHONY NO. 2 IN D MAJOR, op. 73. I. Allegro non troppo. II. Adagio non troppo. III. Allegretto grazioso. IV. Allegro con spirito.

Where Brahms's first symphony had been an epic, the second is an idyllic, pastoral poem. It is, indeed, the warmest of heart, the gentlest and the sunniest of Brahms's four symphonies. To the distinguished conductor Felix Weingartner, "the stream of invention has never flowed so fresh and spontaneous in other works by Brahms, and nowhere else has he colored his orchestration so skilfully."

In the opening movement, a three-note phrase precedes a haunting refrain in horn. This is followed by one of Brahms's most beautiful melodies, an opulent song for cellos and violas. The woodwinds repeat it, after which a vigorous marcato episode ensues. The first theme and an undulating transitional passage between the two main subjects become the material for the development. After a more or less formal recapitulation, the coda devotes itself to the opening theme, then ends quietly.

The slow movement is in three-part song form. The first part consists of a sensitive melody for cellos, with its first six measures repeated by violins. A passage in imitation for horn and woodwind brings us to the graceful middle part, with its subject in flutes and oboes. Following some elaboration and development, the first melody returns, altered and modified.

The third movement is an intermezzo with two contrasting trio sections. The main theme of the opening is a playful tune in two clarinets and bassoons, accompanied by plucked strings in cellos. In the two trios, this theme is varied. The basic theme, however, recurs between the two trios and at the movement's close.

The finale is in sonata form, opening with the principal subject in strings; it faintly suggests the beginning of the first movement. An extended transition brings on the second subject, in A minor, first in strings, then in woodwind with string accompaniment. A vigorous treatment of this melody in the orchestra brings on the development, in which the opening and closing measures of the first theme provide the basic substance. In the recapitulation, the two main themes return much as they had appeared in the exposition. The first measure of each of the two themes is then worked out in a long and effective coda.

1878. COMPOSITIONS FOR SOLO PIANO, op. 76:

4 Capriccios: I. F-sharp minor; II. B minor; III. C-sharp minor; IV. C major.

4 Intermezzi: I. A-flat major; II. B-flat major; III. A major; IV. A minor.

The "capriccio" is a short piano form devised and perfected by Brahms. Here a whimsical mood is projected in fast tempo and in a comparatively light style. Four of Brahms's Capriccios are found in opus 76, which is entitled *Eight Pieces* (the other four being the Intermezzi). The most frequently played Capriccio in this set is the second, in B minor. A sparkling staccato melody is contrasted with a supple lyrical episode. The first Capriccio is the most complex of the group, with involved canonic writing and partiality for inversions. The C-sharp minor Capriccio is a spirited piece with exciting cross-rhythms. The C major is a brilliant technical exercise, which comes to an end with a sober Adagio. Later in life, Brahms wrote three more Capriccios (see 1892).

In a slower tempo, and much more poetic in content than the capriccio, is the piano intermezzo, a free form in which Brahms produced eighteen pieces. "Here," says Ernest Hutcheson, "he reached his long-sought-after perfection, and lovely ideas are expressed with utmost economy of means." Brahms's first four Intermezzi are found in opus 76, all in a romantic style, frequently carrying echoes of Mendelssohn through their charming lyricism. For Brahms's later Intermezzi, see 1892 and 1893.

1878. CONCERTO IN D MAJOR, for violin and orchestra, op. 77. I. Allegro non troppo. II. Adagio. III. Allegro giocoso, ma non troppo vivace.

Like Beethoven before him, Brahms wrote only a single violin concerto, and that one is a glory in the violin literature. Hubert Foss finds that of all the large works by Brahms this is the one that shows the "reconciling of the two opposite sides of his creative mind—the lyrical and the constructive: Brahms the song writer and Brahms the symphonist. For this Concerto is a song for the violin on a symphonic scale—a lyrical outpouring which nevertheless exercises to the full his great powers of inventive development. The substance of it is, throughout, the growth of the themes; they blossom before us like opening flowers in a richly stocked garden."

"The main theme of the first movement is announced at once by the cellos, violas, bassoons and horns," wrote Lawrence Gilman. "This subject, and three contrasting song-like themes, together with an energetic dotted figure, marcato, furnish the thematic material of the first movement. The violin is introduced after almost a hundred measures for the orchestra alone, in an extended section, chiefly of passage work, as preamble to the exposition of the chief theme. The caressing and delicate weaving of the solo instrument about the melodic outlines of the song themes in the orchestra is unforgettable."

The solo violin never plays more than the first three notes of the main melody of the second movement, confining itself mainly to figurations and contrapuntal material. This tune, played by the oboe, is said to have been derived from a Bohemian folk song. The solo violin is heard in the second important theme, which it then embroiders with the most sensitive and fanciful decorations. "Perhaps not since Chopin have the possibilities of decorative figuration developed so rich a yield of poetic loveliness as in this Concerto," says Gilman. "Brahms is here ornamental without ornateness, florid without excess; these arabesques have the dignity and fervor of pure lyric speech."

To Gilman the finale is a "virtuoso's parade. The jocund chief theme, in thirds, is stated at once by the solo violin. There is many a hazard for the soloist: ticklish passage work, double-stopping, arpeggios. Also there is much spirited and fascinating music—music of rhythmical charm and gusto."

1879. SONATA NO. 1 IN G MAJOR, "RAIN," for violin and piano, op. 78. I. Vivace non troppo. II. Adagio. III. Allegro molto moderato.

There are two reasons why Brahms's first violin sonata is known as *Rain.* One is that he quoted in it one of his own Lieder, "Regenlied," or "Rain Song," op. 59, no. 3 (1871–1873). Another is that in the finale there is a running figure in sixteenth-notes for the piano that sounds like the gentle downpour of raindrops.

Walter Niemann described this sonata as a "tender, instrumental idyll, thoroughly intimate in style and in writing, with an elegiac and tenderly melancholy tinge and a prevailing atmosphere of still contemplation and pensive cheerfulness." A motto phrase—a three-time repeated note of D, first heard in the beautiful opening melody of the first movement—recurs in the later movements to provide integration. The slow movement begins with a singing melody in piano alone, evoking a pastoral mood. Midway, in the contrasting più andante section, the three-note motto is reintroduced. In the finale, a rondo, we hear the three-note motto twice immediately before the opening melody of the second movement is brought back by the violin in double stops. The motto is heard for the last time in the last six measures, in augmentation, to bring the sonata to a tranquil end.

1879. 2 RHAPSODIES, for piano, op. 79: I. B minor. II. G minor.

In writing rhapsodies for the piano, Brahms carried out the original Greek concept of the term "rhapsody" by creating music of epic character, passionate in mood, dramatic in impulse. The two Rhapsodies are among Brahms's masterworks for the piano. (Brahms wrote a third rhapsody in E-flat major, op. 119, in 1893, his last solo piano. See 1893.)

Here is how James Gibbons Huneker described the two rhapsodies: "The first Rhapsody in B minor . . . is drastic, knotty, full of insoluble ideas, the melodic contour far from melting and indeed hardly plastic. The mood is sternly Dorian. . . . It is the intellectual Brahms who confronts us with his supreme disdain for what we like or dislike; it is Brahms giving utterance to bitter truths, and only when he reaches the section in D minor does he relax and sing in smoother accents."

The second rhapsody is "magnificent, more ballade-like than rhapsodic, yet a distinct narrative. . . . The bold modulation of the theme, its swiftness, fervor and power are very fascinating. . . . The working-out is famous in its intensity, in its grip; never for a moment is the theme lost, never for a moment is subsidiary material introduced. . . . A hurricane of emotion that is barely stilled at the end, this rhapsody reminds me of the bardic recital of some old border ballad. In it there is tragedy, and the cry of bruised hearts; in it there is fierce action, suffocating passion and a letting loose of the elements of the soul."

1880. AKADEMISCHE FESTOUVERTUERE (ACADEMIC FESTIVAL OVERTURE), for orchestra, op. 80.

TRAGISCHE OUVERTUERE, (TRAGIC OVERTURE), for orchestra, op. 81.

In 1879, the University of Breslau conferred on Brahms the degree of Doctor of Philosophy *honoris causa* in recognition of his leadership in Germany "in music of the more severe order." As a gesture of appreciation, Brahms completed in 1880 what he described as "a very jolly potpourri on students' songs." He himself conducted the première performance—in Breslau on January 4, 1881—before an audience including the leading officials of the city and the University, many of whom were shocked to hear popular melodies favored by students at beer parties used in a concert overture.

The first principal theme is heard without preface—softly in the violins. This is a brisk Allegro tune associated with beer mugs. A more sedate episode in E minor, with the violas prominent, and a return of the opening brisk tune precede the statement of the first student song, "Wir hatten gebauet ein stattliches Haus." The orchestra offers a strong section, of which the first principal theme is a part. Following a change of key to E major, the second violins (over plucked strings in cellos) present the second student song, "Der Landesvater." A third student song, "Fuchslied," is heard after this, given by the bassoons to pizzicati in cellos and violas. An elaborate working out of some of this material ensues. The recapitulation comes to a stirring climax with the most famous college song of all, "Gaudeamus igitur," in wind instruments over scale passages in strings.

Even while he was working on this spirited overture, with its culminating hymn to the joys of the good life, Brahms was deep at work on a second concert overture far different in character. As he explained to his publisher: "I could not refuse my melancholy nature the satisfaction of composing an overture for a tragedy." And to one of his friends, Brahms described his two contrasting overtures as follows: "One of them weeps, the other laughs."

The overture that "weeps" he named *Tragic,* but had no specific program in mind. Two loud chords precede the grim and fever-ridden first theme in the strings. The melancholia deepens as the melody is elaborated. Then relief from this somber mood is brought about by the woodwind with a tender melody. The development of these two subjects has deeply tragic overtones. With a slackening of the tempo, a little march tune in dotted rhythm is given. Earlier material is now recalled, and the overture ends with a forceful statement of the opening subject by strings and brass.

1881–1882. NAENIE, for chorus and orchestra, op. 82.

GESANG DER PARZEN (SONG OF THE FATES), for chorus and orchestra, op. 89.

The shadow of death hovers ominously over Brahms's last two works for chorus and orchestra. In *Naenie* (1881), text by Schiller, death is portrayed, explains Karl Geiringer, "as a kindly genius in whose arms those weary of life find sweet repose." The three sections, all in a major tonality, create throughout "a spirit of perfect harmony, tranquil and serene." An expressive orchestral prelude, highlighted by a melody for oboe, precedes the first chorus, which, says Geiringer, "rises to a sweet intensity at the mention of Adonis. War-like accents hail the name of Achilles, and yet the fundamental content is unaltered." With the appearance of the sea-goddess, Thetis, a more romantic note is introduced, "In particular, the passage 'See How the Gods All Are

Weeping' with its strange octave leaps, is charged with the deepest feeling. This noble composition closes with a delicate repetition of the choral opening."

The *Song of the Fates* is a setting of a text by Goethe, which, in turn, comes out of the Greek tragedy, *Iphigenia in Tauris*. What we encounter here is not gentle serenity but anguish. "The terrible decrees of Fate are inevitably fulfilled," explains Geiringer. The modulations in the prelude suggest a disturbed atmosphere. The chorus enters with a powerfully dramatic utterance, "while a drum motive provides an effective background, and by its very monotony produces an impression of irresistible power." A momentary suggestion of levity intrudes with a dance-like episode. The opening chorus returns slightly altered. Then Brahms felt the need of some relief from earlier tensions. He, therefore, concludes with a "passage of milder and more human tones in order to give the composition a more consoling character. Thus a second episode makes its appearance. . . . The agonized words of the poem are sung to gently transfigured, quietly resigned melodies. The work closes with a finale echo of the beginning . . . and the music dies away in a dreamy, mysterious pianissimo."

1881. CONCERTO NO. 2 IN B-FLAT MAJOR, for piano and orchestra, op. 83. I. Allegro non troppo. II. Allegro appassionato. III. Andante. IV. Allegretto grazioso.

"I have written a tiny, tiny piano concerto with a tiny, tiny wisp of a Scherzo," Brahms wrote to his friend, Elizabeth von Herzogenberg, in 1881. To another friend, Dr. Billroth, he described the new concerto as "some little piano pieces."

In such a modest—and facetious—vein did Brahms launch one of the most monumental in structure and most exacting in technique of Romantic piano concertos; a concerto of such spaciousness and breadth in its orchestral writing that it is sometimes described as a symphony with piano obbligato.

Where Brahms's first piano concerto had pronounced tragic implications, the second is idyllic and serene. It is in four, rather than the more usual three, movements—a Scherzo appearing between the first and slow movements to avoid, as the composer explained, "an Adagio mood." The first movement opens with a suggestion of the main theme in first horn. The piano replies. Then the orchestral tutti presents both main themes. The first, strong and assertive, is in full orchestra; the second, lyrical and feminine, is heard in the violins, accompanied by pizzicati violas and cellos. The piano repeats the vigorous first theme after an octave passage. In the development, the opening horn motive and the second theme are worked out with amplitude of design. The horn motive reasserts itself cautiously in the recapitulation, in which the basic melodic material is heard in fascinating new guises. This material is also altered in the powerful coda.

The Scherzo begins with a forceful statement by the piano. The orchestra now progresses to a subject based on the rhythm of this theme, which the piano soon takes over. A second main theme, in octaves, is later presented by the strings, the piano providing figurations. A completely new melody then is given by the strings in the middle trio section. When the opening part returns, its material is developed and altered rather than repeated.

A rhapsodic song appears in solo cello in the slow movement. Toward its conclusion the piano is heard in a brief comment on this melody. Then a new idea, in F-sharp, is presented by the piano, to an accompaniment by clarinets and cellos. The haunting opening song is then repeated, followed by a brief coda.

The finale is in a happy mood, beginning as it does with an ebullient subject in the piano, followed by a sprightly Hungarian-like tune shared by woodwind and strings. After that, the buoyant feelings are maintained with a whimsical motive in piano, accompanied by plucked strings. "For a lighthearted colloquy," comments Hubert Foss, "the canvas is large; but Brahms has filled every inch of it with a successful as well as entertaining musical design."

1882. STRING QUINTET IN F MAJOR, op. 88. I. Allegro non troppo ma con brio. II. Grave ed appassionato. III. Allegro energico.

Brahms wrote his first string quintet (two violas, two violins, and cello) comparatively late in his career, when he was forty-nine. He, therefore, brought to it his full maturity, as well as his vast technical experience. He was pleased with the result. "I can tell you," he told his publisher, "that you have not as yet had such a beautiful work from me, and probably you have not published one such in the last ten years."

The Quintet is sometimes called *Spring*. "In reality," Brahms's friend, Dr. Billroth explained, "the whole thing is pervaded by the atmosphere of Spring." The first movement opens with a tender melody; but as soon as it is expanded, it changes into a dance tune which suggests the arrival of the vernal season. The second theme, introduced by first viola and carried on by first violin, is in the characteristic Brahmsian rhythmic pattern of contrasting twos and threes. After the development, there comes one of the loftiest pages in this score, the extended dramatic preparation for the return of the main theme.

The middle movement is a compromise between a slow movement and a Scherzo. Alternating sections present, now the slow part (with its solemn melody in the cello, which gains in intensity with each restatement), and now the light-footed Scherzo section.

The finale has the winged flight of a perpetual motion. Effective use is here made of fugal writing within the sonata-form framework. Two loud chords set the stage for the fugal subject in the viola. The subject then passes on to second violin, first violin, cello, and second viola.

1883. SYMPHONY NO. 3 IN F MAJOR, op. 90. I. Allegro con brio. II. Andante. III. Poco allegretto. IV. Allegro.

Six years separate the second and third symphonies. To Hans Richter, the

Third is Brahms's *Eroica*. It opens with a proud motto theme that plays an important role throughout the work: two strong chords for the woodwind. Immediately, we get the bold first theme, a heroic downward stride of the violins. As this subject unfolds, the motto theme is interjected first by the woodwinds, then by horns. A gentle episode in violins and cellos serves as a transition leading to the soft-sensitive melody in clarinet and bassoon that sounds like a lullaby. A new thought now intrudes: a dance tune for the woodwind, to which strings offer a reply. Before the exposition ends, this thematic material gets amplification, the motto theme again and again interwoven into the fabric. This material is further elaborated in the development; the motto gets prominence in a majestic passage for horn over a syncopated accompaniment. This motto also opens the recapitulation and introduces the coda. The latter is built to a climax before it is allowed to subside to a final gentle statement.

A chorale-like melody with religious feeling is presented by clarinets and bassoons in four-part harmony in the second movement. This calm is maintained in the lyrical second subject, for the woodwind. Then the mood grows sensual with two passionate interludes for the strings. Tranquillity returns with a recall of the chorale melody.

The first theme of the third-movement Romanza is a somewhat introspective thought for cellos over string arpeggios. In the middle of the movement, the woodwinds are heard in a hesitant tune in waltz rhythm over syncopations in the cello. To Karl Geiringer, the finale is a "tremendous conflict of elemental forces." It opens in the minor with a theme in octave strings and bassoons; an air of mystery is projected. A solemn melody for strings and wind follows. Now the elemental forces, of which Geiringer speaks, are released, rising toward a stately song for cellos and horns. Calm prevails at last in the coda. "Like a rainbow after the thunderstorm," says Geiringer, "the motto played by the flute, with its message of hope and freedom, spans the turmoil of the other voices."

1885. SYMPHONY NO. 4 IN E MINOR, op. 98. I. Allegro non troppo. II. Andante moderato. III. Allegro giocoso. IV. Allegro energico e passionato.

Brahms had considerable misgivings about the way the public would react to his fourth symphony. His fears were partly justified when he presented this new work in a two-piano arrangement to a circle of intimate friends, most of whom disapproved. Eduard Hanslick remarked after the first movement: "Really, you know it sounds like two tremendously witty people cudgeling each other." Brahms remarked sadly to Max Kalbeck: "If persons like Billroth, Hanslick and you do not like my music, whom will it please?" Brahms then decided to put his symphony to an acid test—in a rehearsal by the Meiningen Orchestra, directed by Hans von Buelow. He insisted that if the work did not go well there he would withdraw it permanently. But the rehearsal was a success, and the conductor was most enthusiastic. He called the symphony "stupendous, quite original, individual, and rock-like. Incomparable strength from start to finish." And it was the Meiningen Orchestra, the composer conducting, which gave the symphony its world première, on October 25, 1885.

There is such a consistent note of melancholy in the Fourth that Walter Niemann was tempted to call it Brahms's *Elegiac Symphony*. In this music he finds "the inward tragedy . . . [and] the resignation of solitary old age," revealing themselves in "the weary, veiled tone, curiously objective and reminiscent of epic or ballad which predominates in it."

Without any introduction, the first theme of the opening Allegro is heard in the violins. It is a serene subject built from a two-note phrase to which woodwind give reply after each two-note sequence. An eloquent horn episode leads to the second theme—a forceful statement, the first part in woodwind and horns, the second part in woodwind and cellos, over a plucked-string accompaniment. Before the exposition ends, the strings engage in a soaring interlude, which rises to ecstatic heights in the highest registers. The development concerns itself mainly with the opening subject and only incidentally with the first part of the second theme. The two-note phrase of the opening subject, in augumentation, introduces the recapitulation; the same material is the basis of the coda.

The four-measure introduction to the slow movement offers the motive of the first theme in horns and woodwind, derived from the old Phrygian mode. In the fifth measure, the woodwinds are heard in a tender song, accompanied by pizzicato strings. This elegiac mood gives way to an impassioned outburst in the strings, only to return again with one of Brahms's highest flights of melodic inspiration, a wonderful song for the cellos. Both these lyrical ideas are elaborated, and the first of these is discussed in the coda.

In the third movement, Karl Geiringer finds that "a sturdy gaiety reigns supreme." He also finds that the orchestration "is broader and more plastic, more calculated to secure massive effects." The full orchestra is heard in the first sprightly subject, while the second theme, in an equally light vein, is heard in the violins.

In the finale, which Geiringer aptly calls "the crowning glory" of the whole symphony, Brahms returns to the old Baroque form of the passacaglia. Brass and woodwind present the stately, sonorous eight-measure theme. This is followed by some thirty variations. "Brahms chose the form of variations on a ground for this finale," Donald Francis Tovey explains, "because dramatic activity (always on the ebb in finales) was fully exploited in the other three movements. He desired a finale that was free to express tragic emotion without being encumbered by the logical and chronological necessities of the more dramatic sonata forms."

1886. PIANO TRIO IN C MINOR, op. 101. I. Allegro energico. II. Andante grazioso. III. Presto non assai. IV. Allegro molto.

The last of Brahms's piano trios is also the most distinguished, a work of extraordinary concentration and compactness. Walter Niemann described it as "defiant, wild and forceful to the verge of asperity." The main subject of the first movement is a four-note motive, built up with cyclonic force in the development. The second theme, in E-flat major, is, on the other hand, "a melody of wonderful intensity," as Niemann said, "both of feeling and tone, which flows forth in a broad full stream of melody from the two stringed instruments in unison." In the second movement, a folk-song combines two 3/4 measures with four 2/4 measures. Such variety of rhythmic interest is maintained in the agitated second theme, whose meter varies from bar to bar from 9/8 to 6/8. To Niemann, the Scherzo is a blend of "the fantastic, spectral elements of the unadorned flowing principal theme with the passionately . . . restrained mood of the second subject." And the finale has a "decided Scherzo character," its second theme once again of interest for its rhythmic variety and subtlety.

1886 1888. SONATA NO. 2 IN A MAJOR, "THUN," for violin and piano, op. 100. I. Allegro amabile. II. Andante tranquillo. III. Allegretto grazioso.

SONATA NO. 3 IN D MINOR, for violin and piano, op. 108. I. Allegro. II. Adagio. III. Un poco presto e con sentimento. IV. Presto agitato.

SONATA NO. 2 IN F MAJOR, for cello and piano, op. 99. I. Allegro vivace. II. Adagio affetuoso. III. Allegro passionato. IV. Allegro molto.

Brahms's second violin sonata came seven years after his first. He wrote it mainly during a summer holiday at Lake Thun, the reason why it is known as the *Thun Sonata*. It is also sometimes described as the *Prize Song Sonata* because the first-movement main theme bears a three-note resemblance to the "Prize Song" from Wagner's *Die Meistersinger*. In the sonata, this melody appears first in the piano, with an echo phrase in the violin. The second movement is a fusion of a slow movement and Scherzo. A mobile melody unfolds in the violin, alternating with a whimsical, scherzo-like section. The light Scherzo mood prevails at the close of the movement. The finale, a rondo, opens with youthful vigor, with a vigorous subject worked out in arpeggio figures. The gentle and introspective second subject introduces an idyllic note.

The third and last of Brahms's violin sonatas is in the key of D minor, a tonality reserved by the composer for some of his most deeply felt and passionate moods. There is feverish unrest throughout the first movement, dominated as it is by a fiery first theme, in which effective use is made of a pedal point on the dominant. The slow movement emphasizes an emotional song to which a sensual gypsy-like section for violin in double stops later provides a change of mood. Dramatic chords introduce the third-movement Scherzo. The main subject here is an expressive thought built from a five-note phrase. The febrile atmosphere of the opening movement returns in this finale. A Hungarian-type melody starts the proceedings; later in the movement, it is magically transformed into a pensive song for the violin. In the development, the music assumes a march-like character. The passion is now intensified, then a momentary silence precedes the outburst of emotion with which the sonata ends.

Over twenty years separate Brahms's two cello sonatas. The first, in E minor, op. 38 (1865), is a pastoral work with elegiac overtones. The second is charged electrically with high tensions. The exclamations of the cello in the first movement was described by Walter Niemann as "outcries, and appeals of wild agitation"; its feverish character often accentuated by turbulent tremolos in the piano. The slow movement opens solemnly, with piano chords and plucked strings. The cello now offers a soaring melody, the heart of the movement. The third movement is unusual for its spacious design, and for the strength of its material. This is a Scherzo conceived along such ambitious lines that the finale that follows almost seems like an epilogue. In this, one of Brahms's shortest finales, the storm of earlier movements gives way to placidity. For a moment, the feeling may become animated—but only for the moment. A quiet and sensitive coda concludes the finale with the same kind of relaxation with which it began.

1887. CONCERTO IN A MINOR (DOUBLE CONCERTO), for violin, cello, and orchestra, op. 102. I. Allegro. II. Andante. III. Vivace non troppo.

In his two early orchestral Serenades, Brahms had reverted to a form favored by such classical masters as Haydn and Mozart. In writing a concerto for violin and cello, he took another glance backwards. This time he returned to the Baroque structure of the concerto grosso. He uses the two solo instruments often as the concertino, setting them off against, or combining them with, the full orchestra (ripieno). The concerto-grosso form had been in discard for many years. This is one of the reasons why the première of Brahms's Double Concerto, in 1887, was a failure. Another reason was the novelty of a concerto for *two* solo instruments; a third, the contradiction between a classical structure and a Romantic style.

The full orchestra is heard at once with the first-movement main theme. Taking over the last three notes of this orchestral preface, the solo cello embarks upon a recitative before woodwinds appear in the compassionate second theme. A powerful build-up of this lovely melody follows. Its last three notes now serve to introduce the solo violin, soon to be joined by the solo cello in an unaccompanied restatement of the main theme. Another forceful climax develops, leading to a recall of the main themes by the orchestra. Later on in the movement, two subsidiary ideas are introduced. The first comes immediately after the orchestral ritornello; it is a variation of the main theme in solo cello. The second is a duet for the two solo instruments.

The slow movement begins with a rising fourth in the horn, in which the woodwind soon join. This is the preface to a soulful song for the two solo instruments. Contrasting material midway in the movement comprises two new ideas, one in the woodwind, the other an exchange between the two solo instruments. The opening melody then returns. The movement ends with a gentle coda devoted to the new contrasting ideas.

The brilliant finale is in rondo form. A racy Hungarian melody is played by the solo cello. Subsidiary themes contribute to the exuberance. One of these is heard in double stops in the solo cello; another in the two solo instruments in double stops and triplets. The return of the lively opening and a vigorous coda bring on an energetic conclusion.

1887. ZIGEUENERLIEDER (GYPSY SONGS), for vocal quartet and piano, op. 103: 1. He, Zigeuner. 2. Hochgetuermte Rimaflut. 3. Wisst ihr, wann mein Kindchen. 4. Lieber Gott, du weisst. 5. Brauner Bursche. 6. Roeslein dreie. 7. Kommt dir manchmal in den Sinn. 8. Horch, der Wind klagt. 9. Weit und breit. 10. Mond verhuellt sein Angesicht. 11. Rote Abendwolken ziehn.

The lighter Brahms is found in his waltzes and *Hungarian Dances*. The gypsy element, so pronounced in these *Dances*, recurs in the songs for vocal quartet and piano. Brahms derived his eleven texts from a collection of Hungarian folk songs selected by Hugo Conrat, the verses translated into German. In 1891, Brahms set four more of these poems, including them in op. 112. They were: "Himmel strahlt so helle," "Rote Rosenknospen," "Brennessel steht am Wegesrand," and "Liebe Schwalbe."

Eduard Hanslick described these songs as follows: "The *Zigeunerlieder* are a little romance, the events in which we are not told, the persons in which are not named, and yet which we understand perfectly and never forget. The first song begins with a wild cry of 'He, Zigeuner' ('Ho, Gypsy!'). The tenor sings his solo, the quartet repeats the strophe. . . . In the following quartet, 'Hochgetuermte Rimaflut' ('Piled High Are the Waters of Rima'), there is still a lingering echo of the passionate mood. But the gypsy lad seems soon to have found another love: the minor mode is followed by the merry key of D major, furious lamentation by lighthearted love making, 'Wisst Ihr, wann mein Kindchen am allerschoensten ist?' ('So you know When My Little One Is Loveliest?'). Whereupon his lady love joins in a merry mood, 'Lieber Gott, du weisst', ('Dear God, You Know'), after which all the voices unite in exuberant jollity: 'Brauner Bursche fuehrt zum Tanze sein blauaeugig schoenes Kind' ('The Swathy Lad Leads Out His Blue-Eyed Maiden to the Dance'). Next follow two of the loveliest numbers, two gems, one full of playful mockery, the other overflowing with serious, deep feeling. Could anything be daintier than the song of the 'Schoenstes Staedtchen Kecskemet' ('Kecskemet, That Fairest of Towns'), or anything more full of soul than the 'Taeusch mich nicht, verlass' mich nicht' ('Deceive Me Not, Oh, Leave Me Not')? An echo of the mood still hovers on the melancholy mood in G minor, 'Horch, der Wind klagt' ('Hark the Wind Wails'), which opens on such a note of sincerity in the major key, in the words of blessing: 'Gott schuetze dich!' ("God Protect You'). The next piece displays the same alternation between G minor and G major, but again with quite a different color. It opens wildly and stormily with all the voices singing in unison, 'Weit und breit schaut niemand mich an' ('Far and Wide No Man Beholds Me'), in the wildest and most exultant czardas rhythm. Once again longing and heartache prevail; a deep, fervent emotion quivers in the song, 'Mond verhuellt sein Angesicht' ('The Moon Veils Her Face'), the accompaniment of which has a suggestion of the distant, metallic tremolo of the dulcimer. And now we come to the last piece in the collection, 'Rote Abendwolken ziehen' ('Red Sunset Clouds Float Overhead'). The melody rushes by, urged on, as it were, at every pause by two powerful, defiant chords. An incomparably poetical conclusion."

1890. STRING QUINTET IN G MAJOR, op. 111. I. Allegro non troppo ma con brio. II. Adagio. III. Un poco allegretto. IV. Vivace ma non troppo presto.

This is the second of Brahms's string quintets, and his last chamber-music work for strings. Completed when the master was fifty-seven, it remains, nonetheless, a work extraordinary for its over-all youthful exuberance, vigor, and optimisim. Tremolos in upper strings serve as a background for the forceful first theme in cello. It starts out in G major, then wanders off into several different tonalities before returning to home base. The violin provides a transition to the second subject, a songful utterance for viola accompanied by a rhythmic background by violins and cellos. This idea is taken over by the first violin before a new theme is heard; it is a pleasing Viennese waltz.

The exuberance of the first movement is succeeded by the tragedy of the second. It is built almost entirely around a single melody, first heard in the violin. This intensely sorrowful music grows into a veritable outburst of uncontrolled grief. But when the disturbed emotions are finally quieted, the main melody reappears.

The more cheerful attitudes of the first movement are recalled in the third-movement Scherzo. It opens with a waltz tune. The main subject of the trio, exchanged between violins and violas, is also in a light manner; but in the coda, this material is made serene and introspective.

A dynamic gypsy-like melody erupts in the viola to open the finale, charging it with an electric current that increases in voltage toward the end of the movement. There the gypsy tune becomes an uninhibited and abandoned Hungarian dance.

1891. CLARINET TRIO IN A MINOR, op. 114. I. Allegro. II. Adagio. III. Andantino. IV. Allegro.

CLARINET QUINTET IN B MINOR, op. 115. I. Allegro. II. Adagio. III. Andantino. IV. Con moto.

The A minor Trio (for clarinet, cello, and piano) is the first of four chamber works by Brahms calling for a clarinet. All four were written for the same performer: Richard Muehlfeld, clarinetist of the Meiningen Orchestra, whom Brahms considered the foremost performer of a wind instrument he had ever heard. All four works reveal a weariness of spirit that tormented Brahms in 1890 and temporarily made him feel he would never again write another piece of music. The lubugrious melodies that pass through all four compositions, like storm clouds that blacken the daylight, are uniquely suited for the plangent voice of the clarinet.

The first movement of the Clarinet Trio opens with a somber melody for the clarinet; it seems to carry a foreboding of death. It is interesting to remark that later in this movement, Brahms reverts to a technique found in the classical masters, almost with the retrospection of somebody who feels life is just about over. This technique is found in the second subject which, in place of new material, is a canonic treatment of the inversion of the first theme. The slow movement has a gravity that once again has funereal overtones. The main melody of the third movement is as touching in its simplicity as it is deeply affecting in emotional content. J. A. Fuller-Maitland finds here a certain *morbidezza,* "a beauty of such ripeness that the slightest touch must make it over-ripe." Polyphonic skill is found in the finale, particularly in the presentation of the second subject in the cello. When the theme is taken over by the clarinet, the cello proceeds canonically with the same subject inverted. To Daniel Gregory Mason the coda that ends this trio is notable for its "noble severity." He adds: "There the shadows are like those we see on snow in a day of blue sky—tinged, whatever their darkness, with lustrous cobalt. Here sky as well as earth is gray; charm is not offered, it is not even expected or desired. In recompense for its absence we find a high, unyielding sincerity, a grave dignity, a kind of stoic Roman virtue."

The Quintet in B minor is the most remarkable of these works with clarinet, in fact one of the most extraordinary of all Brahms's chamber-music works. As a child of the composer's last years, this Quintet is a work of autumnal beauty; here we find the serene contemplations of a man whose life is behind him and thus is given to introspection and quiet reminiscences. There is here a feeling of ineffable sadness, but sadness strengthened by resignation. We find this in the poignant first theme of the opening movement, sung by the clarinet over the strings. The clarinet is also heard in the no less eloquent second theme. Indeed, the gentle and elegiac voice of the clarinet dominates the whole movement.

The second movement opens in an almost elegiac vein—with a melody of incomparable tenderness for the clarinet, to which the violin gives reply before both instruments team up. Midway in the movement comes a rhapsodic section with florid figures for the clarinet and tremolo passages for the strings. This agitation passes quickly, and the tender melancholy of the opening returns. Serenity still prevails in the opening part of the third movement, but the lyric element in this section finds contrast in a light, almost whimsical, section whose staccato theme is a variant of the four notes with which the movement opens. In the finale, a pleasing melody receives five variations, beginning with a solo for the cello. The fourth variation, which shifts from minor to major, is noteworthy for its rich-textured scoring. In the fifth, triple time replaces duple, introducing not only grace but also a touch of pathos. The mood now begins to darken. The finale comes to a tragic denouement with the combination of the variation melody with the principal theme of the first movement.

1892. COMPOSITIONS FOR SOLO PIANO:

3 CAPRICCIOS, op. 116. I. D minor. II. G minor. III. D minor.

4 INTERMEZZI, op. 116. I. A minor. II. E major. III. E minor. IV. E major.

3 INTERMEZZI, op. 117. I. E-flat major. II. B-flat minor. III. C-sharp minor.

The volume of piano pieces, opus 116, was named by Brahms *Fantasias,* but all it contains are three capriccios and four intermezzi. Peter Latham thus describes these pieces: No. 1 (Capriccio in D minor) is a vigorous capriccio of the concert-study type, uncompromising, full of octaves and brusque chords. The G minor Capriccio "begins and ends passionately, with a majestic episode in between," while the D minor is "fast and restless, with characteristic cross-rhythms." The A minor Intermezzo is "whimsical with a fantastic middle section." In the E major, Brahms "adopts a favorite plan of his, developing a piece of fragrant enchantment out of two trifling scraps." In the E minor, Brahms preserves an "intimate mood." This is a "wisp of a thing that looks easy to play and is not." The E major Intermezzo is "the simplest of all . . . and one of the most deeply felt."

The first Intermezzo in opus 117 is mainly a gentle lullaby over which appears a quotation from *Lady Anne Bothwell's Lament,* a Scottish ballad translated by Herder. The next two Intermezzi have even greater sobriety. That in B-flat minor is quietly reflective, with a sinuous falling and rising melody over broken chords. The C-sharp minor Intermezzo, which is in the sonata form, is more melancholy still.

1893. COMPOSITIONS FOR SOLO PIANO, op. 118; op. 119:

7 INTERMEZZI: I. A minor, op. 118, no. 1; II. A major, op. 118, no. 2; III. F minor, op. 118, no. 4; IV. E-flat minor, op. 118, no. 6; V. B minor, op. 119, no. 1; VI. E minor, op. 119, no. 2; VII. C major, op. 119, no. 3.

ROMANZE IN F MAJOR, op. 118, no. 5.

RHAPSODY IN E-FLAT MAJOR, op. 119, no. 4.

BALLADE IN G MINOR, op. 118, no. 3.

The seven Intermezzi in opus 118 and opus 119 are more varied in style and emotional gamut than any of Brahms's earlier pieces in this form. The first, in A minor, is an intense utterance, while the second, in A major, is gentle and melodious. Severity of idiom characterizes the F minor, which features canonic writing. The E-flat minor has overtones of tragedy, the main theme being a lugubrious subject consisting only of three notes. The B minor Intermezzo was described by Clara Schumann as "a gray pearl—veiled and very precious"; it is an Adagio with arpeggio figures and syncopations. The E minor Intermezzo features a light, rhythmic Laendler-like section, while the C major Intermezzo is one of the gayest pieces Brahms produced in this form.

The Romanze in F major, in op. 118—the only such work by Brahms—opens with a four-measure theme which is then subjected to a series of variations. The E-flat Rhapsody is the composer's last piece for the piano—music of extraordinary strength and vitality, though its episodic material is frequently touched, ever so lightly, by the brush of melancholy.

The G minor Ballade, the third piece in the opus 118 set, is a dramatic composition with dynamic sweep; a light melody in G major provides contrast.

1894. SONATAS FOR CLARINET AND PIANO, op. 120:

No. 1, F minor. I. Allegro appassionato. II. Andante un poco adagio. III. Allegretto grazioso. IV. Vivace.

No. 2, E-flat major. I. Allegro amabile. II. Allegro appassionato. III. andante con moto.

With these two clarinet sonatas, Brahms bid permanent farewell to chamber music. The first, in F minor, opens pessimistically, but the spirit gathers its strength and hope as the music progresses to emerge in the end triumphant. "It is remarkable," says Karl Geiringer, "how in each of the three sections of the beautifully proportioned introductory movement the lyrical opening rises gradually to epic strength, leading to final victory in the softer mood of the coda." The pensive slow movement is made up of a single melody, first heard in the key of A-flat in the clarinet over a soft piano accompaniment. The third movement is in the graceful, restrained animation of Brahms's Intermezzo style. In the finale, the jovial mood remains undiluted.

The second sonata has an unusual structure in that it ends with a slow movement—a theme and variations of which only one variation is in fast tempo. "Thus," remarks Geiringer, "Brahms, with a predominantly slow movement, bids farewell to chamber music." The first movement has a gentle, feminine quality, while the middle-movement Scherzo is brusque and impetuous.

1896. VIER ERNESTE GESAENGE (FOUR SERIOUS SONGS), for voice and piano, op. 121: I. Denn es gehet dem Menschen. II. Ich wandte mich und sahe. III. O Tod, wie bitter. IV. Wenn ich mit Menschen un mit Engelzungen.

The *Four Serious Songs,* texts taken from the Bible, was written about a year before Brahms's death. It has overwhelming emotional impact. Here the speech is that of a man who knows he is not far from death; to whom life, difficult though it had been, is still precious; who views the coming end as a stroke of merciless destiny. A bitter *Weltschmerz* courses through these songs, but, at times, a philosophic resignation as well. Simple in structure, these songs are a forthright projection of a consistently tragic mood, sometimes too painful to be contemplated

Here is how Walter Niemann described the four songs: "The first three songs positively steep themselves with a painful pleasure in somber ideas of the crying contradictions between the ideal world of Christianity and that of modern reality." He finds that in the first song (text from Ecclesiastes iii), man is placed "on the same level as the beasts in his mortality transiency . . . and asks in poignant doubt, 'Who knoweth the spirit of man that goeth upward, and the spirit of beast that goeth downward to earth?'" The second song, (Ecclesiastes iv), "exalts the dead above the living, in its recognition of the injustice born of force, which is going on at every moment." The third song (Sirach xli), "praises death as the bitter enemy of those who revel carelessly or thoughtlessly in wealth and luxury," and is a "gentle benediction of the miserable, the poor and the sick." The concluding song (I Corinthians xiii), "points to faith, hope and charity as the way out of the fearful labyrinth of these torturing perceptions."

MILY BALAKIREV 1837–1910

Balakirev was the founder of the "Russian Five," the first significant nationalist school in music; that was his supreme contribution. As Stassov, the eminent Russian critic and one of Balakirev's friends noted: "Had there been no Balakirev to act as leader, educator, champion and helpmate . . . there would have been no new Russian school, and many a page of telling, live, fearless and joyous activity and progress would be missing from the history of Russia's musical life. . . . The importance of the part he played in the evolution of Russian music is so great as to preclude all possibilities of comparison and entitles him to the first place in the history of Russian music after Glinka."

Balakirev himself was a productive composer whose works embrace two symphonies, two piano concertos, and sundry other orchestral pieces of music; an octet, a septet, and a string quartet; several choral works; and a library of piano music including mazurkas, nocturnes, waltzes, a sonata, the famous *Islamey,* and the very popular transcription of Glinka's song, "The Lark"; and about fifty songs. Much of it is good, some of it indestructible. But in the last analysis, Balakirev was a greater influence than he was a composer. He was the one who first crystallized the aims and ideals of Russian nationalism; he was the guiding star of his contemporaries; he was the inspirer of composers like Borodin, Mussorgsky, and Rimsky-Korsakov, and helped them realize their creative identities. Stimulated by Glinka—the man as well as the music—Balakirev made it his all-consuming mission to write music derived from Russian folk songs and dances, drawing its inspiration and strength from Russian backgrounds, history, and culture. Little by little, he drew into his orbit young and idealistic musicians like César Cui (1835–1918), Rimsky-Korsakov, Mussorgsky, and Borodin. These young men met from time to time to discuss Balakirev's ideas. César Cui later recalled: "These informal meetings . . . gave rise . . . to the most interesting and instructive debates, which ranged conscientiously over the whole of the then existing literature of music. . . . In this way, the little brotherhood ended by acquiring fixed convictions and by forming criteria which they applied to a number of questions in the realm of art that frequently lay outside the current ideas of the public and the press. While each member of the group retained his own characteristics and capacity, an ideal common to all soon began to be sharply defined, and an effort was made to imprint on it their compositions."

The "Russian Five," as an integrated group traveling under a single banner, made its official appearance at a concert of the Free School of Music conducted by Balakirev, on May 24, 1867. The program was made up of compositions by Balakirev, Cui, Borodin, Mussorgsky, and Rimsky-Korsakov. Reviewing this concert, Stassov baptized this group as "the mighty five," and from then on the Russian national school has thus been identified.

As a transcriber of Russian folk songs, and as a composer of music influenced by Russian folk art and endowed with a pronounced Russian personality, Balakirev set the example that others followed.

Mily Balakirev was born in Nijni-Novgorod, Russia, on January 2, 1837. His mother gave him some piano lessons when he was a child; later on, he studied in Moscow with Alexandre Dubuque. In 1855, he settled in St. Petersburg, where his debut as composer took place with a performance of a movement from his first piano concerto. It was at this time that he came under the influence of Glinka, who directed his thinking into nationalist channels. Under this stimulus, Balakirev completed the *Overture on Three Russian Themes* in 1858. In 1862, Balakirev helped organize the Free School of Music in St. Petersburg, where for a number of years he served as assistant director and as conductor of its orchestral concerts. In that same year, he visited the Caucasus to make a study of its folk music; and in 1866, he published a collection of folk songs. Emotional instability made him give up his varied activities in 1869. In 1873, he took on a job as a stores-superintendent for the Warsaw Railway. Then in 1878, he returned to music with renewed vigor, completing several important works, including *Tamara*. But physical and mental deterioration eventually made it impossible for him to continue working. After 1887, he went into complete isolation, surrendering to a religious mania that held him a victim for the remainder of his life. He died in St. Petersburg on May 29, 1910.

1858. OVERTURE ON RUSSIAN THEMES, for orchestra.

Balakirev was only twenty-one when he produced his first successful piece of music embodying his nationalist principles, the *Overture on Russian Themes,* introduced in 1859. As the title indicates, the work is based on Russian folk songs, three in number. One is "In the Field Stood the Little Birch Tree," which Tchaikovsky used for the finale of his fourth symphony. A second, "She Went to a Feast," was later quoted by Igor Stravinsky in *Petrouchka*. A third is "Lo, the White Birch Tree Stood Near the Field."

The overture opens with an Allegro energico section in which the song, "In the Field," is only suggested. A slow section follows in which flutes and clarinets offer the song, "Lo, the White Birch." After the tempo is accelerated, the clarinet is heard in "In the Field." This subject is developed before "She Went to a Feast" appears in oboe, over plucked strings and figures in the cello. All three songs are amplified, occasionally with contrapuntal skill. A thunderous climax is followed by tranquillity with a final return of "Lo, the White Birch."

1858–1863. SONGS, for voice and piano:

"Come to Me"; "Georgian Song"; "Hebrew Melody"; "Selim's Song"; "Song of the Golden Fish."

Some of Balakirev's finest songs are found in a collection of twenty, written between 1858 and 1865. All are based on poems by Lermonotov, except for the "Georgian Song" (1863), which has a text by Pushkin. Gerald Abraham notes that Balakirev's songs are "predominantly lyrical" and that in his "emotional warmth" he is "reminiscent of Glinka, but the voice parts are often less singable than Glinka's, and the piano part is often very important." Rosa Newmarch adds: "Nearly all these songs are emotional to a high degree and replete with an ardent sentiment of the triumph of love. . . . Some of them re-create marvelously the very atmosphere of the Orient. . . . They are little gems, cut in innumerable facets, of which each reflects an exquisite and subtle emotion. The accompaniments to these songs resemble the setting of a jewel—they are independent, but they enhance, they complete the musical thought which glistens in the center."

1869. ISLAMEY, fantasy for piano.

In 1862, Balakirev studied the folk songs and dances of the Caucasian region. This research led him to incorporate some of this material into several significant works. The most famous is *Islamey*. The fantasy develops three Oriental melodies freely, richly harmonized, and decorated with brilliant bravura passages. Alfredo Casella orchestrated *Islamey,* a version introduced in Chicago in 1909.

1882. TAMARA, tone poem for orchestra.

The inspiration for this tone poem is a poem by Lermonotov which tells about the beautiful and evil queen who lures travelers to their doom from her castle on the River Terek. In the opening Andante maestoso section, the river Terek is depicted. A drum roll, and a sinister passage for bass trombone and tuba, give warning of dire developments. The Allegro moderato ma agitato section opens with a subject for muted violas. A strong rhythmic figure in unison strings and woodwind, set against chords in the brass, prefaces Tamara's seductive song, in clarinet to a harp accompaniment. This song is developed passionately before a Vivace section unfolds with a brilliant description of a revelry in Tamara's castle, to which a warrior has been lured. That warrior is represented in the ensuing development by a march-like theme in the woodwind. Earlier material is dramatized. We then hear once more Tamara's seductive song and the ominous passage from the opening section. The music ebbs away in a whisper.

1884. RUSSIA, tone poem for orchestra.

In 1864, Balakirev wrote a second *Overture on Russian Themes,* this time with some of the material he had acquired during his then recent visit to the Caucasus. It was published in 1869 under the title of *One Thousand Years*. In 1884, Balakirev revised the overture extensively, revamped it as a tone poem, and gave it the new title of *Russia*. At that time he provided the following programmatic analysis: "The work is founded on three motives borrowed from my book on Russian songs. In it I attempted to express the principal elements of our history: Paganism; the period of Princes and popular government that gave birth to the Cossack regime; and the Muscovite Empire. The struggle among these elements, which ended with the fatal blow struck against Russian nationalistic and religious tendencies by the reforms of Peter I, supplied the subject of this instrumental drama." The folk material used by the composer include two dances from Samara and Simbirsk, and a wedding dance from the region of Nijni-Novgorod.

ALEXANDER BORODIN 1833–1887

Of the five members of the Russian coterie to develop musical nationalism, Borodin was the first to gain international recognition. One can readily understand why. His lyricism is stronger, more personal, more infectious than that of his colleagues. The heroic mold into which he poured these melodies, and the appealing exoticism of the Oriental strains he favored, made his music particularly appealing on first contact. "Borodin's music," said David Lloyd-Jones, "is a remarkable blend of the bold and the original with an almost classical quality of clarity and melodic appeal. The Second Symphony (the first two movements especially), the *Polovtsian Dances* and March, several of the songs, and countless small examples from other works, all serve to earn him a reputation as one of the great nineteenth-century originals and innovators, and his direct influence can be traced not only in the works of his fellow countrymen . . . but also in Debussy, Ravel . . . and even early Stravinsky."

Borodin's preference for the Oriental is one way in which he differs from the other members of "The Five," but there are other ways, too. Though his music, like theirs, derives its identity from Russian folk song, he rarely used material not his own, preferring to create his own melodies rather than borrow them. He also permitted himself the luxury, avoided by the others, of allowing outside influences to mold his style and technique; his indebtedness to Schumann, Berlioz, and Liszt was far-reaching.

Since he divided his life between science and music, he did not produce many compositions. In fact, he looked upon his musical endeavors with a good deal of condescension, relegating science to a far more important place in his life. "It should be understood," he once wrote, "that I do not seek recognition as a composer, for I am somehow ashamed of admitting to my composing activities. This is understandable since, while for others it is a straightforward matter, a duty, and their life's purpose, for me it is a relaxation, a pastime, and an indulgence which distracts me from my principal work." His own set of values notwithstanding, he did succeed in leaving behind him a handful of compositions that place him with Russia's leading musical creators.

Alexander Borodin, the illegitimate son of a Georgian prince and the wife of an army doctor, was born in St. Petersburg on November 12, 1833. As was then the custom, Borodin was registered as the lawful son of one of the Prince's serfs, assuming his name. Though he showed unusual talent for music from boyhood on, undertaking composition when he was fourteen, Borodin was directed to science. He was graduated in 1856 from the Academy of Medicine in St. Petersburg, where he specialized in chemistry. After that, he served as assistant professor there, besides devoting himself to scientific research. Music, however, was not abandoned, though followed for a long time as a hobby.

His first meetings with Balakirev in 1862, and his marriage in 1863 to Catherine Protopopova, a gifted pianist, led him to indulge his interest in music through additional study and first attempts at composition in ambitious forms. Under the stimulation of his association with Balakirev, he completed his First Symphony in 1867, introduced in St. Petersburg on January 16, 1869. This work marked Borodin's debut, both as a serious composer and as a nationalist. He also completed in 1867 his first opera, *The Bogatyrs,* introduced in Moscow on November 18 of that year. From then on, until the end of his life, he devoted himself equally to science and music. Composition took place mainly in the summertime, or during periods when illness kept him away from the medical Academy. His second symphony was completed in 1876, his first string quartet in 1879, his tone poem *On the Steppes of Central Asia* in 1880, and his second string quartet in 1885. During the last eighteen years of his life, he worked on and off on his folk opera, *Prince Igor,* which he did not live to complete. Borodin died in St. Petersburg on February 27, 1887.

1877. SYMPHONY NO. 2 IN B MINOR. I. Allegro. II. Prestissimo. III. Andante. IV. Allegro.

It took Borodin six years to write his second symphony, a period in which the composer was also involved in writing parts of his epic folk opera, *Prince Igor* (which see). The symphony is the brother of the opera. Not only is the over-all character of the musical style similar in both works, but also in the symphony Borodin used some of the material he had planned for the opera. Like *Prince Igor,* the symphony is an epic, heroic in mood, Oriental in orchestral and harmonic colorations. Because of its size and proportions, it has acquired the nickname of *Bogatyr*—a "bogatyr" being a giant in ancient Russian epics.

Stassov, Borodin's friend and a distinguished critic, once described the symphony as a picture of feudal Russia. In carrying out such a program, Stassov saw the first movement as a description of the gathering of ancient Russian princes. In the second movement, he heard the songs of the bayan, the old Russian troubadour. He interpreted the music of the finale as a banquet of old Russian heroes in which the festivities were enlivened by music from such old instruments as the gusla and the bamboo flute.

The main subject of the first movement is presented without any introduction. It is an energetic melody for unison strings, with bassoons and horns coming in for support on alternate measures. This idea recurs throughout the movement, but two other subjects are also discussed. The first of these comes ten measures after the opening, in the woodwind; the second is a nostalgic song first heard in cellos, and then in woodwind. The opening forceful theme becomes the basic material of the powerful coda that ends the movement.

The second movement, a Scherzo, has for a preface several introductory measures. Then two themes are presented: a vigorous statement for the brass, and a syncopated idea for the string. In the trio, we find a pleasing tune for the oboe.

In the slow movement, four introductory measures precede a haunting thought for solo clarinet, accompanied by harp. This is followed by the song of the old troubadours, in horn. The tempo now quickens, and the mood changes dramatically to usher in new material in the strings. Following a thunderous climax, the opening melody returns, this time in the strings; then a solo clarinet brings the movement to an idyllic conclusion.

The principal theme of the finale appears forcefully in full orchestra after a seventeen-measure introduction. The clarinet appears with a contrasting second melody. Then a passage for flute and oboe, accompanied by strings and harp, precede the working-out of this thematic material in an extended development.

1880. ON THE STEPPES OF CENTRAL ASIA, a sketch for orchestra.

For the twenty-fifth anniversary of the reign of Alexander II in 1880, twelve Russian composers were commissioned to write the music for "living pictures" ("tableaux vivants") in which principal events from Russian history were dramatized. Borodin's contribution was *On the Steppes of Central Asia,* a description of the success of Russian arms in Asia. This work became Borodin's most popular one outside Russia; and together with the *Polovtsian Dances* from *Prince Igor,* it is the one heard most frequently at symphony concerts.

In the preface to the published score, the composer appended the following program: "Out of the silence of the sandy steppes of Central Asia come the sounds of a peaceful Russian song. Along with them are heard the melancholy strains of Oriental melodies, then the stamping of approaching horses and camels. A caravan, accompanied by Russian soldiers, traverses the measureless waste. With full trust in its protective escort, it continues its long journey in carefree mood. Onward the caravan moves. The songs of the Russians and those of the Asiatic natives mingle in common harmony. The refrains curl over the desert and then die away in the distance."

The loneliness, the vast expanse of the plains is evoked in the opening measures with a sustained high E played in octaves by two violins. We now hear the "peaceful Russian song" in solo clarinet, and the "melancholy strains" of an Oriental melody in the English horn. Incisive rhythms from plucked strings in cellos and basses suggest the movement of the caravan across the desert. In the development, the two main melodies are treated contrapuntally. The sketch ends atmospherically with the sound of a lonely flute, and the plaintive tones of flute and violins dying away in the distance.

1885. STRING QUARTET NO. 2 IN D MAJOR. I. Allegro moderato. II. Scherzo. III. Notturno. IV. Andante vivace.

If the third movement has a familiar sound today to those hearing this quartet for the first time, it is because this romantic melody was used so successfully for an American popular song, "And This Is My Beloved," by Robert Wright and George Forrest, for their Broadway operetta, *Kismet* (1953), whose entire score is an adaptation of Borodin's music. This music has also been adapted for string orchestra by Sir Malcolm Sargent.

Andrew Porter likens the style of this third-movement Nocturne to that of Chopin's piano pieces "where the melody threads its way over an accompaniment of broken chords, with more and more intricate arabesques."

In the opening Allegro moderato, the first subject is heard in the cello, and repeated by the first violin a fourth higher. After that, a cantabile section for first violin moves over a pizzicato accompaniment. The Scherzo, to Andrew Porter, is "an enchanting movement, as light in touch as one of Mendelssohn's, but harmonically far more interesting." The first theme is made up of quavers, supported by broken chords. A lilting waltz tune enters in the violins after the twenty-first measure. In the Nocturne, the poetic song appears in cello, over syncopated chords in second violin and viola. The finale opens with a recitative-like slow section. In the ensuing Vivace, two themes, says Porter, "are handled as subjects of a quasi-double fugue, which soon gives way to a very long tune."

1887. PRINCE IGOR, folk opera in prologue and four acts, with text by the composer, based on an outline by Vladimir Stassov. First performance: St. Petersburg, November 4, 1890.

In 1869, Stassov brought Borodin the outline of a libretto for a Russian folk opera based on the twelfth-century conflict between Russian forces headed by Prince Igor, and the race of Tartars in Central Asia known as the Polovtsi. The theme entranced Borodin. He immediately made an intensive study of the history of the period, and gathered some of the folk music of Central-Asian tribes. Then he went to work developing the libretto and noting down musical episodes. But the opera went slowly. Time and again, he discarded what he had written to start all over again. At certain times, he stopped working altogether, sometimes because of illness, sometimes to embark on some other project. Then he would return to his opera to write some new numbers. Early in 1887, eighteen years after he first became interested in the project, he was still writing, sketching, and outlining. His death that year left *Prince Igor* incomplete—a good deal of the material still in sketches or in a rough draft, some of the opera entirely missing. Rimsky-Korsakov and Alexander Glazunov assumed the job of restoring order to all this chaos by reassembling the material and completing what Borodin had left unfinished. The final product was produced posthumously, three years after Borodin's death. Though it did not prove to be a consistently inspired work—nor for that matter consistently interesting—the opera did boast some of Borodin's most eloquent pages.

Prince Igor is rarely produced today, mainly because it fails to sustain interest, being more lyrical than dramatic, and lacks a strong central plot. "As static as an oratorio," explains Richard Anthony Leonard, "it needs . . . the splendor of brilliant staging to bring it to life in the theater. Meanwhile, its individual numbers keep it green: many stirring choruses, arias which are in the repertories of all Russian singers, and the incomparable dances."

The best of these individual numbers include the following: the first-act basso aria, "I hate a Dreary Life"; the villagers' chorus, "We Come in Our Distress" and the duet of Yaroslavna and Galitsky; in the second act, the girls' chorus, "The Prairie Flowereth," the *Polovtsian Dances,* the tenor aria, "Daylight is Fading," and the baritone aria, "No Sleep, No Rest"; in the third act, the opening *Polovtsi March;* and in the fourth, the peasants' chorus, "'Twas Not the Furious Tempest Wind," and the duet, "The Surroundings Are Sad."

The second act *Polovtsian Dances* are particularly popular, the main reason why this opera will always be remembered. They appear toward the end of the act, during a lavish feast given by Khan Konchak, the leader of the Polovtsi for his captives, Prince Igor and Igor's son. In the opera, this music is scored for chorus and orchestra, but at symphony concerts today the chorus is dispensed with.

The first dance brings on the procession of the royal captives with an Oriental melody for flute and oboe. Then comes the dance of the savage men, accompanied by a lively tune for clarinet over a descending and sharply accented phrase. In the dance of the boys, war games are simulated, the music for this being a forceful, syncopated melody for strings, interrupted by clashes of the cymbals. Then comes the dance of the young girls in which a tortuous, sensual Oriental melody is shared by violins and cellos. At the end, the dancers salute the Khan Konchak to music that is brilliant in color and dynamic in rhythm.

In the prologue, a Russian army, headed by Prince Igor and his son, set forth to attack the Polovtsi. During their absence, Igor's brother-in-law, Prince Galitsky tries to stir up the people against the Prince, and is denounced by Igor's wife, the Princess Yaroslavna. All this transpires in the first act, which ends with the news that Igor and his army have suffered a terrible defeat. In the second and third acts, Prince Igor and his son are captives in the camp of the Polvtsis. After the Russian warriors are treated with the ceremony and festivities befitting their station, Igor's son, Vladimir, falls in love with the daughter of Khan Konchak. Thus he prefers to remain behind in the camp of the enemy when the father makes his escape. In the last act, Prince Igor returns triumphantly to his palace—and to the arms of his wife.

MODEST MUSSORGSKY 1839–1881

The four other members of the "Five" were more sophisticated, better trained, and more cultured than Mussorgsky. But for all the crudities of his harmonic writing and orchestration, for all his lack of a proper technique, Mussorgsky was the genius of this group. He was the individualist, the original, the one least derived from or indebted to Western musical culture. He was the innovator and the seer, the one opening up new horizons for music. Like his colleagues, he was a nationalist, his music being Russian to the core. But he had another vision, too. He wanted his music to arrive at a truth intimately tied up with life and people. Beauty of sound, richness of emotion, perfection of technique and structure did not interest him. "The quest for artistic beauty for its own sake," he said, "is sheer puerility —it is art in its nonage." His music had to be a reflection of mankind and living as he saw them—crude, raw, undisciplined.

To arrive at this musical truth, he had to devise a new kind of melody modeled after speech inflections. He called it "the melody of life," adding proudly, and somewhat defiantly: "If I succeed, I shall be a conqueror in art —and succeed I must!" What he aimed for in opera was "to make my characters speak on the stage as they would in real life, and yet write music that is thoroughly artistic. . . . If I have succeeded in rendering the straightforward expression of thoughts and feelings as it takes place in ordinary speech, and if my rendering is artistic and musicianly, then the deed is done."

In this passionate, indefatigable search for a new truth in his operas and songs—for these are the two areas in which his genius flourished—he had to open new paths. Sometimes he was far ahead of his own times—with unusual chord sequences, unconventional modulations, unorthodox rhythm patterns, abrupt transitions. Sometimes he returned to the past, to the modal scales and part-writing of the old Russian polyphony. "In the uphill task of discovering the means of expression he required," says M.D. Calvocoressi, "he found guidance in his intuition, in the idiosyncrasies of his nature and even in his prejudices—his mistrust of conventions and of theoretical learning, which might lead him to rely on conventional values, in his acquired views on the realistic function of music; in the native folk music in which, from his earliest childhood, he had been steeped; and above all, in his auditory sensitiveness and imagination."

His strength lay in his capacity to project dramatic values, whether in opera or in song. Indeed, Gerald Abraham maintains, "no musician has been more completely a dramatic composer than Mussorgsky. As a musical translator of words and all that can be expressed in words, of psychological states and even physical movements, he is unsurpassed."

Modest Mussorgsky, son of a prosperous landowner, was born in Karevo, in the district of Pskov, Russia, on March 21, 1839. Though he early received musical training from his mother and Anton Hernke, and though he published a piano piece when he was sixteen, he was directed to a career in the army. After graduating from cadet school of the Imperial Guard, in 1856, he became a member of the Preobrazhensky Regiment. One year later, his friendship with Balakirev, César Cui (1835–1918), and Alexander Dargomyzhsky (1813–1869) reawakened his early and dormant interest in music. He studied with

Balakirev for a brief period, then wrote some songs and two piano sonatas. His reborn passion for music led him to resign his army commission and devote himself completely to that art. Under Balakirev's guidance, he now completed his first mature work, the Scherzo in B-flat for orchestra, whose première was conducted by Anton Rubinstein in St. Petersburg on January 23, 1860.

The emancipation of the serfs in 1861 led to the liquidation of the Mussorgsky estate. Now in financial difficulties for the first time, Mussorgsky was compelled to work for a living. Between 1863 and 1867, he served as clerk in the Ministry of Communications, without deserting composition. In 1864, he completed the first act of an opera, *The Marriage,* in which he made his first significant experiments with speech-like melodies. Between 1865 and 1866, he completed several remarkable songs; and between 1860 and 1866, sketches of his first orchestral work still fresh in the symphonic repertory, *A Night on Bald Mountain*.

He was back in government service in 1869, working for the next eleven years in the department of forestry. But all the time, he was suffering from nervous disorders which had plagued him from 1858 on. In addition, spiritual and moral disintegration had begun to take place, as he yielded more and more helplessly to the addiction of drink, and sought out the society of disreputable people. Nevertheless, he managed to produce a handful of masterworks, among them being his epic folk opera, *Boris Godunov,* first produced in St. Petersburg in 1874; also the song cycles *Sunless* and *Songs* and *Dances of Death,* the *Pictures at an Exhibition* for piano, and two operas he did not live to complete, *Khovanchina* and *The Fair at Sorochinsk*. Mussorgsky died of an apoplectic stroke in St. Petersburg on March 28, 1881. Most of his scores were revised and edited by Rimsky-Korsakov.

1858. SCHERZO IN B-FLAT MAJOR, for orchestra.

Mussorgsky's first ambitious work for the orchestra, the Scherzo in B-flat, originated as a piano piece; it was then orchestrated by the composer, this version being introduced in St. Petersburg in 1860. When Mussorgsky first played the piano version for Borodin, the latter remarked: "I was absolutely amazed at the strange elements in his music. I cannot say that his music pleased me at first, though I was greatly impressed by the novelty of it; but the longer I listened, the more I came to enjoy it."

The principal theme is heard at once in first violins. The middle part was described by the composer as "something in the Oriental style." It opens with a singing tune for flutes and clarinets over a tonic pedal in horns and low strings. Muted and divided strings then take over. A crescendo for trombones leads into a loud restatement by full orchestra of the opening subject.

1867. INTERMEZZO—IN MODO CLASSICO, for orchestra (also for piano).

While spending a winter holiday on his family estate in Pskov in 1861, Mussorgsky became entranced with the sight of peasant lads ploughing through the thick snows. "Suddenly in the distance a crowd of young women appeared, singing as they came along the shining way. The picture at once took shape in my imagination; quite unexpectedly, the first theme of my Intermezzo was born, with its vigorous down and up, Bach-like movement; and the merry laughing young women were transformed into the theme that I afterwards used for the middle part, or trio—all in modo classico in keeping with my musical activities at that time." He wrote it first, in 1861, as a piano piece, then in 1867 orchestrated it. It opens with a downward leaping phrase for unison and octave strings. This is followed by the first principal subject, in clarinets and bassoons. The middle trio, into which Mussorgsky brought the "merry, laughing women" is introduced by a theme for flutes and clarinets over plucked strings in violas and cellos."

1868–1877. SONG CYCLES, for voice and piano:

The Nursery: 1. With Nurse. 2. In the Corner. 3. The Cockchafer. 4. With the Doll. 5. Going to Sleep. 6. On the Hobbyhorse. 7. The Cat 'Sailor.'

Sunless: 1. Between Four Walls. 2. Thou Didst Know Me in the Crowd. 3. The Idle, Noisy Day Is Ended. 4. Boredom. 5. Elegy. 6. On the River.

Songs and Dances of Death: 1. Lullaby. 2. Serenade. 3. Trepak. 4. The Field Marshal.

Mussorgsky created a landmark in Russian song through his search for musical realism and through his rare gift at molding a melodic line to the rhythm and inflections of speech. His songs may be comical or tragic, satirical or tender, charmingly nonsensical or profoundly grim. But in projecting a scene or a mood, in delineating character, and in their theatrical effects, they are all basically the work of a dramatist rather than a melodist.

Some of his individual songs have become popular, most notably the amusing "Song of the Flea," words by Goethe (1879). However, it is in his three song cycles that he attains the heights within the song form. The seven numbers in *The Nursery* (1868–1872), text by the composer, are, as Gerald Abraham points out, a "series of musical transcriptions of a child's speech caught with extraordinary truth and total absence of adult sentiment. All existing musical conventions are thrown overboard; the voice part is often the purest musical prose."

In *Sunless,* words by Golenischev-Kutuzov (1874), realism gives way, says Gerald Abraham, to "subjective, pessimistic emotion. Mussorgsky now speaks to his own person, not as a village idiot, sex-tormented theological student, or little boy, and his utterance is touched by almost lyrical melancholy." Here the composer deserts a national idiom to create a feeling of melancholy, at times desolation, through stark melodies and unorthodox harmonies.

In the *Songs and Dances of Death,* words once again by Golenischev-Kutuzov (1875–1877), the pessimism of *Sunless* is brought within the framework of a miniature musical drama. Here, says Kurt Schindler, "we find a descriptive power uncanny in its visual correctness; melodic lines of undreamed of boldness; harmonies that none other heard or felt before him; and a masterful handling of technical resources and of declamation. A child dies in his mother's arms; death serenades a sick girl; death dances with a drunk peasant lost in a snowstorm; death rides a moonlit battlefield." What we have here, as Richard Anthony Leonard has said, "the paradox of Death, with its irony and degradation, its lacerating cruelty for the living, its spiritual justification. . . . Always there is tenderness, and yet an uncompromising directness and force. The composer evokes the pity and the tragedy of human life and death in the terms of the highest art."

1872. BORIS GODUNOV, opera in prologue and four acts, with text by the composer, based on Pushkin's historical drama and Nikolai Karamazin's *History of the Russian Empire*. First performance: St. Petersburg, February 8, 1874.

Russian national opera, first conceived by Glinka, and then further developed by Dargomyzhsky and by Mussorgsky's colleagues of "The Five," achieved its apotheosis with *Boris Godunov*. This is the supreme national opera, not only because its subject is a segment of Russian history, but also because text and music penetrate so deeply and profoundly into the psyche of Russian characters, into the very soul of the Russian people. "To seek assiduously the most delicate and subtle features of human nature—of the human crowd—to follow them into unknown regions, to make them of our own; this seems to me the true vocation of the artist . . . to feed upon humanity as a healthy diet which had been neglected—there lies the whole problem of art." Thus spoke Mussorgsky. In *Boris Godunov,* he finally fulfilled his own destiny as a musical interpreter of human nature and of the crowd. For as M. Montagu-Nathan has suggested, Mussorgsky's opera does not make Boris Godunov the sole or even central point of interest in his opera. "From the earliest moment in the prologue the People, their sentiments and their actions, are brought well to the fore. Even without a knowledge of Mussorgsky's sympathies, it would require much penetration to perceive that the hero of *Boris Godunov* is the Russian nation and the ostensible protagonists are in reality nothing but objects on which the light of nationalism may shine." Secondary only to the people themselves—and to the complex emotional forces that were brought to play on them—is the panorama of the times, the social conditions and the mores. An entire epoch unfolds in this opera.

The many different versions that exist today of *Boris* deserve some clarification. The first was Mussorgsky's original conception, consisting of seven scenes, which he completed in 1869. "What strikes us when we consider the original version of *Boris,*" says M. D. Calvocoressi, "are its starkness and terseness. It does not, like the later version, afford hearers any opportunity for relief. It pursues its grim course without an instant of intermission, except when the tension is relieved awhile by touches of character-comedy in the dialogue. . . . And even at these points, there is nothing (except Vaarlam's song, 'In the Town of Kazan') that comes as an intermezzo inducing a halt, however brief, of the action. Every one of these touches is part and parcel of the whole."

At the request of the directors of the Maryinsky Theater, Mussorgsky revised *Boris* extensively to make it more palatable. He introduced some love interest and several new attractive airs; he shifted the scenes around for greater theatrical effect; he omitted some material that had proved too provocative or lacked audience-appeal. This is the second version, the one with which *Boris Godunov* made its bow to the world on February 8, 1874. The opera was a huge success; the composer took thirty curtain calls. But the critics were united in their hostility. One called the opera a "cacophony in five acts"; another described it as "unimaginable chaos"; a third found it to be "disorderly, formless, shameless." After twenty-five performances the government censor stepped in and banned all further presentations.

The next time the opera was given—in 1896, fifteen years after the composer's death—it was heard in an edited and reorchestrated version by Rimsky-Korsakov. After that, Rimsky-Korsakov subjected his own adaptation to several revisions. His new adaptation was produced in 1904 with Feodor Chaliapin in the title role. This was the version used for many years throughout the world. It was presented at the Paris Opéra in 1908; in London in 1913; and in the United States for its American première, at the Metropolitan Opera, also in 1913, on March 19.

Many critics have long felt that the refinements and sophistication of Rimsky-Korsakov's editing had robbed *Boris* of a good deal of its elemental power and originality. On February 16, 1928, the Bolshoi Theater presented *Boris* as Mussorgsky wrote it; and a year and a half later, Leopold Stokowski conducted it in a concert performance in the United States. Since then, several important attempts have been made to achieve a compromise between the original conception and Rimsky-Korsakov's edited version—notably by Karol Rathaus and by Dmitri Shostakovich.

The central character of the opera is, to be sure, the Czar of Russia who ruled from 1598 to 1605. The prologue transpires in the courtyard of the monastery Novodievich in Moscow. A crowd begs Boris Godunov to ascend the throne, recently vacated by the death of Czar Feodor ("Why Hast Thou Abandoned Us?"). From the distance come the voices of pilgrims appealing to Heaven to protect Russia. When they come on the scene, they distribute amulets to the people, and urge the widow of Czar Feodor to use her influence to sway Boris's decision. Boris finally relents. In the second part of the prologue, his coronation takes place with pomp and ceremony in the courtyard of the Kremlin. The people, Prince Shuisky at their head, acclaim their hero ("To the Sun in All Splendor"). When Boris finally appears, he invokes the help of the Almighty. As the procession moves into the Cathedral, church bells toll, and the people sing a hymn of rejoicing.

Five years pass. The first scene of the first act takes place in a cell in the Monastery of the Miracles. Pimen is describing the events recently transpired in Russia ("Still One Page More"). Near him, the young monk, Gregory, is crying out in his sleep, tortured by a dream that has come to him three times. When he awakens, he describes it to Pimen; the old monk suggests he seek peace in prayer and fasting. Pimen then tells Gregory how Boris's men have murdered the Czarevitch Dmitri, who was as old as and looked like Gregory. This information fires the young monk with the ambition to avenge Dmitri's murder by assuming his identity.

The scene changes to an inn on the Lithuanian border. Two wandering monks—Vaarlam and Missail—enter, blessing the inn and its hostess. With them is Gregory, disguised as a peasant, in flight from police, who charge him with spreading the false rumor that Dmitri is still alive. Refreshed and invigorated by wine, Vaarlam embarks upon a delightful ditty, "In the Town of Kazan," then falls into a sound sleep. Several guards come for Gregory. He deflects their suspicions towards Vaarlam while making his own escape.

In an apartment in the Kremlin—in the second act—Xenia and Feodor, Boris's two children, are listening to their nurse singing a folk tune, "Song of the Gnat." Upon Boris's appearance, he praises Feodor for having learned his lessons so well, reminding him that some day he will be Czar. Then Boris is tormented by all the conspirators who surround him and for the way he is ever blamed for evils attending his land and people ("I Have Attained Highest Power"). Hardly has he finished his soliloquy when Prince Shuisky informs him that the people are rallying under the leadership of a false Dmitri. This news fills the Czar with the morbid delusion that Dmitri has risen from the grave. He is seized by terror and hallucinations, convinced that the ghost of the murdered Dmitri is haunting him. He prays to God for mercy ("Ah, I am Suffocating").

In the third, or "Polish" act—added by the composer to make the opera more appealing to his audiences through the introduction of a female character—Marina, daughter of a Polish landowner, aspires to be Czarina. She is in her apartment, where maidens entertain her by praising her beauty. After they leave, Marina confesses her dream of interesting Poles in the cause of Dmitri, and at the same time getting him to fall in love with her. A Jesuit, Rangoni, comes to plead with her that, should he ever reach Moscow, she would help convert Russian heretics to the true faith. And now the scene is in a moonlit garden at the castle at Sandomir. Dmitri is waiting for a word from Marina, and as he waits, he sings of his great love for her. The Jesuit, Rangoni, convinces him that Marina is in love with him. This news makes Dmitri determined to make her his Czarina. When several Polish nobles, accompanied by Marina, come into the garden, Dmitri goes into hiding. Music of a polonaise comes from within the castle to accompany their conversation as they contemplate a march to Moscow and as they express their admiration for Marina. One of the Polish noblemen is particularly attentive to Marina. This leads Dmitri to suspect that the Jesuit has fooled him, that she is in love with somebody else. After the nobles re-enter the castle, Gregory has an opportunity to speak to Marina. She insists she can be his, only after he has become the Czar of Russia. But she is in love with him, and a passionate exchange of tender sentiments follows ("Oh, Czarevitch").

The fourth act opens in the forest of Kromy. A boyar has been captured by the peasants. They taunt him, and make sport of the Czar. This byplay is interrupted by the appearance of the village idiot, chanting a little ditty, "In the Moonlight the Cats are Crying." Vaarlam and Missail come upon the scene, denounce Boris, and join the peasants in singing the praises of the false Dmitri. Two Jesuits try to participate, but are beaten by the mob, which resents having the clergy in its camp. Martial music heralds the approach of Gregory and his troops. After they proceed on their way to Moscow, the idiot bewails the tragedy about to befall the Russian people.

The final scene is in the reception hall in the Kremlin. The boyars brand Dmitri a traitor, promising death to all following him. Prince Shuisky arrives with terrifying news: Boris is in a state of agony, having seen the murdered Dmitri in a hallucination. And now Boris himself appears. He is distraught, and talks to himself. Painfully, he mounts the throne and begs the boyars to give him guidance. The monk Pimen asks for an audience to inform Boris of a strange tale about a blind shepherd who recovered his vision magically at Dmitri's tomb. The story fills Boris with horror. Dismissing the boyars, he calls for his son Feodor to bid him farewell ("Farewell, My Son, I Am Dying"). Then he proclaims him the new Czar and prays to heaven to guide and protect him. Bells toll. The offstage chant of the people is audible. With a last whisper to his son to forgive him, Boris collapses and dies.

1872–1875. KHOVANTCHINA, musical drama in five acts, with text by the composer and Vladimir Stassov. First performance: St. Petersburg, February 21, 1886.

It was Stassov who suggested to Mussorgsky the subject of *Khovantchina* for an opera. "It seemed to me," Stassov recalled, "that the contrasting and clashing of the Old Russia with the New, the passing of the former and the birth of the latter, afforded a rich subject." Mussorgsky agreed. The major part of his opera was written between 1872 and 1875. Nevertheless, he kept on working on it until his last days. He did not live to complete it; that job was done for him by Rimsky-Korsakov.

Rosa Newmarch explains that *Khovantchina* is a series a vignettes that add up to a panorama of a period in Russia history rather than an integrated drama with character development. The libretto includes numerous episodes that have little relation to the basic plot. To Paul Rosenfeld, this opera is a "glowing portrait of the collective entity, the Russian people . . . executed with a feeling and truthfulness and a power matched by no other of its musical portraitists and by only a few of the composers who have enriched the world. . . . The music of *Khovantchina* is vocal of the very essences of the people, its forces, its sense of the starkness of life, and of the inevitability of suffering, its Asiatic fatalism."

The opera opens with an evocative prelude entitled *Dawn on the Moskava River*. A folk tune, and five variations, suggest a dreary landscape—a cold winter daybreak over the Kremlin. "Nothing in Russian music," says Rosa Newmarch, "is more intensely or touchingly national in feeling." The curtain rises on Red Square, the bells sounding the approach of dawn. Prince Ivan Khovantsky is arousing the Streltsy, a band of radicals, to rise against the Czar. At the same time, a counterplot is hatched by the boyar Shaklovity, who forges a letter intending to prove that the Prince is a traitor. Meanwhile, Andrei, the Prince's son, becomes interested in a young German girl, Emma, whose arrest is ordered by the Prince. The leader of the Old Believers, Dositheus, rescues her.

In the second act, Marfa, a young widow, reads to Prince Galitzin a horoscope foretelling a tragic future. Terrified, the Prince secretly orders Marfa's death. When Prince Khovantsky appears, Galitzin quarrels with him, but the situation is saved by the sudden appearance of Dositheus.

Marfa's life, however, is spared. In the third act, in a street outside Khovantsky's house, she recalls how she had once been in love with Andrei. Night falls. In a beautiful air, "Yes, the Streltsy Are Sleeping," the boyar, Shaklovity, comments on the surrounding peace and quiet. But the tranquillity is soon shattered with the appearance of the Streltsy; its members exchange heated words with their wives, who object to their activities. When the news comes that the insurrection againt the Czar has been smashed with foreign help, the Streltsy pray for divine assistance.

In the first scene of the fourth act, a lavish feast is taking place at Prince Khovantsky's country house. It is here that the "Dance of the Persian Slaves" takes place—one of Mussorgsky's better-known pieces of orchestral music, rich in Oriental colors and pulsing rhythms. After Shaklovity summons the Prince to a council of State, assassins penetrate the house and kill Khovantsky. A famous orchestral entr'acte—a landscape picture of Siberian plains—separates this scene from the one that follows. In this episode, a lugubrious melody for solo trumpet and violins is the main subject. The second scene takes place in a square before the Church. Prince Galitzin is en route to exile, and Dositheus voices a lament for Russia. In despair at the tragic turn of events, the Streltsy plan to destroy themselves, but are saved when they get the news that the Czar has forgiven them.

In the last act, in a wood near Moscow, the Old Believers plan their self-destruction. Marfa applies a torch to a funeral pyre. Proudly chanting a hymn, the Old Believers march to their death in the flames.

1874. PICTURES AT AN EXHIBITION, suite for piano (orchestrated by Maurice Ravel): I. Promenade. II. The Gnomes. III. Old Castle. IV. Tuileries. V. Bydlo—Polish Oxcart. VI. Ballet of the Chicks in their Shells. VII. Samuel Goldenberg and Schmuyle. VIII. Limoges: The Market Place. IX. Catacombs. X. The Hut on Fowl's Legs. XI. The Great Gate of Kiev.

Mussorgsky wrote this piano suite in 1874, after visiting a posthumous exhibit of paintings and drawings by his friend, Victor Hartmann. The pictures stimulated him. "Ideas, melodies come to me of their own accord, like the roast pigeons in the story—I gorge and gorge and overeat myself. I can hardly manage to put it down on paper fast enough." He chose nine of Hartmann's pictures and sketches for musical delineation; and he caught the essence of each with vivid tonal realism and an extraordinary capacity for uncovering Hartmann's most subtle artistic intentions.

While Mussorgsky's original version for solo piano is occasionally given at concerts, and has been recorded, this work is undoubtedly best known through its orchestral transcriptions. Among those who have translated it into symphonic terms are Lucien Cailliet, Fabien Sevitzky, Leopold Stokowski, Granville Bantock, Sir Henry J. Wood, and Maurice Ravel. Ravel's version is the best known of these versions, and is the one that will be discussed here; it was commissioned by the conductor, Serge Koussevitzky, who introduced it in Paris in 1923.

The work opens with a preface, a "Promenade." The composer is here shown, through a brisk Russian melody, walking through the gallery, from picture to picture. This "walking theme" is repeated throughout the work. The second section describes a picture of a gnome, a design for a nutcracker, with a sprightly melody in halty rhythms. The third part contains a poignant melody inspired by a medieval castle, in front of which stands a troubadour. The opening walking theme now serves as a link to the Tuileries, the famous garden in Paris. Hartmann's painting shows children at play and their nurses. Mussorgsky's music recreates the gay hubbub with a brusque melody and vigorous rhythms. In "Bydlo,"—a Polish cart with huge wheels—we hear the stumbling progress of the vehicle in a heavy-footed melody with an abrupt rhythm. As the wagon approaches, the music grows in sonority; and as it disappears, the music fades away. Hartmann's designs for the costumes and setting for a ballet provides the composer with material for the next part. Another repetition of the walking theme now brings on a witty tonal representation of chicks and canaries within their shells; they are dressed absurdly in suits resembling armor and their heads resemble helmets. The portrait of two Jews follows, that of Samuel Goldenburg and Schmuyle—based on sketches made by Hartmann when he visited the Polish town of Sandomierz. One of these Jews is rich, and is portrayed by a proud, stately melody; the other, poor and humble, is evoked through a weak, indecisive little subject. There follows a brilliant picture of a market place at Limoges, a fluttering melody with leaping rhythms suggesting the gossip of housewives. By contrast, there now comes a somber melody with heavy chords, depicting catacombs. "The creative spirit of the dead Hartmann," wrote Mussorgsky about this section, "leads me toward skulls, apostrophizes them—the skulls are illuminated gently from within." An Oriental design of a clock in the shape of a hut, standing on chicken-feet and boasting two cocks' heads, provided Mussorgsky with his next episode. This picture suggested to Mussorgsky Baba Yaga, the witch, as she soars through the air in pursuit of victims. The basic material here is a melody in simple Russian folk-song style. The suite comes to a sonorous and majestic conclusion with a description of "The Great Gate of Kiev"—sketches by Hartmann for a projected monument in Kiev.

1877. A NIGHT ON BALD MOUNTAIN, fantasy for orchestra.

The subject of a witches' revel, similar to the Walpurgis Night in Goethe's *Faust,* haunted Mussorgsky for many years. In 1860, he made some sketches for a musical setting of a drama called *The Witch,* in which witches and sorcerers performed their rites and do a dance to Satan. When Balakirev proved unenthusiastic over this project, Mussorgsky put his sketches aside. In 1867, he tried adapting them into a fantasy for piano and orchestra. Later on, in 1871, when members of the "Russian Five" planned to collaborate on an opera, *Mlada,* Mussorgsky thought of using his sketches for a second-act prelude about a Witches' Sabbath; but the *Mlada* project never materialized. In 1877, while working on his opera, *The Fair at Sorotchinsk,* Mussorgsky thought of using his Witches' Sabbath music as an intermezzo describing a nightmare of a Ukrainian peasant. But not until after Mussorgsky's death was the composer's music crystallized into its final shape and form. At that time Rimsky-Korsakov assembled the sketches, revised them, reorchestrated them, and developed them into an integrated fantasia. In this new and definitive setting, *A Night on Bald Mountain* was finally introduced in 1886.

"Bald Mountain" is Mt. Triglav in the vicinity of Kiev, where, according to folk lore, witches, sorcerers, and evil spirits, presided over by the Black God, Tchernobog, gather on St. John's Eve for revelry. The published score offers the following program: "A subterranean din of unearthly voices. Appearance of the Spirits of Darkness, followed by that of Tchernobog, Glorification of the Black Gods, The Black Mass. The Revelry of Witches' Sabbath, interrupted from afar by the bells of a little church, whereupon the spirits of evil disperse. Dawn breaks."

An eerie, supernatural atmosphere is immediately introduced in the opening measures with violins in upper register, and phrases in woodwind, trombone, and bassoons. The revelry begins with a savage Russian dance in the violins and clarinets. It begins softly enough, but soon develops with demoniac abandon. The excitement dies down; a quieter atmosphere prevails. A subdued dance is now presented by woodwind, supported by the strings. But the demons once again become uninhibited; shrieks in woodwind and strings describe an orgy. When the revels reach a peak of excitation, a sudden pause takes place. Church bells sound. Muted violins tell of the departing flight of the demons and spirits, while a clarinet, over muted strings, suggests the approach of dawn.

1880. HOPAK (or GOPAK), from THE FAIR AT SOROTCHINSK, for orchestra.

Between 1874 and 1880, Mussorgsky made sketches for an opera based on Gogol's story, *Evenings on a Farm near Diakanka.* He did not complete the project. Three different composers worked out Mussorgsky's materials into a full-length opera—César Cui, I. Sakhonovsky, and Nikolai Tcherepnine. Other versions of the opera were later prepared by Emil Cooper and Vissarion Shebalin, with the collaboration of Paul Lamm. Tcherepnine's adaptation (in which he used music from other Mussorgsky compositions) is the one most widely favored. It was heard for the first time in Monte Carlo on March 7, 1923, and received its American première at the Metropolitan Opera on November 29, 1930. When the world première of *The Fair* was given in St. Petersburg on December 30, 1911, the orchestration of Liadov was used.

The plot concerns the efforts of the peasant, Tcherevik, to marry off his daughter to Pritzko. The girl's mother, however, favors the pastor's son. She finally becomes amenable to having her daughter marry Pritzko when she herself and the pastor's son become emotionally involved.

The most popular excerpt from this opera is the robust, spirited folk dance with two beats to a measure—the Hopak that comes in the third act.

NIKOLAI RIMSKY-KORSAKOV 1844–1908

Rimsky-Korsakov was the youngest of the quintet of Russian national composers. Like the others in the group, with the exception of Balakirev, he was, for a long time, an amateur using more instinct and experiment than trained methods. Indeed, when Rimsky-Korsakov was first appointed professor of composition and instrumentation at the St. Petersburg Conservatory in 1871, he did not even know at that time how to "harmonize a chorale properly," as he himself confessed, and he had "never written a single contrapuntal exercise in my life, and had only the haziest understanding of strict fugue; I didn't even know the names of the augmented and diminished intervals or chords." He took on this teaching post, nevertheless, and proceeded to combine his duties with a study of all phases of musical theory. From such unsatisfactory beginnings, he developed into the recognized dean of the "Russian Five"—a scholar and a craftsman, whose technique in composition was virtually an art all its own. His genius at orchestration, for example, was without equal among his Russian contemporaries.

Of course, his goal was nationalism. He achieved it by drawing deep from the well of old Russian folk songs (whose melodies he edited and imitated) and old Russian church music (whose harmonies and scales intruded into his own writing). But where Mussorgsky digressed into realism and Borodin into Orientalism, Rimsky-Korsakov remained the Russian sophisticate, carrying into his composition an elegance of style, a culture, and a healthy optimism that kept him safe from the melancholia that afflicted so many of his colleagues. He was probably at his best when he allowed his musical imagination to roam unrestricted in the world of fantasy, legend, or fairy tales. "He invented the perfect music for such a fantastic world," says Gerald Abraham, "music insubstantial when it was matched with unreal things, deliciously lyrical when it touched reality, in both cases colored from the most superb palette a musician has ever held.

Nikolai Rimsky-Korsakov was born in Tikhvin, near Novgorod, Russia, on March 18, 1844, to an aristocratic family. From 1856 to 1862, he attended the Naval College in St. Petersburg, a period during which he managed to get some music instruction from private teachers. A meeting with Balakirev in 1861 further stimulated his musical interests. He began a period of study with that composer. But it soon had to be terminated when Rimsky-Korsakov was assigned to the clipper *Almaz*, and embarked on a cruise around the world lasting two and a half years. While thus engaged, he completed his first symphony, introduced in St. Petersburg in 1865, soon after his return to Russia. Then, inspired by his associations with Balakirev, Cui, Mussorgsky, and Borodin, he now dedicated himself to composition. Between 1865 and 1868, he completed several orchestral works, including his second symphony, *Antar*. In 1871, he was appointed professor of composition at the St. Petersburg Conservatory; and on January 13, 1873, his first opera, *The Maid of Pskov*, was introduced at the Maryinsky Theater in St. Petersburg. In that same year of 1873, he finally retired from the Navy, to receive an honorary appointment as Inspector of Naval Bands, which he held until that post was abolished in 1884. From 1874 to 1881, he conducted the orchestral concerts at the Free School; and from 1886 to 1900, he was the conductor of the Russian Symphony Concerts. He also achieved notable successes with the baton in Paris and Brussels. Meanwhile, in 1873, he had married Nadezhda Purgold, an excellent pianist.

Between 1880 and 1890, Rimsky-Korsakov completed several of his most famous compositions. These included the opera *Snegurochka* (*The Snow Maiden*), in 1881; the *Capriccio espagnol* for orchestra, in 1887; and in 1888, *Russian Easter Overture* and *Scheherazade*, both for orchestra. All this while, he was pursuing a highly successful career at the Conservatory, where his pupils included Liadov, Ippolitov-Ivanov, Gretchaninov, and Glazunov, among many others. In 1905, he was dismissed as professor when he objected vigorously to the stringent police supervision of Conservatory students. However, when late in 1905, the Conservatory was reorganized with Glazunov as director, and the police relinquished its authority over students, Rimsky-Korsakov returned to his old teaching post and held it for the rest of his life. Among his later works were some of his finest operas, among these being *The Legend of the Invisible City of Kitezh* in 1905 and *Le Coq d'or* (*The Golden Cockerel*) in 1907. Rimsky-Korsakov died in St. Petersburg on June 21, 1908.

1865–1898. SONGS, for voice and piano:
"In the Silence of the Night," op. 56, no. 2; "It Is Not the Wind," op. 43, no. 2; "The Nightingale and the Rose," op. 2, no. 2; "Oh, if Thou Couldst Only for a Moment," op. 39, no. 1.

"The Nightingale and the Rose," possibly its composer's most popular song, belongs to the early period of his career (1865–1866), when he was strongly influenced by Balakirev and Cui. The song, poem by Koltsov, is sometimes also known as "Eastern Romance." Here, says James Husst Hall, we do not find the "ordinary realism of the poet's lute, or the song of the nightingale, or the East where the scene is fancied," but the fusion of all these elements into "a new intangible poetry."

A strong personal identity and a new approach to vocalism can be met within the many songs Rimsky-Korsakov completed between 1897 and 1898, mainly to poems by A. K. Tolstoy and Maikov. These became apparent in the *Four Songs,* op. 39 (1897), in which the composer returned to songwriting after the absence of a number of years. The most familiar number in this group is "Oh, if Thou Couldst Only for a Moment." Here is how the composer himself described his new approach to writing songs: "The melody, following the turns of the text, poured out from me in a surely vocal form, i.e., it was so in its very origin, accompanied only by hints at harmony and key plan. The accompaniment was devised and worked out after the composition of the melody, whereas formerly—with few exceptions—the melody was conceived as it were instrumentally, i.e., apart from the text and only harmonizing with its general content, or evoked by the harmonic basis which sometimes precedes the melody. Feeling that the new way of composing produced true vocal music, and being satisfied with my first attempts in this direction, I composed one song after another." The finest of these later songs were "It is Not the Wind" in the cycle, *Spring,* text by Tolstoy (1897); and "In the Silence of the Night," from *Two Songs for Soprano,* words by Maikov (1898).

1868. SYMPHONY NO. 2, "ANTAR," op. 9. I. Largo; Allegro giocoso. II. Allegro; Molto allegro; Allargando. III. Allegro risoluto alla marcia. IV. Allegretto vivace; Andante amoroso.

The middle and the most celebrated of Rimsky-Korsakov's three symphonies was written in 1868, but extensively revised in 1875. The composer derived his program from an Arabian tale by Sennkovsky. Antar, an enemy of all mankind, has become a recluse in a desert, where he saves a graceful gazelle from an attack by a bird. Falling alseep, he dreams he is in the palace of Queen of Palmyra. The Queen, the fairy Gul-Nazar, is actually the gazelle Antar has rescued. In gratitude, the Queen permits him the fulfillment of three of life's greatest joys: vengeance, power, and love. Antar accepts these blessings gratefully, then entreats the Queen to take his life if ever the pleasures of love begin to become boring. Antar then falls in love with the Queen, but in time he is weary of his passion. The Queen takes him in her arms and kisses him with such ferocity that his life ebbs away.

This entire legend is interpreted in the first movement; the next three movements are concerned with each of the three delights enjoyed by Antar. Two important melodies recur throughout the symphony. The first suggests Antar, and is given by the violas in the introduction to the opening movement. Later on in the same movement, the flutes and horns offer a melody representing the Queen.

Here is how César Cui described the four movements: In the first, "Antar is in the desert. He saves a gazelle from a beast of prey. The gazelle is a fay, who rewards her deliverer by granting him three pleasures. The whole of this part, which begins and ends with a picture of the desolate and boundless desert, is worthy of the composer's magic brush." The second movement is "the pleasure of Vengeance—a rugged, savage, unbridled Allegro, with crescendos like the letting loose of furious winds." In the third movement we see "the pleasure of Power." This is "an Oriental march, a masterpiece of the finest and most brilliant interpretation." The finale devotes itself to the "pleasure of Love, amid which Antar expires." This is a "delicate, poetic, delicious Andante."

1879. OVERTURE TO MAY NIGHT, for orchestra.

May Night was Rimsky-Korsakov's second complete opera, produced in St. Petersburg in 1880. This work, as the composer revealed in his autobiography, was closely bound up with his courtship of his wife. It also marked the beginning of his desertion of a purely polyphonic style that had characterized (and marred) his first opera, *The Maid of Pskov*. After that, Rimsky-Korsakov's style was intimately related to Glinka's.

The text of *May Night* was prepared by the composer from a tale by Gogol. It placed a good deal of emphasis on pageantry and ballet. The overture opens romantically (Molto andante) with a fanciful episode that carries the listener into the world of fantasy. An atmospheric horn solo (Andantino) leads to the overture's main section. Here the principal material consists of a melody that sounds like a folk song, and a vivacious tune shared by violins and woodwind. Frequent changes of dynamics and tempo dramatize the mood; the overture ends with a whirlwind Presto section.

1881. SNEGUROCHKA (THE SNOW MAIDEN), opera in prologue and four acts, with text by the composer, based on a play by Ostrovsky. First performance: St. Petersburg, February 10, 1882.

Several of Rimsky-Korsakov's finest operas came after 1900, the reason why they are not discussed in this volume. Of the operas completed before 1900, one of the best and most successful was *The Snow Maiden,* the composer's third opera. The text is a fairy tale with flights into fantasy; Ostrovsky's text is based on an old Russian folk story. The Snow Maiden, daughter of King Winter and Fairy Spring, lives in the mythical land of the Berendeys in prehistoric times. The songs of the shepherd Lel, fill the Snow Maiden with the dream of becoming a mortal. As such, she first encounters disappointment and unhappiness when Lel spurns her. Then she is passionately wooed by the merchant Mizguir, who deserts his own wife for her. After the Fairy Spring endows the Snow Maiden with the capacity to fall in love, she responds sympathetically to Mizguir. Just as Mizguir is about to take the Snow Maiden as his bride, the sun touches her, and she melts away. Mizguir's grief drives him to suicide.

Described by its composer as "a legend of Springtime," this opera exploits Russian folk tunes, many of which are used in their entirety, while others contribute mere fragments. Other melodies are of the composer's own invention, though even here the kinship to folk music is readily recognizable.

With *The Snow Maiden,* says Richard Anthony Leonard, Rimsky-Korsakov evolved a new form of lyric drama—a genuine fairy tale in music. Not a little of the charm of the score comes from the composer's skilful use of actual bird calls, those of the merlin, cock, bullfinch, and cuckoo.

The most frequently heard excerpt from the opera is the *Dance of the Tumblers,* or *The Dance of the Buffoons,* from the third act. This is an orchestral episode, accompanying a dance of the Berendey peasants during an Arcadian festival. These are some of the most significant vocal numbers: two songs by the shepherd Lel, "The Forest Gaily Awakens" from the first act, and "Clouds Plotted with Thunder" from the third; the Snow Maiden's first-act air, "How Painful," and her death aria in the last act, "And Yet I Faint"; the beautiful second-act tenor cavatina, "Full of Wonders"; and several choral pages, including "In the Fields a Lime Tree Stood" in the first act, and "Far Upon the Distant Plain" in the third.

What is believed to have been the American première of *The Snow Maiden,* took place at the Metropolitan Opera in New York on January 23, 1922.

1887. CAPRICCIO ESPAGNOL (SPANISH CAPRICE), for orchestra, op. 34. I. Alborada. II. Variations. III. Alborada. IV. Scene and Gypsy Song. V. Fandango of the Asturias.

Rimsky-Korsakov himself explained that the *Spanish Caprice* belonged to that period in his creative life "at the end of which my orchestration had reached a considerable degree of virtuosity and bright sonority without Wagner's influence, within the limits of the usual make-up of Glinka's orchestra." He further explained that the *Caprice* was one of several of his compositions to demonstrate "a considerable falling off in the use of contrapuntal devices, which is noticeable after *The Snow Maiden*." He emphasized that his aim now was to write for the orchestra, solely in terms of orchestral timbre. "The change of timbres," he said, "the felicitous choice of melodic designs and figuration patterns, exactly suiting each kind of instrument, brief virtuoso cadenzas for solo instruments, the rhythm of the percussion instruments, and so forth, constitute here the very essence of the composition, and not its garb of orchestration. The Spanish themes, of dance character, furnished me with rich material for putting in use multiform orchestral effects. All in all, the *Caprice* is undoubtedly a purely external piece, but vividly brilliant for all that."

The five sections are played without interruption. The first movement (Vive e strepitoso) is an "alborada," a morning song or morning serenade. This is not, however, a romantic song but a virile dance section made up of two themes; both are stated by full orchestra, then repeated by clarinet. The movement ends pianissimo, after an orchestral cadenza and a passage for solo violin. The "Variations" section follows (Andante con moto), its main theme presented by horns over string arpeggios. It is followed by five variations. After a flute solo, the music of the opening "Alborada" is recalled, but in the changed key of B-flat (instead of A major), and in different orchestral dress. The fourth part is the "Scene and Gypsy Song" (Allegro), consisting of five dramatic orchestral cadenzas. It opens with a roll in side drums and a syncopated fanfare for horns and trumpets. In the concluding part, the principal subject of the fandango is given at once in trombones, to be followed by a related theme in the woodwind. Some interesting passages for solo violin and solo clarinet ensue. The fandango is now built up with telling effect to achieve a climax with a forceful restatement of the main theme in trombones. Then, suddenly, the fandango music is supplanted by a return of the opening Alborada melody.

1888. SCHEHERAZADE, suite for orchestra, op. 35: I. The Sea and Sinbad's Ship. II. The Tale of the Kalandar. III. The Young Prince and the Princess. IV. The Festival at Bagdad.

This, Rimsky-Korsakov's most celebrated composition, is a setting of several episodes from *The Arabian Nights*. In his published score, the composer provided the following program: "The Sultan, convinced of the faithlessness of women, had sworn to put to death each of his wives after the first night. But the Sultana Scheherazade saved her life by diverting him with stories which she told him during a thousand and one nights. The Sultan, conquered by his curiosity, put off from day to day the execution of his wife, and at last renounced entirely his bloody vows. Many wonders were narrated to the Sultan by the Sultana Scheherazade. For her stories, the Sultana borrowed the verses of poets and the words of folk songs, and she fitted together tales and adventures."

The composer was consciously vague about the specific episodes in *The Arabian Nights* that stimulated his musical imagination. He avoided a definite story-telling program for his music, and though he utilized Leitmotives, he took pains to explain that they are not "linked always and unvaryingly with the same poetic ideas and conceptions. On the contrary, in the majority of cases, all these seeming Leitmotives are nothing but purely musical material, or the given motives for symphonic development. These given motives thread and spread over all the movements of the suite, alternating and intertwining each with the other. Appearing as they do each time under different moods, the self-same motives and themes correspond each time to different images, actions and pictures. . . . In this manner, developing quite freely the musical data taken as the basis of the composition, I had in view the creation of an orchestral suite in four movements, closely knit by the community of its themes and motives, yet presenting, as it were, a kaleidoscope of fairy-tale images and designs of Oriental character."

Two significant musical subjects recur throughout the work. One is a powerful theme for unison brass, woodwind, and strings that opens the first movement. This melody represents the Sultan. The other, portraying Scheherazade, is a romantic melody in triplets for solo violin.

The Sultan theme, with which the first movement begins, is followed by several soft chords for the brass. Now the solo violin appears with the Scheherazade melody over harp arpeggios. Once the principal characters have been introduced, the music proceeds with a vividly realistic description of the sea, on which Sinbad's ship (portrayed by solo flute) is tossed about. The Scheherazade theme for solo violin brings on the second movement. Here the bassoon spins a languorous melody intended to depict the tale of the Kalandar. The third movement comprises love music whose poignant melody is shared by violins and clarinets. The Scheherazade theme closes this section and helps to bring on the next and concluding one—a brilliant picture of a Bagdad festival. This episode is interrupted to bring on a picture of a ship being hurled to destruction against rocks in a stormy sea. The storm ended, the suite—and Scheherazade's wondrous tales—concludes with a quiet recollection of the Scheherazade theme.

1888. LA GRANDE PÂQUE RUSSE (THE RUSSIAN EASTER), concert overture for orchestra, op. 36.

Rimsky-Korsakov borrowed his melodic material for this concert overture from the *Obikhod,* a collection of canticles of the Russian Orthodox Church. The overture is intended to describe a Christian-pagan ritual of old Russia, known as the "Bright Holiday." The composer provides the following analytical commentary: "The rather lengthy slow introduction . . . on the theme "Let God Arise' (in the woodwind), alternating with the ecclesiastical theme, 'An Angel Cried Out' (in solo cello) appeared to me, in its beginning as it were, as the ancient Isaiah's prophecy concerning the resurrection of Christ.

The gloomy colors of the Andante lugubre seemed to depict the holy sepulchre that had shone with ineffable light at the moment of the Resurrection—in the transition to the Allegro of the overture. The beginning of the Allegro (introduced by a cadenza for solo violin), 'Let Them Also That Hate Him Flee Before Him,' led to the holiday mood of the Greek Orthodox church services on Christ's matin; the solemn trumpet voice of the archangel was replaced by a tonal reproduction of the joyous, almost dance-like, bell-tolling, alternating now with the sexton's rapid reading, and now with the conventional chant of the priest's reading the glad tidings of the evangel. The *Obikhod* theme, 'Christ Is Arisen,' which forms a sort of subsidiary part of the overture, appears amid the trumpet blasts and the bell-tolling, constituting also a triumphant coda."

1896. SADKO, opera in three acts (seven scenes), with text by the composer and Vladimir I. Bielsky, based on an eleventh-century legend. First performance: Moscow, January 7, 1898.

Sadko is Rimsky-Korsakov's sixth opera, and one of his best. Here he gives freedom to his particular gift for fantasy; here he re-creates a world which Gerald Abraham once described as "half-real, half-supernatural," in which the "naïvete" is combined with "sophistication," the "romantic with the humorous," and "beauty with absurdity." Here we find some of the composer's most brilliant attempts at tone painting, some of his most poetic lyricism, and some of his most tellingly effective choruses in a national idiom. In addition, his style sometimes simulates that found in the verses of the old bardic poets, particularly in some of his recitatives, which are derived from the old "bylina" ("a sort of conventionally regulated narrative," explains the composer, "of parlando singing").

Sadko is an eleventh-century wandering minstrel. In the first act, he antagonizes the merchants of Novgorod at their banquet, by criticizing their soft life and love of luxury. He then goes off to the shores of Lake Ilmen, where his poignant singing wins the heart of Volkhova, daughter of the Sea King. She informs him that if he will throw his net into the sea, it will be filled with gold fish.

Sadko now comes to the harbor of Novgorod, where he wagers his life against the combined wealth of local merchants that he can catch a net full of gold fish. Some foreign visitors are at hand to witness the scene. One is a Hindu merchant, who sings of the exotic beauty of his homeland in what is undoubtedly the most familiar air in the opera, the "Song of India" (equally famous in transcriptions). Another visitor renders the popular "Song of the Viking Guest," and a third a Venetian barcarolle. Sadko then proceeds to the winning his wager.

In the third act, Sadko, aboard ship, offers himself as a sacrifice to the Sea King in order to save his ship and men. Descending to the bottom of the sea, he wins Volkhova's hand in marriage, amid grand festivities. But when his bride is transformed into a river, Sadko leaves the sea to return home to his wife. The townspeople of Novgorod hail him as a hero, and sing a praise to mighty Russia.

Several other vocal arias, besides those already mentioned are of interest. These include Sadko's first-scene aria, "O Ye Dark Forest"; Sadko's fifth-act air, "Farewell, My Friends"; and the poignant seventh-scene cradlesong, "Sleep Went Along."

PETER ILITCH TCHAIKOVSKY 1840–1893

The early Tchaikovsky gave every indication of serving the cause of Russian nationalism. The second symphony (*Little Russian*), and the early operas (*The Voyevode, The Oprichnik,* and *Vakula the Smith*) made copious, and at times effective, use of Russian folk songs and dances. The national element is still pronounced in the first act of *Eugene Onegin*. Then Tchaikovsky began drawing away from folk sources toward a more cosmopolitan style; he allowed himself to be influenced by German Romanticism; he sought to bring to his writing the elegance, sophistication, and good breeding of the Western world. For these strong European leanings, Tchaikovsky was violently attacked by the die-hard nationalists. They found him too eclectic for their tastes, a negation of the principles for which they stood.

Yet it was Tchaikovsky who was the first to bring about a genuine appreciation of Russian music in the Western world. And it is still Tchaikovsky who to most music lovers represents the epitome of Russian music. For if Tchaikovsky deserted Russian nationalism, nationalism never really deserted him. The Russian identity in his melodies and rhythms remained pronounced until the end of his days, just as the Russian tendency toward brooding and melancholia dominated his moods. Nobody knew better than Tchaikovsky himself how Russian he was. He wrote: "As to the Russian element in my music generally, its melodic and harmonic relation to folk music—I grew up in a quiet place and was drenched from the earliest childhood with the wonderful beauty of Russian popular songs. I am, therefore, passionately devoted to every expression of the Russian spirit. In brief, I am a Russian, through and through."

Many years later, Igor Stravinsky agreed with him by saying: "Tchaikovsky's music, which does not appear Russian to everybody, is often more profoundly Russian than music which has long since been awarded the facile label of Muscovite picturesqueness. This music is quite as Russian as Pushkin's verse or Glinka's song. Whilst not specially cultivating in his art the 'soul of the Russian peasant,' Tchaikovsky drew unconsciously from the true, popular sources of our race."

Attacked by some of his own contemporaries in Russia as being too European, Tchaikovsky was also severely criticized by many Europeans as being too Russian. He has also been taken severely to task for a sentimentality that often descends to bathos; a facility of style that frequently skirts the superficial; a pathos and a pessimism that frequently become hysteria; a tenderness that easily turns cloying; and a melancholia that disintegrates into self-pity. These accusations are not without merit. And yet, the incontestable fact remains that today, as yesterday, Tchaikovsky is the most popular Russian composer who ever lived. He retains this popularity because when he is in his element, he is of the elect—in his capacity to speak straight from the heart to the heart; in the effable beauty and sadness of his melodies; in the telling impact of his subjective moods; and in the powerful impact of his sweeping emotions.

"There is little of the recondite in his art," sums up Richard Anthony Leonard, "and little for the academician to ponder over or the student of classic procedure to imitate. But its great strength, and its great mystery, is the clarity of its thought and at the same time the abundance of the creative ideas which crowd into every line or every measure. Thus it is expressive and communicative in the highest degree. That it is also comparatively easy to absorb and appreciate should be accounted among its virtues intead of its faults."

Peter Ilitch Tchaikovsky was born in Votkinsk, Russia, on May 7, 1840, the son of a mining inspector. When he was ten, his family moved to St. Petersburg, where for nine years Tchaikovsky attended preparatory school, then the School of Jurisprudence. After being graduated from the latter institution, he worked for three years as a clerk in the Ministry of Justice. But by 1861, he started to study music with greater intensity than ever, becoming a pupil of Nicholas Zaremba. One year after that, Tchaikovsky gave up his government post to attend the newly founded St. Petersburg Conservatory. His studies there were completed in 1865; he now assumed the post of professor of harmony at the Moscow Conservatory which Nicolas Rubinstein had recently opened. His first symphony was performed in 1868; and in 1869, his first opera, *The Voyevode,* received its première. By 1870, he had completed a tone poem, *Fatum,* songs, piano pieces, and the initial version of his first masterwork, *Romeo and Juliet.*

In 1868, Tchaikovsky became convinced he was in love with Désirée Artôt, an opera singer. When Désirée deserted him to marry a Spaniard, Tchaikovsky took the disappointment philosophically. But his involvement with two other women left a much deeper impression on his life and career. One of these was Antonia Miliukova, a high-strung, neurotic music student who, in her first interview with the composer, fell on her knees in adoration before him. Following a few more meetings with her, Tchaikovsky asked her to marry him, even though he did not love her. There is documented proof, in the form of a letter from Tchaikovsky to his brother, to prove that the only reason he embarked on this marriage was to silence the well-founded rumors that were beginning to brand him a homosexual. In any event, the marriage —which took place on July 18, 1877—was such a disaster from the very beginning that Tchaikovsky tried to commit suicide. Failing that, he fled from his new wife and Moscow, and spent a year traveling about in Europe. He never returned to her; nevertheless, she remained a continual source of torment to him, and three years after Tchaikovsky's death was consigned to an insane asylum.

Tchaikovsky's second significant relationship with a woman involved Nadezhda Filaretovna von Meck, a patroness and a musical dilettante. She wrote him of her admiration, and he replied, expressing gratitude. Thus began a thirteen-year contact between composer and patroness, a period in which she endowed him with a handsome annual subsidy to make him financially independent. Through all those years, the two exchanged numerous letters while friendship blossomed into love and in which the composer confided his inmost torments, dreams, and aspirations. Yet in all those years, the two never had a face to face meeting, because that was the condition imposed upon Tchaikovsky from the beginning. Many explanations have been offered for this strange request: their difference in social station; her adoration for her children and her refusal to allow anybody to interefere with it.

For Tchaikovsky, the relationship with Mme. von Meck provided the stimulation he needed for the completion of a number of masterworks that gave him a place of first importance in Russian music: the fourth and fifth symphonies; the opera, *Eugene Onegin;* the *Capriccio italien* and the *1812 Overture,* both for orchestra; the Violin Concerto and the first Piano Concerto; some of his greatest songs. His fame now spread throughout the world of music and many honors came his way. In 1884, he received from the Czar the Order of St. Vladimir; and in 1888, the Russian government bestowed on him an annual pension. Beginning with 1888, Tchaikovsky also started making European tours conducting his compositions, during which he gathered further personal triumphs.

His friendship with Mme. von Meck ended as suddenly as it had begun. While in the Caucasus in 1890, he received word from her that due to "financial reverses" she would be unable to continue her subsidy to him any longer. Tchaikovsky hurried to reply that he was no longer in need of her generosity, that he hoped nothing would be permitted to break up their friendship. That and later letters went unanswered. Upon returning to Moscow, Tchaikovsky discovered that Mme. von Meck had not suffered financially at all; she had used finances as a pretext for ending a relationship of which she had grown weary.

In 1891, Tchaikovsky paid his only visit to the United States, helping to open up the newly built Carnegie Hall with a performance of his *1812 Over-*

ture. Back in Russia, his chronic melancholia grew so intense that at times he thought he was going mad. While in the depths of depression, he completed his last work and his greatest symphony, the *Pathétique*. A few days after the première, Tchaikovsky became infected with cholera after drinking some unboiled water; the fact that he drank this water during a cholera epidemic, without taking precautions, has led to the unfounded suspicion that he was trying to commit suicide. He died in St. Petersburg on November 6, 1892. The last words on his lips were the name of Mme. von Meck and the phrase, "the accursed one."

1867–1882. COMPOSITIONS FOR SOLO PIANO:

Souvenir de Hapsal, op. 2: I. The Castle Ruins; II. Scherzo; III. Chant sans paroles.

Romance in F minor, op. 5.

Noctune and Humoresque, op. 10.

Nocturne in C-sharp minor, op. 19, no. 4.

The Months, suite, op. 37: I. By the Hearth; II. Carnival Time; III. Song of the Lark; IV. Snowdrop; V. Bright Nights; VI. Barcarolle; VII. Reapers Song; VIII. Harvest; IX. The Hunt; X. Autumn Song; XI. In the Troika; XII. Christmas.

Chanson triste, op. 40, no. 2.

Valse sentimentale, op. 51, no. 6.

Tchaikovsky was not a particularly distinguished composer for the piano. His writing too often is unpianistic, often suggests string or wind instruments rather than the keyboard. With the exception of his two piano sonatas, Tchaikovsky's solo piano works comprise morsels. Some are tasty confections. What they lack in originality of method or material, they compensate for in pleasing sentiments and touching melodies, and at times in elegance of style. The best of these items have been popular through various transcriptions.

The trio of pieces making up the *Souvenir de Hapsal* (1867) are the composer's recollections of a visit to Finland. We find here one of the composer's most celebrated melodies, the *Chant sans paroles*. This tender melody is the last number in the set, the first two being atmospheric pictures. One gains its musical effect from a steadily repeated bass. The other is a Scherzo suggesting a hunting expedition.

The Romance in F minor (1878) is believed to have been inspired by the composer's brief love affair with Désirée Artôt, to whom the piece is dedicated. It is passionate music and one of Tchaikovsky's most familiar melodies.

In the Nocturne and Humoresque, op. 10 (1871), it is the latter piece that is played most often, one of the composer's rare exercises in whimsy; the middle part of the Humoresque comes from a French folk song.

Among the composer's Nocturnes, that in C-sharp minor, op. 19, no. 4 (1873) is the most significant, a romantic evocation of the mystery of night.

The piano suite, *The Months* (1876) is an interesting attempt by the composer to write an appropriate piece of programmatic music for each month of the year, beginning with January. The best-known movement is the fifth, a barcarolle representing the month of June. If this melody is particularly familiar to lovers of operetta, it is because Sigmund Romberg borrowed it for the middle part of his song, "Lover Come Back to Me." The haunting loveliness of "Autumn Song" representing October, and the vivacity of "Troika" for November also make for pleasurable listening.

The *Chanson triste* (1878) is a slight, sentimental little song, which is the second number in a set of twelve pieces of "moderate difficulty" for children. The *Valse sentimentale* (1882) is one of the composer's most elegant salon waltzes.

1869–1893. SONGS, for voice and piano:

"Again, as Before, Alone," op. 73, no. 6; "Deception," op. 65, no. 2; "Don Juan's Serenade," op. 38, no. 1; "Gypsy's Song," op. 60, no. 7; "I Bless You, Forests," op. 47, no. 5; "If I Had Only Known," op. 47, no. 1; "In This Moonlight," op. 73, no. 3; "It Was in Early Spring," op. 38, no. 2; "A Legend" ("Christ in His Garden"), op. 54, no. 5; "Lullaby," op. 54, no. 1; "None But the Lonely Heart," op. 6, no. 6; "Not a Word, O My Friend," op. 6, no. 2; "Only Thou," op. 57, no. 6; "Pimpinella," op. 38, no. 6; "Tears," op. 65, no. 5; "Was I Not a Little Blade of Grass," op. 47, no. 7; "We Sat Together," op. 73, no. 1; "Why?" op. 6, no. 5.

Tchaikovsky was often criticized by his colleagues and contemporaries for the indiscriminate way in which he altered the texts of his songs to suit his own fancy; for the inadequacy of his musical declamation; for the carelessness; for adherence to antiquated traditions of songwriting. César Cui was in the vanguard of these critics. He insisted Tchaikovsky did not have "the flexibility required for real vocal music. . . . He did not acknowledge the equal rights of poetry and music. . . . In the music, the punctuation is very badly observed. . . . Not particular in the choice of musical ideas, he nevertheless let go of them with difficulty and developed them in every possible way. But more often than not, this development consists of repetition and variation, effected with the skilful craft of the experienced technician."

To these and similar critics, Tchaikovsky gave the following response: "Absolute accuracy of musical declamation is a negative quality, and its importance should not be exaggerated. What does the repetition of words, even of whole sentences, matter? There are cases where such repetitions are completely natural and in harmony with reality. Under the influence of strong emotion a person repeats one and the same exclamation and sentence very often. . . . But even if that never happened in real life, I should feel no embarrassment in impudently turning my back on 'real' truth in favor of 'artistic' truth."

Time has silenced Tchaikovsky's critics and has proved the validity of Tchaikovsky's song methods. Tchaikovsky's best songs are gems, filled with psychological insight, poetic beauty, musical truth. "Tchaikovsky's romantic songs are little poems of the kind that go deeper than merely personal states of mind," says A. Alshvang. "These deeply truthful pages are permeated by a philosophy of life. . . . Artistic simplicity, artlessness of musical language, perfection of form, variety and originality of melody, richness of accompaniment: all these qualities are combined in Tchaikovsky's musical style."

"Tchaikovsky's genius as a songwriter," wrote Edwin Evans, "belongs to the borderland between the Teutonic and the Slavonic. His melodies are in most cases more emotional than a German songwriter would have them, and their beauties of expression savor more of the physical than the intellectual. On the other hand, he was an accomplished lyricist, and though his methods may differ widely from those of a Schubert or a Brahms, he has bequeathed to us many songs of incontestable artistic greatness. It is particularly when dealing with a thought suggesting a certain languor that he is at his best. His Slavonic temperament, without even then shaking off its eclectic trappings, makes itself convincingly felt."

Tchaikovsky's first published set op. 6 (1869) includes what is one of the most popular songs he ever wrote, "None But the Lonely Heart," poem by Goethe. Here the gentle melancholy of the melody is built up effectively into a climax at the words "how I suffer" and achieves a compelling intensity with the phrase "my bosom bursts." Two other fine songs in this set also reflect the melancholia afflicting the composer. "Why?" text by Heine, and "Not a Word, O My Friend," are throughout permeated with pathos.

But elegiac strains were not the only ones sounded by Tchaikovsky in his songs. Already in opus 38 (1878), we encounter a variety of moods: "Don Juan's Serenade" is as dramatic and as theatrical as an opera aria; "It Was in Early Spring" is idyllic; and "Pimpinella" has the forthright simplicity of folk music, based as it is on an Italian street song.

Variety of style, feeling, and atmosphere also characterize some of Tchaikovsky's best later songs. In opus 47 (1880), "I Bless You Forests" has solemnity; the hymn, says A. Alshvang, "resounds majestically, powerfully, inspiringly." "A Legend," in opus 54 (1883), has sweetness and charm. This is the melody used by Arensky as the theme for his theme-and-variations movement in his Second String Quartet. Gravity and sensuality characterize "Gypsy's Song" in opus 60 (1886); here Tchaikovsky's melody echoes a suggestion of the "fate" theme from Bizet's *Carmen*. And all the songs of opus 73 (1893)—Tchaikovsky's last set—are "full of intimate lyricism," explains Alshvang, "psychologically true, human, full of ardent love of life."

1870. ROMEO AND JULIET, overture-fantasy for orchestra.

Of the many attempts to write music for or about Shakespeare's *Romeo and Juliet,* that of Tchaikovsky remains the most popular. "Here for a moment," says Lawrence Gilman, "he captured the very hue and accent of Shakespearean loveliness." The suggestion to write a tone poem based on the Shakespeare drama—and even a basic plan—came from Balakirev. Tchaikovsky started work in early fall of 1869, completing his first version by late November. Balakirev was not satisfied, and advised numerous changes. In the summer of 1870, Tchaikovsky revised the overture extensively. Now Balakirev was able to tell him: "It is your best work. . . . This is the first piece by you which fascinates by the mass of its beauties, and in such a way that one without deliberation can call it good." A decade later Tchaikovsky again revised the overture; this third version is the one played today.

The introductory section (Andante non tanto quasi moderato) represents Friar Lawrence. The main melody here is a religious chant for clarinets and bassoons. A quickening of the tempo brings on the Allegro section. Turbulent scale passages and forceful chords tell of the feud between the Montagues and the Capulets. When the storm has spent its fury, the English horn and muted violins are heard in Romeo's poignant love song to Juliet, over syncopated horns and plucked strings. The second subject is Juliet's passionate response, a rhapsodic melody for muted and divided strings. The spell is broken with a return of the storm music describing the family feud. Soon the love music manages to penetrate through the agitation. At first, it appears in the woodwind. Then, almost as if the emotional dykes had broken down, it spills over in the entire orchestra. The roll of the kettledrums and a sudden silence, however, give warning of impending doom. There is a frenzied outburst in the orchestra, followed by an elegiac episode. The drums beat a funereal rhythm, the love music becomes drenched with melancholia. Chords, and a last dramatic roll of the kettledrums, end the overture on a tragic note.

1871. STRING QUARTET IN D MAJOR, op. 11. I. Moderato e semplice. II. Andante cantabile. III. Allegro non tanto. IV. Allegro giusto.

The popularity of this string quartet is due to its Andante cantabile movement, become famous in transcriptions. When Tolstoy first heard it, he burst into tears at its simple beauty. The familiar serene melody is given by muted strings, a melody Tchaikovsky had heard a carpenter sing outside his window. A pizzicato basso ostinato in the cello leads into the second equally affecting and equally lyrical second subject; this time the melody is Tchaikovsky's own. The first part is then repeated.

The first movement opens with a sixteen-measure syncopated section. The first theme, in the violin, is played over a pedal D and A in cello and viola. This theme is payed twice, over countersubjects in semiquavers. Two measures in viola then lead into the expressive second subject.

The third-movement Scherzo has an Oriental personality. It opens with a syncopated, exotic theme that extends for twenty four measures. The Oriental character persists into the finale, with its dramatic first theme, that later in the movement is treated in imitation. The second theme in B-flat, this time Russian rather than Oriental, is also given in imitation, but in slow tempo, before the end of the movement.

1872. SYMPHONY NO. 2 IN C MINOR, "LITTLE RUSSIAN," op. 17. I. Andante sostenuto; Allegro vivo. II. Andantino marziale quasi moderato. III. Allegro molto vivace. IV. Moderato assai.

Tchaikovsky completed his first symphony, in G minor, op. 13, in 1866. He called it *Winter Dreams*. Here the thematic material frequently has a Russian flavor; the main subject of the slow movement, in solo oboe, sounds like a Russian folk song. Such a national identity is even more pronounced in the second symphony, which makes such extensive use of Malo-Russian folk songs that the critic Kashkin was led to dub the work, "Little Russian."

A melancholy theme for solo horn (restated by solo bassoon over pizzicato lower strings) appears in the first-movement introduction. The main first subject in this movement is a derivation of a folk tune associated with Stenka Razin, "Down By Mother Volga"; it is heard in the strings. A fortissimo climax in full orchestra precedes the entrance of the second subject, in oboe to a wind accompaniment. "The entire movement," said James Gibbons Huneker, "is characterized by a bizarre freedom, even recklessness."

The melody of the second movement is one the composer had previously (1869) utilized as a wedding march in an unpublished opera, *Undine*. It is heard in the clarinets after a two-measure introduction in the kettledrums. The Scherzo that follows opens with a soft staccato episode before proceeding to a more melodious idea. In the trio, an accented theme is given by the winds. Huneker described this Scherzo movement as follows: "It reveals plenty of spirit and there is the diabolic, riotous energy that pricks the nerves, yet never strikes fire in our souls."

Two basic melodies are prominent in the finale, which is generally regarded as the finest movement. A hint of the first one is given in the introductory measures before it emerges forcefully in the violins; this tune is borrowed from the Russian folk song, "The Crane." A more expressive and emotional melody follows in the strings. Both themes are elaborated and varied before they are combined. "The movement," says Huneker, "has the whirl and glow of some wild dance mood, and over all Tchaikovsky has cast the spell of his wondrous orchestration."

1873. THE TEMPEST, symphonic fantasy, op. 18.

The critic Stassov gave Tchaikovsky both the idea and a detailed program for a fantasy based on the Shakespeare drama. The following description is found in the published score: "The sea, Ariel, spirit of the tempest. Wreck of the ship bearing Ferdinand. The enchanted island. First timid beginnings of love between Miranda and Ferdinand. Ariel. Caliban. The amorous pair free themselves to the triumphant spell of passion. Prospero strips himself of the power of enchantment and leaves the island. The sea."

The fantasy is constructed from the following nine elements, singled out by Rosa Newmarch: "(1) The sea, heard in double basses; (2) a second sea motive, given out by the horn; (3) the tempest—violins and cellos; (4) Prospero's spell; (5) the meeting of the lovers, started by the violas; (6) a second theme for the lovers, given to the violins; (7) a semiquaver figure, heard in the strings, connected with Ariel; (8) a heavily accented passage, fortissimo in the basses, the unmistakable Leitmotiv of Caliban; (9) Prospero's departure."

1874. CONCERTO NO. 1 IN B-FLAT MINOR, for piano and orchestra, op. 23. I. Allegro non troppo e molto maestoso; Allegro con spirito. II. Andante semplice. III. Allegro con fuoco.

Tchaikovsky wrote his first, and most celebrated, piano concerto for Nicolas Rubinstein. On Christmas Eve of 1874, he played the work for Rubinstein in an empty classroom in the Conservatory. Throughout the playing, Rubinstein maintained an icy silence. When the performance ended, as Tchaikovsky later recalled, "there burst forth from Rubinstein's mouth a mighty torrent of words. He spoke quietly at first; then he waxed hot, and at last he resembled Zeus hurling thunderbolts. It appeared that my concerto was utterly worthless, absolutely unplayable; passages were so commonplace and awkward that they could not be improved; the piece as a whole was bad, trivial, vulgar. I had stolen this from that one and that from this one; so only two or three pages were good for anything, while the others should be wiped out or radically rewritten. . . . I left the room silently and went upstairs. I was so excited and angry that I could not speak. Rubinstein soon came up, and called me into a remote room, for he noticed that I was heavily cast down. There he repeated that my concerto was impossible, pointed out many passages which needed thorough revision, and added that he would play the concerto in public if these changes were ready at a certain time. 'I shall not change a single note,' I answered, 'and I shall publish the concerto as it is now.' And this, indeed, I did."

Such were the stormy beginnings of a concerto since become one of the most popular in the repertory; a work of such dash, brilliance, and emotional appeal that its impact upon audiences never fails; a score that yielded for Tin Pan Alley tunesmiths not one but two song hits in "Concerto for Two" and "Tonight We Love."

To Hans von Buelow, and not to Nicolas Rubinstein, went the distinction of introducing this concerto to the world. This took place not in Russia, but in the United States—in Boston, on October 25, 1875, where it enjoyed a phenomenal success. When this performance was repeated, the finale had to be encored. Von Buelow played the work across Europe, and so did various other pianists, including Siloti and Sauer. By now, Nicolas Rubinstein realized he had misjudged the work seriously, admitting his error by performing it brilliantly at the Paris Exhibition in 1878.

The concerto opens with one of the most extended introductions in concerto literature—an expanse of one hundred and six measures. Its main subject is a sweeping, majestic theme in strings accompanied by dynamic chords in the piano; this is heard after four introductory measures. The melody is then taken over by the piano, which embarks on a cadenza. After a brief exchange between piano and orchestra, the majestic melody returns. Despite the effectiveness of this subject, Tchaikovsky never repeats it, once the introduction ends. In the main body of the first movement, the two principal themes are first a folk-like tune with a strong rhythmic surge in the piano (believed to have been heard by the composer from a blind beggar in the Ukraine); then a tender melody (molto espressivo) given by horns and woodwinds, and repeated by the piano.

An exquisite, somewhat elegiac song is presented by the flute after four introductory measures, in the poetic slow movement. The romantic mood prevails as the piano takes this melody over, embellishes upon it, then passes it on to the cellos. Later, contrasting material is provided by an opulent waltz in violins and cellos, which Tchaikovsky confessed he derived from a French chansonette.

The finale enters with an outburst of unbridled energy. The first theme is a Russian dance in the piano; the second, a song for the violins, accompanied by horns. This second theme, after it has been repeated by the piano, is given forceful presentation by piano and orchestra. Then the opening dance tune is recalled. A rising octave in the piano, and three strong chords for piano and orchestra, make for a dramatic conclusion.

1875–1878. COMPOSITIONS FOR VIOLIN:
Sérénade mélancolique, for violin and orchestra, op. 26.
Mélodie, for violin and piano, op. 42, no. 3.

These two pieces are noteworthy for their melodic charm and touching emotion. Both are extremely popular, though neither belongs with the composer's major achievements. The *Sérénade mélancolique* in B-flat minor (1875) places its emphasis more on the "melancholy" than on the "serenade." A short introduction leads into a three-part sentimental song. The *Mélodie* in E-flat major (1878) is the last of a set of three pieces for violin and piano, *Souvenir d'un lieu cher*. The tender melody was used by a Tin Pan Alley tunesmith for the song hit, "The Things I Love."

1875. SYMPHONY NO. 3 IN D MAJOR, "POLISH," op. 29. I. Moderato assai; Allegro brilliante. II. Alla tedesca: allegro moderato e semplice. III. Andante elegiaco. IV. Allegro vivo. V. Allegro con fuoco.

It took Tchaikovsky less than two months to write his third symphony. It was named *Polish* by the conductor Sir August Manns (when he performed the work in London in 1899) because the closing movement makes prominent use of a polonaise.

Lawrence Gilman described this symphony as follows: "The work opens with a somber introduction (Tempo di marcia funebre) in D minor, 4/4, which gradually becomes more animated. 'A fine, broad, sunrise effect' leads to a forte outburst on the chief subject in the major key. The oboe brings forward the second subject, at first in G minor (Molto espressivo, poco meno mosso). The exposition is concise, the development elaborate."

The waltz-like second movement was regarded by Tchaikovsky as the first of two Scherzi movements. It begins with "a gracious melody for solo flute and clarinet over pizzicato chords of all the strings. There is a trio, initiated by a vivacious, chattering figure in the woodwind."

The slow movement opens "with a flute melody supported by harmonies of the other wind. The D minor melody, extended by solo bassoon and horn over a pizzicato accompaniment, is succeeded by a more expressive cantilena in B-flat major for the strings (the melody doubled by clarinets), which is worked up to a fortissimo climax, but ends quietly in D major."

The symphony's second of two Scherzi is "an engaging and effective piece of writing with an ingenious Trio in which Tchaikovsky introduces the theme in seven different keys over a sustained D of the horns. The strings are muted throughout."

The finale is the energetic and rousing polonaise movement. At the London concert at which this symphony was baptized *Polish,* the program annotator found in the music of this finale, "Poland mourning in her oppression and rejoicing in her regeneration."

1876. LE LAC DES CYGNES (THE SWAN LAKE), op. 20, dramatic ballet in four acts, with book by V. P. Begitchev and Vasily Heltzer. Choreography by Julius Reisinger. First performance: Moscow, March, 4, 1877.

It may be said with justification that the golden age of Russian ballet dawned with Tchaikovsky's three masterworks, beginning with *The Swan Lake;* that classic Russian ballet and the name of Tchaikovsky are virtually synonymous; that one of Tchaikovsky's greatest contributions was through his ballet music.

Yet the significance of *The Swan Lake* was not recognized at first. A number of unhappy circumstances were responsible for this, all adding up to a fiasco. The conductor had never before directed so complex a score and was incapable of doing it justice; the dancers insisted that much of Tchaikovsky's music was ungrateful to ballet, with the result that some of it was deleted with a good deal of inferior material substituted. The scenery and costuming were slipshod. As a result, the première was a dismal failure, and after a few performances, the ballet disappeared from the repertory. Only after *The Swan Lake* was revived soon after Tchaikovsky's death, did this work finally receive the success it deserved. The parts originally deleted were restored; new choreography was devised by Lev Ivanov and Marius Petipa. First, only the second act in 1894, then the entire ballet in 1895, were triumphs. Today, we know with George Balanchine that this is "undoubtedly the most popular of all classical ballets," a perennial favorite of ballerinas the world over. The first American presentation took place at the Metropolitan Opera in New York on December

20, 1911, staged by Mikhail Mordkin, based on the Ivanov-Petipa choreography.

The music of *Swan Lake* originated as a little dance piece performed for children at the country estate of Tchaikovsky's sister, in 1871. Four years later, when the Imperial Opera in Moscow commissioned Tchaikovsky to write a ballet score, the composer decided to extend his children's dance sequence to full ballet dimensions.

The heroine in this ballet is a beautiful girl, Odette, who with her companions has been transformed into a swan by the magician, Rothbart. They can resume human form every midnight. On one such occasion, when she is human again, Odette meets Prince Siegfried, who falls in love with her. He invites her to his palace for a ball; there he intends to select her as his bride. The magician also attends the ball, accompanied by his daughter, Odile, whom he has made to look exactly like Odette. After dancing with Odile, the Prince announces this is the girl he will marry. By rejecting Odette, he has condemned her to death, much to the delight of the magician. But Prince Siegfried soon discovers his mistake. He rushes back to the lake to seek out Odette, and finds her just as she is about to destroy herself by jumping off a high rock. To prevent a possible union between Odette and the Prince, the magician invokes a storm that causes the waters to overflow, and threatens the lives of all those near by. Prince Siegfried is willing and ready to die with Odette. Through this noble sacrifice, he is able at last to break the evil spell. Nymphs and naiads dance joyfully, and conduct the lovers to the temple of happiness.

There are thirty-three musical numbers in the complete score. Various combinations of the most popular of these pieces are heard as orchestral suites at symphony concerts. These are some of the most favored excerpts: Orchestral introduction to Act I; in Act I, the "Pas de trois" for the Prince, the waltz for the corps de ballet, the Polonaise, and the "Danse des coupes"; in Act II, the Introduction to and the opening scene, the celebrated waltz which the swans dance to at the side of the lake, and the Dance of the Swan Queen; in Act III, the Wedding Dance, the Spanish Dance, the Czardas, the Mazurka and the Waltz; and in Act IV, the Dance of the Little Swans, and the Final Scene.

1876. MARCHE SLAVE, for orchestra, op. 31.

In 1876, there was scheduled a benefit concert for Serbian soldiers wounded in the war against Turkey. For this event, Tchaikovsky wrote a stirring martial composition, reflecting his own sympathies for the Slavs, and in which he prognosticated their ultimate victory. The work is in three uninterrupted sections. A solemn introduction precedes a statement by the strings of the main march melody. This stately melody was expropriated by the composer from an old Serbian folk song. This is followed by a trio section, where two more folk songs are quoted. A climax is reached with a powerful quotation of the Russian national anthem. The anticipation of a Slavic victory over the Turks comes in the closing part, with an exultant repetition of the march melody.

1876. FRANCESCA DA RIMINI, orchestral fantasy, op. 32.

In July 1876, Tchaikovsky wrote to his brother, Modeste: "Early this morning I read through the fifth canto of the *Inferno* and was beset by the wish to compose a symphonic poem, *Francesca da Rimini.*" Three months later he wrote again: "I have just finished the composition, a symphonic fantasia, *Francesca da Rimini.* I have worked at it 'con amore' and believe my devotion has been successful." The première performance in Moscow in 1877 proved so successful that the work had to be repeated twice during the next two months.

Tchaikovsky himself provides a program for his music. He explains that the first section is a description of the gateway to the Inferno, and the agonies suffered by the condemned. The middle part relates the tragic love story of Paolo and Francesca. The third part, a return to the Inferno, is followed by a concluding episode. The composition is played without interruption. In the first and third sections, stormy scale and brio passages paint the turbulent infernal regions. The middle part brings us Francesca's love song in a rapturous melody for clarinet over pizzicato strings (Andante cantabile).

1876. VARIATIONS ON A ROCOCO THEME, for cello and orchestra, op. 33.

Tchaikovsky's affection for Baroque music, and his adulation of Mozart, both find reflection in this composition. The melody heard in the solo instrument after a sixteen-measure orchestral preface has the grace, refinement, and texture of a Mozart theme, in spite of the fact that it is also touched by Tchaikovsky's own personality. Seven variations follow, all of them in eighteenth-century style; an orchestral ritornello separates each of the variations.

1878. CONCERTO IN D MAJOR, for violin and orchestra, op. 35. I. Allegro moderato. II. Andante. III. Allegro vivacissimo.

Tchaikovsky labored long and hard on his only violin concerto, aided by Joseph Kotek, a young virtuoso. The first movement and finale pleased Tchaikovsky; the slow movement proved less satisfying to him. On April 29, 1878, he wrote to Mme. Meck that he had written a completely new Andante. (The displaced movement became the "Meditation" in the suite, *Souvenir d'un lieu cher,* op. 42). "I consider," he said with finality, "that the concerto is now completed."

It took almost four years for the public to hear the concerto. Leopold Auer, to whom the work was dedicated, was discouraged by the technical problems posed by the work, vacillated about playing it, then declined. Adolf Brodsky finally became interested in it, and introduced it in Vienna in 1881. The audience proved apathetic, the critics savage. Eduard Hanslick wrote: "The violin is no longer played, it is yanked about, it is torn asunder, it is beaten black and blue. . . . Tchaikovsky's violin concerto brings us for the first time to the horrid idea that there may be music that stinks to the ear." From such disagreeable beginnings, the violin concerto went on to become one of the most popular ever written.

A short introduction in the violin sets the stage for the first movement. The orchestra then enters with a suggestion of the first major theme, which before long unfolds bountifully in the solo violin. After this melody has been ornamented, and following some passage work, the second theme arrives—a broad, sentimental melody in A major for the solo violin. The first theme provides the material for the development section, which abounds with brilliant passages for the violin. After an orchestral tutti, the solo instrument engages a detailed cadenza. The recapitulation and a brief coda follow.

The slow movement is a canzonetta. A twelve-measure introduction precedes a soulful, melancholy melody in the solo violin. A secondary lyrical subject in E-flat is heard next. A triplet figure leads to the return of the first melody, this time accompanied by clarinet arpeggios. After a recall of the opening measures, the second movement passes into the finale without a break. Sixteen measures of orchestral introduction and a brief cadenza for the solo violin, are followed by the main theme, a spirited Russian dance (trepak) in the solo violin. The second theme is, on the other hand, melodious, soon heard in the violin over a drone bass. After a repetition of the opening dance tune, the thematic material is worked out energetically, creating a momentum that carries the music along to an exciting coda, where the dance tune helps to bring the concerto to a whirlwind finish.

1878. SYMPHONY NO. 4 IN F MINOR, op. 36. I. Andante sostenuto; Moderato con anima in movimento di valse. II. Andantino in modo di canzona. III. Pizzicato ostinato; Allegro. IV. Allegro con fuoco.

The F minor Symphony is the first by Tchaikovsky to win a permanent place in the repertory. It was conceived during a hyperemotional period in the composer's life. The composer had just embarked upon, and fled from, his brief and disastrous adventure with marriage. He had also initiated his friendship with Mme. von Meck. It was the latter circumstance—the relationship with Mme. von Meck—that influenced the writing of the symphony most significantly. He dedicated it to her; he described the symphony to her as "ours"; he confessed that in writing it "how much I thought of you with every bar."

A good many interpretations and analyses of this symphony exist. The most illuminating is still the one Tchaikovsky prepared for Mme. von Meck. In reads in part:

"The introduction [to the first movement] is the kernel, the quintessence, the chief thought of the whole symphony. This is Fate, the fatal power which hinders one in the pursuit of happiness from gaining the goal, which jealously provides that peace and comfort do not prevail, that the sky is not free from clouds—a might that swings, like the sword of Damocles, constantly over the head, that poisons continually the soul. This might is overpowering and invincible. There is nothing to do but to submit and vainly to complain."

The Fate theme is a fanfare for horns and bassoons in octaves, to which trombones and woodwind soon contribute their own voices. In the main part of the movement, first violins and cellos are heard in a syncopated subject—the first main theme. A contrasting lyrical episode follows in clarinets.

"The second movement," continues Tchaikovsky, "shows another phase of sadness. Here is that melancholy feeling which enwraps one when he sits at night alone in the house exhausted by work; the book which he had taken to read has slipped from his hand; a swarm of reminiscences had arisen. . . . One mourns the past and has neither the courage nor the will to begin a new life. One is rather tired of life."

The principal melody appears in the oboe, as strings provide a pizzicato accompaniment. A counter-melody, equally poignant and expressive, follows in woodwind, violins, and cellos. Midway in the movement, lyricism gives way to rhythmic vitality with a lively tune for clarinets and bassoons.

In the third-movement Scherzo, Tchaikovsky explains, "are capricious arabesques, vague figures, which slip into the imagination when one has taken wine and is slightly intoxicated. The mood is now gay, now mournful. . . . Suddenly rush into the imagination a picture of a drunken peasant and a gutter song. Military music is heard passing by in the distance. These are disconnected pictures which come and go in the brain of the sleeper. They have nothing to do with reality; they are unintelligible, bizarre."

The main theme of the Scherzo is a melody played throughout by pizzicato strings. In the trio, plucked strings make way for a spirited Russian dance for the woodwind.

Tchaikovsky explained the finale as follows: "If you have no pleasure in yourself, look about you. Go to the people. See how they can enjoy life and give themselves up entirely to festivity. The picture of a folk holiday. Hardly have we had time to forget ourselves in the happiness of others, when idenfatigable Fate reminds us once more of its presence. The other children of men are not concerned with us. . . . How merry and glad they all are. . . . And you will still say that all the world is immersed in sorrow? There still *is* happiness, simple, native happiness. Rejoice in the happiness of others—and you can still live."

This finale begins with a sweeping subject for woodwind and strings. Soon tranquillity sets in. The woodwinds quote a familiar Russian folk song, "In the Fields There Stands a Birch Tree" (Stravinsky used the same tune in *Petrouchka* many years later.) The strings give a vigorous reply, creating a disturbance that provides the proper setting for a return of the stormy opening theme. And now there comes a majestic march for full orchestra. All this material is worked out powerfully, at times the treatment being canonic. Drum rolls and a return of the march help to bring the symphony to its dramatic denouement.

1879. EUGENE ONEGIN, op. 24, opera in three acts, with text by the composer and Constantine Shilovsky, based on a poem by Pushkin. First performance: Moscow, March 29, 1879.

In a letter to his brother, Modeste, in 1877, Tchaikovsky explained how he first became interested in Pushkin's "novel in verse" as material for an opera. He was at the home of Mme. Lavrosky discussing possible operatic subjects when she suddenly brought up *Eugene Onegin*. "I was enchanted when I read the work. I spent a sleepless night. The result—a sketch of a delicious opera based upon Pushkin's text. The next day I went to Shilovsky, who is now working poste-haste at my sketch. You have no notion how crazy I am about this subject!"

Some of Tchaikovsky's colleagues were far less enthusiastic about the operatic possibilities of *Onegin*. As a satire on Russia's Europeanized aristocracy, as a portrait of a cynical and egotistic Byronic character, and as a poem that stressed introspection and psychological insight, *Onegin* offered few opportunities for dramatic action, spectacle, climaxes. Tchaikovsky was well aware of all this. From the very first, he set out to write an intimate stage work which drew its interest from moods, from beautiful lyrical sequences rather than from theatrical effect. Indeed, he described *Eugene Onegin* not as an "opera" but as "lyric scenes." And he went on to explain: "It is true that the work is deficient in theatrical opportunities; but the wealth of poetry, the humanity, and the simplicity of the story . . . will compensate for what is lacking in other respects."

Since Tchaikovsky was more interested in the romantic aspect of Pushkin's poem than in its satire or characterizations, he made Tatiana, rather than Onegin, the principal character. He saw Tatiana, as he explained to Mme. von Meck, as "a creature of pure feminine beauty, a dreamy nature, ever seeking some vague ideal and striving passionately to grasp it. . . . It needs only the appearance of a man who—at least externally—stands out from the commonplace surroundings in which she lives, and at once she imagines her ideal has come, and in her passion becomes oblivious of self."

The setting is St. Petersburg; the time, 1815. In the garden of Mme. Larina's home, her two daughters, Tatiana and Olga, are singing a little duet to their mother ("Hast Thou Heard?"). As evening descends, harvesters are returning from the fields ("On the Bridge"). Two guests arrive. One is Lensky, who is interested in Olga; the other is his friend, a young dandy named Eugene Onegin. Tatiana becomes deeply impressed by Onegin. Later on, in her bedroom, she is so emotionally disturbed she is unable to sleep. She begs her nurse to tell her a story, then confides to her how much she loves Onegin. Suddenly, she decides to reveal her feelings to Onegin in a letter, in the most famous aria in the opera, Tatiana's "Letter Scene." To this ardent note, Onegin responds by arranging a meeting. Then, in Tatiana's garden, he tries to convince her he is not the man for her ("Written Words"). Distraught, Tatiana runs away from him.

In the second act, a ball is celebrating Tatiana's birthday. The guests are dancing a waltz, one of Tchaikovsky's most famous ones. Overhearing gossip in which his name is linked with Tatiana's, Onegin decides to dispel all rumors by paying excessive attention to Olga. Aroused by jealousy, Lensky challenges him to a duel. This takes place in the next scene, at dawn, by a mill dam. While waiting for Onegin's arrival, Lensky recalls his youth in "Faint Echo of Youth." Then, after Onegin appears, Lensky is killed in the duel.

Six years have elapsed. In the third act, a brilliant reception is taking place at Prince Gremin's palace, the guests participating in a colorful polonaise. Tatiana is now married to Prince Gremin. When she notices that Onegin is one of her guests, she treats him coldly. By now Onegin is made to realize how profoundly he loves Tatiana. He despatches to her a secret message urging her to meet him. As Tatiana awaits him in her boudoir, she is torn by conflicting emotions. She knows she wants to take Onegin in her arms, yet she also wants to remain faithful to her husband. When Onegin comes to plead for her love, Tatiana rejects him and sends him away.

At its première presentation in Moscow on March 29, 1879 (a student performance), and at the first public performance less than two years later, also in Moscow, *Eugene Onegin* was coldly received. The static action, the lack of climaxes and big emotional scenes, invited monotony. The opera once again was poorly received when it was seen for the first time in the United States—at the Metropolitan Opera in New York on March 24, 1920. James Gibbons Huneker described the music as "weak, petty, inconsequential. . . . It is watery, sugary bonbons, mixed with . . . caviar."

Eugene Onegin is not an opera that wears its attractions on the surface. It took many years, and numerous revivals, for the opera public to recognize its subtle beauties. It is now regarded as Tchaikovsky's operatic masterwork, and one of the supreme achievements in Russian opera. To discriminating operagoers, it provides a deeply moving aesthetic experience. Its strength lies in its exquisite lyricism. As Harold C. Schonberg wrote in *The New York Times,* after *Eugene Onegin* had been revived by the Metropolitan Opera for the 1963–1964 season: "What a continuous melodic wash it has! Idea follows idea: the exquisite opening duet (which grows into a quartet); the rapturous duet of Lensky and Olga, followed by what is surely one of the great love arias in all opera, Lensky's 'I Love You, Olga.' Tatiana's letter scene is perhaps the most familiar part of the opera (aside from the orchestral dances), and as one studies it there comes greater and greater respect for Tchaikovsky's powers as a craftsman. How surely he builds to the climax—Tatiana's outcry, 'Here I Am Alone,' with the orchestra welling up to one of those unforgettable Tchaikovskian inspirations. . . . Then there are the quarrel sequences; the bleak duel scene, with Lensky's great aria to his youth; the noble aria of Gremin describing his happiness as Tatiana's husband; the desperation of the final confrontation between Onegin and Tatiana. All this is in a style that owes little to any composer."

In the last analysis, *Eugene Onegin*—as Richard Anthony Leonard remarked —is a "fading, nostalgic picture of a vanished past which suddenly takes on the glow of life; the drama becomes real and moving as the music evokes the atmosphere of Pushkin's story—'young men with romantic, lofty ideas, hypersensitive, schwaermische ladies, desperate passions, and infinite longings.'"

1879. THE SLEEPING BEAUTY (LA BELLE AU BOIS DORMANT), op. 66, ballet in three acts and prologue, with book by Marius Petipa and Ivan Vsevolojsky, based on Charles Perrault's fairy tale. Choreography by Marius Petipa. First performance: Maryinsky Theater, St. Petersburg, January 15, 1890.

AURORA'S WEDDING (or PRINCESS AURORA), one-act classical ballet, which is actually the third act of *The Sleeping Beauty,* made up mainly of divertissements. First performance: Ballet Russe de Monte Carlo, May 18, 1922.

A decade after Tchaikovsky suffered a humiliating failure with his first ballet, *The Swan Lake,* he was commissioned by the director of the St. Petersburg Imperial Theaters to write a score for a new ballet, but this time to a scenario which the director himself had helped devise from a fairy tale. While working on his score, between January and June of 1889, Tchaikovsky spent a good deal of his leisure time in the company of a three-year-old child; this period of play and talk is believed to have given him the child's perspective he needed in writing music for a fairy tale, besides dispelling the morbidity then afflicting him. The writing of the music proved a joy, and when he finished it, he regarded it as one of his finest musical creations. Rosa Newmarch agrees. "Though not deeper than the subject demands, [the ballet score] is melodious in the best sense of the word, fantastic, brightly colored; while it never descends to the commonplace level of the ordinary ballet music."

The première of *The Sleeping Beauty* was a giant success, and finally established Tchaikovsky's fame as an outstanding composer of ballet music; to this day, it remains one of the noblest achievements of the Russian classic ballet. What is believed to have been its American première took place in Philadelphia, Pennsylvania, on February 11, 1937, choreography by Catherine Littlefield.

Here is how Edwin Evans describes the ballet scenario: "The first scene is that of the christening, to which the wicked fairy Carabosse was not invited because nothing had been heard of her for more than fifty years and every one thought her dead. Far from it, she intrudes and utters the terrible curse. In the second scene, the Princess Aurora, now sixteen, pricks her finger and falls asleep. The third begins as a hunting scene, but when the hunt has dispersed the Lilac-Fairy displays the Sleeping Princess in a vision to Prince Charming. The fourth is that of the awakening, and the fifth is taken up by many notable personages from other familiar fairy tales, such as Puss-in-Boots, Little Red Riding Hood, and Hop o' My Thumb. They serve to enhance the color of the divertissement which so often forms the climax of a classical ballet."

Tchaikovsky wrote thirty musical numbers for the ballet. An orchestral suite made up of the most popular of these selections is sometimes given at symphony programs. Such a suite includes the Introduction, the Dance of the Lilac-Fairy, the Adagio of the Princess, Puss-in-Boots, Panorama (an entr'acte), and the popular Valse to whose strains the princess pricks her finger.

Aurora's Wedding, or *Princess Aurora,* which is made up of the divertissements from the third act of *Sleeping Beauty,* includes the following excerpts: Polonaise, Pas de Sept of the Maids of Honors and Their Cavaliers, Dance of the Duchesses, Dance of the Marquesses, Farandole, Florestan and his Two Sisters, Little Red Riding Hood, the Blue Bird, the Porcelain Princess, the Three Ivans, Pas de Deux by Princess Aurora and Prince Charming, and Mazurka.

"The music," said Alexandre Benois of *The Sleeping Beauty,* "really possesses so strong a power of suggestion that those who give themselves up to it are completely transported from reality into the magic world of fairy tale."

1880. CONCERTO NO. 2 IN G MAJOR, for piano and orchestra, op. 44. I. Allegro brilliante e molto vivace. II. Andante non troppo. III. Allegro fuoco.

Tchaikovsky's second piano concerto has been completely dwarfed and obscured by the fame of its giant predecessor. To this day, it is a stranger in the concert hall, yet it contains a wealth of delightful melodies as well as brilliant writing for the piano. It enjoyed a tremendous success when introduced by Taneiev in Moscow in 1882—then lapsed into its undeserved neglect and obscurity. A long work with a symphonic breadth that has led some to describe it as a symphony with piano obbligato, this work overflows with ingratiating materials. Besides exciting virtuoso writing for the solo instrument, this concerto contains so many extended passages for solo violin and solo cello that some musicologists refer to the work as a "triple concerto." The first movement has a dramatic first theme, initially given by the full orchestra, then joined in by the piano. A lyrical second theme is exchanged by clarinet and horn. The slow movement is a Romanza with a poetic song in the piano; to this, solo violin and cello provide embellishments. The finale is a brilliant rondo constructed out of four themes.

On the infrequent occasions when the concerto is given today, it is heard in a revised and truncated version prepared by Alexander Siloti in 1893.

1880. CAPRICCIO ITALIEN (ITALIAN CAPRICE), for orchestra, op. 45.

On February 17, 1880, Tchaikovsky wrote to Mme. von Meck from Rome: "I am working on a sketch of an Italian fantasia based on folk songs. Thanks to the charming themes, some of which I have heard in the streets, the work will be effective." The score was completed in the summer of 1880 after the composer's return to Russia, and on December 18 of the same year it was introduced in Moscow. It opens with an orchestral fanfare, making effective use of a bugle call. This motive was played each night at the barracks of the Royal Cuirassiers; since Tchaikovsky's hotel room overlooked those barracks, he heard the bugle call regularly. The introductory part over, the strings are heard in a gentle Italian melody, soon to be amplified by the orchestra. This is followed by a folk song in the oboes, which is also elaborated. A change of tempo brings on vigorous march music. This, in turn, is followed by a whirling tarantella and a sprightly melody in triple rhythm. An electrifying presto, and a second tarantella provide an exciting conclusion.

1880. SERENADE IN C MAJOR, for strings, op. 48. I. Pezzo in forma di sonatina. II. Waltz. III. Elegia. IV. Tema Russo.

Tchaikovsky explained that he wrote this Serenade "from inward impulse. I felt it, and venture to hope that this work is not without the qualities of a work of art." To Mme. von Meck he further explained: "I wish with all my heart you could hear my Serenade properly performed. It loses so much on the piano, and I think the middle movement, played by the violins, would win your sympathy. As regards the first and last movements . . . they are merely a play of sounds and do not touch the heart. The first movement is my homage to Mozart; it is intended to be in imitation of his style, and I should be delighted if I thought I had in any way approached my model."

That tribute to Mozart in the first movement is in the form of a sonatina. It opens with a chorale-like melody (Andante non troppo), then features a robust theme (Allegro moderato). The second movement is the most famous part of the Serenade, and is often given independently of the other movements. It is a graceful Waltz, with a faint suggestion of Spanish rhythms and colors. The character of the third-movement Larghetto is emphasized by two doleful melodies presented in alternation. The finale opens with a solemn introduction for muted violins. Two Russian melodies follow, the second derived from a street song from the district of Kolomna. The serenade ends with a forceful repetition of this melody, followed by a restatement of the first-movement chorale.

1880. OUVERTURE SOLENNELLE, "OVERTURE 1812," for orchestra, op. 49.

The Temple of Christ the Redeemer was built in Moscow as a memorial to Napoleon's defeat in Russia in 1812. For its consecration ceremonies, planned for 1881, Tchaikovsky was asked to write an appropriate piece of music. He decided upon a programmatic overture relating the historic events surrounding the Battle of Borodino and Napoleon's flight from Moscow. It is doubtful if the *1812 Overture* was actually performed at that consecration of the Temple. What is today accepted as its world première took place in Moscow in 1882.

The overture opens with a subject for woodwind and strings, quoting the Russian hymn, "God Preserve Thy People." The main part of the overture is devoted to a description of the Battle of Borodino. Here we get quotations from the Russian national anthem and the *Marseillaise* to identify the opposing armies. A powerful climax is built up, at its peak the triumphant strains of the Russian national anthem proclaiming Russia's victory.

Since the consecration ceremonies for the Temple of Christ had been planned for the outdoors, Tchaikovsky originally included among his percussion group an actual cannon which was to boom at specified intervals. The cannon is sometimes used today in open-air performances of the overture.

1882. PIANO TRIO IN A MINOR, op. 50. I. Pezzo elegiaco. II. Tema con variazioni. III. Finale.

Late in 1880, Mme. von Meck asked Tchaikovsky to write a chamber-music work for her household trio (its pianist was Claude Debussy). The death of Nicolas Rubinstein in 1881 made it possible for Tchaikovsky to kill two birds with one stone. He complied with Mme. von Meck's request. At the same time, he paid homage to the memory of Rubinstein. The A minor Trio was to become its composer's most distinguished chamber-music work.

There are four themes in the first movement, each partly developed after the initial statement. The music remains consistently elegiac, and ends in a kind of dirge. The second movement is a theme and variations. Each variation is in some set form, such as the mazurka, waltz, fugue, scherzo, and so forth. It is believed that Tchaikovsky intended each of these variations to describe some episode in Rubinstein's life. Homer Ulrich regards the finale as "a tour de force unlike anything else in the literature." First Tchaikovsky develops the theme of his preceding variations movement, carrying it on to climaxes. Then he reintroduces the main theme of the first movement "in the company of thundering chords and flashing arpeggios; only in the last few measures is a degree of restraint and deep feeling introduced. There . . . a dirge-like march restores an air of solemnity to this otherwise brilliant and sentimental trio."

1884. SUITE NO. 3 IN G MAJOR, for orchestra, op. 55. I. Élégie. II. Valse mélancolique. III. Scherzo. IV. Theme and Variations.

The thematic material of the first two movements, as their titles suggest, are elegiac. The two main themes of the first movement are in G major and E-flat major respectively. Both subjects are developed before the movement ends sadly in English horn and solo violin. The elegiac waltz melody of the second movement begins in the strings and continues in the flutes to string accompaniment; other woodwinds join in. In the third-movement Scherzo, trombones and percussion instruments are used in the suite for the first time. Two introductory measures precede the projection of the main subject with a tarantella rhythm, in violins. The trio alternates between soft and vigorous statements, and the movement closes with a quiet statement ending with a forceful chord.

The most significant movement is, however, the finale, a theme and variations, sometimes performed independently of the other movements. The theme is given in the first violins, accompanied by detached chords.

Twelve variations follow, the last a lively Polacca, elaborately embellished. George Balanchine used this theme-and-variations music for a ballet—also named *Theme and Variations*. He introduced it at the New York City Center in 1947.

1885. MANFRED, a symphony "in four pictures," op. 58. I. Manfred Wanders in the Alps. II. The Witch of the Alps Appears to Manfred Beneath the Rainbow of the Cataract. III. Pastorale. IV. The Underground Palace of Arimanes.

While designated as a "symphony," *Manfred* is not one of the six listed as Tchaikovsky's symphonies, but is a seventh independent composition. Balakirev was the one who suggested that Tchaikovsky write a musical work based on Byron's *Manfred*. In following this advice, Tchaikovsky sought to portray the hero's introspective nature, his inner torment, his sense of guilt. "It is the soul of Manfred that I wish to portray," Tchaikovsky said.

Balakirev provided Tchaikovsky with a detailed program, which Tchaikovsky followed with few deviations; it is published in the score. The first movement (Lento lugubre: moderato assai) describes Manfred's wanderings in the Alps. The program explains: "Tortured by the fatal anguish of doubt, racked by remorse and despair, his soul is a prey to sufferings without a name. . . . The memory of fair Astarte, whom he has loved and lost, eats his heart. Nothing can dispel the curse which weighs on Manfred's soul; and without cessation, without truce, he is abandoned to the tortures of the most atrocious despair."

In this first movement, Manfred's torment is suggested by a forceful subject in bassoons and clarinets appearing in the opening measures. This theme recurs throughout the symphony. A second subject is a lyrical passage for the woodwinds, suggesting Manfred's yearning for forgetfulness.

Beyond the title—"The Witch of the Alps Appears to Manfred Beneath the Rainbow of the Cataract"—the score provides no further clue to the program of the second movement. Here, where Manfred invokes the Spirit of the Alps, Tchaikovsky provides us with unforgettable Nature pictures—musical images of the reflecting sunlight, the rainbow, the waters rushing over the rocks. The principal musical subject is a mobile melody for first violins accompanied by harp.

The third movement (Andante con moto) is a "Pastorale" described in the program as "the simple, free and peaceful life of the mountaineers." A bucolic melody dominates this section, first heard in the oboe. A recall of the theme of Manfred's torment introduces an agitated section. A powerful climax is then built up. Tolling bells and a return of the bucolic melody restore serenity.

In the finale (Allegro con fuoco; Adagio ma a tempo rubato), "Manfred appears in the midst of the Bacchanal. Evocation of the ghost of Astarte. She foretells the end of his earthly woes. Manfred's death."

First we hear the Manfred invocation music of the second movement. The orgiastic episode that follows describes the frenzy of the Bacchanal.

Material from earlier movements is now quoted—notably the motives of Manfred's invocation and torment. Suddenly, the solemn tones of the "Dies Irae" are sounded, accompanied by an organ. A climax precedes the vivid description of Manfred's death. Manfred's torment thus finally put to rest, the symphony ends in tranquillity.

1887. MOZARTIANA, suite for orchestra, op. 61. I. Gigue. II. Menuet. III. Preghiera. IV. Theme and Variations.

In *Mozartiana,* Tchaikovsky paid homage to the composer he admired above all others by devoting himself to—and adapting for orchestra—some of the master's less familiar compositions. "The author of the arrangements of the Suite having as its title *Mozartiana,*" Tchaikovsky explained in the published score, "desires to give a new impulse to the study of these little masterworks, whose succinct form contains incomparable beauties." The first movement (Allegro) is based on a gigue for clavier written by Mozart in 1789. This is followed by a miniature minuet without trio, a clavier piece from the year of 1788. The slow movement (Andante con tanto) is the most famous Mozart music used by Tchaikovsky—the motet, "Ave Verum," which Mozart wrote during his last year. (Tchaikovsky prepared his orchestration from a transcription made for piano by Liszt, *À la chapelle Sistine.*) The suite ends with a theme and variations. The theme is by Gluck, "Unser dummer Poebel meint," from the comic opera, *The Pilgrims from Mecca;* Mozart had used it for a set of clavier variations, K. 455.

1888. SYMPHONY NO. 5 IN E MINOR, op. 64. I. Andante; Allegro con anima. II. Andante cantabile, con alcuna licenza. III. Valse: allegro moderato. IV. Andante maestoso; Allegro vivace.

It took over a decade after the Fourth Symphony—and a good deal of doubts and soul-searching—before Tchaikovsky was able to return to the symphonic form. He had lost confidence in his powers; he was weary of spirit. Even after the Fifth Symphony was successfully introduced in 1888, Tchaikovsky was haunted by fears that this work was a failure. "It was obvious to me," he wrote to Mme. von Meck, "that the ovations I received were promoted more by my earlier work and that the symphony itself did not really please the audience. The consciousness of this brings me a sharp twinge of self-dissatisfaction. Am I really played out, as they say? Can I merely repeat and ring the changes on my earlier idiom? Last night I looked through our symphony [No. 4]. What a difference! How immeasurably superior it is! It is very, very sad." But after a brilliant and highly successful performance of the symphony in Hamburg, Tchaikovsky had a sudden change of heart. "I like it better now," he reported to his nephew, Davidov.

The Fifth is the most unified of all Tchaikovsky's symphonies. It is the one that suggests most irresistibly what Ernest Newman noted was "one central controlling purpose." Throughout the symphony a solemn motive, interpreted as Fate, is heard again and again. But the repeated use of the Fate motive is only one of several reasons why this work has such a remarkable unity of purpose and design. The Andante melody of the second movement is repeated in the finale; the first main theme of the finale is derived from the first principal theme of the opening movement; that first-movement theme also recurs in the major key in the closing part of the finale. "Nothing can be clearer," Newman adds, "than that the work embodies an emotional sequence of some kind."

The Fate motive appears in a thirty-seven measure somber introduction to the first movement; it is presented by clarinets and bassoons over a light string accompaniment. The mood lightens perceptibly with the graceful first theme, in clarinets and bassoons, a melody the composer lifted from a Polish folk song. The second theme, however, has the pessimism of the introduction. It is quietly stated by strings in the key of B minor. Both these melodies receive extended development, and are recalled in the recapitulation. The opening theme is the material for the extended coda.

Chords in lower strings precede the beautiful melody of the slow movement in first horn. A secondary melody follows in oboe. The first-movement Fate theme recurs forcefully twice. The second theme closes the movement on a melancholy note.

The third movement is unusual in that in place of a Scherzo we have a Waltz—the lovely "con grazia" melody in first violins. A graceful sixteenth-note figure, first in strings and then in the woodwind, provides the basic material of the middle trio. After a recall of the waltz melody, the movement ends with an ominous recall of the Fate theme.

The finale opens with a triumphant major-mode version of the Fate theme. A powerful new first subject in the strings opens the main part of this movement; in intervallic structure, it is a derivation of the first-movement main theme. A related theme is soon heard in the strings, followed by a passionate woodwind subject that carries a reminder of the horn melody of the slow movement. The Fate theme appears majestically at the peak of each of two climaxes. With a no less grandiloquent restatement of the finale's first theme, the symphony ends in an exalted mood.

1888. HAMLET, overture fantasy for orchestra, op. 67.

Tchaikovsky's friend, the celebrated actor Lucien Guitry, promised he would appear in a production of *Hamlet* if the composer would provide incidental music. Stimulated by Shakespeare and a drama that reflected his own state of melancholia, Tchaikovsky produced not just a few random pieces but a spacious overture fantasy. It opens with an extended atmospheric introduction in A minor (Lento lugubre), suggesting the first-act ghost scene. The fragment of a somber subject in violas and cellos is swept to a forceful climax. Muted horns are heard in twelve G's, crescendo, over syncopated figures and arpeggios. The brass and basses then recall the somber opening fragment. With the introduction over, the Allegro enters with a strong episode, followed by a softer one for oboe, representing Ophelia. The second subject (Moderato con moto) appears in the woodwind, and receives replies by the strings; in its tenderness it reflects the love interest between Hamlet and Ophelia. There is one more important theme, a march tune in E-flat major. There is virtually no development, but the recapitulation gives extended treatment to the Ophelia subject and the love melody. The solemn motif of the introduction returns in the coda.

1890. PIQUE DAME, or THE QUEEN OF SPADES, opera in three acts, with text by Modeste Tchaikovsky, based on a short story of the same name by Pushkin. First performance: Maryinsky Theater, St. Petersburg, December 19, 1890.

At first, Tchaikovsky did not favor the Pushkin story of *Pique Dame* as material for an opera. The text, prepared by Tchaikovsky's brother, had originally been intended for another composer (Klenovsky) who turned it down. Modeste than brought his libretto to his brother, who was cold to it. "A subject like that of *Pique Dame,*" he said, "doesn't move me at all, and I could never make anything worthwhile of it." But two years later, in 1889, the director of the Russian Imperial theaters offered to mount *Pique Dame,* if Tchaikovsky stood ready to write it. This offer brought a change of heart in Tchaikovsky. He went off to Florence, Italy, to work assiduously on his opera, completing the full score in about six months.

When introduced in St. Petersburg in 1890, the opera was a huge success. It forthwith acquired a permanent place in the Russian operatic repertory to become second to *Eugene Onegin* in popularity among Tchaikovsky's operas. On March 5, 1910 it became the first Tchaikovsky opera ever given in the United States, when Gustav Mahler directed a brilliant performance at the Metropolitan Opera (in the German language).

The setting is nineteenth-century St. Petersburg. In a public garden, Herman, a young engineer, confides to his friend Tomski, that he is in love with a girl of unknown identity ("Her Name is Unknown to Me"). She turns out to be Lisa, granddaughter of a Countess, fiancée of Prince Yeletsky. Tomski now reveals how the Countess had acquired the nickname of "Queen of Spades" ("It Happened in Versailles")—by inventing a winning system at cards. The scene changes to Lisa's room. There she and her friend, Pauline, are singing songs ("Already Shades of Night"), and visitors are dancing. When the company leaves, Lisa reveals in a poignant soliloquy that Prince Yeletsky is not the man she loves, but Herman ("O Burning Tears"). Herman makes a sudden appearance through the bedroom window, and speaks out of the depths of his emotion ("Forgive Me, Bright Celestial Visions"). With the arrival of the Countess he must go into hiding; but once the Countess leaves, he learns from Lisa how much she loves him.

In the first scene of the second act, a masked ball is taking place. Yeletsky tells Lisa how deeply he loves her ("I Love You, Dear"). Then a little pastorale interlude, *The Faithful Shepherdess,* is performed for the guests—its music in a pseudo-eighteenth-century style ("Alas, My Chosen Swain"). This is followed by a picturesque polonaise, which celebrates the arrival of the Empress.

Meanwhile, Herman, eager to get the Countess's secret for winning at cards, has secreted himself in that lady's boudoir. Lisa and her maids arrive to put the Countess to bed and to lull her to sleep to the strains of the famous aria, "'Twill Soon Be Midnight." When the Countess is alone, Herman comes out of hiding and tries through threats to wrest the Countess' secret. He threatens her with his pistol. The Countess, terrified, falls back dead.

In the third act, Herman is in his room reading a letter from Lisa in which she has forgiven him and suggests a meeting near the Winter Palace. Putting the letter aside, he succumbs to a hallucination in which he sees the ghost of the Countess come tc him with the card secret. He then goes off to meet Lisa, but what is on his mind is not love but gambling. By raving about the Countess' winning system, he reveals that he has lost his sanity. This is the last blow for poor Lisa. She plunges to her death in the nearby canal.

The final scene is in a gambling establishment where Tomski is discussing women flippantly ("Darling Maidens"), and Yeletski is bitter. Herman, however, is interested only in gambling. Playing for high stakes, he wins twice; but staking all against Yeletsky, he draws the wrong card (the Queen of Spades) and loses. When the ghost of the Countess comes to haunt him, Herman plunges a knife into his bosom and dies.

1892. CASSE NOISETTE (THE NUTCRACKER), op. 71, classic ballet in two acts, with book by M. I. Petipa, based on Alexandre Dumas's version of a story by E. T. A. Hoffmann. Choreography by Lev Ivanov. First performance: Maryinsky Theater, December 18, 1892.

It was a foregone conclusion that, after the tremendous success of *The Sleeping Beauty,* Tchaikovsky would be commissioned to write a new ballet. This time he was not only given a specific text to work with, but also was detailed the moods and dances his music was to fit. The new assignment seemed to inspire very little enthusiasm in the composer, and when he finished the chore, he did not esteem his work very highly. "[It] is infinitely worse than *The Sleeping Beauty*—so much is certain," he wrote to his nephew, Davidov. "If I arrive at the conclusion that I can no longer furnish my musical table with anything but warmed-up fare, I will give up composing altogether."

Tchaikovsky's score received its first hearing as an orchestral suite in 1892, when it aroused so much enthusiasm that five of the six numbers had to be repeated. But the première of the ballet failed to repeat this triumph. The audiences were not accustomed to seeing an entire first act dominated by children, and they did not favor a text derived from a German story. Actually, this ballet never has known the popularity enjoyed by *Swan Lake* and *Sleeping*

Beauty. Its fame rests almost exclusively on the delightful orchestral suite, a staple in the symphonic repertory. The ballet itself had to wait half a century before it was produced in the United States; that première took place in New York on October 17, 1940, in a presentation by the Ballet Russe de Monte Carlo.

Edwin Evans has provided the following summary of the ballet scenario: "Silberhaus and his wife are giving a Christmas party for their children and those of their friends. The guests arrive, the candles are lighted, and the children come in to receive their presents. But Drosselmeyer brings his presents in person. . . . To Clara, daughter of the house, he gives . . . an old-fashioned German nutcracker in the shape of a man who breaks the nuts in his capacious jaw. This pleases Clara more than all her other presents, but her brother Franz, and the other boys, snatch it away from her and break it. Clara bursts into tears, caresses the poor Nutcracker, and fusses over it as an invalid. When the party is over and she has gone to bed, she cannot sleep for thinking of her patient, so she creeps downstairs again.

"At midnight the room is invaded by mice, but all the toys come to life, and a battle royal is engaged in which reaches its climax in a duel between the King of the Mice and the Nutcracker. At the moment when the King seems likely to be victorious, Clara intervenes with a well-aimed slipper and the mice are defeated. The Nutcracker, whose life Clara has saved, now changes into a handsome Prince, who invites her to come with him to . . . the Kingdom of Sweets. They fly over the wintry forest, and to Clara all the snowflakes are living beings dancing around her. Arrived in the Kingdom of Sweets, where the Sugar-Plum Fairy is Queen, they are entertained with a divertissement in which Spanish, Arab and Chinese dancers represent respectively chocolate, coffee, tea; and there are other delectable dances, culminating in the well-known *Valse des fleurs*."

Despite Tchaikovsky's own doubts about his score, the music of *The Nutcracker* is sheer enchantment, its best pages some of Tchaikovsky's most spontaneously inspired creations. These best pages are encountered in the highly popular orchestral Suite. It opens with a "Miniature Overture" scored only for woodwind and higher strings—the delicate voice of a triangle intruding occasionally. Two lively tunes are here present. A piquant "March" follows, its brisk theme given by clarinets, horns, and trumpets; in the trio part, woodwind and strings exchange a lively staccato subject. "The Dance of the Sugar-Plum Fairy" is unusual in that its sensitive melody is assigned to a celesta, one of the rare instances up to that time when this instrument was assigned such importance in the orchestra. Three colorful dances come after that. The first is a dynamic Russian trepak; the second, an exotic Arabian dance whose main theme is presented by the clarinet in the lower register; the third, a Chinese Dance, its oriental melody assigned to flute and piccolo. In the seventh section, the "Dance of the Flutes," a haunting melody appears in flutes, with trumpets providing a robust contrast. The first suite ends with the famous "Waltz of the Flowers," which opens with an infectious waltz tune in horns, which the clarinets soon assume. Two delightful subjects come after that, after each of which the waltz is repeated; the first of these new themes is heard in the strings, and the second in flute and oboe.

1893. SYMPHONY NO. 6 IN B MINOR, "PATHÉTIQUE," op. 74. I. Adagio; Allegro non troppo. II. Allegro con grazia. III. Allegro molto vivace. IV. Adagio lamentoso.

When he first started work on his Sixth Symphony, Tchaikovsky was assailed by the same doubts that had attacked him when he wrote his Fifth Symphony. He destroyed the first sketches of the Sixth because, he said, they "contained little that was really fine—an empty patter of sounds without inspiration." But as he started work again and outlined new sketches, his enthusiasm began to mount. "It goes with such ardor that in less than four days I have completed the first movement, while the remainder is clearly outlined in my head," he wrote to his nephew, Davidov. "You can imagine what joy I feel in the conviction that my day is not yet over, and I may still accomplish much." When his symphony was finally committed to paper, he considered it "the best, certainly the most sincere work I have ever written. On my word of honor," he wrote to his publisher, "never in all my life have I been so satisfied, so proud, so happy in the knowledge that I have written a good work."

Tchaikovsky originally planned to call the work a *Program Symphony,* hinting darkly that it had a personal message to expound, yet refusing to reveal what the message or the program was. At the première performance, in 1893, the symphony was merely listed by its number. Still Tchaikovsky felt the need for some identifying title, and seized upon the suggestion made to him by his brother Modeste that he call it *Pathetic.*

We do not know if Tchaikovsky planned to put into his music all the anguish, torment, and mental stresses that were torturing him when he wrote his symphony. We cannot even be sure that in writing it he was trying to produce his own requiem (even though a passage for first trombone in the first movement quotes from a Russian funeral service, a passage that has no possible relation with the rest of the material). But surely this is one of the most pessimistic documents in all musical literature, a monumental tragedy in tone, the apotheosis of human suffering. It is the most tragic piece of music Tchaikovsky ever wrote and the most personal; he confessed that in writing it he often burst into weeping. It is almost as if he knew that this one was destined to be his farewell.

The Sixth is Tchaikovsky's greatest symphony, as well as his most popular; it is also the most celebrated symphony in all Russian music, and probably in all Romantic music. "Nowhere else," says Donald Francis Tovey, "has he encountered so great a variety of music within so effective a scheme; and the slow finale with its complete simplicity of despair, is a stroke of genius which solves all the artistic problems that have proved most baffling to symphonic writings since Beethoven. . . . All Tchaikovsky's music is dramatic; and the *Pathetic* is the most dramatic of all his works."

The funereal character of the symphony is established at once in the introduction of the first movement. The solo bassoon appears with a lugubrious subject that turns out to be the germ of the movement's main first theme. That first theme, in which the expression of grief is still controlled, is presented by the strings. The melancholia grows deeper with the soaring melody of the second theme in flute and bassoon. Now the tension grows, to be suddenly broken by a vigorous chord. After a recall of the first theme, we hear the quotation from the Russian funeral service. And now the mood becomes alternately melancholy and agitated. A somber melody for the brass, over a descending pizzicato passage for strings, brings the movement to its close.

There is a temporary relief from tragedy in the two middle movements. The second is a Scherzo, featuring an infectious dance tune first in the cellos, and then in the woodwind, in both instances accompanied by pizzicato strings. A more solemn note is interjected in the trio, but this grim mood is dispelled with the return of the first section with its dance melody. The third movement is a stirring march, built up with cyclonic power. The germ of the march melody is given first by the oboe in the eight-measure introduction. Other sections of the orchestra repeat this idea before the march is released by the full orchestra.

Tradition is shattered in the finale. This is one of the rare instances in which a slow movement has been made to close a symphony. Here we get a mighty lamentation from a heart and spirit that are permanently shattered; this is the speech of a man who faces both despair and death. The outcry in the orchestra, with which the movement opens, is the very essence of grief, a grief that gains in intensity and passion as the movement progresses. This, says Richard Anthony Leonard, is "a slow descent into darkness and silence, achieved with such beauty of musical utterance that few listeners may leave this work without feelings of aesthetic satisfaction and emotional surfeit."

HENRI VIEUXTEMPS 1820–1881

Like Paganini, Henri Vieuxtemps was a violin virtuoso in the grand manner: a dazzling technician in full command of all the resources of his instrument; an artist with an aristocratic sense of style and nobility of concept. And, once again like Paganini, Vieuxtemps did not hesitate to charge his own violin compositions with the electricity of pyrotechnics—but usually not at the expense of a deeply felt emotion which asserted itself continually in the most expressive lyricism. Though he wrote many pieces for the violin, of which the *Ballade et Polonaise* is among the most popular, he is most famous for two of the six concertos he wrote for his instrument.

Henri Vieuxtemps was born in Verviers, Belgium, on February 17, 1820. He was a remarkable prodigy who attracted the interest and support of Charles de Bériot, the eminent violinist. De Bériot taught Vieuxtemps for three years, then took him to Paris where the boy created a sensation. Beginning with 1831, and for the next forty years, Vieuxtemps toured the music world. He was acclaimed not only by the critics and the public but also by many world-famous musicians, including Berlioz, Schumann, and Wagner. Vieuxtemps made three tours of the United States, the first in 1845, the last in 1870–1871, after which he retired from the concert stage. In 1871, Vieuxtemps became professor of the violin at the Brussels Conservatory. Paralysis of the side compelled him to give up teaching in 1873. He died in Mustapha, Algeria, where he had come for a rest cure, on June 6, 1881.

1850. CONCERTO NO. 4 IN D MINOR, for violin and orchestra, op. 31. I. Andante; Moderato. II. Adagio religioso. III. Vivace. IV. Andante; Allegro.

Vieuxtemps regarded this concerto as his favorite, and many leading musicians agreed with him. When Berlioz heard Vieuxtemps perform it at its Paris première, he said that the violinist "showed himself no less remarkable as a composer than he was incomparable as a virtuoso."

It differs from most violin concertos in that it has four instead of three movements, the additional one being the third, a scherzo. But the composer took pains to point out that the concerto could well be performed without the third movement, explaining that the performer could pass on "immediately from the Adagio to the final Allegro, omitting the fourteen measures of Andante which serve as an introduction to it." Many present-day violinists prefer to play only the three movements.

An unidentified commentator has said of this work that it is "set forth with a majestic sense of proportion, subscribing quite successfully to Liszt's definition of a concerto as a work which should be clear in sense, brilliant in expression, and grand in style." The concerto opens dramatically with an orchestral preface in slow tempo, another way in which this work differs from other violin concertos. After the violin enters on a sustained high note, it embarks on a virtuoso's mission before settling down to an eloquent melody to which the orchestra provides an effective countersubject. Eloquence is pronounced in the second movement, which is connected to the first by a sustained note in the horn. The main melody, in the violin, has an exalted religious character which gains in intensity and spiritual grandeur when a contrapuntal background is later provided by the orchestra. The optional third movement has a waltz-like melody in its initial section, and a motif in the trio that sounds like a hunting call. A stirring martial character is predominant in the finale where melodic ideas from earlier movements are recalled.

1858. CONCERTO NO. 5 IN A MINOR, for violin and orchestra, op. 37. I. Allegro non troppo. II. Adagio. III. Allegro con fuoco.

Arthur Hartmann, a distinguished violinist, thus described this concerto: "To my critical judgment [it] . . . represents a unique achievement in violinistic art, and is exemplary for its beautiful symmetry, skill and art of construction and for its wealth of noble and musically dramatic utterances."

Though in three movements, the concerto is actually an integrated composition played without interruption. After the opening declaration by the orchestra, the violin appears with arpeggios and proceeds to technical exercises. Only then does it launch upon one of the principal melodies of the work—a beautiful, fully developed song. This subject is then embellished upon by the violin, after which the orchestra expropriates it. A development and cadenza follow, succeeded by a brief but deeply moving section whose main material is a variation of the song. A high tensioned climax leads into a brief coda with which the concerto ends.

HENRI WIENIAWSKI 1835–1880

Wieniawski was one of the foremost violin virtuosos of the late nineteenth century, a technician second to none. Joseph Joachim once said that the flexibility of his left hand would not be believed by anybody who had never heard him play. Wieniawski also produced a tone of rare beauty and variety of color and nuances, made possible by his own method of bowing. To technique, he added the fire of his temperament, the charm of his personality, and the authority of his sound musicianship. And the composer was very much like the performer. Wieniawski wrote exclusively for the violin: two concertos and about thirty other sundry items. A dazzling technical equipment is required for the performance of most of these works, but pyrotechnics is usually subservient to the lyrical content and to a rich Romantic temperament.

Henri Wieniawski was born in Lublin, Poland, on July 10, 1835. A remarkable prodigy, he entered the Paris Conservatory when he was eight. As a pupil of Massart, he made Conservatory history by being the first eleven-year-old to win the gold medal for violin playing. His studies ended in 1848, he embarked on a virtuoso career that eventually brought him to all parts of the civilized world. In 1872 he toured the United States, often appearing in joint recitals with Anton Rubinstein. In 1860 he was made court violinist at St. Petersburg, holding this post for eleven years. In 1874 he was appointed professor of the violin at the Brussels Conservatory. Wieniawski died in Moscow on April 2, 1880.

1870. CONCERTO NO. 2 IN D MINOR, for violin and orchestra, op. 22. I. Allegro moderato. II. Romanze: andante non troppo. III. Allegro moderato à la zingara.

In *Violin Masterworks and Their Interpretation,* Leopold Auer, the distinguished teacher of the violin, remarked that this concerto "shows that the composer intended to write not merely a virtuoso composition for the violin, but to produce as well an interesting musical creation." Bravura passages take second place to an expressive lyricism, which is consistently spontaneous and fresh, and at times even soulful. The sum total is one of the most treasurable works in Romantic violin music.

The first movement opens with a sixty-seven measure orchestral preface in which the first theme is heard in the orchestra and the second in the horn. When the solo instrument finally appears, he discourses on the first theme. After some passage work he provides triplet figures to the second theme when the latter is recalled by the orchestra. After the usual development and recapitulation, a clarinet solo provides a bridge to the second movement which enters without pause. This music is a romance for the violin, rich in poetry and emotion. A cadenza for the solo instrument separates this movement from the finale, whose first theme is a lively gypsy tune in the orchestra, soon repeated by the solo instrument. The violin later remembers the second theme of the first movement. After a change of key, and with the preliminaries of a staccato passage, the violin engages the second important theme of the movement, now heard for the first time. Throughout this movement virtuosity is exploited effectively without any sacrifice of sound musical values.

———. COMPOSITIONS FOR VIOLIN:

Kujawiak, in A minor, for violin and piano, op. 3.
Légende, for violin and orchestra, op. 17.
Polonaise brilliante, in D major, for violin and piano, op. 4, no. 1.
Scherzo—Tarantelle, in G minor, for violin and piano, op. 16.
Souvenir de Moscou, for violin and orchestra, op. 6.

There is more than one string to Wieniawaski's creativity. Some of his compositions are pyrotechnical, making exacting demands on the digital and bowing dexterity of the performer. In this category we find the electrifying *Scherzo-Tarantelle.* In other Wieniawski compositions Russian folk songs provide a point of departure. Of these the most celebrated is the *Souvenir de Moscou,* a set of short variations on two Russian folk tunes, one of which is the popular folk song, "The Red Serafin." At times, Polish folk dances contribute to Wieniawski's pieces their cogent rhythms. This happens in the fiery *Kujawiak,* a variety of the mazurka which got its name from the fact that it was popular in the Kuawy district of Poland; also in the *Polonaise brilliante* in D major, with its exciting accentuations on the half beats and its syncopations. Still another facet of Wieniawski's creativity is his German-Romantic partiality to emotional or poetic utterances. This is particularly notable in the *Légende,* a three-part song of excessive tenderness and sentiment, but with a dramatized middle part for contrast. This *Légende* was inspired by Wieniawski's love affair with Isobel Hampton, the woman who later became his wife.

KARL GOLDMARK 1830–1915

Because he espoused the cause of Wagner so passionately in his criticisms for the *Konstitutionelle Zeitung,* Karl Goldmark was often identified by his fellow Viennese as a Wagnerian. But his relationship with "the music of the future" is tenuous, to say the least. If anything, in his operas, he is closest to Meyerbeer, especially in *The Queen of Sheba.* And here, and in some of his orchestral music, Orientalism and exoticism are his strong suits. The writing of music with the intervallic structure, cadences, and colors of the Orient came naturally to him; and it is in this style that we find his finest works, such as the ballet music in *The Queen of Sheba* and the orchestral overture, *Sakuntala.* Even when he is the German Romantic, who floods his music with sentiment, Oriental mannerisms manage to intrude into his writing.

Karl Goldmark, the son of a synagogue cantor, was born in Keszthely, Hungary, on May 18, 1830. When he was fourteen, he entered the Vienna Conservatory. His studies were permanently ended when the Conservatory closed down during the 1848 revolution. For a while, he earned his living playing the violin in theater orchestras, teaching piano, and writing music criticisms. A concert of his works was given in Vienna in 1857, and another in Budapest in 1859, but neither lifted him out of obscurity and poverty. Not until 1865 did he attract the attention of critics and audiences, when his still popular *Sakuntala Overture* was given for the first time. His fame grew perceptibly after that, with the première of such works as *The Rustic Wedding Symphony,* the A minor Violin Concerto, and *The Queen of Sheba.* Karl Goldmark died in Vienna on January 2, 1915.

1865. SAKUNTALA, concert overture for orchestra, op. 13.

Goldmark's first success as a composer came with this brilliantly orchestrated and melodic overture. When first heard in Vienna in 1865, it received the blessings of Eduard Hanslick who wrote: "Fresh and characteristic in invention and fine in detail, the overture reveals a definite clearing up of the previously confused and fermenting talent of Goldmark. As concerns the relation of the work to the celebrated East-Indian drama, *Sakuntala,* the overture is no sample of dependent descriptive music in the mistaken sense. As a fully comprehensible and independent piece of music, it takes from the play only the poetic suggestion of the action and the mood and local color only in the simplest features of the plot."

The music is based on the drama of Kalidasa, which tells of the love of Sakuntala, the water nymph, for a king. The King presents her with a ring, by which she is to be recognized as his wife, but she loses it. When she comes to the palace, the King does not recognize her; and since she does not have the identifying ring, he repudiates her. In despair, Sakuntala returns to her watery kingdom. Only then is the ring found, and the King is able to recall that she is the one he had chosen as his wife. He finds her and brings her back to his kingdom.

Dark colored harmonies in lower strings and bassoon suggest an eerie setting as the overture opens. Trills bring up the image of playing waters in a spring. After a change of tempo, we hear the principal melody. This is a beautiful song for clarinet and cellos, the love music of the King and Sakuntala. Two other important subjects follow. The first, for first violins and oboes, is juxtaposed against the love melody now assigned to second violins and violas. The other, in a sprightlier tempo, has the character of hunting music. Strong chords help to restore the opening material. The coda opens with the hunt tune in crescendo, after which the other two major subjects are recalled forcefully.

1875. DIE KOENIGEN VON SABA (THE QUEEN OF SHEBA), opera in four acts, with text by Salomon Hermann Mosenthal, based on the Old Testament. First performance: Vienna Royal Opera, March 10, 1875.

The Queen of Sheba is rarely seen today. But in the last quarter of the nineteenth century and in the first decade of the twentieth, it had a tremendous vogue. In Vienna, its première had been a triumph. After that, it was acclaimed throughout Germany and Italy. The American première—also a formidable success—took place at the Metropolitan Opera in New York on December 2, 1885.

Though an avowed Wagnerian, Goldmark did not try here to write a music drama. His aim was an opera in the Meyerbeer tradition. Indeed, when Wagner first heard *The Queen of Sheba* he was severely critical, maintaining it was the kind of opera to which he had always been violently opposed and whose ritual and clichés he had tried to destroy. *The Queen of Sheba* had, for its main attractions, pageantry, ceremonials, storm scenes. The big vocal moments include set arias in the old manner, such as Assad's first-act air, "Magische Toene," the second-act song of Solomon, "Blick' empor zu jenen Raeumen," and the third act aria with chorus of Sulamith, "Doch eh' ich in des Todes Tal." Possibly the highlight of the whole opera came with the sensual Oriental ballet performed for the Queen in the early part of the third act, while the brilliantly scored and theatrical festive march in the second act was hardly less theatrical. All this put *The Queen of Sheba* solidly in the enemy camp, as far as Wagner was concerned.

Mosenthal drew only the bare essentials from the Bible for his libretto. That text was described by Henry E. Krehbiel as a "dramatic story which is rational, which strongly enlists the interest if not the sympathies of the observers, which . . . abounds with imposing spectacles that are not only intrinsically brilliant and fascinating, but that occur as necessary adjuncts to the story."

Assad, the Hebrew warrior, is betrothed to Sulamith, daughter of the High Priest. Assad has seen a strange woman bathing in the stream and forthwith has fallen in love with her. When he learns she is the Queen of Sheba, he arranges a secret meeting. The Queen proves receptive to his amorous advances, in spite of which, he proceeds with his plans to marry Sulamith. At his wedding, however, he impulsively takes the wedding ring he is about to present to his bride and throws it at the feet of the Queen. Sheba insists that Assad is a total stranger. Bitterly, Assad curses Jehovah, for which he is condemned to die. But after the Queen pleads with Solomon to save the young man's life, the sentence is changed to exile. When Assad goes off to the desert, he is followed by Sulamith. She has forgiven him, after which both become the fatal victims of a violent sandstorm.

Here is how Krehbiel described Goldmark's score: "At times his music rushes along like a lava stream of passion; every bar pulsates with eager, excited and exciting life. He revels in instrumental color; the language of the orchestra is as glowing as the poetry attributed to the King whom his operatic story celebrates. Many other composers before him have made use of Oriental cadences and rhythms, but to none have they seemed to come so like native language as to Goldmark. It is romantic music against which the strongest objection that can be urged is it is so unvaryingly stimulated that it wearies and makes the listener long for a fresher and healthier musical atmosphere."

1876. LAENDLICHE HOCHZEIT (RUSTIC WEDDING SYMPHONY), op. 26. I. Wedding March. II. Bridal Song. III. Serenade. IV. In the Garden. V. Dance.

Though designated a symphony by its composer, the *Rustic Wedding* is in reality a suite of five tonal pictures grouped around a Central European wedding ceremony. The musical style ranges from the sentimental to the gay. The charm is on the surface; the lyricism, often cast in the mold of folk music, avoids the subtle.

The symphony opens with a wedding march (Moderato molto), in which a stately melody is followed by thirteen variations. The second episode is a sentimental tune in oboe, played contrapuntally with the opening-movement march (Allegretto). This is followed by a pastoral section (Allegretto moderato scherzando) dominated by the oboe. The dialogue of lovers is suggested in the fourth movement (Andante), while in the finale (Allegro molto) the march subject of the opening movement is given fugal treatment.

1878. CONCERTO NO. 1 IN A MINOR, for violin and orchestra, op. 28. I. Allegro moderato. II. Andante. III. Moderato; Allegretto.

Goldmark wrote two violin concertos, but only the first has taken a permanent hold in the repertory. The first movement side-steps the usual sonata form by introducing a third major subject. This one is given immediately in the orchestra but is deserted as soon as the exposition section begins. It recurs fugally in the development and in the coda. The two main melodies of the exposition are a tender theme for the solo violin over pianissimo second violins, and a song for the solo violin, accompanied softly by the strings. In the slow movement, the solo violin appears with a stately melody after a fifteen-measure introduction. The finale opens with a five-measure introduction before the violin appears with the first main thought. Two other lyrical passages follow, both introduced by the solo violin, the first in octaves.

MAX BRUCH 1838–1920

In his own time, Bruch was esteemed most highly for his choral works, of which he produced an impressive repertory. Hugo Riemann was of the mind that it is here that the true essence of Bruch's creative gift can be found. But this choral music has long since become terra incognita. This is equally true of his two full-scale operas—*Die Loreley* (1863) and *Hermione* (1872)—his three symphonies, two piano concertos, two string quartets, and sundry other compositions. What has remained as gratifying today as when first heard are the first violin concerto (a fruit of early manhood), and the *Scottish Fantasy* and *Kol Nidrei* (both of them products of the composer's full maturity). Here Bruch appears as the German Romantic, who could bring to his writing warmth of heart, attractive lyricism, and technical skill. "It is impossible," Donald Francis Tovey once said in considering the first violin concerto, "to find in Max Bruch any lapses from the standard of beauty which he thus instinctively sets himself. . . . He was the type of artist universally accepted as a master, about whose works no controversy could arise because no doubt was possible as to their effectiveness and sincerity."

Max Bruch was born in Cologne, Germany, on January 6, 1838. In 1852, he received the Mozart Foundation scholarship enabling him to study with Hiller and Reinecke in Cologne. He was only fourteen when he completed his first symphony, and twenty when his first opera, the one-act *Scherz, List und Rache,* was produced in Cologne. From 1858 to 1861, he taught music in that city. His first full-length opera, *Die Loreley* (a libretto originally intended for Mendelssohn) was seen in Mannheim in 1863. During the next few years, he completed his first significant choral works, among these being the *Frithjof Scenen,* op. 23.

In 1865, Bruch became the musical director of a concert group in Coblenz. While holding this post, he completed his first masterwork, the first violin concerto. Two years later, he became the Kapellmeister for the Prince of Schwarzburg-Sondershausen. When he gave up this post, he concentrated on composition. For a number of years he lived in Berlin, where his opera, *Hermione,* was introduced in 1872. Between 1880 and 1883, he served as conductor of the Liverpool Philharmonic; from 1883 to 1890, was director of a musical group in Breslau; and from 1891 to 1910, was professor of composition at the High School of Music in Berlin. Meanwhile, in 1883, he visited the United States. In 1908, he received the Prussian Ordre pour le Merite, and a decade after that was elected a corresponding member of the French Academy. He was also the recipient of a number of honorary degrees from leading universities. From 1910 on, he lived in retirement in Friedenau, a suburb of Berlin, where he died on October 2, 1920.

1867. CONCERTO NO. 1 IN G MINOR, for violin and orchestra, op. 26. I. Allegro moderato. II. Adagio. III. Allegro energico.

Bruch wrote three violin concertos, but it is only the first of these that has stayed in public favor. After the first draft had been introduced in Coblenz in 1866, Bruch revised it extensively. The new and definitive version was given by Joseph Joachim in Bremen in 1868 and has become one of the most popular violin concertos in the Romantic literature.

The first movement is unusual in that the material of the orchestral introduction bears no relation to the main body, and is never heard again. The introduction over, the solo violin embarks on the first main subject, accompanied by tremolos. A second, and more emotional, melody is also introduced by the solo instrument, in collaboration with the oboe. These ideas are enlarged and recapitulated. A cadenza then serves as the link to the second movement. A soaring song for solo violin is the principal subject, while a subsidiary thought is later introduced by the orchestra, with filigree decorations by the violin. The finale opens with a robust march-like tune in solo violin, on the heels of a short orchestral introduction. The full orchestra provides contrasting material in the form of a lyrical second theme, which is soon assumed by the solo violin. There are brilliant virtuoso passages for the violin in the development, and a delightful canonic interlude for the orchestra. An abbreviated version of the opening theme serves as the closing statement.

1880. SCOTTISH FANTASY, for violin and orchestra, op. 46. I. Grave; Adagio cantabile. II. Allegro. III. Andante sostenuto. IV. Allego guerriero.

Several novels by Sir Walter Scott provided the stimulus for the writing of the *Scottish Fantasy,* which was introduced in Hamburg in 1880 by Pablo de Sarasate. In each of the four movements, a popular Scottish air is quoted. The first movement has a solemn introduction for brass, followed by a recitative for solo violin. Then the Scottish melody, "Auld Rob Morris," is presented. In the second movement, another orchestral preface sets the stage for the lively folk-dance tune, "The Dusty Miller," first in the orchestra, then in solo violin. In the slow movement, "I'm Down for the Lack of Johnnie," is first presented by the orchestra to embellishments by the solo violin. The finale enters with a vigorous triple stop passage for the violin, accompanied by harp. Then the Scottish melody "Scots Wha' Hae" is introduced.

1880. KOL NIDREI, for cello and orchestra, op. 47.

The Kol Nidrei is a traditional synagogal chant, intoned on the eve of the holiest of all Jewish holidays—Yom Kippur. It represents on the part of the worshiper an annulment of all vows made the preceding year. The century-old melody is perhaps one of the most familiar in cantorial music. It attracted Bruch, and he used it as the spine of an extended work for cello and orchestra, introduced in Leipzig in 1881. This melody is stated in full by the solo instrument. Several variations follow. A second important melody is then presented by the orchestra and repeated by the solo cello. This theme is Bruch's own, and consequently more German Romantic in style than Hebraic. Because of Bruch's effective and convincing presentation of the Kol Nidrei, and the sincere religious atmosphere of the entire work, he has long and erroneously believed to have been of the Jewish faith.

BEDŘICH SMETANA 1824–1884

Smetana was Bohemia's first nationalist composer, and founder of a school that included Antonín Dvořák. Bohemian music was a distillation of European influences. In opera, it imitated the Italians, and in symphonies and chamber music it echoed the styles of German and Austrian masters. Then in the second part of the nineteenth century, a wave of nationalism swept over Europe and inundated Bohemia. The ferment that followed led the Austrian rulers to grant Bohemia political autonomy in 1860. An aroused patriotism and national consciousness developed, which led Bohemia's younger artists to seek out a national art. This, in turn, led in 1862 to the founding of a national theater (by public subscription), dedicated to Bohemian drama and operas. For this theater, Smetana wrote his first opera, *The Brandenburgers in Bohemia,* which he completed in 1863, though it was not performed until 1866. Its text described a Bohemian rebellion against Teutonic invaders, while the music (though strongly Wagnerian) began to assume something of the identity of Bohemian folk songs and dances. In his next three operas—beginning with his masterwork, *The Bartered Bride,* in 1866, and continuing with two works based on Bohemian legends, *Dalibor* in 1867 and *Libusa* in 1872—Smetana became Bohemia's first and foremost spokesman in the musical theater.

He tapped the rich veins of Bohemian folk music also in his concert works, and most notably in his monumental set of six tone poems collectively entitled *My Fatherland,* of which *The Moldau* (or *Vltava*) is a universal favorite; in his two autobiographical quartets entitled *From My Life,* the first of which is a masterwork; in his *Bohemian Dances* for the piano. What Pitts Sanborn once said of *The Bartered Bride* holds true for all of Smetana's national works. They are, by no means, folk music "in a cramping sense. While distinctively of its native soil . . . [this music] possesses the universal qualities necessary to give it a world-wide currency. We of other countries delight in Czech rhythms, its national dances, the characteristic contour of its melodies, but we also find in this music more than local color and exotic charm; the flowing humanity is there that transcends limits and boundaries."

"Smetana," adds Jan Lowenbach, "was privileged not only to hear and imitate the spirit of the rich melodies and varied rhythms of his nation, but also to invent, to feel, and to express it in a new way and to adapt it to the spirit of modern times."

Bedřich Smetana was born in Leitomischl, Bohemia, on March 2, 1824. His father, manager of a brewery, opposed a musical training for the boy. Nevertheless, Bedřich managed to receive some music instruction from Joseph Proksch before going to Prague. There he studied piano and theory intensively with J. B. Kittl, director of the Prague Conservatory. After completing these studies, Smetana served for four years as a music teacher for the family of Count Thun. Then, with the help of Liszt, he opened up in 1848 his own music school in Prague, which proved sufficiently successful to enable him a year later to marry his boyhood sweetheart, Katharina Kolar, a fine pianist. Meanwhile, he had tried with little success to make his way as concert pianist and composer. His first compositions included sundry pieces for the piano, including waltzes, bagatelles, and impromptus.

Unable to make any headway in his own country either as performer or composer, Smetana went to Göteborg, Sweden in 1856, to serve as conductor of its Philharmonic Society. He stayed in that city five years, and in that time achieved a measure of recognition for his conducting, piano playing, and compositions. In Göteborg, Smetana completed his first three tone poems, of which *Wallensteins Lager* (1859) is the most important.

In May 1861, Smetana returned to his homeland. He now became a leader of the national movement by writing national operas, assuming direction of a chorus and a symphony orchestra, and organizing the Society of Artists to promote native music and musicians. He became first conductor at the National Theater, for which he wrote his later operas.

A victim of nervous disorders that were impairing his health, Smetana was compelled to resign his post at the National Theater in 1874. By the end of that year, he was totally deaf. In spite of this calamity, he was able to create several significant works: two comic operas, *The Two Widows* in 1873 and *The Kiss* in 1876; the cycle of national tone poems, *My Fatherland;* and his first string quartet.

While working on his last opera, *Viola,* in 1884, which he never completed, Smetana lost his sanity and had to be consigned to an asylum in Prague, where he died on May 12, 1884.

1866. THE BARTERED BRIDE (DIE VERKAUFTE BRAUT), comic opera in three acts, with text by Karel Sabina. First performance: Prague, May 30, 1866.

Smetana wrote eight completed operas. The first was *The Brandenburgers in Bohemia* produced at the National Theater in Prague on January 5, 1866; the last, *The Devil's Wall,* was seen at the same theater on October 29, 1882. Some were influenced by Wagner; some were comic rather than dramatic; some were heroic in cast. But all were nationalistic and sometimes with strong political or patriotic overtones. One was a masterwork that the world has taken to its heart—the comic opera, *The Bartered Bride.*

Curiously, the composer looked upon this, his greatest as well as most popular opera with a considerable amount of condescension. He wrote it, as a matter of fact, because he resented those critics who regarded his first opera as too Wagnerian and too pretentious. To demonstrate he could write otherwise if he chose, he immediately set his librettist, Karel Sabina, to work on a light and frivolous text for what he hoped would be an Offenbach-like comic opera. Long after *The Bartered Bride* had achieved world-wide fame, Smetana belittled it in order to throw attention on what he considered were more serious and ambitious operas, and which he also felt were being unduly neglected. But his efforts notwithstanding, *The Bartered Bride* remained a favorite in and out of Bohemia, and it is the only one of his operas to remain consistently in the repertory of the world's foremost opera houses.

There were several versions of this opera. The first, the one that had received its world première in 1866, was more of a musical comedy than an opera, since it was primarily a spoken comedy with interpolations of songs and dances. A second version was planned for the Opéra-Comique in Paris, in which the score was extended through the addition of some more solo numbers and choruses. (The Paris presentation did not materialize.) Having now begun to think in terms of a more expansive setting, Smetana soon decided to include several folk dances (among them a Furiant and the now extremely popular polka). This second adaptation, with new musical material, was seen for the first time in Prague on January 29, 1869. A third major revision followed, when, recognizing that his work was more of an opera than an operetta, Smetana replaced spoken text with recitatives. In this final form, the opera was produced in Prague on September 25, 1870. Though *The Bartered Bride* had been well received in earlier versions, it was now a major triumph. Forthwith, it established itself as a prime favorite of Bohemian audiences among home-made operas. Between 1870 and the outbreak of World War II, the opera had been given almost fifteen hundred times in Prague alone.

Gustav Mahler introduced the opera to the United States when he conducted a performance at the Metropolitan on February 19, 1909. When, in 1936, the Metropolitan Opera revived the work, it presented it in an English translation.

What W. J. Henderson said about this opera when it was first introduced to America still holds true. "The chief charms of the opera are its incessant flow of melody, of fresh and piquant character, its bright and vivacious pictures of Bohemian life, its captivating dances, its excellent character sketches, its simple yet unctuous comedy, and its admirable instrumentation. As a specimen of genuinely artistic comic opera it takes a commanding position." The opera is almost Mozartian in its blend of comedy and tenderness, with its insight into human frailities, and in its penetrating understanding of human motivations. What Smetana had failed to realize was that, though his touch was light and gay, and his purpose was sheer entertainment, he had plumbed more deeply into human psychology and emotion than he was able to do in his more serious and ambitious operas.

The lively overture forthwith establishes a frivolous mood. The effervescent first theme is given at once in strings and woodwind, accompanied by brass. This subject is then treated fugally and is repeated before a second melody is presented by the oboe. Later on, after the first subject has been discussed, a third vivacious idea is projected by violins and cellos.

The curtain rises on a public square in a little Bohemian village a century ago. A festival is taking place, the villagers celebrating the vernal season in the chorus, "See the Buds Burst on the Bush." Everybody is in a holiday spirit except Marie and Hans, for they are in love, and their union is opposed by Marie's parents. They want her to marry Wenzel, a stuttering idiot, son of the wealthy landowner Micha—a marriage arranged by the broker, Kezal. Marie tells Hans that she will love him forever, ("Gladly Do I Trust You"). Upon the arrival of Marie's parents, in the company of Kezal, the marriage broker elaborates on Wenzel's many virtues as a prospective son-in-law ("A Proper Young Man"). But Marie will have none of him, insisting she loves Hans alone. Kezal goes off to try to convince Hans to renounce Marie. The villagers return to the square to dance a polka.

The second act is in the village inn, where the farmers are enjoying drink and talk. Hans and Kezal are also here. Hans speaks of the ecstasy of love, Kezal about the importance of money. As more villagers crowd into the inn, they participate in the peasant dance, the Furiant. Once it is over, Wenzel makes an appearance. He has been instructed by his mother to seek out his future bride, but he does not know where to find her, since he has never met her ("Ma-Ma-Mamma So Dear"). Nor does he recognize her when Maria arrives. To taunt him, Marie tells him his prospective bride is a horrible shrew. The timid Wenzel, shocked out of his senses, promises to avoid her like the plague, then tries to embrace Marie, whom he finds attractive. When Marie eludes him, he chases after her, stuttering all the while of how much she appeals to him. Once they are gone, Hans recalls his far-off home ("Far from Here Do I Live"). At the same time Kezal tries to convince him to give up Marie for good, by telling him about another attractive girl ("One I Know Who Has Money Galore"). But Hans is indifferent. Kezal tries another maneuver—bribery. He is ready to offer Hans three hundred gold pieces if Hans, in turn, renounces Marie. Hans accepts, but only on the condition that Marie be forced to marry Micha's son. Since Wenzel is Micha's son, the condition is willingly accepted.

In the public square, in the third act, a traveling circus is setting up shop. Wenzel is bemoaning his fate. The girl he loves is not interested in him. But when he catches a glimpse of the tightrope dancer, Esmeralda, he quickly forgets his woes and pursues her. He is even willing to play the part of a dancing bear to win her fancy. After the troupe has performed the popular "Dance of the Comedians," Wenzel's parents come to fetch him. They want him to meet his bride who, as it turns out, is Marie after all, a fact that makes Wenzel eager for the first time to go through with the bargain. Marie, meanwhile, has learned that Hans has given her up for a bribe, a discovery that sends her to the depths of despair ("How Strange and Dead"). In retaliation, she stands ready to marry Wenzel. Hans tries approaching Marie to explain why he entered into such a contract with Kezal ("My Dearest Love, Just Listen"), but Marie turns a deaf ear. At this point, Micha recognizes Hans as his long-lost son, and Hans explains how he has perpetrated a trick on the wily marriage-broker. Since he, Hans, is also the son of Micha—and since his contract with Kezal specified that Marie must marry Micha's son—then he can be Marie's husband and keep the bribe. The villagers are delighted; Kezal is shattered.

1874–1879. MÁ VLAST (MY FATHERLAND), a cycle of six national tone poems for orchestra. I. Vitesgrad. II. The Moldau (or Vltava). III. Sárka. IV. From the Fields and Groves of Bohemia. V. Tábor. VI. Blanik.

Smetana's six orchestral tone poems—inspired by Bohemian history, legends, geography, and backgrounds—is his most significant creation for symphony orchestra, and one of the reasons why he has earned the sobriquet of "father of Bohemian music." As Zdenek Nejedly wrote: "Má Vlast is not only Smetana's largest symphonic work, it is one of the greatest of all his works, and forms the culminating point of this brilliantly creative period of his national work, a period in which he appears as the spokesman, singer and prophet of the Czech nation, realizing their highest inspiration and ideals by the medium of his matchless powers as an artist."

The first four tone poems, explains Jan Lowenbach, are "of fiercely musical reflections, impressions of Bohemian nature and reminiscences of Bohemian history filtered through a sensitive musical imagination." *Vitesgrad,* the first tone poem (1874), was inspired by Bohemia's history. Vitesgrad is an ancient citadel near Prague, a stronghold of kings; the tone poem, consequently, is a tonal picture of old Bohemia.

The second tone poem—*The Moldau,* or *Vltava* (1874)—is the most popular work in the set, its place in the symphonic repertory secure. This music is a portrait of the river Vltava (the Germans called it the Moldau), which rises in the forests of south Bohemia and flows past Prague into the Elbe River. The following program, which the music follows faithfully, appears in the published score: "Two springs pour forth their streams in the shade of the Bohemian forest, the one warm and gushing, the other cold and tranquil. Their waves, gayly flowing over their stony beds, join and glitter in the sun. The woodland brook, chattering along, becomes the river Moldau which, as its waters hurry through the valleys of Bohemia, becomes a mighty stream. It flows through the dense wood amid which the joyous sounds of the chase resound, and the call of the hunter's horn is heard ever nearer and nearer. It flows through verdant meadows and lowlands where a marriage feast is being celebrated with song and dance. At evening, in its glimmering wavelets, wood nymphs and naiads hold their revels, and in these waters many a fortress and castle are reflected which bear witness to the bygone splendor of knight-errantry and to martial fame vanished with days of yore. At the rapids of St. John, the stream speeds onward, winds through cataracts, cleaves a path for its foaming torrent through the rocky gorge into the wide river bed in which it rolls on, in majestic calm, toward Prague, where, welcomed by time-honored Vysehrad, it disappears from the poet's gaze far on the horizon."

The gentle ripple of the flowing river is simulated at the opening of the tone poem with an idyllic subject for flute, accompanied by pizzicati strings, then with an undulating figure in the strings. The violins soon offer us a Bohemian folk song, the heart of the entire work. A subject for horns simulates the hunting calls and the chase depicted in the program; a gay peasant tune in the orchestra suggests the celebration of the marriage; and a sprightly theme in the flutes, the revels of nymphs and naiads. Then once again the Bohemian folk song emerges, rising to a climactic peak, then subsiding. The tone poem ends with a final glimpse at the river as it gently winds its way past Prague.

The third tone poem, *Sárka* (1875), describes a rock valley near Prague, which was the setting of an old Bohemian legend. The music then goes on to tell this story: how the chieftain Ctirad was murdered by his sweetheart, an Amazon.

In popular appeal, *From The Fields and Groves of Bohemia* (1875) ranks just below *The Moldau* among these six tone poems. This is the program supplied by the composer in his published score: "On a fine summer day we stand in Bohemia's blessed fields, whose lovely scent of flowers and cool breezes fill us with inspiration. From the general plentitude of enjoyment and gladness resounds the natural, blissful tone of country contentment. Far from the rush of the human wave we are led into a shady, quiet grove. Fanned by the light breeze, the lisping of leaves and twigs is wafted further and louder, until the whole wood resounds with echoes, with which is mingled the twittering song of birds in endless harmony. In this Hymn of Nature sound from afar ecstatic horn tones. . . . We find ourselves in the midst of a brilliant feast of the country folk, who divert themselves with music and dancing and are glad to live. Their gladness and enjoyment of life spread themselves in the shape of the eternally fresh national song, even over the farthest meadows of Bohemia."

Smetana also provided a detailed description of his music. "At the very beginning, this tends to be a powerful impression of the arrival in the country; hence the forcible beginning on accent chords of G minor. Then G major, as the walk of a naïve girl of the fields. At the 3/4 (theme for first violins muted) there is the splendor of Nature in summer at high noon, when the sun falls directly on the head. In the forest, complete shadows; only here and there a luminous ray passes through the treetops. The constant figure (in triplets) represents the twittering of birds. It persists in all the counterpoint that follows when the motive in F major appears in the horns. Here was a great contrapuntal task which I accomplished as if it were mere sport, for I have greatly exercised myself in such things! G minor: it is the festival of the harvest, or in general some peasant holiday."

In *Tábor* (1878) the composer speaks his patriotism and gives voice to his national ideals. Here the composer utilizes the rhythm of the Hussite military tune, "Oh, You Warriors of the Lord God," as a motto theme recurring throughout the work as an expression of the faith, the will to victory, of the old Hussite warriors.

Blanik (1879) is an extension of *Tábor,* and also makes use of the Hussite hymn, "Oh, You Warriors of the Lord God." Jan Lowenbach describes *Blanik* as follows: "The Hussite warriors await, in the interior of the mythical mountain, the hour set for the deliverance of their hard-pressed fatherland. Therefore the recurrence of the same motif." Smetana himself adds: "This melody, this Hussite principle, will serve as the basis for the resurrection of the Bohemian people."

1876. STRING QUARTET NO. I IN E MINOR, "AUS MEINEN LEBEN" ("FROM MY LIFE"). I. Allegro vivo appassionata. II. Allegro moderato à la polka. III. Largo sostenuto. IV. Vivace.

Smetana wrote two autobiographical string quartets, each entitled *From My Life*. The first, and the more celebrated, came when the composer was fifty-two years old; the second followed in 1882. Both were written when the composer was deaf. In the first quartet, the composer suggests his deafness through a high pedal on E, which is heard in the coda in the closing Vivace. But beyond that, the work is optimistic, even vivacious, with occasional excursions into tenderness. Only infrequently do suggestions of morbidity or despair intrude.

The composer himself provided the program for all four movements. In the first, he says, he depicts "the love of art in my youth, the romantic supremacy, the inexpressible yearning for something which I could not clearly define, and also a kind of warning of future misfortune." The movement opens with that warning in a strong chord, followed by a passionate descending passage for the viola, a subject repeated throughout the whole quartet. This strong material is soon contrasted with a romantic song in which the composer tells of his youthful love of art and his romantic tendencies. But agitation returns in the development, and the coda is touched with sadness.

The second movement is in the rhythm of the polka, bringing to mind the "joyful days of my youth when I composed dance music enough to bury the world and was known as a passionate lover of dancing." The main dance subject is heard after a few introductory bars; this vigorous mood is maintained in the appealing trio section. In the third movement, the composer "recalls the bliss of my first love for the girl who afterwards became my faithful wife." An interval of a fifth in the cello precedes a wonderful love song that at times is touchingly melancholy and at times rises to a pitch of ecstasy. When the emotions are spent, a gentle melody hovers over a pizzicato accompaniment in the violin, after which the love song is recalled passionately.

In the finale, Smetana describes "the discovery that I could treat the national elements in music, and my joy in following this path until the catastrophe overwhelmed me; the beginning of my deafness, with the prospect of a wretched future." This movement abounds with gay folk melodies and dance rhythms. Of the two main themes, one is Slavonic in character, the other Russian. The material is treated vigorously, even joyously, until a sudden break brings on the coda. Here a high E in the first violin, over tremolos in the other three strings, tells of Smetana's deafness. "I permitted myself this little joke, such as it is, because it was so disastrous to me. There is a little ray of hope in a passing improvement, but remembering all the promise of my early career, there comes a feeling of painful regret." After that come a recall of main themes from earlier movements, with special attention to the gentle second theme of the opening Allegro. The quartet ends quietly and in a mood of resignation.

George Szell orchestrated the quartet and conducted its première at a concert of the NBC Symphony over the NBC network, in 1941.

ANTONÍN DVOŘÁK 1841–1904

The tide of nationalism that swept over Bohemia in the latter half of the nineteenth century carried Dvořák to fame and greatness. He became the first Bohemian Composer to achieve recognition outside the boundaries of his own country. In his earlier works, Dvořák was an echo of German Romanticism and particularly of Wagner. Only when he used his music as the trumpet to proclaim his national feelings did he finally arrive at individuality. He retained his own Bohemian identity even when he performed the same service for the folk songs of the American Negro and the ritual music of the American Indian that he had previously done for the polka, the Furiant, and other Bohemian folk dances.

Philip Hale finds much in Dvořák that is ingenuous, even childlike. He says: "He delighted in vain repetitions; he was at times too much pleased with the rhythms and colors, so that he mistook the exterior dress for the substance and forgot that after all there was little or no substance behind the brilliant trappings." But Hale then went on to praise Dvořák for his "piquancy, strength, and beauty in thought and expression".

Concentrating on Dvořák's strong points, Vladimir Helfert has pointed to his importance both to Bohemian and to Romantic music. "In him, Bohemian music produced a genius of spontaneous directness. In this, he is related to Schubert, with whom he has much in common. Dvořák's wealth of inspiration is surely unique in Bohemian music. He is always full of fresh ideas and effervescent melodies. . . . In the first place, Dvořák was a man of the common people. . . . His music, therefore, has all the vigor and directness of folk music. Secondly, Dvořák had a passionate and lively temperament which had something elemental about it. It was the temperament of the joy and passion of the common man, often somewhat crude, but always spontaneous. Hence the characteristic Dvořák rhythms which never fail to create an immediate interest and impression. . . . We also find (in Dvořák's music) an expression of piety—simple and sincere—such as only a deeply religious man is capable of. From this piety sprang the touching Adagios and Lentos of his symphonies and chamber-music works. . . . [Finally], Dvořák showed a keen understanding of the popular Romantic element, reflected in folk ballads and in the beauties of

Nature. Such sources provided Dvořák with material enabling him to introduce new and typical elements into Bohemian music."

Daniel Gregory Mason balances the simplicity and directness of Dvořák's speech with his artistic achievements. "His aims in music have always been simple, definite, unsophisticated by intellectualism. . . . Indeed, of all great composers he is perhaps least the scholar, most the sublimated troubadour, enriching the world with an apotheosized tavern music. . . . To him music is primarily sweet sound, and we shall misconceive his aim and service if in looking for something deep in him we miss what is, after all, very accessible and delightful for itself—the simple charm of his combinations of tone."

Antonín Dvořák was born in Muelhausen, Bohemia, on September 8, 1841. His father, an innkeeper, wanted him to become a butcher, but his own inclinations led him to music from boyhood on. Having learned by himself to play the violin, he performed at village fairs; he also sang in church choirs. His first systematic training came from Antonín Liehmann with whom he studied viola, piano, and organ. When he was sixteen, Dvořák entered the Prague Organ School. Completing his studies there in 1861, he played the violin for almost a decade in the orchestra of the National Theater in Prague. There he came under the influence of its conductor, Bedřich Smetana, who impressed on him the importance of musical nationalism.

In 1873, Dvořák became the organist of the St. Ethelbert's Church; in the same year he married his former pupil, Anna Cermakova. He now concentrated more than ever on composition. Realizing how derivative his writing up to now had been from Wagner and other German post-Romantics, he destroyed most of his compositions and embarked upon a new direction leading to Bohemian music. His first success came with *The Heirs of the White Mountains*, a patriotic hymn introduced in 1873. Two years later, he won the Austrian State Prize with his Symphony in E-flat, performed in 1874. His Stabat Mater in 1877 and his *Slavonic Dances* in 1878 spread his fame throughout Europe.

In 1884, Dvořák paid the first of several visits to England, where from then on, he was esteemed as one of the foremost composers of his time. In 1890, he toured Russia and Germany as well as England, received from the Austrian government the Iron Cross of the Third Class, and was elected a member of the Czech Academy of Art and Sciences. In 1891, a year in which he received an honorary doctorate from Cambridge, he was appointed professor of composition, instrumentation and musical form at the Prague Conservatory.

Between 1892 and 1895, Dvořák served as the director of the National Conservatory in New York. During his prolonged stay in the United States he became interested in the folk music of the Negro and the American Indian. This source material inspired him to write some of his most famous compositions, among these being the *Symphony from the New World* and the *American String Quartet*.

Upon returning to Prague, he resumed his professorial post at the Conservatory, becoming its director in 1901. He was now appointed life member of the Austrian House of Lords, the first time a musician had been thus honored. However, his last days were embittered by the fiasco of his opera, *Armida,* introduced at the National Theater on March 25, 1904. He died of an apoplectic stroke in Prague on May 1, 1904, his funeral on May 5 being decreed a day of national mourning.

1877. STABAT MATER, op. 58, for solo voices, chorus, and orchestra.

Dvořák began sketching the Stabat Mater in 1876, then put it aside to work on other projects. But the death of his child in September 1877 led him to seek escape from his grief in the writing of religious music; he completed the Stabat Mater on November 13. It scored a major success when first heard, in Prague in 1880, and was a triumph when introduced to London in 1883.

The work is described as "the first oratorio of modern Czech music," and as "the foundation stone of modern Czech oratorios." According to Otakar Sourek, the Stabat Mater falls into two emotional, as well as musical, sections. The first is realistic and dramatic; the second, spiritual and tender.

"The first number," explains Rosa Newmarch, "seems to lift our eyes to the Christ raised upon the Cross, while the rising and falling of the chromatic passages which swell in steady crescendo depict the heart of the suffering mother, now sinking in anguish, now uplifted in love, until the pent-up emotion bursts forth unrestrained when the whole orchestra crashes down on the chord of the diminished seventh."

Miss Newmarch finds dramatic interest in the "low breathless accents of the chorus with their reiterated 'Stabat Mater dolorsa,'" and profound grief in the lamentation, "Quis est homo" for solo quartet, where "the theme is continually caught up from the voices and imitated by various orchestral groups—sometimes in contrary motion." Realism permeates the "Eia Mater" section, which "with its halting, rhythmic subject has something of the character of a funeral march."

In the section, "Fac ut ardeat," where the female chorus enters accompanied by the organ, Newmarch becomes conscious of "a lamp held up in the darkness; a flame which flickers, but never totally fails us again." The pastoral chorus, "Tui nati vulnerati," and the tender tenor solo with male chorus, "Fac me vere," lead to the duet, "Fac ut portem," where we are "uplifted on broad and noble structural lines from the gloom of Golgotha, and before us lies the freedom and fervor of the 'Inflammatus' which combines clear-cut majestic rhythm with an impassioned and exalted melody." Then Dvořák recalls "the sense of despairing anguish once more in the quartet and chorus, 'Quando Corpus.' But with the words, 'Paradisi gloria,' the light returns, and through the key of G major we are led to the great 'Amen' in D major, and in this Handelian style of rejoicing, the work comes to an end."

1878–1886. 8 SLAVONIC DANCES, for piano duet (also for orchestra), op. 46. I. C major. II. E minor. III. D major. IV. F major. V. A major. VI. A-flat major. VII. C minor. VIII. G minor.

8 SLAVONIC DANCES, for piano duet (also for orchestra), op. 72. I. B major. II. E minor. III. F major. IV. D-flat major. V. B-flat minor. VI. B-flat major. VII. A minor. VIII. A-flat major.

In 1876, Dvořák wrote *Moravian Dances,* for soprano and contralto (op. 32) in which he successfully deployed the idioms of such native Bohemian dances as the polka and the Furiant. This work appealed so favorably to the Austrian Commission that it gave its composer a yearly pension of about $250. Brahms, one of the judges on this commission, persuaded the publishing house of Simrock to issue some of Dvořák's music; also to contract him to write a set of *Slavonic Dances* along the lines of Brahms's *Hungarian Dances*. Dvořák complied, and his *Slavonic Dances* for piano duet proved so successful that Simrock prevailed on him to orchestrate them. "They will make the rounds of the whole world," prophesied Louis Ehlert in the *Berlin Nationalzeitung* when the *Dances* were first published. "This is no pastiche placed together haphazardly from national echoes." It was by virtue of the first set that Dvořák first became known throughout all Europe, and even in the United States. Eight years later Dvořák wrote a second set of eight *Slavonic Dances*.

These dances, says Karel Hoffmeister, "came as a distinct revelation. They were . . . authentic, springing directly from the soul of the people. Something of the Slavic character speaks in every phrase of them—the stormy, high-spirited mood of the Furiants; the whimsical merriment, charm, the touch of coquettry, the ardent tenderness of the lyrical passages."

"There is something utterly elemental about these *Slavonic Dances,*" wrote Paul Stefan, "like a natural phenomenon, so that the listener is entirely unaware of the artistry and craftsmanship that have gone into them. All the good qualities of Czech folk music seem here realized in the most intelligible manner, but it is the genius of Dvořák that leads them on to their ultimate triumph."

The *Slavonic Dances* traverse a wide gamut of emotion. That in G minor (op. 46, no. 8) is vigorous and gay, while those in E minor and A-flat major (op. 72, nos. 2 and 8) are tender and elegiac. The rhythmic vigor of the folk dance contributes excitement to the C major and A-flat major (op. 46, nos. 1 and 6). Dramatic contrasts abound in the E minor (op. 46, no. 2), while whimsy and a coquettish manner are projected in the A major and C minor (op. 46, nos. 5 and 7). Gypsy abandon and sensuality are the keynotes of the B-flat minor, B-flat major, and A minor in op. 72 (nos. 5, 6, 7).

1878. THEME AND VARIATIONS IN A-FLAT MAJOR, for piano, op. 36.

This is one of Dvořák's most ambitious and significant pieces for solo piano. The theme (tempo di minuetto) was probably derived from a subject in the first movement of Beethoven's Piano Sonata, op. 26. Seven variations follow. The most notable of these is the fourth, a Moravian Scherzo, in which the composer makes effective use of the whole-tone scale before Debussy. The sixth, with its eloquent outpouring of fresh lyricism, is also of special interest. This work ends with a grandly conceived and powerful finale.

1878. 3 SLAVONIC RHAPSODIES, for orchestra, op. 45. I. D major. II. G minor. III. A-flat major.

In his three *Slavonic Rhapsodies,* Dvořák evokes for us the distant Bohemian past: the Bohemia of knights, fair ladies, tournaments, and sagas. It was with the first of these works that Dvořák made his debut as conductor, in Prague on November 17, 1878, in a concert made up exclusively of his works. This first rhapsody features two vibrant melodies. The first describes a tournament of knights; the second, more lyrical, tells of a lover's tryst. The most famous of this trio of rhapsodies is the third, in A-flat major, in which a hunt and the service of fair ladies is described. Its main theme is a folk dance, constructed from the fragment with which the rhapsody opens and closes.

1880. CONCERTO IN A MINOR, for violin and orchestra, op. 53. I. Allegro ma non troppo. II. Adagio ma non troppo. III. Allegro giocoso ma non troppo.

Dvořák wrote two concertos for solo instruments and orchestra that have stayed popular. The Concerto in A minor is in a Bohemian vein, while the other —the B minor Cello Concerto—utilizes American Negro folk materials. The first draft of the violin concerto was completed in 1879. But Joseph Joachim, the distinguished virtuoso, suggested so many changes that Dvořák had to spend a year rewriting the complete solo part. Then, in 1883, the work was introduced in Vienna. It opens with an orchestral flourish and the first theme stated in unisons and octaves. The solo violin responds, accompanied by the woodwind. After this material has been developed by the orchestra, the violins present the principal subject—it is in octaves, with a contrapuntal background provided by the woodwind. The solo instrument returns to discuss the first main theme and to introduce a third one, which is more vivacious than the other two. A slackening of tempo brings the second movement without pause. This is a Romanza, built out of three themes. The first is given by the solo violin, accompanied by the woodwind; the second and third are shared by solo violin and orchestra. After this material has been treated in a rhapsodic manner, the first theme in horns brings the movement to a poetic conclusion. In the finale, a rondo, all three main themes are of Bohemian folk origins, and all three are heard first in the solo instrument. The third of these provides the material for the effective coda.

1880. SYMPHONY NO. 5 IN D MAJOR, op. 60. I. Allegro ma non tanto. II. Adagio. III. Furiant. IV. Allegro con spirito.

The D major symphony is now identified as Dvořák's first, because it was the first to get published, and the first of his artistic maturity. He had written a symphony as early as 1865 (*The Bells of Zlonice*), and four more between 1865 and 1875. Only two of these were published, and none is in the permanent symphonic repertory. The now designated first symphony, however, is Dvořák in the ripeness of his powers. As Donald Francis Tovey said, this music "moves with great mastery and freedom. The scale and proportions are throughout noble, and if the procedure is often like Schubert's, unorthodox and risky, it is in this case remarkable."

Otakar Sourek regards this symphony as "a specially characteristic and revealing document. Each movement embodies a masterly stylization of living optimism, courage, rejoicing and good spirits. And at the same time it is in its mood and expression one of his most thoroughly Czech works. . . . In this symphony, the humor and pride, the optimism and passion of the Czech people come to life and in it there breathes the sweet fragrance and the unspoiled beauty of Czech woods and meadows. . . . And just as the mood is one of serenity and unclouded happiness, so, too, the composition is unburdened by any complicated musical problem of form or structure. . . . Its expression is throughout clear and unforced, the form correspondingly simple in outline and transparent in texture, yet at the same time rich and attractive in thematic treatment, the instrumentation still further simplified and remarkably plastic, the tone-coloring gay, varied and fresh."

The main subject of the first movement appears in flute and oboe, after an introductory measure; the second theme is a highly lyrical thought. The development is introduced by sustained chords which become the base on which the composer builds the fragments of his first theme. These fragments are then pieced together and combined with other material in a masterly fashion. The slow movement is a sustained song for first violins and horn that sometimes has the character of an improvisation. The Scherzo has for its main idea a spirited Furiant, a dance in triple time, which Dvořák favored in many of his larger works. The finale, though opening serenely enough, transforms the opening gentle subject into an outburst of agitation, in full orchestra; the rest of the movement maintains this vigor and energy.

1880. GYPSY SONGS, cycle of songs for voice and piano, op. 55. I. I Chant My Lay. 2. Hark, How My Triangle. 3. Silent Woods. 4. Songs My Mother Taught Me. 5. Tune Thy Strings, O Gypsy. 6. Freer Is the Gypsy. 7. The Cloudy Heights of Tatra.

Dvořák produced some fifty songs. While this branch of composition was less grateful to him than others, he did manage to create a number of melodies, rich in dramatic feeling and original in harmonic writing. He had, maintains Alec Robertson, "the born songwriter's feeling for the vocal phrase." But Robertson also adds that only rarely does he demonstrate "the born lieder writer's feeling for a song as a work of art."

One of Dvořák's two greatest achievements in the song form came with the *Gypsy Songs,* in which will be found the highly popular "Songs My Mother Taught Me" (also familiar in various transcriptions). The text of the whole cycle, by Adolf Heyduk, had pronounced national leanings, to which, of course, the composer could respond enthusiastically and sensitively.

Here is how Alec Robertson described these songs: "In the first song, 'I Chant My Lay,' Dvořák . . . uses his dance-like opening measure to bind the verses together and maintains a perfect balance between voice and accompaniment." In the second number, the two verses "are not only connected by a dance measure, but that is taken over by the voice in a charming little coda." "Silent Woods," says Robertson, is sensitive "to the changing mood of the words; there is a cadence at the end of each verse, a rising ninth, of remarkable beauty." Now comes the famous "Songs My Mother Taught Me," of which Robertson says, is "truly inspired writing, a perfect little work of art and a most moving one." Of the remaining three songs, Robertson pays special attention to the last, "The Cloudy Heights of Tatra" as "bold and well-planned. . . . The accompaniment variation is dramatically right and the extended phrase in the voice part of the last verse not only makes a fine climax to the cycle but lies most gratefully for the voice."

1881. 10 LEGENDS, for piano duet (also for orchestra), op. 59: I. D minor. II. G major. III. G minor. IV. C major. V. A-flat major. VI. C-sharp minor. VII. A major. VIII. F major. IX. D major. X. D-flat major.

The "Legend" is a descriptive term devised by Dvořák, among others, for a piece of instrumental music with a narrative character. The *Ten Legends* which Dvořák first wrote as a piano duet and then orchestrated, are among his finest works. Usually Dvořák uses a three-part form, but occasionally the variation technique is deployed. To Alec Robertson, the third, in G minor, has the personality of one of the composer's *Slavonic Dances,* with "a tranquil woodwind middle section." The fourth, in C major, has "heroic pomp"; the seventh, in A major, boasts appealing folk dance rhythms; and the eighth, in F major, has a "dramatic episode with some typical modulations back to the first section." Also of interest are the first, in D minor, an idyllic melody; and the second, in G major, which features a folk-song type of melody contrasted with an animated section.

1883. SCHERZO CAPRICCIOSO, IN D-FLAT MAJOR, for orchestra, op. 66.

Among the most popular of Dvořák's shorter works for orchestra is the *Scherzo capriccioso.* It is in two parts. The first is a fiery Scherzo (Allegro con fuoco), opening with a festive theme for horns that serves as a motto throughout the composition. Next comes a spacious melody for full orchestra and a waltz tune for the violins. In the second part, a trio (Poco tranquillo), a haunting refrain is sounded by the English horn, and a secondary subject is heard in strings and wind. The spacious melody of the first part is now given an extended development; the second theme of the trio returns in a modified form. The opening motto subject is the basis of the concluding coda.

1884. FROM THE BOHEMIAN FOREST, for piano duet, op. 68. I. In the Spinning Room. II. On the Dark Lake. III. Witches' Sabbath. IV. On the Watch. V. Silent Woods. VI. In Troubled Times.

In these descriptive piano pieces, too much attention should not be paid to the titles, which Dvořák supplied *after* the music had been written. All pieces are romantic in mood. "One surrenders," says Alec Robertson, "to the luscious middle section of *On the Dark Lake* (homage to Chopin) and to the languorous tune of *Silent Woods* (homage to Liszt). The horrors of the *Witches' Sabbath* are limited to a few shudders on . . . the diminished seventh, and there is a luscious tune which appears in a more attractive form in the last movement of the A major Quintet, op. 81. In the last piece, a stirring march, the composer quotes from the Scherzo of his early D minor Symphony." In 1893, Dvořák transcribed *Silent Woods* for cello and orchestra.

1885. SYMPHONY NO. 6 IN D MINOR, op. 70. I. Allegro maestoso. II. Poco Adagio. III. Vivace. IV. Allegro.

How highly Donald Francis Tovey regarded this symphony can best be measured from the fact that he put it solidly in the class of Brahms's four symphonies and Schubert's C major, as the most important symphonies produced after Beethoven. Dvořák wrote it at the suggestion of the Royal Philharmonic Orchestra of London (which had made him an honorary member a year earlier); and it was that orchestra, under Dvořák, that introduced the work in 1885.

The first movement embarks on a somber voyage with a theme in lower strings over horns, basses, and drums. After it is repeated fortissimo by the full orchestra, a gentle, elegiac song is heard in the woodwind to a string accompaniment. The development pays more attention to the second subject than to the first; it is characterized by outbursts of agitation, and at times by suggestions of tragedy. A recapitulation section and an extended coda are of heroic dimensions.

In the second movement, we first hear a chorale in the woodwind supported by string pizzicati. This is followed by a stately second theme, introduced by first violins and cellos. The main theme of the Scherzo is heard immediately in the opening measures. Violins and violas present it, to a countertheme in the cellos. An idyllic episode for woodwind and strings is the central thought of the trio.

In the solemn introduction to the finale, a phrase from the first theme of the first movement passes from one group of instruments to the next. This is succeeded by a forceful and dramatic subject in the strings, and a lyrical episode in the cellos. A good deal of attention is paid to the forceful and dramatic theme in both the development and the recapitulation. The symphony ends with a spacious, impressive sounding coda.

1887. PIANO QUINTET IN A MAJOR, op. 81. I. Allegro ma non tanto. II. Andante con moto. III. Furiant. IV. Allegro.

The A major Quintet is in the Slavic idiom of many of Dvořák's best known works completed before his extended stay in the United States. It overflows with the vivid harmonic colors, the vital dance rhythms, the sensual melodies and the quick contrasts of mood of Bohemian folk music. "The first movement," explains John Clapham, "is rich in themes, hovers between major and minor in its opening section, and is peculiar in having more bars in the submediant key than in the tonic in recapitulation and coda combined." The slow movement is a Dumka, or elegy. Following four introductory bars for the piano, the viola is heard in a mournful song in the lowest register, while the piano provides a countertheme in the treble. Two other sections follow, one of them with the high voltage rhythmic charge of one of the more passionate of Bohemian folk dances. The Scherzo is a Furiant, without the displaced accents expected in this form of folk dance. The finale is in the form of a rondo.

1889. SYMPHONY NO. 8 IN G MINOR, op. 88. I. Allegro con brio. II. Adagio. III. Allegretto grazioso; Molto vivace. IV. Allegro ma non troppo.

This symphony has acquired several different identifying nomenclatures. It has been called the *English Symphony*—because it was issued in 1892 by Novello, an English publisher. It was described as a *Pastoral Symphony* by the London *Times* in 1890, which saw in the music "rural sights and sounds, all fresh and charming." Many, however, prefer to call it the *Bohemian Symphony,* for its pronounced and unmistakable national identity, and because it was dedicated to the Bohemian Academy. In any event, its overflowing lyricism, its charming Bohemian verve, and its generally cheerful mood have made it one of the most popular of all Dvořák's symphonies, with the exception of *From the New World.* Karel Hoffmeister described it as "a simple lyric, singing of the beauty of our country for the heart's consolation—a lovable expression of a genius who can rejoice with the idyllic simplicity of his forebears."

A rustic, somewhat melancholy minor-key song for woodwind and cellos opens the first movement. A cadenza, and a change of key, bring on the first main theme, which is in a more optimistic vein; it is first given by the flute. The second major subject, also in a happy frame of mind, is introduced by flute and clarinet over triplet figures in the second violins. The second movement is dominated by a pastoral melody, first in strings, then continued by the woodwind. New material is introduced by the violins over pizzicati violas and cellos later in the movement; this material is subsequently amplified by oboe and first violins. The Scherzo enages a graceful thought for first violins, and a waltz-like tune for the trio. The finale arrives with a stirring trumpet call. This martial mood continues eighteen measures later with a drum roll. The first main theme, unmistakably of Bohemian identity, appears in cellos, then is loudly repeated by full orchestra. This is followed by another captivating thought in flute, accompanied by violins and violas. The tempo then quickens and dramatic impulses are released to bring the symphony to a dynamic conclusion.

1890. REQUIEM, for solo voices, chorus, and orchestra, op. 89.

On February 26, 1964, Dvořák's Requiem was revived in New York after an absence of some sixty years. It turned out to be music of the first significance, one of its composer's most moving compositions, a masterwork whose long neglect in the concert hall proved inexplicable. "It is," reported Harold C. Schonberg in the *New York Times,* "a beautiful score. . . . Dignified, devout, full of calm and spacious melody, the Requiem is a testament to the composer's faith as well as to his inspiration."

The composition is integrated through the use of a two-measure, gentle Leitmotiv (Poco lento) which reappears throughout. (In his tone poem, *Asrael,* Joseph Suk quoted this motive in memory of Dvořák, his father-in-law.) In the beginning of the Requiem, this Leitmotiv is presented by the cellos.

The Requiem has two sections, the first concluding just before the "Offertory." Paul Stefan explains: "The different sections are linked together without breaks. Solo and choir alternate in taking up and continuing the thread so that there is no opportunity for big solo arias."

Here is Paul Stefan's analysis of the Requiem: "Modulations and a soprano solo lend a personal stamp to the very beginning of the work. The 'Dies Irae' recalls us to the traditional sequence of the Requiem. Above the tempest in the orchestra, the choir bursts out in a cry of terror, and the sense of impending doom turns to tender-hearted mourning. Instead of the pathetic orgies in the brass, the alto sings the lament in the 'Tuba mirum.' The theme denoting Judgment is more expressive of sublimity than of fear. The solo quartet sheds the beauty of its melody over the 'Quid sum miser.' The 'Recordare' recalls Dvořák's 'Quis est homo' in Stabat Mater. One theme is the inversion of the other. And throughout the work the Leimotiv plays a leading role."

In the second section, "the soul turns from the horror of Death, the Judgment, and hopes of Salvation to a general expression of confidence and faith in God. An unusual feature is an old, traditional Slav hymn to the words of the text, 'Quam olim Abrahae.' Despair and confidence still alternate; the 'Benedictus' seems to illumine all that bliss to be found after death. In the stirring 'Sanctus,' B-flat is contrasted with B, thus permitting Dvořák's peculiar chromatic ascent to the next higher step. Once again the 'Agnus' reveals Dvořák's diffident contemplation of death, and, at the same time, the reconciling certainty of his unshakable faith."

Stefan sums up: "Rich in sonority, Dvořák's work is one of the most beautiful, original and worthwhile settings of the Mass for the Dead."

1891. DUMKY TRIO, for violin, cello, and piano, op. 90. I. E minor. II. C-sharp minor. III. A major. IV. D minor. V. E-flat major. VI. E minor.

A "dumka" is (in Russian) a "passing thought." Dvořák borrowed the term for a slow movement of elegiac character. Besides writing several dumky for the piano, Dvořák also wrote a significant piano trio in which each of the six movements (the first three played without interruption) is a dumka.

"In the first dumka," explains John Clapham, "there is a thematic link between Lento maestoso and Allegro. A plaintive character is maintained in the first part of the third dumka despite the major key. The fourth dumka starts with a halting accompanying figure for the piano, and in the third bar the violin adds a monotonous quaver figure; two bars later, the cello enters with the melody. . . . The trio as a whole is outstanding for its wealth of themes, its colorful scoring, and its varied treatment of the idea of melancholy."

1891. 3 CONCERT OVERTURES, for orchestra:

In der Natur (*In Nature*), op. 91; *Carneval* (*Carnival*), op. 92; *Othello,* op. 93.

Dvořák planned a cycle of overtures to be performed together as a trilogy, portraying "three great creative forces of the Universe—Nature, Life, and Love." In all three he used a basic melody describing "the unchangeable laws of Nature." He eventually abandoned the trilogy project, and in its place completed three separate concert overtures, with no programmatic relation to each other, and intended to be performed separately.

The most famous of these overtures is the middle one, *Carnival.* The composer provided the following program: "A lonely contemplative wanderer reaches the city at nightfall where a carnival of pleasure resigns supreme. On every side is heard the clangor of instruments, mingled with shouts of joy and unrestrained hilarity of the people, giving vent to their feelings in song and dances."

The brilliant opening theme in full orchestra brings up the picture of a gay carnival. After some episodic material, the violins are heard in a gentle melody, while oboes and clarinets contribute a countertheme. This melody is elaborated upon. Following a return of the vigorous opening, a sensual passage engages flute and violins, while the English horn provides the accompaniment; this episode describes the tender exchange of words between lovers. Earlier material is recalled, after which the overture ends as boisterously as it began—a final presentation of the revelry.

In Nature, says Dvořák, presents "the emotions awakened in a solitary walk through meadows and woods on a quiet summer afternoon, when the shadows grow longer until they lose themselves in the dusk and gradually turn into the early shades of night." A serene melody in bassoons and violas, with answering statements in the flute, is the first subject. After a loud repetition of this theme in full orchestra, the strings present a new sensitive subject. A climax, and a forceful restatement of the first theme, precede a fantasia section where the two melodies are developed freely. The coda is brought in with a loud recall of the first theme in horns and trumpets, but ends serenely.

Othello is a love poem for orchestra. In the opening section, an eloquent melody describes Desdemona, while the beginning of the main section depicts Othello's insane passion and jealousy. The working-out of both these ideas is dramatized by vivid contrasts of mood, for which the tragic dénouement in the Shakespeare play provides a suitable program.

1893. SYMPHONY NO. 9 IN E MINOR, "FROM THE NEW WORLD," op. 95. I. Allegro molto. II. Largo. III. Molto vivace. IV. Allegro con fuoco.

Soon after assuming the office of director of the National Conservatory in New York, Dvořák was visited by Harry T. Burleigh, a Negro Conservatory student, who came to play and sing for Dvořák some Negro Spirituals and plantation songs. "Dvořák just saturated himself with the spirit of these old tunes," Burleigh later recalled. The composer became convinced that Negro folk music could provide Americans with material from which an authentic national musical art could be developed. He said: "These beautiful and varied themes are the products of the soil. They are American. They are all folk songs of America, and your composers must turn to them. . . . In the Negro melodies of America I discover all that is needed for a great and noble school of music."

Putting theory to practice, Dvořák himself created several large compositions inspired by the songs of the American Negro. He never quoted directly, but preferred modeling his melodies from patterns characteristic to American Negro music. Yet at times he wrote with such authenticity that his own melodies sound as if they had been borrowed from folk-music sources.

The *Symphony from the New World* was one of the works that was inspired by the Negro Spiritual. There are, it is quite true, echoes and strains of Bohemia in this symphony, particularly in the Scherzo and finale. This has led some critics to remark that if this is American music it is American music through the ears of a Bohemian. To William Ritter, "the national Czech feeling in this work, quickened by homesickness, is so marked that it is recognized throughout Bohemia, by the learned and by the humblest." Maybe so! But there is also much in the symphony that rings so true of the Spiritual that for a long time it was erroneously believed that some of its themes were quotations—the beautiful melody of the second movement, particularly.

The Symphony from the New World received its world première in the new world—in New York City by the New York Philharmonic under Anton Seidl in 1893. It was formidably successful. "I felt like a king in my box," reported Dvořák.

The American-Negro identity is established in the first movement with its dark-hued Adagio introduction. A somber melody, like a Negro lament about hard times, is sung by the cellos, then carried on by flutes and oboes, with responses of drum beats and chords from the wind. The main theme is then faintly suggested by violas, cellos, and two horns over violin tremolos. Following a climax, this main theme is promulgated by two horns, supported by strings. A transition in flutes and oboes leads to the second theme, introduced by flute, and continued by the violins; the similarity between this tune and the Spiritual, "Swing Low, Sweet Chariot," has often been remarked.

The elegiac song for English horn over string harmonies in the second movement sounds as if it might be a Spiritual; but the melody is Dvořák's own. (William Arms Fisher wrote words for it in the now famous song, "Goin' Home.") A faster, agitated section brings on a new melody (flutes and oboes over tremolo strings) and a lively tune (oboe). Then the earlier mood returns with a recall of the Spiritual-like melody, broken up intermittently. Then the movement ends with several quiet chords.

The lively tune for flute and oboe (with answering phrases in the clarinet) with which the Scherzo opens, sounds more like an American-Indian ritual dance than a Negro tune. A contrasting subject is then heard in flute and oboe. The middle part of the Scherzo contains not one but two trios, each in a different key. The coda makes use not only of the opening Scherzo material but also of the main theme of the first movement.

A syncopated theme sets the finale into motion, followed by a main theme jubilantly exclaimed by horns and trumpets against full chords in the rest of the orchestra. A subsidiary section features a dance tune that sounds like a plantation reel. Then a lugubrious melody is chanted by clarinets over tremolo strings. In the development, the two main themes are discussed; at the same time, a backward glance is given to earlier movements with quotations from the main theme of the Largo, the opening Scherzo melody, and the main theme of the first movement. Earlier material from preceding movements is once again used, with telling impact, in the coda.

1893. STRING QUARTET NO. 6 IN F MAJOR, "AMERICAN," op. 96. I. Allegro ma non troppo. II. Lento. III. Allegro molto vivace. IV. Vivace ma non troppo.

STRING QUINTET IN E-FLAT MAJOR, op. 97. I. Allegro ma non tanto. II. Allegro vivo. III. Larghetto. IV. Allegro giusto.

SONATINA IN G MAJOR, for violin and piano, op. 100. I. Allegro risoluto. II. Larghetto. III. Molto vivace. IV. Allegro.

The songs of the Negro was only one of two areas cultivated by Dvořák in America. The other was the songs and dances of the American Indian. While on a holiday in Spillville, Iowa (where Dvořák went because it had a large Bohemian colony), he was visited by three Iroquois Indians. They performed for him authentic Indian music, whose fascination stimulated him into writing a number of major works in that idiom. But he did not quote directly any actual Indian material. "I have simply written original themes embodying the peculiarities of the Indian music and, using these themes as subjects, have developed them with all the resources of modern rhythm, harmony, counterpoint, and orchestral color."

Haunting refrains with a pronounced Indian identity dominate the first and second movements of the F major Quartet. There are three such subjects in the first movement: the first is in the viola, repeated by first violin; the second is a duet for the two violins; and the third appears in first violin over chords in the other three instruments. An exotic song is the essence of the slow movement. This is the subject with which the movement opens and closes—in the opening, heard in first violin, then repeated by the cello; in the closing, in the cello against plucked strings. The single main melody of the third movement (stated by cello and second violin) is Bohemian rather than Indian; so are the folk-song like tunes and the dance rhythms of the finale.

In the E-flat major String Quintet, insistent drum rhythms endow the first movement with an authentic Indian character. Here the principal theme is first suggested at the very opening—in the viola before it evolves fully in first violin. A subsidiary idea, presented vigorously by the first violin, and a transitional passage, lead into a beguiling Indian melody. Otakar Sourek described the second movement as "one of the most exotic of Dvořák's American creations." A drum-like figure in the viola precedes the principal Indian melody, which unfolds in the first violin. We hear some contrasting material before this theme is repeated to end the movement. The Larghetto once again starts with a poignant Indian tune. Five variations follow. The finale, a rondo, has for its main thought a strongly accented melody, and two subsidiary ideas, all of them with a pronounced Indian personality.

The main interest in the Violin Sonatina in G major lies in its slow movement. This is a tender Indian song, which Fritz Kreisler transcribed for violin and piano, and called *Indian Lament*. Gaspar Cassado arranged this movement for cello and piano.

1894. BIBLICAL SONGS, cycle of songs for voice and piano, op. 99: 1. Clouds and Darkness. 2. Lord, Thou Art My Refuge. 3. Hear My Prayer. 4. God Is My Shepherd. 5. I Will Sing New Songs of Gladness. 6. Hear My Prayer. 7. By the Waters of Babylon. 8. Turn Thee to Me. 9. I Will Lift Mine Eyes. 10. Sing a Joyful Song.

The *Biblical Songs* is second in importance to the *Gypsy Songs* (which see) among Dvořák's vocal compositions. Paul Stefan is of the opinion that Dvořák's stimulation in setting texts of a seventeenth-century Czech translation of the Bible came upon learning that Gounod and Tchaikovsky had recently died. Dvořák continually sought relief in religion when touched by sorrow.

Dvořák took his verses from the Book of Psalms. His writing is consistently sober, and at times suffused with melancholy. But, as Paul Stefan adds, "melody and style are here happily combined with profound spirituality." Alec Robertson singles out the following songs in this cycle for special consideration: "God Is My Shepherd," he says, is "a really charming piece of Baroque decoration of the simpler kind." "I Will Sing New Songs of Gladness," offers "a fine bit of tune, differently harmonized on each of its four appearances and furnished with a good climax." "By the Waters of Babylon," has the semblance of a Negro Spiritual. And "Turn Thee to Me" is "a moving song with beautiful well-contrived modulations and a really lovely use of the major third after leaving the minor key."

1894. 8 HUMORESQUES, for piano, op. 101. I. E-flat minor. II. B major. III. A-flat major. IV. F major. V. A minor. VI. B major. VII. G-flat major. VIII. B-flat minor.

Schumann was one of the first Romantic composers to write a Humoresque. Dvořák's eight Humoresques were his last creations for the piano. The seventh in this set is one of his most famous instrumental compositions and surely the best-known Humoresque of all, by any composer. All of Dvořák's Humoresques are elementary in structure, short, and melodic. As Sir George Grove has pointed out, the Dvořák Humoresques basically have little humor or whimsy to them, as is so characteristic of the Humoresque form; they are more closely related to the Caprice or Capriccio. However, the world-famous G-flat major Humoresque—in Dvořák's original version—is light, airy, and capricious, and in a fast tempo. Fritz Kreisler, in transcribing it for violin and piano—an adaptation that was solely responsible for making this piece of music so famous—utilized a slow tempo in order to sentimentalize the melody. And it is as a sentimental rather than a whimsical piece that this Humoresque is now appreciated.

1895. CONCERTO IN B MINOR, for cello and orchestra, op. 104. I. Allegro. II. Adagio ma non troppo. III. Allegro moderato.

Dvořák's interest in American-Negro folk songs led him to use this material in his famous cello concerto. He completed this work while still in the United States, but its première took place in London in 1896. This concerto opens with an orchestral introduction, offering the two main themes. The first is in clarinets, and the second (more identifiably in the style of a Negro Spiritual) is heard in solo horn accompanied by strings. To Donald Francis Tovey, this second theme is "one of the most beautiful passages ever written for the horn." When the solo cello appears, it engages both principal themes before embellishing them with dazzling virtuoso passages.

A dreamy passage for the woodwind, and a moving melody for the strings, precede the appearance of the solo cello in the slow movement. The cello comments poetically on this first subject before a brief dramatic episode brings on a temporary disturbance. Before long, the reflective mood is restored as cello and orchestra engage in an eloquent dialogue based on earlier thematic material.

A brisk march-like introduction precedes the entry of the solo cello in the finale; it is heard in the movement's first main subject, an enlargement of the subject suggested in the march-like opening. "Dvořák settles down to another glorious series of epilogues," explains Donald Francis Tovey, "in a steady progression of picturesqueness and calm. . . . Eventually . . . the ghost of the first movement appears seraphically in the clarinets. But at last the orchestra rouses itself. The trombones give out the figure of the rondo theme in solemn big notes; and, after all, the work ends Allegro vivo in high spirits."

1896–1897. TONE POEMS FOR ORCHESTRA:
The Wild Dove, op. 110.
The Hero's Song, op. 111.

Between 1896 and 1897, Dvořák devoted himself to the writing of five tone poems, a form with which Richard Strauss had been electrifying the music world for a number of years. The first four were inspired by the folk ballads of K. J. Erben, distinguished Czech poet: *The Water Goblin,* op. 107; *The Noonday Witch,* op. 108; *The Golden Spinning Wheel,* op. 109; one of the finest of this group, *The Wild Dove,* op. 110; and *the Hero's Song*, op. 111.

Dvořák prepared the following program for *The Wild Dove* in his published score. It opens with a funeral march (Andante), to whose solemn strains a widow is accompanying her husband's coffin to the graveyard. This march tune is developed into the principal motive of the tone poem and is meant to represent the "guilt feelings" of the bereaved widow. But she soon forgets her dead husband. In an Allegro-Andante section that follows, she meets a peasant, falls in love with him, and consents to marry him. A Molto Vivace-Allegretto grazioso interlude offers a picture of their wedding. Then there comes a dramatic change of mood with an Andante episode in which a dove coos a gentle song over the husband's grave. The tone poem now offers a new funeral march, and an elaboration of the "guilt" theme. Driven by remorse, the woman commits suicide by drowning. With a brief recall of the opening march music, the tone poems ends in a somber mood.

The Hero's Song was Dvořák's last orchestral composition. Like Richard Strauss's more familiar tone poem, *Ein Heldenleben,* Dvořák's music has strong autobiographical interest. In his hero's triumph, Dvořák sees his own victory after early struggles and frustrations.

There are three principal musical motives in *The Hero's Song.* Paul Stefan characterizes them as "Determination" (a theme with eight variations, each variation virtually a new melodic idea), "Disappointment" and "Consolation and Hope." A description by Jan Lowenbach follows: "A swift opening section, Allegro con fuoco, is followed by a slow movement, Poco adagio lacrimoso. After a brief recall of the introductory theme, there follows first a Scherzo section, then a recapitulation of the opening part, with a brilliant climax leading to the finale. The main motives dominating the scheme alter and develop according to Dvořák's philosophical plan of struggle toward victory, with new contrasts constantly enriching the development."

EDVARD GRIEG 1843–1907

As a musician who had received his basic musical training at the Leipzig Conservatory, Grieg was at first influenced by the German Romantic style of Schumann and Mendelssohn. Then, in 1864, he met and became a friend of young Rikard Nordraak, an ardent Norwegian nationalist, who wrote his country's anthem. Nordraak introduced Grieg to Norwegian folk music, and fired him with his own flaming ambitions to work along the lines of musical nationalism. "It was as if the scales fell from my eyes," Grieg confessed. "From Nordraak I learned for the first time what the Norwegian folk song was, and learned to know my own nature." From then on—beginning with the Humoresques, for piano, op. 6—Grieg aspired to write Norwegian music. He sought to shape his musical writing after the idioms of Norwegian folk songs and dances. The qualities that were henceforth to identify Grieg's music were also those basic to Norwegian folk music: his tendency to construct melodies around the third degree of the scale; his partiality for dotted rhythms and square-cut phrases; his individual colorings; his addiction to modal melodies and harmonies; even his excursions into discords.

Essentially, Grieg was a miniaturist, as he himself recognized. Despite the value and the success of his Piano Concerto, the last two violin sonatas, and the string quartet, he was never completely at ease in the larger forms. His musical ideas seemed to come in short breaths, and were, therefore, at their best in cameo setting. As late as 1877, he confessed he was still waging a fight to win out in the more ambitious structures; but after this third violin sonata in 1887, he admitted defeat. Though he remained productive after that, he preferred working henceforth in more limited dimensions. For in deserting German Romanticism for Norwegian nationalism, Grieg had also renounced the German processes of composition—the massive structures, the complex developments of thematic material, the elaborate and abstruse thinking. "His instinct," says Hubert Foss, "told him to harness the waterfall of his ideas into narrower, more managable—almost more domestic—channels than the spouting seas of Liszt and Wagner. Never touched by the *Kolossal,* Grieg was determined, content, to be a small master; his deliberate smallness is one of his greatest virtues."

But though his world was limited, he was an unqualified master in it. The world he created was of considerable enchantment, and one of his own making. As John Horton said, Grieg found "unsuspected treasures of poetry among rocks and forests . . . rich and delightful sonorities heard in the loneliness of unfrequented places, a lifting of the heart at the touch of a fresh and childlike imagination."

Edvard Hagerup Grieg was born in Bergen, Norway, on June 15, 1843. After preliminary study of the piano with his mother, Grieg was sent, in 1858, to the Leipzig Conservatory, where he was a pupil of Moscheles, Hauptmann, and Reinecke, among others. In 1863, he concluded his music study in Copenhagen with Niels Gade. Friendship with Rikard Nordraak, a dedicated patriot and a passionate advocate of Norwegian folk music, led Grieg to direct his creative forces through national channels, and to help promote the development of music in Norway. Upon returning to Norway, Grieg helped to found the Norwegian Musical Academy, which sponsored concerts of Norwegian music; he also became conductor of the Harmonic Society in Christiana (now Oslo), where once again he was instrumental in performing works by Norwegians. The expression of a Norwegian personality in his own music became crystallized between 1865 and 1867 with the Humoresques and the first book of *Lyric Pieces,* all for the piano.

In 1867, Grieg married his cousin, Nina Hagerup, with whom he had been in love, and for whom he wrote his most famous song, "I Love You." Success as a composer came with the world première of his A minor Piano Concerto in Copenhagen in 1869. His incidental music to *Sigurd Jorsalfar* in 1872, and particularly to *Peer Gynt* in 1876, gave him further recognition. He was now given a government annuity, which made him financially independent for the rest of his life. In addition, in 1872, he was appointed to the Swedish Academy, and in 1873 to the Leyden Academy. In 1890, he was made a member of the French Academy, and his sixtieth birthday in 1903 was declared a national holiday in Norway. Just before his death, he received honorary doctorates from Cambridge and Oxford.

His first appearance in England had taken place on May 3, 1888, in a concert of his own music. It was in England that he was fated to make his last public appearance anywhere, with a program of his compositions in London in May of 1906. On September 4, 1907, he died of a heart attack in Bergen. He was buried in a grotto on the ground of Troldhaugen, a villa near Bergen, where he had been living in comparative seclusion for many years.

1862–1898. SONGS, for voice and piano:

"The Bewitched One," op. 32; "A Bird Song," op. 25, no. 6; "The Fair-Haired Maiden" (no opus number).

Haugtussa, cycle of eight songs, op. 67: 1. The Singing. 2. Little Maiden. 3. Bilberry Slopes. 4. Meeting. 5. Love. 6. Kidlings' Dance. 7. Evil Day. 8. At the Brook.

"I Love You," op. 5, no. 3.

6 German Songs, op. 48: 1. Greeting. 2. Some Day My Thought. 3. The Way of the World. 4. The Discreet Nightingale. 5. In the Time of Roses. 6. A Dream.

"Spring," op. 33, no. 2; "A Swan," op. 25, no. 2; "With a Water Lily," op. 25, no. 4; "The Wounded Heart, op. 33, no. 3.

The almost one hundred and fifty songs published by Grieg place him with the foremost song composers in Scandinavia. They are settings of Danish and German, as well as Norwegian texts. Among his earliest song efforts are his Danish groups; and this includes what is undoubtedly his most popular song of all, "I Love You," text by Hans Christian Andersen. This is the composer's love song to Nina Hagerup, written in 1864 before she became his wife. It is the third in a set of four, *Heart Melodies,* op. 5 (1864).

Grieg's first group of published songs, opus 2 (1862), are to German poems by Heine and Chamisso. Here he revealed a predominantly German personality, and a patently derivative style. In the *Six German Songs,* opus 48 (1889), his Norwegian identity begins to assert itself over German influences. In this group, we encounter "Some Day My Thought" ("Dereinst, Gedanke mein"), poem by Geibel, which Hugo Wolf set later on. "Wolf approaches this song as an intellectual," explains Astra Desmond, who finds that Grieg endows it "with resignation and a simple faith, religious in feeling, that is very moving." "The Way of the World," ("Lauf der Welt"), poem by Uhland, has an infectious gaiety, while "In Time of Roses" ("Zur Rosenzeit"), poem by Goethe, has a poignant melody that soon makes room for passion. The most celebrated number in this opus 48 set is "The Dream" ("Ein Traum"), poem by Bodenstedt, unforgettable for its subtle atmosphere and suggestive nuances.

Grieg's first important Norwegian songs include his setting of Bjoernson's "The Fairhaired Maiden," (1867). "At once," says Desmond, "we see a change in Grieg's style. There is an economy and strength in Norwegian poetry not to be found in Danish, and as Grieg breaks away from foreign influences and begins to find his Norwegian soul, we find a new economy in his music which, used with the mastery of a technique gained from his previous teachers, gives us songwriting of a high order."

Among Grieg's numerous songs to Norwegian texts, we find what Kristian Lange and Arne Ostvedt call "the high tide of his song composition, the Ibsen songs, opus 25 (1876). Here we find "A Swan," "With a Water Lily," and "A Bird Song." Again Grieg scales the pinnacle with the Vinje songs, opus 33 (1873–1880), which includes "The Wounded Heart" and "Spring," which Grieg later orchestrated and retitled *Two Elegiac Melodies* (see 1880). Notable, too, are the *Haugtussa* cycle, poems by Arne Garborg (1896–1898) and "The Bewitched One" (1878), based on an old Norwegian poem. In commenting on this last-named song, Lange and Ostvedt say: "The text is a folk poem describing a mortal who has lost his way into the enchanted forest and is trying in vain to find his way out again. It is one of Grieg's most gripping works. In it he interprets his own tragedy."

1865. IN THE AUTUMN, concert overture for orchestra, op. 11.

This was the composer's first attempt at writing orchestral music. When Grieg first showed it to his former teacher, Niels Gade, the latter told him, "This is trash." "I went home and . . . wept," Grieg later recalled. "I let it lie, arranged it as a duet and played it at home with Nina." In this form, he submitted it in a competition of the Swedish Academy. It won first prize, and was published in Stockholm. One of the interesting footnotes to this successful resolution was that one of the members in the committee that gave Grieg the prize was Niels Gade.

Grieg revised and rescored his overture in 1888. This composition is an extended treatment (with an added introduction and coda) of one of the composer's songs, "Autumn Storm," text by Hans Christian Andersen, the last of four songs in opus 18 (1865). "The strength of the work lies . . . in its Nature impressions," says David Monrad-Johansen. "There is a charming blending of the melancholy and cheerful reflections on the time of the year that the subject—Autumn—gives rise to, and the overture ends very effectively with the joyous dance-song of the harvesters."

1867–1901. LYRIC PIECES, ten volumes of pieces for the piano:

Book I, op. 12: 1. Arietta. 2. Waltz. 3. Watchman's Song. 4. Fairy Dance. 5. Autumn Leaf. 6. National Song.

Book II, op. 38: 1. Cradle Song. 2. Folk Song. 3. Melody. 4. Halling. 5. Spring Dance. 6. Elegy. 7. Waltz. 8. Canon.

Book III, op. 43: 1. Butterfly. 2. Lonely Wanderer. 3. In the Native Country. 4. Little Bird. 5. Erotik. 6. To the Spring.

Book IV, op. 47: 1. Valse-impromptu. 2. Album Leaf. 3. Melody. 4. Melancholy. 5. Spring Dance. 6. Elegy.

Book V, op. 54: 1. Shepherd Boy. 2. Norwegian March. 3. March of the Dwarfs. 4. Nocturne. 5. Scherzo. 6. Bell Ringing.

Book VI, op. 57: 1. Vanished Days. 2. Gade. 3. Illusion. 4. Secrecy. 5. She Dances. 6. Homesickness.

Book VII, op. 62: 1. Sylph. 2. Gratitude. 3. French Serenade. 4. Brooklet. 5. Phantom. 6. Homeward.

Book VIII, op. 65: 1. From Years of Youth. 2. Peasant's Song. 3. Melancholy. 4. Salon. 5. In Ballad Vein. 6. Wedding Day at Troldhaugen.

Book IX, op. 68: 1. Sailors' Song. 2. Grandmother's Minuet. 3. At Thy Feet. 4. Evening in the Mountains. 6. At the Cradle. 7. Valse mélancolique.

Book X, op. 71: 1. Once Upon a Time. 2. Summer Evening. 3. Puck. 4. Peace of the Woods. 5. Halling. 6. Gone. 7. Remembrances.

The sixty-six pieces for the piano that Grieg gathered into the ten volumes of his *Lyric Pieces* are among his most successful writing for solo piano. This, says Kathleen Dale, is a "treasure house of diverse and interesting exhibits," representative of "Grieg's art as a whole." Up to 1867, Grieg did not use descriptive titles for any of his piano works, but from the first of his *Lyric Pieces* on, he found them singularly useful as guide posts to the programmatic content of his music.

These *Lyric Pieces* fall into several different categories. More than half of the total are either impressionistic or subjective pieces in which, says Kathleen Dale, we find "the essential Grieg, [displaying] almost every facet of his personal style." Among these are such atmospheric items as *The Watchman's Song,* op. 12, no. 3 (inspired by a performance of *Macbeth*)*; The Lonely Wanderer, Erotik* and *To the Spring* in op. 43; *Shepherd Boy* and Nocturne in op. 54; *Brooklet* in op. 62 and *Summer Evening* in op. 71.

Some of the pieces are mood pictures. *Melancholy* in op. 47 and *Homesickness* in op. 57 are somber; *Gratitude* in op. 62 and *At the Cradle,* in op. 68, are of a sunnier disposition. Some are highly descriptive. The best of these are *Butterfly* in op. 43 and the highly popular *March of the Dwarfs* in op. 54.

Among the most highly regarded numbers are some of those that give us a vivid picture of Norwegian life and customs. In this genre we find the *Norwegian March* in op. 54, and *Peasant's Song* and *Wedding Day at Troldhaugen in* op. 65.

In 1903, Grieg orchestrated four of his *Lyric Pieces,* identifying the new work as *Lyric Suite,* op. 54. The four movements are: *Shepherd Boy, Norwegian Peasant March, Nocturne*, and *March of the Dwarfs*.

1867. SONATA IN G MAJOR, for violin and piano, op. 13. I. Lento doloroso; Allegro. II. Allegretto tranquillo. III. Allegro animato.

Grieg wrote three violin sonatas. The first, in F major, op. 8 (1865), gave Grieg his first contact with success, since Liszt found it to give evidence of "a powerful, logically creative, ingenious and excellent constructive talent for composition." The second, in G major, was written a month after the composer's marriage to Nina Hagerup. Undoubtedly, Grieg's happiness is reflected in the ardent, romantic spirit that pervades the whole sonata.

This second sonata, in G major, is the only one of the three to open with a slow introduction; it is also the only one in which the main theme of a fast movement is first heard in the piano. That main theme, however, is first foreshadowed by the violin in the slow introduction before it comes fully to life in the piano in the ensuing Allegro. The secondary theme is a tranquil melody treated at some length. The development is comparatively short, and the recapitulation is along familiar lines. The slow movement offers us a spacious melody, which Yvonne Rosketh praises for its "marvelous purity of writing" and describes as "a model of perfection." The finale is vitalized by a spirited Norwegian folk dance that bubbles with vitality and happy spirits.

1868. CONCERTO IN A MINOR, for piano and orchestra, op. 16. I. Allegro molto moderato. II. Adagio. III. Allegro moderato e marcato.

When Grieg received a government stipend in 1869, he had the wherewithal to make a trip to Rome to visit Franz Liszt, who had praised his F major Violin Sonata. He came with the manuscript of his Piano Concerto, which Liszt tried out at the piano. "I admit," Grieg later recalled, "that he took the first part . . . rather too quickly and the beginning lost a little by it, but later, when I made an opportunity to indicate the time myself, he played as only he and no other can play. It is characteristic that the cadenza, which is technically difficult, he played perfectly. . . . At the end he said, with a singularly cordial accent, 'Go on. I tell you that you have the ability, and—don't let anything scare you!'"

When the concerto was introduced—in Copenhagen in 1869—it was a triumph, as the soloist, Edmund Neupart, duly reported to Grieg. "Even as early as the cadenza in the first movement the public broke into a real storm. The three dangerous critics—Gade, Rubinstein and Hartmann—sat in the stalls and applauded with all their might."

The Piano Concerto is Grieg's only successful effort to write within a spacious structure. It is both one of his most ambitious works and one of his most successful, a perpetual favorite at symphony concerts. To Richard H. Stein, the concerto speaks of the "joy of life, longing, and youthful fire." He found the first movement to be something of a self-portrait, the ardent and enthusiastic voice of a young artist ready to realize himself. A crescendo timpani roll culminating in an outburst by the entire orchestra, and descending octaves in the solo piano, sets the stage for the main theme of that first movement. This is a march-like tune given first by the woodwind, then by the piano. The piano then embarks on some new material, including a whimsical subject, lightly supported by the orchestra. The second important theme is introduced by two phrases in the cellos; it is a poetic song in the piano. The development, introduced by a gentle flute passage, gives free play to the two main themes. After a vigorous recollection of the first theme, the cadenza for the piano offers a rhapsodic treatment of that melody, together with a new variation. Descending and ascending octaves carry the movement to a dynamic end.

To Richard H. Stein, the Adagio catches "sounds learned from Nature herself [lifting] the composer out of the church into the free fields of God." A rapt and atmospheric song is heard in muted strings. The piano embellishes it, with a soft commentary by the strings. After a climax in the piano, the song returns, amplified and dramatized. When the agitation subsides, the movement ends peacefully.

The finale enters energetically without pause. Here (with its thoughtful passage in D) Stein sees the "image of the beloved appearing to Grieg, giving reality to his dreams of longing." Two folk tunes are prominent. The first is for piano alone, then is repeated by the orchestra. The other, of lighter texture, also is introduced by the piano. A brief cadenza and a succession of powerful chords conclude this section. A pastoral theme now engages the flute, to be worked out by piano, with flute and clarinet joining in. A good deal of attention is now paid to the first folk tune. A series of scale passages lead into the coda in which that melody is first given softly and rapidly, but is built up with impressive sonorities and considerable rhythmic interest. The momentum grows until, in the concluding section, the second dance tune is given an impressive setting by the woodwind, trumpet, and cellos over fast piano arpeggios. This subject is given a final joyous treatment by the piano, and immediately after that by brass and violin. An extended scale passage and some forceful chords provide a fitting end to a dramatic movement.

1872. SIGURD JORSALFAR, suite for orchestra, op. 56. I. In the King's Hall. II. Borghild's Dream. III. Homage March.

Sigurd Jorsalfar is a drama by Bjoernson, whose hero is a twelfth-century king. He joins the Crusades in the war against the Saracens. The play, with Grieg's music, was produced in Christiana (now Oslo) in 1872; in 1892, Grieg revised his score. The three-movement orchestral suite adapted from the incidental music begins with a three-part description of the king's hall. In the first section, the main theme is a descriptive subject for clarinets and bassoons, accompanied by pizzicato strings. The middle part is a trio, stressing a melody for flute, imitated by oboe. The third section repeats the first. The second movement is a delicate Intermezzo, its main melody contrasted with a dramatic episode. The third movement opens with trumpet fanfares, after which the cellos are heard in a martial tune. A middle trio provides an expressive melody for first violins.

1875. BALLADE IN G MINOR, for piano, op. 24.

Outside of the ten-volume *Lyric Suite,* the Ballade is Grieg's most significant piano work. The form is a theme and variations, the theme being a melancholy sixteen-measure episode with strong folk-song character. Fourteen variations follow. In the first eight, Kathleen Dale explains, "the theme is preserved almost intact either melodically or harmonically, though it is subjected to such elaborate metamorphosis that player and listener are as keenly aware of the intrinsically beautiful piano-writing as of the skill with which the theme is varied." The ninth variation is a transition to "a more symphonic type of composition, and is different from all the others in being the only one which, while referring to the theme, transcends its melodic and structural boundaries and is in itself a complete and independent piece of music." The rest of the variations are "less concentrated in expression and more elaborate in piano technique. They are no longer separate pieces, but form one continuous stream of music."

1875. PEER GYNT, suites for orchestra:

No. 1, op. 46: I. Morning; II. Ase's Death; III. Anitra's Dance; IV. In the Hall of the Mountain king.

No. 2, op. 55: I. Abduction of the Bride and Ingrid's Lament; II. Arabian Dance; III. Peer Gynt's Homecoming; IV. Solveig's Song.

Peer Gynt is Ibsen's symbolic poetical drama, first produced in 1867. The hero is a character out of Norse folklore who, in the Ibsen play, is a vain, boastful egotist, and a chronic liar. He lives alone with his aged mother, Ase. Invading the wedding ceremony of his former girl friend, Ingrid, he abducts her to the mountains. After Ingrid deserts him, Peer becomes an outlaw and goes through various experiences, including one with the troll king's daughter in the hall of the mountain king. When the trolls attack him, Peer is saved, the sound of church bells sending the trolls scurrying away in fright. He sets up home in a hut in the woods where he is followed by the lovely Solveig, who is in love with him. He soon deserts her to return home for Ase's death. Then he is off again, spending the next quarter of a century in America, Morocco, Egypt. When he comes home again, he is an old, wasted man, who finds redemption through the constancy and devotion of Solveig.

In 1873, when a production was being planned for a revised version of Ibsen's play, the dramatist asked Grieg to write the incidental music. At first, Grieg lacked interest, feeling the subject of the play would not stimulate him. But, as his wife recorded, "the more he saturated his mind with the powerful poem, the more clearly he saw that he was the right man for a work of such witchery and so permeated with the Norwegian spirit." The play, with Grieg's music, was introduced in Christiana (now Oslo) in 1876, and was a success of the first magnitude. Soon afterwards, Grieg developed two orchestral suites from his score, of which the first is Grieg's most popular symphonic work.

The opening movement of this first suite is a Nature picture of morning; the music is in the style of a barcarolle. As a background to a bucolic melody, we hear echoes of a mountain yodel and cowbells. This is followed by a poignant elegy for muted strings that accompanied Ase's death in the play. "Anitra's Dance," the third movement, is a rhythmically exciting Oriental dance in the tempo of a mazurka; the exotic atmosphere is accentuated in the orchestration through the use of a triangle. A subsidiary subject in the strings contributes further to the over-all sensual mood. The final movement, speaking of the land of trolls and gnomes, is constructed from a single grotesque-like motive, first heard in bassoons, then passing on to the rest of the orchestra as the sonority develops all the way.

Though the second suite is far less familiar than the first, it boasts one of Grieg's finest melodic pages in "Solveig's Song." This is a simple, eloquent folk melody, one of the infrequent instances when Grieg went to the storehouse of Norwegian folk music for his material. In this second suite, the first movement offers an effective contrast between the agitated music of "The

Abduction of the Bride" and the poignant melancholy of "Ingrid's Lament." The exotic "Arabian Dance" and the serene measures of "Peer Gynt's Homecoming" precede "Solveig's Song" with which the second suite ends.

1878. STRING QUARTET IN G MINOR, op. 27. I. Un poco Andante; Allegro agitato. II. Andantino. III. Allegro molto marcato. IV. Lento; Presto al saltaretto.

Grieg's only string quartet is in a cyclic form. The motto theme, in the first-movement introduction, is the opening measure of that movement's first theme; it later also becomes the source for the movement's second subject. This motto is a quotation from one of Grieg's songs, "Minstrels," the first in opus 25 (1876). It recurs throughout the quartet in various shapes and forms.

The most interesting movement in the quartet is the second, a Romance in which a poignant folk song is contrasted with a stormy episode. The third movement is an atmospheric Intermezzo. In the finale, the motto is introduced in imitation; the entire movement is in the style of a saltarello.

"Here," say Kristian Lange and Arne Ostvedt of the quartet, "he breaks away from the traditional polyphonic style of quartet music, bursting the restricted dynamic range of chamber music with an almost orchestral sonority."

1880. TWO ELEGIAC MELODIES, for string orchestra, op. 34: I. Heart Wounds. II. The Last Spring.

These two episodes are orchestral transcriptions of songs, texts by A. O. Vinje, which Grieg wrote in 1880 and included in his opus 33 set. In that album, the songs are called "The Wounded Heart" and "Spring." For his transcription, Grieg revised the respective titles slightly to provide a better indication of their emotional content. The first (Allegretto espressivo) is in comparative fast time, but is, nonetheless, music deeply tinged with sorrow. The second (Andante) has an even more somber character.

1881. FOUR NORWEGIAN DANCES, for piano duet (also for orchestra), op. 35: I. D minor. II. A minor. III. G major. IV. D major.

In these four lively dances, the composer made singularly effective adaptations of actual folk material. He wrote them originally for piano duet before transcribing them for orchestra. "It is difficult, indeed," maintains Kathleen Dale, "to imagine these folk tunes without Grieg's settings, so appropriate do they appear." In the first dance, in D minor, Kathleen Dale finds an example of the composer's "apparently inexhaustible power of diversifying a melody full of repetitions" through various harmonic treatments. The second dance, in A minor, is one of Grieg's most popular short compositions.

1884. HOLBERG SUITE, for piano (also for orchestra), op. 40: I. Prelude. II. Sarabande. III. Air. IV. Gavotte. V. Rigaudon.

Ludwig Holberg was regarded in his country as the father of Danish literature. Upon the bicentennial celebration of his birth, Grieg paid him tribute by writing a classical suite utilizing the dance forms of the seventeenth century. But though the forms belong to the past, Grieg's melodic and harmonic style is still Romantic. The suite, then, is a happy fusion of the old and the then new, and may well be said to anticipate the later neo-classical trend. Grieg originally wrote this music for piano in 1884, but in 1886, he transcribed it for orchestra. The Prelude offers a strong melody with a restless rhythm. Three graceful seventeenth-century dances are presented in nineteenth-century dress, a Sarabande, Gavotte, and Rigaudon. Between the Sarabande and Gavotte, Grieg introduces an air, a poignant melody in the style of a Norwegian folk song.

1887. SONATA IN C MINOR, for violin and piano, op. 45. I. Allegro molto ed appassionato; Presto. II. Allegretto espressivo alla Romanza. III. Allegro animato; Cantabile; Prestissimo.

The third is the greatest of Grieg's three violin sonatas. Where the earlier ones sparkle with ebullient spirits, the third is more mellow and poetic. There is no introductory material to the first movement. The first main theme is stated at once by the violin, then is given a vigorous chordal accompaniment. The calmer second theme is a change of pace. The Presto, with which the movement ends, is built out of the first theme. In the slow movement, Grieg becomes brooding and introspective. This is mainly a lovely Norwegian folk song. After the melody has been spun, a contrasting section in quick 2/4 time is heard. A scale passage leads to a return of the opening song. An interesting feature about the tonality of this movement is that it is in E major; this is the only instance in Grieg's chamber music in which later movements are not written in a tonality closely related to the first one.

The rhythms of Norwegian folk dances energize the finale. The first principal subject is presented by the violin, then repeated by the piano. Throughout this movement the second subject is the property of the violin. The coda gives a lightning presentation of the first theme's opening measures.

1895. TWO NORTHERN MELODIES, for string orchestra, op. 63: I. In the Style of a Folksong. II. The Cowherd's Tune.

This is possibly the simplest of all Grieg's creations in a national style. The first movement is in a slow tempo. It is based on a folk song chanted by cellos after several introductory measures. The violins then elaborate on this melody, which is finally loudly proclaimed by all the strings just before the concluding coda. The second movement opens with a folk melody, "The Cowherd's Tune," in the strings. From here it progresses to a vigorous, earthy peasant dance.

JULES MASSENET 1842–1912

Jules Massenet was the foremost French opera composer of the late nineteenth century. He covered a wide area in his more than twenty-five operas. He used an Oriental setting for *Le Roi de Lahore* (1877), and a Spanish one for *Le Cid* (1885). He set a Biblical tale in *Hérodiade* (1881) and an ancient Egyptian one in *Cléopatre* (1912). He tried to write a Wagnerian music drama with *Esclarmonde* (1889). *Grisélidis* (1901) and *Le Jongleur de Notre Dame* (1902) are miracle plays, while *Cendrillon* (1899) is a child's opera. In addition, *Manon* takes place in eighteenth-century France, *Werther* in eighteenth-century Germany, and *Thaïs* in fourth-century Egypt.

Though he covered so many different backgrounds and periods, Massenet, nevertheless, always retained his own artistic identity, rooted though his technique and style might have been in Gounod or Wagner. To most of his operas, Massenet brought an eroticism, on the one hand, and a religious exaltation, on the other, through the most tender and exquisite lyricism and the most moving sentiment encountered in the French lyric theater. His main strength lay in his melody, which, as Donald Jay Grout has said, has "a highly personal quality: lyrical, tender, penetrating, sweetly sensuous, rounded in contours, exact but never violent in interpreting the text, sentimental, often melancholy, sometimes a little vulgar, and always charming."

Jules Massenet was born in Montaud, France, on May 12, 1842. When he was eleven, he entered the Paris Conservatory where he stayed until 1863, a pupil of Ambroise Thomas, among others. He received prizes in piano, fugue, and, in 1863, the Prix de Rome. During his three-year residence in Rome, he married one of his pupils, Mlle. de Sainte-Marie; he also completed his first opera, *Esméralda,* which was never published nor performed. *La Grand' Tante,* his first opera to get produced, was seen at the Opéra-Comique on April 3, 1867; later the same year, his first orchestral suite was introduced at a Pasdeloup concert. Success came with his incidental music to *Les Érinnyes,* and the oratorio, *Marie-Magdeleine;* both were heard in Paris in 1873. With *Hérodiade,* produced at the Théâtre de la Monnaie in Brussels on December 19, 1881, and with his masterwork, *Manon,* given in 1884, Massenet became the foremost opera composer in France since Gounod. Meanwhile, in 1878, he became professor of composition at the Paris Conservatory, and was elected to the Académie des Beaux-Arts. In 1899, he was made Grand Officier of the Legion of Honor. His most successful operas after *Manon* were *Werther* in

1892, *Thaïs* in 1894, *Sapho* in 1897, *Cendrillon* in 1899, *Le Jongleur de Notre Dame* in 1902, and *Don Quichotte* in 1910. Massenet died in Paris on August 13, 1912.

1873. LES Érinnyes, suite for orchestra. I. Entr'acte. II. Grecian Dance, III. Invocation. IV. Scène religieuse.

Massenet achieved his first major success as composer through his incidental music to *Les Érinnyes,* a tragedy by Leconte de Lisle. In this drama, a new treatment was given to the old Greek legend of Agamemnon, his murder at the hands of his wife Clytemnestra, and the vengeance sought and achieved by their son, Orestes. The play, with Massenet's music, was given at the Odéon in Paris on January 6, 1873.

One of its sections has since become one of its composer's most popular pieces of music—now known as the "Élégie," but designated in the *Les Érinnyes* score as "Invocation." Massenet renamed this episode "Élégie" when he transcribed it for cello and piano; subsequently, it was adapted into a song, text by E. Gallet.

The opening "Entr'acte" (Andante appassionato) is concerned with a sensual melody, first heard in unison violins, accompanied by the other strings. The main melody of the "Grecian Dance" is given by flutes over plucked strings. After the "Invocation" (or "Élégie"), the suite comes to a close with an eloquent religious melody for solo cello, describing the funeral rites at Agamemnon's tomb.

1873. SCÈNES PITTORESQUES (PICTURESQUE SCENES), for orchestra: I. Marche. II. Air de Ballet. III. Angelus. IV. Fête bohème.

This is the fourth and most familiar of Massenet's seven orchestral suites. The most famous movement is the third, the "Angelus," in which a stately religious melody is accompanied by the solemn tolling of bells. The "Air de Ballet" is in a similarly lyrical character, while the interest in the other two movements lies mainly in its rhythmic energy.

1876. OVERTURE TO PHÈDRE, for orchestra.

This overture is a faithful tonal representation of Racine's tragedy recounting the frustrated love of Phedre for Hippolytus. The tragic mood is projected in the opening measures of the overture with a lugubrious introductory section. A description of Phedre's unrequited love follows in a passionate melody for clarinet. The music gains in dramatic power and intensity as Hippolytus is sent to his doom by his irate father. Phedre's love is then recalled in a glowing passage for violins in unison. Then Hippolytus's tragic end at the hands of Neptune is described stormily. The overture ends in the same solemn manner with which it began.

1881. SCÈNES ALSACIENNES, suite for orchestra: I. Dimanche matin. II. Au cabaret. III. Sous les tilleuls. IV. Dimanche soir: air alsacien, rétraite française.

This is the last of Massenet's seven orchestral suites—made up of four nostalgic pictures of Alsace, lost to France as an aftermath of the Franco-Prussian War, in which the composer had participated actively. Massenet himself provides the program for his music in the published score. In the first movement, "Sunday Morning," the composer recalls with delight "the Alsatian village Sunday morning at the hour of divine service; the streets deserted, the houses empty except for the elderly ones who sun themselves before their doors. The church is full, and the sacred hymns are heard at intervals in passing." The second movement describes "The Tavern," where so many happy gatherings take place. Wine is drunk, and forest rangers raise their voices in song. "Oh, the joyous life and the gay companions!" The third movement is in a pictorial vein, depicting a scene "Under the Linden Trees." The music brings up a picture of "the long avenue . . . in the shadow of which, hand in hand, quietly walks a pair of lovers." The finale is a vigorous presentation of a Sunday evening in the market place. "What noise, what movement!. . . . Everyone at the doorsteps, groups of young gallants in the streets, and dances that embody in rhythm the songs of the country. Eight o'clock! The noise of the drums, the blare of the trumpets—'tis retreat! The French retreat! And when in the distance the sound of the drum dies down, the women call their children in the street, the old men relight their big pipes, and to the sounds of violins, the dance is joyously recommenced in smaller circles, with couples closer."

1884. MANON, opera in five acts, with text by Henri Meilhac and Philippe Gille, based on *L'Histoire du Chevalier des Grieux et de Manon Lescaut,* by Abbé Prévost. First performance: Opéra-Comique, Paris, January 19, 1884.

Of the three operatic settings of Prévost's celebrated romance about the courtesan, *Manon Lescaut,* that of Auber preceded Massenet's by over a quarter of a century, produced in 1856; that of Puccini followed Massenet's by less than a decade, its première taking place in 1893. Auber's opera is rarely heard; Puccini's is still active in the repertory and has much to recommend it (which see). But it is Massenet's *Manon* that is the most universally admired and the most frequently played of these adaptations of Prévost. In this story, Massenet found a text tailor-made to his special gifts as a composer. His surpassing tenderness of lyricism and his uncommon gift in projecting erotic moods could here be exploited to their fullest advantage; so could his rare gift in evoking old-world settings and in characterizing provocative heroines. In *Manon,* the marriage of text and music is heaven-made. The result is a masterwork, one of the most popular operas in the French repertory. At times, we encounter experiment here—as when Massenet uses spoken dialogue over an orchestral accompaniment. At times, there is derivation, such as in Massenet's use of a Leitmotiv technique. But essentially, what confronts us in this opera is neither something borrowed nor something new but something that is essentially "Massenetique"—warmth, charm, voluptuousness, passion, and even poignant melancholy," as Herbert F. Peyser once described that term.

The setting is France in the early eighteenth century, in the cities of Amiens, Paris, and Le Havre. Three melodies from the opera are heard in the brief orchestral prelude: the gay and festive music of the Cours-la-Reine scene; the dramatic exposition of the archers as they lead Manon to her exile in the last act; and the passionate love song of Des Grieux to Manon in the gambling-house scene.

In a courtyard of an inn at Amiens, Lescaut is awaiting the arrival of his cousin, Manon, whom he is seeing for the first time. When she comes by coach, she describes her journey in "Jes suis encore tout étourdie," music in which with vivid strokes the composer provides us with an insight into her character. Lescaut has words of warning about life and the world ("Ne bronchez pas, soyez gentille"). But Manon, who is en route to a convent, is rueful about rejecting the pleasures of life and love ("Voyons, Manon, plus de chimères"). Her feelings become intensified with the appearance of Chevalier des Grieux, for Manon is powerfully attracted to him, just as he is instantly made aware of her fascination and beauty ("Et je sais votre nom"). By the time the coach arrives for Guillot, a French minister, both Manon and Des Grieux have decided to expropriate it and make their escape to Paris.

The second act takes place in an apartment in Paris where Des Grieux and Manon have made their home. With Manon's aid, Des Grieux is writing a letter to his father asking for his consent to their marriage ("J'écris à mon père"). Now Lescaut has come to seek out his cousin, accompanied by the nobleman, De Brétigny. Convinced by the letter that Des Grieux intends to marry Manon, Lescaut becomes more sympathetic to the young man. De Brétigny, meanwhile, reveals to Manon that the older Des Grieux has plans to avoid the marriage by abducting the son. De Brétigny stands ready to place his wealth and protection at Manon's call. Though Manon cannot forget how much she loves Des Grieux, she realizes her future happiness is dependent on her going off with De Brétigny. While Des Grieux goes out to post his letter, Manon bids farewell to the apartment where she has known such great happiness, and to the table where she has shared so many meals with her beloved ("Adieu, notre petite table"). By the time Des Grieux returns she is in tears. He tries to soothe her by describing a recent dream, in which he shares paradise with his beloved Manon ("En fermant les yeux."). Loud knocking is heard. When Des Grieux goes to open the door, he is abducted by his father's men.

A graceful minuet for orchestra precedes the Cours-la-Reine scene in the third act. It is a holiday; Paris is festive. Lescaut is one of the merrymakers, having just known good luck at the gaming tables. He sings a madrigal to a girl named Rosalinde. Now a bevy of lovely girls intrude; One of them is Manon, in whose florid aria she reveals how she relishes her devil-may-care way of life ("Je marche sur tous les chemins"). Then, in a delicate gavotte, she explains that her life's philosophy is to enjoy song and dance ("Obéissons quand leur voix appelle"). The older Des Grieux is also at hand, having come to Paris to visit his son, who is now a priest at St. Sulpice. Overhearing the name "Chevalier des Grieux," Manon discovers that she is still very much in love with him. She rushes off to St. Sulpice. There the elder Des Grieux has come to plead with his son not to renounce life by entering the priesthood. The younger man exclaims vehemently that life has brought him nothing but bitterness, that only in religion can he hope to find peace. After the father has bid his son a tender farewell, the young Des Grieux stirs old memories of Manon. Vainly does he try to rid his mind of her image ("Ah! fuyez douce image!"). Within the church, where a Magnificat is being chanted, Manon is praying for forgiveness, and for an opportunity to see her beloved once more. Des Grieux is also present at the service. Manon pleads with him to return to her. At first Des Grieux resists. But as she becomes more and more supplicating ("N'est ce plus ma main que cette main presse?") Des Grieux sweeps her into his arms ("Ah! Manon! Je ne veux plus lutter contre moi-même!").

The fourth act takes place in a fashionable gaming room at the Hotel de Transylvanie. Lescaut, on whom Dame Luck continues to smile, sings a hymn in praise of the Queen of Spades. Suddenly Manon appears, in the company of Des Grieux. Manon extols the virtue of money in "Ce bruit de l'or ce rire". Des Grieux tries his luck, and proves so fortunate that he is accused of cheating. In the ensuing brawl, Des Grieux is rescued and removed from the gambling establishment. Manon is seized and arrested as a woman of ill repute.

In the last scene, Manon is on a lonely road to Le Havre, en route to exile to an American plantation. Young Des Grieux has followed her, to plead with her that she run away with him. But Manon is too ill to be persuaded. Her growing weakness is emphasized in the orchestra by a roll of the kettledrums, the sound of tambourines and the rhythm of plucked strings. She falls lifeless in Des Grieux's arms, and he is overcome by grief.

The first American performance took place at the Academy of Music in New York on December 23, 1885 (in Italian). When first given at the Metropolitan Opera, on January 16, 1895, the original French text was used.

1885. LE CID, ballet music for orchestra.

Le Cid was an opera Massenet wrote and had produced immediately after *Manon*. It was seen at the Paris Opéra on November 30, 1885, but with so little success that it was rarely given after that. But its ballet sequences, with their exotic melodies, appealing Spanish idioms, and vivid orchestral colors, have become popular.

The libretto was based on Corneille's tragedy, set in twelfth-century Burgos. El Cid (The Conqueror) is the descriptive title given to Rodrigo. He kills Chimène's father in a duel. She vows vengeance, but before she can achieve it she falls in love with her enemy.

The ballet music, the highlight of the opera, appears in the second scene of the second act. A series of colorful Spanish dances takes place in the public square, for whose musical materials Massenet often went to authentic Spanish sources. The first dance, "Castillane," derives its vivacious rhythms from a dance native to Castille. This is followed by "Andalouse" and "Aragonaise," the first an Andalousian gypsy dance, the second a dance come from the Aragon district. By way of contrast, a soft lyrical episode follows in "Aubade." But the dance rhythms are again emphasized in the last sections: "Catalane," native to Catalonia; "Madrilène," a two-part contrasting melody from Madrid; and "Navarraise," a stately dance from Navarre.

1892. WERTHER, opera in four acts, with text by Édouard Blau, Paul Milliet, and Georges Hartmann, based on Goethe's romance, *Die Leiden des jungen Werthes*. First performance: Opera, Vienna, February 16, 1892.

English-speaking audiences have never been particularly partial to *Werther*. But in France, it is regarded with *Manon* as Massenet's greatest opera. This is Massenet's only successful opera where the central character is a male rather than a heroine. He is a young poet who, in the eighteenth-century town of Wetzlar, commits suicide because of his frustrated love for Charlotte. Goethe wrote this sentimental romance after his own tragic love affair with Charlotte Buff in Wetzlar; and for a time, he even contemplated doing away with himself.

A brief, romantic prelude precedes the rise of the first-act curtain in the courtyard of the Bailiff's house. His oldest daughter, Charlotte (though engaged to the long-absent Albert) is planning to attend a party that evening with the poet, Werther. When he appears, he sings an ode to Nature ("O Natur"). After the pair have gone off to the party, Albert comes for Charlotte, and is welcomed by her sister, Sophie. An orchestral intermezzo, with cello obbligato, now points up the fact that at the party Charlotte and Werther have fallen in love. After returning home, Werther expresses his passion for Charlotte in the duet, "Il faut nous séparer". But upon discovering that Albert is back, Charlotte insists to Werther she is bound by honor to return to him. Werther insists that if Charlotte marries Albert, he will kill himself.

Three months have passed. Outside a church, villagers are celebrating the golden wedding anniversary of their pastor ("Vivat Bacchus!"). Werther is desolate; Charlotte and Albert are man and wife ("Un autre est son époux"). In vain does Sophie try to cheer him up by inviting him to dance a minuet with her. When, at last, Werther has the opportunity to speak to Charlotte, he reiterates his undying love. Charlotte insists he must go away for several months and try to forget her. After entreating God for help, Werther announces that he is leaving for good.

For several months Werther has been wandering aimlessly in his attempt to forget Charlotte; his misery and desolateness is vividly described in the third-act prelude. It is Christmas now, and at her home Charlotte is reading some of Werther's letters ("Werther! Qui m'aurait dit"). She has not forgotten the poet, nor can she ignore any longer that she still loves him. Sophie's efforts to soothe her only make her burst into tears and express her true feeling ("Va! laisse les couler!"). Once she is alone, she is startled to see Werther before her. He has come back to beg for her love, to try to reawaken her feelings for him by reading her Ossian's verses ("Pourquoi! me réveiller?"). Impulsively, Charlotte rushes to him; but then, taking command of herself, she orders him from the room and locks the door. When Albert appears, he learns of Werther's return and willingly sends the poet pistols for which he had asked. Learning of this request, Charlotte realizes Werther intends to commit suicide, and prays she is not too late to save the man she really loves.

There is no intermission between the third and fourth acts. An orchestral interlude serves to describe Charlotte's emotions as she begs God to save Werther's life. In Werther's room he is lying mortally wounded after having shot himself. Charlotte rushes in to find him dying, begs for his forgiveness, confesses that he is the one she has always loved. With the distant sound of Christmas carols sung by children, Werther dies in her arms.

"The best music," wrote W. J. Henderson after *Werther* was given for the first time at the Metropolitan Opera on April 19, 1894, "is that which expresses the passion and desperation of Werther. His solos in the first and second acts and his reading of the poems are good music, the last named being a really fine piece of work. The ensuing duet with Charlotte is theatrically strong. . . . If Massenet's opera does not have lasting success it will be because it has no genuine depth."

The American première of *Werther* preceded this Metropolitan Opera production by less than a month—in Chicago on March 29, 1894.

1894. THAÏS, opera in three acts, with text by Louis Gallet, based on Anatole France's novel. First performance: Opéra, Paris, March 16, 1894.

When Vincent d'Indy first heard Massenet's oratorio, *Marie-Magdeleine,* in 1873, he coined a phrase since used frequently to identify Massenet's style: "discreet and semi-religious eroticism." This phrase can also serve to characterize *Thaïs*. The effect of opera comes from its union of the religious and the exotic, the sacred and the profane, in a musical language that at turns is hauntingly tender, frequently sensual, and at times sanctimonious.

When Massenet asked Gallet to prepare for him a libretto based on Anatole France's story, he suggested that the text be in prose. Gallet compromised by producing something he called a "poème mélique" in which "music and poetry each asserts its own inalienable rights," as Ernest Newman explains, "while at the same time politely accommodating toward the rights of the other." While Gallet avoided rhymes, he did achieve a "kind of free rhythm that differentiates it from out-and-out prose, a rhythm designed to help rather than impede the composer."

Massenet wrote the opera with Sibyl Sanderson, the American prima donna, in mind. She appeared in it at its world première in 1894. The opera did not do well then, nor has it ever equalled anything like the success of *Manon*. The American première took place at the Manhattan Opera in New York on November 25, 1907, with Mary Garden in the title role. The role was assumed by Geraldine Farrar when the opera was first mounted at the Metropolitan Opera on February 16, 1917.

If *Thaïs* is less popular than other Massenet's operas it is because it has very little action, because the plot development lacks conviction, and because its big scenes seem out of place. The finer qualities in the opera—its subtle suggestions and nuances, the delicately tinted atmosphere, and the sensitive lyricism—become evident only after the opera has been heard a number of times.

A brief orchestral prelude suggests a peaceful night on the banks of the Nile in fourth-century Egypt. Palemon, a Cenobite monk, is seated around a table with other monks. When the monk Athanaël appear, he is weary and disillusioned: he has just visited Alexandria, which is infected with corruption and degradation, much of it instigated by the beautiful Thaïs. Indeed, even Athanaël momentarily was drawn to this glamorous courtesan. Having thus had a brief taste of temptation, Athanaël vows he would devote himself henceforth toward saving the soul of Thaïs. The monks join him in prayer, and disperse to go to bed. In his sleep, Athanaël sees a vision of Thaïs, half nude, dancing in an Alexandrian theater (the orchestra emphasizing the voluptuousness of her performances with its lavish colors and harmonies). Awakening in a cold sweat, Athanaël is more determined than ever to save Alexandria from Thaïs, and Thaïs from perdition.

We catch a glimpse of Alexandrian gaiety and abandon in the orchestral introduction to the second scene. Athanaël has return to the city, lamenting in an eloquent air how corrupt it has become ("Voilà donc la terrible cité"). Nicias, a wealthy Alexandrian infatuated with Thaïs, is cynical about Athanaël's dream of saving Thaïs. Nevertheless, being a close friend of the monk, he is ready to prove helpful. He dresses Athanaël in handsome attire and jewels to prepare him for a confrontation with the alluring courtesan. Soon Thaïs appears, accompanied by a bevy of actors and actresses. When Nicias reveals to her that a monk has come to redeem her soul, she replies mockingly her only interest is in love. She is even ready, she says, to introduce Athanaël to love's rapture, a suggestion that sends the monk in flight.

The first scene of the second act transpires in Thaïs's house. She is depressed and world-weary ("Ah, je suis seule"). Then, after consulting the mirror to reassure herself she is beautiful, she calls upon Venus for help ("Dis moi, que je suis belle"). Athanaël intrudes upon these reveries, once again to be struck by her dazzling beauty. He tries to convince her that there is a love nobler than the physical. Thaïs, suddenly and inexplicably, is moved by his arguments. The appearance of Nicias points up for her how corrupt her life has been. In spite of these reflections, she takes hold of herself and makes a desperate effort to justify her way of life. But Athanaël is now convinced she is ready for conversion, and waits for her outside her house.

During a change of scene, the orchestra plays the famous "Meditation," its spiritual melody, in solo violin, describing Thaïs's regeneration. Outside her house, the courtesan addresses Athanaël humbly and reverently. She has seen the light; she is ready to obey his commands. Angrily, Athanaël destroys the statue of Eros which Nicias had once presented her, and which Thaïs had said she wanted to take with her. Then he invades her house to smash every other symbol of corrupt living. There he confronts Nicias and his friends in a state of revelry. A ballet is taking place, and other entertainment is provided by jugglers and buffoons. Sternly Athanaël orders them to be silent. He announces that no longer is Thaïs a courtesan but the bride of God. When she appears she gives evidence of her transformation. She is dressed in threadbare simplicity, and her hair is dishevelled. The crowd is so upset that it rushes at the monk to attack him. But Nicias saves the situation by throwing a handful of gold at it. While the crowd scurries to pick up the coins, Athanaël and Nicias make their escape.

The third-act prelude may be interpreted as the suffering and exhaustion of Thaïs and Athanaël as they make their way across the desert. They have come to an oasis, where Thaïs faints with pain and fatigue. Overwhelmed with pity and love, Athanaël kisses her bleeding feet; then he feeds her fruit and water. With the arrival of a procession of nuns, Athanaël turns Thaïs over to them, though tortured by the thought he may never again see her.

Back at his hut, Athanaël confesses to the monk, Palemon, that in converting Thaïs he has lost his own soul. He is continually haunted by a reminder of her beauty. His body is tormented with desire for her ("En vain j'ai flagellé ma chair"). When Palemon leaves, Athanaël prays, then falls asleep. In his dreams he again sees a vision of Thaïs, this time calling to him seductively. A chorus of angels announces Thaïs's imminent death. Awakening suddenly, Athanaël rushes out of his hut into the desert.

Once again we hear the tender strains of the "Meditation" between scene changes. Athanaël has come to the convent where Thaïs is dying. With infinite tenderness, Thaïs recalls her difficult journey through the desert, and the stages by which she arrived at salvation ("Te souvient-il du lumineux voyage"). Overcome by his passion, Athanaël confesses that only physical love is the true one, that nothing exists but life itself. But Thaïs does not hear his protestations. She has caught a glimpse of Paradise ("Deux seraphins aux blanches ailes"). Suddenly she falls back dead; Athanaël gives voice to his fathomless grief.

EMMANUEL CHABRIER 1841–1894

"Chabrier's language," writes Gilbert Chase in *The Music of Spain,* "is marked by great brilliance, exuberant verve and wit and an inexhaustible spontaneity of vivid harmonies, rhythmical and orchestral coloring. His work shows a rare power of combining all the musical materials at his disposal." Though he is most famous for *España,* one of the most successful portraits of Spain by a foreigner—and though he proved himself here to be a master in evoking nostalgic scenes and in re-creating colorful national songs and dances—Chabrier was probably at his best when he could give free rein to his flair for grotesquerie and burlesque. Thus Chabrier's creative identity can be uncovered more clearly in his comic opera, *Le Roi malgré lui* than in his Wagnerian opera, *Gwendoline;* in works like the *Bourrée fantasque* and the *Marche joyeuse* than in atmospheric songs and piano pieces.

Emmanuel Chabrier was born in Ambert, Puy-de-Dôme, France, on January 18, 1841. Though he showed aptitude for music from childhood on, and received some instruction, he was trained in Paris for the law. In 1862, he entered the Ministry of the Interior where he was employed eighteen years. Having meanwhile gone though intensive instruction in counterpoint and fugue with Semet and Hignard, and piano with Édouard Wolf, Chabrier combined his duties at the Ministry with composition. Between 1877 and 1879, he completed two operettas, *L'Étoile,* produced at the Bouffes Parisiens on November 28, 1877, and *Une Éducation manquée,* seen at the Cercle de la Presse, on May 1, 1879. During a visit to Munich in 1879, he heard *Tristan and Isolde,* which convinced him that his life-work lay in music. Returning to Paris, he resigned from the Ministry, and from this time on, he concentrated on composition. In 1880, he completed a set of piano pieces, *Dix Pièces pittoresques,* published a year later. This was followed in 1885 by *Habanera,* for piano. Success came in 1883 with *España,* still his most popular work. His comic opera, *Le Roi malgré lui,* was produced in 1887. Toward the end of his life, Chabrier was the victim of a mental breakdown. He died in Paris on September 13, 1894.

1880. SUITE PASTORALE, for orchestra: I. Idylle. II. Danse villageoise. III. Sous bois. IV. Scherzo-Valse.

This suite consists of four numbers lifted from the *Pièces pittoresques,* for piano. The first movement is in an idyllic mood, a romantic melody being accompanied by plucked strings. A sprightly country dance follows, its main subject first given by the clarinets. The pastoral atmosphere of the first movement returns in the third, while the fourth is at turns dynamic and graceful.

1883. ESPAÑA, rhapsody for orchestra.

The composer's most famous work was the aftermath of a visit to Spain in the Spring of 1883. The country's folk songs and dances exerted such a fascination on Chabrier that he made copious notes while traveling about. Back in Paris, he decided to use some of this material for an orchestral composition. It was a huge success when played for the first time in 1883, in Paris; it became one of the most significant works by a French composer finding stimulation and inspiration in Spain. "Across the seductive and intriguing rhythms of its themes," wrote Julien Tersot, "one seems to perceive the contortions of Spanish dancers carried away as by some frenetic whirlwind. Strange associations of sounds . . . accumulations of harmonies which are overcharged and voluntarily incomplete, chords with free combinations, rhythms either broken or badly superimposed—this is what one perceives in this work which is so different from anything one has heard in France, Germany, or anywhere else."

There are three melodies in this rhapsody. The first is a jota, a dance in quick triple time, usually accompanied by castanets; it originated in the Province of Aragon. The second, a malagueña, is also in rapid triple time; it comes from Malaga and Murcia. A third subject—a forceful theme for trombones—is Chabrier's own. These three ideas are developed freely in the style of a fantasia. These main themes were used by the Parisian waltz king, Emil Waldteufel (1837–1915) for his famous waltz, *España*.

1883. TROIS VALSES ROMANTIQUES, for two pianos: I. Très vite et impetueusement. II. Mouvement modéré de valse. III. Animé.

A few strong chords precede the first waltz, an animated dance movement. The second waltz is more formal and sedate, a Laendler-like introduction preceding an expressive melody. The third waltz, the finest in the set, was described by Robert Brussel as having "almost the accents of passion." The work ends pianissimo. Felix Mottl orchestrated the suite.

1883. OVERTURE TO GWENDOLINE, for orchestra.

In 1879, Chabrier fell under the spell of Wagner. From then on, his ambition was to write a Wagnerian music drama. Catulle Mendes prepared for him such a libretto, based on a medieval legend, and the opera—*Gwendoline*—was produced in Brussels on April 10, 1886. In this drama, Harald, a Viking king, falls in love with Gwendoline, daughter of Arnel, a Saxon captured by Harald. While pretending to be in favor of a marriage between Harald and Gwendoline, Arnel plots and brings about the king's death. Distraught by this tragedy Gwendoline commits suicide.

The dramatic overture to the opera is one of the composer's finest works for orchestra. It is a tone portrait of Harald, opening with a fiery subject (Allegro con fuoco) which represents the king. Midway in the overture, effective use is made of the second-act love duet of Harald and Gwendoline.

1887. LE ROI MALGRÉ LUI (A KING IN SPITE OF HIMSELF), opéra-comique in three acts, with text by Émile de Najac and Paul Burani, based on a comedy by François Ancelot. First performance: Opéra-Comique, Paris, May 18, 1887.

In writing this opéra-comique, Chabrier shed himself of Wagnerian influences and reverted to the opéra-comique tradition of writing set numbers between stretches of dialogue; he also exploited his natural bent for wit and mockery. The result was one of his most important works for the stage, and a minor classic in the French musical theater. The setting is sixteenth-century France. Henri de Valois, about to be crowned king, first allows himself the luxury of a few escapades in Paris. When he finally comes for his coronation, he finds a conspiracy against his life has been hatched by a number of Polish noblemen. Disguising himself as De Nangis, Henri moves with the conspirators, wins their trust, and offers his services in the plot to kill the future king. When the real de Nangis comes to the conspirators' camp, he is confused with the king and threatened by murder. The conspiracy is finally foiled; both de Nangis and Henri are spared; and Henri is finally crowned.

Chabrier's score is full of tuneful episodes: the king's Ceremonial and Romance, "Beau pays!"; the gypsy song, "Il est un vieux chant de Bohème"; Nangis's aria, "Je suis roi"; and such appealing orchestral numbers as the melodious overture, the *Danse slave,* and the *Fête polonaise.* Though his style is consistently light and gay, there is daring in his harmonic writing and orchestration. Maurice Ravel was so fond of this opera that he once maintained he would rather have written it than the *Ring of the Nibelungs.*

Acclaimed at its world première, *Le Roi malgré lui* could anticipate a highly successful season. But after its third performance, the Opéra-Comique theater burned down. The new opera could not be produced until late the following winter when the company found new quarters. However, once the Opéra-Comique acquired a permanent home, *Le Roi malgré lui* became fixed in its repertory.

1888. JOYEUSE MARCHE, for orchestra.

This composition originated as a piano piece, *Marche française,* intended as a sight-reading exercise at the Bordeaux Conservatory. When it was found too difficult for this purpose, Chabrier orchestrated and retitled it. The *Joyeuse marche* is in the composer's most infectious satirical style. It is believed to be a description of the stumbling progress of several drunk musicians as they stagger home after an evening's revel. The work opens with an orchestral flourish. Two gay themes follow. The first, in the oboe, describes satirically the halting advance of the drunks. The second, in the violins, tells of their happy, abandoned spirits.

1891. BOURRÉE FANTASQUE, for piano.

"Mon petit," wrote Chabrier to the pianist, Édouard Risler, in sending him the manuscript of *Bourrée fantasque.* "I am sending you a piece which contains for each note an entire problem to solve." Georges Servières, Charbier's biographer, gives us a clue to this music by suggesting it was the composer's tribute to his native Auvergne, where the bourrée was said to have originated. Desaymard is of another mind. He finds in this music the "macabre imagination and a ballet of death, rustic and danced in wooden shoes, with here and there a touch of mysticism." In any event, much of the writing in this score is distinguished by its humor and grotesque moods.

Both Felix Mottl and Charles Koechlin orchestrated the *Bourrée fantasque.* The music was the inspiration for a classical ballet, also named *Bourrée fantasque,* with choreography by George Balanchine, introduced in New York on December 1, 1949. "This dance spectacle," Balanchine has explained, "has no story, but each of the three parts has its own special character and quality of motion to match the buoyant pieces by Chabrier." The music of *Bourrée fantasque* is used for the ballet sequences, and the overture is Chabrier's *Joyeuse marche* (see above).

ERNEST CHAUSSON 1855–1899

Though there are forceful reminders of Wagner in Chausson's Symphony in B-flat major, and while the shadow of César Franck hovers over so many other of Chausson's compositions, Chausson's own personality shines through bright and clear in the handful of remarkable works he has left us. This man may be influenced but he does not imitate. "It may be said," wrote Pierre de Breville, "that all his works exhale a dreamy sensitiveness which is peculiar to him. His music is constantly saying the word *chèr*. His passion is not fiery; it is always affectionate and this affection is gentle agitation in discreet reserve. . . . If he did not know futile brutality, he nevertheless knew what power is. . . . He has been charged with melancholy, but he was not a sad man. The melancholy that veiled his soul veiled also from his eyes the vulgarity of exterior spectacles."

Ernest Chausson was born in Paris on January 21, 1855. Since he planned to become a lawyer, he did not begin exhaustive music study until comparatively late in life. He entered the Paris Conservatory when he was twenty-five; his teachers included César Franck who influenced him profoundly. Unhappy at the Conservatory with its strict regimen and academic approaches, Chausson left to study privately with Franck. In 1878, Chausson published two songs; and in 1882, he completed his first work for orchestra, a tone poem, *Viviane.* As a man of independent means, he could devote himself completely to creative work without the necessity of earning a living. Nevertheless, he produced only a few compositions, the best of which is music of great distinction. For ten years he was the secretary of the Société nationale, promoting the work of contemporary French composers. Chausson was riding a bicycle in Limay, France, when he lost control and smashed into a wall. A fractured skull and internal injuries proved fatal. He died in Limay on June 10, 1899.

1890. SYMPHONY IN B-FLAT MAJOR, op. 20. I. Lent; Allegro vivo. II. Très lent. III. Animé.

Chausson, like his teacher Franck, wrote only a single symphony; once again, like Franck, he produced a work that has become a treasure in French symphonic music of the late nineteenth century. When first heard, in Paris in 1891, the symphony was not well received. But its importance became evident when Artur Nikisch conducted it in Berlin in 1897.

The work opens with a slow introduction in which an expressive thought is presented by solo clarinet, horn, and strings; this idea will play a significant part in the finale. Glissandi passages for strings and woodwind lead into the Allegro section, where the first main theme is given by solo bassoon and horn over tremolos. As the subject passes to other instruments, the sonority is built up until a climax is reached in full orchestra. Now we hear the second forceful theme, in solo clarinet, violas, and cellos. There is still a third important idea later on, an elegiac melody built up with considerable gusto. A transition to F-sharp minor brings on the development, in which the oboe recalls the first main theme, while the brass repeat the expressive material of the introduction. An ascending chromatic scale in thirds in two clarinets leads into the recapitulation. The coda concerns itself with the first main theme.

The slow movement is bleak, brooding music. A somber passage for strings precedes a haunting and melancholy tune for English horn and clarinet over figures in violas and cellos. The mood is built up passionately and sweeps onward toward a strong conclusion.

Vigor and joy predominate in the finale. Figures in lower strings, calls in the trumpet, and chromatic scales in thirds in the woodwind, set the stage for the principal theme, a virile melody for cellos and double basses. No less powerful is the second subject for full orchestra, a chorale-like melody. After a theatrical elaboration of both ideas, and a dramatic crescendo, the horns and trumpets proudly recall the subject of the first-movement introduction. The chorale-like subject is built up along dramatic lines, but the symphony ends serenely and contemplatively with a last reminder of the expressive theme from the first-movement introduction.

1891. CONCERTO IN D MAJOR, for violin, piano, and string quartet, op. 21. I. Decidé; Calme; Animé. II. Sicilienne: pas vite. III. Grave. IV. Très animé.

Nicolas Slonimsky has noted some of the ways in which this concerto is unusual and unorthodox. "The solo violin and piano often play a duo for long stretches, with but occasional responses from the strings. There is little counterpoint in the writing for the instruments, which infrequently move side by side, in parallel octaves. Arpeggios, trills and tremolos abound. Harmonically, the concatenation of secondary seventh chords, with occasional augmented triads, is the principal scheme. The cadences are all plagal, with the exception of the very end when the common dominant seventh raises its plebian head.

It is this new art of treating an old form that irritated the critics of the 1890's."

The concerto opens with a three-note motto in the piano that recurs throughout the first movement. In the ensuing "Calme" section, the motto evolves into the first theme, a flowing melody for the strings over piano arpeggios. After the tempo quickens, solo violin and piano engage in an unaccompanied duet; this romantic subject is the movement's second theme. A trill on the solo violin, and a descending passage for piano, bring a return of the first theme, in quartet and piano. Now a new section unfolds, with a lyrical subject heard in solo violin and cello, and a second beautiful melody in solo violin.

The second movement is a Sicilienne with classic grace and design. Two main melodies here are assigned to the solo violin. In the third movement, Grave, the composer becomes somber; the heart of this section is an extended brooding duet for violin and piano. A brisk rhythmic passage for the piano, extended by the strings, introduces the finale which Slonimsky describes as a "gigue-toccata." Following a brief vigorous exchange between piano and strings, the piano offers an eloquent melody.

1896. POÈME, for violin and orchestra, op. 25.

As the title suggests, the *Poème* tries to project a poetic mood. "There is no description," the composer explained, "no story, nothing but sensation." The composition is a rhapsody with two main themes. The first embarks on a soaring lyrical flight; the solo violin unaccompanied is involved here, following a brief orchestral introduction. This idyllic mood is shattered as the music gains in intensity and passion. Then the solo violin is heard in the second subject which, while still agitated, nevertheless is also deeply romantic. Trumpet calls precede a return of the first theme, now shared by orchestra and solo violin. The tranquillity of the opening is now restored. The *Poème* ends gently with a succession of descending trills in violin, accompanied by orchestra.

1897. STRING QUARTET IN A MAJOR, op. 30. I. Animé. II. Andante. III. Simple et sans hâte. IV. Animé.

Written two years before the composer's death, this string quartet is to Gustave Samazeuilh, "Chausson's most complete work, most significantly typical of the musician's personality, by the blending of intense lyricism and serene sensibility one finds in it." The first movement is of particular rhythmic interest as 5/4 time alternates with 4/4 and 6/4. The second movement, on the other hand, is outstanding for its emotional and melodic appeal. This is music, now calm and now touched with pathos, which Georges Jean-Aubry said "is not surpassed in emotional content even by that of Debussy's Quartet." In the brisk, vital third movement, Spanish atmosphere is projected. The finale begins dramatically, then is allowed to be built up into an uninhibited expression of joyous feelings.

CAMILLE SAINT-SAËNS 1835–1921

Saint-Saëns was one of the most versatile musicians of all time. Besides his activity as a composer, he was a distinguished organist, pianist, conductor, editor, scholar, and teacher. Even outside music, his versatility was remarkable. He was a linguist; an omnivorous reader, well acquainted with both literature and the stage; an author of essays, poetry, and plays; a student of astronomy, natural history, archaeology.

The same kind of infinite variety governs his musical writing. There is no field of music he did not invade, and his vast output is characterized by an amazing diversity of style. At times he was influenced by Wagner, at times by Verdi. At times he wrote music in the manner of the old masters: keyboard pieces in the style of the sixteenth-century harpsichordists; dance movements in a seventeenth-century idiom; eighteenth-century preludes and fugues. In some of his works, he is unmistakably French; in others, he translated the personalities of foreign lands with uncommon authenticity. He wrote an Algerian suite, Persian songs, an Egyptian concerto, Russian caprices, Portuguese barcarolles.

Many critics lament in Saint-Saëns a lack of individuality, a personal point of view. Yet there is a good deal in his music that commands respect, which justifies his contemporaries regarding him as one of the foremost French composers of his generation. He possessed a fantastic technique, never failing good taste, an aristocratic polish, a beguiling charm, sophistication, breeding, and culture.

Here is how Philip Hale once evaluated the credits and debits of Saint-Saëns's compositions: "Possessing an uncommon technical equipment . . . [he was] French in clearness of expression, logic, exquisite taste; a master of rhythm, with a clear appreciation of tonal color and the value of simplicity in orchestration." Hale adds further: "He is seldom warm and tender; seldom does he indulge himself in sentiment, passion, imagination. With him unorthodox form must always be kept in mind. . . . His wit and brilliancy are indisputable. He seldom touches the heart or sweeps away the judgment. He was not a great creator, yet his name is ever to be mentioned with respect."

His influence on his contemporaries was far-reaching and permanent. As M. D. Calvocoressi once noted, Saint-Saëns was "a pioneer of progress and a champion of instrumental music at a moment when musical France stood in great need of the influence. . . . He played a great part in the formation and toward the recognition of the modern French school of symphony: for his music, though lacking strength of character and imaginative power, and often even seriousness, set high standards in form, style and workmanship."

Camille Saint-Saëns was born in Paris on October 9, 1835. A musical prodigy, he made his first appearance as pianist when he was five, started composition at six, and at eleven gave a remarkable concert in Paris. After preliminary studies of harmony with Pierre Maleden, he entered the Paris Conservatory where, under Benoist and Halévy, he won prizes in organ playing, and started composition. In 1852, his *Ode à Sainte-Cécile* received first prize in a competition sponsored by the Société Sainte-Cécile; and in 1853, his first symphony was introduced and acclaimed. From 1853 to 1857, he was organist of the Saint-Merry Church in Paris; from 1858 to 1877, he occupied the organ bench at the Madeleine Church. His fame as virtuoso and at improvisations spread throughout Europe. He also achieved recognition as teacher and promoter of new music. From 1861 to 1865, he taught piano at the École Niedermeyer; in 1871, he helped found the Société nationale de musique to sponsor modern French music. Meanwhile, he proved himself remarkably industrious, and remarkably successful, as a composer. His first work for the stage—a comic opera, *La Princesse jaune*—was produced in Paris in 1872; his first tone poem, *Le Rouet d'Omphale,* was heard the same year; his second and third piano concertos were given in Paris and Leipzig respectively between 1868 and 1869; and his first cello concerto was heard in 1873.

In 1875, Saint-Saëns married Marie Truffot. Their union was unhappy; after the death of their two infant sons, they separated for good. After 1877, Saint-Saëns gave up most of his musical posts to concentrate on composition. He remained exceptionally productive up to the end of his life. But some of his finest works came before the end of the nineteenth century. These included his opera, *Samson and Delilah;* his fourth and fifth piano concertos; his third violin concerto; two violin sonatas; and his first string quartet. Regarded by many as the leading composer in France of his day, Saint-Saëns was the recipient of many honors. In 1913, he achieved the highest rank in the Legion of Honor, the Grand Croix; and in 1881, he had been elected to the Institut de France.

In 1906, Saint-Saëns paid his first visit to the United States. He returned to America in 1915 to direct the première of his *Hail California* in San Francisco. In 1916, he made his first tour of South America. In 1920, at the age of eighty-five, he made appearances as conductor and as pianist in a festival of his works in Athens, Greece. His last public appearance took place in Dieppe on August 6, 1921, in a piano recital. He died a few months after that—on December 16, 1921—while on a rest cure in Algiers.

1868. CONCERTO NO. 2 IN G MINOR, for piano and orchestra, op. 22. I. Andante sostenuto. II. Allegretto scherzando. III. Presto.

Saint-Saëns wrote five piano concertos, the first (D major, op. 17) in 1858, the last (F major, op. 103), in 1895. The second came in 1868 when Anton Rubinstein, scheduled to conduct a concert in Paris, invited Saint-Saëns to appear as soloist. For this event Saint-Saëns wrote a new concerto, a chore that took him only seventeen days, and he introduced it in 1868. The work opens with a cadenza for solo piano in a free fantasia structure. Arpeggios and chords precede the entrance of the orchestra, which is first heard in a forceful phrase. Then the piano appears with the expressive first theme. Virtuoso passages ensue, after which the orchestra repeats the first theme to a discreet piano background. A climax comes with a powerful restatement by the orchestra of the short forceful phrase introduced at the beginning of the movement.

The second movement is a Mendelssohn-like Scherzo, its main subject a dance tune in the piano, soon supported by orchestra. A change of key to B-flat major leads to the second subject, a lyrical statement by unison violas, cellos, and bassoons against a rhythmic accompaniment by the piano.

An electrifying finale opens with exciting triplets in the piano, repeated by the orchestra. The first theme is a vigorous dance tune in the style of a saltarello. A brief transition in the piano brings contrast with a lyrical second theme in D minor for the piano. A brief recollection of the first theme precedes the development of both ideas. Trills introduce some new material, a choral episode in woodwind and horns accompanied by strings. Virtuoso passages then lead to the recapitulation and to a dynamic coda.

1870. INTRODUCTION AND RONDO CAPRICCIOSO, for violin and orchestra, op. 28.

Long a favorite in the violinist's repertory, the *Introduction and Rondo Capriccioso* (as the title suggests) is in two distinct sections. The first part is slow and melancholy (Andante malinconico). Here the solo violin offers the plaintive principal subject in the second measure to pizzicato strings. After that comes the Rondo capriccioso (Allegretto ma non troppo). The principal theme of this part is heard at once in the solo violin, followed by a contrasting lyrical idea. These two themes are discussed. Then the orchestra gives a new melody, which the solo violin repeats. The first theme of the Rondo capriccioso section comes in the orchestra at the peak of a climax, the background to which is a series of broken chords in the solo instrument. The coda provides the performer with brilliant virtuoso passages.

1871–1877. TONE POEMS, for orchestra:
Le Rouet d'Omphale (*Omphale's Spinning Wheel*), op. 31.
Phaëton, op. 39.
Danse macabre, op. 40.
La Jeunesse d'Hercule (Hercules's Youth), op. 50.

Inspired by Liszt's example, Saint-Saëns set out to produce several works in the then new format of the tone or symphonic poem. Saint-Saëns's own description of what a tone poem is provides us with a clue to his approach and methods. He called it "an ensemble of different movements, depending on each other, and proceeding from a fundamental idea, these being connected in the form of one piece. The plan of a musical poem thus understood can be varied indefinitely."

Between 1871 and 1877, Saint-Saëns completed four tone poems. The first was *Le Rouet d'Omphale*. Its program is the story of Hercules, serving as a slave to Omphale, the Lydian Queen. She humiliates him by having him perform effeminate duties, including spinning. The composer further explained in his published score: "The subject . . . is feminine seductiveness, the triumphant struggle of weakness against strength. The spinning wheel is only a pretext; it is chosen merely from the viewpoint of rhythm and the general aspect of the piece."

The whirr of the spinning wheel is imitated at the opening by figures in the violin. Hercules's anguish and humiliation are then represented by a solemn subject in the bass. This theme gets a mocking treatment from the oboe as Omphale taunts him. The undulating figures return, as the spinning is resumed; now it is punctuated by chords in the woodwind, then in harp and woodwind. Toward the end of the tone poem, the motion of the spinning wheel gets increasingly slower, then comes to a halt.

Phaëton came two years later. In mythology, Phaëton is the son of Apollo. For a single day, he is allowed by his father to guide the chariot of the sun. Proving himself incompetent, he is hurled from the skies into the river Po by a thunderbolt from Jupiter. To M. Baumann this legend represented to Saint-Saëns "a symbol of revolt and chaos," and exalts "rule and order."

After a short introduction, a brisk figure suggests the gallop of the Steeds of the Day. Horns and cellos sound a note of warning. But the rhythm of the first theme is intensified, then becomes confused, as Phaëton tries to direct his steeds. Now we hear Phaëton's ecstasy in four horns as he proceeds on his flight. His delight turns to anguish when he fails to control his chariot. A subject rises from the basses prognosticating doom. Jupiter's thunderbolt comes in the form of a mighty E-flat chord. In the coda, the melody of Phaëton's ecstasy becomes a lament for cellos and flute.

Danse macabre is the most famous of Saint-Saens's tone poems. It was written in 1874. For his program, the composer went to a grotesque poem by Henri Cazalis whose opening lines read:

Zig and Zig and Zig—hark! Death beats a measure,
Drums on a tomb with heels hard and thin.
Death plays at midnight a dance for his pleasure—
Zig and Zig and Zig—on his old violin.

The harp announces the stroke of midnight. A violin is being tuned; it is Death preparing to summon with his music skeletons from their graves for a ghostly dance. The flute introduces a wild dance tune. Then Death offers grotesque music of his own, the xylophone imitating the rattle of bones. Suddenly, the august strains of the "Dies irae" are sounded. The ghostly dance is over. The oboe imitates the cock's crow announcing dawn. Dance music and the skeletons all fade into the mists.

Saint-Saëns's last tone poem, *La Jeunesse d'Hercule,* was completed in 1877. The score bears the following explanatory program: "The fable relates that Hercules on his entrance upon life saw two roads lying open before him—that of pleasure and that of virtue. Insensible to the seductions of nymphs and bacchantes, the hero chooses the paths of struggle and combats, at the end of which he catches a glimpse of the reward of immortality through the flames of the funeral pyre."

A slow introduction (Andante sostenuto) with its main subject in muted violins accompanied by woodwind, describes the awakening emotional life of young Hercules. A roll of the kettledrums prefaces the main first theme, a flowing melody for strings, with oboe and horn providing a counter subject. With a change of tempo and key, the oboe is accompanied by flutes and clarinets in an eloquent melody; this is the call of passion and grows in emotional turbulence as it is enlarged. A climax is reached with a bacchanal. The hero dismisses the revellers in a bold passage for the brass. The Maestoso section that follows—beginning with a slow descending passage for trombones—suggests the victory of manly will and virtue. A fanfare and harp arpeggios lead to a dramatic ending.

1871. MARCHE HÉROIQUE, for orchestra, op. 34.

This impressive march music was written as a tribute to one of the composer's friends—the painter, Alexandre Regnault, killed in the Franco-Prussian War. It originated as a work for two pianos, but the composer subsequently orchestrated it. The stirring march tune is presented by the woodwind accompanied by pizzicato strings. The middle trio utilizes fragments of this march melody to accompany a lyrical passage in trombones. After a return of the opening march section, the composition ends with a forceful coda.

1873. CONCERTO NO. 1 IN A MINOR, for cello and orchestra, op. 33.

Of Saint-Saëns's many works for the cello, the first concerto is the most distinguished—a work notable for compactness and lucidity of its structure, elegant workmanship, charm of style, and richness of melodic material. It is in a single movement, but with three clearly defined sections. In the first (Allegro non troppo), the solo cello gives the main theme—a vigorous melody accompanied by second violins and violas. This is elaborated upon by woodwinds and strings before the cello is heard in the second theme, an eloquent song accompanied by pianissimo strings. The second section (Animato) appears after a hurried review of the first theme. This new part is spirited, the solo cello entering with a vigorous passage in double stops, followed by an equally strong episode for orchestra. A development of the first theme and a recall of the lyrical second one, both from the preceding section, and both in solo cello—precede the concluding part (Allegro con moto). Here a minuet-like tune is whispered by muted strings. The cello follows with a lilting dance theme. Later on, virtuosity and brilliant dynamics provide fireworks. The return of the first theme carries the concerto to its conclusion.

1875. CONCERTO NO. 4 IN C MINOR, for piano and orchestra, op. 44. I. Allegro moderato; Andante. II. Allegro vivace; Andante; Allegro.

The fourth piano concerto followed the second (see 1868) by seven years. This work is unusual in structure, being made up of two divisions. The first is further split up into two parts, and the second into three. Themes recur throughout the work to provide unification. Charles Malherbe explains: "The themes are distinct, peculiar to each movement, but they intermingle at times in the developments, and the return establishes a sort of natural bond between different portions of the work. Thus the Andante in 4/4 time of the first section is transformed into triple time in the second, and the first Allegro reappears with a different measure in the finale."

Malherbe also provides the following analysis: "The work begins with a sort of free prelude. . . . A theme of eight measures is given out alternately by the orchestra and the piano; it is treated now contrapuntally, now in free preluding style, somewhat after the manner of a cadenza. This species of introduction leads to the main body of the movement. . . . There are soft and mysterious harmonies for orchestra with flowing arpeggios for the piano. The chief theme, a simple melody, is developed at some length and enriched with varied ornamental work."

The second movement begins with a scherzando. "The theme of the prelude to the first movement reappears in a faster tempo. There is a short Andante . . . with reminiscences of the first movement. This leads to the finale. . . . A theme that has the character of a folk song is developed energetically and brilliantly somewhat after the manner of a rondo."

1876. PRELUDE TO LE DÉLUGE, for string orchestra, op. 45.

The Deluge is an oratorio, text by Louis Gallet, introduced in Paris in 1876. Only its orchestral prelude is heard today, having become one of its composer's most popular symphonic compositions. While the oratorio is scored for full orchestra, the prelude requires only strings, and highlights a solo violin.

A passage from *Genesis* is believed to have been the composer's inspiration for this atmospheric music: "And God repented having created the world." After a solemn introduction, the violas offer a theme that soon is treated fugally. This whole section has overtones of mysticism. There now comes the heart of the work—a soulful melody for solo violin, which to Arthur Hervey suggests "humanity in its original state of purity."

1877. SAMSON ET DALILA (SAMSON AND DELILAH), opera in three acts, with text by Ferdinand Lemaire, based on the Bible. First performance: Weimar, Germany, December 2, 1877.

Samson and Delilah had to wait thirteen years after its Weimar première to get heard in its own country.

When the composer first submitted it to the Paris Opéra, the director turned it down. He regarded it too Wagnerian, austere, and gloomy. Other French operatic theaters followed the lead of the Opéra. When one act was heard in a concert version in Paris in 1875, the critics complained of the lack of melody and the ponderousness of style. Then at last, the opera found a champion in Franz Liszt, who mounted it in Weimar in 1877 in a German-language presentation. It made a highly favorable impression. Performances in Brussels and Hamburg followed, once again with an enthusiastic response. Finally, the opera returned to its home base, France—not to Paris, initially, but to Rouen, in 1890. The first presentation in Paris took place on October 30, 1890, still not at the Opéra proper, which did not mount the work until November 23, 1892.

Since 1892, *Samson and Delilah* has become a strong favorite both in and out of France. The American première took place in New Orleans on January 4, 1893, followed by a production at the Metropolitan Opera on February 8, 1895. The American success of this opera, however, began, not with these two presentations, but with a magnificent revival at the Manhattan Opera House on November 13, 1908.

Because of its Biblical text and its impressive choruses, *Samson and Delilah* is sometimes given as an oratorio, without scenery or costumes. Indeed, when *Samson* first came to the Metropolitan Opera, W. J. Henderson inquired if this was not the best way to hear the work. "There is so little action in it that it seems hardly necessary to go to the trouble of dressing and setting scenery. The action is almost wholly confined to the ballet." Nevertheless, when attractively mounted, *Samson and Delilah* makes for effective opera. Its pageantry and ballet sequences have striking visual interest, just as Saint-Saëns's sensual musical style is a feast for the ear.

Outside of dance and spectacle—and some highly appealing choral episodes—the main interest of the opera lies in the characterization of the heroine, and in the music the composer wrote for her. "Delilah engages him [Saint-

Saëns] so strongly," say Wallace Brockway and Herbert Weinstock, "that the other figures, including Samson, are secondary, and it is significant that the erring Hebrew has few solo moments of arresting interest, while two of Delilah's arias—'Printemps qui commence' and 'Amour! Viens aider ma faiblesse'—always stop the show. Even the tremendously famous duet, 'Mon coeur s'ouvre à ta voix,' is arranged to give the impression of being primarily a mezzo-soprano solo with tenor chiming in."

The opera opens upon a public square in Gaza, Palestine, in Biblical times. Hebrews are lamenting their bondage to the Philistines. When Samson upbraids his people for complaining to God rather than praising Him ("Arrêtez, o mes frères"), he is taunted by Abimelech. In a fury, Samson kills him. The Philistine High Priest calls on his people to avenge this murder ("Maudite à jamais soit la race"). At the same time, Samson rallies the Hebrews to attack the enemy. The Philistines dispersed, the Hebrews sing a mighty hymn to victory in "Hymne de joie." Suddenly, Delilah emerges from the temple followed by her maidens. They are bringing garlands to the victors, singing "Voici le printemps" as they come. Then Delilah contributes a joyful song of her own, in praise of Spring ("Printemps qui commence"). When Samson realizes how powerfully attracted he is to Delilah, he begs God for strength to resist her.

In the second act, outside her house, Delilah calls upon the powers of love to help her overcome Samson ("Amour! Viens aider ma faiblesse"). She is spurred on by the High Priest, who wants her to uncover the source of Samson's physical powers. After Samson appears, Delilah lavishes her love on him in the famous duet, "Mon coeur s'ouvre à ta voix." Though aware she is a temptress, Samson finally reveals that his strength comes from his shock of hair. Seductively, Delilah lures him into the house, where she manages to cut his hair off. The Philistine soldiers enter and seize him.

In the first scene of act three, Samson is a prisoner of the Philistines at the mill of Gaza. He is in chains; his captors have plucked out his eyes. In anguish Samson calls to God for help ("Vois ma misère, hélas!"). His torment is compounded when from the distance he hears the Hebrews denouncing him for having betrayed them ("Samson, qu'as tu fait?").

The scene shifts to the Temple of Dagon, where the Philistines are celebrating their victory. A spectacular bacchanal takes place. Now a child leads Samson into the Temple, where he is mocked by Delilah and other Philistines. Tied to two huge pillars supporting the temple, Samson prays for a momentary return of his former strength ("Souviens-toi de ton serviteur"). His prayers are answered. Samson brings down the huge pillars. The temple crashes in ruins, bringing death to Samson, Delilah, and the Philistines.

1879. SUITE ALGÉRIENNE (ALGERIAN SUITE), for orchestra, op. 60: I. Prélude. II. Rhapsodie mauresque. III. Rêverie du soir. IV. Marche militaire française.

An inveterate traveler and an admirer of Morocco, Saint-Saëns here offers three travel pictures of Algeria. They are preceded by a Prelude, in which the composer describes his reactions upon catching his first glimpse of land from aboard ship. Brief thematic fragments suggest some of the sights he sees, while a swelling figure represents the gentle swaying of the boat. The "Moorish Rhapsody" is in three parts. The first and last are brilliant in orchestration and harmony; the middle is an atmospheric Oriental song. "An Evening Dream" is a poetic nocturne inspired by the famous majestic Algerian fortress at Blidah. The suite ends with the "French Military March," believed to be an expression of the composer's joy and sense of security in coming upon a French garrison. This last movement is sometimes played independent of the other movements.

1880. CONCERTO NO. 3 IN B MINOR, for violin and orchestra, op. 61. I. Allegro non troppo. II. Andantino quasi allegretto. III. Molto moderato e maestoso; Allegro non troppo.

Saint-Saëns wrote three violin concertos, the third of which is the one played most often today. It was written for and introduced by the distinguished Spanish virtuoso, Pablo de Sarasate.

Without introduction, the solo instrument is heard in a passionate subject over strings and kettledrums; this is the movement's first main theme. After some passage work, the solo violin is heard in the lyric second subject in the changed key of E major. In the development, prominent treatment is given to the first theme, mainly by the orchestra with the violin providing embellishments. The original key of B minor returns for the brief recapitulation, in which the second subject is discussed. This is followed by an extended coda devoted to the first theme.

After three introductory measures in the orchestra, the solo violin engages a song in the rhythm of a siciliano over a string accompaniment. Other instruments repeat the closing phrase of this melody twice. Then a contrasting virile melody, in F major, is given by the solo violin.

The finale opens with a narrative for solo violin, as the orchestra interjects exclamations. After a brief pause, the main part of the movement begins with a brilliant idea for the violin, accompanied by strings and woodwind. Transitional material then brings on the solo violin in the second theme. This is a sensual melody with wind accompaniment, which is elaborated powerfully. Then a new thought is introduced in the form of a chorale melody for muted strings, to which woodwind and solo violin give response. In the recapitulation, the second theme is brought back, but in the key of C major; and the coda makes effective use of the chorale tune in trombones and trumpets.

1881. SEPTET, for string quartet, bass, trumpet, and piano, op. 65. I. Préambule. II. Menuet. III. Intermède. IV. Gavotte et Finale.

The reason why Saint-Saëns wrote a septet for an unusual combination of instruments, with emphasis on the trumpet, is that he wrote it for a society known as *La Trompette,* which gave its' première performance. This Septet, one of its composer's finest chamber-music compositions, is in the form of a suite. The vigorous theme of the opening movement (Moderato) recurs throughout the rest of the work and serves as a catalyzing agent. Because of the prominent use of the trumpet, most of the music has a military character, a fact that is emphasized through the quotation of a French army regimental call. Virility and occasionally a touch of jocosity are even found in the second-movement Minuet (Allegro moderato) and the fourth-movement Gavotte that precedes the Finale (Allegro non troppo). But the third movement (Andante) is by contrast atmospheric.

1883. BALLET MUSIC FROM HENRY VIII, for orchestra.

Henry VIII was Saint-Saëns's fifth opera, text by Léonce Détroyat and Armand Silvestre; it was seen for the first time at the Paris Opéra on March 5, 1883. The opera itself is a stranger today; but the ballet music from the second act has become a staple in the literature of light classics. In that second act, the king at Richmond has arranged a gala evening to honor the Papal Legate. A series of stunning dances is part of the entertainment. The composer derived some of his material from a collection of Scottish and Irish tunes. However, in "The Entry of the Clans," Saint-Saëns makes use of an English folk song, "The Miller of the Dee," through a mistaken notion that the river in that song is Scottish rather than English (there being a Dee River in both places). The "Scotch Idyll" that follows, however, is unmistakably Scottish with its jaunty rhythmic little tune in the oboe. This is followed by a "Gypsy Dance" presenting two dance melodies, the first in English horn and the second in violins. The last of the dances is a robust "Gigue."

1886. SYMPHONY NO. 3 IN C MINOR, op. 78. I. Adagio; Allegro moderato; Poco adagio. II. Allegro moderato; Presto; Maestoso; Allegro.

In 1886, the Royal Philharmonic of London commissioned Saint-Saëns to write a symphony for its seventy-third season. The composer had already produced two such works: the first in E-flat major, op. 2 in 1855, and the second in A minor, op. 55 in 1878. He now went on to produce his most celebrated work in that form, and his last. He dedicated it to the memory of Liszt.

The composer prepared his own analysis for the world première, which took place on May 19, 1886.

"The symphony, divided into two parts, nevertheless includes practically the traditional four movements: the first serves as an introduction to the Adagio; and the Scherzo is connected after the same manner with the finale. The composer has thus sought to shun in a certain measure the interminable repetitions which are more and more disappearing from instrumental music.

"After an introduction Adagio of a few plaintive measures, the string quartet exposes the initial theme, which is somber and agitated. The first transformation of this theme leads to a second motive, which is distinguished by greater tranquillity; after a short development, in which the two themes are presented simultaneously, the motive appears in a characteristic form, for full orchestra, but only for a short time. A second transformation of the initial theme includes now and then the plaintive notes of the introduction. Varied episodes bring calm gradually, and thus prepare the Adagio in D-flat. The extremely peaceful and contemplative theme is given to the violins, violas, and cellos, which are supported by organ chords. After a variation (in arabesques) performed by the violins, the second transformation of the initial theme of the Allegro appears again, and brings with it a vague feeling of unrest, which is enlarged by dissonant harmonies. These soon give way to the theme of the Adagio. The first movement ends in a coda of mystical character, in which are heard alternately the chords of D-flat major and E minor.

"The second movement begins with an energetic phrase which is followed immediately by a third transformation of the initial theme in the first movement, more agitated than it was before, and into which enters the fantastic spirit that is frankly disclosed in the Presto. Here arpeggios and scales, swift as lightning, on the piano, are accompanied by the syncopated rhythm of the orchestra, and each time they are in a different tonality (F, E, E-flat, G). The repetition of the Allegro moderato is followed by a second Presto, which at first is apparently a repetition of the first Presto; but scarcely has it begun before a new theme is heard, grave, austere (trombone, tuba, double basses), strongly contrasted with the fantastic music. There is a struggle for mastery, and this struggle ends in the defeat of the restless, diabolical element. The new phrase rises to orchestral heights and rests there as in the blue of a clear sky. After a vague reminiscence of the initial theme of the first movement, a Maestoso in C major announces the approaching triumph of the calm and lofty thought. The initial theme of the first movement, wholly transformed, is now exposed by divided strings with the piano (four hands), and repeated by the organ with the full strength of the orchestra. A brilliant coda, in which the initial theme by a last transformation takes the form of a violin figure, ends the work."

1886. LE CARNAVAL DES ANIMAUX (THE CARNIVAL OF ANIMALS), for two pianos and orchestra. I. L'Introduction et marche royale du lion. II. Poules et coqs. III. Hémiones. IV. Tortues. V. L'Eléphant. VI. Kangourous. VII. Aquarium. VIII. Personnages a longues oreilles. IX. Volière. X. Le Coucou au fond des bois. XI. Pianistes. XII. Fossiles. XIII. Le Cygne. XIV. Finale.

We find Saint-Saëns in one of his gay moods in this delightful suite. At certain moments he is satirical, as when he places pianists in the category of animals; at points he is amusing, as when he makes sly quotations from the works of other composers; in some pages he is droll, as in his amusing characterizations of some of the animals. The composer himself regarded all this as a minor, playful indiscretion. He wrote it solely for his own amusement. Except for a single private performance for his friends, he did not allow it to be performed, or published, in his lifetime. Today the work is sometimes heard with the addition of brilliant verses by Ogden Nash.

In the opening "Introduction and Royal March of the Lion," rumblings in the piano and a royal fanfare set the stage for the arrival of the lion, whose roar can clearly be heard in the orchestra. In the second section, which devotes itself to hens and cocks, the former are portrayed with cackles in piano and strings, the latter by a figure in the clarinet. The two pianos, accompanied, now bring us the picture of mules, though the composer's purpose here is not so much to describe these four-legged animals as to satirize pianists who insist on playing music in strict time and with unchanging dynamics. In the fourth section about tortoises the composer introduces two brief quotations from Offenbach's *Orpheus in the Underworld*. Paradox and incongruity are the spice of the section about elephants, since a heavy-footed melody, representing that cumbersome animal, is contrasted with a graceful waltz tune; an added dash of satire is injected with a brief quotation of Berlioz's "Waltz of the Sylphs." Kangaroos, described in halting rhythms, offer a mocking commentary on audiences who talk through a concert performance. Sensitive lyricism replaces burlesque and satire in the "Aquarium," where a haunting melody for flute and violins flows over piano arpeggios. A tune with leaping rhythms now portrays the donkey in "Personages with Long Ears." Passages for flute, and tremolos, bring us a picture of birds in flight in "Aviary," while a graceful subject for the clarinets depicts the "Cuckoo in the Woods." At this point, the composer goes on to characterize pianists as animals by sounding keyboard scale passages. In "Fossils," the composer pokes fun at some of his fellow composers by quoting from Rossini's *The Barber of Seville,* and from two French folk songs, as well as from his own *Danse macabre*. Now all wit and malice are brushed aside to make way for a serene song for the cello, whose grace and beauty describe the gentle movement of a swan in peaceful waters. "The Swan" has become so famous that it is often played apart from the rest of the suite; Anna Pavlova's dance interpretation of this music was one of the most famous numbers in her repertory. The finale recalls all the characters in a kind of curtain call.

1887. HAVANAISE, for violin and orchestra, op. 83.

A Havanaise—or Habanera, as it is known in Spanish—is a slow and stately dance in 2/4 time, believed to have originated in Cuba. Saint-Saëns's popular composition for violin, offers the Habanera rhythm in the orchestra over which the solo violin sings a romantic Spanish melody.

GABRIEL FAURÉ 1845–1924

Fauré's music, like his life, passes from the nineteenth to the twentieth century, from Romanticism to modernism. Though he opened new sluices in his art towards the end of his life and produced then, some of his most remarkable works, it is the works of the nineteenth century that most often represent him on the concert programs of our time. Here Fauré created music of a rare serenity, objectivity and contemplation. This is music characterized by beautiful balances and symmetry. Where other Romantics were ready to shout and declaim, Fauré was willing to whisper the most tender confidences and uncover the most sensitive moods. Aaron Copland described Fauré's most characteristic works as "delicate, reserved and aristocratic," possessing "all the earmarks of the French temperament: harmonic sensibility, impeccable taste, classic restraint, and a love of clear lines and well-made proportions." Julien Tierost put it well when he found that in Fauré "the spirit of Hellenism" was reborn.

Gabriel Fauré was born in Pamiers, Ariège, France, on May 12, 1845. From 1855 to 1865, he attended the École Niedermeyer, where he was strongly influenced by Saint-Saëns. While still a student, Fauré published *Trois Romances sans paroles,* for piano, in 1863. After leaving the École, Fauré served for four years as organist of the Saint-Sauveur Church in Rennes. In 1870, he became organist of Notre Dame de Cliqancourt in Paris. With the outbreak of the Franco-Prussian War, he deserted music to join the French infantry. After the establishment of the Third Republic, he assumed the office of organist at Saint-Honoré d'Eylau in Paris. Soon after this, he became assistant organist at the Madeleine Church, where for a number of years he also served as chorusmaster. In 1872, he joined the faculty of the École Niedermeyer; and in 1883, he married Marie Fremiet.

His first significant work was the Violin Sonata, op. 13, introduced at the Paris Exhibition in 1878. This was followed by a symphony (first heard at a Colonne concert on March 15, 1885), and the Requiem (introduced at the Madeleine in 1888). In 1892, Fauré was appointed Inspector of music in Paris. One year after, that he was made first organist of the Madeleine and professor of composition at the Conservatory, where, in 1905, he assumed the post of director. Increasing deafness, which for a long time he tried to conceal from even his closest friends, finally compelled him to give up his Conservatory office in 1920. He spent the last four years of his life in retirement. Nevertheless, he continued to produce significant music. He died in Paris on November 4, 1924.

1865–1897. SONGS, for voice and piano:

"Après un rêve," op. 7, no. 1; "Aurore," op. 39, no. 1; "Les Berceaux," op. 23, no. 1; "Clair de lune," op. 46, no. 2; "En Prière," (no opus number); "En Sourdine," op. 58, no. 2; "Lydia," op. 4, no. 2; "Nell," op. 18, no. 1; "Noël," op. 43, no. 1; "Le Parfum impérissable," op. 76, no. 1; "Poème d'un jour," op. 21; "Les Roses d'Ispahan," op. 39, no. 4; "Le Secret," op. 23, no. 3.

La Bonne chanson, song cycle, op. 61: 1. Une Sainte en son auréole; 2. Puisque l'aube grandit; 3. La Lune blanche luit dans les bois; 4. J'allais par des chemins perfides; 5. J'ai presque peur; 6. Avant que tu ne t'en ailles; 7. Donc ce sera par un clair jour d'été; 8. N'est-ce pas?; 9. L'hiver a cessé.

Fauré was one of the most significant song composers in France in the second half of the nineteenth century and his songs represent one of the most important facets of his art. He was not an exceptional melodist, but he did have a most remarkable gift to project the most subtle moods and nuances in the long flowing line of the voice and the inner voices of his piano accompaniment. He placed so much importance on the piano that, as Eric Blom said, he "did not invent a tune and then suitably harmonize it; he seems to have devised a harmonic scheme and then adjusted melodically to it." One program annotator, unidentified, described Fauré's best songs as "essentially undramatic," then went on to say, "sobriety and equilibrium of poetic and musical elements characterize all of Fauré's Lied compositions."

Two of Fauré's earliest songs—"Lydia" and "Après un rêve" (c. 1865)—are still among his most popular vocal numbers. Eric Blom notes a charming excursion into punning in "Lydia" through harmonic means: by transforming the F major tonality to the Lydian mode through the introduction of B-natural. "Après un rêve" is probably Fauré's most famous song. This is a melody of extraordinary sensitivity and grace, which has enjoyed numerous and varied transcriptions.

E. Burlingame Hill found that songs like "Nell," have the "atmosphere of the salon which presupposes cultivation and receptibility to mood." He singles out "Le Secret" for its "intimate sentiment"; "En Prière," for its delicate mysticism; "Clair de lune" for its "adroit suggestions of Verlaine's Watteauesque text"; and "Les Roses d'Ispahan" for its "impassioned exoticism."

The song cyle, *La Bonne Chanson* (1891–1892) finds its composer at the height of his powers within the song form. This cycle (text by Paul Verlaine) was described as follows by an unidentified annotator: "The first song presents the motive of love. The second song begins very fluently, but gradually calms down as the climax of sentiment is reached. . . . The third song is built . . . on a barcarolle-like motion. The fourth song, beginning in the minor mode, leads to a happy climax in which the love-motive returns, greatly intensified. The fifth song, one of the most beautiful in the series, opens in breathless excitement, after which the climax emerges in a beautiful contrast. The sixth song introduces the nature motive. . . . At the end, complete happiness is expressed in a new motive which immediately is developed in the seventh song, of summer and love. . . . In the sublime eighth song, the spirit of unproblematic deep happiness is maintained in the steady walk of the initial rhythm. The final song is built on the nature-motive, exuberant this time, and ends with the recall of the love-motive."

1876. SONATA NO. 1 IN A MAJOR, for violin and piano, op. 13. I. Allegro molto. II. Andante. III. Allegro vivace. IV. Allegro quasi presto.

Fauré wrote two violin sonatas; the earlier one, in A major, is the more familiar. Florent Schmitt said of this music that it appears "by its beauty and originality, on the one hand, to continue a line of development which seemed to have ended with Schumann and Chopin, and, on the other hand, to foreshadow Franck's work of ten years later; and it marks a red-letter day in the history of chamber music." There is such an intimate relationship between this sonata and the one written by Franck a decade later that Charles Koechlin was led to make the comment that here we must "render unto Gabriel and not unto César that which is Gabriel's."

The sonata opens with a passionate theme for the piano, which is assumed and completed by the violin. The second theme has a more reflective character. This sobriety prevails through the second movement, particularly in a melody of classic design assigned exclusively to the violin. The Scherzo is, for the most part, whimsical; but the middle trio is lyrical and expressive. The finale has agitation and drama, with temporary relief introduced through a song for the violin, described by Schmitt as "Schumannesque.

1881. BALLADE IN F-SHARP MINOR, for piano and orchestra, op. 19.

Fauré's most distinguished work for a solo instrument and orchestra was originally conceived as a piano solo, and only later adapted for piano and orchestra. This is Alfred Cortot's description of the Ballade: "The work is calm and controlled in an atmosphere of quite happiness which emphasizes an instrumental technique, deliberately light and pellucid. . . The grace of the orchestral version, where the added instruments assume part of the original harmonic framework, seems to me greater than that for the piano. The variety of timbres accentuates, yet without allowing it to predominate, the play of translucent, quick-silver virtuosity, the swirl of arpeggios, the rushing flight of scales, the mad ripple of trills, and from this point of view holds several attractive modifications."

1885–1896. COMPOSITIONS FOR SOLO PIANO:

Barcarolle No. 2 in G, op. 41; Barcarolle No. 5 in F-sharp minor, op. 66; Impromptu No. 2 in F minor, op. 31; Nocturne No. 7, in C-sharp minor, op. 74.

Fauré's extensive literature for solo piano embraces impromptus, nocturnes, barcarolles, caprices, preludes, valse-caprices, and variations. Ernest Hutcheson has said that in writing for the piano, Fauré's particular talent lay in the way he enriched "his smooth phrases by some unexpected turn of line or harmony that at a stroke conferred distinction on them." At the same time Fauré made a most effective use of a "subtly evanescent harmony" of appeggios and broken chords; his piano music abounds with "lyrical invention and refinement of taste."

Fauré produced his first nocturne (op. 33), first impromptu (op. 25) and first barcarolle (op. 26), all in 1883. In the first three nocturnes, the influence of Chopin can readily be detected. But with the beautiful Nocturne in C-sharp minor (1898), Fauré's personality emerges through music suffused with sudued melancholy. Henceforth, Fauré would bring to his Nocturnes gloomy, tragic accents, where Chopin's had been poetic and sentimental.

In his barcarolles and impromptus, Fauré's writing combines "sheer lyricism" with "winged fantasy," in André Coeuroy's description. One of Fauré's most notable barcarolles, that in F-sharp minor (1895), brings us the picture of "the sea, on the one hand, and the free passion of Anthony and Cleopatra, on the other." The Impromptu No. 2 in F minor (1883) is distinguished for its extraordinary richness of harmonic colors, the brilliance of its pianism, and the sensitivity of its lyricism.

1886. PIANO QUARTET IN G MINOR, op. 45. I. Allegro molto moderato. II. Allegro molto. III. Adagio non troppo. IV. Allegro molto.

This is Fauré's most significant chamber-music work for piano and strings. To Florent Schmitt, the opening theme of the first movement—a passionate subject for unison strings—would alone "have assured immortality for its composer." The contrasting second theme is affectingly tender. The Scherzo movement is unusual in that it dispenses with a middle trio. Its main theme has the character of a moto perpetuo. The slow movement is in the rhythm of a barcarolle. The viola offers the main theme after a brief piano introduction. Later on in this movement the strings serve to reintroduce the barcarolle melody. The tempestuous finale has for its second theme a subject that Schmitt described as "a long phrase which . . . implores and shrieks like a chorus of lost souls."

1887. MESSE DE REQUIEM, for solo voices, chorus, and orchestra, op. 48.

The death of Fauré's father in 1885 led him to write a requiem to his memory. By the time the work was introduced (in 1888), it also served as a memorial to Fauré's mother.

This Requiem differs from others in being intimate in tone, comparatively slight of structure, and reserved in style. It does not speak of the torment of death but of the tranquillity and serenity death brings. It also maintains deep religious conviction throughout. "No exterior effect," said Nadia Boulanger, "alters its sober and rather severe expression of grief, its spotless faith, its gentle confidence, its tender and tranquil expectancy. . . . With an alternation, a passing note, some special inflection of which he has the secret, Gabriel Fauré gives a new and inimitable character to what he touches. The end, with its linked chords descending in double measures, strangely recalls an adorable Agnus Dei in G major by Claudio Monteverdi."

There are seven sections. The first, "Introit and Kyrie" sounds a prayer for eternal rest and mercy. The "Offertory" is a plea for the delivery of the souls of the dead from hell's tortures. In the "Sanctus," the Lord of Hosts is glorified. An entreaty to Jesus for the granting of eternal rest is again sounded both in "Pie Jesu" and in the "Agnus Dei." "Libera Me" voices the hope of deliverance from "eternal death in that terrible day when the heavens and earth shall be moved." The Requiem ends with the "In Paradisum" section, where the angels and the martyrs receive the dead souls into paradise and lead them into the holy city of Jerusalem, bringing them "eternal rest with Lazarus who once was poor."

1887. PAVANE, for orchestra, op. 50.

Fauré's resurrection of the Baroque form of the Pavane—the slow and stately dance in 4/4 time and usually in three sections—has classic serenity. Its main melody is first assigned to the flute over an insistent rhythm; then it is shared by the other woodwind; finally, it unfolds entirely in the woodwind and violins, while other strings provide a pizzicato accompaniment.

1892. PELLÉAS ET MÉLISANDE, suite for orchestra, op. 80. I. Prelude. II. Les Fileuses. III. Siciliana. IV. La Morte de Mélisande.

There is more than one musical setting of Maeterlinck's Impressionist play. The most celebrated, of course, is the opera of Debussy; but Arnold Schoenberg and Jan Sibelius were two twentieth-century composers to write orchestral subjects on the same subject. One of the earliest musical settings of the Maeterlinck play came from Fauré in the form of incidental music for a production given in England in 1898, starring Mrs. Patrick Campbell.

Fauré's now celebrated orchestral suite drew four basic sections from this incidental music score. The Prelude (Quaso adagio) is an atmospheric tone poem, setting the mood. The two main themes—one in the strings, the other in cello, flute, and bassoons—are both sedate and melancholy. "The Spinners" (Andantino quasi allegretto) is a description of Mélisande at the spinning wheel. Violins and violas suggest the whirring motions of the wheel in triplets, providing a background for a sensitive melody in the woodwind. A stately Siciliana originated as a Sicilienne for cello and piano (op. 78) which

Fauré adapted for the purposes of this play. The suite ends with the death of Mélisande (Molto adagio), the background music for the tragic last scene. The opening is a tender elegy for the wind instruments; the music soon erupts into a passionate outburst of grief.

GUSTAV MAHLER 1860–1911

Mahler's greatest works came in the twentieth century—the last five symphonies, the *Kindertotenlieder,* and *Das Lied von der Erde*. Nevertheless, by 1900, he had become one of the leading, and one of the last, exponents of the German post-Romantic movement. In his first three symphonies (as in his later ones), he was a builder of monumental structures on Wagnerian foundations. Like Wagner, Mahler needed immense musical forces to project his ideas, and sought to make tones convey concepts belonging more rightfully to philosophy, metaphysics, or poetry. In those early symphonies, an attempt is already made by the composer "to make the work cover the whole life," as Ernest Newman said. Here, as later, we confront the same "alternations or fusions of the ecstatic, the tragic, the gay, the naïve, the complex, the philosophic, the ironic, sardonic, frequently achieved by the same technical procedures—the piling of tension on tension, for example, followed by a sudden relaxation and then a recommencement of the process of strain and release." The diversity of style and mood characterizing and individualizing his later symphonies can also be found in the earlier ones. "Here," continues Mr. Newman, "he could veer in a moment from the simplest joys of childhood to the martyr's ecstasy in his sufferings and back again. . . . He can plunge without explanation and without a bar's break, as he does in the third symphony, from a setting of Nietzsche at his most sibylline to a setting of German folk poetry at its most naïve."

Though often dramatic, personal, introspective, and symbolic Mahler was also at times an echo of Schubert. For like Schubert, Mahler was first and foremost a creator of melodies, a symphonist who begins and ends with songs, whether vocal or instrumental.

There are those who regard him as prolix, bombastic, pretentious. There are others who looked upon him as a prophet and a seer. Today, we know that the truth lies somewhere midway between such two extremes. At times, Mahler could be naïve, hysterical, even vulgar; and most of the time, he was diffuse and garrulous. It is possible that too often he tried to make music say more than it can. Yet when the spirit moved him, he achieved a spirituality, a poetic exaltation, an emotional intensity rarely encountered elsewhere, and which endow the post-Brahms symphony with new meaning as well as new dimension.

Gustav Mahler was born in the Bohemian town of Kalischt on July 7, 1860. When he was fifteen, he entered the Vienna Conservatory, where he studied the piano with Julius Epstein, harmony with Robert Fuchs, and composition with Theodor Krenn. He also took courses in history and philosophy at the University of Vienna. His formal academic and musical studies ended, Mahler embarked upon a career as conductor in small opera houses in Ljubljana, Olmuetz, and Cassel. In 1885, he received his first important appointment, at the Prague Opera. In 1888, he was made musical director of the Budapest Opera; and in 1897, he was called to fill a similar post with the Vienna Royal Opera. First in Budapest, then in Vienna, he created a new epoch in opera performances, which placed him with the foremost conductors of all time.

He combined his exacting duties as conductor with composition. His first large work was *Das klagende Lied,* text by the composer based on the Grimm brothers. He wrote this work for solo voices, chorus, and orchestra in 1880. During the next three years, he completed two more song cycles, the more significant of which was the *Lieder eines fahrenden Gesellen* in 1883. His first symphony followed in 1888, a fiasco when introduced. The hostility of the public and critics kept mounting with the premières of his second and third symphonies. But Mahler remained unbowed. "My time will come," he said simply. And while waiting for recognition, he continued producing monumental symphonies in the early 1900's.

In 1907, Mahler left the Vienna Royal Opera for good. He came for the first time to the United States to become conductor of German operas at the Metropolitan Opera in New York, making his bow with *Tristan and Isolde* on January 1, 1908. In the fall of 1908, he combined his activity at the Metropolitan Opera with the office of principal conductor of the New York Philharmonic Orchestra. All this while, he was working on his most gargantuan symphonic concepts: the Eighth Symphony, the so-called "Symphony of a Thousand Voices," introduced in 1910; the Ninth Symphony and *Das Lied von der Erde,* both of which were introduced posthumously under Bruno Walter's direction.

Mahler's health broke down in the United States in 1911. He was brought back to Paris for serum treatment, then transferred to Vienna, where he died on May 18, 1911.

1883. LIEDER EINES FAHRENDEN GESELLEN (SONGS OF A WAYFARER), four songs for voice and orchestra: I. Wenn mein Schatz Hochzeit macht. II. Ging heut Morgen uebers Feld. III. Ich hatt' ein gluehend Messer. IV. Die zwei blauen Augen.

As a young man of twenty-four, serving as assistant conductor at the Cassel Opera, Mahler fell in love with a singer who rejected him. As an outlet for his emotional disturbance, he wrote four poems about love's sorrow and the consolation that can be found in Nature; he then set them for voice and orchestra. The first poem speaks of his sorrow on the day that his beloved became somebody else's bride ("When My Love Is a Bride"). A note of optimism creeps into the second song, as a friend points out to him the beauty of Nature in "As I Walked Abroad This Morn." But the appeasement of pain is ephemeral. In the third song, he describes how never again can he find peace or rest, that a cruel sword is planted in his aching heart ("Deep in My Aching Heart"). In the last song, he recalls the beauty of his beloved's eyes ("My Love's Blue Eyes") and is convinced that having once looked into them, he must grieve for evermore.

1888. SYMPHONY NO. 1 IN D MAJOR. I. Langsam, schleppend wie ein Naturlaust (Adagio comodo). II. Kraeftig bewegt, doch nicht zu schnell (Con moto). III. Feierlich und gemessen, ohne zu schleppen (Moderato). IV. Stuermisch bewegt (Tempestoso).

Though throughout his life Mahler expressed his aversion to programmatic interpretations of his symphonies, and disavowed all poetic or literary explanations of his music, he endowed the first symphony with highly descriptive titles and subtitles, and all kinds of programmatic allusions pointing up his aims in writing this work. When the symphony was heard for the first time, in 1889, Mahler described it as a "symphonic poem in two parts." But in subsequent performances he went one step further by giving the entire work the title of *The Titan* (after a novel by Jean Paul Richter), and endowed specific and detailed indications as to the content of each of the four movements. He now divided the work into two parts, each with its own subtitle. The first he called "Days of Youth, Flowers and Thorns." His program continued as follows. For the first movement: "Spring without end. The introduction represents the awakening of Nature at early dawn." A second movement (permanently deleted from the symphony after its performance in Weimar in 1894) was described as "A Chapter of Flowers," while the ensuing Scherzo had the heading of "Full Sail!" The second part of the symphony —the last two movements—was designated as the "Human Comedy." This part opens with a "Funeral March à la Callot" further described as "Stranded." The funeral march is succeeded by the finale, "From Inferno to Paradise."

This is the way Paul Stefan described the high points of the symphony:

"How beautiful the introduction is, suggesting the melancholy of the Moravian plains over a long-sustained A, down to which the minor theme in oboe and bassoon sinks dreamily! Thereupon the upstriving fanfare of the clarinets; the fourth becomes a cuckoo-call in the woodwind, a lovely song in the horns; then, still over the pedal A, a gradual rolling movement, first in the divided cellos and basses, like the reawakening of the earth after a clear summer's night. The tempo quickens, the cuckoo's call becomes the first notes of the *Lied eines fahrenden Gesellen* (a quotation from Mahler's song cycle), 'Ging heut, morgen uebers Feld." The whole melody, here, in symphonic breadth, is sung softly by the strings, turns into the dominant, mounts in speed and strength, sinks back pianissimo and is repeated. . . . A kind of development section follows, but it really rather confirms the theme. The leap of the fourth now becomes a fifth, developed melodically through major and minor; the 'awakening' is repeated, the harp taking the tune; once again D major over the pedal A. A new tune in the horns; modulation, livelier play of the motives, with many an unrelated succession of ideas. Suddenly in the woodwind, a theme of the last movement, immediately followed by a Brucknerish climax, on whose summit is heard the introductory fanfare, then abruptly the horn theme and the fourths of the commencement. Then comes a kind of reprise.. . . The *Lied eines fahrenden Gesellen* fixes the entire character; no secondary theme, scarcely a development. . . .

"There follows a merry dancing Scherzo, an Austrian Laendler, exquisitely harmonized and scored. A horn leads into the olden time Trio. . . . After a long pause begins the third part with the rugged canon, 'Frère Jacques.' Muted drums beat out the 'fourth'; it sounds like the rhythm of a grotesque funeral à la Callot. A muted double bass begins, a bassoon and cello follow, then bass tuba and a deep clarinet. An oboe bleats and squeaks thereto in the upper register. Four flutes with the canon drag the orchestra along with them; the shrill E-flat clarinet quacks. Over a quiet counterpoint in the trumpets, the oboes are tootling a vulgar street song. . . . But the barrel-organ canon . . . starts again, dies away finally and leads directly into the last movement.

"Raging, a chromatic triplet rushes downward, a theme from the development of the first movement announces itself, everything ferments and fumes, clinging fast to the key of F minor. Over a pedal on D-flat, the cello movement and the 'fourth' motive from the first part now sound triumphantly in D major. This relationship and similarity of the themes in different movements is still more emphatically developed by Mahler than by his predecessors. An even louder climax, where seven horns must be heard above everything, even the trumpets. They sound like a chorale from paradise after the waves of hell. Saved!"

1894. SYMPHONY NO. 2 IN C MINOR, "RESURRECTION," for soprano, alto, mixed chorus, and orchestra. I. Allegro maestoso. II. Andante moderato. III. In ruhig fliessender Bewegung. IV. Urlicht: sehr feierlich aber schlicht; Choralmaessig. V. Finale: Aufersteh'n.

There is a poetical affinity between the first and second symphonies as Mahler himself explained. "I have called the first movement, 'Celebration of the Dead'; and if you wish to know, it is the Hero of my first symphony whom I bear to the grave. Immediately arise the great questions: Why have you lived? Why have you suffered? Has it all been only a huge, frightful joke? We must all somehow answer these questions, if we are to continue living, yes, even if we are only to continue dying. Whoever hears this call must give a reply. And this reply I give in my last movement."

The Second Symphony has been described as "a tonal allegory of the life of man." It opens with his death, continues in the second and third movements in a more reflective vein with occasional reminders of life's vulgarities, and concludes with a picture of Judgment Day. "In the first three movements," said Bruno Walter, [we find] a substratum of moods without any continuity of thought. . . .Moods, emotions and thoughts are here dissolved within the music." Bruno Walter then goes on to explain that the second movement has a gay character, with Mahler himself describing this music as a "friendly episode in the life of the hero." Walter sees the third movement as being in a "sinister frame of mind—as if the chaos of life suddenly appeared unreal and ghostlike." The fourth movement calls for a contralto who sings verses from *Des Knaben Wunderhorn,* beginning with the lines: "Thou red, rose! Ah, man lies in bitter throes." Here, says Walter, man "sings of his trust that the dear Lord may vouchsafe him a little light to show the way into the life beyond." In the finale—scored for soprano, alto, chorus, orchestra with organ—Mahler drew his inspiration from Klopstock's poem, *The Resurrection.* In this movement, to which Mahler gave the name of "The Great Summons," he "replies for the first time to the sorrows, the doubts, and the questions of his soul," as Walter explains.

The first movement, the description of a hero's death, begins with "an extended funeral march," Paul Stefan has explained, "[rising] sharp and trenchant from the restless, declamatory basses." A "consuming lament" follows. "Then suddenly the change from minor to major, so characteristic of Mahler, in horns and strings; very softly, a first promise of consolation. But quick as lightning the convulsion of the beginning returns. . . .A lighter secondary section; modulation; the basses burst through the march rhythm. Development. In the funeral march, a chorale is heard, which sweeps forward from gloomy resolution to joyous promise, and is repeated in the last movement. . . . Harps and basses introduce the coda, which slowly advances, but only to speak an epilogue. . . . The chord of C major immediately goes over to C minor. A swift descending run, and the colossal movement ends."

The second movement is an Intermezzo in A-flat. "The strings begin a dance tune. A horn leads to the key of B, changing E-flat enharmonically to D-sharp. Lively, youthful gay triplets over an unmoving bass. Once more the dance tune, with a counterpoint in the cellos. After a subdued variation fo the mobile theme, the dance melody creeps back for the third time, this time pizzicato in the strings, and lengthened by interpolated imitative measures."

The next movement, in C minor, is in the form of a Scherzo. It is, Paul Stefan explains, "St. Anthony of Padua's sermon to the fishes (from *Des*

Knaben Wunderhorn). A second typical figure; the hero in manhood goes forth into the world, and sees how stupidity and vulgarity, like the fishes of the legend, are incorrigible. The trio, beginning with a fugato, mounts from step to step, reaches a point of repose, and sinks back into C. . . . Return of the Scherzo. An outcry of disgust, and then even the tireless progression of this movement refuses to flow onward."

The fourth movement enters without interruption. It is based on verses from *Des Knaben Wunderhorn,* intoned by a contralto, accompanied by orchestra. The fifth movement, based on Klopstock, also enters without pause. "The storm of the orchestra (a wild, frenetic, terrifying Scherzo), is interrupted by reassurances. Distant horns spread the terror of the Last Day. Softly, march-like, the chorale of the first movement is recalled. . . . The Great Summons is heard; the trumpets of the Apocalypse sound the call. Amid the awful silence, we seem to hear a far, far distant nightingale, like the last quivering echo of earthly life. The chorus of the saints, and the heavenly host begin almost inaudibly: 'Thou shalt arise from the dead.' The splendor of God appears. . . . It is no judgment; there are no sinners. . . . There is no punishment and no reward. An irresistible sentiment of love penetrates us with blessed knowledge and vital glow."

1896. SYMPHONY NO. 3 IN D MINOR, for solo contralto, women's chorus, boys' chorus, and orchestra. Part I: I. Vigoroso. Part II: II. Tempo di minuetto. III. Comodo; Scherzando. IV. O Mensch, Gib Acht. V. Es sungen drei Engel. VI. Adagio.

"My work," Mahler said of the third symphony, "forms a musical poem embracing all the steps in (cosmic) development in regular ascending order. It begins with lifeless Nature and rises to divine Life." Sometimes known as the *Summer Morning's Dream Symphony,* and sometimes as the *Program Symphony,* this work—voice of the composer's Pantheism—is a mighty hymn to Nature.

Donald Ferguson has noted that it is with the third symphony that Mahler established "the essentials of his highly individual method of symphonic composition." Analyzing this structure, Ferguson goes on to explain that "the first part resembles . . . that of an act from a Wagnerian opera. It makes no pretense of organizing its substance after the pattern of the sonata. We find no orderly exposition, setting forth high contrast between two principal themes. . . . There is no pre-appointed time for any 'subject' to appear; no conventional succession of keys; no 'development' in which themes are manipulated for the heightening of their rhetorical interest."

The symphony has two parts. To the first, the composer fixed the following programmatic titles: "Introduction: Pan Awakes, Summer Marches In." It is in sonata form with an extended exposition. "From every side it burgeons," Mahler himself explained. "And in the midst of this there is still something profoundly secret and painful, as lifeless Nature awaits in empty immobility the coming of life. It cannot be expressed in words." Mahler indicated that there should be no intermission after this movement. The second part embraces the five other movements. Each bears some descriptive title, as follows: "What the Wild Flowers Tell Me"; "What the Animals of the Forest Tell Me"; "What Man Tells Me"; "What the Angels Tell Me"; and "What Love Tells Me." The first of these movements is a minuet; the second a Scherzo based on material from one of Mahler's songs which, in turn, came from a German folk song; the third requires a contralto solo for verses from Nietzsche's *Also sprach Zarathustra;* the fifth, in rondo form, calls for a women's and a boys' chorus.

The finale is Mahler's paean to love. Here, the composer explains, he was dealing "with another kind of love than you suppose. The matter of this section runs: 'Father, look thou upon my wounds! Not one soul be lost!' Do you see what that means? Almost I might entitle the movement, 'What God Told Me'—and that in such a sense God is only to be understood as love."

HUGO WOLF 1860–1903

Though he wrote some chamber and orchestral music, and a full-length opera, Hugo Wolf was a genius in just one branch of musical composition—the Lied. He belonged to that royal line of German composers that began with Schubert, and continued on with Robert Franz, Schumann, and Brahms. There are some musicologists who regard Wolf as the greatest of them all. More than all the others, Wolf was most sensitively attuned to poet and text. "Poetry," he once told Humperdinck, "is the true source of my music." Wolf would concentrate on one poet and extract from him the essence of his art and transmute that essence into tones. Then he would go on to the next poet, never to return to the first one, having apparently exhausted all the musical possibilities he had opened up for him. "He allowed the poet," says Ernest Newman, "to prescribe for him the whole shape and color of a song, down to the smallest details. It was not that he was so little a musician that he could not, like the others, bend any poem to his arbitrary will, but that he was so much of a musician that he could accept any condition the poet liked to impose upon him and yet work as easily under them as another man could do without seeming limitations."

Wagner was Wolf's musical god. To his songwriting, Wolf tried to bring some of the ideals and aesthetics of the music drama. Thus stimulated and inspired, Wolf aimed not at beauty of melody or sound but at a fusion of melody and words, so much so that the song might become almost something "spoken." His melodies frequently were merely declamations, so completely at one with the texts that both seemed to be the work of the same man. Wolf's songs, at times, resembled miniature dramas. In the projection of these dramas, he had to devise new modulations, new kinds of piano accompaniments, new harmonies, new intervallic relations and progressions.

He brought an altogether new significance to the piano accompaniment. The title pages of his songs read that these were written not for voice with piano accompaniment but for "voice and piano," a hint that the piano was an equal partner of the voice. With his extraordinary skill at polyphony, Wolf frequently combined voice and melody into a single inextricable texture. "Counterpoint with him," says Newman, "was a living thing; he could scarcely think of a melody without other melodies consanguineous with it spontaneously suggesting themselves to him."

Then Ernest Newman sums up: "To think of his songs one by one is to see defiling before the eye a veritable pageant of humanity in epitome, a long procession of forms of the utmost variety, all drawn to the very life—lovers and maidens in every phase of passion and despair, poets, rogues, humorists, philosophers, hunters, sailors, kings, lovable good-for-nothings, Hedonists, Stoics, religious believers of every shade of confident ecstatic faith or torturing doubt. They are set in every conceivable form of environment; the whole panorama of Nature is unrolled before us—flowers, mountains, clouds, the sunset, the dawn, the dead of night, the salt open sea and the haunted inland waters—together with everything in Nature that has voice or movement—the elves, birds, the wind, the fire. For volume and plasticity and definiteness of characterization there is nothing like it in music outside Wagner. No two characters are the same; each bears about him all the distinguishing signs of his native land, breathes his own atmosphere, wears his own dress, thinks with his own brain."

Hugo Wolf was born in Windischgraz, Austria, on March 13, 1860. His first music instruction came from his father, an amateur musician, and a village schoolmaster. In 1875, he came to Vienna. For two years he studied piano with Wilhelm Schenner and harmony with Robert Fuchs at the Vienna Conservatory. Incapable of conforming to discipline, and severely critical of his teachers, Hugo Wolf was expelled in 1877. For a while, he earned his living teaching the piano to children; then he worked as chorusmaster in Salzburg, and music critic in Vienna. Meanwhile, he had come under the influence of Wagner, having attended a performance of *Tannhaeuser* in 1875. Under the stimulus of Wagner, he began writing his first songs to texts by Heine, Goethe, and other poets.

Because of his passionate espousal of Wagner, and his equally bitter denunciation of Brahms, Wolf made many enemies in Vienna; they joined forces to destroy him. The première of his *Penthesilea* by the Vienna Philharmonic, in 1886, was a fiasco. The two leading string-quartet ensembles in Vienna refused to consider his Quartet in D minor. But neither attacks nor failures could stem the tide of his productivity. Having given up music criticism in 1887, Wolf turned to songwriting with a passion and a concentration matched only by his self-assurance and his awareness of his powers. "Am I the one who has been called—am I of the elect?" he asked. In a few months' time, he set forty-three poems to music. By the end of 1888, he had completed the fifty-three songs of the Moerike song book, the twenty songs of the Eichendorff song book, and in a three-and-a-half-month period, fifty Goethe songs. In 1889, his first published volume of songs made its appearance. Between 1889 and 1890, he completed the forty-five numbers of the Spanish song book; and between 1890 and 1891, the twenty songs of the first volume of his Italian song book. "I work at a thousand horsepower," he exclaimed. "What I write now, I write for the future. They are masterpieces. There has been nothing like it since Schubert and Schumann."

This creativity came to a sudden halt in 1891. Wolf felt he had written himself out. But before that year was over, his old creative strength returned —renewed and revitalized. He now completed the second set of his Italian song book. But once again, between 1892 and 1894, the well ran dry; and once again, in 1895, it overflowed.

Slowly, his genius was being recognized throughout Germany and Austria. Hugo Wolf Societies were formed to promote his music. The world première of his opera, *Der Corregidor,* in Mannheim in 1896, was a *succès d'estime.* But such as it was, his success came too late. Wolf suffered a nervous breakdown in 1897 and had to be confined to an institution. For a while it seemed as if recovery was at hand; but then his mental condition grew worse. After an attempt at suicide, Wolf was placed in an insane asylum in Vienna in October, 1898. He died there on February 22, 1903.

1885. PENTHESILEA, tone poem for orchestra.

Penthesilea is based on a tragedy by Heinrich von Kleist. The heroine is the queen of the Amazons, who becomes involved in a losing battle with Achilles. There are three sections to the tone poem, played without interruption. In the first part ("The Departure of the Amazons"), Penthesilea assumes leadership over the Amazons. Trumpet flourishes introduce a strong march melody; the middle section presents contrasting material. The second section ("Penthesilea's Dream of the Feast of the Roses") describes Penthesilea's revery through a serene melody for flute, oboe, and violins, accompanied by violas. Toward the end of this part, the mood becomes animated. In the finale portion ("Combats, Passions, Frenzy, Annihilation"), two facets of Penthesilea's personality are stressed: her will to conquer and her will to love. The two themes are worked out powerfully. The restoration of her tranquillity is pointed up by a solo viola. Another strong climax is built up, emphasizing her passion for revenge and destruction. Then the storm settles and a soft and peaceful ending speaks of Penthesilea's death.

1887. ITALIENISCHE SERENADE IN G MAJOR (ITALIAN SERENADE), for string quartet.

Hugo Wolf's only successful chamber-music composition, the *Italian Serenade,* started out as the first movement of a projected suite for orchestra. After completing fragments for two other movements, Wolf abandoned this plan, and adapted the first movement for string quartet; in 1892, he transcribed it for small orchestra. The main subject is a romantic melody, derived from an Italian folk song that used to be played in Italy on a pastoral instrument called the "piffero" (an obsolete form of the oboe).

1888. MOERIKE LIEDERBUCH (THE MOERIKE SONG BOOK), fifty-three songs for voice and piano: 1. Der Tambour. 2. Der Knabe und das Immlein. 3. Jaegerlied. 4. Ein Stuendlein wohl vor Tag. 5. Der Jaeger. 6. Nimmersatte Liebe. 7. Auftrag. 8. Zur Warnung. 9. Lied vom Winde. 10. Bei einer Trauung. 11. Zitronenfalter in April. 12. Der Genesene an die Hoffnung. 13. Elfenlied. 14. Der Gaertner. 15. Abschied. 16. Denk es o Seele. 17. Auf einer Wanderung 18. Gebet. 19. Verborgenheit. 20. Lied eines Verliebten 21. Selbstgestaendnis. 22. Erstes Liebeslied eines Maedchens. 23. Fussreise. 24. Rat einer Alten. 25. Begegnung. 26. Das verlassene Maegdlein. 27. Storchenbotschaft. 28. Frage und Antwort. 29. Lebe wohl. 30. Heimweh. 31. Seufzer. 32. Auf ein altes Bild. 33. An eine Aeolsharfe. 34. Um Mitternacht 35. Auf eine Christblume I. 36. Peregrina I. 37. Peregrina II. 38. Agnes. 39. Er ist's. 40. In der Fruehe. 41. Im Fruehling. 42. Nixe Binsefuss. 43. Die Geister am Mummelsee. 44. An den Schlaf. 45. Neue Liebe. 46. Zum neuen Jahre. 47. Schlafendes Jesuskind. 48. Wo find ich Trost? 49. Karwoche. 50. Gesang Weylas. 51. Der Feuerreiter. 52. An die Geliebte. 53. Auf eine Christblume II.

Hugo Wolf wrote his first songs when he was about fifteen. Here, and for the next half dozen years, he was influenced by Schubert and Schumann. Wolf emphasized the lyric line and singing melodies, also strong felt romantic feelings. Among these first fruits, songs of more than passing interest include "Mit Schwarzen Segeln," "Du bist wie eine Blume," and "Sterne mit den golden Fuesslein," all to poems by Heine (1876–1880), and two songs to poems by Lenau, "Herbst" and "Frage nicht" (1879).

Individuality began to assert itself in some of the songs in the Eichendorff group (1888). This was a set of songs to poems by the German Romantic, Baron Joseph von Eichendorff. Schumann had also set some of these verses. But where Schumann had been dreamy and introspective, Wolf is virile and realistic. Some of Wolf's songs are robust in their humor, and some are touching in their melancholy. "Verschwiegene Liebe" is as interesting for its unusual modulations as for its delicacy; "Nachtzauber" is outstanding for its subtle evocation of a moonlit night while retaining elements of strength and humor; "Das Staendchen" is significant for its ingenious interrelationship of voice and piano.

It is in his set of fifty-three songs to poems by the Swabian pastor, Eduard Moerike, that Wolf comes fully into his own as one of the greatest composers of Lieder of all time. Up to now, his writing had been mainly strophic; his accompaniments, formal and conventional. Now his style becomes freer, his point of view more independent, his accompaniment richer in expression and sometimes carrying the brunt of the message. "In der Fruehe," is a masterpiece of concentration in which, Philip Radcliffe explains, "a single short phrase is taken through a variety of keys with a feeling of complete inevitability." "Der Feuerreiter" gives the effect of epic proportions within slight dimensions, pointing to Wolf's uncommon powers to create dramas in miniature. "Verborgenheit" is a compelling emotional experience. Here, says James Husst Hall, "the melody moves in simple dignity, the accompaniment weaving about it, here above, there below, and again with it." "Erstes Liebeslied eines Maedchens" seeks out and translates the erotic mood of the poem, just as "Er ist's" is the musical equivalent of the poem's simple message of love. "Wo find ich Trost?" and "Agnes" have deeply religious overtones. Frank Walker finds in "Auf einer Wanderung" and "Im Fruehling" examples of Wolf's symphonic style within the song form. Here "the voice delivers the poem in a sort of free melodic rhapsody over an elaborate piano part, built up out of one or more themes, somewhat in the manner of symphonic development."

In "Das verlassene Maegdlein," explains Ernest Newman, Wolf "has painted a singularly pathetic picture of a poor little maidservant getting up in the cold morning to light the fire and thinking of the faithless lover of whom she had dreamt in the night. Examine the song carefully and you will realize the consummate art of it—its faultless suggestion of the cold gray atmosphere of the poem, its subtle gradations of feeling, its pure pathos and big humanism."

1888–1889. GOETHE LIEDERBUCH (GOETHE SONG BOOK), fifty-one songs for voice and piano: 1. Harfenspieler I. 2. Harfenspieler II. 3. Harfenspieler III. 4. Philine. 5. Spottlied. 6. Anakreons Grab. 7. Der Schaefer. 8. Der Rattenfaenger. 9. Gleich und Gleich. 10. Dank des Paria. 11. Frech und Froh I. 12. St. Nepomuks Vorabend. 13. Gutmann und Gutweib. 14. Ritter Kurts Brautfahrt. 15. Der Saenger. 16. Mignon: Kennst du das Land. 17. Mignon I. 18. Mignon II. 19. Fruehling uebers Jahr. 20. Mignon III. 21. Epiphanias. 22. Cophtisches Lied I. 23. Cophtisches Lied II. 24. Beherzigung. 25. Blumengruss. 26. Prometheus. 27. Koeniglich Gebet. 28. Grenzen der Menschheit. 29. Ganymed. 30. Was in der Schenke waren heute. 31. Solang man nuechtern ist. 32. Ob der Koran von Ewigkeit sei. 33. Sie haben wegen der Trunkenheit. 34. Trunken muessen wir alle sein. 35. Phaenomen. 36. Erschaffen und Beleben. 37. Nicht Gelegenheit macht Diebe. 38. Hochbeglueckt in deiner Liebe. 39. Wie sollt' ich heiter bleiben. 40. Als ich auf dem Euphrat schiffte. 41. Dies zu deuten bin erboetig. 42. Wenn ich dein gedenke. 43. Komm, Liebchen, komm. 44. Hatt' ich irgend wohl bedenken. 45. Locken, haltet mich gefangen. 46. Nimmer will ich dich verlieren. 47. Frech und Froh II. 48. Der neue Amadis. 49. Genialisch Treiben. 50. Die Bekehrte. 51. Die Sproede.

Wolf's gamut was never more varied than in his fifty-one songs to texts by Goethe. They are at turns gently humorous and poignantly melancholy; turbulent and passionate, and delicate and tender. Here, too, Wolf increases the subtlety of his expression and introduces a new profundity of insight. Some of these songs have great lyric beauty; of these the gentle and peaceful "Anakreons Grab" is particularly celebrated, echoing the mood of the Goethe poem "in a slow, soothing 12/8 measure," remarks James Husst Hall. Also outstanding for their melodic attractiveness are "Fruchling uebers Jahr" and "Gleich und Gleich." But to Frank Walker, the most characteristic note sounded in these Goethe songs is not lyricism but something "stern" and "harsh." "There is an end of carefree singing," Walker adds.

In "Prometheus," Wolf produced one of his most remarkable ballads, comparable only to the "Feuerreiter" in the Moerike set. It contains, says Ernest Newman, "such a volume of mental energy as has never been put into any ballad before; while even in the smaller things—yes, even the smallest of them—we feel that we are watching the cerebration of a man of extraordinary psychological insight."

The writing of songs to Goethe's poems represented a challenge to Wolf. Wolf admired Schubert excessively, but he also felt that with few exceptions Schubert had failed to catch the essence of Goethe. The exceptions to Wolf were "An Schwager Kronos" and "Geheimis"—and these two Goethe poems, Wolf left alone. (Wolf rarely set to music any poem to which he felt another composer had done full justice.) But where he felt Schubert had failed, Wolf stepped in boldly.

Here is how Philip Radcliffe compared the settings by Schubert and by Wolf: "Wolf has produced the more continuous and closely-knit structure. . . . In 'Ganymed,' the texture is beautifully woven and produces an atmosphere of extraordinary serenity." Radcliffe finds that "Nur wer die Sehnsucht kennt" has a "tender and more tortured atmosphere than any earlier setting"; that "Der Rattenfaenger" and "Die Sproede" and "Die Bekehrte" are "vivid character portraits; that "Epiphanias" is "charmingly gay"; and that the first "Cophtisches Lied" reflects perfectly "the sardonic geniality of the words."

1889–1890. SPANISCHES LIEDERBUCH (SPANISH SONG BOOK), forty-four songs for voice and piano: 1. Wer sein holdes Lieb verloren. 2. Ich fuhr ueber Meer. 3. Preciosas Spruechlein gegen Kopfweh. 4. Wenn du zu den Blumen gehst. 5. Alle gingen, Herz, zur Ruh. 6. Nun wandre, Maria. 7. Die ihr schwebet um diese Palmen. 8. Die du Gott gebarst, du Reine.

9. Bedeckt mich mit Blumen. 10. Seltsam ist Juanas Weise. 11. Treibe nur mit Lieben Spott. 12. Und schlaefst du, mein Maedchen. 13. In dem Schatten meiner Locken. 14. Herz, verzage nicht geschwind. 15. Sagt, seid Ihr es, feiner Herr. 16. Klinge, klinge mein Pandero. 17. Herr, was traegt der Boden hier. 18. Blindes Schauen, dunkle Leuchte. 19. Bitt' ihn, o Mutter. 20. Wer tat deinem Fuesslein, weh? 21. Auf dem gruenen Balkon. 22. Sie blasen zum Abmarsch. 23. Fuehr mich, Kind, nach Bethlehem. 24. Wunden traegst du, mein Geliebter. 25. Ach, wie lang die Seele schlummert. 26. Ach, des Knaben Augen. 27. Muehlvoll komm' ich und beladen. 28. Nun bin ich dein. 29. Trau nicht der Liebe. 30. Weint nicht, ihr Aeuglein. 31. Schmerzliche Wonnen und wonnige Schmerzen. 32. Ach, im Maien war's. 33. Eide, so die Liebe schwur. 34. Geh', Geliebter, geh' jetzt. 35. Liebe mir im Busen. 36. Deine Mutter, suesses Kind. 37. Moegen alle boesen Zungen. 38. Sagt ihm, dass er zu mir komme. 39. Dereinst, dereinst, Gedanke mein. 40. Tief im Herzen trag' ich Pein. 41. Komm, o Tod, von Nacht umgeben. 42. Ob auch finstre Blicke glitten. 43. Da nur Leid und Leidenschaft. 44. Wehe der, die mir verstrickte.

Though Wolf never visited Spain, he was deeply interested in the country, its people, and its art. Of all his sets, the *Spanish* is perhaps the most remarkable —"a wonderful series of portrait sketches of men and women in every phase of love's torment and delight," as Frank Walker explained. Walker also points out that Wolf, in writing Spanish songs based on poems adapted by Paul Heyse and Emmanuel Geibel, had a "real feeling for things Spanish, accepted the convention of wide-spread guitar-like chords and impetuous dance-like movements without hesitation, and forged from them, in the fires of his imagination, a new style of remarkable flexibility and power."

We find songs here of an incandescent religiosity and mysticism—something new to Wolf ("Die du Gott gebarst", "Nun bin ich dein," "Herr, was traegt der Boden hier," and "Nun wandre, Maria"). We also find here ecstatic love songs with fire and passion, of which "Geh', Geliebter" is perhaps the most significant example. There are songs here of an infectious gaiety ("Auf dem gruenen Balkon"), of great sobriety ("Alle gingen, Herz, zur Ruh"), of a light and airy lyricism ("Klinge, klinge mein Pandero") and with powerful declamatory lines ("In dem Schatten meiner Locken," which Brahms had also set).

1891–1896. ITALIENISCHES LIEDERBUCH (ITALIAN SONG BOOK), forty-six songs in two volumes, for voice and piano:

First volume (1890–1891): 1. Mir ward gesagt, du reisest in die Ferne. 2. Ihr seid die Allerschoenste. 3. Gesegnet sei, durch den die Welt entstund. 4. Selig Ihr Blinden. 5. Wer rief dich denn. 6. Der Mond hat eine schwere Klag' erhoben. 7. Nun lass uns Frieden schliessen. 8. Dass doch gemalt all deine Reize waeren. 9. Du denkst mit einem Faedchen mich zu fangen. 10. Mein Liebster ist so klein. 11. Und willst du deinen Liebsten sterben sehen. 12. Wie lange schoen war immer mein Verlangen. 13. Geselle, woll'n wir uns in Kutten huellen. 14. Nein, junger Herr. 15. Hoffaertig seid Ihr, schoenes

Kind. 16. Auch kleine Dinge. 17. Ein Staendchen Euch zu bringen. 18. Ihr jungen Leute. 19. Mein Liebster singt. 20. Heb' auf dein blondes Haupt. 21. Wir haben beide lange Zeit geschwiegen. 22. Man sagt mir, deine Mutter woll' es nicht.

Second volume (1896): 1. Ich esse nun mein Brot nicht trocken mehr. 2. Mein Liebster hat zu Tische mich geladen. 3. Ich liess mir sagen. 4. Schon streckt ich aus im Bett. 5. Du sagst mir, dass ich keine Fuerstin sei. 6. Lass sie nur gehn. 7. Wie viele Zeit verlor ich. 8. Und steht Ihr frueh am Morgen auf. 9. Wohl kenn ich Euren Stand. 10. Wie soll ich froehlich sein. 11. O waer dein Haus. 12. Sterb' ich, so huellt in Blumen. 13. Gesegnet sei das Gruen. 14. Wenn du mich mit den Augen streifst. 15. Was soll der Zorn. 16. Benedeit die sel'ge Mutter. 17. Schweig einmal still. 18. Nicht laenger kann ich singen. 19. Wenn du, mein Liebster, steigst zum Himmel auf. 20. Ich hab in Penna. 21. Heut' Nacht erhob ich mich. 22. O wuesstest du, wieviel ich deinetwegen. 23. Verschling' der Abgrund. 24. Was fuer ein Lied soll dir gesungen werden?

The *Italian Song Book* is a setting of forty-six Italian poems that Paul Heyse had adapted into German from the verses of various Italian poets including Leopardo, Giusti, and Carducci. Though the two sets came five years apart, there is a homogeneity of style among all the songs which, for the most part, are more personal and intimate than Wolf's earlier Lieder. The passion, the turbulence of earlier days have been spent. In their places we find humor, gentle and temperate moods, and surpassingly tender expressions of love. Here, too, we encounter greater spontaneity, terseness, economy of means, and slightness of texture than heretofore. Most of these songs are exquisite miniatures. "The *Tristan*-like harmonies that were frequent earlier," explains James Husst Hall, "now rarely appear. Most of the songs are short, twenty measures often being sufficient; but they seem less compressed than some of the earlier songs of equal length."

These are some of the more memorable songs in these sets: "Auch kleine Dinge," which, in Hall's description, is "as lovely a gem as a pearl, as full of substance as an olive, and as sweet as a rose"; the exquisitely tender, "Heb' auf dein blondes Haupt" and "Und willst du deinen Liebsten sterben sehen" with their almost orchestral accompaniments; the depth and subtlety of "Sterb' ich, so huellt in Blumen"; the irony and humor of "Ich hab in Penna"; the organic unity of piano and voice in "Was fuer ein Lied soll dir gesungen werden?" in which, Ernest Newman points out, "the whole conception is one and indivisible."

1895. DER CORREGIDOR (THE MAGISTRATE), opera in four acts, with text by Rosa Mayreder, based on Pedro Antonio de Alarcón's, *The Three-Cornered Hat*. First performance: Mannheim, June 7, 1896.

For many years, there stirred restlessly in Wolf the ambition to write an opera, and thereby prove he could be successful on a canvas larger than the song. He began considering the possibilities of *The Three-Cornered Hat* in 1888.

But after Rosa Mayreder prepared a libretto for him, he rejected the subject and started to look around for something else. At one time, he became interested in Shakespeare's *The Tempest,* then in a life of Buddha, then in a drama based on Pocahontas, and then in Apuleius's *The Golden Ass*. Finally, in 1894, he returned to *The Three-Cornered Hat* and now described it as "the comic opera par excellence." In the Spring of 1895, he went to work with his usual frenzy, writing without interruption day after day, from morning till evening. Except for the orchestration, his score was completed by July 9; the orchestration absorbed him for another few months after that.

Fruitless attempts to get his opera performed in Vienna, Berlin, and Prague almost broke Wolf's heart and spirit. But the Mannheim Opera accepted it, and mounted it on June 7, 1896. That première was a tremendous success—largely due to the efforts of many of Wolf's friends and admirers, who had come en masse from all parts of Germany and Austria. But the Wolf clique was not present at the second performance, and on this occasion the audience reaction was lukewarm, to say the least.

Der Corregidor is rarely produced today because, as Frank Walker said, it is hardly more than "a succession of separate musical miniatures, more or less happily joined together." There are several individual parts that are most attractive. The most popular of these are a delightful orchestral Intermezzo and the famous Lied "In dem Schatten meiner Locken," which Wolf interpolated into his score. But for the most part, Wolf is not at ease writing for the stage. The musical numbers, good though they are by themselves, fail to penetrate beyond the surface of dramatic action and characters; the opera is little more than a stringing together of songs. Besides all this, the Wagnerian influence upon Wolf is ill-suited for the frothy comedy text—the polyphony, the overdressed orchestration, the abundant use of a Leitmotiv technique.

If the plot of *Der Corregidor* is familiar to some, it is because it is the same one used for Manuel de Falla's celebrated twentieth-century ballet, *The Three-Cornered Hat*. Don Eugenio di Zuniga, a magistrate, is pursuing the lovely Frasquita. One day he comes to her door soaked to the skin, having just fallen into a pool. Threatened by Frasquita's gun, he falls into a dead faint and must be put to bed. He is found there by Lucas, Frasquita's husband, who becomes convinced his wife has been unfaithful to him. Taking the magistrate's clothes, Lucas avenges himself by going off to the magistrate's house and making love to the magistrate's wife. For their respective attempts at illicit love-making, both the magistrate and Lucas receive a sound thrashing. This convinces them that it is the better part of wisdom to confine their future love-making to their own wives.

1897. MICHELANGELO LIEDER, three songs for voice and piano: 1. Wohl denk' ich oft. 2. Alles endet, was entstehet. 3. Fuehlt meine Seele.

These are Wolf's last songs, completed in March 1897, several months before he lost his mind. The first, says Philip Radcliffe, has "immense power and dignity and is followed by 'Alles endet,' which is bleak and somber beyond words. The third . . . is less forbidding, and has something of the warmth of the love songs written in earlier years."

ALEXANDER GLAZUNOV 1865–1936

Glazunov represents the end of an epoch in Russian music. He was the final extension of the Romantic tendencies of Tchaikovsky and the "Russian Five." He lived well into the twentieth century, but his music stayed behind in the nineteenth. He neither sympathized with nor understood the upheaval created in music by such younger Russian contemporaries as Stravinsky and Prokofiev. The new sounds horrified him. For a while, he chose to ignore them, and continued writing as if the nineteenth century had never ended. Then when it became painfully apparent that he was just a carry-over of a now-dead age, that he was no longer a voice of his times, he could write no longer. After 1914, Glazunov was silent, even though he lived on for more than two decades longer.

Except for a handful of works, Glazunov's prolific output came in the nineteenth century. (His most important compositions in the twentieth century were the ballet, *The Seasons;* the Violin Concerto in A minor; the suite, *From the Middle Ages;* the seventh and eighth symphonies. And all this music came before 1907.) It is from his production in the nineteenth century that we get most of the works by which he is remembered. Here he was an eclectic whose program music traversed a wide area: Russian, Oriental, Greek backgrounds; antiquated dance forms and ecclesiastical modes. In his symphonies and string quartets, he was most strongly influenced by Brahms. In either case, there is not much in his writing that was either personal or individual. All the same, Glazunov was a distinguished melodist; his harmonic invention and orchestration, while rarely original, always revealed skilful workmanship. Rosa Newmarch pointed out that Glazunov's music was "usually most characteristic in moods of restrained melancholy" and was full of "picturesque suggestion."

Alexander Glazunov was born in St. Petersburg on August 10, 1865. As a boy, he attended technical high school, while taking lessons in music. At fifteen, he became a pupil of Rimsky-Korsakov, under whose guidance he made swift strides. In a year's time, he completed an excellent symphony, which was introduced in St. Petersburg on March 29, 1882. Two overtures on Greek themes between 1881 and 1883, the tone poem *Stenka Razin* in 1884, and his second symphony in 1886 placed him, in spite of his youth, as the most important follower of the nationalist school. His fame soon spread throughout Europe. In 1889, he was invited to conduct his symphonies in Paris; and in 1896–1897, he was acclaimed in London in concerts devoted to his works. In 1899, he was appointed instructor at the St. Petersburg Conservatory, where from 1905 to 1922 he was director. He left Russia for good in 1928, making his home in Paris. In 1929, he paid his first visit to the United States, making guest appearances as conductor with the Boston and Detroit symphony orchestras. Glazunov died in Paris on March 21, 1936.

1885. STENKA RAZIN, tone poem for orchestra, op. 13.

Stenka Razin was the seventeenth-century Cossack who led daring raids on the Czarist regime. Captured, he was given amnesty in return for an oath of allegiance. He broke his promise, and headed an army of several hundred thousand renegades in an attempt to overthrow the government. His despotic nature and his love of violence, finally alienated his followers. Captured once again, he was sentenced to death in 1672.

Glazunov's tone poem dramatizes and romanticizes the Cossack's career. The slow introduction (Andante) suggests the river Volga; we hear a hurried quotation in the trombones of the famous "Volga Boatman." The music describes Stenka Razin's raids on villages along the river; then his abduction of a Persian princess, whom he captures and later drowns in the Volga. In the main section of the overture (Allegro con brio) two main themes are presented. The first represents Stenka Razin; the second, sensual and passionate, describes the Persian princess. The strains of the "Volga Boatman" return in the brass to help bring the overture to a powerful conclusion.

1888. FIVE NOVELETTES, suite for string quartet, op. 15. I. Allegretto alla spagnuola. II. Orientale. III. Interludium in modo antico. IV. Valse. V. Allegretto all'ungherese.

This suite is one of its composer's most popular chamber-music works. It is made up of five atmospheric pieces, each romantic in style, each developed freely. The most famous number is the third, a successful attempt to re-create in Romantic terms an ancient musical style. The Valse is in the graceful salon style exploited so well by the composer in his two *Valses de concert* for orchestra (see 1893–1894). The Orientale and the concluding Allegretto offer an exotic atmosphere through sensual melodies and dynamic rhythms.

1893. SYMPHONY NO. 4 IN E-FLAT, op. 48. I. Andante; Allegro moderato. II. Allegro vivace. II. Andante; Allegro.

Glazunov completed his first symphony, in E major (op. 5) before he was sixteen. He wrote seven more symphonies after that, to become one of the most significant symphonists after Brahms. The fourth, in E-flat, was an immense success when introduced in St. Petersburg in 1894 and is still one of the symphonies by Glazunov most often played.

Here is Herbert Elswell's definitive analysis of the work from his program notes for the Cleveland Symphony:

"After two bars of chordal introduction, the English horn sings a tune whose simplicity and passive melancholy establish the mood. . . . A repetition of the subject in the first violins and flutes [is] now presented with a flowing accompaniment and moving gracefully and easily in a transition towards the main body of the movement. . . . The melodic idea, appearing first in the oboe, is echoed successively by a number of instruments. . . . On the heels of this comes the true second subject, a flowing cantabile song sung by flutes and oboe with a sustained background reverting soon to the rhythmic accompaniment of the first subject. . . . The main theme is thoroughly worked out. . . . A strong climax is reached, and with it the return of the principal theme in its original form. The formal recapitulation continues up to the point where the second subject should normally enter, and it is here interrupted by an insertion of the theme of the introduction, Andante, after which the second subject appears. . . . A brief restatement of the first subject concludes the movement.

"The Scherzo . . . begins . . . with four measures of introduction for the bassoons and second violins, pizzicato. The subject, giocoso, expressive of playfulness and gentle gaiety is allotted to the clarinet. . . . The trio in D-flat major brings forth a more tranquil theme for the clarinet with sustained harmony in the strings and staccato afterbeats in the flute. . . .

"There is no independent slow movement in this symphony, but only a short Andante which serves as an introduction to the finale. Against a soft tremolando in the violins, the third clarinet and violas sing a quietly expressive theme. . . . Below the trills of the woodwind and strings is heard a vigorous rhythmic figure in the trumpets and horns, anticipating the theme of the finale which, after a mighty crescendo, bursts forth. . . . A sudden shift of tonality . . . brings a secondary idea which is also worked over, serving as a transition to the second subject. This bright quiet tune is sung first by the violas and oboe in G major, and then by the violins with counter-melodies in the lower strings."

1893–1894. VALSES DE CONCERT, for orchestra:
No. 1: D major, op. 47.
No. 2: F major, op. 51.

The two Valses are among the composer's most popular works for orchestra. The first (1893) opens with a brief introduction (Allegro) before the main waltz melody is given, first by violas and clarinets, then by violins. A second waltz subject is then assigned to the clarinet, accompanied by string pizzicati. After a return of the first waltz melody, the composition ends with a brilliant coda. The second Valse (1894) gives a warning of its main waltz melody in the introductory Allegro. The waltz is finally heard in the violins, and dominates the entire composition, though fragments of other ideas are introduced from time to time.

1894. CARNIVAL OVERTURE, for orchestra, op. 45.

This is a gay picture of a carnival. In an introductory section, a lively dance for violins and woodwind is contrasted with a sedate subject for woodwind. The main part of the overture also makes use of contrasting material. The first subject is a rhythmic tune for flutes and clarinets, while the second (oboes, clarinets, horns, and cellos) is serene and reflective.

1894. SCÈNES DE BALLET, suite for orchestra, op. 52. I. Préambule. II. Marionettes. III. Mazurka. IV. Scherzino. V. Pas d'action. VI. Danse orientale. VII. Valse. VIII. Polonaise.

This eight-part suite, a concert favorite, opens with an introductory movement (Allegro) in which a graceful tune unfolds in the first violins before being repeated by the woodwind. A playful description of marionettes follows (Allegro), with a saucy idea for piccolo and glockenspiel. In the third part, a lively mazurka (Allegro) dance tune is heard in full orchestra after a twenty-eight measure introduction. The fourth movement (Allegro) consists mainly of a gentle theme for muted strings and woodwind. Now comes an Adagio movement in which an expressive melody is shared by cellos and violins. In the sixth section, the oboe—accompanied by strings and the rhythms of a tambourine—is heard in an exotic Oriental melody. A contrast comes in the seventh movement, with a graceful waltz in the violins. The suite ends with a picturesque polonaise for full orchestra.

1896. SYMPHONY NO. 6 IN C MINOR, op. 58. I. Adagio; Allegro passionato. II. Andante. III. Allegretto. IV. Andante maestoso; Scherzando.

The sixth is one of Glazunov's most famous symphonies. The stately introduction to the first movement presents an effective theme for cellos and double basses. After being treated in imitation, it is carried to a thunderous climax. Chromatic harmonies bring on the main part of the movement. Its first theme is a version of the subject heard in the introduction, but in a changed rhythm. The second melody is a lyrical episode for violins, followed by the woodwind. Both themes are joined contrapuntally with telling effect in the free development section. The concluding coda is a vigorous restatement of earlier material.

There is a simple tune with seven variations in the slow movement. The third movement Scherzo is in reality an intermezzo, its main subject stated by the woodwind accompanied by plucked strings in cello. A trio, and some new thematic material in flute and violin pizzicato, follow before the earlier section of this movement is repeated. The finale has the energy and abandon of a Russian dance. There are two dynamic themes here, which undergo various transformations of tempo and rhythm.

1898. RAYMONDA, ballet suite for orchestra, op. 57a.

Glazunov wrote the scores for two successful ballets. Since the second of these (*The Seasons*) came after 1900, it does not come within the scope of this volume. *Raymonda* preceded *The Seasons* by about two years and was the composer's first work for the stage. It was introduced by the Russian Imperial Ballet in St. Petersburg on January 19, 1898, with choreography by Marius Petipa. The heroine is a girl betrothed to a knight gone off with the Crusades to fight the Saracens. During his absence, Raymonda is wooed by a Saracen who is rebuffed, even after he had offered Raymonda his wealth. The knight returns in time to kill his rival and thus save Raymonda from abduction. The ballet ends with the festive nuptials of Raymonda and her knight.

The following sections from the ballet score go to make up the orchestral suite: Introduction; In the Castle; Dance of the Pages and Young Girls; Arrival of the Stranger; Entrance of Raymonda; Moonlight; Prelude and La Romanesca; Variations; Raymonda's Dream; Spanish Dance; Valse fantastique; Grand Adagio; Raymonda's Variation; Arab Boys' Dance; Entrance of the Saracens; Love Triumphant; Wedding Feast.

AMILCARE PONCHIELLI 1834–1886

"When Ponchielli was struck by the dramatic rightness of a situation," says Robert Lawrence, "he not only sparked—he flamed." Ponchielli wrote nine operas. Only one survives—*La Gioconda*. While it is uneven and not without blemish, it is also an opera whose best pages reveal the composer was on fire. Ponchielli contributed nothing to Italian opera that had not been said before him, and better, by *Aïda*. Ponchielli's main achievement was to create blood-and-thunder opera that seizes the imagination and holds it fast for four acts. It is rather his influence as a teacher, rather than his example as a composer, that set into motion the "Verismo" movement soon to be fertilized by Leoncavallo, Mascagni, and Puccini, the last two of whom were his pupils.

Amilcare Ponchielli was born in Paderno, Fasolaro, in Cremona, Italy on September 1, 1834. For nine years, beginning with 1843, he attended the Milan Conservatory. After completing his studies, he worked as organist at S. Ilario Cathedral in Cremona. Then he was town bandmaster. His first opera, *I Promessi sposi,* was produced in Cremona on August 30, 1856. It was with a revision of this opera, given in Milan on December 5, 1872, that Ponchielli achieved his first success. *La Gioconda,* in 1876, gave him international stature. From 1881 to 1886, he was Maestro di Cappella at the Cathedral of Bergamo; and from 1883 on, he was professor of composition at the Milan Conservatory. His last complete opera, *Marion Delorme,* was produced at La Scala on March 17, 1885. Ponchielli died in Milan on January 16, 1886.

1876. LA GIOCONDA, opera in four acts, with text by Arrigo Boïto (using the pen name of Tobia Gorrio), based on Victor Hugo's drama, *Angelo, tyran de Padoue.* First performance: La Scala, Milan, April 8, 1876.

It was almost as if the creators of *La Gioconda* deliberately set out to incorporate in it all those elements that make opera "grand"; then they went one step better. Boïto's libretto (one of his poorer efforts) embraces infidelity, illicit love, hate, jealousy, suicide, death by strangulation, and a sleep-inducing potion. For spectacular scenes, the opera offers a feast day, a masked ball, a regatta, a ship set afire. For ballet, there was "The Dance of the Hours," one of the most spectacular dance sequences in Italian opera. For lavish settings, there was nothing less than the Doge's palace in Venice. If grand opera profits from a heroine, then *La Gioconda* had not one but three. If grand opera must have a big aria, then *La Gioconda* boasted six—one for each voice range.

There is much in La Gioconda that is unbelievable, confused, vulgar, obvious, and meretricious. But *La Gioconda* has survived to become one of the most popular Italian operas in the second half of the nineteenth century, because it has many items on the credit side. It has sensual lyricism, dramatic reçitatives, tellingly theatrical finales. Here is how Claudio Sartori balanced the scales in measuring the faults and the virtues of the opera: "If Ponchielli's idiom is somewhat lacking in refinement, his characters are full of a hot-blooded vitality. They may be roughly hewn, they may savor of highly colored popular drama, but they are alive with genuine dramatic force, and precisely because of their lack of subtlety they make an immediate impact upon the imagination and the senses. Within this genre, *La Gioconda* is Ponchielli's most successful opera, even if it is the most uneven, with pages of real value side by side with others that are quite worthless."

A short orchestral prelude uses some of the material from the opera. The most important of these melodies comes from La Cieca's first-act air, "Voce di donna," and a subsidiary one, strongly rhythmic, representing Barnaba.

Boïto supplied each act with a title. The first he called "The Lion's Mouth." It is set in a square outside the Doge's palace in seventeenth-century Venice. A festive crowd is informed by Barnaba, a spy of the Inquisition, that the regatta is about to begin. After people rush off to see the race, La Gioconda, a beautiful street singer, appears, leading her blind mother, La Cieca. In an effective trio, "Figlia che reggi," the mother express her gratitude to her daughter for her devotion, the daughter speaks of her tenderness for her mother, and (from a distance) Barnaba plots to win La Gioconda's love. When Barnaba accosts La Gioconda, she brushes him aside rudely. Now Barnaba is bent on destroying her. After the crowd returns, he whispers to Zuane, the loser in the regatta, that La Cieca is a witch who had cast an evil spell over him. Zuane is about to attack the blind woman when Enzo Grimaldo, a Genoese nobleman, comes to her help. La Cieca, however, is rescued by the Grand Duke Alvise, and his wife Laura. In profound gratitude, La Cieca presents Laura with a rosary ("Voce di donna"). Barnaba knows that in years past Laura and Enzo had once been engaged, and he suspects they are still in love. Therefore, Barnaba slips over to Enzo to tell him that Laura plans to visit his ship in the harbor that very night. Though suspicious of the spy, Enzo is beside himself with delight ("O grido di quest' anima"). Later, Barnaba dictates an anonymous letter to the head of the police warning him of the impending rendezvous. La Gioconda has overheard Barnaba. Since she is secretly engaged to Enzo she is in despair.

The second act, "The Rosary," takes place in an island in the lagoon. Sailors aboard Enzo's ship are singing a nautical tune as they work ("Ho! He!"). Disguised as a fisherman, Barnaba offers a barcarolle. ("Pescator, affonda l'esca"). On the deck of his ship, Enzo is contemplating the beauty of sea and sky in one of the opera's most famous arias, "Cielo e mar." It is not long before Laura, conducted by Barnaba, appears. The lovers embrace ecstatically, than plot to flee. As Enzo orders his sailors to set sail, Laura prays to the heavens for protection ("Stella del marinar"). Soon La Gioconda is at hand —come to threaten Laura with a dagger, and at the same time to warn Enzo that the Duke is arriving. Terrified, Laura seeks the protection of La Cieca's rosary. The sight of her mother's rosary, and a recollection of the way Laura had helped save her from danger, brings a change of heart in La Gioconda. She is now determined to help Laura all she can. Pushing her into a nearby boat, she sends Laura off to safety. Then, when the roar of guns reveals to Enzo he is about to be attacked by the Duke's fleet, he orders his ship to be set aflame.

The third act, "The House of Gold," has two scenes. The first is a chamber in the Doge's palace. Aware that his wife is faithless, the Duke is planning to punish her ("Si! morir ella de"). He calls to Laura, then orders her to drink a vial of poison. But La Gioconda has substituted a sleep-producing potion for the poison. Upon returning to the chamber and seeing Laura stretched out, the Duke is convinced she is dead.

The scene changes to the grand ballroom of the palace where a huge party is taking place. After the guests have sung the praises of their host in "Alla cà d'oro," a colorful ballet takes place. It is "The Dance of the Hours," symbolizing the victory of right over wrong; the dancers, emerging in groups of six, impersonate the hours of the dawn, day, evening, and night. After the dance is over, Barnaba drags La Cieca into the room and accuses her of being a witch; he also tells the guests that bells are now tolling for Laura's death. At this point, Enzo is discovered; his arrest is ordered by the Duke. La Gioconda steps forward with a bargain. She is ready to give herself up to Barnaba if he can effect Enzo's escape. Hardly has Barnaba agreed when the Duke dramatically pulls aside the curtain to reveal the outstretched Laura. He confesses that it is he who has murdered her. Grief-stricken, Enzo rushes towards the Duke with a drawn dagger, but is stopped by the guards, and arrested.

The dénoument of the opera takes place in the fourth act, "The Orfano Canal." La Gioconda has brought Laura for safety to a lonely island off Venice. In her magnificent scena, "Suicidio!" La Gioconda laments the fact that she has nothing more to live for, now that she has lost the man she loves, and that she must give herself up to Barnaba. When Enzo, released from prison, comes for Laura, she awakens from her drugged sleep. The lovers voice their gratitude to La Gioconda ("Sulle tue mani l'anima"), then effect their escape in a boat. When Barnaba comes to claim La Gioconda, she plunges a dagger into her breast. The enraged Barnaba shouts at the dead La Gioconda that the day before he had killed her mother.

Upon receiving its American première, *La Gioconda* became the only "unfamiliar work" seen during the opening season of the Metropolitan Opera; this performance took place on December 20, 1883. The opera did not meet with favor, and was dropped after only three performances. It was not seen again at the Metropolitan Opera for another two decades, until its revival in 1904.

PIETRO MASCAGNI 1863–1945

The most significant movement in Italian opera after Verdi was "Verismo." Verismo, for the most part, was partial to everyday settings, characters and situations—as distinguished from historical materials. But the most significant tendency in Verismo was to treat passionate, violent, sometimes even sordid episodes in a realistic manner. Musically, Verismo preferred melodramatic arias to florid ones, or to those with soaring flights of lyricism. It placed a considerable importance on naturalistic recitatives, orchestral tone-painting, and choral episodes establishing a mood.

It was Mascagni who set this movement into motion with *Cavalleria rusticana*. This was the composer's third opera, and consequently an early one. One of the tragedies in Mascagni's career was that, though through the years he wrote and produced over fifteen operas, he was never able to repeat either the quality or the success of *Cavalleria*. *L'Amico Fritz* in 1891, and *Iris* in 1898, were moderate successes and of some endearing qualities. But Mascagni's career, nonetheless, represented a consistent downward descent from the heights of *Cavalleria* to the valley of his pro-Fascist opera in 1935, *Nerone*. Mascagni recognized this sad fact when he remarked at the end of his life: "It is a pity I wrote *Cavalleria* first, for I was crowned before I became king."

Pietro Mascagni, son of a baker, was born in Leghorn, Italy, on December 7, 1863. While attending the Instituto Luigi Cherubini, he wrote a symphony and a Kyrie which were performed at the school in 1879. In 1880, he completed his first opera, *Pinotta*; this score was lost for half a century, then found and given its world première in San Remo in 1932. In 1881, he received praise for a cantata, *In Filanda*. A wealthy amateur of music now financed his studies at the Milan Conservatory where Mascagni came under the influence of Ponchielli. But, unhappy with the strict discipline and formal ways of the Conservatory, Mascagni abandoned his studies to become the conductor of a traveling opera company. For the next few years, he lived in poverty and obscurity, directing a music school, conducting a town band, and giving piano lessons.

In 1889, he received first prize in a competition conducted by the publisher, Sonzogno. The opera was *Cavalleria rusticana,* and it proved a sensation when introduced in Rome in 1890. Performed soon thereafter throughout the world of music, *Cavalleria* made its composer famous and wealthy. He was never destined to repeat that success; most of his operas were dismal failures. In 1902, Mascagni toured the United States directing *Cavalleria;* because this visit had been badly managed it proved a financial fiasco. A tour of South America, in 1911, was far more successful. From 1895 to 1902, Mascagni was director of the Rossini Conservatory in Pesaro. He also distinguished himself as conductor. In 1929, he was elected to the Royal Italian Academy. Because of his close ties to the Fascist regime, Mascagni was rejected by most of his one-time friends and admirers after World War II. His last days were spent in disgrace and poverty. He died in Rome on August 2, 1945.

1889. CAVALLERIA RUSTICANA, opera in one act, with text by Guido Menasci and Giovanni Targioni-Tozzetti, based on a play by Giovanni Verga. First performance: Teatro Costanzi, Rome, May 17, 1890.

The idea for *Cavalleria rusticana* had been revolving in Mascagni's mind long before the announcement of an opera competition sent him into action.

He then completed his whole score in less than three months. He thought the result was so poor that he refused to submit it to the contest. His wife got possession of the score and without his knowledge sent it to Sonzogno. It won the first prize, and in 1890 was mounted at the Costanzi Theater in Rome.

That première was a triumph with few parallels. The composer had to take forty curtain calls. Upon returning home late that night, he found the entrance to his house besieged by hundreds upon hundreds of opera lovers; he had to sneak into his apartment through a window. Before the year was over, the opera was given in Hungary, conducted by Gustav Mahler. Then it was produced in all parts of Europe. Its American première took place in Philadelphia on September 8, 1891, with performances in Chicago, Boston, and New York coming soon thereafter. On December 30, it was produced at the Metropolitan Opera. There, in 1893, the opera was paired with *Pagliacci* for the first time to fill out the evening bill—a partnership that has proved more or less traditional.

It was due to *Cavalleria* that honors came to its composer from all directions. The town of Cerignola made him an honorary citizen; in 1890, he was made Knight of the Crown of Italy. Medals with his image were sold in the shops of Milan. In 1940, the fiftieth anniversary of the first performance of *Cavalleria* was celebrated with festive performances in Venice, Rome, and Milan, directed by the composer.

The action takes place in a public square of a Sicilian village toward the end of the nineteenth century. The orchestral prelude opens with a stately melody (Andante sostenuto) describing the peace of Easter Day. The mood is dramatized, then brought to a climax with a fortissimo chord. The return of a more subdued mood is followed by a quotation of the melody sung in the opera by Santuzza to Turiddu. Before the prelude ends, Turiddu's offstage voice is heard extolling the praises of Lola in the passionate siciliana, "O Lola." The overture ends with a repetition of the Santuzza melody.

It is Easter morning. The townspeople are on their way to church. Santuzza, a village girl, stops Mamma Lucia, Turiddu's mother, for information about him. Soon Alfio, a teamster, makes his appearance in the company of his cronies. He presents a gay song about the joys of his profession ("Il cavallo scalpita"). The religious strains of "Regina coeli" summon the people to church. Santuzza, left behind, confesses to Mamma Lucia how much she loves Turiddu ("Voi lo sapete"). When Mamma Lucia goes off to church, Turiddu appears. Bitterly, Santuzza denounces him for having been unfaithful to her with Lola, Alfio's wife. Just then Lola appears, a gay song on her lips ("Fior di giaggiolo"). Lightly, she informs Turiddu that she has no intention of taking him from Santuzza, a fact that so enrages the young man that he throws Santuzza to the ground in his haste to follow Lola. Her heart broken by this treatment, Santuzza reveals to Alfio that his wife and Turiddu are having an affair. Bitterly, Alfio vows to get revenge before that day is over.

The curtain goes down to suggest a brief lapse of time. The orchestra plays the celebrated Intermezzo ("Intermezzo sinfonico")—its serene and spiritual music projecting the Easter spirit. At the rise of the curtain, the villagers are emerging from church. Turiddu, with Lola on his arm, makes for the nearby tavern where he joins his friends in a drinking song ("Viva il vino"). He then offers a glass to Alfio, who spurns it contemptuously. Insulted, Turiddu challenges him to a duel. In a repentant mood and filled with a sense of doom, Turiddu bids his mother farewell and asks for her blessings ("Mamma, quel vino"). When he rushes off his mother tries to follow him but is stopped by Santuzza. From behind the scenes, shouts announce that Turiddu has been killed. Surrounded by the excited villagers, Santuzza and Mamma Lucia give way to their grief.

Herbert F. Peyser has said that "if there is such a thing as an Italian folk opera, *Cavalleria rusticana* is its very model. . . . Its melodic idiom does not perceptibly owe anything to anyone unless it be to Italian folk song. . . . Mascagni grasped the deep artistic truth that action on the stage is not so important in opera as action in music. It is the seething action in the score cunningly punctuated with periods of repose or alleviation that resolves whatever problems *Cavalleria* may offer."

1891. L'AMICO FRITZ, opera in three acts, with text by Nicola Daspuro (using the pen-name of P. Suardon), based on a novel by Erckmann-Chatrian. First performance: Teatro Costanzi, Rome, October 31, 1891.

L'Amico Fritz was the immediate successor of *Cavalleria rusticana* among Mascagni's operas. Where *Cavalleria* was dramatic and emotional, *L'Amico* was refined and idyllic. When first produced, the opera was a success—though, of course, not of the dimensions of *Cavalleria*. After that, it became Mascagni's only opera besides *Cavalleria* to be regularly performed in Italy. Its American première took place at the Metropolitan Opera on January 10, 1894.

The setting is an Italian village; the time, the latter part of the nineteenth century. Fritz Kobus, a farmer, is a confirmed bachelor. At the prodding of Rabbi David, he provides a handsome dowry for one of his tenants. Laughingly, the Rabbi insists that someday he will find a girl to suit Fritz's tastes. Just then Suzel, a village girl, appears. She has flowers in her arms, and she is singing about the loveliness of Spring ("Son pochi fiori"). Though she appeals to Fritz, he wagers with the Rabbi that he will never get married. The rest of the opera concerns itself with the machinations of Rabbi David to bring Fritz and Suzel together and to get them to fall in love with each other. Having found happiness in Suzel, Fritz is only too happy to pay the wager—a vineyard, which the Rabbi then turns over to the bride as his wedding gift.

The musical highlights of the opera, beyond the already-mentioned Spring Song of Suzel, include the following: the second-act duet of Fritz and Suzel, sometimes known as the "duet of cherries" ("Suzel, buon dì"); the melodious orchestral intermezzo between the second and third acts; Fritz's third-act aria, when he finally realizes he is in love ("O amore"); and Suzel's rapturous song in the same act ("Non mi resta").

RUGGIERO LEONCAVALLO 1858–1919

There is poetic justice in finding the opera houses of the world coupling Mascagni's *Cavalleria rusticana* and Leoncavallo's *Pagliacci* so frequently for an evening's fare. Between them, these two operas crystallized the Verismo movement in Italian opera (see Mascagni). Like Mascagni, Leoncavallo wrote many other operas besides *Pagliacci.* Though *Zaza* (1900) is occasionally revived, it is through *Pagliacci,* and *Pagliacci* alone, that its composer has won world fame. It is the only one of his operas whose emotional intensity, high drama, and richness of musical invention have assured its permanence in the repertory.

Ruggiero Leoncavallo was born in Naples, Italy, on March 8, 1858. After studying with private teachers, he attended the Naples Conservatory, His first opera, *Chatterton,* was written soon after his studies ended; but the production Leoncavallo had arranged with an unscrupulous impresario failed to materialize when he absconded with Leoncavallo's money. For a number of years after that, Leoncavallo traveled in Europe and the Near East, earning his living mainly by playing the piano in cafés. Returning to Italy, he completed the first opera of a projected trilogy about the Renaissance, *I Medici.* While waiting for this work to get performed, Leoncavallo wrote *Pagliacci,* which established his reputation, following its sensational première in 1892. Now a composer of consequence, Leoncavallo was able to get his earlier operas mounted. *I Medici* was seen in 1893, *Chatterton* in 1896, and both were failures. *La Bohème,* introduced in Venice in 1897, was a success and probably would have become Leoncavallo's most popular opera next to *Pagliacci* but for the fact that Puccini wrote an opera on the same subject and threw Leoncavallo's into a complete shade. Of Leoncavallo's later operas, only *Zaza,* given in Milan in 1900, made any sort of an impression. In 1906, Leoncavallo toured the United States and Canada, conducting *Pagliacci.* For America he wrote a new opera, *La Jeunesse de Figaro,* which proved such a dud, he made no attempt to get it mounted in Europe. He revisited the United States in 1913; and on December 13, 1920, one of his last operas, *Edipo Rè,* received a posthumous world première in Chicago. Leoncavallo died in Montecatini, Italy, on August 9, 1919.

1892. PAGLIACCI, opera in prologue and two acts, with text by the composer. First performance: Teatro dal Verme, Milan, May 21, 1892.

Failing to get a production for his ambitious grand opera, *I Medici,* Leoncavallo soon came to the conclusion that, if he was ever to reach the stage, it would have to be with a work of a more modest design. He decided on an incident he had witnessed in Calabria in his youth, in which a jealous actor murdered his wife during an actual performance. The fact that *Cavalleria rusticana* had recently become a sensation, convinced Leoncavallo of the wisdom of using an opera text involving human emotions passionately and realistically.

He played the completed score for the publisher, Sonzogno, who midway in Leoncavallo's performance went over and threw his arms around him. Sonzogno not only purchased the publication rights but arranged for its brilliant première. The cast was headed by Victor Maurel in the part of Tonio, and Arturo Toscanini was the conductor. The enthusiasm that followed the final curtain was stormy. "The crowded Dal Verme theater was literally in a frenzy," Claude Trevor later recalled. "A scene of such wild enthusiasm took place as is only to be seen rarely." Immediately after that, *Pagliacci* made a triumphant sweep around the world. It came to America for the first time on the stage of the Metropolitan Opera, on December 11, 1893.

The orchestral prelude is built from three motives. The vigorous opening theme suggests the life of strolling players. This is followed by a plangent subject (Largo); in the opera, it describes Canio's grief. The third theme (Appassionato) represents Silvio, the lover. When the prelude ends, Tonio, a hunchbacked clown, comes through the curtain for his famous prologue ("Si può!"). He has come to explain to the audience that the play they are about to witness is a real episode with real people. He then calls for the curtain to rise. It is the feast day of the Assumption of the Blessed Virgin in a Calabrian village. The villagers welcome the arrival of a group of strolling players ("Viva Pagliaccio!"). Canio, head of this troupe, announces a performance for that evening. When the villagers invite Canio for a drink in the nearby tavern, Canio asks Tonio to come with him. When Tonio refuses, the crowd maliciously warns Canio that the only reason Tonio wants to stay behind is because he is waiting for Canio's wife, Nedda. Canio brushes off this gossip with a brief explanation that theater and life are not one and the same thing; it would not be wise for Tonio or Nedda to play a theatrical game ("Un tal gioco"). The tolling of church bells summon the villagers for Vesper services ("Din, don, suona vespero"). Left to herself, Nedda worries over what Canio has just said. She soon throws aside her fears and becomes as lighthearted as the flight of birds, which she describes picturesquely in the Ballatella, "O! che bel sole"). Tonio now emerges from a hiding place to tell Nedda of his feelings for her. Nedda shows her contempt for the deformed clown. Undaunted, Tonio tries to kiss her. When Nedda strikes him with a whip, he stalks off angrily, swearing he will have his revenge. A passionate melody in the orchestra accompanies the appearance of Silvio, a peasant with whom

Nedda is in love. Tonio happens to overhear their passionate exchange of sentiments; hurriedly, he summons Canio to witness what is taking place. Canio arrives in time to see Silvio escape, but is unable to identify him. In vain does he try to get Nedda to reveal who her lover is. When he menaces her with a dagger, Tonio and a fellow clown, Beppe, intervene and save her. Canio then gives vent to his grief by remarking that though his heart is breaking he must soon appear in a comedy. This lament, to be sure, is "Vesti la giubba," not only the melodic high point of the opera, but one of the most famous tenor arias ever written.

Canio's misery is reflected in the lubugrious intermezzo separating the two acts. In the second act, we see the play performed by the strolling players —a play that curiously follows the lines of the true-to-life problems besetting the main performers. Harlequin (played by Beppo) serenades Columbine (enacted by Nedda) with "O Colombina." Taddio (Tonio) comes on the scene and tries to make love to Columbine ("È casta al par di neve"), but is driven off by Harlequin. The love scene of Harlequin and Columbine that follows is interrupted by the arrival of Columbine's husband, Pagliacci (Canio). Harlequin flees. At this point in the performance, Canio suddenly forgets he is playing a role. Savagely he attacks Nedda, demanding to know the name of her lover. When she refuses, he plunges a dagger into her breast. Silvio, who is in the audience, suddenly realizes that this is play-acting no longer. He rushes to the stage to help Nedda, only to be killed by the maddened Canio. Then, turning to the audience, Canio remarks tragically: "The comedy is ended." The knife falls from his hand. The orchestra cries out in anguish with a fortissimo recollection of a phrase from his "Vesti la giubba" aria, and the curtain falls.

Cecil Smith has pointed out that the music of *Pagliacci* is not derived from the traditions formerly established by the school of Bellini, Donizetti, and Verdi. "The musical forerunner of *Pagliacci*," he explains, "is Ponchielli's *La Gioconda,* which first promulgated the vehement vocal style that was adopted by the veristic composers. . . . *Pagliacci* might be called one of the first examples of musical yellow journalism."

GIACOMO PUCCINI 1858–1924

When Puccini invaded the arena, Italian opera was subjected to two powerful influences. On the one hand the impact of Wagner was being felt so strongly that some of the newer Italian composers were beginning to assume many of the mannerisms and ideals of the music drama. On the other hand, Verismo—established with Mascagni and Leoncavallo—was luring other Italians into its fold.

There is some Wagner in Puccini, and more than an occasional touch of Verismo. But Puccini essentially belonged to neither camp. He early recognized his strength. He possessed a lyricism of a haunting melancholy, encompassing tenderness, a winning gentleness—"naked emotion," is the way Donald Jay Grout described it, "crying out, and persuading the listener's feelings by its very earnestness." In addition, Puccini boasted an aristocratic style, whether writing for orchestra or voice. He knew the theater well, was a master of stage effects. He was always able to summon the musical materials he had at hand for the dramatic end he wished to serve; and when those materials were not available, he was capable of uncovering new ones of his own—for Puccini was also an innovator. "The expression of silence, of humble speech, the portraying of intimate, charming characteristics . . . are new contributions to the lyric stage," says George R. Marek. "So is his peculiar melody." Finally, Puccini was incomparable in the delineation of frail, simple, lovable, and exciting heroines.

He was never intended for vast operatic concepts, for dramas on a large scale, and he knew it. "The only music I can make is of small things," he once said. But in writing of small things he was a genius. And through the writing of small things he became the foremost Italian operatic composer after Verdi.

Most of the Puccini operas that hold the world's opera stages came after 1900, and consequently are not within the scope of this volume. These include *Tosca, Madama Butterfly, Gianni Schicchi,* and *Turandot* among other works.

But by 1900, Puccini had written two important operas in which his personality and style were fully realized. These were *Manon Lescaut* and *La Bohème.* And it is with these two immensely successful works—the latter possibly the most popular of all Puccini operas—that Puccini appeared as the logical successor to Verdi's throne.

Giacomo Puccini was born in Lucca, Italy, on December 22, 1858. Early music study took place at the Istituto Musicale of Lucca, where he showed such talent that a subsidy was raised to send him to the Milan Conservatory. Puccini stayed there three years, a pupil of Ponchielli and Bazzini among others. For his graduation he wrote *Capriccio sinfonico,* which was well received. His first opera, *Le Villi,* was submitted in a contest sponsored by the publisher Sonzogno. It did not win the prize, but was produced with minor success in Milan on May 31, 1884. On the strength of this work, the publisher Ricordi commissioned Puccini to write a new opera, *Edgar,* produced with moderate success at La Scala on April 21, 1889. Puccini's first triumph came with his third opera, *Manon Lescaut,* in 1893. His fame was further solidified throughout the world of music with *La Bohème* in 1896, *Tosca* in 1900, and *Madama Butterfly* in 1904.

In 1907, Puccini visited the United States for the first time, to assist at the Metropolitan Opera production of *Madama Butterfly*. In America, Puccini was commissioned by the Metropolitan to write *The Girl of the Golden West,* whose première—in New York on December 10, 1910—was a gala event.

Puccini did not live to complete his last opera, *Turandot*. A victim of cancer of the throat, he submitted to an operation in Brussels that induced a fatal heart attack. Puccini died in Brussels on November 29, 1924.

1893. MANON LESCAUT, opera in four acts, with text by Luigi Illica, Marco Praga, and Domenico Oliva, based on the romance of Abbé Prévost. First performance: Teatro Regio, Turin, February 1, 1893.

Having suffered failures with his first two operas, Puccini came to the conclusion he would have to seek out texts more grateful to his artistic personality and musical endowments. Thus he came upon Prévost's romance of Manon Lescaut—which Massenet had already set to music and with which he had realized a masterwork that had won the admiration of the world. Puccini fell in love with the story. The heroine was somebody who could inspire him, and whom he could bring to life with his individual sensitive lyricism. It took an act of courage to write an opera on the same subject that Massenet had used and with which he had won world acclaim. Then a comparatively inexperienced and unknown composer who still had to prove himself, Puccini was coming to grips with a champion. But Puccini was not afraid of the challenge. His *Manon Lescaut* turned out to be, not an echo of Massenet, but pure Puccini, with its own charm, grace, and poignancy. He flooded Prévost's story with unforgettable Puccini melodies. "They keep coming," as George R. Marek explained, "one after another with a prodigality that is the prodigality of youth. From Edmondo's first carefree tune to Manon's last lament, they crowd upon us, some gay, some capricious, some flashing, but the best of them sighing, set in a melting mood, real Puccini melodies."

If there were any eyebrows raised in Turin in 1893 that Puccini should dare to write an opera in competition with Massenet, they were lowered quickly enough. The first-night audience was stunned by the beauty of Puccini's opera. No effort was made to compare it with Massenet, for it was *sui generis*. As one unidentified reporter wrote in a Milan newspaper after the première: "The echo of the last notes of the orchestra, epilogue to a drama of human suffering, has just died away, and I am here, confused, stunned, and wondering; and, what is of more importance, profoundly moved: moved even to tears. And I am not alone in this. The public has wept with me, and even the Turin musical critics, known for their reserve and their coldness, confess that they were moved, and tomorrow they will say it themselves in the papers." They did. "*Manon,*" said the *Corriere della Sera,* "is the work of a genius conscious of his own power, master of his art, a creator and perfecter of it. *Manon* can be ranked among the classical operas." Bernard Shaw said prophetically after first hearing *Manon:* "Puccini looks to me more like the heir of Verdi than any other of his rivals."

Manon Lescaut was first seen in the United States, on May 27, 1898 in Philadelphia. Its first appearance at the Metropolitan Opera took place on January 18, 1907, a performance which Puccini attended. He reported: "*Manon's* first night was almost beyond description. Enthusiastic reception by a theater filled to overflowing. . . . Extraordinary ovations—I've never had anything like it."

The first act transpires in the courtyard of an inn at Amiens. Manon Lescaut has arrived by coach—en route to a convent—in the company of her brother, and a Parisian galant, Geronte, who is interested in her. The young and handsome Chevalier des Grieux is also present. His sadness is noted by his companions who taunt him that he must be in love. To this, Des Grieux replies lightly with the aria, "Tra voi, belle." The moment Des Grieux catches a glimpse of Manon, he falls in love with her. He is ecstatic over her beauty ("Donna non vidi mai"). When Des Grieux uncovers a plot hatched by Geronte to abduct Manon, he entreats her to run off with him to Paris in Geronte's own coach. After the pair have left, Geronte vows to use his wealth and influence to get vengeance. Manon's brother consoles him with the thought that she will surely desert Des Grieux before long.

Lescaut's prophecy comes to pass. Manon has deserted Des Grieux to live with Geronte, at whose apartment we find her in the second act. But Manon has not forgotten Des Grieux. She bewails the fact to her brother that luxury is no substitute for real love ("In quelle trine morbide"). To provide her with distraction, Geronte summons a group of singers to entertain her with a madrigal ("Sulla vetta tu del monte"). Later on, he encourages her to dance a minuet with him and with some of his friends. After the company has gone, Des Grieux appears. He severely upbraids Manon for having deserted him ("Ah, Manon, mi tradisce"). It is not long before their one-time passion is reawakened. When Geronte arrives, he finds them in each other's arms. Angrily, he rushes off to fetch the police. Manon's brother urges the lovers to escape, but before Manon can gather her valuables, she is trapped and arrested.

An atmospheric orchestral intermezzo separates the second and third acts; it describes Manon's journey to Le Havre, on the way to permanent exile in Louisiana. In the third act, in a square in Le Havre, Lescaut and Des Grieux have come to save Manon from deportation, but in their attempts to bribe the guards they prove unsuccessful. Des Grieux now pleads for permission to go with Manon to Louisiana ("No! pazzo son!"). His eloquence breaks down the resistance of the guards, who smuggle him aboard ship.

In the final act, Des Grieux and Manon are on a desolate plain near New Orleans. They have come in search of shelter, and are in a state of complete exhaustion. Manon poignantly speaks her regret at having reduced the man she loves to such a pitiable state ("Tutta su me ti sposa"). When Des Grieux leaves her momentarily, she is haunted by terror ("Sola, perduta, abbandonata"). By the time Des Grieux returns, she is dying.

1896. LA BOHÈME, opera in four acts, with text by Giuseppe Giacosa and Luigi Illica, based on *Scènes de la vie de Bohème* by Henri Murger. First performance: Teatro Regio, Turin, February 1, 1896.

Puccini had not hesitated to write *Manon Lescaut,* even though he had to challenge the supremacy of Massenet's *Manon.* It could, then, hardly be expected that he should have avoided the subject of *La Bohème* upon learning that Leoncavallo (recently become famous for *Pagliacci*) was planning such an opera. Murger's romance of Bohemian artists in Paris's Montmartre and his tender characterization of Mimi had made a strong impression on Puccini. He knew that this was his kind of material, and envisioned an opera that would portray Bohemians and Bohemian life in Paris with compassion and sensitivity.

One day, at a Milan café, Puccini revealed to Leoncavallo his intention of writing *La Bohème.* Leoncavallo, planning to do a similar opera was stunned. Neither Puccini nor Leoncavallo would withdraw from the project. "Very well, then," Puccini told Leoncavallo, "then there will be two *La Bohèmes.*"

There were two—and Puccini's came first. Leoncavallo's came a little more than a year after Puccini's, in Venice on May 6, 1897. Though the Leoncavallo opera was highly esteemed, and though much in it was attractive, it could not help being completely overshadowed by Puccini's masterwork. Leoncavallo never forgave Puccini. To the end of his life, the composer of *Pagliacci* expressed only hatred and contempt for Puccini at every conceivable occasion.

Peculiarly enough, at their respective premières, Leoncavallo's opera did far better than Puccini's, even though the Puccini première was a gala affair. Toscanini conducted. The audience came with expectancy and anticipation to see how far the composer of the wonderful *Manon Lescaut* had developed. The audience reaction to *La Bohème* was reserved, and most of the critics sent in a negative report. The reason for all this may have been that the audience expected something Puccini had no intention of supplying. The naturalism of the story and characters did not permit big scenes or stirring spectacle. Puccini, instead, had emphasized human values and subtle characterizations in a way few operas had done before this. "We ask ourselves," inquired the critic of the *Gazzetta del Popolo,* "what pushed Puccini on this deplorable road of Bohème." The critic of *Stampa* insisted: "It will not leave much of a mark on the history of our lyric theater." But one or two other critics were more perceptive. Said *La Perseveranza:* "Because of the importance of the subject, the elegance of its workmanship, the quicksilver quality of its comedy, supported by a very fine libretto which does its duty well, because of the vivaciousness of the music, which alternates with delicate, pathetic, and persuasive episodes, because of the variety of the action, *Bohème* will become a strong work in our national repertoire, a precious document to attest that our art still holds high its ancient and glorious banner."

It did not take long for opera audiences to be won over completely to the charms and subtleties of *Bohème*. This happened first in Palermo, on April 13, 1896, when *La Bohème* received a thunderous ovation. After its première in England in 1897, *La Bohème* became a strong favorite in that country, especially after 1899, when Melba began to assume the role of Mimi. The American première took place in Los Angeles on October 14, 1897; the first Metropolitan production followed on December 26, 1900. From then on, *La Bohème* was seen at the Metropolitan every season except one; by 1962, it had been given there over four hundred times.

A short orchestral introduction with a vigorous motive that courses throughout much of the first act leads into a scene in an attic, in Bohemian Paris—the humble abode of Rodolfo, a poet, and Marcello, a painter. The place is cold. Marcello suggests making a fire by burning a chair, but Rodolfo instead offers a sheaf of unpublished manuscripts. Schaunard, a musician, bursts in with the news that he has just acquired a patron; his arms are overflowing with food, drink and fuel. In a jubilant mood, the Bohemians decide to continue their celebration in the Café Momus in the Latin Quarter. Rodolfo stays behind to finish some work. A soft knock at the door disturbs him. It is Mimi, his neighbor, seeking a light for a candle. When she is seized by a coughing fit, Rodolfo attends to her solicitously; then, after she recovers, he escorts her to the door. But she is back again soon, having lost her key. As Rodolfo and Mimi go on hands and knees to look for it, their hands touch. Rodolfo, finding her hands cold, offers to warm them; and as he does so he tells her about his life as a poet, in the opera's most famous tenor aria, "Che gelida manina." Upon the completion of his narrative, Mimi reciprocates by detailing something about herself, how hungry she is for the warmth of springtime ("Mi chiamano Mimi"). Shouts of Rodolfo's friends from the street call the pair to join them at Café Momus. When Rodolfo opens his attic window, the moonlight streams into the room. This leads Rodolfo to rhapsodize over Mimi's beauty as the two give voice to sentiments of love ("O soave fanciulla"). Then the two go off to Café Momus.

The second-act curtain rises on Café Momus in the Latin Quarter; it is Christmas Eve. The square is filled with people in a holiday mood. Rodolfo and Mimi join their Bohemian friends. Musetta, one-time sweetheart of Marcello, arrives with Alcindoro, a wealthy councilor. A coquette by nature, Musetta describes how men are attracted to her—in the charming waltz, "Quando m'en vo' soletta." As Marcello listens to her, he realizes he still loves her, just as Musetta is aware she really has never gotten over Marcello. On the pretext that her shoe is tight, she sends Alicindoro to a cobbler's shop. Then she rushes to Marcello. When the bill for the refreshments is presented, Marcello instructs the waiter to make Alcindoro pay. The Bohemians then disappear in the crowd. Returning with a new pair of shoes for Musetta, Alcindoro realizes he has been jilted.

Tragedy now begins to penetrate into the lives of the Bohemians. Rodolfo has quarreled with Mimi, and Marcello with Musetta. Mimi, shivering and coughing, has come to a tavern at one of the city gates. Finding Marcello, she reveals that she and Rodolfo have come to the parting of ways, Rodolfo's insane jealousy having made their life together intolerable. When Rodolfo appears, Mimi hides behind a tree where she overhears his bitter complaints about her; at the same time, he expresses concern over Mimi's delicate health ("Mimi e tanto malata!"). When Mimi comes out of hiding, Marcello tries to bring her into the tavern. The sound of Musetta's gay laughter inside makes him stop. When he realizes Musetta is flirting with somebody, he rushes inside, leaving Mimi with Rodolfo. The sight of poor Mimi, coughing and wan, revives Rodolfo's tenderness. He takes her in his arms. But Mimi insists he must leave her for his own good ("Donde lieta usci"). At first they bid each other farewell ("Addio, dolce svegliare"), but soon find they cannot separate, and go off together.

In the fourth act we are back in the attic room. Marcello and Rodolfo, having now been separated for some time from Musetta and Mimi, recall the happiness they had once known with their respective sweethearts. Rodolfo is particularly affected by his memories of Mimi ("Ah, Mimi tu più"). With the arrival of Colline, the philosopher, and Schaunard, the gloom is dispelled. Food and drink revive the spirits of the Bohemians. Hilarity sets in with a mock duel and a quadrille. At the height of the merrymaking, Musetta bursts in; she has brought Mimi with her, who is sick and emaciated. Rodolfo has Mimi put to bed, then sends his friends to get some medicine. Alone, Rodolfo and Mimi confess that their love for each other has never really died. Passionately they embrace. Upon their return, Rodolfo's friends are in gloom, for they know Mimi's end is near. As Rodolfo goes to the window to cover it and shield Mimi from the light, Schaunard takes one look at the bed and realizes at once that Mimi is dead. Turning around from the window, Rodolfo instantly guesses what has happened. Crying out the name of "Mimi," he falls sobbing on her prostate body.

UMBERTO GIORDANO 1867–1948

A younger contemporary of Puccini, Giordano was one of the last significant exponents of Verismo. His equipment included a varied fund of ingratiating melodies and a strong bent for theatrical effects. But his weakness for the obvious and the meretricious, a somewhat old-fashioned harmonic language, and a lack of genuine distinction in his workmanship give him a secondary place in the Verismo movement. Nevertheless, his masterwork, *Andrea Chenier,* is unquestionably a work of great power, of dramatic strength and of universal appeal. Its place in the permanent repertory is assured. And the best pages in Giordano's lesser operas (*Fedora* in 1898, *Madame Sans-Gêne* in 1915, and *La Cena delle beffe* in 1924) make their occasional revivals welcome events.

Umberto Giordano was born in Foggia, Italy, on August 27, 1867. After receiving his preliminary instruction in music in his native city, he attended the Naples Conservatory where he was a pupil of Paolo Serrao. While still a student he completed his first opera *Marina,* which he submitted to the competition in which Mascagni won first prize for *Cavalleria rusticana. Marina* made such an impression on the publisher Sonzogno (who had sponsored that competition) that he commissioned Giordano to write *Mala vita,* produced in Rome in 1892. This and the opera that followed it (*Regina Diaz* in 1894) were failures. But *Andrea Chenier* in 1896 made Giordano a world figure in opera. Two years after that came *Fedora,* second only in popularity to *Andrea Chenier* among Giordano's operas. After several successive failures Giordano once again attracted world interest with *Madame Sans-Gêne* which received its world première at the Metropolitan Opera in New York on January 25, 1915, Toscanini conducting. Giordano's last success was *La Cena delle beffe,* first performance at La Scala in Milan on December 20, 1924. Giordano died in Milan on November 12, 1948.

1896. ANDREA CHENIER, opera in four acts with text by Luigi Illica. First performance: La Scala, Milan, March 28, 1896.

Giordano's first successful opera was set in Paris during the time of the French Revolution. Its hero was the famous French poet of the Revolution, André de Chenier, who was guillotined. Giordano had written two operas before this which were failures. Of *Andrea Chenier* he said: "This is my last card. If this opera is not a success, I shall play no more." The last card won the stakes. The world première proved such a triumph that forthwith Giordano was placed with Mascagni, Leoncavallo and Puccini as Italy's most popular composers in the post-Verdi era. *Andrea Chenier* soon made the rounds of Italy's leading opera houses, gathering successes wherever it went. Its American première took place at the Academy of Music in New York on November 13, 1896. The opera was produced for the first time at the Metropolitan Opera on March 7, 1921, when W. J. Henderson reported: "*Andrea Chenier* seems to stand upright and carry a proud crown of foliage."

In *Andrea Chenier,* says Katherine Griffith McDonald, Giordano is "at his best when most colloquial, and least effective when attempting expansive melodies in the Verdi-Puccini manner. Too often the soaring line seems to be the first that came to mind, chosen without much sensitivity to situation or character; sometimes, as in 'La Mamma morta' and the final love duet, it becomes a Procrustean bed into which the text is forced. The effect is curiously square and unconvincing in comparison with the techniques used for most of the opera." Mrs. McDonald then adds: "*Andrea Chenier* is largely an aria opera, for better or worse; even conversations resolve quickly into soliloquies. . . . When the text makes sense, and especially when it moves away from the heroic, Giordano is . . . successful. Moments of ironic humor scattered through the score are underlined by mockingly formal tunes in the eighteenth-century manner. . . . Giordano is clearly a musician of action. When he feels compelled to let the singers vocalize he can turn out grandly lyrical melodies, though they fall somehow short of the perfect appropriateness that makes memorable opera. When, true to his own nature, he lets the music follow the drama and create its own patterns—as an improvisation does—*Andrea Chenier* is fast moving and impressive musical theater."

The first act takes place in the ballroom in De Coigny's palace in Paris. Gerard, a servant, is contemptuous of the decadent French aristocracy, and makes his sentiments known to a sofa ("T'odio casa dorata"). The Countess de Coigny, who is planning a gala party, enters accompanied by her daughter, Madeleine, with whom Gerard is in love. Later on, Madeleine laments the plight of a young girl who must always be fashionable ("Si! io penso all' tortura"). With the party about to begin, guests begin to file into the ballroom, one of whom is the poet, Andrea Chenier. After a pastoral masque has been presented for the delectation of the guests, Madeleine scornfully invites Chenier to speak about love. He does so in the celebrated improvisation, "Un di all' azzurro spazio," in which he sings the praises of France but denounces the church and the aristocracy for their greed and tyranny. The guests are horrified, but their shock and embarrassment become dissipated when they begin to dance a gavotte. Suddenly a group of starving peasants intrude to beg for alms. When the Countess orders their removal, Gerard strips off his livery and announces his allegiance to the downtrodden in "Si, me ne vo, Contessa"). The party continues after Gerard and the peasants have been ejected.

The Revolution is in full swing in the second act; the reign of terror has begun. Chenier is at Café Hottot, a rendezvous for revolutionists, where he is regarded with suspicion since he has denounced Robespierre. Roucher, Chenier's friend, warns him to flee from Paris, but Chenier refuses. One of the things that keeps him in Paris are the mysterious letters he has been receiving from an unknown Parisian woman, whom he is eager to meet ("Credo a una possanza arcana"). The writer of these notes is Madeleine, who soon appears in the café in disguise. She reveals her true identity to Chenier in "Eravate possente." Now realizing they love one another, Chenier and Madeleine plot to run off together ("Ora soave, sublime ora d'amore"). But before they can effect their escape, Gerard, now an important revolutionary figure, appears. When he tries to seize Madeleine, Chenier attacks and wounds him, then flees. Gerard, however, refuses to reveal to the angry mob the identity of his assailant.

Chenier has been caught and arrested. In the third act he is being brought to trial before the revolutionary tribunal. Gerard describes the sad plight of France as, from outside the courtroom, the people are heard singing the revolutionary song, the "Carmagnole." Compelled to denounce Chenier, Gerard is torn by inner conflict, since he cannot forget his friend's nobility and loyalty ("Nemico della patria"). Nevertheless, he signs the paper that seals Chenier's doom. When Madeleine comes to plead for Chenier, Gerard tries to convince her she belongs to him alone, and to forget Chenier forever ("Perchè ciò volle il mio voler possente"). In an effort to save Chenier's life, Madeleine offers herself to Gerard in return for the poet's freedom. She then describes bitterly how her mother had been murdered ("La Mamma morta"). Moved by her narrative, Gerard promises to help Chenier. The courtroom now becomes filled for the trial. Chenier defends himself eloquently in "Si, fui soldato." Despite Gerard's efforts, the poet is condemned to die.

In the last act, Chenier is awaiting execution in prison. He writes an eloquent poem of farewell, "Come un bel di di maggio." Madeline now appears, having bribed one of the jailers; she has come to die with her love. They embrace, repeat their eternal devotion ("Vicino a te s'aqueta"), then hand in hand go to the guillotine.

1898. FEDORA, lyric drama in three acts with text by Arturo Colautti, based on the drama of the same name by Victorien Sardou. First performance: Teatro Lirico, Milan, November 17, 1898.

Fedora, which followed *Andrea Chenier* by two years, was a monumental success at its première and immediately thereafter. Time, however, has robbed *Fedora* of much of its one-time appeal. The blood and thunder play by Sardou on which the opera is based lacks conviction, and its intense passions stir the blood no longer. But a handful of Giordano's arias, together with the effective characterization of the heroine, make a revival of *Fedora* a rewarding experience. As Philip Hope-Wallace has said: "Giordano's best melodies . . . are real inspirations, even though they may be 'immediate' pleasures rather than hidden treasures which linger teasingly in the mind all your life. When the Russian Princess Fedora is introduced to the anarchist who bombed her fiancé and is passionately attracted to him. . . Giordano writes his tenor that brief 'Amor ti vieta.' Could anything be more effective in its place?. . . *Fedora* is not, of course, epoch making. But it does not deserve oblivion."

The action in the opera shifts from St. Petersburg to Paris to Switzerland in the last years of the nineteenth century. The heroine, Fedora, is a Princess about to marry Count Vladimir. She reveals how much she loves him by addressing his photograph ("O grandi occhi"). Soon the Count is carried into the palace; he has been fatally wounded by an assassin believed to be Count Loris Ipanov, a Nihilist. Fedora vows to get revenge.

In the second act, Fedora has come to Paris. As part of her plot to avenge the death of her beloved, she contrives to get Count Loris to fall in love with her. At one of her receptions, the Count confesses to her how much she has come to mean to him ("Amor ti vieta"). Taking Fedora into his confidence, he now reveals that it is true that he is the slayer of Vladimir. Angrily, Fedora summons the police, only to discover before their arrival the true reason for Loris's crime: Vladimir had seduced Loris's wife. This revelation makes Fedora lose all enthusiasm for her vengeance. She now helps Loris escape.

The third act, in Fedora's villa in Switzerland, finds Fedora and Loris now married. But a dark shadow covers their lives. Having previously denounced Loris's brother, Valerian, as an accomplice to Loris's crime, Fedora has been responsible for Valerian's execution and for Valerian's mother's death through grief. All this turns Loris's love for Fedora to hate. In vain does Fedora plead for forgiveness. Failing to receive it, she takes her life with poison. As she dies in Loris's arms, she hears him exclaim with uncontrolled grief that he has forgiven her.

The American première of *Fedora* took place at the Metropolitan Opera in New York on December 5, 1906. The opera was revived by the Metropolitan in 1925 for Maria Jeritza.

ENGELBERT HUMPERDINCK 1854–1921

It is not difficult to relate Humperdinck's music to Wagner. Humperdinck's harmonic writing, orchestration, chromaticism, use of the Leitmotiv technique, all betray his allegiance to the "music of the future." But in the larger scheme of things, Humperdinck was no imitator of Wagner but the innovator of a new species of opera—the fairy opera based on fairy tales. It was his extraordinary success in this field that encouraged several important German composers after him to write similar works. But even within such a limited sphere, Humperdinck was able to cover a wide range of style. On the one hand, in his masterwork *Hansel and Gretel,* he is as simple and as unpretentious as a folk song; in fact he drew copiously from the well of German folk music. And on the other hand, in *Koenigskinder* he is a modernist who anticipated the song speech (*Sprechstimme*) of the atonalists.

Engelbert Humperdinck was born in Siegburg, near Bonn, Germany, on September 1, 1854. He was a student of architecture when Ferdinand Hiller recognized his talent for music. Hiller convinced Humperdinck to attend the Cologne Conservatory. There, in 1876, Humperdinck won the Mozart Scholarship. Later study took place in Munich, first privately with Franz Lachner, and after that at the Conservatory. In 1879, Humperdinck received the Mendelssohn Prize and in 1881, the Meyerbeer Prize, enabling him to travel to France and Italy. In Italy he became acquainted with Wagner for the first time. He accompanied Wagner to Bayreuth where he assisted in copying out the score of *Parsifal* and helped in the productions. Between 1885 and 1887, Humperdinck was professor at the Barcelona Conservatory; and in 1890, he assumed a professorial post at Hoch's Conservatory in Frankfort-on-the-Main. *Hansel and Gretel,* in 1893, made him a world-famous composer. Humperdinck could now give up his teaching chores and devote himself completely to composition. But in 1900, he returned to pedagogy by becoming director of the Akademische Meisterschule in Berlin. He visited the United States in 1910 on the occasion of the world première of his opera *Koenigskinder* at the Metropolitan Opera. Humperdinck died in Neustrelitz, Germany, on September 27, 1921.

1893. HAENSEL UND GRETEL (HANSEL AND GRETEL), opera in three acts, with text by Adelheid Wette, based on a fairy tale by the brothers Grimm. First performance: Weimar, Germany, December 23, 1893.

Hansel and Gretel is the most successful attempt to carry the fairy tale into the opera house. It had unassuming beginnings. Humperdinck's sister planned a little entertainment for the children of the Humperdinck family. For this purpose she made a dramatization of *Hansel and Gretel* for which Humperdinck supplied a few musical numbers. So pleased was he with his effort and so enchanted with the project as a whole, that he decided to write additional material and make *Hansel and Gretel* into an opera. When he sent his score to Richard Strauss, Strauss unequivocally described it as a masterwork. And it was Strauss who directed the world première of the opera in Weimar. It was a triumph. In less than a year, it was produced virtually in every city in Germany. Many audiences in Germany were weary of Wagner's gargantuan dramas with their political and social symbolism. A simple little opera, in which text had no message to propound and in which the music had the charm and spontaneity of folk music, proved a welcome antidote.

An English opera company, headed by Sir Augustus Harris, brought *Hansel and Gretel* to America for the first time—in an English-language presentation at Daly's Theater in New York on October 8, 1895. The first performance at the Metropolitan Opera (this time in German) took place on November 25, 1905. The opera has since become a children's classic, usually given at Christmas time—though precisely why the opera should be a Yuletide attraction remains a mystery.

The overture is based on material from the opera. The opening religious theme in horns and bassoons is the children's second-act prayer. A dramatic change of mood describes the children's fright in the presence of the Witch. The overture then proceeds to the Dewman's third-act song and the children's dance after they destroy the Witch. It ends with a recall of the prayer melody.

The first act takes place in the hut of Hansel and Gretel. The children are cold and hungry. In an attempt to distract her brother from his troubles, Gretel teaches him a little song and dance, the tune in the style of a German folk song ("Bruederchen, komm tanz' mit mir"). The mother, back from her chores, is disconcerted to find them playing instead of doing housework. Angrily, she sends them off to the woods to pick strawberries for the evening meal. When the father returns home, he is apprehensive over the children's prolonged absence and goes off with his wife to look for them.

In the woods, Gretel stops to rest under a tree and sing a little folk song ("Ein Maennlein steht im Walde"). Hansel catches up with her, a basket full of strawberries in hand. Hungry, the children cannot resist the temptation to gobble up the strawberries. As night falls, the children lose their way and are seized by terror. But terror gives way to fatigue. As they grow drowsy the Sandman comes to lull them to sleep with a haunting lullaby, "Der kleine Sandmann bin ich." The children say their prayers ("Abends will ich schlafen gehen") and fall asleep. To protect them, angels descend and form a ring around them, to the atmospheric music of the "Dream Pantomime."

The next morning the Dewman sprinkles dewrops on the children ("Der kleine Taumann heiss' ich."). The children rouse themselves from their sleep and discover they are outside a gingerbread house. Fearfully they enter and begin to consume pieces of the house when a witch seizes them. Hansel is imprisoned in a cage while Gretel is made to do housework. All the while the witch's chant can be heard, "Hurr, Hopp, Hopp, Hopp." Stealthily Gretel steals the witch's magic wand. With it she is able to free her brother from his cage. Then, upon being ordered by the witch to look into a hot oven, Hansel and Gretel manage to push her into the leaping flames. They dance and sing with joy when they realize the witch is dead ("Gingerbread Waltz"). Suddenly, the gingerbread figures come to life. They are children who had been victimized by the witch's evil powers. By the time the parents of Hansel and Gretel arrive, the children are involved in a noisy celebration.

1898. MAURISCHE RHAPSODIE (MOORISH RHAPSODY), for orchestra. I. Tarifa. II. Tangier. III. Tetuan.

Humperdinck's finest work for orchestra is a set of three portraits of Moorish towns, inspired by three poems of Gustav Humperdinck that appear in the published score. "Tarifa," is "an elegy at sunset" (Langsam). This movement begins with a brief passage for muted violins. After that, a Moorish melody is presented by the English horn, with counterfigures in the violins. Several lesser subjects appear later, the most important being a pastoral tune for oboe and an expressive melody for strings. "Tangier" is a picture of "a night in a Moorish café" (Lebhaft). This is a lively section in which the main subject in the woodwind arrives after a surging string passage placed over chords in the wind. "Tetuan" is a description of a "ride in the desert" (Maessig schnell). Here we get a realistic picture of galloping horses over burning sands and under a hot desert sun. The first-movement Moorish melody is repeated, decorated with contrapuntal material. The coda depicts an oasis—a mirage.

1910. DIE KOENIGSKINDER (ROYAL CHILDREN), opera in three acts, with text by Ernst Rosmer (pen-name for Elsa Bernstein). First performance: Metropolitan Opera, New York, December 28, 1910.

In 1897, Humperdinck wrote incidental music for the play, *Die Koenigskinder*. Once again (as had happened with *Hansel and Gretel*) he became convinced that his score could be extended into an opera. *Die Koenigskinder,* like *Hansel and Gretel,* is a fairy tale set to music. The Goose Girl, who lives in the woods with an evil witch, chances to meet the king's son come disguised as a humble beggar. She falls in love with him. He promises her that she will see him again only when a star falls into a certain lily. This strange event occurs; the two meet again. But the Goose Girl is not fated for happiness. The evil witch destroys her with a poisoned pastry.

In his score Humperdinck experimented with song speech: declamations in prescribed rhythms and pitches juxtaposed to an orchestral accompaniment. By doing this, Humperdinck anticipated the Sprechstimme of such twentieth-century atonalists as Arnold Schoenberg and Alban Berg. But lyricism, rooted in the German folk song, is also present here—found in such episodes as the first-act aria, "Vater, Mutter, hier will ich knien" and in the moving third-act hymn, "O du Lieb' heilige."

The composer was in attendance when the opera received its world première at the Metropolitan Opera. Henry E. Krehbiel reported: "Though the composer hews to a theoretical line, he does it freely, naturally, easily and always with the principles of musical beauty as well as that of dramatic truthfulness and propriety in view. His people's voices float on a symphonic stream, but the voices of the instruments, while they sing in the endless melody, use the idiom which Nature gave them. There is an admirable characterization in the orchestral music, but it is music for all that."

GUILLAUME LEKEU 1870–1894

Though Lekeu was only twenty-four when he died, he nevertheless succeeded in completing several remarkable works—so original in their melodic gift, so sensitive in style, so delicate in emotion, so high-minded in purpose, and so touching in sentiment that he remains a significant figure in French Romantic music. The greatest influence upon him had been that of César Franck; but Lekeu's writing and thinking also betrayed the impact of Beethoven and Wagner. All the same, he reveals his own image. "I do not like pretty music, nor any music that is not deeply felt," he once said. "I am impelled to put my whole soul in my music."

Martin Cooper explains that Lekeu's ideal was "to make every note *alive,* not merely well placed in a pattern, but emotionally *speaking.*" Lekeu also aimed to abolish "all 'accompaniment.' . . . It was a dream of idealistic egalitarianism—each part, each voice, each instrument contributing to the grand emotional effect. . . . He was intensely emotional. . . and acknowledged no other criterion of excellence in music."

Guillaume Lekeu was born in Heussy, near Verviers, Belgium, on January 20, 1870. When he was five his family moved to Poitiers where he attended high school. Hearing some music by Beethoven when he was fourteen inflamed Lekeu's musical interests. He started studying piano and solfeggio and to dissect and analyze the masterworks of Bach, Beethoven and Wagner. In 1889, he completed the *Chant de triomphale déliverance* for orchestra, performed in Verviers. Meanwhile, in 1888, he had settled in Paris to begin there an intensive period of music study, first with Gaston Vallin, then with César Franck and finally (after Franck's death) with Vincent d'Indy. In 1891, Lekeu received the second Belgian Prix de Rome for the cantata, *Andromède.* This work made such an impression on Eugène Ysaÿe, that he commissioned Lekeu to write for him a violin sonata, which Ysaÿe introduced in 1892. In January 1894, Lekeu was stricken by typhoid that proved fatal. He died in Angers, on January 21, 1894, one day after his twenty-fourth birthday.

1891. ADAGIO FOR STRINGS (also for string quartet).

A motto lifted out of a poem by Georges Vanor appears at the head of the published score to provide a clue to the mood of the music. It reads: "The pale flowers of memory." The Adagio opens with an elegiac subject for the violins. This melancholy feeling is intensified with a touching melody for the violin; then the opening elegy is repeated. In his scoring, Lekeu divides his violins into a solo violin and into first, second, third and fourth violins; the violas, into first and seconds; the cellos into solo cello and first and second cellos. In certain places even these subdivisions are split into smaller segments.

1891. SONATA IN G MAJOR, for violin and piano. I. Introduction; Vivo con passione. II. Molto lento. III. Finale.

O. G. Sonneck finds in this sonata—written for and introduced by Eugène Ysaye—the "freshness and joyousness of youth in the first movement," which is continually electrified through the use of "bold, biting dissonances." The second movement is music of "the utmost calm [in which] sadder chords are touched." Sonneck further explains: "The themes of the sonata show a remarkable lung capacity. They possess breadth. . . . Instead of dissecting, doubling, telescoping, breaking up his themes and juggling them with their component parts . . . Lekeu preferred to leave his themes more or less intact and sought to make the thematic narrative more convincing by repetition of important phrases at different pitches."

1892. FANTAISIE SUR DEUX AIRS POPULAIRES ANGEVINS (FANTASY ON TWO POPULAR ANGEVIN AIRS), for orchestra.

Lekeu's Fantasy is based on two tunes he heard whistled in Angers. He apparently had a program in mind in writing this composition. In a letter describing d'Indy's enthusiasm, he added: "He finds the *fête populaire* at the beginning most infectiously gay, the impression of night on the plain at the end 'exquisite' and the love scene 'charming.'"

Martin Cooper explains that neither one of the two folk songs is in itself appealing, but he finds this to be an advantage. "Lekeu . . . takes the last phrase of his second melody and plays about it, naïvely but pleasantly, until he gets it into a rhythmic shape which will combine with his first tune. . . . He then tries transferring the rhythm of the second theme to the notes of the first, returns to what had originally been merely a bridge between themes one and two and varies his own variations, all with a skill which is not that of a master but of a gifted apprentice who is already at ease in handling musical ideas of a simple order."

1892. TROIS POÈMES, for voice and piano. I. Sur une tombe. II. Ronde. III. Nocturne.

Lekeu's only work for voice and piano is a setting of his own texts; a quoted epigraph heads each of the three numbers. Vernon Duke, in his program notes to a recording of the Society of Forgotten Music, goes on to say; "The first of the *Poèmes* . . . (epigraph by Lamartine) is a touching elegy, remarkable for its scrupulous economy of means. The second . . . (prefaced by Verlaine's 'And we loved that dupe's game') is a gay, outgoing romp with flavorsome folksy overtones—the carefree ritornello, shot through with meditative interludes. The last song . . . (the romantic epigraph is by Victor Hugo) suggests an enchanting landscape, extravagantly colored and requiring the utmost fluency and ease on the singer's part."

1893. PIANO QUARTET IN B MINOR. I. Dans un emportement douloureux; Très animé. II. Lent et passionée.

Lekeu did not live to complete his piano quartet; this chore was done for him after his death by Vincent d'Indy. The first movement is in a free sonata form. A forceful first subject appears in the piano supported by passionate accompaniment of unison strings. After this thought is repeated by the cello and then by the violin, a spacious melody unfolds in the piano. A calm codetta ends the exposition before the appearance of an extended development section. In the recapitulation, the second theme is discussed before the first. The second movement is one of Lekeu's highest flights of lyricism. A fifteen-measure introduction precedes an expansive and expressive song, first heard in the cello, then in the viola and finally in first violin. A recitative for piano is the transition to a second noble melody. Temporary agitation, with spirited passages for the piano, yield to a section of wondrous calm, the mood in which this movement ends.

ERIK SATIE 1866–1925

By the time the nineteenth century ended, Erik Satie had become one of music's most influential iconoclasts. Already he had produced a number of piano pieces whose experiments and unorthodox idioms branded him one of the earliest of France's modernists. Later on, in the twentieth century, Satie would outrage his contemporaries by using outlandish titles and including in his compositions whimsical instructions for the performers. But he was also a rebel before 1900. Here, as later, he carried on his one-man onslaughts against the overstuffed Romantic tendencies of the post-Wagner era; against those self-appointed high priests of music who moved about in a rarefied atmosphere and concerned themselves exclusively with grandiose concepts. In his rebellion Satie was seeking a simpler kind of music—music that was human, witty, down to earth.

This editor has written in *David Ewen Introduces Modern Music:* "Many of the later French composers who were either his contemporaries or his successors were able to write the kind of music they did and to adopt their brand of musical principles, because of Satie. With Satie came an invigorating breath of fresh air, a revitalizing burst of warm sunlight, into the dank and stuffy living room of the post-Wagnerian idiom. Satie represented youth and rejuvenation for modern music—where the music of post-Wagnerism could only lead to decadence." By their own admissions, both Debussy and Ravel were given direction by Satie—even though later in his own career Satie also revolted against the preciousness of Impressionism. In the twentieth century Satie was the spiritual godfather to two modernist schools: the "French-Six" which included Arthur Honegger, Darius Milhaud, and Francis Poulenc; and the "Arceuillists" which embraced Roger Desormière and Henri Sauguet.

Erik Satie was born in Honfleur, France, on May 17, 1866. He received his first lessons in music from the town organist, who aroused his interest in old polyphonic methods. In his thirteenth year, Satie entered the Paris Conservatory. There he came into conflict with both his teachers and his fellow students: with his teachers because of his esoteric and discordant pieces; with his fellow students because of his partiality for medieval plain-chants and modal music. After about a year, Satie quit the Conservatory to proceed on his own with his musical experiments. His first important piano pieces appeared between 1886 and 1890, their novelty and unique approaches arousing considerable antagonism among his contemporaries. Meanwhile he earned his living playing the piano at a Montmartre café, *Le Chat Noir,* where he first met and influenced Debussy.

After the turn of the twentieth century, Satie's innovations grew bolder. Many French musicians regarded him as a charlatan and buffoon; a few recognized him as a significant creative force. Then, dissatisfied with his technique, Satie returned to music study just before his fortieth birthday. He enrolled in the Schola Cantorum where his teachers included Vincent d'Indy and Albert Roussel. Following this three-year period of re-education, Satie embarked on several ambitious projects, including a satirical ballet, *Parade,* in 1916 and a lyric drama, *Socrate,* in 1918. To the end of his days, Satie refused to accept the status quo in music; to the end of his days he remained a humorist, an eccentric, and a revolutionary. He died in Paris on July 1, 1925.

1887–1897. COMPOSITIONS FOR SOLO PIANO:
Sarabandes; *Gymnopédies; Gnossiennes.*
Pièces Froides: I. Airs à faire fuir. II. Danses de travers.

Satie's first composition for the piano was *Ogives* in 1886. In the three Sarabandes that followed in 1887 the classic and stately dance is dressed in modern harmonies: chords of the ninth and eleventh are here used that anticipate Debussy. This music is a break with the chromatic harmonies of the late nineteenth century, opening up new areas which many of Satie's contemporaries and successors would cultivate so fruitfully.

Satie's most significant piano music of this early period is a set of three *Gymnopédies* (1888), dances for the piano. A "gymnopedia" was a religious festival in ancient Sparta in which naked youths worshiped their Gods in song and dance. Satie was stimulated into writing this music by a decoration on a Greek vase. Each of the three pieces is in slow 3/4 time; each opens with a four-measure introduction; each presents a grave and serene melody in the right hand. In simplicity, economy, and directness this music represents another important rupture with the inflationary methods of post-Romanticism. But here, too, we encounter advanced thinking—particularly in the use of unusual harmonic progressions. "The strangeness of his harmonic coloring," said Constant Lambert, "is due, not to the chords themselves, but to the unexpected relationships he discovers between the chords, which in themselves are familiar enough. . . . His progressions have a strange logic of their own, but they have none of the usual sense of concord and discord, no trace of the *point d'appui* that we usually associate with the word progression. They may be said to lack harmonic perspective in much the way that a cubist painting lacks spatial perspective."

The first and third of the *Gymnopédies* were orchestrated by Claude Debussy.

Satie's experiments grew even more daring in the three *Gnossiennes* (1890) suggested by Flaubert's *Salammbô*. Here for the first time Satie used barless notation. Much of the effect of these pieces comes from the use of continually repeated melodic phrases against a persistent fundamental bass.

In the two *Pièces Froides* (1897) the style, says W. Wright Robert, is "classical in a true sense, classical in their firmness and economy of workmanship, and in their broad impersonality."

CLAUDE DEBUSSY 1862–1918

As the father of musical Impressionism, Debussy was one of the most significant generative forces in twentieth-century music. He had been a rebel from his Conservatory days on. There he had shocked his teachers with compositions flaunting the textbook with unresolved seventh chords, parallel fifths, and counterpoint in parallel motion. The "envois" he sent back from Italy as a Prix de Rome winner were so new in style and idiom that the academicians of the Paris Conservatory denounced them in no uncertain terms. "I can only make my *own* music," was Debussy's reply. Once back in Paris, where he was influenced by that *enfant terrible* of French music, Erik Satie (see above)—and where he came into personal contact with the Impressionist painters and the Symbolist poets—Debussy was able to direct his lifelong revolutionary tendencies into constructive, creative channels. He now aspired consciously to write music freed from restrictions imposed upon it by classicism and from the emotional excesses to which the Romantics had subjected it. He renounced realism, programmatic writing, or the dramatic aims of composers like Wagner. He dreamed of an altogether new kind of music that would achieve through tones what Manet, Renoir, and Cézanne had accomplished with paints and Stéphane Mallarmé with poetry. He sought out a music in which light and color, nuance and atmosphere were all-important, where subject matter was of lesser significance. The Impressionists had freed painting from the bondage of representation, and the Symbolists had liberated poetry from slavery to ideas. This same kind of revolution Debussy hoped to realize in music. "Chords became for him," this editor has written elsewhere, "a means of projecting color and thus were used individually for their own specific effect rather than for their relationship to chords that preceded or followed them. Unresolved ninths and elevenths, moving about freely without concern for a tonal center, evoked for Debussy a world of shadows and mystery, just as the forbidden fifths, the avoidance of formal cadences, and the use of rapidly changing meters and rhythms helped him create elusive moods and evanescent sensations. A new kind of melody—sensitive, refined, seemingly remote—was realized through the use of exotic Oriental scales, church modes, and, most of all, through the whole-tone scale. The last—though appearing in the works of earlier composers—is always identified with Debussy, for it is Debussy alone who used it so extensively and with such extraordinary artistic effect. The whole-tone scale (as the term indicates) is made up entirely of whole tones, the octave being divided into six equal parts. Its unusual intervallic structure is uniquely suited for melodies of a nebulous and haunting character. Thus Debussy became music's first great painter, the first to arrive at new textures, sensations, images, and nuances in sound."

Achille Claude Debussy was born in Saint-German-en-Laye, near Paris, France, on August 22, 1862. After receiving piano instruction from Mme. Mauté de Fleurville (a pupil of Chopin), Debussy entered the Paris Conservatory when he was eleven. He stayed there seven years, studying with Marmontel, César Franck, Émile Durand, and Léo Delibes. Though an iconoclast who infuriated some of his teachers with his unorthodox ways, Debussy was a brilliant student and won numerous prizes. After graduating from the Conservatory, Debussy worked as a household pianist and teacher at the Russian estate of Mme. Nadezhda von Meck, Tchaikovsky's patroness and "beloved friend." In 1884, he received the Prix de Rome for *L'Enfant prodigue*. Unhappy in Rome, and dissatisfied with the way officials were reacting to his "envois," Debussy left Italy without completing his three-year residence. Back in Paris, he completed his first major work, *La Demoiselle élue,* together with some highly gifted songs and piano pieces. Influenced by Satie, the Impressionist painters, and the Symbolist poets, Debussy now began to evolve and crystallize his own manner and style, and by doing so, gave birth to musical Impressionism. His first masterworks in a fully realized Impressionist style were the String Quartet in G minor and the orchestral prelude, *L'Aprés midi d'un faune,* between 1893 and 1894. This was followed by the works that helped make Debussy one of the most influential composers in post-Wagnerian music: the three Nocturnes for orchestra, introduced in 1900; the opera *Pelléas and Mélisande,* first seen at the Opéra-Comique on April 30, 1902; the symphonic sketches, *La Mer,* in 1905; and between 1905 and 1913, the two volumes of *Images* and the two books of Preludes, all for piano. Only those works written before 1900, however, are discussed in the pages that follow.

In 1899, Debussy married Rosalie Texier. He left her five years later to elope with Emma Bardac, then the wife of a banker. Debussy and Emma were married as soon as she got her divorce; they had one child, a daughter, for whom Debussy wrote his delightful *Children's Corner* for piano, and who died when she was only fourteen.

Plagued by cancer, Debussy lived the last years of his life in physical torment. He died in Paris on March 25, 1918.

1877–1900. SONGS, for voice and piano:

"Beau soir"; "Il Pleure dans mon coeur"; "Mandoline".

Chansons de Bilitis, song cycle: La Flûte de Pan. 2. La Chevelure. 3. Le Tombeau de Naïades.

Fêtes galantes, first series: 1. En Sourdine. 2. Clair de lune. 3. Fantoches.

It was in the song form that Debussy first fulfilled himself. His early production in this area contains remarkable melodic invention and extraordinary sensitivity to a poetic text. "Beau Soir" (1878) is a work of Debussy's youth, and reveals him to be still under the influence of Massenet. The song, like the poem by Bourget, is filled with the wondrous beauty and mystery of nighttime at the banks of a river; the melody is touched gently with the sadness of death. "Mandoline," poem by Verlaine (1880) is one of Debussy's most popular songs before 1900. Lightly, spontaneously, it touches on the exchanges of serenaders and their fair ladies. To "Il Pleure dans mon coeur," poem by Verlaine—the third of five numbers in a cycle entitled *Ariettes oubliées* (1888)—the composer appended a line from Rimbaud: "It rains gently on the city." The restrained harmonies and the fluid lyric line carry over the feeling of the rain that is descending not only on the city but in the poet's heart.

To Oscar Thompson, the songs in *Chansons de Bilitis,* (1897), poems by Pierre Loüys, "place Debussy beside Wolf and Mussorgsky as supreme masters of word setting. . . . *Chansons de Bilitis* must be regarded as among the ripe fruits of an art at once sensitive and voluptuous, reticent and sybaritic."

Debussy produced two sets of *Fêtes galantes* to Verlaine's poems, the first in 1892, the second in 1904. "En Sourdine," which opens the first set, begins and ends with the chirping of a nightingale in a song of love, which hovers over the forests. "Clair de Lune"—not to be confused with the far more popular piano composition of the same name (see 1888–1900)—finds the composer freed of influences, and emerging as the Impressionist poet of subtle mood and landscapes. "A sustained melody," explains Oscar Thompson, "moves in an atmosphere of moonlight to an ending of haunting loveliness." "Fantoches" has intriguing touches of irony.

1887. LA DEMOISELLE ÉLUE (THE BLESSED DAMOZEL), lyric poem for women's voices, solo soprano, and orchestra.

During his residence in Italy as a winner of the Prix de Rome, Debussy read and fell under the spell of Dante Gabriel Rossetti's *La Demoiselle élue.* The poem had been published in 1850 in the pre-Raphaelite journal, *The Germ,* and had come to Debussy in 1885 in a translation by Gabriel Sarrazin. Debussy set for himself the task of setting fourteen of Rosetti's stanzas; but not until after he had returned to Paris, in 1887, did he actually get around to the project. Under the laws of the Prix de Rome, Debussy was required to submit compositions ("envois"). *La Demoiselle élue* became the third such exercise he dispatched to the authorities. His earlier "envois" had been repudiated as "bizarre, incomprehensible, and impossible to execute." The academicians were somewhat kinder to *La Demoiselle élue,* though they were hardly in favor of his use of successive fifths, fluctuating rhythms and shifting tonalities. They felt that this music "still bears the marks of that systematic tendency toward vagueness of expression and form" which they had denounced in earlier Debussy compositions. But they were willing to concede that "these propensities and processes . . . seem to some extent justified by the very nature of the subject and its indefinite character." However, they did not permit the work to get performed. The première finally took place at a concert of the Société nationale in Paris on April 8, 1893.

The exquisite orchestral prelude opens with a serene subject for divided strings and woodwind. An extended song appears first in strings, then in woodwind. This is followed by a pastoral episode for the flutes. The chorus then enters with "The Blessed Damozel leaned out from the gold bar of Heaven."

Of the work as a whole, Léon Vallas has written: "It exhales a curious, delightfully fragrant perfume. . . . The succession of fifths in the very first bars proclaim the young composer's audacious personality. . . . The spirit of Wagner—the Wagner of *Parsifal*—hovers over the entire work; there is a faint suggestion of César Franck . . . and Massenet's caressing charm greets one at many a turn." Then Vallas adds: "One notices Debussy's constant care to subordinate the symphony to the poem, to interpret the latter in a flowing style resembling the words and, by means of syllabic diction and a choral treatment free from contrapuntal interlacing, to bring out all the words clearly, even those that occur in the united choral parts. There are some attractive and novel effects in the treatment of the female voices, and the instrumentation is light and delicate, though varied throughout."

1888–1900. COMPOSITIONS FOR SOLO PIANO:

2 Arabesques: I. E major. II. G major.

Rêverie.

Petite suite, for piano duet (orchestrated by Henri Busser). I. En Bateau. II. Cortège. III. Menuet. IV. Ballet.

Pour le piano. I. Prélude. II. Sarabande. III. Toccata.

Suite bergamasque. I. Prélude. II. Menuet. III. Clair de lune. IV. Passepied.

Among Debussy's earlier compositions for the piano, the most popular by far is the *Clair de lune* from the *Suite bergamasque*. Though completed in 1905, this suite was begun in 1890, and most of it was written before 1900. Debussy here tried to recreate seventeenth-century clavecin music in terms of his own concepts of harmony, melody, and tone coloring. The third movement, the popular *Clair de lune,* is one of the most sensitive tonal representations of a moonlight night to be found in piano literature. Here is how Guido M. Gatti described this music: "What an airy flowering of arpeggios ascend the keyboard, to leap up again like a fountain jet which scatters its waters on the air then relapses into calm again in solid tonic and dominant undulations, on which the theme spreads out, ample, sonorous, expressive."

The two Arabesques (1888) are among Debussy's first pieces for the piano. They have proved of greater pedagogic value than aesthetic, and are familiar to most piano students. There is little here that suggests Debussy's later idiom and artistic personality.

The *Petite suite* (1889) is also a look back into the past, rather than a glimpse toward the future. It is mostly a child of the French Romantic movement that preceded Debussy, and not a product of Impressionism. The first movement, "In the Boat," presents a gentle barcarolle melody that suggests the graceful movement of a boat in placid waters. A more vigorous section provides contrast, then the barcarolle tune is recalled. A brilliant "March" and a "Minuet" of classic grace follow. The concluding "Ballet" has a strong rhythmic pulse.

The *Rêverie* (1890), despite its unusual harmonic structure and atmospheric melody, was not regarded highly by the composer. He protested its publication, fifteen years after the piece had been written, on the grounds that he had written it hastily. More than a half-century later, this piece of music gained a new lease on popularity in the United Stated as the popular song hit, "My Revery."

Though completed in 1901, most of *Pour le piano* was realized between 1896 and 1900. The first movement Prelude, (in A minor) which makes use of the whole-tone scale, was described by Oscar Thompson as having a "rapid martellato theme, encircled by reiterated figures or reinforced by brilliant overlaid chords." The melody of the Sarabande is to Thompson one of the most serene melodies Debussy ever wrote, and one of the composer's earliest successful realizations for the piano of an Impressionist style. The Toccata (in C-sharp minor) is "a highly colored work, with decorative arpeggios and an adventurous exploration of sonorities."

1893. STRING QUARTET IN G MINOR, op. 10. I. Animé et très decidé. II. Assez vif et bien rhythmé. III. Andantino doucement expressif. IV. Très modéré.

The G minor String Quartet is the first composition in any medium in which the composer's Impressionist style emerges fully developed; and, by the same token, it is the first of his unqualified masterworks. The structure is traditional—the classic moulds of the sonata, the scherzo, and the three-part song form. The impact of César Franck, particularly in the use of a unifying subject within a cyclic form, is evident. But apart from such influences with the past, the Quartet is throughout singularly Debussy in its use of color, in the subtlety of its effects, in its nebulous harmonic texture. The work opens with a motto theme that recurs throughout. It is a strong accented subject for the four instruments. The contrasting theme is a sensitive song for violin and viola. In the second movement, a Scherzo, the motto theme (altered in rhythm, tempo, and intervallic structure) is first heard in viola over a pizzicato accompaniment; later it is taken over by the violin. The third movement is in the three-part song form. The first section consists mainly of a passionate song for muted strings. In the middle part, violin and cello are heard in a haunting lyrical episode. Then the passionate music of the first section returns. The motto theme receives considerable attention in the powerful finale. It is first heard, inverted, in the violin, and then is made the basis of a fugato section.

1894. L'APRÈS MIDI D'UN FAUNE (THE AFTERNOON OF A FAUN), prelude for orchestra.

In 1892, Debussy planned an orchestra triptych comprising a prelude, interlude, and finale based on the Symbolist poem of Stéphane Mallarmé, *The Afternoon of a Faun,* published in 1876. Eugène Ysaÿe consented to give this music its world première in Brussels early in 1894. But this performance did not materialize because by concert time not only was Debussy still revising his music, but by then he had abandoned the idea of a three-part composition for one comprising only the first-movement prelude. That prelude was completed late in 1894, and its world première took place in Paris on December 23, of the same year. The audience proved so enthusiastic that the prelude had to be repeated. Mallarmé expressed his own enthusiasm as follows: "This music prolongs the emotion of my poem and fixes the scene more vividly than color could have done."

The distinguished English writer, Edmund Gosse, prepared the following admirable synopsis of the Mallarmé poem, which can serve as a program for Debussy's prelude. "A faun—a simple, sensuous passionate being—wakens in the forest at daybreak and tries to recapture his experiences of the previous afternoon. Was he the fortunate recipient of an actual visit from nymphs, white and golden goddesses, divinely tender and indulgent? Or is the memory he seems to retain nothing but the shadow of a vision, no more substantial than the 'arid rain' of notes from his own flute? He cannot tell. Yet surely there was, surely there is, an animal whiteness among the brown reeds of the lake that shines out yonder. Were they, are they, swans? No! but the naiads plunging? Perhaps! Vaguer and vaguer grows that impression of this delicious experience. He would resign his woodland godship to retain it. A garden of lilies, golden-headed, white-stalked, behind the trellis of red roses?

Ah! the effort is too great for his brain. Perhaps if he selects only one lily from the garth of lilies, one benign and beneficent yielder of her cup to thirsty lips, the memory, the ever-receiving memory, may be forced back. So when he has glutted upon a bunch of grapes, he is wont to toss the empty skins in the air and blow them out in a visionary greediness. But no, the delicious hour grows vaguer; experience or dream, he will never know which it was. The sun is warm, the grass is yielding; and he curls himself up again, after worshipping the efficacious star of wine, that he may pursue the dubious ecstasy into the more hopeful bondages of sleep."

The extended melody for solo flute, with which the prelude opens, forthwith evokes the half-real, gossamer world inhabited by the faun. A chord in the woodwind, followed by horn calls and harp arpeggios, contribute an air of mystery. The faun's opening flute melody returns and is expanded. We now hear a passionate melody for the oboe. A climax is preceded by a brief subject for woodwind and horns, followed by a monologue in solo violin. Once again the opening flute melody is given, but it soon passes over to flute and solo cello, and then (somewhat altered) to muted horns and violins. A sensitive chord for the flute dissolves into mist the unreal word of fauns and nymphs.

The music of this prelude was used for one of the most successful ballets in the repertory of the Ballet Russe de Monte Carlo, and became one of the supreme achievements of the famous dancer, Nijinsky, who conceived the choreography, and was principal dancer. The ballet was seen for the first time in Paris on May 29, 1912.

1897–1899. THREE NOCTURNES, for orchestra. I. Nuages. II. Fêtes. III. Sirènes.

When the idea to write a set of nocturnes for orchestra first occurred to Debussy he planned a work for solo violin and orchestra to be played by Eugène Ysaÿe. He intended it to be an experiment in instrumental timbres by employing only strings in the first nocturne; horns, flutes, trumpets, and harp for the second; and a combination of both groups for the third. While working on these ideas, Debussy had a sudden change of heart. He decided to score the first two nocturnes for full orchestra, and for the third he interpolated female voices. Here is how the composer himself described his purpose: "The title 'Nocturnes' is intended to have a more general, and above all, a more decorative meaning. We, then, are not concerned with the form of the Nocturne, but with everything that this word includes in the form of diversified impression and special lights."

The following program was appended by the composer to the first nocturne, *Clouds:* "The unchanging aspect of the sky, and the slow, solemn movement of the clouds, dissolving in gray tints, lightly touched with white." The moving clouds are suggested by soft chords in the woodwind. In this section, the principal motives are an atmospheric subject for the English horn; a passage for solo viola; a melody for flute and harp.

The composer thus described the second nocturne, *Festivals:* "The restless dancing rhythm of the atmosphere, interspersed with sudden flashes of light. There is also an incidental procession (a dazzling imaginery vision) passing through and through and mingling with the aerial revery. But the background of uninterrupted festival is persistent, with its blending of music and luminous dust participating in the universal rhythm of all things." A dance rhythm appears in the violins, followed by a lively melody in English horn and clarinets. Calls in trumpet and oboe lead to an important melody for the woodwind which receives detailed treatment. After a climax, a march rhythm makes a dramatic entrance in harp, drums, and plucked strings. The mood later becomes subdued with a gentle melody for the oboe. Then the nocturne fades into mist.

The concluding nocturne, *Sirens,* calls for a chorus of eight mezzo-sopranos performing a wordless chant. This is Debussy's program: "The sea and its innumerable rhythms; then amid the billows silvered by the moon, the mysterious song of the sirens is heard; it laughs and passes." The principal subject is built from two tones, one rising and the other falling over changing harmonies.

EDWARD MACDOWELL 1861–1908

Edward MacDowell was the first significant composer of concert music produced by the United States. A Romantic, nurtured on German music, MacDowell tried to achieve a national identity early in his career. As a young man in Europe he thought of doing a tone poem using the technique of ragtime, but popular music did not stimulate him, and he abandoned the project. Then he completed several works utilizing American-Indian melodies and rhythms, the most notable of which is the *Indian Suite,* for orchestra. But he was at his best adapting the Romantic equipment he had mastered in Germany to his American personality and experiences, as in his deservedly famous second piano concerto; also when his sensitive responses to American Nature scenes sought and found an outlet in delicate pictures for the piano. "He suggested at his best no one save himself," said Lawrence Gilman. "Vitality—an abounding freshness, a perpetual youthfulness—was one of his traits; nobility of style another." Finding MacDowell's best works "charged with emotion," Gilman went on to say: "Yet it is not brooding or hectic, and it is seldom intricate or recondite in psychology. It is music curiously free from the fervors of sex."

Edward MacDowell was born in New York City on December 18, 1861. He began music study early, receiving instruction at the piano from Juan Buitrago and Teresa Carreño. From 1876 to 1878, he attended the Paris Conservatory; and from 1878 to 1879, he completed his music study in Wiesebaden and the Frankfurt Conservatory. After his studies were over, MacDowell stayed on in Germany, earning his living teaching the piano; in 1881, he joined the faculty of the Darmstadt Conservatory. Through Liszt's influence, MacDowell's first *Modern Suite* for piano was heard in Weimar in 1882. MacDowell then settled in Wiesebaden to devote himself to composition. He completed a tone poem (*Hamlet and Ophelia*), the second Modern Suite for piano, and his first piano concerto. Meanwhile, in 1884, he returned briefly to the United States to marry an American, Marian Nevins, one of his pupils. In 1888, MacDowell finally left Europe to make his home in Boston. During the next few years, his reputation as composer was established with performances of his two piano concertos by the Boston Symphony and premières of some of his tone poems and orchestral suites. In 1896, by a unanimous decision of the trustees, MacDowell was appointed to fill a chair of music just created at Columbia University in New York. He held this professorial post for eight years. Toward the end of that period he came to a bitter disagreement with the authorities on how a music department should be run. Frustrated and disillusioned, MacDowell handed in his resignation, but not without airing his grievances in the press. As an aftermath of this unpleasant controversy with the trustees of Columbia, MacDowell developed melancholia. Disintegration of health developed by 1905 into insanity. During the last years of his life, he was like a child, oblivious of his identity, career, or surroundings. He died in New York City on January 23, 1908. Just before his death, his summer home in Peterborough, New Hampshire, was endowed as a summer retreat for creative people, come to be known as the MacDowell Colony; it was directed by MacDowell's widow until her death in 1956.

1885. CONCERTO NO. 2 IN D MINOR, for piano and orchestra, op. 23. I. Larghetto calmato; Poco più mosso e con passione. II. Presto giocoso. III Largo; Molto allegro.

MacDowell's second piano concerto is his most famous concert work, and one of the most significant American representatives in piano-concerto literature. He wrote it while living in Germany, and while being influenced by the German Romantic movement in music. But some of the material of his second movement was also stimulated by a performance of Shakespeare's *Much Ado about Nothing,* starring Henry Irving and Ellen Terry—a performance he had attended in London during his honeymoon. At that time, he thought of writing a tone poem, *Beatrice and Benedick.* Upon deserting that project, he used some of its material for his concerto.

When the concerto was heard for the first time—in New York City on March 5, 1889, with the composer as soloist, and Theodore Thomas conducting—Henry E. Krehbiel reported that the work was "so full of poetry, so full of vigor as to tempt the assertion that it must be placed at the head of all works of its kind by either a native or adopted citizen of America."

The concerto opens with a serene, almost melancholy, introduction. After the piano enters with a powerful statement, it engages the orchestra in a subdued dialogue. The woodwinds then set the stage for the main subject—a broad, romantic melody in the piano. This matter is discussed before the cellos are heard in a broad lyrical second theme. In the development, effective contrasts appear between dramatic and lyrical moods, but the concerto ends with the same kind of melancholy serenity with which it had begun.

The second movement is a graceful, elfin, Mendelssohn-like Scherzo. The first sprightly subject is given by woodwind and strings; the more vigorous second theme comes in the horns. The finale has a slow and deeply moving preface in which the main thought is spoken by cellos and bassoons, while the piano and woodwind offer a reply. The piano then embarks upon an effective soliloquy, which becomes the transition to the main section of the movement. Its principal subject is a vigorous melody for the woodwind. The rest of the movement remains virile and energetic, highlighting sparkling virtuoso passages for the piano together with electrifying episodes for the orchestra.

1892. SUITE NO. 2 ("INDIAN"), for orchestra, op. 48. I. Legend. II. Love Song. III. In War Times. IV. Dirge. V. Village Festival.

The second *Indian Suite* is one of several works in which, searching for a national identity, MacDowell made use of American-Indian melodies and rhythms. The basic material in this work was taken by the composer from Theodore Baker's *Die Musik der Nordamerikanischen Wilden,* which one of MacDowell's pupils (and later the gifted composer), Henry F. Gilbert, brought to his attention. But, as Gilbert took pains to point out, although MacDowell made many basic changes in the themes, these changes "have been in the direction of musical beauty, and enough of the original tune has been retained to leave no doubt as to its barbaric flavor."

The first movement is based on an Iroquois theme, and is believed to have been inspired by Thomas Bailey Aldrich's Indian legend, *Miantowona.* In the opening sections, horns present two contrasting melodies, the second of which is amplified in the main part of the movement. The second movement is a plaintive love song of Iowa Indians. A martial atmosphere prevails in the third movement, its main thought being a savage melody popular with Indian tribes along the Atlantic coast. This is followed by a dirge—a woman's song of mourning among Kiowa Indians. This melody is introduced by tolling bells and is presented by muted unison violins. In the finale, two themes of Iroquois Indians are used. The first is a war dance (plucked strings); the second is a woman's dance (flute and piccolo, accompanied by strings and woodwind).

1896. WOODLAND SKETCHES, suite for piano, op. 51. I. To a Wild Rose, II. Will-o'-the-Wisp. III. At an Old Trysting Place. IV. In Autumn. V. From an Indian Lodge. VI. To a Water Lily. VII. From Uncle Remus. VIII. A Deserted Farm. IX. By a Meadow Brook. X. Told at Sunset.

MacDowell's two most popular piano pieces—*To a Wild Rose* and *To a Water Lily*—are both found in a set of mood and Nature pictures collectively entitled *Woodland Sketches*. Side-stepping American-Indian influences, which had affected some of his earlier works, MacDowell here set out to write music inspired by American scenes and natural beauties, one of the first composers to do so. What John F. Porte said about MacDowell's piano music in general applies forcefully to the *Woodland Sketches* in particular: "His piano poems are absolutely responsive to elemental moods, unaffected in style and yet distinguished, free from the commonplace. Speaking with a personal note that is inimitable, they are mature Nature poems of an exquisitely charming order, beautiful not only for their outward manifestations, but for the deeper significance they give to their sources of inspiration."

RICHARD STRAUSS 1864–1949

Richard Strauss's monumental contributions to opera was a twentieth-century development, beginning with *Salome* in 1905, and continuing with *Elektra* in 1908, and *Der Rosenkavalier* in 1910. For this reason, his dramatic works cannot come under consideration in this volume. But even before 1900, Strauss emerged as an unqualified master in two other fields of musical creativity: the tone poem and the Lied. Even before 1900, he proved himself to be one of the most original, strongly endowed, influential—and villified—composers since Wagner. A composer who lived to see himself become a classic, Strauss produced some of those classics comparatively early in his career.

His cyclonic impact on the world of music was made mainly through his tone poems, all of them completed before 1900. Here Strauss was an outgrowth of the German Romantic movement. In the apprentice compositions that had preceded the tone poems, Strauss was an imitative voice. Finally freeing himself from Brahms, Strauss started to charter a new course for himself. Wagner now became his Northern star. The new course led him (by way of Liszt) to the tone poem. That form was certainly nothing new in 1888, when Strauss wrote his first such work. But Strauss's approach, idiom, techniques, and methods *were* certainly new. His cacophonies, his tonal realism, his introduction of unorthodox instruments (a wind machine and a thunder machine, for example), his unorthodox modulations, his extravagantly sensual melodies, and his lush orchestration and harmonies—all this startled and shocked his contemporaries. "This is not music," César Cui said firmly, "this is a mockery of music." Even Debussy, himself a heretic, could describe one of Strauss's tone poems as "an hour in an insane asylum."

The novelty has vanished; the shock is no more. What remains are masterworks with a grandeur of speech, an incandescent beauty, a wizardry of technique, a cataclysmic dramatic power, and a gift at program writing that found few rivals in the late nineteenth century. Here Strauss "touched life with generous daring," as Lawrence Gilman once wrote, "and at every side—at its lowliest and noblest, at its most disordered and pitiable and grotesque. He had learned how to convey experience still drenched in its essential colors, pungent with veritable odors, rich with all its implications. But Strauss, the orchestral tone poet, concerned himself less with the voicing of elemental emotions through heroic types than with the expression of human experience through the most direct and realistic processes of musical psychologizing. . . . It was not Grief nor Desire that engrossed him, but Don Quixote's grief and Don Juan's desire."

If the songs produced by Strauss before 1900 are less iconoclastic than his tone poems, they are, nevertheless, no less lofty in inspiration, poetic in concept, noble and elegant in speech.

Richard Strauss was born in Munich, Germany, on June 11, 1864. His father was a horn player who was a member of the orchestra conducted by Wagner for the première of *Tristan and Isolde;* his mother was the daughter of the wealthy brewer, Pschorr. Richard began taking piano lessons from his mother when he was four, and made his first attempts at composition at six. Later music study took place with Benno Walter, August Tombo, and F. W. Meyer. At the same time, he received an academic education in a Munich high school and at the University of Munich. While attending University, he completed several compositions—including a string quartet and a symphony, both performed in Munich. Hans von Buelow, conductor of the Meiningen Orchestra, became impressed with Strauss's talent and commissioned him to write some works for his orchestra. In 1885, Strauss became von Buelow's assistant conductor with the Meiningen Orchestra; and in 1886, he succeeded him.

After completing several major works in a post-Romantic style, Strauss was stimulated by his enthusiasm for Wagner and his friendship with the philosopher-poet, Alexander Ritter, to veer in a new direction. Between 1888 and 1900, he completed eight tone poems which gained him international fame (and notoriety), and which made him the most publicized and provocative composer in Germany. Before the nineteenth century had ended, he also completed several songs that were masterpieces. He also directed his energies to opera, a field in which he acquired supremacy with such masterworks as *Salome, Elektra,* and *Der Rosenkavalier*.

Strauss paid two visits to the United States. In 1904, he toured the country as conductor of the Wetzler Orchestra. During this visit to America, on March 21, 1904, he led the world première of his *Sinfonia domestica*. He returned to the United States in 1921 as guest conductor of several major orchestras in programs devoted entirely to his works.

By the time the Nazis rose to power in Germany, Richard Strauss was recognized as one of the greatest composers of his generation (as well as one of its most distinguished conductors). For a while, Strauss embraced the Nazi cause by becoming President of the Kulturkammer. But he soon came to grips with the new regime, and disassociated himself from it as best he could. During World War II, he lived partly at his home in Garmisch-Partenkirchen, and partly in Switzerland. After the war, he completed several new works, including an oboe concerto, a double concerto for clarinet, bassoon, and strings, and *Metamorphosen* for twenty-three solo strings. In 1947, he visited London to attend a Strauss festival where he directed one of the concerts. In 1952, his opera, *Die Liebe der Danae* (completed in 1940) was given its world première at the Salzburg Festival. His last opera was *Capriccio,* completed in 1941, and introduced in Munich in 1942.

Strauss's eighty-fifth birthday in 1949 was celebrated throughout the world with festivals and single performances of his music. Strauss died in Garmisch-Partenkirchen, in Bavaria, on September 8, 1949.

1882–1896. SONGS, for voice and piano.

"Allerseelen," op. 10, no. 8; "Caecilie," op. 27, no. 2; "Heimliche Aufforderung," op. 27, no. 3; "Ich trage meine Minne," op. 32, no. 1; "Morgen," op. 27, no. 4; "Die Nacht," op. 10, no. 3; "Ruhe, meine Seele," op. 27, no. 1; "Staendchen," op. 17, no. 2; "Traum durch die Daemmerung," op. 29, no. 1; "Zueignung," op. 10, no. 1.

It did not take Strauss long to take a commanding position in the world of the Lied. He was in his teens when he created and published his first group of songs for voice and piano, the *Eight Songs,* op. 10, based on Hermann von Gilm's *Letzte Blaetter*. Here we find "Zueignung," "Die Nacht," and "Allerseelen," three exquisite gems, which to this day are among the composer's finest creations in the song form. Here the song style that made Strauss the foremost song composer after Hugo Wolf is already crystallized and perfected. "Strauss," says James Husst Hall, "could write in a broad, flowing line, and be suave and full of glittering sensuous charm." He is a master of the expansive lyric line. His accompaniment, which often has an orchestral texture, continues Hall, "almost invariably commands the chief interest . . . is the principal agent in the expression of moods behind the text."

Elena Gerhardt, one of the greatest Lieder singers of her generation, points to some of the salient technical qualities of Strauss's greatest songs before 1900. "In a gay song he suddenly breaks into a few bars of recitative, as in his delightful 'Staendchen' (1886). This often brings out the following legato phrase to even greater effect. . . . Strauss . . . has a genius for drawing the most beautiful legato line. For instance, how wonderfully he lets the voice take over the lovely line . . . in 'Morgen' (1886). If the singer is a fraction late in taking it up, all is spoiled. And how mystically he creates atmosphere in 'Traum durch die Daemmerung' (1895). One feels drawn through the dusky twilight toward the beloved, and how caressing is the downward almost breathtaking line when he sings of her beauty. The poem speaks of the ribbon drawing one to the land of love. I cannot imagine this sentiment more warmly and irresistibly expressed. . . . In 'Ruhe meine Seele' (1894), how intense the expression of a tortured soul in the climax of the song, followed by the quiet comforting end, bringing peace to all suffering. But in 'Heimliche Aufforderung' (1894), he breaks out in jubilation, lightheartedness and the enchantment of love."

1885. BURLESKE IN D MINOR, for piano and orchestra.

Strauss completed *Burleske* when he was twenty-one. He did not hold a high opinion of it, regarding it as so much "nonsense." He put it aside (after Hans von Buelow had judged it "unplayable") and made no effort to get it either published or performed. Then in 1890, he relented, and directed its première in Eisenach, with Eugen d'Albert, soloist. Even then, he was doubtful of its value. When a publisher offered to pay Strauss an attractive price for publication rights, Strauss turned him down; not until 1894 did he finally give his approval.

The work, for all its composer's unfavorable reactions to it, is charming for its humor and burlesque moods. It opens (Allegro vivace) with the ground rhythm of the principal theme in four kettledrums. (The kettledrums play an important role throughout the work; occasionally they enter into a discourse with the piano.) The orchestra replies. Now the piano enters with the first theme. The second theme—derived from the second bar of the first subject—also comes in the piano. After an effective climax, the horn offers some new material. All this is worked out, varied, and repeated in an elaborate improvisation-like section. The coda features a piano cadenza, but it is the kettledrums that, in the closing measures, have the final word.

1888–1898. TONE POEMS, for orchestra:

Macbeth, op. 23; *Don Juan,* op. 20; *Tod und Verklaerung,* op. 24; *Till Eulenspiegel's lustige Streiche,* op. 28; *Also sprach Zarathustra,* op. 30; *Don Quixote,* op. 35; *Ein Heldenleben,* op. 40.

Strauss's friendship with the poet-philosopher, Alexander Ritter, was responsible for making him change his course as a composer. Up to that time, Strauss had written a symphony, a violin sonata, and a piano quartet, all derivative from Brahms, adhering to Brahms's principles of absolute music within classical structures. Ritter, a passionate Wagnerite—he was married to Wagner's niece—used his influence to steer Strauss toward dramatic, programmatic music in the style of Wagner. He fired Strauss with his own enthusiasm for the Wagner cult. "His influence," Strauss later confessed, "was in the nature of a storm wind." The direct result of that influence was the writing of Strauss's tone poems—and his first masterworks for orchestra.

Following a trip to Italy in 1886, Strauss made a break with his creative past by writing *Aus Italien,* a symphonic fantasy in which his impressions of Italy were reported programmatically and realistically. *Aus Italien,* introduced in 1887, was a fiasco; its discords disturbed many listeners. "Does my age make me so reactionary?" asked Hans von Buelow. "I find that the clever composer has gone to the extreme limits of tonal possibilities (in the realm of beauty) and in fact has even gone beyond those limits without real necessity."

But Strauss could not be deflected from his mission. Unfalteringly, he progressed from *Aus Italien* to his first tone poem—*Macbeth.* (Though it bears a later opus number than *Don Juan,* it preceded that work by a year.) And *Macbeth* was followed by a succession of tone poems that made their composer a world figure in music, and one of the most controversial.

Macbeth (1887) carries no detailed program. It is believed Strauss intended it as a character study of the two principal protagonists in the Shakespeare tragedy—Macbeth and his wife. At the beginning, the violins offer the subject representing Macbeth; this idea dominates the entire work. A dramatic passage for flute and clarinets portrays Lady Macbeth. It soon gives way to a passionate melody for the violin. A dramatic working-out of this material is followed by a hasty recall of the Lady Macbeth subject. Then a soaring song for the violins becomes enmeshed contrapuntally with this Lady Macbeth theme.

Don Juan (1888) was based on a poem by Nikolaus Lenau. Lenau explained: "My Don Juan is no hot-blooded man eternally pursuing women. It is the longing in him to find a woman who is to him incarnate womanhood, and to enjoy, in the one, all the women on earth, whom he cannot as individuals possess. Because he does not find her, although he reels from one to another, at last disgust seizes hold of him, and this disgust is the devil that fetches him."

This tone poem opens breathlessly with an upward surge of the strings at whose peak there comes a tempestuous subject descriptive of Don Juan's ardor. His longing for womankind is then remarked in a sensitive, tender episode for strings. Don Juan himself makes an appearance with a strong melody for the horns. In the passionate music that follows, Don Juan's love escapades are described. Here a principal thought consists of a romantic interlude for oboe, soon repeated by clarinet. The mood quickly develops from love to passion to debauchery. A shattering discord precedes an ominous silence. Shuddering figures in the orchestra tell of Don Juan's disgust as the tone poem ends.

Death and Transfiguration, or *Tod und Verklaerung* (1889), follows so literally and realistically a poem by Alexander Ritter that surely it must come as a shock to discover that Ritter wrote his poem *after* Strauss had completed his score. Here is a translation of that poem: "In the little room, dimly lighted by only a candle end, lies the sick man on his bed. But just now he has wrestled despairingly with Death. Now he has sunk exhausted in sleep. But Death does not long grant sleep and dreams to his victim. Cruelly he shakes him awake, and the fight begins afresh. Will to live and power of Death! What frightful wrestling! Neither bears off the victory, and all is silent once more. Sunk back, tired of battle, sleepless, as in fever-frenzy, the sick man now sees his life pass before his inner eye. First the morning red of childhood. Then the saucier play of youth, till he ripens to the man's fight, and now burns with hot lust after the higher prizes of life. Cold and sneering, the world sets barrier upon barrier in the way of his achievement. And so he pushed forward, so he climbs. Then clangs the last stroke of Death's iron hammer, breaks the earthly body in twain, covers the eye with the night of death. But from the heavenly spaces sounds mightily to greet him what he yearningly sought for here: deliverance from the world, transfiguration of the world."

There are four sections to the tone poem, played without interruption. The introduction, entitled "Sleep, Illness, Revery," starts off with a syncopated idea for second violins that suggests Death. The dying man recalls his youth through a haunting melody for the oboe. An agitated section, "Fever and Struggle with Death" follows. First there come strong chords, then a feverish crescendo, then the Death motive, and finally the epical struggle with Death. Suddenly, trombones, cellos, and violas present the opening strains of the "transfiguration theme." In the third part—"Dreams, Childhood, Memories, and Death"—the victim recalls episodes of his youth and manhood struggles. A frenetic interlude reveals that Death's struggle is about to begin again. The dying man tries to make a protest; it is a feeble one, in ascending harmonies. Harp and tam-tam pronounce the inevitability of his defeat. Death has triumphed; transfiguration is about to begin. This is the concluding part —the "Transfiguration"—where the transfiguration theme is proclaimed by the horns, and asserts itself, as the victim's childhood is being reviewed. The theme grows ever more dramatic and passionate; then it receives a final exultant statement by the strings over harp arpeggios.

Till Eulenspiegel's Merry Pranks (1895) is based on an old German legend about a rogue. Here is how Wilhelm Mauke retells the story: "Once upon a time there was a prankish rogue, ever up to new tricks, named Till Eulenspiegel. Now he jumps on his horse and gallops into the midst of a crowd of market women, overturning their wares with a prodigious clatter. Now he lights out with seven-league boots; now conceals himself in a mousehole. Disguised as a priest, he 'drips with unction and morals,' yet out of his toe peeps the scamp. As a cavalier he makes love, at first in jest, but soon in earnest, and is rebuffed. He is furious, and swears vengeance on all mankind, but, meeting some 'philistines' he forgets his wrath and mocks them. At length his hoaxes fail. He is tried in a Court of Justice and is condemned to hang for his misdeeds; but he still whistles defiantly as he ascends the ladder. Even on the scaffold he jests. Now he swings; now he gasps for air; a last convulsion. Till is dead."

It should be remarked that in the original German legend Till succeeds in eluding his final fatal punishment; but Strauss does not permit him this victory.

A simple statement in the violins at the opening is the musical equivalent of "once upon a time" with which fairy tales begin. A puckish little tune in French horn, followed by a no less insouciant one for small clarinet, tells about Till and his bent for mischief. The scene of the market place, with its hubbub, is re-created in a disturbed and noisy episode for oboes and clarinets. A solemn theme brings Till upon the scene, astride a horse. The disaster he soon brings on is told through a crash of timpani. In his next escapade, Till has put on the garb of clergy, described by a religious melody. With a glissando of the violin, Till tears the holy garment from his body. Sensual music now describes Till in love; loud exclamations in unison horns speak of his anger in being rejected. Soon Till forgets his disappointment by joining the village girls in a peasant dance. A drum roll brings a sudden halt to his roguish pranks. He is being brought to justice. His final doom is pronounced solemnly by a descending major seventh interval in bassoons, horns, trombones, and tuba. All is still. Then the tone poem ends as it began, with a simple folk-like statement by the orchestra informing us that "once upon a time" there was a rogue named Till Eulenspiegel.

Thus Spake Zarathustra (1896) is based on Nietzsche and may be regarded as a philosophical tone poem, the first of its kind. This is in spite of the fact that the composer disavowed any intention of writing "philosophical music" or of portraying "Nietzsche's great work musically." Strauss explained further: "I want to convey by means of music, an idea of the development of the human race from its origin, through the various phases of development, religious as well as scientific, up to Nietzsche's idea of the Superman." He further added that he wished to "embody the conflict between man's nature as it is and man's metaphysical attempts to lay hold of his nature with intelligence—leading finally to the conquest of life by the release of laughter."

The following quotation from Nietzsche's *Thus Spake Zarathustra* appears in the published score: "Having attained the age of thirty, Zarathustra left his home and went into the mountains. There he rejoiced in his spirit and his loneliness and, for ten years, did not grow weary of it. But at last his heart turned. One morning he got up with the dawn, stepped into the presence of the Sun, and thus spake unto him: 'Thou great star! What would be thy happiness, were it not for those on whom thou shinest? For ten years thou hast come up here to my cave. Thou wouldst have got sick of thy light and thy journey but for me, mine eagle, and my serpent. But we wait for thee every morning, and, receiving from thee thine abundance, blessed thee for it. Lo! I am weary of my wisdom, like the bee that hath collected too much honey. I need hands reaching out for it. I would fain grant and distribute, until the wise among men could once more enjoy their folly, and the poor once more their riches. For that end I must descend to the depths, as thou dost at evening, when sinking behind the sea, though gives light to the lower regions, thou resplendent star! I must, like thee, go down, as men say—men to whom I would descend. Then bless me, thou impassive eye, that canst look without envy upon overmuch happiness. Bless the cup which is about to overflow, so that the water, golden-flowing out of it, may carry everywhere the reflection of thy rapture. Lo! this cup is about to empty itself again, and Zarathustra will once more become a man.' Thus Zarathustra's descent began."

The tone poem is divided into an introduction and eight sections, played without interruption. Each section is given an identifying title. The introduction opens resplendently, with an ecstatic subject with which Zarathustra greets the sunrise; it culminates with a grandiose C major exclamation for full orchestra and organ. Here we encounter a motto theme (C-G-C) that courses throughout the tone poem and is identified as the "Nature" or "World Riddle" theme. The first section, "Of the Dwellers of the World in the Rear," consists of a religious subject in horns derived from the Gregorian chant, "Credo in unum deum." The second section, "Of Great Longing," also quotes a Gregorian chant in the solemn peals of the organ; at the same time the horns recall the "Credo" motive. In this and the preceding section Strauss points up man's awe in the presence of the power of God. Religious grandeur turns to ascetism, then to physical passion in "Of the Great Longing." Here we find an ardent song for strings against harp glissandi. The ecstasy spent, the trombones give voice to disgust in loud unison. There follows a mournful episode, "Song of the Grave," where oboe and English horn are heard in an elegiac chant. In "Of Science," Zarathustra seeks solace in science. The solution of life's riddle through scientific music receives musical translation in a canonic imitation in fifths. This science motive is amplified and extended through contrapuntal devices in "The Convalescent." The "Longing" motive is represented in an altered form by cellos and violas, succeeded by a triumphant outcry by the trumpet and a wryly humorous recall of the motif of "Disgust" by the clarinet. Man's indefatigable striving for earthly and sensual pleasures is depicted in "Dance Song" through a soaring waltz. Twelve strokes of the bell pronounce the coming of midnight. In the concluding section, "The Song of the Night Wanderer," the opening motto theme of C-G-C is heard in the plucked strings of the double basses against discords in the trombones; thus the key to life's riddle is provided.

Don Quixote (1897) was described by the composer as "Fantastic variations on a theme of knightly character." There are ten variations. There are preceded by an Introduction and Theme, and concluded by a Finale. The program, of course, comes from characters and incidents in the classic by Cervantes. Throughout the work, Don Quixote is represented by solo cello; his squire, Sancho Panza, appears first in tenor tuba and bass clarinet, and later on in solo viola.

In the Introduction, Don Quixote de la Mancha, having lost his mind and heart to the study of chivalric lore, decides to set forth on adventures as a knight errant. The first subject, in the woodwind, and an eloquent melody for the strings that follows, bring up suggestions of knight-errantry and chivalry. The fair Dulcinea, the Ideal Woman, appears to him in an eloquent theme for the oboe accompanied by harp and muted strings. This episode concludes with unrelated chords and piercing discords to tell us that Don Quixote's mind has begun to wander.

Don Quixote's two-part theme is given in the solo cello (Moderato), while Sancho Panza's melody is presented by tenor tuba and bass clarinet.

In the first variation, Don Quixote and Sancho Panza set forth on their adventures, the first being Don's attack on the windmills which he mistakes for giants; he is unceremoniously unseated from his horse by the mill's sails. The second variation finds Don in another battle, this time with sheep, who to the befuddled Don appear to be the army of Emperor Alifanfaron. The woodwind are heard in a pastoral subject, to which muted brass contribute the sound of bleating sheep. The Don charges on the sheep and disperses them. In the third variation, Don and his squire discuss the pros and cons of chivalry. When Sancho Panza finds greater virtue in a comfortable life than in a search for an Ideal, Don Quixote takes him soundly to task and bids him hold his tongue. The fourth variation presents a religious chant in bassoons and muted horns. A band of pilgrims is approaching. The Don mistakes them for robbers, attacks them, and is soundly thrashed. While Sancho sleeps, Don Quixote muses about the Ideal Woman and addresses the Dulcinea passionately. The Dulcinea is here represented first by a bass, then by an ardent song for solo cello, to which strings and harp contribute cadenzas. A peasant woman, portrayed by woodwind and tambourine, approaches Don Quixote and Sancho Panza in the sixth variation. Sancho tries to convince his master that the peasant is actually the Dulcinea in disguise. At first Don is incredulous, then is led to believe that his Ideal Woman has been transformed through evil magic. In the seventh variation, Don and Sancho Panza are astride a wooden horse, imagining they are flying through the air. To portray the rush of the wind during the flight, the composer introduces into his orchestra a wind machine. But the riders are soon made aware that they have indulged in fantasy. A sudden halt on a sustained note in the bassoon brings their flight to a halt. A graceful barcarolle now describes Don's voyage on the river Ebro on a mission to save a distressed knight. The boat overturns, but the Don and his squire are saved. This leads them to speak their gratitude in a chant for woodwind and horns. In the ninth variation, the adventurers come upon two monks whom they mistake for magicians about to abduct a princess. The Don attacks them, a fight vividly described in a dramatized passage for the strings, while the bassoons continue to personify the monks. The monks are sent into rout. In the concluding variation, the knight meets his doom in a struggle with the Knight of the White Moon. Scale passages for low strings and woodwind depict the fight. When the Don is defeated, he promises to withdraw into the peace and safety of his own home. A poignant tune for the English horn reveals that the Don is ready to resume his old calling of shepherd. In the finale, we are witnessing Don Quixote's death. The theme that identifies him now assumes the character of a lament. Consonant chords create an atmosphere of serenity and normalcy, as Don Quixote leaves the world peacefully.

Strauss's eighth and last tone poem, *A Hero's Life,* or *Ein Heldenleben* (1898) tells the biography of a hero who surmounts all obstacles and triumphs over all enemies in his struggle to build a new world. Strauss was speaking about himself. If there is any doubt on this point, it is dispelled in the fifth section, where, in summing up our hero's "Works of Peace," Strauss quotes from a number of his own works.

The tone poem is in six uninterrupted sections. In the first, "The Hero," he is introduced with a bold, proud subject in horns and low strings. This theme is worked out to reveal different facets of the hero's personality—his ambition, pride, idealism, imagination, inflexible will. This section ends in a stirring fortissimo. Next we are told about the "Hero's Adversaries." Curt phrases in flutes, oboes, piccolo, English horn, and clarinets bring us a picture of this malevolent crew. The hero theme, stated at first quietly in muted cellos and basses reinforced by clarinets, bass clarinet, and later horns, arises in quiet protest. A brass fanfare sends the hero to action. A solo violin brings up the image of the hero's beloved, in "The Hero's Courtship." At first, she is capricious and flirtatious, but soon her feelings become more sincere and intense. Then the entire orchestra erupts into a wondrous love song. With the dying out of the ecstasy, the malicious voices of the enemy are heard from afar. Distant fanfares summon the hero to battle in "The Hero's Battlefield." A monumental struggle unfolds in the orchestra, with consistent reminders of the theme of the Beloved as the Hero's inspiration. A mighty outburst then tells of the hero's victory. His struggles ended, the hero can embark upon achievements of peace in "The Hero's Works of Peace." At first the trumpet offers a motive suggesting the peace-time accomplishment. Then brief excerpts from various Strauss compositions point up his own contributions. These include quotations from *Don Juan, Death and Transfiguration, Don Quixote, Till Eulenspiegel, Macbeth, Thus Spake Zarathustra,* the music drama *Guntram,* and the song, "Traum durch die Daemmerung." The tone poem ends with "The Hero's Retreat from the World and Fulfillment." The voice of the hero's enemies speaks in the tubas, over which rides the monumental anger of the hero, and recollections of the storm and strife of his career.

Presently, the solo violin recalls the Hero's beloved. A wonderful serenity now surrounds the hero. As the solo embarks on a radiant melody, the hero's soul takes flight. For the last time we hear the hero's motive. At first it is solemn, but then is built up into a tremendous climax. In the end the mood is funereal; the hero is being put to his final rest.

SOURCES

ABRAHAM, GERALD, *Borodin*. London: Reeves (no date).
———, *A Hundred Years of Music*. 2nd edition. London: Duckworth, 1949.
———, "The Song in Russia" in *A History of Song*, edited by Denis Stevens.
———, *Studies in Russian Music*. New York: Scribner's 1936.
ABRAHAM, GERALD (editor), *Grieg: A Symposium*. Norman: University of Oklahoma Press, 1950.
———, *Handel: A Symposium*. London: Oxford University Press, 1954.
———, *The Music of Tchaikovsky*. New York: Norton, 1946.
———, *The Music of Schubert*. New York: Norton, 1947.
———, *Schumann: A Symposium*. London: Oxford University Press, 1952.
APTHORP, WILLIAM F., *The Opera, Past and Present*. New York: Scribner's, 1905.
ARRAU, CLAUDIO, "Mozart's Piano Music." *Musical America*, February 15, 1956.
Balanchine's Complete Stories of Great Ballets, edited by Francis Mason. New York: Doubleday, 1954.
BARBAUD, PIERRE, *Haydn*. New York: Grove, 1959.
BARRICELLI, JEAN-PIERRE, and WEINSTEIN, LEO, *Ernest Chausson*. Norman: University of Oklahoma Press, 1955.
BARZUN, JACQUES, *Berlioz and the Romantic Century*. Boston: Little Brown, 1950.
BEAUMONT, CYRIL W., *Complete Book of Ballet*. Garden City: Garden City Co., 1941.
BEDBROOK, G. S., "The Genius of Giovanni Gabrieli." *Music Review* (London), January 1947.
BEDFORD, HERBERT, *Schumann*. New York: Harper, 1925.
BEKKER PAUL, *Beethoven*. New York: Dutton, 1925.
———, *Richard Wagner*. New York: Norton, 1931.
BENEDICT, JULIUS, *Sketch of the Life and Works of Felix Mendelssohn*. London, 1853.
BERLIOZ, HECTOR, *Memoirs*, edited by Ernest Newman. New York: Knopf, 1948.

BIANCOLLI, LOUIS (editor), *The Analytical Concert Guide*. New York: Doubleday, 1951.
———, *The Mozart Reader*. New York: World, 1954.
———, *The Opera Reader*. New York: McGraw-Hill, 1953.
BLOM, ERIC, *Mozart*. New York: Pellegrini and Cudahy, 1949.
———, "Mozart's Chamber Music" in *Chamber Music,* edited by Alec Robertson.
———, "Mozart's Symphonies" in *The Symphony,* edited by Ralph Hill.
BONAVIA, F., *Verdi*. London: Dobson, 1947.
———, "Verdi" in *The Heritage of Music,* Vol. II, edited by Hubert J. Foss.
BONAVIA, F. (editor), *Musicians on Music*. New York: Robert McBride, 1957.
BOROWSKI, FELIX and UPTON, GEORGE P., *The Standard Concert Guide*. Garden City: Blue Ribbon Books, 1940.
BORREN, CHARLES VAN DEN, *Orlande de Lassus*. 3rd edition. Paris: Alcan, 1930.
BOUCOURECHILEV, ANDRE, *Schumann*. New York: Grove, 1959.
BROCKWAY, WALLACE, and WEINSTOCK, HERBERT, *Men of Music*. 2nd edition. New York: Simon and Schuster, 1950.
———, *The World of Opera*. New York: Pantheon Books, 1962.
BRODER, NATHAN, Essays on Mozart's Operas in *The Great Operas of Mozart*. New York: G. Schirmer, 1962.
BROWN, M. J. E., *Schubert*. New York: St. Martin's Press, 1958.
BUKOFZER, MANFRED, *Music in the Baroque Era*. New York: Norton, 1947.
BURK, JOHN N., *The Life and Works of Beethoven*. New York: Random House, 1943.
———, *Mozart and His Music*. New York: Random House, 1959.
BURNEY, CHARLES, *A General History of Music*. New York: Dover, 1957.
CALVOCORESSI, M. D., *Mussorgsky*. London: Rockliff, 1956.
CALVOCORESSI, M. D. and ABRAHAM, GERALD, *Masters of Russian Music*. New York: Knopf, 1936.
CAPELL, RICHARD, *Schubert's Songs*. New York: Macmillan, 1957.
CARDUS, NEVILLE, *A Composers Eleven*. London: Jonathan Cape, 1958.
CARNER, MOSCO, *Puccini*. New York: Knopf, 1959.
———, "Schubert's Orchestral Music" in *The Music of Schubert*, edited by Gerald Abraham.
CHASE, GILBERT, *The Music of Spain*. New York: Dover, 1959.
CHISSELL, JOAN, *Schumann*. London: Dent, 1948.
———, "Schumann's Chamber Music" in *Chamber Music*, edited by Alec Robertson.
CLAPHAM, JOHN, "The Chamber Music of Antonin Dvořák" in *Chamber Music,* edited by Alec Robertson.
COATES, HENRY, *Palestrina*. New York: Pellegrini and Cudahy, 1949.
Cobbett's Cyclopaedic Survey of Chamber Music. Revised edition. London: Oxford University Press, 1963.
COLLES, H. C., *The Growth of Music*. New Edition. London: Oxford University Press, 1959.

———, *Symphony and Drama*. Vol. VII of the Oxford History of Music. London: Oxford University Press, 1934.

Cooper, Martin, *French Music*. London: Oxford University Press, 1951.

———, *Gluck*. London: Oxford University Press, 1935.

———, "The Songs of Schumann" in *Schumann: A Symposium,* edited by Gerald Abraham.

Copland, Aaron, *Our New Music*. New York: Whittlesey House, 1941.

Cortot, Alfred, *French Piano Music*. London: Oxford University Press, 1932.

de Courcy, G. I. C., *Paganini*. 2 vols. Norman: University of Oklahoma Press, 1957.

Craft, Robert, "The Murderous Prince of Madrigalists" (Carlo Gesualdo). *High Fidelity Magazine,* September 1961.

Cross, Milton, *Complete Stories of the Great Operas*. New York: Doubleday, 1951.

Crowest, Frederick J., *Cherubini*. London: Reeves, 1890.

Cui, César, *La Musique en Russie*. Paris: Fischbacher, 1893.

Curtiss, Mina, *Georges Bizet*. New York: Knopf, 1959.

Dale, Kathleen, "Grieg's Piano Music" in *Grieg: A Symposium,* edited by Gerald Abraham.

———, "Schubert's Piano Music" in *The Music of Schubert,* edited by Gerald Abraham.

———, "Schumann's Piano Music" in *Schumann: A Symposium,* edited by Gerald Abraham.

Dannreuther, E. G., *The Romantic Period*. Vol. VI of the Oxford History of Music. London: Oxford University Press, 1905.

Da Ponte, Lorenzo, *Memoirs*. New York: Orion Press, 1959.

David, Hans T. and Mendel, Arthur (editors), *The Bach Reader*. New York: Norton, 1945.

Dean, Winton, *Georges Bizet*. London: Dent, 1948.

The Decca Book of Opera. London: Werner Laurie, 1956.

Demuth, Norman, *César Franck*. New York: Philosophical Library, 1949.

———, *Introduction to the Music of Gounod*. London: Dobson, 1950.

Dent, Edward J., *Alessandro Scarlatti*. London: Edward Arnold, 1960.

———, *Mozart's Operas*. London: Oxford University Press, 1947.

———, *Opera*. London: Penguin, 1940.

Desmond, Astra, "Grieg's Songs" in *Grieg: A Symposium,* edited by Gerald Abraham.

Dickinson, A. E. F., *The Art of Bach*. Revised edition. London: Hinrichson, 1950.

———, "The Chamber Music of Schumann" in *Schumann: A Symposium,* edited by Gerald Abraham.

Downes, Olin, "Chopin" in *The World of Great Composers,* edited by David Ewen.

Dumesnil, Maurice, *Claude Debussy*. New York: Washburn, 1940.

EINSTEIN, ALFRED, *Essays in Music*. New York: Norton, 1936.
———, *The Italian Madrigal,* 3 vols. Princeton: Princeton University Press, 1949.
———, *Mozart and His Character*. New York: Knopf, 1945.
———, *Music in the Romantic Era*. New York: Norton, 1947.
———, *A Short History of Music*. New York: Knopf, 1937.
ENGEL, GABRIEL, *The Life of Bruckner*. New York: Roerich Museum, 1931.
———, *Gustav Mahler: Song Symphonist*. New York: Bruckner Society, 1932.
EVANS, EDWIN, *Brahms' Vocal Works*. London: Reeves, 1912.
———, *Chamber and Orchestral Music of Johannes Brahms*. 3 vols. London: Reeves (no date).
———, *Tchaikovsky*. New York: Pellegrini and Cudahy, 1949.
EWEN, DAVID, *The Book of European Light Opera*. New York: Holt, Rinehart and Winston, 1962.
———, *David Ewen Introduces Modern Music*. Philadelphia: Chilton, 1962.
EWEN, DAVID (editor), *From Bach to Stravinsky*. New York: Norton, 1933.
———, *The World of Great Composers*. Englewood Cliffs: Prentice-Hall, 1962.
FERGUSON, DONALD N., *A History of Musical Thought*. New York: Appleton-Century-Crofts, 1948.
———, *Piano Music of Six Great Composers*. New York: Prentice-Hall, 1947.
FINCK, HENRY T., *Grieg and His Music*. New York: Dodd Mead, 1909.
———, *Song and Song Writers*. New York: Scribner's, 1900.
FLOWER, NEWMAN, *George Frideric Handel*. New York: Scribner's, 1948.
FORKEL, JOHANN NIKLAUS, *Johann Sebastian Bach*. London: Boosey, 1820.
FOSS, HUBERT, J., "Grieg's Orchestral Music" in *Grieg: A Symposium*, edited by Gerald Abraham.
FOSS, HUBERT, J. (editor), *The Heritage of Music*. 2 vols. London: Oxford University Press, 1927, 1951.
FRANKENSTEIN, ALFRED, "Beethoven" in *Music and Western Man,* edited by Peter Gravie.
FULLER-MAITLAND, J. A., *The Age of Bach and Handel*. Vol. IV in the Oxford History of Music. London: Oxford University Press, 1902.
———, *Masters of German Music*. New York: Scribner's, 1894.
GARVIE, PETER (editor), *Music and Western Man*. London: Dent, 1958.
GEIRINGER, KARL, *Brahms: His Life and Work*. Revised edition. New York: Oxford University Press, 1947.
———, *Haydn: A Creative Life*. New York: Norton, 1946.
GILMAN, LAWRENCE, *Phases of Modern Music*. New York: Harper's, 1904.
———, *Wagner's Operas*. New York: Farrar and Rinehart, 1937.
GIRDLESTONE, CUTHBERT, *Jean-Philippe Rameau*. London: Cassell, 1957.
———, *Mozart's Piano Concertos*. London, 1948.
GLINKA, M. I, *Memoirs*. Norman: University of Oklahoma Press, 1963.
GLYN, MARGARET H., *About Elizabethan Virginal Music and its Composers*. London: Reeves, 1924.

GRAY, CECIL, *A History of Music*. London: K. Paul, Trench, Trubner, 1928.
———, "Liszt" in the *Heritage of Music,* Vol. II, edited by Hubert J. Foss.
GROUT, DONALD J., *A History of Western Music*. New York: Norton, 1960.
———, *A Short History of Opera*. New York: Columbia University Press, 1947.
Grove's Dictionary of Music and Musicians, Fifth edition, edited by Eric Blom. St. Martin's Press, 1955.
Hadden, J. Cuthbert, *Haydn*. New York: Pellegrini and Cudahy, 1905.
HADOW, W. H., *Collected Essays*. London: Oxford, 1928.
———, *Studies in Modern Music*. London: Seeley, 1893.
———, *The Viennese Period*. Vol. V of the Oxford History of Music. London: Oxford University Press, 1905.
HALE, PHILIP, *Boston Symphony Program Notes*. Garden City: Doubleday, Doran, 1935.
HALL, JAMES HUSST, *The Art Song*. Norman: University of Oklahoma Press, 1953.
HALL, LELAND, "César Franck" in *The World of Great Composers,* edited by David Ewen.
HANSLICK, EDUARD, *Vienna's Golden Years of Music:* 1850–1900. New York: Simon and Schuster, 1950.
HARRISON, F. Ll., "Choir and People in the Later Middle Ages," in *Choral Music*, edited by Arthur Jacobs.
HEDLEY, ARTHUR, *Chopin*. New York: Collier, 1962.
HELFERT, VLADIMIR, "Dvořák," in *The World of Great Composers,* edited by David Ewen.
HENDERSON, W. J., *Richard Wagner: His Life and His Dramas*. New York: Putnam, 1901.
HERVEY, ARTHUR, *Masters of French Music*. New York: Scribner's, 1894.
———, *Meyerbeer*. New York: Stokes, 1913.
———, *Saint-Saëns*. New York: Dodd Mead, 1922.
HILL, E. BURLINGAME, *French Music*. Boston: Houghton Mifflin, 1924.
HILL, RALPH (editor), *The Concerto*. London: Pelican, 1952.
———, *The Symphony*. London: Pelican, 1952.
HOFFMEISTER, KAREL, *Antonín Dvořák*. London, 1928.
HOLLAND, A. K., *Henry Purcell*. London: Penguin, 1932.
HOLST, IMOGEN (editor), *Henry Purcell: Essays on His Music*. London: Oxford University Press, 1959.
HOOVER, KATHLEEN, "Claudio Monteverdi: Prophet of Music." *Opera News,* March 10, 1962.
HORTON, JOHN, *Grieg*. London: Duckworth, 1950.
———, *Some 19th Century Composers*. London: Oxford University Press, 1950.
HUGHES, DON ANSELM and ABRAHAM, GERALD, *Ars Nova and the Renaissance*. Vol. III of the New Oxford History of Music. London: Oxford University Press, 1960.

HUGHES, ROSEMARY, "The Chamber Music of Haydn" in *Chamber Music,* edited by Alec Robertson.

HUNEKER, JAMES GIBBONS, *Chopin: The Man and His Music.* New York: Scribner's, 1900.

———, *Liszt.* New York: Scribners, 1931.

———, *Mezzotints in Modern Music.* New York: Scribner's, 1925.

HUSSEY, DYNELEY, *Verdi.* New York: Pellegrini and Cudahy, 1949.

HUTCHESON, ERNEST, *The Literature of the Piano.* New York: Knopf, 1949.

HUTCHINGS, A. B., *The Baroque Concerto.* New York: W. W. Norton & Co., Inc., 1961.

D'INDY, VINCENT, *César Franck.* New York: Dodd, Mead, 1931.

JACOB, H. E., *Felix Mendelssohn and His Times.* Englewood Cliffs: Prentice-Hall, 1963.

———, *Haydn: His Art, Times and Glory.* New York: Rinehart, 1950.

———, *Johann Strauss.* New York: Greystone, 1940.

JACOBS, ARTHUR (editor), *Choral Music.* London: Penguin, 1963.

JAHN, OTTO, *Mozart.* London: Novello, Ewer, 1889.

JEAN-AUBRY, GEORGES, *French Music Today.* London: K. Paul, Trench, Trubner, 1919.

JOHANSEN, D. M., *Edvard Grieg.* New York: Tudor, 1945.

KING, A. HYATT, *Chamber Music.* New York: Chanticleer, 1948.

———, "Mozart's Concertos" in *The Concerto,* edited by Ralph Hill.

KIRKPATRICK, RALPH, *Domenico Scarlatti.* Princeton: Princeton University Press, 1953.

KRACAUER, S., *Orpheus in Paris* (Offenbach). New York: Knopf, 1937.

LAMBERT, CONSTANT, *Music Ho.* London: Faber and Faber, 1934.

LANDON, H. C. ROBBINS, "The Baffling Case of Anton Bruckner." *High Fidelity Magazine.* February 1963.

LANDON, H. C. ROBBINS and MITCHELL, DONALD (editors), *The Mozart Companion.* New York: Oxford University Press, 1956.

LANDORMY, PAUL, *A History of Music.* New York: Scribner's, 1934.

LANDOWSKA, WANDA, *The Music of the Past.* New York: Knopf, 1924.

LANG, PAUL HENRY, *Music in Western Civilization.* New York: Norton, 1941.

LATHAM, PETER, *Brahms.* New York: Pellegrini and Cudahy, 1949.

———, "The Chamber Music of Brahms" in *Chamber Music,* edited by Alec Robertson.

LEICHTENTRITT, HUGO, *Music, History and Ideas.* Cambridge: Harvard University Press, 1938.

LEONARD, RICHARD ANTHONY, *A History of Russian Music.* New York: Macmillan, 1957.

———, *The Stream of Music.* New York: Doubleday, 1948.

LEWIS, ANTHONY, Article on Heinrich Schuetz in *Grove's Dictionary of Music and Musicians,* edited by Eric Blom.

LEYDA, JAY, and BERTENSON, S. (editors), *The Mussorgsky Reader*. New York: Norton, 1947.

LISZT, FRANZ, *Chopin*. London: Reeves, 1913.

LLOYD-JONES, DAVID, "Professor Borodin's Indulgence." *High Fidelity Magazine,* June 1963.

LOCKE, ARTHUR WARE, *Music and the Romantic Movement in France*. London: K. Paul, Trench and Trubner, 1920.

LOCKSPEISER, EDWARD, *Debussy*. New York: Pellegrini and Cudahy, 1949.

LOWENBERG, ALFRED (editor), *Annals of the Opera*. Revised edition. Geneva: Societas Bibliographica, 1955.

MACKINLAY, STERLING, *The Origin and Development of Light Opera*. London: Hutchinson, 1927.

MAREK, GEORGE A., *A Front Seat at the Opera*. New York: Allen, Towne and Heath, 1948.

———, *Puccini*. New York: Simon and Schuster, 1951.

MASON, DANIEL GREGORY, *Beethoven and His Forerunners*. Revised edition. New York: Macmillan, 1940.

———, *Chamber Music of Brahms*. New York: Macmillan, 1933.

———, *From Grieg to Brahms*. New York: Macmillan, 1927.

———, *The Romantic Composers*. New York: Macmillan, 1930.

MAY, FLORENCE, *The Life of Brahms*. 2 vols. London: Reeves (no date).

McDONALD, KATHERINE GRIFFITH, "Giordano." *Opera News,* March 2, 1963.

McKINNEY, HOWARD D., and ANDERSON, W. R., *Music in History*. New York: American Book Co., 1940.

MANN, WILLIAM, "Chamber Music of Schubert" in *Chamber Music,* edited by Alec Robertson.

MELLERS, WILFRID, *Couperin*. New York: Roy, 1951.

———, *Man and His Music: The Sonata Principle*. London: Rockcliff, 1957.

———, *Man and His Music: Romanticism and the 20th Century*. London: Rockcliff, 1957.

MORGENSTERN, SAM (editor), *Composers on Music*. New York: Pantheon, 1956.

MURDOCH, WILLIAM, *Chopin: His Life*. New York: Macmillan, 1935.

MYERS, ROLLO H., *Erik Satie*. London: Dobson, 1948.

NEWMAN, ERNEST, "Hugo Wolf." *Contemporary Review* (London), May 1904.

———, *Hugo Wolf*. London: Methuen, 1907.

———, *The Life of Richard Wagner*. 4 vols. New York: Knopf, 1933–1946.

———, *More Stories of Great Operas*. New York: Knopf, 1943.

———, *Stories of Great Operas*. New York: Knopf, 1930.

———, *Wagner as Man and Artist*. New York: Vintage, 1960.

NEWMARCH, ROSA, *The Concertgoers Library of Descriptive Notes*. 6 vols. London: Oxford University Press, 1928–1948.

———, *The Music of Czechoslovakia*. London: Oxford University Press, 1943.

———, *The Russian Opera*. New York: Dutton, 1914.

NIECKS, FREDERICK, *Frederic Chopin as Man and Musician*. London, Novello, Ewer, 1888.
———, *Robert Schumann*. London: Novello, Ewer, 1888.
NIEMANN, WALTER, *Brahms*. New York: Knopf, 1947.
PAHLEN, KURT, *Music of the World*. Revised edition. New York: Crown, 1953.
PARRY, C. HUBERT, *The Evolution of the Art of Music*. New York: Appleton, 1930.
———, *Johann Sebastian Bach*. Revised edition. New York: Putnam, 1934.
———, *The Music of the 17th Century*. Vol. III in the Oxford History of Music. London: Oxford University Press, 1902.
PELTZ, MARY ELLIS (editor), *The Opera Lover's Companion*. Chicago: Ziff-Davis, 1948.
PEYSER, HERBERT F., "La Forza del Destino," "Lakmé," and "Tales of Hoffmann," in *The Opera Lover's Companion,* edited by Mary Ellis Peltz.
PINCHERLE, MARC, *Corelli*. New York: Norton, 1956.
———, *Vivaldi*. New York: Norton, 1957.
PIRRO, ANDRÉ, *Johann Sebastian Bach*. New York: Orion, 1957.
PORTE, JOHN F., *Chopin: The Composer and His Music*. New York: Scribner's, 1935.
PORTER, ANDREW, "The Chamber Music of Mendlessohn" in *Chamber Music,* edited by Alec Robertson.
POUGIN, ARTHUR, *Adolphe Adam*. Paris, 1876.
———, *Musiciens du XIX siècle*. Paris: Fischbacher, 1911.
POURTALES, GUY DE, *Chopin*. New York: Holt, 1927.
PRUNIERES, HENRI, *A New History of Music*. New York: Macmillan, 1943.
———, *Claudio Monteverdi*. London: Oxford, 1952.
PULVER, JEFFREY, *Johannes Brahms*. New York: Harper, 1926.
PYNE, ZOË KENDRICK, *Giovanni Pierluigi Palestrina*. London: John Lane, The Bodley Head, 1922.
RADCLIFFE, PHILIP, *Mendelssohn*. London: Dent, 1954.
———, "The Song in Germany and Austria" in *A History of Song,* edited by Denis Stevens.
REDLICH, HANS. F., *Claudio Monteverdi*. London: Oxford University Press, 1952.
REESE, GUSTAVE, *Music in the Middle Ages*. New York: Norton, 1940.
———, *Music in the Renaissance*. Revised edition. New York: Norton, 1959.
RIESEMANN, OSKAR VON, *Mussorgsky*. New York: Knopf, 1935.
RIMSKY-KORSAKOV, NIKOLAI, *My Musical Life*. 3rd Edition. New York: Knopf, 1942.
ROBERTSON, ALEC, *Dvořák*. New York: Pellegrini and Cudahy, 1949.
———, "Schubert's Songs" in *The Music of Schubert,* edited by Gerald Abraham.
ROBERTSON, ALEC (editor), *Chamber Music*. London: Pelican, 1957.
ROLLAND, ROMAIN, *Beethoven the Creator*. New York: Harper, 1929.
———, *Essays on Music,* edited by David Ewen. New York: Dover, 1959.

———, *Handel*. New York: Holt, 1916.
———, *Some Musicians of Former Days*. New York: Holt, 1915.
ROSE, GLORIA, "The Cantatas of Carissimi." *Musical Quarterly*, April 1962.
ROSKETH, YVONNE, *Grieg*. Paris: Rieder, 1933.
SACHS, CURT, *Our Musical Heritage*. 2nd edition. New York: Prentice-Hall, 1955.
SAINT-FOX, GEORGES DE, *The Symphonies of Mozart*. New York: Knopf, 1949.
SAINT-FOX, GEORGES DE and WYZEWA, T., *Wolfgang Amadeus Mozart: Sa Vie Musicale*. Paris, Oesclée, 1912.
SANBORN, PITTS, *The Metropolitan Book of the Opera*, New York: Simon and Schuster, 1937.
SARGENT, MALCOLM (editor), *The Outline of Music*. New York: Arco, 1962.
SAUNDERS, WILLIAM, *Weber*. London: Dent, 1940.
SCHAUFFLER, ROBERT HAVEN, *Beethoven: The Man Who Freed Music*. New York: Tudor, 1947.
———, *Florestan: The Life and Works of Robert Schumann*. New York: Holt, 1945.
———, *Franz Schubert: The Ariel of Music*. New York: Putnam, 1949.
SCHNEIDER, MARCEL, *Schubert*. New York: Grove, 1959.
SCHUMANN, ELISABETH, *German Song*. New York: Chanticleer, 1948.
SCHUMANN, ROBERT, *On Music and Musicians*. New York: Pantheon, 1946.
SCHWEITZER, ALBERT, *Bach*. London: Breitkopf and Haertel, 1911.
SELTSAM, WILLIAM H. (editor), *Metropolitan Opera Annals*. New York: H. W. Wilson, 1947.
SEARLE, HUMPHREY, *The Music of Liszt*. London: Williams and Norgate, 1954.
SEROFF, VICTOR I, *The Mighty Five*. New York: Allen, Towne and Heath, 1948.
———, *Debussy: Musician of France*. New York: Putnam, 1956.
SMITH, LEO, *Music of the 17th and 18th Centuries*. London: Dent, 1931.
ŠOUREK, OTAKAR, *Dvořák*. New York: Philosophical Library, 1954.
———, *The Chamber Music of Dvořák*. Czechoslovakia: Artia (no date).
———, *The Orchestral Works of Dvořák*. Czechoslovakia: Artia (no date).
SPECHT, RICHARD, *Brahms*. New York: Dutton, 1930.
———, *Puccini*. New York: Knopf, 1933.
SPITTA, PHILIPP, *Johann Sebastian Bach*. New York: Dover, 1951.
STEFAN, PAUL, *The Life and Works of Anton Dvorák*. New York: Greystone, 1941.
———, *Mahler*. New York: Schirmer, 1913.
STEVENS, DENIS (editor), *A History of Song*. New York: Norton, 1960.
STEVENSON, ROBERT, *Music Before the Classic Era*, New York: St. Martin's Press, 1955.
STREATFEILD, R. A., *Handel*. London: Methuen, 1909.
———, *The Opera*. London: Routledge (no date).
SULLIVAN, J W. N., *Beethoven: His Spiritual Development*. New York: Knopf, 1927.

TERRY, CHARLES SANFORD, *Bach: The Historical Approach.* London: Oxford University Press, 1930.

———, *John Christian Bach.* London: Oxford University Press, 1929.

THAYER, A. W., *The Life of Ludwig van Beethoven.* 3 vols. London: Centaur, 1960.

THOMPSON, OSCAR, *Debussy: Man and Artist.* New York: Dodd Mead, 1937.

TIERSOT, JULIEN, *Un Demi Siècle de Musique Française.* Paris: Alcan, 1924.

TITCOMB, C., "From Ockeghem to Palestrina" in *Choral Music* edited by Arthur Jacobs.

TOVEY, DONALD FRANCIS, *Essays in Musical Analysis.* 6 vols. London: Oxford University Press, 1935–1939.

———, "Schubert," in *The Heritage of Music,* Vol. I, edited by Hubert J. Foss.

TOYE, FRANCIS R., *Rossini: A Study in Tragi-Comedy.* New York: Knopf, 1934.

———, *Giuseppe Verdi: His Life and Works.* New York: Knopf, 1946.

TURNER, W. J., *Beethoven: The Search for Reality.* London: Dent, 1927.

———, *Berlioz: The Man and His Work.* London: Dent, 1934.

———, *Mozart: The Man and His Music.* New York: Knopf, 1945.

———, "Mozart" in *The Heritage of Music,* Vol. I, edited by Hubert J. Foss.

ULRICH, HOMER, *Chamber Music.* New York: Columbia University Press, 1948.

VALLAS, LÉON, *César Franck.* London: Harrap, 1951.

———, *Claude Debussy: His Life and Works.* London: Oxford University Press, 1933.

VEINUS, ABRAHAM, *The Victor Book of Concertos.* New York: Simon and Schuster, 1948.

WALKER, ERNEST, *A History of Music in England.* Oxford: Clarendon Press, 1907.

WALTER, BRUNO, *Gustav Mahler.* Revised edition. New York: Knopf, 1957.

WEBER, MAX, *Carl Maria von Weber.* Boston: Ditson, 1865.

WEINSTOCK, HERBERT, *Chopin.* New York: Knopf, 1949.

———, *Donizetti.* New York: Pantheon, 1963.

———, *Handel.* Revised edition. New York: Knopf, 1959.

———, *Tchaikovsky.* New York: Knopf, 1946.

WERFEL FRANZ, and STEFAN, PAUL (editors), *Verdi: The Man In His Letters.* New York: L. B. Fischer, 1942.

WESTERBY, HERBERT, *Liszt and His Piano Works.* London: Reeves, 1936.

WESTRUP, J. A., *Purcell.* New York: Collier, 1962.

———, "Schubert's Chamber Music" in *The Music of Schubert,* edited by Gerald Abraham.

WOLFF, WERNER, *Anton Bruckner: Rustic Genius.* New York: Dutton, 1942.

WOOLDRIDGE, H. E., *The Polyphonic Period.* Vol. I of the Oxford History of Music. London: Oxford University Press, 1901–1905.

YOUNG, PERCY, *Handel.* New York: Pellegrini and Cudahy, 1947.

———, *An Introduction to the Music of Mendelssohn.* London: Dobson, 1949.

ZWEIG, STEFAN, *Tides of Fortune.* New York: Viking, 1936.

INDEX